EMILIA-ROMAGNA

GW00994812

**FUTURE
ON A HUMAN SCALE**

www.regione.emilia-romagna.it

Regione Emilia-Romagna

AUTHENTIC
Italy

Touring Club Italiano
President and Chairman: *Roberto Ruozi*

Touring Editore
Editorial Director: *Michele D'Innella*
Head of cartographic-tourist sector: *Fiorenza Frigoni*

Editorial coordination: *Cristiana Baietta*
Technical coordination: *Maurizio Passoni*
Senior Editor: *Paola Pandiani*
Editor: *Monica Maraschi*
Maps: *Touring Editore*

Texts by the editing team of Touring Editore
Translation: *Studio Queens, Milano*
Design: *Studio Queens, Milan*

Cover photo: *G. Carfagna*

Advertising Office: *Caterina Indelicato*
Local Advertising: *Progetto*
www.progettosrl.it - info@progettosrl.it

Printing and Binding: *Giunti Industrie Grafiche, Iolo (Prato)*

Distribution
USA/CAN – *Publishers Group West*
UK/Ireland – *Portfolio Books*

Touring Club Italiano, Corso Italia 10, 20122 Milano
www.touringclub.it

© 2008 Touring Editore, Milan
www.touringclub.com

Code HK8AAM
ISBN-13: 978 – 88365 – 4489 – 9

Printed in May 2008

AUTHENTIC
Italy

TOURING CLUB
OF ITALY

SUMMARY

6 Italy: instructions for use

HERITAGE

This section explores the key places to visit in Italy, providing information about the most interesting sites or points of interest as well as giving a more detailed description of some cities and towns. The main cities are covered in specific sections of their own.

ITINERARIES

This selection of theme itineraries offers an unusual way to explore often unknown aspects of Italy. Not only can one learn more about a range of aspects, but also enrich one's knowledge of regional intricacies.

FOOD

*Italy is famous for its good food and wine: each region –
even each zone – has its own dishes and products that go
best with local wines. This section contains a wealth of
interesting information, covering all the different flavors
and tastes – often unexpected – of the various regions.*

PRACTICAL INFO

*This section is divided into two parts: the first part has
the addresses, telephone numbers and websites of the
museums in the guidebook; the second part contains a
selection of hotels and restaurants in the main centers
described in the other sections.*

ITALY: INSTRUCTIONS FOR USE

Italy is known throughout the world for the quantity and quality of its art treasures and for its natural beauty, but it is also famous for its inimitable lifestyle and fabulous cuisine and wines. The information and suggestions in this brief section will help foreign tourists not only to understand certain aspects of Italian life, but also to solve the everyday difficulties and the problems of a practical nature that inevitably crop up during any trip. This practical information is included in brief descriptions of various topics: public transport and how to purchase tickets; suggestions on how to drive in this country; the different types of rooms and accommodation in hotels; hints on how to use mobile phones and communication in general. This is followed by useful advice on how to meet your everyday needs and on shopping, as well as information concerning the cultural differences in the various regions. Lastly, there is a section describing the vast range of restaurants, bars, wine bars and pizza parlors.

TRANSPORTATION

From the airport to the city
Public transportation in major cities is easily accessible and simple to use. Both Malpensa Airport in Milan and Fiumicino Airport in Rome have trains and buses linking them to the city centers. At Malpensa, you can take a bus to the main train station or a train to Cadorna train station and subway stop.

Subways, buses, and trams
Access to the subways, buses, and trams requires a ticket (tickets are not sold on board but can be purchased at most newsstands and tobacco shops). The ticket is good for one ride and sometimes has a time limit (in the case of buses and trams). When you board a bus or tram, you are required to stamp your previously-acquired ticket in the time-stamping machine. Occasionally, a conductor will board the bus or tram and check everyone's ticket. If you haven't got one, or if it has not been time-stamped, you will have to pay a steep fine.

Trains
The Ferrovie dello Stato (Italian Railways) is among the best and most modern railway systems in Europe. Timetables and routes can be consulted and reservations can be made online at www.trenitalia.com. Many travel agents can also dispense tickets and help you plan your journey. Hard-copy schedules can be purchased at all newsstands and most bookstores. Automated ticket machines, which include easy-to-use instructions in English, are available in nearly all stations. They can be used to check schedules, makes reservations, and purchase tickets.
There are different types of train:
Eurostar Italia Trains *ES★* : fast connections between Italy's most important cities. The ticket includes seat booking charge;
Intercity *IC* and Espresso *E* Trains: local connections among Italy's towns and cities. Sometimes *IC* and *E* trains require seat booking. You can book your seat up to 3 hours before the train departure. The seat booking charge is of 3 euro.
Interregionale Trains *iR* move beyond regional boundaries. Among the combined local-transport services, the *iR* Trains are the fastest ones with the fewest number of stops. No seat booking available.
Diretto *D* and Regionale *R* Trains can circulate both within the regions and their bordering regions. No seat booking available.
Do not forget: You can only board trains in Italy with a valid ticket, which must be time-stamped before boarding; there are numerous time-stamping machines in every station. You cannot buy or stamp tickets on board.
If you don't have a ticket - or did not stamp before boarding - you will be liable to pay the full ticket price plus a 25 euro fine. If you produce a ticket that is not valid for the train or service you're using (i.e. one issued for a different train category at a different price, etc.) you will be asked to pay the difference with respect to the full ticket price, plus an 8 euro surcharge.

Taxis
Taxis are a convenient but expensive way to travel in Italian cities. There are taxi stands scattered throughout major cities. You cannot hail taxis on the street in Italy, but you can reserve taxis, in advance or immediately, by phone: consult the yellow pages for the number or ask your hotel reception desk or maitre d'hotel to call for you. Taxi drivers have the right to charge you a supplementary fee for luggage, as well as evening surcharges.

Driving
Especially when staying in the countryside, driving is a safe and convenient way to travel. And while it is best avoided for obvious reasons, driving in the cities is not as difficult as it may seem. It is important to be aware of

street signs and speed limits, and many cities have zones where only limited traffic is allowed in order to accommodate pedestrians. Although an international driver's license is not required, it is advisable. ACI and similar associations provide this service to members.

The fuel distribution network is reasonably distributed all over the territory. All service stations have unleaded gasoline ("benzina verde") and diesel fuel ("gasolio"). Opening time is 7am to12:30 and 15 to 19:30; on motorways the service is 24 hours a day.

Type of roads in Italy: The Autostrada (for example A14) is the main highway system in Italy and is similar to the Interstate highway system in the US and the motorway system in the UK. Shown on our Touring Club Italiano 1:200,000 road maps as black. The Autostrada are toll highways; you pay to use them. The Strada Statale (for example SS54) is a fast moving road that may have one or more lanes in each direction. Shown on our Touring Club Italiano 1:200,000 road maps as red. Strada Provinciale (for example SP358) can be narrow, slow and winding roads. They are usually one lane in each direction. Shown on our Touring Club Italiano 1:200,000 road maps as yellow. Strada Comunale (for ex-

ample SC652) is a local road connecting the main town with its sorrounding.

Speed limits: 130 kmph on the Autostrada, 110 kmph on main highways, 90 kmph outside of towns, 50 kmph in towns.

Do not forget:
- Wear your seat belt at all times;
- Do not use the cellular phone while driving;
- Have your headlights on at all times when driving outside of cities;
- The drunk driving laws are strict - do not drink and drive;
- In case of an accident you are not allowed to get out of your car unless you are wearing a special, high-visibility, reflective jacket.

ACCOMMODATION

Hotels

In Italy it is common practice for the reception desk to register your passport, and only registered guests are allowed to use the rooms. All hotels use the official star classification system, from 5-star luxury hotel to 1 star accommodation.

Room rates are based on whether they are for single ("camera singola") or double ("camera

WHAT IS THE TOURING CLUB OF ITALY?

Long Tradition, Great Prestige

For over 110 years, the Touring Club of Italy (TCI) has offered travelers the most detailed and comprehensive source of travel information available on Italy. The Touring Club of Italy was founded in 1894 with the aim of developing the social and cultural values of tourism and promoting the conservation and enjoyment of the country's national heritage, landscape and environment.

Advantages of Membership

Today, TCI offers a wide rage of travel services to assist and support members with the highest level of convenience and quality. Now you can discover the unique

charms of Italy with a distinct insider's advantage. Enjoy exclusive money saving offers with a TCI membership. Use your membership card for discounts in thousands of restaurants, hotels, spas, campgrounds, museums, shops and markets.

How to Join

It's quick and easy to join. Apply for your membership online at www.touringclub.it Your membership card will arrive within three weeks and is valid for discounts across Italy for the entire year. Get your card before you go and start saving as soon as you arrive. Euro 25 annual membership fee includes priority mail postage for membership card and

materials. Just one use of the card will more than cover the cost of membership.

Benefits
- Exclusive car rental rates with Hertz
- Discounts at select Esso gas stations
- 20% discount on TCI guidebooks and maps purchased in TCI bookstores or directly online at:
www.touringclub.com
- Preferred rates and discounts available at thousands of locations in Italy: Hotels - B&B's - Villa Rentals - Campgrounds -TCI Resorts - Spas - Restaurants - Wineries - Museums - Cinemas - Theaters - Music Festivals - Shops - Craft Markets - Ferries - Cruises - Theme Parks - Botanical Gardens

doppia") occupancy. In every room you will find a list of the hotel rates (generally on the back of the door). While 4- and 5-star hotels have double beds, most hotels have only single beds. Should you want a double bed, you have to ask for a "letto matrimoniale". All hotels have rooms with bathrooms; only 1-star establishments usually have only shared bathrooms.

Most hotel rates include breakfast ("prima colazione"), but you can request to do without it, thus reducing the rate. Breakfast is generally served in a communal room and comprises a buffet with pastries, bread with butter and jam, cold cereals, fruit, yoghurt, coffee, and fruit juice. The hotels for families and in tourist localities also offer "mezza pensione", or half board, in which breakfast and dinner are included in the price.

It's always a good idea to check when a hotel's annual closing period is, especially if you are planning a holiday by the sea.

Farm stays

Located only in the countryside, and generally on a farm, "agriturismo" – a network of farm holiday establishments – is part of a growing trend in Italy to honor local gastronomic and wine traditions, as well as countryside traditions. These farms offer meals prepared with ingredients cultivated exclusively on site: garden-grown vegetables, homemade cheese and local recipes. Many of these places also provide lodging, one of the best ways to experience the "genuine" Italian lifestyle.

Bed & Breakfast

This form of accommodation provides bed and breakfast in a private house. There are over 5,000 b&bs, classified in 3 categories, and situated both in historic town centers, as well as in the outskirts and the countryside. Rooms for guests are always well-furnished, but not all of them have en suite bathrooms. It is well-recommended to check the closing of the open-all-year accommodation services and restaurants, because they could have a short break during the year (usually no longer than a fortnight).

COMMUNICATIONS

Nearly everyone in Italy owns a cellular phone. Although public phones are still available, they seem to be ever fewer and farther between. If you wish to use public phones, you will find them in subway stops, bars, along the street, and phone centers generally located in the city center. Phone cards and pre-paid

phone cards can be purchased at most newsstands and tobacco shops, and can also be acquired at automated tellers. For European travelers, activating personal cellular coverage is relatively simple, as it is in most cases for American and Australian travelers as well. Cellular phones can also be rented in Italy from TIM, the Italian national phone company. For information, visit its website at www.tim.it. When traveling by car through the countryside, a cellular phone can really come in handy.

Note that when dialing in Italy, you must always dial the prefix (e.g., 02 for Milan, 06 for Rome) even when making a local call. For cellular phones, however, the initial zero is always dropped. Freephone numbers always start with "800". For calls abroad from Italy, it's a good idea to buy a special pre-paid international phone card, which is used with a PIN code.

Internet access

Cyber cafés have sprung up all over Italy and today you can find one on nearly every city block. The Italian national phone company, TIM, has also begun providing internet access at many of its public phone centers.

EATING AND DRINKING

The bar

The Italian "bar" is a multi-faceted, all-purpose establishment for drinking, eating and socializing, where you can order an espresso, have breakfast, and enjoy a quick sandwich for lunch or even a hot meal. You can often buy various items here (sometimes even stamps, cigarettes, phone cards, etc.). Bear in mind that table service ("servizio a tavola") includes a surcharge. At most bars, if you choose to sit, a waiter will take your order. Every bar should have a list of prices posted behind or near the counter; if the bar offers table service, the price list should also include the extra fee for this.

Lunch at bars will include, but is not limited to, "panini," sandwiches with crusty bread, usually with cured meats such as "prosciutto" (salt-cured ham), "prosciutto cotto" (cooked ham), and cheeses such as mozzarella topped with tomato and basil. Then there are "tramezzini" (finger sandwiches) with tuna, cheese, or vegetables, etc. Often the "panini" and other savory sandwiches (like stuffed flatbread or "focaccia") are heated before being served. Naturally, the menu at bars varies according to the region: in Bologna you will find "piadine" (flatbread similar to pita) with Swiss chard; in Palermo there are "arancini" (fried rice balls stuffed with ground meat); in Genoa you will find that even the most unassuming bar serves some of the best "focaccia" in all Italy. Some bars also include a "tavola calda". If you see this sign in a bar window, it means that hot dishes like pasta and even entrées are served.

A brief comment on coffee and cappuccino: Italians never serve coffee with savory dishes or sandwiches, and they seldom drink cappuccino outside of breakfast (although they are happy to serve it at any time).

While English- and Irish-type pubs are frequented by beer lovers and young people in Italy, there are also American bars where long drinks and American cocktails are served.

Breakfast at the bar

Breakfast in Italy generally consists of some type of pastry, most commonly a "brioche" – a croissant either filled with cream or jam, or plain – and a cappuccino or espresso. Although most bars do not offer American coffee, you can ask for a "caffè lungo" or "caffè americano", both of which resemble the American coffee preferred by the British and Americans. Most bars have a juicer to make a "spremuta", freshly squeezed orange or grapefruit juice.

Lunch and Dinner

Wine is generally served at mealtime, and while finer restaurants have excellent wine lists (some including vintage wines), ordering the house table wine generally brings good results (a house Chianti to accompany your Florentine steak in Tuscany, a sparkling Prosecco paired with your creamed stockfish and polenta in Venice, a dry white wine with pasta dressed with sardines and wild fennel fronds in Sicily). The most sublime culinary experience in Italy is achieved by matching the local foods with the appropriate local wines: wisdom dictates that a friendly waiter will be flattered by your request for his recommendation on what to eat and drink. Mineral water is also commonly served at meals and can be "gassata" (sparkling) or "naturale" (still).

Whether at an "osteria" (a tavern), a "trattoria" (a home-style restaurant), or a "ristorante" (a proper restaurant), the service of lunch and dinner generally consists of – but is not limited to – the following: "antipasti" or appetizers; "primo piatto" or first course (i.e., pasta, rice, or soup); "secondo piatto" or main course (i.e., meat or seafood); "contorno" or side-dish, served with the main course (i.e., vegetables or salad); "formaggi", "frutta", and "dolci" (i.e., cheeses, fruit, and dessert); caffè or espresso coffee, perhaps spiked with a shot of grappa.

The pizzeria

The pizzeria is in general one of the most economical, democratic, and satisfying culinary experiences in Italy. Everyone eats at the pizzeria: young people, families, couples, locals and tourists alike. Generally, each person orders her/his own pizza, and while the styles of crust and toppings will vary from region to region (some of the best pizzas are served in Naples and Rome), the acid test of any pizzeria is the Margherita, topped simply with cheese and tomato sauce. Beer, sparkling or still water, and Coca Cola are the beverages commonly served with pizza. Some restaurants include a pizza menu.

The wine bar (enoteca)

More than one English-speaking tourist in Italy has wondered why the wine bar is called an enoteca in other countries and the English term is used in Italy: the answer lies somewhere in the mutual fondness that Italians and English speakers have for one another. Wine bars have become popular in recent years in the major cities (especially in Rome, where you can find some of the best). The wine bar is a great place to sample different local wines and eat a light, tapas-style dinner.

CULTURAL DIVERSITY

Whenever you travel, not only are you a guest of your host country, but you are also a representative of your home country.

As a general rule, courtesy, consideration, and respect are always appreciated by guests and their hosts alike. Italians are famous for their hospitality and experience will verify this felicitous stereotype: perhaps nowhere else in Europe are tourists and visitors received more warmly. Italy is a relatively "new" country. Its borders, as we know them today, were established only in 1861 when it became a monarchy under the House of Savoy. After WWII, Italy became a Republic and now it is one of the member states of the European Union.

One of the most fascinating aspects of Italian culture is that, even as a unified country, local tradition still prevails over a universally Italian national identity. Some jokingly say that the only time that Venetians, Milanese, Florentines, Neapolitans, and Sicilians feel like Italians is when the national football team plays in international competitions. From their highly localized dialects to the foods they eat, from their religious celebration to their politics, Italians proudly maintain their local heritage. This is one of the reasons why the Piedmontese continue to prefer their beloved Barolo wine and their white truffles, the Umbrians their rich Sagrantino wine and black truffles, the Milanese their risotto and panettone, the Venetians their stockfish and polenta, the Bolognese their lasagne and pumpkin ravioli, the Florentines their bread soups and steaks cooked rare, the Abruzzese their excellent fish broth and seafood, the Neapolitans their mozzarella, basil, pizza, and pasta.

As a result of its rich cultural diversity, the country's population also varies greatly in its customs from region to region, city to city, town to town. As you visit different cities and regions throughout Italy, you will see how the local personality and character of the Italians change as rapidly as the landscape does. Having lived for millennia with their great diversity and rich, highly heterogeneous culture, the Italians have taught us many things, foremost among them the age-old expression, "When in Rome, do as the Romans do."

NATIONAL HOLIDAYS

New Year's Day (January, 1), Epiphany (January, 6), Easter Monday (day after Easter Sunday), Liberation Day (April, 25), Labour Day (May, 1), Italian Republic Day (June, 2), Assumption (August, 15), All Saints' Day (November, 1), Immaculate Conception (December, 8), Christmas Day and Boxing Day (December, 25-26). In addition to these holidays, each city also has a holiday to celebrate its patron saint's feast day, usually with lively, local celebrations. Shops and services in large cities close on national holidays and for the week of the 15 of August.

EVERYDAY NEEDS

State tobacco shops and pharmacies

Tobacco is available only at state licensed tobacco shops. These vendors ("tabaccheria"), often incorporated in a bar, also sell stamps. Since 11 January 2005 smoking is forbidden in all so-called public places – unless a separately ventilated space is constructed – over 90% of the country's restaurants and bars.

Medicines can be purchased only in pharmacies ("farmacia") in Italy. Pharmacists are very knowledgeable about common ailments and can generally prescribe a treatment for you on the spot. Opening time is 8:30-12:30 and 15:30-19:30 but in any case there is always a pharmacy open 24 hours and during holidays.

Shopping and Tax Free

Every locality in Italy offers tourists characteristic shops, markets, and even boutiques. Iin general, shops are open from 9 to 12:30 and from 15/16 to 19/20, but in large cities they usually have no lunchtime break.

Non-EU citizens can obtain a reimbursement for IVA (goods and services tax) paid on purchases over €155, for goods which are exported within 90 days, in shops which display the relevant sign. IVA is always automatically included in the price of any purchase, and ranges from 20% to 4% depending on the item. The shop issues a reimbursement voucher to present when you leave the country (at a frontier or airport). For purchases in shops affiliated to 'Tax Free Shopping', IVA may be reimbursed directly at international airports.

Banks and post offices

Italian banks are open Monday to Friday, from 8:30 to 13:30 and then from 15 to 16. However, the afternoon business hours may vary. Post offices are open from Monday to Saturday, from 8:30 to 13:30 (12:30 on Saturday). In the larger towns there are also some offices open in the afternoon.

Currency and Credit cards

Effective 1 January 2002, the currency used in many European Union countries is the euro. Coins are in denominations of 1, 2, 5, 10, 20 and 50 cents and 1 and 2 euros; banknotes are in denominations of 5, 10, 20, 50, 100, 200 and 500 euros. All the main credit cards are generally accepted, but some smaller enterprises may do not provide this service. Foreign tourists can obtain cash using credit cards at automatic teller machines.

Time

All Italy is in the same time zone, which is six hours ahead of Eastern Standard Time in the USA. Daylight saving time is used from March to October, when watches and clocks are set an hour ahead of standard time.

Passports and vaccinations

Citizens of EU countries can enter Italy without frontier checks. Citizens of Australia, Canada, New Zealand, and the United States can enter Italy with a valid passport and need not have a visa for a stay of less than 90 days. No vaccinations are necessary.

Payment and tipping

When you sit down at a restaurant you are generally charged a "coperto" or cover charge (1.5 to 3 euros), for service and the bread. Tipping is not customary in Italy. Beware of unscrupulous restaurateurs who add a space on their clients' credit card receipt for a tip, while it has already been included in the cover charge.

This guidebook moves from region to region and from north to south, exploring the most beautiful places in Italy, including some spectacular art, delightful mountain landscapes and places of natural wonder. The "Heritage" section (red) looks at the main tourist destinations. Each chapter opens with an overview of the key features of the zone and then, in the "Not to be missed" paragraph, the main places are highlighted. In many cases, this is followed by more detailed information on the main town in the area. The major Italian cities and places have their own chapter. There are also city plans for Milan, Venice, Florence, Rome and Naples. Heritage is the biggest section and it is followed by two smaller sections, also divided by region. First, there is the "Itineraries" section (light blue), which has suggestions for artistic or nature tours, often taking one off the beaten track. Then, there is "Food" (green), which contains a brief but comprehensive overview of the region's food and wine, including famous dishes, special products and excellent wines. The last section contains practical information and useful addresses: museums mentioned in the guide and a carefully chosen selection of hotels and restaurants in the main towns and cities.

Heritage

- **The most interesting places to visit**
- **Not to be missed**
- **Key towns and cities**

NOTE: stars are used in the text to emphasize the importance of places and art-works:
** **very important**
* **important**

(➡ see below)
(see below)
indicates places described in detail

Itineraries

- **Historical and artistic itineraries**
- **Nature parks**
- **Ski areas and beaches**

Food

- **Traditional regional dishes**
- **Cured meats, cheese and local products**
- **The best wines from each region**

NOTE: European Quality Labels
DOP (Protected Designation of Origin)
IGP (Protected Geographical Indication)

Around 1750, a physician from Bern, J. Georg Zimmermann, wrote that when standing before mountains, "the imagination soars to greater heights." In the face of the "grandeur of nature, amid vast masses of ice, when dangling over bottomless chasms or wandering past thundering torrents and through deep forests," the mind "begins to ponder the nullity of human strength." It is hard to say whether any of us today would be able to summon such a pre-Romantic vision, but this may be as close as we get: the sight of Cervino (also called the Matterhorn). Cervino was first climbed, up the Swiss side, on 14 July 1865,

The wonderful location of Breuil-Cervinia.

by English mountaineer E. Whymper, with a party of six (four died on the way down). On the Valle d'Aosta side, on the same day, Abbot A. Gorret, J. A. Carrel, and J. B. Bich were just beneath the peak, which they attained, a close second, on the 17th century. Along this route, for many reasons, getting there is as enthralling as actually arriving due to the stark Alpine landscape of the lower Valle d'Aosta and the feudal, late-Gothic atmosphere of the castles; then, as if you were climbing a staircase, you go from lake to lake, through meadows, villages, through the lovely Valtournenche.

NOT TO BE MISSED
Pont-Saint-Martin the bridge over the Lys is Roman (1C BC), as is the stretch of road just beyond **Donnas**, with an arch cut into the rock. **Bard**, locked in a narrow gorge, over which towers a spectacular fortress, was rebuilt in the 19th century. **Verres**, with the square 14th century. Castello degli Challand, atop a lofty crag. **Issogne**: the castle may be the loveliest in the entire Valle d'Aosta. **Montjovet**: looming over the town are the ruins of a castle. **Saint-Vincent** (➡ see below), an elegant spa resort which hosts one of Italy's four municipal casinos; its popularity dates back to 1770, when an abbot discovered the curative properties of the springs. **Châtillon** is a market and manufacturing town at the mouth of the Valtournenche. On a rocky crag overlooking the Dora stands the Ussel castle. **Valtournenche** is perched high in the valley of the same name; you can descend to the Gouffre des Busserailles, a gorge of the Marmore River. **Breuil-Cervinia** (➡ see below), renowned mountain resort, is surrounded by rocky peaks sheathed in ice and has a fine view of Cervino.

SAINT-VINCENT
Famed since Antiquity for the beneficial effects of its thermal water, it also has fine monuments. Some of a **Roman bridge*** has survived, including a ramp at one end. The water of the **spa complex**, set in a panoramic position, has given the town a reputation as a spa center, attracting many famous people. The **Fons Salutis spa complex** still has a 20th-century facade whereas the interior and the infrastructures are of later date. From the garden terrace in front of the building there is a splendid view over Saint-Vincent and up the Dora Valley. The **parish church*** stands on the site of a large Roman building (4-5C, the remains can be seen underground) and is built on a Romanesque plan. The oldest part (11C) is the crypt. The imposing **bell tower** has a Romanesque base, with additions higher up (16-17C). At the beginning of the left

aisle, the windows belong to the **Museo Parrocchiale di S. Vincenzo**. Its collection includes wooden statues, a stained-glass window of Flemish origin and sacred objects. Finally, the **Casino** can be reached by walking along the pedestrian Via Chanoux, then along Viale Piemonte. Near the Casino is the **Grand Hotel Billia**, a beautiful Art-Nouveau building.

BREUIL-CERVINIA
The town is one of Italy's most prestigious resorts. It is situated below the highly spectacular peak of **Cervino****, a mountain which is unique in terms of its shape and beauty. Higher up, near the top of the cablecar of the Little Mt Cervino, is the highest and largest **ice-cave** in the world (with a diameter of 26 m, and an average height of 5 m). The cave can be reached by walking along a tunnel 50 m long, dug out of the ice.

THE AOSTA AREA

In the Valle d'Aosta region the landscape, whether natural or manmade, varies widely. The main valley, fed by the Dora Baltea, ranges from a valley floor, at Pont-Saint-Martin, just over 300 m, to the 1,000 m of Pré-Saint-Didier. On either side, ranks of mountains are dotted with fields, vineyards, and warehouses; then there are tiny villages, perched high on mountain slopes, with no apparent means of reaching them. There are patches of high mountain meadows, set amidst forests, naked boulders, little waterfalls that freeze solid in winter, and ice raking the sky. Castles and once-mighty ruins line the valley and rise on dizzying ridges, guardians of an ancient and violent history. Trade between France and Italy continues to flow through this valley, along with hikers, mountaineers, and skiers. Mont Blanc, or Monte Bianco, towers at the end of this route; scaled for the first time on 8 August 1786, it can be reached by a cableway.

NOT TO BE MISSED

Chambave is a small town surrounded by vineyards. Just north, on the road to Saint-Denis, are the ruins of the Cly castle, atop a panoramic crag. The 14th-century Fenis castle is certainly the most intact of Valle d'Aosta's castles. Further on, at Nus, the 13th-century Pilato castle; another castle stands at Quart (2 km along the road that runs off to the right of the quarter of Villair). **Aosta** (➡ see below), with its walls virtually intact, the collegiate church of S. Orso with its Romanesque cloister, and its odd mountain-urban air, is a city of remarkable artistic, architectural, and historical value. **Sarre:** the castle, rebuilt in the 18th century, has remarkable interiors; another castle, at Saint-Pierre, has a museum of natural science. **La Salle** houses vineyards that climb up to 1,000 m, and produces fine white wines. **Pré-Saint-Didier** from the hot springs, renowned among the ancient Romans, you can walk down to the dramatic steep gorge, of the Dora di Verney. **Courmayeur** (➡ see below): the oldest and best known ski resort in the Italian Alps, is also a capital of mountaineering; the peak of Mont Blanc is 9 km from town as the crow flies; excursions first took place in the 19th century. **Entreves:** from La Palud take a cableway up to the Punta Helbronner (3,642 m), and then up over the dizzying rock spires of Mont Blanc, to Chamonix (France).

AOSTA

All around rises a majestic mountain landscape. In the outskirts of town are signs of recent development, the product of the tourist industry linked to the mountain resorts of the upper valley. International traffic with France and Switzerland has grown greatly since the completion of the Monte Bianco (Mont Blanc) and the Gran San Bernardo (Great St Bernard) tunnels. Further growth has come about through the city's status as capital of this autonomous region. From the outskirts, you proceed to the city's ancient heart, amid the timeworn stones of the "Rome of the Alps," ancient "Augusta Praetoria." Here we also find remarkable relics of the Middle Ages, a "borderland" artistic culture, and the stern, tranquil atmosphere of a mountain town.

Aosta: Arch of Augustus.

Arch of Augustus**, located outside the walls, this Roman arch was built at the time of the founding of the city (25 BC), and was dedicated to Augustus Caesar. It has a single vaulted passageway framed by Corinthian pilasters. The Crucifix under the arch is a copy of a 14th-century original set and now in the Treasury of the cathedral. The square has a fine panoramic view of the surrounding mountains. Not far off, beyond the Buthier River, is a single-span Roman bridge that once crossed a mountain torrent, which shifted its course in the 13th century.

S. Orso*, the largest medieval complex in Aosta, in a secluded corner of town, is dominated by a Romanesque bell tower* (1131), with a century-old linden tree. Note the collegiate church and the Priory. The collegiate church, founded in early times (994-1025), was rebuilt more than once, most recently in the 15th century. The facade has a pointed-arch portal. The interior is Gothic, with handsome cross-vaults and frescoes; fragments of older frescoes (11C) in the high areas of the nave can be seen in the attic (enquire in sacristy). In the presbytery is a carved wooden choir* (late 15C). Note the 11th-century crypt, with five little aisles. The Treasury has a rich collection of precious medieval objects. From the right aisle (or from a passageway to the right of the church) you can enter the Romanesque cloister** (12C): arches and vaults (15C), set on slender columns with intricate carved capitals.

Priory of S. Orso, a picturesque priory, built between 1494 and 1506, has elegant crossed terracotta windows and an octagonal tower.

S. Lorenzo, a passageway behind the church of S. Lorenzo, facing S. Orso, leads to the remains of an Early Christian complex from the 5th century, which have been roofed over.

Porta Pretoria*, this gate formed part of the ancient city walls (1C BC). It is made of enormous square-hewn blocks, forming a double curtain wall with three openings (buried about 2.5 m deep by the rising level of the streets). To the left, note the massive Torre dei Signori di Quart.

Parco Archeologico del Teatro Romano*, the ruins of this Roman theater include a stretch of the tall facade wall (22 m) with several rows of windows, and the lower section of the tiers and the skene. To the north of the theater, in the courtyard of the convent of S. Caterina, dating from the 13th century, you can see ruins of the Roman Amphitheater.

Terme Pubbliche Romane, situated in an area behind the city hall, these Roman Baths include apsidal rooms, a calidarium, and a tepidarium.

Piazza della Cattedrale, occupies in part the old site of the Roman Forum, remains of which can be seen in the enclosure alongside the Cathedral: below street level you can see the left side of the podium of a temple; you can descend into the cryptoporticus, which runs around three sides of the Forum, part of which is under the church.

Cathedral*, surviving from the original Romanesque version of this cathedral (11-12C) are two apsidal bell towers; the rest of the church was rebuilt repeatedly from the 15th century, the facade dates from 1526. The interior is Gothic: note the stained glass windows, the mosaic floor of the presbytery (12-13C), the Gothic wooden choir* (ca. 1469),

and the funerary monument to Count Tommaso II of Savoy (14-15C), in the apse.

Beneath the arches of the apse – where, under a glass floor, you can also see the remains of one of the five Romanesque apses – is the Museo del Tesoro (Treasury Museum), with collections of architectural fragments and artworks from the Cathedral and other structures, including an ivory diptych depicting the Emperor Honorius (406), reliquaries (silver reliquary of S. Grato, 15C), a wooden altar frontal with 20 carved panels, a Crucifix (14C) that once stood beneath the Arch of Augustus, sculptures in stone and wood, goldwork, glass, enamel, and so on. From the aisle you can enter the cloister* (1460).

Museo Archeologico Regionale. In Piazza Roncas, near the former Convent of the Visitazione, this archeology museum houses a collection ranging from the Neolithic to Roman times, from digs in surrounding areas.

Mura, these Roman city walls date from the reign of Augustus and form a rectangle (727.5 x 574 m). They were punctuated with 20 towers, which are particularly well preserved on the west side (Torre del Lebbroso and the Tour Fromage (Cheese tower), near the Teatro Romano, both used for temporary exhibitions), and on the south side, with the medieval Torre Bramafam (13C) and, near the railway station, the Roman Torre del Pailleron.

Area Megalitica, in the quarter of Saint-Martin-de-Corléan, to the east of the center, near the church of S. Martino, there stretches an archeological site with megalithic tombs, lines of anthropomorphic steles, and altars from the 3rd millennium BC.

Villa Suburbana Romana, recently discovered to the north of town, in the area called Consolata, this Roman villa from the last republican period features remains of mosaic floors and walls.

THE COGNE VALLEY

This is one of the most charming valleys in the area and becomes obvious as you drive towards it. The road climbs gradually higher between the forested slopes on either side. The sharp ridges and the jagged peaks of Mt La Grivola and Mt Grand Nomenon appear up ahead above a succession of outcrops and expanses of forest. We are in the eastern part of the Graian Alps. After crossing the Grand Eyvia Stream, the road passes the ruins of two disused iron foundries, which formerly played an important role in the valley.

Cogne lies in a broad, sun-kissed hollow surrounded by woods, on the northern edge of the Parco Nazionale del Gran Paradiso. This is one of the places where you can access the park. One of the delightful features of the town is the lovely and unspoiled **field of Sant'Orso**, a triangular piece of land that has been saved from the clutches of the developers. In the oldest part of the **historic center**, slightly higher up than the rest of the town, are some traditional rural houses which have central courtyards with earth floors. Some of them have pointed doors and windows and wrought-iron decoration. Near the parish church of S. Orso, the statue of the saint on the facade dates from the early 17th century. The church contains late 17th-century Baroque altars and an aluminum statue of St Barbara. In Piazza del Municipio (where there is an incredible view of Mt Gran Paradiso), the iron fountain was cast in 1809. The **Museo Minerario Alpino**, housed in the former mining village, describes the long-standing relationship between Cogne and the local mines which exploited the vast local deposits of magnetite (possibly the most prized of all the iron-ore minerals). The mines certainly existed in the 15th century and are possibly even older. They were finally closed down in 1979.

COURMAYEUR

Situated in the upper reaches of the Valdigne, where the presence of the gigantic Mt Blanc massif is overwhelming, **Verrand** is an old town with marvelous views and an interesting setting. Not far away is Courmayeur, the local skiing and mountaineering capital . It is situated below Mount Blanc in a beautiful valley of fir trees and larches. The **old center** has the **church of Ss. Pantaleone e Valentino** and a fine Romanesque bell tower with a spire with one-, two- and three-light windows. Inside the church is a Neo-Classic black marble altar and two fine Baroque wooden altars with twisted columns. The building opposite the church is also interesting and is the headquarters of the Alpine Guides. It also houses the **Museo Alpino Duca degli Abruzzi** where you can find out everything you ever wanted to know about mountaineering, including equipment, photographs, diaries and other information about climbing in the Alps and international expeditions. In the town center, **Via Roma** is a busy shopping street with restaurants and cafés, while **Via Marconi** is an old street that has been saved from the developers. In the piazza, **Torre Malluquin**, is all that survives of the 14th-century castle.

HIGHLIGHTS

THE WALSER

A wave of migration that lasted 300 years, ending in the 15th century, brought groups of farmers from an area of Switzerland on the far side of the Alps, to the valleys on the south side of the Monte Rosa. Laden with household goods, farm tools and equipment, families of farming folk crossed the Alps by narrow mule-paths in search of land to cultivate and colonize. This was the beginning of the epic of the Walser, as these people were called by the people with whom they came into contact, after their land of origin (Valais). In the Valle d'Aosta the Walser settled mainly in the Gressoney Valley and the Val d'Ayas, in unused land, in areas which were inaccessible and unpopulated. It was precisely the fact that the Walser communities remained isolated that enabled them to preserve their language, traditions and culture for centuries. Even today, exploring the lands of the Walser means taking a step back in time. Their houses are striking in their simplicity. They have broad balconies which were used for drying and storing hay. The ground floor was used as a cowshed, the first floor contained the bedrooms, and the top floor was used for storage. The elegant costumes traditionally worn by women were made of black and red fabric, and were worn with a white blouse decorated with beautiful lace trimmings and hats embroidered with gold filigree. Their language is also very interesting. Philologists have traced it back to an early branch of modern German. At Issime they still speak a dialect known as Töitschu, whereas, at Gressoney, they speak Titsch, which resembles modern German more closely. In order to preserve their sense of identity and in memory of the great migration which spread the Walser people all over the southern edge of Monte Rosa, today, many young people from the Walser villages follow the route known as the Great Walser Footpath. Using very old paths, they make an interesting tour of the mountain massif not only in Italy, but also making forays into Switzerland, Austria and Liechtenstein.

SKIING IN VALLE D'AOSTA

LA THUILE

The last ski resort before the French border, La Thuile stands in the center of a vast bowl trapped between the Venoise and Mont Blanc massifs and within sight of the majestic outline of the Testa del Rutor. It is one of the most popular winter resorts in the Vallée area, with good accommodation and modern facilities. However, the hamlet has maintained its traditional mountain identity, with a welcoming and pleasant feel. The skiing is on the southern slopes of Chaz-Dura and is part of one of the largest ski areas in the Alps. The cross-border link to the French resort of La Rosière means it is possible to ski on two sides of the Alps with a single skipass. In total, including both the Italian and French sides, there are 150 km of ski runs, accessible via a series of modern lifts. In addition, there is a free skibus (shuttle service) and children can enjoy themselves either at the 'baby park in the snow' or the 'miniclub'. La Thuile also has something for cross-country skiers. Besides the training area, there are four trails (of 3.5, 7.5 and 10 km) near the resort and in the Petosan bowl that head through thick woods and across sun-drenched plateaus where one can enjoy the majestic view of Mont Blanc.

COURMAYEUR

This elegant ski area at the foot of Mont Blanc sits in the shadow of four soaring mountains, Grand Golliaz, the Léchaud point, Aiguille des Glaciers and Mt Dolent, and runs along the two deep valleys of Veny and Ferret, where there are six large glaciers. It is one of the most famous ski resorts in the world, largely because of the spectacular, varied ski runs and lifts, and the high standard of the accommodation. This ski area in the Mont Blanc Valley includes La Salle, a relaxing hamlet where there is good downhill skiing and lovely excursions, Morgex, which has some lovely cross-country skiing trails in the Arpy Valley, and Pré-Saint-Didier, home to one of the most spectacular ravines in Valle d'Aosta. The skiing is on two slopes, both with different characteristics: Veny has wide, wooded runs while Checrouit cuts across vast, grassy plateaus. Indeed, lovers of the snowboarding can try a special cross-border run at Plan de la Gabba: 500 m of cambered turns, jumps and moguls. For lovers of heli freeriding, Courmayeur has a range of options on Mont Blanc.

BREUIL-CERVINIA

Lying at the foot of the pyramid-shaped granite mass of Cervino (Matterhorn), Breuil-Cervinia is one of the best known ski resorts in the Alps, a white expanse that runs from 3,480 m at Plateau Rosà, touches the 3,883 m of Piccolo Cervino and climbs the 4,478 m of the summit of Cervino. Breuil-Cervinia, a trendy, modern and innovative skiing capital, has an excellent network of lifts.

The Breuil-Cervinia ski area is one of the most beautiful in the Alps, with 60 snow-covered, well-groomed runs (many are covered by artificial snow spraying) that wind for over 350 km across the Breuil bowl, Valtournenche and Zermatt in an area straddling the Swiss-Italian border. The modern network of lifts makes it possible to get from Plan Maison to the Bontadini-Colle del Teodulo area and Plateau Rosà. From here, it is possible to take the Klein Matterhorn cableway, the highest in Europe, to Zermatt, or to head to Piccolo Cervino. From the Cime Bianche saddle, the Goillet chairlift takes you to the runs in the Valtournenche ski area, while the Bardoney and Cieloalto chairlifts take you up to some wonderful runs. Next to the Fornet di Plan Maison is the Indian Park, a true fun park on the snow that is aimed at snowboarders who love grooving to music. There is a 3 km cross-country skiing circuit, at 2,050 m, in the shadow of the

HIGHLIGHTS

MONTEROSASKI

This is one of the largest ski areas in the Alps, at the foot of Monte Rosa massif and between the peaks of three valleys: Ayas and Gressoney, in Valle d'Aosta, and Valsesia, in Piedmont. This area has 200 km of ski runs, ensuring a range of trails for all types of skiing. There is also a network of runs that takes in the major towns and villages, such as Champoluc, Gressoney-la-Trinité and Alagna Valsesia, and the more compact resorts of Brusson, Gressoney-Saint-Jean and Antagnod.

splendid Grandes Murailles and Cervino. The ski-mountaineering is also notable, with some good full day itineraries that explore the pristine, fresh snow. Finally, Cervinia has a proud history of professional Alpine guides – the ideal people to help you learn about winter mountaineering and ice-climbing.

VALTOURNENCHE

This ski resort is dominated by the imposing, easily identifiable bulk of Cervino (the Matterhorn) and the Grandes Murailles mountain chain. Since the 19th century, Valtournenche has been closely tied to some major mountain-climbing exploits: it was the starting point for the discovery of various, memorable routes to scale Cervino. The resort slowly became an increasingly important downhill skiing resort and, today, it is one of the largest ski areas in Valle d'Aosta. The skiing is in the vast bowl between Mt Roisetta and Gran Sometta, with the routes generally being easy or moderate. The useful skibus (shuttle) makes access to the lifts easy. Valtournenche has numerous runs, but there is also the link from the Superiore (upper) hill of Cime Bianche to the snowfields and lifts of Breuil-Cervinia and Zermatt, on the Swiss side of Cervino. Taken all together, this is one of the largest skiing zones in the Alps and makes it possible to spend entire skiing holidays without ever repeating a run. In addition, if you want to get in some summer skiing, you should head to the the Italian-Swiss Plateau Rosà glacier. The options for ski-mountaineers are plentiful.

VAL D'AYAS

Val d'Ayas is dominated by the Monte Rosa mountain chain and has 14 peaks that soar over 4,000 m. As you head up the valley, you come to Brusson, home to international cross-country skiing competitions, the village of Antagnod, famed for its wide, sunny runs, and Ayas. Champoluc, the last village in the Evançon Valley, stands in a lovely bowl in the shadow of the Monte Rosa massif. The skiing at Champoluc-Frachey is on the western slope of the Bettaforca hill, which has numerous runs, including the Contenerey one and the taxing Larici. Beyond the hill lies the Gressoney Valley, and then Staffal. In addition to the Champoluc lifts, there are the Palasinaz ski runs, at Brusson, and the Antagnod lifts. There are many ski-mountaineering trails, especially on the Palasina point, which can be reached using the Estoul lifts, not far from Brusson. The glaciers in Val d'Ayas are the setting for the famous Trofeo Mezzalama, the oldest race in the whole Alps.

THE GRESSONEY VALLEY

The Gressoney Valley, also known as the Lys Valley, is located at the foot of the imposing Testa Grigia and surrounded by a glacier. It is also the central valley in the vast Monterosaski area. There are two main resorts: Gressoney-la-Trinité, at the head of the valley, and Gressoney-Saint-Jean, which achieved fame as early as the last century and was chosen by Queen Margherita of Savoy as the setting for her castle. The Gressoney-la-Trinité resort has 53 km of runs, including some covered by artificial snow spraying; there are modern lifts on the Bettaforca hill (connection to Val d'Ayas), the Gabiet slope and the Jolanda point, leading up to 3,000 m at the Salati pass, which is the starting point for the link to the Alagna Valsesia lifts. Staffal is the starting point for thrilling ski-mountaineering trails (and off-piste skiing) that go up Monte Rosa to the Gnifetti point and the Regina Margherita refuge hut, the highest in the Alps.

PILA

The Pila bowl lies in a delightful natural setting, amid endless larch and fir forests. Many of the main mountains in the western Alps are visible: Mont Blanc, Grand Combin, Cervino and Monte Rosa. The bowl is almost like a natural balcony overlooking Aosta from beneath a chain of mountains that includes Mt Emilius, the Valletta point and the Tza Setze Couis and Drinc hills. This winter resort was built specifically for skiing, that is, it was created basically from scratch as a ski resort, and has various forms of accommodation (hotels, self-catering apartments and other resort accommodation) right behind the ski runs. The 70 km of well-groomed runs make this a skiing paradise. There are 25 runs encompassing most levels of difficulty. In addition, there are comfortable lifts and snow cannons, ensuring artificial snow can be sprayed, if needed. Pila is also an ideal location for skiers who love carving (Bosco, Bellevue run) and for those who are fans of telemarking or boarding. There are some ski-mountaineering trails, of varying difficulty and length, that start from the hermitage of S. Grato or the slopes of Mt Emilius. For snowboards there is a snowboard park with a funbox, rails and jumps for daring acrobatic flights as well as slides and a spectacular halfpipe made with permanent structures dug into the ground.

GRAN PARADISO NATIONAL PARK

PARCO NAZIONALE DEL GRAN PARADISO

PROVINCES OF AOSTA AND TURIN

AREA: 70,318 HECTARES. INCLUDES THE MOUNTAINS OF THE GRAIE ALPS AND THE SURROUNDING VALLEYS SLOPING DOWN TO THE DORA BALTEA AND ORCO RIVERS.

HEADQUARTERS: ENTE PARCO NAZIONALE GRAN PARADISO, VIA DELLA ROCCA 47, TORINO, TEL. 0118606211

VISITORS' CENTERS: NOASCA TOWN HALL, PARK TOURIST OFFICE, TEL. 0124901070

WEB SITE: WWW.PNGP.IT

The controversial road between lakes Agnel and Serrù leading to Colle del Nivolet.

Seldom has a name, Great Paradise, been so apt in describing this imposing slice of mountain scenery with its spectacular glaciers, one foot in Piedmont and the other in the Valle d'Aosta region. It was the first, and perhaps the most famous, Italian national park. Over 70,000 hectares of untrammelled and mainly mountainous nature hedged by four valleys. The southern limits of the park are marked by the long Orco Valley, to the east the well-wooded slopes of Val Soana, to the north the Cogne Valley

(with the Vallone dell'Urtier), and to the west the Val di Rhêmes, while the Valsavarenche is driven like a wedge between the other two Aosta valleys and lies completely within the park. The snow-covered Mt Gran Paradiso peak (4,061 m) occupies pride of place, surrounded by a halo of equally impressive peaks and glaciers.

3,000 M FROM HEAD TO TOE

The park covers a vast area with a dramatic altitude difference of over 3,000 m from its peaks to its valleys. The valleys themselves are well-wooded with evergreen larch, spruce, Scotch pine and the occasional silver fir extending to the tree line at just over 2,000 m. Higher up the woods give way to Alpine pastures, the lonely 'hanging valleys' (basins of glacial origin suspended at the head of many alpine valleys) and sweeping scenery against the dramatic background of the gleaming glaciers. The sheer variety of natural environment is even more marked on the Piedmont side of the park, where the boundaries dip down to below the 1,000 m mark and include deciduous woods of chestnut trees, ash, maple and beech. Water is one of the park's signature tunes, with a wealth of rushing streams that have carved out whole valleys, waterfalls and lakes, some of them with dams to produce hydroelectric power.

The easiest place to catch a glimpse of the normally shy, but supremely elegant, chamois are the quiet valleys towards Canavesa. The true symbol of the park, the majestic ibex, is much easier to spot: they graze peacefully all over the park, including its more popular parts, supremely indifferent to parties of eager camera-toting tourists. The ibex are the uncrowned kings of the pastures and the peaks, mountain goats whose cloven hooves are perfectly adapted to rock climbing. Another animal that can often be spotted in the park is the marmot, a born lazybones who only rushes into his den when he feels danger threaten. Among the other species of wildlife in the park are the roe deers, hares, foxes, badgers, pine martens and stoats. Birds are another familiar sight; golden eagles, goshawks, owls, kestrels, Alpine choughs, eagle owls, buzzards, ptarmigans and sparrowhawks. Sightings of the bearded vulture have also become increasingly frequent.

FOOD IN VALLE D'AOSTA

When one thinks of cheese from Valle d'Aosta, one thinks of Fontina, the regional leader both in terms of quality and quantity. The popularity of this cheese cannot merely be understood in the taste, but also in its association with flowering meadows and pristine skies. Of course, such a setting has not only produced one tradition-filled, high-quality product, but a range of them, including a ham known as jambon de Bosses and Arnad lard. The most emblematic dish for the region is simply known as "soupe", a rich vegetable soup combining many regional flavors.

THE DISHES

Fondue. This dish is a combination of milk, butter, egg yolk and, most importantly, Fontina cheese. It is rich enough to be simply eaten with croutons, polenta, rice or vol-au-vent.

Soupe valpellinentze. This dish gets its name from Valpelline, a valley on the way up to the Great Saint Bernard Pass. It consists of bread, chopped cabbage, Fontina cheese and meat broth, all cooked in the oven. Traditionally, it is given to people during convalescence.

Carbonade. The original recipe called for salted beef with herbs, but that is practically impossible to find now. As such, a good cut of beef chopped into cubes is more common. This meat is cooked in wine, with onion, salt and pepper. It is accompanied by polenta.

Caffè valdostano. This coffee, with sugar, a good helping of grappa and lemon rind, is the classic end to any regional meal. It is served, after being lit, in a low wooden cup with multiple spouts that is known as the Coppa dell'Amicizia or Friendship Cup.

THE PRODUCTS

Fontina DOP. This cheese is the standard bearer for local gastronomy and is produced across the region. It is made using full-cream milk from Valdostana cows, especially those that graze in the high-mountain pastures, where the rich forage helps flavor the cheese.

Valle d'Aosta Fromadzo DOP. In the local dialect, 'fromadzo' indicates a compact cheese made with cow's milk and, potentially, some goat's milk. There are various types of these cheeses that fall into this category.

Valle d'Aosta Jambon de Bosses DOP. This ham is seasoned in Alpine huts in the Saint-Rhémy-en-Bosses (1,600 m) municipality in the upper Great Saint Bernard Valley. The ham is slightly salty to taste, with sweet and aromatic hints. The appearance is more akin to game cold meats than processed ones.

Valle d'Aosta Lardo di Arnad DOP. This lard is often eaten on black bread as an appetizer, sometimes with a touch of honey. It is made using meat from the back and shoulder of so-called 'Pesante Italiano' pigs that weigh over 160 kg.

Miele Valle d'Aosta. Bee-keeping in this region involves transporting the bees from the valley floor up into the mountains to allow the bees to collect pollen from both types of flowers. The result are: a 'multi flower' honey with hints of the woods and pastures; a chestnut honey that is a dark amber with a balsamic smell and a slightly bitter taste; and a rhododendron honey that is light in color and delicate in taste.

THE WINES

The wines are the fruit of the heroism of the valley dwellers, who 'stole' space from the mountains, cut it into terraces and planted vines on the sunny slopes. Petit-Rouge and Nebbiolo (of Piedmont origin and known locally as Picoutener) account, in equal parts, for over half of the vines. The remainder consists of either local varieties or ones imported from France. All this variety has led to a notable quantity of Valle d'Aosta DOC wine. The main reds are Donnas, Enfer d'Arvier and Chambave Rosso; the key whites are Blanc de Morgex et de La Salle, Petit Arvine and the more international Chardonnay and Pinot Grigio. All this wine has also encouraged the production of grappa and other distilled spirits. The spirits made with white berries are notably aromatic due to the changes in temperature that characterize the valley.

Fontina, with the label showing that it is protected.

"Langa," the singular of Langhe, means, in local dialect, the narrow ridge of a chain of hills. Following the "langa" means staying in the highlands, avoiding the valleys, and in fact this route offers fine views of vineyards and castles, perched on the higher hills. Alba, where the route comes to an end, has a famed annual truffle fair; there are also excellent mushrooms, vegetables, fruit, rabbits, pheasants, and partridges. The wines are classic Piedmontese varietals.

NOT TO BE MISSED

Bra is a handsome town full of Baroque architecture, and was once known as "Brayda." **Cherasco** boasts an improbable Visconti castle, dowry for the Visconti bride of Louis d'Orléans (1387), and used as a pretext a century later when Louis XII of France laid claim to the duchy of Milan. **La Morra**, a medieval hilltop village, offers a fine view. Along the road to Grinzane Cavour, note the former Abbey of the Annunziata, with private wine cellar and museum. **Barolo,** in the Castello Falletti, you can visit the Museo della Civiltà Contadina, featuring exhibits of rural life. **Dogliani** is a wine-making town with a high medieval section; take a detour down to the Tanaro River, and then to Carrù, with a Baroque parish church by F. Gallo, and then to Bastia Mondovì, where you can see late Gothic frescoes in the church of S. Fiorenzo. **Murazzano** is a resort with excellent views. **Bossolasco** is another resort with a view from the central square. **Serralunga d'Alba** is a hilltop town, with the elegant Castello Falletti di Barolo. **Grinzane Cavour** you can see the regional wine-cellar in the Castello Cavour, residence of Camillo Cavour, the 19th-century statesman who united Italy. **Alba** is a little town with medieval architecture, towers and tower-houses; sections are strongly redolent. It is renowned for its white truffles and its wines.

CUNEO

The oldest part of the town is concentrated on the peninsula between the rivers in Contrada Mondovì. Piazza Duccio Galimberti, which has elegant 19th-century buildings with long porticoes, is the heart of the town and acts as a link between the old town and the new.

Cathedral. At the beginning of Via Roma, lined by characteristic porticoes, stands the cathedral of Nostra Signora del Bosco, rebuilt in 1662 on the site of a medieval chapel with a Neo-Classic facade. Inside the church, built on a Greek-cross plan, the dome (1835) is decorated with frescoes. In the apse is a remarkable Purification. Notice also the wooden choirstalls and the pulpit (1668).

S. Chiara, this deconsecrated church, now used for exhibitions, was completed in 1719. Altered in the 19th century, it has a curved facade divided into two tiers. The quiet, striking interior contains interesting frescoes .

S. Sebastiano, the church stands in Via Mondovì, a medieval street lined with porticoes. On the same street is the synagogue, which was modernized in 1884 and is decorated in the late-Baroque style. The facade of the church dates from 1880. Inside there are some remarkable works by Giovanni Antonio Molineri (in the vaults and the apse), choirstalls dating from 1595 and some 16th-century paintings.

S. Ambrogio, the original church dates from 1231 but it was rebuilt between 1703 and 1743. The apse was frescoed in 1870-80. The striking, elegant interior is built on a Greek-cross plan, with a marvelous interplay of arches, vaulting and ribbing. Above the crossing of the transept is a dome with a lantern.

Former church of S. Francesco is the town's most important example of medieval architecture. The building, built on Gothic lines, has a 15th-century facade divided into three parts by two pilaster strips and decorated with terracotta friezes and pinnacles. The fine marble doorway dates from 1481. Above it is a tympanum with a rose-window. The mighty bell tower, with its octagonal pyramidal spire, dates from 1399. The adjoining cloister with frescoed lunettes leads into part of the monastery, now the **Museo Civico**. It has sections devoted to archeology, the Middle Ages, an ethnographic collection and a beautiful collection of rag dolls dressed in local Cuneo costume.

S. Croce: on the same street stands this magnificent church, built between 1709 and 1715. It has an unusual concave facade with two tiers, ending in an elegant curved tympanum with the remains of frescoes. The interior consists of two intersecting elliptical halls. In the apse is a fine carved wooden bishop's throne in the French Gothic style and an altarpiece in a marble frame (18C). Don't miss the painting in the first chapel of the left aisle, a splendid Madonna and Child with Sts Bernardino of Siena and St Augustine.

MONFERRATO, ASTI AND ALESSANDRIA

In the 13th century a manuscript praises the wines of Monferrato, a highland over the Po, at the foot of the Ligurian Apennines, north of the Langhe, and mingling with it. This is the northern Monferrato, high in elevation, stretching north from Asti and the Turin-Piacenza freeway running through it to the Po, arching between Moncalieri and Valenza. These highlands are dotted with vineyards, towns perched on ridges and peaks, and views that change with each curve in the road.

NOT TO BE MISSED

Moncalvo: home of 17th-century painter G. Caccia; from the tower in Piazza Carlo Alberto, a fine 360-degree view of Monferrato, the Po, and the Alps. Sanctuary of Crea (16C), with 23 chapels scattered in the woods. **Murisengo**, with a fine castle and a Piedmontese-Rococo parish church. **Montiglio**,

The typical vineyards of the Monferrato area.

with a noted series of frescoes (14C), in the park of the castle. **Cocconato**, a hilltop town with a Gothic town hall and noted for its fine food. **S. Maria di Vezzolano**, noteworthy Romanesque-Gothic abbey, said to have been founded by Charlemagne but in fact built in the 13th century. **Castelnuovo Don Bosco**: birthplace of a noted Italian man of the cloth, Don Bosco. **Cortazzone** boasts a handsome Romanesque church, S. Secondo, perched on a hilltop outside of town. **Asti**: (➡ see below) a town of red brick, yellow tufa and medieval architecture.

ASTI

A fascinating town renowned for its wines and delicious food, it lies in the heart of the Monferrato hills, on the right bank of the Tanaro River. The old town center, with its narrow, winding medieval streets is very picturesque.

Piazza Vittorio Alfieri. The square was named after one of the town's most famous sons, poet and playwright Vittorio Alfieri. Palazzi with porticoes line three sides of the square, which was laid out between 1860 and 1870 above the old military parade ground. In the center is the monument to Vittorio Alfieri (1862) and, opposite, Palazzo della Provincia (1958-61).

S. Secondo*. According to tradition, the church stands where the saint was martyred in 119. This fine Gothic building was rebuilt between the second half of the 13th century and the mid-14th century on the site of a 7-10th-century church. The facade, completed in 1462, is divided into three parts. Three doors with embrasures are framed by columns with capitals. Only the central apse belongs to the earlier church (late 13C). The splendid 10th-century Romanesque bell tower is visible from the courtyard of Palazzo di Città, left of the church. Built on a Latin-cross plan, the nave and side-aisles are separated by pillars. Flights of steps on either side of the presbytery lead down to the crypt, which was part of the original building (possibly 7C). The short aisles are divided

by six small columns with sandstone capitals, and converge on a small apse, shrine of the 16th-century silver reliquary containing the remains of St Secondus.

Corso Vittorio Alfieri, the elegant, paved, slightly sloping main street is overlooked by some of the town's most elegant 18th-century palazzi. In Piazza Roma, just off the Corso, is a late 19th-century Neogothic building and the 13th-century Torre Comentina. Buildings of note on the Corso include: Palazzo di Bellino, a medieval fortified house restored in 1751; Palazzo Ottolenghi, a medieval building restructured in 1740; the Cripta (crypt) and Museo di Sant'Anastasio, an archeological park-cum-museum. Finally Palazzo Alfieri, where Alfieri was born, is an 18th-century transformation of a 13th-century palazzo, with a magnificent central courtyard.

Roman Tower. Continuing along the main street, inside Palazzo del Michelerio, is the former church of Gesù (1549) and, more particularly, the cloister of Gesù, a masterpiece of local 16th-century architecture, with perfect lines. Further on, stands the Torre Romana or Torre Rossa, dating from the Augustan period (1C). It has 16 sides and was possibly once part of an old gate. The top of the tower, decorated with small arches and columns (late 11C).

Cathedral*. This majestic brick cathedral is one of Piedmont's most important Gothic buildings. It was built between 1309 and 1354 above the remains of an earlier church and has been altered several times over the centuries. The lower part of the facade is decorated with narrow blind arches and three Gothic doorways (ca. 1450). The upper facade is divided into three sections by two pilaster strips ending in pinnacles. It has three rose-windows and is crowned by a cornice of small intersecting blind arches. In the right-hand wall of the church, is a remarkable porch in the flamboyant Gothic style (post-1450), with delicate reliefs and exquisitely carved statues. The Romanesque bell tower was rebuilt in 1266 and the height of the tower was lowered in the 17th century. The well-illuminated nave and slender side-aisles are built on a Latin-cross plan. The walls and ceiling are entirely covered with late-17th-century frescoes. The treasury is worth visiting and contains some very valuable objects. Opposite the cathedral stands the late 17th-century church of S. Giovanni, built on the site of a 9th-century church. Below the church is the interesting crypt of St John (8C), with four splendid columns made of Egyptian granite and syenite with anthropomorphic carved capitals.

S. Maria Nuova. The church was rebuilt in the 14th century on the site of an earlier Romanesque church, and altered again in the 17th and 19th centuries. The lower part of the bell tower dates from the original church (11C). Inside is a remarkable *Madonna Enthroned with the Child and Saints* by Gandolfino d'Asti (1496) in its original frame. The beautiful Chiostro dei Canonici Agostiniani adjoining the church dates from 1591.

Rotonda di S. Pietro and S. Pietro in Consavia*, in Piazza I Maggio is an unusual museum complex consisting of the Battistero or Rotonda di S. Pietro, the church of S. Pietro in Consavia and the cloister. The Rotonda, one of Asti's most important Romanesque monuments, was built in the 12th century and was based on the Church of the Holy Sepulchre in Jerusalem. Used as a baptistery, it is a low, octagonal building surrounded by mighty buttresses. Above is an octagonal drum crowned with small arches. The interior of the building is round with eight short columns with alternating bands of brick and sandstone and square capitals. These support the octagonal dome, the walls of which were frescoed in the 17th century. You walk through the baptistery to enter the church of S. Pietro in Consavia, an example of 15th-century architecture between the Gothic and Renaissance styles. Note the terracotta friezes around the

windows and on the cornices. The cross-vaulting of the cloister of the Pilgrims' Hospice is supported by columns. A door leads into the Museo Archeologico e Paleontologico, which has exhibits dating from the Roman, Barbarian and Medieval periods, an Egyptian collection and a fossil collection.

ALESSANDRIA

Renowned historically as a military stronghold, over the centuries, thanks to its strategic position on the Tanaro River, it attracted the attention of many military men. From Frederick Barbarossa to Napoleon Bonaparte, the town's history is dotted with military events which have influenced the development of the town on the plain between the Tanaro and Bormida rivers. A case in point is the Cittadella (fortress), built between 1733 and 1745, a fine example of military architecture.

Piazza della Libertà. A vast rectangular square bordered with trees, it is the heart of the town. To the east side, lies Palazzo della Prefettura e della Provincia, one of the town's most important Baroque buildings. The reception rooms are still decorated in the 18th-century style with ornamental panels above the doors, mirrors, fireplaces and frescoed ceilings depicting mythological themes.

Cathedral. Built in 1810 on the site of the previous church, it overlooks Piazza Giovanni XXIII. It has a fine Neo-Classic facade (1822-23) and a tall bell tower with a spire which was only completed in 1922. The drum is decorated with statues of the patron saints of the 24 cities of the Lombard League (an alliance formed in 1167 by most of the cities in northern Italy to counter the attempts of Holy Roman Emperor Frederick Barbarossa to bring Italy within his sphere of influence).

S. Maria di Castello. This church, founded in 1470 (although not completed until 1545), was built on the site of two earlier churches (some ruins can be seen under the floor). Its lines are mainly in the late Gothic style. Inside the church is a wooden Crucifix (ca. 1480) and a 16th-century polychrome terracotta Deposition. In the presbytery are some late 16th-century carved wooden choirstalls and the high altar (1640). In the left transept is a Madonna, a polychrome stone carving in high relief (15C). In the refectory of the adjoining monastery is a Crucifixion dating from 1520.

S. Lorenzo. Work on the church began in 1770-72. The magnificent interior was decorated by the Lombard mural painters Giovanni Pietro and Pietro Antonio Pozzo, and there are two interesting paintings by A. Lanzani.

TURIN/TORINO

Founded in ancient times at the confluence of the Dora Riparia with the Po, Turin now extends along the left bank of the Po, from the confluence with the Stura di Lanzo, downstream, to that of the Sangone, upstream. On the opposite bank rise the Alpine foothills, forming a very pleasant background for the lives of the Turinese. In the distance, one can make out the silhouette of the Alps. Turin is a major city, the fourth largest in Italy; it is thoroughly up-to-date, busy, and courteous. In the heart of the city, both architecturally and historically, is the ancient capital of the Savoy dynasty. Turin is known best as an industrial metropolis and as Italy's car-manufacturing capital; socially, it has a reputation of formal "drawing-room" entertaining, in the neighborhoods of Piazza San Carlo, Via Roma, and surrounding areas. The city, however, also boasts a surprisingly rich artistic and cultural life, and a wealth of monuments.

TURIN THE CAPITAL

The oldest buildings along this square-shaped route through the heart of the city are largely of the 17th century. Some of the most illustrious sites in this capital city – first of a Savoy duchy and later of a Savoy kingdom – are found here, many of them by the hands of the "court architects" Guarino Guarini and Filippo Juvarra. This was also a Roman colony many centuries ago, and traces of that period can be seen in the regular checkerboard pattern of streets. The Roman walled perimeter, within the bounds of which Turin remained until the 17th century, also enclosed the medieval city.

Piazza Castello. This large square, surrounded by regular porticoed palazzi (the 90 m skyscraper that stands on the western side dates from 1934), is the heart of Turin. Isolated at the center of the square stands Palazzo Madama. A wrought-iron gate separates it from Piazza Reale, beyond which you can see the dome of the Holy Shroud chapel and the bell tower of the Duomo; opposite Palazzo Madama rises the dome of the church of S. Lorenzo. On the eastern side of the square is the facade of the Teatro Regio, the only surviving 18th-century part of a building which has been recently rebuilt and reopened. On the western side of this square, opposite Palazzo Madama, are the offices of the regional government of Piedmont.

Palazzo Madama**. This great palazzo in the center of the square sums up in its long process of construction the history of Turin itself. It incorporates the remains of an ancient Roman gate (front towers), which was transformed in the Middle Ages into a castle; this castle, enlarged in the 15th century by the House of Savoy, with corner towers and mullioned windows, became the home of Madama Reale (hence its current name) Maria Cristina, the widow of Vittorio Amedeo I and the regent of C. Emanuele II; in 1721 F. Juvarra designed and built the monumental Baroque facade. The palazzo now holds the Museo Civico di Arte Antica*, featuring artwork largely from Piedmont, including sculpture (T. di Camaino*), wooden carvings, paintings (A. da Messina, Pontormo, M. Spanzotti, M. d'Alba, D. Ferrari, and G. Jaquerio), illuminated manuscripts (*Les très belles Heures* du Duc de Berry**, illustrated by J. van Eyck and

Palazzo Reale and Palazzo Madama, the strongholds of Savoy power, overlooking Piazza Castello.

his school), furniture*, tapestries, glass, ceramics, ivory, and embroidery.

S. Lorenzo*. This small church, of great architectural interest, is one of the loveliest in Turin. Devoid of the facade – it has the elevation of a palazzo instead – it was built between 1668 and 1680 and is one of the major works by G. Guarini. Note the complex structure of the central plan interior and the cupola.

Armeria Reale*, beneath the portico to the right of the fence around Palazzo Reale, is the entrance to one of the most notable collections of arms and armor in Europe. Note: the weapons of E. Filiberto (1561); parade arms and armor (16C); firearms from the finest German smiths (17C); firearms from Brescia and the other leading European armsmakers.

Palazzo Reale*, built in 1660, this enormous royal palace with its stern facade was, until 1865, the residence of the House of Savoy. The interior features spectacular examples of furnishing and decoration from the 17th-19th centuries. Note especially the painted and carved coffered ceilings and wooden floors, and the collection of large vases from the Far East. The Scala delle Forbici*, a stairway that runs from the entry hall to the upstairs apartments, is a remarkable creation of F. Juvarra, who also designed the decorations in the remarkable little Chinese room. Behind the palace extend the royal gardens, created in the French style in the late 17th century.

Palazzo Chiablese, on the left of Piazzetta Reale, palace refurbished in the 18th century, once housed the cinematography museum that is now in Mole Antonelliana.

Duomo*. This cathedral was built in 1491-98, and has a Renaissance facade, the only one in Turin, made of white marble, with three portals in the Tuscan style; standing alone to the left of cathedral is the mighty bell tower, built in Romanesque style around 1470, and made even taller in 1720. The interior contains the columned nave and aisles, simple and austere; on the wall, near the entrance, note the tomb of Anna de Créquy. To the side of the presbytery, you can go up to the Holy Shroud chapel*, a remarkable chapel designed by G. Guarini (1668-94), entirely faced with black marble and with a conical cupola comprising six stacked rows of arches. On the walls, note four monuments to members of the House of Savoy; above the sumptuous altar is a silver urn containing the Shroud (Sindone), the shroud that is believed to have been used to wrap the body of Jesus after it was taken down from the Cross; it supposedly bears the miraculous impressions of his face and hands. This pre-

cious relic, which became a possession of the House of Savoy in 1430 and was first placed here in 1694, is displayed to the public only on rare occasions; in the left aisle of the Duomo you can see a life-size photograph.

Piazza Cesare Augusto, a square there are a number of items of archeological interest: remains of walls, a stretch of Roman road (between the two statues of Caesar and Augustus), and the Porta Palatina* (1C AD), a gate with four vaults topped by two rows of windows and flanked by two polygonal towers, forming part of the city walls. To the left of the Duomo, beyond a fence that runs along the NW wing of the Palazzo Reale, are the remains of the Roman theater (1-3C).

Museo di Antichità, at no. 105 Corso Regina Margherita is the entrance to this museum of antiquities. It occupies what were once the greenhouses of Palazzo Reale, and contains archeological material, ranging from prehistoric times to late Roman and barbarian times. Of particular importance: Cypriot and Greek ceramics; the Etruscan collection; silver from the treasure of Marengo, with a portrait of Lucius Verus; collection of Roman glass.

S. Domenico, a Gothic church, restored in 1906-08, has a single portal. In the chapel at the end of the left aisle, note the frescoes.

Corso Regina Margherita. On the right side of this avenue, in Via Cottolengo, is the Cottolengo, or Piccola Casa della Provvidenza, a hospital founded by S. Giuseppe Cottolengo in 1828, a celebrated institution of Christian charity, and the headquarters of the Opere Salesiane, the organization founded by S. Giovanni Bosco (1846); note the adjoining church of Maria Santissima Ausiliatrice (1868), where the body of the saint is kept.

Sanctuary of the Consolata*, formed by the union of two churches, this sanctuary was built in 1678 by G. Guarini, who transformed the existing church of S. Andrea into a vestibule of the new sanctuary. To the right of the Neo-Classic facade (1860) is the 11th-century Romanesque bell tower, part of the original structure. The interior is built to a hexagonal plan, and is surrounded by elliptical chapels and decorated with lavish marble and gilt stucco; in the chapel to the left of the presbytery, note the kneeling statues of the queens Maria Teresa and Maria Adelaide, by V. Vela (1861). As you continue along Via della Consolata you will see, at the corner of Piazza Savoia, the Palazzo Martini di Cigala (1716), attributed to Juvarra, with a handsome atrium opening out onto the courtyard. The church of tha Carmine,

HIGHLIGHTS

THE HOLY SHROUD

The Shroud ('Sindone' in Italian) is a yellow piece of woven linen cloth with a herring-bone motif, 4.37 m long and 1.11 m wide. Impressed on it is the figure of a man who has been tortured and killed by crucifixion. It shows signs of wounds to his face, head and body, and a more obvious knife-wound between the ribs on the right-hand side of the body. There are many obvious coincidences linking the trials of this man to the Passion and death of Jesus Christ, as described in the various versions of the Gospels. Despite scientific objections to the authenticity of the relic, for centuries, this mysterious object has been a subject of great fascination. The first certain news of the Shroud appears in the mid-14th century, in France. From 1694 it is placed in the chapel between the royal palace and the Duomo, designed specially for the relic by Guarino Guarini.

designed by F. Juvarra, with an austere 19th-century facade, has a luminous interior, with a barrel vault ceiling. Not far off, at no. 1 in Via della Consolata, stands the Palazzo Paesana di Saluzzo, with a loggia-lined courtyard, once one of the most luxurious homes in Turin. Also of note is Palazzo Faletti di Barolo, in Via delle Orfane 7.

Via Garibaldi, a shopping street, off-limits to automobiles, and lined with 18th-century houses and palazzi. Continuing along it toward Piazza Castello you will see, on the right, the church of the Ss. Martiri, built to plans by P. Tibaldi after 1577, with decorations inside of marble, stucco, and bronze. Next to the church is the Cappella della Pia Congregazione dei Banchieri e Mercanti (chapel of bankers and merchants), a fine example of Baroque architecture of the late 17th century, with many canvases by A. dal Pozzo. Further along, on the left, is the Palazzo di Città, 1659-63, whose main facade overlooks the Piazza di Città, with a monument to the Conte Verde (1853).

Corpus Domini, a short detour to the left, along the narrow Via Porta Palatina, leads to the church of Corpus Domini, built to plans by A. Vittozzi (1609-71) on the site of a miracle that supposedly occurred 150 years previous (the miracle involved a mule and a stolen monstrance, or ostensory).

Santissima Trinità. Continuing further along the Via Garibaldi, just before you reach Piazza Castello, note (on the left) the Neo-Classic facade of the church of the Santissima Trinità, designed by Ascanio Vittozzi (1606), with an interior built to a circular plan and dome, lavishly faced with marble by F. Juvarra (1718).

THE MODERN HEART OF TURIN

The late 16th-century citadel and the fortifications with which Turin defended itself against a French siege in 1706 were demolished under Napoleon. In the spaces thus left free (this route runs along them in part), these avenues, or Corsi, and the broad tree-lined boulevards, laid out before the invention of the automobile, interpreted in a new architectural language the aristocratic image of Turin. This route ends along Via Roma, the best-known road in Turin: central thoroughfare of a Baroque addition, renovated in questionable style in the early 20th century, it remains, with the Baroque square that lies across its middle, the "drawing-room" of Turin.

Via Pietro Micca, lined by buildings in eclectic architectural style, it starts from the western corner of Piazza Castello and is one of the most elegant streets in Turin, with porticoes along the right side; it was built with a diagonal line of demolition in 1894 through an old neighborhood.

S. Maria di Piazza, set back along a cross street of Via Pietro Micca, this small church was rebuilt in 1751 to plans by A. Vittone, but the facade dates from 1830. The interior is interesting; note the cupola and the theatrical altar.

Cittadella, at the beginning of the Corso Galileo Ferraris, in a garden, stands the keep of the Cittadella, all that remains of the enormous fortress built by E. Filiberto of Savoy in 1564-68. It houses the Museo Storico Nazionale dell'Artiglieria, which features a collection of firearms and memorabilia of the Piedmontese corps of artillery and engineers.

Museo Pietro Micca, not far off, to the west, at no. 7 in Via Guicciardini, in the area once occupied by the fortress, stands this museum with models, maps, and memorabilia of the Cittadella di Torino (Turin Citadel) during the time of the French siege, in 1706. A custodian will take you into the underground chambers beneath the building (they once extended 14 km under the city). Here, Pietro Micca, an Italian national hero, sacrificed his life to save the town. Follow the porticoes of Corso Vinzaglio and you will reach the broad and tree-lined Corso Vittorio Emanuele II, a central thoroughfare in the modern section of Turin; once

you reach Largo Vittorio Emanuele II, in which looms a monument dating from 1899, you will take a right into Corso Galileo Ferraris, and will soon reach the Galleria d'Arte Moderna. **Galleria d'Arte Moderna e Contemporanea***, at no. 31 Via Magenta, this is one of the leading collections of modern art in Italy, occupying a modern building with 19th-century art on the first floor. The works are predominantly by Piedmontese painters (M. d'Azeglio, Fontanesi, Avondo, Delleani, Grosso, Quadrone, Reycend, and G. Pellizza), although the Lombards (Hayez, Cremona, Induno), Tuscans (Fattori, Lega, Signorini), Venetians, and painters from other parts of Italy are also well represented. The second floor is devoted to the Futurists, early 20th-century painters (Spadini, Modigliani, De Chirico, Carrà, Tosi, Casorati, Morandi, Scipione, Rosai, and De Pisis) and painters of later generations (Mafai, Menzio, Paulucci, Spazzapan, Birolli, Guttuso, Cassinari, Morlotti, and Santomaso) all the way up to the modern avant-gardes. Among the sculptors, we should mention Canova, Marocchetti, Vela, Gemito, Medardo Rosso, Andreotti, Martini, Marini, Manzù, Fazzini, and Mastroianni. European art is present with works by Courbet, Renoir, Léger, Utrillo, Pascin, Klee, Ernst, and Chagall, as well as the contemporary artists Tobey, Hartung, Le Moal, Manessier, Gischia, Tal Coat, and Tamayo.
Museo Civico di Numismatica, Etnografia e Arti Orientali, not far from the Galleria d'Arte Moderna, at no. 8 Via Bricherasio, is this collection of Greek, Roman, Byzantine, and Italian coins, from the Middle Ages to modern times, along with plates, seals, and medals; there are also collections of material from Africa, the Americas, and Oceania, archeological finds from Gandhâra, in India, and items of Chinese art.
Piazza S. Carlo*, is linked with Piazza Carlo Felice, on one side, and Piazza Castello, on the other, by Via Roma, Turin's main thoroughfare, lined with porticoes and elegant shops. This square was given its current appearance – with symmetrical porticoed palazzi along the main sides – in the 17th century. The southern end features the two churches of S. Cristina (Baroque, by F. Juvarra) and S. Carlo, whose 19th-century facade reproduces many of the architectural motifs found in S. Cristina. In the center of the square is an equestrian monument to E. Filiberto, by C. Marocchetti (1838).
S. Teresa, a Baroque church (1642-74) may have been built to plans by A. Costaguta; the facade dates from 1764. Inside, note the rich marble decoration and the spectacular altar of S. Giuseppe* by Juvarra (1735). Alongside the church, at no. 5 Via S. Teresa, is the Museo della Marionetta, with puppets, marionettes, backdrops, and costumes created by the Lupi brothers for the traditional Teatro Gianduia.

THE GALLERIA SABAUDA AND THE MUSEO EGIZIO

When the city was still enclosed within its fortified walled perimeter, expansion took place through well-planned projects, beginning with the shift outward of bastions and ramparts. The district to the SE of Piazza Castello, explored by this route, was added from 1673 on, and still shows the stern style of the Piedmontese Baroque, illuminated by the brilliant flashes of architectural genius of Guarino Guarini. Marks of cultural continuity can be seen in the two most prestigious collections of art in Turin, the Galleria Sabauda and the Museo Egizio.
Palazzo Carignano, overlooks Piazza Carignano, with a statue of the Turin-born Italian philosopher and politician Vincenzo Gioberti (1859). Among the stern buildings that surround it is the Teatro Carignano, where, in 1775, Vittorio Alfieri's first tragedy, Cleopatra, was performed. Built by G. Guarini (1679-85), the palazzo belonged to the Carignano branch of the House of Savoy; Carlo Alberto (1798) and V. Emanuele II (1829; later king of Italy) were born here. The kingdom of Italy was proclaimed in the courtyard, on 14 March 1861; Italy's first parliament met here, until the capital was moved to Florence (1865). A new wing that closes off the courtyard and the monumental facade overlooking Piazza Carlo Alberto were built in the 19th century. The palazzo contains the Museo Nazionale del Risorgimento Italiano, with a major collection of documents, memorabilia, and other material concerning the period of the struggle for Italian unification, with manuscripts by Garibaldi, Cavour, Mazzini, and V. Emanuele II; a section is devoted to the Italian Resistance movement in WWII.
Palazzo dell'Accademia delle Scienze, a imposing brick Baroque building, by G. Guarini (1678), houses two of the most important collections in Turin: the Museo Egizio and the Galleria Sabauda.
Galleria Sabauda**, housed on the second and third floors of the Palazzo dell'Accademia delle Scienze. This is a first-rank collection of paintings, boasting, among other things, remarkable paintings of the Flemish and Dutch schools. There are works by Piedmontese painters of the 15th-16th centuies: M. d'Alba,

Spanzotti, G. and D. Ferrari, Sodoma, and Giovenone. There is a notable group of works by Tuscan painters: B. Daddi, Fra' Angelico, Pollaiolo, L. di Credi, and Bronzino. Among the Venetians we should mention Mantegna, B. Montagna, Veronese, Tintoretto, Bassano, Schiavone, and Savoldo. There are many works by Italian painters (17-18C): Carracci, Reni, Guercino, B. Strozzi, O. Gentileschi, G.B. Tiepolo, Magnasco, Bellotto, Piazzetta, Ricci, and Guardi. Particularly noteworthy is a group of Flemish and Dutch paintings by J. van Eyck, R. van der Weyden, Memling, Petrus Christus, Van Dyck, G. Dou, Rembrandt, J. van Ruisdael, P. Potter, and others. The collection of the princes of Savoy includes portraits by F. Clouet and Van Dyck. Also worthy of note is the Gualino Collection, comprising a major group of paintings by early Italian masters, including a painter active prior to Giotto, Botticelli, E. de' Roberti, and Veronese, as well as Chinese sculpture and medieval furniture.

Museo Egizio**, in the Palazzo dell'Accademia delle Scienze, this is one of the most notable collections of Egyptian antiquities in all Europe. On the ground floor is the statuary section, with remarkable material: 10 seated statues and 11 standing statues of the lion-headed goddess, Sachmis; the pharaohs Tuthmosis I (1505-1493 BC), Tuthmosis III (1490-1436 BC), Amenophis II (1438-1412 BC), Haremhab (1333-1306 BC), and Ramesses II* (1290-1224 BC). Of special note is the re-assembled "speos"* (little cliff temple) of El-Lesiya, with bas-reliefs dating from 1450 BC, a gift (1966) from Egypt to Italy. On the first floor are collections of various material: sarcophagi, mummies, canopic vases, statuettes, weapons, tools, papyrus (Book of the Dead), and paintings, illustrating various aspects of Egyptian civilization (daily life, culture, religion, the funerary cult, etc.). Especially noteworthy is a small room with material from the tomb of a married couple, Kha and Merit (1430-1375 BC), uncovered intact.

S. Filippo Neri, begun in 1675, this church was completed in 1772 by F. Juvarra. Before it is a classical pronaos (1835); note the vast interior, with stuccoed relief, marble, and paintings. Alongside the church

A statue of Amenhotep I.

is the Oratory of S. Filippo, also designed by Juvarra; facing it is the Palazzo Carpano, built in 1686 to a design by M. Garove, pupil of Guarini. Note the spiralling columns.

Piazza Carlo Emanuele I, built at the end of the 17th century, this square has, at its center, a monument to Cavour (1873). Not far off are the Museo di Antropologia e di Etnografia (Museum of Anthropology and Ethnography, at no. 17 Via Accademia Albertina; and the Museo di Scienze Naturali (Museum of Natural Sciences; , at no. 36 Via Giolitti).

Piazza Cavour, a square, with little hillocked flowerbeds, dotted with trees and 19th-century homes, is adjacent to the so-called Aiuola Balbo, a large garden created in 1835 on the site of ancient fortifications. From Piazza Cavour, continuing further along the Via Giolitti, you will soon reach Piazza Maria Teresa, a quiet tree-lined square in a residential neighborhood, which has retained the appearance of early 19th-century Turin.

Piazza Vittorio Veneto, a large rectangular square, surrounded on three sides by porticoes, was designed and built between 1825 and 1830 in the area in which the 17th-century Porta di Po once stood. Overlooking the Po River, it has as a backdrop in the large church of the Gran Madre di Dio (see below) and the hills behind it.

Via Po, this broad thoroughfare is lined with uniform rows of buildings and porticoes; built in 1675, it links the enormous Piazza Vittorio Veneto with Piazza Castello. In a cross street on the right, Via Montebello, stands the Mole Antonelliana*, a remarkable construction by A. Antonelli, now an emblem of the city. Begun in 1863 and completed toward the end of the century, it was originally built entirely in masonry and stone. It stands 167.5 m tall; the spire, torn down by a hurricane on 23 May 1953, has since been rebuilt. Originally built as a synagogue, it has a huge single hall some 85 m tall; the original structure has been fortified by a skeleton in reinforced cement. Take an elevator up to a broad terrace above the cupola for a remarkable view of Turin and the surrounding area.

Museo Nazionale del Cinema, situated in the Mole Antonelliana, the museum illustrates the technical and artistic development of the cinema industry and of photography. The first rooms are devoted to forms of entertainment which preceded cinema, based on the vision of moving images.

Pinacoteca dell'Accademia Albertina di Belle Arti, located in the Palazzo dell'Accademia Albertina, at no. 6 Via dell'Accademia Albertina, this museum contains paintings and drawings by G. and D. Ferrari, Spanzotti, F. Lippi, and 17th-century artists from Italy (O. Gentileschi; Cavarozzi) and elsewhere in Europe (P. Brill; S. Vouet). On the Via Po, just before Piazza Castello, on the right you will see the stern facade of the University, built in 1713 to plans by M. Garove, with a porticoed courtyard and a loggia decorated with statues and busts of illustrious historical figures.

THE BANKS OF THE PO RIVER

The Po River, and the surrounding hills, which rise verdant over the opposite bank, are some of the most distinctive features of Turin, deeply rooted in the mindset and customs of its population. All the same, the city discovered the delights of the banks of the Po fairly late; aside from the Castello del Valentino, a princely outlying villa, Turin did not turn to the riverbanks until the 19th century. It then made the riverbanks into a public park, as well as a showcase: the medieval "Borgo," Torino Esposizioni, and the buildings of the Centennial Celebrations of the Unification of Italy (1961) are three approaches to the concept of "showing the city's best face," in three different times and three different cultural contexts.

Gran Madre di Dio, from Piazza Vittorio Veneto (see above) the V. Emanuele I bridge (1810-15), the oldest masonry bridge in Turin, leads up to this large church, built to commemorate the return of the House of Savoy in 1814, following the Napoleonic period. Built between 1818 and 1831 by F. Bonsignore in Neo-Classic style (modelled on the Pantheon), the church houses, in the crypt, a sanctuary for Italians who died in WWI. To the side of the bridge are the Neo-Classic 19th-century Murazzi, built to contain the river.

Monte dei Cappuccini. This isolated wooded hill served as a fortified position protecting the city. On the hilltop (284 m) stands the church of S. Maria del Monte; this church, with a luminous interior richly decorated with marble, was built by A. Vittozzi (1583-96), who also designed the adjoining convent. Alongside it is the Museo Nazionale della Montagna Duca degli Abruzzi*, with a vast array of documentary material concerning mountains, the history and techniques of climbing, geology, landscapes, culture and peoples of the mountains, and expeditions outside of Europe. From the square in front of the building, remarkable view* of the city and the Alps, from Monviso to Monte Rosa.

Parco del Valentino*, a public park, on the left bank of the Po, built in 1830. On the grounds, lined with boulevards and paths, is the large Castello del Valentino, built in 1630-60 by C. di Castellamonte on the model of French castles of the 16th-17th centuries, with a broad rectangular courtyard opening out to the city, and a majestic terracotta facade overlooking the Po River. To the left of the castle is the entrance to the University's Botanical garden, one of the leading botanical gardens in Italy, and one of the first (1729). Further along, near the banks of the Po, is the Borgo Medievale, a remarkable array of faithful reproductions of medieval houses and castles from the Valle d'Aosta, built for the International Exposition of 1884. The Palazzo Torino Esposizioni (1948), at the southern edge of the park, on Corso D'Azeglio, is a complex of exhibition pavilions, some designed by P. Nervi and R. Morandi.

Museo dell'Automobile Carlo Biscaretti di Ruffia*. At no. 40 Corso Unità d'Italia, this car museum offers a remarkable assortment of material on the history and development of the automobile in Italy, and a survey of world production. Among the many cars on exhibit, note the "Itala" that won the race from Peking to Paris in 1907, the earliest steam-driven cars, the first Fiat (1899), the cars that raced in the first Giro d'Italia (1901), racers, and limousines; there is also a section devoted to the early years of the Touring Club Italiano. Not far from the museum, in a park area overlooking both Po and hills, stand various buildings, including the Palazzo del Lavoro, by P.L. Nervi, now the headquarters of the Organizzazione Internazionale del Lavoro and other professional institutions, and the Palazzo delle Mostre, an exhibition hall with a remarkable "sail" roof; both buildings were erected to commemorate the Centennial of Italian Unity, for the "Italia 61" Expo.

Corso Agnelli, this road is lined by FIAT factories, built in 1938 and later enlarged; to one side of the complex is the auto test track. In Via Nizza stands the old FIAT Lingotto factory, built after WWI, and now used for art exhibits. Note the multi-storey construction; cars can drive on any storey and from one storey to another, culminating in the remarkable test track on the roof of the factory.

LAKE MAGGIORE AND LAKE D'ORTA

One somewhat excitable geographer wrote of these lakes that they are "isolated depressions and valleys, in which the rushing waters of land and sky finally find peace, unable to thunder off elsewhere." These lakes are of glacial origin. The Lake Orta comes from the glacier of Ossola or the Toce River. The little lake of Mergozzo was separated from Lake Maggiore a thousand or more years ago. The remarkable views should be understood in the context of a climate that allowed the introduction of exotic species, of mountains rearing straight up from the lake shore, and distant snow-capped peaks, of a history of churches, castles, and sanctuaries, surrounded by compact little villages. In recent centuries, noble villas and imposing middle-class hotels have been built up along the lakefront. Literary travellers have provided descriptions; the Isole Borromee – perhaps the jewel of this route – are called "art playing with nature" (J. Cambry, 1788); while E. Quinet (1832) said that they "resemble a creation of Ariosto. They have the same inventive grace as the Orlando Furioso, with an added pinch of the savage...."

NOT TO BE MISSED

In the old part of **Arona** there is still a flavor of the ancient lake-front marketplace; note the nearby gigantic 17th-century statue of St Charles Borromeo, the "S. Carlone." **Massino Visconti** has a castle that was the origin of the Visconti, lords of Lombardy until the mid-15th century. **Carpugnino** has a handsome Romanesque-Gothic parish church, S. Donato. **Gignese**: this town produced many master umbrella-makers, who emigrated throughout Europe; now there is a Museo dell'Ombrello e del Parasole (Museum of Umbrellas and Parasols). **Alpino**: 1,500 species and varieties of Alpine plants and medicinal herbs, in the Giardino Alpinia. **Mottarone**, with the 1,491 m peak looming above the road. When the sky is clear, the view is spectacular: Monte Rosa and all the western Alps, seven lakes, and the Po Valley. **Orta San Giulio** has ancient houses, loggias, Baroque facades, and lovely narrow lanes. Behind it is the Sacro Monte d'Orta, a series of spectacular hilltop chapels; take a boat to the **Isola di S. Giulio***, with its fine Romanesque basilica. **Omegna**, at the northern tip of the Lake d'Orta, is a manufacturing town with medieval and Renaissance structures. **Mergozzo**: a high road above the isolated little lake leads to Montorfano, with the Romanesque church of S. Giovanni. **Baveno**: aristocratic homes and gardens overlook Lake Maggiore from the southern shore of the Golfo Borromeo. **Stresa***, an exclusive lake-side resort, with a strong Belle Epoque flavor; from here you can take a boat to the renowned **Isole Borromee***, three small islands called Isola Bella, Isola dei Pescatori and Isola Madre. **Belgirate**: distinctive houses, with porticoes and loggias, in the upper, older part of town.

The little village on Isola di San Giulio on Lake d'Orta.

PIEDMONT, CROWNED WITH MOUNTAINTOPS

Piedmont literally means the foot of the mountain and it is a good indication of the type of landscape that abounds in these parts. On a clear day, the mountains are visible from the plain, forming a majestic natural frame and offering some spectacular views. In south-west section of these mountains, the valleys are almost in a radial pattern with Turin in the center, while to the north, they tend to be slightly less regular and more Alpine, adding to the overall glacial appearance. To the south, by contrast, the Maritime Alps are located close to the Mediterranean coast, but are not lacking in soaring mountains. This is truly the type of destination loved by hikers and those who enjoy superb landscapes. In addition, there are plenty of relatively unknown stunning spots with excellent views, ensuring this is a genuinely pristine natural area.

CASA DELL'ALPINO REFUGE HUT

DIFFERENCE IN HEIGHT: 571 M
TIME: 1 HOUR AND 30 MINUTES
DIFFICULTY: NONE WHATSOEVER
PERIOD: FROM APRIL TO NOVEMBER
TRAIL MARK: SIGNS AND MARKED STONES
ALTITUDE: 1,303 M
LOCATION: PRA ALPS
OPEN: SUMMER AND WEEKENDS,
TEL. 032353326

Near Lake Maggiore, you can find the most vast wilderness in Italy. In a unique valley, encompassed by silence, nature becomes sovereign with deep, steep, narrow valleys and gorges protected by an overhanging rockface at the bottom, from which clear water runs. The hike enters into the territory of the Parco Nazionale Val Grande along a nature trail and continues among forests and pastures until it reaches the grassy summit, where the Casa del'Alpino refuge hut is found.

PIAN CAVALLONE REFUGE HUT

DIFFERENCE OF HEIGHT: 500 M
TIME: 1 HOUR AND 30 MINUTES
DIFFICULTY: NONE WHATSOEVER
PERIOD: FROM MARCH TO NOVEMBER
TRAIL MARK: SIGNS AND MARKED STONES
ALTITUDE: 1,530 M
LOCATION: PIAN CAVALLONE
OPEN: LAST WEEK IN JULY TO AUGUST,
TEL. 03234022852

On the grassy slopes of Mount Todano, on the eastern boundary of the Parco Nazionale Val Grande territory, the rise of Pian Vallone forms a natural balcony that overlooks Lake Maggiore. The Pian Cavallone refuge stands above the dense forests that cover the crests all the way to the villages below.

PASTORE REFUGE HUT

DIFFERENCE IN HEIGHT: 271 M
TIME: 30 MINUTES
DIFFICULTY: NONE WHATSOEVER
PERIOD: FROM MARCH TO NOVEMBER
PASTORE REFUGE ALTITUDE: 1,575 M
LOCATION: PILE ALPS
OPENING: FROM MAY TO SEPTEMBER,
TEL. 016391220

The path in the Parco Nazionale dell'Alta Valsesia territory, the highest park in Europe, unwinds in a mild environment in the presence of the Monte Rosa massif.

The little house of the Casa dell'Alpino refuge is immersed in greenery.

SKIING IN PIEDMONT

SESTRIERE

Around the world, Sestriere is largely synonymous with skiing, which is no surprise since this hill saw the creation of one of the first Italian ski resorts in the 1930s. The key elements for the creation of the resort were the notable altitude (2,035 m), the natural ski runs where it was easy to design pistes without pulling down hundreds of trees and the vast open views. Sestriere is at the heart of the largest ski area in Italy, the Vialattea, which also includes Sauze d'Oulx, Sansicario, Cesana Torinese, Claviere and Montgenèvre (France), amounting to an impressive total of 400 km of ski runs and over 80 lifts. This is a true skiing paradise, with ski runs for first-timers and average skiers, who can choose from an array of moderate runs, as well as some of the best black and competition level runs in Europe. The comprehensive artificial snow-spraying program ensures skiing even when there is minimal snow. The best area for beginners is the section between Borgata and the hill; at the summit, on the Sises slope, there are some lifts for young children. The options are endless for the average skier. Imagine immense, snow-covered hills that invite you to 'carve' them up. The entire Banchetta area, which is accessible from Borgata, is wonderful and was host to the men's speed skiing (downhill and SuperG) at the Winter Olympics in 2006. The show piste for the races was the Kandahar Banchetta-Giovanni Nasi, a challenging technical run that goes from the top of Banchetta down to the village, passing walls, sharp turns and spectacular jumps. The technical events for the men and women were held on the slopes of Sises, where the floodlit Giovanni Alberto Agnelli ski run is one of the best in the world for the special slalom. Those taking on the Giant Slalom had to start from higher up, at the Sises summit. This includes a super wall, but it should only be attempted by more advanced skiers. An interesting option for relatively good skiers is to head down from here towards Sansicario, along the ski runs used for the women's races at the 2006 Winter Olympic Games, and then up to the Fraiteve summit and on towards Jovenceaux along the lovely red 12 ski run. The total vertical drop for this route is over 1,000 m. To head back up from Jovenceaux towards Col Basset, you cross the Sauze d'Oulx ski area, which is one of the largest in Vialattea. Finally, there are 10 km of circuits for lovers of cross-country skiing.

SANSICARIO

Sansicario was born out of nothing to become a ski resort and, although 40 years later, it followed the same model as nearby Sestriere. Once again, the plan was to create an ideal ski resort, although this time it was designed to meet the needs of more modern skiers and to cater for the advances in skiing. The result was a resort where the ski runs end right in the village and the preferred means of getting around is walking, or using escalators, rather than the car. Sansicario owes much of its success to its location on a sunny, scenic balcony overlooking the Val di Susa. The slopes that loom above the resort lead to the summit of Mt Fraiteve and are covered by a large ski area with notable vertical changes. Sansicario is an integral part of the Vialattea ski area and is largely on the northern side of Mt Fraiteve, between 2,700 and 1,700 m. The nature of the slopes, where the gradient changes and wooded areas alternate with open fields, means there are wide, enjoyable ski runs. Most of the runs are of moderate difficulty, but there are some easier ones that glide down the sun-drenched slopes. The resort is also the ideal place for children to learn more about winter sports, especially at the "fun park", which has a special conveyor lift that is ideal for the youngest learners. The skiing links to Sestriere and Sauze d'Oulx take just a few minutes and open up a range of options; the lifts can also be used to get to Cesana Torinese and then head up the opposite slope of Luna and Claviere Mountains. The main ski runs are covered with artificial snow spraying if necessary. For cross-country skiers, there is a 10 km circuit.

CESANA TORINESE

Cesana Torinese is strategically located in one of the most important hubs of the Vialattea, which is a massive ski area where you can go to Sestriere, Sauze d'Oulx, Sansicario, Cesana, Claviere and Monginevro, without ever removing your skis. It has a bob, skeleton and sledge track, which made it a key destination during the Winter Olympics in 2006. Two chairlifts upstream of the village climb towards Sansicario and the Monti della Luna area, one of the best options for people looking for a ski holiday on the move. By heading towards Sansicario, you reach the Sauze d'Oulx/Sestriere sector: a large area with a rich array of ski runs for everybody. The climb towards the Monti della Luna and the Claviere/ Montgenèvre ski area is equally interesting. A series of lifts takes you up to 2,293 m at the Bercia hill: from here, you head back down towards Claviere and Montgenèvre, via the pass with the same name. The Monti della Luna/ Claviere/Montgenèvre ski area is one of the best for panoramic views and has numerous red and blue runs for average skiers, firsttimers and those who are still finding their skiing legs. There are also some interesting black runs. For lovers of cross-country skiing, there are 22 km of trails to be explored.

CLAVIERE

Claviere is the final village before the French border. As the resort is in the heart of the Monti della Luna/Montgenèvre ski area, it is an ideal base for exploring the Vialattea skiing zone. To reach the Sestriere/Sauze d'Oulx/ Sansicario sector of this zone, you need to pass through Cesana Torinese and take two chairlifts that do not provide access to any particular runs. There are two chairlifts and one for younger children starting from the resort and leading to some lovely runs, including two black trails and a long blue one that heads all the way back to the resort. You can reach France along a link that includes a red run and some lifts. The ski area runs as far as the Bercia hill, which is the point where you meet the lifts that go from Cesana to Col Saurel, at 2,409 m, and it is also one of the loveliest spots in the Vialattea. The upper section tends to have moderately difficult ski runs, but there is also a simple run that takes you down into the valley from the Gimont refuge hut. The only section without any blue runs is the final one, near the Bercia hill and Col Saurel. By taking the red run that links this area to the French side of Montgenèvre, you find a series of easy runs in the Prarial and Col de l'Alpet sections. Claviere is a good destination for cross-country skiers: a charming 16 km circuit takes you to Montgenèvre and then back to the resort. The altitude ensures good snow even beyond the season's end.

SAUZE D'OULX

This scenic natural balcony overlooks the Val di Susa and is dominated by the peaks of Genevris, Moncrons and Triplex. The location makes Sauze an ideal ski area, with various runs in both open and wooded stretches, wide-open panoramas and many hours of delightful sun. It is also home to some of the most formidable runs in the Vialattea and, during the 2006 Olympics, these were used for the freestyle events. It is possible to reach, without having to remove one's skis, Sestriere and Sansicario. From Sansicario, it is then possible to reach the Monti della Luna area and Claviere, although this link is much longer and is better for a ski-touring holiday than a single run. The Sauze ski area has a total vertical drop of over 1,000 m, with the main lifts being chairlifts and draglifts. If the two black runs are not included in the equation, then this ski area is ideal for average skiers and beginners, with red runs and long blue trails connecting just about everywhere in the ski area. Two consecutive chairlifts, with the first leaving from the center of the resort, take you up the mountains and then you can, for example, return to the resort on either red or blue runs. It is also possible to get back to the resort from the Col Basset area using only blue trails. More generally, the whole sector between Sauze d'Oulx, Sportinia and Jovenceaux is covered with exciting red runs. Of course, Sauze d'Oulx is one of the best bases for an excursion towards Sansicario or Sestriere, where you can try out some of the 400 km of runs. From Col Basset, you head towards Sestriere on a red run, while from Fraiteve, you would need to head to Sansicario along the taxing route 21, which is one of the loveliest in the entire Vialattea area, or on one of the interesting red trails. For lovers of cross-country skiing, there are 13 km of trails.

BARDONECCHIA

Bardonecchia is a pleasant village that can be seen as the birthplace of Italian skiing. It is home to more then 20 lifts and 110 km of runs. The ski area is large and divided into two parts: Jafferau and Mélezet-Colomion. At Jafferau, the vertical drop is greater, with skiing between 1,300 and 2,800 m, and the slopes face west. In the other section, the vertical drop is around 1,000 m and the slopes face north. There is something for all levels of skier, with some notable trails in the wood that are ideal for average skiers. The easiest runs are found at Campo Smith, Mélezet and in the middle of the Jafferau section. There are also some challenging trails for advanced skiers, such as the interesting ones reached on the Clos, Chesal-Selletta, Chesal-Seba and Mélezet-Colomion lifts as well as the one accessible via the Fregiusia-Plateau and Testa del Ban chairlifts at Jafferau. The altitude and the exposure ensure the skiing is good, and the use of artificial snow also helps when needed. The nature of the Bardonecchia runs has made them very popular with snowboarders.

Indeed, this ski area was chosen for the Torino Winter Olympics in these events, with runs 23 and 24 of Mélezet being used. Run 23 is ideal, in terms of width and vertical drop, for a parallel giant slalom event: the run is wide and fast with gentle changes in slope. Run 24, by contrast, is best used as a halfpipe.

MACUGNAGA

The resort of Macugnaga is protected by the imposing east face of Monte Rosa, which could be called the Hymalyan Alp because of its vertiginous drops and the sheer size of the expanses. The resort, moreover, is one of the most intact in the Alps. The Macugnaga ski area is divided into two sectors: Alpe Burky and Mt Moro. Both have an interesting range of runs that are given an extra special touch because of the panoramic views you can enjoy. The roughly 40 km of runs are equally divided in terms of difficulty and thus there is something for just about everyone. From Pecetto, two consecutive chairlifts take you to Alpe Burky, which lies right under the imposing wall of Monte Rosa. Here, there are various long and enjoyable blue runs: the Belvedere run, over 3 km long, will satisfy even more demanding skiers. The other sector, namely Mt Moro, is connected to Macugnaga by two cableways. In this section, if you ignore the higher runs accessible by the S. Pietro lift (also giving access to a "snowpark" for snowboarders), the trails are largely for moderate to good skiers. Some of the red and black runs that head down into the valley are 7.5 km long with an impressive vertical drop of over 1,000 m. The altitude ensures good snow cover and Alpe Burky can also rely on artificial snow spraying, if needed. For lovers of cross-country skiing, there are about 20 km of trails, with the most notable probably being the circuit through the various districts that takes you past old Valais houses (that is, the interesting houses built by former inhabitants of Canton Valais in Switzerland) and through some woods. For those looking for the thrill and excitement of off-piste ski-

A view of the Sauze d'Oulx hamlet.

ing, then there are helicopter rides to take you to the best spots for powdery snow: you head to the east face of Monte Rosa and then down towards the bottom in the direction of the distinctive Cervino (normally known as the Matterhorn outside of Italy).

LIMONE PIEMONTE

Located at 1,009 m above sea level, Limone Piemonte is the main resort in Val Vermenagna. This valley starts out as open and gently rolling, but then becomes more Alpine in appearance and shape. In the early years of the 20th century, this village was the setting for some of the very first skiing in the Alps and it soon became a winter resort. Since those early days, it has grown in fame, and indeed this gracious resort is at the top of the ranks of Italian ski resorts and it plays host to World Cup skiing events. A true highlight is the Riserva Bianca ski area. This is one of the best such areas in the world with carefully chosen, snow-covered runs. This formidable ski area has 80 km of runs and is ideal for average skiers, although there is also plenty for people who love more trying runs that test one's technique. There are also options for true first-timers or relative beginners, with a nice training slope in the town. For those who have just left the training slopes, though, the options are limited. Despite the upper limit being 2,000 m, the climate remains relatively mild. In addition, Riserva Bianca receives plenty of snow thanks to the microclimate and it often has good skiing conditions right throughout the season. Should there be limited snow, then there is a substantial network of artificial snow spraying that keeps the main runs open as well as the connections with the main hubs in the lift network. The best run, which is one of the most charming in the Italian Alps, is the Olimpica: the upper and lower sections are red, while the middle stretch is black, making it ideal for competitions. For those who like snowboarding, there is a "snowpark", while cross-country skiers can make use of the 6 km of runs.

FOOD IN PIEDMONT

The natural resources present in this region mean that top-quality cuisine is to be expected. The white truffle is the undoubted standard bearer of the region. Indeed, the mere addition of 'alla piemontese' suggests the dish is made with white truffle. Rice, vegetables, dairy products, meat, game and wine are the other pillars of regional gastronomy. These ingredients are combined to make rich and sumptuous – but never overdone – dishes. The cuisine evokes dishes such as risotto, boiled meat in sauce, mixed fish dishes, jugged hare and snails cooked in Barbera wine.

THE DISHES

Vitello tonnato. This starter is typically made with rump boiled with herbs and then thinly sliced. The meat is then covered with a sauce made of tuna, capers and anchovies.

Agnolotti. The exact filling of this stuffed pasta varies from place to place. The basis, though, is always some form of chopped, salted meat combined with eggs and cheese.

Risotto dishes. The region has great expanses of rice paddies, making risotto a key culinary proposition. The most common variants are Barolo; Finanziera (a butter sauce with herbs, sweetbread, chicken livers, mushrooms and Marsala); Fonduta (a white risotto with fondue and, in season, truffle); and Piemontese (with a roast meat sauce and, possibly, some truffle shavings).

Tajarin. Originally from the Langhe area, this egg pasta is like little tagliatelle and is the only 'indigenous' pasta and sauce dish from the region. The pasta is boiled and then dressed with a roast meat sauce (al brucio), with butter and sage or with, occasionally, a tomato sauce.

Fonduta. Cheese – Fontina or Toma – melted to a cream. The cheese needs to be chopped into cubes and then soaked in fresh milk for a few hours. It is then heated and stirred with a wooden spoon until a velvety cream is obtained. It should be served piping hot with some sliced truffle on the top.

Bagna caôda. This well-known combination of oil, garlic and anchovies has a rich taste. It is served in a single bowl or in individual bowls for each person. Raw cardoons, peppers or celery are then dipped in.

Fritto misto. In Piedmont, this mixed fry dish is made with sweetbreads, brains, slices of veal and beef fillet, liver, cubes of chicken, mushrooms, macaroons and sweet and savory semolina.

Salame cotto. This salami is one of the ingredients of a traditional *gran bollito alla piemontese* (Piedmont's classic dish of boiled meats). It is a large sausage made with prime pork meat, lard, pancetta and herbs which vary depending on the recipe. This

Salame cotto resembles its more famous cousin from Emilia, mortadella.

salami, produced mainly around Alessandria and Asti, is eaten when it is fresh, either warm or cold. When sliced, the salami is dry and pink with large grains of lard.

Bicerin. Typical of Turin, it is a drink made with coffee, milk and chocolate that is served in a special chalice-like glass.

Bonet. This pudding made of cocoa and almond biscuits gets its name from the Bonet hat, which has a similar shape and color.

Krumiri. These are the most famous local biscuits, having originated with the House of Monferrato. Made with short pastry, their shape is said to be inspired by Victor Emanuel I's moustache – the biscuits were created in his honor in the year of his death.

Marron glacé. For centuries – and still today – Cuneo is synonymous across much of Europe with top-quality chestnuts, whether fresh, dried, processed or as flour. There are an amazing 21 varieties, with the most representative being a sugar coated one known as the marron glacé. These chestnuts delights go wonderfully with candied violets made with flowers picked fresh in the early morning.

THE PRODUCTS

Bra DOP. The name is tied to the small town of Roero, which was the major market where this cheese was traded. It is made with semi-skimmed milk (especially using cow's milk from local breeds) from the valleys and mountains of the Cuneo area. The cheese is light in color, with small holes and a generally rounded shape.

Castelmagno DOP. This medium-fat cheese is flavored with herbs and, for the most part, cow's milk is used. The flavor ranges between delicate and strong, sometimes even spicy hot.

Murazzano DOP. The name comes from a town in the Belbo Valley that is the epicenter of production, but it is made in various places in the Cuneo section of the Alta Langa. The delicate flavor is lightly scented, becoming spicy if matured for more than the normal 10 days.

Raschera DOP. This medium-fat cheese is made mainly with cow's milk, although some goat's and sheep's milk is sometimes added in. It is made in the entire Cuneo province, with the 'di alpeggio' variant being applied to some of the cheese made in the Alta Langa.

Robiola di Roccaverano DOP. This fresh cheese is made in 19 towns in the Monferrato area. It is made with various types of milk, giving the cheese a delicate, slightly sharp taste. It is often preserved in oil with herbs.

Toma Piemontese DOP. This semi-cooked cheese is made in most Alpine areas in the region. It is made entirely with cow's milk, making it white and soft with a sweet taste when young and harder with yellowish touches and a stronger taste when seasoned.

Tartufo bianco. Mainly found in the Roero and Monferrato sections of the Langhe, this is the king of a whole range of edible mushrooms. It has a strong, unmistakable smell.

Fassone del Piemonte. This name can be applied to meat from the Bianca Piemontese breed that have the so-called 'double leg'. This meat is mainly boiled or stewed in Barolo, but it can also be eaten as carpaccio or as 'carne all'albese' (sliced very thinly, tenderized with a knife and eaten raw, perhaps with some white truffle shavings).

Nocciola del Piemonte. This is the name for the Tonda Gentile delle Langhe hazelnuts. These nuts are widely used in chocolates and sweets, especially the famous Gianduiotto and the nougat from Asti and Alba.

THE WINES

Piedmont has 42 DOC recognized wines and 8 DOCG ones, making it a leader – perhaps the leader – in Italy and certainly one of the most famous regions internationally. It is a land where the vineyard is synonymous with culture, hard work and an age-old artisan tradition. Despite all this past, it is also looking forward to create new opportunities linked to food and wine tourism and based on the major regional wine shops, the numerous special wine shops and the private wine farms.

Wine making in this area is generally based on local grape varieties that have been cultivated for centuries and are ideally suited to the terrain. About 70% of the grapes are red and the remaining 30% white. The most famous grape is Nebbiolo, which has a history dating back to at least the Middle Ages and is part of some famous Piedmont wines, including Barolo, Barbaresco, Gattinara, Ghemme and Roero (all DOCG). The most widespread vine, though, is Barbera, which accounts for roughly half of production. Other notable reds include famous names like Dolcetto, Freisa, Grignolino, Bonarda and Brachetto. Moscato is the best known white grape and the leader in terms of production volume accounting for 80 million bottles of Asti DOCG. The other traditional white vines are Cortese (used for Gavi DOCG), Erbaluce and Arneis. More recent introductions include Pinot Bianco, Pinot Grigio, Riesling Italico and Renano, Chardonnay, Sylvaner and Müller Thurgau, some of which have been used to produce impressive results. All this high quality wine production is matched, especially between Langhe and Monferrato, by excellent grappa, often derived from already famous wine labels.

One wine that deserves a special mention is Vermut, which has its origins in 18th-century Turin. The name comes from the old German word Wermuth, meaning wormwood (Artemisia absinthium). Vermut is made using white wine – usually Moscato. Alcohol is then added to bring the percentage up to 17.5% (or more). Finally sugar cane and some secret ingredients are mixed in. One of the attractions of Vermut is that it is associated – especially in Turin – with aperitifs in splendidly decorated bars.

A wine-cellar at Costigliole d'Asti.

LAKE COMO

The magnolia tree, with its dense shadow of glistening leaves, the delicate wisteria, clinging to a gazebo, dark cypresses standing against the bright sky or the soft light colors of the mountain slopes, azaleas, rhododendrons, and, in the words of Stendhal, "groves of stunningly green chestnuts, bathing their branches in the lapping waves"; 16th-century villas, late-Baroque and Neo-Classic estates, parks built and defended over the centuries; venerable lakefront towns, their houses clustered together, with the whisper of the lapping wavelets; Romanesque parish churches made of grey stone. The blend of natural beauty, art and history is perfectly balanced here. Merged with the gentle climate, the "manmade" landscape attains something close to perfection. From the shore roads and the lakefront promenades, shaded by ancient trees, you can always see the opposite banks; thus, each place you visit will first be seen from across a silvery sheet of lakewater. And this preliminary view is linked with the preconceptions provided by literature and fame. Indeed, sometimes the view is even superfluous. For example, one morning in 1865, H.A. Taine, the French critic and historian, boarded a steamboat in Como. The white boat with black smokestack and thundering wheels took him for a tour of the lake, and the French writer spent the entire day amidst the red velvet of the salon, reading, researching, and writing about Venice. He emerged on deck only in the evening, but later wrote of the trip: "All day long, thoughtlessly, effortlessly, we sailed across a goblet of light...."

NOT TO BE MISSED

Lasnigo: along the climb from Asso to the Ghisallo, note the Romanesque church of S. Alessandro, with its handsome 12th-century bell tower and late-15th-century Lombard frescoes. **Passo del Ghisallo**, with the little church of the Madonna del Ghisallo, patron saint of bicyclists; splendid views of Lake Como during the descent to Civenna. **Civenna** offers another spectacular view from the tree-lined plaza of the Belvedere Grigne. **Bellagio*** is well located, at the juncture of the three basins of Lake Como; it has an old center with narrow lanes, hotel parks, and noble villas. **Torno** has two centers: one down near the marina, and another up toward the church of S. Giovanni; the 16th-century. Villa Pliniana graces the view from the far bank. **Como**: (➡ see below) in this "city of silk," exquisite relics of the age of the medieval communes and of the Lombard Renaissance stand side-by-side with notable buildings from the early 20th century. **Cernobbio**, practically a residential suburb of Como, has grand villas and a fine lakefront promenade; from the sanctuary atop Mt Bisbino is a panoramic view of the lake, the plains, and the Alps. **Sala Comacina**: take a boat to the Isola Comacina, the only island in the lake. **Ossuccio**: the church of S. Maria Maddalena has an impressive late-Gothic bell tower. **Tremezzo**: visit the early 18th-century **Villa Carlotta***,with its azaleas and rhododendrons blooming in April and May. **Gravedona**: fine views of this lovely town, and the church of S. Maria del Tiglio, a major Lombard Romanesque work. **Colico**: follow the shore of the lacustrine gulf, called the Lake Piona; a short detour takes you to the Abbey of Piona, an ancient monastery (a fine 13C cloister). **Corenno Plinio**: this village is clustered and perched on a lakefront crag. **Bellano**, a pleasant health resort which boasts the renowned gorge of the Pioverna Stream. **Varenna** boasts the lakefront promenade and the stairs leading up between houses, with fine views of the old center. **Fiumelatte**, named after the river that tumbles down, from spring to fall, white with foam; it is only 250 m in length.

COMO

The city is cupped in a small hollow, surrounded by an arc of hills, at the base of the Mount of Brunate, overlooking the southernmost tongue of its lake, the Lario or Lake Como. This is the city of the Maestri Comacini, or Romanesque master artisans of Como, and of both Plinys, Elder and Younger, who are immortalized in the statuary on the facade of the Duomo. It is also the home of the silk industry, ancient but still thriving, and of the Italian Rationalist architecture of the early 20th century. More than for the city itself, Como is beloved and frequented for "the enchanting loveliness, the light, and the expressive mobility of the lake." (Maurice Barres). By noticing only the lake, however, one is deprived of the pleasure of many discoveries, of noteworthy monuments and remarkable atmospheres.

Lungolario, a lakefront drive and promenade. The northern part of the city curves around the gulf at the base of the lake. Off Piazza Cavour – the heart of Como –are the docks of the boats and hydrofoils that carry passengers across the lake.

Piazza del Duomo is the monumental center of the city and home to Torre del Comune, the Broletto, and the Duomo.
Broletto*, once the center of Communal government, this Romanesque-Gothic town hall was built in 1215; note the marble facing, with white, grey and pink stripes, the portico, the mullioned windows and 15th-century balcony. The tower, or Torre del Comune, was built in 1215, and rebuilt in 1927.

A splendid view of Como on the lake riverside.

Duomo**. This monument traces its origins to the architectural culture of the Maestri Comacini. Begun in 1396, work continued until the 17th century, when the dome was added, designed by F. Juvarra (1740). The Gothic-Renaissance facade, split in three by slender pilaster strips, features portals, high windows, and a large rose window, and is enlivened by sculptures, mostly by G. and T. Rodari (15-16C). On either side of the central portal are two aediculas with statues of Pliny the Elder (who died in the eruption of Mt Vesuvius in AD 79) and Pliny the Younger, his nephew. Also note the two portals, one on the right side and the other on the left (called Porta della Rana), by Rodari, and the apse (1513). The interior is a mix of Gothic (nave and aisles) and Renaissance (transept) styles, with a 75-m dome. Tapestries adorn the nave. The side altars have reliefs by Rodari and canvases by Ferrari and Luini.

Casa del Terragni, once used by the Fascist party, this building stands in the Piazza del Popolo, facing the apse of the Duomo; built by G. Terragni in 1932-36, this is one of the most notable pieces of Rationalist architecture in Italy.

S. Fedele, a basilica was originally Como's cathedral, and dates from the early 12th century. The polygonal apse is crowned with a small loggia; note the portal with reliefs, in Via Vittorio Emanuele. In the little square are two interesting buildings, with terracotta and wood sections, now being restored.

Musei Civici. The town museums are the Museo Archeologico Paolo Giovio in Palazzo Giovio, and the Museo Storico Giuseppe Garibaldi in Palazzo Olginati, both linked by a gallery. The former contains collections of archeological finds; the latter, exhibits of local history, from the Renassiance to the present. Now being installed are halls that will exhibit Greek, Etruscan, Phoenician-Punic, Assyro-Babylonian, and Egyptian artifacts, as well as a portrait gallery.

Pinacoteca di Palazzo Volpi, art gallery housed in the Palazzo Volpi; it has a collection of 17th-century Lombard canvases, frescoes and bas-reliefs from the 14th century, and work by abstract artists living in Como.

Piazza Vittoria, note the monument to Garibaldi, by V. Vela. On one side of this square stands the Porta Torre, also known as the Torre di Porta Vittoria (1192), a gate with two passageways and large windows on the interior, once part of the city walls, rebuilt by the emperor Barbarossa; at the corners, note the two five-sided towers. In the cellar of a nearby school are ruins of the Torre Pretoria, a tower dating from the Roman Empire (3C); in the cellars of another school in Via Carducci are ruins from the walled perimeter that dates from the Roman Republic. Yet other Roman ruins (baths and library of Pliny the Younger, 2C) are found along Viale Lecco; recently, ruins of a Roman villa were uncovered at the corner of Via Tommaso Grossi and Via Zezio.

S. Abbondio*, this basilica, built in the 11th century, is one of the masterpieces of Lombard Romanesque architecture. Note the facade, adorned with pilaster strips and cornices in relief, and the two bell towers. The interior features a four-aisle nave divided by columns and tall piers, with a deep presbytery. In the loggia over the entrance and in the apse, there is a vast frescoed *Life of Christ* by Lombard painters of the mid-14th century To the left of the altar is a marble statue of S. Abbondio (1490) attributed to C. Solari. On the western shore of the port is the public garden; at the water's edge is the Temple Voltiano; this Neo-Classic-style building (1927) contains memorabilia and documents concerning Alessandro Volta, Como's most illustrious son, inventor of the electric battery (1745-1827). Continuing along past the War Memorial (1933), there is a tower designed by Futurist architect A. Sant'Elia. On the left is the Sinigaglia Stadium.

THE LODIGIANO AND CREMONESE AREAS

The 15th-century Bolognese architect A. Fieravanti (who later went to Moscow to build cathedrals in the Kremlin) worked on the irrigation and reclamation of southern Lombardy for the duke F. Sforza (1460). He noted that this area is not blessed by nature, and that hard work and organization were needed to make it the rich agricultural region that it has since become. This route invites you to perceive how humans have changed this landscape, sunny in summer, foggy in winter, vast, flat, and abundant. The subtly varied riverside views of the last part of the route are dotted with distinctive Lombard features: farmland, churches, town squares, castles, and cities – such as Lodi and Cremona – that form part of this agrarian world with its long and venerable history.

NOT TO BE MISSED

Lodi (➡ see below) is a distinctly medieval Po Valley town, picturesque and monumental; in the Renaissance Sanctuary of the Incoronata are four exquisite panels by Bergognone; in the Romanesque Duomo, note the relief from the wealthy old town of "Laus Pompeia," attacked and leveled by Milan in 1158. **Lodi Vecchio** has an isolated Romanesque-Gothic basilica (S. Bassiano), with notable frescoes. **Sant'Angelo Lodigiano**: the restored castle has fine art collections. **San Colombano al Lambro** is an ancient farming village at the foot of a hill studded with grapevines. **Casalpusterlengo** still has a few traces of its rural origins and a large town tower, a relic of the feudal castle. **Codogno**, now a modern manufacturing town, has fine paintings in the 16th-century parish church. **Pizzighettone** is surrounded by the bastions of its venerable fortifications, defending the bridges across the Adda River. **Cremona** (➡ see below), a modern bustling city, has a splendid monumental center, with much surviving intact from the Middle Ages.

CREMONA

The Po River, flowing within the massive earth embankments, runs past the edge of Cremona, while the Adda is just a short way upstream. The surrounding countryside is well watered and fertile. A considerable portion of the city's industry and trade is linked to agriculture. The Gothic crown of the Torrazzo tower, visible from the surrounding fields for quite a distance, amid the low-lying Lombard plain, stands in one of the loveliest medieval squares in Italy.

Piazza del Comune**. This is the artistic center of Cremona and one of the loveliest medieval squares in Italy. Note the array of monuments lining the square: the Torrazzo, the Duomo, the Battistero, the Loggia dei Militi, and the Palazzo del Comune.

Torrazzo, an exceedingly tall bell tower (111 m), a symbol of Cremona, was built around 1267; the massive brick shaft has an octagonal marble top, added between 1284 and the early 14th century. A stairway (487 steps) leads to the top, with a fine panoramic view*. The Renaissance Loggia della Bertazzola (1525; under the arcades, medieval marble carvings and 14th-century sarcophagus, by B. da Campione) links the Torrazzo with the facade of the Duomo.

Duomo**. This is one of the most notable pieces of Lombard Romanesque architecture, built during the 12th century and en-

larged (transept) in the 13th and 14th century. The marble facade has two orders of loggias, a handsome rose window (1274), and a 15th-century crown, as well as a 13th-century arched entranceway (in the front, note the strip of reliefs, depicting work in the fields*, sculpted by the school of Antelami), surmounted by an aedicula with three statues by M. Romano (1310). Overlooking Via Boccaccino is the northern end of the late 13th-century transept, with an arched entranceway, mullioned windows, rose windows, and terracotta ornamentation. As you continue to walk around the church, you will note the complex of three apses, and the southern end of the transept (1342). The interior has a nave and two aisles and is divided by pillars. The rich decoration softens the somewhat stern architecture. Along the walls of the nave and the central apse is a series of frescoes depicting the lives of Mary and Jesus*, by a number of Lombard-Venetian painters (1506-73), including Boccaccino, Romanino, and Pordenone. Note the Renaissance sculpture in the two pulpits* in front of the presbytery, with reliefs attributed, in part, to Amadeo. In the crypt is the Arca dei Ss. Marcellino e Pietro, once attributed to B. Briosco (1506), and reassembled here in 1609. The octagonal Romanesque baptistery*, crowned by a small loggia, dates from 1167.

Loggia dei Militi, built in 1292 as a meeting

The bell tower, a symbol of Cremona.

hall for the captains of the city's militia. Notable portico and high mullioned windows.

Palazzo del Comune*. The headquarters of government in early Cremona, it was rebuilt in 1206-46, and has been greatly renovated since. The central pillar of the ground-floor portico bears an "arengario," or external pulpit, built in 1507. Upstairs, there are a Renaissance portal, a marble fireplace (1502) in the Sala della Giunta, where the city authorities meet; and, in the smaller Saletta dei Violini, five of Cremona's finest violins – by Stradivarius, Amati (two), Pietro Guarneri, and Giuseppe Guarneri del Gesù.

S. Agostino*. Church built in 1345, with a monumental Gothic facade; interesting frescoes in the 3rd and 5th chapels at right. **Museo Civico Ala Ponzone***. Housed in the 16th-century Palazzo Affaitati (entrance at no. 4 in Via Ugolani Dati), this museum features an art gallery, collections of fine craftwork, the collection of Cremona history and iconography, and the archeological section. The noteworthy Pinacoteca, or art gallery, features many halls decorated with medieval frescoes and paintings of the Cremonese school, dating from the 15th to 18th century, as well as other Italian and foreign artists, and a collection of modern Italian art. The same building contains the Museo Stradivariano, with collections of documents and objects linked to great musicians and instrument makers of Cremonese history. In particular, original drawings, mod-

els, and tools, made or used by Stradivarius; manuscripts by Ponchielli.

Corso Garibaldi. This avenue is lined by noteworthy buildings, especially Palazzo Raimondi (no. 178), built in 1496, now housing associations of study of ancient music and violin making. On the right, midway along the Corso, Palazzo di Cittanova, built in 1256 (heavily restored in the 1920s).

Palazzo dell'Arte. This modern building overlooking Piazza Marconi contains the school for violin-makers (Istituto Professionale Liutario e del Legno) and the Museo Civico di Storia Naturale, dedicated to natural history.

LODI

On 24 April 1158, the long and bitter rivalry between Lodi and Milan came to a head with the destruction of what is now called Lodi Vecchio by an army from Milan. However, on 3 August of the same year, the go ahead was given to create what would become modern-day Lodi. By 1160, construction had begun on the cathedral and major land reclamation work was in the process of turning the surrounds into some of the most fertile land in Lombardy. The castle was built in 1370 over an earlier construction. Later, during the Hapsburg reign, it was enlarged and then turned into a barracks. In recent years, the southern part has been restored, bringing to life a double entrance overlooking a moat.

Piazza della Vittoria*, heart of the old center, remains an important part of city life. The buildings around the side are fairly uniform, except for the cathedral and the city hall. The arcades are a typical architectural feature of the Po Valley.

Duomo*. This is the oldest religious building in the city. The lunette shows the *Redeemer with the Virgin Mary and St Bassian*, while the jambs have an unusual depiction of *Adam and Eve* with crossed legs*. Grotesque figures function like atlases. The bell tower built into the facade and the Lombard porch (1284) is supported by column-bearing lions. Inside, the cathedral is shaped like a basilica with a nave and two aisles. This is the result of major work in the 20th century that restored the Romanesque brick- and stone-work that was hidden behind an 18th-century facing.

Tempio civico dell'Incoronata**. This is an early example in Lombardy of Bramante's notion of a building built around a central point. **Inside***, the effect – especially the colors – of the decorations and paintings is quite something. The Museo dell'Incoronata is housed in the basement.

S tands of tall poplars, irrigation canals, and embankments bordering the fields, a landscape of carefully tended, low-lying farmland: Sabbioneta is just 25 m above sea level; San Benedetto Po, 19. The immense volume of silt borne by the river continually raises its waters; near Pavia the Po is already higher than the surrounding farmland. Reclamation, drainage, and construction of banks along the Po began in the early Middle Ages and continues to this day. The embankments tower as high as 10 m; climb the banks, or cross a bridge, and you will note that vast expanses of land lie within the embankments, sometimes dry in the hot Po Valley summers, sometimes wreathed in heavy fog or blanketed with snow, and sometimes lying under by a flooded river (high-water season in May-June and October-November; low-water in January-February and August-September). The two key art centers – aside from Mantua – are San Benedetto Po and Sabbioneta, representing two different phases in the construction of this riverine realm. Benedictine monks undertook the first drainage and reclamation, beginning in 1007, while Sabbioneta was one of the "little Gonzaga capitals" during the Renaissance, with a sophisticated court and remarkable architectural treasures.

NOT TO BE MISSED

Mantua (➡ see below), this city's superb architecture is matched by the charm of its silent streets. It was the birthplace of Virgil. **Villa Pasquali** is a small town whose spectacular parish church is one of the most significant creations of the late Baroque in the Mantua region, both in terms of size and inventiveness. **Sabbioneta** (➡ see below) is a fortified, complete "ideal city" of the 16th century, the dream of a Gonzaga prince, splendid and perfectly useless. **Viadana**: the ruins of extensive settlements of stilt-dwellings, dating from the Bronze Age, discovered in 1885, are on display in an 18th-century palazzo. **Pomponesco** has a large, late-Renaissance porticoed square. **Guastalla** still has a few relics of its past as a "minor Gonzaga capital"; the monument to Ferrante I Gonzaga (L. Leoni, 1564), the Palazzo Ducale, and the Cathedral, both 16th-century, are noteworthy. Nearby, **Gualtieri** has a handsome porticoed square and the 16th-century Palazzo Bentivoglio. **Luzzara** has Palazzo della Macina, a Gonzaga residence. **Suzzara**: the Galleria d'Arte Contemporanea features the artworks awarded the "Premio Suzzara" (1948 to the early 1970s). **Pegognaga** has a handsome Romanesque church, S. Lorenzo. **San Benedetto Po** dates back to the foundation of the Benedictine abbey of Polirone: church, re-built by G. Romano in 1539-47, refectory, and three cloisters, all 15th-century. **Motteggiana**: the Corte Ghirardina*, a 15th-century country home, possibly by L. Fancelli, is an interesting blend of palazzo-court-villa-castle.

MANTUA/MANTOVA

The Mincio River flows around the city, spreading out into the three lakes, crossed by two bridges, the Ponte dei Molini and the Ponte di S. Giorgio. All around is the low-lying plain; the Po is only 12 km away. This city is marked by quiet streets, lovely colors, an overall Neo-Classic patina, with the sharply distinct monuments of the Middle Ages and the Renaissance. Mantua was an ancient "capital" (of the Gonzaga state), one of those towns with the signs of a centuries-old conjunction of culture, power, wealth, high-minded patronage of the arts and sickly decay. The lakes warded off industrial development; the city is tied to the land, in a very prosperous agricultural area.

THE OLD CENTER

In the NE part of the city, the oldest section of Mantua, near the Ponte San Giorgio that divides the Lake Mezzo from the Lake Inferiore, contains the most noted places and works.

The walking tour that links them covers the masterpieces by L.B. Alberti and Mantegna, who painted the Camera degli Sposi in the Castello di S. Giorgio.

Piazza Mantegna, the basilica of S. Andrea looms over this little porticoed square at the end of Via Roma and at the beginning of Mantua's three monumental squares (Piazza delle Erbe, Piazza Broletto, and Piazza Sordello).

S. Andrea**, this Renaissance masterpiece, designed by L.B. Alberti, was begun in 1472; work was continued in 1597-1600 and again in 1697-99; in 1732-65 the dome was added (F. Juvarra). The classical facade comprises a majestic arcade topped by a pediment; on the left side is a Gothic bell tower (1413), with large mullioned windows. Note the early 16th-century portal, with reliefs. **The vast interior***, grand and classical, has an aisleless nave and transept; six of the chapels are monumental, with 16th-century frescoes and altarpieces. The first chapel on the left commemorates Andrea Mantegna: the tomb of the artist, with a bronze bust, paintings and decorations is by his own followers. In the left-hand transept is the Cappella Strozzi*, probably designed by G. Romano.

Piazza delle Erbe*, the length of the square, dating from the late Middle Ages, is a balance between the enfilade of late Gothic and Renaissance porticoes of Via Broletto, flanking S. Andrea, and a remarkable series of monumental structures, like the house of the merchant Giovan Bonforte da Concorezzo, with the 14th-century Torre del Salaro. At the corner of Piazza Mantegna, just past a 15th-century house with terracotta decorations, is the slightly recessed Romanesque Rotonda di S. Lorenzo*, the rotunda dates from the 11th century but was later absorbed into the structure of the houses in the Jewish ghetto. It resurfaced in 1908 following a radical renovation; inside, ambulatory with arcades, loggia and dome. To the left of the rotunda, the **Torre dell'Orologio**, or clock tower, built by L. Fancelli in 1473; the astronomical-astrological clock, from that period, by B. Manfredi, was restored in 1989. Adjacent is the 13th-century **Palazzo della Ragione**, with battlements and mullioned windows, and 15th-century portico. At the end of the square is the 12th-century **Palazzo del Podestà**, rebuilt in the 15th century. The facade on the adjacent Piazza Broletto has a tower and a 13th-century statue of Virgil. The mullioned windows and loggia over the vault are remains of the Arengario (ca. 1300).

Museo Tazio Nuvolari e Learco Guerra, at no. 9 in Piazza Broletto (entrance under the loggia), this museum features trophies and memorabilia of these great champions.

Piazza Sordello*, this rectangular square, unusually large for the historic center, still preserves much of its medieval appearance. Follow the short stretch of Via Broletto, through the passageway of S. Pietro, by G.B. Bertani. On the left, crenelated 13th-century palazzi, on the right, the facade of Palazzo Ducale; at the far end, the Duomo.

Palazzo Ducale*, the two late 13th-century porticoed buildings on Piazza Sordello to the right of the Duomo, along with many other buildings erected from the 13th to the 18th century, make up the Ducal Palace of the

Torre del Salaro, piazza delle Erbe.

Gonzagas, one of the most lavish creations of Italy under the seigneurs. This "city within a city" extends toward the shores of the Lake Inferiore, or lower lake, enclosing palazzi, churches, inner squares, gardens, and porticoes, eloquent indications of the artistic and architectural fertility of the age of the Gonzagas. You should, however, be able to see paintings by D. Morone, V. Foppa, F. Bonsignori, G. Romano, G. Mazzola Bedoli, Tintoretto, Rubens, D. Fetti, G. Bazzani, and others, as well as Greek and Roman sculptures, sarcophagi, inscriptions, medieval and Renaissance sculptures (bust of F. Gonzaga*, attributed to Mantegna). The most notable halls and apartments are: the Sala delle Sinopie, with an exhibit of the preparatory drawings found on the plaster beneath the frescoes by Pisanello, discovered in 1969-72; the adjacent Sala di Pisanello, with the unfinished **fresco cycle*** painted for G.F. Gonzaga; the Appartamento degli Arazzi, with copies of **nine tapestries** made in Flanders to cartoons by Raphael; the Appartamento Ducale, with inlaid decorated ceilings (late 16-early 17C); Appartamento dei Nani (dwarfs, 17C), actually a miniature reconstruction of the Scala Santa in Rome; the Appartamento delle Metamorfosi; the Appartamento Estivale (Summer Apartment), by G. Romano, renovated by G.B. Bertani (16C); the Cortile della Cavallerizza (16C); and a series of halls, frescoed and stuccoed by G. Romano and his school, by Primaticcio, and other 16th-century artists, going from the Hall of Months to the majestic Salone di Manto. While touring the palace, you will also see the Castello di S. Giorgio (see below); in a corner tower is the famous **Camera degli Sposi**** (tour limited to a few minutes, to preserve the works), frescoed by A. Mantegna (1465-74) with scenes from the everyday life of the Gonzagas.

Museo del Risorgimento. This museum of the Italian unification movement occupies four rooms at no. 42A in Piazza Sordello.

Duomo*. Built in the Middle Ages, this cathedral still has an immense Romanesque bell tower and Gothic sections on the right side; most of the cathedral now standing dates from the 16th century. The facade reveals the influence of Roman Mannerism and

The castle of S. Giorgio.

Baroque; the interior, by G. Romano (1545), shows classical influence, with the aisles and the nave featuring flat, coffered ceilings. In the right aisle, sarcophagus, Gothic baptismal chapel with frescoes fragments; in the left aisle, the 15th-century Cappella dell'Incoronata, by L. Fancelli (1480). Walk past the Duomo and the 15th-century Casa del Rigoletto, and at the northern tip of Piazza Sordello you will see the large 19th-century Mercato dei Bozzoli, adjacent to Palazzo Ducale. **Castle of S. Giorgio**, this splendid urban castle, part of the Palazzo Ducale complex, dominates the waters between Lake Mezzo and Lake Inferiore. Built in the late 14th century by B. da Novara, it has four crenelated towers and a broad deep moat. Beyond the castle, along the Lungolago Gonzaga, is the outer facade of the "Rustica" by G. Romano; further along, off Piazza Arche, is the **Galleria Storica dei Vigili del Fuoco**, a museum on the history of firefighting.

Teatro Scientifico* or Accademia Virgiliana. The theater, at no. 47 Via Accademia, has a luminous facade designed by Piermarini (1771-75), which can be seen on the left from Piazza Arche. The interior, a jewel of Baroque theater architecture, was built by A. Galli Bibiena (1769) and has four tiers of boxes. Upstairs is the Library, with a collection of editions of Virgil's work and one of 18th-century surgical instruments. Leave Piazza Arche, turning right into Via Teatro Vecchio, along Via Scuderie Reali and Vicolo Ducale, among the secondary buildings of Palazzo Ducale, and take a passageway to the porticoed Piazza di S. Barbara, with the church of **S. Barbara**, built by G.B. Bertani in 1562-72. Another passageway, to the left, leads to the porticoed **Piazza Castello**, also by Bertani, and then to the Castello di S. Giorgio; a monumental 16th-century frescoed corridor leads to Piazza Sordello.

THE "CIVITAS NOVA" AND RENAISSANCE MANTUA

Setting off from the center, you will pass through the districts that belonged to the "city of the second walled perimeter," or the "Civitas Nova," the new district laid out at the end of the 12th century; after you cross the Rio, you will be in the later expansion of Mantua, until you reach Palazzo Te, created by the remarkable genius of G. Romano for the pleasure of the court of Federico II Gonzaga. **Museo Diocesano Francesco Gonzaga**, at no. 55 in the huge Piazza Virgiliana, this museum of the diocese is in a former monastery. It has paintings (15-17C), sacred goldwork* from the Duomo and from the basilica of S. Barbara. **Piazza Matilde di Canossa** set behind the large red Palazzo Barbetta, built on what is now Via Cavour in 1784, this cozy little square is dominated by the impressive grotesque-work facade of **Palazzo Canossa**, built in the late 17th century, with one of the most interesting monumental staircases* of all Italian Baroque. In the square there is also a typical 19th-century newspaper stall made of wrought-iron, wood and glass, restored by FAI (Fondo per l'Ambiente Italiano). Follow Via Fratelli Bandiera, and at no. 17 is a 15th-century house with a carved portal and frescoes on the facade; further along, at the corner with Via Arrivabene, **Palazzo Arrivabene**, in poor condition and much renovated, but with the original late 15th-century porticoed courtyard.

S. Francesco, a 14th-century Gothic church was heavily damaged in WWII and was restored to its original appearance; inside, frescoes by T. da Modena and others.

Palazzo d'Arco, the long neoclassical facade overlooks Piazza Carlo d'Arco. Donated to the city in 1973, this building is a fine example of a noble residence. Note the furnishings and paintings by F. Pourbus the Younger, F. Boselli, J. Denys, N. da Verona, and L. Lotto. Pass through the courtyard to reach a 15th-century palazzo; the Hall of the Zodiac*, has frescoes by G.M. Falconetto (1520).

Piazza Martiri di Belfiore, one of the focal points of Mantua's traffic, this square was built between 1925 and 1955 as part of the project that resulted in the filling in of the central stretch of the Rio and the demolition of the convent of S. Domenico. It extends toward Via Matteotti with an expanse of greenery that features the isolated Gothic bell tower of S. Domenico; behind the tower is the double portico of the **Pescherie**, built in 1535 by G. Romano, across the Rio.

Palazzo Sordi. Standing near the eastern end

of the Via Corridoni, lined by 17th- and 18th-century buildings, this palazzo extends its vast rusticated facade at no. 23 in Via Pomponazzo. It is by the Flemish architect F. Geffels (1680); note the courtyard and monumental staircase, with statues and stuccowork.

Palazzo Valenti. This 17th-century palazzo on the left side of Via Frattini (no. 7) has a handsome porticoed courtyard. Also, at no. 9, Casa Andreasi and, at no. 5, a 15th-century palazzo decorated with terracotta statues.

Via Chiassi. Lined with palazzi from various periods, is notable for the 18th-century Baroque facade of the **church of S. Maurizio**, built in the early 17th century by A.M. Viani. Just beyond, at the mouth of Via Poma, is the monumental **church of S. Barnaba**, with facade by A. Galli Bibiena. At no. 18 Via Poma is the **Casa di Giulio Romano**, designed by the artist (1544), in a Neo-Classic style; facing it is the **Palazzo di Giustizia** (Hall of Justice), with its massive structure and caryatids on the front.

Casa di Andrea Mantegna, no. 47 Via Acerbi, may have been designed and built by Mantegna himself, and has a circular courtyard.

S. Sebastiano*, a beautiful classical church was built in 1460 to plans by L.B. Alberti; the facade was modified in 1925. Note the crypt, altar beneath a 16th-century baldachin, and the monument to the Martyrs of Belfiore.

Palazzo Te**, a suburban villa is one of the best preserved examples of 16th-century architecture, built and decorated by G. Romano as a holiday home for Federico II Gonzaga. Made up of four low buildings around a courtyard, it is faced with imitation plaster ashlars: inside, the halls are lavishly decorated with frescoes and grotesque work, largely by G. Romano and followers: the Hall of Psyche*, has noted Manneristic frescoes, and the Hall of Giants*, was praised by Vasari for its effect on the viewer. Also note the Loggia di Davide, linking the main courtyard and the garden, which in turn is bounded by a 17th-century exedra and an orchard. Also suggestive is the Appartamento della Grotta which, beyond the secret garden, opens up in an artificial cave encrusted with shells and mosaics. The building also houses the **Museo Civico di Palazzo Te**, broken up into various sections: Donazione Mondadori, with paintings by A. Spadini and F. Zandomeneghi; Donazione Giorgi, with work by this 20th-century painter; Sezione d'Arte Moderna (Mantuan artists, 1850-1950); Sezione Gonzaghesca, with medals, coins, et al., 1328-1707; Collezione Egizia Acerbi, with ancient Egyptian art and artifacts.

S. Maria del Gradaro. This 13th-century Gothic church, with pointed portal and rose window, was used as a barracks from 1775 till 1917, and was then restored to its original form in 1952-66.

SABBIONETA

It is said that the duke Vespasiano Gonzaga, a valiant soldier wounded time and time again in battle, carried Vitruvius' renowned architectural treatise with him at all times, even during hard campaigning. When the 16th-century duke drew up the plans for his little capital, he imagined it as perfectly finished in every detail, within the star-shaped walls. Sabbioneta – honored as a 'small latter-day Athens' for the enlightened court – is an exemplary model of an 'ideal city', conceived and built to suit its prince, in perfect accordance with the canons of Renaissance urban planning.

Piazza Ducale* (or Garibaldi). This is the center of Sabbioneta. Partly bounded by small portico-fronted palazzetti, this square preserves its ancient appearance. Note the Palazzo Ducale and the parish church, 1581, which contains the 18th-century chapel of the Sacro Cuore by A. Bibiena.

Palazzo Ducale*. The ducal palace was built in 1568 with a ground-level portico. The "piano nobile" has marble windows, and there is a turret in the center of the facade. In the interior are halls with carved wooden ceilings and frescoes by B. Campi, A. Cavalli, and others. Note the four wooden equestrian statues of the Gonzagas, and the Galleria degli Antenati, with busts of the dynasty. Behind the palazzo is the church of the Incoronata (1588), with the mausoleum of Vespasiano Gonzaga by G.B. Della Porta (1592) and the bronze statue of the duke, by L. Leoni (1588).

Teatro Olimpico*. A masterpiece by V. Scamozzi (1588). The interior has a rectangular plan, with tiered steps and loggia. Note the excellent frescoes by the Venetian school.

Piazza d'Armi or Castello. This is the ancient parade ground, with a Roman column in the center. It is surrounded on one side by the long buildings of the Galleria degli Antichi (1584). **Palazzo del Giardino***. Built between 1577 and 1588 as a pleasure palace for the prince, this holiday home is filled with halls and antechambers, decorated with frescoes, stuccoes, and grotesques by the Campi brothers and the school of G. Romano; from here you pass into the Galleria degli Antichi*, 97 m long, with a wooden ceiling and frescoes.

LAKE ISEO, VALCAMONICA AND VAL SERIANA

The lake, the petroglyphic "stories" carved into rocks, the hardworking people of the foothills, and fine paintings: there are numerous attractions in the course of this route. The traveller is free to choose those found most appealing. Writing about the Lake Iseo in the early 19th century, one author cited the "beaches crowded with olive groves" and the "theatrical savagery of certain points, which contrast so well with the glittering shoreline" ... This region was also the birthplace of Italian industry: the low and middle Valcamonica, traversed by the Oglio River, are forbidding pre-Alpine valleys; the slopes are dotted with vineyards and chestnut groves, while the valley floors feature farmland and factories. All around are iron mines; in this region, the highest point, physically, is the Passo della Presolana, with a fine distant view. The artistic high points are Capo di Ponte, with prehistoric petroglyphs, and the gallery of Lovere, with Venetian paintings.

A view of the green fields and Alpine peaks in the Val Seriana.

NOT TO BE MISSED

Sarnico is a summer resort, with some medieval architecture in the town center. **Tavernola Bergamasca** is an old harbor, from the days when there were no coast roads. There are houses with loggias and fine frescoes, including a youthful effort by Romanino, in the church of S. Pietro. Steamers will take you out to Sensole, on Monte Isola; walking tours of the island. **Lovere**, overlooking the lakefront, has noteworthy medieval architecture. Do not miss the Galleria dell'Accademia Tadini. **Pisogne**: note the frescoes by Romanino in the 15th-century church of the Madonna della Neve. **Breno**: go see the frescoes by Romanino in the former church of S. Antonio and in the town parish church. **Capo di Ponte** boasts over 100 boulders with rock-carvings, in the Parco Nazionale delle Incisioni Rupestri di Naquane*; do not miss the Romanesque church of S. Salvatore and, in the village of Cemmo, the 11th-century parish church of S. Siro. **Boario Terme**, an important spa since the 19th century; as you drive up the Val di Scalve, beyond Angolo Terme, the "Via Mala" – an old mountain road, which you can take, though you may prefer the more modern detour – penetrates into the Dezzo deep gorge. **Clusone** has a handsome old town center, in a tranquil setting. A Triumph of Death and a Danse Macabre are frescoed (1485) on the walls of the Oratory of the Disciplini. **Albino**: this was an early manufacturing center; don't miss the paintings by G.B. Moroni, who was born here, in the church of S. Giuliano and the Sanctuary of the Madonna del Pianto.

BERGAMO

The distinctive silhouette that can be seen from the surrounding lowlands, etched out against the mountainous background, is that of Bergamo Alta, or upper Bergamo, aloof, hushed, and ancient. This is one of the most perfect stratified assemblies of urban construction and historical memory in Lombardy, and perhaps in all of Italy. Roughly one hundred meters below, at the edge of the plain, near the mouth of the Brembana and Seriana valleys, lies the thriving town of Bergamo Bassa, or lower Bergamo, the modern section, even though it has centuries of prosperous trading, banking, and manufacture behind it. In Bergamo you are going to meet the forbidding gaze of the equestrian monument to Bartolomeo Colleoni, great condottiere, but even greater self-aggrandizer; the merchants who look out from portraits by G.B. Moroni; the baleful, disapproving eye that the artist Fra' Galgario cast upon the aristocrats of the 16th-century provinces; the airy, "musical" still-lifes by E. Baschenis; mellifluous romantic airs by G. Donizetti, or the rough jokes and rapid banter of Arlecchino – Harlequin – both native sons of Bergamo.

BERGAMO ALTA

From the modern center of town you climb up to the heart of old Bergamo, with its famous monuments and exquisite architecture. After an excursion to the panoramic Colle S. Vigilio and a tour of the secluded and silent Borgo Canale, this route runs along a stretch of the old Venetian walls, with remarkable views.

Piazza Vittorio Veneto. This square, with the adjoining Piazza Matteotti, Piazza Dante, and Piazza della Libertà, forms the heart of Bergamo Bassa, the lower town. This orderly system of squares, built in the area of the demolished Fiera di S. Alessandro, is a modern piece of urban planning, laid out in the early 20th century to designs by M. Piacentini (1914-34).

Viale Vittorio Emanuele II. This road forms part of the long straight avenue built between 1837 and 1857 with the name of Strada Ferdinandea, linking Bergamo Bassa with Bergamo Alta, now the chief thoroughfare in the city. Midway, where the road turns beneath the walls, is the lower station of the funicular running up to Bergamo Alta, built in 1886-87.

Porta S. Agostino. Comprising a double curtain wall, this gate dates back to the time when the walled perimeter itself was built (16C). The gate takes its name from the nearby former **convent of S. Agostino**, founded at the end of the 13th century and suppressed in 1797; the church of this convent has a late-Gothic sandstone facade and, inside, fragments of frescoes.

Via Porta Dipinta. This street runs steep and winding among palazzi and old houses, going past the Romanesque **church of S. Michele al Pozzo Bianco**, renewed in the 15th century and again later; in the nave and crypt, note the fine frescoes (12-14C): those in the chapel to the left of the presbytery are by Lorenzo Lotto (1525). Further along is the Neo-Classic **church of S. Andrea** with a notable altarpiece* by Moretto in the right-hand chapel. Across the street is the 17th-century Palazzo Moroni, with frescoed interiors and a garden on the hill.

Rocca, from Piazza Mercato delle Scarpe (the upper terminus of the funicular) a narrow lane runs up and off to the right to the 14th-century fort, with a glacis now used as a park (Parco della Rimembranza); from atop the donjon, a fine view of Bergamo, the surrounding plain, and the Alpine foothills (Prealpi).

Via Gombito. Narrow and winding, this road runs up from the Piazza Mercato delle Scarpe to the heart of Bergamo Alta. Along this distinctive road you will see a 16th-century fountain, medieval ruins, old houses, and the 12th-century Torre di Gombito. In the nearby Piazza Mercato del Fieno, at the former convent of San Francesco, is the Museo Storico di Bergamo, a historical museum which houses finds and mementoes of Bergamo from the period of the Cisalpine Republic to the 20th century.

Piazza Vecchia* and the adjoining Piazza del Duomo, form the monumental center of Bergamo Alta. Built in 1440-93, it is adorned with an 18th-century fountain. It is bounded by the late-12th-century **Palazzo della Ragione***, a venerable town hall with a large ground-floor loggia and three-light Gothic windows; above the 16th-century balcony stands a lion of St Mark, a relic of former Venetian rule; adorning the upper hall are frescoes (14-15C) from churches and palazzi in Bergamo. In particular, note the Three Philosophers, by Bramante. To the right is the 12th-century Torre del Comune, a tower with much-rebuilt crowns. Facing the Palazzo della Ragione is the Palazzo Nuovo, designed in 1593 but built in stages; the facade was not completed until 1927-28. This building houses the Biblioteca Civica (town library), with major collections of manuscripts and antique printed material.

Piazza del Duomo. The square contains, in picturesque asymmetry, the most noted religious monuments of Bergamo: from left to right, the **Duomo**, S. Maria Maggiore, the Cappella Colleoni, and the Battistero, or Baptistery. The Duomo, with its 19th-century facade, features paintings by A. Previtali, G.B. Tiepolo, and G.B. Moroni; behind the main altar is an inlaid 18th-century choir.

S. Maria Maggiore*, a complex Romanesque construction, with no facade, dates from the second half of the 12th century. In the left transept, note the portal with the superb porch by G. da Campione (1353), with columns set on carved lions. Walk around the church toward the left to appreciate its intricate and lively architecture. You should also note another portal by G. da Campione (1367); the Renaissance structure of the Sagrestia Nuova (or New Sacristy, 1491); the apse with archwork and loggia above the stairway; the bell tower (14-16C); the right transept with two apsidioles and portal with porch, by G. da Campione (1360); an ancient fountain; and, isolated above the rest, the little 11th-century church of S. Croce. The **interior**, with gilding and stuccoes, was renovated in the late 16th and 17th century. Along the walls, note the exquisite tapestries, made in Tuscany (16C) and Flanders (17C). In the right transept, Tree of Life, fresco by followers of Giotto (1347); in the presbytery, six bronze candelabra from 1597, inlaid benches and choir*, in part to designs by Lotto (1522-55). Across from the presbytery: Baroque confessional, carved by A. Fantoni (1704); tomb of the composer G. Donizetti, by V. Vela (1855); monument to Cardinal Longhi, by U. da Campione; tapestry of the Crucifixion (1698), and a large painting by L. Giordano. **Cappella Colleoni****, built by B. Colleoni, a condottiere who served the Venetian Republic, as his own funerary chapel, the space is a jewel of architecture and decoration, a masterpiece by Amadeo (1476), and a crowning creation of the Lombard Renaissance. All the features that make up the exquisite facade – pilaster strips, portal, windows, rose window, and loggias – blend in the chromatic interplay of the pink-and-white marble facing. Inside, amidst the decoration (18C), note the Tomb of Colleoni* and the tomb of his daughter Medea, adorned with statues and reliefs; both are by Amadeo. In the lunettes and the spandrels beneath the cupola and in the votive chapel, are frescoes* by G.B. Tiepolo (1733). **Battistero***. This small octagonal baptistery, enclosed by a wrought-iron fence and crowned by a gallery with slender columns in red Verona marble, is a 19th-century reconstruction of the original building by G da Campione (1340). The 14th-century statues are by the Maestri Campionesi.

Museo Donizettiano, museum located in the Palazzo della Misericordia (15-16C), headquarters of the Civico Istituto Musicale, in Via Arena 9. It houses a collection of memorabilia and documents of the Bergamo-born composer Gaetano Donizetti. Not far off, in Piazzetta Terzi, is the 16th-century Palazzo Terzi, one of the most important private homes in the historical center; the terraced courtyard has a fine view of the plain below. At no. 3 in Via Donizetti is the Renaissance structure of the Casa dell'Arciprete by the Bergamasque architect P. Isabello (1520); note the marble facade* with the lovely central window on the ground

Piazza Vecchia: the Torre del Comune.

floor; elegant courtyard, with loggia opening out onto a vast view.

Via Colleoni. Setting off from the Piazza Vecchia along the Via Colleoni, you will find at no. 9-11 the Casa Colleoni, home of the great condottiere, and headquarters of the charitable institution he founded; 15th-century frescoes. A bit further along is the church of the Carmine, rebuilt in the 18th century, with canvases from the 16th and 17th century.

Piazza Mascheroni. This square features the **Cittadella**, originally built in the 14th century (note the surviving large tower), which was taken by the Venetian commanders of the occupying forces as their residence. On the eastern side of the square is the entrance to the **Museo di Scienze Naturali Enrico Caffi** (Museum of Natural Science), while under the northern portico is the entrance to the **Museo Civico Archeologico**, with archeological material ranging from prehistoric times to the Longobard period. From here, walk under an arch onto the esplanade known as the Colle Aperto, with **Porta S. Alessandro**, a gate through which you can walk out to S. Vigilio and the surrounding hills.

Botanical garden, you enter this botanical garden along a stairway that runs from Viale Beltrami, beyond Colle Aperto; it is especially rich in Alpine plants.

Colle S. Vigilio. A funicular runs up to to the top of this hill from the Porta S. Alessandro; from the terminus at the top, you can walk to the summit, with the **Castello**, a simple fortress with remains of walls and four round towers. The esplanade, now a public park, affords a fine panoramic view* of Bergamo and the surrounding plain. Not far from the Porta S. Alessandro, on the slopes of the hill, extends the distinctive **Borgo Canale**, still rural in flavor. At no. 14 in Via Borgo Canale is the birthplace of G. Donizetti.

Viale delle Mura runs down from the Colle Aperto along the 16th-century walls built by the Venetians, ending at the Porta S. Agostino. The walls* and the four gates that open into each side of the old town offer a vivid image of a 16th-century citadel; inside the walls and gates is a series of rooms, with internal access roads, garrison halls, and gunports. Along this ring of stone, which forms a sort of terrace overlooking Bergamo Bassa and the surrounding plains, is a panoramic promenade.

BERGAMO BASSA

This circuit runs through ancient streets, exploring the part of Bergamo that, ever since Roman times, stood here on the plain. Setting out from the Porta S. Agostino for a tour of the nearby Accademia Carrara, the route then reaches the modern heart of Bergamo and runs through its most elegant streets; it then ventures into the western sections of Bergamo, with small shops and the workshops of fine craftsmen; going up to Bergamo Alta, it ends at the Porta S. Giacomo.

Pinacoteca dell'Accademia Carrara**. This art gallery is housed in a Neo-Classic palazzo which is the headquarters of the Accademia Carrara, founded at the end of the 18th century by Giacomo Carrara. Currently the gallery, one of Italy's finest in terms of both quality and cultural depth, possesses about 1900 paintings (especially from the Venetian and Lombard schools), as well as major collections of prints and drawings and lesser, but notable, collections of medals, bronzes, sculpture, porcelain, and miniatures. The most outstanding works are on permanent public display in 15 halls on the second floor, arranged by date and historical consequence, from International Gothic to late-18th century Venetian painting. There are celebrated masterpieces by such painters as B. Bembo, Botticelli, Pisanello, G. Bellini, Mantegna, Carpaccio, Raphael, Bergognone, Lotto, Cariani, Titian, Tintoretto, El Greco, Moroni, Dürer, Clouet, Brueghel the Elder, Baschenis, Fra' Galgario, Ceruti, Pitocchetto, Longhi, Piazzetta, Guardi, Canaletto, Bellotto, and Tiepolo. On the first floor, in 8 halls that can be toured by request are works from the Venetian, Lombard, and Piedmontese areas, (15-17C), as well as Baroque works from elsewhere in Europe, and Italian paintings (18-20C).

The Galleria d'Arte Moderna e Contemporanea is housed in the buildings overlooking the Accademia Carrara, once part of a 15th-century convent. On permanent exhibit are the Spajani and Manzù Collections, while several temporary exhibitions offer the visitors insights into 20th-century Italian art.

Via Pignolo*, the street descends steeply down from Bergamo Alta, and is lined with 16th-18th-century palazzi. A short distance from the corner of Via S. Tommaso, near the lovely Piazzetta del Delfino (note the 16C fountain that gives this square its name) is the **church of S. Alessandro della Croce**: inside, note the 18th-century altar* by A. Fantoni and the paintings by Bassano, Lotto, Costa, and A. Previtali. At no. 75 is the Museo di Arte Sacra Adriano Bernareggi, a museum of sacred art which includes archeological finds, paintings, and church furnishings formerly in the Museo Diocesano. At no. 80 is the 15th-century Palazzo dei Tasso. At the corner of Via S. Giovanni stands the church of S. Bernardino in Pignolo, founded in the 16th century; in the apse is an altarpiece by Lotto (1521). At the corner of Via T. Tasso is the **church of S. Spirito**, with a rusticated facade; note the bronze sculptures on the facade (1972). Inside, paintings by Lotto, Previtali, and Bergognone.

The Sentierone, in Piazza Matteotti, is a handsome tree-lined avenue, with porticoes on one side, built by the merchants of Bergamo in 1620 and today a popular promenade and meeting spot. Note the Teatro Donizetti, with its late-19th-century facade, and the church of S. Bartolomeo, in the apse of which is an altarpiece* by Lotto (1516), also known as the "Pala Martinengo"; also note the choir with 16th-century inlay work.

Via S. Alessandro: this road runs down from Bergamo Alta, forming the central thoroughfare of one of the old "borghi" that radiate out from the old center; you reach it by following the shopping street, Via XX Settembre. Just before the intersection with Via Garibaldi is the **church of S. Alessandro in Colonna**, rebuilt in the 18th century, with paintings by Bassano, Romanino, Lotto and Moretto. At the corner of Via Botta is the church of S. Benedetto, with a terracotta facade and small Renaissance cloister with frescoed lunettes. The last stretch of Via S. Alessandro is like a viaduct, running over large stone arches; this tour ends with the monumental Porta S. Giacomo, the southern gate of Bergamo Alta.

In the heart of the mountain fastness, the Alpine range extends endlessly. As impressive as the length of this great mountain range – running from the Colle di Cadibona all the way to Augsburg and Vienna, sloping down to the Danube – is, so to speak, its "breadth": about 150 km, on a line with Mont Blanc, and more than 330 km, on a line between Verona and Augsburg. Since Italy's northern border, as is well known, runs nearly entirely along the high crest of the Alps, save for in the Canton Ticino, the steeper and short slopes, facing south, are part of the Italian landscape; every stream runs down to the Po River and to the Adige. The route suggested here, which runs across the Swiss border, allows you to enjoy views of the far side of the watershed, to the other edge of the Rhaetian Alps, and, in particular, to the north slope of one of the most notable Alpine mountain groups, the Bernina, a mighty colossus of rock and ice, with the highest summit (4,049 m, therefore constituting the last 4,000 to the east of the Simplon Pass), and watered by torrents and rivers which will flow all the way through Europe, to the Black Sea. The names of the valleys through which you will travel or which you will cross are evocative of so many different faces of the Alpine world: Val Chiavenna, Val Bregaglia, Val Bernina, Val Poschiavina, Val di Livigno (a little patch of Italy just jutting over the watershed), Val Viola, and Valtellina. Along the way, there are a few artistic landmarks, but the enjoyment of this route lies chiefly in the variations of landscape through which you will travel, as you head over passes and drive down into valleys. Note another feature of this route: cableways take you quickly up to high altitudes and spectacular views.

NOT TO BE MISSED

Colico, overlooking the water, with a 19th-century landing embarcadero, offers a last glimpse of Lake Como. **Chiavenna** is well located, with fine views, excellent scenery, historic heritage, and much art (church of S. Lorenzo, Baptistery, and treasury). **Casaccia**: at the first ramps of the steep climb up to the Passo Maloja, note the path to the gorge and waterfall of Orlegna. **Passo Maloja**, with a fine view of the Val Bregaglia; in the small town, visit the house of the artist Segantini and a castle dating from 1885. **Silvaplana**: from nearby Surlej you can take a cableway up to Piz Corvatsch (3,303 m), amidst glaciers; there is a spectacular view of the Engadine Alps. **Pontresina** lies surrounded by a great Alpine arc. On your way up to the Passo del Bernina you will pass by the base-stations of two high cableways: one leads to the Diavolezza (2,973 m), a remarkable high-elevation viewpoint overlooking the glacier of Morteratsch, the Bernina,

A view of Bormio.

and the Piz Palù; the other runs up to the Piz Lagalb (2,959 m), with an equally fine view of the Bernina group. **Livigno** lies on the broad valley floor; its houses were all once made of wood, widely separated for fear of fires. The old part of **Bormio** is still a typical Alpine village; L. Sforza "the Moor" and Beatrice d'Este lived in the Torre degli Alberti for a while in 1496.

SONDRIO

The most dynamic center in Valtellina, it is at the heart of a wine area. The city probably has Roman origins, sitting near the Mallero Stream and the first slopes of the Rhaetian Alps.

Piazza Garibaldi, built in the first stage of Austrian domination, is the heart of the city. It is flanked by elegant Neo-Classic buildings, such as the Pedretti cinema/theater (built in 1820 by L. Canonica) and Palazzo Martinengo, a residence (16C) redone in Neo-Classic style. On the other side of the Mallero lies Palazzo Carbonera (16C), with a charming courtyard and a double loggia over the portico.

Piazza Campello: this square is flanked by Palazzo Pretorio, a 16th-century building with a lovely entrance, and the collegiate church of SS. Gervasio e Protasio (11C, but redone in 18C). The facade is a 19th-century facing. The large bell tower stands alone on the side.

Museo valtellinese di Storia e Arte: this local art and history museum is housed in Palazzo Sassi de' Lavizzari. The art gallery section has some 14th-18th century paintings. The upper floors are divided into 2 sections: archeology and contemporary art. The annexed Museo diocesano has paintings, pieces of frescoes (14-18C), altar cloths and holy vessels.

LAKE GARDA

To quote a 17th-century author: "delightful gardens, full of lemon trees, orange trees, and cedars, lush and flowering throughout the year, offer an exceedingly agreeable view, amidst laurel and myrtle, in a temperate and fragrant climate." He was describing the microclimate of Italy's largest lake, a slice of the Mediterranean amidst the Alps: the cypress became common here under Venetian administration, the grapevine dates back to remotest times, the olive tree may have been introduced by the Etruscans, but the Austrians developed it as a business. The mulberry has long vanished. Citrus trees were first grown by Franciscan brothers under Venetian rule; there are ruins of ancient winter greenhouses on the terraced slopes. Under Austrian rule, many towns without roads were served by a steamer called the "Archduke Ranieri"; on the Lombard side, a coastal road was not built until 1931. This route runs through a varied succession of landscapes: steep slopes and villas below, then even steeper rocks; the breathtaking view from the highlands of Tremosine, overlooking Mt Baldo; the colors of Venetian architecture, venerable little ports along the east shore; vast views, more like an arm of the sea than a lake, lie beyond Punta di S. Vigilio. Last comes Sirmione, frequented and described by Catullus: "Paene insularum, Sirmio, insularumque ocelle," the "delight of peninsulas and islands."

NOT TO BE MISSED

Salò*, with a handsome historical center, lies in an inlet, amidst green hills: the beauty of the site is the reason for its renown. **Gardone Riviera***: a lovely lakefront promenade embellishes this exclusive resort; also worthy of attention is the remarkable Vittoriale, home of the early-20th-century poet G. D'Annunzio. **Maderno** lies on the delta of the Toscolano River, with the Romanesque church of S. Andrea. Pieve, center of the township of Tremosine, has a remarkable overlook; to reach it you must take a detour up a twisting mountain road, into the gorge of the Brasa River. **Limone sul Garda**, set amidst abandoned olive, cedar, and lemon groves, has lovely homes in the old center, at the end of the lakefront promenade. **Riva del Garda**: this little town is a perfect combination of Alpine, Tridentine, and Venetian flavors (for a few brief decades, in 15C, it was ruled by Venice). **Torbole** has an enchanting lakefront. "Marmitte dei Giganti," notable geological formations, line the road to Nago and from Nago to Arco. **Malcesine**: the most remarkable features of this old town are the Palazzo dei Capitani del Lago and the Castello; you can also take a cableway up to Tratto Spino (1780 m), on the crest of Mt Baldo, with a twofold vista of Lake Garda and the Adige Valley. **Torri del Benaco**: a Scaliger castle dominates this lovely little village. **Punta di S. Vigilio***, among olive and cypress trees, deserves its reputation as the most romantic place on the lake. **Garda**: again, an enchanting lakefront, lined with fine old houses. **Bardolino** lies amidst vineyards whose grapes are used to produce the wine of the same name; in the town, visit the Romanesque church of S. Severo and the little church of S. Zeno, surrounded by small quaint houses. **Lazise** has a nearly intact ring of medieval walls. In the lovely panorama of the broad basin of the southern lake, note the enchanting – though often overcrowded – setting of the marina. **Peschiera del Garda** was a Venetian outpost fortress, the stronghold of the Austrian Quadrilateral: the town's military function can be seen in the fortifications that surround the markedly Venetian center, where the Mincio River flows into Lake Garda. **Sirmione***: the spectacular medieval walls of the Rocca Scaligera, the remarkably twisting streets of the "borgo", and the fine views of the lake are all well known, printed on too many postcards, perhaps, but still eminently enjoyable. The celebrated, so-called Grottoes of Catullus are actually the ruins of the largest existing ancient Roman villa from imperial times in northern Italy.

Sirmione: the Grottoes of Catullus.

BRESCIA

Brescia is the second largest city in Lombardy, both in terms of population and economic power. Located between the Po Valley and the Alpine foothills, it is a large and modern city, with renowned and noteworthy monuments and considerable art collections. Brescia is also seen as the gateway to Franciacorta, a famed wine zone – often associated with sparkling wines – that runs as far as the shores of Lake Iseo.

Piazza della Loggia*. Largely surrounded by Venetian-style buildings, this square is a vast and harmonious architectural complex. The dominant structure is the **Loggia***: now Palazzo del Comune, or city hall, this building was erected between 1492 and 1574 as a meeting hall. The ground floor (1492-1508) is partly porticoed; the upper floor (1554-74) was designed by many illustrious architects of the time, including Sansovino, Alessi, and Palladio, but probably chiefly by L. Beretta. A stairway climbs to the upstairs halls, partly decorated with 16th-century paintings.

Rotonda*. Brescia's premiere Romanesque monument is circular, topped by a dome surrounded by small pilastered arches. The interior* comprises a central space covered by a hemispherical dome, ringed by an ambulatory. A presbytery and two chapels were added in the 15th century; the left-hand chapel holds a rich, rarely shown array of treasures; the right chapel has paintings* by Moretto. Note the mosaic floor, dating from the 1st century BC, and two 14th-century sarcophagi*.

Broletto*. One of the most notable town halls in Lombardy, built between 1223 and 1298, and extensively enlarged and rebuilt in later centuries, this building is flanked by the Torre del Popolo, a tower dating from the 11th century. Note the courtyard, a mixture of medieval, Renaissance, and Baroque.

Castello. This immense fortress, which crowns the Colle Cidneo, dates from the time of the Communal government, though its current appearance dates from the 16th century. In the Grande Miglio is the Museo del Risorgimento, devoted to Italy's movement for independence and unification, covering the period from the 18th century to Italian unity in 1870.

Piazza del Foro*. Covering the ancient Roman Forum only in part, this square is surrounded by the Tempio Capitolino, a number of sections of the eastern portico, the Teatro, and the Basilica. These ruins, which harmonize perfectly with the square's medieval and Renaissance architecture, are Lombardy's most important Roman complex.

Tempio Capitolino*. This ancient temple was built in AD 73 under the emperor Vespasian; part of the steps, a partly rebuilt Corinthian colonnade, and the pediment, likewise reassembled, survive. Under the pronaos are the ruins of a sanctuary from the Republican period (1C BC); of the two porticoed wings, only the base of the eastern one remains, from which a passage leads down to a space known as Aula dei Pilastrini. On one of its ends are the portals which go into the three cellae. A fourth cella gives access to the impressive ruins of the Teatro Romano, an ancient theater partly covered by Renaissance and modern buildings.

Complesso museale di S. Salvatore e S. Giulia. This monastery was founded in AD 753 and suppressed in 1797, when it became a barracks; it houses the Museo della Città*, with documentation on archaelogical, historical, artistic, architectural aspects of Brescia. Among the Roman finds, noteworthy is the Vittoria Alata*, or winged victory, a huge bronze statue (1C AD) from the Hellenistic world. It also contains three churches: S.Giulia, begun in 1466 and enlarged in 1599, with frescoes by F. Ferramola; S. Maria in Solario*, a Romanesque structure containing frescoes (16C) by local artists; and S. Salvatore*, a piece of architecture from the high Middle Ages built in the 11th century on the site of an 8th-century church and Roman ruins: it has capitals from the 6th century and a crypt, as well as frescoes and stuccoes (8C); in the chapel at the base of the bell tower, frescoes by Romanino.

Pinacoteca Tosio Martinengo**. One of Lombardy's largest collection of paintings. Among the artists: Veneziano, Civerchio, Foppa, Solario, Raphael, Moretto, Romanino, Lotto, Savoldo, Piazza, G.B. Moroni, Tintoretto, Ceruti, Zuccarelli, and Hayez.

S. Maria dei Miracoli. Built between the 15th and 16th century, this church has a marble facade* (1488-1500) with bas-relief decorations and marble bas-reliefs inside.

Ss. Nazaro e Celso*. This church, with an 18th-century facade, contains fine paintings by Moretto (1541), Pittoni (1740), and Romanino, and a masterpiece by the young Titian, the Averoldi polyptych (1522).

S. Francesco. This Romanesque-Gothic church (1265) has a marble portal and rose window; inside frescoes (13-15C) and paintings by Moretto and Romanino. In the sacristy, wooden intarsias by F. Morari, 1511; also, note the cloister.

MILAN/MILANO

T hriving, open-handed, forward-looking: the Milanese pride themselves on their city's wealth, international ties, and metropolitan sophistication. Milan is Italy's second-largest city; the population swells each day by 20 percent as commuters and travellers flock into the city. Even so, the number of residents has declined in recent years. The city proper is relatively small (extending just 8 km from the golden spire of the Duomo); its influence extends over the surrounding plain, which is densely populated and heavily industrialized, especially to the north. Milan is a city of executives, marketers, and financiers. It is the capital of Italy's "service industry," and boasts more than 100,000 local businesses. It stands on the brink of the brave new "post-modern" world, as it quickly sheds the last remnants of its "blue-collar" past. Culturally, La Scala, the fabled opera house, is perhaps Milan's best-known landmark, but is only a small part of the city's rich artistic heritage. Milan is vast and hard-working; were business to disappear entirely from the landscape, however, a remarkable "art city" would still stand on the Lombard plains. On a clear, windy day, from the roof of the Duomo, or any other vantage point, one can clearly see the Alps glittering with snow to the north (and, beyond them, all of Central Europe), to the south, east, and west, the broad rolling expanse of the Po Valley, one of the wealthiest regions on earth.

Galleria Vittorio Emanuele II, in the heart of Milan, has lovely art-nouveau glass ceilings.

THE "CENTRAL CORE"

The Duomo, Corso Vittorio Emanuele, La Scala, Palazzo Marino, the Galleria, Palazzo della Ragione: famed and little-known city sights, in a stroll through memories and high society, never more than 400 m from the golden statue of the Madonnina (the small Virgin Mary) high atop the Duomo's central spire.

Piazza del Duomo. This vast rectangle that fronts the Duomo is the city's geographic core, the hub of the great avenues that run outward like so many spokes, in line with the 19th century urban plan. Working just after Italy's Unification, G. Mengoni gave this piazza much of its modern-day appearance, designing the porticoes that run its length as well as the great portal that opens into the Galleria Vittorio Emanuele II (1878), to the left of the facade of the Duomo. In the center of the square stands an equestrian statue of this sovereign, who was Italy's first king. Opposite the Galleria are the loggia-structures of the Arengario (1939-56), to the left of which is the Piazzetta Reale, fronting Palazzo Reale, the site of some

of the most important temporary exhibitions in town. Beyond the palace lies **Piazza Diaz**.

Duomo**. This cathedral, above all others, has come to symbolize Milan. Tradition states that the church was founded in 1386, under the rule of Gian Galeazzo Visconti, dedicated to "Santa Maria Nascente." It magnificently dominates the eastern side of the piazza, a vast and intricately fashioned marble structure, straw-yellow in color. The seemingly interminable process of construction began under the direction of the "engineer general" S. da Orsenigo, assisted by other Lombard masters; he was succeeded by G. de' Grassi, and in the first half of the 15th century – when plan and elevation took final form – in turn by M. da Carona and F. degli Organi. Over the ensuing centuries, the supervision of construction fell to the leading "Visconti" architects, among them Giovanni and Guiniforte Solari and G.A. Amadeo (who designed the tambour) in the second half of the 15th century, V. Seregni and P. Tibaldi in the 16th century, L. Buzzi and F.M. Richini in the 17th century. In 1765-69 F. Croce completed the

HIGHLIGHTS

O MIA BELA MADONINA

The statue of the Holy Mother (4.46 m tall and weighing 3 tons), built between 1769-1774, is affectionately known by everybody as the "Madonnina", notably in the popular song by Giovanni D'Anzi. There is a memorial plaque to maestro D'Anzi at the entrance to the Galleria del Corso, in Piazza Beccaria, also commemorating the most famous line from his best known song: "O mia bela Madonina..." To make sure it is pronounced properly, the plaque is actually engraved with the word "Madunina", since the "u" is rendered as an "o" in the written dialect; although this was argued over for a while, everything eventually sorted itself out in the usual good spirits of the Milanese.

tambour with the main spire, on the top of which was placed in 1774 the gilded statue of the "Madonnina." Napoleon ordered the completion of the facade (1805-13), for which one plan after another had been submitted since the 17th century, and in 1811-12 the remarkable forest of spires was finished. As huge as the piazza itself may be, it does little to diminish the Duomo's vast size: 158 m long, 93 m wide at the transept, with an interior of 11,700 m²; the tallest spire rises 108 m. The church boasts more than 3400 statues, largely distributed over the 135 spires. The side view, from Piazzetta Reale, and the rear view, from Corso Vittorio Emanuele, standard fare of 19th-century view painters, help us to appreciate to the full the sheer mass of Candoglia marble employed, punctuated by buttresses and topped by dizzying spires. In the rear, the massive transept and polygonal apse are pierced by three enormous stained glass windows.

The interior, with a four-aisle nave, is crossed by a short three-aisle transept with a deeply recessed presbytery and ambulatory. In the shadowy coolness, 52 colossal engaged piers line the nave, transept, and apse, surmounted by huge capitals adorned by statues of saints and prophets. Most of the spectacular stained-glass **windows*** date from the 15th and 16th century, though some date from the 19th and 20th century; especially noteworthy are the windows in the first, fifth, and sixth bays on the right and at the end of the right arm of the transept. Also, note the immense Gothic Trivulzio candelabrum at the end of the left arm of the transept.

Overlooking the ambulatory are the 14th-century **portals*** of the vestries; the portal on the left vestry is believed to be the earliest piece of sculpture in the Duomo, and is attributed to G. da Campione (1389). The stairway facing the south vestry leads down to the crypt, which contains the remains of Saint Charles Borromeo. Adjacent is the Duomo's **Treasury***, which features remarkable goldwork, the earliest dating from the 4th and 5th century. On the inner side of the facade a stairway leads down to the **Scavi paleocristiani**, a series of Early Christian excavations where you can find the remains of the Battistero di Giovanni alle Fonti (AD 378) with an octagonal plan. Here St Ambrose, patron saint of the town, is said to have baptized St Augustine. From the left side, outside the cathedral, you can climb up to the roof. Here you will see a second, "open-air" cathedral, over which looms the elaborate tambour; from here you can enjoy a splendid view of the city*. Near the elevator is the oldest spire on the Duomo, the **Guglia Carelli**, built in 1397-1404.

Palazzo Reale. Although it was first built in the 14th century, its final, Neo-Classic form is the work of Piermarini (1778). It was the residence of Spanish and Austrian governors and was damaged by bombing in 1943. It now houses the Museo del Duomo and the Civico Museo d'Arte Contemporanea (museum of contemporary art), and various exhibition spaces.

Museo del Duomo*. This ground floor museum features 600 works, largely sculpture and architecture taken from the Duomo. There are also fragments of ancient stained glass pieces, tapestries, sketches, architectural models, and wooden carvings.

Civico Museo d'Arte Contemporanea. This museum features 20th-century Italian artworks, ranging from Futurism, the school of metaphysical painting, Novecento, early abstract artists, the Roman school, "Corrente," and others. There are halls devoted to the work of Boccioni, De Chirico, Sironi, Morandi, De Pisis, Fontana, and others.

Piazza Fontana. This piazza takes its name from the 18th-century fountain; a commemorative plaque reminds us that the square was the site of a terrorist bombing that killed 16 people in 1969. The **Archbishop's Palace** (no. 2) dominates the square.

Corso Vittorio Emanuele II. This pedestrian zone lined by porticoes and modern architecture, movie theaters and stores, was rebuilt after the bombing of 1943. At the beginning of the Corso, on the left, overlooking Piazza del Duomo, is La Rinascente (rebuilt in 1950), a famous Italian department store. Worth noting along the Corso is the Art Nouveau Piazza del Liberty (no. 8), and the Neo-Classic **church of S. Carlo al Corso**, built in 1839-47.

Piazza S. Babila. The result of extensive urban rebuilding in the 1930s and after WWII, this portico-lined piazza takes its name from the ancient **church of S. Babila**, with its 17th-century column at the corner of Corso Monforte and Corso Venezia. The church was completely rebuilt between 1853 and 1906.

Corso Matteotti. Carved out as a Fascist avenue in 1926-34, this is an outstanding example of state architecture of the era. It culminates in a large disk-shaped statue by A. Pomodoro (1980); to the right, note Piazza Belgioioso, with **Palazzo Belgioioso**, by Piermarini (1772-81). At the corner of Via Morone is the house of the great writer A. Manzoni, now the **Museo Manzoniano**. The brief Via Omenoni features the **Casa degli Omenoni***, with its telamons underpinning the facade.

Piazza S. Fedele. This pedestrian square features a monument to A. Manzoni (1883) and the **church of S. Fedele**, built to plans by P. Tibaldi (1569) but completed only in 1835. It has remarkable paintings and, in the 17th-century vestry, handsome carved cabinets. To the left of the church, is the rear facade* of **Palazzo Marino**, built by G. Alessi (1553) in late Renaissance style and left unaltered by the reconstruction. From Via Marino (no. 2), you can view the inner courtyard*, with two orders of loggias, through the former main ceremonial portal. Nowadays Palazzo Marino, whose main facade is in Piazza della Scala, opposite the theater, is Milan's Town Hall.

Piazza della Scala. A city block was torn down in 1858 to make way for this square, designed by Luca Beltrami, who also rebuilt the facade of Palazzo Marino. In the center of the square stands a monument to Leonardo da Vinci (1872), overlooking La Scala.

Teatro alla Scala*. Italy's premier opera house, possibly the world's finest, La Scala was built in 1776-78 by G. Piermarini, in linear Neo-Classic style, on the former site of the church of S. Maria della Scala, hence the name. The hall seats 3,000, has four tiers of boxes and two galleries, and is nicely finished in Neo-Classic style; partially destroyed by bombing in 1943, it was rebuilt and inaugurated with a legendary concert, directed by A. Toscanini.

Museo Teatrale alla Scala. It houses major collections of operatic and theatrical memorabilia; the Raccolta Verdiana is noteworthy. **Galleria Vittorio Emanuele II***. Traditional meeting place of the Milanese, as well as one of the most remarkable pieces of the architecture of Milan after the Unification of Italy, the Galleria links Piazza del Duomo with Piazza della Scala. Built by G. Mengoni in 1865-78, it is crowned by a distinctive glass-and-steel roof that culminates in a central "octagon." There are four grand portals; the one facing the Duomo is connected to the porticoes of the piazza.

Palazzo della Ragione*. Also called Broletto Nuovo, it stands on what was once a large square, eliminated by the creation in 1867-78 of both Via and Piazza Mercanti. Built in 1233, this was the largest medieval town hall in Lombardy. The facade overlooking the piazza features a Romanesque relief* of O. da Tresseno – its builder – on horseback (13C). Facing the Palazzo della Ragione along Via Mercanti is Palazzo dei Giureconsulti, with a portico and notable windows, almost entirely rebuilt since 1561, as have been many of the buildings along this street, from 14th to 17th century.

BRERA AND THE "QUADRILATERO DELLA MODA"

In the northern part of town, enclosed within the Cerchia dei Navigli, this route takes you to the Pinacoteca di Brera, one of Italy's finest art galleries, through streets studded with aristocratic mansions and smart boutiques. The understated elegance of this neighborhood has made it a capital of Italian fashion designers.

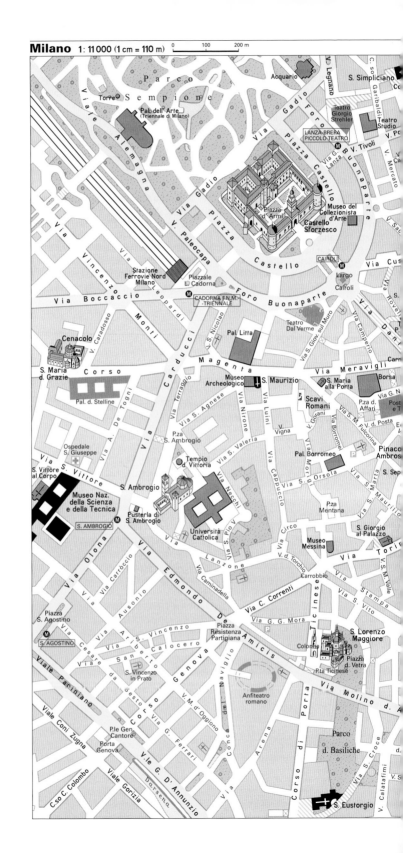

Milano 1: 11 000 (1 cm = 110 m)

0   100   200 m

Parco Sempione

Acquario

S. Simpliciano

Torre

Pal. dell' Arte
(Triennale di Milano)

Teatro Giorgio Strehler

Teatro Studio

LANZA-BRERA
PICCOLO TEATRO

V. Tivoli

Piazza Castello

Piazza d'Armi

Museo del Collezionista d'Arte

Castello Sforzesco

Castello

CAIROLI

Via Cus

Stazione Ferrovie Nord Milano

Piazzale L. Cadorna

Largo Cairoli

CADORNA F.N.M. -TRIENNALE

Via Boccaccio

Foro Buonaparte

Via Dan

Teatro Dal Verme

Via Campério

Cenacolo

Pal. Litta

S. Maria d. Grazie

Corso

Magenta

Via Meravigli

Carr

Museo Archeologico

S. Maurizio

S. Maria alla Porta

Borsa

Pal. d. Stelline

Scavi Romani

P.za d. Affari

Via G. N

Via S. M. Fulcorina

V. d. Posta

Post e T

P.za S. Ambrogio

V. Vigna

Ospedale S. Giuseppe

Tempio d. Vittoria

Pal. Borromeo

Pinaco Ambros

S. Vittore al Corpo

S. Ambrogio

Via S. Orsola

S. Sep

Museo Naz. della Scienza e della Tecnica

Pusterla di S. Ambrogio

S. AMBROGIO

Università Cattolica

P.za Mentana

S. Giorgio al Palazzo

Museo Messina

Via Tori

V.S.M-Valle

Otona

V. d. Torchio

Carrobbio

Via C. Correnti

Via S. Vito

Piazza S. Agostino

Via C. Correnti

Via Stampa

S. AGOSTINO

Piazza Resistenza Partigiana

Via G. G. Mora

S. Lorenzo Maggiore

Colonne

S. Vincenzo in Prato

Piazza d. Vetra

P.ta Ticinese

Via Molino d. A

Anfiteatro romano

Parco d. Basiliche

P.le Gen. Cantore

Porta Genova

V.le G. D'Annunzio

S. Eustorgio

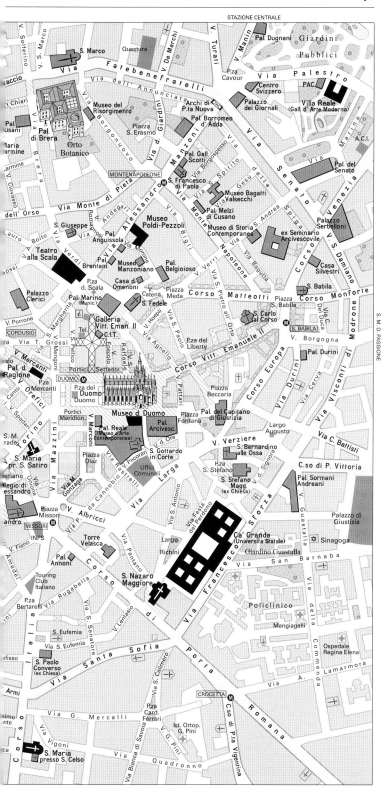

STAZIONE CENTRALE

S. Marco
Questura
Pal. Dugnani
Giardini
Pubblici

V. Solferino
V. S. Marco
V. De Marchi
V. Manin
V. Cavour

Via Fatebenefratelli
Via Palestro

Via dell'Annunciata
Centro Svizzero
PAC

Archi di P.ta Nuova
Palazzo dei Giornali
Villa Reale
(Gall. d' Arte Moderna)

Museo del Risorgimento
Pal. Borromeo d'Adda

Piazza S. Erasmo
A.C.I.

Pal. di Brera
Orto Botanico

MONTENAPOLEONE
Pal. Gall. Scotti

S. Francesco di Paola
Pal. del Senato

S. Giuseppe
Museo Poldi-Pezzoli
Museo Bagatti Valsecchi

Pal. Anguissola
Pal. Melzi di Cusano

Museo di Storia Contemporanea
Palazzo Serbelloni

Teatro alla Scala
Pal. Brentani
Museo Manzoniano
Pal. Belgioioso
ex Seminario Arcivescovile
Casa Silvestri

Casa d. Scala
Museo Omenoni
S. Babila

Palazzo Clerici
Pza. Meda
Piazza Meda
Corso Matteotti
Piazza S. Babila
Corso Monforte

Pal. Marino (Munic.)
S. Fedele
Piazza S. Babila
Pal. Durini

Galleria Vitt. Eman. II
S. Carlo al Corso
S. BABILA

CORDUSIO
Via T. Grossi
C.I.T.
Pza. del Liberty
V. Borgogna

Pal d' Ragione
Portici Settentr.
Corso Vitt. Emanuele II
Corso Europa

Pza. Mercanti
DUOMO
Pza. del Duomo
Duomo
Pal. Durini

Portici Merid.
Piazza Beccaria

Museo d. Duomo
Piazza Fontana
Pal. del Capitano di Giustizia
Largo Augusto

Pal. Reale (Museo d'Arte Contemporanea)
Pal. Arcivesc.
V. Verziere

S. M. rade
Piazza Diaz
S. Gottardo in Corte
S. Bernardino alle Ossa

S. Maria pr. S. Satiro
Uffici Comunali
Hza. S. Stefano

legio di essandro
S. Stefano Magg. (ex Chiesa)
Pal. Sormani Andreani

Piazza Missori
MISSORI
V. Albricci
C.so di P. Vittoria

INPS
Torre Velasca
Largo Richini
Ca' Granda (Università Statale)
Palazzo di Giustizia

Pal. Annoni
Sinagoga

Touring Club Italiano
S. Nazaro Maggiore
Giardino Guastalla

Via San Barnaba

S. Eufemia
Policlinico

S. Paolo Converso (ex Chiesa)
Mangiagalli

Santa Sofia
Ospedale Regina Elena

CROCETTA
Pza. Card. Ferrari

S. Maria presso S. Celso
Ist. Ortop. G. Pini
Quadronno

Piazza della Scala, with the famous theater on the right, is a symbol of Milan.

Piazza Cordusio. Oval in shape, with a statue to the 18th-century poet Parini, this piazza is Milan's "business center," and features the official turn-of-the-century architectural style. Via Broletto. This lovely old street, which continues as Via Ponte Vetero and then Via Mercato, is lined with office buildings, old working-class Milanese row houses, and small storefronts and business establishments.

S. Maria del Carmine. Although the slightly fanciful "Lombard-Gothic" facade dates only from 1880, the church itself was founded in the 15th century. Running off to the left from the square is the narrow Via Madonnina, intersecting with Via S. Carpoforo and Via Fiori Chiari. Longago a neighborhood of ill repute, these narrow lanes now teem with expensive shops and elegant nightspots; there is a fine Mercato dell'Antiquariato, or antiques market (3rd Sat. of each month).

Palazzo di Brera*. This impressive building, at Via Brera no. 28 was headquarters of the Milanese Jesuits for two centuries (1572-1772); it then became home to many of the city's most important cultural institutions, including the Pinacoteca di Brera, the Biblioteca Nazionale Braidense, and the Accademia di Belle Arti. Built in the 15th century, it was renovated by F.M. Richini (1651) and completed by Piermarini (1774). The elegant courtyard with two rows of arcades features a heroic bronze statue of Napoleon Bonaparte I, by A. Canova (1811).

Pinacoteca di Brera**, spread out through the forty or so halls of the first floor, this is one of the leading collections of paintings in Italy; it chiefly features works of the Lombard and Venetian schools of the 15th to 18th centuries. Founded two centuries ago as a resource for the students of the Accademia, opened in 1803, the galley grew rapidly throughout the

19th century and the more recent acquisition of the Donazione Jesi (1976-84) gave Brera a 20th-century dimension as well. More than 600 works are on display: 15th-16th-century Venetian, Lombard, and Emilian artists (J. Bellini, his two sons, G. and G. Bellini, Mantegna, Crivelli, Carpaccio, Lotto, Titian, Veronese, Tintoretto, and J. Bassano, B. Luini, Correggio); central Italian painters from the 14th-16th century (A. Lorenzetti, G. da Fabriano, D. Bramante, P. della Francesca, Raphael, L. Signorelli); non-Italian artists (Van Dyck, Rubens, and El Greco); 17th-century Italians (Ludovico, Agostino, and A.Carracci, Guercino, and Caravaggio); 18th-century Italians (Tiepolo, G.B Piazzetta, A. and P. Longhi, F. Guardi, Canaletto, Bellotto); and 19th-century Italians (A. Appiani, F. Hayez, S. Lega, G. Fattori, G. Pellizza da Volpedo). A major collection of 20th-century work, the Donazione Jesi, includes paintings by Modigliani, Boccioni, Severini, Carrà, Campigli, Morandi, Sironi, De Pisis, Scipione, Picasso, and Braque; and sculpture by M. Rosso, A. Martini, and M. Marini.

Via Brera. With Via Solferino and Via S. Marco, this street runs through the heart of one of Milan's most interesting neighborhoods; here art galleries vie with fine restaurants, bars, and cafés.

S. Marco. Once overlooking the intersection of two canals, this church now faces out over the corner of Via S. Marco and Via Fatebenefratelli, just behind the Palazzo di Brera. It features the original portal, bell tower, and several statues upon the facade, dating from the 13th and 15th century; in the interior are a number of paintings, frescoes, and other works.

Civico Museo del Risorgimento, this museum of Italian history is housed in the Neo-Classic Palazzo Moriggia, at no. 23 in Via

Borgonuovo. Along the way back to Via Manzoni, overlooking Via Verdi, is a particularly fine Baroque **church S. Giuseppe**, designed by F.M. Richini (1630).

Via Manzoni this venerable Milanese street is lined with handsome villas, many with large rear gardens. On your left, in Largo Croce Rossa, is a controversial monument to the late Italian president and Resistance leader Sandro Pertini (Aldo Rossi, 1990); beyond this is the tree-lined **Via dei Giardini**, with the remains of a 15th-century monastic cloister, in Piazza S. Erasmo. Past Via Monte Napoleone, Baroque and Neo-Classic palazzi and churches line the road. Via Manzoni ends with the **Arco di Porta Nuova**, a city gate dating from the 12th century.

Museo Poldi Pezzoli*, this is an outstanding example of Milanese home-cum-museum, and its 23 halls give a sterling indication of the tastes of a private collector of the 19th century, in this case, Gian Giacomo Poldi Pezzoli. The collection includes 14th- to 19th-century paintings and decorative arts: goldwork, enamels, Murano glass, Italian and European ceramics, furnishings, textiles (Persian carpet, signed and dated, 1542-43), lace and tapestries, mechanical clocks (Falck Collection) and sundials (Portaluppi Collection), weapons and armors. There are some masterpieces by artists such as P. del Pollaiuolo, Botticelli, P. della Francesca, Mantegna, Cosmè Tura, and F. Guardi; and a wide range of work by Lombard painters of the 15th and 16th century (Bergognone, Boltraffio, C. da Sesto, Foppa, Luini) and 18th-century Venetians (Tiepolo, Canaletto).

Via Monte Napoleone. Almost entirely rebuilt in the Neo-Classic style, lined with aristocratic palazzi, this street – with the last section of Via Manzoni, Via della Spiga, and Via S. Andrea – encloses the "Quadrilatero della Moda," the fashion district featuring antique shops, jewelry stores, and leading fashion designers' retail outlets.

Museo Bagatti Valsecchi, this late 19th-century home in Via S. Spirito no. 10 offers a fine view of the home of a collector. The furnishings include 16th-century Flemish tapestries, stained glass, hope chests, and a bed decorated with bas-reliefs of Bible scenes. There are also paintings and other works.

Museo di Storia Contemporanea. Located in an 18th-century palazzo, at no. 6 Via S. Andrea, this museum of contemporary history is the seat of temporary exhibitions; upstairs is the **Museo di Milano**, with 600 18th-19th-century paintings and prints regarding Milan.

S. AMBROGIO AND QUARTIERE MAGENTA

The centuries have left their mark in Milan, and this walk goes to the churches of S. Ambrogio, a Romanesque archetype, and Santa Maria delle Grazie, where Leonardo da Vinci painted his Last Supper, and then goes past the Biblioteca Ambrosiana and the Pinacoteca Ambrosiana.

Piazza S. Ambrogio. This oddly shaped square was once a broad thoroughfare – Stradone di S. Ambrogio – running alongside the basilica. One end of the square is marked by the **Pusterla di S. Ambrogio**, built in 1939 in imitation of the medieval city gates (12C) and decorated by an authentic tabernacle with statues of patron saints (1360). Behind the basilica stands a military monument called the **Tempio della Vittoria**, an octagonal tower (1927-30), and the **Università Cattolica del Sacro Cuore**, one of the most important universities of the town, which features two cloisters by Bramante*.

S. Ambrogio**. One of Milan's most distinctive landmarks, this basilica, dedicated to the city's patron saint, is a remarkable mixture of restoration and a founding monument of Lombard Romanesque. Built in AD 379 as the "Basilica Martyrum," it is the final resting place of St Ambrose, who was buried here in AD 397. It was rebuilt extensively in the 9th and 10th century, and has undergone almost constant renovation since then. Standing before the basilica is a solemn rectangular **atrium***, with porticoes (1088-99) resting upon composite columns with carved capitals. On the far side of the atrium is the sloped-roof facade*, consisting of two storeys of loggias: the upper loggia features five arches of declining size. On either side is a bell tower, the one on the right dating from the 9th century, the one on the left, with pilaster strips and little arches, dating from 1128-44. On the left portal, note the pre-Romanesque relief of St Ambrose*; the central portal is adorned with minute carvings of monstrous figures and a grapevine motif (8-9C). The interior is laid out with a nave with two aisles, terminating in apses and separated by piers, roofed by broad cross vaults, with galleries along the aisles, tambour, and the deep central apse. In the third bay of the nave, on the left, above the sarcophagus of Stilicho (4C), is a **pulpit*** made of 11th-century fragments. At the center of the presbytery, set on four porphyry columns from Roman times, is the ciborium*, decorated with Lombard-Byzantine polychrome stuccoes (10C). Beneath the ciborium is the altar frontal known as **Altare d'Oro****, a precious work of goldsmithery

HIGHLIGHTS

THE FASHION DISTRICT

Aristocratic streets embellished with elegant Neo-Classic buildings, where there were still food stores until not so long ago, are now lined with the shop windows of prestigious stores, in summer displaying the cuts and colors which will be fashion in autumn and in winter diplaying the bright colors destined to be in vogue the following spring. Here, between via Monte Napoleone and via Della Spiga, all the most famous names in italian and world fashion – like Prada, Moschino, Dolce&Gabbana, Armani, Valentino – have their stores. Jewelry (such as Cartier, Tiffany and Bulgari) and perfume shops as well as antiques stores abound, but are always tied to the world of luxury and elegance.

from the Carolingian period in gold and silver sheet (Stories of Christ and St Ambrose) with decorations in enamel and gems, by the Maestro Volvinio (835). In the apse, note the carved Gothic wooden choir (1469-71); in the vault is an enormous mosaic, with sections dating from the 4th and 8th century and portions redone in the 17th and 20th century; in the crypt, silver urn (1897) with the bodies of St Ambrose and two other saints. In the right aisle, fresco attributed to G. Ferrari; detached frescoes by Tiepolo; canvases and frescoes by Lanino. The seventh chapel leads into the **Sacello di S. Vittore in Ciel d'Oro*** (4C), a chapel whose cupola is decorated with mosaics with figures of saints. From the left aisle (first chapel, Christ and Angels* by Bergognone) you emerge under the Portico della Canonica*, by Bramante (1492), rebuilt with original materials after heavy damage suffered in WWII. Under the portico of the rectory is the entrance to the **Tesoro di S. Ambrogio**, which features goldwork, fabrics, tapestries, and other artwork from the basilica.

S. Vittore al Corpo. Set back on a small rectangular piazza, this Early Christian basilica was rebuilt in the late 16th century. The interior features paintings (17C) and a remarkable wooden choir. To the left of the basilica is the former Monastery of S. Vittore, now the site of the Museo della Scienza e della Tecnica (see below). Founded by Benedictines in the 11th century, the monastery was rebuilt in the 16th century and repeatedly renovated; part of the cloisters and a few rooms survive from the original structure.

Museo Nazionale della Scienza e della Tecnica Leonardo da Vinci*, opened in 1953 as a museum documenting the development of science and industrial technology, the building extends over a vast area between Via Olona and Via S. Vittore (entrance from the Piazza, at no. 21). With more than 35,000 m² of exhibition space in three adjoining buildings, the museum has 28 sections. Temporary

exhibits and conferences are held here; it also has a notable specialized library (about 40,000 volumes). In the monumental building (once a monastery) is a great gallery devoted to Leonardo da Vinci, forming a considerable part of the museum, with extensive documentation concerning Leonardo, both as a scientist and as a technician and scholar of nature; other rooms given over to other areas of science and technology (computer science, timekeeping, acoustics, astronomy, telecommunications) and, in the basement, land-based transportation, and metallurgy. There is a rail transport building, with about twenty antique locomotives (steam and electric), railroad cars, signals, and other material documenting the technological development of trains in Italy. In the air and sea transport building, there are sections concerning air transport (twenty antique airplanes, including a Bleriot 11 from 1909) and maritime transport (the training ship "Ebe", the bridge of the trans-Atlantic liner "Conte Biancamano"); also, a section devoted to agriculture. In this same complex is the **Civico Museo Navale Didattico**, a museum on the history of ships, now being renovated.

Porta Magenta. The city gate was demolished in 1885, but the name persists, a name that describes the elegant neighborhood stretching along Corso Magenta, Via Ariosto, Via Pagano, and the Parco Sempione. Remarkable buildings date from the turn of the century.

Cenacolo Vinciano**, on the far wall of the huge refectory of the former Dominican convent, to the left of the church of Santa Maria delle Grazie (see below), is Leonardo da Vinci's renowned fresco of **The Last Supper**** (1495-97), now completely restored after heavy damage during WWII.

S. Maria delle Grazie**, this church is one of the greatest monuments of the Milanese Renaissance. Built in Gothic style (1466-90), the church was given its apse in 1492, based on the design by Bramante, in the shape of a huge three-apse cube, topped by a polygonal tambour with a gallery. The elegant marble and terracotta decorations of the apse, and the 15th-century marble portal in the facade are worthy of note. The nave and two aisles are flanked by chapels, the bays divided by broad pointed arches resting on columns. The chapels and piers feature remarkable works by such artists as Gaudenzio Ferrari and Paris Bordone.

The Renaissance **tambour**** was meant to be a Sforza family mausoleum, and features a cupola set upon a drum held up by four spectacular arches. The dignified "graffito" decoration* (discovered in 1934-37 and restored in 1984-87) is attributed to Bramante; in the presbytery is a carved wooden choir (1470-1510). On the left is the lovely little **cloister****, again believed to be by Bramante. Then you enter the **Sagrestia Vecchia**, or Old Sacristy, with inlaid cabinets* and early 16th-century paintings.

Corso Magenta. This main thoroughfare runs through the heart of the Quartiere Magenta. In the first stretch only the facades survive from the 18th-century buildings that once lined it; just past the Cerchia dei Navigli (ring of canals, many now covered over), or what is now Via Carducci, on the left (no. 24) stands the **Palazzo Litta** by F.M. Richini (1648), now the offices of the State Railroads, with a Rococo facade (1763) and a splendid porticoed courtyard. Facing it is the former **Monastero Maggiore**, once an enormous Milanese nunnery, built in the 15th century, partly demolished in 1864-72 and badly damaged in WWII; the church of S. Maurizio and the entry cloister survive, part of the Museo Archeologico.

Civiche Raccolte Archeologiche e Numismatiche, at Corso Magenta no. 15, it features remarkable archeological and numismatic collections. Of special interest are the sculptures (Aphrodite-Aura), portraits (Maximin the Thracian*), mosaics, ceramics, oil lamps, glass, bronzes, silver, barbarian funerary objects. There are also remarkable collections of Attic and other ancient pottery as well as a large Etruscan collection. From the garden, there is a fine view of two Roman towers.

S. Maurizio*, this Renaissance church was begun in the 16th century and completed in 1872-96. The interior features a remarkable fresco, attributed to B. Luini.

S. Maria alla Porta. This church, built after 1652 by F.M. Richini, overlooks Via S. Maria alla Porta, which followed the Roman "decumanus maximus." Inside, note 17th-century canvases and sculpture. Heading back toward the beginning of Corso Magenta, you can follow the narrow Via Brisa (left) to the excavations of a large Roman building. Just behind the church is the "Quartiere degli Affari," or Financial District, the heart of which is the **Palazzo della Borsa**, the Stock Exchange building by P. Mezzanotte (1931), which stands on the site of the ancient Roman theater (relics in the basement). In nearby Piazza Borromeo, at no. 7, is the **Palazzo Borromeo**; in the inner courtyard are frescoes* in the International Gothic style (first half of the 15C).

Piazza S. Sepolcro, this is the site of the ancient Roman Forum, though no traces survive. Overlooking the piazza is the church of S. Sepolcro, founded in 1030, but rebuilt in 1894-97.

Pinacoteca Ambrosiana*, this is one of the most important cultural institutions in Milan, dating from the early 17th century, with collections, chiefly Lombard and Venetian, of works by Botticelli, Bergognone, Luini, Bramantino, Leonardo, G.A. De Predis, Raphael, Tiepolo, Caravaggio, Moretto, Titian, and Bassano.

THE CASTELLO SFORZESCO AND CORSO GARIBALDI

The northwestern section of the historical center of Milan lies around the majestic structure of the Castello, its courtyards, great walls, and mighty towers redolent with the history of the Visconti and Sforza dukedom. Behind the castle lies the Parco Sempione.

Via Dante. One of the finest legacies of Milan under King Umberto (1890), this street provides a fitting link between Piazza Cordusio and the Castello Sforzesco. At no. 2 is the Palazzo Carmagnola, all that survived of the wholesale demolition of the 19th century Next to it, in Via Rovello, is the Piccolo Teatro, a prestigious Milanese theater founded in 1947. The Nuovo Piccolo Teatro by M. Zanuso is in Piazzale Marengo. At the end, Via Dante opens out into L**argo Cairoli**, with a monument to Garibaldi (1895). This is the spot marking the convergence of the two tree-lined semicircles of Foro Buonaparte and Piazza Castello, part of the unfinished Neo-Classic design by Antolini (1801) for a huge circular square around the Castello Sforzesco.

Castello Sforzesco**, this huge fortified complex – perhaps the most significant Renaissance monument still standing in Milan, despite its troubled history – has housed the city museums and other major cultural institutions since the end of the 19th century.

The castle was commissioned by F. Sforza (1450), and was built on an existing 14th-century structure. It became the home of Galeazzo Maria Sforza, duke of Milan, in 1466. The new duke summoned artists to turn the castle into a stately home; among them were V. Foppa, C. Moretto, and B. Ferrini. L. il Moro, in turn, summoned Leonardo da Vinci, Bramante, Filarete, Zenale, and Butinone. After the Spanish took Milan in 1535, the Castello became one of the largest and best-served citadels in Europe (early 17C). It was heavily damaged by a French siege under Louis XV (1733); Napoleon Bonaparte ordered the castle demolished in 1800, though his orders were only partly carried out. It was used as a barracks by the Austrian occupying army. In 1893 L. Beltrami undertook a fairly rough-and-tumble restoration, demolishing and rebuilding freely to recreate the "original" appearance of the Castello. The outer ramparts were demolished at the orders of Napoleon. The Castello is now a vast square building made of brick, with long curtain walls and huge windows framed in terracotta, massive corner towers, battlements, and a moat. In the center of the facade is the so-called Torre del Filarete, a reproduction (1905) of the 15th-century tower. The arch at the foot of this tower opens out into a vast courtyard, the Piazza d'Armi, enclosed by three buildings (from the left): the Rocchetta, the Torre di Bona di Savoia (1477), and the Palazzo della Corte Ducale, with large terracotta Gothic windows. To the left of the entrance is the Raccolta delle Stampe A. Bertarelli, a collection of over 600,000 prints, ranging from the homeliest woodcuts to the most exquisite etchings. On the side of the Piazza d'Armi opposite the Torre del Filarete, you enter the Corte Ducale, or ducal courtyard, through a door surmounted by the Sforza crest, with a portico and Renaissance loggia on the left; to the right is the entrance to the Civici Musei (see below). A passageway on the left leads into the porticoed courtyard called Cortile della Rocchetta, with the entrance to the Archivio Storico Civico and to the Biblioteca Trivulziana, originally the private library of the Trivulzio family, purchased in 1935 by the City of Milan, with rare books and incunabula. Back in the Corte Ducale, the Porta del Barco is the gate which leads out into the Parco Sempione (see below); follow the moat off to the right, and you will reach the NE side of the Castello, with the Ponticella di Ludovico il Moro, a small bridge attributed to Bramante, but largely rebuilt during the 19th-century reconstruction.

Musei del Castello**, these museums comprise collections of sculpture, painting, and the applied arts; they are divided into three major sections, respectively of ancient art, decorative arts and archeology, and musical instruments, largely arranged in chronological order. Other important sections include the Sala del Gonfalone, with frescoes of heraldic devices of Spanish royalty and viceroys, and a gonfalon* of Milan, painted and embroidered (1566); the Sala delle Asse*, with a frescoed vault, and heavily restored cartoons by Leonardo da Vinci, as well as the Belgioioso Collection of Dutch and Flemish 17th-18th-century paintings; the Cappella Ducale, a chapel with 15th-century frescoes; the Sala della Balla, with **tapestries** depicting the months*, begun in 1503, designed by Bramantino and woven in Vigevano; and the Sala del Tesoro, the treasury hall with a fresco representing Argo.

Castello Sforzesco-Museo d'Arte Antica e Pinacoteca. Collections of statuary, largely from Milanese and Lombard monuments: sculpture from Early Christian, Longobard, Romanesque, and Gothic periods, as well as 15th-16th-century sculpture and architecture by A. di Duccio, A. Mantegazza, M. Michelozzi (Portal of the Banco Mediceo* in the hall of 16-17C weapons), Bambaia, and Michelangelo (**Pietà Rondanini****). On the first floor are the 15th-18th-century collection of furniture*, along with tapestries, paintings, statues, and wooden bas-reliefs; note the reconstruction of a hall from the Castello di Roccabianca (Parma) with a detached series of 15th-century frescoes*. Your next stop is the **art gallery** with paintings by: Mantegna, Bembo, G. Bellini, Foppa, Bergognone, Bramantino, C. da Sesto, Correggio, Lotto, Tintoretto, Fra' Galgario, Cerano, Magnasco, G.B. Tiepolo, and F. Guardi.

Castello Sforzesco-Museo delle Arti Decorative e Museo degli Strumenti Musicali. This museum of applied arts has a ceramic section, with porcelain and majolica, enamels, Renaissance bronze figurines, religious fabrics and clothing. It also includes the Museo degli Strumenti Musicali, with a collection of 640 musical instruments in five sections; also note the 18th-19th-century costumes.

Civiche Raccolte Archeologiche e Numismatiche. This is a branch of the Museo Archeologico in Corso Magenta, and features a prehistoric section, with much material on early Lombard cultures; an Egyptian section, with everyday objects and funerary material; an epigraph section, with more than 100 pieces. The medal collection includes roughly 230,000 items, from 6th century BC to modern times.

Parco Sempione. Extending over an area of 47 hectares behind the Castello, this park was arranged in the English style in 1893 by E.

Alemagna, with trees planted to offer a perspective on to the Arco della Pace.

To your left, as you leave the Castello through the Porta del Barco, you will find the **Palazzo dell'Arte** (1932-33), housing the exhibition quarters of the Milan Triennale and of other events. Note the Torre del Parco, formerly Torre Littoria, built in 1932 by Gio' Ponti, in steel tubing, 109 m tall, and the small bridge which was once on the Naviglio. At the end of the park, in the center, stands the **Arco della Pace** (Arch of Peace), one of the most distinctive monuments of the Neo-Classic period, by L. Cagnola, begun in 1807 to honor Napoleon, and dedicated in 1838 to Francis I of Austria, and in 1859 rededicated to the independence of Italy. It directs the gaze out over the Corso Sempione, the first stretch of the great Napoleonic road running toward the Lake Maggiore; note the old palazzi at no. 25, 27, 33, and 36. In the park to the right of the Castello is the **Arena Civica**, a Neo-Classic construction from Napoleonic times, built by L. Canonica (1807), where sport events are held. Overlooking Via Gadio (no. 2) is the **Acquario Civico** (aquarium), with 48 tanks holding freshwater and saltwater fish, reptiles, amphibians, and invertebrates. The building is the only surviving construction from the International Exhibition of 1906 and is a rare example of Art Nouveau in Milan.

Piccolo Teatro di Milano-Teatro Strehler. Set back between Via Tivoli and Piazzale Marengo, the theater is a work by M. Zanuso (1984). Nearby, at no. 50 Foro Buonaparte, is the Fondazione A. Mazzotta, a private exhibition space with an interesting program of art shows.

Corso Garibaldi. The central thoroughfare of one of the oldest and most distinctive Milanese districts, this street runs along the ancient Roman "Way to Como," through a working-class neighborhood, only partly changed by the arrival of the underground. On the left (no. 17), note the facade of the Teatro Fossati (1858-59), refurbished by M. Fossati.

S. Simpliciano*. Set back on the Piazza S. Simpliciano, to the right of Corso Garibaldi, this Romanesque basilica was founded in the 4th century but was drastically renovated in the 19th century. Some of the outside walls date back to 16 centuries ago, but in the facade only the central portal and some arches date back as early as the 12th century Inside, note the large fresco* in the vault of the apse, by Bergognone (ca. 1515) and the carved wooden 16th-century choir. To the right of the basilica (Piazza delle Crociate no. 6) is the former **convent of S. Simpliciano**, now occupied by

the Facoltà Teologica Interregionale, with a small 15th-century cloister and a larger mid-16th-century cloister*, possibly by V. Seregni.

S. Maria Incoronata. Erected in the late 15th century, this church has a facade divided into two sections which correspond to its interior spatial organization. According to certain sources, the twin structure, with two identical aisles, was built at the behest of Francesco Sforza and his wife Bianca Maria as a symbolic seal of the happiness of their marriage. Inside, on the right, on the walls of the chapels, are 15th-century funerary plaques and remains of frescoes in the apse (late 16C).

Cimitero Monumentale, at the end of Viale Ceresio, this monumental cemetery was built in 1863-66 by C. Maciachini; in the middle of the long front facade is the Famedio, a sort of Milanese Pantheon, where leading citizens are buried. Chapels and monuments constitute an interesting gallery of Lombard architecture and sculpture of the late 19th and 20th century (M. Rosso, E. Butti, L. Bistolfi, A. Wildt, and F. Messina).

PORTA TICINESE AND PORTA ROMANA

Along the perimeter of the Spanish bastions, there once stood ten mighty town gates (late 16C); their names are still used for the districts into which they gave access, and five of them are still standing. In the southern part of Milan, between Porta Ticinese and Porta Romana, there are relics of early Christian times (S. Lorenzo), Renaissance monuments (S. Satiro, Cappella Portinari, Ca' Granda), and the surprising cityscape of the Navigli.

Piazza Missori. A tangled welter of older and more recent architecture, this square marks the western extremity of the demolition done after WWII. At the beginning of Via Albricci, in the middle, are the remains of the church of S. Giovanni in Conca, founded in early Christian times and rebuilt in the 11th century To the right of the Palazzo dell'INPS (no. 8-10) by M. Piacentini (1929-31), is the brick facade of the 17th-century Collegio di S. Alessandro (now part of the university); also note the **church of S. Alessandro**, behind Piazza Missori, begun in 1601 by L. Binago, continued by the Richini, father and son, and completed in 1710. Inside, late 17th-century canvases and frescoes.

S. Maria presso S. Satiro*. This church, an architectural gem of the early Renaissance, was built in 1476-86, with much work by Bramante, who worked on it after 1478. The facade, some distance from Via Torino, was rebuilt in 1871. In the rear, visible from Via Mazzini, is a late

10th-century Romanesque bell tower, behind which stands the older Cappella della Pietà*, a chapel with an elegant 15th-century exterior. The small interior has an aisleless nave and a transept covered with broad barrel vaults; note the cupola. The asymmetrical plan resulted in the famous false painted **presbytery***, behind the main altar, the work of Bramante. At the end of the left transept is the Cappella della Pietà, a chapel that was once a separate structure (Basilica di Ansperto, 9C), with a Greek-cross plan; on the altar, note the group of the Pietà, by A. de' Fondutis (1482-83). From the right side, you can enter the octagonal **Battistero*** (or baptistery), with two rows of pilaster strips and a dome, also by Bramante, decorated with a handsome frieze, also by de' Fondutis (1483).

Via Torino. This major shopping thoroughfare follows the medieval road that led to the Duomo, or Cathedral. Set back at no. 3-5 in Via Spadari is the Art Nouveau facade of the **Casa Ferrario** by E. Pirovano (1904). Not far away, Via Torino is dominated on the right by the tall cylindrical structure of the **church of S. Sebastiano** (1577-95), built to fulfill a vow made in the hopes of halting an outbreak of the plague (1576). Designed by P. Tibaldi, but heavily modified since its construction, the interior has a circular plan and is crowned by an 18th-century dome. Further along, and also on the right, is the **church of S. Giorgio al Palazzo**, founded in AD 750, but rebuilt in Neo-Classic style by L. Cagnola (1800-21); inside, note the frescoes and panels by B. Luini (1516). At the end of Via Torino is the **Carrobbio**, an ancient intersection of Roman origin (the name is believed to derive from the Latin word for "intersection"). Set back in Via S. Sisto (no. 10), in the former church of S. Sisto, is the **Museo-Studio Francesco Messina** with numerous works by this artist (bronzes, polychrome statues, paintings, drawings, sketches).

S. Lorenzo Maggiore**. This basilica is one of the most important and the oldest monuments in Milan, of considerable significance in the history of western architecture. Before the church lies a broad square, with a bronze copy of a statue of the emperor Constantine, in commemoration of the Edict of Milan (AD 313), which gave civil rights and toleration to Christians throughout the Roman Empire. Note the 16 Roman **columns*** dating from the Imperial Age, once part of a temple (2-3C), transported here in the 4th century, and inserted in the great quadriporticus (later destroyed) in front of the facade.

In its basic features, this is a late 16th-century church, which incorporates the Early Christian church, built at the end of the 4th century as a Palatine basilica and transformed into a Romanesque church in the 12th century. The church still preserves the central plan of the original structure, with four corner towers and three chapels (best seen from behind).

The interior, with its central plan, can be compared to S. Vitale in Ravenna; the majestic circular hall, with exedrae, galleries, and an immense dome, is lined with a broad ambulatory. On the right, through an atrium with traces of 4th-century mosaics and a Roman portal (late 1C), you enter the 4th-century **Cappella di S. Aquilino****, an intact original chapel, octagonal in shape, with niches, a loggia, and dome: in two niches, more 4th-century mosaics*; to the right of the entrance, 3rd-century sarcophagus; on the altar, a silver urn with the relics of S. Aquilino. A little stairway behind the altar leads down to the foundations, probably built with blocks of stone from the amphitheater. Behind the main altar of the church is the Cappella di S. Ippolito; on the left side of the church is the Cappella di S. Sisto.

Parco delle Basiliche. Extending from Piazza della Vetra, behind S. Lorenzo, all the way to S. Eustorgio, this park offers a visual sweep encompassing both remarkable churches. To the right of the Basilica di S. Lorenzo stands the medieval **Porta Ticinese** gate, built in the 12th century, rebuilt in the 14th century, and further modified in 1861-65. On the outer facade, note the tabernacle with reliefs of saints, by the school of G. di Balduccio (14C). Beyond the gate, Corso di Porta Ticinese continues out of town through the heart of the working-class Quartiere Ticinese, with much of the flavor of the original medieval "borgo."

S. Eustorgio*. One of the most notable monuments in Milan, this basilica has a complex and stratified structure, with fragments from the 7th century and pieces of the Romanesque structure (12C), set in a building that was being modified and revamped until the late 15th century. Surrounded by a broad tree-lined area, the Neo-Romanesque facade dates from 1862-65; only the little loggia is intact (1597), in the left corner; at the end of the right flank, with its 15th-century chapels, near the apse, stands the tall bell tower* (1297-1309), behind which you can see the handsome exterior of the Cappella Portinari. Inside, in the nave and aisles, divided by piers with 11th-12th-century capitals, note the deep apse. In the chapels on the right, 14th- and 15th-century funerary monuments and frescoes (in the vaults; in the 1st chapel, triptych by Bergognone; in the 4th, funerary monuments to S. Visconti by G. di Balduccio). In the right transept, note the Cappella dei Magi, with a large Roman sarcophagus which held the supposed relics of the saint until 1164. On the main altar, note the unfinished marble frontal, possibly designed by G. de' Grassi (early 15C) and M. da Campione. Behind the apse (where you can see the foundations of the original 5C basilica), from the pseudo-crypt you can enter the **Cappella Portinari****, a gem of early Renaissance Tuscan-style architecture (1466). Long thought to be the work of Michelozzo, this chapel is square in plan, covered by a dome, with a sacellum in which stands the altar. It has elaborate and lavish decoration; especially fine is the polychrome Procession of Angels* holding festoons in the tambour beneath the dome, designed by a Tuscan master, and perhaps executed by V. Foppa. The **frescoes**** high on the walls are a masterpiece by V. Foppa (1468); in the middle is the marble Arca di S. Pietro Martire**, an urn carved by G. di Balduccio (1339). The little Museo di S. Eustorgio features 17th-century paintings and sacred furnishings from the 17th and 18th century; it also has underground rooms, the remains of a Roman and Early Christian cemetery.

Porta Ticinese. Do not confuse this gate with the medieval gate of the same name; this one stands isolated in the center of Piazzale XXIV Maggio. One of the most notable works of Milanese Neo-Classicism, it was built by L. Cagnola (1801-14) as an arch of triumph to commemorate Napoleon's victory at Marengo. Nearby is the **Darsena** an old town port and the only basin to survive from the complex system of canals that once ringed Milan; it now marks the convergence of the Naviglio Grande, running from Abbiategrasso and the Naviglio di Pavia, which flows into the Ticino River. Overlooking the water is a distinctive district of old Milan, once quite working-class, now as fashionable and expensive as can be, with restaurants, bars, and nightspots. In early June, the popular Festa dei Navigli is held here, and, on the last Sunday of each month, also the noted Mercatone del Naviglio Grande, with merchandise ranging from fine antiques to bric-a-brac. At no. 27 Ripa Ticinese is the **Museo del Giocattolo e del Bambino**, a museum of toys, with a rotating exhibition of items from the 18th to the 20th century

S. Maria presso S. Celso*. Also known as S. Maria dei Miracoli, this church is a fine example of 16th-century architecture; it was designed by Dolcebuono (1493) and completed in 1506. Before it stands a solemn quadriporticus*, a masterpiece by Cesariano from the early 16th century; the four-register facade is by G. Alessi and M. Bassi (late 16C).

The interior has a nave with two aisles, 16th-century decorations, fine dome, and presbytery surrounded by ambulatory. Beneath the dome, on either side of the cross-vault, statues by S. Lorenzi and A. Fontana, who also did the statue of the Assunta (Annunciate, 1586) on the altar of the Madonna (to the left of the presbytery), to which Milanese brides traditionally pay their respects on their wedding day; in the presbytery, note the handsome inlaid choir (1570). On the altar of the right transept and in the ambulatory are sculpture and paintings by P. Bordone, G. Ferrari, and Il Moretto; the altar in the left transept incorporates a 4th-century sarcophagus; in the 1st chapel on the left, note the painting by Bergognone. To the right of the church of S. Maria dei Miracoli stands the Romanesque **church of S. Celso**, built in the 10th century but rebuilt by Canoni-

At night, the canal area comes to life.

ca (1851-54), with a Lombard-Romanesque bell tower and the original portal.

Corso Italia. This broad thoroughfare, running out from the center, was builtaround 1900; in part it goes along the ancient "Corso di S. Celso"; roughly halfway along this broad street is the former **church of S. Paolo Converso,** now the headquarters of an auction house. Across the street is a 17th-century column. The church was built between 1549 and 1580; the facade is by Cerano (1613); the handsome interior is by the Cremonese architects Antonio, Giulio, and Vincenzo Campi. Further along (no. 10) is the Palazzo del Touring Club Italiano (1914-15), with the bookshop and offices.

Corso di Porta Romana. Linking Piazza Missori with Porta Romana, this street, built in 1598, runs along the course of what was originally the Roman "decumanus maximus," which was lined with monumental porticoes (2-3C; you can see traces in the Missori station of the Metropolitana underground railway, line 3). In its first stretch, the Corso alternates modern buildings with ancient palazzi (at no. 6, the 17C Palazzo Annoni) and is dominated by the **Torre Velasca** (1958), a 26-storey office and apartment building, outstanding creation of postwar Milanese architecture.

S. Nazaro Maggiore*. This basilica was founded by St Ambrose (AD 386); much of the cross-structure dates from the 4th century It was rebuilt in the 11th century (apse and tambour), and renovated extensively in later centuries. A notable work is the octagonal **Cappella Trivulzio***, built by Bramantino (1512-50), containing the family tombs in a simple room, including the Arca di G.G. Trivulzio, with the noteworthy Latin inscription: "Qui numquam quievit quiescit; tace" (He who never had rest is now resting; silence). From the chapel you can descend into the basilica proper. In the right arm of the transept is a Last Supper by B. Lanino. To the right of the presbytery, note the 10th-century Basilichetta di S. Lino; from the left arm of the transept, you can enter the 16th-century Cappella di S. Caterina d'Alessandria, with a fresco* by Lanino (1546).

Ca' Granda*, this is the former Ospedale Maggiore, used for health care until 1939 (now part of the state university); it remains one of the most noteworthy monuments of 15th-century Milan. It was founded in 1456 by Francesco Sforza and his wife Bianca Maria, and was enlarged between the 17th and 19th century. Devastated by bombing and subsequent fires in 1943, it has been radically restored. The 15th-century wing, on the right side of the long facade, shows a style in transition from Gothic to Renaissance; built by Filarete, it consists of an arched portico below and a floor of handsome terracotta mullioned windows. The central section is a lavish imitation of the 15th-century wing; along with the vast inner courtyard* with portico and loggia, it was built in the 17th century by F.M. Richini, F. Mangone, and G.B. Pessina. To the right of this courtyard, note the lovely little late 17th-century Cortiletto, a small courtyard with two rows of arcades. The notable Quadreria dei Benefattori*, a portrait gallery, is being moved to the old stables of the abbey of Mirasole.

Piazza S. Stefano. This oddly shaped space is dominated by the Baroque facade and the tall bell tower (17C) of the **church of S. Stefano Maggiore**, now headquarters of the Archivio Storico Diocesano, a religious archive; also note the 17th-century former church of S. Bernardino alle Ossa, which takes its name (Ossa, or bones) from a macabre chapel lined with human bones.

PORTA VITTORIA AND PORTA VENEZIA

In the NE area of Milan, starting from the Verziere and continuing on beyond the walls, you will encounter relics of the Baroque age, marks of 19th-century opulence, streets and houses decorated with "floral" motifs and the scars of a metropolis undergoing constant rebuilding.

Largo Augusto. Standing in this small square is the Colonna del Verziere, a column erected in the 17th century as a votive offering after the end of the plague in 1577, by Ricchino, among others. Running into this square is **Via Durini**, lined with aristocratic palazzi, including, at no. 20, the Casa Toscanini (18C) and, at no. 24, the Baroque **Palazzo Durini**, also by F.M. Richini (1648). At the intersection between Corso di Porta Vittoria and the Cerchia dei Navigli (ring road along the course of the old canals) is the 18th-century **Palazzo Sormani Andreani**, now housing the Biblioteca Centrale Comunale, or main library. Further along is the massive Palazzo di Giustizia (Hall of Justice) by Piacentini and Rapisardi (1932-40). Set back on the Via Besana is the **Rotonda della Besana**, a rotunda that was originally the cemetery of the Ospedale Maggiore (1713-25) and which is now used for exhibitions, with the former church enclosed by a circular portico.

S. Pietro in Gessate. We are not sure who built this church (attributed either to P. Antonio or G. Solari), but we do know it was built from 1447 to 1475, in a transition style from Gothic to Renaissance. The facade was redone in 1912, and only the central portal survives. Inside, Lombard frescoes and paintings (15C). The left transept is covered with frescoes by B. Butinone and B. Zenale (1490).

S. Maria della Passione*. This large church, second only to the Duomo, was begun to a Greek cross plan in 1486, while the dome was completed by Cristoforo Lombardo in 1530. Transformed to a Latin-cross plan at the end of the 16th century, it was given a Baroque facade in 1692-1729. In the interior, on the piers of the

The arcade of Ca'Granda, home to the state university.

nave and in the enormous octagon of the dome, are paintings* by D. Crespi, who also created the doors of the twin organs in the niches of the presbytery (the organ on the right is an Antegnati, 1558; the one on the left dates from 1610). In the right transept is a Deposition, attributed to Luini; in the left transept, Last Supper by G. Ferrari. From the niche between the apse and the transept, you enter the **Sala Capitolare**, or Chapter House, with marvelous frescoes by Bergognone. To the right of the church, in a former convent (early 16C courtyard, attributed to C. Solari), is the **Conservatorio di Musica Giuseppe Verdi**, a conservatory with a remarkable library of musical scores (18-19C). To the left of the church (Via Bellini no. 11) is the **Casa Campanini**, one of the most remarkable examples of Milanese Art Nouveau; 1909).

Corso Monforte. This chief thoroughfare of what was once the "Borgo di Monforte" features (no. 35) the **Palazzo Isimbardi**, built in the 15th century and repeatedly renovated; it is now headquarters of the Amministrazione Provinciale, or provincial government; the vault of the Sala della Giunta is decorated with a large painting by G. B. Tiepolo.

Corso Venezia. This major thoroughfare has a series of aristocratic palazzi and parks, giving it the dignity of a major urban boulevard. It ends with the two massive structures of the **Caselli di Porta Orientale**, custom houses which flank the gate, by R. Vantini (1827-28). On the right in the first stretch of this street (no. 10), **Casa Silvestri** is a fine example of a small Renaissance palazzo (1475), with an elegant courtyard and 14th-century fragments. Almost directly across the street (no. 11), note the portal (1652) of the **Seminario Arcivescovile**, done in 1565-77 by P. Tibaldi and V. Seregni, with a courtyard built in 1602-8 by A. Trezzi and F. Mangone. At the corner of Via S. Damiano

(no. 16), note the enormous **Palazzo Serbelloni** with a Neo-Classic facade (1793).

Palazzo del Senato. This noteworthy creation of the architecture of the Counter-Reformation (1608-30) has a facade by F. M. Richini and two majestic courtyards by F. Mangone. Restored after the bombing of 1943, it is now the headquarters of the Archivio di Stato, one of Italy's leading state archives.

Villa Reale Belgiojoso Bonaparte*. One of the finest creations of Milanese Neo-Classicism, built in 1790 by L. Pollak for the counts of B. di Belgiojoso. It was the residence of Napoleon and of E. de Beauharnais, viceroy of Italy; the Austrian soldier Count Radetzky lived here (1857-58). Note the rear facade, overlooking the garden; inside is the Museo dell'Ottocento, an exposition of modern art.

Museo dell'Ottocento*, this museum has a select collection of painting and sculpture, particularly Lombard, from the Neo-Classic period (A. Canova, A. Appiani), the Romantic era (Piccio, F. Hayez) and the late 19th century (D. Ranzoni, T. Cremona, G. Segantini, M. Rosso). Note the Vismara Collection, with work by Tosi, Modigliani, De Pisis, and Morandi; **Il Quarto Stato** (Fourth Estate) by G. Pellizza da Volpedo, purchased with a public subscription in 1920; the Museo Marino Marini, with a collection assembled by the sculptor himself, of his own work. The Raccolta Grassi is a collection comprising objects of art, fabrics, Oriental carpets, and especially 19th-20th-century paintings of the French (Corot, Sisley, Manet, Cézanne, Gauguin, Van Gogh, Vuillard, Bonnard, Toulouse-Lautrec, Utrillo) and Italian (Lega, Ranzoni, Boldini, De Nittis, Mancini, Spadini, Pellizza, Segantini, Balla, Boccioni, Morandi) schools. Annexed to Villa Reale is the **Padiglione d'Arte Contemporanea** (PAC) by I. Gardella (1954), where temporary exhibitions are held.

Piazza Cavour. Situated between the arches of Porta Nuova and the Giardini Pubblici (public park; see below) this square is dominated by the Palazzo dei Giornali, or press building, built in 1937-42 by G. Muzio, and by the tall building of the Centro Svizzero (1952). Set back on the right in Via Manin (no. 2) is the 18th-century **Palazzo Dugnani**, with porticoes and loggias; inside, the central hall was frescoed* by G.B. Tiepolo. The building houses the **Museo del Cinema della Cineteca Italiana**, with documents, memorabilia, and materials on the history of film-making.

Via Turati. At the beginning of this street, back on the left, at no. 5 Via Carlo Porta, are the headquarters of the Fondazione Corrente, with the Collezione Studio Treccani, on either side of Via Turati, on a line with Largo Donegani, is the sober complex of the former Palazzi della Montecatini (no. 2 dates from 1936-38 and no. 1 from 1951), both by the architect Gio' Ponti and associates; on the far side of Via Moscova is the eclectic residential complex called Ca' Brütta (1919-22). In a further stretch of Via Turati, at no. 34, is the **Museo della Permanente** (1886), where major art exhibits are held. At the end of the street, two twin tall buildings (1960s) mark the transition to the huge, tree-lined Piazza della Repubblica, built in the 1930s and rebuilt after WWII.

S. Angelo. At the beginning of Via Moscova adjoining a Franciscan convent, this church is one of the principal 16th-century monuments in Milan, with a 17th-century Mannerist facade. Inside, on the altars and in the sacristy, 16th-17th-century canvases by A. Campi, the Fiammenghini, and by G.C. and C. Procaccini.

Giardini Pubblici. Completely enclosed by a long fence, this is the oldest public park in the city; with an area of 17 hectares, it comprises a Neo-Classic section (toward Corso Venezia), designed by Piermarini (1783-86), with a later English-style garden (1857-81). In these gardens, aligned along Corso Venezia, are the **Planetario** (Planetarium; 1930-55), where lectures and astronomical slide shows are held; and the Museo Civico di Storia Naturale.

Museo Civico di Storia Naturale*, founded in 1838 with the donation to the city of the collections of the naturalists G. and G. J. De Cristoforis, this museum is housed in an immense Neo-Romanesque building (1888-93). Despite heavy damage in 1943, it remains one of the leading museums of natural history in Europe, with a thriving research division (specialized library, with over 30,000 volumes;

huge research collections). More than 20 halls on two floors feature minerals, fossils, and stuffed animals, as well as models, dioramas*, and explanatory panels. Of particular interest to the history of science, note the surviving material from the 17th-century naturalistic Museo Settala*; also, dinosaur skeletons and eggs; the skeleton of a 19 m whale; skeletons of extinct vertebrates (*Equus quagga, Alca impennis*); a single giant crystal of colorless topaz (40 kg.); and a stuffed specimen of the Tridacna gigantea.

Corso Venezia (second stretch). This monumental Neo-Classic boulevard is lined with solemn facades overlooking the park of the Giardini Pubblici; note, at no. 40, Palazzo Saporiti (1812) and, at no. 51, Palazzo Bovara (1787); at no. 47, **Palazzo Castiglioni**, by G. Sommaruga (1900-1904), emblem of Italian Art Nouveau. Other interesting examples of the early 20th-century Milanese style can be found in the area between Corso Venezia and Viale Majno: in particular, at Via Cappuccini no. 8, **Palazzo Berri-Meregalli** by G.U. Arata (1911-14); further along, in Via Malpighi (no. 3), is the Casa Galimberti, by G.B. Bossi (1903-4).

Corso Buenos Aires. This busy thoroughfare of the "zona Venezia", one of Milan's largest and most crowded neighborhoods, is also a major shopping streets. This is a continuation toward the outskirts of town of Corso Venezia, along what was in the 18th century the "Strada Regia detta di Loreto," in a densely populated late 19th-century neighborhood, now marked by episodes of urban blight.

Grattacielo Pirelli. Since 1978 this skyscraper has been the headquarters of the Lombardy regional government; it is safe to call this the most prestigious creation of postwar Milanese architecture. Built in 1955-60 by Gio' Ponti and associates, with the consultation of P.L. Nervi, it dominates Piazza Duca d'Aosta (127 m tall, the highest building in Milan), facing the colossal building of the **Stazione Centrale**, massively imposing, covered with decorations, designed by U. Stacchini and built in 1912-31; from the main gallery you can enter the Museo delle Cere (Wax Museum).

Centro Direzionale. Established by the town plan drawn up after WWII, in the area between Via Fabio Filzi and Via Melchiorre Gioia, but left unfinished, this office district constitutes a hodge-podge of tall office buildings, mostly from the 1960s, and vacant lots; the easternmost point is **Stazione Porta Garibaldi**, a railway station built in 1963, with adjacent twin skyscrapers of the railroad corporation.

THE ROMANESQUE IN BRIANZA

he splendid landscape of Brianza, much praised by foreign travelers visiting Italy in the 19th century, was the setting for the magnificent villas built in the 18th and 19th centuries by nobles and the rich bourgeoisie of Milan, who loved to holiday here. But this area around Lecco and Lake Como also has many well-preserved medieval buildings, particularly from the Lombard Romanesque period. In Brianza, since most of the domestic architecture from this period has either been incorporated into later buildings or disappeared, the art of the 11th and 12th centuries is mainly represented by religious buildings. The Romanesque period has left a particularly rich artistic heritage: country churches, bell towers, baptisteries and religious complexes. Much of Brianza lies within the diocese of Milan. In fact, these monuments were built and preserved by the clergy of the metropolis. Particularly on the routes used by early travelers, the Romanesque churches are of a magnificence that makes this area a very special center of medieval art. They fit naturally into the local landscape in a way that enhances even further the exploration of the area's artistic and architectural treasures.

ARCHITECTURE

One of the most important examples of Romanesque is the church of S. Vincenzo di Galliano, now in the town of Cantù, rebuilt in 1007 at the wishes of Ariberto d'Intimiano, who was deacon at the time. Some of the original features have disappeared, but the proto-Romanesque character of the building remains: its nave and two aisles ending in apses, the crypt, raised in order to create an oratory, and its wooden tie-beam roof. While the carved capitals of the crypt convey the simplistic style of the early Middle Ages, the painted decoration still owes much to the great Byzantine tradition, as in the great Maestà in the apse. Below the figure of Christ surrounded by a mandorla, we can see Bishop Ariberto who commissioned the painting.

The basilica of Ss. Pietro e Paolo in Agliate Legata, in the municipality of Carate Brianza, was built on the remains of a basilica dating from Late Antiquity. It was restored in the late 19th century. The nave is separated from the aisles by arches resting on columns, many retrieved from classical sites, with Roman capitals.

To the north, in the Alpine foothills, at Civate, lies the largest Romanesque complex of the Brianza, consisting of the churches of S. Calocero, S. Pietro al Monte and the nearby oratory of S. Benedetto. This group of buildings is unique in terms of its complexity, its structural characteristics and the fine decoration. In particular, in S. Pietro, there are fine stuccoes and frescoes dating from the early 12th century.

SCULPTURE

Of all the examples of Romanesque sculpture, the best-preserved are the expressive stuccoes of S. Pietro at Civate. Since local marble quarries (on Lake Como) were exploited very little during the central period of the Middle Ages, sculptors often resorted to reworking ancient statues or, where possible, and especially for the decoration of interiors, using stucco. Not only did stucco resemble marble when hard, but it was easier to work.

PAINTING

Examples of painting from this period are few and, apart from the ones at Civate, usually in a bad state of repair. One of the most important examples, dating from the first half of the 11th century, is the great Maestà in the apse of S. Vincenzo di Galliano, with a predella depicting scenes from the life of St Vincent. There are more paintings from this period in the chapel of S. Martino di Carugo, near Giussano, where two tiers of frescoes depict stories from Genesis and the life of St Martin.

The basilica of Ss. Pietro e Paolo in Agliate.

FOOD IN LOMBARDY

From the Ticino to the Mincio River, the Po Valley is one of the most fertile farming areas in Europe. This productivity has its origins in reclamation work begun around the year 1000 by monks and continued over the centuries, resulting in a dense network of canals that keep even the driest parts fertile. Animal breeding – and thus dairy farming – has ancient roots here and is the basis for a series of products that bring justified pride to the region. In the areas around Pavia and Mantua, rice farming is a specialty, while fruit and vegetable farming abounds all the way along the Po.

THE DISHES

Risotto alla milanese. A traditional saffron risotto dressed with butter and grated Parmesan. In Monza, there is a variant in which pieces of a local type of sausage are added in.

Cassoeula. This filling winter dish is a cabbage and pork stew. Although a truly Milanese dish, it is found in other towns, often with small variations.

Costoletta alla milanese. Veal loin is used for this classic chop that can either be cooked as is or tenderized. The meat is dipped in egg and then bread crumbs, before being fried in butter that is, in the most opulent version, so abundant it is frothy.

Polenta. This classic Lombard dish is generally made with maize flour although in Valtellina buckwheat can be used. It can be served with butter and garlic, a meat sauce or a traditional game bird sauce.

Panettone. This has become the classic, mass produced Christmas dessert, although artisan production remains important. It is made with flour, yeast, butter, sugar, eggs, candied citrus fruit and sultanas.

THE PRODUCTS

Bitto DOP. This rare cheese from high in the mountains is made in the section of Valtellina facing the Orobie Alps. It is made with cow's milk and, sometimes, a touch of goat's milk. It can be matured for a number of years.

Gorgonzola DOP. The name comes from a town near Milan where, supposedly, the process for making this cheese was discovered in the 12th century. It comes in both sweet and spicy versions.

Grana Padano DOP. This is one of the world's great cheeses. It was invented in around the year 1000 by Cistercian monks from the Abbey of Chiaravalle near Milan. The cheese is made with cooked semi-skimmed cow's milk. The cheese has a grainy texture, but the taste is soft and clear.

Taleggio DOP. The name comes from the Taleggio Valley, in the Bergamo area, where this soft, square cheese originated. It has a strong, distinct smell.

Salame Brianza DOP. This salami is made with minced pork. The smaller version is finely minced, while the large one is less so. It is lightly scented with spices and an animal gut casing is used.

Salame di Varzi DOP. This pork salami is made with relative large pieces of meat. Salt and peppercorns are added as are garlic and red wine. The salamis weigh 500 g to 2 kg and they need to season for a number of months.

The Bresaola is a speciality of Valtellina.

Bresaola della Valtellina IGP. The flagship of gastronomy in Valtellina, it is actually from the nearby Val Chiavenna, where one can find smoked and deer bresaola. It is made with the best leg cuts of beef, which are separated, cleaned and salted. Finally it is covered and seasoned, potentially for 6 months.

THE WINES

Barbera is the strongest regional wine, being produced across much of the area, but especially in the Oltrepò Pavese zone. In Valtellina, nebbiolo is quite common, being used to make top quality wines like Sfursat. Interestingly, this name comes from 'sforzato' (forced), indicating the ripening of the grapes in the cellars for about 3 months. To the south-east, Lambrusco is quite common, indicating the presence of Emilia, while in the north Marzemino is often found, highlighting the proximity of the Adige Valley. In terms of whites, the bubbly ones from Franciacorta (in the Brescia area) are the undoubted leaders, being made from Pinot Bianco, Pinot Nero and Chardonnay grapes.

BRENTA DOLOMITES

There is an odd similarity in the history of the two towns on either end of this route, Riva del Garda and Merano; both were "patches of southern sun" for the Austro-Hungarian Empire and its client states. There, however, the similarities end. Riva del Garda is dotted with olive trees, lemon groves and cypresses, and overlooks a glittering blue lake; Merano blooms with apple trees against a backdrop of snowcaps and crags. Moreover, these two extremes are just the beginning and end of a startling array of mountain landscapes, following a route that links Trentino with Alto Adige: chestnut groves and stands of beech trees line the turquoise waters of the Lake Tenno; in the Val Rendena, beneath slopes dark with conifer forests, are delicate green fields of good earth – one etymology holds that the name "Rendena" means "land of generous yields." Then there is the broad and sunny Anaunia, or Val di Non, where hidden torrents rush through deep gorges. The high notes of this symphony of landscapes, at any rate, come from the two mountain groups on either side of the Val Rendena. They differ even in their component rock: the Adamello-Presanella, crystalline, to the west, the limestone Brenta Dolomites, to the east. The latter can be seen from Madonna di Campiglio, while the former can be viewed from a detour to Val Genova. These are exquisitely Alpine mountains, with high ridges looming well above tortuous

glaciers, jagged rock arenas, titanic stairways of seracs, little lakes, unexpected waterfalls thundering in the silence. The Adamello (3,539 m; the highest peak) stands to the left of the valley; the Presanella (3,558 m) is at the right. The valley itself forms part of the Parco Naturale Adamello-Brenta: this is a haven for ermines, marmots, martens, and grouse. Overhead soars the golden eagle, and moving timidly through the forests are the last brown bears in the Alps. Here, we have spoken almost exclusively of nature; in the Val Rendena you can admire a number of paintings by the Baschenis family, a 15th-century dynasty of artists from Averara near Bergamo.

The imposing sight of Adamello.

NOT TO BE MISSED

Riva del Garda* this little town is a blend of Alpine, Tridentine and Venetian qualities; at the start of the road to Tenno you can admire the waterfall of Varone, where the water plunges 80 m into a narrow gorge. **Tenno**: the old village lies in the shadow of a castle; from the church of S. Lorenzo (with 14-16C frescoes) is a fine view of the plain between Riva and Arco. **Lake Tenno:** a small tree-lined island lies amidst calm waters. Fiavè, a panoramic resort; during the Bronze Age, a large settlement of lake-dwellings was built here. **Stenico:** the castle is one of the oldest in the Trentino, with sections from the 13th century. **Pelugo:** the church of S. Antonio has exterior frescoes by D. Baschenis (1493). **Pinzolo** has a "Danza Macabra," or 'dance of death,' by S. Baschenis (1539) on the side of S. Vigilio, a small cemetery church; inside is another fresco by the same artist. **Val Genova***, mantled with woods, is a majestic landscape that leads up to the Adamello and the Presanella: 4.5 km from Carisolo is the waterfall of Nardis* with a sheer drop of over 100 m, 19.5 km away is Pian di Bedole (1,578 m) in an amphitheater of rock and ice. **Madonna di Campiglio*** is an elegant mountain resort, with skiing and mountain climbing; take a cableway up to the Mt Spinale (2,104 m), with a breathtaking view of the Brenta group; another fine view from the Grostè (2,348 m), accessible by cableway from Campo Carlo Magno, a mile or so further along. **Malè**, main center of the Val di Sole, boasts much old architecture; go see the remarkable S. Valentino chapel, next to the parish church. **Senale**: situated in a lonely valley, this village is called Unsere Liebe Frau im Walde in German, after the ancient hospice of S. Maria in Silva; you reach it by leaving the Palade road just before the pass. **Lana**: the houses are scattered among the vineyards and apple orchards; don't miss the carved gilt 16th century altar in the parish church of Lana di Sotto, or Niederlana; a fine view of the Adige Valley, as far as the Dolomites, can be had by taking a cableway up to the Mt S. Vigilio/Vigiljoch (1,486 m). **Meran/Merano*** (➡ see below) the ancient center is typical of the Alto Adige; hotels, parks, and promenades, all with a flavor of Central Europe.

MERANO/MERAN

The Passirio River crosses Merano, on its way to join the Adige; in the surrounding valley, hills teem with vineyards and orchards, with castles and mountains in the background. A gentle climate, fine strolls, neat parks and gardens, hotels where Hapsburg noble ladies once spent the summer, and cafés where Danubian pastries and sweets tempt one to laze away the day: the cosmopolitan mountain spa preserves some of the Austro-Hungarian flavor of bygone eras. Take the waters which bubble from Mt S. Vigilio and S. Martino. Merano is a true garden city, with an eclectic architectural style, and despite the increasing number of tourist initiatives – one of the most recent being the building of the Merano 2000 ski resort – it has managed to preserve its original feel.

Piazza del Teatro, the square opens next to the Ponte del Teatro overlooking the Passirio River; it is the heart of Merano, where all the main streets in town meet.

Corso Libertà, running from the railway station to Piazza della Rena, passing the Kursaal (1914) and the Pavillon des Fleurs (1874), meeting places in town.

Duomo*, this 14th-century Gothic cathedral, dedicated to St Nicholas, is Merano's main monument, with its over 80 m bell tower, and buttresses. Note, along the sides, 14th-century reliefs and frescoes. Inside is a 15th-century carved altarpiece. Behind the cathedral is the little octagonal Gothic church of S. Barbara, with a fine fresco of St Christopher.

Via dei Portici*, this is Merano's most distinctive street, lined by porticoes and shops. At no. 68, note the **Museo della Donna Evelyn Ortner**, with collections of historical womenswear from 1870 to 1970, including hairpins, buttons, and paper figurines. At no. 192 is the modern Palazzo Municipale, or town hall (1929).

Museo Civico, this museum has collections ranging from natural science and archeology to folklore and art, both medieval and modern.

Castello Principesco, this princely castle stands in Via Galilei; built in 1480 by Archduke Sigismund of Austria, it boasts original furnishings and a collection of ancient musical instruments. Note the chair lift to Mt Benedetto (475 m).

Passeggiata Lungo Passirio*, running along the right bank of the Passirio, in the shade of the poplars, this promenade runs downstream from the Ponte del Teatro to the Lido di Merano; upstream is the Casinò Municipale. At the Ponte della Posta, it changes its name to the **Passeggiata d'Inverno**, partly roofed, pushing through lush vegetation across the Ponte Romano, to the ruins of Castel S. Zeno.

Passeggiata d'Estate, along the left bank of the Passirio, this promenade runs from the Ponte della Posta (note 15C Gothic church of S. Spirito), up the tree-shaded river to Ponte Passirio. Note the marble statue of the empress Elizabeth, or "Sissi," as she is known here. You may continue to the villas, hotels, and parks of Maia Alta.

Passeggiata Tappeiner*, this promenade begins at Via Galilei, winding 4 km over the hills to Quarazze, just below Castel Tirolo; fine views of the Conca di Merano, a valley dotted with vineyards and orchards.

Ippodromo, from Piazza del Teatro, south along Via Piave, you will reach the race track, or Ippodromo di Maia Bassa, where horse races and steeplechases are held.

A glimpse of the center of Merano.

STILFSER JOCH AND THE UPPER VAL VENOSTA

The first person to reach the peak of the Ortles (3,905 m) was Joseph Pichler, known as Passeyer Josele, a hunter of chamois from Sluderno, in Val Venosta, in September 1804; the local peasants said that he couldn't have made the climb without the help of the devil. As you drive up the 48 hairpin turns of the Stelvio road, at each turn a little higher with respect to the glaciers on the Ortles, you can lazily imagine the sensations of that first climb. The road climbs to an elevation of 2,758 m – at Rocca Bianca, one of the finest viewpoints, you pass an obelisk commemorating the climber – and was built for military reasons, with no help from the devil, between 1820 and 1825, at the behest of the emperor Francis I, father of Marie Louise, the second wife of Napoleon. The road was meant to link the Val Venosta in Alto Adige with the Valtellina and Lombardy, which had just been recovered from the wreckage of Francis's son-in-law's enormous empire. Stagecoaches passed here in the summer; the rocks and ice echoed with bells and snapping whips. In winter, sleighs whisked past on the snow. After 1859, the pass marked the border between Austria and Italy for 60 years. Aside from the Stelvio, the rest of this route has all the allure of high-mountain landscapes: the Val di Solda, with its glittering icy peaks, high above the meadows of the valley floor; the Val Monastero, eastern corner of the Grisons; the vast green expanses and lakes on the way up to the Passo di Resia and the source of the Adige River (in Val di Solda and Val di Trafoi you are in the Parco Nazionale dello Stelvio). All this is expected, given the location of the tour; perhaps more surprising is the art, especially the Carolingian paintings at Malles and Müstair and the medieval frescoes at Tubre and Mt Maria.

NOT TO BE MISSED

Solda/Sulden resort famed for skiing and mountain climbing; take a cableway up to the Rifugio Città di Milano (2,573 m), an Alpine hut with a fine view of the glaciers of the Ortles-Cevedale group. Trafoi: take a cableway up to the Rifugio Forcola (2,153 m, an Alpine hut), with another view of the Ortles; from the town, walk (2 km) to the Sanctuary of the Madonna delle Tre Fontane (1,605 m), with many votive offerings. **Passo dello Stelvio/ Stilfser Joch** (2,758 m): the surrounding National Park extends into the Ortles-Cevedale group and along the Valtellina and Val Venosta; take a cableway up to the Nuovo Albergo Pirovano, and another up to the Rifugio Livrio (3,174 m), an Alpine hut in a high mountain setting surrounded by glaciers. **Müstair** (Monastero), in the Val Monastero, Switzerland, descends from an abbey founded in Carolingian times, the Abbey of S. G. Battista: the museum and fine frescoes in the church are well worth a visit. **Tubre/Taufers im Münstertal**, on the Swiss border, has frescoes from the early 13th century and others dating from 1370, in the church of S. Giovanni. **Glorenza/ Glurns***, enclosed by sober, intact walls. **Sluderno/Schluderns**: armory, art, and furnishings in the towering Castel Coira (13-16C). **Malles Venosta/Mals im Vinschgau** the village is studded with towers, bell towers, and structures of great antiquity; note the exceedingly rare Carolingian frescoes in the little church of S. Benedetto. Abbey of Monte Maria/Kloster Marienberg founded in the 13th century, a luminous white building with Gothic cloister (16C), set in the spruce forest on the mountainside, with 12th century frescoes in the crypt. **Curon Venosta/Graun in Vinschgau** the bell tower of the old town rises from the waters of the manmade lake of Resia, which flooded the village in 1950; in the new church are altarpieces from the old one.

HIGHLIGHTS

SPRING IN VAL VENOSTA: MAGIC OF FLOWERS AND ICE

The Val Venosta is the kingdom of apple farming par excellence. The farmers here use organic farming methods, insects, to combat parasites. In fact, the ladybird has become the symbol of this high-quality production area. In spring, when the apple orchards begin to flower, this valley offers a fascinating spectacle of rare beauty. High up, the peaks are still covered in snow, while down in the valley, the delicate pinkish-white flowers of the apple-trees emanate their sweet, intense perfume, particularly in the evening. The irrigation system used to defend the crops is quite amazing. During the cold nights, the delicate flowers would otherwise be damaged by the frost. The method is known as "freezing heat": water which freezes produces heat which, below a thin layer of ice, prevents the temperature of the buds from falling below one degree below zero. Seen with the naked eye, the effect is unforgettable: an enchanted forest of frozen flowers sparkling in the early-morning sun.

THE GREAT DOLOMITES ROADS

The Grande Strada delle Dolomiti was built between 1895 and 1909, during the reign of the Austro-Hungarian emperor Francis Joseph; note the Belle-Epoque hotels along the road. Back then, people traveled these mountain roads in open coaches called "torpedoni"; as protection against the great clouds of white dust they wore dusters, helmets with earflaps, and goggles, cheerfully turning in every direction to see the spectacular Dolomites. This route has few rivals on earth, and is spectacular for the skyline and the steep climbs. Consider these vertical distances: 1,745 m from Bolzano to the Passo di Costalunga, 904 m from the Val di Fassa to the Pordoi, 691 m from the Val Cordevole to the Passo di Falzarego, for a total of 3,074 m. The descents are considerable as well: from Pordoi to Arabba, 638 m in less than 10 km. And you can see, or take pictures of many peaks in the Dolomites along the road: the Catinaccio, Latemar, Sassolungo, Sella, Marmolada, Sorapiss, Antelao, Pelmo, Civetta, Nuvolau, Tofane, and Cristallo. If you take the cableway up to the Sass Pordoi (2,950 m), the entire vast mountainscape lies before you, beneath the bright sky, as if in a geographic model, all the way to the Alps.

The imposing sight of Marmolada.

NOT TO BE MISSED

Sanctuary of the Madonna di Pietralba/ Maria Weissenstein a traditional pilgrimage site in the Alto Adige, this sanctuary dates back to the 17th century, and is set among spruce trees and Alpine views. **Nova Levante/ Welschnofen**: a ski resort amidst the craggy Dolomites. **Lake Carezza/Karersee*** the bright blue water, with hints of cobalt, reflects the dense, dark stands of fir trees, white slides of gravel, and ridges of the Latemar; this is the first "picture-perfect" setting in the Dolomites along this route, heartbreakingly lovely. At the **Passo Nigra/Nigersattel** (1,690 m) between Carezza al Lago and the Passo di Costalunga, a road runs off to the left, beneath the Catinaccio; the pass at the end of the detour is 6 km away; on the way back there are fine views of the Latemar. **Passo di Costalunga/Karerpass**, 1,745 m this marks the boundary between Alto Adige and Trentino. **Vigo di Fassa** is a mountain resort town, with winter sports; in the San Giovanni quarter, note the 15th-century Gothic church of San Giovanni, with fine frescoes; take the cableway up to the Ciampedie meadows (1,997 m), with panoramic views of the Catinaccio, the Pale di S. Martino, the Latemar, and the Marmolada group. **Rifugio Gardeccia** (1,948 m), in the high valley of Vaiolet, with a view of the jagged rocks of Larsec; you can walk or take the summer minibus from **Pozza di Fassa** or from the fork in the road between Pera di Fassa and Mazzin; continue on foot for an hour to reach the Rifugio Vaiolet (2,243 m), an Alpine hut situated in the heart of the Catinaccio beneath the celebrated Torri del Vaiolet. **Campitello di Fassa**, a renowned winter sports center; take the cableway up to the **Col Rodella*** (2,387 m), an astonishing overlook with a far-reaching view of the Dolomites. **Canazei**, a resort with skiing and mountain climbing; follow the high Avisio Valley to the Lake Fedaia, and from there take a cableway up to the Marmolada glacier. **Passo Pordoi** (2,239 m) is the highest point along the Great Dolomites Road; this marks the shift of the watershed from the Adige to the Piave; take a cableway up to the Sass Pordoi* (2,950 m), where the 360-degree view is one of the most breathtaking in all the Dolomites. **Arabba**, in the Val Cordevole, is the first location in the Cadore in the route; take a cableway up to the Porta Vescovo (2,550 m), a balcony overlooking the icy slopes of the Marmolada. **Passo di Falzarego** (2,477 m) the Swiss stone pine dots the high meadows; take a cableway up to the Piccolo Lagazuoi (2,746 m), with another panoramic view of the Dolomites. **Pocol**: the nearby viewpoint offers a fine view of the fabulous hollow of Cortina d'Ampezzo; at sunset, before stretching shadows swallow them in darkness, the mountains glow in nuanced shades from pink to violet. **Cortina d'Ampezzo**** set in a spectacular location, this world-renowned resort is justly famous.

BOLZANO/BOZEN

On his way south, Goethe noted the vineyards where "light-blue bunches of grapes dangle on high, ripening in the heat of the earth below," the fruit vendors in the main square, peddling peaches and pears, thriving trade, and the "bright cheerful sunshine." From the south, you are more likely to notice the Gothic appearance of the old town, at the confluence of the rivers Talvera and Isarco, and the sense of a mixture of two worlds, Latin and Germanic, beneath the distant skyline of the Dolomites.

Piazza Walther, the center of Bolzano is bounded on one side by palazzi now serving as hotels, and on the other by the impressive Gothic cathedral. In the middle is a monument to the great German medieval poet, Walther von der Vogelweide. Beneath the square is a parking lot.

Duomo*. This Gothic cathedral has a fine apse and colorful steep-pitch roof, with a bell tower (16C). Outside, 14th century portals and reliefs; inside, frescoes and a notable pulpit (1514). **Church of the Domenicani**, this Gothic church, once the place of worship for Italians in Bolzano, was rebuilt after heavy bomb damage in WWII. Inside, note frescoes, an altarpiece by Guercino (1655), and the chapel of S. Giovanni*, a chapel with remarkable frescoes by the Giotto Paduan school (note the Triumph of Death; ca. 1340). In the adjacent Gothic cloister (entrance through no. 19 A), frescoes by F. Pacher and paintings by local 16th-century artist S. Müller; also 14th century frescoes in the Sala Capitolare, or chapter house, and the Cappella di S. Caterina. **Via dei Portici***, this straight road has been the heart of Bolzano for many centuries and is still lined with elegant shops. Note the porticoed houses, esp. no. 39 (main facade in Via Argentieri), and the Baroque Palazzo Mercantile (1708).

Piazza delle Erbe, the square is lined with handsome homes and is the site of the fruit market; on one side is the Fountain of Neptune (18C), with bronze statue by G. Mayr.

Church of the Francescani. This Gothic Franciscan church has a noteworthy main altar, carved by H. Klocker (1500), and a lovely 14th-century cloister, as well as good frescoes.

Museo Provinciale di Scienze Naturali. At the corner of Via Bottai and Via Hofer. This museum of natural science features an exhibition on the landscape and ecosystems of Alto Adige. **S. Giovanni in Villa**, confined to a narrow little square is a church, with an immense bell tower. Inside are two series of frescoes (14C). **Museo Civico***, this town museum is located in the former Casa Hurlach, at no. 14 in Via Cassa di Risparmio. It features archeological material dating from the Mesolithic (note the menhir of Lungostagno, or Renon; the mid-Bronze Age sword of Hauenstein; and a milestone from the reign of the emperor Claudius, AD 46); a collection of folk costumes and domestic objects; and a gallery of local art.

Ponte Talvera, uphill, along the left bank of the river, runs the Lungotalvera Bolzano, a handsome riverside promenade, which passes the Castel Mareccio (13-16C), with four massive round towers with conical roofs, now a conference center; the promenade then joins the Passeggiata S. Osvaldo, which runs up the slopes of Mt Renon.

Monumento della Vittoria, majestic triumphal arch built in 1928 by M. Piacentini; sculptures by L. Andreotti, A. Dazzi, P. Canonica, and A. Wildt. This monument has been bombed by German-speaking terrorist groups, and is entirely cordoned off.

Abbey of the Benedettini di Gries, this Bendictine abbey lies on the main square of this suburb which is popular as a spa, and is amidst gardens and vineyards. On the square is also the Baroque church of S. Agostino, built in 1771; note frescoes and the altarpiece by Tyrolean painter M. Knoller. Nearby, Gothic parish church (15-16C), with a noteworthy altarpiece by M. Pacher (1475).

Piazza Walther, with the Gothic apse and bell tower of the cathedral.

VAL GARDENA AND THE CIRCUIT AROUND THE SELLA

The Sella group (3,152 m) is a magnet for mountaineers, and its architecture is described in terms more typical of military architecture: bastions, curtain walls, towers... Straight and sheer,

the mountain appears at the head of four valleys (Fassa, Gardena, Badia, Livinallongo). The color of the rock changes by the hour, as clouds hide the sun or reflections reverberate from the snow that drifts onto the "cenge," or high ledges, that dot the cliff face – this is the classic image of the Dolomites. It is ringed by roads that, from valley to valley, go over four famous passes: Pordoi, Campolongo, Gardena, and Sella; the "Giro del Sella," along these passes, is as classic a climb in the Dolomites as the Great Road (and coincides with that route, briefly, over the Pordoi Pass). On these passes, each year, you will see young men in colorful tops, pedalling furiously: on walls and

The unmistakable shape of the Sella massif.

bare rock you will see painted messages of encouragement. In the "magic ring" of the passes you begin with the Val Gardena, taking it from Bolzano along a route that soon leaves the Isarco Valley and runs up to the Alpe di Siusi. When Montaigne passed through here, he had his secretary note: "Beyond the first mountains, we could see other, taller mountains, cultivated and inhabited, and we learned that still further up there were vast lovely meadowlands that provide wheat to the towns below..." Between the Passo di Campolongo and the Passo Gardena, the route wanders through meadows and forests, in the upper Val Badia and San Cassiano valleys.

NOT TO BE MISSED

Siusi/Seis, a resort surrounded by pine forests; about 10 km to the east is the **Alpe di Siusi/Seiser Alm***, rolling and serene. **Castelrotto/Kastelruth** is another highland resort. **Ortisei/Sankt Ulrich***, a famed ski resort, is the capital of the Val Gardena; the Museo della Valle in Cësa di Ladins is noteworthy in terms of the history of local wood-carving. **Plan de Gralba/Kreuzboden**: a cableway runs up to the Rifugio Piz Sella (2,240 m), below the Sassolungo, with a fine view of the upper Val Gardena, the Sella, and the Odle. **Passo di Sella**: a rather tortuous yet spectacular pass which links the Val Gardena and the Val di Fassa; it is certainly one of the most celebrated passes in the Dolomites. **Passo Pordoi**: in a harsh and grandiose setting, you cross the watershed between the Adige and Piave. **Corvara in Badia/Corvara** is a winter sports resort; in the Gothic parish church, note the 15th-century frescoes. **La Villa/Stern**, another ski resort, lies in a broad hollow at the foot of the Sasso Lungo. **San Cassiano/Sankt Kassian** is the chief town of the idyllic San Cassiano Valley, which runs into Badia Valley. **Passo di Gardena/Grödnerjoch**: like the other high passes on the "Sella Ronda," it offers remarkable variations on the landscapes and panoramas of the Dolomites.

VAL BADIA AND VAL GARDENA

The Badia and Gardena valleys are a paradise for skiers in winter and hikers in summer. Surrounded by the Dolomites, they are home to numerous woods, lush fields and plenty of mountain animals.

La Villa/Stern: This is the largest town in the northern Val Badia and home to World Cup skiing. In the bowl below Gardenaccia and Piz La Villa, stands Castel Colz, a square 16th-century manor surrounded by walls with round turrets. **Corvara in Badia/Corvara**: in the

late Gothic church of S. Caterina, with a neo-Gothic loggia, 15th-century frescoes have been discovered below layers of decoration in the nave, the choir and the triumphal arch.

Selva di Val Gardena/Wolkenstein in Gröden, is situated in a hollow surrounded by conifer forests, which provide a contrast with the dolomitic rocks of Sella and Sasso Lungo. There are plenty of cable cars. At the edge of the town are the ruins of the 13th-century Castello Wolkenstein, an unusual building which was a fortified cave.

PALE DI SAN MARTINO AND VAL DI FIEMME

The taste for exploring mountains, of course, is historically a fairly recent development. It is part and parcel of a mentality and attitude that date from the late 18th century, when the Enlight-enment was in the throes of yielding to early Romanticism, the age in which men and women first began to climb mountains for pleasure and inspiration rather than personal profit. Of this route through the Dolomites, an ancient traveler would un-doubtedly have noted the im-portance of the mines (long since abandoned) of Fiera di Primiero, the amount of fine wood to be cut in the spruce forest of Pan-eveggio, in the upper Val Travig-nolo, the hay in the Val di Fiemme, and the annual tribute that the high valleys paid to the bishop-prince in the plains be-low. Certainly, it is possible our ancient traveler might not even

The famous Pale di San Martino.

have mentioned the Pale; the Camaldolites, who made their way up to San Martino di Castrozza centuries ago, were interested only in finding solitude and something resembling a certain closeness to God. These historical "interferences" certainly add an extra dimension to this rap-id mountain foray from the upper Cismon to the middle Avisio, two Tridentine valleys that are trib-utaries, respectively, of the Piave and the Adige rivers, through the three passes of Rolle (1,970 m), Valles (2,033 m), and S. Pellegrino (1,918 m). Nowadays, most people would seem to agree, however, that the objective and chief place of interest certainly remains the group of the Pale di S. Martino – the highest point being the Cima di Vezzana (3,192 m), while the sharp triangular pin-nacle of the Cimon della Pala (3,185 m) dominates the landscape of San Martino – with sheer un-broken walls, perpendicular bastions, deep fissures and crannies, and the broad hidden uplands, inconceivable when viewed from the valley below, entirely made of rock, blanketed in snow, pocked with pools of fresh water that springs from the rock, and with patches of glacier in the rough rolling surface. The alternatives among which you are forced choose, between the Passo di Rolle and the Passo di Valles, feature a descent into a forest of towering Norway spruce trees, as far as Paneveg-gio, and Alpine silence amidst the rock arena of the Pale, from the Baita Segantini (an Alpine hut).

NOT TO BE MISSED

Fiera di Primiero: resort, with skiing and mountain-climbing, once a mining town; in the Gothic church of S. Maria Assunta is the old altar of the miners. **San Martino di Castrozza***: a famed mountain re-sort; take the chairlift up to the Col Verde (1,965 m), then a cableway to the Cima Rosetta (2,609 m), at the edge of the rock upland of the Pale di S. Martino. **Paneveggio Forest**: this is the largest for-est in the Italian Alps; you pass through it on the route from the Passo di Rolle to the Passo di Valles. **Falcade** is a widespread town in the Biois Valley; the first little community you reach, as you descend from the Passo di Valles*, just beyond the fork for the Passo di S. Pellegrino, is Falcade Alto, with-in sight of the Civetta. **Passo di S. Pellegrino** (1,918 m), between the Biois Valley and the Val di Fas-sa: take a cableway up to the Col Margherita (2,511 m), fine view; just beyond the pass, a detour takes you through the larch forest to the lake of S. Pellegrino. **Moena** is a noted ski resort with the little ancient church of S. Volfango. **Predazzo** is another ski resort that has a museum of geology and pa-leontology. **Tesero**, with frescoes on houses and churches; go see the frescoes on the little church of S. Rocco, including one that deplores working on Sunday. **Cavalese** is the chief town of the **Valle di Fiemme**: art collection in the Palazzo della Magnifica Comunità; medieval in origin, the Palazzo retains a marked 16th-century appearance; take a cableway up to the Alpe Cermis (2,000 m), in the Lagorai chain; fine view.

A lake, a sheer rock face, idyllic nature, and a fearful challenge. Every mountain has a personality all its own; these are features of the Dolomites. A little, brilliant lake, a flat narrow lakeshore, fragrant with the aroma of spruce trees, the gaze hemmed in by a round arena of ridges high above the treetops – an overall sense of tranquil serenity. When faced with a bare rock face, a climber coolly calculates the grip, the route, the ledges, the transits, balancing difficulty against strength (anyone else simply gazes in astonishment, admiration, and perhaps a little fear). Lakes and rock faces are the protagonists of a number of the episodes of this route through the inexhaustible Dolomites, which runs from Cortina d'Ampezzo to Brunico, from the hollow of Cadore, in the shadows of the Tofane and the Cristallo to the broad, open, green Pusteria, over the Passo Tre Croci and the Landro Valley. Among the lakes of the Dolomites, it seems that the smaller they are, the greater their fame, aside from the really small ones – the lake of Landro, almost dry now; Dobbiaco, surrounded by woods; Anterselva/Antholzersee, with green waters. An example, however, is the Lake Misurina, surrounded by such peaks as the Sorapiss, the Cadini, the Marmarole; another is the Lake Braies/Pragser Wildsee, reflecting the Croda del Becco in solitary splendor. As for the rock face, the Rifugio Auronzo, an Alpine hut, faces the Tre Cime di Lavaredo, one of the greatest challenges in climbing in the Dolomites: even if you are not about to climb it, with rope, pitons, and crampons, and are only gazing up from below, it is a daunting sight.

Brunico, with its castle and the churches.

NOT TO BE MISSED

Rifugio Lorenzi (2,948 m): from the road to the Passo Tre Croci via the Cristallo chairlift at Som Forca (2,230 m), then take a long-distance cableway to the Forcella Staunies (2,989 m); the Alpine hut is nearby. **Lake Misurina***, 1,745 m: the peaks surrounding the hollow in which the lake lies form one of the classic settings in the Dolomites; a walk around the lake takes 40 minutes. **Rifugio Auronzo** (2,320 m): it is surrounded by the legendary, mighty Tre Cime di Lavaredo; you can proceed to the Rifugio Lavaredo and then, on foot, to the Forcella Lavaredo, with a notable view of the Tre Cime. **Lake Landro/Dürrensee** (1,403 m); just beyond, on the right, a view of the Tre Cime di Lavaredo. **Dobbiaco/Toblach** (➧ see below): the ancient center of this renowned mountain resort has a strong flavor of the Alto Adige. **Lake Braies/Pragserwildsee*** (1,493 m): this is another of the motionless lakes of the Dolomites; it reflects the dark green fir trees and luminous rocks of the Croda del Becco and the Sasso del Signore; in one hour you can walk around it. **Lake Anterselva/Antholzersee** (1,642 m): the dark green waters of this lake, surrounded by woods, is the destination of the detour from Valdaora to the Alpine watershed, along the tranquil Anterselva Valley, with a fine view of the Vedrette di Ries. **Brunico/Bruneck** an old road, typical of the Alto Adige, lies at the heart of the little town; the castle and the nearby war cemetery are noteworthy; in the quarter of Teodone/Dietenheim, visit the Museo degli Usi e Costumi della Provincia Bolzanina, focusing on local folkways.

DOBBIACO/TOBLACH

Situated below the Landro Valley/Höhlensteintal, between 1800 and 1900, Dobbiaco became a favorite holiday place for the Hapsburg nobility and bourgeoisie. The old town lies to the north, in the short San Silvestro Valley, clustered around the **parish church of S. Giovanni Battista***. The church was built between 1764 and 1774 in a particularly harmonious Baroque style, with clear architectural lines and refined stucco and fresco decoration. The Herbstenburg castle, built around a medieval tower, was enlarged in the 16th century conserving the appearance of a fortress. Just outside the town, the Stations of the Cross, comprising five shrines and a chapel with polychrome stone reliefs. The Landro Valley is popular with hikers bound for the Lakes Dobbiaco and Landro. Many places in the valley have spectacular **views** of the ridges and peaks of the Dolomites.

THE HIGHLANDS OF TRENTINO AND ASIAGO

A little museum in Roana, in Val d'Assa, just a few kilometers from Asiago, on the highland of the Sette Comuni, is devoted to "Cimbrian traditions." The Cimbrians were a tribe swept away by complex migratory patterns in the ancient world. They lived in what is now Schleswig, between the Baltic and the North Sea; they entered Italy over the Norico pass, defeating the Romans in the Adige Valley, and then pouring into ancient "Venetia," until Marius defeated them at Campi Raudii, near Vercellae (Vercelli), in 102 BC. Northern tribes did settle on the highland of the Sette Comuni and other nearby highlands, but only the scholars of the Renaissance truly thought they were the Cimbri; in fact, Germans colonized this area in the high Middle Ages. In this mountain region, between the Adige, the plains, and the large oxbow curve of the Brenta as it runs through the Valsugana, the highlands of Folgaria, Tonezza, Sette Comuni, and Lavarone, to name them in the order of this itinerary, wander from Veneto to Trentino. All share the same lovely landscape, with rolling pastures, immense forests, high terraces, hills, nearby mountains, spruce trees and beech groves, dizzying views from the ridges overlooking broad valleys, and the clear signs of centuries of back-breaking labor (before resorts and ski slopes came into being). Then came WWI: Austrian offensives were met by Italian counterattacks; ancient Asiago was wiped away, and shells and bombs were so scattered through the valleys that some mountain folk made a precarious, risky living for decades, picking them up carefully and selling them to other people as scrap metal.

NOT TO BE MISSED

Rovereto: the city, typically Tridentine, with patches of the Venetian, is dominated by the castle erected by the Castelbarco family in the 14th century, which houses a war history museum; another museum boasts works by the Futurist F. Depero, who was born here. **Volano**: this village has the small church of S. Rocco, with frescoes by local artists. **Serrada**: take a long-distance cableway to the Dosso della Martinella (1,604 m). **Tonezza del Cimone**, winter sport resort; detour of 4.5 km to the Piazzale degli Alpini (1,109 m), then a 15-min. walk takes you to the Ossuary a top Mt Cimone (1,230 m). **Velo d'Astico**: in the village of San Giorgio, a Romanesque-Gothic parish church with frescoes (12C). **Asiago**, center of the uplands of the Sette Comuni, resort town; you can tour the astrophysics observatory; a 360-degree view of the upland can be had by taking the chairlift up Mt Caberlaba (1,221 m). **Forte Belvedere**, an intact stronghold of the Austrian defenses during WWI; to get there, you take a walk from the village of Cappella, on the Lavarone upland. **Orrido della Fricca***: this gorge offers a spectacular view of jagged rocks, worn by water, along the route, after Carbonare.

TRENT/TRENTO

The town stands at the convergence of the valleys that run through Trentino amidst the Alps. It has always been the focal point of the region and is surrounded by mountains drained by the Adige, a river linking the Po Valley to the Alps and beyond. Trent is a town of stern medieval and Renaissance architecture, where mountains constantly greet one's gaze.

Piazza di Fiera. This square is lined with 100 m of crenelated walls, built in 1230; at the end of Via Mazzini is the Torrione, ruins of a tower (16C), now used as living quarters.

Museo Tridentino di Scienze Naturali. Housed in the 16th-century Palazzo Sardagna, in Via Calepina at no. 14, with halls frescoed by Fogolino, this museum of natural science has collections of geology, prehistory, zoology, and botany. Note the prehistoric art from the Tridentine region.

Piazza del Duomo*. The monumental center of Trent, adorned by the 18th-century Fontana del Nettuno, this square is surrounded by noble residences and buildings. On the south is the long side of the Duomo. To the east is the 13th-century Palazzo Pretorio, with mullioned windows, site of the Museo Diocesano, and the Torre Civica. To the NE, the two 16th-century Case Cazuffi, with facade frescoes by Fogolino; note the small Fontana dell'Aquila.

Duomo**. This cathedral, a stern mixture of Romanesque and Gothic (12-13C), with a powerful bell tower, is flanked by charming little loggias, with large rose windows in facade and transept, lavish portals, and a handsome apse (adjacent to which is the so-called Castelletto, a battlemented 13th-century building, with mullioned windows). Inside, a high nave with aisles, polystyle piers and cross vaults. Note the flying staircases cutting diagonally across the walls at the foot of each aisle. Along the walls, various 16th-century funerary monuments. Note the Altar of S. Anna with the

Frescoed houses on Piazza Duomo.

altarpiece by Fogolino; nearby, the Cappella del Crocifisso contains a historic wooden Crucifix (16C) by the German sculptor S. Frey. Here, the decrees of the Council of Trent were promulgated. At the head of the left aisle, stone statue of the Madonna degli Annegati (named after the fact that those drowned in the Adige River were brought before the statue to be identified, when it still stood in a niche outside the church). Beneath the church, remains of the Early Christian basilica, with mosaic walls and sculpture fragments.

Palazzo Pretorio. This building lines on the east side of Piazza del Duomo and houses the Museo Diocesano. Next to it is the 13th-century Torre Civica (the civic tower, 41 m tall).

Museo Diocesano Tridentino*. This museum features the most precious cathedral treasures: seven Flemish tapestries*, executed in Brussels by P. van Aelst at the turn of the 16th century; carved altars and statues, panels and paintings, are on display.

Via Belenzani*. This lovely broad road is lined with Renaissance Venetian-style palazzi, some with frescoed facades. In particular, note at no. 20 the 16th-century Palazzo Geremia; at no. 32, the Casa Alberti Colico, with frescoes by Fogolino. Across the street, Palazzo Thun, now the town hall. At the end of the street is the church of S. Francesco Saverio, the finest Baroque church in Trent.

Via Manci. This street is lined with remarkable palazzi, among them no. 63, the Baroque Palazzo Galasso, 1602; no. 57, the 16th-century Palazzo Pedrotti, headquarters of the Società degli Alpinisti Tridentini (SAT, an association of mountaineers), with the small Museo SAT about the mountains; just beyond, Palazzo Salvadori (16C), once a synagogue. At the end of the road is the early 16th-century Palazzo del Monte – note the frescoes of the Labors of Hercules, executed around 1540.

Castello del Buonconsiglio**. Ancient residence of the bishop-princes, this castle is within a wall studded with low keeps. The castle comprises several wings: to the north, topped by the round Torre Grande, the battlemented 13th-century Castelvecchio, modified in 1475, with a central courtyard with stacked loggias; note the frescoes by Fogolino and others. In the center, the so-called Giunta Albertiana, a wing built to join the north and south wings; to the south, the Magno Palazzo, Renaissance in style, with a broad loggia overlooking the Cortile dei Leoni, Note the splendid frescoes by G. Romanino (1531-32).

Inside is the **Museo del Castello del Buonconsiglio-Monumenti e Collezioni Provinciali***, with sections also in Castel Beseno, Castel Stenico and Castel Thun. It has ancient, medieval, and modern art. From the entrance, you cross the garden, and on the right you can see the cells of Italian heroes D. Chiesa, C. Battisti, and F. Filzi, executed here in 1916. The museum, with artifacts, coins, codices, sacred objects, and paintings, occupies many rooms in the Magno Palazzo and Castelvecchio; note the wooden ceilings and frescoes by D. Dossi, Romanino, and Fogolino and the frescoes of the *12 Months** (15C) by anonymous artists.

Piazza Raffaello Sanzio. Note the yellow-and-green tiled Torre Verde (13C), with remnants of the walls of which it was a part.

Piazza Dante. Located between the modern Palazzo della Regione (A. Libera, 1954-62), the train station and Palazzo della Provincia, this square boasts a public garden with a famed monument to Dante, by C. Zocchi (1896), a symbol of Italian resistance under Austrian domination. To the west, note the 12th-century Romanesque church of S. Lorenzo, rebuilt in 1955 after heavy damage in WWII.

S. Apollinare. Across the Adige, this Romanesque-Gothic church has a portal and rose window in red Veronese porphyry.

Palazzo delle Albere. This square "suburban" villa with corner towers and moat was built around 1535 by the bishop-prince C. Madruzzo. It is the site of the Tridentine section of the Museo d'Arte Moderna e Contemporanea di Trento e Rovereto with documentation of fundamental phases of Italian art, from Romanticism and Divisionism, and the Ca' Pesaro period to the Novecento movement, and from Spatialism to the Informal. Among the Trent-born artists are E. Prati, U. Moggioli, L. Bonazza, T. Garbari, and F. Depero.

Torre Vanga. Square and crenelated, this tower was built in the 13th century to protect a bridge over the Adige River.

SKIING IN TRENTINO-ALTO ADIGE

T rentino-Alto Adige is one of Italy's most ski-focused regions, often making it taxing to decide which of the many ski resorts to head to. The selection of ski areas covered below starts from those around Bolzano, that is, in Alto Adige, and then moves on to those in Trentino. This list is by no means exhaustive, but is designed to offer a taster of what the region has to offer snow lovers.

PROVINCE OF BOLZANO

Val Senales/Schnalstal

The Val Senales is one of the few Alpine skiing areas that is regularly open for more than 10 months a year. The core is the Croda Grigia-Giogo Alto Glacier. It is enclosed by imposing massifs, such as the Tessa Mountains and Silmilaun to the northeast and Palla Bianca to the west, and opens into the Val Venosta via an inaccessible 3 km gorge a little upstream from Naturno. The snowboarding scene is lovely, with a well-equipped center at Maso Corto. A well-known ski-mountaineering expedition leaves from Vernago and heads to the Tisa ridge and Similaun, near where the famous mummified body of a Copper Age resident of the zone, known as Ötzi, was found. One final aspect to note in the Val Senales are the 86 *masi chiusi* (literally, closed farmhoues, but indicating a farmstead that cannot be divided up among heirs), which are some of the highest and oldest permanent settlements in the Tyrol.

Bressanone-Plose/Brixen

Bressanone lies at a mere 560 m, but it is the cultural and religious center for the Tyrol area, with its own flourishing culture and trade. The Bressanone ski runs are a little higher, with the ski-lifts departing from Sant'Andrea (about 1,050 m). The area, along with Maranza-Gitschberg and Valles-Jochtal, forms part of the northwestern edge of Dolomiti Superski (81 km of ski runs), with a single ski pass and the spraying of artificial snow as needed. The skiing area lies on the southwest facing slopes of Plose and on the adjacent Mt Fana.

Brunico-Olang/Bruneck/Valdaora

Not long after the beginning of the Val Badia at San Lorenzo di Sebato is Plan de Corones, a white natural dome with gentle slopes, woods and various ski runs. Brunico, enhanced by a lively pedestrian zone, is an important tourist center. The second major center from which you can reach Plan de Corones is Valdaora, about 10 km to the east at the start of the small Furcia

Valley. The third and no less important center is San Vigilio di Marebbe. The Plan de Corones skiing area has some hotels and numerous family-run bars and restaurants, creating a typical Dolomite feel. The flat summit of Plan de Corones makes this an ideal place for children.

Corvara in Badia/Corvara
Colfosco/Kollfuschg

The Alta Badia phenomenon is created by an amazing combination of Nordic efficiency, Ladin warmth, hospitality and professionalism, everything set in the marvelous landscape of the Dolomites. Corvara is full of tourist resorts and well-positioned ski-lifts that blend in to the landscape. Colfosco is practically a satellite of Corvara, lying at the bottom of the pass. Its church, with Sella as a backdrop, is one of the classic images of the Dolomites. A network of lifts covers all of the slopes, making Alta Badia (and Corvara) the hub of the Sella Ronda area. The Corvara-Colfosco system is well connected both to the villages of Alta Badia and the nearby Arabba and Val Gardena (a total of, at least, 450 km of ski runs).

Selva di Val Gardena/Wolkenstein in Gröden

Selva di Val Gardena is a giant of the ski industry, with ski runs and lifts at every corner, and a modern infrastructure with shops, bars, restaurants, hotels and other types of accommodation that spread across the valley floor. Of the three Ladin towns in Val Gardena, one of the major skiing zones in Europe in the heart of Sella Ronda and Dolomiti Superski, Selva is probably the one with the most notable winter sport soul: it is the hub of 175 km of ski runs (about 10% are classed as difficult, 60% moderate, and 30% easy; nearly all are covered by snow canons) in the valley and a point on the Sella Ronda ski tour.

Altopiano dello Sciliar/Schlern Hochgebiet/
Alpe di Siusi/Seiser Alm

This natural balcony is located at 1,000 m and lies between the Isarco Valley and the rocky cliffs of the magnificent Sciliar. It is al-

The beautiful landscape around Alpe di Siusi.

so the wonderful, sunny setting for Fiè allo Sciliar, Siusi and Castelrotto, three typical Tyrolean settlements characterized by old, solid houses decorated with wrought iron. The plateau itself is dominated by the bulky, yet beautiful mass of Scilia. From the settlements, a series of steep mounds hides Alpe di Siusi, which can practically be considered as a second section of this tourist area. This mythical alp is the true "white" heart of Fiè allo Sciliar, Siusi and Castelrotto.

PROVINCE OF TRENT
Canazei-Campitello di Fassa

Canazei and Campitello di Fassa lie beneath the imposing walls of the Sella massif and within sight of the inspiring Gran Vernel and Marmolada peaks. This is a major skiing area in the eastern Alps, with over 170 hotels. Set amid the best known Dolomites, Canazei is central for Trent, Bolzano and Cortina d'Ampezzo. The lively town is spread out along the main roads lined with many different hotels, houses, rooms-to-rent and sports shops. Campitello di Fassa and Canazei are the hubs of the large, connected skiing area covering the valleys that surround the Sella massif. They are also the only places in Trentino from which you can access the Sella Ronda skiing area directly.

Moena-Passo di San Pellegrino-Bellamonte

Known as the fairy of the Dolomites, Moena stands at the start of the Val di Fassa and the opening of the San Pellegrino Valley. Moena still has its Ladin heart. The Latemar system is close, and to the east and northeast, things are dominated by Monzoni. The Skiarea Tre Valli del Dolomiti Superski has 100 km of trails divided into two sections: Alpe di Lusia-Bellamonte and San Pellegrino Pass-Falcade. In addition, given

the proximity, many skiers spend time in the Val di Fassa, which has a total of 9 areas and 147 km of trails (200 km, if you include the adjoining areas).

Madonna di Campiglio

For over 50 years, this resort has hosted one of the classic stops on the World Cup circuit. It is also one of the places to go for all winter sport lovers. The figures for the skiing area are impressive (60 km of ski runs, which become nearly 120 km if you include the 30 km of the Folgarida-Marilleva area and the 27 km of Pinzolo) but the real attraction lies in the nature of Madonna di Campiglio's ski runs: panoramic, winding, open and clearly marked. The zone receives more snow than anywhere else in the central and eastern section of the Alps and, although there are high-powered artificial snow machines should the need arise, you often ski through fir trees and chalets immersed in snow. In addition, the town lies at 1,550 m, making it an integral part of the skiing area and ensuring you can always ski back. The various connecting trails, with bridges, tunnels and little roads make it easy to move around.

Fai della Paganella-Andalo-Molveno

This is a plateau cloaked in woods and enclosed by two of the major mountain groups in Trentino. Andalo, Fai della Paganella and Molveno are the main skiing areas, although Molveno is also a summer destination, largely because of its wonderful lake, and was once favored by a jet-setting crowd. Andalo, located on a watershed between the Noce and Sarca basins, is characterized by pleasant tourist structures. Fai della Paganella, standing on a natural balcony overlooking the Adige Valley, is slightly less touristy. Each of the towns on the plateau has its own identity, but in skiing terms, they combine to form the Paganella skiing area (nearly 50 km of runs). The hubs are Andalo and Fai della Paganella, both with high-capacity lifts.

Folgaria-Lavarone

Folgaria, on the gentle slopes of Becco di Filadonna and Cornetto, and Lavarone are situated amid rolling plateaus, snow-covered meadows and pastures, dwarf-pines and fir trees. The area is covered by a single brand, Skitour dei Forti. There are 70 km of ski runs divided between two hubs, Folgaria-Serrada (the main one) and Lavarone.

NATIONAL PARK STILFSER JOCH

Parco Nazionale dello Stelvio

Provinces of Bolzano, Brescia, Sondrio, Trent

Area: 134,620 hectares. Ortles-Cevedale Mountain massif and side valleys.

Headquarters: Piazza Municipio 1, Glorenza (Bolzano), tel. 0473830430

Via Roma 65, Cogolo di Peio (Trent) tel. 0463746121

Website: www.stelviopark.it

Park gates: Laces/Latsch (Bolzano), for the SS38 road. Pejo and Rabbi (Trent), A22 highway, San Michele dell'Adige-Mezzocorona exit, for the SS12, 42 and 43 roads.

The **Parco Nazionale dello Stelvio** is part of one of the largest reserves in Italy. The northern border extends to the Engadina National Park in Switzerland, while the southern one touches Lombardy's Parco Adamello-Brenta, which is connected, in turn, to the Parco Naturale Adamello-Brenta in Trentino. This creates one of the largest protected areas in Europe (over 260,000 ha), with the Parco dello Stelvio right at the heart, in all senses. The mountainous nature of this zone is evident, with roughly 70% being above 2,000 m.

The center of the park is the mountainous mass of Ortles-Cevedale. This massif is home to nearly 100 glaciers, including the largest in Italy (Forni, 20 km²), and 25 valleys running off in all directions. The main valleys are the Pejo and Viso, heading south, the Rabbi to the east and, to the north, the Solda, Trafoi and Martello. The park is a haven of pristine nature where the green of the fields and larch and fir forests contrast with the white of the peaks and the bright blue of the lakes. The wealth of the park, aside from the great diversity of plants and animals, lies in the numerous landscapes where you can see glaciers, Alpine pastures, forests, farmed fields, farmstead settlements and villages.

The park covers an enormous range of altitudes, from 650 m at Laces in the Val Venosta to 3,905 m at the summit of Ortles, and thus numerous different plant species. Despite this, the woods are dominated by firs: spruces, especially in the valleys of Trentino and Alto Adige, larch and Swiss stone pines. The latter, along with dwarf mountain pines, can be found as high as 2,300 m. As you go higher, up to 3,500 m, the vegetation consists of "specialized" species, such as the glacier crowfoot, that can resist the harsh climate and especially the cold, snow and ice.

The variety of terrains and environments (including peat-bogs, high-altitude pastures and snow-covered valleys) means that over 1,200 plant species can be found in the park, including the extremely rare lady's slipper orchid, *Paludella squarrosa* and *Soldanella pusilla*, and over 600 other vegetal species (mushrooms, moss and lichen).

All of the typical Alpine animals can be found in the park. The chamois, numbering over 4,500, is the most common small hoofed-animal. The present deer population, descendants of animals from the Engadina park, is the largest in Italy with nearly 2,500 animals. The best places to try and spot them are the Val Venosta forests. If you are looking for roedeer, the best option is the valleys of Trentino. The ibex was reintroduced to the park as part of project begun in 1968 and now there are a few hundred animals, which can be seen as far north as the border with the Engadina park. In terms of other mammals, the most widespread is the marmot, although there are numerous foxes, small rodents and martens, such as the stoat and the beech marten.

The symbol of the park is the golden eagle, of which there are at least 10 recorded nesting pairs. The sizeable beak, the predatory look, the powerful talons and a wingspan of over 2m have always fascinated man. In the park, they are often seen circling high above the Martello or Rabbi valleys. Other birds-of-prey in the park include the goshawk, sparrowhawk, eagle owl and pygmy owl.

In total, there are about 130 species of bird in the park, many of which nest there, including the Alpine grouses (wood, black, hazel and snow grouses), five species of woodpecker, nutcrackers, Greek partridges, ring ouzels, and treecreepers and other passerines. In recent times, the bearded vulture has been spotted, despite not being seen in the Alps for over a century. The reason for this wonderful development is that, in the 1980s, a program was launched to reintroduce this impressive bird that can fly hundreds of kilometers a day.

FOOD IN TRENTINO-ALTO ADIGE

Vineyards and orchards are commonplace in the whole of Trentino-Alto Adige, practically forming the backdrop for the various products that indicate this is a border area: the common crops of the Po Valley and the Veneto plain are found in Trentino, while more Alpine elements are to be seen in Alto Adige. As one climbs up through the Dolomites, the contrast between the crops of the valley floor (vineyards and orchards) and the animal rearing and dairy farming of the mountains becomes more noticeable. The highlight of the latter is a type of cured meat like bacon that is called speck (Speck altoatesino Igp).

THE DISHES OF TRENTINO

Polenta di patate. This polenta is made with maize flour combined with fried onions and potatoes. This is then turned into a purée and served with meat stews or cheese.

Beans and salted meat. This is a typical dish, especially in Valsugana. Leg cuts of beef are kept in brine, then sliced and heated in a frying pan before being served with boiled beans.

Pinza trentina. A classic homemade dessert, it is made by soaking stale bread in milk and then adding in chopped, dried figs, sugar and flour. It is baked in the oven and often served at tea time.

THE DISHES OF ALTO ADIGE

Knödeln. These large, rounded gnocchi are served in broth or with a sauce. They are generally a first course, although sometimes they are served with a meat stew. There are various types of Knödeln: a simple form made with stale bread, flour, milk, butter, eggs, parsley and onion; a richer version that also includes speck, veal or beef liver, salami and so on.

Sauerkraut. The German name for finely sliced cabbage, it is placed on wooden dishes, with salt, saffron, cumin and other spices. It is traditionally eaten with German sausage.

Strudel. The flagship of desserts in the Alto Adige area, it consists of a layer of puff pastry filled with fruit, cream and poppy seeds. It comes in various forms, but the most common filling is apple.

THE PRODUCTS OF TRENTINO

Grana Padano Trentino DOP. The word "Trentino" printed on the cheese indicates it is the real deal from the area, guaranteeing that it has been made following the correct procedure, including what the cows were allowed to eat (only fresh grass, hay and feed based on cereal crops and pulses).

Puzzone di Moena. This medium-fat cheese is white or pale yellow with some small holes in it. The damp crust, sharp smell and strong, unmistakable taste make this cheese easy to recognize.

Mela Renetta. This is the most traditional apple from the area and was key to the success of local fruit growing. In Val di Non – the ideal setting – it now accounts for 20% of production. Golden Delicious and Red Delicious are the other two major types.

THE PRODUCTS FROM ALTO ADIGE

Graukäse. This is one of the oldest dairy products in the region and is typical of the Aurina Valley. Semi-skimmed milk is used. The cheese has a distinct grey color, with a soft texture and a clear, spicy flavor.

Speck dell'Alto Adige/Südtiroler Speck IGP. This cured meat is made with pork from the leg that is cold smoked and seasoned. Speck is red with some whitish-pink parts. It smells of smoke and the spices used in the seasoning. The flavor is distinct and quite strong.

To preserve the aroma of speck, it should be stored in a cool place, wrapped in parchment paper.

THE WINES

Local wine production includes Marzemino – a red with delicate traces of violet – the white Müller Thurgau, Teroldego Rotaliano – a robust red with raspberry hints – and the sweet, scented Vino Santo Trentino. The region is also a true leader for sparkling wine.

Alto Adige is the homeland for Gewürztraminer, an aromatic white, and Lagrein and Santa Maddalena (reds). There are also many wines made with more international grapes: Pinot Nero, Pinto Bianco, Cabernet, Merlot, Pinot Bianco, Sauvignon, Chardonnay, Riesling, Müller Thurgau and Sylvaner.

THE EUGANEI HILLS

The Euganei hills rise up from the flat Venetian plain in the form of regular green cones; the Mt Venda (601 m) is the tallest among them. On the southern slopes there are many Mediterranean details; elsewhere, you will be able to find a wide variety of trees such as chestnut, hornbeam, manna-ash, and durmast; here and there you will come across orchards and vegetable gardens, vineyards and olive groves. The region had volcanic origins. History has scattered the landscape with jewels: 12th-century hermitages cunningly arranged with spectacular views, medieval castles, villas, gardens, and parks of the Venetian nobility. The waters here have curative properties, as the Romans already knew many centuries beforehand; over time, it was forgotten, but by the 13th century, the city of Padua was passing new laws regulating the use of these waters. The route begins just entering the northern foothills, up to Teolo, then it runs west and south around them, passing through the historic cities of the Paduan area – Montagnana, Este, Monselice – and returns to the starting point, entering the famous locations of the highlands: Arquà, Valsanzibio, the hermitages of Monte Rua.

NOT TO BE MISSED

Abbey of Praglia**: a boulevard lined with plane trees leads to the solemn Benedictine monastery founded in the 12th century and almost totally re-built in the 15th-16th century, with a church and four cloisters. **Teolo** is believed to be the birthplace of the Roman historian Livy; fine view from the 13th-century parish church of S. Giustina at the highest point in town; from the square in front of the church, a road enters the Parco Lieta Carraresi, a nature reserve with excellent scenery and views. **Noventa Vicentina**: Villa Barbarigo, at the center of a small town that grew up around it, is now the town hall; in the parish church is a canvas by Tiepolo. **Poiana Maggiore**: of the three villas that belonged to the Pojana family, one was designed and built by A. Palladio. **Montagnana***: girt with intact medieval walls, among the finest in Europe; in the Duomo are good paintings, one by Veronese; Palazzo Pisani, just outside town, was built by Palladio. **Este***: still intact are the walls of the Castello Carrarese around the holiday home of the Mocenigo family (visit the museum on Venetia prior to the Romans); canvas by Tiepolo, among others, in the Duomo. **Monselice***: along the walk on this hill are the Castello, the Duomo Vecchio, the Sanctuary of the Sette Chiese, the Villa Duodo, and fascinating views of the plains. **Arquà Petrarca**: here the great 14th-century poet Petrarch lived in his old age and died; his tomb is in the church courtyard. **Battaglia Terme**: Stendhal frequented this spa; around it are the Villa Selvatico Capodilista high on the Colle di S. Elena and, along the road to Padua, the Villa Cataio. **Valsanzibio**, with the Italian-style garden of the Villa Barbarigo. **Eremo di Rua**: this hermitage is inhabited by Camaldolite monks, who live in cloistered seclusion; the setting is green and silent, the view extends to the hills, the plain, the Alps, and Venice. **Monteortone***: this sanctuary (15C) is supposedly the site of a miracle. **Abano Terme***: the large Venetian "ville d'eaux" is typical of the turn of the 20th century.

PADUA/PADOVA

This active provincial capital with its medieval layout and artistic wealth has become a focus for tourism. The presence of a university here since 1222 made Padua one of Europe's great cultural centers. Padua's strong Roman Catholic tradition is rooted in the preaching of the Fransciscan monk Anthony (1195-1231), who spent the last years of his life here and was proclaimed saint shortly after his death. The presence of Giotto, Donatello and Mantegna qualifies Padua as capital of Italian art in the 14th and 15th centuries. According to Virgil, the city was founded by Antenor of Troy. Local archeological finds point to civilization dating from the 11th to 10th centuries BC. It came under full Roman rule in the 2nd century AD, and became one of the Empire's richest cities. The earliest permanent markets date from the 12th century, roughly where Piazza delle Erbe and Piazza della Frutta are today. In 1318, the da Carrara family came to the fore, providing the town with a solid set of walls, but were overwhelmed by the Visconti of Milan (1388-90). In 1406 they were ousted by the Venetians who ruled Padua until it was invaded by Napoleon in 1797. The city became part of the Kingdom of Italy in 1866.

Palazzo della Ragione separates Piazza delle Frutta from **Piazza delle Erbe**, closed on the east side by 15th-century **Palazzo Comunale** and site of a colorful daily market.

The palazzo was built on a rectangular plan in 1218-19 as a lawcourt. Enlarged in 1306-09 by adding external loggias and a ship's keel roof, a fire in 1420 destroyed Giotto's frescoes. Subsequently restored, the frescoes cover more than 200 m of walls and are divided into 12 sections. The huge wooden horse (1446) is a copy of Donatello's equestrian statue of Gattemelata.

Piazza dei Signori, named after the da Carrara family, the square is overlooked by the 17th-century church of S. Clemente and the elegant marble **Loggia del Consiglio*** (1496-1553), with a ground-floor portico and a broad staircase; at the far end is Palazzo del Capitanio (1605), whose facade incorporates the **Arco dell'Orologio** (1532), with Italy's earliest clock (1344). Beyond, the Corte Capitaniato is surrounded by 16th-century buildings and the **Liviano** (1939), the seat of the University Arts Faculty; in the atrium, frescoes by M. Campigli and a statue of Livy by A. Martini (1942). A **monumental staircase*** leads up to the first floor to the vast Sala dei Giganti, decorated in the 16th century with frescoes of kings and heroes (in one corner is a 14th-century portrait of Petrarch). The Liviano houses the **Museo di Scienze Archeologiche e d'Arte**, with a fine collection of ceramics, votive and domestic objects from pre-history to late Antiquity, and a plaster-cast museum Greek and Roman sculpture.

Battistero. The 12th-century Baptistery is built on a square plan with a broad dome. The interior is covered with exceptional **frescoes*** (1374-76), the masterpiece of G. de' Menabuoi. He also painted the polyptych at the altar: a prime example of Italian 14th-century painting. The font in the center dates from 1260.

Duomo. Founded in the Early Middle Ages, re-built in the 9th and 10th centuries and again before 1124, its present appearance reflects the reconstruction begun in 1551, to a design by Michelangelo. The warm brick facade is unfinished. The interior is bare and majestic, dominated by mighty pilasters. In the walls of the transept: monumental tombs of the 14th to 16th centuries. In the Sagrestia dei Canonici: 14th-century panels and fine paintings.

Museo Diocesano. Housed in the prestigious **Palazzo Vescovile** (Bishop's Palace), the museum (visitors should book) contains precious examples of painting, sculpture, gold- and silver-ware, codices, incunabulae and vestments from the diocese of Padua.

Highlights include a 9th-century ink-well, an 11th-century panel depicting Christ making the sign of benediction, the 12th-century cover of a book of the the Gospels, a cycle of paintings depicting the Stories of St Sebastian (1367), panels by G. Schiavone and paintings by G.B. Tiepolo (S. Francesco di Paola). The S. Maria degli Angeli chapel (1495), with frescoes, is now part of the museum.

Piazza Insurrezione lies in the heart of the modern city. Nearby, the 18th-century **church of S. Lucia** has a harmonious interior decorated with statues and fine paintings, and, high up, monochrome paintings, with works by G.B. Tiepolo (**St Luke***). Not far away, in Via Marsilio da Padova is the 13th-century Casa di Ezzelino. I Carmini, the complex of the church of S. Maria del Carmine, documented as early as 1212, was re-built in the late 15th century. For centuries, it was the fulcrum of the town north of the city walls. Badly damaged by bombs in WWII, the sacristy and the nearby **Scuola del Carmine***, built in the 14th century, and decorated with 16th-century frescoes, survived. The school was re-built in the early 16th century.

Palazzo Zuckermann contains a new museum complex, inaugurated in June 2004, that comprises the Museum of Art and Applied and Decorative Arts. The first contains more than 2,000 objects from the collections of the Civic Museum of Medieval and Modern Art: glass, inlay work, ceramics, silver, ivories, jewelry, fabrics and furniture used in Padua from the Middle Ages until the late 19th century. The second museum has an exhibition of coins and medals, paintings, furniture, sculptures, Chinese ceramics, antique weapons and other items collected by N. Bottacin, a merchant who donated his art and coin collection to the city in the mid-19th century.

Museo di Mineralogia, the museum contains various collections (systematics, mineral deposits, genetics, and the "G. Gasser" regional collection) and is the most important mineralogical collection in the Veneto. There are also smaller collections of gemstones, geological phenomena, crystals, meteorites, and fluorescent minerals. It also has displays of equipment used in the 19th and 20th centuries for analyzing and studying minerals, models of crystalline structures and early illustrated books on mineralogy.

Scrovegni Chapel, named after the man who commissioned it, stands in the Giardino Pubblico dell'Arena, named after the 1st-century Roman amphitheater which once

The Basilica of Sant'Antonio.

stood on this site. The little church, also called S. Maria dell'Annunciata, was consecrated in 1305. Inside are the **famous frescoes by Giotto****, executed with the aid of his assistants and completed by 1305. They constitute one of the finest examples of Italian painting. On the wall above the entrance is the Last Judgement. On the side-walls (below) are the 7 vices and 7 virtues, and above are 38 panels depicting the Life of Christ and the Life of Mary. The frescoes reflect the special characteristics of Giotto's art: monumental composition, simplicity of representation and great use of melodrama. In the presbytery, the statues above the altar are a **Madonna and two Angels*** by G. Pisano.

Eremitani. The church of the Eremitani, dedicated to St Philip and St James, was built between 1276 and 1306. Half-destroyed by bombs in 1944, it has been lovingly restored. Inside, the single nave has a wooden ceiling. On the walls of the nave are tombs and sculptures from the 14th and 16th centuries: the tomb of J. da Carrara, with an inscription by Petrarch, and the tomb of Ubertino da Carrara (both 14C). At the far end, on the right is the **Cappella Ovetari***. The chapel's famous frescoes by Andrea Mantegna and other artists were destroyed by the bombs. Some of Mantegna's works have survived: the **Assumption*** (behind the altar), two scenes of the Martyrdom of St Christopher (on the right) and the Martyrdom of St James (on the left, partly destroyed).

Musei Civici agli Eremitani, housed in the restored cloisters of the monastery of the Eremitani monks, the **Museo Archeologico** has pre-Roman, Roman, Egyptian, Etruscan and paleo-Christian exhibits. Highlights include the 88 items, including some finely decorated candle-sticks, from the tomb of the embossed Vases (700 BC) and various Roman remains: a head of Augustus (1C AD), a bust of Silenus (2C BC), and an aedicular tomb.

The **Pinacoteca** has a splendid range of paintings from the Venetian School (14-20C) and important works by Giotto (Christ on the Cross, from the Scrovegni Chapel), Tintoretto (Dinner at the house of Simon) and Veronese (Martyrdom of St Primus and St Felicianus). The **Emo Capodilista Collection** has a nucleus of 543 paintings by Venetian and Flemish artists. Highlights include paintings by Giorgione (Leda and the Swan), Titian (Mythological Scenes) and Giovanni Bellini (Portrait of a Young Senator).

Museo di Storia della Fisica. The museum contains a collection of scientific apparatus dating from the 16th to 20th centuries. The exhibits include 16th-century astronomical instruments, some extremely rare microscopes from the 17th and 18th centuries and a collection of instruments (18-9C) used in the study of physics.

S. Sofia, the oldest church in Padua. S. Sofia was possibly founded in the 9th century. It was altered and rebuilt several times. It has an interesting facade (11-14C) and a beautiful **apse*** with three overlapping tiers of blind arcading. The somber interior has a nave and two side-aisles and an ambulatory around the far end of the presbytery.

Piazza Cavour, is the liveliest square in the city. In a small square nearby is **Caffè Pedrocchi**, an elegant Neo-Classic building dating from 1831. It was once known as the "café with no doors", because it stayed open all night. It was a popular meeting-place for intellectuals, writers and politicians and the focus of the life of the city.

Via VIII Febbraio, on its left is the University and on the right, Palazzo del Municipio. The **University**, known as Palazzo del Bo' (from "bue" *ox*, the name of an inn which once stood on the spot) is one of the oldest in Europe (1222) and has many cultural traditions. Frequented by students from all over Europe (Galileo Galilei taught here), it is regarded as the cradle of modern medicine. Palazzo del Municipio (16C) has a very fine **courtyard*** with a portico and loggias. From here, steps lead up to the upper floor, where the most interesting rooms are located: the **anatomy theater***, the first of its kind (1594), the Sala dei Quaranta (with Galileo's wooden "cattedra") and the Aula Magna (Great Hall), which is decorated with numerous coats of arms.

Via S. Francesco, in Piazzale Antenore, which is crossed by this street, is the **Tomb of Antenor**, a spired aedicule (1283). It stands above the tomb traditionally regarded as that of Antenor, the mythical founder of Padua. In fact, it is the tomb of a warrior of the 2nd or 4th century. Further on is the 15th-century **church of S. Francesco**, which has a porticoed entrance. Gothic in style, it has a nave and two side-aisles.The Ascension above the doorway is attributed to Paolo Veronese.

Via Roma, one of Padua's busiest streets, is overlooked by the side of the church of S. Maria dei Servi (1372-92), with its 16th-century doorway. Inside are some fine frescoes (the Pietà in the right aisle) and Renaissance sculptures.

Museo "La Specola" INAF Osservatorio Astronomico di Padova, in the late 18th century, the University of Padua converted the Great Tower of the old castle into an astronomical observatory. "La Specola" was divided into two parts. The lower observatory, called the Sala della Meridiana (Room of the Sun-dial), was used for making observations at midday using the sun-dial incorporated in its floor and for observing stars at the celestial meridian. The octagonal upper observatory has large windows which enabled students of astronomy to observe the stars in every direction. The museum also has an exhibition room (Sala Colonna) with astronomical instruments from the 18th and 19th centuries. **Museo del Precinema – Collezione Minici Zotti,** the museum focuses on the pre-cinema age and the "magic lantern", an optical instrument invented in 1650 for projecting images painted on glass onto a screen. There are numerous magic lanterns, hand-painted panes of glass used in magic-lantern shows, a photography and stereoscopy section and optical games. Almost all the exhibits are original, except the ones which have been reproduced to give visitors a "hand's on" experience.

Prato della Valle, one of Europe's largest squares, was laid out in 1775-76. In the center of the square is an island planted with trees, Isola Memmia, surrounded by a pool and 78 statues.

S. Giustina. Corner of Prato della Valle, the grand 16th-century **church of S. Giustina** has a bare facade and eight domes. Its vast interior has a nave and two side-aisles separated by pilasters. The right transept leads into the **sacello di S. Prosdocimo*** (church of St Prosdocimus), the remains of a primitive church of the 5th and 6th centuries, which still has part of the old marble iconostasis (6C) on one side. In the **old choir*** (1462), formerly the apse of the previous church, are wooden choir-stalls with fine inlay work (1477). In the adjoining rooms is a 15th-century terracotta statue (Madonna and Child), and the lunette and architrave from the Romanesque doorway of the earlier church (ca. 1080), with fine sculptures. In the apse is the **choir***, made of walnut, carved and inlaid in 1566, and the **Martyrdom of St Giustina***, a large altar-piece by P. Veronese. In the 2nd chapel on the left, the painting *St Gregory the Great frees Rome from the Plague* is by S. Ricci.

Botanical garden, created in 1545 for acclimatizing and studying plant species of potential pharmacological value, this is the oldest university botanical garden in the world. The layout of the garden is original: a circular walled garden with four sectors containing numerous, mainly perennial, botanical species. Outside the walls are the glass-houses and the arboretum. The collection of carnivorous and acquatic plants is particularly interesting. Since 1997, it has been a UNESCO World Heritage Site.

Piazza del Santo and Monumento al Gattamelata, heart of the so-called "Cittadella antoniana", Piazza del Santo is a vast square decorated with a bronze equestrian statue, the **monument to Gattamelata***, a mercenary soldier of the Republic of Venice (ca. 1370-1443). This masterpiece of the Italian Renaissance is by Donatello (1453), who also designed and created the pedestal. Site of the Basilica of the Santo, the Oratory of S. Giorgio and the Scuola di S. Antonio, part of the historic square is lined with porticoed houses and shops selling souvenirs and religious mementoes.

S. Antonio/St Anthony's Basilica, or, simply, **Il Santo,** is one of Italy's most famous sanctuaries. It was built between 1232 and the mid-14th century to enshrine the tomb of St Anthony of Padua (who was born in Lisbon in 1195 and died in Padua in 1231). The exterior has eight domes arranged in the form of a cross. Inside, in the right transept is the 14th-century **chapel of S. Felice***, decorated with frescoes (Legend of St James, Crucifixion) by Altichiero (1374-78). In the presbytery, the high altar is decorated with fine **bronzes by Donatello*** (1443-50) and his assistants. On the left of the altar is a bronze candle-stick (1515). The ambulatory leads around behind the presbytery, with chapels leading off its outer edge. The fifth chapel, the Chapel of the Reliquaries, contains a fine **treasury***, with some unusual reliquaries: little incense-burners in the shape of ships (15C) and the wooden boxes which once contained the bones of the Saint. At the end of the ambulatory, the chapel of the Black Madonna lies next to the Chapel of the Blessed Luca Belludi (1382), which is decorated with **frescoes*** by G. de' Menabuoi. In the left transept, the **chapel of the Tomb of St Anthony*** was begun in 1500. On the walls are nine reliefs depicting the Life of the Saint, by 16th century sculptors including J. Sansovino (*St Anthony revives a drowned woman*, 1563). In the middle of the chapel is an exquisite altar from 1593, behind which lies the tomb of St Anthony. The right aisle leads to the **cloisters** (13-15C). The first, the Cloister of the Chapter is the oldest part of the monastery (1240). It leads to the Consiglio della Presidenza dell'Arca, where there is a fresco of *St Anthony and St Bernard in Prayer* by A. Mantegna.

Museo Antoniano and Mostra Antoniana della Devozione Popolare. Founded in 1895, the Museum of St Anthony's Basilica was reopened to the public on the occasion of its centenary having had its collection re-organized to highlight two main themes: first, testimonials of popular veneration for St Anthony over the centuries and the many artworks created for the basilica and the Scuola which, for various reasons, were removed from their original setting. The gold- and silver-ware section is particularly interesting, with some valuable 18th-century altar-pieces and numerous fabrics.

Scuola del Santo/School of St Anthony was begun in 1427 and the height was raised in 1504-1505. An 18th century staircase leads up to the council chamber, which has some very fine early 16th-century **frescoes*** (the most important works from that period in Padua), depicting the miracles of the saint. Starting at the bottom on the right, the 1st, 12th and 13th scene are by Titian.

S. Giorgio. This 14th-century oratory stands to the right of the basilica, next to the Mausoleum of Rolando da Piazzola. The interior of the oratory is entirely covered with **frescoes*** (*Stories from the Lives of St Catherine and St George*) by Altichiero (1379-84). The cycle, organized in horizontal tiers similar to Giotto's frescoes in the Scrovegni Chapel, is one of the most interesting examples of Italian 14th-century painting.

Galleria Guglielmo Tabacchi – Safilo. This museum of eyewear and optical equipment is arranged on three floors. The imaginative interior has been created through the juxtaposition of different thicknesses of glass and metal. The first room has optical equipment from the 16th to 20th centuries: eye-glasses, eye-glass cases, telescopes, binoculars and other optical accessories. Another focuses on the history of the Safilo company and traces the history of the Italian eyewear industry, from its simple Cadore origins to its modern international scale. The exhibition is enhanced by photographs, documents and advertisements. There is also a section devoted to eye-glasses worn by famous personalities and goggles worn by top ski champions. Upstairs, there is a display of protective equipment worn during WWII, a more scientific section with instruments and charts used for testing eyesight, and an artistic section with early paintings and prints of eye-glasses from the 17th to 20th centuries.

"**B**eyond the handsome fields that extended on either side, we would pass through merry little villages, and at every hour we saw noble houses, many of them quite splendid, belonging to the powerful of Venice, who come to spend the summer and part of the fall here...." This is the Riviera del Brenta, the first part of this route that Spanish traveler Leandro Fernandez de Moratin described in his "El Viaje de Italia," 1793-96. Even if you leave aside the cities, with their universal culture of art, architectural style, and atmosphere – Padua, Vicenza and Treviso are exquisite – a great deal can be learned from the Venetian countryside: from the fragments of combative medieval culture and the 16th-18th-century "villa culture" – the nobility was moving inland, farming, living in the pleasant countryside, studying, socializing, or simply whiling away the newly civilized rustic day. This route links the two eras: the former can be found in the Castello di Castelfranco Veneto and the menacing walls of Cittadella, the latter along the Riviera del Brenta and on the Terraglio (the road from Mestre and Treviso), in Villa Foscari alla Malcontenta, Villa Emo a Fanzolo, or Villa Contarini a Piazzola. As Andrea Palladio put it: "The true gentleman will draw great benefit and consolation from the country home..."; today those gifts can be had by the unassuming tourist as well.

NOT TO BE MISSED

Stra: Villa Pisani, with its palatial interiors, fresco by Tiepolo, park, and labyrinth, is the sumptuous introduction to this trip along the Riviera del Brenta. **Dolo**, main center of the Riviera in the 18th century: near the surviving fragments of the 16th-century locks, note the old plaque with inscribed boat tolls. **Mira**: go see Villa Widmann, a fine piece of Venetian rococo dating back to 1719. **Malcontenta** is the name of the place, as well as of the Villa Foscari, both built by Palladio, at the end of the Riviera del Brenta, near the lagoon. **Treviso** (➡ see below) is an alluring city with fine art and architecture; here the setting counts as much as monuments, canvases, and collections. **Istrana** boasts the 18th-century Villa Lattes with noteworthy artwork. **Villa Emo** di Fanzolo: you pass through Vedelago to reach this Palladian villa. **Castelfranco Veneto**: this dignified Venetian town is the birthplace of Giorgione; you can tour his home and, in the Duomo, admire a celebrated altarpiece of his. **Cittadella** still has its elliptical ring of walls intact. **Piazzola sul Brenta**: visit the spectacular Villa Contarini.

VICENZA

This town stands in the gentle green Venetian plain, now an industrialized area, at the foot of the Berici Mountains; other mountains loom on the horizon. Vicenza is linked to the name of the 16th-century architect A. Palladio. His "new", classicizing beauty, pervades the city, harmonizing with the fragments of Venetian Gothic, and with another face of Vicenza, with bridges, canals, haunting vignettes, and sudden views of hills and alpine foothills.

Piazza dei Signori*. This is the monumental center of Vicenza including, on the south side, the Basilica, with the adjacent slender 82-m Torre di Piazza (12C); at the far end, the two columns of the Piazza, one topped by the Lion of St Mark's (1520), the other by a statue of the Savior (1640); on the NE side, the Loggia del Capitaniato*, also known as Loggia Bernarda, an unfinished work by Palladio (1571), and the long facade of Palazzo del Monte di Pietà, with the Baroque facade of the church of S. Vincenzo in the center (1614; inside, marble Deposition* by O. Marinali).

Basilica**. The most important monument in Vicenza, one of the outstanding buildings of the Venetian Renaissance, built between 1549 and 1617, the basilica is a masterpiece by A. Palladio, who enclosed the existing 15th-century Gothic Palazzo della Ragione in a sumptuous marble sheath, featuring a classical portico and loggia. The term "Basilica," first used by Palladio himself, here means a building in which justice was administered. On the right side, a stairway leads up to the loggia, and from here you enter the Gothic hall, which occupies the entire upper floor of the building. Nearby, in the Piazza delle Erbe, stands the medieval Torre del Girone, or Torre del Tormento. **S. Maria in Foro**. This 15th-century church overlooks Piazza delle Biade; inside altarpiece by B. Montagna.

Casa Pigafetta. Located at no. 9 in Via Pigafetta, this house was built in a Venetian Gothic style in the 15th century. It was the birthplace of A. Pigafetta, who sailed with Magellan on the first circumnavigation of the earth (1519-22), and wrote an account of the journey. **S. Nicola da Tolentino**. This oratory is decorated with stuccoes that frame numerous paintings by F. Maffei, G. Carpioni, A. Zanchi, and others. From the nearby bridge of S. Michele (1623), you have a fine view of the center of Vicenza; in the Contrà Piancoli, note the buildings at no. 4, 6, and 8.

Piazza del Duomo. The square is overlooked by the Duomo and the bishop's palace, rebuilt in Neo-Classic style in 1819 and partly after being damaged in WWII; in the courtyard of the palace is the splendid Loggia Zeno*, a Renaissance creation by B. da Milano and T. da Lugano. On the south side, next to the Palazzetto Roma, is a Roman cryptoporticus, part of a 1st-century AD Roman house.

The solemn classical facade of Palladio's Basilica in Vicenza.

Duomo*. Still in its original forms (13-16C), the Vicenza Cathedral has a Gothic facade (1467) in polychrome marble, attributed to D. da Venezia, and an elegant Renaissance apse (1482-1508). The Romanesque bell tower (11C), built on Roman foundations, is across the street. The Gothic interior, with a vast nave and cross vaults, features paintings by F. Maffei, L. Veneziano, and B. Montagna.

Piazza Castello. This square features Palazzo Piovini (1656-58), now a warehouse, and the unfinished Palazzo Porto, built by V. Scamozzi to plans by Palladio (late 16C). At the end of Corso Palladio stands a mighty tower, the only relic of the medieval castle of the Della Scala family. Outside the Porta Castello are the public gardens, once belonging to Villa Salvi, with the Loggetta Valmarana, a small loggia in Palladian style (1592), set alongside a stream of running water.

Ss. Felice e Fortunato*. This basilica is a mainstay in the religious history of Vicenza. It was built in the late 10th century, and restored to its Romanesque forms in the early 20th century. Worthy of note are the mosaic floors, from an earlier building on the same site; also, the distinctive little bell tower.

Corso Andrea Palladio* (first stretch). This main street runs through Vicenza, east to west, amidst a series of monumental homes and churches, dating from the 14th-18th century. At no. 13, the enormous Palazzo Thiene, later Bonin-Longare, attributed to Palladio and completed by V. Scamozzi; at no. 45, the Renaissance Palazzo Capra-Clementi (late 15C); at no. 47, the Venetian Gothic Palazzo Thiene, with handsome five-light mullioned window; at no. 67, the elegant Venetian Gothic Palazzo Braschi-Brunello, with a portico. **Corso**

Fogazzaro. One of Vicenza's liveliest streets, it has fine Baroque and Renaissance residences. On the right, at no. 16, the solemn Palazzo Valmarana-Braga (1566) by Palladio; further along, the Palazzo Repeta, by F. Muttoni (1711).

S. Lorenzo*. Impressive Franciscan church, in brickwork and Gothic style (13C). On the facade, note the portal* decorated with statues (1344). Inside, amidst round piers, various funerary monuments dating from the 14th-16th century, an altar relief by Pojana, and a fresco by B. Montagna. The cloister (1492) features a round-arch portico.

Carmine. In Corso Fogazzaro, this Neo-Gothic construction preserves portals and other elements from the long-demolished 14th-century church of S. Bartolomeo (14-15C). Inside, paintings by Veronese, Bassano, and B. Montagna.

Galleria d'Arte Municipale. Set in a 16th-century former church, in a nook in Corso Palladio, this city art gallery features paintings by local artists such as S. Prunato, and G.A. Fumiani.

Palazzo Trissino-Baston*. At no. 98 in Corso Palladio, the palace, which now houses the city hall, is lined with a tall portico with Ionic columns. A masterpiece by V. Scamozzi (1592), it has a handsome courtyard and, on the second floor, are the Council Hall, adorned with a frieze by G. Carpioni, and the Sala degli Stucchi.

Contrà Porti*. This road runs past a number of splendid palazzi: at no. 6-10, the 15th-century Venetian Gothic Palazzo Cavalloni-Thiene; at no. 11, the vast Palazzo Barbaran-Porto, by Palladio (1571), soon to become the Museo Palladiano; at no. 12, the Renaissance Palazzo Thiene (head office of the Banca Popolare), designed by Palladio, with facade by L. da Bologna (1489); at no. 14, the Gothic Palazzo Trissino-Sperotti (1450-60), with an elegant balcony; no. 17, the Venetian Gothic

Palazzo Porto-Breganze (1481), with a handsome Renaissance portal and a porticoed courtyard; at no. 16, the Renaissance Palazzo Porto-Fontana; no. 19, the magnificent Venetian Gothic Palazzo Porto-Colleoni (late 14C); at no. 21, Palladio's unfinished Palazzo Iseppo da Porto, later Palazzo Festa.

S. Marco. This 18th-century church, with a lavish facade, is worth a visit for the painting of the Ecstasy of St Theresa by S. Ricci.

Contrà Zanella. This street is lined with notable buildings: at no. 2, Palazzo Sesso-Zen, a rare piece of Vicentine Gothic; at no. 1, on the Piazzetta S. Stefano, the crenelated Renaissance Palazzo Negri De Salvi; to the left, the Baroque church of S. Stefano (painting* by Palma the Elder); further along, the Palladian rear facade of Palazzo Thiene.

Corso Palladio*. At no. 147, Palazzo Dal Toso-Franceschini-Da Schio*, known as Ca' d'Oro, a gem of Venetian Gothic architecture (14-15C); to the left, the garden of the 13th-century church of S. Corona; at no. 165-67, the Casa Cogollo, inaccurately but frequently called Casa di Palladio, with a late Renaissance facade (1559-62), possibly by G.A. Fasolo.

S. Corona*. This Dominican church, built from 1261 on, has an imposing marble central portal and an elegant bell tower. The interior has Gothic nave with aisles, with a deep, raised Renaissance presbytery (1489), built by L. da Bologna. On various altars throughout the church are paintings by P. Veronese (1573), Giovanni Bellini, L. Bassano, and B. Montagna. Also, note the high altar (1669), the inlaid wooden choir, and the handsome reliquary, which contains a Thorn from the Crown of Christ, displayed only on Good Friday. In the adjacent convent are the Museo Naturalistico, with exhibits of natural history, and the Museo Archeologico, with collections ranging from the Stone Age to the High Middle Ages. No. 25 of Contrà S. Corona is the Baroque Palazzo Leoni Montanari, the seat of a private museum featuring an interesting art collection. The paintings, of the Venetian school, are by artists such as Longhi, Canaletto, Carlevarijs, Guardi.

Piazza Matteotti. This broad green space is flanked by Palazzo Chiericati, site of the Museo Civico, and, to the left, in a garden scattered with carved marble pieces, by the Teatro Olimpico; behind the theater rises a medieval tower.

Pinacoteca Civica di Palazzo Chiericati*, located in Palazzo Chiericati*, a work by Palladio (1550), opened in 1855. This art gallery includes a section of medieval art, and one with works from the Venetian school (16-18C).

In the first section, 13th-century Venetian painting is represented by P. Veneziano, B. da Vicenza, G. Buonconsiglio, and others. In the second section are works by 15th-16th-century artists such as C. da Conegliano, B. Montagna, P. Veronese, J. Tintoretto, J. Bassano, and 17th-18th-century artists such as G. Carpioni, F. Maffei, S. and M. Ricci, P. della Vecchia, G. Zais, G.B. Tiepolo; there are also still-lifes and landscapes from the 17th-18th century. Also works by B. Boccaccino, F. del Cairo, L. Giordano, and the Flemish artists H. Memling and Van Dyck; note the Virgin and Child*, a terracotta by J. Sansovino. The museum also has a collection of drawings by A. Palladio.

Teatro Olimpico**. The theater is the last creation of Palladio (1580), completed by his son Silla in 1582-83. The largest of the reception halls is the so-called *Odeo* or *Odeon*, a meeting place for the Accademia degli Olimpici, built by V. Scamozzi in 1608, with frescoes by F. Maffei. Then comes the Antiodeo; from here, along stairways that lead to the upper loggias, you enter the theater proper. Built in wood and stucco, it imitates the forms of classical theaters with a semielliptical auditorium made up of thirteen rows and crowned by columns and a balustrade with statues. The lavish stage features an imposing permanent set on two registers, adorned with 95 statues; its three arches open up towards the architectural perspectives of the seven roads of the ancient city of Thebes, designed by V. Scamozzi.

S. Maria in Aracoeli. The church is one of Vicenza's few Baroque monuments, designed by G. Guarini and built by C. Borella (17C) to an elliptical plan. **S. Pietro**. This Gothic church has a late 16th-century facade and fine paintings inside. The nearby hospice (note the monument to its founder, in theatrium, by A. Canova) includes a 15th-century cloister*.

TREVISO

Narrow porticoed streets, lovely vignettes, and astonishing monuments, a welter of medieval lanes set within the old walls, Gothic and Renaissance paintings – Treviso is set at the confluence of the Botteniga and Sile rivers.

S. Nicolò**. This Gothic church (13C) is made entirely of brickwork, with tall windows and apses. The interior has a nave with two aisles, transept, and five chapels. Note the colossal round piers. Among the artists whose work adorns the church, we should mention: T. da Modena, L. Bregno, A. da Treviso, M. Pensaben, G. Savoldo, and Andrea da Murano. Note the remarkable organ, built by A. Palma, with doors painted by G. Lauro. In the chapel to the right of the presbytery, 14th-century frescoes; on the altar is a canvas by the Anonymous Venetian. Also note the Monument to the Senator A. Onigo*, by the sculptor G. Buora and the painter L. Lotto.

Seminario Vescovile. Adjacent to the church, in a former convent, is the Sala del Capitolo dei Domenicani, decorated with frescoes by T. da Modena (1352), and three small museums: Museo Etnografico degli Indios del Venezuela, with tribal objects from Amazonia; Museo Zoologico Giuseppe Scarpa, with Italian vertebrates and exotic reptiles; Museo di Archeologia e Paleontografia Precolombiana del Sudamerica featuring pre-Columbian culture.

Museo Civico Luigi Bailo. Located at no. 22 in Borgo Cavour, this museum houses the archeological and art collections of the town of Treviso. In the archeological section are objects from the Copper, Bronze, and Iron ages (axes, buckles, swords), Roman artifacts (urns, plaques, sculptures, portraits, bronzes), as well as sculptures from early Christian times and the High Middle Ages. In the gallery are paintings and statues: in particular, by Venetian and local artists. Special note should be given to the works by G. da Fabriano, G. Bellini, C. da Conegliano, L. Lotto, Titian, P. Bordone, J. Bassano, R. Carriera, F. Guardi, P. and A. Longhi. Also, works by painters F. Hayez, I. Caffi and a sculpture by A. Canova.

Museo della Casa Trevigiana. Located in the Casa da Noal, at no. 38 Via Canova, this late Gothic building houses a collection of medieval and Renaissance marble sculptures, terracotta, wooden statues, ancient weapons, and musical instruments. Next door, at no. 40, is the Renaissance Casa Robegan.

Duomo. Originally built in the Middle Ages (Romanesque sections on the left side, column-bearing lions on either side of the pronaos): the apse of this cathedral was rebuilt in the 15th-16th century, and the rest in the 18th century. Before it stands a Neo-Classic six-pillar pronaos, built in 1836. The interior, divided into three spaces, with seven cupolas, includes artworks by noteworthy painters and sculptors. Among them are A. Vittoria, A. Lombardo, P. Bordone, G. da Treviso the Elder, Titian, G. A. Pordenone, P. and T. Lombardo, and L. Bregno. Note the crypt, with a forest of columns and re-used capitals (possibly 8C). **Battistero.** To the left of the Duomo, this Romanesque baptistery (11C) has a bas-relief on the pediment, Roman friezes on either side of the portal, and, inside, fragments of frescoes (12C) in the apses. Note the large tower.

Museo Diocesano di Arte Sacra at no. 9 Via Canoniche. Note the various marble reliefs*, the fresco by T. da Modena, the tapestries and other objects from the Cathedral Treasury.

Calmaggiore. This lovely and busy main street of the old town is lined by 15th and 16th-century porticoes and homes.

Piazza dei Signori*. In the middle of Treviso, the medieval flavor of this square is due to the complex of Communal buildings on three sides. To the east, Palazzo dei Trecento*, from about 1210 (wholly rebuilt), then Palazzo del Podestà with the Torre Civica, and, on the west side, the ancient Palazzo Pretorio.

Loggia dei Cavalieri. Romanesque arcaded structure (1276-77), once a meeting place for Treviso's nobility.

Piazza del Monte di Pietà. Behind Piazza dei Signori is the ancient Palazzo del Monte di Pietà, with the Cappella dei Rettori*, a small 16th-century room, richly adorned with paintings and decorated leather walls (17C).

S. Lucia and S. Vito. In Piazza S. Vito, these two medieval churches have been joined into one. Of the two, S. Lucia, with frescoes by T. da Modena, is the more interesting.

Pescheria. This islet on the Botteniga River is the site of the fish market; note the welter of canals and little lanes that converge here.

S. Francesco*. This Gothic church, built in 1230, was rebuilt in 1928; note the frescoes by T. da Modena, the tombs of Francesca, daughter of Petrarch (d. 1384), and Pietro, son of D. Alighieri (d. 1364).

Porta S. Tomaso. The most monumental of the three gates in Treviso's Venetian-built walls, it is from 1518 (G. Bergamasco); note the lion of St Mark's, emblem of Venice.

S. Caterina dei Servi di Maria. This church was devastated by bombing in 1944, restored, and made into an art gallery. Note the paintings, by T. da Modena and others.

S. Maria Maggiore. This Gothic church was built in 1473 and has a handsomde cloister.

Villa Manfrin. As you head to Conegliano, note this estate (1783), with vast gardens.

Old Treviso reflected in the Buranelli canal.

Roman from AD 49, Verona became an important hub of consular roads and a key defensive outpost, a role it continued to play for centuries. The rise to power of the Della Scala (or Scaligeri) family, in 1262, marked the start of a new building phase, with the construction of Castelvecchio and new fortifications (1283 to 1329). As a result of the town's newfound prosperity, Piazza delle Erbe and the Piazza dei Signori were laid out: the former the symbol and center of commercial power, the latter of political power. The Scaligeri were driven out by the Visconti (1387), who, in turn, were ousted by the Venetians (1405), under whom, in the 16th century, the city's fortunes generated a wave of artistic excellence. The first major changes came in the 18th century due to increasing friction between the local nobility and the Venetian overlords. After the French interlude (1796-1814), a brief period of "co-existence" with the Austrians (1801-1805) under Hapsburg rule (1814-66) restored Verona's defensive role: the city was encircled with a massive set of fortifications. When Verona became part of Italy in 1860, its military role diminished, and disappeared entirely in the 20th century.

THE CITY OF GIULIETTA AND ROMEO

Piazza delle Erbe is on the old *Roman forum*. The rectangular piazza is surrounded by medieval houses and towers: the **fountain*** (1368) in the center incorporates a Roman statue. On the right is Palazzo del Comune with the high Torre dei Lamberti and the Arco della Costa (1470), so called because of the whale's rib dangling from its vault. The arch leads into Piazza dei Signori.

Piazza dei Signori. This square surrounded by monumental buildings joined by arcades, once the seat of the city's institutions, looks more like a courtyard. **Palazzo del Capitanio**, with a tower built by the Scaligeri and a doorway by M. Sanmicheli, was altered in the 19th century. **Palazzo della Prefettura**, formerly called Palazzo del Governo or di Cangrande, is an early residence of the Scaligeri (both Dante and Giotto stayed here). Built in the 14th century, restored in 1929-30, the doorway is by Sanmicheli (1533). **Loggia del Consiglio**, built in the late 15th century as the Town Hall, is an elegant expression of Renaissance architecture. An arch joins it to the Casa della Pietà, rebuilt in 1490.

Arche Scaligere. The little Romanesque church of S. Maria Antica (12C) and the *Arche Scaligere* (the monumental tombs of the lords of Verona) are situated in Piazzaletto delle Arche. A 14th-century wrought-iron grille with the heraldic symbol of the Della Scala family ("scala" means "ladder") surrounds the tombs. They are portrayed as recumbent or equestrian figures covered with elaborate carved stone canopies. Inside the grille (on the left) is the **tomb of Mastino II** (died 1351), the sumptuous **tomb of Cansignorio**, the richly decorated **sarcophagus of Albert I** (died 1301) and, at the back, the hanging memorial tablet of Giovanni della Scala (died 1359). Above the doorway of the little church

is the **tomb of Cangrande I** (died 1329). The equestrian statue of Cangrande is a copy of the original.

S. Anastasia. The church of St Anastasia was built between 1290 and 1481 (restored late 19C); it has an unfinished facade with a 14th-century **doorway*** and a bell tower (1481). *Inside*, the holy-water stoups date from the 16th century; the 1st altar on the right is by Sanmicheli (1565); in the first chapel of the right apse, a large fresco, *The Cavalli family being presented to the Virgin by Three Saints* by Altichiero (ca. 1370); in the 2nd chapel, two Gothic tombs and some terracotta bas-reliefs (1435); in the presbytery, a large 14th-century fresco (*Last Judgment*), and the tomb of Cortesia Serego, attributed to Florentine N. di Bartolo (1429). The left transept leads into the Giusti chapel, with a detached fresco of **St George at Trebizond***, an early work by Pisanello.

Galleria d'Arte Moderna Palazzo Forti. Housed in 18th-century Palazzo Emilei-Forti, it has about 1,000 works by Italian 19th-century artists (Hayez, Fattori, Bianchi, Savini and others) and 20th-century artists (De Pisis, Birolli, Casarini, Casorati, Boccioni, Vedova and others).

Duomo. The cathedral is Romanesque with 15th-century and Renaissance additions. The front has a two-tiered monumental **porch*** decorated with reliefs (1139); the 16th-century bell tower is unfinished. The 12th-century **apse*** is made of tuff. Left of the cathedral is the Romanesque **cloister** (ca. 1140), with part of the mosaic floor of a paleo-Christian basilica; from it you enter the little church of S. Elena (Romanesque, built on paleo-Christian foundations) and the old baptistery of S. Giovanni in Fonte with its 13th-century octagonal **marble font***, both 12th-century. Behind the cathedral,

Palazzo del Vescovado has a Renaissance facade (1502).
Museo Canonicale and Biblioteca Capitolare. The Chapter Library, housed in Palazzo del Canonicato (built 1673, rebuilt 1948) is one of the finest ecclesiastical libraries in Europe. It also houses the Museo Pinacoteca Canonicale, with sculptures and paintings from the

Piazza delle Erbe is still the home of a popular market.

12th to 19th centuries: highlights include a relief of *St Hermagorus and St Fortunatus* (ca. 1120) and an edicule with *Christ giving the Blessing and Saints* (15C). The collection focuses on the Verona School of the 15th and 16th centuries, with enamels, ivories, bronze figurines, coins, medals and musical instruments from the Roman period.

S. Giorgio in Braida. The church of St George and its majestic dome by M. Sanmicheli dominate the loop of the Adige River. Built between 1477 and 1536, the white marble facade was added in the 17th century. Inside are many fine paintings: **Baptism of Christ*** by Jacopo Tintoretto, **Madonna appearing to Saints*** by Moretto da Brescia, **Martyrdom of St George*** by Paolo Veronese. Opposite is Sanmicheli's Porta S. Giorgio (1525).

S. Stefano. The church, one of Verona's most important early-Christian buildings, was a bishop's seat until the 8th century. The facade and apse are 12th century. The interior has a nave and two aisles separated by massive pilasters, with a raised presbytery and transepts. The apse has early-Christian and medieval features: the 10th-century ambulatory, and the capitals from the 5th- and 6th-century church; the bishop's throne (8C) with 12th-century decoration.

Area archeologica del Teatro romano. Built into Colle di S. Pietro is the Roman theater (early 1C) and the church of Ss. Siro e Libera (rebuilt in the 14C and altered since). The theater is used for summer performances.

Museo Archeologico al Teatro Romano. The Archeology Museum is housed in the former convent of St Jerome (15C). It has Roman finds from Verona and the surrounding area, and Greek and Etruscan finds from private collections and acquisitions.

S. Giovanni in Valle. The church dates from the 8th and 9th centuries, was rebuilt in 1120 and has been altered since. The interior has a nave and two side-aisles with traces of 14th-century frescoes. Below the church is

a crypt with two paleo-Christian sarcophaghi: one is the tomb of St Simon and St Jude (4C). Next-door to the church is the 12th-century Canon's house.

Palazzo Giusti del Giardino. Built after 1572 on a U-shaped plan, is decorated with 18th-century frescoes. It has a magnificent Italianate garden. An *avenue of ancient cypresses* crosses the garden to the rock-face below the Colle di S. Zeno. By following the avenue and climbing some steps you come to a **grotto** originally decorated with stalactites, shells and mirrors, creating optical illusions. Finally, a steep winding staircase leads up to a small bell tower on the summit of the hill, with a viewpoint on the top, with wonderful views over Verona. A valuable collection of Roman finds is scattered around the beds of the garden.

S. Maria in Organo. The present church dates from 1481, but is the result of additions to the original 8th-century church. The lower part of the **facade*** was re-designed by M. Sanmicheli, who covered it with marble and added the three arches; the top still has its original 14th-century blind arcading in tuff and brick. The interior, built on a Latin-cross plan, with a nave and two side-aisles separated by columns, has beautiful Renaissance frescoes: in the nave, stories from the Old Testament; in the apse, frescoes by Giolfino, and magnificent inlaid wooden **choir-stalls*** by Fra' Giovanni da Verona, who also carved the panelling in the sacristy. Below the church, a rare example of a pre-Romanesque crypt with a nave and two side-aisles, and the remains of an early medieval church.

S. Tomaso Cantuariense . The church of St Thomas Becket lies on the far side of the Ponte Nuovo. Begun in the first half of the 15th century, consecrated in 1504, a marble doorway adorns its unfinished facade. Nearby, the church of Ss. Nazaro e Celso (1483) contains some fine paintings by Venetian Renaissance painters. In the left transept is the Renaissance-style S. Biagio chapel.

Museo Civico di Storia Naturale. Since 1926, the 15th-century Palazzo Lavezola Pompei, a masterpiece by Sanmicheli, has housed the town's scientific and natural history collections. Its sections on botany, geology, paleontology, prehistory and zoology give visitors an insight into the evolution of our planet.

Mostra Ferroviaria Didattica Permanente. Housed in Porta Vescovo station, this railway museum has a collection of parts of 20th-century Italian and Austrian railway superstructure, prototypes of locomotives, models of steam trains, locomotives and carriages.

S. Fermo Maggiore. The church of St Fermo is really two superimposed buildings: the lower church dates from the 11th and 12th centuries, the upper one from the 14th century. The apses (the smaller ones are Romanesque and the larger one is Gothic) are remarkable. The interior of the **upper church** has a single nave with a ship's keel ceiling (1314), frescoes from the 14th and 15th centuries and sculptures from the 15th and 16th centuries; next to the ambo, a detached fresco by Stefano da Verona of *Angels with Scrolls*; halfway up the left side of the church, a Baroque chapel dedicated to the Virgin Mary with a fine altar-piece (*Madonna and saints*) (1528). First altar on the left, an altar-piece by B. dal Moro and the Brenzoni tomb by Florentine N. di Bartolo (1439) are framed by a famous fresco of the **Annunciation*** by Pisanello. The right transept leads into the remains of the old Romanesque cloister. From here, steps lead down to the **lower church**, with frescoes dating from the 11th to 13th centuries.

Casa di Giulietta. The 13th-century house stands in Via Cappello; its only connection with Shakespeare's heroine is the famous balcony overlooking the courtyard, added during restoration work in 1935. The building is also interesting because it is a fine example of Gothic domestic architecture in a Roman part of the town. If you proceed from here into Via Leoni, you come to the remains of the Roman **Porta dei Leoni***, dating from the 1st century BC and restored in 1959.

Museo degli Affreschi "Giovan Battista Cavalcaselle". Named after an art historian, Giovan Battista Cavalcaselle (1819-1897), this fresco museum is housed in the monastery of S. Francesco al Corso. It includes architectural fragments and about 50 frescoes removed during the 19th century from palaces and churches in Verona.

Highlights include the sinopias by Altichiero, paintings of the Verona School of the 16th-18th centuries, Roman amphoras, medieval and modern marbles and inscriptions.

Arena. The third-largest amphitheater in Italy (with a seating capacity of 25,000), is one of the symbols of the city. Since 1913, it has been the venue of a highly prestigious

The famous balcony tied to Romeo and Juliet.

international opera festival. Built in the 1^s century BC, only four arches of the north wing of the outermost arcade of the amphitheater are still standing. The 2nd tier of the inner arcade is almost intact.

Piazza Bra, once a suburban field ("braida") today, this square is the most popular meeting-point of the city. Part of it is laid out as a garden: to the north-east is the Arena; to the south-east, the Neo-Classic **Gran Guardia Nuova** or Palazzo Municipale (1848); to the south, the Gran Guardia (begun in 1610, completed in 1836) and the two archways, joined to a pentagonal tower, of Portoni della Bra' (ca. 1480). Porticoed palaces line the north-west side of Piazza Bra and the Listón, the elegant and lively paved street where the people of Verona like to stroll.

Museo Lapidario Maffeiano. This museum is one of the oldest in Europe. Created in 1732 by Scipione Maffei to house his vast collection of inscriptions, it was donated to the city in 1882. The collection, completely reorganized in 1982, has Latin inscriptions, milestones from the Via Postumia, carved stone material, mainly from the Greek and Roman periods, but also of Etruscan and paleo-Venetian origin.

Palazzo del Comune (or Palazzo della Ragione) dates from the late 12th century, but was considerably altered in the 16th century. The **courtyard***, Mercato Vecchio, is Romanesque. The palazzo incorporates the Torre dei Lamberti, 84 m high, begun in 1172 and completed in the mid-15th century.

Porta dei Borsari, built in the mid-1st century, was the main entrance to the Roman town. Its current medieval name refers to the "bursarii", who collected taxes for the bishop.

Corso Cavour, is one of the most elegant streets in Verona. It stretches from Piazzetta di Castelvecchio, from the reconstructed arch of the **Gavi** (1C) to Porta dei Bórsari. Palaces once owned by Verona's nobles line the street: No. 44, Palazzo Canossa by M.Sanmicheli (1537); No. 19, **Palazzo Bevilacqua***, a masterpiece by Sanmicheli with an interesting facade (ca. 1534). Opposite, the 12th-century church of S. Lorenzo with a Gothic archway over the entrance.

Castelvecchio, is the most important example of civic medieval architecture in Verona. It was built by Cangrande II della Scala as a residence-cum-fortress in 1354-57. The keep dates from 1375. An imposing brick building with towers and merloned walls, it is bisected by the bridge: the rectangular part on the right, with towers at the corners and a courtyard, was the parade-ground; on the left, the residence of the Scaligeri is surrounded by a double set of walls, with two courtyards and drawbridges. A section of walls (first half of the 12C) incorporated within the structure runs between the two parts of the castle. The gate of Porta del Morbio (12C) leads onto the bridge. Inside the castle, the **Fondazione Museo Malchi-Erizzo**, still feels like a noble residence. The 16 rooms of the museum house the collections of the Miniscalchi-Erizzo family, including drawings, especially by artists of the Venetian School of the 16th and 17th centuries, Renaissance bronzes, sacred art, archeological finds, early weapons and armor, examples of the decorative arts, coins and paintings.

Museo Civico di Castelvecchio. The museum is housed in the rooms of the castle (mid-14C), the Torre Maggiore and the Napoleonic wing. The entrance to the museum leads to the ground-floor rooms where early medieval and Romanesque reliefs and inscriptions are kept, with sculptures from the Verona area from the 14th and 15th centuries. The exhibits in the rooms of the noble residence include detached frescoes, paintings from the medieval and Renaissance periods, 14th-century sculptures and jewelry. Highlights include the separated parts of the Polyptych of the Holy Trinity by Turone, the Madonna of the Rose-garden by Stefano di Francia, the **Madonna of the Quail** by Pisanello, and works by G. Bellini, Carpaccio, Crivelli, Mantegna and Rubens. The Torre del Mastio (keep), where the armory is situated, leads into the Napoleonic wing, with large paintings by Venetian painters from the 16th to 18th centuries, including works by Tintoretto and Veronese. The last room concentrates on 18th-century works, with works by L. Giordano, G.B. Tiepolo, F.Guardi, P. Longhi and others. On your way around the museum, note the equestrian statue from the tomb of Cangrande I della Scala (14C) on a pedestal, moved here from the Arche Scaligere.

S. Zeno Maggiore, a masterpiece of Italian Romanesque architecture. The church dedicated to Verona's patron saint stands in a large, quiet square between a tower (13-14C) of the old abbey and the bell tower (12C). Built in the 9th century to enshrine the remains of the city's first bishop (died 380), it was rebuilt in the 12th century after the earthquake of 1117 (the apse dates from 1398). Its elegant tuff facade, decorated by an early 13th-century rose-window, has an elegant **porch*** with reliefs (1138) and a west *door* decorated with 24 12th-century bronze **panels*** (Stories from the Old and New Testaments and the Life of St Zeno). The simple, majestic interior has a nave and two side-aisles separated by columns, with a raised presbytery over the crypt and a ship's keel ceiling (1386). On the inner wall of the west facade: a Crucifix (ca.1360); at the top of the right aisle, an octagonal late 12th-century baptistery; in the right aisle and the presbytery, frescoes from the 13th to 15th centuries; above the balustrade of the presbytery, 13th-century statues of Christ and the Apostles; above the high altar, a triptych of the **Madonna and Saints**** by A. Mantegna (1459); wooden choir-stalls (15C). In the left apse: a polychrome statue of St Zeno laughing. The 13th-century **crypt** houses the (modern) tomb of St Zeno. The left aisle leads into the Romanesque cloister (13-14C). A door on the left leads into the 12th-century Oratory of the S. Benedetto.

S. Bernardino. The church was built in the mid-15th century; a cloister surrounded by small columns precedes the facade, with a doorway dating from 1474. The two naves are decorated with paintings of the Verona School from the 15th and 16th centuries; the organ dates from 1481. Upstairs is the **Sala Morone***, an old frescoed library (1503).

Viale Dal Cero. On the right is the Baluardo dei Riformati and the Bastione di S. Spirito, built by the Austrians (19C) to replace sections of the Scaligeri walls, which still encircle the town and are about 10 km long.

Built on piles, it has more than 100 islands, more than 400 bridges, and one piazza, Piazza S. Marco (the others are 'campi' or 'campielli'). Its glorious political and artistic history lasted 1,000 years. Settlements in the lagoon date from Roman times. Venice is laid out differently to mainland towns: there is no central focus but clusters of islands separated by canals. Each island has a square ('campo') with a church. In the 13th century, Venice was much as it is today. In the 14th century, it had a population of more than 130,000, roughly the population at the end of the Venetian Republic. During the intervening centuries, Venice set out across the sea, its main concern being that its ships should have free transit in the Adriatic when Pisa and Genoa posed a constant and serious threat. After the political and military victory of the Sack of Constantinople in 1204 by a Crusader fleet, the Republic became master of "a quarter and a half of the (Byzantine) empire". In the early 13th century, Venetian power in the Levant was at its height. For at least a century, from 1381 until 1498, Venice traded all kinds of goods: gold and silver from Africa, pepper and other spices, cotton and silk. For security, in the 15th century, Venice expanded into the mainland, adding Padua, Vicenza, Verona, Belluno and Udine to its possessions around Treviso. In the 16th century, its status was confirmed for ever: on the mainland by the alliances formed by European and other Italian states against Venice; at sea by the wars against the Turks; with regard to trade, by the forging of new trade routes, shifting the focus from the Mediterranean to the oceans. In the 16th century, Venice invested part of its wealth in a new image. A great fire destroyed the Rialto in 1513 and the whole area was rebuilt, including the Rialto Bridge (1588-1591). In S.Marco, in 1514, work started on the Procuratie Vecchie; in 1582, on the Procuratie Nuove; in 1537, on the Zecca (mint) and the Libreria. In the second half of the 17th century, Venice began to decline. It reacted to the decline of its productive, mercantile and military role by becoming a center for festivals and theater. After many carnivals, Napoleon arrived in 1797, ending an aristocratic republic which had outlived its purpose. For Venice, no longer a capital, a period of transition began under Austrian rule, until it joined Italy in 1866. After Unification, between 1868 and 1871, a broad new street, the Strada Nuova, was laid out parallel to the Grand Canal, linking the Rialto to the station. Between 1880 and 1882, large hotels sprang up on the Riva degli Schiavoni and the Lido. In 1922, work began on the pavilions of the Biennale.

THE CENTER AROUND ST MARK

Piazza S. Marco and bell tower. Symbol of the city and center of its public life throughout, this famous square has slowly adapted to the functional and representational needs of Venice. Not quite a rectangle, its backdrop is St Mark's Basilica with its tall, free-standing bell tower. The **Procuratie Vecchie** on its north side were built in the 12th century and re-built after 1514. To the east is the **Torre dell'Orologio** (clock tower), built in 1496-99. On the south side stand the **Procuratie Nuove**, begun in 1582 by V. Scamozzi and completed in about the mid-17th century by B. Longhena. Under the portico is the 18th-century Caffè Florian, refurbished in the 19th century. The **bell tower** is 96.8 m high. Built in the 12th century on the base of an old lookout tower and restructured in the 16th century, it was rebuilt completely in 1912 after it collapsed on July 14, 1902 (fortunately with no victims). The view over the lagoon from the top is stunning. The elegant marble **loggetta*** below the tower is by J. Sansovino (1537-49).

Basilica di S. Marco and Tesoro della Basilica. Fulcrum of the religious and public life of the city, the place where its doges were consecrated, the basilica is one of the symbols of Venice. Founded in the 9th century to enshrine the body (stolen from Alexandria in 828) of Mark the Evangelist, adopted as the city's patron saint, it has a complex structure. Gothic and Renaissance features were added to its early Byzantine and Romanesque forms. Rebuilt several times, it eventually took on the characteristic profile of Byzantine churches: a large central dome and four semi-spherical domes, capped by onion-shaped domes. The atrium in front of the main doorway has a marble mosaic floor from the 11th and 12th centuries. The walls are adorned with marble and columns, the vaults and domes with gleaming **mosaics*** (stories of the Old Testament) in the Venetian Byzantine style of the 12th and 13th centuries. Three doorways with bronze doors from the 11th and 12th centuries lead into the Basilica. The **interior**** is typically Byzantine: a Greek-cross plan, with three

The view from Riva degli Schiavoni of Palazzo Ducale with St Mark's Square in the background.

aisles in each arm separated by rows of columns supporting the matroneums; mighty arches support the five domes. The **mosaics**** on a gold background decorating the upper walls and domes, executed by Byzantine and Venetian artists in the 12th to 14th centuries, are one of the Basilica's main treasures. Many were replaced in the 16th and 17th centuries based on cartoons by Titian, Tintoretto, Veronese and others. A marble balustrade with statues (1396) divides the raised **presbytery** over the crypt from the rest of the church. Four alabaster **columns*** decorated with 12th-century capitals support the high altar above St Mark's tomb. Behind is the famous **Pala d'Oro**** (Golden altar piece), a masterpiece of Byzantine and Venetian craftsmanship (10-14C). Made of silver, gold and gemstones, its small enameled panels depict religious scenes. Left niche of the apse: the bronze **door*** of the sacristy, J. Sansovino's last work (1546-69). The **Treasury** housed in the Basilica is a sumptuous collection of sacred art, mainly objects from the east from the 6th to 10th centuries, brought to Venice after the 1204 Sack of Constantinople, but also later works by gold- and silversmiths from Venice and Western Europe. The Treasury, (about 300 objects), occupies three rooms: the Anteroom (a silver statue of St Mark, 1804), the Sanctuary (110 reliquaries and a rare back to an alabaster altar-piece decorated in the Eastern style), and the Treasury proper (restored 1938). The exhibits include Egyptian, Roman, Byzantine and Asian vases, amphorae, and bowls; Byzantine icons; glass and rock-crystal chalices; reliquary caskets from the 13th to 18th centuries; sacred furnishings; a 13th-century back altar-piece by a Venetian

goldsmith; bindings for sacred books (St Mark's Gospel is particularly elaborate). At the entrance, the 6th-century marble Chair of St Mark is decorated in the Eastern style.
Palazzo Ducale. The Doge's residence and the highest seat of the magistracy, the Doge's Palace is the symbol of the power and splendor of the ancient Republic. Founded as a 9th-century castle, it gradually assumed its current appearance in the 14th and 15th centuries, resulting in one of Venice's finest examples of Gothic architecture. The Porta della Carta (1438), a Gothic arch linking the palace to St Mark's Basilica, leads into a beautiful **courtyard****, with two 16th-century bronze well-heads. To one side is the Foscari arch, a Gothic arch (1470); opposite, the late 15th-century **Scala dei Giganti*** (Giants' Staircase), with J. Sansovino's statues of Mars and Neptune (1554), where newly-elected doges swore allegiance to the city's laws. **Interior.** A staircase on the south-east side of the portico leads up to the Gothic loggia. From it, the **Scala d'Oro*** (1559) leads to the "piano nobile" and the private apartments of the doge, decorated by G. Bellini, Titian and Carpaccio. On the floor above, the first room is an atrium: on the wooden ceiling (16C), paintings by Jacopo Tintoretto; on the walls, paintings by Veronese. *Sala delle Quattro Porte*: a famous work by Titian: **Doge Grimani kneeling in front of Faith*** (1556). In the Anticollegio: four **wall panels*** by Tintoretto; **Rape of Europa*** by P. Veronese. *Sala del Collegio*: on the walls, works by Tintoretto and Veronese; the elaborate wooden ceiling (1577) has **panels*** by Veronese. *Sala del Consiglio dei Dieci*: the gilt wooden ceiling has **panels*** by Veronese and his assistants. *Sala dei tre Capi del Consiglio dei*

Venezia 1:7000 (1 cm = 70 m)

0   50   100   150 m

Veneto/Venice

HERITAGE

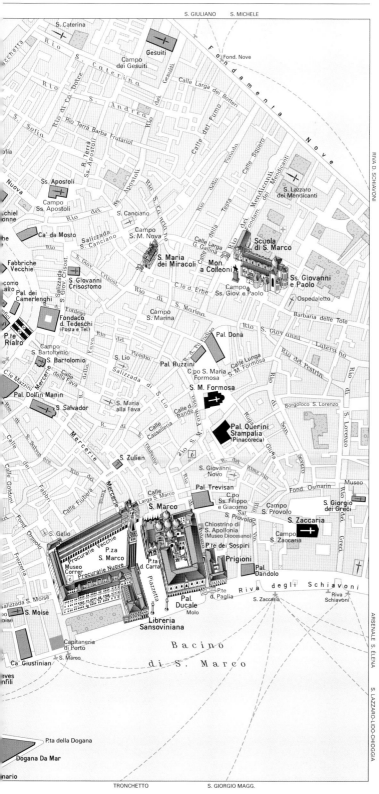

101

Dieci: a ceiling decorated with **panels*** by Veronese and his assistants. Stairs lead down to the *Andito del Maggior Consiglio*, the *Sala della Quarantia Civil Vecchia*, and the *Sala dell'Armamento*, where the remains of Guariento's famous fresco of Paradise, ruined by a fire in 1577, is displayed; in the loggia, the original **statues*** of Adam and Eve by A. Rizzo (1464) for the Foscari arch. *Sala del Maggior Consiglio* (Hall of the Great Council): on the walls, paintings by Tintoretto and assistants (including Paradise), and a frieze of portraits of 76 doges (that of Marin Faliero, executed for treason in 1355, has been obscured), by the Tintoretto; in the center of the ornate ceiling, **Triumph of Venice*** by Veronese. By descending to the Loggia, you can see part of the Prigioni Vecchie (old prisons), with their small, dark, damp cells. Across the **Ponte dei Sospiri** (Bridge of Sighs) the *Prigioni Nuove* date from the late 16th century.

Piazzetta S. Marco. This square overlooks the quay facing the island church of S. Giorgio. Near the water, two 12th-century granite columns support the lion of St Mark and St Theodore, Venice's first patron saint. The space between was once used for public executions. On the square is the **Museo Archeologico Nazionale**, founded in 1523 to house a bequest by Cardinal Domenico Grimani. The museum is based on donations from important Venetian families: in 1593, Giovanni Grimani donated a group of original Greek statues (mainly female statues of 5-4C BC); Piero Morosini donated his medal collection in 1646 and Gerolamo Zulian left his famous cameo of Jove to the museum. In addition to numerous Greek sculptures, the collection contains Roman architectural fragments and sculpture, inscriptions, marbles and busts, bronze figurines, pottery, jewelry, Etruscan, Egyptian and Mesopotamian artifacts, as well as precious stones, ivories and a coin collection (3-1C BC). The museum, owned by the State, also houses part of the Museo Correr's archeological collection (Neolithic and Bronze-Age finds; Egyptian, Assyrian and Babilonian artifacts; Greek, Etruscan and Roman art). Next-door is the **Libreria Sansoviniana**, a masterpiece of 16th-century Venetian architecture, designed by J. Sansovino and completed after his death (1570) by V. Scamozzi. This airy building with a portico and a loggia crowned by a fine balustrade once housed the Biblioteca Marciana (St Mark's Library); a monumental staircase leads to the vestibule,

with a frescoed ceiling by Titian (**Wisdom***). The Zecca (mint), just off the Piazzetta, with rusticated decoration, designed and built by Sansovino (1537-66), now houses the Biblioteca Nazionale Marciana. Created to house a bequest from Cardinal Bessarion in 1468 of about a thousand Greek and Latin manuscripts, it was enlarged by incorporating the libraries of suppressed convents and monasteries; its most precious possession is the late 15th-century illuminated Grimani Breviary. Across Piazza S. Marco the **Museo Correr** occupies the Ala Napoleonica and part of the Procuratie Nuove. Created from the collection which Teodoro Correr left to the city in 1830, it offers various options: rooms in the Neo-Classic style with important sculptures by A. Canova (1757-1822); historical exhibits associated with Venice's institutions; the city's development over the centuries; aspects of daily life; its art gallery, one of the finest collections of Venetian painting, from its beginnings to the early 16th century, with works by the Bellini, Carpaccio, C. Tura, A. da Messina, and L. Lotto, in an imaginative setting by C. Scarpa. Annexed to the museum: the Biblioteca d'Arte e Storia Veneziana, with its fine collection of manuscripts and historical documents, the famous Gabinetto di stampe e disegni with its print and drawing collection, a Photographic Archive, and a Center for Catalogues and Multimedia Products.

CAMPO S. MOISÈ TO PALAZZO GRASSI

The square is overlooked by the **church of S. Moisè** (1668), a fine example of the luxuriant Venetian Baroque style. Another example of exuberant decoration is the facade of the **church of S. Maria del Giglio**, built in 1683, in the eponymous square, with paintings by Rubens, S. Ricci and J. Tintoretto. Close by is **Teatro La Fenice**, one of the world's most famous opera-houses, destroyed by fire on January 29, 1996. Reconstruction work was completed in 2004. Sansovino's masterpiece, **Palazzo Corner della Ca' Granda**, (ca. 1533-53), with a classical three-storey facade, is now the police headquarters for the Venice area. The **church of S. Stefano**, with a flamboyant Gothic-style doorway, dates from the 14th and 15th centuries. The vast interior has a nave and two side-aisles separated by columns, a ship's keel ceiling and many funerary monuments. In the sacristy: *Crucifix* by Paolo Veneziano; polyptych by B. Vivari-

A sunset view of the Rialto bridge over the Grand Canal.

ni; *Holy Family* by Palma the Elder and three large works by Tintoretto (*The Last Supper*, *Washing of the Feet**, *Prayer in the Garden**). **Palazzo Grassi** with its imposing classical forms, built in the 18th century, used for major exhibitions, is now the headquarters of the Palazzo Grassi Foundation. Close by, the 11th-century **church of S. Samuele**, with its small, picturesque Venetian Romanesque 12th-century bell tower, is used for temporary exhibitions.

Palazzo Corner Spinelli, Fortuny and Grimani. Palazzo Corner Spinelli is an early Renaissance building with two storeys of two-light windows, designed by M. Codussi (late 15C). The Gothic facade of this 15th-century palazzo overlooks Campo S. Beneto. It houses the **Museo Fortuny**, converted by the Spanish painter and interior designer M. Fortuny and Madrazo (1861-1949) from his studio (used for photography, designing stage sets, stage machinery, textiles and painting). The museum also hosts exhibitions on the ground floor and the "piano nobile". **Palazzo Grimani** is an imposing three-storey Renaissance building with broad arches supported by pilaster strips and columns. A masterpiece of M. Sanmicheli (1556-75), it is now the seat of the judiciary. Not far away is **Campo Manin**, dominated by the offices of the Cassa di Risparmio di Venezia, a new building noted for its flexible interior design features and its facade, which employs traditional Venetian motifs in a modern context. Just behind the square is the late-Gothic **Palazzo Contarini del Bovolo**, famous for its external spiral stair-

case ("bovolo" in local dialect), connecting several storeys of superimposed loggias.

Ponte di Rialto and Canal Grande. A. da Ponte rebuilt Venice's most famous bridge in 1591. 48 m long and 22 m wide, it has a single arch 7.5 m high and a maximum width of 28 m. Until the 19th century, it was the only bridge linking the two sides of the city. Three parallel staircases lead from one side to the other, the central one lined by arcades with shops. The sides of the bridge are adorned with 16th-century reliefs. The **Canal Grande**. Venice's main internal waterway, flows through the city uniting its various parts. 3,800 m long and between 30 m and 70 m wide, the shape of an upturned S, it owes its current form to the continuous alignment and consolidation of its banks since the 14th century. Originally used to transport goods between the port and the Rialto market, in the 16th century, the Venetian nobility chose it as a site for their luxurious mansions. It is lined with a virtually uninterrupted sequence of palaces dating from the 13th to 18th centuries.

S. Salvador and Mercerie. This church with its white Baroque facade (1663) overlooks the eponymous square. In the right aisle: monument to Doge F. Venier by Sansovino (1561) and a late work by Titian (**Annunciation***) (1566); above the high altar, another Titian (**Transfiguration***) (1560) hides a precious 14th-century silver altar-piece Divided into several parts, the **Mercerie** runs between Piazza S. Marco and Rialto. One of Venice's busiest streets, the shops on either side sell all kinds of

THE MAIN FOLKLORE FESTIVALS IN VENICE: THE CARNIVAL, THE "FESTA DELLA SALUTE" AND THE "REDENTORE"

Carnevale (Piazza S. Marco and center. Carnival week).
The traditional Venice Carnival has witnessed a surprising rebirth since the 1970s, so much so that it has become a really international affair. Apart from the theatrical events the real center pieces of the carnival are the masks, all based on imaginative re-makes of bygone costumes. The carnival centers around Saint Mark's square with jugglers, acrobats and artists of all sorts.
Festa della Salute (Canal Grande. 21 November).
The Festa della Salute (Health Festival) is in memory of the awful Venice plague of 1630. When the plague had been eradicated the Republic had the wonderful church built. For the inauguration, a floating bridge on boats was built for the religious procession. The square throngs with stalls selling a sort of doughnut called frittelle and sweets.
Festa del Redentore (Third Sunday in July).
This is a thanksgiving pilgrimage to the church, which was built in 1592 after the doge vowed he would build it if the plague ended. Tradition has it that a floating bridge was built across the Canal Grande on eighty boats and that the procession walked across the bridge. A floating bridge is still built to connect the Zattere side of the Canal Grande with the Giudecca side. Thousands of boats gather in front of the island ready for the firework display.
Information: www.comune.venezia.it

goods. At the end of the first section (Merceria dell'Orologio), the ancient **church of S. Zulian** overlooks the square named after the church. Rebuilt in its present form (1553-55) by J. Sansovino, it has paintings by P. Veronese and Palma the Younger.
Ca' Pesaro to S. Giacomo dell'Orio. Near Ca' Pesaro, **Ca' Corner della Regina** is an impressive building with classical motifs by D. Rossi (1724) and a facade decorated with two tiers of loggias. It houses the Archivio Storico della Biennale di Venezia. **Ca' Pesaro**, one of the most important palazzi on the Grand Canal, has an open courtyard with a well-head attributed to Sansovino and a splendid entrance-hall. The first and second floors house the **Galleria internazionale d'Arte moderna***, the city's 19th- and 20th-century painting and sculpture collections, including works by Klimt, Chagall, Kandinsky, Klee, Matisse and Henry Moore, as well as works by Italian artists and a graphic art display. The third floor, the **Museo d'Arte orientale*** has one of the world's largest collections of Japanese Edo art (1614-1868). Other sections focus on China and Indonesia, with an important collection of weapons from the 12th to 19th centuries.
Nearby, **Campo S. Maria Mater Domini**, named after the **church of S. Maria Mater Domini** (1502-40), has a facade attributed to Sansovino and a harmonious interior with a Greek-cross plan. It has a Martyrdom of St Cristina by V. Catena (1520) and an early Tintoretto, **Invention of the Cross***. To the west, **Palazzo Mocenigo** is a noble residence with original 18th-century furnishings and paintings. It houses the Centro Studi di Storia del Tessuto e del Costume, a rich and varied display of exhibits from several different collections. Of these, the **Museo di Storia del Tessuto e del Costume** has some particularly rare pieces (fabrics and costumes). The museum also allows scholars access to its library of specialized books on the sector. Overlooking the Grand Canal, the **church of S. Stae** (St Eustace) has an imposing facade by D. Rossi (1709), a single nave and fine works by some of the foremost artists of the early 18th century (Tiepolo and Ricci). On the same side of the canal, the **Fondaco dei Turchi** (heavily restored in 1858-69) with its Venetian Byzantine motifs, was used by Turkish traders. Today it houses the **Museo Civico di Storia Naturale**, an important institution, with many collections and a large library. It also monitors and collects information about the lagoon and its fauna. A long, narrow street leads to **Campo S. Giacomo dell'Orio**, one of the few planted with trees. The

eponymous church, one of the oldest in Venice, contains precious artworks, including Lotto's **Madonna and Saints*** (1546) in the presbytery.

S. Simeon Grande and S. Simeon Piccolo, a cemetery once preceded the facade of the old **church of S. Simeon Grande**, heavily restored in the 18th century. Inside, it has a basilica plan, a nave and two side-aisles separated by ancient columns with Byzantine capitals, a *Presentation in the Temple* by Palma the Younger and a *Last Supper* by Tintoretto. The **church of S. Simeon Piccolo**, built in 1718-38 by G. Scalfarotto, has an elegant Corinthian pronaos at the top of a flight of steps. Its design combines several themes: the Pantheon in Rome, Palladian influences and the church of the Salute.

S. Rocco and Scuola Grande di S. Rocco. Not far from from S. Rocco stands the **Scuola Grande di S. Giovanni Evangelista.** Suppressed by Napoleon in 1806 and deprived of its most precious artworks, and altered several times from the 14th to 18th centuries, it reflects various architectural styles. Restored between 1969 and 1974, it has a splendid monumental staircase (1498) and frescoes by G.D. Tiepolo and Tintoretto. In the *Sala dell'Albergo*, four paintings by Palma the Younger depict the *Apocalypse*. The **church of S. Rocco**, rebuilt in the 18th century, has six remarkable **paintings*** by Tintoretto. The **Scuola Grande di S. Rocco**, begun in 1478, was completed in 1560. The interior is decorated by Tintoretto: his **cycle of paintings** (1564 to 1587) includes more than 60 canvases. To follow the chronological sequence, start upstairs in the Sala dell'Albergo, begun in 1564, with the enormous Crucifixion, one of the few works signed and dated by Tintoretto; the others depict the Passion. The 21 canvases on the ceiling and walls of the upper hall, painted from 1575 to 1581, depict scenes from the Old and New Testaments. A double flight of stairs leads to the lower hall (1583-1587), where Tintoretto painted the last eight scenes from the Life of Mary: the *Annunciation*, the *Flight into Egypt*, *St Mary of Egypt* and *St Mary Magdalene* are particularly fine. Other works in the Scuola include *Christ carrying the Cross*, attributed to Giorgione.

S. Maria Gloriosa dei Frari and Campo S. Polo. Marked by its massive 14th-century bell tower, one of the tallest in Venice, this is one of Venice's most important churches, together with Ss. Giovanni e Paolo. Built by Franciscans in 1340-1443, its majestic Goth-

ic forms end in a complex apse. The vast **interior**, a long nave with two aisles separated by pointed arches resting on massive columns, contains many monuments to doges and illustrious Venetians of the 14th to 19th centuries, and other treasures. In the center of the nave: the **choir***, decorated in the Renaissance and Gothic styles, with a marble choir-screen (1475) and carved wooden choirstalls with fine marquetry (1468). In the sacristy: G. Bellini's **triptych of the Madonna and Saints**** (signed and dated 1488). In the chapel to the right of the high altar: a fine sculpture of **John the Baptist*** by Donatello (ca. 1450). In the presbytery: behind the high altar, Titian's famous altar-piece of the **Assumption**** (1518); on the right wall, the monument to Doge F. Foscari (ca. 1457); on the left wall, the marble tomb of Doge N. Tron (ca. 1476). Left aisle: 2nd altar, the **Pesaro Altar-piece**** by Titian (1526); in the last bay, the pyramidal monument to A. Canova, to his own design (1827). In a narrow lane near Campo S. Polo, Palazzo Centanni is the **birthplace of C. Goldoni**, the comic playwright. It is now a small museum about his life and work, with a famous puppet theater, an extensive archive and a library of scripts and theatrical sketches with more than 30,000 original manuscripts. **Campo S. Polo**, one of Venice's largest squares, was once used for popular festivals. Around it are palaces from the 14th to 18th centuries and the apse of the **church of S. Polo**, of Byzantine origin, with important works by Tintoretto and Stations of the Cross (1747-49) by G.D. Tiepolo.

Ponte dell'Accademia and Gallerie dell'Accademia. The Accademia Bridge was built in 1934 as a "temporary" measure to replace a 19th-century metal bridge built by the Austrians. On one side of it, the **Gallerie dell'Accademia**, founded in 1807 to house paintings from churches and ecclesiastical foundations suppressed by Napoleon have grown as a result of donations and acquisitions.

The first rooms have panels and polyptychs of the 14th and early 15th centuries (P. and L. Veneziano, G. da Fabriano, Pisanello). The next rooms contain eight canvases depicting the **Miracles of the True Cross** (1494-1501) by G. Bellini and V. Carpaccio and nine huge paintings by Carpaccio depicting the **Legend of St Ursula** (ca. 1490-1495). G. Bellini's unforgettable Madonnas, Giorgione (*The Tempest*), C. da Conegliano, Mantegna (*St George*), P. della Francesca and C. Tura mark the progression from the 15th to the 16th century, represented by Titian (*Pietà* and *Presentation of the Virgin*), Veronese (**Christ in the House of Levi**), L. Lotto, Palma the Elder, Palma the Younger and Tintoretto. B. Strozzi and L. Giordano represent the Baroque and Rococo periods. The 18th century is represented by G.B. and G.D. Tiepolo, S. Ricci, the "vedutisti" F. Guardi and Canaletto, pastels by R. Carriera, domestic scenes by P. Longhi and sketches by A. Canova. The Gabinetto di Disegni is next to the main gallery.

Palazzo Venier dei Leoni, designed in 1749, this palace was bought in 1949 by American heiress Guggenheim to house the **Peggy Guggenheim Contemporary Art Collection**, associated with the S. R. Guggenheim Foundation in New York. It has paintings and sculptures of the leading art movements of the 20th century. Artists represented include P. Picasso, R. Magritte, G. De Chirico, G. Severini, M. Duchamp, G. Braque, F. Leger, P. Mondrian, P. Klee, M. Ernst, J. Miró, C. Brancusi, G. Balla, H. Moore, S. Dalí, M. Chagall, Y. Tanguy, P. Delvaux, V. Brauner, J.Pollock, F. Bacon, G. Sutherland and J. Dubuffet. The museum organizes temporary art exhibitions. Just beyond the gallery is the Renaissance-style **Palazzo Dario** (1487) with a triple loggia, four-light windows and an elaborate marble facade.

S. Maria della Salute and Punta della Dogana. This masterpiece of Venetian Baroque by B. Longhena (1631-87) was built by the Senate in thanks for deliverance from the plague. This imposing white marble church built on an octagonal plan is decorated with a statues and topped by a huge semispherical dome; above the presbytery, a smaller dome and two bell towers. Visually flamboyant, it dominates the Venetian landscape. Inside, the slender dome rises above the vast round central area with a circular aisle. A passage leads to the Great Sacristy: above the altar, **St Mark and Saints***, an early work by Titian (1512), who also painted the three **canvases*** in the ceiling; to the right of the altar, a large painting by Tintoretto depicts the **Wedding at Cana***. The Patriarchal Seminary, built by Baldassarre Longhena in 1671, houses the **Pinacoteca Manfrediana**, created from the bequest of M. F. Manfredini (1743-1829). It has works by Italian and Venetian painters (15-18C), sculpture (13-17C) and illuminated manuscripts (14-16C). The **Museo Lapidario** (in the cloister) has archeological

finds from the Roman period, and architectural features from churches, monasteries and convents suppressed by Napoleon. The **Punta della Dogana** juts out between the end of the Grand Canal and the Canale della Giudecca, opposite the island of S. Giorgio. This long, low building shaped like a ship's prow was the **Dogana da Mar** (1677), and already existed in the 15th century as the customs post for all goods arriving in Venice by sea.

Zattere and S. Trovaso. The Zattere is a long promenade running beside the Canale della Giudecca, the waterway separating the city from the island of the Giudecca. The long (almost 2 km) "fondamenta" (running alongside a canal) is divided into four sections, each named after its most salient feature: Zattere al Ponte Lungo, Zattere ai Gesuati, Zattere allo Spirito Santo and Zattere ai Saloni. The Zattere ai Gesuati is named after the church of the **Gesuati**. Built in 1724-36, it incorporates Palladian features. Inside, beyond the rectanguar nave, is a light-filled oval apse. The **church of S. Trovaso** is the result of reconstruction begun in 1585; two almost identical facades conceal an interior with a single nave and a broad presbytery, with works by Tintoretto.

Ca' Rezzonico and Ca' Foscari, This imposing Baroque palazzo on the Grand Canal (1649-1750) houses the **Museo del Settecento Veneziano***. Its luxuriously decorated rooms (some frescoed by G.B. Tiepolo) give a fascinating insight into the life and customs of 18th-century Venice: tapestries, furniture, lacquer furniture, costumes, furnishings, paintings (P. Longhi, Rosalba Carriera, Canaletto, F. Guardi) and **frescoes*** by G.A. Guardi and G.D. Tiepolo.

Palazzo Giustinian and **Ca' Foscari** (begun in 1452), now the main offices of the University, are some of the best examples of architectural uniformity in large 14th-century patrician residences on the Grand Canal. The long facades of the two buildings form a single block overlooking the Grand Canal.

Scuola Grande dei Carmini, i Carmini and S. Sebastiano, was built by the confraternity of the Carmelites, founded out of devotion to St Mary of Carmel: the facade (1668-1670) is attributed to B. Longhena. It contains works by G.B. Tiepolo, who, between 1739 and 1749, decorated the nine sections of the ceiling of the Sala del Capitolo. Next to it stands the 14th-century church of the **Carmini**, with a Renaissance facade, a curved pediment (early

16C) and a 14th-century doorway (left of the church). The works by C. da Conegliano, F. di G. Martini and L. Lotto are particularly fine. The **church of S. Sebastiano**, rebuilt in the first half of the 16th century in the elegant Renaissance style, is famous for the spectacular decoration executed between 1555 and 1565 by P. Veronese (buried here in 1588). A fine series of canvases and frescoes adorns the ceiling, the walls of the nave, the sacristy and nun's choir. The canvases by Titian are also remarkable.

Ponte degli Scalzi and gli Scalzi, rebuilt in 1934 (the first iron bridge dated from 1858), is one of three bridges spanning the Grand Canal. Baldassarre Longhena began building the church in 1654 for a barefooted Carmelite community which had moved to Rome. The exterior is Baroque, the interior has a single nave with three chapels on each side: the vaults of the 2nd chapel on the right and the 1st chapel on the left were frescoed by G.B. Tiepolo.

S. Giobbe. The church, built in the Gothic style in 1450, was finished by P. and T. Lombardo in the Renaissance style. The beautiful doorway, the marble decoration in the presbytery and the two niche chapels on either side of it are by P. Lombardo. At the other end of the same fondamenta, facing the Grand Canal, is **Palazzo Labia**, a luxurious 18th-century residence, now the seat of the RAI. The interior was frescoed by G.D. Tiepolo, who left an extraordinary testimonial of his artistic genius here. Assisted by G. M. Colonna, between 1745 and 1750, he painted two great scenes: *The Arrival of Cleopatra* and *The Banquet of Anthony and Cleopatra*.

Ghetto Nuovo, is part of the ghetto where, from 1516 until 1797, Venetian Jews were forced to live. A small island surrounded by canals and fringed by tall buildings, it is now the location of the **Museo Ebraico di Venezia**, opened in 1953. Recently restored, the museum has a collection of ritual and household objects, sacred furnishings, tapestries, precious bindings for books, manuscripts, silverware, containers for scrolls, curtains for the doors of the Holy Ark, pulpit drapes and old manuscripts of marriage contracts.

Madonna dell'Orto and S. Maria della Misericordia, built in the 15th century, the **church of Madonna dell'Orto** overlooks a charming little square. Statues and a doorway with Renaissance and Gothic features adorn its brick facade. The interior, with a nave and two side-aisles, has **paintings*** by J. Tintoretto (buried in 1594, in the chapel to the right of the presbytery): in the right aisle, 1st altar, **John the Baptist*** by C. da Conegliano (1493). Fondamenta dell'Abbazia leads to the quiet square before the abbey, where the original terracotta pavement lends it a particular old-worldly charm. It is overlooked by the **church of S. Maria della Misericoria**, founded with the abbey in the 10th century and restructured several times, and, in the corner, with a Baroque facade, the 14th-century Scuola Vecchia di S. Maria della Misericoria, one of the largest confraternities in Venice.

Strada Nuova and Ca' d'Oro. Before you turn into Strada Nuova, the elegant Renaissance-style **Palazzo Vendramin Calergi** was designed by M. Codussi and completed by the Lombardo (1509). The composer R.

The Punta della Dogana, with the church of the S. Maria della Salute.

A typical venetian "calle".

Wagner died here on February 13, 1883; it is the winter seat of the Casinò Municipale (in summer it moves to the Lido). Strada Nuova is a wide street laid out in 1871 to link the station to the Rialto. Many buildings were demolished to make this possible. It runs along behind the rear facades of the palazzi overlooking the Grand Canal. Built in the Gothic style (1422-40), the name **Ca' d'Oro** (Golden House) refers to the gold decoration of the facade overlooking the Grand Canal; it has a handsome portico on the ground floor supported by columns, two open loggias with intersecting arches and balconies on the upper floors, and a distinctive row of merlons. This and the adjoining Palazzo Giusti are now the **Galleria "Giorgio Franchetti"**. In 1916, this musician from Turin donated his private collection and the Cà d'Oro to the State. The collection includes paintings by Italian and foreign artists, marbles, bronzes, and Venetian ceramics from the 15th to 18th centuries. Highlights include, on the 1st floor: works by A. Vivarini (**polyptych of the Passion***), A. Mantegna (**St Sebastian****), V. Carpaccio, G. da Rimini, L. Signorelli and C. Braccesco. The sculptures include bronzes and marble busts by T. Lombardo (*Double Portrait*). A fine 14th-century wooden staircase leads to the second floor: works by Titian and Tintoretto, and views of Venice by F. Guardi.

Gesuiti, the original church, S. Maria dei Crociferi, was rebuilt for the Jesuits (1715-30). The elaborate Baroque facade is based on Roman models. The interior is a riot of Baroque. Above the altar left of the entrance, the **Martyrdom of St Laurence*** is by Titian (1558).

S. Giovanni Crisostomo and S. Maria dei Miracoli, The Renaissance church of S. Giovanni Crisostomo was built by M. Codussi (1497-1504). Inside, 1st altar on the right, **St Christopher, St Jerome and St Augustine***, a masterpiece by Giovanni Bellini (1513). This small, isolated **church of S. Maria dei Miracoli** is one of the most eloquent expressions of the early Renaissance in Venice. The masterpiece of P. Lombardo, aided by his sons Antonio and Tullio (1489), polychrome marble decoration enhances its elegant sides and facade, crowned with a semi-circular pediment. The interior is also faced with marble, with an extraordinary marble tribune by T. Lombardo.

Campo and chiesa dei SS. Giovanni e Paolo. Situated in front of the great church dedicated to St John and St Paul is Venice's second-finest monumental square. In the center is a well-head dating from the 16th century. Its focal point is the **equestrian monument to Bartolomeo Colleoni****, a masterpiece of Renaissance sculpture. Modelled by A. Verrocchio in 1481-88, the statue of this Venetian mercenary general was cast by A. Leopardi. From the mid-15th century onwards, the church of **Ss. Giovanni e Paolo**, built by the Dominicans between 1246 and 1430, was used for the funeral ceremonies of the Doges. Note the polygonal **apses*** in the right side of the church. The high slender Gothic interior is similar to that of the church of the Frari, and, like it, contains innumerable funerary monuments of doges, captains and illustrious figures of the Venetian Republic from the 14th to 17th centuries. Back of the main facade: monument to Doge P. Mocenigo by P. Lombardo (1481). Right side-aisle: 2nd altar, polyptych of St V. Ferrer, an early work by G. Bellini (ca. 1465). At the end of the aisle, the chapel of St Dominic (1716), with a carved gilt ceiling and a St Dominic in Glory by G.B. Piazzetta (1727). On the walls of the presbytery, on the left, monument to Doge

A. Vendramin by P. and T. Lombardo (15C), and the Gothic monument to Doge M. Corner, with statues of the Madonna and saints by G. Pisano. At the end of the left transept is the 16th-century **chapel of the Rosario***: the ceiling was rebuilt after a fire and has **paintings*** by Veronese. Next to it, the building which once housed the Scuola Grande di S. Marco is the city hospital. The masterpiece of Pietro, A. and T. Lombardo and G. Buora (1487-90), its long façade with polychrome marble decoration dates from the early Renaissance. The curved pediments were added by M. Codussi in 1495.

S. Maria Formosa and Palazzo Querini Stampalia, according to tradition, the church was built in 639 after a miraculous apparition of the Virgin Mary and rebuilt in 1492 by M. Codussi. The **interior*** has numerous treasures, including a famous polyptych by Palma the Elder of *St Barbara and Saints* (right transept). The bell tower (1678-88) stands on the side facing Campo S. Maria Formosa. Behind the church, **Palazzo Querini-Stampalia** is accessed by a metal bridge by Carlo Scarpa, who also designed the ground floor (it had to be waterproof) and the garden (1959-63). The palazzo was built in about 1528 and, since 1869, has been the seat of the Querini Stampalia Foundation. (As well as a library, it has a fine art gallery with art-works from the 14th to 18th centuries.) The **garden** has a lawn with a series of pools and fountains, an original wellhead, a stone lion, capitals and fountains, creepers and various flowering shrubs.

Campo and church of S. Zaccaria. Situated near Campo S. Zaccaria, the **Museo Diocesano d'Arte Sacra di S. Apollonia** is worth a visit. The museum belongs to the Diocese of Venice and was created by Pope John Paul I (A. Luciani, 1912-1978) when he was Patriarch of Venice. It includes restored art-works from churches in Venice. One room is devoted to silverware; another has objects donated by priests working in Venice (statues of the Virgin Mary in traditional Venetian costume). Quiet **Campo S. Zaccaria** is dominated by the facade of the church and, to the right, its 13th-century brick bell tower. To the left of the church, the arcades (now occupied by shops) belong to the 16th-century cloister of the old convent. The **church of S. Zaccaria** was built in the Gothic style in the 15th century and completed by Mauro Codussi (1483-90), who designed the white stone tiered fa-

cade. It is one of the finest examples of early Venetian Renaissance architecture. The interior has a nave and two side-aisles separated by vast columns; the walls are decorated with large canvases from the 17th and 18th centuries. The most significant work graces the second altar on the left: G. Bellini's famous altar-piece of the **Madonna Enthroned with Saints*** (1505). In the apse of the chapel of S. Tarasio are some important **frescoes*** by A. del Castagno and Francesco da Faenza (1442). There are also three polyptychs in the Gothic style by A. Vivarini and G. d'Alemagna (1443).

Riva degli Schiavoni. The name of the broad, busy promenade beside the Basin of St Mark refers to the sailors from Schiavonia (now eastern Croatia), who used to moor their ships and do business here. Walking towards St Mark's Basilica, you pass the 18th-century **S. Maria della Visitazione** or *Pietà*, the interior of which was designed partly with the performance of concerts in mind. Beyond the Ponte del Vin, the promenade is thronged with tourists and souvenir-sellers. Overlooking it is the Gothic Palazzo Dandolo (15C), now the exclusive Danieli hotel. Nearby, the **church of S. Giorgio dei Greci** is part of the complex which belonged to the Greek Orthodox community of Venice, the city's largest ethnic group during the Renaissance. The tall, narrow façade of the church, divided into two levels overlooks the center of the area – almost a courtyard – acquired in 1526. Behind it, a harmonious, solemn rectangular interior, richly decorated with Byzantine paintings and icons, separated from the presbytery and its triple apse by a marble iconostasis with late-Byzantine paintings on a gold background. Next to the facade stands the **bell tower** (1587-92), which has been leaning ever since it was built. Other buildings of the Greek community include the Istituto Ellenico di Studi Bizantini e Postbizantini (a research institute) and, in the former **Scuola di S. Nicolò dei Greci**, the **Museo delle Icone Bizantine e Postbizantine**. The museum has illuminated manuscripts, embroidered sacred vestments and small craft objects, and the most important collection of icons in Western Europe (14-18C), many of them by Greek artists who settled in Venice, from Constantinople, or from the workshops of painters from Crete.

Campo Bandiera e Moro. Tucked away

from the busier streets in Campo Bandiera e Moro is the Gothic **church of S. Giovanni in Bragora**, rebuilt in 1475, with an unusual brick facade. The interior, with a nave and two side-aisles, has important **paintings*** by A. Vivarini, B. Vivarini and C. da Conegliano.

Scuola di S. Giorgio degli Schiavoni. The little Scuola di S. Giorgio degli Schiavoni was built in the early 16th century by the confraternity of the Dalmatian community ('Schiavoni'). It's famous for the **paintings by Carpaccio**** which adorn the ground floor. The cycle of paintings, regarded as one of Carpaccio's masterpieces (1501-11), depicts scenes from the life of St George, St Jerome and St Tryphone.

S. Francesco della Vigna. This large 16th-century Franciscan church, designed by the Tuscan architect, J. Sansovino, has a classical temple-front facade by A. Palladio (1564-70). The left transept leads into a chapel with a **Madonna and Child with Saints*** by G. Bellini.

Arsenale and Museo Storico Navale. A high merloned wall surrounded by canals marks the perimeter of this great ship-building complex from the 12th and early 13th centuries. It was enlarged several times and continued to develop over the centuries. From this ancient center of maritime power, the Venetian fleet used to set sail. The land entrance to the Arsenale is a **gateway*** (1460), often regarded as the earliest work of the Venetian Renaissance. Above the gateway is a splendid lion of St Mark, attributed to B. Bon. The **Museo Storico Navale** (Naval History Museum), owned by the Italian Navy since 1923, is housed in the former granaries of the Venetian Republic, a 15th-century building close to the Arsenale. The collection includes a 'human torpedo' used very successfully by the Italian Navy during WWII. One section of the museum focuses on the achievements, the vessels and the men of the Serenissima and the Italian Navy. A highlight on the first floor is the model of the Bucentaur, the ceremonial barge used by the Doge during the ritual marriage with the sea. The third floor houses a collection of traditional wooden boats of the Venetian lagoon. One room focuses on the gondola (Peggy Guggenheim's was donated to the museum after her death). The Ship Pavilion contains Venetian vessels and ships belonging to the Italian navy.

S. Pietro di Castello. At the eastern end of Via Garibaldi, the only "via" in the city, lies the island of S. Pietro and the church of S. Pietro di Castello. Its simple facade has a majestic doorway. The broad flat ceiling inside is decorated with 17th-century frescoes.

Public Gardens, were laid out during the Napoleonic period and altered in the mid-19th century to suit the romantic tastes of the time. They are the setting for the pavilions of the Biennale d'Arte, the two-yearly international exhibition of painting, sculpture and decorative arts held here since 1895. The pavilions of the individual countries reflect the architectural trends of different nations over the course of almost a century (1907-95).

S. Giorgio Maggiore. This church designed by A. Palladio stands on the island of S. Giorgio opposite Piazzetta S. Marco. The church, with its noble, classical-style facade, was begun by Palladio in 1566 and completed in 1611. Its somber gray and white interior is composed of a nave and two side aisles. On the walls of the presbytery are two works by Tintoretto: a **Last Supper*** and the *Shower of Manna* (1594). Above the altar of the winter choir: a painting by V. Carpaccio: **St George killing the Dragon*** (1516). From the top of the bell tower, built in 1791 to replace a 15th-century tower, there are magnificent **views*** over the city and the lagoon. The **Monastery of S. Giorgio Maggiore** is now the headquarters of the Fondazione G. Cini. The complex surrounds two lovely **cloisters***. Some of the greatest architects of the late 14th- to 17th centuries worked here: A. Palladio, G. and A. Buora, and B. Longhena.

Giudecca. The name of this long, narrow island situated between the Canale della Giudecca and the southern part of the lagoon may derive from the fact that some Jews ("giudei") established a settlement here in the Middle Ages. Thanks to its position, removed from the city center yet close to the Basin of St Mark, from the 16th century onwards, it became a place of leisure, where noble residences alternated with orchards, monasteries and gardens. In the 19th century, when the Venetian nobility had declined and the convents and monasteries had been suppressed, it was increasingly used for military and naval barracks, prisons, housing for factory workers and factories. The sole remaining testimonial, located in the far east of the island, is the neo-Gothic Mulino Stucky

(1896). On April 16, 2003 a fire destroyed some of the building, causing the collapse of a tower.

Il Redentore. The votive church on the Giudecca was built at the wishes of the Senate to give thanks for deliverance from a serious Plague. It was conceived as the culminating step in the solemn procession of the Redentore (Redeemer) which crossed the canals each year on a bridge of boats. One of A. Palladio's masterpieces, it was begun in 1577 and completed after the architect's death by A. da Ponte in 1592. Its noble facade is based on classical lines. The somber, majestic interior has a colonnade running down the single nave and round the back of the presbytery, crowned by a dome. Above the altar, paintings from the Venetian School (16-17C).

Fondamenta di S. Biagio and ex Mulino Stucky. Fondamenta San Biagio is lined with low buildings dating from the 15th century to the end of the Republic, and was consolidated to enable the large ships of the late 19th-century to moor when factories began to spring up here. The high merloned walls belong to a former beer and liqueur factory, while the Tessuti Fortuny textile factory (No. 805), built in 1919, is still operating. The fondamenta peters out at a metal bridge now closed to the public. In a scenario which is reminiscent of the fog-bound cities of the north, across the Canale della Giudecca is the imposing neo-Gothic **Mulino Stucky**. It was built to the design of the German architect Ernest Wullekopf (1896) at the wishes of a Swiss entrepreneur, Giovanni Stucky.

HIGHLIGHTS

CHIOGGIA

The piazza is a wide street with porticoes on one side and public buildings on the other, bisecting the town from its lagoon entrance on the Bacino di Vigo to the land entrance, Ponte Lungo. Parallel to the main street, Canale della Vena, the brightly-painted houses overlook the sails of the fishing boats moored below the quay. Perpendicular to the piazza and the canal is a dense network of narrow streets, dotted with little squares and courtyards straight out of a Goldoni play. Tucked away in the southern corner of the Venetian lagoon, the town has a large fishing fleet. Although you see cars here, this miniature version of Venice is still an important fishing town and, with the nearby beaches of Sottomarina and Isola Verde, also a popular seaside resort. The Duomo, which already existed in the 11th century, was rebuilt in the Baroque style by Baldassarre Longhena in the first half of the 17th century. Its tall bell tower (64 m high) dates from the mid-14th century. Inside, there is a marble pulpit (1677), a high altar with marble inlay and, in the chapel* to the left of the presbytery, an 18th-century painting of the Venetian School.

Corso del Popolo, known as the piazza, with an average width of 24 m, crosses the town from north to south, parallel to Canale della Vena. Walking in this direction, note: on the left, the Baroque church of S. Andrea, with its Veneto-Byzantine bell tower; the Gothic building with a portico is the Granaio (granary), dating from 1322, with a Madonna by Jacopo Sansovino in a tabernacle on its facade; the 19th-century Palazzo Comunale (Town Hall); the 16th century Loggia dei Bandi with a colonnade in the Doric style, and the church of S. Giacomo, with an 18th-century interior. Further down, on the right, is the Gothic oratory of S. Martino dating from 1392, built entirely of bricks and crowned with a polygonal lantern; inside, a polyptych* dating from 1349 attributed to Paolo Veneziano. The church of S. Domenico, altered in the 18th century, has a 14th-century bell tower; inside, a St Paul, the last known work of Vittore Carpaccio (1520), half-way up the right aisle; a wooden 15th-century Crucifix above the main altar; and a Crucifixion and Saints attributed to Jacopo Tintoretto, left of the presbytery. The Museo Civico della Laguna Sud "S. Francesco Fuori le Mura", housed in a former monastery, traces the historical and environmental development of the area since Roman times and during the Venetian Republic. One section of the museum is devoted to marine activities, fishing and the shipyards, a feature of Chioggia since the 18th century. The display shows how boats have evolved, especially the 'bragozzo', the typical boat of this area. Finally, there is a section for temporary exhibitions.

Between 1915 and 1917, a war within the War was fought on the Belluno Dolomites, the likes of which had never been seen before, nor since. The deep marks that that war made on these mountains left traces that can still be seen today.

THE DOLOMITE FRONT

Starting from the north, the plains of Lavaredo (2,350 m) are the first place we encounter related to the history of the Great War. Amidst the peaks of some of the world's most beautiful mountains you can still visit the remains of Italian bases on the road from the Auronzo refuge to the Longeres mountain pass, south of the Three Peaks. Moving on, we come to the Lavaredo mountain pass, from which the Locatelli/Drei Zinnen refuge can be seen to the north. From the Auronzo refuge, it is easy to reach the area of the Arghena mountain pass (2,036 m), with remnants of trenches, and the Val de l'Aga, along which we come across an Italian fort built in the late 19th century.

The heroic dimension of the battles around the Tre Cime di Lavaredo withered on Mt Piana, where more than a thousand soldiers died in the vain attempt to occupy the mountain dominating the access to the Landro Valley. Today, the peak is reached by a shuttle from Lake Misurina, and you travel along the ring that linked Monte Piana to Monte Piano through tunnels and posts. The route then moves to the area of the Falzarego Pass and the Val Travenanzes. Be sure to visit the open-air museum at Cinque Torri (2,255 m), reached by a chairlift from Bai de Dones up to the Scoiattoli refuge, from where a signed route leads visitors through trenches, artillery stations, barracks and lookouts. Another open-air museum is at Piccolo Lagazuoi (2,778 m), one of the theatres of battle. A favorite target of the Italians, who were clinging to the Martini Ledge, was the Austrian fort, Tre Sassi (2,197 m), which defended the Valparola Pass and Val Badia. Today a museum is housed in the fort (built between 1897 and 1901), displaying objects from both fronts. Trips can be taken from the fort through trenches and tunnels and two cemeteries.

From Valparola Pass, you can also reach a place that evokes the bloodiest images of the conflict on the Dolomites at the Col di Lana (2,209 m), or as the soldiers called it, the "Mountain of Blood". This was a mountain which, despite its low height, the Italian state (perhaps mistakenly) considered, from the start of the war, essential to have full dominance of the area. For almost a year, from July of 1915 to April of 1916, Italian troops were sent to the attack on the mountain's grassy slopes, where Austrian machine guns mowed them down. Thousands of soldiers were killed, until it was decided to blow up the mountaintop and the Austrian positions with an enormous mine placed under the southern peak. This also proved futile as the Austrians were entrenched on the nearby Sief peak to the north where they continued to block the pass to the Alps.

The history museum at Serauta-Marmolada (2,950 m, the highest in Europe) is full of documents of the battle fought on the "Queen of the Dolomites", one of the rare places in which Italians enjoyed an advantageous position, dominating the entire glacier. This is why the Austrians adopted an extraordinary solution, digging dozens of kilometers of tunnels under the glacier. The remains of this incredible "city of ice" are shown in the museum.

GRAPPA

After Caporetto, at the end of October of 1917, the Italians abandoned the Dolomite front. The troops retreated beyond the Piave and to Mt Grappa, where they successfully fought off two major Austrian offensives in the following months and then went on to a victorious counterattack that ended at Vittorio Veneto. The entire area affected by these events is part of the "Museo Diffuso del Grappa dal Brenta al Piave" project. In the Province of Belluno, parts of this museum include Fort Leone at the Campo di Arsiè peak, a mighty fortress built between 1908 and 1912; the Museo Civico Storico Territoriale at Alano di Piave, with an impressive photographic collection; the Museo Storico della Madonna del Piave at Vas, which has pieces from the conflict as well as items related to the river; the church of San Luigi at Seren del Grappa, where a viewpoint on the Grappa is now located; and finally, the former Austrian point of command, which has been restored in the Val Schievenin near Quero.

ROVIGO AND THE PO DELTA

THE PO DELTA

As the Po River approaches the sea, it wanders into six branches, forming a myriad of expanses of water and little islands. In short, it is a natural paradise.

The northern Delta. Following the bank of the Canal Bianco, the SS 443 leads from Adria to **Loreo**, a historic river port on the eponymous canal. Since 1963, the coast at nearby **Rosolina** has been developed as a tourist resort, especially Rosolina Mare. The most important town in the northern delta is **Porto Viro**. At Ca' Venier, with its eponymous rambling palazzo, a ferry crosses over to **Porto Tolle**. Further on still, Ca' Zuliani and Pila are situated where the valle landscape gives way to that of the Bocche di Po (Po Estuary), now protected, underlining the importance of this wetland habitat.

The southern Delta. **Taglio di Po** is named after the cut of Porto Viro, started in 1600. Further east, the old pumping station of Ca' Vendramin (1903, now derelict) lies just before **Ca' Tiepolo**, seat of the scattered municipality of Porto Tolle, which includes most of the delta area. This is the Isola della Donzella and most of it is reclaimed land. At **Scardovari**, the local economy is based on fishing. From here, you can drive around the peninsula at the mouth of the Po delle Tolle, passing the mussel farms of Sacca degli Scardovari. After the mouth of Po di Gnocca and the bridge of boats at **Santa Giulia**, lies **Goro Gorino Veneto**, on the Po di Goro.

The Po Delta in Scardovari.

HIGHLIGHTS

Po Delta Regional Park

The Parco Naturale Regionale del Delta del Po includes one of Italy's most biologically dynamic environments, formed by sedimentation from the Po and the wandering of its branches. It has the features of a wilderness but a landscape strongly conditioned by human presence. These are the reproductive habitats of countless bird species. The coexistence of fresh and salt water diversifies the fauna as well (www.parcodeltapo.org).
Visitors' centers: Centro turistico culturale San Basilio, tel. 042671200; Rifugio Parco del Delta del Po, Via Gorino Sullam 43, Taglio di Po, tel. 042688254.

ROVIGO

This local 'capital' is where Ferrara meets Venice, resulting in interesting churches and some delightful little corners.

Piazza Vittorio Emanuele II. This irregularly shaped square in the heart of the town is decorated by a column of Istrian stone (1519) with the Lion of St Mark (1881). **Palazzo del Municipio** (16C), with a portico, a loggia and a niche with a statue of the Madonna and Child (1590) overlooks the square.

Duomo. The Cathedral was rebuilt in the late 17th century; its facade is unfinished and the dome was added in the 18th century. It contains sculptures and paintings (at the altar, *Resurrection* by Palma the Younger). Near the cathedral, **Torre Donà** (one of the tallest medieval buildings in Italy) and a truncated tower, both of which are leaning, are all that remains of the castle founded in 920.

Accademia dei Concordi. Conceived in 1580 as an association for lovers of music and literature, in the 18th century, the Accademia dei Concordi created a special farming section to find a scientic solution to the hydraulic problems of the Polesine. In this format, between 1833 and 1901, it received bequests of art collections from many local landowners, particularly works of the Venetian School from the 14th to 18th centuries. They now form the **Pinacoteca dei Concordi***. Highlights include: **Madonna and Child*** and **Christ carrying the Cross*** by Giovanni Bellini, and a set of portraits by G.B. Piazzetta, G.B. Tiepolo and A. Longhi.
Beata Vergine del Soccorso. "La Rotonda", the church is built on a central octagonal plan (1594-1613) with a portico around the base; the imposing bell tower beside it is by B. Longhena (1655-73). Inside, the wooden altar dates from 1607 and there are some 17th-century paintings of the Venetian School.

FOOD IN VENETO

Every part of the region has brought something to the rich panorama of Veneto food. The mountains are home to some famous dairy products, like Asiago cheese, as well as some lesser known delights, like Lamon beans from Vallata Bellunese. The hilly zones are famed for their wines and grappas as well as some cured meats, such as Prosciutto Veneto Berico-Euganeo, and olive oil (even here, the taste differs from the Garda to the Mt Grappa zones). On the plain, the most famous items are Treviso Radicchio Rosso (chicory), Vialone Nano Veronese rice and the white asparagus from Bassano. All in all, there are over 30 products – many of which already have official recognition – that combine to make a rich, traditional cuisine.

THE DISHES

Pesce in saòr. Fried fish in a sauce made of onion, vinegar, sugar, pine nuts and sultana grapes. Sardines and sole are most commonly used. This starter is found across the region.

Bigoli co' l'arna. The bigoli – large spaghetti-like pasta made using a press – are cooked in a duck broth and then served in a sauce made of giblets (from a water bird) fried in oil and butter. This dish is typical in the Vicenza area.

Brodetto. In dialect, 'broeto'. This is a basic Venetian (or even Adriatic) fish soup that has small changes across the region. The broth is made with small fish like goby and then large fish are cooked in it.

Risi e bisi. This rice and peas dish is made with a broth of pea shells. In the Padua area, it is often eaten with goose in sauce (made using goose preserved in its own fat). In the Vicenza area, the broth is made using mutton neck and the dish is called 'risi e bisi e colo de castrà'. Rice is prepared in many different ways in this region, for example, with eel, with beans, with 'bruscandoli' (hops shoots) and with mutton (risi in cavroman).

Risotto alla trevigiana. A traditional risotto made with a base of onion and celery fried in oil. While the risotto is being cooked, a sausage from Treviso called 'luganega' (made with pork shoulder and cheek) is added in. There are other varieties of risotto, including one with radicchio, one with eel and one mixed seafood version known as 'alla chioggiotta'.

Baccalà alla vicentina. This is the most famous type of cod fish from the region. The dried cod is boned, cut into pieces and cooked with onion, garlic, parsley, anchovies, Parmesan, oil and milk. It is served with fresh or fried polenta.

Fegato alla veneziana. This famous liver dish is one of the few Venetian dishes to make it on the international scene. Thin slices of veal are cooked in oil, butter and plenty of chopped onion. Finally, chopped parsley is sprinkled on top.

Polenta e uccelli. Birds are pushed onto skewers and cooked in sage with oil and some lard. These are either served with fresh or fried polenta.

Fugazza. This might be the oldest Venetian dessert and it has a curious list of ingredients. The dough includes iris roots, orange rind, cloves, ginger, cinnamon, vanilla and almonds.

Pandoro. This classic Christmas cake from Verona is very light, being made only with flour, yeast, eggs and butter.

The famous pandoro.

THE PRODUCTS

Asiago DOP. This semi-cooked cow's milk cheese originated on the Asiago plateau. Today, it is also made on the surrounding plain, in the province of Trento and parts of the provinces of Padua and Treviso. It comes in two types: "d'allevo", seasoned, and "pressato", fresh. The former, which is more like the original version, is called 'mezzano' if seasoned for 3 to 5 months and 'vecchio' if seasoned for more than 9 months. The fresh version is sweeter than the seasoned one.

Monte Veronese DOP. This cheese is made with full cream or semi-skimmed cow's milk. It is made in the northern section of the province of Verona, in the Lessini Mountains. The version eaten at the table is seasoned for 3 months, while the one to be grated requires at least 6 months. It is white, with a few holes in it. The flavor is strong, becoming slightly spicy when seasoned.

Prosciutto Veneto Berico-Euganeo DOP. This ham is made in over 20 municipalities in the Padua and Vicenza areas. The legs – from adult Italian pigs – are trimmed and salted. They are then cured before being seasoned for 10 months.

Sopressa vicentina. Produced with top quality pork from locally-farmed pigs, this salami is made by mincing the meat roughly and then pushing it into beef gut casings. It is then seasoned 5 months to over a year in a cellar, eventually becoming covered in grey mold. The most famous type is from the Pasubio valleys, in the northern Vicenza area, although it is also made across the region.

Fagiolo di Lamon della Vallata Bellunese IGP. This broad bean only comes from the Lamon plateau. The exceptional soil and climate have meant that 4 main types have been cultivated since the 16th century: 'spagnolit', the most prized; 'spagnolo', the rarest; 'calonega', the most common; 'canalino', the least prized.

Radicchio rosso di Treviso IGP. The most famous chicory from Veneto, it was also the first Italian vegetable to get EU recognition. The elongated form is the result of a special cultivation method. It comes it two variants: early, being collected around 1 September, it has small leafs; and late, being collected around 1 December, with redder leafs and a more bitter taste. It is grown in the provinces of Treviso, Padua and Venice.

Radicchio variegato di Castelfranco IGP. This type of chicory is sometimes called 'the flower that you eat' because, when ripe, it looks like a giant set of red petals. The taste is delicate and sweet with occasional bitter hints. It is made is the same areas as Radicchio di Treviso.

Asparagus. The best known asparagus comes from the Vicenza area: Asparago bianco di Bassano del Grappa. Other key variants are: Asparago bianco di Cimadolmo IGP, in the Treviso area, and Asparago del Medio Adige.

Riso Vialone Nano Veronese IGP. Grown in the southern part of the Verona area, the presence of spring water gives the rice something special.

Garda Extra-Virgin Olive Oil DOP. Made around Benaco, it comes in sub-varieties: 'Veronese', 'Bresciano' and 'Trentino'. This cold-pressed oil has very little acid content, but plenty of chlorophyll, a strong fruity flavor and a delicate taste.

THE WINES

The word Veneto makes one think of a great variety of wines, starting with Merlot, which accounts for over a third of regional wine production. In the Lake Garda region, there is Bardolino, while the glacial foothills are home to Bianco di Custoza.

The hills around Verona are the setting for a prized red, Amarone, with a full-bodied and velvety taste, and Recioto, which is a raisin wine (red in the Valpolicella version, white in the Soave one). Soave is also the zone of a famous white, Soave, made from an autochthonous grape, garganega, which is also used for the Gambellara DOC. On the north-eastern border of the province, you find vineyards for the Monti Lessini DOC wines, made from another autochthonous grape, Durello, which is used for sparkling wines. In the province of Vicenza, there are two wine areas: north of Vicenza lies the Breganze DOC area, which is home to more white grapes, including vespaiolo (used to make a famous raisin wine, Torcolato); to the south, rising out of the plain, are the Berici hills, which have a Mediterranean micro-climate that favors red grapes.

In the Padua area, the Euganei hills are famed for the Moscato fior d'arancio while a top class red, Friularo, comes from the so-called Dominio di Bagnoli. The eastern part of the region is home to the rolling hills connecting Conegliano to Valdobbiadene. The most international wine from the region is Prosecco, one of the most famous bubbly wines in Italy. Finally, the flood lands of the southern Treviso area are home to Piave DOC and, further inland, Lison-Pramaggiore DOC.

Veneto is also the region from which grappa gets its name. Grappa is no longer a poor man's drink, having become a refined product made with top quality raw materials and a carefully controlled distillation process.

FOOD

❝ **J**oyous view, cheerful, and lovely appearance/Such is the sea when, tranquil and calm/It murmurs, whitening, up to the shore." These words are from Torquato Tasso's "Il Mondo Creato." The "lieta vista" appears roughly midway through the route and especially in the last stretch, along the luminous shore of the Gulf of Trieste. The route, which goes from Portogruaro along the littoral, may seem distant from the sea (in atmosphere, culture, and history, if not in actual miles), when it passes through the vineyards and intensive farming of the Friulian plain or past the grassy bastions of the Venetian citadel of Palmanova. In reality, the ties to the sea are close and fertile: observe the landscape of the lagoon of Grado and the all-encompassing relationship between sea, people, and history. Beginning with Portogruaro itself, an ancient market town, greeting boats and goods; then Aquileia, where the cypress adorns the ruins of the Roman city, another fine river harbor; not to mention cosmopolitan Trieste.

NOT TO BE MISSED

Portogruaro, a small town on the Lemene River, with a marked 15th-16th-century. Venetian influence, is largely intact; at Concordia Sagittaria, go see the solitary ruins of the late-Roman/high-medieval settlement (cathedral, baptistery, excavations); at Sesto al Reghena is the Romanesque-Byzantine abbey of S. Maria in Sylvis, with frescoes dating from the 12th-13th-century above the entrance and in the vestibule. **Latisana**: in the Duomo of this little town on the Tagliamento River is an altarpiece by P. Veronese. **Palmanova**, with a radial plan, is a star-shaped fortress with bastions, ramparts, and embankments, truly a city-cum-citadel; the Venetians built it (1593) to protect their open eastern frontier; take an 8 km detour from Cervignano del Friuli. **Aquileia** (➠ see below): Roman ruins, museums, and the basilica with its Early Christian mosaics are all eloquent commemorations of the centuries of late antiquity and the High Middle Ages when this was a prosperous and powerful center of a vast region. **Grado***, with its medieval center of narrow lanes and "campielli" and its Early Christian churches. San Giovanni di Duino, with the Bocche del Timavo, where the waters of this river return to the light of day, after their long passage underneath the Carso, or Karst. **Duino**: in this former fishing village are two castles of local siegneurs, with the legend of the ill-fated Dama Bianca, who was turned to stone; also, literary history tells us that Dante Alighieri spent much time pondering, seated on the rocks overlooking the sea, and that Rainer Maria Rilke took inspiration here for his "Duino Elegies." **Sistiana**: beach resort, in a small rocky inlet, surrounded by woods. **Miramare castle**: it stands between the waters of the Gulf of Trieste and the dark holm-oaks, fir trees, and cypresses inland, a Romantic and princely Hapsburg residence. If you have time to add in a little detour, head to **Udine** (➠ see below), with its castle, and **Gorizia** (➠ see below), historically a meeting place for cultures and peoples.

AQUILEIA

Friuli Venezia Giulia, province of Udine. Along the road to Grado, just before the last patch of plain gives way to the lagoon, is the Romanesque basilica of Aquileia. The 73-meter-tall bell tower no longer towers over the solitary lands that were once so dear to Italy's Nobel laureate, the poet G. Carducci. Aquileia is now a thriving small town in prosperous farmland; it also boasts one of Italy's most interesting archeological sites. In the shade of tall cypresses, the ruins of a Roman river port evoke ancient trade in exotic merchandise, brought from all over the Mediteranean, and in precious amber, gathered on distant Baltic beaches and transported across the European continent.

Basilica**. Among Italy's proudest Romanesque monuments, the basilica looks

A view of the Basilica in Aquileia.

much the same as it was when the patriarch Poppone built it in the 11th-century. The first religious structure to stand here dates from AD 313, following the Edict of Milan. In 1031, the new Basilica was completed after ten years of construction. An earthquake caused extensive damage in 1348, and restoration gave it a more Gothic appearance. Later, the Venetians added elements of Renaissance style. The simple facade is joined by a portico, which links the building to the 9th-century church of the Pagani and the ruins of the 5th-century baptistery. To the left, the massive 11th-century bell tower stands alone. The solemn interior features 14th-century Gothic arcades, raised on columns, and a spectacular 4th-century mosaic floor** from the original church, discovered in 1909-12. Split into nine large panels, this is the largest surviving sample of Early Christian mosaics in the West. In the right-hand apse, there are frescoes, also from the 4th-century church. At the center of the stairway leading into the presbytery is an elegant Renaissance tribune* by Bernardino da Bissone (1491). To the right of the central altar, part of a late-5th-century mosaic, discovered in 1970, is visible. Beneath the presbytery is the crypt, with walls and vaults decorated with frescoes*, perhaps from the late 12th century. At the end of the left aisle is the entrance to the Cripta degli Scavi*, or crypt of the excavations, where fragments of the 4th-century early Christian basilica are visible, as well as fragments of 1st-century Roman homes with mosaic floors*.

Museo Civico del Patriarcato. This museum of the municipality, in Viale Patriarca Popone, casts light on the religious history of Aquileia, mainly through slabs and sacred furnishings.

Case Romane and Oratori Paleocristiani. The site near Viale Patriarca Popone includes a complex of Roman houses, some from the late Republic, with mosaic floors, pipes, wells, and two small early-Christian oratories. Another archeological area lies to the left of the Basilica, of Piazza del Capitolo.

Museo Archeologico Nazionale*. It is located in the Villa Cassis, Via Roma 1. One of Italy's leading museums of Roman antiquities, it boasts impressive collections from archeological digs in and around Aquileia. Inaugurated in 1807, it has been enlarged and renovated several times in the past two centuries. Among the items on display are inscriptions and reliefs concerning the foundation of Aquileia; statues and busts; a Venus; a superb collection of glassware, amber, and carved stones; and many remarkable mosaics.

Museo Paleocristiano. North of the center, a vast former Benedictine convent stands on the remains of a 4th-5th-century Christian basilica, with extensive remains of 5th-century mosaic floors*. In the former convent a museum has been set up, with extensive artifacts of Early Christian Aquileia: mosaics, sarcophagi, and an early depiction of the Baptism of Jesus.

UDINE

The castle was probably built to defend the area during the Hungarian incursions (5C). In a document of 983, Emperor Otto II ceded the castle of Udene to the Patriarch of Aquileia, Rodoaldo, for this purpose. In the 13th century, Patriarch Bertoldo of Andechs moved back to Udine, abandoning Cividale. For Udine, this was the start of a period of growth of which little remains, apart from the little church of S. Maria di Castello. From now on, Udine was the capital of Friuli. In 1420, Udine and the rest of Friuli became part of the Republic of Venice. After the fall of the Venetian Republic and the short period of Napoleonic rule, Udine became part of the Austrian region of Lombardy-Veneto and was then incorporated in the Kingdom of Italy (1866). Only after WWI did the town begin to expand beyond the old walls, and only very recently has it begun to spread in terms of urban development.

Piazza della Libertà. Situated below the castle hill, Piazza della Libertà, the focal point of the town, is surrounded by Venetian-style buildings. Notice the Loggia del Lionello and the Portico di S. Giovanni: to the left of it, an archway marks the way up to the castle.

Civici Musei and Gallerie di Storia e Arte. Udine's Municipal Museums were inaugurated in 1865. There are five main parts: the Donazione Ciceri (a private collection donated to the town), the Archeology Museum, the Gallery of Early Art, the Gallery of Drawings and Prints, and the Friuli Museum of Photography. Finally, the town's cultural heritage includes an Art Library of 30,000 volumes about the area's historical and artistic heritage.

Civica Galleria d'Arte Moderna. The gallery contains more than 4,000 works dating from the late 19th century to the 20th century (Modigliani, A. Martini, Fontana) and the present day (Vedova). The Astaldi Collection includes masterpieces of Italian 20th-century painting by De Chirico, Savinio, Severini, Carrà, Sironi, Morandi and others, and also works by foreign painters.

Duomo. The cathedral has retained its Gothic, 14th-century appearance, particularly the central doorway and the doorway* on the left (1390). The interior contains altar-pieces by G.B. Tiepolo. A door on the left of the presbytery leads to the Museo del Duomo, which includes the 14th-century chapel of S. Nicolò and the old baptistery, situated below the bell tower, with fine Gothic arches, and the tomb of the Blessed Bertrando, with reliefs dating from 1343.

Palazzo Patriarcale. The complex was built in the early 16th century. The first floor of the palace houses the Museo Diocesano d'Arte Sacra*. A spiral staircase leads up to the second floor and the reception rooms: the Blue Room, the Yellow Room, and the Red Room, formerly the old ecclesiastical courtroom. This theme features in the huge ceiling fresco by Tiepolo: The Judgement of Solomon. Next is the Throne room*, or Portrait Room (containing portraits of the bishops, patriarchs and archbishops from the foundation of the church of Aquileia to the present day) in which the Galleria degli Ospiti** is Tiepolo's masterpiece.

GORIZIA

Scene of conflict between different peoples and cultures, its language and culture are Italian. Its past is mainly Austrian and its territory stretches from the Friuli plain to the Slovenian mountains beyond a border which, since 1947, has run around its town center. It owes its medieval development to the fortunes of the Counts of Lurngau who controlled access to the peninsula. As a crossroads of trade with Central and Eastern Europe it grew fast. During WWI, the town was destroyed by bombing. Reconstruction under Fascism was rapid, but other problems arose at the end of WWII, when the border decided in 1947 with Yugoslavia, which ran around part of the town, proved to be an "iron curtain" between the Soviet and Western blocks.

Duomo. Dedicated to the Christian martyrs Hilary and Tazianus, patron saints of the town, the cathedral is an amalgamation of the churches of St Hilary, recorded in 1342, and St Acazio. It became a cathedral (1752) and was restored in the late 19th century and again between 1925 and 1928, to repair damage from the bombs of WWI.

Musei Provinciali di Gorizia a Borgo Castello. The museum complex has several parts. Artworks from various periods are housed in

one art gallery and another focuses on 20th-century art. There is an exhibition of pieces from the Palazzo Attems-Petzenstein museum. The Museo della Moda e delle Arti Applicate has exhibits including yarns, fabrics and costumes from the 18th-19th centuries, tools and looms. Casa Formentini has other exhibitions on folk traditions and customs in the basement. The Museo storico della Grande Guerra describes in detail the 12 battles fought on the Isonzo (1915-1917) to capture Gorizia.

The castle in Gorizia was rebuilt in the 20th century.

Castle. It dates from the 11th century and was rebuilt after WWI. It houses collections of medieval furniture and objects, some paintings of the Venetian School and fragments of 16th-century frescoes. The Sala della Didattica on the second floor is devoted to Gorizia's medieval history.

Sant'Ignazio. This church is one of the most important Baroque buildings in the Gorizia area. Its imposing facade has two domed bell towers. The complex marble decoration includes a statue of St Ignatius. In the left-hand niche: a statue of Joseph. In the right-hand niche: a statue of John the Baptist. Inside, the single nave has a barrel vault. The length and height of the nave and the presbytery are identical, adding to the grandeur of the church. At the far end is a trompe l'oeil fresco of the Glory of St Ignazius by Christoph Tausch.

Palazzo Coronini Cronberg. The garden of Palazzo Coronini Cronberg is one of many gardens and parks which give Gorizia the appearance of a "garden-city". In 1870, Count Alfredo Coronini designed the garden at the palazzo, using the lie of the land to create romantic view-points, and perspectives which reflected the tenets of the English garden in vogue at the time. The late 16th-century palazzo contains paintings, furniture, porcelain, jewellery, silverware, carpets, prints, drawings, coins and period costumes.

TRIESTE

Trieste's origins date from the Roman colony of Tergeste, founded 2,000 years ago. In 1382 it submitted to the Hapsburgs. Three and a half centuries passed in obscurity before Emperor Charles VI declared the city a free port in 1719, giving Trieste a competitive advantage. This measure was renewed by the more systematic reforms implemented by Charles VI's daughter, Maria Theresa, whose reign (1740-80) was a turning-point for the mercantile fortunes of the city. In Trieste, the crisis of the Hapsburg Empire in the 19th and 20th centuries was manifested as a growing desire to be freed from Austria rule. Fascism, with its expansionism towards the Balkans, worsened relations between Italians and Slavs. The Italo-German Axis declared war on nearby Yugoslavia (April 1941) and invaded it. As a result, Istria and Trieste itself were occupied (May-June 1945) by Tito's partisans. The Trieste area did not return to Italy until 1954.

Having welcomed about 60,000 refugees from Istria after WWII, between the end of the 20th century and the dawn of the 21st, the city concentrated on reviving its former role as mediator between cultures and markets in the fields of services for research, commerce and finance.

Castle of S. Giusto. The castle was built between 1470 and 1630 over an earlier fort, which, in turn, was probably erected above a pre-Roman stronghold. Restored in the 1930s it was converted into a museum and a setting for outdoor performances. There are marvelous views over the city and the Bay of Trieste from its bastions. The **Civico Museo del Castello di S. Giusto-Armeria-Lapidario tergestino al Bastione Lalio** has a valuable collection of chests, furniture, paintings and weapons dating from the 14th to 19th centuries from private collections. Highlights include 12th-century swords, suits of chainmail, late 16th-century Venetian halberds, crossbows, rifles from the Napoleonic period, sabers and bayonets. Artworks include a 15th-century wooden statue. The recently restored Bastione Lalio of the castle of St Justus houses the Lapidario Tergestino: limestone material from the Roman period including inscriptions from monuments and tombs, bas-reliefs, full reliefs and architectural fragments.

Basilica Cathedral of S. Giusto. This church dedicated to St Justus is the symbol of the city. It was created by amalgamating (in the 14C) two Romanesque basilicas (5-11C) dedicated to St Justus (on the right) and the Assumption (on the left). The simple brick facade and sloping roof is enhanced by a magnificent 14th-century rose-window. The jambs of the main doorway are from a Roman funerary stele. The bell tower (14C) left of the church was built over the remains of a Roman temple. There is a Romanesque statue of St Justus in a niche on the right-hand side of the bell tower. The interior of the church comprises five asymmetrical naves and aisles separated by columns with fine capitals. The central nave has a 16th-century painted ship's keel ceiling, replaced in 1905. The right apse has blind arcading and 13th-century frescoes; in the vault, a fine late 13th-century mosaic. In the floor are remains of a mosaic from the 5th-century basilica. In the vault of the left apse is a Madonna between the Archangels Michael and Gabriel and, below, the Apostles, both 12th-century mosaics*. On the wall of the left aisle is a *Virgin and Child with Saints*, by B. Carpaccio (1540). The left aisle leads to the Baptistery, where there is a 9th-century font for total immersion.

Civico Museo di Storia e Arte and Orto Lapidario. The museum, created in 1925, contains collections of finds from Egypt, Magna Grecia, Africa, Etruria and Greece, and Maya exhibits from El Salvador. There is also material from Trieste itself, Aquileia and Istria: bronze artifacts from the Tolmino necropolis (8-5C BC), marble statues and busts, glass- and earthenware, gold, silver and amber from the Roman period and Greek pottery. The Orto Lapidario outside, formerly a cemetery, contains architectural fragments and inscriptions from Trieste and Aquileia.

S. Maria Maggiore. Behind the Town Hall, from the hill of S. Giusto the church overlooks an area where many buildings were demolished in the 1930s. Built in 1627-82, it has a fine Baroque facade. The altar to the right of the high altar has a revered image of the Madonna della Salute. To the right of the church, slightly lower down, is the little 11th-century **church of S. Silvestro**, restored to its original lines in the 1920s.

Arco di Riccardo. The arch, erected in 33 BC, was once one of the gates of the Roman town. Restored by FAI (the Italian Fund for the Protection of the Environment), it has a single arch, decorated with pilasters.

Museo della Comunità Ebraica "Carlo e Vera Wagner". The museum, opened in 1993, has examples of Jewish culture and art of the Jewish community of Trieste, and religious fabrics from its synagogues. The collection includes richly-decorated 18th-century Venetian silverware, books and documents.

Teatro Romano. In 1938, the cavea and the stage of an early 2nd-century Roman theater were discovered below the hill of S. Giusto. The theater had a seating capacity of 6,000.

Civico Museo Mario Morpurgo de Nilma. Ceramics, glassware, porcelain, exotic furnishings, silverware, crystal, books, prints, drawings and paintings were donated to the city in 1943 by Mario Morpurgo de Nilma, a passionate collector. They are displayed in part of a beautiful late-19th century palace, now the Municipal Morpurgo Museum. Sadly, much of the collection was lost during WWII.

Civico Museo Teatrale Fondazione Carlo Schmidl. The Carlo Schmidl Municipal Theater Museum has recently been created on the second floor of Palazzo Gopcevic, as the result of a bequest by a local music publisher (1859-1943) and, in terms of the sheer size, is second only to the La Scala Theater Museum in Milan. It includes costumes, posters, photographs, prints, librettos, scores and musical instruments from Europe and further afield.

Viale XX Settembre is crossed by Via Carducci, created in 1850 by covering the river carrying the springwater from the hills above Trieste to the sea, and Via Battisti, which leads to the 19th-century public garden. On Viale XX Settembre, an elegant promenade lined with cafés, theaters and cinemas, is **Teatro Eden**, now a cinema, a notable example of Art Nouveau decoration, and the **Politeama Rossetti** (1878), important in the theatrical and patriotic life of Trieste.

Piazza Oberdan. Conceived as a dramatic entrance to the city in the 1930s, Piazza Oberdan lies on the site where, in 1882, Trieste patriot Guglielmo Oberdan was hanged by the Austrians. It is also the terminus for the popular *Opicina tram*, a rack tramway dating from 1902.

Civico Museo del Risorgimento and Sacrario Oberdan. The museum has a collection of historical memorabilia, photographs, documents, uniforms and paintings illustrating local events of the Risorgimento from 1848 up to WWI. Outside is the *Sacrario*, a monument to patriot G. Oberdan, and the cell where he was detained.

Galleria Nazionale di Arte Antica. The main nucleus of the gallery is the Mentasti collection, about 50 paintings dating from the 15th to 19th centuries, including works by G. Antonio and F. Guardi, a series of drawings by Canaletto and some paintings attributed to L. Cranach the Elder and J Tintoretto.

A view of the Canal Grande and out to sea from Ponte Rosso.

Piazza della Libertà has retained its monumental late 19th-century appearance. Surrounded by elegant buildings of eclectic style including Palazzo Economo, it is dominated by the broad facade of the Stazione Centrale (1878). To the left, the former grain depot (1890) has been converted into the main bus terminus (1986-1989).

Canal Grande. Dug in 1750-56, the Canal Grande provided a safe haven for sailing ships and enabled them to unload their cargoes, destined for the warehouses of the newly-emerging *borgo teresiano* in the 18th century, created by filling in the salt-pans west of the old city. On the right of the sea end of the canal is **Palazzo Carciotti** (1802-05), one of the city's best examples of Neo-Classic architecture, with a facade decorated with six columns, a balustrade and statues. Close by is the former Hôtel de la Ville (1839). At the top of the canal stands the Neo-Classic **church of Sant'Antonio Nuovo**.

Piazza Ponterosso (red bridge) was named after a wooden drawbridge, replaced in 1840, which spanned the Canal Grande. This square, adorned by an 18th-century fountain, and nearby Piazza Sant'Antonio Nuovo are dominated by the shining **church of SS. Trinità e S. Spiridione Taumaturgo**. Built by the Serbian Orthodox community and opened in 1868, its interior has silver furnishings and mosaics with a gold background.

S. Nicolò dei Greci. The church built in 1784-87 for the Greek Orthodox community, has a facade with twin bell towers (1819-21). Inside, the iconostasis is richly decorated with worked silver.

Molo Audace. This quay where the people of Trieste like to stroll takes its name from the torpedo boat which brought the first battalions of Italian soldiers on November 3, 1918.

Teatro Comunale Giuseppe Verdi. Overlooking Piazza Giuseppe Verdi, the theater is a Neo-Classic building (1801), whose facade is reminiscent of La Scala in Milan. In 1850, Giuseppe Verdi staged the first performance of *Stiffelio*, conceived and written in Trieste.

Piazza dell'Unità d'Italia. Heart of the old town, Piazza dell'Unità d'Italia faces the sea (the buildings on the front were knocked down) like a sort of enormous stage, with the facade of the **Palazzo Comunale** (Town Hall) (1875) as a backdrop.

Civico Museo Pasquale Revoltella – Galleria di Arte Moderna. The Civic Museum and Modern Art Gallery, founded in 1872, is housed in the palazzo built by Baron P. Revoltella (1852-1858). There are three main parts to the collection. The first is the palazzo itself, with many works from the early 19th century, including Neo-Classic sculptures by A. Canova; the second consists of works from the second half of the 19th and early 20th centuries; finally, the third part, designed in the 1960s by C. Scarpa, focuses on 20th-century art.

Museo Sveviano. Created in 1997 by the daughter of writer I. Svevo, the museum is a place where the work of the writer can be studied through an exhibition of manuscripts, photographs, books and letters, which are available for consultation along with translations of his work.

Museo Petrarchesco Piccolomineo. The museum houses art and book collections relating to two great men: F. Petrarca (Petrarch) (1304-1374) and E. S. Piccolomini (1405-1464). The collection includes 5,500 printed books, 79 manuscripts, about 700 examples of iconography and ancient documents.

Civico Museo di Storia Naturale. The museum, opened in 1846, is divided into two main parts: the function of the first is primarily educational, with collections of animals and plants, while the second is only open to scholars. The paleontological and mineral exhibits come from caves and breccia of the Carso and Istria, like the fossil remains of a dinosaur found at Duino. A Mammal Room has recently opened, focusing on local mammal species.

Civico Museo Sartorio. Housed in a villa where the Sartorio family lived from 1838 to 1947, the museum offers the chance to see rooms with their original furnishings and some very fine art collections, including a collection of Italian ceramics from the 16th to 19th centuries. The museum, which is constantly being restored, contains a magnificent triptych attributed to P. Veneziano (*Triptych of St Clare**), and a valuable collection of drawings by G.B. Tiepolo. The Quadreria (art gallery) has more than 1,200 paintings from Trieste's Municipal Museum of History and Art. There is also a plaster-cast collection of more than 350 works (sculptures and busts of plaster, marble and different types of stone) from the 16th to the mid-20th centuries.

Civico Museo del Mare. The museum provides a complete picture of Trieste's maritime history, with models of boats and ships, scale models of the harbors of Trieste and Dalmatia, nautical maps, photographs and prints. The museum began in 1904, when the School of Fishing and Fish-farming set up a permanent marine exhibition, subsequently enriched with other material.

Museo della Farmacia Piccola. The museum has seven rooms containing a collection gathered over 200 years which traces the history of this old, family-run city pharmacy (1799). It includes more than 2,000 pharmaceutical objects, 800 scientific books and documents. Since 1999 it has belonged to the European Association of Museum of the History of Medical Sciences in Paris.

Civico Museo di Guerra per la Pace "Diego de Henriquez". The Museum of War for Peace, created in 1997, contains the collection of D. de Henriquez (1909-1974), comprising military objects, early and modern weapons, tanks, uniforms, photographs, prints, scale models and a collection of paper soldiers.

Risiera di S. Sabba. This former rice refinery, built in 1913, was converted by the Fascists and Nazis after September 8, 1943, into a depot for confiscated possessions and a prison camp for partisans, political prisoners and Jews. Thousands of people were deported from here to the death camps in Poland. Many were eliminated here, the only place on Italian soil with a cremation oven, between June 1944 and April 1945. In 1965 S. Sabba was declared a national monument and, now restored, houses the Museo della Resistenza (Museum of the Resistance).

CASTLES AND FORTIFICATIONS

For many centuries, from the Roman Age to the Modern Age, the Friuli and Giulia areas were the site of profuse fortification building. It was vital to defend travel routes and the rivers' fords. The situation was highly diversified and grew increasingly complex. Structures with military functions were joined by abbeys, villages and walled cities, growing to today's total of over 300 structures. The Romans built the first systems of fortifications and watchtowers. Castles in Gemona, Venzone and Udine were built between 1077 and 1420. The city of Palmanova (1593) is the sole example of a fortress built from scratch. After the 16th century, castles in isolated areas were often abandoned, while those near main roads became mansions.

IN VENEZIA GIULIA

The region's most famous castles are on the coast of Trieste. The castle of San Giusto overlooks Trieste. It was built in the early 15th century and renovated after WW I, adapted into a museum. The nearby 19th-century Miramare castle was built at the behest of Archduke Maximilian of Hapsburg. In keeping with the fashion of that era, every room is inspired by a different style. The dining room features Rococo furniture; the chapel is Gothic; the sitting rooms are Japanese and Chinese; and the archduke's bedroom is set up like a ship cabin. A similar variety is seen in the park. Its romantic scenery includes a lake of swans, mountain pavilions, grottos, Greek statues, a Sphinx and hundreds of plant species.

Moving west, we come to the castle of Duino: a group of buildings from various eras distributed within a courtyard that includes a tower partly built by Romans. There are nearby ruins of an earlier castle, destroyed by the Turks in the 15th century.

Gorizia is also loomed over by a hulking fortress, originally from the 11th century and expanded many times. The complex fell into disrepair starting in the 17th century, was bombed during WW I and rebuilt with its 16th century features, rendering it today a sort of castle/museum. The fortification works in Gradisca date from the 15th century. The Venetians fortified this city as a bulwark against Turkish raids; it fell into the hands of the Hapsburgs in the early 16th century. The fortress at Monfalcone was the stronghold of the Aquileia patriarchate. Surviving is a square tower within circular walls, which are surrounded by the remains of pre-Roman castelliere settlement. In Spessa (Capriva del Friuli), underground passages dug into the rock are all that remains of its 13th-century fortress. Ruins of a 7th-century fortification are found near Cormons.

IN FRIULI

On the way to Carnia, the first castle is the Bernarda (Premariacco) fortress, turned into a residence in 1567. Today, it holds a wine producer, as does the nearby abbey of Rosazzo, a fortified medieval complex. The fortified sanctuary, Castelmonte in Cividalese, is the grandest of its kind. Continuing northwest, the rises controlling the valleys and roads were extremely well fortified. A visit to the Attimis medieval archeology museum is well worthwhile, illustrating the nature of the settlements, their construction types and the military needs that the castles of this area met. A short way to the northeast, the fort of Osoppo, the castle of Gemona and the walled city of Venzone clearly announce their importance given their position in the Tagliamento Valley on the road to Austria.

The hills surrounding Udine are no less important. The castle of Udine, already documented in 983, sits atop the hill over the city. It was destroyed by an earthquake in 1517 and rebuilt with residential and diplomatic functions; it is currently home to the city museums. Castles around the city include Tricesimo, Cassacco, Colloredo di Monte Albano, Susans, Arcano and the ruins of the upper castle of Brazzacco. Villalta boasts one of Friuli's most majestic medieval castles, which includes a residence, a crenellated wall, towers and a keep. On the plain, the fortress city of Palmanova is noteworthy; and there are two 14th-century castles in Strassoldo.

The greatest example of a fortified construction in the Pordenone Friuli area is the abbey of Santa Maria in Sylvis at Sesto al Reghena, first documented in 762. It was destroyed in 889 and then rebuilt. The travails of history have brought it to us in its current form, slowly developed since the 15th century. Other important sites include the castles of Porcia, Cordovado and Zoppola (with a 15th-century tower and an 18th-century chapel) and the castle of Spilimbergo, consisting of a series of structures gathered around a courtyard of particular interest.

FOOD IN FRIULI VENEZIA GIULIA

The mainstays of the food of Friuli Venezia Giulia are a cheese, Montasio DOP, and a locally cured ham, Prosciutto di San Daniele DOP, both renowned for their excellent quality and long tradition. Montasio is a mountain cheese produced in the Carnia, an area with fascinating food and culture. San Daniele ham is made in the hills, near the vineyards which provide another important mainstay of the local economy. Other traditional products are coming to the fore. Certain cured meats and cheeses have been brought back from the brink of extinction, and are still made using artisanal methods, whereas others are long and well established products like some of the local grappas.

TRADITIONAL LOCAL DISHES

Cialzons. A local kind of ravioli, and typical of the Carnia. Filled with meat, eggs and cheese and lots of aromatic herbs. Other versions of the same dish are stuffed with calves' brains, roast chicken and various herbs.

Iota. A classic soup very common throughout the region. In Friuli it's made with beans, milk, brovada (pickled turnips) and polenta flour, whereas, in Venezia Giulia the beans are cooked with potatoes, crauti, pork skin and smoked pork chops.

Brovada. White turnips fermented with winepressings for 3 months. They are cut into very thin strips and used to make iota but they are also stewed with lardo to accompany the traditional muset or cotechino.

Frico. From the Friuli peasant tradition, bursting with taste and simple to prepare, made with potatoes and soft cheese fried together, with onion, salt and pepper.

Muset. This is a local cotechino made with parts of a pig's head, pigskin and pork shin, flavored with cinnamon, coriander and other herbs. It is then boiled and served with brovada or polenta.

Gubana. A specialty from Gorizia, a sweet dough filled with walnuts, zibibbo raisins, sultanas, pine nuts, chocolate and other ingredients and rolled up before baking. It is sprinkled with grappa before serving.

TYPICAL LOCAL PRODUCTS

Montasio DOP. This compact cheese with sparse, uniformly distributed eyes is made with full-fat cow's milk. It is matured for various lengths of time: fresco, with its mild, delicate flavor from 60 days to 5 months; up to 12 months for the mezzano, with a rounded taste and a more crumbly body; and more than a year for the stravecchio, which is used for grating and has quite a strong flavor. Another non-DOP variety of Montasio, called ubriaco, is matured in grape-pressings.

Prosciutto di San Daniele DOP. One of Italy's most extraordinary foods. The area of San Daniele has always been renowned for its marvelous cured meats. Now only made in San Daniele del Friuli, with top-quality meat. After at least 12 months of aging, this results in tender reddish-pink ham with pure-white fat. It has a strong perfume and mild taste, with a stronger after-taste.

Prosciutto di Sauris. This ham made with artisanal methods comes from a town in the Alta Carnia. It is made with the haunches of locally reared pigs, seasoned with juniper and spices, and smoked over resinous wood or beech wood. Finally it is matured for 10 months in ventilated maturing sheds.

WINE

This region is known for its excellent white wine, but also makes some very good reds. The two DOCGs made here are the whites Ramandolo and Picolit from the Colli Orientali del Friuli, whereas the 9 DOC and 3 IGT wines of the region are made from other grapes. The most common reds are Merlot, Friulano (once called Tocai Friulano but recently changed),

Prosciutto di Sauris, a ham with a very ancient tradition.

Cabernet Franc and Sauvignon, Refosco and Schioppettino; white wines include Verduzzo, Ribolla Gialla, Pignolo, Malvasia Istriana and Vitouska. Great wines means excellent winepressings and consequently excellent grappa: this is so in Friuli Venezia Giulia, which leads the field in the production of this distillate. In fact, in the early 'seventies, it was here that grappa was first made with pressings of one grape variety. A completely new grappa is distilled with honey, and, they make other distillates with fruit that are common throughout Central Europe: Sliwovitz (prunes), Williams (pears) and Kirsch (cherries).

FOOD

La Spezia was transformed from a small seaside town into a prosperous city almost overnight in 1808 when Napoleon Bonaparte arrived, declared the gulf a naval base and the town a Maritime Prefecture. New construction methods meant that defensive fortifications could be built on the seaward side, and that the medieval landing-stages, located in naturally protected little bays, could be replaced with larger, modern ones. Later, La Spezia became the newly-created Kingdom of Italy's main naval base. In the late 19th century, the medieval fabric was largely destroyed to make way for a new arsenal and a new town layout, which is mainly what you see today. In La Spezia, whether you are visiting its array of interesting museums, climbing up to the imposing castle of San Giorgio on a sunny day or strolling along its bustling, well-kept seafront, there are unexpected delights in store.

Corso Cavour. This long street is the result of the "expansion plan" worked out in 1862, which swept away most of the medieval town. This period of town planning is perhaps what characterizes most the appearance of the town center, which is elegant, tidy but without many memorable landmarks. The most interesting buildings on this long street and the squares which intersect it are the church of Nostra Signora della Salute (1900) in Piazza Brin, Palazzo Crozza (No. 251), now the municipal library, with the Musei Civici (city museums) behind, and the church of S. Maria Assunta, in Piazza Beverini.

Museo Civico di Etnografia e Antropologia Giovanni Podenzana. Now that the archeological collection has been moved to the S. Giorgio castle, the museum at No. 9 Via Curtatone is divided into two sections: a natural history section and an ethnographical section, which is excellent and comprises costumes, tools and equipment used in everyday life and by the farming community of the area around Luni.

Museo Civico d'Arte Antica, Medievale e Moderna Amedeo Lia. The meticulous restoration of the 17th-century Paolotti convent, with the aim of converting it into a suitable showcase for the town and the art it was to house, has resulted in a museum that is worthy of the outstanding collection donated by the collector Amedeo Lia to the town of La Spezia. This is one of Europe's most important collections of paintings from the 13th-15th centuries. The 13 rooms also contain liturgical objects from various periods, medieval ivory, fragments from windows, a rare and precious collection of miniatures, medals, rock crystals worked by Milanese craftsmen, Venetian glass, and a large number of archeological artifacts from the Mediterranean area. The paintings make up the largest collection and include several masterpieces by such painters as P. di Giovanni Fei. Some of the other major

artists represented in the collection are G. Bellini, S. del Piombo, J. da Pontormo (Self-portrait, the symbol of the museum) and Titian (Portrait of a Gentleman*). Finally, don't miss the magnificent collection of bronze figurines* from the Renaissance, Mannerist and Baroque periods.

San Giorgio castle. The first 13th-century fortress was gradually demolished, rebuilt in 1371 and enlarged in the 17th and 18th centuries. The Museo del Castello di S. Giorgio has a very good archeological section, famed above all for its 19 precious anthropomorphic sandstone statue-stelae* dating from the Bronze and Iron Ages.

Arsenale. This was one of the first and most important public works undertaken by the newly-united Italy. In just a few decades, the naval arsenal transformed the social and economic structure of the city, as well as its physical layout. The architect behind the design of the industrial and military complex and the new town plan was D. Chiodo. Having been severely damaged by allied bombing raids, after WW II, the Arsenal was carefully and painstakingly reconstructed. To the left of its monumental entrance is the Museo Tecnico Navale della Marina Militare (navy museum).

CINQUE TERRE

Visiting the Cinque Terre, listed since 1998 as a UNESCO World Heritage Site, means taking a dive into one of the most unspoiled corners of the coast in terms of history and landscape. Like the exquisite Sciacchetrà *passito* wine made here, the little towns are the result of centuries of hard work under conditions rendered even more difficult by the steepness of the land. Many are of the opinion that the best way to explore the Cinque Terre is to walk its demanding but well-maintained network of footpaths which are highly rewarding in terms of views, smells and sea breezes.

RIOMAGGIORE

The main street lies above the final, covered-over section of the Rivus Major Stream, after which the town is named. Tall, narrow houses stand on either side, forming two compact, parallel terraces. Monuments in the town include the parish church of S. Giovanni Battista (1340), with a Neogothic facade (but the rose window is original). Riomaggiore lies in the middle of a protected area which, amongst other things, regulates scuba diving activities in the stretch of sea offshore, one of the richest in Italy in terms of marine flora and fish species. The headquarters of the recently created **Parco Nazionale delle Cinque Terre** is in Riomaggiore. A panoramic footpath leads to the ruins of the castle (15-16C). A more demanding route leads to the sanctuary of the Madonna di Montenero (341 m), built on a hill above the town overlooking a broad stretch of sea. It can also be reached by car or by using the rack tramway known as the *trenino del vino* (wine train), normally used by local farmers to transport grapes. Recently, an Environmental Education Center was established at Torre Guardiola, on the Montenero promontory. There is a botanical route where you can learn all about the species of the Mediterranean scrubland, a birdwatching hide and an innovative "writing route", which encourages visitors to observe and write about the local wildlife. One of the most famous walks in the Cinque Terre starts at Riomaggiore: the **Via dell'Amore***, a footpath carved out of the rock in the 1920s. Poised above the sea, it winds its way past geological formations and wonderful views to Manarola.

Riomaggiore is the start of the Via dell'Amore.

MANAROLA

Dramatically situated on a huge black rock with a sheer drop down to the sea, the town spreads gradually down to a tiny port. The perimeter of the houses on the outer edge of the town, unusually striking on account of its shape and colors, corresponds to the original size of the castle, destroyed in 1273. The **church of S. Lorenzo** (or of the Natività di Maria), built in 1338, is a remarkable building and stands in a fine position dominating the town. The Gothic facade has a rose window while, inside, there are three good 15th-century artworks.

CORNIGLIA

This delightful little town, built on the ridge of a promontory about 100 m above the sea, has the atmosphere of a hill-town rather than a seaside town, apart from its magnificent view, of course. 365 steps connect the town to the sea and the train station. The layout of the town, the traditions of its inhabitants and their relationship with the neighboring hills have resulted in a town based on farming, especially growing vines.

VERNAZZA

The town, situated at the mouth of the Vernazzola Stream (now covered up) boasts the only little yacht harbor in the Cinque Terre. The medieval town was built around it and is still in place, with fine architectural features testifying to the fact that the town was richer than its neighbors. The view of the town includes two mighty Genoese lookout towers, and the charming Ligurian Gothic **church of S. Margherita d'Antiochia**, arranged, unusually, on two levels.

MONTEROSSO AL MARE

There are two parts to Monterosso. The old town, although its appearance has been marred somewhat since the railway was built between the town and its beautiful beach, has the typical atmosphere of other towns in the Cinque Terre, with narrow streets winding up the hill. The seaside resort area of **Fegina**, on the other hand, looks like any other resort, but has a noble and longstanding tradition. For example, it was here that the Montale family from Genoa used to come on holiday. The old town has two fine churches. The parish church of S. Giovanni Battista, on the little square, has a typical Gothic facade with horizontal stripes and a magnificent carved rose window. The **church of S. Francesco** (1619), situated at the top of the hill next to a Capuchin monastery, contains some good paintings: a *Crucifixion* and a *Mocking of Christ* by B. Castello, *La Veronica* by B. Strozzi, a *Penitent St Jerome* by L. Cambiaso and a *Pietà*, possibly by the same artist.

PORTOFINO AND GULF OF TIGULLIO

When you think of the word "riviera," this elegant section of the Riviera di Levante is probably what comes to mind: once a watering hole of high society, now a popular resort area, made lovely by nature and tirelessly improved upon by man. They've been seen a thousand times, yet they never grow old – sun, sea, palm trees, colorful houses, jagged rocks, dishes laden with seafood. Generations of the leisured class have planted exotic plants here. The olive tree is a symbol of the Mediterranean landscape, but it was introduced to these dizzying terraced slopes 300 years ago; just 150 years ago, odd to say, the farmers here planted "grapevines beneath the olive trees, and between the rows of vines wheat and rye..." (D. Bertolotti, 1838). Seaside villas are girt with medieval towers and a vast array of eclectic styles; a few are authentic mansions of Genoan nobles. There are also turn-of-the-century hotels and many noteworthy monuments, such as the 13th-century basilica, S. Salvatore dei Fieschi.

NOT TO BE MISSED

Nervi* is a famed resort town with an enchanting marina, waterfront promenade, and the Serra-Gropallo park. **Camogli***: this ancient fishing village has tall, colorful houses, facing the sunny waterfront; on the second Sunday in May, the chararteristic annual Fish Festival takes place here. Portofino Vetta, a fine panoramic viewpoint (416 m), is the starting point of many paths that pass through the Monte di Portofino nature reserve. **San Lorenzo della Costa**: in the parish church, is an exquisite late-15th-century Flemish triptych. **Santa Margherita Ligure***: straddling two inlets, this little seaside resort town still has the

Portofino is a favored destination of the rich.

dignified elegance of the 19th century, when it was developed; it is surrounded by villas with parks. **Paraggi**, a small cluster of houses once inhabited by fishermen and millers, who ran its 20 mills; note the landscape around the inlet. **Portofino** (➡ see below): the tall houses overlooking the little marina are no longer inhabited by sailors and fishermen, but by celebrities and society folk; by boat or via a footpath, you can reach **San Fruttuoso di Capodimonte***, a remarkable little village. **Monte di Portofino***, a unique promontory on the Ligurian coast, is crisscrossed by trails through the Mediterranean maquis, or underbrush, with fine views of jagged coastline. **San Michele di Pagana** has colorful houses lining the beach; in the parish church is a canvas by A. Van Dyck. **Rapallo** is an elegant resort town which has expanded in recent years, though the waterfront is still intact. **Chiavari** is a historical little town with a lively center lined with low porticoes and dignified 19th-century architecture; at a distance of 4.5 km, across the Entella River is the 13[th]century **Basilica dei Fieschi***, one of the most important Romanesque-Gothic buildings in Liguria. **Sestri Levante**: the promontory shelters the delightful hidden inlet to the south known as the Baia del Silenzio, an important holiday resort.

PORTOFINO

This town lies on the southernmost extremity of the Monte di Portofino. Around a little seaside square and along the natural port is a fringe of Ligurian houses, tall, narrow, and brightly colored. In the water, during the high season, are luxury yachts flying every imaginable flag and elegant parties are the rule here. Inland, among the pines and holm-oaks, are the villas that were exclusive and elegant at the turn of the 20th century.

The port. As you stroll through the main square and then along the waterfront, you will enjoy remarkable scenes and landscapes of all sorts. The natural setting becomes even more spectular if you go to a corner of the square and take the Salita S. Giorgio up to the church of S. Giorgio, which grandly surveys two bodies of water (on one side the open sea, on the other the bay). From the church courtyard you can enter the **S. Giorgio** castle, a 19th-century adaptation of an existing building; beneath the church, a little lane runs out among the Mediterranean pine trees of the promontory, leading to the lighthouse at the tip of the Cape; from here you will enjoy a majestic view of the Gulf of Tigullio and the coast as far south as Sestri Levante.

RIVIERA DI PONENTE

Landscape and climate vary considerably as you follow this stretch of the Ligurian Riviera; Bordighera is considerably south of Genoa. Contrary to common belief, the "tall palm trees" were introduced much earlier than the 19th century, when the English first discovered this part of Italy; L. Alberti wrote about them in 1550, describing the vegetation as "lovely to behold and fragrant as well," adding that there are "delightful gardens, in which to rest and banish all melancholy." And the description holds true. If you expect this coast road to offer a continual view of the sea, "as it murmurs and whitens the length of the shore" (Tasso), bear in mind that the sight, smell, and sound of the sea can be had only on beaches and waterfront promenades. This road offers only a few fine views, mainly from the capes and points (Noli, Mele, Cervo, Berta, for example). Along the so-called "Riviera dei Fiori," or Riviera of Flowers, in the westernmost section of the route, there is a profusion of greenhouses. There are many places to stop and enjoy the sights and artworks, but they must be sought out with patience and skill.

NOT TO BE MISSED

Savona (➡ see below): the Priamar fortress and the church of Nostra Signora di Castello, with a splendid polyptych of the Madonna and saints**. **Noli***: an ancient village beneath the fortified Ursino castle. **Varigotti**, with singular terrace-roof Ligurian houses. **Finale Ligure**: don't miss the 15th-century town walls at Finalborgo, the historical section of town. **Loano**, with the renowned caverns of Toirano*. **Albenga*** is the centerpiece of this route, in terms of atmosphere and monuments; note the Museo Navale Romano. **Alassio***: an extensive and elegant beachside resort; take a boat to the Isola Gallinara. **Laigueglia**, with the nearby Colla Micheri (162 m; 3 km away), a perfect little village with olive groves. **Cervo***, an intact Ligurian fishing village. **Imperia** (➡ see below). **Oneglia** and **Porto Maurizio**, two towns with two ports flanking the city. **Taggia***, a well preserved ancient village, dotted with lovely sights; there are paintings by L. Brea in S. Domenico church. **Bussana Vecchia**, partly destroyed in 1887, is now an art "colony." **Sanremo***: the Pigna, the medieval center of town with steep narrow streets overlooks the 19th-century resort town. **Bordighera*** is an elegant sunny town shaded by palm trees; the petroglyphs in the Museo biblioteca Clarence Bicknell are worth seeing. **Ventimiglia** still has a medieval air; to the east are Roman archeological excavations. **Mortola Inferiore** boasts the celebrated Giardini Hanbury, a botanical garden on the steep slopes. **Balzi Rossi***, or red cliffs, the tower over the sea; the caverns inhabited by humans in the Paleolithic epoch and the museum are noteworthy.

SAVONA

Some towns become famous tourist destinations regardless of their real merits whereas others, having established themselves in economic or productive sectors, have treasures which nobody even knows exist. Savona is one of these. In fact, Savona keeps its attractions well hidden, revealing them only to people who are really interested and are willing to pay more than a flying visit. A passing visitor is likely to focus on the quays of the port and the industrial complexes (many now abandoned) which have engulfed the seaward side of the old town, making it look rather ugly and off-putting. They conceal the town's considerable artistic and architectural treasures, which can only be discovered by exploring the streets of the old town on foot. Indeed, in the post-war period the productive areas of Savona were at the center of a debate as to whether the city was a trading/port town, a crossroads or a tourist hub. Historically, the city was

a port and a military fortress, although it has always had a duplicity: on the one hand, it was a seaward looking rival of Genoa, on the other, it looked inland to Piedmont.

Priamar. This great fortress, begun by the Genoese in 1542 (as a base for its garrison), stands on the hill where the first town of Savona was established, and was then destroyed, together with the old *castrum* and the first cathedral. It was then altered many times, and was recently converted into a major museum complex. We particularly recommend visiting the castle, since it offers not only a splendid example of military architecture (with magnificent views from the ramparts), but also the excellent museums described below.

Pinacoteca Civica. Situated on the third floor of Palazzo della Loggia, the gallery gives an insight into Ligurian painting from the Middle Ages to the 18th century. Undoubtedly, the most interesting section is the one devoted to art of the 14th-15th centuries, which includes two splendid **Crucifixions***, respectively by D. de' Bardi and G. Mazone, who also painted the magnificent polyptych depicting the *Annunciation*, *Calvary and Saints*. The rooms devoted to 17th-18th-century painting contain works by painters whose art is to be found in many of the churches and oratories around Genoa and Savona. The ceramics section has some excellent examples of the ancient local pottery tradition, whose fame spread far beyond the local area.

Civico Museo Storico-Archeologico del Priamar. Also located in Palazzo della Loggia, the exhibits refer to the original settlement of Savona that was established on this hill. Archeologists have excavated a necropolis dating from the 5th-6th centuries AD, and the route includes a visit to the excavations. Other items of interest include some mosaic floors made by North African craftsmen (3-4C AD). There are also artifacts from the Bronze Age, some Etruscan bucchero ware (7-6C BC) and a Greek skyphos (5C BC).

Torre di Leon Pancaldo. This small tower looking out to sea, decorated with a statue of the Madonna of Mercy, was erected in the 14th century. It is named after the navigator from Savona who accompanied Magellan on his voyages and died tragically in 1537 on the Rio de la Plata. On the side facing the sea is a couplet dedicated to the Madonna which sounds the same in both Italian and Latin: *In mare irato, in subita procella, invoco Te, nostra benigna stella* (Amid an angry sea, surrounded by misfortune, we invoke Your name, our benign star). Next to it is Via Paleocapa, the town's lively, busy main street, whose elegant porticoes on either side shelter several shops.

Via Pia. This narrow street, packed with shops of all kinds, yet retaining its monumental dignity, is the hub of Savona's old town. Its medieval origins are still very apparent. Notice the many beautiful slate doorways (15-16C) with carved lintels. no.1, Palazzo Sormani, dates from the 16th century and is decorated with frescoes; no.5, Palazzo Della Rovere-Cassinis, has the typical lines of the Ligurian Renaissance. Beyond the old square of Piazza della Maddalena, no. 26 is Palazzo Pavese Spinola (16C), which still has a few frescoes of grotesques in the atrium. Palazzo Della Rovere, begun in 1495, is now the Police Headquarters at no. 28 Via Pia. From 1673 onwards, it was the convent of the Clarisse (Poor Clares), so that it was given the name of "Palazzo S. Chiara", but it has lost its beautiful interior decoration which was plastered over for religious reasons. At the beginning of the 19th century, it became the Prefecture under Napoleon Bonaparte.

Duomo. A walk along Via Sansoni and Via Vacciuoli brings us to the cathedral dedicated to St Mary of the Assumption, built in 1589-1605 (although the facade is 19C). Inside, against the back of the facade, is a marble **Crucifix*** dating from the late 15th century and a font made out of a Byzantine capital, with carved balustrades; it has a remarkable *pulpit of the Evangelists* (1522) and even better carved **wooden choirstalls*** (1500). In the chapel to the right of the high altar is a **Madonna and Child Enthroned with Sts Peter and Paul***, a masterpiece by A. Piazza, and a 16th-century marble relief depicting the *Presentation of the Virgin*. Notice the harmony of the Mannerist decoration of the fourth chapel on the left, and, near it, the 14th-century bas-relief of the *Assumption*.

Nostra Signora di Castello. In Corso Italia, this oratory, which is quite well hidden, contains a **Madonna and Saints****, a splendid monumental late 15th-century polyptych by Vincenzo Foppa, completed by L. Brea. Notice also the tallest existing set of carved figures used in processions, a *Deposition* by F. Martinengo (1795). Along with Via Paleocapa, the long, straight Corso Italia, with its elegant shops, is the other main thoroughfare in the area into which Savona expanded in the 19th century.

IMPERIA

In 1923, Oneglia and Porto Maurizio were combined to form a single administrative unit called Imperia. Almost 80 years on from then, the two parts of Imperia still look like two quite distinct towns. Indeed, the difference is magnified by the very different layouts, which is partly the result of geography. Oneglia, prevalently modern, lies at the mouth of the Impero Stream, while Porto Maurizio, which is full of historical interest, is situated on a hill overlooking the sea. The hinterland is extremely varied in terms of landscape. The terraced hills around the town are covered with an endless expanse of olive groves, the main resource of the area since early medieval times. There are plenty of sites to visit in the surrounding area. Most of these date from the medieval and Baroque periods, sometimes hidden away in picturesque mountain villages and in the towns dotted along the coast. However, the coastal towns are often busy and tend to be dominated by tourism.

ONEGLIA

The admiral A. Doria and writer E. De Amicis are the town's most famous sons. During the 20th century, a thriving industrial zone boosted the town's traditional resources, based on its port and the cultivation of olives, yet it is still pervaded by a small-town atmosphere. No. 4 of the centrally located Piazza Dante is overlooked by the eclectic pseudo-medieval facade of the former Palazzo Comunale (1890-91). Palazzo del Tribunale, in Piazza De Amicis, dates from almost the same time (1891-92) and is the birthplace of E. De Amicis. Near the harbor, fish shops and restaurants are sheltered by the characteristic porticoes of Calata G. B. Cuneo. Behind them stands the collegiate church of S. Giovanni Battista, begun in 1739. It has a large dome and is divided into a nave and two aisles, separated by pillars. The marble tabernacle on the left of the presbytery is by the Gagini family (1516). In the fourth chapel of the left aisle is a late 17th-century crucifix, while the first chapel contains a Madonna of the Rosary. The **Museo dell'Olivo***, in the Fratelli Carli olive-oil plant in Via Garessio sums up 6,000 years of olive cultivation in this area.

PORTO MAURIZIO

Apart from the Palazzo Municipale (Town Hall, 1932), there is not much else of interest in Viale Matteotti, the main road connecting Oneglia to the western part of the town. In Porto Maurizio, on the other hand, there is no shortage of interesting buildings. For example the cathedral, completed between 1781 and 1838, is a building with majestic proportions, designed according to the tenets of the Neo-Classic style. The pronaos, with its eight Doric columns, leads into the church proper, built on a central plan. It contains a rich collection of 19th-century paintings in addition to works from the former parish church of S. Maurizio, now demolished. They include a statue of the Madonna of Mercy (1618), in the second chapel on the right, and, in the third chapel on the left, a crucifix in typical Genoese style. In Piazza Duomo, which was laid out when the church was built, stand the Pinacoteca Civica (art gallery) and, at No. 11, the Museo Navale Internazionale del Ponente Ligure.

Although the exhibition space available is somewhat limited, the museum has an interesting display of nautical objects, with an excellent section about life on board a ship.

Porto Maurizio is a residential area of Imperia.

Parasio name*. The old port of Porto Maurizio, comes from the palace of the ruler of Genoa ("Paraxu"). In the late 20th century, after a long period of decline, foreign investment poured into the town to improve its commercial status. Starting in Piazza del Duomo, Via Acquarone leads up towards Palazzo Pagliari (14-16C), with its portico of pointed arches. Further up, at the top of the hill, is Piazza Chiesa Vecchia, named after the church of S. Maurizio, which was demolished in about 1838. The "Paraxu" stood on the same square. The three churches on the seaward side of the Parasio are all decorated in the Baroque style. The 17th-century oratory of S. Leonardo contains a painting by G. De Ferrari (*Our Lady of Sorrows with Souls in Purgatory*) and two by D. Bocciardo (*Death of St Joseph and Tobias Buries the Dead*). The house next to the oratory is the birthplace of the titular saint. The convent of S. Chiara (14C), on the other hand, is of medieval origin. It was rebuilt in the 18th century. Inside there are several good artworks: *St Domenico Soriano and the Madonna* and a *Madonna and Child with St Catherine of Bologna*. Behind the church, the convent has a beautiful portico* with spectacular views on to the sea. The church of S. Pietro, a 17th-century reworking of an earlier church, belonged to a confraternity of merchants. The facade (1789) is very dramatic, with three arches on coupled columns, and a small belfry made from a converted lookout tower. The cycles of paintings (depicting the *Life of St Peter*) inside the church are by T. and M. Carrega.

In 1358 the Italian writer, poet and Humanist F. Petrarca (whom we know in English as Petrarch), described Genoa as follows: "You will see a regal city built on the mountainside, superb for its men and its walls: the mere sight of the city is enough to merit the title signora del mar (lady of the sea)...". Genoa was founded on the sea in about 500 BC. Right from the beginning (and still today) it was a crossing-point between two important transport networks: maritime routes, which led from here across the waters of the Mediterranean, and land routes, which wound up over the Apennines into the north of Italy and thence to the rest of Europe and beyond. These two networks were mainly used for trade, but, over the centuries, they also enabled people of different cultures to travel widely and foreigners to reach Genoa. Today, the city stands in a charming setting with all the fascination and the thousand faces of a city of art and architecture with a long, complex history. Genoa is currently going through a phase of regeneration that will take the city into a new and dynamic future.

Palazzo Doria Pamphilj. This building, also known as Palazzo del Principe, was built for Admiral Andrea Doria. It has an elegant entrance designed by the Florentine Perin del Vaga, to whom the admiral entrusted the decoration of his entire residence (1528-33). The artist amply repaid this trust, as we can see in the frescoes of Andrea Doria's magnificent apartments: starting in the atrium (*Stories of the Roman Kings and Triumphs*), we continue to the Loggia of the Heroes (ancestors of the Doria family) and the great hall of the Fall of the Giants (*Zeus Hurling Thunderbolts at the Giants*). In the hall is the famous portrait of A. Doria dressed in the uniform of the papal fleet. The Galleria contains a series of splendid **tapestries** made in Brussels in 1582-91. The south facade is just as grand: its porticoes and patios overlook the garden, laid out on a series of terraces at the end of the 16th century. In the center of the park stands the Fountain of Neptune (1599).

D'Albertis Castle. Not far from the Porta Principe train station is D'Albertis castle which was given to Captain E. Alberto D'Albertis, a famous navigator, and now houses the collections of the Museo delle Culture del Mondo. In addition to the captain's legacy, which includes ancient weapons, nautical instruments and geographical publications, there is a collection of items exhibited by the American Catholic missions at the Great Exhibition of 1892. By walking along Via Gramsci, we see the church of S. Giovanni di Pré, built in 1180, and the adjoining Commenda, a convent dating from 1508 which now houses temporary exhibitions.

Palazzo Ducame/Royal Palace. The building was given its name by the Savoys, who took possession of the palazzo in 1824. Everything inside the main entrance is worthy of a royal palace, including the brightly-painted facades surrounding the main courtyard. At the far end of it, beyond the three-arched gateway, a hanging garden overlooks the sea, with a two-color mosaic pavement made with cobbles recovered from the demolished convent of the Turchine. The staircase on the left leads to the *piano nobile*, which houses the **Museo di Palazzo Reale**. 17th-century frescoes and fine furnishings (18-19C) enhance the setting of many important artworks. This juxtaposition is particularly striking in the Gallery of Mirrors, with its four fine statues (**Hyacinth**, Clitie, Amore and Venus). The Hall of Audiences contains two very valuable paintings: the *Rape of Proserpine* by V. Castello and the portrait of Caterina Durazzo by A. Van Dyck, who also painted the Crucifix in the King's Bedroom. The silk hangings in the Hall of Peace were painted by G. F. Romanelli to look like tapestries. Behind Palazzo Reale is Palazzo dell'Università. This palazzo has a similar structure: an atrium, a raised courtyard and a double staircase in the refined 17th-century style (note the coupled columns of the portico). The whole palace was restored to its former glory in the 1980s and 1990s and is now open to the public.

Church of the SS. Annunziata del Vastato*. Via Balbi leads to Piazza della Nunziata, site of the church of SS. Annunziata del Vastato, rebuilt in 1591-1625, above a late-Gothic church. The facade is graced by two bell towers. The spectacular interior is built on a Latin-cross plan, splendidly decorated with inlaid red and white marble, gold-painted stuccoes and frescoes executed by the finest Genoese artists. From here we walk down Via Campo, and across Piazza Fossatello to visit the **church of S. Siro**. This was Genoa's first cathedral and dates from the 4th century. When S. Lorenzo became the city's cathedral (9C), it was rebuilt in the Romanesque style. In 1580 the basilica was destroyed by fire, and rebuilt in the form we see today. The splendid doorway on the right facade dates from this period. The bell tower, the last vestige of the Romanesque church, was demolished in 1904 because it was thought to be unstable. The interior, divided into a nave and two aisles by coupled columns, is richly decorated with polychrome marble and frescoes. It has a splendid black marble and bronze **high altar**. **Palazzo S. Giorgio**. This building dating from 1260 was the city's seat of government for only two years. In 1407, the palazzo became the headquarters of the Bank of S. Giorgio, hence its present name. In

The facade of the Cathedral of S. Lorenzo.

1570, the wing on the seaward side was added and, in 1606-08, the facade was decorated with splendid frescoes. It was altered in 1912, and carefully restored in 1990. In the majestic **Salone delle Compere** note the *Statues of the Bank's Protectors* and some fine paintings, such as the *Madonna depicted as the Queen of Genoa with St George*, by D. Piola (17C), Genoa's coat-of-arms and the *Symbols of Justice and Fortitude*. This is the area known as the Porto Antico (Old Port) which has been given a new lease of life by the famous architect R. Piano. The **Aquarium** is one of Genoa's greatest attractions and the third most visited monument in Italy. A few figures will explain why it is the biggest in Europe: more than 6,000 specimens of 600 marine species, 62 tanks and almost 10,000 m² of exhibition space. One of them is the *Grande Nave Blu* (Big Blue Ship), with exhibits of fish, crustaceans and rare reptiles and plants from Madagascar.

Close by is **Porta Siberia** or **Porta del Molo**, the mighty bastion designed by G. Alessi (1553), part of the city's 16th-century fortifications. It was important as the stronghold of the port area and was also the customs office. **Cathedral of S. Lorenzo**. The city's cathedral for more than 1,000 years. Founded in the 9th century, it was preferred to S. Siro because it stood within the city walls. In the early 12th century, it was rebuilt in the Romanesque style but never completed. The two **side doors**, known respectively as the doors of St John and St Gothard, date from this period. The cathedral began to take on its current appearance in the early 13th century, when the first tier of the facade was added with its motif of grey and white horizontal stripes. Other features dating from this period include the column-bearing lions and the so-called *arrotino* (knife-grinder) which actually depicts a saint with a sundial. At the end of the same century the second tier of the facade with its two-light windows was added. The upper tier, decorated with mullioned windows and a rose window, was added in the 15th century, along with the loggia of the left tower. The bell tower and the dome were completed in the 16th century. When Via S. Lorenzo was laid out and the level of the square lowered, the front steps were added. The interior has a nave and two aisles. On the back of the facade is a remarkable early 14th-century fresco of the *Last Judgement* and the *Glorification of the Virgin*. In the left aisle, just beyond the entrance to the baptistery, is the **chapel of St John the Baptist***, with an elaborate front dating from 1451. At the end of the aisle, the Lercari chapel is decorated with frescoes. In the right aisle, in the Senarega chapel has an altar-piece (*Crucifixion with the Virgin, St John and St Sebastian*) painted in 1597 by F. Barocci. Also worthy of note are the wooden choirstalls and the frescoes in the vault of the apse. Beyond the sacristy (door on left of presbytery) is the **Museo del Tesoro della Cattedrale di San Lorenzo**. Steps lead down to four rooms lined with black stone from Promontorio, an interesting setting for the objects on display: the **Sacro Catino*** (holy bowl), a symbol of the cathedral, traditionally identified with the Holy Grail but actually a work of Islamic origin; the **Reliquary of the Ashes of St John the Baptist*** by T. Danieli and S. Caldera (1438-45), still used in the annual procession of June 24. The fine **Zaccaria Cross*** is a Byzantine reliquary dating from the 10th century but remodelled in the 13th century, decorated with gold leaf, pearls and oriental gems. According to tradition, the fragments of wood inside are from the True Cross.

Piazza S. Matteo. This square was surrounded by the mansions and the church of the Doria family. Their power is reflected in the buildings around its edge, for example Palazzo Andrea Doria (no. 17). On the left side of the square are Palazzo di Domenicaccio Doria (no. 16) and Palazzo Branca Doria (entrance at no. 1 Vico Falamonica). Their characteristic light and dark striped facades date the buildings to the second half of the 13th century.

Church of S. Matteo*. The church was founded earlier (1125), but rebuilt in 1278. The Doria used it as their private chapel and the inscriptions around the base refer to the military successes of members of the family. The interior, richly decorated with frescoes, stuccoes and marble, was commissioned in the 16th century by Andrea Doria, whose remains lie in the sarcophagus below the crypt. Partly concealed, to the left of the church, is the cloister, with pointed arches resting on coupled columns (1308-10).

Palazzo Ducale/Ducal Palace. Designed by Vannone (1591-ca. 1620), the facade overlooking Piazza De Ferrari is decorated with colorful frescoes while the Neo-Classic facade overlooking Piazza Matteotti has a double order of coupled columns and, on top, an attic storey topped with statues and trophies. The interior, now used for temporary exhibitions and other cultural events, has two courtyards surrounded by columns. Two flights of stairs lead up to the loggia above, where the state rooms are arranged around the west courtyard. There is also a chapel with frescoes (Glories of Genoa) painted in about 1655 by G. B. Carlone, and the halls of the Great and Small Councils, which were rebuilt in 1780-83 after a fire.

Porta di S. Andrea or Porta Soprana**. Today this door marks the dividing line between the historic center and the modern city. The gateway stands in a position which, together with its beautiful lines has become one of the city's most famous views. The bastion, formerly part of the 9th-century fortifications, was rebuilt in 1155. Set between the two towers and built on a semi-circular plan, the bastion has

A narrow street in the heart of Genoa.

a pointed arch with small blind arches, merlons and a chemin-de-ronde. Not far away is the church of S. Agostino, adjoining a former Augustinian monastery dating from before 1260. Its facade, divided into three parts, has the recurring motif of dark and light-colored stripes. Above the right transept, the fine 15th-century **bell tower** has a spire and four pinnacles decorated with polychrome majolica tiles. In 1995, the church was converted into an auditorium, whereas the former monastery now houses the Museo di S. Agostino. It contains architectural features and artworks such as the remains of the **funerary monument of Margaret of Brabant*** (1313-14) and a **Penitent St Mary Magdalene*** by A. Canova (1796).

S. Donato. this church is one of the finest examples of the Genoese Romanesque style (early 12C). It has a splendid octagonal bell tower** with two tiers of two-light windows (the third was added in the 19C). During restoration work in the late 19th century, a rose window and the pseudo-porch with columns were added. The doorway with the deep embrasure and the arch are original. On the right side of the church is a small shrine with a dove representing the Holy Spirit, containing a statue of the Madonna and Child. The interior is divided into a nave and two aisles by columns, six of which are re-used Roman columns. Above the colonnade is a fake matroneum spanned by two-light windows. The chapel of St Joseph situated halfway down the left aisle contains a fine **triptych*** with doors dating from 1515.

S. Maria di Castello. The word "Castello" refers to the fortifications built on the hill in pre-Roman times. The first church to be built on the site of the present one dates from the 10th-11th century. The Romanesque church we see today was begun in the early 12th century. It has a basilica plan with a nave and two aisles and a fake matroneum above the arches. Many of the columns and capitals are re-used Roman material (2-3C AD). In 1441, the church was given by Pope Eugenius IV to the Dominicans, who built the chapels of the great Genoese families and the convent next door. The dome, built on an octagonal plan, dates from the following century. Inside the church (4C chapel on the right) note the *Martyrdom of St Peter of Verona*. However, the finest artworks are kept in the **Sale dei Ragusei**. These rooms can be accessed from the sacristy (door in right transept). Amongst other works, they contain a *Madonna and Child* by B. da Modena and a *Coronation of the Virgin* by L. Brea (1513). The convent is also very interesting and has a superb **fresco** painted in 1451 by "Iustus de Alemania". Left of the church, 41 m high, is the **Torre degli Embriaci** (12C): this is the sole tower to survive an edict issued in 1296 limiting the height of towers in the city.

S. Maria Assunta in Carignano. The church stands on the top of the hill which gives it its name. G. Alessi designed it and oversaw the building work which lasted 50 years (1552-1602). It has a Greek-cross plan and consists of a cube with a central dome resting on pillars and four smaller domes at the corners. It should also have had four bell towers, but only two were built on the main facade, which was altered in 1722. Inside, the niches in two of the pillars supporting the dome contain two magnificent statues (**Blessed Alessandro Sauli*** and **St Sebastian***), dating from 1668. It has many fine paintings, including the **Martyrdom of St Blaise** above the second altar on the right and the **Pietà*** above the third altar on the left. Note also the painting of *St Francis receiving the Stigmata* by Guercino, and the organ (1656) with its painted organ-doors. Not far away is the Museo Civico di Storia Naturale Giacomo Doria, founded in 1867 and in its present location since 1912. It has one of the finest collections in Europe, especially its splendid zoological collection. It has many exhibits from outside Europe and is particularly proud of its entomological collection, the largest in Italy.

S. Stefano. Without wishing to do an injustice to the facade, the church is best approached from the rear, because the steps leading to it from Viale IV Novembre have lovely views of the **apse***, a masterpiece of Romanesque art, sitting on a base punctured with the small windows of the crypt. The facade, almost suspend-

ed over Via XX Settembre, features that motif so common in Genoa's churches of black and white stripes, as well as a large rose window. It has a gable roof, another common feature in Genoa, and the bell tower stands behind. Inside, note the superb **Martyrdom of St Stephen***, painted in 1524 by G. Romano. Also look out for the choir on the back of the facade and the **Martyrdom of St Bartholomew** in the presbytery. By walking along Via XX Settembre you come to Piazza De Ferrari, the center of 20th-century Genoa, with its equestrian monument of Garibaldi. Facing it, the Teatro Carlo Felice (theater) has an extraordinary stage, with four mobile platforms controlled by sophisticated computer systems.

Via Garibaldi. Originally the "Strada Nuova" was laid out in 1551 by architect Bernardino as a residential street. There was no external access at the time. Only very wealthy families could afford to build mansions there in the years between 1558 and 1583. The street was opened to traffic at the end of the 18th century. In the two centuries that followed, the houses built by the great families of Genoa were gradually taken over by the city's banks, antique shops and exclusive private clubs, which were able to maintain this considerable artistic and architectural heritage. It is now a pedestrian precinct and the street and the houses on either side of it have been declared a UNESCO World Heritage Site. The rooms of the *piano nobile* of **Palazzo Cambiaso** (No. 1), are decorated with Mannerist frescoes. P. Orsolino carved the reclining figures (*Prudence and Vigilance*) on the marble doorway of the house opposite, **Palazzo Gambaro** (No. 2), built in 1558-64. The nearby **Palazzo Carrega Cataldi** (no. 4) was completed in 1561, and designed by B. Cantone and G. B. Castello: the latter also painted the frescoe in the atrium; the splendid Rococò gallery. **Palazzo Lercari Parodi** (no. 3) has an unusual courtyard in front of the main building, making it look even more splendid, and suggests that it was built later than the houses nearby, which all follow the "enclosed block" pattern. **Palazzo Spinola** (no. 5) has particularly fine decoration on the *piano nobile*. There is a splendid hall on the *piano nobile* of **Palazzo Doria** (no. 6), with an ornate 18th-century fireplace. The facade of the building dates from the late 16th century, another work by the team of Cantone and Castello (1563-67). Between 1563 and 1566, they also built **Palazzo Podestà** (No. 7), still privately owned, with a magnificent Mannerist facade: three tiers decorated with figures and a delightful atrium decorated with stuccoes. There is even a nymphaeum in the courtyard. Nearby **Palazzo Campanella** (no. 12) was altered in the late 18th century, but was badly damaged by air raids in 1942.

Palazzo del Municipio**. The first things that catch the eye in Palazzo del Municipio are the extraordinary dimensions of the front of the building, the length of which is three times as long as the symmetrically equal facades of the other palazzi. Its splendid staircase leads up to the colonnaded courtyard where two flights of steps climb up to a loggia. The decoration of the facade is enhanced by motifs of white and pink marble and slabs of grey slate. In 1596, the palazzo was bought by the Doria family, who began to build the loggias at the side and to landscape the garden. More additions were made in 1820, when the clocktower was erected. Although the palazzo is splendid architecturally, the actual decoration is comparatively restrained.

Palazzo Rosso*. The palace took six years to build (1671-77). Its name is supposed to derive from the red stones decorating the facade. One of the first works in the **art gallery** housed in the palazzo is a **Portrait of a Man*** ("Principe moscovita") formerly attributed to Pisanello, and now thought to be by Giambono; the **Portrait of a Young Man*** painted in 1506 by A. Dürer bears his signature. In the next room is a **Judith with the head of Holophernes**** by Veronese, also an **Annunciation*** by L. Carracci and a **St Sebastian*** by G. Reni; the **Death of Cleopatra**** is by Guercino. There are also works by O. Gentileschi (**Madonna and Sleeping Child***), M. Preti (**Clorinda frees Olindo and Sofronia***), B. Strozzi (**The Cook, Madonna and Child and the young St John***), the **Allegories of the seasons*** by De Ferrari (*Spring, Summer*) and D. Piola (*Fall, Winter*).

Palazzo Bianco*. Although the palace is not so fine architecturally, it has a charming **art gallery**. One section of the gallery is devoted to the works of Caravaggio (**Ecce Homo***) and his followers. Not far from here, Piazza della Meridiana is named after the sundial (18C) on the facade of the palazzo of the same name, built in 1541-45. Inside (entrance at no. 4 Salita S. Francesco), there are two fresco cycles by L. Cambiaso.

Spianata Castelletto. A rack tramway connects Piazza Portello to the **Belvedere Montaldo****, which has marvelous views over the old city and the old port. The Art-Deco windows of the station at the top have an old-fashioned charm.

Port. In the 10th-12th centuries work began to build the port on a site that had been used as a natural harbor in Roman times (and was probably used even before that by the local inhabitants). In the second half of the 14th century, a dockyard was built with an arsenal attached. At the beginning of the 17th century, the first quantum leap forward was achieved with the construction of the Molo Nuovo (new mole) and the establishment of a "free port". More building work was undertaken under the House of Savoy in the second half of the 19th century, when the whole complex was reorganized. Between the Molo Nuovo and the Molo Vecchio, 11 long jetties and 18 quays were built, protected by the 1,500 m-long Duca di Galliera breakwater. Boat tours of the port leave from Ponte Spinola and Calata Zingari. Beyond the old port and Porto della Darsena (docks) is the area reserved for ferry traffic: cruise liners moor at Ponte dei Mille and Ponte Andrea Doria. Behind them, the modern tower-blocks of the San Benigno district, built in the last two decades of the 20th century, are more reminiscent of North America. A New York studio designed the unmistakable "Matitone" (Big Pencil), based on the bell tower of the church of S. Donato.

NERVI

So close and yet so different from the city of Genoa, Nervi is connected to it by the panoramic, winding Via Aurelia and the busy Corso Europa. In 1959, restoration work partially restored the original appearance of the church of S. Siro, erected in the first half of the 12th century and rebuilt in the 17th century. A charming 2 km walk called the **Passeggiata Anita Garibaldi**** winds along the coast past pink and yellow houses, beached boats, the mouth of a stream, crossing the occasional medieval bridge. A characteristic corner of Liguria is the little harbor at Nervi, protected by a dyke and the starting-point of a famous coastal walk. The English-style gardens of Villa Gropallo, Villa Serra and Villa Grimaldi are now incorporated in a large park called the **Parchi di Nervi***. The park has typical Mediterranean plant species as well as numerous exotic varieties. The setting is delightful by itself but the resident squirrel population and cultural references add to the overall feel. Another "must see", so to speak, is the garden of Villa Serra, now the Modern Art Gallery, with its magnificent **rose-garden***: there are incredible 800 species, which flower from May to November.

GENOA AQUARIUM

NEAR THE OLD PORT (PORTO ANTICO) AND SPINOLA BRIDGE

TEL. 0102345678

WEBSITE: WWW.ACQUARIO.GE.IT

OPEN: ALL YEAR (OPENING HOURS ON WEB-SITE)

ADMISSION: ADULTS € 15, CHILDREN (4-12 YEARS) € 9 AND DISABLED PEOPLE € 13.

HOW TO GET THERE:

BY CAR: A7 MILANO-GENOVA HIGHWAY, GENO-VA OVEST EXIT.

BY TRAIN: GENOVA PORTA PRINCIPE OR GENOVA BRIGNOLE STATIONS, THEN THE BUS.

The Genoa Aquarium, designed by R. Piano and P. Chermayeff and built in 1992, looks like a ship ready to set sail. It is easy to reach (only 10 minutes on foot from the Genova Porta Principe train station) and has good access for disabled people. It is located in the heart of the old port area and is one of the most popular outings in Italy. The aquarium covers most ocean and sea environments in the world, faithfully rebuilding numerous ecosystems. It is one of the largest aquariums in Europe, often attracting visitors because of the giant tanks that one can explore from various angles. You need at least two hours to visit it, but the numerous rest areas, toilets and snack bars make it a good day out for children as well. The visitors route takes you through two levels and the Great Blue Ship (Grande Nave Blu), an exhibition area that was opened in 1998, adding 2,700 m² to original 10,000 m². This new area is used to recreate some interesting environments, including one of Madagascar. The aquarium has over 6,000 animals and 600 different species, as well as plenty of vegetal species. The animals, housed in over 70 tanks, include various jellyfish and other invertebrates, fish, seals, sharks, dolphins and numerous other animals that are carefully looked after by a series of biology experts and vets. The tanks themselves are interesting, with some shaped unusually (like the cylindrical jellyfish tank), others extremely large and others designed so that visitors can actually touch the animals: the one with the rays is very popular among children, who seem unable to believe that they are actually allowed to touch the animals. Some of the tanks are enticing merely for the names: Neptune grass, ancient pier, moluccan islands, mangroves, central American forest, giant Japanese spidercrabs, waves on the reef and the flooded forest.

There never seems to be enough time for the dolphin tank, as they play and jump endlessly. In 2002, one of the dolphins, Bonnie, become a mom for the second time, causing the number of visitors to increase yet again (roughly 1.2 million annually). In the same year, the Genoa Aquarium became home to numerous homeless animals following the closure of the Marseilles aquarium. Some of these new arrivals, like the guitar-fish, were added to the new Mediterranean reef touch tank, an open display area that is designed to spread awareness about the problems linked to conserving and managing the eco-systems in our seas. In 2002, the 10th anniversary of the aquarium was celebrated by adding yet another display area, this time dedicated to the smallest birds in the world, namely hummingbirds. These birds are housed in a reconstruction of a lush rain forest and it costs a little more to see them (€ 2 for adults; € 1 for children). To help raise public awareness about marvelous but scary creatures like the shark, the aquarium has recently renewed the tank housing this sea predator. One of the elements the tank tries to highlight is that of the roughly 400 known species of shark, only 4 are known to attack man without provocation. Thus, to create a more realistic picture of sharks, the tank has a scenic backdrop that includes well made fiberglass rock and special lighting. Two sawfish swim with three species of shark (bull, gray, angel) and amberjack, gilthead, short sunfish and grouper. In short, the aquarium is an excellent, diverse outing.

Genoa's aquarium is one of the city's main attractions.

BEACHES

Italy's two main mountain ranges are the Alps and the Apennines, and Liguria is where they meet, resulting in a narrow region that hugs the coast amid a mountainous embrace. These are the elements that characterize the Riviera, perhaps seeming a little narrow for those more akin to open spaces, but charming nonetheless. As such, Liguria's beaches are often thin and pebbly, trapped between rocky cliffs that fall sharply into the sea. Yet, this landscape is precisely where the beauty of this coastline lies, especially when the sheer cliffs are broken by little bays and gulfs, although all too often these have been turned into harbors or jetties. The climate is mild thanks to the warm and humid winds that arrive from the sea and the mountainous barrier that blocks the cold northern winds. Finally, the region can also boast two marine protected areas: Portofino and Cinque Terre.

Balzi Rossi beach. Near France, along the Via Aurelia road, you find a lighthouse with a path that leads to a splendid, rocky stretch of coast. At the foot of one of these cliffs lies a series of caves and shelters that has been used since prehistoric times. You reach the beach from road to the Museo Preistorico. After passing the privately-managed beach – also called Egg Beach after the oval-shaped rocks – you need to continue until you come to a number of large, flat rocks that are ideal for lying in the sun. This is also a good scuba-diving spot.

Capo Verde seaside. This beach lies on the eastern side of Sanremo. To get there, you need to leave your car or bike on Via Aurelia near the roadman's house (parking is limited and it is easy to be fined). You then need to jump over the guardrail and head down the steep path to the reef: 150 m of relatively well preserved rocky beach, with small, crystal clear inlets that are filled with sea grass. The hidden nature of this beach means it is popular with nudists. There is no sand, only rocks and gravel. The only real downside is the purification plant.

Riva Ligure beach. Over the last few years, the main Italian environmental group, Legambiente, has organized the "Clean Beaches"

initiative on the last Sunday in May. The aim is to clean up as many of Italy's beaches as possible. Riva Ligure has a lovely reef with a shallow, pebbly seabed. The only facilities available for bathers are the showers.

Bergeggi isle. An ideal place for diving, you can get there by dinghy or boat, mooring at the little jetty on the northern side of the island. Along the coast, you can go to Punta delle Grotte (Cave Point) from Via Aurelia. In the various underwater caves, scuba divers can see stalactites and stalagmites. The zone is a regional reserve and it might become a national marine protected area.

Cinque Terre beaches. The two villages on the edges of Cinque Terre (Monterosso to the west and Riomaggiore to the east) are the only two beaches that can easily be reached by car. The others can be reached by boat (from Genoa or La Spezia) or on foot, following the "Azzurro Trail". Monterosso has a lovely sandy beach. A little before Punta Linà lies the Frate (or friar) reef. The point itself has a small natural tunnel, *Pertuso del Diavolo*, just on the water line, making it accessible for small boats. The beaches between Vernazza, Manarola and Corniglia lie along an impervious path. The Guvano beach deserves a mention alone as it is one of the most beautiful in the Cinque Terre park. You can reach it by following the very taxing path or, from the Corniglia station, by heading through a tunnel (although you must pay a toll).

Palmaria island. Also on the island, but this time facing Portovenere, you find an amazingly beautiful beach that is washed by the current that constantly flows through the Portovenere Channel. The beach is a mixture of rocks and gravel.

Monterosso beach in the Cinque Terre.

FOOD IN LIGURIA

The Ligurian landscape is dominated by olive groves. This region may not produce large quantities, but it has an extraordinary variety. For example, the vegetables and herbs grown here (like the basil used for pesto alla genovese), the foods produced in the mountains: salamis and cured meats, cheese, mushrooms and chestnuts, and fish and shellfish from the sea.

TYPICAL LOCAL DISHES

Focaccia genovese. Wheat flour, water and yeast are the ingredients of the famous Ligurian focaccia, flavored with rosemary, sage, origano, onions and even whitebait. The focaccia made in Recco is filled with soft fresh cheeses such as stracchino or crescenza.

Pansoti. The pasta dough is made with flour, water and white wine with a pinch of ground

garlic. The filling consists of borage, beet, herbs, ricotta and parmesan, and egg. Always served with a walnut sauce.

Trenette al pesto. Genoa's most famous dish. Pasta served with classic pesto made with basil, olive oil, garlic, parmesan, and pine nuts. In the classic version, the pasta and pesto are served with lightly-boiled thinly-sliced potatoes and young green beans.

Stoccafisso accomodato. Dried cod is cooked in olive oil, anchovies and herbs, before olives, pine nuts and potatoes. In Sanremo, it is called stoccafisso brand de cujun: other boiled cod is cut into small pieces, added to boiled potatoes and onions, and tossed with olive oil, garlic and parsley.

Tomaxelle. Delicious rolls of veal stuffed with calf's udder, minced veal, marjoram, parsley, garlic, mushrooms, pine nuts, cheese and egg cooked in white wine, tomatoes, a rich meat sauce and stock.

Amaretto di Sassello. A soft, light, friable biscuit made with ground almonds. In the classic recipe sweet and bitter almonds are mixed with egg whites and sugar.

TYPICAL LOCAL PRODUCTS

Olio Extravergine di Oliva Riviera Ligure DOP. There are three geographical labels according to where the oil comes from: Riviera dei Fiori from around Imperia, Riviera di Ponente (oil made mainly with Taggiasca olives), and Riviera di Levante, with the three cultivars Lavagnina, Razzola and Pignola. The first two are yellow with a mature fruit aroma and a fruity flavor with a hint of sweetness; oil from the Levante area is distinctive because of its greenish color, mild flavor and sweetish taste, with a strong, bitter after-taste.

Basilico genovese DOP. A special variety of basil with small leaves and a very strong smell. The main ingredient of pesto, Liguria's most famous sauce, is sold in bunches with the roots still attached. Basil from Prà is particularly good.

Acciughe sotto sale del Mar Ligure IGP. Anchovies are fished in the traditional way with the lampara¸ a small boat with a lamp at the front. Considerable quantities are caught, especially near La Spezia, and preserved in salt.

Oliva Taggiasca. This black or greenish-purple olive is named for a town in the Province of Imperia: Taggia. This is one of the most highly-prized olives in oil production. The tradition of keeping them in brine derives from the need to have olives all the year round. Often eaten as an 'appetizer' with drinks before a meal.

WINE

The mild marine climate of Liguria is ideal for growing grapes, although the jagged coastline has little land suitable for farming. Traditionally a land of sailors and traders, a great variety of grapes are grown, resulting in wines such as the white Vermentino, the most common wine in the region, or the red Dolcetto, locally called Ormeasco. With seven areas of DOC wines, two of Liguria's traditional wines reflect the dual nature of this land. To the east, the Riviera di Levante produces Sciacchetrà delle Cinque Terre, grown in vineyards that slope down to the sea, a wine with an extraordinary bouquet, as famous as it is sweet; in the west, in the Riviera di Ponente they make Rossese di Dolceacqua, a wine of the hinterland, the only red from the region with any character. It turns into a characteristic rich ruby-garnet red with aging, and is smooth on the tongue.

ITINERARIES

PIACENZA AND BOBBIO

Situated on the western edge of Emilia, Piacenza has always been a land of transit, a land of beginnings and ends, set in a key strategic position between the Po, the great northern-Italian plain and the Apennines. It attracts mainly business tourism and weekend visitors who often ignore the opportunities offered by a city where there is much to explore. Its old town center has buildings dating from Roman times to the present day, including many fine churches and palazzi. Bobbio lies quite close to Piacenza and is the best known town in the Trebbia Valley, normally associated with spas and watersports on the river.

S. Savino. One of Piacenza's earliest churches (founded early 5C), S. Savino was rebuilt in 1107, altered in 1630 and later restored to its Romanesque lines (early 20C); a Baroque portico (1720) with pairs of columns obscures the facade. The interior is representative of the Romanesque Lombard style; the nave is separated from the side-aisles by granite pillars decorated in various styles. Fine capitals carved with animal and plant motifs support the round arches. In the presbytery, an interesting floor mosaic (12C); the black-marble altar with bronze decoration (1764) contains a sarcophagus with the relics of St Savinus.

Duomo. The complex structure of the Duomo was built in two stages: the first between 1122 and 1160, the second between the beginning of the 13th century and 1233. It has a gable roof, and the facade is built of red Verona marble and sandstone, divided into three sections by pillars; in the center is a large 14th-century rose-window, whereas, on each side, small blind loggias echo the loggias at the top which, in turn, emphasize the lines of the sloping roof. Above each doorway is a porch with a loggia (the central one is decorated with the signs of the Zodiac), supported by lions and telamones, decorated with carvings by masters of the Piacenza School. On the left, the solid **bell tower*** (1333), 71 m high, has a tapering spire with a gilt copper weather-vane on the top in the form of an angel. The octagonal dome cladding above the crossing of the transept has frescoes (1625-27) by Guercino in the segments. Guercino also painted the **Sybils** in the lunettes below. In the presbytery, at the high altar, there is a remarkable wooden polychrome **altar-piece** (1447).

S. Antonino. Founded *extra moenia* (outside the city walls) between 350 and 370, rebuilt in the first half of the 11th century, the church was later altered several times (15-16C) and subsequently restored (19-20C). As a result, it is a combination of many different styles. However, two architectural features domi-

nate the building: the imposing octagonal tower (1004) with three tiers of two-light windows, built above the crossing of the transept, and the tall, graceful Gothic pronaos known as '*il Paradiso*' (Paradise, 1350), which stands in front of the left wing of the transept; it shelters a marble doorway (1172) with high-reliefs on the jambs by masters of the Piacenza School (12C). The **interior**, in the neo-Gothic style, is built on an interesting upside-down Latin-cross plan, with a nave and two side-aisles, each with an apse; it has a remarkable gilt wooden organ gallery on the right of the nave and frescoes in the vaults of the apses; at the third altar on the right, a fine 15th-century polychrome terracotta **Crucifixion**.

Piazza dei Cavalli. Laid out in the 13th century, the square is the civic heart of the city. In the middle are two **bronze equestrian statues**** (1620-25) depicting *Duke Ranuccio I* and his father *A. Farnese*, set on pedestals adorned with bas-reliefs. The way the horses have been expressed is particularly striking. The monument to Ranuccio is more static and composed, while that of his father throbs with the expressive vitality created by the flow of his cloak and the horse's mane. The square is dominated by Palazzo Pubblico, known as **il Gotico**** (the Gothic), one of the most significant examples of 13th-century civic architecture in Italy. It has the typical structure of a Lombard *broletto* (town hall) with an open ground-floor area supported by broad pointed arches; the pillars are faced with white marble but, higher up, the white marble alternates with stripes of red Verona marble and eventually meets the warm colors of the of the brick upper floor. Set back slightly is the former Palazzo dei Mercanti (1676-97); opposite is the elegant Neo-Classic facade of Palazzo del Governatore (1787), with a large sun-dial and a perpetual calendar (1793), the top of which is decorated with statues of pagan gods. Just off the east side of the square, the **church of S. Francesco**, erected in 1278.

Palazzo Farnese. This is one of Piacenza's most important buildings. It comprises two adjoining but separate parts: the remains of the **Cittadella Viscontea** (1373) and the actual palazzo. With regard to the old fortress, the remaining parts include the west part, with a loggia, two corner-towers and the curtain-wall running between them. The palazzo houses two important cultural institutions, including the **Musei Civici**, which has an interesting display with works of great artistic importance, and the **Pinacoteca**, which contains works mainly from churches in and around Piacenza, the *Fasti Farnesiani* (frescoes depicting the Life of the Farnesi) and a beautiful collection of paintings by Genoese and Flemish masters. In the basement is the marvelous **Museo delle Carrozze***, a collection of 40 carriages (18C and 19C).

S. Sisto. This very old complex dates from the 9th century, but was completely restructured during the Renaissance. The church (1499-1511) dedicated to St Sistus was radically changed by the innovations wrought by Bramante and B. Rossetti. A massive 17th-century doorway in the 'rustic' style leads into a courtyard with a portico on three sides (1591-96), masking the late-Renaissance facade. The **interior**, adorned with frescoes, wrought-ironwork and 18th-century decorative features, is built on a Latin-cross plan. The first transept near the entrance makes it possible to see the nave and two side-aisles almost in cross-section: the side-aisles with their smaller domes and the nave with a barrel vault decorated with painted recessed panels; at each end of this first transept are two unusual models of churches built on a Greek-cross plan, decorated with niches and five small domes; above the crossing between the nave and the second transept is the tiburium, surrounded by a loggia of small columns. In the presbytery, note the lovely wooden **choirstalls** (1514-25) with wonderful carvings and marquetry work; at the far end, the original *Sistine Madonna* painted by Raphael in 1512 has been replaced by a copy. Notice the large gilt carved wooden gallery, and the organ (16C) by the Facchetti.

Madonna di Campagna. This church, documented as early as 1030, is a very important example of Renaissance art. Rebuilt in 1522-28, the solid main part of the church is built on a Greek-cross plan, (the shape was altered when the presbytery was extended in 1791), with exactly the same features inside and outside; the height of the brick building is emphasized by the large octagonal tiburium, made taller and more slender by the lantern and the four smaller tiburia above the chapels at each corner. The harmonious space inside the church is divided up by four central pillars, which support the dome and the barrel vaults of the four arms of the building. The whole interior is covered with painted decoration, dominated by figurative scenes.

BOBBIO

Bobbio is a holiday resort for people who come to visit the nearby river and spa. The town's history is closely linked to the **abbey of S. Colombano**, founded by the Irish missionary monk in 614. It was one of the most important medieval centers of religious culture in Italy, with a famous scriptorium and library. The network of narrow streets and paved alleys, with its old houses and noble palazzi, lends a medieval atmosphere to this town, which grew up around the monastery, and has been awarded the TCI's "Bandiera Arancione" (Orange Flag). Piazza Fara, the heart of the town, is overlooked by the apse of the basilica and the long loggia (1570) of the monastery which now houses the **Museo dell'Abbazia and Museo della Città**, a collection of archeological material and works associated with the figure of St Colombanus (from 4 to 18C).

Outside the town, the unusual twisted outline of the **Gobbo bridge**, one of the symbols of Bobbio, attracts the eye; its eleven arches of varying dimensions have been restored to provide a pedestrian route across the Trebbia River. Possibly of Roman date, it is documented from 1196 onwards and was restructured in the 16th and 17th centuries.

The medieval Gobbo bridge is a symbol of Bobbio.

Perhaps the true sites of Verdi's past are the boards and the backdrops of the stages, the "mystic gulf" of the orchestra pit, the seats, the boxes of the theaters, or La Scala where the composer's first work, "Oberto," was presented when he was 26; the Queen's Theater of London, where "I Masnadieri" was acclaimed; the theater of the Khedive in Cairo, where "Aïda" was produced; the Teatro La Fenice of Venice, the S. Carlo of Naples, the Argentina or the Apollo in Rome; Florence's La Pergola or the Opera in Paris. Or perhaps we should travel, in our imagination, to other lands, historical times, and settings: those evoked by the props, the Babylon of "Nabucco," Paris of "La Traviata," the grim Hapsburg Spain of "Don Carlos," the bittersweet England of "Falstaff," which the maestro composed at the age of 80 ("I am just writing for my own enjoyment," he commented). But if we are going to tour the land of his youth, where he returned as a grown man, then we will visit the plains between Parma and the Po, farmland, a handsome countryside with distinct seasons, silence and snow, trees like shadows in the fall mists, as the swifts dart back and forth in the sunset, cities, towns, and villages with rich aromatic cooking and a tradition of "bel canto." Those towns are three, to be exact: Verdi's birthplace, Róncole; Busseto, the dignified little town where he learned music and forged his destiny; and Sant'Agata: the maestro, already successful, bought a house and land there, encouraged by his second wife, G. Strepponi, an opera singer. In the route that we recommend, these places are parentheses along the way: do not miss the three portals of the facade of Fidenza's Duomo, a masterpiece of Po Valley Romanesque architecture. Then there is the blend of the Middle Ages and Renaissance in the castles of Fontanellato and Soragna. Lastly, the magic landscape of the Po, glimpsed through the trees, or from secluded roads along the banks.

NOT TO BE MISSED

Fidenza: the Duomo is one of the finest Romanesque monuments in the Po Valley. **Fontanellato** boasts the Rocca, or fort, with frescoes by Parmigianino; it stands, pale red and battlemented, facing the broad square of a farming village. **Soragna**: another farming village, another Rocca, the sumptuous princely home of the Meli Lupi family. **Róncole Verdi** has the birthplace of Giuseppe Verdi, a modest enough place, and, in the church of S. Michele, the organ on which Verdi first practiced music. **Busseto** (➡ see below): the cult of Verdi does not interfere with the history and dignity of what was once the capital of the little state of the House of Pallavicino; there is a museum in the Villa Pallavicino; in the church of S. Maria degli Angeli is the *Lament for the Death of Christ* terracotta group by G. Mazzoni (1476-77). **Villa Verdi a Sant'Agata**: the maestro spent his summers here, composing opera; you can tour his living quarters. **Roccabianca**: the Po flows by, slow and majestic, just a few hundred meters away; the 15th-century Rocca, or fort, was built by P.M. Rossi for his beloved, Bianca Pellegrini, hence the name Rocca-Bianca. **Colorno**: restoration has helped to recover some of the charm and allure of the ducal palazzo and estate, hunting grounds and holiday spot of the dukes of Parma, upon which many architects worked for long years.

PARMA

Parma shows many aspects of its personality in the medieval monuments upon which Antelami worked, and in the delightful works created by Correggio. The city is also a treasure trove of opera and "bel canto," Stendhalian in the refinement of its culture, and then, primarily, ducal, if we may use the term (referring to the three centuries, before Italian Unity, of Farnese and Bourbon rule, with the interlude of the ruler that the people of Parma still like to call, with affectionate pretension, "la nostra Maria Luigia," known to us as Marie Louise of Austria).

Piazza del Duomo*. Intimate and silent, this square truly preserves its medieval character; surrounded by the cathedral, the baptistery, and the Palazzo del Vescovado.

Duomo**. This cathedral is certainly one of the masterpieces of the 12th-century Romanesque architecture of the Po Valley. Its austere facade is enlivened by three superposed rows of loggias; the central portal extends into a porch surmounted by an aedicula, by G. da Bissone (1281). The tall terracotta Gothic bell tower (1294) is noteworthy. The interior features piers with lovely capitals. The walls of the high nave are frescoed (G. Mazzola-Bedoli, 16C); note the copper statue of the Archangel Raphael (1294). There are 15th-century frescoes in various chapels, and an inlaid Baroque pulpit (1613). In the cupola is the majestic

*Assumption of the Virgin**, by Correggio (1526-30). On the right wall of the right transept, the relief of the *Deposition** by B. Antelami (1178). In the apse, note the 12th-century episcopal throne*, with excellent high-reliefs by Antelami, and the inlaid choir by C. da Lendinara (1473).

Battistero**. This lively Romanesque-Gothic baptistery (1196-1270) with an octagonal plan is combed with lovely architraved loggias. In the lower section, the reliefs* on the three portals and the decorative fillets and the statues* in the niches, by B. Antelami, are one of the masterpieces of Italian Romanesque sculpture. The octagonal interior, with niches, two rows of small loggias, and high ribbed cupola, contains Antelami's high-reliefs of the *Months**, the *Seasons**, and the *Signs of the Zodiac**; the frescoes with a Byzantine flavor, in the lunettes and dome, are largely from the late 13th century; in the center of the baptistery is a double baptismal font (13C).

S. Giovanni Evangelista*. This Renaissance church (1510) has a facade and bell tower dating from the early 17th-century. Inside, set in exceedingly elegant architecture, is a renowned cycle of frescoes** by Correggio and Parmigianino. The vaults and candelabra were decorated by M. Anselmi (1520-21) under the guidance of Correggio; the painted lacunar ceiling and frieze are by F. M. Rondani, after drawings by Correggio (1522-23). In the apse, note the inlaid and carved choir* by M.A. Zucchi (1512-13), and paintings by G. M. Bedoli (ca. 1556). In the Sala Capitolare (enter from second cloister), there are two detached frescoes* by Correggio.

Piazza Garibaldi. Called Piazza Grande in the 19th century, this square lies in the center of Parma, with the monument to Garibaldi, Palazzo del Governatore with its Torre (1673), or tower, and the porticoed Palazzo del Comune (1627). Also, to the right, the former Palazzo del Podestà (13C).

Strada Garibaldi. This road runs past the Neo-Classic Teatro Regio (1829), one of Italy's most renowned opera houses (hall with four tiers of boxes). Almost directly across the road is the church of the Madonna della Steccata (see below). From Piazza Garibaldi, the Strada Mazzini leads to the Ponte di Mezzo, a bridge over the Parma River; take the underpass along the right bank to see the remains of the Roman bridge on Via Emilia, built during the reign of Augustus and used until the course of the river shifted in the 12th century.

Madonna della Steccata*. This church, designed by B. and G.F. Zaccagni (1521-25), is a

The Cathedral bell tower and baptistery.

Renaissance structure, with large semicircular apses and cupolas adorned with loggias. The majestic interior is decorated with frescoes by artists of the 16th-century Parmesan school, among them B. Gatti, M. Anselmi, G. Mazzola-Bedoli, and Parmigianino. Also, note the funerary monument by L. Bartolini and, in the sacristy, the inlaid wooden armoires. Beneath the church are the tombs of the Farnese, dukes of Parma.

Camera di S. Paolo or del Correggio**. A major center of Parmesan culture, adjacent to the former Benedictine nunnery of S. Paolo, it can be reached from the Strada Macedonio Melloni. Originally part of the private apartment of the abbess, it was renovated and decorated from 1514 on, at the behest of Giovanna da Piacenza. Correggio worked here in 1519, in his first major project, achieving one of the masterpieces of the mature Italian Renaissance. The hall is covered with an umbrella vault, divided into 16 gores, set on lunettes: Correggio painted a pergola with putti set in tondos, and in the lunettes* he painted Neo-Classic monochrome figures. In an adjacent room there are frescoes by A. Araldi (1514).

Palazzo della Pilotta. Impressive building erected by Farnese in 1583-1622, unfinished. Its name comes from the game of "pelota," played in a courtyard. It houses the Museo Archeologico Nazionale, the Galleria Nazionale – one of Italy's finest art galleries – and the Biblioteca Palatina.

Museo Archeologico Nazionale*. Founded by Philip I of Bourbon in 1760, in conjunction with the dig at Veleia, this is one of Italy's earliest archeological collections, stocked largely with local finds. Note sculpture from the great Farnese and Gonzaga collections; an Egyptian collection; Greek, Italiot, and Etruscan ceramics; Greek and Roman coins; a fine 1st-century BC bust of the head of a youth; the slab of the Lex de Gallia Cisalpina, and the tabula alimentaria, from Trajan's time. Moreover, there are local collections of prehistoric material, and Celtic artifacts as well. All sorts of Roman material (amphorae, bronzes, marble, mosaics) come last.

Galleria Nazionale di Parma and Teatro Farnense**. Of special importance in terms of Parmesan painting from the 15th-18th century, this gallery boasts a number of masterpieces by Correggio, among others. As a surprising and theatrical atrium to the Gallery you will pass through the magnificent Farnese teather* (1617-18), one of the most attractive theaters on earth, rebuilt in the 1950s, following the damage from bombing in 1944. The collections are arranged in sections, by school and chronological order. In the medieval section you will find capitals and sculptural fragments, including three capitals by B. Antelami. Early painting of the 14th-15th century includes works by A. Gaddi, P. Veneziano, Fra' Angelico, and B. Daddi. Then come frescoes and paintings by A. and B. degli Erri, F. Francia, and L. da Vinci. In the section of 17th-century Emilian painters are F. Mazzola, D. and B. Dossi, and Garofalo; among the 16th-century Italian paintings are several *Virgins* and *Child* (by M. Anselmi, G. Gandini del Grano) and canvases by S. del Piombo and G. Romano. The section featuring the Parmesan school of the 16th-17th century includes works by G.M. Bedoli, G.B. Tinti, and L. Spada; there are also works from the Flemish school (J. Sons, D. Calvaert), the Venetian (Tintoretto, Palma the Younger, El Greco), the Emilian (the Carracci) and the Lombard (G.C. Procaccini) schools. The 17th-century section features works by painters of various schools: Bolognese (C. Aretusi, Guercino), Genoan (Genovesino, G.A. De Ferrari), Spanish (Murillo, Giobbe*), Flemish (A. van Dyck), and Lombard (C.F. Nuvolone). From 18th-century Venice, works by G.B. Tiepolo, G.B. Piazzetta, Canaletto, and S. Ricci. The 19th-century halls are noteworthy for some important works by Correggio and Parmigianino.

Palazzo Ducale. The ducal palace is situated in a lovely park, created in 1561 on 20 hectares of land along the left bank of the Parma River. The palace was designed by Vignola, and enlarged by Petitot in 1767. Note the halls frescoed by A. Carracci, A. Tiarini, G. Mirola and with 18th-century stuccowork.

Casa di Toscanini. At no. 13 Borgo Tanzi, birthplace of the great conductor Toscanini; memorabilia.

BUSSETO

The historic center of Busseto, which has been awarded the TCI's Orange Flag, is partly surrounded by walls with towers at the corners. The whole length of Via Roma, Busseto's main and oldest street, is porticoed. On each side are old shops and historic buildings, many of which are associated with the memory of Giuseppe Verdi. At the end of it is the square named after the town's most famous citizen. Set around **Piazza Giuseppe Verdi** are the Rocca, the collegiate church of S. Bartolomeo and Palazzo Comunale Vecchio. In the center is the bronze monument to Giuseppe Verdi. The **Rocca**, founded in the 13th century, is a combination of late-Gothic and Renaissance motifs. It now houses the **Teatro Verdi**, built between 1856 and 1868. Nearby is the **collegiate church of S. Bartolomeo**, erected in 1437-50. The facade is adorned with beautiful terracotta decoration in the Lombard style. The interior, decorated in the mid-18th century with rocaille stucco-work, has some important paintings and **frescoes** dating from the 16th/18th centuries. The **Treasury of the collegiate church,** kept partly in the 17th-century sacristy and partly in the church, comprises sumptuous vestments, hangings, 15th-century illuminated choir-books, ivories (early 15C) and splendid embossed sculpted silver-ware. On Via Roma, stands **Casa Barezzi**, where Verdi lived for many years, and taught the daughter of the house, Margherita, whom he later married. The late 18th-century *salone* of the house is possibly the place most closely associated with Verdi in Busseto. On the same street, the Neo-Classic **Palazzo Orlandi** and **Palazzo del Monte di Pietà*** were built between 1679 and 1682. Inside are frescoes detached from the portico (1682), antique furniture and some fine silver-ware. Outside the old walls of the town stands the austere Gothic church of **S. Maria degli Angeli** or **dei Frati** with its Franciscan monastery, built between 1470 and 1474. The facade has a beautiful doorway with a terracotta frieze, a large rose-window and polygonal apses. The interior is plain and bare. Nearby is **Villa Pallavicino**, which stands alone at the end of an avenue of poplars, surrounded by a square fish-pond. This is one of the most splendid villas in the Parma area, built on a five-module checkered plan. The villa now houses the **Museo Civico**. The exhibits include mementos of G. Verdi, antique furniture, exhibits associated with local history, and paintings and ceramics from the 17th and 18th centuries.

HILL COUNTRY BETWEEN REGGIO AND MODENA

The Via Emilia is a single straight road, centuries old, linking Parma, Reggio nell'Emilia (cities located in different states until 1859) and Modena. The land this road runs through is relatively homogeneous, in terms of dialect, accent, and cordial hospitality. Outside of the cities – with their many relics of long and illustrious histories, with perfect settings and remarkable monuments – everything is farmland, the pride of the plains of northern Italy. The broad sweeping landscape is sealed off to the south, however, by broad rolling verdant hills, climbing up to the Apennines, flanking the long river valleys. This route passes among these hills. The scenery varies widely; it rolls by peacefully, at times solitary and even harsh, invariably abounding in harmonies of color, ranging from tender greens and electric greens in the springtime, sere burnt yellows in the full heat of summer, under a dizzying blue sky, or the majestic array of autumn, with the red and antique-gold leaves of chestnut trees withering, preparing for winter. This place is overflowing with history, which tangles and catches at the castle towers, just as valley-bound fog wraiths and snags at the wizened branches of brier bushes and leafless trees on winter mornings. There are stout castles: Torrechiara, Rocca dei Rossi, Montechiarugolo dei Sanvitale, Rossena, Canossa (stronghold of the powerful countess of Tuscany, Matilda, the "gran contessa"), a castle built a thousand years earlier by a certain Azzo of Longobard descent. Quattro Castella owes its name to four fortresses that once surrounded it, overlooking the forests beneath from atop four different peaks: Mt Vetro, Mt Bianello, Mt Lucio, and Mt Zane (one survives; the three others lie in ruins). Many local place names seem like a list from the counter of an Italian delicatessen: Felino, synonymous with exquisite salami; Langhirano (on the Parma River, which is slightly neglected in this route) is known for the excellence of its prosciutto (ham), rivalled perhaps only by that of Parma. Mentioning them, however, may help to transport all these castles and the ruins and memories of such castles out of their romantic haze, and present them as genuine military instruments, designed to rule – and defend – this land, made fruitful by backbreaking labor.

NOT TO BE MISSED

San Biagio di Talignano is a Romanesque parish church which can be reached from Sala Baganza along a detour of 3 km through the Parco Regionale dei Boschi di Carrega, a regional park. **Castello di Torrechiara*** is a 15th-century castle, one of the largest and best preserved in the region; make sure to see the renowned Camera d'Oro, or Room of Gold, with its rare fresco cycle dealing with profane subjects, attributed to B. Bembo (1463). **Villa Magnani** is located in Corte di Traversetolo, and boasts

The hills aroud Reggio seen from Rossena castle.

a notable collection of paintings. From Traversetolo, you will then continue on to Montechiarugolo with its Rocca, or fortress, with notable frescoes in the interior. **Rossena castle** is a 13th-century fortress perched on a high crag, with fine views. **Canossa castle** stands on a white rock base in a barren panorama of badlands: note its remarkable history, the view, the ruins, and a small museum. **Quattro Castella**: these four fortresses were an outpost of Canossa, though only the Bianello survives (privately owned); in town, there is a 16th-century palazzo and a parish church of Romanesque origin.

REGGIO NELL'EMILIA

A city with a down-to-earth, generous nature, rooted in the farming tradition, its people are hard-working, combining quality of life with great civic commitment: the culture of Reggio is based on study, solidarity, sociability and services. Situated on the Via Emilia, the old town is enclosed within the hexagon formed by its circular roads, which follow the almond-shape of its old walls. City of art, it has a strong cultural tradition and an important historical and artistic heritage. Its many layers of building reflect various styles, so that Roman remains mingle with medieval, masterpieces of the Renaissance with Baroque and Neo-Classic monuments.

Piazza Camillo Prampolini. This large rectangular square is the city's main public space and is closed and surrounded on all sides by buildings; access points are not noticeable, as they are hidden or concealed under large vaults. The overall impression is somber, the only decoration being the statue of Crostolo from Palazzo Ducale di Rivalta. The east side is occupied by a complex of religious buildings: **Palazzo Vescovile**, the facade of which incorporates the profile of the **Baptistery of S. Giovanni Battista**, dating from the 11th century, the Duomo and Palazzo dei Canonici. The square is also overlooked by **Palazzo del Comune**, built in 1414-94 and rebuilt 1583, with a composite architecture resulting from gradual additions. It has a graceful 18th-century facade, decorated with large arches, and a three-arched portico. Inside, the **Sala del Tricolore** is a magnificent oval hall with three tiers of balconies (1774-75). Towering above **Palazzo del Monte**, the hub of the city, is the Torre dell'Orologio (clock-tower). 47 m high, it reflects the crenellated tower erected in 1216.

Duomo. Dating from the Romanesque period (9C), the cathedral has been modified several times over the centuries. The facade with its gable roof, decorated by small hanging arches, is crowned by an original octagonal tower with a niche containing an image of the *Madonna Enthroned and Child and Donors*, in gilt, embossed copper, by B. Spani (15C). The structure resembling a westwork (a northern architectural model used in the Romanesque period), on an axis with the nave, gives a vertical dimension to the facade. The partial marble decoration dates from the Renaissance. The interior is built on a basilica plan with a nave and two side-aisles; the crypt below the transept has cross-vaulting supported by 42 columns.

Basilica of S. Prospero*. The church, founded in the 10th century, is one of the oldest in the city. Reconstructed in 1514-23, it is adorned with a striking carved facade (1748-53) with mixtilinear cornices, a play of niches and eleven statues (18C) portraying the patron saints of the city and the Doctors of the Church. On the edge of the parvis are six large lions of red Verona marble (1504). There is a strong contrast between the 18th-century forms of the church (in brick) and the adjacent **bell tower** (in gray stone), a remarkable octagonal construction, one of the most significant local Renaissance buildings. The interior of the church is built on a Latin-cross plan, illuminated by an oculus and divided by

Doric columns covered with imitation marble stucco-work. It displays several works by local artists of the 16th and 17th centuries. A riot of form and color draws visitors to the splendid cycle of **frescoes** in the choir and presbytery. Above the high altar 'del Santissimo' is the **altar-piece of the Assumption,** a masterpiece by T. Laureti and L. Carracci (1602).

Musei Civici. The atrium has mosaics of Roman date and figurative floors (12-13C) from the Duomo and other local churches. The **Museo Spallanzani di Storia Naturale*** has zoological, mineralogical and paleo-ethnology collections, as well as anatomical and botanical collections. The **Museo di Paletnologia "Gaetano Chierici"*** is a priceless example of late 19th century museological culture, preserved with its original furnishings and as arranged immediately after Chierici's death; it has good ethnographical collections of native American material from the great plains of North America. The **Galleria dei Marmi** (Marble Gallery) has a large collection of cippi, epigraphs, marbles, miscellaneous pieces, sculptures and decorations of local origin, dating from Roman times to the 18th century. In the adjacent cloister is a recomposition of Roman architectural marbles including some funerary monuments of centurions. The **Museo di Reggio in Età Romana** has finds dating from the town's foundation to Barbarian times; the archaeology of late Antiquity is illustrated by the Roman-Barbarian treasure (late 5C) with gold-work and coins of the Imperial and Barbarian periods, and from Constantinople. The **Raccolte di Preistoria e Protostoria fino all'Età del Ferro** include material from prehistoric times up to the Iron Age, such as the famous neolithic *Venus* and *cippi* from Rubiera, and Etruscan funerary tablets (5-7C BC) with friezes and inscriptions.

Teatro Municipale "Romolo Valli". Standing imposingly in the tree-lined public gardens is the impressive Neo-Classic theater, erected in 1852-57. One of the most beautiful and functional in Europe, this is the hub of the city's cultural life. Inaugurated in 1857, it is dedicated to a famous local actor (1925-80). The facade, composed and elegant, lends distinction to the long architraved portico; its upper order is divided by pilaster strips, and crowned with allegorical statues. Inside is the magnificent horse-shoe-shaped hall, with four tiers of boxes and a balcony; white and gold decorations and a splendid chandelier contrast with the dark red wall covering. Note the famous **curtain** by A. Chierici. A visit backstage shows the rigging, balconies and winches for the scenery and special effects. The foyer areas include the notable *Hall of Mirrors*, adorned with mirrors featuring carved gilt frames.

Civica Galleria Anna e Luigi Parmeggiani. This is in an eccentric building by A. Ferrari (early decades of the 20C), which stands in the south-west corner of Piazza della Vittoria. An unusual example of eclectic architecture, it was designed as a museum, in a combination of French and Spanish forms, a mixture of Gothic and Renaissance styles. The gallery presents a collection formed in France, between the late 19th and early 20th centuries, by the Asturian painter and benefactor I. Leòn y Escosura, the painter C. Detti (1848-1919) and Parmeggiani himself. The arms, gold-work, fabrics, paintings and furnishings are mostly 19th-century fakes in medieval and Renaissance style. In the atrium are marbles, terracottas and stone capitals; next is the *Sala dei Gioielli*, with Limoges enamels (12-13C); the *Sala delle Armi*, containing bayonets, firearms and armor (15-17C); of note among the paintings in the central hall is a **Christ of the Benediction** by D. Theotocopulos, known as El Greco and, in the center, works formerly attributed to Velázquez and Van Eyck; the *Sala Detti* has family paintings and self-portraits in historic costumes, and the *Sala Escosura* has paintings based on historic subjects; the *Flemish, English and French rooms*; the Spanish room exhibits the most comprehensive collection of Spanish art in Italy; the *Sala dei Costumi* and the *Sala dei Velluti*, with 18th-19th-century garments and clothing accessories.

Sanctuary of Beata Vergine della Ghiara. Built to a design by A. Balbi (1597-1619) and completed by F. Pacchioni, the church is preceded by a large parvis. The facade, in brick with marble adornments, is in two rows, animated by pilaster strips and serlianas, and crowned at the top by acroterions. The whole culminates in a soaring dome and the unfinished bell tower. Three doorways lead into an interior built on a Greek-cross plan with a deep apse. The decorative unity of the interior highlights the chromatic contrast between the decorations and the architectural space. Sumptuous 17th-century decoration in gilt stuccowork frames a fine cycle of frescoes that covers the vaults. Beside the convent cloister is the Museo della Ghiara, with the rich legacy of the lay vestry consisting in silverware, fabrics, votive offerings, sacred furnishings of the 17th-19th centuries and a drawing of the **Madonna of the Ghiara** by L. Orsi (1569). In the Sala del Tesoro (treasury room) is a remarkable painting, the *Salvation of Laura da Correggio* by Luca Ferrari and a precious 17th-century crown of the Virgin.

MODENA

"The immense ocean of the horizon is broken, to the west, only by the towers of Modena": Stendhal described the landscape as he saw it from the hill above Bologna. The towers he described still stand: the Torre dell'Orologio, atop Palazzo Comunale, but especially the 88-m-tall Ghirlandina, a military structure more than a bell tower. In the ancient center of town are the Duomo (Romanesque masterpiece by Lanfranco and Wiligelmo), the curving porticoed streets of the Middle Ages and the geometric grid of streets built by the d'Este family, who held Modena for 250 years after losing Ferrara (1598). The town is also famous for its wine (Lambrusco), food (tortellini and zampone), and tradition of fast cars (the Ferrari factory, at nearby Maranello).

Piazza Grande. This square forms a monumental complex with the cathedral and its tower. The 17th-century building with porticoes, with a 13th-century clock tower in the middle, is the Palazzo Comunale, or town hall; from the courtyard, you can climb to the upper floor, with handsome rooms, decorated with frescoes and paintings by N. dell'Abate, E. dell'Abate, and B. Schedoni, and with coffered ceilings. In the small loggia, note the wooden bucket, subject of a local feud, immortalized in the mock-heroic poem, "La Secchia Rapita," by A. Tassoni.

Cathedral**. Modena's most important monument, and a masterpiece of Romanesque architecture, this cathedral was begun in 1099 under the direction of the Lombard master Lanfranco with the help of the sculptor Wiligelmo, and was completed in the 13th century by Campionese masters. It features a handsome tripartite facade, with three ornate portals (note the central portal*), a handsome loggia, and a 13th-century Gothic rose window. Of particular interest are the four bas-reliefs* by Wiligelmo (12C), among the earliest examples of Romanesque sculpture. Along the sides are fine carved doors and bas-reliefs by A. di Duccio. Adjacent to the three handsome apses is the massive bell tower, called **La Ghirlandina*** (86 m tall), with a Gothic crown, a symbol of Modena. The austere interior, powerfully designed in brick, has a nave with two aisles and cross vaults. At the end of the nave is a fine gallery* set on slender columns, with parapet decorated with reliefs by A. da Campione (ca. 1180); above it is a 14th-century wooden Crucifix; to the left, a 13th-century carved ambo. Midway on the left, a pulpit by A. da Campione (1322). Huge crypt with 60 small columns (late 11C capitals); on the right, a group of five polychrome statues, called the *Madonna della Pappa**, by G. Mazzoni (1480). In the presbytery, a 13th-century screen of slender columns bounds the main altar; note the inlaid choir by C. and L. Canozzi da Lendinara (1465). In the left apse, 15th-century Tuscan bas-relief; marble statue attributed to A. di Duccio; intarsias* by C. da Lendinara (1477), and polyptych by S. Serafini (1384). On the left side of the cathedral, at no. 6 in Via Lanfranco, is the Museo Lapidario with Roman, medieval, and Romanesque stonework, including eight splendid 12th-century metopes**.

S. Pietro*. A Renaissance church (1476-1518) with an elegant facade, and inside, fine paintings* by G. Romanino and F. Bianchi Ferrari, statues by A. Begarelli, and an inlaid choir (1543).

S. Francesco. This Gothic church, built in 1244, and since restored, has a group of terracotta sculptures by A. Begarelli (1523).

Palazzo dei Musei. A vast 18th-century building that houses the many collections of the city of Modena; foremost among them, the Galleria Estense and the Biblioteca Estense.

Biblioteca Estense*. On the first floor, this is one of the richest libraries in Italy, with illuminated codices of great note, including the 15th-century Bible* of Borso d'Este, illuminated by T. Crivelli.

Musei Civici. The municipal museums include various sections: the Museo Civico di Storia e Arte Medievale e Moderna has objects of sacred art and goldwork, weapons, musical and scientific instruments, fabrics and embroidery, and more; 17th-18th-century paintings in the Galleria Campori. The Museo Civico Archeologico Etnologico has collections that range from prehistoric artifacts and exhibits to Roman objects, as well as ethnographic material from New Guinea, Amazonia, Africa, and so on.

Galleria Estense.** Located on the top floor of the palazzo, this is one of the finest art galleries in Europe, particularly rich in works of the Emilian and Po Valley schools of the 14th-

Modena Cathedral and the Ghirlandina.

18th-century. As you enter, you will see various ancient Etruscan and Roman objects, as well as a marble bust of Francesco I d'Este* by Bernini. Among the paintings, at the beginning, are works by early Emilian artists, including paintings* by T. and B. da Modena, S. dei Crocifissi, and by Tuscans, including G. di Paolo. Among the 15th-16th-century Ferrarese and Modenese painters are C. Tura, A. and B. degli Erri, B. Bonascia, F.B. Ferrari, G. da Carpi, D. Dossi. Bronzes by B. di Giovanni; majolicas by S. da Ravenna. Works by 16th-century Florentines and Emilians include art by L. di Credi, Correggio, and L. Orsi. Non-Italian painters include: J. van Cleve, C. de Lyon, Velázquez, El Greco. Painters of the Venetian school include: Montagna, G. F. Caroto, J. and D. Tintoretto, J. Bassano, Veronese, and Palma the Younger. There are excellent medals, made for the d'Este family, by Pisanello and G. delle Corniole. Lastly, among the 17th-century Emilian artists are Scarsellino, the Carracci, Guercino, G. Reni, L. Ferrari, and C. Cignani.

S. Agostino. This 17th-century church features a terracotta group by A. Begarelli and a fresco by T. da Modena. Take the Via Emilia, Modena's main strolling street, and on the left you will see the church of S. Giovanni Battista, built in 1730, with a handsome polychrome terracotta group by G. Mazzoni.

Palazzo Ducale*. In Piazza Roma is the massive, lavish ducal palace of the d'Este family; note the courtyard and facade. Construction began around 1630, incorporating a castle built in 1288. Since 1862 it has housed the Italian Accademia Militare, or military academy.

BOLOGNA

I n the urban landscape of Bologna, the monumental buildings blend into the fabric of minor buildings, hidden behind their red and ochre-colored walls and rows of porticoes. The porticoes, which, end-to-end, amount to almost 38 km in length, lend harmony to the city landscape, attenuating the breaks between buildings with different architectural styles. Its nicknames, Bologna "the Learned" and Bologna "the Fat", refer to the city's famous university and its gastronomic tradition. Traces of the Roman and medieval origins of this city of art and culture, built at the foot of the Apennine foothills, can still be perceived today, but the predominant impression is of architecture of the 17th and 18th centuries, interspersed with buildings erected in the following two centuries. The history of Bologna begins with Roman colonization and the building of the Via Aemilia, which still forms the backbone of the modern city. In the 11th century, Bologna's reputation as a center for law led to the founding of the oldest part of the university (1088). In medieval times, many towers and tower-houses were built by feudal lords who came to live here and the newly-emerging merchant classes, as were the porticoes, which provided a setting for craft and commercial activities. The city's appearance changed radically in the 15th century under the rule of the Bentivoglio family. When Bologna was incorporated into the Papal States, an oligarchy of nobles, the Senate, held economic power and ruled the city. Bologna now began to take on the appearance which still predominates today, with its senators' palaces, its convents and monasteries being made even more beautiful. After Italian Unification (1861), there was an attempt to recover Bologna's image as a Gothic commune, in contrast to the Baroque city, and restoration work was carried out in an endeavor to emphasize its medieval character. Bologna is a city with a human dimension, a place where past and present live side by side. The streets of the city center are pervaded by an atmosphere of days gone by. The noises of the city are muffled and fade into the background. What predominates is the feeling of being in a medieval town, but, walking under the porticoes, you encounter the university city. Jolly groups of students, street musicians and the colorful signs above the trattorie are indications of a relaxed and hard-working city.

Fontana del Nettuno. The famous bronze statue in the center of the Fountain of Neptune depicting the god in the process of placating the waves, popularly known as *"il Gigante"* (the Giant), is the work of Giambologna (1563-66). It stands on a base designed by Tommaso Laureti. Giambologna also executed the four *putti* (cherubs) with dolphins and the four mermaids. The square named after the fountain was laid out in 1564 to provide access to the city's largest square, Piazza Maggiore, which the people of Bologna refer to as *"la piazza"*.

Piazza Maggiore. The noble monumental center of the city was laid out between 1200 and 1203, and assumed its current appearance in the first half of the 15th century. It has always been the setting for the city's most important civic and religious ceremonies and festivals. Until 1877, it was also the market square. Splendid public buildings overlook the square: **Palazzo del Podestà***, **Palazzo Comunale*** and the **basilica di S. Petronio****.

Palazzo del Podestà. This palazzo adjoins the Palazzo di Re Enzo behind, forming a single block, situated above the crossroads of two passageways. The tall Torre dell'Arengo (1212) was built daringly above the crossroads of the

passageways below; the large bell at the top of the tower, called the *Campanazzo* by the locals (brought here in 1453), is rung to mark important civic occasions. The porticoed facade of the building overlooking the square was re-designed with Renaissance forms in 1485.

Palazzo Comunale, also known as Palazzo d'Accursio. This palace was built and added to subsequently. The original part of the palazzo (13-14C) is the porticoed building with the tower. The rest is the result of defenses added in 1365 which, on three sides of the building, give it the appearance of a fortress. The facade is graced by large 15th-century windows and a terracotta *Madonna and Child* by N. dell'Arca (1478). The former municipal offices are now a cultural center for the city. The central part of these facilities is the impressive former Stock Exchange: below the glass floor you can see Roman and early medieval remains. The building is entered through a 16th-century doorway; beyond the courtyard, a large sloping ramp with long, shallow steps leads up to the first floor and the Sala d'Ercole, with a statue of Hercules by A. Lombardi (1519) and a fresco of the *Madonna of the Earthquake* by F. Francia (1505). On the sec-

Piazza Maggiore. On the right stands the basilica of S. Petronio.

ond floor, the Sala Farnese leads into the Farnese chapel. Off the Sala Farnese is the entrance to the **Museo Giorgio Morandi***, which contains 281 works (paintings, watercolors, drawings, etchings and two sculptures) by the great Italian 20th-century artist. It also contains the entrance to the **Collezioni comunali d'Arte***, which include paintings from the 13th-19th centuries of the Bologna and Emilia Schools, furniture from the 17th and 18th centuries, 17th-18th-century miniatures, tapestries, ceramics, clocks, decorations and frescoes from the 16th-19th centuries and 19th-century paintings.

S. Petronio. Dedicated to Petronius, bishop and patron saint of Bologna, but never a cathedral, the church is proof of the city's ideals of independence. In fact, it was the civic authorities who decided to erect the church at the end of the 14th century. The construction of the basilica, designed by A. di Vincenzo, began in 1390 and was not completed until the mid-17th century. The three doorways are decorated with marvelous **sculptures**** by J. della Quercia (1425-38), a masterpiece of the transition between the Gothic and Renaissance styles. On the right of the church is the bell tower, erected in 1492. The side-chapels inside the church have carved marble or wrought-iron screens (15-17C). In the right aisle, the second chapel has 15th-century frescoes and a polyptych attributed to T. Garelli; in the third chapel, a frescoed polyptych of the Lombard School (15C); in the fourth chapel, stained-glass windows by James of Ulm (1466); in the fifth chapel, a **Pietà** by A. Aspertini (1519) and a wooden Cru-

cifix (1462); in the sixth chapel, **St Jerome**, a panel by L. Costa (1484); in the eighth chapel, carved and inlaid **stalls** (1521); opposite the eleventh chapel, a painted terracotta group of figures depicting the **Lamentation of the Dead Christ** by V. Onofri (late 15C). In the left aisle, the first chapel has a **St Roch** by Parmigianino. A little further on is the beginning of the meridian line which stretches as far as the west wall, traced by G. D. Cassini (1655). This feature was regarded by travelers on the Grand Tour as one of the most curious sites of the city. In the seventh chapel, a **Madonna and Saints** by L. Costa (1492); in the fifth chapel, a **Martyrdom of St Sebastian** of the Emilia School (second half 15C); in the fourth chapel, frescoes by G. da Modena and assistants (1410-15). The pilasters are decorated with early 15th-century frescoes; the beautiful second chapel, where the relic of the head of St Petronius is kept, has rich decoration by A. Torreggiani (1750); in the first chapel, frescoes by G. da Modena. The **Museo di S. Petronio**, accessed from the far end of the left aisle, has two rooms containing drawings and designs for the facade of the basilica.

Museo Civico Archeologico**. Via dell'Archiginnasio runs along the left side of S. Petronio. On the opposite side of the street, the *Portico del Pavaglione* is always crowded. At No. 2 is the entrance to the Museo Civico Archeologico, one of Bologna's most prestigious institutions, housed in the former hospital of S. Maria della Morte, a 15th-century building converted by A. Morandi (1565). It has a vast and very prestigious collection. The prehistoric section contains objects dating from the Paleolithic to the Bronze Age, mostly from the Bologna area. The finds from the Villanova culture (a modern name applied to a prehistoric culture, dating from the 9th century to the mid-6C BC, it refers to the town of Villanova, where the remains of a necropolis were found in the 19C) consist of groups of grave goods. The museum's **Etruscan finds** include the *Certosa situla*, a bronze-plated bucket with reliefs depicting scenes from daily life and religious processions, and some votive bronze statuettes (early 5C, BC). The museum has some good Greek and Roman displays and the **Egyptian collection** is one of the finest in Europe.

Palazzo della Mercanzia, erected in the late-Gothic style under the supervision of A. di Vincenzo and L. da Bagnomarino (1384-91), was originally a customs house. Built of brick and Istrian stone, it has a splendid loggia with two pointed arches and three pilasters decorated in various architectural styles with flowers on the capitals.

S. Maria della Vita. This Baroque church overlooks Via Clavature (no. 10). Built on a central oval plan, the space inside the church is dominated by its height. To the right of the high altar is a wonderful sculpture of the **Lamentation of the Dead Christ***, composed of seven life-size polychrome terracotta figures, a work by N. dell'Arca (1463). In the adjoining oratory (1617) is another fine composition of 14 statues depicting the **Transito della Madonna**, by A. Lombardi (1522).

Due Torri**. The Two Towers (Due Torri), also called the *Torri Pendenti* (Leaning Towers), are the most famous of the many towers built during the medieval period and are the best-known site in the city. The **Torre degli Asinelli*** (97.20 m high) was named after the family who built it in the early 12th century; the small fort at the bottom of the tower was added in 1488. Those who wish to brave the 498 steps of the tower, which leans west 2.23 m off the perpendicular, will be rewarded with magnificent views over the city. **Torre Garisenda*** (48.16 m), built in the same period and owned by the Garisendi family, was originally 60 m high. The height was reduced amid fears that it might collapse (1351-60); a plaque recalls the verses written by Dante Alighieri inspired by the tower.

Chiesa Metropolitana di S. Pietro. The original church of the Metropolitana di S. Pietro was altered several times, but the present structure dates from the re-building work executed in 1605 by F. Ambrosini. Its imposing brick facade with marble decoration was

designed by A. Torreggiani (1747). Inside, the nave is flanked by communicating side-chapels, and the presbytery was designed by D. Tibaldi in 1575. The terracotta figures of the **Pietà** by A. Lombardi (1522) and the Romanesque (12C) holy water stoups on each side of the main doorway and the side entrance in the right wall of the church are worthy of note; in the large lunette above the apse is an *Annunciation* by L. Carracci, his last work (1619). The Museo del Tesoro della Cattedrale has a fine collection of superb early examples of sacred art. Outside the church, the **bell tower*** is important both from an architectural and historical point of view; it was begun in 1184 and the pinnacles on the top were added in 1426.

Museo Civico Medievale**. No. 4 Via Manzoni, the majestic **Palazzo Ghisilardi-Fava**, is a typical example of local late 15th-century architecture. Today, it houses the city's medieval collection, with material dating from the Middle Ages and the Renaissance. Highlights of the museum include sculptures from the 14th-17th centuries, bronze figurines and plaquettes dating from the Renaissance, sacred vestments, Byzantine ivories (10-12C), fibulas, military bracelets and early medieval gold-and-silver-work; various works of figurative art from the period of rule of the Bentivoglio (15C) and a fine weapon collection dating from the 16th and 17th centuries. The museum also has many interesting exhibits relating to natural history and the exotic from private collections made in previous centuries.

S. Francesco. This Franciscan chrurch was built between 1236 and 1263, restored in the 19th century and re-built after the WW II. The larger bell tower, by A. di Vincenzo, was erected in about 1402 while the other dates from the 13th century. The most interesting feature of this building is the apse, with a choir and deambulatory with chapels arranged around the edge and rampant supporting arches, in the late-Gothic style. The facade, the lines of which are Romanesque (completed in about 1250), rises to a point, and has a doorway with a porch. Inside, Renaissance tombs decorate the base of the walls, including the monument to Pietro Fieschi (second on right, 15C), the tomb of Pope Alexander V (fourth on left), and the tombs of N. Lamberti and S. di Bartolomeo (1424-82). At the high altar is a precious **altar-piece*** with marble bas-reliefs, statues and fretwork sculpted by P. P. dalle Masegne (1392). The sacristy, dating from the late 13th century, is by A. di Vincenzo. The adjoining monastery, where, in the 13th century, the "Universitas Artistarum" (University of Artists) used to meet, contains the Chiostro dei Morti (late 14C), and the tombs of the rectors of the university.

Palazzo Sanuti-Bevilacqua. This palazzo is one of the finest expressions of early Renaissance architecture in Bologna. Built between 1477 and 1482, it is completely decorated with rusticated ashlars, with two tiers of elaborate one- and two-light windows. The porticoed **courtyard**, with its loggia and double tiers of arches, has worked columns and capitals and a frieze around the edge.

S. Domenico. The church of S. Domenico overlooks **Piazza S. Domenico**, an irregularly-shaped cobbled square in the urban fabric, the site of two votive 17th-century columns and the **tombs*** of two doctors of law. The church, with a monastery attached, was built in the late-Romanesque style between 1228 and 1238 and altered in 1727-33. Inside, the nave and two side-aisles reflect the tenets of Neo-Classic 18th-century elegance. Half-way up the right aisle is the chapel of St Dominic, built in 1597-1605 on a Greek-cross plan, with a dome and a *Glory of St Dominic* by G. Reni (1613-15) in the vault; below is the **tomb of St Dominic****, a startling sculptural composition executed by artists from different periods. The sarcophagus is by N. Pisano, assisted by A. di Cambio, Pagno di Lapo and Fra' Guglielmo (1265-67). In the chapel in the right transept, a *St Thomas Aquinas* by Guercino (1662); in the chapel on the right of the presbytery, a **Mystic Marriage of St Catherine** by F. Lippi (1501). In the presbytery are beautifully inlaid wooden **choirstalls***. In the left transept, a painting of the **Crucifix** by G. Pisano (1250) and a *funerary monument to Taddeo Pepoli*, the work of a Tuscan sculptor dating from the 14th century. In the left aisle, in the chapel of the Rosary, at the altar, is a *series of small paintings by* L. Carracci, B. Cesi, G. Reni, F. Albani and others; in the vestibule beyond it, the **monument to Alessandro Tartagni**, an elegant work by F. di Simone Ferrucci; in the second chapel, **Raymond of Peñafort** by L. Carracci. At the end of the right aisle is the entrance to the **Museo di S. Domenico**, which contains gold- and silverwork, holy vestments, reliquaries, codices and illuminated choir-books (from the 13C) belonging to the church, and some important paintings and sculptures. The right transept leads into the Chiostro dei Morti (14-15C),

dominated by the Romanesque Gothic bell tower of S. Domenico.

Archiginnasio. Palazzo Archiginnasio is a long, porticoed building with a square internal courtyard and a double loggia. Like almost all the rooms, the walls of the courtyard are decorated with painted or sculpted coats-of-arms of rectors, priors and students who attended the *Studio* (as Bologna University is called) between 1500 and 1700. Off the courtyard on the ground floor is the chapel of S. Maria dei Bulgari and, on the first floor, the **anatomy theater**: the design is by A. Levanti (1649), and the 18th-century wooden sculptures are by E. Lelli and S. Giannotti. Since 1835, the palazzo, which was the main part of the university until 1803, has housed the prestigious **Municipal Library**, which contains more than 650,000 volumes, 12,000 manuscripts, letters, maps and prints.

S. Maria dei Servi. The Gothic church of S. Maria dei Servi, begun in 1346 and finished in 1545, has an elegant four-sided portico dating from different periods (late 14C to mid-19C). The interior, consisting of a nave and two side-aisles, is late-Gothic in style. The most interesting part of the church is the ambulatory, decorated with fragments of frescoes by Vitale da Bologna (1355). On the walls: a *Madonna Enthroned with Saints*, attributed to L. di Dalmasio, and a *Madonna and Child with Saints*, a polychrome terracotta altar-piece by V. Onofri (1503); in the third chapel, a **Maestà**** by Cimabue and a fresco by L. di Dalmasio. In the presbytery are some fine wooden inlaid choirstalls (15-17C) and, on the left wall, a *Virgin with the Seven Founder Saints* by G. M. Crespi (1734). In the left aisle, at the sixth altar, an *Annunciation* by I. da Imola and frescoes by Bagnacavallo.

Complesso di S. Stefano**. Via S. Stefano is one of the most characteristic streets of the old city of Bologna. The square is overlooked by **Palazzo Bolognini** (16C), which has unusual anthropomorphic decoration on the facade, the picturesque group of houses of **Case Tacconi**, where Renaissance features blend with Gothic, and Palazzo Isolani, with its 18th-century facade, and Palazzo Bolognini (15C), also decorated with faces of animals and monsters. The complex of S. Stefano is one of Bologna's most important religious centers and dates back more than a thousand years. It incorporates a series of religious buildings, also known as the Sette Chiese (Seven Churches), which were built and altered in different periods, with features

The cloister of the church of S. Stefano.

Chiostro dei Benedettini (Cloister of the Benedictines) (12-13C), with two tiers of loggias: the lower tier has arches resting on large pillars and groups of four small columns, while the upper tier is supported by pairs of small columns and capitals with plant, animal and human motifs. Off the cloister lies the **Museo di S. Stefano**, with a remarkable collection of paintings of the Bologna School from the 14th-15th centuries, statues, bas-reliefs, reliquaries and church furnishings (14-18C).

Strada Maggiore. For centuries, as its name suggests, Strada Maggiore, the part of the Via Aemilia which crosses the city center, lay on the main route to Rome. Cutting straight through the city, it has porticoes on each side in the section below the Torre degli Asinelli. Almost every building on the street has some feature of interest, whether medieval houses, palaces or churches. The senatorial **Palazzo Hercolani** dates from the 18th century. On the ground floor is an atrium, a loggia, a grand courtyard and an English-style garden; a Neo-Classic monumental staircase leads up to the piano nobile (upper floor). Facing Piazza di Porta Ravegnana, on the right, beyond Palazzo Poggi Tartagni, with its 15th-century capitals, the Neo-Classic facade of the 16th-century Palazzo Sanguinetti incorporates the medieval Torre Oseletti. Beyond **Casa Isolani** (13C) with its tall wooden piers are the Neo-Classic 16th-century facades of Palazzo Fantuzzi and Palazzo Gessi, and Casa Valori and Casa Bonfanti, which date from the 15th and 14th centuries respectively.

S. Giacomo Maggiore. This church dedicated to St James the Greater, one of the city's most important monuments, was built by Agostinian monks between 1267 and 1343. In the second half of the 15th century, the interior was re-designed in the Renaissance style. An elegant **portico** decorated with terracotta friezes and grooved sandstone columns was added to the side of the church. The Gothic facade of the church culminates in a small shrine containing a statue of the saint. It has a rose-window (replaced in 1954), two tall two-light windows,

which date back to late Antiquity. Much of what you see today is the result of restoration work conducted between 1870 and 1930. From left to right, the following buildings overlook the square: the church of the Crocifisso, the octagonal church of S. Sepolcro and the church of Santi Vitale e Agricola. The **church of the Crocifisso** has a Romanesque facade culminating in a single point and a pulpit dating from 1488. Inside there is a single nave and a raised presbytery dating from the 14th century, altered in 1637. Suspended from the arch above the choir is a wooden painted *Crucifix* by S. dei Crocifissi; below the presbytery is the crypt. A door on the left of the church leads into the **church of S. Sepolcro** (12C). Built on a dodecagonal plan, the church has an ambulatory, matroneums and incorporates a number of re-used Roman capitals. The **church of Santi Vitale e Agricola**, which dates from the 11th century, has a nave and two side-aisles divided by cruciform pilasters alternating with Roman columns. The side-apses contain the tombs (11C) which once held the remains of the proto-martyrs Vitale and Agricola. From the church of Santo Sepolcro you can access the rectangular **Cortile di Pilato (Pilate's Courtyard):** in the center is an 8th-century marble bowl with a Lombard inscription; the two side-chapels contain 16th-century frescoes. From the courtyard you enter the church of the Trinità, with a nave and transepts, restored in 1924. The chapel on the left contains a wooden sculpture of the **Adoration of the Magi** (14C) by Simone dei Crocifissi. The courtyard also leads into the a doorway with two lions supporting columns, and niches with tombs on either side. The interior has a single nave, and side-chapels in groups of three, under large arches joined at the top by a gallery adorned with statues. In the seventh chapel on the right, a *Mystic Marriage of St Catherine* (1536) and other frescoes by Innocenzo da Imola; in the ninth chapel, a **St Roch Consoled by an Angel** by Ludovico Carracci; further on is the **Poggi chapel**, designed, decorated and frescoed by P. Tibaldi (mid-16C). The ambulatory contains several works (14-15C): in the second chapel, a **polyptych** by P. Veneziano and a Crucifix by J. di Paolo; in the third chapel, a *Coronation of the Virgin and Saints* by J. di Paolo and, on the left, a *Crucifix* by S. dei Crocifissi (1370); the sixth chapel is the **Bentivoglio chapel****, built on a square plan with a dome (1486): above the altar, a **Madonna Enthroned with Child and Saints**, a painting by F. Francia (ca. 1494), in the upper lunette, the *Vision of the Apocalypse* is a fresco by L. Costa; on the walls, also by Costa, are (on the left), a **Triumph of Death and Triumph of Fame** (1490) and (on the right) a *Madonna and Child with the Bentivoglio family* (1488). Opposite, next to the edge of the presbytery, is the **tomb of A. G. Bentivoglio** executed by Jacopo della Quercia and his assistants (1435). The portico outside leads into Via Zamboni, and the *oratory of S. Cecilia* which contains a remarkable **fresco cycle*** depicting scenes from the life of Sts Valerian and Cecilia, by F. Francia, L. Costa and others. The church overlooks **Via Zamboni***, an old street which was altered in the second half of the 15th century by the Bentivoglio, where the street widens out is the Neo-Classic facade of the 16th-century Palazzo Manzoli. Opposite, Palazzo Malvezzi de' Medici has a large staircase which leads up to the first floor. Beyond it, Palazzo Magnani was designed by D. Tibaldi (1577-87) and belonged to a family of blacksmiths (*magnano* in the dialect of Padua means blacksmith).

Università, The heart of the cultural city is **Palazzo Poggi** (1549); originally the seat of the Institute of Sciences (1711) it became the seat of the university in 1803. Founded in 1088, **Bologna University**, called the "Studio", is regarded as the oldest in Europe. Palazzo Poggi is dominated by the two parts of the *Torre della Specola* (1721). The headquarters of the Academy of Sciences has frescoes depicting **stories of Ulysses** by P. Tibaldi (1549). In the main seat of the university, the **Musei di Palazzo Poggi** incorporate the old laboratories of the 18th-century Istituto delle Scienze. The rooms of the museum, which was conceived in a way that links teaching, research and conservation, focus on the following themes: *Boats and seafaring; Military architecture; Human anatomy; Obstetrics*. The *Museo Storico dello Studio*, housed in the same building, has a multimedia section which, with documents and memorabilia, tells the story of the university. Further along Via Zamboni is the interesting **Museo Geologico Giovanni Capellini***, with the largest paleontological collection in Italy. It includes early collections, fossilized plants and vertebrates, and geological specimens. There is a remarkable life-size (24 m) model of a Diplodocus (species of dinosaur).

Pinacoteca Nazionale**. The gallery is housed in a palazzo in Via delle Belle Arti which dates from the second half of the 17th century. The collection began as the private collection of the Accademia di Belle Arti, established here in 1804. It was subsequently enhanced in the second half of the 19th century and mainly contains paintings by artists from Bologna and Emilia from the 14th-18th centuries. The collection reflects the artistic development of the city. Highlights of the collection include: **St James at the Battle of Clavijo**** by P. J. di Francesco (first half of the 14C); a polyptych of the **Madonna and Child with Saints*** by Giotto and his workshop (1333-34); a number of works by V. da Bologna: a **Last Supper** (a fresco fragment), a **St George and the Dragon**** and four panels depicting the **stories of St Anthony Abbot**. There are also works dating from the late-Gothic and Renaissance periods, works of the Ferrara School, including the **Merchants' altar-piece*** by F. del Cossa (1474), and by painters from Bologna, such as the **Ecstacy of St Cecilia**** by Raphael. Works from the Emilian Mannerist School include a **Madonna and Child with Saints*** by Parmigianino. Other works document the Golden Age of the Bologna School between the late 16th century and the second half of the 17th century, including a **Madonna degli Scalzi*** by L. Carracci; a **Madonna of St Louis*** by A. Carracci; **Slaughter of the Innocents****, **Samson Victorious**** and **Portrait of a Mother**** by G. Reni. The 18th century is mainly represented by the works of G. M. Crespi (**Courtyard Scene***), D. Creti and the three Gandolfi: Ubaldo, Gaetano and Mauro.

FERRARA

Ferrara's geographical position in the territorial context of Emilia Romagna has influenced its destiny in historical terms with regard to both its social and economic development. Ferrara is out of the way in relation to the important route of the Via Aemilia on which virtually uninterrupted urban development took place all the way from Milan to Rimini, resulting in an unusual and constant pressure to develop. The position of Ferrara, removed from the area from which much of the rest of the region has benefited, and almost subordinate to it, has had positive repercussions, particularly from a physical and environmental point of view. In fact, the area of Ferrara and its province has avoided the scourge of industrialization and has thus been spared the often negative consequences of such things. As a result, the area has been able to preserve its natural environment, the high quality of which led to Ferrara to being designated a UNESCO World Heritage Site in 1995. In 1999, this prestigious award was extended to the Po Delta and the Delizie Estensi (as the summer palaces built by the Estes are called). Thanks to extensive restoration work and considerable human effort, the city's urban and architectural resources have made it possible to launch an impressive cultural initiative based on a program of urban quality. Gradually, the city has built up an image which now attracts a discerning and assiduous type of tourism. Ferrara, the "bicycle city", is pervaded by the peaceful atmosphere typical of its province, but is enlivened by its cultural and historical heritage.

The majestic Castello Estense.

Palazzo dei Diamanti. The 'diamonds' in the name refer to the pointed, faceted ashlars which decorate the facade. As the light changes, they alter the appearance of the building. This is certainly one of the most famous palaces of the Italian Renaissance. It houses the **Pinacoteca Nazionale****, which plays an important role in conserving and reconstructing that 'lost paradise' which once constituted Ferrara's artistic heritage. The left wing contains works (14-15C) including two tondi with **Stories of St Maurelius*** by C. Tura. The grand hall houses the gallery's larger works, such as the magnificent frescoes depicting the **Slaughter of the Innocents***, a beautiful **polyptych of St Andrew **** (ca. 1530) and a **Death of the Virgin***, dated 1508. Works from the 16th and 17th centuries include a **Madonna and Child*** by G. da Fabriano, **Christ with the Soul of the Madonna***

by A. Mantegna and a **Madonna and Child in the Rose Garden*** (ca. 1480). **Castello Estense,** from Palazzo dei Diamanti, **Corso Ercole I d'Este***, which marks the transition from the Renaissance to the medieval part of the city, leads to the castle. The Corso has the aura of a princely street reflects the Renaissance concept of what a city should be. There are many gardens between the noble palazzi, including the majestic **Palazzo di Giulio d'Este** (late 15C), with its fine terracotta **cornice**. The castle's evolution from being a powerful military structure to a sumptuous ducal residence has resulted in the Castello Estense being the city's most emblematic monument. It was built with four towers and is surrounded by a wide moat which not only reminds us of its original function but has the effect of isolating it from its urban context. The visit begins under the portico at the entrance to the Museo Provinciale del Castello. The Gothic rooms, in the oldest part of the complex, and the other rooms, have exhibits associated with the history of this castle-palace. The itinerary includes the dungeons. An artillery ramp leads up to the first floor to the *Loggia delle Duchesse*, the *Loggia degli Aranci* and the **Giardino pensile degli Aranci***, a small terrace-garden with citrus trees in pots; from the loggia, cross the frescoed *Stanzino dei Baccanali*, to the **Ducal chapel*** (1590-91), traditionally called the **chapel of Renée de France**: small and compact, it is decorated with polychrome marble and devoid of images, except for the Evangelists on the ceiling. Next to it is the **Ducal** apartment, (ca. 1570), with richly decorated rooms (Sala dell'Aurora, Saletta dei Veleni, Saletta and Salone dei Giochi). The visit includes climbing the 13th-century **Torre dei Leoni**, from the top of which there are marvelous views over the city.

Cathedral. Its bottom is Romanesque and the top Gothic, has a handsome central **doorway*** and a **porch**, crowned by a loggia. On the right-hand side of the cathedral, which faces Piazza Trento e Trieste is the **Loggia dei Merciai** (built in 1473 to house the shops which, in the 13-14C, had been set up under the cathedral wall). The **bell tower** (1441-42), designed partly by L. B. Alberti, is unfinished. It has a beautiful **apse*** (1498) and, at the foot of the cathedral, is a long inscription of the city statutes carved in stone (80 m long). The interior, preceded by a narthex, with objects in stone and marble, is a fascinating mixture of different periods and styles. In the right transept, an altar with a **Martyrdom of St Lawrence***, by Guercino, and another with a bronze statue of **Christ on the Cross, the Virgin Mary, St John, St George and St Maurelius*** (1450-56) by N. Baroncelli and D. di Paris. Around the curved apse are wonderful **wooden choirstalls** (1500-25), while the fine late 16th-century stuccoes draw attention to the vault of the apse, where there is a visionary **Last Judgement*** painted by Bastianino in 1577-80. In the sixth chapel of the left aisle, a splendid **Coronation of the Virgin** by F. Francia. Close to the cathedral is the deconsecrated **church of S. Romano** (15C). It now houses the important **Museo della Cattedrale***. The collection includes interesting **tapestries**, four **panels**** by C. Tura (1469) and other interesting works. On the walls are fine marbles, including the twelve **reliefs of the months*** (13C). On the first floor are 22

splendid **illuminated choir-books*** (executed between 1477 and 1535), together with an illuminated hymn-book and psalter (1472), and precious marbles. By walking west we come to the *ghetto*, created around the mid-15th century. Under the rule of Ercole I d'Este (1471-1505), Ferrara became a veritable center of Jewish culture in Italy. The old synagogue is in Via Mazzini. The streets of the ghetto and the places associated with the Jewish community and references to the cultural peculiarities of some of its inhabitants are described throughout the works of G. Bassani, author of the famous book "The Garden of the Finzi Contini", on which the film by De Sica was based.

Basilica di S. Francesco, The formal quality of this church, with its vast brick facade, finds expression inside, where the Brunelleschian dimensions seem to "breathe" the light and the atmosphere of the Ferrara Renaissance. However, this equilibrium was affected in 1956 by the replacement of the terracotta floor with a floor in *botticino* marble. Amongst others, G. da Carpi worked on the triple fresco cycle with a Franciscan theme painted on the ceilings between the 16th and 19th centuries. On the pilaster between the sixth and seventh chapel of the right aisle, a terracotta *Flagellation*, attributed to N. Baroncelli; in the eighth chapel, a 14th-15th-century fresco of *St Anthony of Padua*. In the right transept is the *tomb of Ghiron Francesco Villa*, a military man; in the chapel to the right of the presbytery, a *Madonna Glykophilousa* (Madonna of the sweet embrace), a Venetian icon by a Cretan painter, and a ciborium in the form of a temple (ca. 1636). In the left transept, a Roman sarcophagus in the Ravenna style, re-used as the tomb of F. Ariosto, uncle of the famous poet. In the first chapel on the left, a good fres-

co by Garofalo depicting the **Arrest of Jesus in the Garden of Gethsemane** (ca. 1524).

Casa Romei, dominated by the high transept of S. Francesco, begun in 1442, was built for G. Romei, a rich noble at the Este court. It is one of the best examples in Ferrara of a 15th-century aristocratic residence, although the facade is very simple. Conversely, the interior is richly decorated. The grand central courtyard is dominated by a large *Monogram of Christ* surrounded by terracotta angels. On three sides of the courtyard is a portico and a loggia with remains of wall painting. On the ground floor, the **Sala delle Sibille** (named after the sybils depicted in the paintings in the mid-15C), has a monumental fireplace decorated with terracotta; next-door, and similar, the *Saletta dei Profeti*. Some rooms on the first floor have wall paintings dating from the second half of the 16th century, figurative works and grotesques by C. Filippi and his sons: in particular the *Chapel of the Principesse*, the *Salone d'Onore* and the *Studiolo* of G. Romei. The rooms of Casa Romei also contain precious objects such as marbles, sculptures and detached frescoes from abandoned churches and palaces around Ferrara.

Palazzo Schifanoia, close to Palazzo della Schifanoia, which overlooks **Corso della Giovecca***, the street connecting the medieval and Renaissance parts of the city, is **Palazzina di Marfisa d'Este**, daughter of F. d'Este, a good example of Mannerist architecture (1559). Palazzo della Schifanoia, the most famous of the palaces built by the Este family, houses part of the collection of the **Musei Civici di Arte Antica**; these museums, dotted about the city, include the Lapidario Civico in the former church of S. Libera, the Palazzina di Marfisa, *Palazzo Bonacossi*, the *Cella di T. Tasso* (the cell where the poet was confined) in the Arcispedale S. Anna, the house of the poet L. Ariosto and the Museo della Cattedrale. The palace was built in the late 14th century but altered in the next century by L. d'Este to *schivar la noia* (prevent the duke from getting bored, hence its name). The marble **doorway*** has bas-reliefs, some of which depict the achievements of Duke Borso d'Este, who had the palace enlarged to make room for his grand new apartments. The hall contains the delightful **frescoes of the months**** (ca. 1470), the most eloquent expression of the Renaissance in the Ferrara area. By 1467, the magnificent **ceiling of the Sala degli Stucchi** had been completed. The *Sala delle Imprese*

contains numerous heraldic crests of the Este family. Palazzo Schifanoia houses some important collections: archeological finds, medals and coins, Renaissance ceramics with graffito decoration, prints, paintings and bronzes. The collection of **illuminated codices***, with choir-books and an incunabulum is particularly interesting. There are also some fine terracotta **statues**, an English alabaster **polyptych** depicting the *Passion* (early 15C) and a collection of Gothic and Renaissance ivories.

Chiesa di S. Maria in Vado of medieval origin. The church once stood next to a ford (*guado* in Italian, hence *vado*) on the Po. Built on a Latin-cross plan with a nave and two side-aisles, the focal point of worship is the **chapel of Preziosissimo Sangue** in the right transept: this is the site of the altar cloth over which, on March 28, 1171, blood spurted out of a wafer broken by a priest who had doubts about the Sacrament of the Eucharist. The richly decorated little church with a pronaos dates from the late 16th century. Between 1617 and 1630, the painter C. Bononi came here to work on one of the important decorative projects in the history of the art of Ferrara. His painting of high quality can be found on the arches and ceiling above the nave, in the presbytery and in the vault of the choir. There are other important paintings by D. Mona (sixth chapel of the left aisle and the presbytery) and C. Filippi, who painted the *Annunciation with St Paul* above the fine wooden choirstalls.

Palazzo Ludovico il Moro, also known as **Palazzo Costabili**. It is a majestic and very harmonious architectural complex. It now houses the **Museo Archeologico Nazionale***. Its beautiful square **courtyard** is decorated with porticoes and loggias with recurring pairs of windows. From it, a grand staircase leads into the museum. This contains a huge number of finds, including grave goods from 21 burials (500-400 BC), most of which are of Attic origin and some of Italic origin. The painted vases depict scenes from the Greek myths, with which the Etruscans were also familiar. Nearby is the Museo dell'Architettura, located in the *Casa di Biagio Rossetti*, the house which the architect designed for himself (note the double-window motif and the terracotta decoration). Not far away you can see the old **walls*** of Ferrara, which still run almost all the way round the city. Not only are they of historical and environmental importance, but they add to the city's charm.

THE STRADA ROMEA AND RAVENNA

The SS 309 road, or Strada Romea, between Mestre (in Veneto) and Ravenna (in Emilia-Romagna) follows one of the routes used by "Romei," or pilgrims headed for Rome. Our route is not haunted by these phantoms, however; rather it wanders among images of reclaimed farmland and untouched wetlands. In the late 17th century, one traveler was moved by the fertility of the newly drained Ravenna territory, "once so sterile and waterlogged" (Misson); modern sensibilities are different, and the terms "marsh" or "wetlands" have lost their negative connotations. There are rivers (Reno, Po, Adige, Brenta) and branches of the sea as well, and everywhere signs of the impetuous modifications made by man: dry land where water once was. The changes in the littoral can be seen on the map: Ravenna once sat between lagoons and the harbor of the Roman fleet; where ships once rode at anchor, fields now sprout green. In Etruscan times, for instance, the waves of the Adriatic broke against sandy dunes at a point midway between Pomposa and Codigoro (now Taglio di Po). Today, the lighthouse of Bocca del Po di Pila is 25 km eastward, while the estuaries of Comacchio stretched some 20 km inland. The Valli di Comacchio and the Po Delta are joined, of course, by the Laguna Veneta, or Venetian Lagoon, another realm of water and land, "nature" preserved by the wisdom of the Serenissima, a world of colors that change with the sky. The architecture of Comacchio, Pomposa, Mesola, Chioggia, or La Malcontenta is all worth seeing, whether monumental or minute, all part of the landscape in which it is immersed.

NOT TO BE MISSED

Comacchio was once surrounded by "valli," or water barriers, and has now been thoroughly reclaimed, crisscrossed by canals, unassuming yet charming; the remarkable landscape can be seen by following the embankment, or Argine Agosta, along the road to Alfonsine. **Volano** is a village on the banks of the Po di Volano, a branch of the Po, whose delta is a nature reserve. **Abbazia di Pomposa****: the bell tower dates from the year 1000; it rears up to mark the site of the abbey, solitary on the vast plain, a notable achievement of Romanesque architecture and art; don't miss the precious series of frescoes in the refectory of the monastery. **Riserva Naturale Bosco della Mesola**, a nature reserve, was once part of a vast Este hunting park; you can tour it now only on foot or by bicycle. **Mesola** is a 16th-century Este hunting lodge. **Ca' Tiepolo**: on the island of the Donzella, this is the seat of the township of Porto Tolle; you get there by following the Po of Venice, a branch of the Po, with privileged views of the endless universe of nuances of water textures of the Po Delta. **Chioggia*** is a town wedged into the southern edge of the Laguna Veneta, or Venetian Lagoon, with the houses, "calli" or lanes, canals, colors, and sounds of a working-class Venice, as C. Goldoni must have known it in the 18th century. La Malcontenta or Villa Foscari, built around 1555 for the Foscari brothers by A. Palladio, lies just a few hundred meters from the Strada Romea (right at the fork for Fusina). **Mestre**: Piazza Ferretto, the Duomo, the Torre dell'Orologio, and a few other fragments of ancient architecture show that this town is more than just a manufacturing outpost of Venice and a bedroom community for those who have moved away from the Serenissima.

RAVENNA

Ravenna, the mosaic city, has a host of architectural masterpieces and mosaic art dating from the times of Galla Placidia, Theodoric and Iustinian (ca. 400-550). The 'Byzantium of the West' has retained its unique appeal in its treasure of early-Christian basilicas, its baptisteries, its cylindrical 10th-11th-century bell towers, its Romanesque churches with examples of Renaissance architecture left by the Venetians and its 17th-18th-century palazzi. The city has a surprising vitality which would make it interesting even if it did not have a great, albeit distant, past; even if it had not preserved the monuments that have made it famous the world over, eight of which have been designated UNESCO World Heritage Sites; even if it were not situated in the great basin of the Romagna Riviera. However, the discerning tourist will soon discover that the city has many surprises in store and that, behind its mask of art and history, there is much more to see beyond the great early-Christian and Byzantine remains. Here, the impetuous wind of modernization, which has destroyed much and which has brought much that is new, has spared the 'soul' of the historic city. Not only the soul jealously preserved inside the basilicas and baptisteries, protected and exalted, strangely, by their ancient, rough brick walls; not only its 'nocturnal' soul, which is to be found in the most secluded corners of the city (Galla Placidia, the area associated with Dante). But also the more familiar soul, which is to be found all over the historic center. The old and the new live side by side, forming an unusual symbiosis, creating an atmosphere which is not only fascinating but difficult to put into words.

Mausoleo di Galla Placidia. The most famous Placidian monument deserves special attention. This small squat building on a Latin-cross plan demonstrates its function as a tomb through the symbolism of its **mosaics****. Despite being almost certainly some of the oldest in the city, possibly dating from before 450, they are in an excellent condition. The quiet, dark setting of the tomb and feeble light filtering through the alabaster windows enhance its beauty and charm. In the lunette above the doorway is a depiction of the *Good Shepherd*; in the opposite lunette, *St Laurence with his gridiron in front of a cupboard with the four Evangelists*. In the four arms of the building are three large *sarcophagi*: the one on the left is late 5th century, the one on the right, early 6th century, and the undecorated middle one is of Roman times.

Basilica di S. Vitale. The new entrance leads to steps down which you can enter the basilica through its oldest ceremonial entrance: the monumental narthex, which formerly widened into the original, and now lost, four-sided portico. The basilica was built on the site of an earlier oratory (5C), visible in the submerged enclosure. In the famous **mosaics*** in the *vault of the apse*, the most prominent figure is Bishop Ecclesius who stands to the left of Christ, while, to the right of the Savior is the soldier martyr, St Vitalis, patron saint of Ravenna, after Apollinaris, its first bishop. The four main parts of the mosaic cycle in the apse and the dividing arch are: 1. The scene of the *Theophany of the Heavenly Christ*, assisted by archangels Michael and Gabriel, giving the crown of glorious martyrdom to St Vitalis *while Bishop Ecclesius presents a model of the church*, as if to Christ; 2. The *Imperial procession of Justinian and Maximian*, with magistrates, soldiers and clergy, bearing bread for the Holy Communion (Justinian is holding the paten) in the church towards the altar; 3. The *Imperial procession of Empress Theodora* bearing the chalice of wine for the Holy Communion, in the ceremonial act of entry led by officials with a following of court ladies; 4. The Imperial significance of the apse arch where *two Imperial eagles*, to the

right and left of the central Christological clipeus, with unfolded wings, support the clipeus containing a stylized monogram (Imperial Constantinian) of Christ. In the presbytery, the **mosaic cycle*** is divided into two pictures of Biblical sacrifices: on the right, the

The basilica of S. Vitale.

sacrifices of Abele and Melchizedech; and, on the left, the *sacrifice of Abraham*.

Museo Nazionale. Ravenna's leading cultural institutions include the national museum, known as S. Vitale after the monastic complex in which it is housed, although it originated and developed in the monastery of Classe. A complement integration and extension of Ravenna's whole monumental heritage, the Museo Nazionale occupies the former monastery's first and second cloisters. The first, Renaissance one contains the most important materials of Roman Ravenna (and Classe). In the large refectory of the monastery, is the entire 14th-century cycle of frescoes from the choir of the medieval convent church of S. Chiara – masterpieces by P. da Rimini.

Domus dei Tappeti di Pietra. This is one of the most important archaeological sites uncovered in Italy in recent decades. It is the only private dwelling found so far in the city, a large noble mansion, the full layout of which has been reconstructed. A succession of different construction phases (at least ten) ranging from the 4th-3rd century BC to the 16th century AD are revealed down to a depth of about 7 m. Of these, it was decided to highlight the one illustrating city life in the 6th century AD. The Domus has 14 rooms and two courtyards paved with geometric marble mosaics (*opus sectile*). Access to the site, situated three meters below the present road level, is via the **church of S. Eufemia** (1742-47). The circular-plan church hall leads, to the left of the main altar, into the sacristy, or *Sala dei Cento Preti*, which conserves the well-head used as a baptismal font by the bishop of the city, Apollinaris; the painting above the niche and the frescoes in the lunettes are attributed to A. Barberini (1757) and his School. The remains of St Euphemia are in a Greek marble sarcophagus in the center. A short staircase descends to the rooms of the Domus. The visitor route winds along a raised walkway that roughly follows the perimeter of the ancient walls and crosses all the rooms in the house, allowing you to admire the floor mosaics. Note the mosaic of the *Good Shepherd*, which does not really belong to the mansion but to a domus that stood on the same spot in a previous period (4-5C).

Duomo. Visitors are invited to search for evidence of Ravenna's older Ursiana basilica beneath today's large cathedral, commenced in 1732. The materials (24 columns, floor marble, four columns in the atrium and the entrance) came from the Ursiana cathedral and the monumental **ambo of Archbishop Agnello*** (556-569) is the most notable work to have survived from that time. Also old (5C) are the sarcophagi of Esuperanzio (and Maximian) and the **sarcophagi of Barbaziano and Rinaldo***. The high altar, a fine work dated 1760, has a dual mensa, just like the earliest altars. The **bell tower*** of the Duomo (9-10C) is perhaps, from a historical point of view, the most important of all the round bell towers; certainly, it seems to be the oldest and it was probably the prototype for the other bell towers of Ravenna.

Battistero degli Ortodossi. The baptistery is well preserved and famous for the splendor of its **mosaics**** and the cultural symbolism of their cycles. There are five iconographic registers: three are found in the dome, one in the tambour and the fifth in the base wall structures. 1. **Christ being baptized by John the Baptist** 2. The **Group of Apostles**, depicting the main Christian preparatory rite for baptism, the so-called *traditio symboli*, i.e. giving the catechumen candidates the Creed. 3. The **Heavenly Paradise**, an iconographic description of the garden of the Heavens, the place where those who pass through the shadow of death, via baptism, to enter the realm of light and life will be eternally blessed. 4. The **Sixteen Prophets**. 5. The **bottom register** of the building, in keeping with its square foundation structure, was decorated with

marble *tessellae* (*opus sectile*), *vine* tendrils, human figures in mosaic, four apses containing the Biblical scenes (lost) described by the four Latin inscriptions. As well as the baptismal font which is a mixed blend of the 16th-17th centuries, be sure to see three other important features: the original marble ambo of the baptistery; the bronze cross ordered by Archbishop Theodore (ca. 688); and the altar, dating from the 5th century, which was not associated with the original use of the building. **Museo arcivescovile.** This museum is famous both for its precious collection and because it is housed in the historic **Episcopate** of Ravenna, an extremely old building foundation (pre-396) comprising the fine 5th-century Arcibishop chapel (see below). It houses numerous relics, including one of the most precious monuments of all Christian antiquity: the **chair of Maximian****, an Episcopal throne commissioned by the famous theological archbishop of Ravenna (546-556).

Arcibishop chapel. Also known as the St Andrew's chapel, this is the old oratory of the bishops of Ravenna, built at the beginning of Ostrogoth rule in the city as a response by the Orthodox Catholic Episcopate to the massive presence of the Arian Church. Arianism, condemned as heresy by the Councils of Nicaea (325) and Constantinople (381), was named after Ario, a priest of Alexandria (280-336). This heresy denied the divine nature of Christ, that he was of the same 'substance' as God and the fact that he was eternal. Christ was regarded as a man of high moral standing, but only a man. Despite being condemned by the Church of Rome, Arianism spread throughout the Christian world and the Barbarian tribes who occupied the territories of the fallen Roman Empire (Visigoths, Ostrogoths, Vandals, etc.) became Arians. In fact, the controversial message is obvious in the symbolism of the atrium with *Christ the Warrior driving out the beasts of heresy*. The cross vault is decorated with splendid **mosaics*** which have been gleaming since the early 6th century.

Museo d'Arte della Città di Ravenna (MAR). Housed in the former *Lateran Canons Monastery* (1496-1508), this is of special worth for its beautiful **Renaissance cloister***, and, overlooking the public gardens, the **Loggetta Lombardesca***, thus called for its general attribution to the circles of the Lombardo family; an elegant construction with two rows of arches constructed after 1503. The gallery is particularly interesting because of the insight it gives to painters from Romagna: N. Rondinelli da Lugo, F. Zaganelli da Cotignola and B. Ramenghi, known as 'il Bagnacavallo'; but there are also paintings by Marco Palmezzano and Baldassarre Carrari from Forlì; and others, of the Ferrara, Bologna, Venetian and Tuscan schools. The Basilica of S. Francesco provided the most famous work in the collection: the **funerary monument of Guidarello Guidarelli*** (a military man from Valentino, mortally wounded in Imola in 1501), by Tullio Lombardo (1525). Of no lesser importance are the modern and contemporary sections of the museum, which offer a rich collection of artists from Ravenna and Romagna datable to around the second half of the 19th century and the first half of the 20th century. Also linked to the city's great mosaic tradition is the *collection of contemporary mosaics* (produced in the second half of the 20C) on permanent display on the ground floor, in the setting of the cloister of the Loggetta Lombardesca.

Basilica di S. Apollinare Nuovo. Historically and culturally, this is perhaps the most important monument of the Imperial and early-Christian Roman period in Ravenna. Here, in fact, two impressive walls covered with **mosaics**** (unique in the art history of Antiquity) represent both the Catholic faith of the great ancient Church and the Arian faith. The commissioning Arian bishops of court had the two series of pictures of the life of Christ placed in the register above the windows.

Inside S. Apollinare Nuovo.

The series should be observed starting from the apse, i.e. the altar. In this way, the first scene on the right and the first scene on the left correspond perfectly; they show the two suppers that prompt respective sequels: the supper in Cana that marks the beginning of the Saviour's public life, and the Jewish Easter supper that starts the '*historia*' of the Passion, Death and Resurrection, i.e. the mysteries of the Christian Easter celebrated in Holy Week. The cycle of mosaics is completed by two large facing panels of *Christ the King* and the *Virgin Mother seated on the throne and assisted by the four archangels, Michael, Gabriel, Raphael and Uriel.*

S. Giovanni Evangelista. In assessing the historical and cultural value of the monumental complex of the Palatine basilica of St John the Evangelist, the visitor should not only bear in mind that he/she is in Ravenna's oldest church, but that he/she is entering the Roman basilica which, in the ancient mosaics (destroyed in the 16C), celebrated the pomp of the Roman-Christian Empire. Important monuments apart from the *protesi* and the *diaconicon* (chapels on the right and left of the apse) include the original marble altar with a Latin inscription from the same period, the medieval bishop's chair, the 10th-century bell tower, the mosaic floor dating from 1213 in the large fragmented squares next to the perimeter walls, the main **doorway** with sculptures in the Romanesque-Gothic style (13-14C), and the beautiful 16th-century Benedictine **cloister**.

Mausoleo di Teodorico. The Tomb of Theodoric is the only monument in Ravenna without wall mosaics. This recognition is well deserved, not only for its uniqueness (it is the only religious building in Ravenna built entirely in stone) but also because it is of remarkable historical importance within the context of Ostrogoth monuments. This can be seen by interpreting the perfect Greek-cross plan of the lower cell and a perfect circle in the upper cell, a true funerary chamber. This round cell is, moreover, crowned with a perfectly round 'capstone', an whole monolith that acts as a roof; a unique architectural feature. Admire in particular the Barbarian frieze, i.e. a tongs-shaped frieze: the most striking of the two rings of decoration on the upper part of the building. At the top, in the center of the monolithic capstone, is a cross in clipeus with colored traces of what appears to be mosaic decoration. On the outside, high up, are the names of some of the Apostles and Evangelists.

The remarkable Sigismondo Malatesta, an accomplished soldier and ruler of Rimini, summoned L. B. Alberti to transform a Gothic church into a Neo-Classic "temple," a mausoleum for himself and his third wife, Isotta degli Atti ("O lovely sweet light, proud soul," as he described her in his poetry; but he murdered his previous two wives, poisoning one, strangling the other); we see him depicted by P. della Francesca, kneeling between two greyhounds. This route passes almost entirely through lands of his family, in a distant corner of Romagna, bordering the Marche, here and there venturing into that region (Marecchia Valley, and then up into the lovely green hills of the Conca Valley). Amidst the lands and forts of the Malatesta family, however, the route passes through two other major landmarks. One is San Leo, high overlooking a tributary of the Marecchia; Federico da Montefeltro ordered the fort built by F. di Giorgio Martini in the 15th-century. The other is San Marino, with its rocky ridge of Mt Titano, crowned with fortifications. Why this little medieval town, no different from many others, should have survived as a sovereign state, is a strange twist of history.

NOT TO BE MISSED

Rimini (➡ see below) is a city of manifold attractions, of which the beach is only the best known. **Santarcangelo di Romagna**: this little farming town has an old section, perched on a hill, with twisting streets; the fortress dates from the 15th century; the "grottoes" are remarkable underground warehouses whose remote origins are subject to debate; and there is a museum devoted to the folkways of Romagna. **Verucchio**: the hills that form bookends for the "borgo" were once topped by menacing forts, of which one survives; the Museo Archeologico is notable for its collections of artifacts from the Villanovan culture, centered here in the early Iron Age. **San Leo***: this town is inaccessible, or practically so, on its limestone crag; the rustic parish church and the Duomo are Romanesque, while the renowned fort has the severe 15th-century perspective and volume given it by F. di Giorgio Martini; after Rimini, this is the artistic focus of the route. **San Marino***: leave the capital town of the tiny republic, a lofty village straddling the crown of the Mt Titano, and follow the ridge for a pleasant stroll to the Guaita, the Cesta, and the Montale, three impressive towers. **Montefiore Conca** surveys the valley from atop a hill, with a ring of walls enclosing the old section, in the shadow of a 14th-century fortress built by the Malatesta (with detached frescoes of figures from the past, and battles). **Saludecio** is a medieval hamlet enclosed by walls and tapering in plan along the hill road, with terracotta buildings; note the Neo-Classic parish church of S. Biagio. **San Giovanni in Marignano**: you can still see the 14th-century layout; in the Biblioteca are archeological finds from imperial Rome. **Cattolica** (➡ see below) is a fishing town and a beach resort; the old part sits on a terrace, 1 km inland, on what was the shoreline.

RIMINI

Long sunny days on the beach, warm nights on the dance floor: Rimini is the heart of Romagna's Riviera, the spectacular playground of Europe. This was just a fishing village when the first adventurous bathers ventured into the waves, in hats and ample suits. The 18th-19th-century breakwaters changed the shape of the beach, increasing the eastern shores with fine iridescent sand, and eroding the western ones. And overlooking the eastern beach is the luxurious Grand Hotel, so dear to the film director Fellini. Rimini itself dates back to the 3rd century BC; 17 centuries later, the local ruler, Sigismondo Malatesta (1429-1468), had P. della Francesca paint his portrait, and asked L. B. Alberti to transform a little local church into the majestic Tempio Malatestiano, a major masterpiece of the early Renaissance.

Piazza Cavour. Historically the heart of Rimini, this square has a statue of Pope Paul V (1613) and a 16th-century fountain. On the NW side are the 16th-century Palazzo Comunale and the 13th-century Palazzo dell'Arengo (note loggia and mullioned windows; upstairs are the large detached frescoes), and, at the end, the 14th-century Gothic Palazzo del Podestà. Also note the 19th-century Teatro Amintore Galli.

S. Agostino. This Romanesque-Gothic church dates from 1247 and has a fine tall bell tower*; inside, 14th-century frescoes, paintings by G. da Rimini, frescoes by the Maestro dell'Arengo, and a large 14th-century Crucifix*.

Piazza Tre Martiri. This square lies on the ancient Roman Forum, where Julius Caesar exhorted his troops in 49 BC after crossing the Rubicon. Also note the Torre dell'Orologio, or clock tower (1547), and the 17th-century octagonal church of S. Antonio.

Arco d'Augusto*. Oldest of the surviving Roman arches, with medieval crenelations, it was built in 27 BC in honor of Augustus, who

Arco d'Augusto at night.

rebuilt the Via Flaminia which joined the Via Emilia at Rimini.

Tempio Malatestiano**. This church symbolizes Rimini, and is considered one of the masterpieces of the early Renaissance. A 13th-century chapel stood here, and was almost entirely rebuilt by L.B. Alberti (1447-60), at the behest of Sigismondo Malatesta. Heavily damaged in WWII, the church was restored in the 1950s. The majestic facade (unfinished) takes its style from Roman triumphal arches, along the side, solemn arches house the tombs of famous men and women. The Gothic interior was renovated by the Veronese architect M. de' Pasti. The decoration is by A. di Duccio. The tomb of S. Malatesta is to the right of the entrance. Note the detached fresco** by P. della Francesca (1451), the tomb of Isotta degli Atti*, perhaps by M. de' Pasti, and a Crucifix** on panel, by Giotto (ca. 1312). Also, bas-reliefs* and tomb* by A. di Duccio (1454).

Museo della Città. Set in a huge ex-convent still being restored (entrance at no. 1 in Via Tonini), this museum has Roman epigraphs, a Pinacoteca, or art gallery, and archeological and naturalistic sections. In the Lapidario Romano, note: colossal Augustan milestone* from the "Via Emilia," two altars* to Iuppiter Delichenus, mosaic floors. The Pinacoteca features works by 14th-century Riminese artists such as: G. da Rimini, as well as G. Bellini, D. Ghirlandaio, and G. Cagnacci.

Ponte di Tiberio*, or Tiberius's Bridge, originally spanned the Marecchia River (since shifted northward). Begun by Augustus and completed under Tiberius (AD 14-21), it has five arches. Nearby is the 16th-century church of S. Giuliano, with paintings by P. Veronese and B. da Faenza (1409).

RICCIONE

The 'Green Pearl of the Adriatic' is one of the most famous and popular holiday spots along the Romagna coast. The image of this small town is inextricably linked to the idea of summer holidays, sea and fun, and this notion is reinforced by its numerous restaurants, shops, hotels, bars and night clubs. **Viale Ceccarini*** is the throbbing heart of Riccione, one of the most famous places in the whole Rimini Riviera, with elegant boutiques and other shops, attractive cafés and trendy venues: a veritable cross-section of the 'sweet life' for which the Romagna Riviera is renowned. The **Museo del Territorio*** is housed in the Centro Civico della Pesa and shows how human colonization has evolved in and around Rimini, focusing on the physical transformation of the area from a natural environment to an environment dominated by human intervention. The **Agolanti** castle stands isolated on a hill and is now used for important exhibitions and other events. There are also a number of **theme parks**.

CATTOLICA

In the center of **Piazzale I Maggio** is the **Fontana delle Sirene** (Mermaid Fountain), a symbol of the city. This is the heart of the tourist resort of Cattolica. On summer evenings, the square with its park and water features become the setting for a show in which the water of various fountains, set on a raised platform, dances to the notes of symphonies and waltzes. The tree-lined Viale Bovio, a famous shopping street, leads to Piazza Nettuno, surrounded by lines of trees. From here, Via Mancini is another popular street with holiday-makers and tourists, which leads to Piazza Mercato. This is the commercial hub of the town, dominated by the **covered market**. Nearby, the church of **S. Pio V** and the 13th-century church of **S. Apollinare** are worth a visit. The **Museo della Regina*,** housed in the Ospedale dei Pellegrini (1584), has an interesting collection. The display is divided into two sections: the archeological section contains everyday objects from the 1st century BC, and the marine section, with models of boats of different periods and an extensive collection of boat-building tools, fishing equipment, ex-votos and nautical charts. The **Parco "Le Navi"*** is worth a visit.

BEACHES

With its 120 km of coastline Emilia-Romagna is an ideal destination for beach-lovers. The resorts on the shores of Romagna were among the first to have water purification plants and all those infrastructures required for making a stay at the beach more comfortable and fun. Despite the pressure exerted on them by the number of tourists, the coasts still offer precious natural areas such as the lagoons and reclaimed land of Comacchio or the pinewood of Ravenna, representative of the typical coastal vegetation. The low-lying, flat and sandy Romagna coast lends itself to tourism providing amenities and facilities which satisfy the demands of all age groups.

Lido di Volano. This is in one of the most picturesque spots on the Adriatic coast, at the south-east end of Mesola wood, between Emilia-Romagna and Veneto. Lido di Volano is a precious natural oasis with its characteristic gentle, sandy beach, its system of dykes, its many saltwater inlets, islands and Mediterranean vegetation. It can be reached from Ferrara, by heading east and taking the Via Romea and then continuing for about 18 km until you find the sign for the beach. Once you have arrived, it is worth continuing to the lake called Taglio della Falce, a true gem. Don't forget the pinewood of Volano and the Bertuzzi Valley which stretches for about

A beautiful sandy beach on the Riviera.

2,000 hectares, with its rich fauna of nesting birds, such as the dwarf heron, the stilt-plover and the purple heron.
Ancona di Bellocchio Beach. Over 3 km of public beach north of the mouth of the Reno River, in the park of the Po Delta, lying between the territories of Ferrara and Ravenna. The beach, a favorite of nudists, is surrounded by a solid dune belt and entrance is from the foreshore of Lido di Spina. Behind it you will find Ancona di Bellocchio and Lake Spina, different biotopes in a precious wetland. Both zones, which have large bird populations, can only be observed from the outside.

Porto Corsini Beach. A southern extension of Marina Romea beach, this public beach (400 m long and 70-80 m wide) has a lovely pinewood to the rear with interesting tree species and undergrowth. The dune between the shore and the pinewood is part of the perimeter of the Parco Regionale del Delta del Po and is 100-120 m wide in parts. The protected dune belt is accessible on foot from the north and south and by a footpath through the wood.
Ex Colonia Varese Beach and Park. In Milano Marittima holidays center on two things – the beach and the pinewood – and there are still some areas that have not been developed. This former summer camp is a wonderful example of 1930s architecture. The surrounding park and beach have been left to grow wild. In the dunes opposite, you can find dropwort, wormwood, sea rocket, soldanella, sea fennel, salwort, common evening primrose and a strong-smelling grass: the cocklebur, once found on all the dunes along the coast of Cervia. Conservation has enabled this area to be restored to its former glory.
Bassona Beach. At Fosso Ghiaia, between Ravenna and Cervia, it is part of the Riserva Naturale della Foce del Bevano and protected to the rear by a large pinewood. Just a few meters from the sandy shore, there is a 1 km-long dune belt, partly shaded by pine trees. There are no facilities or organised entertainment. To reach the area follow the gravel road which, after the SS 16 road at Fosso Ghiaia, turns east towards the mouth of the Bevano. Continue to the end, following the river, and you come to the sea. To get there from the north, follow the signs for Lido di Dante.
Pinarella di Cervia Beach, the beach stretches for about 2,600 m with a lovely pinewood to the rear with fossil dunes. From the naturalistic point of view we recommend the salt

marshes of Cervia, beyond the SS 16 road. The salt marshes, in the heart of the southern part of the Parco del Delta del Po are European Union conservation sites and home to numerous and important bird species such as herons, pink flamingos and spoonbills.

Cesenatico Public Beach. In the home of beach resorts, discos, water parks and beach hotels, you can still find a few grains of sand which are unspoilt and some short stretches of semi-natural coast. In Cesenatico for example there is about 1 km of public beach where you can treat yourself to a few hours of leisure, much better if it is in low season. Avoid July and August when the shore is crowded with kids on organised holidays. Instead, at the end of May or the beginning of June or September the area is quiet and pleasant with its wide sandy beach and shallow waters. To reach the beach exit the A14 highway at Cesena Sud and then follow the signs.

Beach life. Since the first seaside resorts dating back to 1843, principally conceived to offer spa treatments exploiting the thalasso-therapeutic properties of the Adriatic Sea, the Rimini Riviera has been a testing ground for every new idea that has been dreamt up to improve the quality of "beach life". Such attention, with the intent to offer tourists the best possible welcome, is the result of a veritable philosophy of life, which sees in hospitality and entertainment two of the cornerstones on which to base a professional approach brimful of surprises. The highest concentration of hotels in the world. The highest number of workers in the hotel industry per number of inhabitants.

Rimini, the city most visited by Italian tourists. These impressive figures are partly the result of 40 km of fine sandy beach, which in some places reaches a width of 200 m. This natural heritage has produced a fair number of public beaches as well as 700 bathing resorts. A paradise of entertainment and efficiency, a place to relax where the facilities on offer cleverly combine tradition and technology. And so here we have "technological" beaches alongside the inevitable sun loungers and parasols. Here we have environmentally friendly beach resorts where technology goes hand in hand with nature. In recent years ad hoc resorts have sprung up. Their plans for the environment, beginning with recycling waste, aim to make the impact on the environment of the huge mass of tourists who crowd the beaches less burdensome. The resorts, built from environmentally friendly materials, are equipped with technologies for saving water and energy as well as sound proof structures for reducing noise pollution. As well as protecting nature, the novelty of beaches aimed at improving well-being has been successfully launched in recent years. On the seashore you can get into physical and spiritual shape through art, gymnastics, dance, song, martial arts and health food. There is also space for books. For people who love reading, be it magazines or novels, there are resorts with small libraries. As ever a great deal of attention is given to families with small children. Every bathing resort has a play area for kids that is often fenced off, with swings, roundabouts and inflatable toys. Some have beach huts with facilities for warming babies' bottles and nappy changing. If the family also has a pet there are specially equipped areas (beaches are, generally speaking, strictly off limits to animals). As well as being a great place for kids (there are numerous swimming, windsurf and canoe lessons designed for little ones) the beach is the ideal setting for all sports enthusiasts. Everywhere beaches are equipped for beach tennis, and often have beach soccer and beach volleyball courts now that Olympic sports are very much in vogue in Rimini (the city hosts one of the legs of the Italian championships). You can also play bowls, frisbee and basketball. There are many open air gyms for body building enthusiasts. Not to mention pleasure-boating and pedalo-rides, surfing, canoeing or jet-skiing. The Riviera is a veritable breeding ground of new fashions in sports and beach games. And so we have cheecoting (dear old marbles; the first championship on giant tracks made by a sand artist was held in Rimini), tchoukball (a combination of handball and Basque pelota), beach polo, beach boxing (where qualified instructors reveal the secrets of boxing and kick boxing), kite surf (the board is pulled along by the kite which flies over the waves). After so much effort why not treat yourself to something naughty but nice? There are lifeguards who regularly bring down local specialities for you to try on the sea shore. And beach life doesn't stop when the sun goes down. Dusk makes the atmosphere even more pleasant and picturesque. Numerous bathing resorts become the ideal spot for happy hours, aperitifs, dinners on the beach, or open air cinema. And the latest craze is dancing barefoot on the sand, turning the beach into an open air disco.

FOOD IN EMILIA ROMAGNA

The region has several gastronomic highlights. In the south, the pig reigns supreme. We are talking about very special foods, like culatello, Prosciutto Crudo di Parma, coppa piacentina, salama da sugo, spalla cotta and many other specialties. But this is also prime cheese country, where Parmigiano-Reggiano comes from. Wines too. Lambrusco is made between Reggio Emilia and Modena, and a wine called Bosco Eliceo is made in the Po Delta. Many vegetables are grown here: tomatoes, which play such an important role in the local cuisine, and refined specialties like the green asparagus from Altedo. Fruit, too, with great expanses of pear and peach orchards, and fields of melons and water melons. There is plenty of fresh water too. The choice of traditional local foods reflects the considerable variety of landscape.

TYPICAL LOCAL DISHES

Erbazzone di Reggio Emilia. This savory dish is made with boiled beet and spinach flavored with lardo and herbs, grated parmesan and egg. There is also a sweet version.

Gnocco fritto. This is the Emilian alternative to bread. Made with wheat flour, warm water, suet and salt, mixed together, rolled flat and cut into diamonds. It is then cooked in suet (recently replaced by olive oil) and is eaten either hot, or cold the following day. Excellent with hams, salamis and cold meats or cheese.

Cappelletti and tortellini. This tiny jewel of Emilian cuisine has different names in differ-

Cappelletti are one of the symbols of Emilia-Romagna's gastronomic tradition.

ent places but the substance is much the same. Every chef has their own recipe but all agree that the pasta must be made with wheat flour and eggs, and rolled out by hand. For the filling: pork meat, turkey meat, ham, mortadella, eggs, cheese and nutmeg. Tortellini should be cooked in proper meat stock, and should also be served in it (although eating them 'dry' with cream or meat sauce is also allowed). In Romagna the filling is made with lean meat and cheese.

Lasagne alla bolognese. This is the classic dish of Bologna. The rectangular lasagne made with fresh pasta are par-boiled, then laid in a flat dish. Then alternate layers of ragù (Bolognese sauce), bechamel sauce, grated Parmigiano-Reggiano and pasta are added, ending with a generous sprinkling of parmesan. Then the dish is baked in a hot oven.

Pisarei e fasö. Pisarei from Piacenza are small gnocchi made with stale bread, flour and milk. They are served with boiled Borlotti beans, some of which have been passed through a sieve.

Piadina. Flour, water, salt, oil or suet are the ingredients of this typical flat, round unleavened bread from Romagna. The dough is rolled flat and cut into circles that were traditionally cooked on terracotta (now on hot plates). Usually eaten filled with salamis or cured meats, cheese or vegetables. In Rimini they make a flaky version of the piadina.

Salama da sugo. This is a typical food of Ferrara, made especially at Christmas. It is a tasty salami which is cooked for a long time and served with mashed potatoes.

Pan speziale or certosino. A Christmas specialty from Bologna: sweet and bitter almonds, pine nuts, sultanas, cedar or candied orange peel, cocoa, honey, rum and aniseed.

Spongata. A flat, round cake, with an outer layer of thin, crunchy pastry, covered with icing sugar, with a soft, tasty, spicy filling.

Torta di riso reggiana. This cake traditionally celebrates the arrival of spring. The main ingredient is rice cooked in milk, to which beaten egg, sugar, almonds and lemon zest are added.

TYPICAL LOCAL PRODUCTS

Coppa piacentina DOP. Coppa is made from the round piece of meat between the bottom of the head and the fourth vertebra. Coppa is matured for between 6 months and a year.

Culatello di Zibello DOP. The finest of all cured meats made in Emilia. The slices are unmistakably round and lean, since it is made with the best part of the best pig's haunch. The maturing process, in which the foggy climate of the area plays an important part, sharpens its sweet, delicately herby flavor.

Parmigiano-Reggiano DOP. The flagship of Italian cheese with an annual production of 95,000 tons. It is made with the milk from two milkings from dairy herds fed on high-quality fodder. After aging (up to 3 years), the cheeses have a compact and slightly granular body, and a strong but not spicy flavor.

Pancetta piacentina DOP. One of the fattest cuts of pork, usually rolled with traces of bright red meat and white fat. It has a pleasant, sweet, slightly spicy smell and a characteristic flavor.

Prosciutto di Modena DOP. Haunches of the Pesante Padana pig breed are cut and trimmed, rubbed with salt and hung up to mature. The meat is bright red, has a sweet smell and a delicate flavor.

Prosciutto di Parma DOP. This famous ham which, after 10-12 months of maturing, bears the mark of the five-pointed ducal crown, has a distinctive delicate, sweet flavor and smell.

Salame piacentino DOP. Made with lean pork meat. Bright red when cut, with traces of white fat, it has a fragrant smell and a sweet, delicate flavor.

Mortadella Bologna IGP. This famous cooked salami is made from a smooth mixture of second-quality cuts of pork, fat from the throat of the pig cut into cubes, and herbs. The meat is a distinctive pink color and has a delicate perfume.

Cotechino Modena IGP. This popular salami is made by finely mincing lean cuts of pork with parts of the head and neck.

Zampone Modena IGP. This is made with the front trotters of the pig which are filled with a mixture of lean cuts of pork, pigskin and fat from the throat. It is boiled before serving.

Aceto Balsamico Tradizionale di Modena DOP. This, the best-quality balsamic vinegar, is made with the must of top-quality Trebbiano grapes, which is drawn off, filtered and boiled until the volume is reduced by 50%. Then it is aged in casks of different woods of diminishing size, located in attics exposed to varying temperatures. The manual process takes years and the level of dedication justifies the high price. The same applies to Aceto Balsamico Tradizionale di Reggio Emilia DOP.

Asparago Verde di Altedo IGP. The tips of this asparagus grown between Bologna and Ferrara are green and streaked with purple, and it has a pleasantly bitter smell.

Fungo di Borgotaro IGP. This label applies to fresh mushrooms of several varieties of the genus Boletus (normally referred to as 'porcino') that grow in the broad-leaved deciduous woods and coniferous forests of the Appenines.

Pera dell'Emilia-Romagna IGP. There is a long tradition of growing pears in the Lower Po Valley, especially between Modena and Ravenna. The main types are William, Kaiser, Abate, Fétel, Conference and Decana del Comizio.

Pesca and Nettarina di Romagna IGP. These peaches are grown mainly between Ferrara and Forlì, while nectarines are grown between Ravenna, Forlì and Bologna. Other top-quality fruits grown in Romagna include strawberries, kiwi fruit and lotus.

Ciliegia and Susina di Vignola. Several varieties of cherry (Durone, Mora etc.) are eaten fresh, preserved or made into juices or jams.

Marrone di Castel del Rio IGP. These chestnuts from the local 'domestico' cultivar.

WINE

The whole region is split diagonally by the Via Emilia which runs its length. On one side lie the low hills of the Apennines, perfect vine-growing country, both in terms of exposure to the sun and climate. On the other side the plain slopes gradually down towards the Po and the Adriatic, and has proved to be unexpectedly successful as a wine area. The area can be divided roughly into four parts which have similar traditions and ampelographic characteristics. In the Colli di Piacenza e di Parma, the prevalence of Barbera and Bonarda is obviously influenced by the nearby Oltrepò Pavese and Piedmont further west. The area of Lambrusco extends from the hills to the banks of the Po in the Provinces of Reggio Emilia and Modena. In the Colli Bolognesi and the lower Reno Valley, they traditionally grow white wines such as Pignoletto. Finally there is the huge wine area of Romagna, dominated by Sangiovese, Trebbiano and Albana. There is also a small area near Ferrara where the vines are planted on the silt of the Po Delta, where the local red is Fortana.

Romagna is also the home of Italian brandy. Similar to Cognac and Armagnac, the local brandy is made by distilling wine slowly in copper stills similar to the ones used for grappa (which is made from distilling grape-pressings). In Romagna they use Trebbiano, which is particularly well-suited to making brandy because it is white, not very aromatic, has a low alcohol grade, a good level of fixed acidity and is resistant to oxidation. Another home-made liqueur from the region is Nocino, a digestif made from infusing green walnuts in alcohol with sugar, cinnamon and lemon zest.

FOOD

66... while the Apuan peaks/are shrouded with a sunlit vermilion mist,/and the rays glitter against the distant/glass panes of Tiglio;/come to this new fountain, with/ewers balanced on your heads, shining like a mirror,/delicately balanced, o maidens/of Castelvecchio..." (Pascoli, "La Fonte di Castelvecchio"). While he was teaching Latin and Greek in the towns of Matera, Massa, and Livorno, Professor G. Pascoli often submitted Latin poetry to competitions held in Amsterdam, and more than once he was awarded first place; with his winnings, the great poet was able to purchase a home in this land on the far side of the Apennines, in the Garfagnana, at Castelvecchio di Barga. The tour of Pascoli's home is a literary parenthesis in this route, which is chiefly focused on mountain landscape, hill country and valleys. High elevations, forests, endless vistas: the many and steep climbs and descents only contribute to the excitement of this route. In the first leg, on the Pistoia slopes of the Apennines, for example, you begin close to sea level, then you cross the Passo di Oppio at 821 m, at La Lima you are at 454 m, at Abetone at 1388 m. During all these climbs, you have passed from one valley to another, and though you have never left Tuscany, you have driven some distance alongside the course of the Reno River, which then flows down to the Adriatic through the plains of Romagna. The Reno and its valley are adjacent to other tributaries bound for the Tyrrhenian Sea, in the intricate mountain topography over Pistoia. The eye wanders over craggy silhouettes, amidst the green of alders, beech, white and red deal trees. After Abetone you head down the Modena slopes as far as Pievepelago, and the climbs and descents continue: after going over two high passes, the mouths of the Radici and the Terrarossa, you enter the Serchio Valley – Garfagnana, part of Tuscany but for three centuries ruled by the Este family, dukes of Ferrara, later reduced only to Modena and Reggio Emilia. You can make out the rolling crests of the Apennine watershed and the sere, jagged peaks of the Apuans. The circle is closed as you follow the valley of the Lima River, a tributary of the Serchio, running through steep gorges.

NOT TO BE MISSED

Maresca is a resort at the edge of the Teso Forest, and can be reached via a detour just after the Passo di Oppio. **Gavinana**: in a small museum, you can see documents regarding the battle of 1530 between the Florentines under F. Ferrucci and the imperial troops of the Prince of Orange; the Florentine defeat marked the end of the republic and the return of the Medici to Florence. **Cutigliano** can be reached via a 1.5 km detour from Casotti, on the road to Abetone, after La Lima; a cableway takes you up to the 1,715 m crest of the Apennines, between Libro Aperto and the Corno alle Scale, with a panoramic view. **Abetone** (1,388 m), is a noted ski resort near a large forest; fine views from the Rifugio Selletta, a mountain hut at an elevation of 1,711 m (take a chairlift up) and from Mt Gomito at 1,892 m (another cableway up). **Pievepelago** is a resort town in the Modenese Valley of the Scoltenna; take an 11.5 km road up to the little Lago Santo (1,501 m) at the foot of Mt Giovo. **Foce delle Radici** (1,529 m) is a pass between Emilia and Tuscany with a fine view. At **San Pellegrino in Alpe**, via a 2.5 km detour, you have a vista that reaches the sea, as well as an ethnographic museum. **Castiglione di Garfagnana** lies within the walls of a 14th-century Lucchese fortress, in the 15th-century church of S. Michele with a Madonna by G. di Simone (1389) and a 15th-century wooden crucifix. **Castelnuovo di Garfagnana**: from 1522-25 the great epic poet L. Ariosto lived, as governor, in the 12th-century fortress here. **Grotta del Vento**: known as the cave of wind, it is much loved by European scientists, with 4 km of tunnels, sinkholes, ponds, lakes, underground rivers and numerous natural features. It is like an encyclopedia of the karst world and can be visited along a special path with qualified guides. **Castelvecchio Pascoli**: the house that belonged to G. Pascoli, a great 19th-century Italian poet, is outside the town, among the houses of Carpona. **Barga**: the Romanesque Duomo stands on the high meadow of the Arringo, towering over the ancient village, with a panoramic view over valley and mountains. **Bagni di Lucca** is a spa with a venerable reputation, founded by E. Baciocchi, sister of Napoleon and princess of Lucca; as the 19th century wore on, an elect international clientele would come here, including celebrated authors and in 1840 the first casino to be built in Europe was established here. **Vico Pancellorum** is a secluded village high in the valley of the Lima, at the end of a 2.5 km detour, a few km past Fabbriche and just before Popiglio. **Popiglio**: note the ancient towers in the village's skyline, and the medieval parish church of the Assunta. **Pistoia** (➡ see below): this city rivals Lucca and Florence, both in the history of art and of politics; you can spend more than one intensely interesting day examining art, collections, monuments, and the old city itself.

PISTOIA

Situated within the diamond shape of the 14th-century walls, the juxtaposition of light-and-dark striped marble, so typical of the medieval architecture of Pisa, Tuscany, and Liguria, here becomes more minute and subtle, setting a forest green against the pure white. Thus, the architecture here is perfectly matched with the surrounding landscape, and the stone blends with the plain of the Ombrone River and the nearby spurs of the Apennines. This harmony may seem surprising from a city that spawned so much art yet so much violence: the medieval chronicler, G. Villani, recalls "the bad seed that came from Pistoia, engendering black and white factions," the source of the raging factions that drove D. Alighieri, a member of the "white" faction, into lifelong exile; another poet, C. da Pistoia, was of the "black" faction, and was also exiled. This "stilnovista" wrote that he liked to "see others smitten in the face by blows of a sword, and ships sent to the bottom of the sea."

Piazza del Duomo*. The historical and artistic center of Pistoia, bounded by medieval buildings, this square holds, of course, the Duomo, with its tall bell tower, the Palazzo Vescovile, and the baptistery, with the Palazzo del Pretorio and Palazzo del Comune facing each other. At the corner of Via Tomba stands the medieval Torre di Catilina, whose name marks the fact that Catiline, a Roman conspirator denounced by Cicero, fled here and was defeated (62 BC), and then buried near Pistoia's walls.

Duomo**. This Romanesque cathedral was built in the Pisan style in the 12th-13th century, and has a stone facade with three rows of loggias, with a marble portico (late 14C). The lunette over the central portal has an enameled terracotta bas-relief* by A. della Robbia (1505), who also did the decorations of the barrel vaults. Note the enormous bell tower. The interior is majestic, and you should observe numerous artworks. Among them: in the right aisle, the early 14th-century funerary monument of C. da Pistoia; Crucifix on panel by C. di Marcovaldo (1275); monumental silver altar panel of S. Jacopo**, begun in 1287 and finished in the mid-15th century. At the end of the aisle is the entrance to the sacristy, mentioned by Dante in his "Inferno." Note the S. Atto chapel, with painting by M. Preti; also, a fine bronze candelabrum by M. di Bartolomeo (1440). In the chapel to the left of the presbytery, canvas* by L. di Credi (1485), and stele commemorating the bishop D. de' Medici

by A. Rossellino. At the foot of the left aisle, the monument to Cardinal Forteguerri (1419-73): the statues of Faith and Hope are by A. Verrocchio, those of Christ and angels are by Verrocchio's pupils, among them L. di Credi. Note the baptismal font by A. Ferrucci da Fiesole, designed by B. da Maiano.

Battistero**. An admirable piece of Gothic architecture, octagonal in shape, this Baptistery was begun in 1338 by C. di Nese, to plans by A. Pisano, and completed in 1359. With white-and-green marble facing, it is surmounted by a blind gallery and has three fine portals, with reliefs and statues. Inside, 14th-century full baptismal font, restored in 1960.

Palazzo dei Vescovi. This 14th-century building with loggia and mullioned windows is a major piece of Pistoian civil architecture of the Middle Ages, renovated in later centuries. It houses the Museo Capitolare di San Zeno,

The facade of the baptistery in Pistoia.

with exquisite artwork and sacred objects from the Treasury of the Duomo, as well as frescoes and paintings. Also note the archeological section documenting the origins of Pistoia.

Palazzo del Podestà. This stern building dates from 1367 and was enlarged in the mid-19th century. Note the mullioned windows and porticoed courtyard, studded with family crests in marble and terracotta; to the left of the entrance is a stone "judge's bench," restored in 1507, where the accused were tried. **Palazzo del Comune***. This austere and majestic town hall, built with local Tuscan stone called "pietra serena" was begun in 1294 and enlarged in 1348-85. To the left of the large central window, crowned by a Medici crest, with papal keys honoring Leo X (1513), is an odd head carved of black marble, probably depicting Musetto, the king of Majorca, defeated by the Pistoian G. de' Ghisilieri (1113-14). This palazzo now houses the Museo Civico; in the courtyard, sculpture by M. Marini.

Museo Civico. Pistoia's city museum is housed on the two upper floors of the Palazzo del Comune, where the handsome public halls feature frescoes and carved ceilings. Note especially, in the main hall, the wooden ceiling, the long 16th-century bench, and the city crest, in marble, by the workshop of A. Verrocchio. In the museum proper, 13th-14th-century paintings are on display. Note the rare panel with scenes from the life of St Francis (1260-70), and a polyptych dated at 1310, and the wooden sculpture by F. di Valdambrino. From the 15th-16th century are the altarpieces from local churches, by L. di Credi, G. Gerini, R. del Ghirlandaio, Fra' P. da Pistoia, G.B. Volponi, and B. del Signoraccio. A section features canvases from the 17th-18th-century by such artists as G. Gimignani, F. Vanni, M. Rosselli, P. Batoni, L. Cigoli, and others. Also note the Puccini collection, with works ranging from 17th-century. Florence to 19th-century furniture. A hall is also devoted to contemporary local painters.

Madonna dell'Umiltà*. This basilica, a major piece of Renaissance architecture, was built by V. Vitoni (1494-1522) and may have been designed by G. da Sangallo; it has an octagonal plan and is surmounted by a vast dome, by G. Vasari. On the main altar, fresco by P. Tacca; chapels decorated by B. Ammannati.

S. Francesco. Begun in 1289 and completed in the 15th century, this large church was greatly renovated over the centuries, especially in Baroque times; the white-and-green striped marble facade dates from 1717. Inside, fragments of frescoes from the 14th-15th-century: work by P. Capanna, and others of the school of Giotto and local schools; in the sacristy, frescoes in the manner of N. di Pietro Gerini; also, 14th-century Sala Capitolare.

S. Andrea**. A 12th-century church with a Romanesque facade in the Pisan style; over the architrave of the central portal, reliefs by Gruamonte and Adeodato (1166). Inside is one of the masterpieces of 12th-13th century. Italian sculpture: the pulpit** (1298-1301) by G.

Pisano, who also carved the wooden Crucifix* in a 15th-century tabernacle, midway up the right aisle. Also note the frescoes by G. da Pistoia, and the 14th-century baptismal font.

Ospedale del Ceppo*. This 13th-14th-century hospital was named after a stump used to collect alms. Note the Florentine-style portico (1514), with medallions and a frieze* in polychrome terracotta, by G. della Robbia and S. Buglioni (1525-26).

Palazzo Rospigliosi. This palazzo is a combination of several buildings from different eras, the oldest of which is adjacent to the cathedral. The entrance is from Ripa del Sale, up a double staircase. Upstairs is a lavish apartment, named after Clement IX, a Pistoian pope believed to have lived here. Note the 17th-century furniture and paintings. Also, visit the Museo Diocesano, with sacred objects and artwork from local churches.

S. Paolo. A Pisan-style church built in 1291-1302, with a handsome facade and a portal with carved lunette; note the Gothic tombs. Inside is a 14th-century wooden Crucifix.

S. Domenico. Built in the late 13th century and enlarged in 1380, this church holds a funerary monument to Filippo Lazzari by B. and A. Rossellino (1462-68).

S. Antonio del Tau. Named after the "tau," or Greek "T," worn by its monks on their habits, this church was built in 1340 by Fra' G. Guidotti; it has not been used for worship for two centuries. Inside there are the 14th-15th-century frescoes*. In the former convent, restored in 1987, is the Centro di Documentazione e Fondazione Marino Marini, with collections of the work of the Pistoian artist, including etchings, lithographs, and sculptures.

S. Giovanni Fuorcivitas**. Begun in the 12th century and completed in the 14th-century, this is one of Pistoia's largest Romanesque churches. Note the facing with bands of travertine and greenish marble; in the portal, architrave by Gruamonte (1162). Inside, note the marble pulpit* by Fra' G. da Pisa (1270); holy-water stoup* with reliefs by G. Pisano. In the presbytery, polyptych* by T. Gaddi (1353-55), fragments of frescoes from the early 14th century, and terracotta group* by the Della Robbia school.

Via Roma. At the beginning of this street, note the imitation-Renaissance Palazzo della Cassa di Risparmio (1905); nearby, on the opposite side of the street, is the Palazzo del Capitano del Popolo (late 13C), at the corner of Via della Straccería, lined with medieval homes and workshops.

VALDINIEVOLE AND LUCCA

The Nievole is a short mountain stream that flows down from the Apennines to sink into the Padule di Fucecchio, but the Valdinievole (or Nievole Valley) is a world to itself: a high hilltop meadowland, fading into hillocks topped by cypresses, chestnut trees, grapevines, light-colored expanses of olive trees, and, in the valleys, fields dense with flowers. The Valdinievole includes the valleys of the Pescia and the Pescia di Collodi, as well as Montecatini Terme and the town of Pescia. The route runs from west to east. The Florentine author of "Pinocchio," C. Lorenzini, took his pen name from the town of Collodi, where he spent part of his childhood. We may suppose that this was the landscape in which Pinocchio "rolled his eyes around to see, amidst the dark green of the trees, a white speck in the distance: a little house as white as snow," the house of the "little girl with light-blue hair." At any rate, the town of Collodi perennially celebrates the little boy carved of wood. Mt Albano is a forest-covered chain of hills, running NW to SE, between Montecatini Terme and the Arno, sealing off the plain of Pistoia and Prato to the south. And these two cities, with their remarkable ancient quarters, certainly offer the artistic highlights of this route: in Pistoia, the silver altar frontal of S. Jacopo (mentioned by Dante); in Prato, Donatello's dancing cherubs on the pulpit of the Sacro Cingolo, to mention only two.

NOT TO BE MISSED

San Gennaro can be reached by taking a detour from the SS 435 road, about 12 km from Lucca; it boasts a remarkable Romanesque church. **Collodi** requires another detour, soon after, from the SS 435 road; it is notable for the Parco di Pinocchio and the garden of Villa Garzoni. **Pescia**: in the church of S. Francesco is a panel by B. Berlinghieri (1235); flowers are grown intensively. **Montecatini Alto** has medieval quarters; to get here, you must detour 2 km from the road; noteworthy view. **Montecatini Terme***: parks, Art-Nouveau (or "liberty," in Italian) architecture and the high-society elegance of a spa town. **Serravalle Pistoiese** has ruins of medieval fortifications; in the former Romanesque church of S. Michele are 14th-century Florentine frescoes. **Vinci** has a 13th-century castle, with a museum devoted to L. da Vinci; continue along till you come to the Romanesque parish church of San Giusto, on the ridge of Mt Albano. **Poggio a Caiano** features a Medici villa by Giuliano da Sangallo. **Prato***: it is best known as a thriving wool-manufacturing town, but the old area, enclosed by 14th-century hexagonal walls, has a venerable air and great monuments of Italian art. The church of S. Giovanni Battista, near a major highway interchange, the Firenze Nord, is a masterpiece of modern architecture by G. Michelucci (1960-64). **Sesto Fiorentino** has the Museo delle Porcellane di Doccia, or museum of shower tiles, and, in the outlying neighborhood of Quinto, the Etruscan tomb of Montagnola. Continue along through the outskirts of Florence, and stop by the Medici villas of Castello and Petraia.

LUCCA

The marble sleep of the lovely statue of Ilaria del Carretto, carved by J. della Quercia, in the church of S. Martino, seems a perfect symbol for this dignified city, enveloped in its proud past. Lucca is a thriving and modern town, but it jealously preserves the timeless image of the ancient city enclosed within its red walls. It stands on the left bank of the Serchio River, in an exceedingly fertile alluvial plain, enclosed between the Apennine slopes of the Pizzorne and Mt Pisano, in a landscape of olive groves and rolling hills.

The monumental center. Piazza Napoleone, a square whose name reveals its date of foundation, was built at the same time as the tree-lined avenues along the walls; note the unrivalled monumental church of Ss. Giovanni e Reparata and the Duomo, as well as the nar-

The walls of Lucca.

row, attractive streets in the heart of Lucca.

Piazza Napoleone. This vast square, lined with plane trees, is adorned by a Neo-Classic monument to the duchess Maria Luisa, by L. Bartolini (1843). It is flanked by the Palazzo della Provincia, formerly della Signoria or Ducale, begun in 1578 by B. Ammannati; interior by L. Nottolini, who also built the spectacular, stucco-adorned staircase* (19C).

Ss. Giovanni e Reparata*. Built in the 12th-century and rebuilt in the 17th century, this church still has its original portal (1187). Recent archeological excavations (1969-90) have uncovered a series of fascinating structures, among

Facade of the church of S. Michele in Foro.

which is the ancient Baptistery, a vast square room with a Gothic vault.

Piazza S. Martino with the adjacent Piazza Antelminelli. This square forms a handsome medieval setting dominated by the marble Duomo (see below) and bounded by low houses: left, Palazzo Bernardi, by B. Ammannati (1556); right, against the bell tower, the medieval Casa dell'Opera del Duomo (13C).

Duomo*, dedicated to San Martino (St Martin), this is Lucca's main church. It was built in Romanesque style in the 11th-13th century, but the interior was rebuilt in the 14th-15th century. The remarkable asymmetrical marble Romanesque facade* (1204), largely by G. da Como, comprises a portico supported by three broad arches and three rows of small light loggias, with polychrome casing and small varied columns; to the right is a stout 13th-century bell tower, adorned with parapets. Under the portico, note the reliefs*, begun in 1233, by a Lombard master; the reliefs on the left portal are attributed to N. Pisano; the doors of the central portal were carved by M. Civitali (1497). The sides of the cathedral date

from the 14th century; note the impressive apse*, which shows late Pisan influence. The elegant Gothic interior features sculptures and paintings by artists such as Civitali, Zuccari, Tintoretto, D. Ghirlandaio, P. di Noceto, D. Bertini da Gallicano, Giambologna, Juvarra, and Fra' Bartolomeo. In the center of the second chapel of the left transept is the justly renowned funerary monument to Ilaria del Carretto**, a masterpiece by J. della Quercia (1408) and one of the finest pieces of 15th-century Italian sculpture.

Complesso museale e archeologico della Cattedrale. Piazza Antelminelli, this museum features religious treasures from the Duomo and the church of Ss. Giovanni e Reparata, including: a 14th-century Flemish reliquary, a painting by F. Marti, and a handsome gilt cross, called the Croce dei Pisani*. Note the paintings and sculpture from the Duomo, by J. della Quercia and M. Civitali.

S. Maria della Rosa, directly behind the Palazzo Arcivescovile, or archbishop's palace, this church was originally a Pisan-Gothic oratory (1309). The Renaissance portal is by Matteo Civitali; inside, fragments of the 2nd-century BC Roman walls. From the nearby bastion known as Baluardo S. Colombano, at the end of Via della Rosa, there is fine view of the Duomo.

Via Guinigi*, among the most attractive of Lucca's roads, this one still seems medieval. It features the Case dei Guinigi*, a compact set of towers and brick houses (14C), the palazzo at the corner of Via S. Andrea, and the Torre Guinigi, topped by holm-oaks (entrance to the top of the tower from Via S. Andrea).

Ss. Simone e Giuda. This small 13th-century church overlooks Via Guinigi; it has a simple grey stone facade, with three portals and an elegant window. In Via S. Andrea, after the entrance to the Torre Guinigi (see above), is the 13th-century church of S. Andrea; facing it is the late 14th-century Casa Gentili.

Piazza del Salvatore. In the square are a Neo-Classic fountain by L. Nottolini, the medieval Torre del Veglio, and the 13th-century church of the Misericordia, with fine reliefs.

Piazza S. Michele*, on the site of the Roman Forum, this square is a pulsing center of life in Lucca. Surrounded by 13th-century buildings, its focal point is the marble church of S.

Michele in Foro (see below); at the corner of Via V. Veneto is the Palazzo Pretorio, begun in 1492, possibly by M. Civitali, and enlarged in 1588 by V. Civitali. Around the corner, in Via di Poggio, is the birthplace of G. Puccini.

S. Michele in Foro**. This church was built between 1143 and the 14th century, and is an outstanding example of Pisan-Luccan architecture. The tall facade is surmounted by four rows of small loggias, with a lavish decoration* of marble inlay; note the colossal Romanesque statue of the Archangel Michael; low on the right corner is a statue of the Virgin with Child, by M. Civitali (1480). The left side, with its pronounced arches and 14th-century loggia, is particularly handsome. Then there are the stout bell tower, decorated with small arches and the Pisan-influenced apse*. The interior features frescoes, terracottas, paintings, and marble reliefs by such artists as G. di Simone, A. della Robbia, F. Lippi, A. Marti, and R. da Montelupo.

S. Paolino. In a widened part of Via S. Paolino is this church, with a marble facade and handsome sides. Begun in 1522 by B. da Montelupo on the site of a huge Roman building, it was completed in 1536, and is Lucca's only example of a Renaissance church. Inside, two holy-water stoups by N. Civitali, a painted wooden sculpture by F. Valdambrino (1414), the choir stalls by N. and V. Civitali, a 14th-century painted wooden Crucifix, a 15th-century panel of the *Coronation of the Virgin* with a depiction of medieval Lucca, and a panel by A. Marti.

Palazzo Mansi*, at no. 43 Via Galli Tassi. This 17th-century building has a handsome porticoed courtyard. The interior is largely intact, with 18th-century furnishings. Note the Salone della Musica, frescoed in 1688 by G. G. Del Sole, and the Camera dell'Alcova*, with silk embroideries, stuccowork and gilded inlaid wood; Flemish tapestries (1665). The palace houses the Pinacoteca Nazionale.

Pinacoteca Nazionale di Palazzo Mansi. This art gallery possesses paintings, from Italy and elsewhere, dating from the Renaissance to the early 18th century, arranged so as to imitate the collection of the Guardaroba Mediceo, a gift made to Lucca by Leopoldo II. Particularly noteworthy, among the Tuscan paintings, are works by: Beccafumi, Bronzino, V. Salimbeni, Pontormo, A. del Sarto; among the painters from other schools, mention should be made of Veronese, J. Bassano, Ligozzi, Tintoretto, S. Rosa, R. da Tivoli, J. Sustermans, Barocci, Zacchia the Elder, C. Dolci, Domenichino, Borgognone, Reni, P.

Brill, J. Miel, G. Terborch, L. Carlevarijs, and D. Calvaert. On the second floor, two more sections are dedicated to 19th-century artists from Lucca, including P. Batoni, B. and P. Nocchi, A. Tofanelli, and M. Ridolfi, and historic fabrics, dating back to the 16th century, especially damasks, a local specialty. Note the Tongiorgi Collection of 6th-10th-century Coptic fabrics.

S. Romano. This 13th-century church has traces of its Gothic appearance (on the sides, especially) and a lively apse (1373). Inside, note the tomb* by M. Civitali (1490).

S. Alessandro. This notable piece of early Luccan Romanesque architecture (11C) has a marble facade, a 13th-century apse, and, inside, handsome Romanesque and re-used capitals (3-4C).

S. Frediano and the northern districts. Via Fillungo is the medieval backbone of the historic center, with the handsome facade of the church of S. Frediano, the oval of Piazza del Mercato, the unrivalled treasures of Luccan art, displayed in the Museo di Villa Guinigi.

S. Giusto, overlooking Piazza S. Giusto, a late 12th-century Romanesque church has a marble facade and a stuccoed interior.

Via del Battistero, the handsome street runs from Piazza S. Giusto passing by Palazzo Tegrimi Mansi. At the corner of Via S. Donnino.

Via Fillungo*, the main street of the historic center of Lucca is lined with fine shops but still has a medieval look, with old houses and towers. First, note the early 16th-century Palazzo Cenami, by N. Civitali, and, across from it, the 13th-century Pisan-style church of S. Cristoforo, with portal and rose window. At no. 43 is the 13th-century Casa Barletti Baroni, with mullioned windows with terracotta casements also the 13th-century Torre delle Ore.

Via C. Battisti. This winding street is lined with fine 17th-18th-century palazzi, ending with the startling presence of the large crenelated bell tower* of S. Frediano (see below). At no. 33, Palazzo Controni-Pfanner, 1667, with an outside staircase* and 18th-century statue-bedecked garden.

S. Frediano**, built in 112-47 and renovated in the 13th century, this church has a simple and noble facade, with a small loggia with architrave, surmounted by a Byzantine-style mosaic*. The lovely interior, with a nave with two aisles, ancient columns, and vast apse, features works by A. Aspertini, A. Ciampanti, A. della Robbia, M. Civitali. Note the richly carved 12th-century Romanesque font* at the foot of the right aisle. In the left aisle are the funerary slabs of L. Trenta and wife. In the presbytery, 12th-century Cosmatesque mosaic floor, and the last chapel in the left aisle features reliefs** by J. della Quercia. Alongside the church are the relics of the 13th-century cemetery of S. Caterina, in the form of a three-sided cloister.

Piazza Anfiteatro, former Piazza del Mercato. This square, just off Via Fillungo, was opened in 1830 on the site of a 2nd-century AD Roman amphitheater, hence the elliptical shape. Parts of the original walls of the theater can be seen; the houses that had been built in the arena were demolished. The houses now enclosing the square were built around the shape of the arena. Via Fillungo ends with the medieval Portone dei Borghi, a city gate with two passages and round towers.

S. Pietro Somaldi, this 12th-century church has a Pisan facade with grey-and-white stripes, a handsome portal, and a solid terracotta bell tower. Nearby, at the intersection with Via del Fosso (see below), is a tall column with ancient capital, crowned by a 17th-century statue of the Madonna dello Stellario; note also the Neo-Classic fountain by L. Nottolini.

S. Francesco. This church was begun in 1228, rebuilt in the 14th-17th-century, and restored in the early 20th century. The white limestone facade has a portal and two aediculae, one dating from 1249. Inside, 15th-century Florentine frescoes; choir with lectern by L. Marti (16C); on left wall, funerary plaques honoring the Luccan composers Boccherini and Giminiani.

Museo Nazionale di Villa Guinigi*. This museum is set in the 15th-century villa that once belonged to P. Guinigi (lord of Lucca from 1400 to 1430), a vast brickwork construction, with a ground-floor loggia and handsome mullioned windows restored to its original appearance following WWII. Recently, it was thoroughly restored and modernized. The museum contains almost exclusively art works produced for the city or surrounding territories, either by local artists or outsiders. The collections therefore give one an excellent idea of Lucca's artistic history through the centuries; the collections were established mainly following the Unification of Italy, through the confiscation of ecclesiastical holdings.

Ground floor. Archeological section, with local finds dating from prehistoric to late Roman times: furnishings from Ligurian and Etruscan tombs, Roman inscriptions, architectural fragments, mosaics, a Greek-Hellenistic relief from Vallecchia, and a huge altar uncovered (1983) in Piazza S. Michele. Halls with collections of coins and ceramics are followed by rooms of medieval art: fragments of archi-

tectural decorations, church furnishings, and rare examples of Longobard jewelry and metalwork (note the shield found near the church of S. Romano), and 12th-13th-century sculpture and paintings. First floor: sculpture from the late 13th to the 15th-century, by artists including D. Orlandi, L. Marti, P. della Quercia, V. Frediani, M. and A. Ciampanti, M. da Lucca, M. Civitali, F. Marti, A. Aspertini, Fra' Bartolomeo, Zacchia the Elder, A. Marti, G. Vasari, P. Guidotti, G. Reni, P. da Cortona, Lombardi, Brugieri, and Luchi. Two rooms are devoted to the work of P. Paolini and G. Scaglia, interesting 17th-century Luccan artists. The gardens contain archeological finds and medieval relics, including a 2nd-century mosaic floor. Note the medieval lions from the city walls.

Via del Fosso. One of Lucca's loveliest streets, it takes its name from the moat ("fosso"), that once lay east of the 13th-century walls. Along Via del Fosso is the handsome park of the 16th-century **Villa Buonvisi**, with frescoes by V. Salimbeni; across from the villa is the little **church of the Santissima Trinità**, built in 1589. Nearby, the 13th-century **Porta dei Ss. Gervasio e Protasio**, handsome city gate with two semicircular towers; also, against the walls, the Orto Botanico, the botanical gardens established in 1820.

S. Maria Forisportam. This Romanesque, Pisan-style church (13C) has a marble facade with fine carved portals. In the square is a granite Roman column, once used as the finish line in town horse races (Palio). Inside, an early Christian sarcophagus and two paintings by Guercino. In the right transept, note the 17th-century ciborium.

Via S. Croce. This road runs straight, past medieval houses and aristocratic palazzi, from Porta dei Ss. Gervasio e Protasio to Via Fillungo. In the middle, note the 16th-century **Palazzo Bernardini**, by N. Civitali. Behind the palazzo is the 17th-century church of the Suffragio, built in a plague-year burial ground (1630). To the left, the 13th-century oratory of S. Giulia; inside is a 13th-century painted Cross.

The walls*. Ancient and intact, these walls were one of the outstanding pieces of fortification in all Tuscany; they form a tree-lined ring around Lucca (built 1504-1645). With 11 bastions, these walls are about 21 m tall, offering charming views of the city. In summer, concerts and performances are held here; the Baluardo **S. Paolino** is the site of the Centro Internazionale per lo Studio delle Cerchie Urbane, with the summer Museo Virtuale.

LOWER VALDARNO AND PISA

Although the course of the Arno River from Florence to Pisa and on to the sea is anything but straightforward, it does tend westward. This route runs through the Arno Valley, upstream from Pisa and Florence, and almost entirely forsakes the two more common roads on either bank of the river, in favor of less well known routes, overlooking the winding Arno from the high roads. This route heads north over Mt Pisano, then south through the Valdera and over the hills between Palaia and San Miniato, and lastly north, through C. Guidi and Vinci, over Mt Albano. The thriving and prosperous valley shows the hand of man nearly everywhere. This route offers remarkable vistas, exquisite art and architecture, and lovely stretches of scenery. Let us mention two, which formed subjects for two lost masterpieces of Tuscan art. At Cascina, the Florentines, who had pushed thus far in their war against Pisa, risked it all on a toss of dice (and won) on 28 July 1364, battling fiercely against the 800 men-at-arms under the Pisan commander-general, G. Acuto (the Italian version of the name of the English soldier John Hawkwood, who fought for Florence as well; see the funerary monument painted by P. Uccello in S. M. del Fiore). When commemorating this past glory of Florence, at one point, the G. P. Soderini commissioned Michelangelo to paint a fresco of the event. Michelangelo "filled the painting with nude men, who were cooling off from the summer heat in the Arno River, at the very moment that the battle began in the field" (Vasari): that work is now lost, as is its companion piece, the Battle of Anghiari, by L. da Vinci – once they both could be seen in Palazzo Vecchio. Drive on through olive groves and vineyards to the town of Vinci, where the great artist was born, an "illegitimate son" (according to the town records) of a notary and property owner in Anchiano, and a certain Caterina, who later married Attaccabriga di Pietro del Vacca.

NOT TO BE MISSED

Calci: the Certosa, or Charterhouse, of **Pisa** (➡ see below) is here, as is an 11th-century parish church; take a 12 km detour over Mt Serra to the highest peak on Mt Pisano (917 m): there is an immense vista, with the sea, the Apuans, Valdarno, and the Apennines. **Cascina**: you take a 3 km detour from Lugnano to get here; go see the 14th-century frescoes in the Oratory of S. Giovanni and the Romanesque parish church of S. Maria. **Vicopisano**: a maze of medieval lanes, a Pisan Romanesque parish church, and the ruins of the fortifications restored by Brunelleschi, following the Florentine conquest of 1407. **Palaia** boasts the parish church in the old town and the church of S. Martino just outside of town, both dating from the 13th century. **San Miniato** has very fine monuments and collections of art; the views and medieval quarters are noteworthy. A theater festival takes places in the square at the end of July, and there is a national market exhibition of white truffles in November. **Fucecchio** stands on the outlying ridges of the Mt Albano; the collegiate church of S. G. Battista is at the top of a stairway (a fine view from a square to the left). **Cerreto Guidi**: a splendid stairway by B. Buontalenti leads up to the Medici Villa (1576), where P. G. Orsini strangled his wife Isabella. **Vinci**: L. da Vinci took his name from this village, although he was probably born in Anchiano; visit the Museo Vinciano in the castle. **Artimino**: amid olive groves and vineyards; facing the town is the Medici Villa, La Ferdinanda. **Signa** is a town in which straw and terracotta objects are manufactured; in the upper part of town are a 15th-century baptismal font and frescoes depicting the life of S. Giovanna in the parish church of S. G. Battista.

PISA

The columns of the Battistero, or Baptistery, were brought across the sea from Elba and Sardinia; the Camposanto, or Cemetery, encloses earth brought by galleon from Golgotha, in the Holy Land (1203). Even before the architect Buscheto began designing the Duomo, in the 11th century, he had been influenced by the Islamic architecture of the Levant, as well as by architecture from Armenia. The breezes from the sea are a fundamental component of this city – straddling the Arno River – which certainly holds a place of high honor in Italian art.

THE MEDICI CENTER AND PIAZZA DEL DUOMO

From the Ponte di Mezzo, the sight of the imposing ranks of venerable palazzi overlooking the Arno River foreshadows – after you make your way through the 16th-century Medici center of Pisa – the spectacular geometric perspective of the Campo dei Miracoli, a must for any visitor.

Ponte di Mezzo. This oldest bridge in Pisa was rebuilt after WWII. It crosses the Arno in a single span, opening north onto Piazza Garibaldi. Note the bronze monument (1892).

Borgo Stretto. One of the main streets of the old district, lined with handsome porticoes. In a 17th-century tabernacle at the head of the right portico, there is the copy of a wooden sculpture by Nino Pisano (the original is at the Museo di S. Matteo). A bit further on is the church of S. Michele (see below).

S. Michele in Borgo*. Built in the 11th-century, modified in the 14th century, this church has a Pisan-style facade (14C); note the portals and loggias. Inside, 13th-century fresco and a 14th-century marble Crucifix.

Piazza dei Cavalieri*. Once the center of Pisa, during the Republic, this square was renovated under the Medici to accommodate the 16th-century headquarters of the Order of the Knights of St Stephen. Many of the buildings on the square are by G. Vasari, but one of them stands out: Vasari's Palazzo dei Cavalieri* (1562), which features a massive curving facade, a double stairway, a statue and a fountain by P. Francavilla (1596); on the right, the church of S. Stefano dei Cavalieri (see below). Note also Vasari's Palazzo dell'Orologio, a building which is said to stand on the site of the captivity of Count Ugolino della Gherardesca, whose horrible death is recounted by Dante in his "Inferno".

S. Stefano dei Cavalieri*. The church and bell tower are by G. Vasari (1569); the marble facade dates from 1606. Inside: on the walls, three fragments of a 17th-century processional ship; canvases and ceiling by Cigoli, Allori, Empoli, and Ligozzi. Note the painting by Bronzino (1564).

Via S. Maria. Perhaps the most distinctive of Pisa's streets, lined with 17th-18th-century buildings, some of which belong to the university. Toward the Arno River, at no. 26, is the Domus Galileana, with a major library of works by and about G. Galilei. Note, at the corner of Via Volta, a 13th-century tower-house; also, the church of S. Giorgio dei Tedeschi, and the 15th-century Ospizio dei Trovatelli*.

Orto Botanico dell'Università; entrance from Via Ghini no. 5. This botanical garden was moved here from its previous site on the Arno in 1595 by Ferdinando I. It occupies over 2 km², with greenhouses and open plantings.

Piazza del Duomo**. Also known as Campo dei Miracoli, this square holds the finest masterpieces of Pisan Romanesque art, and is one of the best known and most popular monuments in Italy. On the broad meadow, against the backdrop of crenelated medieval walls, stand the cathedral, baptistery, tower, and cemetery. Built in different periods, they are wonderfully homogeneous in color and style.

Bell tower**. Also known as the Torre Pendente, or Leaning Tower, it is the emblem of Pisa and one of the most famous towers in the world, both for its elegant white marble and for its decidedly odd tilt. Construction began in 1173, was halted as the ground began to sink, and was begun again in 1275, to be finished after 1350. Cylindrical, it has the same decorative motif as the apse of the Cathedral. Inside is a 294-step winding staircase, leading to the 54-m-high top of the tower. From here, Galileo is said to have performed his experiments concerning the pull of gravity on falling objects.

Duomo**. This impressive white building, with its elegant decoration, was built between 1064 and the 12th century by Buscheto and Rainaldo, and is the crowning creation of Pisan Romanesque architecture. The facade is spectacularly adorned with four rows of small loggias, and decorated with marble statues and inlay. Followers of Giambologna made the bronze doors of the three portals. To the left of the apse is the Portal of S. Ranieri, with lovely bronze doors* by B. Pisano (1180). The interior, solemn and beautifully lit, dressed in black-and-white marble, has a nave with four aisles divided by close-set columns, an elliptical dome, and a deep apse. In the nave, note the handsome bronze holy water stoups by F. Palma (1621); at the end of the nave is the marble pulpit** by G. Pisano (1302-11), a complex masterpiece of Italian Gothic

The Cathedral and the dome of the baptistery.

G. di Simone. An inner gallery surrounds the meadow of the ancient cemetery. Of the two simple portals, the right one is surmounted by an elegant Gothic tabernacle (school of N. Pisano, 1350). Ravaged in July 1944 by a fire sparked by combat, its current appearance is the result of painstaking restoration. Intended for the burial of noble and illustrious citizens of Pisa, from the 15th century on many funerary monuments were moved here (most are now restored to their original locations), along with a collection of mostly Roman sarcophagi*. The walls were decorated with frescoes, often destroyed by time or fire; many of those that survive are protected in a room, which can be reached from the north arm.

West arm: several remarkable Roman sarcophagi; a large marble Etruscan vase; the family tomb of the Conti della Gherardesca (1315-20), by a follower of G. Pisano; on the wall, chains from the ships of the Battle of Meloria. **North arm**: Greek and Roman funerary objects. In the Ammannati chapel, monument to L. Ammannati (died in 1359), from the school of G. Pisano. To the left of the chapel is a hall of frescoes* by the so-called Maestro del Trionfo della Morte (1360-80; some identify this Master as B. Buffalmacco): *Triumph of Death***, *Last Judgement*, *Hell*, and a *Massacre of Anchorites**; also a *Landscape* by T. Gaddi. In a huge hall next to the chapel, a series of large prints show the frescoes as they originally were. Also, note the 2nd-century BC Greek marble vase*. In the Aulla chapel, note the 2nd-century AD "sarcophagus of Countess Beatrice"*, and the sarcophagus of the Sponsali*. **East arm**. Completely stripped of its original frescoes; note the tomb of G. Buoncompagni by B. Ammannati (1574); the tomb of O. Massotti, with a female figure by G. Duprè; and the renowned statue of the "Inconsolable Woman," by L. Bartolini (1842).

South arm: tablets concerning the original Roman colony of Pisa, mosaics, two headless 2nd-century statues, and Roman and medieval sarcophagi.

Museo delle Sinopie*. This museum in Piazza del Duomo has collections of preparatory drawings (usually ocher in color) of the frescoes that once decorated the cemetery. It is the largest and most interesting collection of drawings by great 14th-century artists. Note the work* by the Maestro del Trionfo della

sculpture. Almost directly across from it is the "lamp of Galileo," made of bronze, and designed by B. Lorenzi (1587); its swinging motion was long believed to have inspired Galileo's discoveries concerning the pendulum (it is now known, however, that these discoveries were made six years before the lamp was installed). Right aisle: note the paintings by A. del Sarto and G.A. Sogliani. Right transept: 14th-century mosaic, partly hidden by the chapel of S. Ranieri; also note the tomb of the Holy Roman Emperor Henry VII* by T. di Camaino. Cross vault of the transept: remarkable 13th-century Cosmatesque mosaic floor.

Presbytery: two bronze angels by Giambologna (1602); 15th-century inlaid stalls*; and paintings by A. del Sarto and Sogliani. On the altar, bronze Crucifix by Giambologna. In the vault of the apse, note the large 13th-century mosaic of the Savior between Mary and St John the Evangelist* (the head of the latter is by Cimabue); below, paintings by Beccafumi, Sodoma, and Sogliani.

Baptistery**. This majestic round Romanesque building, made of white marble, girded by arches and loggias with elegant Gothic crowning ornamentation, was begun in 1152 by Diotisalvi, continued in the next century by N. and G. Pisano, and completed around 1350, with a pyramidal eight-sided dome* by C. di Nese. The Baptistery has four exceedingly fine portals*: particular note should be given to the one facing the Cathedral. Inside, note the octagonal baptismal font* by G. da Como (1246); on its left, supported by carved stone lions bearing columns on their backs, is the pulpit** by N. Pisano (1260). Before the altar, 13th-century Cosmatesque marble floor. Along the walls, large statues* by N. and G. Pisano and school, formerly set on the exterior of the Baptistery.

Camposanto**. This perfect rectangular structure with blind arcades was begun in 1277 by

Morte, and the large Crucifixion*, for the first fresco done in the cemetery (1320-30), by F. Traini; also, works by T. Gaddi, P. di Puccio, S. Aretino, B. Gozzoli, and A. Bonaiuti.

Museo dell'Opera del Duomo*. This large museum comprises collections of art from the monuments of the Campo dei Miracoli, and stands at the far eastern side of Piazza del Duomo. On the ground floor and in the cloister is the core of the collections: 11th-14th-century statuary. Note the Islamic bronze griffon; 12th-century Burgundian wooden Christ; masterpieces by N. and G. Pisano, T. di Camaino, N. Pisano, A. Guardi, and M. Civitali. Moreover, in the Duomo's Treasury: ivory carvings by G. Pisano and fine religious metalwork. Upstairs, a vast array, from illuminated codices to Egyptian and Etruscan artifacts.

Piazza dell'Arcivescovado. The 15th-century Palazzo Arcivescovile stands here. Continuing along Via Maffi, with a fine view of the Duomo's apse and bell tower, and along Largo del Parlascio, you will see ruins of 2nd-century AD Roman baths; on the left is the Porta a Lucca (1544); from outside the gate, a fine view of the medieval walls* (1155).

S. Caterina*. Built in the late 13th century, this church has a Pisan-style marble facade and a large rose window; the terracotta bell tower is decorated with ceramic bowls. Inside are marble statues* by N. Pisano (1360); in the sacristy, paintings by Fra' Bartolomeo (1511) and F. Traini (ca. 1350).

S. Zeno. Standing at the end of Via S. Zeno, alongside the 13th-century Porta di S. Zeno, outside of which is a fine view of the medieval walls*, this church was founded before the year 1000, rebuilt in the 13th century, deconsecrated in 1809, and used as a warehouse until 1972. The interior is usually closed.

S. Francesco*. Construction of this convent church first began in 1211, was then undertaken again by G. di Simone in 1265-70 and completed in the 14th century; the facade is from 1603. Inside, Baroque altars and large canvases by Empoli, Passignano, and S. di Tito, frescoes by T. Gaddi (1342) and marble altarpiece by T. Pisano (14C). In the left transept, note the structures supporting the bell tower. In the sacristy, frescoes by T. di Bartolo (1397).

S. Pierino. This Romanesque church was built between 1072 and 1119; inside, fragments of frescoes, and a 13th-century mosaic floor. Behind the main altar is a 13th-century Crucifix.

Piazza Cairoli. This cozy square has a column with a statue of Abundance (16C). Note the Via delle Belle Torri, one of Pisa's loveliest streets, despite damage done in WWII. Along it are 12th-13th-century tower-houses.

S. Andrea Forisportam. This simple 12th-century Pisan-style church is decorated with hanging arches and terracotta bowls (copies). Handsome, original Romanesque interior.

Museo Nazionale di S. Matteo**. Overlooking the Lungarno Mediceo, since 1949 this museum has occupied part of the convent of the Benedictine nuns of S. Matteo, a building adjacent to the 11th-century bell tower, with a 13th-century porticoed courtyard. Among the museum's vast collections, we should make special note of the collections of Pisan sculpture, Tuscan paintings of the 12th-15th-century, and Pisan and Islamic medieval ceramics. A separate section in the former Palazzo Reale will house the works from private donations and from the collections

The small church of S. Maria della Spina, on the banks of the Arno.

of the Houses of the Medici, Lorraine, and Savoy. **Ground floor**. Remarkable collection of medieval ceramics: series of ceramic basins*, some of 11th century. Islamic origin, others from 13th century. Pisa, used as ornaments on the exterior walls of Pisan churches; also, ceramic archeological finds from all over Pisa. Armor from the Gioco del Ponte, an example of rough sport begun in Pisa by the Medici in the 16th century; also, one of the most important European collections of antique metal arms and armor (about 900 pieces). **First floor**. Sculpture from the 12th-14th century: eloquent examples of Pisan art with fragments of Romanesque buildings and statues; works by follower of G. Pisano, T. di Camaino, N. Pisano,

F. Traino, A. and N. Pisano, F. di Valdambrino, A. di Giovanni; a rock-crystal cross from the late 13th-century Venetian school. Sculpture from the 15th century: works by Donatello**, a follower of Michelozzo*, workshop of Verrocchio* della Robbia. Painting from 12th-13th century: works by Berlinghiero, E. di Tedice, G. Pisano, Maestro di S. Martino. Painting from the 14th century: works by D. Orlandi, S. Martini, G. di Nicola, L. di Tommè, B. Daddi, Maestro di S. Torpè, L. Memmi, C. di Pietro, B. da Modena, S. Aretino, M. di Bartolomeo, T. di Bartolo. Painting from the 15th century: works by G. da Fabriano, Masaccio, Fra' Angelico, G. da Milano, A. Veneziano, D. Ghirlandaio, B. Gozzoli, P. Schiavo, N. di Bicci, and L. di Bicci.

Lungarno Mediceo. This riverfront quay runs from Ponte alla Fortezza to Piazza Garibaldi: at the corner of Piazza Mazzini is the 13th-century Palazzo dei Medici, modified by restoration in the early 20th century. Further along is the 16th-century Palazzo Toscanelli.

S. MARIA DELLA SPINA AND THE DISTRICTS ON THE LEFT BANK

Here you can admire the miracle of the little church of S. Maria della Spina, seemingly floating upon the waters of the Arno River, the simple facade of the church of S. Paolo, and the lively left bank, a district which sprang up in the 19th century.

Lungarno Pacinotti. Stretching from Piazza Garibaldi to Ponte Solferino, this quay offers handsome views of the opposite bank. At no. 26, Palazzo Agostini, and at no. 43, Palazzo Upezzinghi, designed by C. Pugliani (1594).

S. Frediano. Not far from the university campus is this 11th-century Pisan Romanesque church. Inside, note the 12th-century Crucifix and a painting by A. Lomi (1604).

Museo Nazionale di Palazzo Reale. It is housed in the huge building at no. 56 on Lungarno Pacinotti, which was begun in 1559 by Cosimo I de' Medici, and later enlarged. The museum includes part of the collections of the Museo Nazionale di S. Matteo, especially items from the collections of the Houses of the Medici, Lorraine, and Savoy, becoming a museum of court life and art. Among the most important pieces are Flemish tapestries, a series of ivory miniatures, Medici portraits and the Collezione Ceci, with works by B. Strozzi, A. Magnasco, F. Francia, A. Canova.

S. Nicola. Behind Palazzo Reale, part of this church's lower facade and the remarkable bell tower* are 13th century. Note Traino's painting and statues by G. and N. Pisano.

S. Maria della Spina**. This exquisite piece of Romanesque-Gothic architecture and art, originally a small church on the banks of the Arno River, was enlarged in 1323. It was named after a thorn ("spina") believed to be from the true crown of thorns (now in S. Chiara). Disassembled and moved to higher ground to save it from the flooding of the river (1871), the church is girt by arcades enclosing mullioned windows and portals. Note the statues* on facade and spires by T. Pisano.

Lungarno Sonnino. Across from this riverbank boulevard you can see the brick sheds, once boat yards of the Cavalieri di S. Stefano. At the end of Lungarno Simonelli, at the Ponte della Cittadella, is the Cittadella Vecchia, the ruins of a Florentine fortress (1405).

S. Paolo a Ripa d'Arno*. This handsome Pisan Romanesque church of the 11th century has the same decorative pattern as the Duomo. Inside (much restored after damage of WWII), note the handsome columns, supporting pointed Arab-style arches, and a painting by T. Vanni (1397). Behind the apse is the separate, octagonal chapel of S. Agata* (12C)

S. Antonio. Only the lower order of the facade survives from the original 14th-century church. To the left, in Via Mazzini, is the Domus Mazziniana, commemorating Giuseppe Mazzini, a father of Italian Unity.

Corso Italia. This lively pedestrian street links the railway station to the historic center of Pisa. Along the way are two churches: S. Domenico (14C) badly damaged in WWII; and the S. Maria del Carmine, with paintings by Allori, A. Lomi, and B. Lomi Gentileschi. When the Corso reaches the Arno, on the left, note the vast Loggia di Banchi, built in 1603-05 by C. Pugliani, for wool and silk traders. At the mouth of the Ponte di Mezzo, fine view of the north banks of the Arno.

Lungarno Galilei. Between Ponte di Mezzo and Ponte alla Fortezza, this boulevard offers fine views of the Lungarno Mediceo. Note the octagonal church of S. Sepolcro*, by Diotisalvi (1153). Inside, the tombstones of Pisan aristocrats, and painting by the school of B. Gozzoli.

Via S. Martino. Main street of the old district of Chinzica, once inhabited by Arab and Turkish traders. In a square is the church of S. Martino, built in 1332. Inside, frescoes and paintings by G. di Nicola, A. Veneziano, A. Lomi, and E. di Tedice.

Bastione Sangallo. The bastion and nearby walls are all that survive of the 15th-century Cittadella Nuova, built by the Florentines, destroyed by the Pisans, and rebuilt by G. da Sangallo. Visit the lovely park (Giardino Scotto).

"...si dice in galea o nave o altra fusta, quando fussino stati alcuno giorno sanza vedere terra..."
This is an old chantey from the second half of the 15ᵗʰ-century, and it translates roughly: "They say in ships or galleys, or any other vessel, when they have gone several days without sighting land..." At the end of each verse, the chantey returns to call on the help of the Lord and the saints, naming a patron saint or a sanctuary, with specific references to stretches of shoreline or points on the coast. This "pilot's log" of the Catholic faith describes – for the short stretch that corresponds to the beginning of this route along the coastline of northern Tuscany, between Viareggio and Livorno – the Volto Santo Lucchese, San Ranieri, Santa Maria del Ponte Nuovo, and San Piero a Grado (Pisan), Santa Giulia and Montenero (Livornese). Here is a typical verse: "Die' n'aì (meaning "God help us") e Santa Maria delle Grazie di Monte Nero di Livorno..." The chantey clearly refers to the route that we are suggesting here: the lovely thing about driving along the coastline, for that matter, is the endless series of glimpses it offers of the sea, parallel to the glimpses of land that so comforted the terrified ancient sailors. Leaving aside the marvels of Pisa, there are attractions in this route: the alternating distance and approach to the sea, long beaches and a jagged coastline, little coves with crashing waves and gurgling undertow, and, far above, the Mediterranean maquis, pine trees, holm-oaks, ash trees, elms, the northwest wind or "maestrale" redolent of resins and sap, clouds scudding across the windy sky, the "flocks of black birds" that flap their way "through the vespertine sky" (there are many verses by Nobel laureate G. Carducci that seem to describe this region). In this exchange between earth and sea along the coast, the most beautiful section lies between Antignano and Cecina. And if you look inland instead of out to sea, what draws nearer and further away is the outline of hills and blue hazy mountains; you will see grapevines and olive groves, cypresses, Etruscan ruins, hilltop towns. Lastly, as you move south, the climate becomes slightly milder in winter. The last stretch of road, where you begin to see Elba, is the coast of the Maremma, specifically the so-called Pisan Maremma: from here you can take a lovely inland detour.

NOT TO BE MISSED
Torre del Lago Puccini, near the Lake Massaciuccoli, with the stately home and the tomb of G. Puccini. **San Piero a Grado***: this 11ᵗʰ-century Pisan church with early 14ᵗʰ-century frescoes can be reached by taking a detour from the road linking Pisa with Marina di Pisa. **Livorno** (➡ see below): this harbor city is a thriving port with venerable old quarters. It was the first outlet to the sea of the Tuscan grand-duchy; from **Antignano** you will drive up to the Sanctuary of Montenero (collection of votive offerings from those who survived perils of land and sea). **Castiglioncello**: this quietly elegant beach resort stands on a promontory, dense with pine trees and holm-oaks; nearby are inlets and little beaches. **Rosignano Marittimo**: detour from Rosignano Solvay, 2 km inland; the old town stands on a scenic rise. **Marina di Cecina**: take a 2.5 km detour; the beach is on the other side of the pine forest. **Bolgheri**: in order to get here, you must leave the Via Aurelia at the 18ᵗʰ-century octagonal chapel of San Guido, driving a little less than 5 km along cypress-lined boulevards described by 1906 Nobel laureate and poet G. Carducci, truly a lovely sight (as a child, Carducci lived in a house in town here). In the variant that we recommend for the last part of this route: **Castagneto Carducci**, a hillside resort area; the poet lived here as a youth. **Suvereto** may take its

name from the groves of cork-trees that once surrounded it; the Romanesque church of S. Giusto, and the 13ᵗʰ-century Palazzo Comunale are worth seeing. **Campiglia Marittima**, for the most part, still has a medieval appearance; on the Venturina road is the cemetery, with the parish church of S. Giovanni (note the late-12C carving on the architrave over the portal). **Baratti**: on the bayshore, note the Etruscan necropolis. **Populonia** still has its 14ᵗʰ-century "borgo," unchanged by time, perched on the promontory; this was the powerful Etruscan town of "Pupluna" and has the small Collezione Gasparri, which contains finds from the Etruscan necropolis.

Aerial view of Venezia Nuova in Livorno.

LIVORNO

"Imagine a delightful, pocket-sized, brand-new town, that would fit nicely into a snuff-box; that's Livorno". This is how Charles de Brosses (1739) described the new town – a late Renaissance 'ideal city' which was very successful. It was founded in 1577 by the Medici Grand-duke Francesco I, at the southern edge of the Arno flood plain, beside an old Pisan fortified village. Its prosperity was the result of the seaport and the famous 'constitution' of 1593, which encouraged immigration by protecting the freedom of newcomers, and particularly Jews. It was, as De Brosses noted, inhabited by "all kinds of nations of Europe and Asia". Modern Livorno is a thriving commercial and industrial city. In the old center, the five-pointed Medici fortress can still be seen, with its surrounding moat, and beyond, traces of the enlargement carried out under the Dukes of Lorraine in the early 19th century. In 1881 Livorno was chosen as the location of the Naval Academy.

Santo Stefano. This 14th-century church that has been heavily modified. In the 1st chapel on the right, Leggenda della Vera Croce (Legend of the True Cross), 1424; in the right transept, lunette and Madonna and Child*.

Venezia Nuova. This colorful district was once inhabited by fishermen and sailors. It was called New Venice because it was built using Venetian workers and techniques, under the Medici (1629). It still maintains features of the original layout, with a dense network of canals and bridges, narrow lanes, and shops and houses built over the water. Standing in the central Piazza dei Domenicani is the 18th-century, octagonal church of Santa Caterina.

The **Bottini dell'Olio** in Viale Caprera were built in 1705 as warehouses for storing oil. These two large spaces, with vaults supported by stone columns, now house a library. Not far away is the church of San Ferdinando, built in 1707-14 by G.B. Foggini, with a Baroque interior richly decorated with stucco, marble and statues.

Duomo. this late Gothic building (1594-1606) was rebuilt after being totally detroyed by bombs in 1943. It has a simple facade with marble portico on Doric columns. The *nave* houses tombs and ceiling paintings by J. Ligozzi, by Empoli and by Passignano.

Piazza Grande, this square in the heart of the old Medici town, surrounded by porticoed palazzi, is the city's center. It was complete-

ly reconstructed after the second world war. Opposite the Duomo, behind Palazzo Grande, is Largo Municipio. On the right is Palazzo Comunale, built in 1720, with a double marble staircase. On the left is the 16th-century Palazzo della Camera di Commercio, by the Pistoia architect A. Cecchi.

Piazza della Repubblica. This rectangular-shaped square, built between 1844 and 1848, features two Neo-Classic style statues: Ferdinand III, towards the Fortezza Nuova, by F. Pozzi (1837); on the opposite side, Leopold II by E. Santarelli (1885). The neo-Classical Cisternino is almost on the corner with Via Grande. Designed by Poccianti, it was built as a water cistern between 1837 and 1842. However it was never used for this purpose, and today houses exhibitions, especially of figurative art. On the flanks there are architraved open galleries, and at the back a small apse; in front of this, is a monument to D. Guerrazzi by L. Gori and the facade of the 18th-century Palazzo del Picchetto.

Fortezza Nuova (New Fortress). It is surrounded by a moat dug by thousands of slaves and peasants at the beginning of the 17th century. In the upper part there is a beautiful park with a fine view of the city.

Fortezza Vecchia. This massive fortified complex with three bastions and two entrances was built in 1521-34 to a design by A. da Sangallo il Vecchio. It was seriously damaged during the second world war. It incorporates the so-called *Mastio della Contessa Matilde* , a solid 11th-century tower surrounded by a fortress dating from 1377, known as the *Quadratura dei Pisani*, attributed to P. di Landuccio.

Piazza del Cisternone takes its name from the large cistern, with Doric-columned portico, built here in the first half of the 19th century. It is reached from Piazza della Repubblica along the broad Via de Larderel, where the Neo-Classic facade of the 19th-century Palazzo de Larderel stands out at no. 88.

Monumento dei Quattro Mori. This most well-known of Livorno's monuments is in Piazza Micheli, and was built in honor of Grand-duke Ferdinand I in 1595. It is named after the four powerful, realistic, bronze figures of Moorish slaves, by P. Tacca, which were added to the base in 1626. The square looks onto the *Darsena Vecchia,* the old dock. Beyond stretches the *Porto Mediceo*. On the right, the 16th-century reddish walls of the Fortezza Vecchia can be seen.

VAL DI PESA AND CHIANTI

In 1838, Baron Bettino Ricasoli, 29, later the absolute ruler of Tuscany and prime minister of the Kingdom of Italy, took up residence in his castle at Brolio, in Chianti, to devote himself to farming. He wrote that "agriculture in Tuscany takes heart and it takes brains, it is almost a calling." One of the results of that "calling" was Chianti, a wine that had existed since 1716 – along with the now less famous Pomino, Carmignano, and Valdarno – but which Ricasoli made both great and renowned. In the route recommended here, Chianti comes in the latter part, though all of the landscape is enchanting. From Florence you continue on to the Val di Pesa, with its venerable tradition as an aristocratic holiday spot; after driving through this valley for a stretch, you climb through hills in the Valdelsa (the Pesa and the Elsa flow into the lower Arno, from the left bank). After Siena, you return to Florence, with a pause in the land of Chianti. Experts distinguish an aroma of violet in this wine; it is made with Sangiovese grapes, from 75 to 90 percent, while the rest is a blend of black Canaiolo grapes, Tuscan Trebbiano grapes, and Malvasia del Chianti. In the landscape, which varies from grim to lovely, with an endless combination of villas, holm-oaks, farm houses, scrub brush, villages, towers, steep hills, winding roads, parish churches, venerable oak trees, cypresses, and olive trees, you will often see vineyards as well, occupying only the sites that receive plenty of sun and with the finest soil. Save for the secluded Certosa del Galluzzo, with paintings by Pontormo, the turreted skyline of Monteriggioni and, of course, Siena, this tour is of lesser sites, with domesticated nature, and the brilliant clear light, the clear distilled magic essence of Tuscany.

The medieval hamlet of Radda in Chianti.

NOT TO BE MISSED

Certosa del Galluzzo*: church, cloisters, monks' cells, and paintings by Pontormo. To get here, turn off the Via Cassia at Galluzzo and drive for 1 km past cypresses and olive trees. **San Casciano in Val di Pesa**: a fine Crucifix by S. Martini in the Misericordia church. **Poggibonsi** is a thriving modern town; 1.5 km south is the convent of S. Lucchese amid the olive groves. Monteriggioni* was a Sienese outpost; Dante's description – "di torri si corona," or "crowned with towers" – still applies. **Castello di Brolio**: built in the 12th century by the Ricasoli family, it was later restored in 1860. **Gaiole in Chianti** lies amid hills covered with vineyards; you can admire the Romanesque parish church of S. Maria a Spaltenna, the Castello di Meleto, a fortified medieval farm, just 2.5 km away, and the Romanesque church, the remaining part of the nearby Badia a Coltibuono (5 km north). **Radda in Chianti** has an elongated elliptical layout, a relic of the Middle Ages. **Castellina in Chianti** has stood on its hilltop since the Renaissance; it lies between the valleys of Arbia, Elsa, and Pesa and has retained much of its Renaissance atmosphere, with a 14th-century fortress. **Greve in Chianti** has a porticoed asymmetrical square; note the terraces. From here, a 6km detour takes you to **Lamole**; here is the Villa di Vignamaggio, birthplace of the woman who sat for Leonardo's Mona Lisa (La Gioconda). **Impruneta**, on the Florentine hills, is known for its venerable October fair, its pottery kilns (here, Brunelleschi fired the bricks used to build the dome of S. Maria del Fiore), and the basilica of S. Maria.

VALDELSA AND VOLTERRANO

The literary references here are of the highest quality: Certaldo was the birthplace of the 14th-century author Boccaccio, and here he returned as a bitter old man, to die and be buried. When he returned, he said: "Comincianmi già i grossi panni a piacere e le contadine vivande" – "I am happy to wear rough clothing and eat peasant food." Certaldo lies in the Valdelsa. The Elsa River which runs through it flows down from the Montagnola, a small mountain west of Siena; it then flows into the Arno near Empoli. This valley road, which once ran high on the hillcrests before the malarial riverside plain was reclaimed, was the route of the "Romei," pilgrims bound for Rome; it was a main leg of the Via Francigena, a much-used route in medieval Europe. That may explain the ferocity with which Florentines and Sienese fought over it (the Florentines triumphed in the late-14C). The route runs from Florence and enters and goes up the Valdelsa after descending the Arno; it is perhaps at its most intensely Tuscan when it leaves that valley, at Certaldo, and then twists west into valleys and over hills, before ending once again near the Elsa. Along this route, you pass through two exquisitely Tuscan places, different in surroundings and atmosphere. Volterra, with Etruscan and medieval heritages, austere, a clear light silhouetting surrealistic hills, with clayey slopes torn away in desolate washes, and the chasms of the Balze; and San Gimignano, immersed in a landscape with all the gentle lines and delicate colors of Siena's finest painters.

NOT TO BE MISSED

Badia di S. Salvatore a Settimo: restored following damage inflicted during WWII, this abbey is enclosed by crenelated walls. You must turn off, just outside of Florence, right after the Autostrada. **Lastra a Signa** still has part of its old walls; nearby, at Gangalandi, is the 11th-century parish church of S. Martino, with 13th-century paintings and frescoes. Montelupo Fiorentino has the Museo Archeologico e della Ceramica, in Palazzo del Podestà. **Empoli**: Palazzo Ghibellino hosted a council that met to decide the fate of Florence after its disastrous defeat in the 13th-century battle of Montaperti; there are frescoes by Masolino da Panicale in the Museo della Collegiata and in the church of S. Stefano; also local glass-making industry. **Oratory della Madonna della Tosse**: 2 km detour from Granaiolo, with chapel that once contained frescoes by B. Gozzoli (1484), now in Castelfiorentino. **Castelfiorentino**: in the old town center are lavish Baroque churches with 14th-15th-century artwork. The Raccolta Comunale d'Arte has the two series of frescoes by B. Gozzoli. **Certaldo**: strongly medieval in flavor; visit Boccaccio's house, rebuilt, set high on the hill. **Montaione** is an old village with a view; it can be reached by a 3 km detour, at a fork just past Gambassi Terme; another 4.5 km (from a crossroads just before Montaione) takes you to the convent of S. Vivaldo (404 m), with 20 chapels containing Della Robbia terracottas; it is in the forest of Boscolazzeroni, a nature reserve. **Volterra** (➡ see below) is a windswept hilltop town, austerely alluring; the atmosphere is medieval, with towers and grey buildings. Relics of its Etruscan origins can be seen at the Museo Guarnacci. **San Gimignano** (➡ see below) is a perfectly intact town of medieval Tuscany: city gates, houses, squares, and roads, as well as the 14 surviving towers, and works by great artists in the churches and the Pinacoteca. In particular, the collegiate church has major works by G. and B. da Maiano, B. di Fredi, and J.della Quercia. **Colle di Val d'Elsa**: you may reach the old "borgo" by taking the Via del Castello, up high. Don't forgot the birthplace of A. di Cambio, born here in 1232; an exhibit on his work is in the Palazzo Pretorio.

SAN GIMIGNANO

In the 13th century there were nine "hospitatores," or hotels, for the merchants who flocked here; the pride of the newly rich families were 72 tall towers (by law, none could overtop the Rognosa, the tower of the town government). Saffron, too, was worked here, and sold throughout Europe. Nowadays, of the original towers, only 15 survive and create a skyline typical of a medieval hill town.

Porta S. Giovanni. This 13th-century gate has a distinctive Sienese flathead arch, and is part of the medieval walls* that surround the center (rebuilt in 1262) and open onto the Via Francigena, the main axis of the little town.

Via Quercecchio. On this road, note the Oratory of S. Francesco, now a small ornithology museum. A series of stairways leads up to the Rocca di Montestaffoli, a fortress built in 1353 and dismantled in 1558. Note the pentagonal plan and surviving walls; the sole surviving tower affords a fine view** of the town.

Piazza della Cisterna**. Triangular in shape, this square is linked to Piazza del Duomo by an open passageway, forming a harmonious set of spaces that have been the center of San Gimignano since the 13th century. The cistern, in the middle of the huge space paved with herringbone brickwork, dates from 1237 and was enlarged in 1346. To the right of the Becci arch, entering the square, are Casa Razzi, Casa Salvestrini (now a hotel), and the 13th-century Palazzo Tortoli-Treccani (no. 22). Across the square, Palazzo dei Cortesi (no. 5), with the tall Torre del Diavolo; also note the twin towers of the Ardinghelli, built in the 13th century and diverging slightly.

Piazza del Duomo*. Linked to Piazza della Cisterna, and paved with the same herringbone brickwork, this square is lined with medieval houses and towers. Overlooking it is the collegiate church, to the left of which is the facade of Palazzo del Popolo (see below). Across the square is the ancient **Palazzo del Podestà*** (1239), with its handsome loggia and massive tower called the Torre Rognosa (51 m tall); nearby, at the mouth of Via S. Matteo, are the Torre Chigi (1280) and the twin towers known as Salvucci.

Collegiate church**. This 12th-century Romanesque building, with a simple 13th-century facade, has been renovated and restored many times. Inside are paintings and sculpture by great artists: G. and B. da Maiano, T. di Bartolo, B. Gozzoli, J. della Quercia, B. da Siena and G. da Asciano, B. di Fredi, D. Ghirlandaio, and A. da Colle. Of particular interest is the chapel of S. Fina* (closed during mass), a chapel which is one of the most significant works of the Tuscan Renaissance. From the left aisle, you enter the small 14th-century cloister of S. Giovanni, open on Piazza Pecori.

Museo d'Arte Sacra. In the tiny Piazza Pecori, the museum comprises five halls inside Palazzo della Propositura, with mullioned windows. Note 16th-century an Egyptian floral-pattern carpet*, a marble bust by B. da Maiano (1493), the 15th-century altar frontal of the "golden doves;"* the panel of the Madonna della Rosa by B. di Fredi, a painted wooden Crucifix* by G. da Maiano.

Palazzo del Popolo*. Built in 1288 and enlarged in 1323, this building has lost its crenelation but preserves its mayoral crests and three rows of windows; note, at left, two large arcades* and, at right, the Torre Grossa* (54 m; 1311). Fine view from top*. In the courtyard is a cistern (1361), and under the portico a fresco by Sodoma (1507). An exterior stairway leads up to the Museo Civico.

Museo Civico*. On the first floor of Palazzo del Popolo is the enormous Sala di Dante, adorned by the Maestà*, a fresco by L. Memmi (1317); an inlaid door leads to the Sala delle Adunanze Segrete (Hall of Secret Assemblies; note the chairs, from 1475) and another adjacent room, with pharmacist's vases from Faenza (16-17C), Florence, and Siena. Second floor: Camera del Podestà, frescoed by M. di Filippuccio, and three halls used as a gallery, with Tuscan school paintings (13-15C): C. di Marcovaldo, B. Gozzoli, F. Lippi, Pinturicchio, N. di Ser Sozzo, T. di Bartolo, and M. di Filippuccio.

Via S. Matteo*. Northernmost stretch of the Via Francigena that went through San Gimignano, it is lined with medieval houses and palazzi. First, note the twin towers, the Torri Salvucci, Palazzo Pettini and Torre Pettini (no. 2); pass through the Cancelleria arch, once a city gate. The 13th-century Palazzo della Cancelleria and the Romanesque church of S. Bartolo are interesting. At no. 12-14 is a late 13th-century tower-house, the Casa Pesciolini, and at no. 52, the slightly rusticated 15th-century Casa Francardelli. At no. 60-62, Palazzo Tinacci and at no. 97, Palazzo Bonaccorsi. Last comes Porta S. Matteo (1262).

S. Agostino*. This imposing Romanesque-Gothic church, built in 1280-98, has a stark brick facade with four Gothic windows on the right side. Inside, note artwork by S. Mainardi, B. da Maiano (1494), P. F. Fiorentino, B. di Fredi, P. del Pollaiolo (1483), and frescoes by B. Gozzoli and G. d'Andrea (1465), L. Memmi (1320). From the left transept, you can enter the cloister of the adjacent convent.

Spedale of S. Fina. Built in the 13th-century and still used as a hospital, this building overlooks Via Folgore da S. Gimignano: inside, frescoes by S. Mainardi and busts of saints by P. Torrigiani. Further on, to the left, is the 13th-century church of S. Jacopo, and from there, you can turn right to follow the city walls, reaching Porta alle Fonti, and from there climb down to the Fonti, which are springs covered with Gothic arches (12-14C, restored in 1852).

VOLTERRA

"At the summit of a high hill," recalls Stendhal, Volterra surveys the surrounding heights between the valleys of the Era and the Cecina. The landscape mingles lush greenery with hard white lines of ridges and erosion. This city is stern and medieval in its skyline. All around are workshops where craftsman shape the alabaster taken from the ground here. The Museo Guarnacci features fine alabaster work from Etruscan times.

Piazza dei Priori*. This square has been the site of markets since AD 851. One of Italy's loveliest medieval squares, it is lined with handsome buildings, some of which are original. **Palazzo dei Priori***. Built in 1208-54, this massive crenelated building is punctuated by three rows of mullioned windows, and a lovely tower. Still serving as the town hall, on the first floor are the Sala del Consiglio, with frescoes and paintings, and the Sala della Giunta, with an inlaid 15th-century desk.

Duomo*. Behind Palazzo dei Priori, overlooking Piazza S. Giovanni, this Romanesque cathedral dates from the 12th century; the facade is simple and understated, while the interior is rich and lavishly covered with marble. Among the artists who worked on the cathedral: R. Cioli, M. da Fiesole, F. di Valdambrino, M. Albertinelli, and B. Gozzoli. Worthy of note are the finely wrought pulpit* on four

Palazzo dei Priori is on the square with the same name.

columns, assembled in the 16th century with 13th-century sculptures; the 13th-century gild and silver-plated polychrome wooden group; and the handsome Gothic wooden choir (1404). Facing the Duomo is the Battistero, or Baptistery, a fine octagonal 13th-century building with a Romanesque portal and green-and-white striped front; inside, baptismal font* by A. Sansovino (1502).

Museo diocesano di Arte Sacra. Entrance at no. 1 in Via Roma, from the portico behind the bell tower of the Duomo. This museum has collections of sculpture, architectural fragments, metalwork, and paintings of a religious nature. Note the works by A. della Robbia, A. Pollaiolo, Giambologna, and R. Fiorentino.

Quadrivio dei Buomparenti*. This fascinating crossroads in the historic center features the very tall Casa-Torre Buomparenti*, a 13th-century tower-house, connected by a catwalk to the Torre Buonaguidi.

Pinacoteca* and Museo Civico. At no. 1 in Via dei Sarti, the art gallery and town museums are located in the Palazzo Solaini, attributed to A. da Sangallo the Elder. The fifteen halls feature Florentine, Sienese, and Volterran artists, from the 14th-17th century; among them are T. di Bartolo, B. di Giovanni, F. di Val-

dambrino, D. Ghirlandaio, L. Signorelli, R. Fiorentino, P. de Witte, B. Franceschini, D. da Volterra; also medals and coins.

Palazzo Incontri-Viti. This 16th-century palazzo, with the entrance at no. 41 in Via dei Sarti, has a facade attributed to B. Ammannati. The interior is worth touring; note the Volterran alabasters*.

S. Michele Arcangelo. Overlooking the "piazzetta" of the same name, this church has a handsome Romanesque facade and, inside, a Della Robbia terracotta and a painting by Il Pomarancio. Note the 13th-century Tuscan tower-house.

Teatro Romano. This Roman theater, built under Augustus, can be clearly seen from Via Lungo le Mura del Mandorlo, at the outer end of Via Guarnacci.

Fortezza. Not open to the public. Still used as a prison, this is one of the most formidable fortresses built during the Italian Renaissance. From Piazza XX Settembre, you can enter the public gardens; note the interesting Parco Archeologico Enrico Fiumi.

Museo Etrusco Guarnacci*. Entrance at no. 15 Via Don Minzoni; the museum has collections** of Etruscan cinerary urns made of tufa, alabaster, and terracotta, Etruscan sculpture*(among which the famous Ombra della Sera*, a very slender human figure in bronze), and a collection* of more than 3000 Etruscan, Greek, and Roman coins.

Via Matteotti*. A charming road through the most medieval section of Volterra. It is lined with 13th-century tower-houses; at the end (no. 25), the stern Palazzo Maffei, 1527.

Porta all'Arco*. The center of some alabaster workshops, this gate has Roman and Etruscan parts; note the Etruscan heads.

Florence actually purchased this town twice (the second time, in 1384, for 40,000 gold scudi). From the westernmost slopes of the Alpe di Poti, Arezzo looks out over the narrow plain where the valleys of Valdarno, Casentino, and Valdichiana converge. The center of Arezzo still has a medieval appearance, which overlies its earlier incarnations (Etruscan and Roman). In this setting, Arezzo runs the Giostra del Saracino, with Aretinians in medieval dress riding horses, pounding through Piazza Grande, past a menacing, whip-wielding eastern monarch, Buratto, King of the Indies.

A TOWN RICH IN ART TREASURES

Piazza S. Francesco. At the edge of the oldest part of town, this square was enlarged in the late 19th-century, at the expense of a wing of the Franciscan convent.

S. Francesco**. This 13th-century Gothic church, with an unfinished facade, was heavily restored at the turn of the 20th century; the bell tower dates from the 16th century. The interior has a nave and a beam roof. The overall impression, amidst frescoes and austere Franciscan Gothic architecture, is one of grandeur. In the rose window, note the stained glass by G. de Marcillat (1524). Along the right wall are Gothic and Renaissance aediculas and frescoes, some badly damaged. Note the frescoes by L. d'Arezzo, inspired by P. della Francesca; the Crucifix attributed to the Maestro di S. Francesco; and work by S. Aretino, N. di Pietro Gerini, and B. di Lorenzo. Along the walls of the choir is the Legend of the True Cross**, the marvelous cycle frescoed by P. della Francesca probably between 1453 and 1466: in their stylistic discipline and exquisite color, these are towering masterpieces of the Italian Renaissance. In the chapel to the left of the choir are works by S. Aretino, N. di Bicci, and L. Signorelli (attributed).

Chiesa di Badia. On the elegant Via Cavour, the 13th-century Badia di Ss. Flora e Lucilla was enlarged around 1550 by G. Vasari (bell tower, 1650); the Neo-Gothic facade dates from 1914. Inside, paintings and frescoes by B. della Gatta (1476) and S. di Bonaventura and a ciborium by B. da Maiano. The trompe-l'oeil ceiling simulating a vault is by A. Pozzo (1703). In the nearby former monastery are glazed terracotta by the Della Robbia and a 15th-century cloister attributed to G. da Maiano.

Corso Italia. The historic backbone of medieval Arezzo (then called Borgo Maestro), it has been the main street for centuries, with old buildings and fine shops. Toward the center, on the right, is the church of S. Michele (13C), with a Neo-Gothic facade but 14th-century bell tower. Inside, a wooden Crucifix and a panel by N. di Bicci (1466). At the corner of Via Cavour, note the Palazzo Bacci (no. 78-72), and on the right, the Palazzo Altucci. Across from the Pieve (see below) are the 13th-century tower-house (no. 24-26), the 14th-century Palazzo Camaiani-Albergotti (no. 4), and the Torre della Bigazza, 1351.

Pieve di S. Maria**. One of the most impressive pieces of Tuscan Romanesque, this great sandstone church was begun around 1140, as a renovation of a century-old church. Construction continued into the early 14th century, and G. Vasari turned his hand to it in the next century. It was heavily restored in the late 19th century. The Romanesque facade* is noteworthy, as is the central portal, with reliefs of the Months* (1216). The bell tower* dates from 1330. The interior is vast, and features fine bas-reliefs of the Epiphany (11-12C) and a carved baptismal font by G. di Agostino. On the main altar is the large polyptych** by P. Lorenzetti (1320-24). Also noteworthy are the gilt-silver reliquary of S. Donato, the polychrome terracotta Madonna by M. da Firenze, and the 13th-century marble bas-relief of the Crib.

Piazza Grande*. One of Italy's most spectacular and charming squares, this is the site of the Giostra del Saracino (end of June and early September), and, monthly, of a renowned antiques fair. In the square are the Romanesque apse of the Pieve S. Maria, the 16th-century public fountain, the 17th-century Palazzo del Tribunale and the elegant Palazzo della Fraternita dei Laici*. This latter has a Gothic ground floor, portal (1377) and a Renaissance upper floor, by B. Rossellino (1434) – the facade was completed in 1460 by G. and A. da Settignano with balustrade and loggia. Lastly, note the enormous Palazzo delle Logge, with its shop-lined portico, designed by Vasari in 1573. On the other sides of the square are old houses, some with walkways and towers. **Via dei Pileati**. This uphill extension of Corso Italia overlooks on the left the 14th-century Palazzo Pretorio; at no. 28 in Via dell'Orto is the Casa di Petrarca (Petrarch's birthplace), rebuilt in 1948 and now the headquarters of the Accademia Petrarca.

Passeggio del Prato. In the huge expanse of public gardens, note the monument to Petrarch of 1928; behind it is what is left of the Fortezza Medicea, or Medici fortress, by A. da Sangallo the Younger, with a fine view from the battlements.

Duomo*. Set above a flight of 16th-century steps, this impressive Gothic structure was built between the late 13th-15th century. A Neo-Gothic facade (1901-14) replaced the unfinished original; along the right side is the Romanesque-Gothic portal (1319-37), with a group of terracotta sculptures in the lunette; the bell tower dates from 1859. The interior, with a broad nave and two aisles, gives an impression of great soaring height. The large stained glass windows are largely the work of G. de Marcillat (16C). The two marble pulpits in the nave date from the same period. In the presbytery, on the main altar, note the 14th-century Tuscan Arca di S. Donato*, a handsome Gothic marble urn. In the left aisle, fresco* by P. della Francesca; near it is the cenotaph* of the bishop G. Tarlati (1330).

Museo Diocesano. On exhibit in this museum of the diocese are pieces from the Duomo and other churches. Of note are the 13th-century polychrome wooden Crucifix; three frescoes by S. Aretino; 15th-century terracotta bas-relief by Rossellino; panel by A. di Nerio; fresco by B. della Gatta; paintings by L. Signorelli and G. Vasari.

Palazzo del Comune. Built in 1333 as the Palazzo dei Priori, the present-day town hall has been heavily rebuilt over the years; tower (1337), courtyard, and, inside, paintings by local artists. If you take Via Ricasoli toward the church of S. Domenico, at no. 1 you will see the Neo-Classic Palazzo delle Statue (1793).

S. Domenico*. Isolated in a small tree-lined square, this Gothic church has been heavily modified; it has a Romanesque portal and small bell tower, with 14th-century bells. Inside, badly damaged frescoes, by 14th-15th-century painters from Arezzo and Siena; note the Gothic Dragondelli altar (1350). In the middle of the apse is the huge Crucifix**, youthful masterpiece by Cimabue (1260-65).

Museo and Casa Vasari*. At no. 55 in Via XX Settembre, a handsome piece of Mannerist domestic architecture, the home that G. Vasari built, furnished, and frescoed for himself (1540-48). Now it is the Museo e Archivio Vasariano, and features numerous panels and frescoes by the great Renaissance artist and critic; also paintings and other objects dating from the same period.

S. Maria in Gradi. Rebuilt in the Mannerist

The Town Hall is from the 14th century.

style (1592) by B. Ammannati, the church dates from the 11th century. Inside, two wooden choirs and a terracotta *Madonna del Soccorso* by A. della Robbia.

Museo statale d'Arte Medievale e Moderna*. The museum of medieval and modern art is located at no. 8 in Via S. Lorentino, in the 15th-century Renaissance Palazzo Bruni-Ciocchi, at the Canto alla Croce, a monumental crossroads lined with lovely and venerable buildings. Note the courtyard, attributed to B. Rossellino. Arranged in about 20 halls on three floors (some feature Renaissance portals and fireplaces), the collections offer a thorough view of the art of Arezzo and Tuscany, from the 14-19th century. **On the ground floor**: sculpture from the high Middle Ages to the early Renaissance. First floor, overlooking the Renaissance garden, works by G. Vasari, M. d'Arezzo, the Maestro della Maddalena, A. di Giovanni, S. Aretino, P. di Spinello, B. della Gatta, and the splendid collection of majolica and porcelain (14-18C) from the main Italian workshops. On the second floor are paintings by L. Signorelli and by modern Tuscan painters: G. Fattori, T. Signorini, A. Cecioni.

Santissima Annunziata. Overlooking Via Garibaldi, a long curving road around the old part of Arezzo, this Renaissance church was begun in 1490-91, possibly by B. della Gatta, and continued by A. da Sangallo the Elder (1517). The facade is unfinished, with a 14th-century fresco by S. Aretino. Inside, stained glass windows by G. de Marcillat; painting by P. da Cortona; terracotta sculpture by M. da Firenze (ca. 1430).

Museo Archeologico Nazionale "Gaio Clinio Mecenate"*. Located at no. 10 in Via Margaritone, it is set in a semi-elliptical 16th-century monastery, partly standing upon and partly overlooking the southern portion of the Roman amphitheater (built under Hadrian, AD 117-138). With more than 20 rooms, it comprises private archeological collections and many finds from digs in Arezzo, its region and elsewhere in Italy.

In the Etruscan section are Aretinian pieces from archaic and Hellenistic (note the krater* with Hercules and the Amazons by Euphronius) periods; also note the quincussis*, one of the best preserved Etruscan coins. In the Roman section, a considerable collection of the so-called coral vases** (ancient ceramic tableware, varnished red with reliefs). On the first floor are the special sections and collections, especially those of ceramics (amphora with black figures and goblet* with red figures), glass and jewel, as well as the Gamurrini Collection*, with finds from the Agro Falisco, the territories of Chiusi and Orvieto, and Lake Bolsena.

S. Maria delle Grazie*. Out of the city grid, this church stands at the southern tip of Viale Mecenate, where the ancient "Fons Tecta" once flowed. Built in 1435-44, it is a solemn Gothic church, with an elegant portico* by B. da Maiano (15C). Inside, the main altar is a marble work by A. della Robbia; fresco by P. di Spinello.

CASENTINO

Mastro A. Guidi was a counterfeiter of Florentine coins. Burned at the stake for this crime, he later appeared in Dante's "Divine Comedy", punished in the "Inferno" by a burning unslakable thirst, and tormented by visions of the sparkling streams of his homeland. Mountain streams and brooks indeed water these slopes (Pratomagno to the west, Alpi di Serra and Alpi di Catenaia to the east), running down eventually to the Arno. The landscape of the Casentino is framed by mountains of sandstone and limestone, with squat ridges and low peaks (Falterona, 1,654 m), snowcapped for much of the year. Their slopes are covered with emerald meadows, dark dense stands of fir trees, and forests of ash, holm-oaks, oak trees, and chestnut trees. In the valleys are fields of wheat, orchards, tobacco, hemp, and – dotting the land – mulberries, olive groves, and vineyards. Woodcutters and shepherds once pre-

dominated here, following their flocks down to the Maremma in winter. This is a land of ancient churches, castles, and silent hermitages: Vallombrosa, Camaldoli, and La Verna.

Le Sieci boasts the Romanesque parish church of S. Giovanni Battista a Remole, some 12 km outside Florence, on the road to Pontassieve. Vallombrosa: the landscape of the fir forest and the more-than-900-year old convent are remarkable. Take a 10 km detour through the forest, up to the Mt Secchieta (1,449 m); fine view.

Pieve di Romena* is the most interesting parish church in the Casentino (10-12C); take a short detour past the ruins of the Romena castle, descending from Consuma to Poppi.

The hermitage of La Verna is a major pilgrim destination.

Piano di Campaldino: where the road from Stia intersects with this route, there is a column commemorating the great Battle of Campaldino (11 June 1289), in which the 24-year-old Dante Alighieri fought. Poppi: turn off at Ponte a Poppi; in the 13th-14th-century Castello (good artwork) you can sense the power of the Counts Guidi, a noble ruling family. Hermitage and Monastery of Camaldoli: the hermitage is at an elevation of 1,104 m, the monastery at 816 m; both stand in a dense fir grove. The monastery was founded by Saint Romualdo and is nearly 1000 years old. Bibbiena is the largest town in the Casentino, with an old center, high on the hill: the panel by A. di Cola in the church of Ss. Ippolito e Donato and the intense Tuscan vista from the terrace of Piazza Tarlati are noteworthy. Palazzo Dovizi belonged to a cardinal, known as Il Bibbiena, a friend of Raphael and a noted playwright. La Verna*: a limestone peak, a forest, and a convent founded by St Francis of Assisi.

FROM SIENESE CRETE TO VALDICHIANA

In the springtime, the landscape to the SE of Siena becomes green with clover and early wheat; in other seasons, the sere bareness of this land is dramatically evident, amidst an almost tree-less landscape. These are the Sienese "Crete," easily eroded hillocks with deceptively gentle silhouettes, rutted by washouts of clay. Other colors appear between the Ombrone and Orcia rivers and the Valdichiana, later along the route. The Ombrone rises in Chianti and flows down to the Tyrrhenian across the plain of Grosseto; the Orcia pours down from Mt Cetona, south of Chiusi, and into the Ombrone some distance west, where the rivers flow erratically among gentle peaceful hills. Cypresses stand around the secluded monastery of Monte Oliveto Maggiore, olive trees alternate with vineyards on hilltops. Downhill, little towns stand as they have for centuries, stranded by long-vanished ebb tides of history. Montalcino still remembers how the white-spotted banner of the Sienese Republic fluttered high over the town for four years, after the surrender in 1555 following a siege, starvation, and disease: 650 families survived the siege. Pienza, solitary and silent, stands as a visible dream of Humanistic perfection. Montepulciano is an alternation of Renaissance spaces and palazzi with far more ancient and venerable roots. As you reach the former Etruscan town of Chiusi, you are venturing into the Valdichiana: there is a topographic map drawn by L. da Vinci (1502-1503) with shaded mountains, the round, grey-blue lake of Trasimeno, and even larger and elongated, the ancient marsh of the Chiana plain. Chiusi marks the southern edge of this expanse. This route comes to an end with a jog into Umbria: Città della Pieve is your first taste of this region, a cluster of red brick between the green slopes, distant mountain outlines and the blue sky.

NOT TO BE MISSED

Asciano is a medieval "borgo"; adjacent to the Romanesque collegiate church is the Museo d'Arte Sacra; less than a km from the hill of Montepertaccio, the Guelphs of Florence were defeated by the Ghibellines of Siena, led by P. Salvani and F. degli Uberti (this was the Battle of Montaperti, 4 September 1260, described by Dante in his Inferno). **Monte Oliveto Maggiore***: this noted Benedictine abbey, secluded amidst cypresses on a hilltop, was founded in 1313 by B. Tolomei; in the cloister are fine frescoes by Signorelli and Sodoma. **Buonconvento**: girt by a ring of medieval walls, this town has noteworthy artworks in its Museo d'Arte Sacra. **Montalcino**: the fine red Brunello produced here is considered by many to be Italy's best wine; the fortress was the last bastion of Sienese independence. At a distance of 8 km is the solitary Romanesque abbey of S. Antimo, said to have been founded by Charlemagne at the end of the 8th century. **San Quiri-co d'Orcia**: a lovely Romanesque collegiate church. **Pienza****: here the Renaissance architect B. Rossellino interpreted the scholarly concepts of E. Silvio (or Aeneus Silvius) Piccolomini, Pope Pius II, in renovating the village in which the pope was born; no other place in Europe came so close to attaining the status of "ideal city" dreamed of by the 15th-century Humanists. **Montepulciano****: the architecture of the Renaissance, which is set amidst the medieval buildings of this ridge-top village between Chiana and Orcia, is by Michelozzo, Vignola, and A. da Sangallo the Elder (who also built the lovely, solitary, Neo-Classic church of S. Biagio). **Chianciano Terme***: this renowned spa stands on foothills; the old town is secluded. **Chiusi**: originally an Etruscan town with artworks and finds in the Museo and an Etruscan necropolis in the nearby countryside. **Città della Pieve**: the Renaissance artist Perugino was born here, and the countryside reappears in much of his work (paintings by him are in the Cathedral, in S. Maria dei Bianchi, and other churches).

A view of the cathedral and the hamlet of Pienza.

SIENA

Certainly the most distinct and homogeneous of all Tuscany's cities, Siena lies in a hilly landscape similar to that seen in the famous 14th-century fresco in the Palazzo Pubblico, "Assedio del Castello di Montemassi da parte di Guidoriccio da Fogliano". Located in the heart of the Tuscan highland, on the rises that separate the valley of the Arbia River, tributary of the Ombrone, from the valley of the Elsa River, tributary of the Arno. Compact and clearly 14th-century in style, Siena is a city of a single era, with a single past, a city that never ventured down from the three hills along which its steep streets slope, safely girded by the perimeter of its walls. From Duccio di Buoninsegna to Sassetta, the Sienese artistic tradition has always been separate from, and in some sense counterposed to the art of Florence. It is said that the finest Italian spoken is the version found here.

THE PALIO

This remarkable, centuries-old horse race takes place in the heart of Siena, twice a year. Held in the Piazza del Campo, the race is run to commemorate the holidays of the Madonna di Provenzano (2 July) and the Assumption (16 August). This is the deepest-rooted, and, in a sense, the most authentic of Italy's folk events. Competing, by turn, are ten of the city's seventeen historic "contrade," or neighborhoods. The names of these "contrade" are: Aquila, Bruco, Chiocciola, Civetta, Drago, Giraffa, Istrice, Leocorno, Lupa, Nicchio, Oca, Onda, Pantera, Selva, Tartuca, Torre, Valdimontone (literally, Eagle, Caterpillar, Snail, Owl, Dragon, Giraffe, Porcupine, Unicorn, She-Wolf, Shell, Goose, Wave, Panther, Forest, Tortoise, Tower, and Valley of the Ram). Each has a banner with an image corresponding to its name. Before the race, as the excitement builds among the townspeople (understandable excitement; the horses are raced bareback, ridden by jockeys who will do nearly anything to eliminate their rivals), a spectacular historical procession takes place, in costume, in which each "contrada" marches, with banners, followed by the Carro del Trionfo, or Carroccio, literally the Carriage of Triumph, with the "palio," a splendid silk drape awarded to the winning "contrada."

THE CAMPO
AND THE TERZO DI S. MARTINO

Siena branches out into three hilltop ridges, or "terzi," urban districts each of which is then split up into "contrade." From the Campo, in the shadow of the Palazzo Pubblico, the Terzo di S. Martino extends east to Porta Romana. **Piazza del Campo****. This outstanding testimony to the city's medieval harmony of layout and composition, the Piazza – called Campo by the Sienese – with its remarkable shell shape, has always lain at the heart of life in the city. First paved with elaborate brickwork in 1347, the square is dominated by the facade of the Palazzo Pubblico and the elegant silhouette of the Torre del Mangia, the tower which marks the perspectival vanishing point. Along the other sides of the square extends a line of ancient palazzi, some of them crenelated and turreted, interrupted by narrow lanes and "chiassi" leading to the broader streets behind. The square was first laid out in 1169. As early as 1297, a decree of

The Palio di Siena is an age-old competition held annual between 2 July and 16 August.

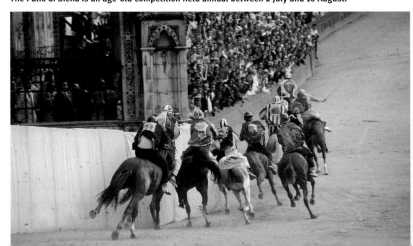

the Republic, one of the first zoning regulations known to history, established standards for buildings facing the Campo. These palazzi were continually improved and beautified over the centuries; some were radically rebuilt in the 18th century, and then restored to their original Gothic style in the 19th century. **Fonte Gaia**, a rectangular basin in the center of the Campo, was created in 1419 by J. della Quercia; the original exquisite marble panels are now in the Museo Civico. Note, to the right of the fountain, the curving facade of Palazzo Sansedoni and, to the left, the crenelated Palazzo d'Elci.

Palazzo Pubblico**. Symbolic of the independence and wealth of Siena's oligarchic ruling class, this town hall is certainly one of the finest achievements of Gothic civil architecture in Tuscany. As if to underscore the shift from a fortress to a residential palazzo, the popular government "of the Nine" had the central, taller wing of this building erected between 1284 and 1305; the two side wings were completed in 1310, with another storey added in 1680. The lower stone section of the facade, once lightened by great doors, balanced the upper brick section, still punctuated by two rows of elegant, three-light, mullioned windows. It is crowned by parapets and the vast disk known as "monogramma di Bernardino" (1425). As work continued on the exterior, the greatest painters of Sienese art were summoned to decorate the interior, in celebration of the wisdom and taste of the leaders of the Republic. The works they created now form the collections of the Museo Civico (see below); a number of halls, used by the city government, are generally closed to the public. Above the left wing rises the soaring profile of the Torre del Mangia* (102 m), built in 1325-48. The sober brick shaft is crowned by a stone corbel structure, probably designed by L. Memmi; it in turn works as the base for a stone structure which serves as the belfry. At the base of the tower, the so-called Cappella di Piazza is a marble loggia joined to the facade of the Palazzo Pubblico; built from 1352 to 1376 to fulfill a vow taken during the Black Death of 1348, its upper section was completed in 1461-68. The sadly deteriorated fresco over the altar was by Sodoma (1537-39). The portal to the right of the Piazza Chapel leads to the porticoed courtyard of the Podestà (1325). At the far side, on the right, is the Teatro dei Rinnovati, once the hall of the Gran Consiglio della Repubblica, rebuilt as a theater in 1560, and once again rebuilt, after two fires, by A. Gal-

li Bibiena in 1753. On the left, entrance to the 503-step stairway to the top of the Torre del Mangia with its fabulous view* of Siena. Further to the right, the entrance to the Magazzini del Sale, partly subterranean rooms with brick vaults, used for temporary shows, and for the exhibitions organized by the Museo per Bambini.

Museo Civico**, this museum comprises an impressive gallery of paintings as well as the monumental halls of the Palazzo Pubblico. From the courtyard of the Podestà, you climb first of all to the 19th-century. *Sala del Risorgimento* (late 19C frescoes by Tuscan artists, including C. Maccari). A steep staircase leads up to the loggia (see below), followed by the *Sala di Balia*, with 15th-century frescoes; the *Sala dei Cardinali*, with sculptures by a student of J. della Quercia and detached frescoes; the Sala del Concistoro, featuring a carved portal* by B. Rossellino (1446) and frescoes by D. Beccafumi in the vault. The room before the chapel, with frescoes by T. di Bartolo (1414), contains ancient gold jewelry, including the mid-15th-century gold rose of Pope Pius II; the chapel*, features a wrought-iron gate (1437), an inlaid wood choir** (1415-28) by D. di Niccolò, fine frescoes by T. di Bartolo (1407), and an altarpiece* by Sodoma. In the Sala del Mappamondo, a great hall where the Council of the Republic met, is the renowned fresco of the Maestà** by S. Martini (1315). Facing it is the Siege of the Montemassi castle by G. da Fogliano** (1328-29), a fresco whose long-standing attribution to Martini is being debated. The hall contains other fine works by S. di Pietro, Sodoma, and D. di Buoninsegna. In the Sala della Pace is the remarkable Allegory of Good and Bad Government**, frescoes painted for the Government of the Nine by A. Lorenzetti in 1338-40. Next comes the Sala dei Pilastri, with 13th-15th-century Sienese paintings, including works by G. da Siena, A. Lorenzetti, N. di Bartolomeo, and M. di Giovanni. The gallery features Italian and especially Sienese paintings from the 16th-18th century, notable among them works by J. Roos and B. di David. Upstairs, the Loggia dei Nove, overlooking the Piazza del Mercato and the Sienese countryside, displays the fragments of the Fonte Gaia*, by J. della Quercia, reassembled in 1904 (undergoing restoration, to be moved).

Università degli Studi. At the corner of Via S. Vigilio, overlooking Via Banchi di Sotto (no. 55-57), this former convent was founded in the 11th century and repeatedly renovated until the Neo-Renaissance version of 1891.

Now the office of the Rector of the University of Siena, this building has, since 1816, been the headquarters of the ancient Sienese Studio, which dates back to the 13th century. Note the Gothic funerary monument in the courtyard. If you follow Via S. Vigilio, a covered entrance (on the left, after Via Angiolieri) leads into the courtyard of the Castellare degli Ugurgieri, a medieval fortress-home. On Via Bandini are the Renaissance palazzi of the Bandini Piccolomini family (no. 25-29).

Palazzo Piccolomini*. This impressive piece of architecture from the later Florentine Renaissance was built from 1469 on by P.P. del Porrina, probably to a plan by B. Rossellino, and enlarged in the 17th century. The light rustication of the facade overlooking Via Banchi di Sotto (no. 52) is crowned by a broad cornice: note the two large marble crests over the main doorway, with the heraldic device of the Piccolomini family. This building contains the State Archives, with vast collections of historical documents, and, especially, the records of the Sienese Republic. Four halls on the second floor contain the Museo dell'Archivio di Stato*, featuring the collection of the Biccherne**, 103 painted wooden tablets which served as covers for books of public records, commissioned from 1258 to 1659, and painted by great artists as A. and P. Lorenzetti, G. di Paolo, Vecchietta, S. di Pietro, F. di Giorgio Martini, and D. Beccafumi. The Archives also contain documents concerning episodes or persons mentioned in Dante's Divine Comedy, the will of Boccaccio, and writings of St Catherine of Siena.

Logge del Papa, this elegant Renaissance loggia with three arcades marks the eastern end of Via Banchi di Sopra; it was built by A. Federighi (1462) at the behest of Pope Pius II Piccolomini.

S. Martino, nearby is one of Siena's oldest churches, which gave its name to the Terzo di S. Martino. Built in 1537, with a solemn facade dating from 1613, the church has nothing of the original, much-older structure. Inside, note the Baroque ciborium by G. Mazzuoli (1649) and the marble altars, with paintings by G. Reni and D. Beccafumi.

Basilica dei Servi*. This immense church, whose full name is San Clemente in Santa Maria dei Servi, was begun in the 13th-century and was not completed and consecrated until 1533, with the 15th-century facade still unfinished. Alongside it stands a 14th-century bell tower (completely restored in 1926). From the broad stairway before it, you have a fine view* of the walled city. The luminous interior, with a nave with two aisles and slender marble columns, preserves the original Renaissance plan, though it is sadly marred by 19th-century "restorations." Of special interest, among the many artworks by the Sienese school between the 13th-16th century, are the Madonna del Bordone** by C. di Marcovaldo, and works by M. di Giovanni, N. di Segna, S. di Bonaventura, P. Lorenzetti, B. Fungai, T. di Bartolo, and G. di Paolo.

Via Roma. This twisting road links Via di Pantaneto with Porta Romana. Set back at the end of Via del Refugio is the church of S. Raimondo al Refugio, with a Baroque travertine facade and works by F. Vanni, S. Folli and R. Manetti. Further along is the little church of the Santuccio, founded in the 14th-century and rebuilt in the 16th century. Note the 17th-century frescoes by V. Salimbeni. In the sacristy is the Museo della Società di Esecutori di Pie Disposizioni, with work by 14th-16th-century Sienese painters.

Porta Romana*, built after 1328, this is the largest of the gates in the 14th-century walls. Going down beyond the gate, along Via Piccolomini, is the church of S. Maria degli Angeli in Valli, a 15th-century building with an elegant marble Renaissance portal.

S. Spirito, overlooking the oddly shaped Piazza S. Spirito, with its handsome 16th-century fountain known as "de Pispini," this solemn brick Renaissance church features a portal believed to be by B. Peruzzi (1519). Inside, paintings by Sodoma and D. Beccafumi, and a terracotta crèche by A. della Robbia.

The Mangia tower and Palazzo Pubblico.

THE DUOMO, NATIONAL ART GALLERY, AND TERZO DI CITTÀ

Its skyline marked by the 13th-century dome of the cathedral and by its white- and black-striped bell tower, the Terzo di Città is the oldest district of Siena. With the paintings of the Pinacoteca, the pulpit by N. Pisano in the cathedral, and the *Maestà* by D. di Boninsegna in the Museo dell'Opera, this route becomes a short course in some of the finest art that Italian history has to offer.

Loggia della Mercanzia*. This elegant Gothic-Renaissance structure (1417-44) is made of three broad arcades, with statues in niches and 16th-century frescoes and stuccoes beneath its vaults; note the two 15th-century marble benches, with carved reliefs. The loggia stands near Siena's central crossroads, where Via Banchi di Sotto and Via Banchi di Sopra, once part of the medieval Via Francigena, meet Via di Città, which leads to the Spedale and the Duomo.

Via di Città*. The refined main avenue of the section of ancient Siena where the Longobard Gastaldo once lived, is still distinctly medieval in flavor; it climbs in a gentle curve, lined with elegant stores and 14th-15th-century aristocratic palazzi. Just past Chiasso del Bargello, with a charming view of the Palazzo Pubblico, the 14th-century Palazzo Patrizi (no. 75-77) is the headquarters of the Accademia degli Intronati, a celebrated Sienese cultural institution founded in the 16th century. Further on is the vast curving facade of the 13th-century Palazzo Chigi-Saracini*, featuring archeological artifacts, sculptures, furniture, ceramics, and Tuscan paintings from the 14th-17th-century, including works by Sodoma, Sassetta, and Beccafumi. Practically facing it is Palazzo Piccolomini o delle Papesse* (no. 126), almost certainly built by B. Rossellino (1460). Since 1998 it has housed the Centro di Arte Contemporanea "Le Papesse" a cultural center for the promotion of the arts. On the other side, also note the 14th-century Palazzo Marsili (no. 132), heavily restored in the 19th century.

Piazza del Duomo*. Dominated by the black-and-white marble mass of the Duomo, high atop its stepped platform, the asymmetrical piazza features some of Siena's oldest and most important buildings. To the left of the cathedral is the Palazzo Arcivescovile, built in 1718-24 in 14th-century Gothic style; facing it is the long facade of the Spedale di S. Maria della Scala (see below) and, to the right of the cathedral, the 16th-century Palazzo del Governatore dei Medici, now the seat of police ad-ministration and provincial government. Further on is Piazza Jacopo della Quercia, originally planned as the site of the enormous, but unbuilt, Duomo Nuovo; relics of this project can be seen in the colonnade and the surrounding buildings, as well as in the "facciatone," the unfinished facade of the "new cathedral."

Duomo**. The pride of Siena, intended to be the "the greatest monument in Christendom," this is one of the most successful creations of Italian Romanesque-Gothic. An earlier cathedral was built here around the 9th century; a larger one was built in its place and consecrated in 1179, but beginning in 1215-20 the building was rebuilt and enlarged; only the crypt remained intact. All scholars now agree that the architect was N. Pisano. Work began on the facade in 1284. In 1339 work began on the ambitious – even overweening – project to make the Cathedral merely a transept of another, immense cathedral, the Duomo Nuovo; the Sienese gave up this folly in 1357. Between 1377 and 1382 the facade and apse were completed. The majestic facade, largely the Romanesque-Gothic creation of G. Pisano, stands out for its exquisite decoration and many sculptures, largely by Pisano and his school. Many of the originals are now in the Museo dell'Opera Metropolitana. Note, on the right side of the Cathedral, the large Gothic windows and the Porta del Perdono: in the lunette, a copy of a bas-relief by Donatello; the original is in the Museo dell'Opera. The tall Romanesque bell tower* was built in the late 13th century. White- and black-striped, it has a progression of mullioned windows, ranging from one-light to six-light, at the top. The interior, built to a Latin cross plan, has a huge nave and aisles; the grandiose proportions are underscored by the black-and-white stripes of the walls and by the marble floor** with color decoration and etched depictions. This immense artwork, with its 56 panels depicting sacred and profane scenes, unique in art history, is covered for protection, and can only be seen during solemn occasions. Among the artists who worked on it, from 1373 to 1547, were G. di Stefano, N. di Bartolomeo, A. Federighi, Pinturicchio, Beccafumi, and F. di Giorgio Martini. Worn down by the shoes of the faithful, part of the floor was completely redone in the 19th century by A. Maccari. A noteworthy counter-facade, with central portal and columns attributed to G. di Stefano. Above it, over the arcades, along the nave and the presbytery runs a 15th-16th-century cornice with terracotta busts of the popes. The transept, with its double aisle, has hexagonal cross vaults and a great dome, with a twelve-sided base. Six large gilded statues of saints (G. di Stefano, 1488) stand beneath a blind gallery, adorned with depictions of patriarchs and prophets. At the opening of the right transept is the circular Baroque Cappella del Voto, attributed to G.L. Bernini (1662), who also did the two marble statues. Inside the chapel, the 13th-century Madonna del Voto, and a masterpiece by M. Preti (1670). In the middle of the presbytery is the high altar by B. Peruzzi (1532), topped by a bronze ciborium* by Vecchietta, which replaced Duccio's Maestà in the early 16th century; on the nearby pillars, the various angels are by G. di Stefano (1489), F. di Giorgio Martini (1490) and Beccafumi (1548-51). In the apse, note the 14th-century wooden choir,* partly inlaid by Fra' G. da Verona (1503), assembled here in the 19th century but originally from Monte Oliveto Maggiore; on high is the exquisite circular stained glass* of 1288 (one of the earliest made in Italy) to cartoons by D. di Buoninsegna. To the left of the presbytery, note the fine holy-water stoup* by G. di Turino (1434) at the entrance to the sacristy, with frescoes by B. di Bindo (1412). From here, you can reach the Chapter House, with portraits of Sienese popes and bishops, and two paintings by S. di Pietro. In the left transept, the octagonal marble pulpit** by N. Pisano (1266-68), a masterpiece of Italian Gothic sculpture (also by his son Giovanni, and others, including A. di Cambio); the stairs are by B. Neroni, Il Riccio (1543). At the beginning of the left transept is an elegant portal by Marrina, through which you enter the Renaissance chapel of S. Giovanni Battista* (1492), with paintings by Pinturicchio (1504-06), partly redone by Rustichino (1615-16); throughout, sculpture by Donatello (1457), A. Federighi (ca. 1460), G. di Stefano, N. di Bartolomeo (1487), T. di Camaino (1317), and F. Vanni (1596). At the end of the left aisle is the entrance to the Libreria Piccolomini**, a Renaissance library built beginning in 1492 by the future pope Pius III, to hold the books of his uncle, Pope Pius II. The marble facade was decorated in Neo-Classic style by Marrina (1497), and bears a fresco by Pinturicchio, note the polychrome wooden group of sculptures by A. di Betto (1421). The walls of the library are frescoed with the Scenes from the Life of Pius II** by Pinturicchio (1502-1509): in the middle is the group of the Three Graces*, a 3rd-century Roman copy from a Hellenistic original; on display are exquisite illuminated choir books*. Next to the entrance, in the aisle of the cathedral, note the huge Piccolo-

mini altar*, begun by A. Bregno in 1481: four of the statues of saints are by Michelangelo (1503-04), while the Virgin with Child (center, top) is attributed to J. della Quercia.

Spedale di S. Maria della Scala*. This huge medieval hospital complex was built to serve pilgrims and the poor, between the 9th-11th century; the facade was renovated repeatedly through the 13th-15th century, and features large mullioned windows. Of particular note, inside is the vast infirmary, or "Pellegrinaio," with a series of frescoes* depicting the hospital's history and everyday operation, by D. di Bartolo, P. della Quercia, and Vecchietta (1440-44). Part of the facade is the flank of the 13th-century church of the Santissima Annunziata, rebuilt in 1466; inside, note the Crucifix (ca. 1330) and impressive organ; also, a statue* by Vecchietta (1476) and a fresco by S. Conca (1732). As Siena's new polyclinic is completed, the Spedale is being retired as a working hospital; there are plans to convert it into a "cultural citadel".

Museo Archeologico Nazionale with a separate entrance at the beginning of the Via del Capitano. This archeology museum reinstalled in two huge halls in the Spedale di S. Maria della Scala. Its collections comprise material (vases, urns, kraters, coins, and jewelry) from prehistoric, Etruscan, and Roman periods, largely drawn from the 19th-century private collections that constitute the museum's historical core; these are found in the antiquarium. In the topographic section are archeological finds, mostly tomb furnishings, found in Siena and its territory.

Museo dell'Opera Metropolitana.** Housed in a building in Piazza Jacopo della Quercia, built as early as the 15th century in what had been intended as the right aisle of the planned Duomo Nuovo, or New Cathedral, this museum comprises artworks from the decoration and furnishing of the cathedral. On the first floor, the Sala di Duccio features, on the facing wall, the front of the Maestà** by D. di Buoninsegna (1308-11), a masterpiece of Sienese art, commissioned for the main altar of the cathedral; on the other side of the room, the back of the altarpiece. On the right wall, a notable triptych** by P. Lorenzetti (1342), and a Madonna* by the young Duccio (ca. 1283). In the three other rooms on this floor, wooden statues, golden reliquaries, ivory crosiers, and illuminated choir books outdo one another in splendor. Note the small wooden Crucifix* by G. Pisano; also, three wooden busts of saints*, by F. di Valdambrino (1409). **Second floor.** In the middle of the first hall, an early 13th-century *Madonna dagli Oc-chi Grossi** (named for her outsized eyes); four saints by A. Lorenzetti; and various works by such artists as G. di Paolo, S. di Pietro, a follower of Sassetta, G. di Cecco. In the other rooms are works by M. di Giovanni, D. Beccafumi (*St Paul Enthroned**), Pomarancio; also altarpieces, liturgical garb, and other objects. From the last room, you can climb up to the top of the unfinished facade of the Duomo Nuovo, known in Siena as the "facciatone," or "great facade" (fine view*). **Ground floor**. At the center, a relief** by J. della Quercia and a bas-relief tondo** by Donatello; along the walls, ten statues** by G. Pisano (1284-96), once on the facade of the cathedral, masterpieces of Gothic sculpture.

S. Giovanni Battista*. This is Siena's baptistery, and is located beneath the apse of the Duomo, on Piazza S. Giovanni. You take a 15th-century staircase down to it, through the portal* by G. di Agostino, intended to be part of the right side of the giant Duomo Nuovo (1345); midway down is the Crypt of Statues, used for exhibitions. **The church**, built amid the arches that support the extended apse of the Duomo over Valle Piatta, has a Gothic facade, with three large splayed portals. Inside, amid frescoes by many mid-15th-century artists, including Vecchietta, note the great hexagonal baptismal font** (1416-34), a masterpiece of the early Tuscan Renaissance, believed to have been built under the overall direction of J. della Quercia. This sculptor also did the marble ciborium with the statue of John the Baptist and bas-reliefs; the bronze angels are by Donatello and G. di Turino, who also did the bas-reliefs, along with G. di Neroccio, J. della Quercia, T. di Sano, and L. Ghiberti.

Pinacoteca Nazionale**. On the left side of Via S. Pietro, this art gallery is located in the early 15th-century Palazzo Buonsignori (no. 29), and the adjacent Gothic Palazzo Brigidi, both of which have been restored in the Romantic style of the 19th century. This gallery dates from the 18th century, when a great scholar named G. Ciaccheri began to collect the work of Sienese "primitive" artists, and it has been in the present location since 1930, filling some thirty rooms. This is certainly one of the most important collections for an understanding of Sienese painting as it developed from the late 12th-17th century. From the elegant courtyard of Palazzo Buonsignori, a stairway (right) leads to the second floor. Sienese painters featured include, from the 13th century: G. da Siena, Maestro del S. Pietro, Maestro del S. Giovanni; from the 14th century: D. di Buonin-

segna (*Virgin of the Franciscans***), N. di Segna, U. di Nerio, B. di Fredi , L. di Tommè, S. Martini (*Virgin and Child***), L. Memmi, A. Lorenzetti (*Annunciation***), P. Lorenzetti, P. di Giovanni Fei, B. Bulgarini, D. di Bartolo, M. da Besozzo, L. Monaco, S. Aretino, and T. di Bartolo; from the 15th century: G. di Paolo (*Our Lady of Humility***), Sassetta, Maestro dell'Osservanza, M. di Giovanni, N. di Bartolomeo, F. di Giorgio Martini, P. di Domenico, G. di Benvenuto, S. di Pietro, and Vecchietta. You descend to the first floor, where there are other works by Sienese painters of the 15th century: G. da Cremona, P. degli Orioli, G. Genga, Pinturicchio, and B. Fungai; and of the 16th century: D. Beccafumi, Sodoma (*Christ at the Column***), and Brescianino. On the third floor is the Collezione Spannocchi, featuring works by northern Italian and central European artists of the 15th-16th century.

S. Pietro alle Scale. Founded in the 13th century and rebuilt in the 18th century, this church has fragments of frescoes by L. da Verona and segments of a polyptych by A. Lorenzetti; on the main altar, note the canvas by R. Manetti.

S. Agostino. Built in the 13th century and renovated in 1747-55 by L. Vanvitelli, this church overlooks the Prato S. Agostino; before it extends a 19th-century portico by A. Fantastici. The luminous, Neo-Classic interior has works by Perugino, A. Lorenzetti (Piccolomini chapel), F. di Giorgio Martini, L. Signorelli, R. Manetti, and Sodoma. Also note the marble altar by F. del Turco (1608), majolica floors, and 15th-century wooden Virgin.

Accademia dei Fisiocritici. This respected academy for the study of science was founded in 1691 by P.M. Gabrielli, and still does extensive research. Located at no. 5 in Prato S. Agostino, across from the church, the academy has many collections of the life sciences, with part of the Museo dell'Accademia dei Fisiocritici installed in the cloister, and on the ground and first floor; outside is a botanical garden.

S. Niccolò al Carmine. This church overlooks the vast semicircular expanse of Piano dei Mantellini, and can be reached from Prato S. Agostino along the distinctive Via T. Pendola, with its venerable homes, and then down along Via di S. Quirico, past the 16th-century Palazzo Pollini (no. 39-41). The church was founded in the 14th century and renovated often in the 15th-16th century; note the bell tower attributed to B. Peruzzi (1517). Inside are paintings by Beccafumi, Sodoma, A. Casolani (1604), and G. del Pacchia; the high altar is by

T. Redi. To the right of the church (no. 40), note the Neo-Classic facade of Palazzo Incontri, designed by S. Belli (1799-1804). Via Stalloreggi, this road twists and turns past craftsmen's workshops with a medieval flavor, extending Via di Città along the hill of Castelvecchio; at the far end, near Piano dei Mantellini, is the Due Porte arch, an old city gate incorporated in the surrounding buildings; on the inner side, a 14th-century fresco by B. di David. Returning toward Piazza Postierla, on the right, Via di Castelvecchio passes by a series of houses and lanes that make up a medieval district; at the intersection of Via Stalloreggi and Via di S. Quirico, note the tabernacle, with a Pietà by Sodoma.

Siena has some wonderful views.

THE TERZO DI CAMOLLIA AND S. DOMENICO

In the northern part of town, extensively modified in the 19th-20th century, you can still find the memories of two great, eloquent Sienese saints: St Bernardino would preach in the oratory near S. Francesco; the son of a washerman, C. Benincasa, or St Catherine of Siena, lived near the Fonte Branda, in a house that had been turned into a sanctuary as early as the 15th century. Banchi di Sopra, the backbone of the Terzo di Camollia, this road climbs with a slight curve from the Croce del Travaglio, breaking off at Piazza Tolomei, with its column crowned by the she-wolf of Siena (1610). On the left, the 13th-century Palazzo Tolomei* (no. 11). On the right side of the palazzo, in Vicolo della Torre, a plaque bears the verses from Dante's Divine Comedy concerning Pia dei Tolomei, believed to have lived in this house.

S. Maria di Provenzano. This majestic basilica, with a fine view of the surrounding walls and hillsides, was built immediately after the Medici conquest, in 1595-1604; inside, marble floor (1685) and immense main altar by F. del Turco (1617-31), with the 15th-century terracotta image of the Madonna di Provenzano.

S. Francesco. This huge 14th-century Franciscan basilica, flanked by the oratory of S. Bernardino (see below) stands on a large square overlooking a panoramic landscape stretching to the hills of Chianti, in the distance. It was completed in 1482, partly destroyed by fire in 1655, and restored to the original Gothic form by G. Partini in 1885-92; the Neo-Gothic facade dates from 1894-1913. Inside, note the fragments of frescoes that once adorned Porta Romana, by Sassetta and S. di Pietro (1447-50), and other frescoes** by P. Lorenzetti, A. Lorenzetti, and L. Vanni. Also note the portal, by F. di Giorgio Martini.

Oratory of S. Bernardino*. Built in the 15th century on the site where St Bernardino da Siena once preached, this two-level oratory has a fine Renaissance portal (1574). In the rooms adjacent to the oratory is the Museo Diocesano di Arte Sacra with precious collections from the churches and convents of the diocese. A vestibule with an exquisite relief* by G. di Agostino (ca. 1336) precedes the upper oratory*, which today is the heart of the museum and one of the most interesting examples of Renaissance architecture; there are 15th-century inlays and stuccoes as well as frescoes* and panels by Sodoma, G. del Pacchia, and Beccafumi (1518-37).

Porta Ovile. Built in the 13th century, this gate was incorporated in the 14th-century walls; from S. Francesco take the steep Via del Comune. In the small aedicula, is the fresco by S. di Pietro. Then, outside the walls, note the 13th-century Fonte d'Ovile (fountain). Climb back up Via di Vallerozzi toward the center, and you will pass, on the right, the Oratory of S. Rocco, with paintings by R. Vanni and V. Salimbeni and frescoes by R. Manetti, B. Mei, and S. Salimbeni. Behind the Oratory, in Via del Pian d'Ovile, is the Fonte Nuova d'Ovile, a fountain built in 1295-1303, a fine medieval blend of monumental form and practical function. As you walk from Via di Vallerozzi to Via dell'Abbadia, you will see the church of S. Michele al Monte di S. Donato, built in 1147, and extensively renovated since; inside, a wooden group by Vecchietta. Facing the church is the enormous Rocca dei Salimbeni, a 13th-century fortress rebuilt in Gothic style in 1883-87 (see below).

Piazza Salimbeni. "Invented" at the end of the 19th century by the architect G. Partini as part of a greater Sienese "Gothic revival," at its center is a monument to Sallustio Bandini (1880); on the left is the mid-16th-century Palazzo Tantucci, by Riccio. On the right side is the Neo-Renaissance facade, by G. Partini (1877-82), of Palazzo Spannocchi, an imitation of the original, by G. da Maiano (1473), in Via Banchi di Sopra. At the far end stands Palazzo Salimbeni, once part of a fortress; the 14th-century Gothic facade is largely the fruit of 19th-century restorations by Partini (1871-79). The entire complex serves as the offices of Monte dei Paschi, an important Sienese bank dating from the Middle Ages: noted historical archive and fine art collections.

Biblioteca Comunale degli Intronati, at no. 5 in Via della Sapienza, in the building where Siena's Studio, or university, was founded, is this major city institution, based on an 18th-century donation. The library now has more than half-a-million volumes, including codices illuminated by 12th-15th-century Sienese artists (L. Vanni, Sassetta, S. di Pietro) and a major collection of drawings and prints. A bit further along, the steep Costa di S. Antonio offers a fine view of the Duomo and its area; continue down, along the Vicolo del Tiratoio, to the Sanctuary of the della Casa di S. Caterina and the Fonte Branda; then return to the center of town along the Via della Galluzza, renowned for the succession of medieval arches through which it passes.

Sanctuary of the Casa di S. Caterina. The sanctuary includes a complex of buildings that have grown up around the birthplace of Caterina Benincasa – Sienese mystic and saint (St Catherine of Siena, 1347-1380), patron saint of Italy (with St Francis) – along the Portico dei Comuni d'Italia (1941), where there is a fine 15th-century well. An atrium with loggia, attributed to B. Peruzzi, leads to the right to the church of the Crocifisso, with a 13th-century Crucifix, before which the saint supposedly received her stigmata; facing it is the Oratorio Superiore, with a gilt lacunar ceiling and majolica floors (16C), adorned with 16th-17th-century paintings by A. Casolani, A. Salimbeni, F. Vanni, R. Manetti, and B. Fungai. Continue down to the Oratorio della Camera, with frescoes by A. Franchi (1896); on the altar, a 16th-century masterpiece by G. di Benvenuto; adjacent is the cell of the saint. Further down is the Oratory of S. Caterina in Fontebranda (1465-74), still in use; in the interior are frescoes by Sodoma, G. del Pacchia, and others; on the altar, a wooden statue* of the saint by N. di Bartolomeo (1475).

Fonte Branda. At the end of Via S. Caterina,

this is the best-known of Siena's fountains, standing in the shadow of S. Domenico. Mentioned by Boccaccio, and documented as early as 1081, it was rebuilt in 1246, entirely in brick; the merlons and cornice of small arches are modern. Nearby is the panoramic Vicolo di Camporegio, with steps leading up to S. Domenico.

S. Domenico*. The nucleus of the huge brick Gothic basilica, still standing, was built between 1226 and 1262-65. Enlarged around 1350, the church had a difficult existence: badly damaged by fire (1443 and 1531), war (1548-52), and earthquake (1798), it was extensively restored and modified in 1941-62. Devoid of its facade, the basilica has a 15th-century bell tower, lopped short in 1793, and still has much of its Cistercian apse. Inside, note the high mullioned windows; the huge transept has six apsidal chapels (from the apsidal terrace, fine view* of central Siena, the Duomo, and the Fonte Branda). On the right as you enter, is the chapel of the Vaults, with a fresco of St Catherine by A. Vanni, believed to be the only accurate portrait of her. Along the right wall of the church, a 14th-century wooden Crucifix and marble portal to the S. Caterina chapel, with frescoes* by Sodoma and paintings by F. Vanni; the marble tabernacle (G. di Stefano; 1466) contains a reliquary with the saint's head. In the sacristy, standard by Sodoma; at the end of the nave, painting by F. di Giorgio Martini and fresco by P. Lorenzetti. On the modern main altar, note the elegant marble ciborium* and the candle-bearing angels* by B. da Maiano (1475). Note the paintings by M. di Giovanni, B. di Giovanni, F. di Vannuccio, Sodoma, R. Manetti, S. di Pietro, and B. Salimbeni.

Fortezza di S. Barbara or Medicea. This huge square fort with corner bastions was built for Cosimo I de' Medici and designed by B. Lanci (1561). Now a public park, it offers a fine view of the hills and city. Inside is the Enoteca Italiana, a wine shop featuring local wines and delicacies. Nearby is the garden of La Lizza, established as a park in 1779 and enlarged at the turn of the 20th century.

Porta Camollia. This 17th century reconstruction of a 14th-century gate still bears an inscription honoring Ferdinando I de' Medici, a symbol of Sienese hospitality: *Cor magis tibi Sena pandit* (Siena opens its heart to you, wider than this gate). Outside the gate, along Viale Cavour, is the tall crenelated Antiporto di Camollia (1270); at the end of the road, near where it meets the Via Cassia, is the medieval Palazzo dei Diavoli, restored in 1859.

It is said that Elba is a precious stone that fell into the sea, when one of Aphrodite's necklaces broke. Elba is an island with coves, bays, promontories, reefs, and crescent-shaped beaches – the 118 km of coastline is four times the extent one would expect of an island this size – steep slopes dotted with olive and almond trees, silent lofty villages, holm-oaks, and sunny vineyards, producing sweet wines, palm trees, agave plants, eucalyptus trees, and cork-oaks. On the eastern beaches, the sand is mixed with pyrite, and a rusty iron-red dominates in the rocks. The Greek name was "Aethalia," or "place of soot," because of the smoke from the ironworks here; "Ilva," the Roman name, refers to the early lords of the island, the Ligurian Ilvates. Porto Argoo (so-called because

Jason, sailing the Argo, landed here during one of his quests), now called Portoferraio, was many centuries ago the main town of Elba. Another name it once bore is Cosmopoli, for the following reason: Cosimo I de' Medici had defended the entire Piombino territory against the wrath of the Barbary pirate and admiral Khair-ed-Din, known also as Barbarossa, or Redbeard. Cosimo then persuaded the Holy Roman Emperor Charles V to let him protect, and rule, the mainland and islands of this patch of what he considered maritime Tuscany, sweetening the pot with a loan of 200,000 ducats. Later, Charles's only son and heir Philip II bestowed Piombino and most of Elba to the Appiani family, leaving Cosimo with Portoferraio. Here, on the site of a modest village, the architect G. Bellucci had built a

A view of Isola Paolina.

city and fortress for the Medici (1548-59): an efficacious piece of military architecture, but also the translation into concrete form of the last tattered dreams of the Renaissance "ideal city." This relic of utopian ambitions, epitomized in the name Cosmopoli, can still be seen.

NOT TO BE MISSED

Portoferraio: note the strategic position guarding the little bay, the dignified architecture, and the late-Renaissance city layout, the creation of Cosimo I de' Medici; the town also contains the Foresiana art gallery boasting works from the 16th-19th-century, and an archeology museum with local finds. **Capo d'Enfola**: here are the clear waters, abounding in fish, around the promontory. **Villa di Napoleone**: take a detour from the fork of Bivio Boni; this was Napoleon's summer home. **Marciana** is a village on the slopes of Mt Capanne, 1,018 m (you can reach the peak by cableway and footpaths); on Mt Giove (a bit of a hike is required) is the Sanctuary of the Madonna del Monte. **San Piero in Campo**: take a detour just before Marina di Campo; this village dating back to Roman times lies at the foot of an old fort. **Penisola di Lacona**: this peninsula can be reached by a detour from a fork near the Golfo della Stella; forest landscape and beaches of exceedingly fine sand. **Capoliveri**: there is a spectacular view from the "borgo," which can be reached from a turnoff just before Porto Azzurro; lovely secluded beaches at Morcone. **Porto Azzurro**: the Spanish built the fortress (now a prison) which looms over the town and the little gulf; from the road to Rio, you can detour to the Sanctuary of Monserrato (also founded by the Spanish, and dedicated to the Virgin of Monserrat, near Barcelona). **Rio nell'Elba** is a mining town in iron country. **Rio Marina** has a small mining museum in the town hall. **Cavo**: there are ruins of a Roman villa on the promontory of Capo Castello.

VALDICHIANA AND LAKE TRASIMENO

Every village and town is perched on a hill, overlooking the plain, like a broad green sea, and across that plain to the opposite shore of hills and highlands. The Valdichiana, indeed, is a great rift running north-south across Tuscany, between Arezzo and Chiusi and, following the collapse of the Roman reclamation project in the Middle Ages, was immersed in swamps, marshes, and shallow lakes until the beginning of the 19th century. All around, the background color is provided by the leaves of the olive trees that shade houses, villages, walls, towers, and castles. This route is simple: from Arezzo it runs south, first along the western hills, with Monte San Savino and Lucignano, then on the other side of the valley, with fine views of Cortona, proud on its high perch, with medieval keeps, Etruscan artifacts, and remarkable art (note the 15C clarity of the church of the Madonna del Calcinaio, by F. di Giorgio Martini). Once away from the Chiana, you enter Umbria. Gentle slopes, bedecked with olive groves and vineyards, surround the silence and reeds of Lake Trasimeno; the three islands, Polvese, Maggiore, Minore, stand quietly enveloped in turquoise light. You travel almost all the way around the lake, then other hilltop roads take you to lovely Perugia, star-shaped, with long arms of walls and houses reaching out across the ridges. Throughout this trip, history lies at every stop, on every hillside. History is present, in sinister garb, at the Magione, on a rise between Lake Trasimeno and Perugia: in the Magione, or castle of the Knights of Malta, then held by Cardinal G. Orsini, in September of 1502 a number of local lords angry at and fearful of C. Borgia, son of Pope Alexander VI and brother of Lucrezia, met to conspire against him. Within three months, Borgia had foiled the conspiracy, and four plotters – V. Vitelli, O. da Fermo, P. and F. Orsini – were killed in Senigallia with what Machiavelli enthusiastically described as a "rare and wondrous deed" (they were poisoned after being invited to dinner). Cardinal Orsini, meanwhile, was dying – or being killed – in Rome's Castel Sant'Angelo.

NOT TO BE MISSED

Monte San Savino: the feudal holding of the Dal Monte family (Pope Julius III was a Dal Monte), a medieval town now rich in Renaissance art. **Lucignano** is a medieval village with a remarkable layout; nearby is the Renaissance sanctuary of the Madonna delle Querce. **Foiano della Chiana**: this thriving hilltop town has old churches and small 16th-century palazzi; a fine panel by L. Signorelli in the collegiate church of S. Martino. **Castiglion Fiorentino**: amid the walls of this medieval town, you can still see the keep of the castle, now the Pinacoteca Comunale, with a notable collection of fine art; further along, to the left of the Valdichiana road, is the large castle of Montecchio Vesponi. **Cortona** (➡ see below): you take a fork at Camucia; landscape, history, and Etruscan relics, medieval townscape, and artworks (by P. Lorenzetti, L. Signorelli, and Fra' Angelico) make this the jewel of the route, one of Italy's artistic capitals. Make a small detour to Madonna del Calcinaio, and visit the Etruscan hypogeum of Tanella di Pitagora; a detour from the road to Città di Castello takes you to the Convento delle Celle. **Castiglione del Lago**: the old town sits amidst olive trees on a promontory overlooking Lake Trasimeno. **Castel Rigone**: take a 6 km detour from a fork at San Vito; the Sanctuary of the Madonna dei Miracoli is one of the masterpieces of the Umbrian Renaissance. **Passignano sul Trasimeno**: also perched on a lakefront promontory, this town has an old center of steep little lanes; on the nearby Isola Maggiore is the 14th-century Gothic church of S. Michele Arcangelo with a crucifix by B. Caporali. **Corciano** is a turreted medieval village, the last detour on the road from Magione to Perugia.

CORTONA

Clean air whispering through the olive trees, and a city the color of the sandstone from which it is largely carved, clustered on the steep slopes once enclosed by the vast Etruscan walls, at the edge of the plain of Valdichiana. The medieval past survives here, in the air and the buildings; for two centuries archeologists have been delving into the more distant Etruscan past thanks to the foundation of the Accademia Etrusca.

THE HISTORIC CENTER

In the 15th century Fra' Angelico came here to paint; a generation later, L. Signorelli, great Cortonese painter, began his career here. This Tuscan hill town is unforgettable in the melting light, when seen from high above, from the Medici fortress.

Piazza della Repubblica. Heart of Cortona, the square is lined by the 13th-century Palazzo Comunale, and the 12th-century Palazzo del Capitano del Popolo; nearby is Piazza Signorelli, with the Palazzo Casali, the site of the Museo dell'Accademia Etrusca.

Museo dell'Accademia Etrusca*. Founded in 1727, with library, as a branch of the Etruscan Academy, this museum has remarkable collections of Etruscan artifacts. Note the great bronze lamp** with satyrs and sirens (5-4C BC); it also exhibits Egyptian and Roman objects, a 12th-century mosaic, medieval and modern pieces of the applied arts (note the little porcelain temple by the Manifattura Ginori at Doccia; 1750-51), coins*, gems, medal-

The old center of Cortona.

lions, seals, miniatures and costumes. Among the paintings, work by N. di Pietro Gerini, B. di Lorenzo, F. Signorelli, Pinturicchio, and L. Signorelli; a hall is dedicated to the work by the modern painter Severini, who was born in Cortona. On the upper floors, three rooms display finds from the Tumulo II of the digs in the so-called Etruscan "meloni" from Il Sodo (see below), including late-Archaic jewelry*.

Duomo. Rebuilt in the 15th century, some Romanesque features survive in the facade of this cathedral; note the 16th-century portal of Cristofanello, under the portico.

Museo Diocesano del Capitolo*. The Diocesan museum is located in the former Gesù church (1498-1505) and adjacent buildings, facing the Duomo. In one section, works by P. Lorenzetti, L. Signorelli, and a Roman sarcophagus*. In the former church, works by Sassetta, P. Lorenzetti, Fra' Angelico, B. della Gatta; in the sacristy, more Lorenzetti and the celebrated Vagnucci reliquary*, by G. da Firenze (1457), and other 13th-century paintings. Downstairs, in the lower church, 16th-century frescoes, partly attributed to G. Vasari.

S. Francesco. This 13th-century church was rebuilt in the 17th century; inside is a fine 10th-century Byzantine ivory reliquary*.

Via Berrettini. This steep street goes up to the 16th-century church of S. Cristoforo, while Via S. Croce leads further up to S. Margherita, with fine views. Along the way is the little church of S. Nicolò.

S. Nicolò. This 15th-century church stands amidst the cypresses; note the standard* of the Compagnia di S. Nicolò painted on both sides by L. Signorelli.

Sanctuary of S. Margherita. This Neo-Gothic sanctuary (1856-97) is renowned for the spectacular view from the square before it. Just uphill is the Medici fortress, 651 m, built in 1556 (view*); take Via S. Margherita back to town; note the mosaic Via Crucis* by G. Severini.

MONUMENTS OUTSIDE THE CITY WALLS

The geometric architecture by F. di Giorgio Martini in the church of the Madonna del Calcinaio contrasts pleasingly with the gentle views of Tuscan countryside, dotted with cypresses and olive trees.

S. Domenico. Just outside the Porta Beralda is this late Gothic church with a triptych by L. di N. Gerini (1402). Take Viale Giardini Pubblici, for a walk with splendid views*.

Madonna del Calcinaio**. Standing some 3 km downhill from the town, near the local road from Camucia, this elegant Renaissance church was an archetype for the sanctuaries built between the 15th-16th century. Built in 1485-1513 to a plan by F. di Giorgio Martini, it has a luminous interior, in the style of Brunelleschi, with stained glass windows by G. de Marcillat (16C); the main altar, from the same period, is by B. Covatti.

Tanella di Pitagora. Some 3 km, SW of town, near the Madonna del Calcinaio, is this Etruscan hypogeum, perhaps dating from the 4th-century BC, set among the cypresses.

S. Maria Nuova. Outside the walls, north of town, this mid-16th-century church is reached by exiting the Porta Colonia. It was drastically rebuilt by G. Vasari.

Convento delle Celle or Convento dei Cappuccini. This convent stands 3.5 km NE, out of Porta Colonia, in a handsome hillside setting, and was founded by St Francis between 1211 and 1221. **"Meloni"**. At Il Sodo, 2 km NW of town, near the SS 71 road, are 4th-3rd-century BC Etruscan hypogea, or underground burial chambers, carved or dug out of sandstone. Some of the finds here are now on display in the Museo dell'Accademia Etrusca.

FLORENCE/FIRENZE

Dante Alighieri and the birth of the Italian language, great artists such as Giotto and Michelangelo, monuments and museums, local wars and civic virtues, Chianti and the great food, the lively character of the people: these are just some of the reasons why the most important Tuscan city, situated on the Arno River at the foot of the Fiesole hills, is associated to such an extent with Italian national identity.

The city first began to distinguish itself in medieval times, as the arts and crafts began to thrive. But as early as Roman times – the Latin name of the city "Florentia" means flourishing – Florence's position on trade routes had benefited it. The city really came into its own in the Renaissance, under the rule of the Medici, great patrons of the arts and founders of the city's museums collections.

For centuries Florence was an obligatory stop on the Grand Tour, the educational travels of young aristocrats from all over Europe. Today it is still a top tourist destination. Florence is truly an open-air museum, because of its unique treasures and architecture. At the same time, it has kept its identity as a modern city, with its economy and local population, despite the impact of crowds of tourists. Indeed tourism is a fundamental part of the economy.

The craft activities so important in the past still flourish: furniture restoration, gold production, lace-making and the famed Florentine straw-plait. Florentine food and cooking has maintained past traditions, and features deliciously good simple country cooking, as well as sophisticated modern adaptions of time-honored recipes. Likewise, 20th-century urban and industrial development has not spoilt the large historic center; here it is possible to wander along loggias and past noble facades, to marvel at squares which look as they did in medieval and Renaissance times, and to rest in centuries-old gardens blending nature and culture.

Duomo or Basilica di Santa Maria del Fiore. This exceptional cathedral, with the Battistero opposite, features the large simple lines of the Gothic style typical of Florence. At first sight a harmonious whole, the impressively massive Duomo is in fact the result of numerous additions over the centuries. Building was started in 1296 by A. di Cambio, suspended when he died (ca. 1310), and then continued on a larger scale in 1331 and again in 1357, under the direction of F. Talenti. In 1378 the central nave vault was completed, and in 1380 the side aisles. The octagon tribunes were finished by 1421, and on thes Brunelleschi's cupola was constructed between 1420 and 1436. The half-completed original **facade** by A. di Cambio was demolished in 1587 and rebuilt at the end of the 19th century. The original colored marble flanks are fundamental to the magnificence of the building. When you enter through the Porta dei Canonici*, the vast tribune* opens out, with three large polygonal apses, and smaller intermediate ones. Above rises the lofty octagonal drum supporting the enormous ribbed **Cupola**** by Brunelleschi. On the left flank is the early 15th-century richly decorated Gothic-Renaissance Porta della Mandorla (Almond Door)*. In the gable, *Assumption of the Virgin*, a high-relief by N. di Banco (1414-1421), and in the lunette, **Annunciation**, a mosaic by Domenico and Davide Ghirlandaio (1491). The simple, harmonious lines of the Latin-cross **interior** create an impression of majesty and austerity, illuminated by stained glass windows by L. Ghiberti in the apses. A staircase descends from the 2nd bay of the right aisle to the remains of **St Reparata**, the ancient cathedral demolished in 1375. The great **Cupola*** by Brunelleschi, soaring to a height of 91 m above the octagon, is decorated by a fresco of the *Last Judgement* by G. Vasari and F. Zuccari (1572-79); below, eight 16th-century statues of the apostles. To the left of the octagon is the Mass Sacristy; here Lorenzo the Magnificent took refuge from the Pazzi conspiracy, on the day that his brother Giuliano was killed (26 April 1478). The sacristy has a bronze door* and a lunette (*Resurrection**) by L. della Robbia (1444). The climb up to the cupola (*463 steps*) starts from the end of the left aisle. It is worth it: the dome structure can be seen more closely, and the view* from the walkway around the lantern (107 m) is fantastic. In the 3rd bay , **equestrian memorial to John Hawkwood****, painted by P. Uccello (1436); in the 2nd, equestrian memorial to N. da Tolentino*, painted by A. del Castagno (1456).
Giotto's bell tower, 84.7 m high, stands away to the side of the Duomo. It is famed

The Duomo or basilica of S. Maria del Fiore.

for its Gothic gracefulness, its magnificent colored marbles, and its fine sculpture work. It was started in 1334 by Giotto; A. Pisano continued with the base, and F. Talenti (1350-59) completed the upper levels with double and triple divided windows, and projecting crowning cornice. The base is decorated with two tiers of 14th-century bas-reliefs (copies: originals in the Museo dell'Opera del Duomo). The first tier reliefs are attributed to A. Pisano and completed on the side nearest the Duomo by L. della Robbia. The second tier reliefs are attributed to A. Pisano, to his school and to A. Arnoldi. Above, in niches, stand statues of patriarchs, kings, prophets and sibyls by A. Pisano, D. and N. di Bartolo (copies; originals in the Museo dell'Opera del Duomo). A staircase with 414 steps climbs up to the terrace with a great view* over the city.

Battistero di San Giovanni, a religious focal point and one of Florence's oldest buildings, the baptistery was described by Dante as his "bel San Giovanni" (lovely St John). It was built between the 11th and 13th centuries over Roman buildings. Its octagonal Romanesque structure, with a double tier of pilasters on white and green marble sides, is surmounted by an octagonal pyramidal roof over a cupola. The famous bronze **doors**,** placed at the cardinal points of the compass, constitute a kind of large-scale illustrated Bible. The oldest *South Door** is the work of Andrea Pisano (1330), and depicts *Scenes from the Life of*

John the Baptist. The most famous is the *East Door*, opposite the Duomo, called the **Porta del Paradiso**** (Door of Paradise) by Michelangelo. This Renaissance masterpiece by L. Ghiberti (1425-52) illustrates scenes from the *Old Testament* in ten panels. The original panels were restored after being damaged in the 1966 flood, and are now in the Museo dell'Opera del Duomo. The **interior,** below the octagonally segmented cupola, has a marble inlay floor* and marble walls bedecked with pilasters, linteled columns and a gallery with double divided arches. The cupola shimmers with 13th-century Byzantine-style mosaics* (*Last Judgement*; *Stories of Genesis*, the *Baptist and Christ*), by Venetian and Florentine artists, including possibly Cimabue. In the apse, other Byzantine-style mosaics* by J. da Torrita (1225), as well as the tomb of the anti-Pope John XXIII*, attributed to Donatello and Michelozzo (1427).

Museo dell'Opera di Santa Maria del Fiore. The museum, founded in 1891, features important 14th-15th-century Florentine works of sculpture, including originals from the Battistero, the Duomo and the bell tower. In the former courtyard, the **panels**** from Ghiberti's Door of Paradise. In the old facade room, sculptures from the old facade of the Duomo: Madonna and Child*, St Reparata*, Boniface VIII*, and relief with Madonna of the Nativity*, all by A. di Cambio; St John*, by Donatello; and St Luke*, by N. di Banco. There is also a section devoted to Brunelleschi and his cupola, with the artist's death mask, a wood model of the cupola and the lantern, and apparatus used in the construction of the cupola.

On the mezzanine floor, the **Pietà**,** a dramatic, unfinished group of figures sculpted by Michelangelo (1550-53), formerly in the Duomo interior. On the upper floor, in the *sala delle cantorie*: **cantoria**** (singing gallery) by Donatello (1433-39), with a procession of dancing putti; below, *Mary Magdalene**, a disturbing wood statue, one of Donatello's later works (1453-55), formerly in the baptistery; **cantoria**** by L. Della

Robbia (1431-38), with reliefs of children singing and making music; 16 **statues**** , formerly in niches in the bell tower, by Andrea Pisano (*Sibyls and Prophets*), Donatello (*Habbakuk**, also referred to as 'Pumpkinhead', because of the statue's baldness; *John the Baptist*; *three Prophets*) and N.di Bartolo (*Abraham and Isaac**, partly by Donatello). Next door, in the *sala delle formelle* are the relief **panels**** removed from the bell tower: the lower tier ones are by A. Pisano, probably partially to a design by Giotto, although the last five are by L. Della Robbia (1439); the upper tier panels (*Sacraments*) are by Andrea Pisano, his school and Alberto Arnoldi. In the *Sala dell'Altare*, **altar frontal**** in silver and enamel with Scenes from the *Life of the Baptist*, by 14th-15th-century Florentine goldsmiths, with a richly worked *Crucifix* in silver above.

San Lorenzo. One of the great masterpieces of early Renaissance church architecture in Florence, the basilica is also inextricably linked to the memory of the Medici family. It was built by F. Brunelleschi in 1442-46 and completed in 1461 by A. Manetti. Standing on the site of the ancient cathedral consecrated by St Ambrose in 393, it was reconstructed in Romanesque style in the 11th century. The facade, which Michelangelo presented a design for, remains unfinished in rough stone. The **interior**, with columned central nave and side aisles, is still today extremely harmonious and exceptionally unmodified, a fine display of the great Brunelleschi's genius. At the beginning of the right aisle, *Marriage of the Virgin**, by R. Fiorentino (1523), and at the end, the marble altar of the Sacrament*, by D. da Settignano (1460). Opposite, one of two bronze pulpits* by Donatello (ca. 1460) and pupils.

The left transept leads into the 15th-century **Sagrestia Vecchia**** (Old Sacristy), a great Renaissance creation designed by Brunelleschi (1421-26) and decorated by Donatello (1435-43). Square in shape with a hemispherical cupola, the stone ribbing stands out cleanly against the white walls. Donatello designed the colored stucco medallions in the pendentives of the cupola (*Life of St John**) and lunettes (*Evangelists**), and the frieze of cherubs. To the left of the sacristy entrance, the sarcophagus of G. and P. de' Medici*, in porphyry and bronze, a masterpiece by Verrocchio (1472).

Cappelle Medicee. The Medici Chapels consist of the chapel of the princes in the dome of San Lorenzo, and the Sagrestia Nuova (New Sacristy).

The octagonal **Cappella dei Principi*** is an elaborate, self-celebratory, Medici mausoleum. Planned by Cosimo I, it was built under Ferdinando I and designed by M. Nigetti. The Opificio delle Pietre Dure (Semi-precious Stone Factory) was created in 1588, to prepare the stone required for it. The final result has been described as a grandiose funereal mantle, because of the gloomy tones of the porphyry and granite used.

The **Sagrestia Nuova**** is a masterpiece by Michelangelo, and prototype of Mannerist architecture. Called "new" to distinguish it from Brunelleschi's "old" sacristy, it is the funeral chapel of Lorenzo the Magnificent's family. It was commissioned from Michelangelo in 1520 by Pope Leo X and his cousin Cardinal Jiulio. The artist worked there until 1534: it was then completed by Vasari and Ammannati (1554-55). The chapel, with frame in *pietra serena*, holds **works sculptured**** by Michelangelo. The tomb of Lorenzo the Magnificent and his brother Giuliano is formed of a simple base supporting the statue of the Madonna and Child*. The tombs of Giuliano Duke of Nemours and Lorenzo Duke of Urbino are opposite each other. Respectively they bear the allegorical figures of Giorno* (*Day*) and Notte* (*Night*) on one side, and Aurora* (*Dawn*) and Crepuscolo* (*Dusk*) on the other.

Biblioteca Medicea Laurenziana. The library is reached through a Brunelleschi-style first cloister (left of the facade of the basilica of San Lorenzo). One of the most interesting 16th-century Florentine buildings, it was designed by Michelangelo, and houses one of Italy's most important manuscript collections. At the entrance is an extremely original staircase: built in 1559 by Ammannati, to a design by Michelangelo, it consists of three flights side by side. The reading room is a spacious peaceful place, with large wood benches, also designed by Michelangelo. The superb carved ceiling echoes the pattern of the brickwork floor.

Orsanmichele. This impressive building is one of Florence's most interesting examples of 14th-century architecture. Built as a grain market in 1337, it was then modified. Intricate divided windows were fitted in the arcades on the ground floor; two floors were added on top, with divided windows. In the

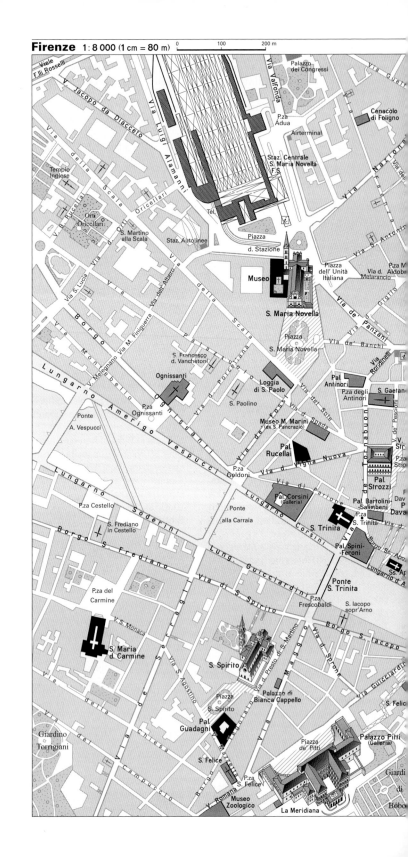

Firenze   1:8 000 (1 cm = 80 m)

0   100   200 m

Viale F.lli Rosselli

V. Jacopo da Diacceto

Via Luigi Alamanni

Via Valfonda

Via Guel

Palazzo dei Congressi

Via Nazionale

Via de

Cenacolo di Foligno

P.za Adua

Airterminal

Tempio Inglese

Via della Scala

Oricellari

Staz. Centrale S. Maria Novella F.S.

Via S. Antoni

Orti Oricellari

S. Martino alla Scala

Staz. Autolinee

Tel.

Piazza d. Stazione

Via de' Panzani

Pza M. Aldobr

Via d. Melarancio

Via S. Lucia

Via

Via

della Scala

Piazza dell' Unità Italiana

Museo

S. Maria Novella

Borgo

Monte

Via della Scala

Piazza S. Maria Novella

Via de' Banchi

Via Roi

Ognissanti

Via M. Finiguerra

Via Melegnano

Via dell'Albero

S. Francesco d. Vanchetoni

Via della Porcellana

Loggia di S. Paolo

Pal. Antinori

P.za degli Antinori

S. Gaetan

Lungarno Amerigo Vespucci

P.za Ognissanti

S. Paolino

Via dei Sole

Via della Spada

Via de' Pesci

Ponte A. Vespucci

Museo M. Marini (ex S. Pancrazio)

Via de' Tornabuoni

V. Sfr

Lungarno Soderini

Via degli Ognissanti

Pal. Rucellai

Via della Vigna Nuova

P.za Stro

P.za Goldoni

Pal. Strozzi

Borgo S. Frediano

P.za Cestello

S. Frediano in Cestello

Ponte alla Carraia

Via di Parione

Pal. Corsini (Galleria)

Lungarno Corsini

Pal. Bartolini-Salimbeni

Dav P

P.za S. Trinita

Dava

S. Trinita

Via d.

Lungarno Guicciardini

Pal. Spini-Feroni

Borgo SS. Apo

Lungarno d. A

SS. Ap

P.za del Carmine

Via di S. Spirito

Ponte S. Trinita

P.za Frescobaldi

S. Iacopo sopr'Arno

Borgo S. Iacopo

V. S. Monaca

Via di Presto di S. Martino

Via d. Sprone

Via di Guicciardin

S. Maria d. Carmine

Via S. Agostino

S. Spirito

Palazzo di Bianca Cappello

Maggio

S. Felic

Giardino Torrigiani

Via della Chiesa

Piazza S. Spirito

Pal. Guadagni

Via Romana

S. Felice

Piazza de' Pitti

Palazzo Pitti (Galleria)

Giardi

Via del Campuccio

Borgo S. Romana

P.za S. Felice

Museo Zoologico

La Meridiana

di

Bobo

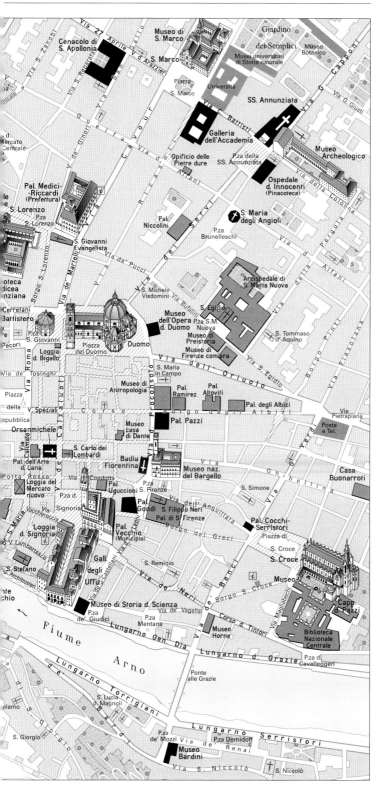

late 1300s it became a church (*San Michele in Orto*) for the city's guilds. Outside, in the pilasters between the arcades, in niches or **tabernacles***, statues of the patron saints of the various guilds were commissioned from the greatest artists working in the city in the 15th-16th centuries. From left to right along Via dei Calzaiuoli: *St John the Baptist* by L. Ghiberti (1412-16); *Incredulity of St Thomas** by A. del Verrocchio (1483); and *St Luke* by Giambologna. In Via Orsanmichele: *St Peter*, attributed to Brunelleschi (1413); *St Philip and statues of four martyr saints**, by N.di Banco; and *St George*, and bas-relief with *St George and the princess*, both by Donatello (copies; originals in the Bargello Museum). In Via dell'Arte della Lana: *St Matthew and St Stephen** by Ghiberti; *St Eligius* by N. di Banco; and in Via de' Lamberti: *St Mark*, copy of an early work by Donatello. In the rectangular **interior**, at the end of the right aisle, is the famous tabernacle* by A. Orcagna, in marble bedecked with mosaics and decorated with reliefs, one of the most beautiful artworks created in Gothic Florence (1355-59).

Piazza della Signoria. Just as Piazza del Duomo is the religious focal point of Florence, this square, created in the 13th-14th centuries, has always been the center of political power and of the city's civic life. Vast and imposing as it is, it is towered over by the massive Palazzo Vecchio; in the background, the three lofty arches of the **Loggia della Signoria*** (also known as the *Loggia dei Lanzi*). The square's original Gothic form (1376-1382) by Benci di Cione and S. Talenti was designed for the Seigniory's assemblies and public ceremonies. Later it became a workshop for sculptors and then basically an open-air art gallery, featuring two masterpieces: **Perseus*** by B. Cellini (1554) and **Rape of the Sabine Women***, by Giambologna (1583). In the open space of the square, copies of well-known sculptures stand near the monumental *Fonte di Piazza* or Neptune Fountain, by B. Ammannati (1563-75), with Neptune, nicknamed "il Biancone" (or "Big White Man") by Florentines, and graceful, dynamic bronze figures of sea deities and satyrs. In addition to Michelangelo's famous David (original in the Galleria dell'Accademia), there is the Marzocco, or the lion which is the symbol of Florence, by Donatello (original in the Museo del Bargello), and Judith and Holofernes, a bronze sculpture by Donatello (original in Palazzo Vecchio).

Palazzo Vecchio. The main civil building in Florence and one of the most important medieval public palazzi in Italy. It has served many purposes over the centuries, always related to the city's political life. A. di Cambio designed it in 1299 as *Palazzo dei Priori*. In the 15th century it became *Palazzo della Signoria* and subsequently a residence of the Medici. From 1865 to 1871, when Florence was the capital, it housed the Chamber of Deputies of the Kingdom of Italy, and since 1872 it has been the seat of the Municipality. Many alterations have been made, but the original nucleus is a solid trapezoid mass in austere ashlarwork, with two tiers of elegant divided windows, crowned by a battlemented gallery. The tower, known as the *Torre d'Arnolfo** (94 m) was built in 1310. **Inside***, in the 15th-century first courtyard, a 16th-century fountain with a copy of the bronze *Putto with Dolphin* by Verrocchio (original now on the Juno Terrace). The monumental *great staircase* designed by Vasari ascends to the upper floors; the **Salone dei Cinquecento*** is a vast grandiose room built by A.da Sangallo and assistants (1495-96) for meetings of the Consiglio Generale del Popolo. It features paintings by Vasari and his school on the ceiling, and the marble group sculpture **Victory***, by Michelangelo (1533-34). To the right of the entrance is the *Studiolo di Francesco**, entirely covered with late Mannerist 16th-century Florentine paintings, and decorated with bronze statuettes. Left of the Victory is the entrance to the *quartiere di Leone X*, with the *room of Leo X* (G. de' Medici, son of Lorenzo, the family's first pope) decorated by Vasari and assistants. On the second floor, two rooms decorated by Vasari: the *quartiere degli Elementi* and the *quartiere di Eleonora*. The Eleonora chapel* was decorated by Bronzino (1545). Beyond the Cappella dei Priori is the Sala dell'Udienza*, with gilded lacunar ceilings by G. da Maiano and frescoes by F. Salviati; next, the sala dei Gigli*, with a magnificent carved and gilded ceiling – again by G. da Maiano (1478) – and a large fresco by D. Ghirlandaio (1485). Also here is the restored bronze group by Donatello, **Judith and Holofernes***. An interactive **Children's Museum** has recently opened in the Palazzo Vecchio, where children can play, dress up and make models. **Galleria degli Uffizi and Corridoio Vasariano.** Possibly the most important art

HERITAGE

gallery in Italy, the Uffizi houses Italian masterpieces from all ages and a selective representation of foreign artists. It is also the oldest museum in Europe. It was founded at the end of the 16th century, and was then expanded, by the Medici family, to include objects of technical and scientific interest. The collection of paintings once included only 16th-century artists (those defined by Vasari as "modern"). It was later

1423), Masaccio and Masolino (*Madonna and Child with St Anna**, 1424), B. Angelico, P. Uccello (Battle of San Romano*), D. Veneziano (Madonna and Child with Saints*, ca. 1445), P. della Francesca (*Portraits of the Dukes of Urbino**, ca. 1465), Filippo Lippi (*Coronation of the Virgin*, 1441-47, *Madonna and Child with Angels*), H. van der Goes (**Portinari Triptych****), S.Botticelli (**Birth of Venus****, **Spring****, *Adoration*

A bird's-eye view with, to the right, the imposing mass of Palazzo Vecchio.

extended with works by Venetian and Flemish painters, and donations. Then the scientific section was separated off, to concentrate on painting and sculpture again. Since the second half of the 19th century, with the acquisition of 14th-15th-century paintings, the gallery has formed the most complete collection of great Italian paintings. At present around 2000 works are displayed; a radical renovation is planned, to enable the public to see the 1800 works currently in storage. On the **ground floor** is the **cycle**** of Eminent Men (including Petrarch, Boccaccio and Dante) by A.del Castagno (ca. 1450), and a detached fresco (*Annunciation**) by S. Botticelli (1481). **First corridor**. This area, occupied by the original gallery, houses a large first section on 13th-15th-century Tuscan painting: D. di Buoninsegna (*Madonna Rucellai**, 1285), Cimabue (*Maestà** from Santa Trinita), Giotto (*All Saints' Madonna**, ca. 1310), S. Martini and L. Memmi (*Annunciation**, 1333), A. and P. Lorenzetti, B. Daddi, Taddeo Gaddi, Giottino (*Deposition**), L. Monaco, G. da Fabriano (*Adoration of the Magi**,

of the Magi), Leonardo (**Adoration of the Magi****, *Annunciation**), Verrocchio (*Baptism of Christ**), Perugino, and L. Signorelli. The next rooms are the oldest in the Uffizi; room 18 is octagonal, and interesting because it shows the gallery's traditional approach of combining ancient works (statues) with modern works (paintings). It contains Neo-Classic statues such as the *Medici Venus** (1C BC) and 16th-century Florentine paintings, including portraits by Bronzino and works by Vasari, Pontormo, R. Fiorentino, and A. del Sarto. The other rooms feature 15th-16th-century paintings by other schools (Venetian, Lombard, Emilian, German, Flemish): L. Signorelli (*Madonna and Child**, ca. 1490, *Holy Family**), Perugino (Monks, *Portrait of Francesco delle Opere*, 1494), A. Dürer (Portrait of Father, 1490, Adoration of the Magi, 1504), G. Bellini (**Sacred Allegory****, ca. 1490), Giorgione (*Judgement of Moses, Judgement of Solomon*), A. Mantegna (*Madonna delle cave**, triptych), V. Foppa, Correggio (*Madonna in Adoration**, Rest during the *Flight to Egypt*). **Second and third cor-**

ridor. Here the first rooms are given over to Florentine painting of the early 16th century: Michelangelo (**Tondo Doni****, an unconventional representation of the holy family), Raphael (portraits of the *Dukes of Urbino* and of *F. M. della Rovere**, **Madonna 'del Cardellino'**** or 'of the Goldfinch', 1506, portrait of **Pope Leo X****), A.del Sarto (*Madonna of the Harpies**, 1517), Pontormo (*Supper at Emmaus**, 1525), R. Fiorentino (*Moses Defending the Daughters of Jethro*, 1523 ca.). Further rooms are devoted to the Venetian school, the Emilian school, and central Italy: Titian, with a whole room (*Flora**, ca. 1520, **Venus of Urbino****, *Venus and Cupid**, ca. 1550), Parmigianino (*Madonna of the long neck**), D. Dossi, Mazzolino, S. del Piombo (*Death of Adonis*), L. Lotto (*Susannah and Old Men*), P. Veronese (*Holy Family*, ca. 1564), J. Bassano, Tintoretto, and F. Barocci (*Madonna of the people**, 1579). The next section features 17th-18th-century Italian and non-Italian artists: P. P. Rubens (*Portrait of Isabella Brant**, 1626); Caravaggio (**Bacchus***, Medusa, *Sacrifice of Isaac*), A. Carracci (*Venus*, 1588), Rembrandt (*Old Man**, *two Self Portraits**, ca. 1634 and 1664), Canaletto (*Views of Venice*) and F. Guardi. The **Corridoio Vasariano** completes the visit to the gallery. The walkway was built in 1565 by Vasari, and joins the Uffizi to Palazzo Pitti over the Ponte Vecchio. It is hung with some very important 17th-18th-century works by both Italian and non-Italian artists, starting with the famed collection of self-portraits, and including works by painters from the 16th century up to today (Vasari, Bernini, Rubens, Rembrandt, Velázquez, Canova, and Delacroix).

Ponte Vecchio. The oldest and most famous bridge in Florence, it was built in 1345 by N. di Fioravante on a previous structure first mentioned in 996. It was also the only bridge in Florence not to be destroyed when the German army retreated in August 1944 (though access to the bridge was heavily mined). Built on three arches, it is lined with shops, in the past wool merchants and greengrocers, today jewelers. Above the shops on the upstream side of the bridge, is the Corridoio Vasariano linking the Uffizi with Palazzo Pitti. There is a great view of the river, the Ponte Santa Trinita and the embankments of the Arno from the terraces halfway across the bridge.

Palazzo Pitti. This monumental palazzo was built around 1458 by the Pitti, a family of Florentine merchants and bankers, probably to a design by Brunelleschi. Simple but imposing, its three floors are in ashlar-work, with arches. It was enlarged in the 16th century, and the two 'rondos' were added between 1764 and 1839. Today, together with other buildings in the Boboli Gardens, the palazzo houses some important Florentine museums: the Galleria Palatina, the Appartamenti Reali, the Galleria d'Arte Moderna, the Museo degli Argenti (Silver Museum), the Museo delle Carrozze (Carriage Museum), the Galleria del Costume and the Museo delle Porcellane. The central doorway leads to the magnificent *courtyard** by B.Ammannati (1570): on the side opposite the entrance is the 17th-century Grotto of Moses; the terrace above features the delightful

Ponte Vecchio is the most famous bridge in Florence.

late 16th-century *Fontana del Carciofo (*Artichoke Fountain*)*. A staircase on the right leads from the courtyard to the Galleria Palatina, the Appartamenti Reali and the Galleria d'Arte Moderna.

Galleria Palatina. The collection is displayed in Palazzo Pitti in magnificent rooms with vaults frescoed by P. da Cortona (1637-47) and C. Ferri (1665). It includes remarkable works, particularly of the 16th 17th centuries, notably by Raphael, A. del Sarto and Titian. The Sala di Venere takes its name from the marble statue of the **Venus Italica**** by A. Canova. The room features four masterpieces by Titian (**Concert****, ca. 1510, **Portrait of Julius II****, 1545, Portrait of a Lady or 'La Bella'*, **Portrait of Pietro Aretino****), as well as works by Rubens (Landscapes) and S. Rosa. In the following rooms, masterpieces by R. Fiorentino (*Holy Conversation**, 1522), Titian (**Portrait of a Gentleman**** and *Mary Magdalen**), Rubens (*The Four Philosophers**, *Consequences of War**), Antonie Van Dyck (*Portrait of Cardinal Bentivoglio**), Tintoretto (*Portrait of Luigi Cornaro**), and Veronese (*Portrait of a Man**). There are also works by Giorgione (**The Three Ages of Man****, ca. 1500), Fra' Bartolomeo (*Mourning on the Dead Christ**), A. del Sarto (*St John the Baptist**, 1523), and Bronzino (*Guidobaldo della Rovere**). The Sala di Psiche (Cupid's Room) is given over to works by S. Rosa. There is an important group of masterpieces by Raphael; **La Velata** or Portrait of a Lady (1516), **Madonna 'del granduca'****, ca. 1506, Portraits of Agnolo Doni* and of **Maddalena Doni** *, Madonna 'del Baldacchino' ('of the Canopy'), unfinished, Portrait of Tommaso Inghirami*, **Madonna 'della Seggiola'**** ('of the Chair'), and **La Gravida**** (Pregnant Woman).

Santa Maria del Carmine. This originally medieval church is located in the square of the same name. It is famous for its frescoes by Masaccio and Masolino decorating the *Brancacci Chapel*, at the end of the right transept. The cycle of **frescoes**** was begun by Masolino and Masaccio in 1424 and completed by F. Lippi after 1480. The frescoes, illustrating the life of St Peter, were much studied by Renaissance painters and, in the words of Vasari, were considered a true "school of the world". The human figures are depicted with great realism and psychological insight, and the use of perspective is masterly. The neighbouring Gothic *sacristy* houses paintings and frescoes attributed to Lippo d'Andrea (1400) and Agnolo Gaddi.

Santa Maria Novella. This is one of Florence's most famous churches and a Gothic masterpiece. It was built by architects of the Dominican Order from 1278 and completed in the mid-14th century. The 14th-century marble *facade** was modified in 1458 by Leon Battista Alberti (commissioned by Giovanni Rucellai) who designed the Neo-Classic doorway and the part above the central cornice with two side volutes. To the right of the facade is the old cemetery, with family tombs of Florentine nobles, lined with arcades. The graceful, harmonious, Gothic **interior** is in the form of a Latin cross; the central nave and two side aisles feature polystyle pilasters, large arches and ogival cross vaults. At the end of the right transept, the Rucellai chapel features the tomb slab of Fra' Dati*, a bronze bas-relief by L. Ghiberti (1426), and a marble statue at the altar (*Madonna and Child**) by N. Pisano (14th century). The 1st chapel to the right of the high altar is the Strozzi chapel, with frescoes by F. Lippi (*Scenes from the Lives of St John and St Philip**, 1502) and the Tomb of Filippo Strozzi*, by B. da Maiano (1491-95). In the Cappella Maggiore, the famous **fresco*** cycle (*Scenes from the Life of the Madonna, Coronation of Mary, Scenes from the Life of St John the Baptist and Evangelists*) by D. Ghirlandaio and assistants (1485-90); at the altar, a bronze *Crucifix* by Giambologna. The Gondi chapel, designed by G. da Sangallo (1503), features a famous wood **Crucifix**** by **Brunelleschi**. At the head of the left transept, the Strozzi chapel* (6) has detached and restored frescoes (*Last Judgement, Paradise**, *Inferno**) by N. di Cione (1350-57). In the nearby *sacristy*, a lavabo in glazed terracotta by G. della Robbia (1498) and **Crucifix** **, a panel by Giotto. *Left aisle*: in the 3rd bay, a remarkable **fresco**** by Masaccio (*Trinity with the Madonna, St John, and the Lenzi donors*), an important innovative work of the early Renaissance.

Basilica di Santa Croce. An important example of Florentine Gothic architecture, the basilica is famous as the resting place of some eminent Italians. It was built to a design by Arnolfo di Cambio between 1295 and 1385, but the marble facade and bell tower date from the 19th century. The large, simple **interior**, is divided into a spacious, light central nave and two aisles by ogival arches on large columns, and has an open beamed ceiling. The walls are lined with tombs, monuments and plaques in memory of celebrities. Along the right aisle is the 16th-century tomb of Michelangelo, Dante's cenotaph (1829), the monument to V. Alfieri by A. Canova (1810), and the tombs of N. Machiavelli, Gioachino Rossini and Ugo Foscolo. Also found on this side are the magnificent marble pulpit* by Benedetto da Maiano, a high-relief *Annunciation** by Donatello (ca. 1435) and the **monument to Leonardo Bruni*** a work by B. Rossellino (1444-45), and prototype of Florentine Renaissance tombs. At the end of the right transept is the Baroncelli chapel, frescoed with Scenes from the *Life of the Virgin**, a masterpiece by T. Gaddi (1332-38). The apse chapels feature two masterpieces of medieval painting by Giotto: the Peruzzi chapel

The neo-Gothic facade of the basilica of S. Croce.

houses a fresco cycle with scenes from the life of St John the Baptist* and St John the Evangelist*, painted in the artist's prime (ca. 1320-25); in the nearby Bardi chapel are **scenes from the life of St Francis***, again by Giotto. At the end of the left transept, above the altar, is the famous wood Crucifix* by Donatello, criticised by Brunelleschi for its excessive realism. Along the *left aisle*, monuments to the musician L. Cherubini, to L. B. Alberti, Galileo's tomb and the monu-

ment to C. Marsuppini*, by D. da Settignano, one of the most remarkable tombs of the 15th century.

Museo Nazionale del Bargello. The museum is housed in the austere Palazzo del Bargello*, built in various stages between the 13th-14th centuries. It was the headquarters first of the Podestà (or governing magistrate) and then, from 1574, of the Captain of Justice, or 'Bargello'. It opened in 1865 with support from the Uffizi, the Mint and the State Archives, as well as considerable private bequests. Today the museum is one of the best in the world, for its collections of sculpture and various art objects, especially for its Tuscan Renaissance sculpture and medieval French ivories. On the **ground floor**, the *Sala del Trecento* (14C Room) houses works originally in Orsanmichele, as well as a Madonna and Child by T. di Camaino and a sculpture group by Arnolfo di Cambio. The *Sala del Cinquecento* (16C Room) features works by Michelangelo and other important 16th-century works including Mercurio Volante* (*Winged Mercury*) by Giambologna. Other works here by Michelangelo are the *Pitti Tondo** (ca. 1504), with the *Madonna, Child and infant St John, Bacchus** (1496-97), the **David-Apollo*** (1530-32) and the bust of **Brutus*** (1539). On the **first floor**, the *Salone del Consiglio Generale** features famous works by Donatello: a bust of N. da Uzzano*, in polychrome terracotta; the Marzocco (1418-20), or lion supporting the Florentine lily, symbol of the city; Atys-Amor*, an intriguing bronze of a winged cupid; a marble David* (1408-09) and the famous bronze **David*** (ca. 1440); **St George*** (1416) and a bas-relief of *St George and the Princess*, both once in Orsanmichele. There are also works by F. Brunelleschi and L. Ghiberti (the two **panels*** of the *Sacrifice of Isaac* made as trials for the famous competition in 1401 for the north door of the baptistery), by Michelozzo (*Annunciation*), by L. Della Robbia (*Madonna 'della Mela'** and *Scenes from the Life of St Peter*), and by D. da Settignano (*Infant St John**). Next come the *Sala Islamica*, with carpets, fabrics, and other Arabian works; the *Sala Carrand* (paintings, sculptures, and especially applied art objects from the 1888 Carrand donation); the *Chapel of St Mary Magdalen*, frescoed by Giotto's workshop, with carved and inlaid choir stalls (late 15C); the *Sala degli Avori*, with 265 ivory works (5-17C); the *Sala Bruzzichelli*, with 16th-century furniture and a Madonna and Child* by J. Sansovino; and the *Sala delle Maioliche*, with a collection of Italian majolica dating from the 15th century. On the **second floor**: the Della Robbia rooms, with a collection of glazed terracottas by Giovanni and Andrea; the *Sala dei Bronzetti*, with works by B. Cellini (*Ganymede** and Greyhound), and by A. Pollaiolo; the *Sala del Verrocchio*, with the famous bronze David*, the marble *Lady Holding Flowers** and the terracotta bust of Piero di Lorenzo de' Medici*. The visit ends with the *Medagliere* section, an extremely rich collection with works by Pisanello, M. de' Pasti, Michelozzo, Cellini and others.

Museo di San Marco. The museum occupies the splendid and carefully restored Dominican convent of St Mark. The convent was largely rebuilt by Michelozzo (1439-44), who established an important center of culture and learning here, hosting among others B. Angelico, St Antonino, Savonarola and Fra' Bartolomeo. The collection of works by B. Angelico is outstanding: in the *Cloister of St Antonino**, St Dominicus Kneeling before Jesus on the Cross*; the *Sala del Capitolo* is frescoed with the magnificent **Crucifixion****. Fra' Angelico's most famous frescoes (1442-45) are found in the cells and corridors of the first floor. At the head of the stairs **Annunciation**** and Crucifix with St Dominicus*. In the first corridor: Noli Me Tangere; Deposition; **Annunciation****; Crucifixion; Nativity; **Transfiguration****; Christ Scorned; and Coronation of the Virgin*. In the *Pilgrim's Hospice*, among frescoes by B. Angelico, is the famous **Deposition of Christ**** started in 1424 by L. Monaco; and the **Tabernacle of the Linaiuoli**** with the Virgin and musician angels (1433) in a marble frame designed by Ghiberti. At the end of the second corridor is the *Prior's quarter*, inhabited by Savonarola, and a portrait of him, by Fra' Bartolomeo.

San Miniato al Monte. On a hilltop square with a beautiful view* over the city, this church, like the Battistero, is a superb example of Florentine Romanesque architecture. The *facade* in white and green marble has a geometrical design; below, there are five round blind arcades on Corinthian half-columns, and above, a niche window surmounted by a 13th-century mosaic. The interior has a central nave and two side aisles, columned, with beamed roof and raised choir above the crypt. At the end of the nave, with its fine marble inlay floor, is the chapel of the Crocifisso* by Michelozzo (1448), with glazed terracotta vault by L. Della Robbia and painted panels by A. Gaddi (1394-96) at the altar. The presbytery, behind a marble screen*, has a pulpit* dating from 1207. In the beautifully arcaded apse, a magnificent 13th-century mosaic showing Christ between the Virgin and St Minias.The crypt with six rows of slender columns (11C) has frescoes* by T.Gaddi (1341) in parts of the vault.

HIGHLIGHTS

Calcio in costume

Florence's traditional version of football ("calcio storico") is revived in June on the feast day of Florence's patron saint, St John the Baptist. Four teams from the city's four quarters compete in the tournament. Before the match, there's a procession with music, flag-throwers, soldiers in costume, artisans and artists, the page bearing the prize or "paliotto", cowherds with the heifer (the prize in the old days), and the "field master", who referees the match. Each team has twenty-seven "kickers", consisting of: "onward passers" (full-backs), "back passers" (goalkeepers), "bunglers" (halfbacks), and "runners" (forwards).
The field – in Piazza della Signoria – is covered with a layer of sand; the players try to score by getting the ball past the opposing team's back line, in any possible way.
The match lasts 50 minutes, and is very rough-and-tumble, a bit like a mixture of rugby, American football, and Greek and Roman wrestling.
For further information:
tel. 0552616051, www.comune.fi.it

VERSILIA

The glittering blue sea spreading out below the jagged Apuan mountains, studded with white fragments of marble amidst high-elevation forests: this is the setting of a small but ancient principality that once lay along the boundary between Tuscany and Liguria. Between the Magra and Serchio rivers, low sand dunes roll up to stands of pinasters and holm-oaks. Versilia ranges from the lake of Massaciuccoli to the mouth of the Cinquale, stretching inland to the Apuan crest. In the mid-19th-century, the first bathing establishments were built, precursors to today's resorts. The swimsuits were far more ample and clumsy then, but the light, the air, and the sparkling water were the same as today. Rising sharply behind green hills, the high Apuans are riven with "canali," as the locals call the narrow and jagged high valleys. They are also a treasure trove of fine marble. Once this was the principality of Massa and Carrara, named for its two capital towns. From the 15th century until the unification of Italy (1861), these two cities feuded, proud of their marble, mountains, and seacoast. The route ends with the Lunigiana, a land of subtle and melancholy charm. Watered by the Magra River, Lunigiana is a blend of Tuscany, Liguria, and Emilia. This farmland set among terraced mountain slopes and chestnut groves was once so poor that there was only one alternative to eating chestnuts and the occasional bowl of polenta: to emigrate, sailing toward distant shores.

NOT TO BE MISSED

Viareggio (➡ see below), with its broad beaches, pine groves, and maritime air, has been a prominent beach resort for the past century-and-a-half, as well as a social and cultural watering spot. **Camaiore** boasts a Romanesque collegiate church and a backdrop of lovely hills. **Pietrasanta** is a town of marble carvers and sculptors, with handsome monuments lining the Piazza del Duomo. **Castelnuovo di Garfagnana** proudly surveys a green expanse of mountains; here two great Italian poets ruled as governors for the Este family: L. Ariosto and F. Testi. **Forte dei Marmi***, set amidst the Mediterranean maquis and pine groves, is the most elegantly exclusive beach in Versilia. **Massa**: the medieval village clusters around the old fortress; beneath it, the 15th-century town features the palace of the Cybo-Malaspina family, facing a square dotted with orange trees. **Carrara** is a venerable capital of the marble trade (spectacular quarries at Colonnata, 8.5 km to the east), renowned as well for its rebellious history. **Fosdinovo**: Dante is said to have looked out from the Malaspina castle over the Gulf of La Spezia. **Sarzana** is a town with an intricate history, its buildings a blend of Ligurian and Tuscan style, especially its 13th-century cathedral. **Santo Stefano di Magra**, a Ligurian village, still boasts earmarks of a fortified medieval "borgo." **Villafranca in Lunigiana** features an Ethnographic Museum which documents local culture. **Pontremoli** is a town with an ancient flavor; on the Piagnaro hill, the castle houses the remarkable museum with a collection of local stelae-statues and other items of archeological interest.

VIAREGGIO

Viareggio first developed in the 15th century around an earlier fortification. For centuries the only sea outlet for Lucca, it was a town of sailors and shipbuilders. Until, that is, it discovered the fashion for bathing that swept Europe in the 19th century. Today Viareggio is an extremely well-established seaside resort. But it hasn't forgotten its more traditional past: fishing and especially shipbuilding are still important activities. Its shipyards are renowned for the pleasure boats they produce.

The city comes alive in the winter, during the famous Carnival, with its float procession which arouses interest nationwide. The skilful work of the artisans who build the floats all through the year can be admired in their hangar-workshops in the north of the city.

Viareggio is an appealing place, not so much for individual buildings or monuments, but as a whole, with its elegant avenues, its pinete (pine groves), and the beautiful seafront with gardens. It also has many fine examples of Art Deco architecture: the Savoia cinema with a neo-Classical touch; the Art Nouveau Duilio '48 stores; the Galleria del Libro, which began life in 1929 as a fashion atelier; Caffè Margherita with decorations by G. Chini; and the Balena baths. The seafront walk leads to the Burlamacca Canal, and continues on along the long mole which starts here.

MAREMMA AND GROSSETO

This is an exploration of the Maremma, along the coast, or inland, beginning in Grosseto and returning to Grosseto. You immediately sense the sea. Stretching from the mouth of the Ombrone and extending to Talamone, the coastline of the Monti dell'Uccellina comprises the Parco Naturale della Maremma. The shore is jagged and wild, the hills are covered with dense Mediterranean underbrush, the solitary towers are old watch posts, built to warn the inhabitants of pirate raids. You must apply to visit the park; further along, however, the so-called Via Aurelia Etrusca runs along the shore of a gulf, with the promontory of the Argentario in the background. In the lagoons of Orbetello, sheets of water separate the necks that link the Argentario

to the mainland; this was once an island. More than 150 bird species have been sighted here. Travel around the promontory via a road which gives views both of rocks, inlets, and little harbors, and views of the islands of Giglio and Giannutri. Claudius Rutilius Namatianus sailed these waters, on his way home to Gaul, from Rome, a few years after the sack of Alaric, in 417. His little poem ("De Reditu Suo") tells of his homeward journey; a few verses seem like snapshots. About the promontory, he wrote: "the Argentario plunges down into the midst

Porto Santo Stefano is a famed resort in Argentario.

of the waves, laying a two-fold yoke around bright-blue bays" ("Tenditur in medias mons Argentarius undas/ancipitique iugo caerula curva premit"); of Porto Ercole at sunset: "the light breeze follows gently upon the declining day" ("vergentem sequitur mollior aura diem"); and at Cosa, "the shadow of the pines wavers at the edge of the waves" ("pineaque extremis fluctuat umbra fretis"). The coastal route ends at the fork for Capalbio. Heading inland, on the way back, you go past Capalbio, Magliano in Toscana, and Istia d'Ombrone; it is hard to imagine these lands when they were malarial swamps, before their reclamation. Now they are farmland, forests, or wild grass, with colors ranging from green to reddish brown and ocher; along the embankments, amidst the old red farmhouses, there is a reigning silence and brightness of light that make this land unique.

NOT TO BE MISSED

Marina di Alberese: take a 14 km detour from Rispescia and you have fine view of the Uccellina coast. **Monti dell'Uccellina**: these are within the Parco Naturale della Maremma, a great nature reserve; the visitor center is at Alberese, not far from the Via Aurelia. **Talamone**: the old part is a port-side village, overlooking the bay; take a 5 km detour from Fonteblanda. **Porto Santo Stefano** is an ancient town, elegant and popular, on an inlet of the Argentario. **Porto Ercole** is a harbor town with a large citadel and three old Spanish forts. **Orbetello** occupies a remarkable site between the two lagoons. **Ansedonia** overlooks the sea from atop a promontory; high up are the Roman ruins of Cosa. Take a 3 km detour from the Via Aurelia; nearby is the Tagliata Etrusca, a piece of ancient Roman engineering designed to keep the port free of sand. **Capalbio**: this medieval hilltop village is now an exclusive resort of Italy's rich and powerful personages; the parish church of S. Nicola contains Roman relics and frescoes from the 15th-16th-century. **Magliano in Toscana**: medieval in appearance, it stands on an olive-bedecked hill in the Maremma landscape. **Istia d'Ombrone** is an old village on a riverside rise. **Rovine di Roselle**: these are the remains of what was long ago one of the main towns of northern Etruria; notable Etruscan and Roman ruins have been found here.

GROSSETO

This market center is the capital of the Maremma region, a flourishing agricultural area, once plagued by malaria, whose marshes have been reclaimed over the centuries. After the ancient Etruscan city of Roselle was abandoned in 1138, Grosseto became a bishopric. The town was subject to Siena and later Florence until its decline between the 18th and 19th centuries. In modern times the city has expanded beyond its walls and become an important center for the hinterland and coast. The coastal area is one of the most beautiful and unspoiled in the whole of Tuscany, largely because of the Parco della Maremma. The attractive old town within the fine hexagonal 16th-century town walls can be admired from the walkway along the ramparts.

former Palazzo del Tribunale (Courthouse), contains Etruscan, Roman and medieval archeological finds, and an Etruscan section which includes the large Chelli collection, a bequest from the museum's founder (1860), with objects largely from the areas around Chiusi and Volterra. It also houses antiquities from the Etruscan and Roman city of Roselle, and archeological finds from the whole Maremma area. The Museo Diocesano, a museum within the museum, contains an equally rich collection of paintings and sculptures from the Duomo and other churches in the diocese, mostly by the Sienese school of the 13th-17th centuries.

San Francesco, the brickwork church, built in the 13th century by the Benedictines, has a simple facade. Only the rebuilt clois-

The Duomo of Grosseto and Palazzo della Provincia on the right.

Duomo, built between 1294 and 1302 on the site of the original 12th-century church, has been restored a number of times. The pink and white marble facade was added in the 19th century, but retains the original symbols of the Evangelists above the capitals of the columns, and on the right flank, two divided Gothic windows with 15th-century stained glass. The Latin-cross interior, contains a large font by A. Ghini (1470); the richly decorated altar-frontal (1474) at the altar of the Madonna delle Grazie is by the same artist. The right transept features a 15th-century panel (*Madonna of the Assumption**) by M. di Giovanni.

Museo Archeologico e d'Arte della Maremma – Museo d'Arte Sacra della Diocesi di Grosseto, the museum, in the

ter remains of the convent, and a well (1590) known as the Pozzo della Bufala (Buffalo Well). Inside, above the high altar, is a painted Crucifix*, thought to be an early work by D. di Buoninsegna.

Museo di Storia Naturale. The museum, founded in 1961, is a fine showcase for the area's natural history. It contains interesting collections of paleontological finds, minerals, coleoptera and mammals.

Mura. The ramparted hexagonal city walls were built by the Medici between 1564 and 1593, replacing the old medieval walls; in 1835 the bastions were turned into walkways and gardens. At the north-east bastion, is the Fortezza Medicea, the rather dilapidated late 16th-century fortress built around a 14th-century Sienese construction.

VIA FRANCIGENA: MEMORY, MYTH AND REALITY

The Via Francigena was the most traveled of the «Romee», the medieval roads that pilgrims followed to Rome. From the 8th century, it was the route through France (hence the name) that linked Canterbury Cathedral and Rome, the heart of Christianity. It was also widely used by soldiers, travelers and merchants.

We know about the ancient route mostly from the churches and castles built along it that still survive today, and partly from the writings of medieval travelers. Perhaps the best-known is the diary written by Archbishop Sigericus of Canterbury, on his journey to Rome in 990. The itinerary is 340 kilometers long. It passes through many towns, both small and large, whose fame and prosperity depended on the Via Francigena in the Middle Ages.

FROM THE LUNIGIANA TO VERSILIA

In Pontremoli, high in the Lunigiana, the village and castle of Piagnaro date from the 9th-10th centuries. Lower down, in Filattiera, the small Romanesque church of San Giorgio preserves an unusual inscription. Also of interest, in the Lunigiana plains, are Sarzana, with two important medieval churches, and the remains of the Roman town Luni, which the region takes its name from.

Carrara (4 km from the Aurelia Highway) with a fine Romanesque-Gothic Duomo, and Massa, which developed as a result of the Via Francigena between the 11th-12th centuries, are situated before Versilia, an area featuring the high Apuan Alps. Pietrasanta was founded in 1255, and the Francigena was the main road through the town. Camaiore has the ancient abbey of San Pietro and a Longobard church.

FROM LUCCA TO SAN GIMIGNANO

From Lucca, with its splendid Romanesque architecture, the road moves on towards other towns in interesting landscapes: Altopascio, which developed as a hopitaller center in the 11th century; Fucecchio, with an abbey founded in the 10th century; and San Miniato, where the Francigena met with the Florence-Pisa road.

The route begins to climb in Valdelsa; it first passes through Castelfiorentino, with a church dating from 1195, and then turns towards Gambassi Terme, with the Romanesque church of Santa Maria a Chianni. It then reaches Certaldo, which features

a 12th-century Palazzo Pretorio. Towards the south, standing out on the horizon are the unique towers of San Gimignano, another wonderful town. It was a center of international fame which developed between the 9th-12th centuries because of its position on the route.

LANDSCAPES AND COLORS AROUND SIENA

The Sienese 13th-century architectural style can be seen in the Fonte delle Fate (Fountain of Fairies) at Poggibonsi, in the tower-house of A. di Cambio, in Colle di Val d'Elsa, in the monastery of Abbadia Isola, and in the splendid town walls of Monteriggioni. Siena, a superb city with a strongly medieval flavor, was described as «daughter of the road» because its fortunes were so closely linked with the Via Francigena.

Continuing past Siena, the medieval past can be seen in the fortress-farm of Cuna, the walls of Buonconvento, in San Quirico d'Orcia with its delightful collegiate church), and in the turreted and battlemented castle complex of Spedaletto. It's worth doing a detour to see the abbey of Sant'Antimo, which did not lie on the Via Francigena but is the most beautiful Romanesque church in the province of Siena. The road then climbs through the magnificent countryside around Mont'Amiata, to Radicofani with its fortified castle.

FOOD IN TUSCANY

Tuscany is one of the regions that is most successful in promoting its food and wines. This is obvious from the sheer number of typical products listed here. They range from well-known specialties like pecorino, Chianina beef and olive oil, to hams, spelt from the Garfagnana and chestnuts from the Mugello, and much less renowned specialties like saffron from San Gimignano or zolfino beans from Pratomagno. The sheer variety of the offering is quite amazing.

TYPICAL LOCAL DISHES

Crostini alla toscana. Common throughout the region, these are slices of Tuscan bread, toasted and spread with a mixture of fried calf's spleen flavored with onion, anchovies, capers and pepper. There are infinite variations made with liver, chicken giblets, clams and other toppings.

Panzanella. A summer starter. The main ingredient is stale Tuscan bread softened in water and vinegar. The salient flavors are of freshly chopped tomatoes, onion, salted anchovies, olives and fresh basil. All the ingredients are blended with really good olive oil.

Acquacotta. The basis of this dish from the Maremma is a stock of mushrooms and tomatoes to which a mixture of egg and grated parmesan is added. Cooked and served on slices of toasted bread.

Cacciucco. A marvelous fish soup made with fish from the rocks and the open sea, with a high proportion of mollusks. The fish is cooked first with olive oil, chopped onions and chili, then tomatoes, red wine and

garlic are added. It is served on slices of bread rubbed with garlic in traditional terracotta bowls. Livorno is the place to go for cacciucco.

Pappa al pomodoro. This soup, common throughout Tuscany, shares with ribollita the nomination for a classic poor man's dish which has become a local specialty. Made with bread, stock and tomatoes cooked with oil, garlic, basil and pepper.

Ribollita. Also known as zuppa di fagioli alla fiorentina. A soup made with beans and black Tuscan cabbage, traditionally made in winter since, to achieve the best results, the leaves must have had the first touch of frost. Usually it is cooked, left to rest and put into the oven the following day (hence its name) with the addition of thinly sliced onions.

Bistecca alla fiorentina. One of the hallmarks of Tuscan cuisine. The best meat for this is Chianina beef – half a kilo or more of loin is used – cooked on the grill, without any fancy additions, just a sprinkling of salt before serving.

Fagioli all'uccelletto. White toscanelli beans are used for this dish. They are boiled slowly and flavored with oil, sage and tomato sauce. Ideal with local sausages, either cooked on the grill or with the vegetables.

Trippa alla fiorentina. A favorite in trattorias all over Italy. First the tripe is boiled, cut into thin strips, fried in olive oil and herbs and then cooked with tomatoes. Basil is added at the end. Served with grated parmesan.

Biscotti di Prato or Cantucci. These famous biscuits often appear at the end of a meal with a glass of Vin Santo. Made with flour, egg yolks, sugar, almonds and pine nuts.

Castagnaccio. The Tuscan cake *par excellence*, often displayed in bakers' windows. Made with chestnut flour, water and salt, baked in the oven without any sugar, and sprinkled with pine nuts and rosemary. The town version, called pattona, includes sugar and raisins.

Panforte. The classic cake from Siena. Made by mixing flour, sugar, lots of candied fruit and spices.

Ricciarelli. Almost as famous as panforte, these biscuits also come from Siena and belong to the marzipan family. Made with flour, sugar and ground almonds.

TYPICAL LOCAL PRODUCTS

Pecorino Toscano DOP. The character of this cheese made with ewe's milk comes from the sweet-smelling meadows of the Tuscan hills. It comes in two types, for eating or grating, with a soft or semi-hard body. The color varies from white (in the first case) to straw-yellow (in the second). It has a decisive, fragrant, balanced flavor.

Prosciutto Toscano DOP. After 10-12 months of maturing, this ham is bright or light re-with very little fat. It has a delicate, but distinctive taste thanks to the use of berries and vegetable flavorings during the salting process and the traditional method of maturing the cheese in the cool valleys and hills of Tuscany.

Lardo di Colonnata IGP. Few people in this little town in the Apennines know how to make this special lardo, which is matured for at least 6 months in marble pits with spices and herbs of the Mediterranean maquis. It is sliced very thinly and served on warm Tuscan bread.

Finocchiona. This salami is made around Florence and Siena. It is made with lean and fat meat minced together and flavored with wild fennel seeds.

Vitellone Bianco Appennino Centrale IGP – This prime beef with an unmistakable flavor comes from Chianina cattle aged between 12 and 24 months, reared on their mother's milk and fed thereafter on fresh grass.

Cinta Senese. Tuscany's oldest breed of pig (black with a pink ring around the forequarters). It fares well in the wild or semi-wild and is reared not only for pork but also for making typical local hams and salamis.

Cantucci are a delicious way to end a meal.

Olio Extravergine di Oliva Toscano IGP. This quality oil is produced all over the region. The regulations stipulate that the olives must be picked right off the tree. The oil varies from golden yellow to green, and has a fruity taste with nuances of almond, artichoke and mature fruit. The Region also produces three DOP olive oils: Olio Extravergine di Oliva del Chianti Classico, Olio Extravergine di Oliva Lucca and Olio Extravergine di Oliva Terre di Siena.

Farro della Garfagnana IGP. Spelt is an ancient form of wheat and the Garfagnana has its own organically grown variety.

Farina di neccio della Garfagnana DOP. Part of the chestnut crop is dried over a wood fire and stone-ground, resulting in a flour for making pasta, polenta and cakes.

Pane toscano. The most distinctive characteristic of Tuscan bread is that it contains no salt. It takes a long time to make, involves several kneading and rising processes and should ideally be baked in a wood oven.

Zafferano di San Gimignano DOP. The cultivation of crocuses, from which saffron derives, dates back to the 13th century and is making a comeback. There is a traditional recipe for saffron soup.

Marrone del Mugello IGP. These chestnuts come from woods between 300 m and 900 m asl, from Marrone Fiorentino trees, which are common locally.

Miele della Lunigiana DOP. Much of the honey production is organic. Acacia and, higher up in the Apennines, chestnut flavors.

WINES

In Tuscany, wine lovers like to visit the areas of the most important wines – Chianti Classico, the revered Brunello di Montalcino, the white Vernaccia di San Gimignano, Morellino di Scansano and Vino Nobile di Montepulciano – but they are invariably distracted by the niche wineries which have built up the myth of the 'Supertuscans': for example Sassicaia, made in Bólgheri. On the other hand, the importance of Tuscan wine can be seen in the figures: 7 DOCGs, 36 DOCs and 14 Strade del Vino (wine routes) are indicative not only of a strong wine tradition but a whole culture and civilization based on wine. The symbol of Tuscan wine production is Chianti, made in Italy's largest wine area: in addition to Chianti Classico, produced in nine 'historic' towns between Florence and Siena, there are seven sub-denominations. Another important fact is that Chianti is made with Sangiovese grapes, grown in three quarters of the vineyards of the region. The most common white grape is Trebbiano, which has always been in good supply, and which is used to make the famous Vin Santo, the ubiquitous 'passito' wine that has become one of the icons of the Tuscan wine business. Other wines are produced in the region: in the Colli Fiorentini they make Pomino and Carmignano; in the Colli Settentrionali, around Massa-Carrara, Lucca and Pistoia, they make Bianco della Valdinievole, Montecarlo and Vermentino Candia dei Colli Apuani; in the Costa Etrusca, between Pisa and Livorno, Bianco Pisano di San Torpè il Montescudaio, Ansonica and Aleatico dell'Elba; finally, around, Grosseto, in the volcanic area surrounding Mt Amiata, they make Bianco di Pitigliano, Sovana and Monteregio di Massa Marittima.

FOOD

URBINO

The location, a hilly spur on the reliefs dividing the Metauro and Foglia valleys, midway between the Adriatic and the Apennines, was inhabited in prehistoric times. Today, Urbino, with its "astonishing palace" (Vasari), "so expensive and daunting to build," as Raphael's father once wrote, is a university town rich with memories of an illustrious court (among the artists and architects who worked here, let us mention L. Laurana, F. di Giorgio Martini, P. della Francesca, and perhaps S. Botticelli). It seems that every detail of this town was carved, painted, or planned by a superior mind. Raphael and Bramante both came from here (the latter from Fermignano, 5 km south).

A MEDIEVAL PEARL

Piazza del Mercatale. This enormous square, at the foot of the town walls, is now a parking lot. With the sandstone gate of the Porta Valbona (17C), this is the main entrance to Urbino. Note, inside the semicircular bastion, the spiral ramp of steps, designed by F. di Giorgio Martini, which leads directly into the center, to the porticoes of Corso Garibaldi.

Corso Garibaldi. Flanked by a long portico and overshadowed by the three apses of the Duomo and the west side of Palazzo Ducale – with two slender towers and three stacked loggias – this road runs past the brick Teatro Sanzio (1853). Designed by Ghinelli, this fine opera house stands on the semicircular bastion overlooking Piazza del Mercatale.

Piazza della Repubblica. At the center of Urbino, situated between the two hills, this square is the hub of all roads. On the north side, note the stern Collegio Raffaello (1705).

Duomo. Designed by F. di Giorgio Martini and built at the behest of Federico da Montefeltro, this cathedral was almost entirely rebuilt in Neo-Classic style by G. Valadier, following the earthquake of 1789; the facade is by C. Morigia (1802). Inside, note paintings by C. Maratta, C. Cignani, and C. Unterpergher; in the left aisle, painting by F. Barocci. From the right aisle, you can enter the Museo Diocesano Albani, with paintings from the 14th-16th centuries (Barocci, A. da Bologna), an English bronze lectern* (13C) and a Paschal candelabrum* by F. di Giorgio Martini.

Piazza Rinascimento. Bounded on one side by the mullioned windows of the long facade of Palazzo Ducale, this square boasts an Egyptian obelisk, brought here from Rome in 1737; opposite is the Gothic former church of S. Domenico, now a gallery, with elegant portal (1451; in the lunette, copy of terracotta by L. della Robbia, original in Palazzo Ducale). Note also the Palazzo dell'Università, once the residence of the Montefeltro family.

Palazzo Ducale**, the palace constituted the model for the unfortified princely residence of the Renaissance. The palazzo houses both the Galleria Nazionale delle Marche and the Museo Archeologico Urbinate.

The building was the creation of the Dalmatian architect L. Laurana, who was summoned in 1465 by Duke Federico da Montefeltro to enlarge the original structure, the part with elegant twin-light mullioned windows, overlooking Piazza Rinascimento. Laurana concentrated the building around the courtyard*, and gave it the famed facade overlooking the valley, with small stacked balconies flanked by slender towers*. The two wings facing Piazza Duca Federico were completed by F. di Giorgio Martini, while the elegant decoration of portals and windows was done by A. Barocci.

Galleria Nazionale delle Marche**. Housed in the Palazzo Ducale since its foundation in 1912, this is the region's leading museum. On the ground floor, adjacent to the Museo Archeologico, are 71 panels depicting the machinery of war and peace built by A. Barocci (15C) to plans by F. di Giorgio Martini. The monumental stairway* leads up to the loggias, where handsome inlaid doors lead into the various rooms of the Galleria Nazionale.

Apartment of Jole. In the older eastern wing of the palazzo, this suite comprises seven rooms, foremost among them the Sala della Jole. Note the carved fireplace, by M. di Giovanni da Fiesole; also worthy of note are the lunette in glazed terracotta by L. della Robbia, and works by A. di Duccio, and F. di Giorgio Martini. In the other rooms, there are badly damaged frescoes attributed to G. Boccati; in F. da Montefeltro's bedroom* are rare examples of 15th-century furnishings, with decorations by G. da Camerino, and paintings by G. Boccati and G. di Giovanni.

Apartment of the Melaranci. In these three rooms you find an array artworks (14C), as well as frescoes* by the Maestro di Campodonico; a polyptych* by G. Baronzio (1345); a Crucifix by the Maestro di Verucchio; a triptych by the Maestro dell'Incoronazione di Urbino; a *Virgin with Child* by A. Nuzi.

Apartment of the Ospiti. Here we have wooden sculptures (15C), ceiling stuccoes by F. Brandani, 103 gold coins (15C), and works by C. and V. Crivelli, A. Vivarini, and G. Bellini.

Apartment of Duke Fedrick*. This apartment includes some exquisite rooms: the Sala delle Udienze, a reception hall with stone decorations, as well as the Flagellation** and the Madonna of Senigallia**, by P. della Francesca; the *Studiolo** of Duke Federico, with inlays by B. Pontelli, executed to drawings by Botticelli, F. di Giorgio Martini, and Bramante, and 14 small panels** by J. van Gand and P. Berruguete, with Portraits of Illustrious Men (there were 28 portraits, but 14 are now in the Louvre); the Cappellina del Perdono* (spiral staircase), a chapel with marble decorations; the Duke's Bedroom, with carved fireplace, attributed to D. Rosselli and F. di Simone Ferrucci, portrait of F. da Montefeltro and his son Guidobaldo* by P. Berruguete, and a *Virgin with Child*, school of Verrocchio. The duke's apartment is completed by the spectacular Sala degli Angeli, overlooking the hanging garden, with its immense fireplace with a frieze of putti* by D. Rosselli, fine inlaid doors* attributed to S. Botticelli, and the artworks: Communion of the Apostles* by J. van Gand, Miracle of the Profaned Host* by P. Uccello, View of an Ideal City*, attributed to L. Laurana; a bas-relief by T. Fiamberti and a carved inlaid chest with a view of a city. The Sala delle Veglie has works by L. Signorelli and G. Santi.

Apartment of the Duchess. Here are a number of rooms, decorated later than the rooms toured so far, with 16th-century works. In the vestibule, see the stained glass by T. Viti, and a fine Florentine bas-relief. In the Salotto della Duchessa (note the stucco ceiling* by F. di Simone Ferrucci) are works by Raphael (La Muta**), Bramantino, and T. Viti; in the bedroom are works by various artists, Titian (Last Sup-

per*), R. del Colle, and V. Pagani, and notable Flemish tapestries. In the wardrobe and adjacent room there are works by Tibaldi, Zuccari, and Brandani (ceiling). In the immense Sala del Trono, or Throne Room (35x15 m), seven handsome tapestries based on cartoons by Raphael.

Apartment Roveresco. The second floor, completed under Guidobaldo II della Rovere, using B. Genga's design, is devoted to the paintings of F. Barocci, early 17th-century artists, and ceramics. Note the work of Barocci and his pupils (Vitali, Marini) and works by O. Gentileschi, G.F. Guerrieri, A. Lilli, Mastelletta, S. Cantarini, and C. Ridolfi. In the last rooms, terraces that were enclosed in the 16th century, you can see work by F. Barocci, A. De Carolis, and ceramics from Faenza, Deruta, Siena and other centers. Last comes the long Galleria del Pasquino (note the battlements, built into the enclosure walls) with the furnishings for the wedding of Federico Ubaldo della Rovere and Claudia de' Medici (1621), the work of C. Ridolfi and G. Cialdieri.

Museo Archeologico Statale. This archeological museum is accessible from the courtyard of Palazzo Ducale. It has a collection of funerary epigraphs. Note the Lastra del Marmorarius Eutropus* (early 4C AD) and a relief of Ulysses and the Sirens (1C AD).

Oratory of S. Giuseppe. This church has a fine old crèche* by F. Brandani; fine paintings.

S. Giovanni Battista*. This oratory, just beyond the one of S. Giuseppe, is late 14th century (the facade is modern). The nave with a handsome wooden ceiling is decorated with a series of frescoes* by the Salimbeni brothers (1416). From the stairs on the left of the building, a fine view of Palazzo Ducale and its towers.

Via Raffaello. This distinctive road has fine views. It begins at the church of S. Francesco (14C); inside, note the reliefs in the Sacramento chapel and a canvas by F. Barocci in the apse. Uphill is the Casa di Raffaello, birthplace of Raphael, with copies of work by the great artist, and a few paintings by Raphael's father, G. Santi, G. Romano, and T. Viti; note a fresco by the young Raphael.

Piazzale Roma. Atop one of Urbino's hills, this square has a vast panorama*. Note the monument to Raphael (1897). From here, along Viale Buozzi, you have a fine view of the 16th-century walls, with Fortezza Albornoz.

Panoramic view of Urbino.

PESARO

Pesaro's heritage begins with pre-Roman and Roman remains, and continues with the Malatesta gateways, the splendors of the city under the Sforza family, the lavish legacy of the Della Rovere seignory, through to the composed neoclassical architecture produced during papal rule in the 18th and 19th centuries. Pesaro boasts a harmonious urban layout, which derives from the organization of the ancient town that grew up in successive layers over the basic Roman grid plan. But the city has, of course, also produced "harmony" of a musical kind, through the works of Gioacchino Rossini.

ROSSINI'S BIRTHPLACE

Piazza del Popolo. The historical and political hub of the city is graced with a fountain with tritons and sea horses (L. Ottoni, 1685). Behind the Municipio (20C) is the little church of Sant'Ubaldo (1605). But the square's and indeed the city's most impressive building is **Palazzo Ducale***. The Renaissance lines of the facade echo in one respect at least the ducal palace in Urbino: the five windows, framed and crowned by festoons (D. Rosselli) of the piano nobile. The portico below has six arched openings between imposing pillars; the top of the facade is crenelated.

The fountain in Piazza del Popolo.

Conservatorio Gioacchino Rossini. The interior is given over entirely to the composer's memory: in the courtyard is the Monument to the Composer (C. Marocchetti, 1864), the Fondazione Gioacchino Rossini and adjoining Tempietto Rossiniano (admission on request, apply at the Foundation), with scores, manuscripts and memorabilia; the Auditorium Pedrotti retains a 19th-century appearance.

Museo Archeologico Oliveriano. Hidden away in the 17th-century rooms of Palazzo Almerici is a collection of ancient works that deserve to be discovered. They include Italic, Roman, and Greek bronzes, a bilingual inscription* in Etruscan and Latin; the 2nd-3rd century ad Boscovich anemoscope*, an instrument used extensively to establish conditions before putting out to sea. But the prize exhibits at the museum are unquestionably the stelae from the necropolis of Novilara, an expression of Picene culture between the 8th-5th century BC, richly decorated with geometric patterns and human figures. In the same building, the Biblioteca Oliveriana has a collection of over 150,000 books. There are 5,000 16th-century volumes as well as documents bearing the signatures of Tasso, Leopardi, and Carducci.

Sant'Agostino. Despite the alterations made in the 18th century, the church still displays its early 15th-century origins in the Venetian Gothic portal*, in Istria stone and decorated with lions and statues in niches and tabernacles.

Exquisitely carved, inlaid choir stalls (beautiful views of the city) from the late 15th-early 16th-centuries enclose the presbytery.

Musei Civici: Pinacoteca and Museo delle Ceramiche*. The art gallery has works from the Venetian, Tuscan and Bolognese schools, including V. da Bologna, G. Bellini (Coronation of the Virgin, known also as the Pala di Pesaro, dated 1474, generally recognized as his masterpiece), M. Zoppo, J. del Fiore and G. Reni The exhibits in the Museo delle Ceramiche come from Urbino, Castel Durante, Faenza, Deruta, Gubbio, Castelli, and Pesaro itself.

Casa di Rossini. The simple home in which the composer came into the world in 1792 – in the street that was named after him – has been transformed, in his honor, into a small museum. Displayed along with various memorabilia are the home's original furnishings.

Rocca Costanza*. This stronghold has all the typical elements of 15th-century military architecture: a deep moat, four imposing round towers and a square plan; these are also the distinguishing features of the style of L. Laurana, who built it between 1474 and 1487.

Sanctuary of the Madonna delle Grazie. Although the revered image to which the complex is dedicated did not arrive here until 1922, the church itself dates back to the 13th century, as the Gothic portal decorated with reliefs and sculptures testifies. The interior is Baroque, but traces of 14th-15th-century frescoes can be seen on the wall behind the facade and the first arches of the right-hand aisle. The 16th-century Image of the Madonna delle Grazie, protectress of the city and believed to have miraculous powers, is in a marble temple in the apse.

ANCONA

This active and courageous town (badly damaged by bombs in WWII and an earthquake in the 1970s) extends like an amphitheater at the foot of Monte Conero beyond which, as Goethe wrote, you can see the "loveliest sunsets on earth." It is divided into two parts: the old section, beneath the Basilica di S. Ciriaco, a landmark for sailors; and the modern area, spilling over to the eastern shore. Its importance as a maritime center dates back to Trajan's time, when the emperor sent his architect Apollodorus of Damascus to build a mole and a new port after Colle Guasco had eroded.

A PORT AND THE CONERO

Lazzaretto. Pentagonal in shape, this fortress-hospital was begun in 1733 by L. Vanvitelli. It has an internal courtyard with a small Doric temple. The building was originally designed to be a multi-purpose building for the port, but it is now used for cultural events.

Piazza della Repubblica, in the heart of Ancona, it opens out over the port between the 16th-century church of the Santissimo Sacramento and the Teatro delle Muse (1826).

Loggia dei Mercanti*, with a lovely Venetian Gothic facade by G. da Sebenico (1451-59), restored by P. Tibaldi. The huge interior hall is also by Tibaldi, as are most of the statues.

S. Maria della Piazza*, a 13th-century Romanesque church has a notable facade*, with several orders of blind arcades (1210-25), and a large portal. Under the church (visible through slabs of glass in the floor) are remains of the 5th-6th-century churches that once stood here, with mosaic fragments.

Piazza del Plebiscito, this elongated square is flanked on one side by a tower, the handsome **Palazzo del Governo**, now the Prefecture, designed by F. di Giorgio Martini (1484): at the end of the square, a spectacular stairway leads up to the **church of S. Domenico** (1761-83), built on the site of a 13th-century church and damaged by earthquakes. Inside are paintings by Titian and Guercino.

Pinacoteca Comunale Francesco Podesti and Galleria d'Arte Moderna. In the Palazzo Bosdari, the two art galleries include works by

C. Crivelli, Titian, L. Lotto, A. del Sarto, S. del Piombo, Pomarancio, Guercino and, among the modern artists, M. Campigli, B. Cassinari, C. Levi, F. Menzio, V. Guidi, and L. Veronesi.

S. Francesco delle Scale. Set high atop a stairway, this church overlooks Piazza S. Francesco d'Assisi. Rebuilt in the 18th century, it has a Venetian Gothic portal* by G. da Sebenico (1454); inside, works by L. Lotto, A. Lilli, and P. Tibaldi.

Piazza Stracca, with a panoramic view of the port, this square is flanked by the Neo-Classic church of Gesù (1743) designed by L. Vanvitelli, and by the 13th-century Palazzo degli Anziani: in the rear are Gothic-Romanesque elements and 15th-century windows.

Museo Archeologico Nazionale delle Marche*, located in the Palazzo Ferretti (16C). The archeological museum features tomb furnishings; magnificent red-and-black Attic vases*; a 5th-century BC "dinos" on a bronze tripod from Amandola*; splendid Etruscan bronzes*; Hellenistic and Roman items that range from fine gold and silver to household implements; a group of gold-plated bronzes (two women and two men on horseback).

Roman Amphitheater, seated 8,000; now only the main entrance and, in the square, stretches of Roman walls and a vault are still visible.

S. Ciriaco**. The church is the pride of Ancona, and certainly one of the most interesting medieval buildings in the Marche. It was erected in Romanesque style with some Byzantine influence and a few Gothic features. The dome, white-and-pink facade, and impressive Gothic portal* with reliefs are remarkable.

Museo Diocesano. To left of S. Ciriaco, this museum of the diocese features fragments of architecture and sculpture from old local churches; note a sarcophagus of F. Gorgonius*.

Trajan's Arch, overlooks the port, at the foot of the Colle Guasco; the architect was Apollodorus of Damascus (AD 115), and the arch was built to commemorate the construction of the wharf. Not far off is the Arco Clementino, another arch honoring Pope Clement XII, designed by L. Vanvitelli (1738).

The pentagonal-shaped Lazzaretto.

THE CONERO HEADLAND

The Conero Riviera is an area of outstanding natural beauty with a wealth of prehistoric sites that is quite unique on the Adriatic coast. The key such places on this stretch of coast, with is lovely headland, are Numana and Sirolo.

A DRIVE AROUND THE CONERO

This extremely picturesque seaside road offers splendid views of the coast.

Lovely beaches at Sirolo.

PORTONOVO

The beach, surrounded by modest bathing establishments and excellent restaurants overlooking the sea, is one of the gems of the regional park of Mt Conero. Above is the Napoleonic Fortress (refurbished and now a hotel), a coastal battery and military bulwark for 600 soldiers built in 1808 to defend the supplies of drinking water during Napoleon Bonaparte's naval blockade of the British fleet. Further along is the Torre Clementina, built by Pope Clement XI in 1716 to defend the coast against marauding pirates. This tower was restored at the end of the 19th century by A. De Bosis, who converted it into a quiet, secluded home. On a spur of the harbor, against the imposing backdrop of Mt Conero, sits the church of Santa Maria di Portonovo*, with dazzlingly white limestone walls. This combination of a basilica and Greek cross plan with dome and trumpet arches was built before 1050 using Lombard building methods (suspended arches and pilaster strips) by Benedictines possibly of Franco-Norman provenance and is a minor masterpiece of Romanesque architecture. Enlarged in 1225 to accommodate a convent (now destroyed), it was abandoned in 1320 following a landslide; after looting by the Turks, it was restored in 1897 and reconsecrated in 1934.

POGGIO

This is one of the small inland historic towns (186 m) that grew up between the 11th and 12th centuries to protect the coast and was the scene of countless raids by marauding Turkish pirates, who plundered the town.

SIROLO

One of the most picturesque corners of the Adriatic coast, this village was fortified in the 11th century by the Franco-Teutonic Cortesi family and ceded to Ancona in 1225.
This resort retains the old castrensian layout. The characteristic bell tower belongs to the church of the Madonna del Rosario. Note also the churches of SS. Sacramento (with 15C portal) and the parish church of San Nicolò (1765). Sections of the medieval wall can be seen in Piazza Teatro including the Torrino rampart; the Cortesi Theater (1908). Sirolo is also a known bathing resort, like the Urbani or Delle due Sorelle beaches. The cleanliness of the sand and the crystal water have ensured environmental recogonition through the awarding of the 'Blue Flag of Europe'.

NUMANA

An ancient Picene port (8C BC), the town was refounded by the Syracusans (4C BC), then became a Roman colony (269 BC) and later a municipium (91 BC). In 558 and 1292 it was ravaged by an earthquake and plundered by the Saracens, and gradually declined until it came under the control of Ancona in 1404. The Shrine of the Crucifix was reconstructed in a somewhat pretentious modern style (1969) over the previous 1561–66 shrine (P. Tibaldi?). Visitors come to see the miraculous late 12th-early 13th-century Romanesque Crucifix. In the same square is the former Bishop's Palace (1773). The Antiquarium has a rich collection of funerary offerings from recently-excavated Picene tombs. Via Roma, from which the characteristic flight of steps of Via IV Novembre known as the Costarella rises, leads to a small square with the Pincio Tower (decapitated in 1930 and with remains of an ogival arch), part of the medieval fortifications.

SIBILLINI MOUNTAINS NATIONAL PARK

This bewitched, fatal place once drew the attention of wizards and necromancers; it is a land of bare mountain tops ravaged by the wind. Over 50 peaks soar above the 2,000 m barrier, with rocky cliffs, moraine, sinkholes and sweeping slopes. In spring, these areas are covered in Apennine flora, attracting hundreds of butterfly species. The most unusual of these, known as Erebia pluto beelzebub, is found on the highest mountain. One of the best bases for visiting the park is the nearby Ascoli Piceno, which also has a lovely square and some wonderful medieval remnants.

SPECTACULAR APENNINES

The Sibillini Mountains are one of the parts of the Apennines with the most limestone, forming a sort of prelude to the highest peaks in the chain in Abruzzo. The mountains are rough in these parts, tending to lie in parallel bands, but mainly, they tower solemnly above the hills of Marche and the valleys and rises that flank the Tiber. The landscape is less rolling here, becoming much harsher at times, as can been seen in the impressive section of the park that juts out above Piano Grande at Castelluccio. Piano Grande, amazingly green in spring and blotted by the colors of cultivated fields, especially lentils, comes as something of a surprise to just about every visitor because of its enormity and the altitude of the plateau – standing at 1,500 m it is remarkably high for the Apennines. This sense of size is added to by the Vettore ridge, which rises for nearly 1,100 m above the plateau.

Exploring the park. The diversity of habitats ensures that any walk is interesting. To start, there are the riverside areas of the Nera, Fiastrone, Tenna and Ambro rivers. Here, a combination of tectonic ruptures and erosion has created awe-inspiring gullies, (e.g. Infernaccio), where you can find medieval hermitages or unusual vegetation. The Canatra Valley is like a storybook of the relationship between wood, pasture and field. The Castoriana Valley, north of Norcia, is a world unto itself where medieval notions such as brotherliness still ring true. This is so at the Guaita di Sant'Eutizio abbey, named after a Syrian monk who founded the first monastic settlements here and encouraged the study of medicinal herbs. The tops of the valleys are crowned by beech woods, like the Macchia Cavaliera or Frondosa woods. In these woodlands, you might hear the call of the eagle-owl or catch a glimpse of the elusive marten or wild cat. Above the tree line, you find the open spaces of glacial valleys, such as the Lago or Panico ones, that are like geomorphologic repositories. Finally, it is necessary to mention the highest peaks in the Sibillini Mountains, Mt Vettore (2,476 m) and Mt Bove, which is a wonderful natural limestone climbing wall with two peaks (each just over 2,000 m) separated by a glacial cirque. This is very much a nature reserve, but not one where man is forgotten. Many old centers bring nobility to this reserve: Visso, home to the park's headquarters, is wedged between the Nera and Ussita rivers, and has numerous interesting buildings; Norcia, with its stylish piazza; Castelluccio di Norcia, on Piano Grande, a magnificent mountain settlement; Montemonaco, a hamlet on the Ascoli Piceno slope with some Romanesque architecture; and finally, Amandola, perched on the remnants of its three old castles.

ASCOLI PICENO

Located at the confluence of the Castellano and Tronto rivers, in a steep hollow, 25 km from the Adriatic, this town is a sort of peninsula, protected on the land side by the Colle dell'Annunziata. Ascoli is stern, noble, and compact: a medieval cloth thrown over Roman bones, with the warm glow of the travertine of which its houses, churches, towers, and bridges are built.

Piazza Arringo*. Rectangular and monumental, this is the oldest square in Ascoli Piceno; in the shadow of the Duomo, and flanked by the Palazzo Vescovile and the nearby Palazzo Comunale (which houses the Pinacoteca Civica), a complex of buildings, joined by a Baroque facade.

Pinacoteca Civica. Occupying 14 rooms, the art gallery's best known piece is the 13th-century cope of Pope Nicholas IV*. In the other

The 'crown' in the Sibillini Mountains.

halls are paintings by: Crivelli, P. Alemanno, C. dell'Amatrice, Titian, Guercino, C. Maratta, O. De Ferrari, S. De Magistris, C. Allegretti, L. Giordano, S. Conca and others. Italian artists of the 19th-20th century include D. Morelli, F. Palizzi, A. Mancini, E. Ximenes, Pellizza da Volpedo, and D. Induno.

Duomo. Standing on the remains of a Roman basilica, the cathedral preserves its 15th-century sides, with Gothic mullioned windows set between tall pilaster strips. The facade is unfinished. Inside, the 15th-century wooden stalls, the 14th-century altarpiece, and the large polyptych* by C. Crivelli (1473) are noteworthy.

Battistero*. This 12th-century octagonal baptistery stands near the left side of the Duomo; note the blind loggia and fine dome. In the Via dei Bonaparte, at no. 24, is the 16th-century Palazzetto Bonaparte, with interesting friezes.

Piazza del Popolo*. Monumental heart of the city, is lined by low, simple Renaissance palazzi, battlemented and porticoed. Looming over the square is the Palazzo dei Capitani del Popolo and one of the sides of the church of S. Francesco. A lively evening strolling ground, especially for the young, this may have been the Forum in Roman times.

Palazzo dei Capitani del Popolo*. Built with its tower in the 13th century, the palazzo has a statue over the portal of Pope Paul III (by S. Cioli, 1549); noteworthy courtyard with portico and loggia. Inside, in 1982, archeologists uncovered Roman and medieval ruins.

S. Francesco**. Construction on this Gothic church continued from 1258 into the 16th century. Two slender bell towers rise between its lively polygonal apses; along its right side runs the elegant five-arched Loggia dei Mercanti* (1513). The facade features three Venetian-Gothic portals, the central one particularly rich in ornament. In the majestic and spare interior, the complex apse is particularly noteworthy. On the left side of the church is the Chiostro Maggiore, built between 1565 and 1623; this cloister is now used as a marketplace; nearby (entrance from Via Ceci) is the 14th-century Chiostro Minore.

S. Maria Inter Vineas. In a small square overlooking the Tronto River is a 13th-century church, partly rebuilt in 1954, with a massive bell tower; inside, 13th-14th-century frescoes and a handsome Gothic-style funerary monument (1482). Nearby, adjacent to the Ponte Nuovo, is Porta Tufilla (1553).

S. Pietro Martire. This monumental Gothic church was begun around 1280 and completed in the early 14th century. On the left side are the portal designed by C. dell'Amatrice (1523) and the three apses. Inside, fragments of 15th-16th-century frescoes.

Piazzetta di S. Pietro Martire. This little square is set at the junction of lanes that run into a notable quarter: Via delle Torri, Via dei Soderini, and Via di Solestà*. This latter street, lined by medieval towers and houses, much rebuilt in the 16th century, leads to the single-arched Roman bridge, or Ponte di Solestà*, from the early Imperial Age, with a medieval gate (1230) and tower.

Via dei Soderini. This fine street still has a medieval feel to it; at no. 26 stands the tall 11th-century Torre Ercolani, the most notable of Ascoli's aristocratic towers; next to it is the 11th-century Palazzetto Longobardo. Facing it, at no. 11, is another tower-house; further along, in Largo della Fortuna, is the church of S. Giacomo, in travertine; interesting bell tower and decorated portal on the left side.

Piazza Cecco d'Ascoli. At the western tip of the city is the small Roman 1st-century Porta Gemina, where the ancient Via Salaria entered Ascoli. Beyond the gate is a stretch of Roman wall, and at the mouth of Via Angelini are the ruins of the Roman theater.

Piazza S. Agostino. At the western end of Corso Mazzini, this square is lined by two tall medieval towers and the facade of the church of S. Agostino; inside, the 14th-century panel of the Madonna dell'Umiltà. On Corso Mazzini, at no. 90, is the Galleria d'Arte Contemporanea, with 20th-century art works and an interesting section devoted to graphic art.

Colle dell'Annunziata. This hill is partly occupied by the shaded Parco della Rimembranza, with fine views of Ascoli and the valley of the Castellano. Note the 15th-century former convent, with church and two cloisters; in the refectory is a fresco by C. dell'Amatrice (1519). Just beneath the square of the church (view) are Roman ruins, commonly called the Grotte dell'Annunziata. Climb the hill to the Fortezza Pia, a fort built by Pius IV in 1560. **S. Angelo Magno**. Take the quaint Via Pretoriana uphill to this church, founded in 1292, on Roman ruins. Note the bell tower and Renaissance interior; the cloister has polygonal pilasters.

Palazzo Malaspina. At no. 224 in Corso Mazzini, which crosses Ascoli from west to east, is this stern 16th-century palazzo, with rustication and a high loggia.

S. Gregorio. Romanesque 13th-century church 17.5 km south of the city that incorporates fragments of a 1st-century BC Roman temple (Corinthian columns on the facade, walls).

FOOD IN MARCHE

Top products in the Marches are a cheese, Casciotta di Urbino, and a local ham, Prosciutto di Carpegna, both of which have been awarded the DOP label. The region shares the IGP label awarded to the beef known as Vitellone Bianco Appennino Centrale with the region next-door. This top trio is the tip of an iceberg of agricultural production which excels in many other sectors. There is extensive cereal production, resulting in pasta made with durum wheat flour; vineyards producing wines of international renown, like the famous Verdicchio; olive oil production and fruit plantations.

TYPICAL LOCAL DISHES

Olive all'ascolana. The large olives grown around Ascoli Piceno are stuffed with a mixture of various types of minced meat, ham, mortadella, cheese and egg. They are dipped in beaten egg and breadcrumbs and then fried.

Passatelli. These hand-made noodles can be made with or without meat. Usually cooked in meat or vegetable stock, in Pesaro, passatelli are made without meat and are sometimes cooked in fish stock or served with sauce.

Vincisgrassi. This lasagne are made with a sauce containing chicken giblets, brains, vegetables, ham and various herbs.

Coniglio farcito. This stuffing for rabbit is made with bread and grated cheese mixed with the liver and heart of the rabbit, quickly fried and finely chopped, lard, garlic, nutmeg, herbs, olive oil and an egg.

Sarde alla marchigiana First the sardines are cleaned and their heads are removed, then they are marinated in oil, salt, pepper and chopped rosemary, sprinkled with breadcrumbs, arranged on a tray with the tails in the center and baked in the oven.

Bostrengo. There are various recipes for this cake made with boiled rice, adding: dried fruit, chestnut flour, raisins and citrus zest.

Cicerchiata. There are several versions of this compact, crumbly dessert, traditionally made for carnival. The ingredients are flour, eggs, butter or olive oil, Mistrà or Cognac, sugar, lemon zest, honey and (optional) candied peel, pine nuts and almonds.

TYPICAL LOCAL PRODUCTS

Casciotta di Urbino DOP. These cheeses weigh about 800g and are matured for 90 days. Made with mixed ewe's and cow's milk inoculated with liquid rennet.

Formaggio di fossa. The mature cheeses are packed into cloth sacks and 'buried' with straw in special holes dug out of tuff, closed with wooden covers and sealed with chalk paste, where they remain for more than 3 months. Mainly made with ewe's milk but some with mixed ewe's and cow's milk. The body is straw-yellow. Eaten young or mature.

Prosciutto di Carpegna DOP. Made in the area wedged between Romagna, Tuscany and the Marche, this is one of the region's most famous hams. Now it is produced in Carpegna on an industrial scale. The quality is high, it has a delicate flavor, and juniper is sometimes used to add flavor.

Ciauscolo. This most distinctive of salamis is usually eaten spread on bread. It is made with minced pork flavored with garlic, herbs, thyme and fennel, mixed together.

Vitellone Bianco Appennino Centrale IGP. The animals reared to produce this top-quality meat belong to a gigantic indigenous Marches breed of cattle.

Olio Extravergine di Oliva Colli Pesaresi – Cartoceto DOP. One of the first oils to be awarded the DOP label. There are various types but the oil is light green, with a strong flavor and a strong hint of almonds.

Tartufo bianco di Acqualagna. These truffles have a smooth, pale-yellow rind, a dark or pale-brown center, and an intense bouquet. The truffle-hunting season lasts from October to December.

WINES

The hilly landscape of the Marche with its clay subsoil provides a uniform habitat for growing vines, except Monte Conero where the bedrock is limestone. This region is usually associated with Verdicchio (especially the wine made in Castelli di Jesi and Matelica), one of the world's great white wines. Reds made here include Rosso Conero and Rosso Piceno, both made with Montepulciano and Sangiovese grapes. Lacrima di Morro d'Alba deserves a special mention. It comes in a passito version and the sparkling red Vernaccia di Serrapetrona, which can be drunk as an aperitif but may also accompany a meal.

MOUNT AMIATA AND ORVIETO

H ere, on the Mt Amiata, they call it "latte di luna," or "moon milk": it is fossil dust, or organic silica, formed by the deposit of countless myriads of diatom algae; it is found in the area around Santa Fiora and is used in the manufacture of dynamite, filters, and insulation. Among the resources of the mountain, it is less well-known than cinnabar, from which mercury is obtained; the Etruscans used it as a dye. Mt Amiata rises in Tuscany and then crosses over the border into Umbria, which is why the itinerary starts in Tuscany. It is the tallest peak in Tuscany south of the Arno River, looking like an isolated cone, mantled on its upper slopes by beech and chestnut forests. On the north slope, a patch of snow endures through spring; in May the mountain explodes in blooming snowdrops (*Galanthus nivalis*), violets (*Viola odorata*), and broom (*Cytisus scoparia*); the crystal-clear springs that run off this mountain provide drinking water for the areas around Siena, Grosseto, Viterbo, and in the Maremma. Midway up the slopes, where grain, grapes, and olives are grown, the towns ring the mountain like a wreath: you will be exploring them, their dark clustered houses, their narrow steep lanes, the castles, the walls, the abbeys, and the medieval atmosphere. Before you reach Mt Amiata, from Chiusi in Valdichiana, you will join the Via Cassia beneath Radicofani on its basalt crag. After the circuit around Mt Amiata, you enter the Paglia Valley; the route, which thus far has remained in Tuscany, proceeds downriver, jogging into Lazio for a short distance, passing through Acquapendente, and then enters Umbria. From crag to crag: the second major crag in this tour is the flat and isolated plateau of tufa upon which stands Orvieto; at its base you find the Paglia again.

NOT TO BE MISSED

Chiusi (Tuscany): the Etruscan origins and heritage (see the museum) are not the only attractions. **Sarteano** lies in the shadow of a 15th-century castle, and is renowned as a holiday and spa resort. **Radicofani**: medieval houses with rustication, along narrow lanes; Montaigne and Chateaubriand stayed at La Posta, an old hotel here. **Abbadia San Salvatore**: the medieval village is virtually intact; all around are dense chestnut groves. A road runs nearly to the peak of Monte Amiata (stopping at 1,651 m), and you can walk on up to enjoy the immense vista from the peak (1,738 m); nearby is the largest mercury mine on earth. **Arcidosso** is a resort with a well-preserved medieval center. **Santa Fiora**: the town has a medieval air; the remains of the castle and the Romanesque parish church are interesting. **Castel Viscardo** is a hill resort with great views; the castle dates from the 15th century. **Orvieto** (➡ see below): perched atop a tufa plateau, this town is deserving of its renown; the Duomo, by L. Maitani, is one of the most exquisite examples of Gothic architecture in Italy.

ORVIETO

The bluff of yellowish tufa on which Orvieto is built rises like a shoal, at the head of the green valley of the Paglia. An island in time, just as it may long ago have been an island in a gulf along the Tyrrhenian coast, Orvieto soars above the surrounding countryside. L. Maitani was summoned from Siena in 1290 when the walls of the Cathedral seemed about to collapse; he repaired them and began to design the remarkable facade, which was later completed by A. Pisano and A. Orcagna. The golden Gothic "triptych" of the facade should be seen from a distance, glittering in the sunset – words hardly suffice to describe it. **Piazzale Cahen**. Across from the Rocca (see below), it can be reached from the railway station via the cableway, built in 1880 and recently restored to service. Near the square is the ancient gate known as Porta Postierla. **Rocca**. This fortress was built at the orders of Cardinal Albornoz (1364), destroyed by the

townspeople in 1390, and rebuilt in 1450. Used as a fort until the 18th century, it is now a park (fine view of the Paglia Valley). Visit the tufa ruins of the Etruscan Tempio del Belvedere, late 5th century BC.

Pozzo di S. Patrizio*. This well, a unique and daring piece of architecture, was built, along with other cisterns and wells, at the order of Pope Clement VII after the Sack of Rome, to ensure that Orvieto would have an adequate water supply during a siege. Begun by A. da Sangallo the Younger in 1528, it was completed in 1537. It comprises a cylindrical chamber (diameter 13 m) that drops to a depth of 62 m; around it are two broad staircases, stacked in a double spiral, illuminated by 72 large windows along their length. In this way, men and mules could efficiently descend and climb with loads of water.

Corso Cavour. This main street winds its way through the center of Orvieto, lined with 16th-century palazzi and medieval houses. At the beginning, a small lane on the right leads to the 13th-century church of S. Maria dei Servi, entirely rebuilt in Neo-Classic style. On the left is the Romanesque church of S. Stefano, and on the left, the medieval church of S. Angelo, one of Orvieto's oldest, rebuilt in 1828. A little further on, facing the Teatro Mancinelli (1864), is the facade of Palazzo Petrucci (16C), begun, but not finished, by M. Sanmicheli.

Torre Civica. This medieval tower is 42 m high, and is topped by a bell, cast in 1316 for Palazzo del Popolo, with the 24 symbols of the Arts. At the base lies Via del Duomo. Next to it is Palazzo dei Sette, built around 1300, partly rebuilt in the 16th century, and now used as a cultural center.

Piazza del Duomo. This cozy square with its odd shape and proportions emphasizes the massive Duomo. The northern end of the square is bounded by low medieval houses;

A detail from the decoration adorning the cathedral.

at the corner with Via del Duomo stands the Torre del Maurizio (1349), a tower whose name derives from the bronze figure that strikes the hours, originally designed to ensure steady work on the Duomo. Across the little square is Palazzo Faina, with the Museo Civico; to the right of the Duomo is Palazzo Soliano, site of the Museo dell'Opera del Duomo and the Museo Emilio Greco.

Duomo**. Begun in 1290 and carried on (1308-30) by L. Maitani, who worked especially on the facade and the terminal section, this cathedral is certainly one of the finest creations of Italian Gothic architecture. The facade, which

was completed in the 16th century, is shaped like an immense triptych, glowing and glittering with polychrome marble, statuary, and mosaics (it was redone in the 17-18C). The central portal and the rose window* – by A. Orcagna – are particularly noteworthy. Also note the statues of prophets and apostles. The four pilasters that frame the portals are lined with reliefs** based on the Bible, by L. Maitani and assistants (early 14C); the same artists made the bronze symbols of the Evangelists above the pilasters and the group in the lunette over the central portal.

In the majestic interior the nave and aisles are still Romanesque, while the transept and presbytery are Gothic in style. Note the baptismal font and holy-water stoups, wrought-iron, and reliefs by R. and F. da Montelupo. At the end of the right arm of the transept is the early 15th-century New chapel, renowned for the frescoes of the End of the World** by Signorelli. Originally begun by Fra' Angelico (1477), with the help of B. Gozzoli, G. d'Antonio Fiorentino, and G. da Poli, the frescoes – outstanding masterpieces of Italian art history – were completed by Signorelli (1477-1504) with the theme of the Last Judgment. In the vault, the prophets shown with Christ the Judge are by Fra' Angelico and helpers, 1447; in the lunette, on the left, in the scene of the Antichrist preaching, the two figures in black are portraits of Signorelli and Fra' Angelico; also note the figures of poets from Homer to Dante. The raised presbytery is decorated with 2,500 m² of frescoes by U. di Prete Ilario (1370-80), unusual in both size and subject (Glory of Mary). Note the majestic inlaid wooden choir* by G. Ammannati (1331-40). On the right wall of the left arm of the transept is a panel*, 1320, by L. Memmi. On the altar, a marble Gothic tabernacle (1358) contains a famed reliquary** with a blood-stained cloth, supposedly from a host that bled to confound a Bohemian priest doubtful about the dogma of Transubstantiation (the Mass of Bolsena, 1263). The reliquary, by the Sienese U. di Vieri (1338), is a masterpiece of Italian goldwork. Nearby is a fresco* by G. da Fabriano (1425).

Palazzo Faina. This palazzo opposite the Duomo houses the Raccolta Archeologica Civica and the Museo Claudio Faina, comprising the city's collection and the archeological collections of Count Claudio Faina, a gift to Orvieto. Among the more notable items: 6th-4th-century BC Attic vases*, and a 4th-century BC Etruscan sarcophagus*.

Palazzo Soliano*. This austere tufa building, with a large exterior staircase and three-light windows, was built at the behest of Pope Boniface VIII (1297-1304); the upper section was left unfinished, and was completed in the 16th century. The Guelph-style crenelations date from the late 19th century. Upstairs, it will permanently house part of the Museo dell'Opera del Duomo*. The ground floor houses the Museo Emilio Greco; it features sculpture and paintings, donated by the artist himself (1947-present). Nearby, the Manneristi Palazzo Buzi (1580), by I. Scalza.

Museo dell'Opera del Duomo*. The museum has collections of sculpture, painting, liturgical objects, jewelry, largely from the Cathedral and other churches of the diocese. Palazzo Soliano will house the Renaissance section, while the medieval one is already in Palazzo Papale, a complex of three buildings from the 13th century, on the right-hand side of the Duomo. Among the artists whose work is present in this museum: C. di Marcovaldo, S. Martini, L. Signorelli, A. Pisano, L. Maitani; reliquary of S. Savino* by U. di Vieri and V. di Lando.

Museo Archeologico Claudio Faina. This archeological museum is in Palazzo Papale and has state collections and the collections of the Opera del Duomo, which document the process of its construction. Note the Etruscan funerary furnishings and the frescoes from the necropolis of Settecamini, with life-size figures; also, intact Etruscan suit of armor.

Parco delle Grotte. The bluff of Orvieto is made largely of tufa, and over the centuries countless chambers have been carved into the soft stone; they are referred to as the "Grotte," or caves. They constitute a sort of underground city, now being studied systematically for the first time. An network of passages and galleries links the many cavities, dating from different eras. The Etruscans built the narrow oval tunnels, storerooms for crops, and a number of deep wells, along with more than 100 cisterns. In the Middle Ages, the "butti" were dug and used to toss rubbish in; the cisterns with grey plaster, the furnaces, and the ruins of Orvieto's first aqueduct also date from the Middle Ages. Many rooms date from the Renaissance as well. The tours are limited to the safest and most accessible areas.

S. Francesco. Founded in 1240 at the highest point in Orvieto, the walls and facade are original (note the rose windows and portal). Inside is a 14th-century wooden Crucifix.

S. Lorenzo de' Arari. This little church has a lovely interior, with 14th-century frescoes; the main altar features an Etruscan panel and a ciborium (12C). Nearby is the Porta Romana

(1822), built on the site of the ancient Porta Pertusa (ruins); from the park area, with the medieval Palazzo Medici, fine view of the Povero River, spanned by the medieval aqueduct. If you skirt the western edge of the bluff, you will reach the octagonal church of S. Giovanni; and, in the adjacent convent, a fine Renaissance cloister.

S. Giovenale. This church was founded in 1004. It has a simple Romanesque facade and fortified bell tower. The interior, with tufa columns, was modified in the 13th century; note fragments of frescoes, and the carved altarpiece from 1170. Nearby, charming medieval homes and the former church of S. Agostino (13C), with a Baroque interior.

Via Malabranca. This handsome road runs along a slope on the surface of the bluff. At no. 14-18, notable old houses; at no. 22, the Renaissance Palazzo Simoncelli (by B. Rosselli-no); at no. 15, the 16th-century Palazzo Caravajal. Turn onto Via della Cava, running downhill between rows of medieval houses to Porta Maggiore. Next to the church of Madonna della Cava, note the well, a deep cylinder drilled into the tufa, used from 1428 to 1546.

Piazza della Repubblica. The center of Orvieto ever since the Middle Ages, this square is dominated by the long facade of the 16th-century Palazzo Comunale, by I. Scalza; on the same square is the simple facade of the 11th-century church of S. Andrea*, with a 12-sided tower. The portico on the left side was built during restoration (1926-30). The interior has fragments of 14th-century frescoes; beneath the church, Villanovan and Etruscan remains and 6th-century mosaic floors.

Palazzo del Popolo**. Begun around 1250, with a huge meeting hall over an open loggia, this building was enlarged at the end of the 13th century with the addition of the residence of the Capitano del Popolo – equivalent to mayor – and a bell tower. As the politics of Orvieto changed, this building fell into neglect, and was used variously as a prison, workshop, warehouse, and silo. Restored recently and now used for conferences and meetings; digs have uncovered Etruscan temples, a medieval aqueduct, and a large cistern. In the upper hall, note the 14th-century frescoes. On the square is the little church of S. Rocco, built by M. Sanmicheli around 1525, as well as the 16th-century Palazzo Simoncelli.

S. Domenico. This church (1264) was drastically changed in 1934; only the transept survived. Inside, note the monument to Cardinal Braye*, by A. di Cambio (1285); beneath the apse is a fine chapel by M. Sanmicheli.

THE UMBRIAN VALLEY AND ASSISI

When M. Boschini used the Italian term for "picturesque" in the title of his book "Carta del Navegar Pitoresco," it simply meant "of or about painting." In time, it came to indicate a wealth of nuance, and then to describe a style of painting devote to secluded and evocative landscapes. Nowadays it means "visually charming," "quaint," "graphic," or "vivid." However commonplace the term has become, it may fairly be applied to the Valle Umbra, or Umbrian Valley, watered by the rivers Ose, Topino, Chiona, Clitunno, and Teverone, ringed by hills, farmland, maple trees, vineyards, silvery olive groves, and towns such as Perugia, Assisi, Spello, Trevi, Spoleto, Montefalco, and Bevagna. The "visually charming" and "quaint" are unquestionable; as for the "graphic" and "vivid," they apply to the overall panorama, made up of such elements as lovely patches of scenery; remarkable art, ancient and modern; poplars and willows reflected in the clear rippling chilly waters of the Fonti del Clitunno; the wooded Monteluco behind grey Spoleto with its ancient stones; the dreamy medieval air of Bevagna; the glittering color of paintings by Pinturicchio, at Spello, or in the Collegio del Cambio in Perugia; the frescoes by Giotto at Assisi; the pink stones of Assisi, seen from Monte Subasio; the reliefs and statuettes by the Pisano family around the Fontana Maggiore of Perugia, with the white-and-red marble flanks of the cathedral, the Etruscan and Roman fragments, part of an architecture that blends perfectly with the landscape, with masterpieces of fine art side-by-side with jewels of the applied arts. Everywhere is power and restraint. It is not often that Italy, as rich as she is, showers so lavish and enchanting a treasure on so small a space.

ASSISI

The Roman city of Assisi – Asisium – was built on a series of terraces which "climbed the mountainside like a great stairway," as it was described in the words of its native son Propertius. The ancient Roman poet would still recognize the landscape, if not the architecture. And Assisi still stands, wrapped in silence and solitude, on a ridge of Mt Subasio, overlooking the Chiascio and Topino plains.

Piazza del Comune in Assisi.

BASILICA OF S. FRANCESCO
AND PIAZZA DEL COMUNE

The basilica is the most important monument in Assisi and one of the best known artistic and religious landmarks in Italy; its counterpoint is the medieval Piazza del Comune, center of the earliest Assisi, at the far end of Via S. Francesco.

Porta S. Francesco. This 14th-century crenelated gate is the main western entrance to Assisi; it affords a fine view* of the Convento di S. Francesco, with the massive arched buttresses that make it look like a great grim fortress.

Piazza Inferiore di S. Francesco*. Entirely surrounded by low 15th-century porticoes, this lower square lies in the shadow of the basilica, with its mighty bell tower* (1239). On the left, note the Oratory of S. Bernardino, the main entrance to the Sacro Convento, and, facing it, the entrance to the lower basilica.

S. Francesco**. The basilica, begun in 1228, two years after St Francis's death, was consecrated in 1253. It is a monument that was designed to perpetuate Francis's message throughout Christendom. The greatest advocate, and perhaps the mastermind behind this complex was Frate Elia, vicar general and architect of the Franciscan Order; apart from a few 14th-century additions, the church is as he built it. It comprises two churches, one atop the other. In the lower one the saint was buried in 1230 and still rests. Both basilicas house cycles of frescoes that are virtually unrivalled in 13th-14th century Italian art.

Basilica Inferiore. You enter the Lower Basilica through a late-13th-century twin portal.

The interior, on a Greek cross plan, has a single nave. Low arches divide it into five bays, with side chapels added at the end of the 13th century. In the first bay, 17th-century frescoes, two huge Gothic tombs, and a pulpit. On the left, chapel of St Sebastian; beyond it, chapel of St Catherine, with frescoes by A. de' Bartoli (1368) and stained glass windows. From here you can enter an attractive little cloister* (1492-93), on the right side of the church. On the walls of the nave, frescoes – partly destroyed by alterations – with scenes of the Passion (right) and stories from the life of St Francis* (left), works by the Maestro di S. Francesco (ca. 1253). Various frescoes by the workshop of Giotto surround the entrance to the crypt, with the stone urn containing the remains of the saint. In the first chapel on the left is an exceedingly fine series of frescoes of the Life of St Martin**, by Simone Martini (1321-26). In the vault are the renowned frescoes* by the Maestro delle Vele, follower of Giotto (1315-20). In the apse is a carved wooden choir^.

In the right transept, frescoes by Giotto's workshop, and a majestic fresco of the Virgin Enthroned with Angels and St Francis**by Cimabue (1280); a fresco* by S. Martini. In the left transept, an astonishing cycle of frescoes with the Passion of Christ** by P. Lorenzetti and his workshop (ca. 1320).

From the transepts, two stairways lead up to the great cloister (1476), with portico and loggia, in the shadow of the tall apsidal section of the basilica. From the terrace of the cloister, you can enter the Treasury; a stairway leads on to the upper church.

Museo-Tesoro e Collezione Perkins*. The Treasury museum contains precious reliquaries, manuscripts, liturgical garb and a fine Flemish tapestry*. The collection includes 14th-15th-century paintings on panel with subjects relating to St Francis; among the artists are Beato Angelico, N. Alunno, A. Romano.

Basilica Superiore. Gothic in style, with French influence, the Upper Basilica has a single nave with four bays. The visit starts from the transept, entirely decorated by a vast cycle of frescoes by Cimabue^, begun in 1277, and sadly deteriorated. In the apse, note the wooden choir*, carved by D. Indivini (1491-1501); in the vault above the main altar and on the walls are various frescoes by Cimabue. The upper part of the walls of the nave are covered with frescoes* considered to be by Roman painters and by followers of Cimabue and, perhaps, by the young Giotto. In the lower part, beneath the gallery that runs all the way around the nave, is the renowned cycle of frescoes by Giotto**, depicting in 28 panels episodes from the life of St Francis. Giotto began working on these frescoes probably in 1296. Also worthy of note are the medieval stained glass windows. Despite restoration, they constitute one of the most complete sets to be found in Italy. The oldest, in the apse, may date from before 1253.

Piazza Superiore di S. Francesco. You exit the church onto the upper square, which is dominated by the simple 13th-century facade*. Adorned with a French-style twin portal, the facade has an enormous rose window with the symbols of the Evangelists.

Sacro Convento. Built with the basilica, the massive buttressing pylons were added later; inside, note the Chapter House, with a fresco by P. Capanna; the enormous portico; and the monumental Refectory (53x13 m), with a *Last Supper* by Solimena (1717).

Via S. Francesco. This medieval road climbs from the basilica to the center and is lined by medieval houses and patrician palazzi.

At no. 14 is the Loggia dei Maestri Comacini (15C); at no. 12, Palazzo Giacobetti, and the former hospital (15C), the Oratory of the Pellegrini, with frescoes. At no. 10 is Palazzo Vallemani, which houses the Pinacoteca Comunale, including works by the followers of Giotto, P. Capanna, O. Nelli, N. Alunno, Andrea d'Assisi, Tiberio d'Assisi, D.Doni. At no. 3 is the Portico del Monte Frumentario, and the Oliviera fountain (1570). Past an arch and up Via del Seminario, you see the Seminario Diocesano; Via Portica leads past the Museo Civico to the Piazza del Comune.

Museo del Foro romano e Collezione archeologica. Located in the Romanesque crypt of S. Nicolò (11C; entrance at no. 2 in Via Portica), this is all that now survives of an old church. The municipal museum features ancient Umbrian and Roman items and art works from the local area. A corridor leads to what is thought to have been the Roman forum, with original paving.

Piazza del Comune*. At the center of Assisi, on the site of the ancient Roman forum, this is a typical medieval square, with a 16th-century fountain, with three stone lions. Note Palazzo dei Priori (1337); this heavily rebuilt complex of buildings features a handsome 16th-century painted passageway, the Volta Picta. The opposite side of the square, marked by the tall crenelated Torre del Popolo, features the 13th-century Palazzo del Capitano del Popolo, victim of a 20th-century architectural travesty. Next to it is the Tempio di Minerva, or Temple of Minerva, a handsome building from the 1st century BC, now a Baroque church inside.

Chiesa Nuova. This Baroque church (1615) stands on the remains of a medieval building said to have been the home of St Francis's father, P. Bernardone. To the left of the presbytery is the entrance to the supposed house of the Saint, which has been restored.

DUOMO AND ROMAN SECTION; S. CHIARA AND BORGO S. PIETRO

From the Duomo, you continue into an area with clearer signs of Roman influence, until you reach the Basilica of S. Chiara, with its fine art works. Borgo S. Pietro is a handsome late medieval district.

Via S. Rufino. Steep and twisting, it has a medieval appearance. From Piazza del Comune it passes old houses to Piazza S. Rufino; note the fountain and the Duomo facade.

Duomo*. Dedicated to S. Rufino, its construction began in 1140; the Romanesque facade is majestic and austere, with three richly carved portals and three rose windows ringed by reliefs. The mighty bell tower belonged to the basilica that previously stood here; it stands on a Roman cistern.

Inside, note the 17th-century stuccoes, the ancient baptismal font where Sts. Francis and Claire were baptized, and the three 16th-century paintings by D. Doni. In the apse, a noteworthy wooden choir* (1520).

Museo Diocesano and Cripta di San Rufino. You enter the cathedral museum by a corridor next to the right aisle. The collections include illuminated codices and detached frescoes. Among the paintings, work by P. Capanna and N. Alunno. From outside the Duomo you can also visit the ancient crypt*, with fragments of 11th-century frescoes and a 3rd-century Roman sarcophagus.

Via S. Maria delle Rose. Along this road, from the Duomo, you will see the Romanesque Palazzo dei Consoli (1225), and, in a linden-shaded square, the ancient former church of S. Maria delle Rose.

Porta Perlici. This 12th-century gate in the medieval walls, at the end of the twisting Via Perlici, which runs from Piazza S. Rufino, has a double arch. The surrounding district has a Roman layout; note the old houses along Via del Comune Vecchio, the amphitheater (in Via Anfiteatro, terrace with overall view) and theater (three arches in Via del Torrione), both from the late Roman Imperial Age.

Rocca Maggiore*. This medieval fortress, built in 1356, stands on a peak overlooking Assisi and the valley; a road winds up from Porta Perlici. The fort is a trapezoidal wall with towers and a keep with a tall square tower (view* of the Umbrian Valley).

Basilica di S. Chiara**. Just outside the medieval gate of S. Giorgio, this church overlooks an immense square, with a fine view of the Umbrian Valley (to the right you can see the apse and bell tower of S. Maria Maggiore). Built in pure Gothic style (1257-65), it has a sober pink-and-white striped facade, with a single portal and a rose window; on the left are three large flying buttresses (late 14C). Alongside, overlooking the valley is the ancient monastery of the Clarissan nuns.

In the severe interior are frescoes and paintings (13C) and a Crucifix which, according to tradition, spoke to St Francis in the church of S. Damiano.

Piazza del Vescovado. In this square stands the church of S. Maria Maggiore (see below); from the garden, you can see ruins of the Roman walls. Near here, in the since-rebuilt Palazzo Vescovile, St Francis renounced his father's wealth.

S. Maria Maggiore. Assisi's early cathedral (10C) has a simple Romanesque facade and a notable semicircular apse. Inside, fragments of 14th-century frescoes.

S. Pietro*. The church was rebuilt in the 13th century and consecrated in 1253. It stands on the edge of the district of S. Pietro. The facade has three portals and three rose windows; inside, note the funerary monuments and fragments of frescoes, all dating from the 14th century. From the square, a fine view of the Assisi Valley; note nearby Porta S. Pietro, a city gate.

THE PLACES ASSOCIATED WITH ST FRANCIS OUTSIDE ASSISI

Outside the town walls are a number of sites of early Franciscan history: Convento di S. Damiano, Eremo delle Carceri, Monte Subasio, the ruins of the Abbazia di S. Benedetto, and the Basilica di S. Maria degli Angeli.

S. Damiano**. Outside of Porta Nuova, some 2.5 km south of the town, this convent was built around a country chapel where, according to tradition, a Crucifix (now in S. Chiara) spoke to St Francis. In 1212 St Claire and her sisters took up residence here. There are frescoes by T. d'Assisi, P. Mezzastris, E. da S. Giorgio and D. Doni. There is a garden where St Francis wrote his "Cantico delle Creature" and the dormitory where St Claire died.

S. Maria di Rivotorto. 3.5 km SE on the SS road to Foligno, this church was rebuilt in Neo-Gothic style (1853); it is on the site where

Francis and his companions lived in 1208-11.

Eremo delle Carceri*. In an oak forest, on the slopes of Monte Subasio, 4 km east of Porta dei Cappuccini, along a panoramic road that climbs through olive groves, is this Franciscan hermitage. The convent was built by St Bernardino of Siena in 1426. Note the "Grotta di S. Francesco," the saint's little cell cut into living rock; stroll through the forest.

The hermitage of the Carceri, immersed in the woods.

Abbey of S. Benedetto. Further along on the same road is this 10th-century abbey (729 m). The original structure was largely destroyed in 1399. Further, at the peak of Mt Subasio (1,290 m), is a fine view* of Lake Trasimeno, Monte Amiata, and the Apennines.

S. Maria degli Angeli*. At 5 km from Assisi, in the plain (218 m) at the foot of the city; leaving the historical center, the view of this church is notable. One of Italy's greatest sanctuaries, this basilica stands on the site where St Francis founded his Order in 1208, and later died. This monumental Mannerist building, designed by G. Alessi, was built between 1569 and 1679. A Neo-Baroque facade was added in 1928. The solemn interior has a nave and two aisles, side chapels, and a deep choir. Beneath the dome is the chapel of the Porziuncola*, a simple 10th-century oratory. The exterior is frescoed. Inside, amidst the lamp-black stains, painting by I. da Viterbo (1393). In the presbytery, on the right, is the Transito chapel*, the cell in which St Francis died on 3 October 1226; inside, frescoes by Spagna, a statue of the saint by A. della Robbia, and, above the altar, the cord the saint wore at his waist. To the right of the basilica is a rose garden with thornless rose bushes. In the refectory of the little convent is a museum with a portrait of St Francis by the Maestro di S. Francesco and a Crucifix* by G. Pisano (ca. 1236).

SPOLETO

Spoleto's charm derives not only from its many remarkable monuments, but also its rather unusual setting. The hill of Monteluco not only functions as a scenic backdrop, but has also played a leading role in Spoleto's history. Special laws have protected its holm-oak forests from felling since Antiquity. Our visit to the town follows two itineraries: the Traversa Interna and the higher part of the town. Afterwards we describe the churches lying beyond the river. The 'Traversa Interna', which runs from Piazza Garibaldi to the church of S. Paolo inter Vineas, cutting through the town from north to south, was really designed for cars, and has virtually no shops or restaurants. Having admired the broad, tree-lined Piazza della Vittoria and having inspected the remains of **Ponte Sanguinario**, with its three arches built of square blocks of travertine, much of which is now below ground, we enter **Piazza Garibaldi**. Porta Garibaldi, through which we access the square, was first rebuilt in the 15th century, and again in 1825. Destroyed by the retreating Germans in 1944, it was subsequently rebuilt as a two-span bridge. Many Roman remains are to be found in the foundations of the square's public buildings. Often, Christian churches were built on earlier sites of cult worship, like the Romanesque **church of S. Gregorio Maggiore***, built in 1079 over an earlier church, near a cemetery. Opening onto the portico that was added in the 16th century is the 14th-century frescoed chapel of the Innocenti, whereas the mighty bell tower was erected in the late 15th century. Medieval frescoes adorn the interior walls. Built in the 2nd century outside the perimeter wall, the **Roman amphitheater** was probably built with two tiers of arches, as you can see from the remains of broad sections of the structure's outer covered passageway. In the Middle Ages, this area was occupied by the former monasteries of the Madonna della Stella and San Gregorio Minore or del Palazzo, which has two impressive cloisters: one late-medieval and the other late-16th century. The Stella monastery church, dedicated to Ss Stefano e Tommaso, dates from the late 18th century. At the beginning of tree-lined **Via Cecili** you can see the tall polygonal apse of the 14th-century **church of S. Nicolò**, which you can access via the steep, cobbled Salita della Misericordia. Erected in 1304 at the same time as the Augustinian monastery, today, its interior houses a convention center and an exhibition hall. Having returned to Via Cecili and passed the church of the Misericordia, an oratory belonging to the Augustinian complex above, you can see an impressive section of the first **town walls**, and the tower built to defend a postern. If you look carefully, you will notice three layers of different wall-building techniques: large limestone blocks form the most ancient stratum (4C BC); above that is a squared buttressing section dating from 241 BC; and then elongated rectangular sections dating from restoration work carried out in the 1st century BC. The **Piazza Torre dell'Olio** is overlooked by a secondary facade of **Palazzo Vigili**, a combination of 13th- and 16th-century structures, including the tall, slender Torre dell'Olio. Continuing beyond the square through Via Pierleone, which has a characteristic medieval tower with megalithic stone walls, we reach a tree-lined square overlooked by the Dominican **church of S. Domenico**, which was built in the 13th and 14th centuries. In 1915, the Franciscans took over the church and restored its Gothic interior. This involved removing its 17th-century decoration and altars. The first altar features an important early 15th-century fresco (**Triumph of St Thomas Aquinas**); the frescoes in the St Mary Magdalene chapel date from the same period. Similarly noteworthy is a silver *reliquary* (1726), supposed to contain a nail from the Holy Cross, which, according to tradition, was brought here by the Blessed Gregorio. The underlying *crypt* is decorated with 14th- and 15th-century frescoes. As with other squares in the city, **Piazza Collicola** results from the nobility's desire to create areas suited to the prestige of their residents. The square is, in fact, dominated by the grand **Palazzo Collicola** (1737), rich in artworks and now the seat of the **Galleria Civica d'Arte Moderna**. It has paintings and sculptures by artists of international renown. From the steps facing the palazzo it is a short walk to the former Romanesque **church of S. Lorenzo**, which conserves frescoes of the Umbrian School from the 15th and 16th centuries. Near **Via Filitteria**, paved in the 19th century, set back a little in Vicolo Corvino, stands the **church of Ss Giovanni e Paolo**, a plain 12th-century structure. The interior has one of the earliest representations of St Francis and a Martyrdom of St Thomas Becket (12C). After a bend with views, we come to **Palazzo Zacchei-Travaglini**. From here, proceed to Via Walter Tobagi, overlooked by **Palazzo Pianciani** (18C). An impressive stairway links Piazza Pianciani to the Via di Fontesecca higher up, for which Palazzo Leoncilli, with its loggia and small balcony, provides a graceful backdrop. At the beginning of Corso Mazzini stands the **church of S. Filippo Neri**, with a grand travertine facade and a Roman-style dome. Its interior is enhanced by frescoes and an elegant 18th century sacristy. On **Corso Mazzini**, the first building we encounter is the former monastery of the Filippini. This area contains some of the town's earliest streets, such as Via del Mercato and the narrow Via San Gregorio della Sinagoga, where the Jewish community lived and worshipped. Especially interesting is the 20 m long corridor of a Roman building, together with a mosaic-paved room, the purpose of which, however, remains a mystery. Almost at the end, on the right, Vicolo III leads down to Palazzo Rosari-Spada (17-18C), the first floor of which now houses the **Pinacoteca Comunale***. Highlights of the collection include a **Crucifix** on canvas fixed onto wood by an Umbrian painter of the late 12th century, and two painted **Crucifixes**, one dating from the 13th century, the other by the Maestro di Cesi (late 13-14C). There are two frescoes by Spagna, especially the **Madonna and Child with Saints**, while 16th- and 17th-century works include a fine **Mary Magdalene**. There are also illuminated codices, gold- and silver-ware, and a selection of 19th-century paintings by local artists. Corso Mazzini ends at **Piazza della Libertà**, court of the noble Ancaiani family, once Umbria's most powerful landowners. In this square is **Palazzo Ancaiani** (late 17C), now the seat of the Italian Center for Medieval Studies. Not far away is the **church of S. Agata**, built as a Benedictine monastery at the end of the 14th century next to a *former church* of the same name (11C). The limited space afforded by the hillside inevitably meant that buildings had to be constructed on several levels. The monastery incorporated the medieval houses of the Corvi family, and now only the palazzo remains. Today the complex houses the **Museo Archeologico Nazionale**. Displayed in chronological order are rare Bronze Age finds from recent digs in the vicinity of the cave at Campello and the Rocca of Spoleto. The museum's Roman section (from the Republican to the Imperial period) features an interesting series of busts from the 1st to the 3rd century. Built within the town perimeter in the second quarter of the

1st century, the **Roman theater** was subsequently concealed and altered by the building of S. Agata, the houses of the Corvi family and the extension to the Benedictine monastery (14-16C). The theater has been restored. Beyond the town walls, the **church of S. Paolo inter Vineas*** was rebuilt together with the convent in the 10th century and remodeled before 1234, when it was consecrated. Through its plain arched doorway you pass into the aisled interior, where the broad transept contains **frescoes** of the Prophets and Scenes from the Creation.

This second itinerary explores the upper part of the town, where the most significant remains of the Roman town are situated, including the Arco di Druso. The visit starts in **Via Brignone,** a palimpsest of the town's history, dotted with the remains of structures from Roman times, preserved in the basements of houses. If you look inside one of the upper town's public buildings, you will see an unusual combination of architectural features. To the left, the street leads to Piazza Fontana, with its elegant 16th-century fountain. Nearby is the **Arch of Monterone** (3C BC), the massive limestone blocks of which span the street of the same name. Further on, *Arco delle Felici* is another structure built with huge blocks featuring fragments which possibly date from the 4th century. The **church of S. Ansano** was built in the 12th century above an earlier oratory dedicated to Sts Isaac and Martial (7C). The oratory was built above part of the Roman forum. The church was renovated in the late 18th century. In the side of the church, you can see sections of the earlier building. A stairway to the left of the main altar leads down to a Roman temple and the crypt of St Isaac. The **temple** was probably built by the second half of the 1st century along the south side of the *forum*, and, according to a traditional layout, comprised a *cella* preceded by a four-columned portico. The **crypt of St Isaac*** dates from the 12th century. Built on a rectangular plan, it has columns with roughly-hewn capitals and interesting fresco fragments on the walls. Yet another tangible remain of Roman Spoleto is the **Arch of Drusus*.** It was the monumental entrance to the *forum*, built in the year 23 in honor of Drusus Minor and Germanicus (the son and nephew of Tiberius) and was covered over in the Middle Ages. The arch is simply decorated with pillars topped with Corinthian capitals. On the left-hand side of Via dell'Arco di Druso, which is a Roman street, is Palazzo

Leti (17C). Beyond Palazzo Parenzi, another 17th-century palazzo set slightly back from the road, we are in the heart of the Roman town. The fact that, in the Middle Ages, **Piazza del Mercato** was still called Piazza del Foro, sheds light on the importance of this area over the centuries, even if, after the intensive building phase during the Middle Ages, very little remains of its broad Roman perimeter wall. The ornate **Fonte di Piazza**, in the Romanesque style, dates from 1746-48 (its coats-of-arms belonged to a previous structure of 1626). The charm of **Via del Palazzo dei Duchi** stems from the medieval-looking shops on either side. They actually date from the 16th century, when the arcades beneath the surviving bays of the church of S. Donato were converted into shops. Goods are still displayed on the original display counters. To the left stands the *Casa Spiga* (14C). Via del Palazzo dei Duchi intersects with **Via Fontesecca**, site of the *Casa dei Maestri Comacini*, with its characteristic pointed-arch doors and arched windows. Passing a number of aristocratic dwellings, renovated between the 15th and the 16th century, we move towards the cathedral and the fortress. To the right, Via di Visiale affords access to a **Roman house** below the 20th-century Palazzo Comunale. This was a wealthy 1st-century residence looking onto the *forum*. The rooms are arranged around a central atrium with an impluvium, with wings on either side and cubicula and a raised triclinium opposite the tablinum. The remains of the black and white floor mosaics show that it was a wealthy household. At the **Bishop's Palace**, beyond the 16th-century portico, is the **Museo Diocesano**. Its collection includes a **bust of Pope Urban VIII** by Bernini (1640). Beyond the Sala del Passetto, where there is a display of 17th-century silver-ware and liturgical vestments, is the **Basilica of S. Eufemia***, which seems even more solemn and splendid when seen from the women's galleries, high above the nave. The church dates from the 10th century but was made wider in the 12th century. The interior is composed of a nave and side-aisles separated by columns and pillars using material from classical and early-medieval buildings. The marble altar is decorated with an **altar-piece** (13C) in the same material, with ornate Cosmatesque decoration and *reliefs*.

Piazza del Duomo* has fine views of the cathedral. On the right-hand side is the 15th-century *Casa Fabricolosi* and a *sarcophagus* featuring a hunting scene (3C), which has

The cathedral in Spoleto.

been converted into a fountain. To the left, the red and white molded stone slabs of the *Casa dell'Opera del Duomo* (1419) and the small but elegant **Teatro Caio Melisso**. The following (former) **church of S. Maria della Manna d'Oro** was built on an octagonal plan in 1527, with Bramantesque influences, and was completed in 1681. Today, it is used for exhibitions. The Romanesque **Duomo****, erected in the late 12th century upon the former S. Maria del Vescovato, is immediately notable. You cannot fail to admire the large rose windows gracing the facade, surrounded by *symbols of the Evangelists*. Equally remarkable is the majestic Byzantine-style mosaic (*Christ Giving the Blessing between the Virgin and St John*), dated 1207, located in the central blind arch of the upper tier. Completing the picture, to the left, stands the massive **bell tower**, built in the 12th century, with material recovered from Roman structures. The magnificent Romanesque **doorway***, with its impressive jambs and architrave decorated with a vine-leaf motif, and preceded by an elegant Renaissance portico, leads into the Latin-cross interior and to the semi-circular apse, which was extensively modified (17C). The nave conserves most of the original 12th-century floor mosaic. On the right is the *Eroli chapel*, with frescoes by Pinturicchio (**God the Father with Angels, the Virgin and Child with Sts John the Baptist and Stephen***, and a *Pietà* on the front of the altar). The chapel is connected to the nearby frescoed *chapel of the Assumption*, by a vaulted chamber which was supposed to hold the tombs of the Eroli family. The **frescoes of the Life of the Virgin**** adorning the apse (1467-69) by Fra' F.Lippi

are truly magnificent. In the left aisle, the chapel of Relics (1540) houses a **Virgin and Child**, a finely crafted polychrome wooden sculpture (early 14C) and a rare autographed letter (to Brother Leone) from St Francis. At the beginning of the aisle is the **Crucifix***, a splendid painting on canvas fixed to a wooden panel (1187). The *priest's house* contains the **Archive**, a collection of important documents. From here, you can visit the **crypt of St Primianus**, a rare example of a semi-circular crypt containing fresco fragments from the same period.

To the left of the Caio Melisso theater, a brief detour from Via del Duomo takes you to Via dello Spagna, where recent restoration work has unearthed a **deambulatory** (1C) consisting of a 30 m curved passageway with a sharp bend and imposing arches overlooking the valley. The vast sloping **Piazza Campello** stretches from the walled city to the Rocca. The trees planted in the 20th century have altered the square's original perspective, concealing its complex access routes. On it stands the former **church of Ss Simone e Giuda**. Next to it is the *Fontana del Mascherone* (1763). **Palazzo Campello** (1597-1600) was erected on the site of medieval buildings belonging to the family after which it is named. At the top of Piazza Campello is the lane leading to the **Rocca/Fortress***. In 1359, Cardinal Albornoz decided to erect a castle here as a stronghold of papal power. The architect entrusted with this task was M. di Giovannello, known as 'Gattapone'. He designed a massive rectangular structure with six towers. It was divided into two quadrangles by an imposing wing, with the parade ground to the north and the courtyard of honor to the south. The fortress contains painted decoration dating from the late 14th to 18th centuries, including the **Camera Pinta**, inside the main tower, a room frescoed with scenes of chivalry and courtly love. The rooms of the first and second floors looking onto the courtyard of honor will house the **Museo Nazionale del Ducato di Spoleto**. The collection, which is displayed in chronological order and according to particular topics, includes inscriptions and archeological finds from Late Antiquity to the late Middle Ages, previously on display in the Museo Civico. The display will also include fresco cycles detached from the church of S. Paolo inter Vineas (12-13C) and the former monastery of Palazzo (late 13C), and a group of altarpieces, now on display in the Pinacoteca Co-

The fortress in Spoleto.

munale. A splendid walk starts from Piazza Campello and proceeds down **Via del Ponte**, flanked by a stretch of polygonal Roman walls. First we pass an open area with marvelous *views* of forest-covered Monteluco, and then the breathtaking **Ponte delle Torri***, which joins the Rocca to the hill of Monteluco spanning a deep gorge. With its nine pillars connected by ten arches, this imposing limestone structure dominates the valley. The function of this bridge-cum-aqueduct was to convey water to the upper part of the town and to the Rocca, while at the same time providing access to Monteluco and to the Mulini fortress. Its two tallest towers (hence the name) are hollow: one consists of two superimposed rooms with windows, and the other contains a room with an arched doorway, and was probably a guard post.

From Porta Monterone, along Via San Carlo, we cross the Tessino River and the main road where there is a magnificent view of the Rocca and the bridge-acqueduct. Steps lead up to a 5th-century panoramic terrace and the **church of S. Pietro***, built by Bishop Achilleus to house a relic from the chains used to bind St Peter. The facade is a masterpiece of Umbrian Romanesque sculpture. Magnificent **reliefs**** adorn the three bands of the facade. Above the central doorway is a horseshoe-shaped tympanum flanked by two eagles. The door-jambs and the architrave feature ornamentation of a more classical type, with two small side columns, and stylized animal and geometric motifs alternating with pairs of symbolic reliefs. The church's aisled interior, restructured in 1699, features a votive fresco on the entrance wall portraying the patron kneeling in prayer. From Piazza della Vittoria take the road that leads to Norcia. Having

crossed the Tessino River, you come to the so-called **Basilica di S. Salvatore***. This is a most interesting early Christian structure (late 4-5C), which has preserved its original architectural features – similar to those of the Tempietto del Clitunno, a blend of classical and oriental motifs. The lower level of its **facade*** has three marble doorways decorated with floral motifs, while the upper level is decorated with three broad windows. The central window is surmounted by an arch, while the ones on either side have tympanums. Its narrow nave and aisles, divided by Doric columns, produce a marked sense of verticality. The quadrilateral plan of the presbytery is quite separate from the nave, the ceiling of which has preserved its original beamed structure. At its four corners are pairs of tall grooved Corinthian columns. The central portion of the apse features a fresco of a monogrammed and jeweled cross. The top of the apse is decorated with fresco fragments (13C) and there is a *Crucifixion*.

The **church of S. Ponziano** is said to stand on the site where St Ponzianus, patron saint of Spoleto, was buried in 175 AD. The saint is depicted in the town's crest on horseback with a crossed shield (in a niche at the entrance to the monastery). The jambs on either side of the doorway are supported by two lions resting on Roman urns. The rose windows are encircled by *symbols of the Evangelists*. A room in its interior houses a sarcophagus from the early-Christian cemetery. In the crypt are three other sarcophagi, and some votive paintings.

The famous ascent of **Monteluco**, with wonderful views, has the added attraction of going to the Romanesque **church of S. Giuliano** (12C) and the **sanctuary of Monteluco**, which contains an oratory where St Francis used to pray. The woods below are dotted with magnificent viewpoints and small caves with a mystical atmosphere which evoke the ancient holy aura of this area.

Finally, the **fortified villages** dotted around the area between the fertile plain of the Maroggia Stream and the Martani mountains deserve a mention. This part of Umbria is rich in beautiful landscapes and history. Villages like **Pontebari**, **S. Brizio**, **Castel S. Giovanni**, **Castel Ritaldi**, **Montemartano**, **S. Angelo in Mercole** and **S. Giovanni di Baiano** are well worth seeing.

PERUGIA

Perugia, Umbria's largest city, dominates a maze of valleys and major communication routes between the Tiberina and Umbrian valleys from its hill, 493 m above sea-level. Here the visitor is afforded various sights, the best being the view when arriving from the direction of Cortona. The historic center appears like the cavea of a theater, from which areas of modern expansion have crept along and down the hill. To get a proper feel of the city, you should approach it by the ancient roads which wind up along the hill into the center of the town. Perugia is, first and foremost, a city of culture. Its state university and its university for foreigners attract large numbers of young people who enliven the historical center. This cultural vitality translates into high-level events, such as: Umbria Jazz (July) and the Sagra Musicale Umbra (September). The city's monumental center, situated in the higher part of town within the Etruscan walls, with the medieval Baglioni district, now completely underground, has a rich artistic heritage. To the north, lie the town's charming medieval districts of Porta Sant' Angelo, Porta Sant' Antonio and Fonte Nuovo. Although they have now all been encompassed within later city walls, they have nevertheless maintained their "low-class" dimension in contrast with the higher noble part of the city. The elongated, narrow medieval district of Porta San Pietro, partly surrounded by fortifications (13-14C), is the southern arm of the historic center, which is itself surrounded by the fortifications of later date (14-15C) which enclose the caracteristic Borgo XX Giugno.

WITHIN THE ETRUSCAN WALLS

Piazza IV Novembre*. This square has been the heart of Perugia since Etruscan times, the center of religious and political power and of artistic achievement, with the Fontana Maggiore, Palazzo dei Priori, the cathedral, and the Loggia di Braccio Fortebraccio.

Fontana Maggiore**. Emblematic of the medieval "Commune" and symbol of Peru-

A birds'-eye view of Perugia.

gia, this fountain was built in 1275-78 to plans by G. and N. Pisano, as the outlet of the aqueduct from Mt Pacciano. It comprises two concentric marble basins, adorned with sculptures, and a bronze cup with a group of three Nymphs, or Theological Virtues. Note the beautiful reliefs depicting the Months of the Year** and the 24 statuettes on the upper basin.

Loggia di Braccio Fortebraccio. This loggia was built in the 15th century, under the rule of Fortebraccio. Note the fragment of Roman wall as well as the Palazzo Arcivescovile, with

the Museo di Storia Naturale with collections of natural history.

Via Maestà delle Volte*. Leading down from Piazza IV Novembre to Piazza Felice Cavallotti, this street passes before 13th-century houses and beneath dark passages, in what is one of the most evocative settings in medieval Perugia. The white-and-red striped Gothic arch is all that remains of the 14th-century oratory of the Maestà delle Volte.

Cathedral*. Begun as a Gothic church in 1345 on the site of a Roman building, work on this cathedral went forward by fits and starts (1437-1587) but was never finished. The unfinished left side, partly covered in pink and white marble, overlooks the square. Dominating the steps on this side is a statue of Pope Julius III, by V. Danti (1555); to the right of the 16th-century portal (G. Alessi) is a pulpit from which Bernardino da Siena once preached. Inside you will find a wide range of styles and decorative approaches. In the chapel of S. Bernardino is a Deposition by F. Barocci. Across from it is a chapel which holds the revered relic of the Virgin's supposed wedding ring (1498), which can be seen only on 30 July. In the apse, note the carved and inlaid choir* by G. da Maiano and D. del Tasso (1486-91).

Museo Capitolare di S. Lorenzo. Adjacent to the Cathedral, this museum features paintings and frescoes by Umbrian and Sienese artists of the 14th-16th century, including B. Caporali and M. di Guido da Siena, and a magnificent *Madonna Enthroned* by L. Signorelli.

Palazzo dei Priori**. Built in several stages (1293-1443) in a rigid Gothic style, this is one of the largest and most impressive "palazzi pubblici" in medieval Italy, a combination of courthouse and town hall. It is now Perugia's Town Hall. The oldest section comprises the three mullioned windows on the left, overlooking the piazza, and the first ten mullioned windows overlooking Corso Vannucci. Note the fine portal (ca. 1326) on the Corso, and the staircase and large Gothic portal, surmounted by bronze statues of the Guelph lion and the Perugian griffin (1281). This portal leads into the large Sala dei Notari*.

Galleria Nazionale dell'Umbria**. On the third floor of Palazzo dei Priori, this gallery has one of the most important collections of 13th-18th-century art of Central Italy, especially Umbria, Tuscany, and the Marche. Founded in 1863, it was given to the Italian State in 1918 as the Regia Pinacoteca Vannucci and includes the art works from religious institutions closed after the Unification of Italy, and the works owned by Perugia's Accademia di Belle Arti. It has been located in the Palazzo dei Priori since 1879. Since 1918, the collection has grown constantly, through donations and acquisitions, and the museum now owns over 1500 works. Among the artists whose work is on display, the most important (in chronological order) are: A. di Cambio, M. da Perugia, M. da Siena, D. di Boninsegna, F. da Rimini, O. Nelli, L. Salimbeni, L. di Velletri, B. Gozzoli, and G. Boccati. Thoroughly represented here is Perugian painting of the late 15th century, including: B. Bonfigli, N. Alunno, F. di Lorenzo, Fra' Angelico, F. di Giorgio Martini, P. della Francesca, and Pinturicchio. There are many paintings by Perugino and his followers of the 15th and 16th centuries, among them G. di Paolo, B. di Giovanni, D. Alfani. Then come works by painters of the Mannerist period, especially those of Central Italy. Among them are: V. Danti, G.B. Naldini, and M. Venusti. Up the spiral staircase, you can see works by artists (17-19C), including P. da Cortona, O. Gentileschi, V. de Boulogne, S. Conca, P. Subleyras, C. Giaquinto, and F. Trevisani.

Collegio della Mercanzia*. On the ground floor of Palazzo dei Priori, the entrance to the right of the main portal, it was the headquarters of the powerful guild of the merchants. Inside, the richly inlaid wood of the Sala dell'Udienza is particularly impressive.

Collegio del Cambio**. Headquarters of the powerful guild of moneychangers, this building was built in 1452-57 at the far end of the Palazzo dei Priori. From the vestibule (Sala dei Legisti) with its Baroque wooden benches, you enter the Sala dell'Udienza*, one of the great bequests of Renaissance culture. The magnificent wooden tribunal was carved and inlaid by D. del Tasso (1493); the walls and ceiling were frescoed by Perugino** and workshop (possibly Raphael among them). In the adjacent St J. Baptist chapel, note the frescoes by G. di Paolo (1513-28), and the altarpiece by M. di Ser Austerio (1512), a pupil of Perugino.

Corso Vannucci. Perugia's most elegant street, and the main one since Etruscan times; note the Palazzetto dei Notari (1438-46), and, at the other end, the 18th-century Palazzo Donini.

Piazza Italia. This 19th-century square was laid out after the destruction of the 16th-century papal fortress, the Rocca Paolina (1860); the far end is occupied by the porticoed Palazzo del Governo (1872), behind which are the Giardini Carducci, gardens with a spectacular view** of the heart of Umbria.

Piazza Matteotti. Built in the late 13th century on artificial terracing, it faces the long facade of the Università Vecchia, or Old University (1490-1514), and the elegant Palazzo del Capitano del Popolo* (1472-81), with fine portals, windows, and balcony. The arch at no. 18 leads to a covered market (1932) and a panoramic terrace. Note the 14th-century porticoed Via Volte della Pace.

Chiesa del Gesù. At the north end of Piazza Matteotti is this 16th-century church, with a splendid Baroque altar, frescoes, and paintings by S. Amadei; see the three oratories below the church, with frescoes.

Via dei Priori. This road passes under the Palazzo Comunale, through the Arco dei Priori, and descends through a district with a strong medieval flavor. On the left is the little 14th-century church of Ss. Severo e Agata, with fine frescoes; facing it is the odd, twisting Via Ritorta. Further along, on the right, is the Baroque church of S. Filippo Neri (17C), with an altarpiece by P. da Cortona (1662); then, the church of Ss. Stefano e Valentino, built in the 12th century. Last, on the left, the high tower of the Sciri* (13C); then the road ends at the medieval Porta Trasimena. Note the 16th-century church of the Madonna della Luce*.

S. Bernardino**. This church is a gem of Renaissance architecture and sculpture; it was built in honor of a saint who often preached in Perugia. The harmonious facade is by A. di Duccio (1457-61); note the statues and reliefs. Inside, the high altar is a 4th-century Roman sarcophagus.

S. Francesco al Prato. This immense Gothic church was built in the mid-13th century and rebuilt often thereafter. Next door is the Accademia di Belle Arti, or Academy of Fine Arts, founded in the 16th century; the Museum has a large collection of statues, paintings from the 19th and 20th centuries, drawings, and prints.

THE NORTHERN DISTRICTS

This route covers the expansion of Perugia northward, beyond the Etruscan walls. From Piazza Danti, you follow Corso Garibaldi to Porta S. Angelo; then, from Piazza Fortebraccio, you continue to the church of S. Maria Nuova and Corso Bersaglieri, heart of the medieval Borgo di S. Antonio. You then return to the center along the Colle del Sole, enjoying a fine view from Piazza Rossi Scotti.

Piazza Danti. Stretching along the right side of the Cathedral, this was Perugia's marketplace in the Middle Ages. At n. 18 is the entrance to the Pozzo Etrusco, or Etruscan Well, a 3rd-century BC structure of notable size: 37 m deep, 5.6 m across. Via Cesare Battisti, a terrace road built in 1901, runs past a long stretch of Etruscan walls (fine view to the north), and drops down to Piazza Fortebraccio. Next to the Arco Etrusco (see below) is the 17th-century church of S. Fortunato.

Arco Etrusco*. The Etruscan Arch was built in the 3rd century BC and was the main gate of the Etruscan walls. Note the later Doric frieze, with the Roman inscriptions "Augusta Perusia" and "Colonia Vibia." The loggia and fountain on the left side date from the 16th century.

Piazza Fortebraccio. This square is dominated by the Baroque Palazzo Gallenga Stuart (1748-58), now the Università Italiana per Stranieri. In nearby Via S. Elisabetta, note the large 2nd-century Roman mosaic.

Corso Garibaldi. This narrow street climbs through a medieval neighborhood lined with small, old buildings. On the right, the church of S. Agostino has several fine artworks: 14th-16th-century frescoes, wooden choir by B. d'Agnolo (1502), and altarpiece by G. di Paolo. Along the Corso, at no. 179, is the monastery of S. Caterina, built in 1574, perhaps by G. Alessi; at no. 191, the monastery of the Beata Colomba – note the paintings by G. Spagna; nearby, is the monastery of S. Agnese, with a fresco* by Perugino.

S. Angelo*. This remarkable Early Christian church (5-6C), with a central plan, has a 14th-century Gothic portal. Inside, an ambulacrum, marked by 16 columns with Roman capitals, runs around a central space. On the walls are detached frescoes; in the baptistery there are frescoes by a 15th-century Umbrian painter. Porta S. Angelo. The largest of Perugia's medieval gates, with parapets and loopholes, it marks the end of the long Corso Garibaldi; beyond it, in Via Monte Ripido, is the 13th-century church of S. Matteo degli Armeni.

Via Pinturicchio. Return to Piazza Fortebraccio and follow this road to the church of S. Maria Nuova. The portal on Via Pinturicchio and the bell tower date from the 16th century; possibly by G. Alessi. Inside, banner painted by B. Bonfigli (1471); wooden choir* (1456); and frescoes by L. Vasari. Then take the Arco dei Tei to Corso Bersaglieri which leads through the Borgo di Porta S. Antonio, the last fragment of medieval Perugia, running past the church of S. Antonio, Porta di S. Antonio (14C) .

S. Maria di Monteluce. Rebuilt in 1451, this church has a handsome twin portal and a marble facade in red-and-white panels. Inside, note the frescoes, including one by F. di Lorenzo. The adjacent monastery is now a hospital.

S. Severo. In the small and isolated Piazza Raf-

HIGHLIGHTS

THE MODERN LANDSCAPE

In the Adoration of the Magi (*see picture*) painted in Perugia in 1504 by Il Perugino, the procession of horses converging on the shed is set against one of the most elaborate landscapes ever created by the artist. The countryside slopes gently towards the center, perfectly framed by gently rolling hills, the horizon flattening out into a stretch of water, recalling the view from Città della Pieve towards Lake Trasimeno, in one of Il Perugino's typical figurative settings. This "almost modern manner", as Giorgio Vasari defined it in the 16th century, turned its back on the tormented Gothic visions of landscape, and marked a decisive change in taste. The rural scene thus took on new organic forms prompting a reappraisal of the ideal landscape, which was later captured so beautifully in Renaissance art.

faello, this ancient church, traditionally said to have once been a temple to the Sun, now has an 18th-century appearance. The adjacent chapel has a fine fresco* by Raphael (1505-08), completed in the lower half by Perugino (1521).

Le Prome. The highest square in Perugia, once the acropolis, set high atop a retaining wall with great arches (1374). Excellent view. Note the little church of S. Angelo della Pace (1545) and the 17th-century Palazzo Conestabile della Staffa, now a library.

THE SOUTHERN DISTRICTS

From Porta Marzia, in the eastern bastion of the long-destroyed Rocca Paolina, the route follows Corso Cavour, through the historic Borgo di Porta S. Pietro. The district first extended to the Porta S. Pietro, enclosed by 13th-century walls and a few centuries later extended to Porta di S. Costanzo, just past the church of S. Pietro. One then returns, after various excursions, up the stairs of Paradiso and through the Arco della Mandorla.

Porta Marzia. Set alongside the Via Porta Marzia, this Etruscan gate probably dates from the 2nd century BC; it is now part of the Rocca Paolina, a fortress built by A. da Sangallo the Younger in 1540 and destroyed in 1860. The gate is one of the entrances to the subterranean Via Bagliona, which runs through the remains of the medieval district upon which the fortress was erected.

S. Ercolano. Set against the ancient walls, this Gothic church (1297-1326) has a Roman sarcophagus as its main altar. To the right of the church, a stairway leads up to the Etruscan arch of S. Ercolano, rebuilt in Gothic times.

S. Domenico*. This impressive church was built during the 14th century, perhaps after a design by G. Pisano. Construction continued until 1482; note the truncated bell tower. The interior shows clear marks of the 17th-century renovation by C. Maderno. The altar-frontal* by A. di Duccio (1459) and the funerary monument to Pope Benedict XI* (early 14C), by a follower of A. di Cambio, are noteworthy.

Museo Archeologico Nazionale dell'Umbria*. Largely housed in an ancient Dominican convent, this museum comprises a Roman-Etruscan section and a prehistoric section. The collections originated with a gift in 1790, and include an impressive array of artifacts uncovered in Umbria and other parts of Italy. Apart from major finds from the Bronze and Iron ages, there is a substantial collection of documents concerning the history of Perugia under the Etruscans. Note the Cippo di Perugia* (3-2C BC), the lengthy Etruscan text of a property agreement.

Porta S. Pietro*. This gate has two faces: the interior is a simple construction (14C); the exterior is an elegant monumental arch, built in the Renaissance by A. di Duccio and P. di Stefano (1475-80) but left unfinished.

Borgo XX Giugno. This district is dominated by the church and monastery of S. Pietro; the street was widened in the 19th century.

S. Pietro**. This basilica, located in a convent complex (10C), preserves part of the original structure and, beneath it, a small Early Christian temple. Over it towers an elegant polygonal bell tower; before it is a handsome 17th-century cloister. Inside, the nave and aisles with ancient columns are splendidly decorated; the original basilica structure has been maintained. In the nave, a wooden 16th-century ceiling and a series of large paintings by Aliense (1592). On the walls and altars of the aisles are paintings by E. da San Giorgio, Sassoferrato, Guercino, Perugino, G. Reni, and others; in the 15th-century sacristy are four small paintings* by Perugino. In the presbytery, two carved chairs (1556) and a remarkable inlaid wooden choir*, considered to be among the finest in Italy (1525-26).

The former Benedictine monastery is now part of the university, and has two cloisters, the smaller one being a work by G. Alessi (1571). Inside is the interesting Orto Botanico Medievale a reconstruction of the medieval monastery garden of herbs.

Giardino del Frontone. Once an Etruscan necropolis, this area was laid out as a garden in the 18th century. The handsome tree-lined avenues end in a small amphitheater, and there is a fine view of Assisi and Mt Subasio.

Porta S. Costanzo. This gate (16C) marks the end of the Borgo XX Giugno. Just beyond it is the church of S. Costanzo, dating from the 11th century but rebuilt in the 19th century.

S. Giuliana. This church, built in 1253, has fragments of frescoes (13-14C); in the adjacent former convent, a 14th-century cloister.

Porta Eburnea. This unadorned town gate dates from 1576; a stairway leads from the church of S. Spirito (1579-1689), not far from a Franciscan convent. Nearby is the ancient church of S. Prospero, first built in the 7th century, with 13th-century frescoes.

Arco della Mandorla. This pointed arch, at the top of the stairs of Paradiso, is a medieval version of an ancient Etruscan gate. The narrow but charming Via Caporali takes you back to the center of Perugia.

MEDIEVAL UMBRIA

The Middle Ages was a flourishing time for Umbria, causing a growth in artistic and political activity. From the 11th century through to the mid-14th century, it was a time of rebirth and glory for the walled settlements. From the 13th century on, these towns became places where the mendicant orders built churches and other structures, leaving a mark on local architecture. At the forefront of this was the Order of St Francis, which often built in a combined Umbrian Romanesque and International Gothic style. What follows is a selection of some of the best examples of medieval Umbrian architecture. Of course, all this architectural beauty lies against a backdrop of gently rolling hills and harsh, steep mountains, often topped by small treasures from the Middle Ages.

Abbey of S. Eutizio. It is said that the grottoes near the abbey were once home to hermits who would occasionally meet under the guidance of Spes and later of Eutitius. By the 10th century, the abbey was the political and economic hub of the region and, until the 12th century, the Benedictine monastery increased its estates and influence over the surrounding areas. Interestingly, the Abbey of S. Eutizio was the origin of one of the oldest known documents (late-11C) written in early Italian (rather than Latin, which was the language of writing in those days). The entrance courtyard is surrounded by various monastic buildings, which are now home to a small Benedictine community, and leads to the church, built in 1190 by Maestro Pietro, as is indicated on the lunette. The church doorway has a double arched lintel and a rose window decorated with two rows of small columns (1236). The bell tower is from the 17th century, although it stands on the site of a medieval structure.

Abbey of S. Salvatore. The Abbey of S. Salvatore or Montecorona, near Umbertide, is one of the most important Benedictine abbeys in Umbria. It was a cradle of the Order of Camaldoli and was probably founded by the creator of the order, St Romuald, in 1008-09. The crypt was part of that original Romanesque building. It consists of five aisles and three apses, with groin vaults supported by Roman columns that were probably part of an earlier pagan structure.

The Abbey of S. Salvatore.

The upper church, altered in the Baroque period, has some 14th-century frescoes by the Umbrian school, an 8th-century ciborium and a Gothic apse.

Bettona. This ancient Umbrian settlement was an autonomous city-state during the Middle Ages. As a result, various private buildings and houses are from that period, especially the 14th century. The collegiate church of S. Maria Maggiore is from the 13th century, with its simple, rough facade and single-nave interior. Palazzo del Podestà is from 1371, while the church of S. Crispolto, with a small Romanesque bell tower topped by a spire, was built in the 13th century and altered in the late 18th century.

Castel San Felice. The old settlement of Castel San Felice lies not far from Sant'Anatolia di Narco. It stands surrounded by an oval ring of walls on a hill by the church of S. Felice. The building is one of the most interesting examples of Romanesque architecture in the Spoleto area. The lovely facade is topped by a tympanum with a dentil band and decorated with blind arches and pilaster strips. The rose window is surrounded by a decorative frame (once colored) filled with shapes and figures (the Evangelists) in full relief. The bottom of this frame has a frieze depicting the legend of Sts Felix and Maurus. The combination of these elements is a clear reference to the farming and land reclamation efforts of the local Benedictine monks as well as to their evangelical mission.

Cerreto di Spoleto. sits like a sentinel guarding the most rugged part of the Valnerina. It once had a castle, but only parts of the 13th-century fortifications remain along with a tall tower. The parish church has some frescoes by F. Damiani (Our Lady of the Rosary, 1583) and the so-called Painter from Poreta (Adoration of the Magi). The town hall houses a Virgin Mary with Child and Sts Anthony Abbot and Lucy by F. Damiani and a Visitation by C. Angelucci (1573). The lower section of the town is home to the fortified monastery of S. Giacomo. This 14th-century complex was refurbished, at least internally, in the 16th century. Fortunately, the wonderful 15th-century frescoes were kept.

Montone. This wonderful, elliptical hamlet still has much of its medieval layout intact. Montone lies between two "centers", the political one and the religious one, each located on a hill. Here, the Dark Ages were dominated by the Colle and Del Monte families and then, from the 13th century, by A. Fortebraccio, known as Braccio da Montone, a mercenary leader and Lord of Perugia. His residence, now Palazzo Comunale, is in the heart of the hamlet, near the Gothic church of S. Francesco (14C), at the end of some steps from where the view is quite superb. Both the church and the adjoining Franciscan convent have partially been turned into a museum and art gallery. In the church, there are some frescoes, generally votive, by the Umbrian school. Note, especially, the frescoes in the Gothic-style apse depicting the Life of St Francis. Just outside the hamlet lies a lovely little country church (11C) dedicated to St Gregory. In Romanesque-Byzantine style, it has a nave, two aisles and some frescoes by the Umbrian school.

Ponte. This former Lombard *gastaldato* (a type of administrative district that is not unlike a viceroyalty) was the local military and economic power during the Dark Ages. Some ruins from this period can be seen atop the rocky outcrop (441 m). The next dominant local force was the parish church of S. Maria. As late as the 14th century, this church still commanded notable influence over the surrounding area. The actual church building is 12th-century and is in Romanesque style, with a rectangular facade decorated with an ornate rose window framed by mosaics and symbols of the Evangelists. The single-nave interior is decorated with frescoes from the Umbrian school (14C and 15C) and the baptistery's font is a reused large, monolithic Roman slab. The design cut into the wall to the right of the entrance replicates the rose window on the facade.

Sassovivo. The Abbey of Sassovivo lies in front of a thick ilex wood and was built around the middle of the 11th century, using an old, fortified residence as the basis. The abbey rose to prominence soon after it was completed, eventually controlling an impressive 92 monasteries, 41 churches and 7 hospitals. It continued to dominate the area under the Benedictines, who occupied the complex from the mid-15th century until the Napoleonic suppression in 1860. The church was rebuilt in 1832 following an earthquake. The Romanesque cloister, created by a Roman maestro called P. De Maria, is from 1229 and is the undoubted highlight. It has 128 coupled and spiral columns supporting 58 arches in a classic trabeated system that is made more lively through the use of colored marble. In the center of the cloister stands a cistern that was built in 1340. The cloister also leads to the monastery, with its lovely vaulted dormitories from the 13th century. Next, you should head down to the inner courtyard to see the Loggia del Paradiso, with the remnants of some single-color frescoes (early 15C). After that, continue to the 11th-century crypt, also known as the chapel of Blessed Alano.

Stroncone. This evidently age-old town lies on a hill covered with olive trees and is still partly enclosed by a 10th-century ring of walls. Before reaching there, you should visit the church of S. Francesco, which is said to have been founded along with the adjoining convent by the saint in 1213. A chapel on the left of the porch has a fresco by Tiberio d'Assisi from 1509. The entrance to Stroncone is marked by a 17th-century fountain and the old hamlet gate, which leads onto a small, charming piazza. Here, you find the church of S. Giovanni Decollato, a 1604 enlargement of a building from 1435. The church of S. Nicolò dominates from above, with its Romanesque portal (1171) decorated with a Byzantine-style bas-relief. A flight of steps leads up to the 13th-century Palazzo Comunale (town hall), with nine choir parchments originally from the churches of S. Michele and S. Nicolò.

Vallo di Nera. The hamlet, located roughly 20 km from Spoleto, is still relatively medieval in appearance. The streets are narrow and, often quite steep because the hamlet lies on a hill and is enclosed by a ring of walls. The houses are linked by arched bridges that make it possible to go directly from one house into another across the street. The ring of walls, protected by towers, was created in the 12th century. The 13th-14th-century parish church of S. Giovanni Battista was altered in the 16th century. The church of S. Maria, from the late 13th century, still has clear Romanesque Gothic elements. The simple facade is enlivened by a Gothic portal with small columns that reach up to leafed capitals. The apse has frescoes from the schools of Umbria and Marche with the *Stories of Christ, the Virgin Mary and the Saints* (late-14C).

FOOD IN UMBRIA

O live oil and meat – beef, from Chianina cattle, and pork, especially the salami and sausage tradition of Norcia – are the flagships of this region's typical food. However, another famous Umbrian specialty comes from the mountains, Castelluccio lentils, which owe much to the exceptional geological and climatic characteristics of the place where they are grown. We mustn't forget the noble truffle – black around Norcia and Spoleto, and white in the area of Gubbio and the Eugubino-Gualdese (the area around Gubbio and Gualdo Tadino) – star of the local cuisine.

TYPICAL LOCAL DISHES

Ciriole. Home-made tagliatelle boiled and served with fried olive oil and garlic, or a meat and fresh tomato sauce.

Risotto alla norcina. This is the Umbrian version of risotto alla parmigiana, with black truffle grated over the top at the end.

Cardi al grifo. A speciality of peasant cuisine: the cardoons are cut into pieces, parboiled, dipped in egg and breadcrumbs and then fried. Then they are placed in a baking tray in alternate layers with minced veal and chicken livers fried in butter. Lastly the dish is covered with tomato sauce and baked.

Palombacci. One of Umbria's most traditional dishes. Wild doves are cooked on the spit and basted continually with *ghiotta*, a mixture of red wine, oil, capers, sage, chopped ham and other ingredients, which is placed in the dripping-pan and constantly enriched with fat dripping from the birds.

Ciaramicola. A traditional ring-shaped Easter cake with a cross in the center and, above it, five mounds representing the main square and the four gates of Perugia. Usually covered with meringue.

Rocciata. This belongs to the family of cakes called *spongate*, *pan speziale* and *panforte* even though it resembles a strudel. It is made with almonds, walnuts, raisins, prunes, dried figs, apples, cinnamon and others.

TYPICAL LOCAL PRODUCTS

Prosciutto di Norcia IGP. This is the top product of the famous local *norcineria* (the local term for charcuterie). Haunches of Italian Landrace pigs are treated with salt, pepper and garlic for about a month, then matured for a year.

Pecorino di Norcia. Cheese made with milk from ewes grazed on local mountian pastures. It is eaten fresh after 60 days of maturing, or used for grating after 8-12 months.

Vitellone Bianco dell'Appennino Centrale IGP. This label certifies meat of the Chianina, Romagnola and Marchigiana breeds which have been reared here for centuries. The meat is of high nutritional value.

Lenticchie di Castelluccio di Norcia IGP. These lentils are grown in small areas of the plateau, where the land and the climate give them a unique taste and make easy to cook.

Tartufo nero pregiato. Black truffles are found all over the region but Norcia is where most of them are found. They have a black, wrinkled skin, black-purplish pulp with fine white striations and a delicate smell.

Olio Extravergine di Oliva Umbria DOP. This label will also bear one of the following denominations: Colli Assisi-Spoleto, Colli

Martani, Colli Amerini, Colli del Trasimeno or Colli Orvietani, depending on where it comes from. Depending on the type of olive, it varies in color from green to yellow and has a fruity taste with a spicy flavor.

WINES

We find the first evidence of vine cultivation in Umbria in Etruscan necropolises. Today, the Umbrian wine tradition produces small volumes of high-quality wine. The influences of nearby Tuscany are obvious in the vineyards: Trebbiano and Sangiovese grapes alone account for three quarters of the production and constitute the basis for most Umbrian wines. These include the white Orvieto, historically an ambassador of Italian wine, and the red Torgiano Riserva DOCG. The indigenous wines are also good and result in wines of character like the white Grechetto and the red Sagrantino di Montefalco DOCG.

FOOD

TOLFA MOUNTAINS AND LAKE BRACCIANO

In the Roman "campagna," or countryside, the days of shepherds wearing fleecy vests and leaning on knobby sticks are long gone; also long vanished are the skittish, unshod ponies of the "butteri," the mounted cowherds of this region, wearing leather chaps and a rifle slung around their neck; no longer do the "seasonal" workers sleep in a circle in the fields. Still, you may glimpse fragments of that lost world now and again: the gritty farmhouse, perhaps, or a stand of pinasters, an ancient clump of ruins, or the gentle curve of the meadowland. Starting from and returning to Rome, this route runs through four different landscapes, redolent with nature and history. The first follows the crescent-shaped Tyrrhenian coastline as far as Capo Linaro and Civitavecchia. You will follow the Via Aurelia, as you head toward the first encounter with the ancient Etruscans: Cerveteri, withdrawn from the shore, with its burial grounds of rounded hillocks, tufted with grass, humping across the countryside around the medieval "borgo," and the ancient ports along the seacoast. After Civitavecchia and its harbor, the route turns inland, and the second landscape is that of the Tolfa Mountains. In the seaside maquis, or among the inland forests, you may still chance upon a wolf, lone descendant of the wolves that were forced down out of the Apennines by the icy winter of 1956.

A view of Lake Bracciano.

Geologists will find ores such as blende, galena, pyrite, alumite, kaolin, and cinnabar, all of which prompted ancient mining operations here. The third landscape surrounds Lake Bracciano: looking down from the high ridge, you will see the lake at the bottom of its funnel-shaped depression, houses crowded along the banks amidst clumps of alders, willows, and poplars; perched on poles, improbable seagulls watch as coots dive into the tranquil waters. Sometimes a sharp-taloned kite will soar overhead. Last comes the solitary landscape of long-lost Veio, and the rustic promenade across fields to the ruins of the Temple of the Vulcan Apollo (the god's statue is now in Rome, in the Museo Etrusco di Villa Giulia).

NOT TO BE MISSED

Cerveteri*: the stern medieval center of town, high on a tufa spur, stands on the site of the Etruscan town of Kysry, a wealthy trading port and sea power; in the castle, you can visit the Museo Nazionale Cerite. Nearby, in the empty landscape of pinasters and cypresses, is a necropolis, with circular barrow tombs. **Santa Severa**: south of the distinctive castle here, archeologists have excavated Pyrgi, the largest port-of-call of ancient Caere (antiquarium). **Santa Marinella**: beach resort; the Odescalchi castle, set amidst pine trees near the little marina of "Punicum," another port-of-call of ancient Caere. **Civitavecchia**: Michelangelo built the eight-sided keep of the high fort that bears his name; this city is now Latium's most important port. In the Museo Nazionale Archeologico are finds from earliest times to the Roman Empire; the nearby Terme Taurine are the baths of a huge Roman villa, owned by the emperor. **Allumiere** lies on the slopes of the Monte Le Grazie; as the town's name indicates, this was once a quarry for rock alum, used in dyeing wool.

Tolfa gave its name to the surrounding mountain group; the papal state mined iron ore here for three centuries. The shafts are now abandoned. **Bracciano**: vast view of the Lake Bracciano from the stern 15th-century Orsini-Odescalchi castle, with fine furnishings. **Trevignano Romano** is a village founded in the remote past on the northern lakeshore; the Museo Archeologico houses material from the necropolises of an Etruscan-Roman center. **Anguillara Sabazia** stands on a point of the shore of Lake Bracciano; it is one of the 13 castles that Pope Paul II seized in the 15th century from the Anguillara family during a 12-day war. **Vigna di Valle**: alongside airplanes of every era, this Italian Air Force museum, the Museo Storico dell'Aeronautica Militare, has exhibits on the history of flight and the polar expeditions of the dirigibles Norge and Italia. **Isola Farnese**: this hamlet stands high on a crag over two gorges; around it are scattered the ruins of Etruscan Veio in a lovely setting.

ROMAN ETRURIA

Roman Etruria coincided with what is now northern Latium, amongst the Volsini, Cimini and Saba-tini Mountains, and the Tyrrhenian coastline. There are four noteworthy Etruscan sites, illustrious and timeworn: Norchia, Tuscania, Vulci, and Tarquinia. At Norchia, the atmosphere is remote, surreal, among the architectural facades of the cliffside tombs and the medieval ruins of the town. At Tuscania, rather than the much faded Etruscan memories, it is the two early Romanesque churches that attract the eye: these are prototypes of the glorious Italian architecture that blends the Mediterranean style with northern European rigor. The beautiful landscape of Vulci, not far from the sea – on a tufa highland on the right bank of the Fiora River – was the site of a heartbreaking act of plunder. In 1828, Luciano Bonaparte, the grasping younger brother of Napoleon, and the papal prince of nearby Canino, excavated in the Etruscan necropolis here, and in four months carried off 2,000 vases. Others followed in the treasure hunt, opening 6,000 tombs, and destroying everything which was not immediately salable, including countless priceless terracottas.

NOT TO BE MISSED

Vetralla: village medieval in appearance, is a point of departure for visiting Norchia*, whose Etruscan necropolis features tombs carved out of the tufa, with architectural facades. **Tuscania***: within the medieval walls of this town is a secluded atmosphere; the town was rebuilt after the earthquake of 1971. On a hillside outside of town are the churches of S. Pietro and S. Maria Maggiore, masterpieces of Italian architecture of the High Middle Ages. **Valentano**, on the lip of the crater hollow of Latera, with hues of emerald in spring, sere and yellow in summer; note the vista, which extends beyond the great round hollow of Latera, Lake Bolsena and, in the distance, Mt Amiata. **Ischia di Castro** is a medieval borgo on a tufa-stone crag, with the Palazzo Ducale by Sangallo and Etruscan artifacts from Castro in the Museo Civico. **Farnese**, where medieval buildings and Renaissance palazzi stand side-by-side; a fine gilded wooden tabernacle in the church of S. Salvatore. **Rovine di Castro**: *Qui fu Castro* (here stood Castro) is inscribed upon a solitary column on a great mass of tufa-stone; the city, once capital of the Farnese duchy of Castro and Ronciglione, was leveled in 1649. **Acquapendente**: notable relics in the mortuary cathedral chapel. **Vulci**: architecture and landscape are very old friends here, as you may note from the bridge, which reuses fragments of earlier Etruscan and Roman structures; also visit the Abbadia, originally a medieval castle, the ruins of the long-vanished Etrusco-Roman town, and the vast Etruscan necropolises.

TARQUINIA

The great Etruscan city of "Tarxuna" stood on a strategic highland, now the plain of Civita. The city appears predominantly medieval, dense with towers and buildings dotted with dark volcanic tufa. It is set on a hill not far from the original settlement; close by is an Etruscan necropolis, unrivalled for its tomb paintings.

Palazzo Vitelleschi. This palazzo (1436-39), now houses the Museo Nazionale Tarquiniense. A mixture of Gothic and Renaissance styles, it boasts a handsome loggia and an elegant inner courtyard* adorned with sarcophagi and carved slabs. Little of the original interior decoration has survived.

**Museo Archeologico Nazionale **. The collections include funerary slabs and sarcophagi, both Etruscan and Roman (note the Magnate, the Obeso, and the Sacerdote), the so-called Winged Horses, a relief from the temple known as the Ara della Regina; Villanovian tomb furnishings and early ceramics; the Vase of Bochoris*, from the tomb of an Egyptian

pharaoh, proof of trade between Etruria and the eastern Mediterranean; Greek vases* of Corinthian and Attic production; and bronze mirrors. Yet to be displayed are frescoes* removed from the tombs of the Olimpiadi, the Letto Funebre, and the Triclinio.

Palazzo Comunale. Originally Romanesque, rebuilt in Baroque style.

Palazzo dei Priori. Situated near the former church of S. Pancrazio (13C), in the heart of the intricate medieval district – note the church of S. Martino* and the Duomo (17C), which worth a visit for the frescoes by Pastura. The Palazzo dei Priori houses the Museo della Ceramica which exhibits medieval ceramic pieces found in two wells in the center of town.

S. Maria di Castello**. A church in the oldest part of Tarquinia, castle overlooking the Marta River and still enclosed by medieval walls with towers. Inside, note the lovely capitals on the pillars, the mosaic floors**, the octagonal baptismal font**, the pergamon by G. di Guittone (1209), and the ciborium.

THE CIMINI MOUNTAINS

The ambiguous term "Mannerism" was first used by L. Lanzi in the late 18th century to designate a 16th-century style in the fine arts, "characterized by a complex system of perspective, elongation of forms, strained gestures or poses of figures, and intense, often strident color." It tended to include the bizarre, the capricious, the fantastic, and a tormented restlessness. This style is found in this route in three exemplary sites: Bagnaia, Bomarzo, and Caprarola. At Bagnaia, Cardinal Gambara had the architect Vignola create, for what is now Villa Lante, an Italian-style garden replete with ornate fountains. Bomarzo, more than the other two places, is disquieting, causing intellectual shivers with its Parco dei Mostri, or Park of Monsters. At Caprarola, it was again Vignola who transformed an old fort into the Palazzo Farnese, with a round central courtyard and a profusion of virtuoso decorations. And the surrounding countryside, dominated by the Cimini Mountains, SE of Viterbo, is gently rolling, with extinct volcanoes, sere landscapes, steep bluffs, high tufa cliffs, and dense forests of oak and chestnut, beneath the beech groves atop the Mt Cimino, overlooking the solitary Lake Vico.

NOT TO BE MISSED

Viterbo (➡ see below): area provincial capital, this town has two noteworthy features: an abundance of cheerful fountains, and an intense, exquisite medieval atmosphere. **S. Maria della Quercia***: the sanctuary, a lovely piece of Renaissance architecture, appears at the end of a long avenue, with a Della Robbia terracotta portal. **Bagnaia**: the medieval section lies on a rocky promontory between two rushing streams; the 16th-century addition lies uphill and culminates in the Villa Lante, designed by Vignola, with the fountains and streams in the garden. **Vitorchiano**: this largely intact medieval village has houses overlooking a precipice; the 14th-century church of S. Maria has been largely rebuilt. **Bomarzo**: dominating the old village is the 16th-century Palazzo Orsini; in the surrounding area, the Parco dei Mostri, the enigmatic creation of V. Orsini, a soldier and man of letters of the late 16th century. **Soriano nel Cimino**: there are two major attractions in this medieval town – the Orsini castle and the Mannerist Papacqua Fountain in the Palazzo Chigi-Albani. **Monte Cimino**: among the beeches that cover the mountain, there is a 250-ton trachyte boulder that will rock back and forth if you pull on a lever; it is called the Sasso Menicante, "naturae miraculum" according to Pliny the Elder. **Vallerano** has a 17th-century sanctuary dedicated to a miracle of the Virgin Mary. **Vignanello**, a town that produces flavorful wines, with a view of the Tiber Valley, lies beneath Palazzo Ruspoli rebuilt in the 16th century. **Corchiano**: 15th-century frescoes in S. Biagio church. **Civita Castellana**: the Cosmatesque portico of the Duomo is the most renowned monument of the town, but hardly the only one: in the fortress by Sangallo is a notable archeological museum, and nearby are the ruins of the Roman "Falerii Novi"*. **Castel Sant'Elia**: pilgrimages are made to the nearby sanctuary of S. Maria ad Rupes, carved out of the rock; tourists instead visit the Romanesque basilica di S. Elia. **Nepi**: 16th-century walls enclose the village, extending along a tufa ridge, dating back to the Middle Ages and the Renaissance. **Sutri**: here too the village is built on tufa stone, along with the Etruscan, Roman and medieval monuments; dark holm-oaks stand around the amphitheater; the shrine to the Madonna del Parto dates back into the mists of time. **Ronciglione**: the streets and aristocratic 16th-18th-century palazzi of this town overlook the Lake Vico; visit the compact medieval "borgo." **Caprarola**: the Renaissance village lies at the base of the five-sided Palazzo Farnese (with a circular courtyard), built by Vignola for the nephew of Pope Paul III; late-16th-century frescoes recall the splendor of this powerful family. **San Martino al Cimino**: medieval walls enclose the 17th-century town and the abbey of S. Martino, built by the Cistercians of Pontigny.

VITERBO

Set on an irregular plain at the foot of the Cimini mountains, along the Via Cassia, this was the historical capital of Upper Latium, the ancient Tuscia of the Romans. It still has turreted city walls, with seven gates. The Palazzo dei Papi is a reminder of the looming papal presence in Viterbo's history.

Piazza del Plebiscito. The square is the political heart of the city since it is flanked by the medieval Palazzo del Podestà and the 18th-century Palazzo della Prefettura, both adorned by columns with the lion symbolizing Viterbo. The adjacent **Palazzo dei Priori**, now city hall, was built in the 15th century under Pope Sixtus IV and later renovated. The 15th-century facade conceals a courtyard with a fine view of the river valley below. Also overlooking the square is the church of **S. Angelo in Spatha**, Romanesque but rebuilt; on the fa-

Piazza della Rocca, home to an archeology museum.

cade is a copy of the sarcophagus of the *Bella Galiana* (the original is in the Museo Civico) and, inside, a fragment of a triptych (14C). In Via Ascenzi, note the handsome portal* of the Gothic church of S. Maria della Salute.

Via S. Lorenzo. Linking the political heart of Viterbo with the religious heart, this street runs through a dense medieval district. The 15th-century Palazzo Chigi and the medieval Torre di Borgognone are noteworthy. Just beyond is the Piazza del Gesù, with the 11th-century Romanesque church of the same name.

S. Maria Nuova*. This Romanesque church, one of Viterbo's oldest (1080), features – at the left corner of the facade – the pulpit from which St Thomas Aquinas once preached. The interior* is basilican; note the 15th-century ceiling with tempera panels. Also worthy of note are a 13th-century Crucifix; from the same period, a triptych* on leather; and artwork by Balletta, M. Giovannetti, and Pastura.

Palazzo Farnese. Beyond the Ponte del Duomo, a bridge with Etruscan blocks (on the right), you can recognize the palazzo by the twin-light mullioned windows on its right side, 14th-century features which were employed in this Renaissance residence.

The **Cathedral** was built in the 12th century, and the bell tower*, revealing Tuscan influences, a century later, while the facade was completed in 1570. Inside, note the columns on the capitals and the Cosmatesque floors; the late 15th-century baptismal font by F. da Ancona; 14th-century fragments of frescoes; and the late 13th-century Madonna della Carbonara*. Housed in some recently restored rooms adjacent to the Cathedral is the **Museo storico-artistico del Colle del Duomo**; on exhibit are church furnishings, reliquaries, paintings and sculptures.

Palazzo dei Papi**. Built in 1255-67 as a papal residence, this is Viterbo's best known monument and the most important example of Viterbese Gothic architecture. Some ex-

ceedingly lively conclaves took place here. A staircase leads up to the battlemented facade; to the right runs the elegant loggia**; the fountain dates from the 15th century. Note the Museo d'Arte Sacra, with 17th-century paintings and sculptures in wood and stone.

Via S. Pellegrino*. This is the main street of the medieval district**, dotted with towers, mullioned windows, and elevated walkways. In the handsome little **Piazza S. Pellegrino*** note the Palazzo degli Alessandri, a 13th-century home with balcony, next to two medieval towers. .

Fontana Grande. Beyond the 15th-century. Case dei Gatti* is the most famous fountain in Viterbo, functioning since 1279.

S. Sisto*. Built in the 9th century on the site of a pagan temple, enlarged in the 12th-13th century, and rebuilt after WWII, the church boasts an ancient apse and two bell towers, one based on the transept, the other rising from the city walls. Note the unusual columns near the triumphal arch and the main altar.

S. Maria della Verità. Built in the 12th century just outside the city walls, this church was damaged in WWII; inside, note the Mazzatosta Chapel, with frescoes by L. da Viterbo (1469).

Museo Civico*. It is located in a former convent; note the Gothic cloister*. Among the archeological finds displayed here are sarcophagi, in particular the Roman one, known as the Sarcophagus of the Bella Galiana*, with hunting scenes. Among the painters: S. del Piombo and G. F. Romanelli. Noteworthy collection of pharmacy vases.

S. Giovanni in Zoccoli. This 11th-century church, rebuilt after the war, features a rose window surrounded by the symbols of the four Evangelists. Inside, a polyptych by Balletta.

S. Rosa. This church and the 13th-century saint's nearby home form the saint's sanctuary; inside, another polyptych by Balletta.

Rocca Albornoz. Cardinal Albornoz began work on this fortress in the mid-14th century Numerous popes carried on construction, at one point summoning Bramante (he designed the courtyard). Restored in the 1960s, now houses the Museo Archeologico Nazionale.

Museo Nazionale Etrusco*. The museum provides documentation of the Etruscan architecture of Viterbo and surrounding areas, through material excavated at San Giovenale (1956-65) and Acquarossa (1966-78). Providing, respectively, material from the Stone Age to the Middle Ages, and the structure of an entire Etruscan city of the 7th century BC, the finds offer such fascinating details as painted tiles from pitch roofs, an entire portico, and primitive siding as well as terracotta fixtures.

Over mountains and through valleys to the east of Rome: the Tiburtini Mountains line the left bank of the Aniene River, from the point where the river turns sharply from NW to SW. Beyond that sharp turn, the river borders the Simbruini Mts: this is Subiaco. The Ernici Mountains, which you will cross as you leave the Aniene Valley, crossing the uplands of Arcinazzo and then heading down to Fiuggi, are much taller (Pizzo Deta, 2,041 m). They stretch from west to east as far as Sora in the Liri Valley, north of the broad cut of the Sacco River. The Prenestini Mountains, lastly, stretch from north to south, between the basins of the Aniene and Sacco rivers, behind Palestrina; with Monte Guadagnolo, they reach an altitude of 1,218 m. The landscape is still that of the Apennines: sere hills, clustered villages, stretches of woods. You begin with the Villa Adriana, or Hadrian's Villa, then Tivoli with the sound of water amidst the crags. On the way back, at Palestrina, you can see the terraces of the Roman sanctuary, where the oracles foretold destinies; at the halfway point, Subiaco, where the Benedictines founded a world of medieval monasteries.

NOT TO BE MISSED

Villa Adriana** (➟ see below): a mirror of ancient style, physical catalogue of culture, repository of souvenirs from the travels of the Emperor Hadrian, who devoted long years to its construction; they are now some of the most significant and varied ruins of antiquity. **Tivoli** (➟ see below), overlooking the Roman countryside ("campagna"), was an aristocratic watering hole, surrounded by jagged rocks, lush greenery, a circular Temple of Vesta, villas, gardens, parks, waterfalls, and fountains. **Vicovaro**, atop a hill on the Aniene's right bank, features ruined walls and a 15th-century eight-sided church, S. Giacomo. S. Cosimato is a Franciscan hermitage set among cypresses and pines; it stands high on a crag overlooking the Aniene, over the ruins of a Roman villa. **Subiaco***: this small, intensely medieval town, set amidst mountains dense with woods, is redolent with the heritage and memory of St Benedict of Norcia (or Nursia), his brother monks, and the monastic world they created; the monasteries of S. Scolastica and the Sacro Speco stand in seclusion in the narrow Aniene Valley. **Fiuggi*** was already famous for its mineral waters in ancient times, one of the finest spas in Italy; the greenery of Fiuggi Fonte (or, springs of Fiuggi) contrasts with the medieval flavor of Fiuggi Città (the town of Fiuggi). **Genazzano**, on the slope of an isolated hill, boasts the Sanctuary of the Madonna del Buon Consiglio, Gothic houses, and the Colonna castle, stronghold of the famed family. In the ruins of the nymphaeum, strewn across the fields, it is said that Ovid was smitten with the love that ultimately caused Augustus to exile him to the Black Sea, where he died; in reality they are the ruins of a Renaissance building. **Castel San Pietro Romano** is a country village lodged on the site of the ancient acropolis of "Præneste" ; crowning the hill are the ruins of the Rocca dei Colonna, the Colonna family stronghold, and the immense vista of the Albani Hills and the Sacco Valley. **Palestrina***: the medieval city merges, in the most remarkable way, with the Roman sanctuary of Fortuna Primigenia; in the 17th-century Palazzo Barberini is the Museo Archeologico Prenestino. The medieval castle of Passerano stands in an inspired setting.

VILLA ADRIANA

Hadrian's Villa was the largest of the ancient Roman imperial villas. Hadrian oversaw the project for over 20 years, building theaters and libraries as well as tributes to places he had seen in his extensive travel through the eastern provinces. Work ended only four years before Hadrian's death.

Pecile. This huge rectangular quadriporticus was used as a gymnasium; it also contained a garden and had a large pool in the center. Its western side stands atop a tall buttressing, containing the so-called Cento Camerelle, small rooms distributed over four storeys, used either as warehouses or slave quarters.

Terme*. This huge bath house is divided into two sections: the Grandi Terme and Piccole Terme, or Large and Small Baths. The Piccole Terme may have been for women, and were surrounded by courtyards with exedrae and gardens; they comprised a large oblong room, an hall surrounded by smaller roooms, and a "frigidarium," or cold bath. In the Grandi Terme, for men, are the rests of the "frigidarium," with a large open-air rectangular pool and a semicircular basin; the adjacent hall has fine stuccoes in the vault. Grouped around a circular hall in the same complex are various rooms, one of them, the "calidarium," with a pool and three furnaces to heat it.

Canopo. Set in a little man-made valley girt by a wall to the east and by a two-storey row of

A lovely view of Canopo, a long and narrow tank adorned with statues.

rooms to the west, this is an architectural tribute to the Egyptian town of Canopus, famed for its huge Temple of Serapis. Along the edge of the long pool (119x18 m) are column fragments and casts of statues, among which are four caryatids and two Sileni. At the northern extremity, two sculptural groups, the Tiber and the Nile. The Serapeo, or Serapeum, was possibly used as a banquet hall.

Palazzo Imperiale. The ruins of the imperial palace, believed to be the emperor's winter residence because of the discovery of a sophisticated heating system, covers a total area of 50,000 m², comprising three complexes of residential and official rooms, distributed around three peristyles. To the SE is the Piazza d'Oro, or Golden Square, named for the lavish artifacts found here. On the central line of the square is the monumental semicircular Ninfeo di Palazzo, or Palace Nymphaeum, which may have been used as a summertime dining area. Adjacent to it is the Sala dei Pilastri Dorici, or Hall of the Doric Pillars, with a courtyard and fluted pillars.

Teatro Greco. This Greek Theater, near the Ninfeo, the little Tempietto di Venere, and the 18th-century lodge called the Casino Fede, still possesses a few features of the original theater.

TIVOLI

Overlooking the Roman countryside from a ridge of the Tiburtini Mts, Tivoli stands among centuries-old olive groves; the Aniene River runs around it in an oxbow curve, plunging from rocky heights in romantic waterfalls. In Roman times this was a famed vacation spot, with fine climate and natural scenery (among those who spent their summers here were Sallust, Catullus, Horace, and Maecenas); after the 16th century, aristocratic villas gilded the lily, with fountains, grottoes, overlooks, terraces, statues, and brooding rows of cypress trees. Hadrian's Villa lies beneath it.

Villa d'Este**. Built by P. Ligorio in the 16th century for Cardinal Ippolito II d'Este, this building was originally a Benedictine convent; Ligorio also designed the park and many fountains. The fairly rigorous palazzo features halls frescoed by such 16th-century Roman painters as L. Agresti, F. Zuccari, and G. Muziano. From the superb loggia you enjoy a fine view of the garden**, which drops away in symmetrical terraces, clad in rich vegetation and enlivened by numerous fountains and sprays. From the stairway, you climb down past the Fontana del Bicchierone, a fountain perhaps by Bernini (on left, the stuccoed Grotta di Diana), to the entrancing Viale delle 100 Fontane, with fountains and statues. Everywhere are fountains: among them the Fontana di Tivoli, probably by P. Ligorio; Fontana di Roma, with miniature reproductions of Roman buildings; Fontana dei Draghi, also by Ligorio; and the great Fontana dell'Organo. The central avenue ends at the Rotonda dei Cipressi, with its centuries-old cypresses.

S. Maria Maggiore. Founded in the 13th century and rebuilt in the 16th century, this church has a late Gothic portal and rose window; inside, artworks by B. da Montelupo, J. Torriti, and B. da Siena.

S. Pietro alla Carità. Founded in the 5th century, this church boasts handsome columns, possibly taken from Hadrian's Villa, and a Romanesque facade and bell tower. The district in which it is located is dotted with late medieval houses.

S. Silvestro. Situated in the small oblong Piazza del Colonnato, named after its portico of Roman columns, this Romanesque church has an apse decorated with 13th-century frescoes. Not far off, facing the 16th-century church of S. Nicola, is a group of two-storey medieval houses.

Duomo. With a portico dating from 1650 and a medieval Romanesque bell tower, this church possesses some fine artwork, including a large 13th-century group of wood-

Villa d'Este, Tivoli.

en statues of the Deposition* and an exquisite 12th-century triptych (covered, visible only on solemn occasions). Next to the Duomo is an 18th-century washing tank and the Mensa Ponderaria, an ancient Roman public scale, with weights and marble slabs with measures of capacity. Along the steps of the Via del Duomo, lined with medieval houses, you will reach the Palazzo Comunale, rebuilt at the end of the 19th century.

Temple of Vesta*. On the site of the ancient acropolis, on a rocky ridge overlooking the valley with its waterfalls, is a small, round, well-preserved 2nd-century temple, dedicated either to Vesta or to Hercules. Near it is the Tempio di Tiburno, the mythic founder of Tivoli.

Villa Gregoriana*. This immense park is laid out around the waterfall** of the Aniene River (vertical drop of 160 meters). First you descend to the overlook of the Grande Cascata, or great waterfall, where the water plunges from a man-made channel, inaugurated in 1835 by Pope Gregory XVI. Next you tour the Grotta delle Sibille and two other waterfalls – the Cascatelle Piccole and the Cascata Bernini – before reaching the astonishing and deafening main overlook* of the Grande Cascata. Then you continue on to two more grottoes: the Grotta della Sirena, where the water rushes straight down, and the Grotta di Nettuno, heavily encrusted with mineral deposits.

Rocca Pia. This powerful fortress, built by Pius II (1461), dominates Viale Trieste. Near it are the ruins of a huge Roman Imperial Age amphitheater (2C AD). Further east is the 15th-century church of S. Giovanni, with frescoes attributed to A. Romano (1475).

PALESTRINA

When you go to the museum in Palazzo Barberini to see the mosaic depicting the flooding Nile, you will climb the same stairs up which people once climbed to consult the oracle. Medieval in appearance, this site is actually a combination of medieval architecture and the relics of the temple of Fortuna Primigenia, a venerated ancient Roman sanctuary. On the southern slope of Mt Ginestro, a ridge of the Prenestini Mts overlooking the Roman countryside, this complex stands on an ancient road running between the valleys of the Sacco and the Tiber.

Piazza Regina Margherita. This central square probably occupies the site of the Forum in Roman Praeneste. Overlooking it is a monumental, multistorey building, in which you can see remains of ancient walls and four Corinthian semicolumns; a 2nd-century BC inscription identifies the Aerarium, in the basement. From the square, through the door to the left of the seminary, you enter the Area Sacra, a huge basilican space. On the right is the hall with apse, identified as the hall of the oracle. Once the great mosaic of the Nile stood here; it is now in the Museo Archeologico (see below). On the opposite side of the Area Sacra is the so-called Antro delle Sorti, or Cave of Destinies, a natural cavern that has been enlarged and built up, adorned with a mosaic floor depicting the bottom of the sea (1C B.), of which only fragments survive.

Duomo. This cathedral was built on the site of a Roman building made of tufa (possibly the "Iunonarium"), of which some relics survive. Only the facade and the bell tower remain of the original Romanesque structure. In the left aisle is a copy of Michelangelo's Pietà.

Sanctuary*. This monumental complex, dedicated to the goddess Fortuna Primigenia, dating from the mid-2nd century BC was built on man-made terracing. Three terraces rise one above the other: the terrace of the Emicicli, the terrace of the Fornici, and the terrace of the Cortina. Overlooking the last terrace is the spare Palazzo Barberini, built in 1640 and now the site of the Museo Archeologico.

Museo Nazionale Archeologico Prenestino*. This museum comprises collections of artifacts found in the sanctuary and the territory. Particularly interesting pieces are a 4th-century relief (Triumph of Constantine); a large 2nd-century BC statue,* perhaps of Fortune, badly damaged; bronze mirrors* and toiletries, including cylindrical recipients. However, the best piece is the renowned mosaic* of the flooding of the Nile, probably 80 BC.

ANAGNI AND CIOCIARIA

The Ciociaria area extends along the Sacco River between the Mts Ernici and Lepini. The towns through which this route passes – Segni, Anagni, Ferentino, and Alatri – will surprise you with their intense character: all of them are pre-Roman, and seem like a rustic symphony. The land takes its name from Cicero – though the name Ciociaria only appears in the 18th century – who described it as *aspera et montuosa et fidelis et simplex* (harsh, mountainous, faithful, simple).

NOT TO BE MISSED

Palestrina*: the Roman sanctuary of Fortuna Primigenia, perched high on the slope, constitutes the backdrop of the medieval town; even higher, in Palazzo Barberini, is the Museo Archeologico Prenestino. **Valmontone** is partly medieval and sits high on a tufa rise at the confluence of two valleys; the 17th-century Palazzo Doria and the nearby collegiate church of Assunta, rebuilt in 1685-89, are worth a visit. **Segni** lies dark amidst the chestnut groves, staggered down the slope of a spur of the Mts Lepini, with stretches of complex walls, and the renowned Porta Saracena, or Saracen Gate. In the lofty acropolis is a 13th-century church occupying the cella of an ancient temple. **Anagni** (➡ see below) sits high atop a spur overlooking the Sacco Valley; one part of the town has a markedly medieval atmosphere, particularly intense in the "Quartiere dei Caetani. **Ferentino***: pre-Roman walls hold up the old acropolis and the Duomo that occupies its "platea," or plaza; the town is a trove of ancient and medieval structures, including S. Maria Maggiore, a Cistercian Gothic church. **Alatri***: this little medieval city stands on a hill blanketed with olive groves; note the Duomo in the silent tree-lined "piazzale" atop the hill, as well as 2 km of intact polygonal walls. Continue on to Collepardo, with the nearby Grotta dei Bambocci, full of stalactites and stalagmites; there is also the Certosa di Trisulti, an old charterhouse, founded in the 13th century and restored in the 18th century. **Frosinone**, chief town of the Ciociaria, is mostly modern; the old quarter high on the hill overlooks the Piana del Sacco.

ANAGNI

Tradition has it that the god Saturn founded this ancient city perched atop a ridge overlooking the valley of the Sacco River. Later, it became a sort of papal capital. Here a supporter of the French king Philip IV slapped Boniface VIII, who later died of mortification, and another pope, Alexander III, excommunicated the Holy Roman Emperor, Frederick I Barbarossa.

Casa Barnekow. Best known of the many medieval-style houses of Anagni, it actually dates from the 16th century. The name was given by a Swedish nobleman who bought it in the mid-19th century, decorating it with frescoes.

Piazza Cavour. Created around 1560, this handsome square overlooks, like a broad balcony, the city center and the distant valley of the Sacco and has the elegant church of S. Maria di Loreto (1750).

Palazzo Comunale. This building has a Lombard-Romanesque appearance (12C). On the ground floor, a majestic vault leads to the square behind, where markets were held and justice was once meted out.

Cathedral**. One of the most important pieces of Romanesque architecture in Latium, built in 1072-1104 and renovated in the 13th century with Gothic accents, this cathedral stands alone high above the town. The magnificent and lively left side features a loggia topped by a statue of Boniface VIII Caetani, and the outer walls of the Caetani chapel. Note also the baptistery and apses, and a bell tower. Inside is a Cosmatesque floor (1231). In the presbytery, a handsome ciborium* above the altar, a tortile paschal candelabrum*, and the bishop's seat at the end of the apse, are all by P. Vassalletto (1267). In the left nave is the Caetani Gothic chapel. The **crypt**** is decorated with fine frescoes* executed between 1231 and 1255 by Benedictine painters. The chapel of St Thomas Becket was perhaps originally a Roman Mithreum. Adjacent to the Cathedral is the Museo del Tesoro, with a rich treasury.

Palazzo di Bonifacio VIII. Built by Pope Gregory IX, it passed into the hands of the Caetani family in 1295. Note the loggia and mullioned windows on the front, and the high arched buttresses in the back. Inside are numerous halls, some frescoed; in one of these, the famed "Slap of Anagni" took place, when Sciarra Colonna, a supporter of the French king Philip the Fair, struck the pope, Boniface VIII, so roundly despised by Dante. The palazzo also houses a Museum with archeological exhibits and documentation on the history and monuments of Anagni. Not far away is Palazzo Traietto, once the home of Boniface VIII.

Today, the sheer size of Rome and its truly unique urban landscape never fail to astonish visitors and tourists. Rome, the Eternal City, is pervaded by a magical, special atmosphere. Once the capital of the world's largest and longest-lasting empire, today, it is a metropolis where one can 'live' a truly extraordinary cultural experience. The uninterrupted sequence of archeological and Roman Imperial remains and early-Christian, Romanesque, Gothic, Renaissance, Baroque and modern buildings conjure up an overall image of this City of a Hundred Churches, the outward sign of the continuity of a city which, for almost three millennia, has developed basically on the same area of land. You still find the letters S.P.Q.R. (an acronym of the Latin phrase Senatus Populusque Romanus – the Roman Senate and People) imprinted on the seats of the public transport buses and the man-hole covers! This is Rome, a place where time has, in many ways, stood still. Visitors to Rome have many treats in store. Here you can tread in the footsteps of the Caesars, you can kneel before the Pope, you can stroll in places where history was made. Lovers can hold hands in its romantic streets and splendid gardens. The streets are full of music day and night, making the atmosphere in the squares and around its fountains even more delightful. Rome is one of Italy's greenest cities. Life here has an unexpectedly human dimension. There are quiet areas where the air still smells of the countryside and osterie where you can still eat cheaply and sample the very tasty, genuine local cuisine. In Rome, you can feel at home, in a truly majestic setting.

THE HOLY CITY

Il Gesù. Reaction to the Reformation demanded a new model for places of worship, because the new liturgical requirements prescribed settings where the attention of the worshippers focused on the high altar. The prototype was the church of the Santissimo Nome di Gesù, begun in 1568 and based on a design by Vignola. Another architect, G. Della Porta, was entrusted with the facade (1571-77), which also became a model, and it was he who completed the church, consecrated in 1584. Inside, the long nave leading to the presbytery and the apse is crossed by a transept of equal width, dominated by a semi-spherical dome resting on a drum. The triumphal architectural language of late Baroque decorates the interior (1672-85). The fresco by Baciccia (1679), the **Triumph of the Name of Jesus***, uses an unusual aerial perspective technique which seems to ignore the limitations of the dome. A. Pozzo designed the **chapel of St Ignatius Loyola** (in the left transept), where the remains of the Jesuit saint are buried.

Area Sacra dell'Argentina. It is very probable that it was here, on the Ides of March of the year 44 BC, that Julius Caesar was murdered, since Pompey's Curia, where the crime was committed, was also discovered here during excavations in 1926-29. This is the largest archeological complex dating from the Republican period. The remains of four temples were discovered on the site. The round temple in the center is called Temple B and some scholars believe it is the "Aedes Fortunae Huisce Diei" built in 101 BC. Above Temple A, built in the 3rd century BC and restored during Domitian's reign, to the right of the previous one, stands the little church of S. Nicola de Calcarariis, dating from the 8th century. To the left of the round temple are the remains of Temple C, the oldest of the four (early 3C BC). Finally, the road now conceals most of the remains of Temple D (early 2C BC), which was rebuilt in the late Republican period.

S. Andrea della Valle. Rome's tallest dome after that of St Peter's was designed in 1622 by C. Maderno, while the travertine facade was designed by C. Rainaldi and C. Fontana (1656-65). Olivieri was responsible for the luxuriantly decorated, light-filled interior in the shape of a Latin cross, like the Gesù. The *frescoes* in the dome and the apse were the object of fierce rivalry between two painters, G. Lanfranco (Glory of Paradise 1625-28) and Domenichino (*Scenes from the Life of St Andrew and the Six Virtues*). Together, they form one of the finest examples of Baroque decoration in Rome, together with the gigantic frescoes in the tribune by M. Preti (especially the *Crucifixion*).

Palazzo Massimo "alle Colonne". The location of this building, which was B. Peruzzi's last work, on the corner with Via del Paradiso, highlights the *chiaroscuro* effect of the colonnade on the ground floor. The convex rusticated facade follows the line of the Odeon of Domitian which once stood here. The building has a fine horizontal entablature over the **doorway**. The building is still occupied by the original family, who have lived in Rome since the late 10th century and whose founder was none other than Quintus Fabius Maximus the Hesitant, depicted in the frieze in the entrance-hall.

Museo Barracco. The purpose of the collection is to provide an overview of ancient sculpture through works that are representative of their culture. All the most important schools of ancient sculpture are represented (Egypt, the Assyrian Empire, Etruria, Phoenicia, Greece, Rome), with particular emphasis on Egyptian sculpture. In fact, Egyptian art makes up the lion's share (the sculptures date from between 3000 and 30 BC), but the smaller Etruscan section has some fine cippi from Chiusi from the 5th century BC. Many of the sculptures in the Greek section are copies of the originals, from the late 6th century BC to the late 3rd century BC. Roman art is represented by

floor of the courtyard are attributed to Michelangelo. Sangallo also designed the magnificent **atrium**, divided into three aisles, which lead through the building to the **courtyard**. This is surrounded by an arched portico resting on pilasters faced with Doric engaged columns. The famous gallery was frescoed in 1597-1604 by A. Carracci and Domenichino. The frescoes, which depict the **Triumph of Love over the Universe**, represent the transition from the Mannerist to the Baroque style.

Galleria Spada. has retained the typical appearance of private collections of the 17th century. The works are displayed in one or two rows, according to purely decorative criteria. The works, almost all by Italian artists working in the 16th and 17th centuries, are displayed in four large frescoed rooms furnished with antique furniture and marbles. The most interesting works include Boreas

A panoramic view of the Imperial Forums, one of the classic sights in Rome.

sculptures made on the Italian peninsula and from provinces of the Roman Empire.

Palazzo Farnese. Standing on the same square, where the twin fountains are attributed to G. Rainaldi, this splendid building, commissioned by Cardinal A. Farnese (afterwards Paul III), was begun in 1517 by A. da Sangallo the Younger. On his death, supervision of the building work passed to Michelangelo (1546-49) and Vignola (1569-73), but it was under G. Della Porta (1589) that the work was completed. Vignola and Della Porta were responsible for the rear facade, whereas Sangallo designed the facades overlooking the side-roads and the square. However, the **cornice** and the loggia with the Farnese crest above it, together with part of the second floor and the upper

abducting Oreithytia by F. Solimena, the Death of Dido by Guercino, Anthony and Cleopatra by F. Trevisani and a sketch for the frescoes in the church of the Gesù by Baciccia. Look out for the Pietà by O. Borgianni and Masaniello's Revolt in Naples by M. Cerquozzi. The Gallery and the Council of State are housed in **Palazzo Spada**, built in the mid-16th century by G. Merisi, G. da Carpi and G. Mazzoni. Mazzoni was responsible for the fine decoration on the outside of the palazzo and the stuccoes in the courtyard. Here you can see F. Borromini's ingenius *trompe l'oeil* **gallery**, which looks much longer than it actually is (in fact it is only 9 m long). This has been achieved by accentuating the perspective by depicting the floor sloping upwards and the ceiling slop-

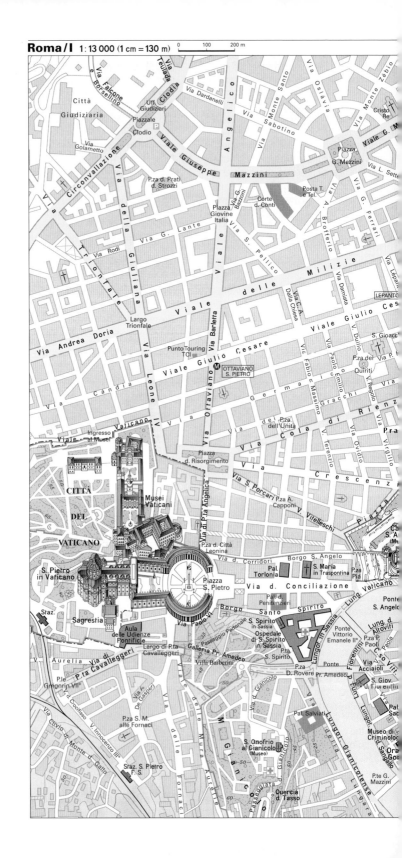

Roma / I 1:13 000 (1 cm = 130 m)

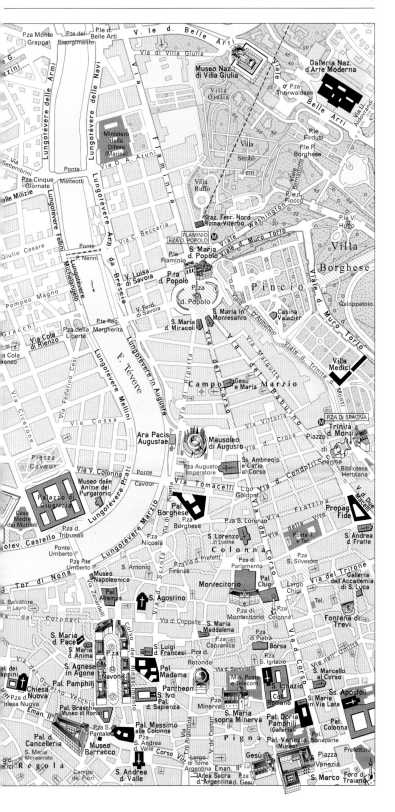

Roma/II 1 : 13 000 (1 cm = 130 m)

0   100   200 m

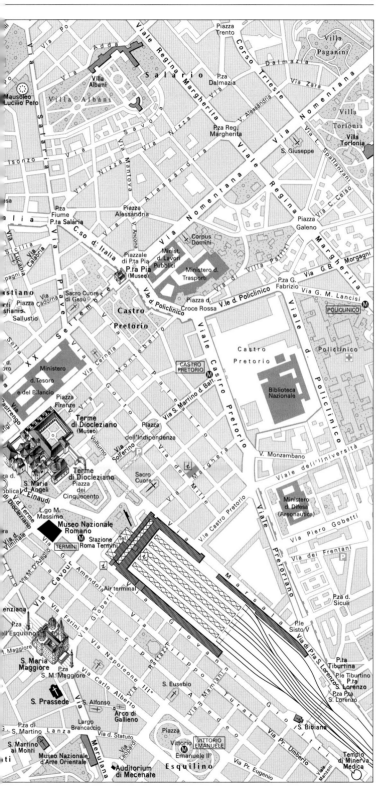

Roma/III

1:13 000 (1 cm = 130 m)

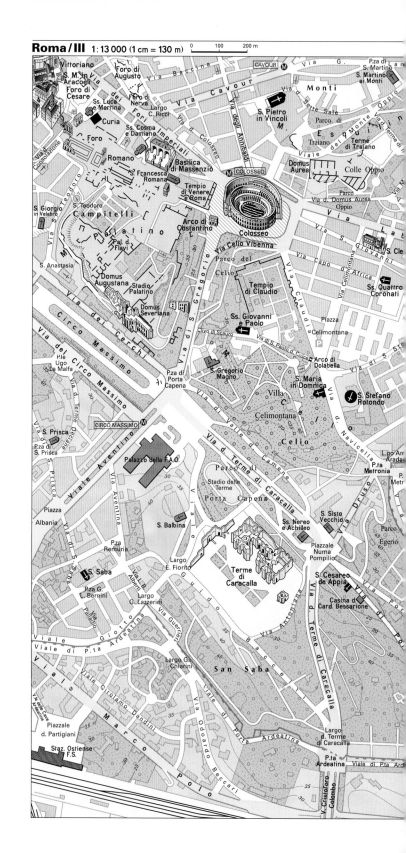

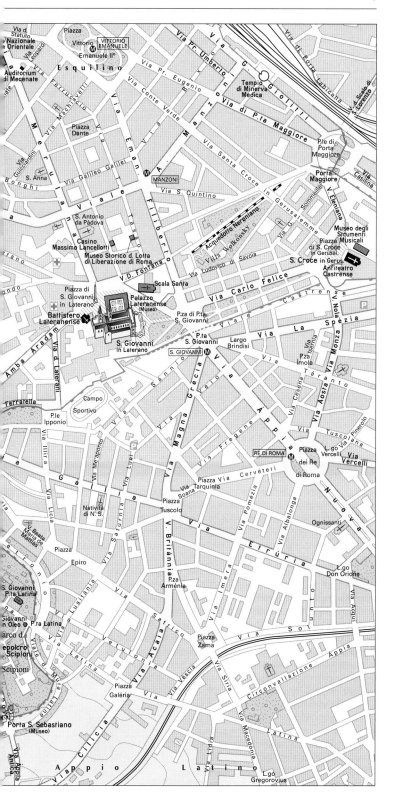

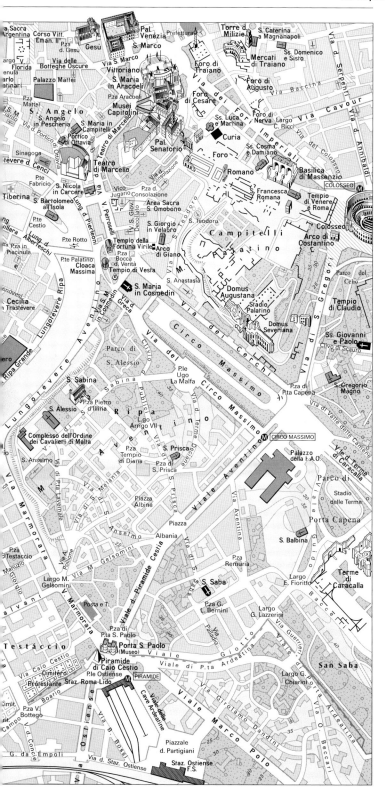

ing downwards between converging walls.

Via Giulia. The long straight road designed in the early 16th century by Bramante was commissioned by Julius II, who imagined it as the setting for the most important buildings of the Holy See. His plan was never fulfilled, but the street has become one of the most noble and beautiful in Rome. This is partly because of the elegant residences on either side, the numerous churches, often linked to the nationalities present in Rome since time immemorial, and its exclusive antiques shops. Like all the historic streets in the capital, the numbers of the houses and shops gradually increase on the left-hand side and decrease on the right-hand side.

Campo de' Fiori. G. Bruno, commemorated in the statue (1887) in the center of the square, was burnt at the stake on February 17, 1600 and was one of many condemned men to be executed here. Although, traditionally, it is thought that the name of the square comes from Flora, Pompey's beloved, the square, which has been a market-place since 1869, probably acquired its name in the late 14th century, when it was abandoned and became a meadow.

Palazzo della Cancelleria. To be sure of having a residence worthy of his rank, Cardinal R. Riario summoned Bramante, who worked mainly on the splendid courtyard. Possibly in the hope that the popes might forget that the Roman Republic of 1849 was proclaimed from this very building, in the Lateran Treaties of 1929 it was declared an exclave of the Vatican, not subject to Italian sovereignty. It still houses the Papal Chancellery and the pope also established the seat of the Tribunal of the Roman Rota here. The most striking feature of the facade is its length, and the fact that it is completely faced in travertine. An elegant **balcony** adorns the curved part of the facade facing Campo de' Fiori and Via del Pellegrino. Inside the building, the **courtyard** mentioned above has three orders of arcades, typical of palazzi in the Urbino area. The first two orders rest on granite columns with Tuscan capitals with rosettes and marble strips with reliefs between series of medallions; the third order consists of a brick wall with alternating pilaster strips and windows.

Museo di Roma in Trastevere. The museum was founded to illustrate the history and life of the city from the Renaissance to the present day through a highly diverse range of exhibits. Sedan chairs used for carrying popes are found alongside works by Baci-

ccia, P. Subleyras, F. Mochi, A. Canova, Roman views by *vedutisti* of the Flemish School, tapestries from Gobelins, costumes dating from the 17th-19th centuries and the famous collection of **watercolors** by E. Roesler Franz depicting views of the Eternal City. The Gabinetto delle Stampe is a valuable collection of prints and drawings showing how the city and the surrounding territory has changed over the centuries. The Gipsoteca Tenerani is a collection of plaster-casts of works by the sculptor.

Chiesa Nuova. Until 1924, the strange fountain of the Terrina which stands in front of the church stood in Campo de' Fiori. When the church was rebuilt, it was based on the church of the Gesù, which was under construction at that time. However, this church differs in many ways from the Gesù prototype. Not so much in terms of the facade (1594-1606) as its interior, where the dome does not stand above the intersection of the transepts, and the side-chapels are connected by a passageway, effectively adding two side-aisles to the single-nave plan. The Baroque decoration of the interior also outstrips in sheer flamboyance that of the church on which it was based. P. da Cortona painted the **frescoes** on the ceiling and designed the stuccoes which frame them. The presbytery contains several masterpieces by P. P. Rubens, painted during his time in Rome (1606-1608). To the left of the presbytery, an extraordinary range of precious marbles adorns the chapel of San Filippo Neri, 1600-1604, where the saint is buried, while the chapel in the **left transept** contains a Presentaion of the Virgin in the Temple by F. Barocci. In the sacristy, the ceiling *frescoes* by P. da Cortona date from 1633-34.

S. Giovanni dei Fiorentini. Leo X consulted all the important architects of the time to work on a design for this church. A. da Sangallo the Younger, B. Peruzzi, Michelangelo and Raphael all competed for the design, but it was J. Sansovino who began to work on the church in 1519. C. Maderno (1602-1620) designed the dome and the transept and A. Galilei (1734) the facade. An imposing row of pillars divides the nave from the side-aisles, and there are five side-chapels on each side. The presbytery is flooded with light from an invisible source. A Baptism of Christ by A. Raggi occupies the center of the huge altar by F. Borromini, who was buried in this very church, as a memorial stone on the third pillar on the left testifies.

Castel S. Angelo. Castel Sant'Angelo began as a grand mausoleum (known as the *Hadrianeum*). It was built at the wishes of the Emperor Hadrian who wanted his remains to be buried there, along with those of his family. Begun in about 123, the mausoleum may have been designed by the emperor himself. He had the *Pons Aelius*, subsequently called **Ponte S. Angelo**** (133-134), built across the Tiber to provide access. The finishing touches to the bridge were added by G. L. Bernini and his school (in the 17th century, Bernini designed the statues and decided how they should be arranged). The mausoleum was completed by Antoninus Pius. It began as a round building on a square base, on top of which was another smaller round tower. Inside, three great superimposed halls, which you can still see, were built to house the Imperial tombs, with a double spiral ramp, part of which has survived. Aurelian transformed the mausoleum into a fortified stronghold, surrounding it with defensive walls and towers. It continued its defensive role, and was also used as a prison, in the following centuries. During the revolt of 1379, the Romans occupied it with the intention of razing it to the ground and the popes transferred their most secret archives there, along with the treasury of the Church. The outward appearance of the complex is the result of restoration work carried out in the late 19th century and in 1933-34. Note the four large corner towers set into the square defensive walls, added by Nicholas V and Alexander VI. If you stand at the end of Ponte S. Angelo, the tower on the right is that of San Giovanni and the one on the left is that of San Matteo. On the far side, the two corresponding corner towers are those of San Luca and San Marco. The curtain wall between the towers of San Giovanni and San Luca contains the reconstructed entrance to the castle. Inside, the old round base of the castle, with the square tower above, stands next to the papal apartments built in the Renaissance, facing the Tiber River. Up on the terrace stands the statue of the Archangel Michael sheathing his sword. The **Museo Nazionale di Castel S. Angelo**** certainly contains interesting collections of ceramics, ancient weapons, furnishings and Renaissance paintings. But the most fascinating aspect of the museum (rather like participating live in a virtual game) is that you are walking about in buildings which, in some cases, are more than 2,000 years old. One minute you are in a room of Roman Imperial date and the next you find yourself in one that was frescoed in

the 16th century in the Mannerist style. Just beyond the entrance is the **ambulatory** which Boniface IX had built between the rounded wall of the castle and the square defensive walls. But, in no time, you are taken back at least ten centuries, when, at the gateway opposite Ponte S. Angelo, a flight of steps leads down to the **dromos**, on the same level as the *Hadrianeum*. A scale model shows which are the oldest parts of the building. Another very early feature is the **spiral ramp** which leads up to the right to the **straight passageway**. Beyond the **sepulchral cella** where the urns containing the Imperial ashes were kept, you come to the **Cortile d'Onore** or dell'Angelo and the statue of the Archangel Michael created by R. da Montelupo in 1544. To the right is the **Armeria Antica (Museum of Arms and Armor)**, while, on the left, the **Rooms of Clement VI-II** and the **Hall of Apollo** are decorated with grotesques. From here, you can also access the **Hall of Justice**, which is the second of the three rooms above the *Hadrianeum*. The **Rooms of Clement VII**, next to the Hall of Apollo, house a small art gallery, including paintings by N. di Liberatore, C. Crivelli, L. Signorelli and M. Fogolino. From the **Cortile del Pozzo**, where there is a charming 15th-century well, a narrow flight of stairs leads up to the beautifully decorated **bathroom of Clement VII**. Another doorway marks the entrance to the **historical prisons**, and a staircase descends to the castle's **provisions stores**, with 84 oil jars and 5 round grain silos. Stairs lead up from the courtyard to the elegant **Loggia of Paul III**, decorated with grotesques (1543). This is possibly the best place to observe the pentagonal outer defensive walls, with their bastions, and the castle moat. The **Giretto of Pius IV (views)** lead to the **Loggia of Julius II**, attributed to G. da Sangallo and facing Ponte S. Angelo, the entrance to the elegant rooms of the **Apartments of Paul III*** which were frescoed in 1542-49. Beyond the **Hall of the Library**, where dignitaries were received, the **Room of the mausoleum of Hadrian** was named after the frieze showing an idealistic depiction of the mausoleum in 1545. Nearby, the **Room of the Festoons** leads to the **Cagliostra**, formerly the loggia of the apartment of Paul II. In the **Room of the Treasury**, which is accessed from the Hall of the Library and which corresponds to the third room of the Roman mausoleum, the secret papal archives were kept in the walnut-wood cabinets set into the walls. The last part of the

Imperial monument is the **Round Hall**, which can be reached by an ancient staircase. At the top is the large terrace situated below the bronze statue of the Archangel Michael, placed here in 1752 to replace the marble statue by Raffaello da Montelupo. To the left, the Campana della Misericordia used to be rung to announce the execution of capital sentences. The **views**** from the terrace are breathtaking.

S. Pietro, Many say that **Via della Concilia-zione***, the broad, straight approach to St Peter's, is the most beautiful street in Rome. It leads symbolically into Piazza S. Pietro and the heart of the Eternal City.

Piazza San Pietro** (St Peter's Square), is one of the places where the Pope appears in public, a huge area enclosed by the double *colonnade* designed by G. L. Bernini. Occupied by churches and oratories at the time of the old basilica, the oval square was laid out in 1656-67. Each of the two colonnades has a quadruple row of columns (there are 284 of them, and 88 pillars), converging on a central point so that anyone standing there sees only one row of columns, so perfectly are they aligned. Many of the wax models for the 140 statues of saints crowning the portico also bear Bernini's signature.

Enormous efforts were required when, on the orders of Sixtus V, the great **Obelisk** was placed in the center of the square. Domenico Fontana was put in charge of the operation. Ordinary ropes were used for lifting the obelisk into place and, once the spectators had been silenced, work began. Caligula had brought it to Rome from Alexandria in 37 AD, to adorn the Circus of Nero. The crowd should have remained silent until the operation was completed, but a sailor called Bresca, who realized that some of the ropes were about to give way, interrupted, shouting "*acqua alle funi*" (put water on the ropes), thus preventing the huge stone from falling. The Pope rewarded him by granting his family the privilege of supplying the Vatican with palms for Palm Sunday.

The bronze lions are by P. Antichi, The fountain on the right of the obelisk is by C. Maderno (1613) and the one on the left by C. Fontana (1677).

The **Basilica of S. Pietro****, the revered heart of the Papacy and all Christianity, is the first and most important church of the city known as the "City of a Hundred Churches". A few figures may help the visitor to comprehend its awesome proportions. It covers a total area of 22,067 m², making it the largest church in the world. From the ground to the top of the cross above Michelangelo's dome, it is 136 m high, and the diameter of the dome is 42 m. The historical events which, over the centuries, led to the church we see today, date back to the beginnings of Christianity. The first basilica, built during the reign of Emperor Constantine, was begun in about 320 and, having been consecrated by Pope Sylvester I in 326, was completed in 349. In the mid-15th century, Nicholas V entrusted B. Rossellino (1452) with the radical rebuilding of the church. But it was Julius II who, in 1506, launched the building work in earnest. He summoned Bramante, and other architects who opted alternately for a new church built on a Greek-cross (Bramante himself, B. Peruzzi and Michelangelo) or a Latin-cross plan (Raphael and A. da Sangallo the Younger). It was Paul V who eventually decided in favor of the Latin-cross plan. The job of extending the basilica was given to C. Maderno, who completed it in 1614. On November 18, 1626, on the 1,300th anniversary of its first consecration, it was officially opened for worship by Urban VIII. G. L. Bernini, who succeeded Maderno, would have liked to add two bell towers to the facade, but various problems made this impossible. As far as the **exterior** of the church is concerned, G. L. Bernini designed the broad, triple **flight of steps**. At either side stand the two large statues of St Peter and St Paul. Carlo Maderno's **facade** is crowned in the middle by a tympanum and spanned by eight columns with pillars at the sides. A portico forms the lower part of the facade, with archways at each end (the left archway leads into the Vatican City). The upper part of the facade is decorated by a balustrade with 13 statues of the Redeemer, St John the Baptist and eleven of the Apostles, except St Peter, and has nine large windows with balconies. The name of the newly elected Pope is announced from the central balcony and is where the new Pope gives his blessing (it is known as the Loggia delle Benedizioni). Michelangelo never saw his **dome**** finished. When he died, only the drum had been completed. The double shell of the dome, divided by trusses into 16 sections, was completed by G. Della Porta and D. Fontana (1588-89). Vignola added the two side-domes, which are purely decorative. In the **portico**, beyond the door on the far right which leads into the Vestibule of the Scala Regia, you can see the equestrian statue of Constantine (Bernini, 1670). The original inscription with the papal seal of Boniface VIII proclaiming the first Jubilee, or Holy Year, (1300) can be seen above the Porta Santa. The bronze **doors** in the central doorway, decorated by Filarete (1439-45), are from Constantine's basilica. Above the central doorway of the portico is the mosaic of the Navicella, executed by Giotto in 1298 but completely reworked in the 17th century. **Inside** the basilica, the artistic masterpieces and the places associated with particular historical events are part and parcel of the fabric of the building.

On Christmas night in the year 800, Charlemagne knelt on the large porphyry disk in the **nave** to receive official approval and the Imperial crown from Leo III. The bronze **statue of St Peter** sits below the huge **dome***. Four pentagonal piers sustain the massive arches supporting the drum. The pilaster strips between the 16 windows support a cornice at the base of the top of the dome which is divided into 16 segments. The six orders of mosaic decoration and the statues at the base of the piers are extraordinary. Above them, four balconies by Bernini have the church's most precious relics.

"*Quod non fecerunt barbari, fecerunt Barberini*" (What the Barbarians didn't achieve was achieved by Barberini). This gibe refers to the fact that Urban VIII Barberini removed the bronzes from the pronaos of the Pantheon and had them melted down to construct the imposing **canopy** (29 m high) above the high altar of St Peter's. Bernini was assisted in this task (1624-33) by Duquesnoy, G. Finelli and, for the architectural part of the project, F. Borromini. Among the vine-tendril decoration

The facade of St Peter's Basilica.

of the spiral columns are the bees of the Barberini family (the sun and bees are the symbols of the Barberini family, to which Urban VIII belonged). 99 eternal flames illuminate the "tomb of Peter" in the **confession** below. In the first chapel of the **right aisle**, decorated like many others and like the transept with 18th-century mosaics, a glass screen protects the **Pietà****, the white marble sculpture (1498-99) considered to be one of Michelangelo's finest works, carved when he was only 25. Under the first arch of the right aisle, below the statue of Leo XII (1836), is Bernini's chapel of the Reliquaries, also called the chapel of the Crucifix because of the beautiful wooden crucifix attributed to P. Cavallini. To the left is the funerary monument to Queen Christina of Sweden by C. Fontana. The second chapel contains the monument to Pius XII, while, under the arch of the aisle, the tomb of Innocent XII is situated opposite the monument to Countess Matilda of Canossa, designed by Bernini. The Neapolitan artist is also responsible for the gilded bronze *ciborium* (1674) in the large chapel of the Blessed Sacrament, decorated by gilded stuccoes and barred by a gate (by Borromini). On the right, under the third arch of the aisle is the monument to Gregory XIII (1720-23); on the left, the tomb of Gregory XIV. The four chapels below a dome mark the corners of the **ambulatory** in the style of Michelangelo, which winds its way around the piers supporting it. The **monument to Clement XIII** (1784-92) is one of A. Canova's best works. To complete the symbolic and dramatic effect of the canopy, Bernini placed the **Chair of St Peter*** in the **apse** (or tribune). This enormous gilded bronze throne is supported at the corners by statues of the Fathers of the Church, and

a gilded stucco gloria draws attention to the symbol of the Holy Spirit. It encloses an old wooden chair which may have been the throne of Charles II the Bald (9C). Bernini also executed the **monument to Urban VIII** (1627-47), while the **statue of Paul III** (1551-75) is by G. Della Porta. A marble altar-piece stands above the altar with relics of Pope Leo the Great. The sacristy leads into the **Sacristy of the Canonici**, next to a chapel with a painting by Giulio Romano of the Madonna and Child and St John the Baptist by G. Romano. Would you expect to find a work by a Protestant artist in St Peter's? Believe it or not, the tomb of Pius VII (1823) in the Clementine chapel is by the Danish sculptor B. Thorvaldsen. There is a copy of Raphael's Transfiguration on the pillar of the dome on the corner of the **left-hand aisle**. The dome of the chapel of the choir by C. Maderno is richly decorated with gilded stuccoes. The chapel contains the gilded bronze **tomb of Innocent VIII**.

The upside-down porphyry lid of an old sarcophagus, which was

Sistine Chapel, detail of the Creation of Adam.

probably used for the tomb of Hadrian and then that of Otto II, forms the font of the baptistery. Although visitors to St Peter's should not miss the **Museo Storico Artistico-Tesoro di S. Pietro* (Treasury)**, it was seriously depleted by the raids of the Saracens in 846, the Sack of Rome in 1527 and the treaty concluded with Napoleon in 1797. It contains the Colonna Santa, once thought to be the column against which Christ leaned in the Temple of Solomon (actually dates from the 4C); the so-called dalmatic of Charlemagne, which is actually Byzantine; the famous Crux Vatcana, a gift from the Emperor Justinian II of the Eastern Empire to Rome (6C); the **monument to Sixtus IV*** signed by Pollaiolo (1493); the **sarcophagus of Junius Bassus**, Prefect of Rome in 359. It was the excavations of the **Sacred Vatican Grottoes**** which threw light on the foundation of the first basilica. Traditionally it was thought that the first church had been built above the ruins of the Circus of Nero, where Peter was

martyred, but the excavations conducted by Pius XII found no trace of the circus but necropolises dating from the 1st to 4th centuries. However, it is the chapel of St Peter, built above the Apostle's tomb, that forms the nucleus of the **New Grottoes**, created when the floor of the church was raised to build the new church and arranged in a semi-circle around St Peter's tomb. Extensions from a later period lead to the oratories situated at the base of the piers supporting the dome and the five chapels. The **Old Grottoes** date from 1606 and consist of three corridors with low ceilings supported by massive pillars, which extend for about 50 m below the nave of the church. In the right-hand aisle, a small, round chapel contains the tomb of Pope John XXIII, next to those of Queen Christina of Sweden and Queen Charlotte of Cyprus; at the end of the same aisle are the tombs of Boniface VIII and Nicholas III, who was laid to rest in an early-Christian sarcophagus. The central aisle contains a monument to Pius VI (1821-22).

Visitors wishing to make the **ascent to St Peter's dome**** may either climb the stairs or take advantage of the lift to the terrace, which has **views** over St Peter's Square and the city beyond. From here, 330 steps lead up to the round corridor inside the dome where you can almost touch the mosaics. A steeper spiral staircase leads up to the loggia at the top of the lantern, where there are marvelous **views**** over Rome and, on a clear day, to the Apennines and the sea.

Vatican City. This city of museums is proof of the fact that the popes were some of the most prodigious patrons of Italian art. The **Cortile della Pigna** is named after the huge bronze **fir-cone** which now stands in front of the niche designed by Bramante on a floor of the double staircase. Dating from Roman times, it is mentioned in D. Alighieri's "Divine Comedy". The courtyard, in the center of which is a contemporary sculpture called Sphere within a Sphere, is part of the much larger Cortile del Belvedere, designed by Bramante to connect the palace of Innocent VIII to the Vatican Palace. The courtyard was divided in 1587-88 when D. Fontana built a new wing for the library. The first of the papal art collections is in the **Pinacoteca Vaticana****, the gallery opened by Pius VI in 1816. It contains paintings with mainly religious themes from the various papal palaces, which are now arranged chronologically and according to the various schools of painting. Early paintings include the *Last Judgement* (11-12C) and the *Legend of St Stephen* by B. Daddi; paintings by Giotto and his School are represented by the famous **Stefaneschi polyptych***, painted by Giotto for the Basilica of St Peter, along with works by P. Lorenzetti, S. Martini, G. da Fabriano and Sassetta. The Tuscan painters F. Lippi, B. Gozzoli and B. Angelico precede masterpieces by M. da Forlì, E. de' Roberti, L. Cranach the Elder and a group of *polyptychs* and *works* by the 15th-century Umbrian School. Visitors to the gallery tend to cluster around Raphael's masterpieces: the 10 **tapestries*** commissioned from him by Leo X for the Sistine Chapel (1515-16); the **Transfiguration****, his splendid **Madonna of Foligno***, painted in 1512-13, and his **Coronation of the Virgin** (1503). L. da Vinci's **St Jerome** (ca. 1480) precedes works executed in the 16th-17th-century works include Caravaggio's **Deposition*** (1602-1604), Domenichino's *Communion of St Jerome* and G. Reni's *Crucifixion of St Peter*, an expression of the Baroque style which was to permeate many 18th-century works, such as the paintings by G. M. Crespi and F. Mancini. When ancient finds began to emerge from excavations across the Papal States, there was a veritable stampede on the part of the popes to claim them. Much of the Greek and Roman material displayed in the five sections of the **Museo Gregoriano Profano*** comes from this source. Greek originals in the collection include the Attic **stele by Palestritos*** (mid-5C BC), **fragments of sculptures from the Parthenon** and a **head of Athena** in the style of Magna Graecia (mid-5C BC). Perhaps the most important example of copies and re-stylings of Greek originals is the **Chiaramonti Niobid**. Roman sculpture of the 1st and 2nd centuries is represented by a relief depicting personifications of the Etruscan cities of *Tarquinia*,

Vulci and *Vetulonia*, as well as the relief of the **altar of Vicomagistri** (ca. 30-40) and the 39 **fragments** from the sepulchral monument of the Haterii.

The **Museo Pio Cristiano** contains other interesting architectural features, sculptures and mosaics. The **Museo Gregoriano Egizio*** puts the exhibits into context by relating them to the dynasties which succeeded each other on the throne, with inscriptions ranging from 2600 BC to the 6th century. There are numerous sculptures, sarcophagi and funerary steles, documents and other finds associated with funeral rituals and many works from the Roman period inspired by Egyptian art. The **Museo Chiaramonti**, which occupies about half of the gallery (300 m long) designed by Bramante, contains Roman copies of Greek originals as well as original works. The **Galleria Lapidaria** comprises about 4,000 pagan and Christian inscriptions collected by Clement XIV, Pius VI and Pius VII. The **Braccio Nuovo (New Wing)**, the floor of which incorporates some 2nd-century **mosaics**, contains the most interesting works, nearly all of which are copies of original Greek sculptures: the **statue of Augustus of Prima Porta***, a copy of a bronze original, the *Wounded Amazon*, a Roman copy of a Greek original, **The Nile**, a statue dating from the 1st century, and the **Doryphoros**, a Roman copy of a Greek original by Polikleitus. The **Museo Pio-Clementino*** has some remarkable Greek and Roman sculptures including the famous **Apoxyomenos***, a Roman replica of a bronze original by Lysippos (4C). From the room behind the statue, you can see **Bramante's spiral staircase**. In the Octagonal Courtyard, the recesses at the four corners of the portico contain some fine statues: the **Apollo Belvedere****, created in the Roman Imperial period and based on an original dating from the 4th century BC, attributed to Leochares, the famous **Laocoön****, a 1st-century Greek marble copy of a Hellenistic original, a **Hermes**, and a **Perseus** by Canova. The Galleria delle Statue contains more ancient statues, including the **Apollo Sauroctonos**, a Roman copy of a bronze by Praxiteles; the **Barberini candelabra** (2C) are a splendid pair. Portraits of Roman emperors and divinities crowd the Sala dei Busti (Gallery of Busts). The Gabinetto delle Maschere (Mask Room) has 2nd-century polychrome *mosaics* of theatrical masks in the floor, as well as the beautiful **Venus of Cnidos**, a fine replica of a work by Praxiteles. Another masterpiece in these museums is the famous **Belvedere Torso*** (1C BC). It was discovered in the early 15th century and influenced many Renaissance artists, especially Michelangelo, who used it as a model for his frescoes of decorative nude figures (the *Ignudi*) in the Sistine Chapel. Other exhibits worth noting are the **Jupiter of Otricoli**, a 1st-century copy of a 4th-century BC Greek original and the two large, 4th-century red-porphyry **sarcophagi of Costantina** (Constantine's daughter) and **St Helena**, Constantine's mother. Few other museums in the world illustrate so completely the mysterious culture of the Etruscans. The finds displayed in the **Museo Gregoriano Etrusco***, come mainly from tombs and other graves found in the north of Lazio (19C). And, completing the cultural overview of the period between the Early Iron Age Etruscan finds from Lazio (9-8C BC) and the Hellenistic period, is a fine collection of Greek and Italiot vases. Some of the pieces are unique: the famous **Mars of Todi***, a late-5th-century BC bronze statue, the **Guglielmi collection** of Etruscan and Greek bronzes and vases, and about 800 pieces dating from the Villanova culture and the Hellenistic period, as well as the **black-figure amphora** of Exekias. The collections in the **Galleria degli Arazzi** and the **Galleria delle Carte Geografiche**, which precede the Raphael Rooms, are named after the exhibits they contain. The first has tapestries made in Brussels in the 16th century. The second gallery was frescoed in 1580-83 with maps which provide interesting insight into geographical knowledge in the late 16th century and Rome's role as the geographical center of the whole Italian peninsula. The **Raphael Rooms**** are one of the things you must see in the Vatican Museums since they represent one of the most important phases of Italian painting. In 1508, Julius II commissioned the young Raphael to decorate this part of the Vatican. After his death, his assistants continued the work until 1525. The painter from Urbino left drawings and instructions for the decoration of the **Sala di Costantino** for G. Romano, R. del Colle and G. F. Penni. Beyond the **Sala dei Palafrenieri**, the room after the Sala di Costantino, and the **chapel of Nicholas V**, where there are **frescoes** by B. Angelico, is the first room frescoed by Raphael himself (1512-14). This is the **Stanza di Eliodoro**, where the **subject-matter of the painting**, which glorifies the Church, was probably suggested by Julius II. The **Stanza della Segnatura** was also entire-

ly decorated by Raphael (1509-11), except for some of the ceiling decoration which was executed by Il Sodoma and Bramantino. The **frescoes**, in which the Humanist ideas associated with the Neo-Classic tradition converge with 15th-century probings into perspective, are among his finest masterpieces. In the **Stanza dell'Incendio**, completed during the pontificate of Leo X, Raphael's assistants based the wall **frescoes** on the cartoons and drawings of their master. The paintings on the ceiling are by Perugino. When Sixtus IV decided to build the **Sistine Chapel**** (1475-81), he could not have imagined that this rectangular space with a low ceiling would become the setting for one of the finest expressions of Renaissance painting. Having commissioned M. da Fiesole, A. Bregno and G. Dalmata to make the *rood screen* and the *balustrade* of the chancel, the Pope summoned (1481-83) some of the most skilful masters of the time (S. Botticelli, L. Signorelli, P. di Cosimo, Perugino, D. Ghirlandaio and Pinturicchio) to paint the frescoes on the side-walls and opposite the altar. In 1506, Julius II took over the project, entrusting its completion to Michelangelo who, between 1508 and 1512, frescoed the ceiling and, under the pontificate of Paul III, the back wall of the chapel. The bottom of the side-walls and the wall opposite the altar are decorated with *fake drapes*. The tapestries by Raphael, now in the Pinacoteca of the Vatican Museums, used to hang above them. The middle part of the side-walls are decorated with *Scenes from the Life of Moses* (right) and *Scenes from the Life of Christ* (left). Between the windows, the top of the side-walls and the wall opposite the altar are decorated with 24 *portraits of popes*. A vast painting cycle covers the ceiling, an extraordinary fusion of architectural and sculptural features, emphasized by the brilliant use of color. The composition is organized into three superimposed registers. The central part of the ceiling illustrates nine of the **Stories of Genesis***. Starting at the panel above the altar: *The Separation of Light from Darkness, the Creation of the Sun, the Moon and the Planets, the Separation of the Land and the Sea and the Creation of the Fishes and the Birds*, the magnificent **Creation of Adam***, *the Creation of Eve, Temptation and Expulsion from Paradise, the Sacrifice of Noah, the Flood* and *the Drunkenness of Noah*. Between the panels, framed by a marble structure, are decorative male figures (called **Ignudi***) holding medallions. On the lower, curved part of the

Raphael's School of Athens in the Stanza della Segnatura.

vault are the powerful *figures of Sybils and Prophets* enthroned. Other *Biblical scenes* are depicted in the triangular spaces at the corners of the ceiling of the lower register, while the *forerunners of Christ* are depicted in the vaults and lunettes above the windows. A majestic composition moving within a space without limitations: this is how Michelangelo painted the frescoes on the back wall in 1536-41. In his magnificent and awesome **Last Judgement****, he exceeded every iconographic ideal and every concept of perspective of Renaissance art. The composition is dominated by the majestic figure of **Christ the Supreme Judge**, next to the *Virgin Mary* surrounded by the *Saints*, *Patriarchs* and *Martyrs* who throng Paradise; on the right, the *Elect ascend into Heaven*, while, on the left, the *Damned are cast into Hell where Charon and Minos await them*. In the lower part of the composition: on the left, the *Resurrection of the Dead*, in the center, *Angels blowing the Trumpets of Judgement*, and, above, in the lunettes, *Angels with the Symbols of the Passion*. (The nude figures were covered in 1564 by D. da Volterra at the wishes of Pius IV, who found their nudity distasteful). It is also interesting to visit the **Biblioteca Apostolica Vaticana (Vatican Library)**. The richly decorated **Salone Sistino*** contains 75,000 manuscripts, 70,000 documents from the archives, 100,000 separate autographs, and more than 800,000 volumes. These form the basis of the library created by Sixtus IV in 1475.

AROUND VIA DEL CORSO

S. Maria sopra Minerva. In 1280, the church was rebuilt on Gothic lines, although it has been altered many times since. In the 17th century, the original Gothic facade was replaced with one with three doorways. The interior (a nave and two side-aisles with cross-vaulting, a transept and two chapels at either side of the presbytery) is the result of work done in 1848-1855. The **furnishings** are some of the richest in Rome and reflect the development of art in the city from the late 13th century to the turn of the 17th century. In the right transept, the archway over the entrance to the **Carafa chapel** and the **fresco decoration** by F. Lippi (1488-93) are quite remarkable. The **statue of the Resurrected Christ*** (1519-21) by the left-hand pillar of the presbytery is by Michelangelo, near the choir are the **funerary monuments of Clement VII** and **Leo X**, by A. da Sangallo the Younger in 1536-41.

The Pantheon, This remarkable building is one of the most famous ancient monuments in the world and the best-preserved in Rome. It constitutes a brilliant example of building technique, an ingenius combination of the domed rotunda often used in Roman bath-complexes, and the traditional pronaos with a tympanum often used to front Neo-Classic temples. It was built by Marcus Vipsanius Agrippa, the son-in-law of Augustus, in 27 DC, but was later rebuilt by Hadrian in 118-125. With the fall of the Roman Empire, the temple was abandoned until 608, when Boniface IV decided to dedicate it to the Madonna and all the Martyrs. Subsequently it was used as a fortress. In 1625, Urban VIII Barberini removed the bronze from the beams of the portico to make 80 canons for Castel Sant'Angelo and the 4 twisted columns supporting the canopy in St Peter's. When Rome became capital of Italy, it was designated as the burial place of Italy's sovereigns. The 16 monolithic columns of the pronaos are of gray and pink granite. Beyond them is the doorway (the bronze *doors* were repaired by Pius IV in the 16C) and two niches which probably contained statues of Augustus and Agrippa. Inside, there are seven rectangular and semi-circular recesses, preceded by pairs of grooved columns of *giallo antico* and *pavonazzetto* marble, and interspersed with shrines; an eighth recess preceded by an archway stands opposite the entrance. The concrete ceiling is decorated by five orders of coffers, the bronze-rimmed oculus being the only source of daylight in the building. Most of the marble *floor*, with its square and circular motifs, is original. The church contains the *tombs of Victor Emmanuel II* (last king of Sardinia, first king of Italy) and *Raphael*, a re-use of a Greek marble sarcophagus. It was Raphael himself who commissioned Lorenzetto to carve the statue of the **Madonna del Sasso** to his own design.

Piazza Navona. If you view it from above or look at a plan of this famous square, so dear to the heart of Italian and American movie directors, who have used it for many scenes in their movies, you can see what it was originally. In fact, it stands above the *stadium of Domitian*, built in about 86 AD, with a seating capacity of about 30,000. From roughly the 13th century onwards, small houses and fortified buildings were erected here, and were subsequently joined by churches and palaces. In 1477, the market previously held on the Capitoline Hill was moved here. Its name probably derives from the athletic games once held here, the *Agoni Capitolini*: *agone*, meaning competition, was transformed into *nagone* and then *navone*. However, it is also possible that it comes from the shape of the square, which vaguely resembles a ship (*nave*) and the fact that, in the 17th-19th centuries, its concave floor used to be flooded for the processions of the retinues of prelates and princes in August. The tradition of selling sweets and toys between December and Epiphany is still alive today. One of the square's most famous features is the famous **Fountain of the Four Rivers****. The proverbial rivalry between G. L. Bernini and F. Borromini gave rise to the saying that the allegorical figures of the great rivers at the corners of Bernini's fountain (the *Nile*, the *Ganges*, the *Danube* and the *Rio de la Plata*) look appalled at the sight of Borromini's

church of S. Agnese in Agone. Set on a rock, (1651) the obelisk brought to Rome under Domitian was originally located in the Circus of Maxentius. Bernini also designed the *Fountain of the Moor*, named after the central figure, an Ethiopian, who is wrestling with a dolphin. G. Della Porta (1576) designed the *Fountain of Neptune*, to which decorative sculptures were added in 1878.

S. Agnese in Agone. According to the legend, when the saint was exposed to public ridicule on this spot, her hair miraculously fell down, covering her body. The church was reputedly built on the site of the miracle between the 8th century and 1123. However, the present church was begun in 1652 by G. and C. Rainaldi, and was completed in 1653-57 by F. Borromini. He gave it a concave facade with a single order of pillars and columns, a dome and twin bell towers. Baciccia worked on the *pendentives* (1665) and C. Ferri frescoed the inside of the *dome* in 1689. The monument above the entrance is dedicated to Innocent X, who is buried, along with other members of the Pamphilj family, in a crypt to the left of the *high altar* (1730). Below the church you can see some remains of Domitian's stadium, a Roman mosaic floor, a marble relief by A. Algardi depicting the miracle of St Agnes and some medieval frescoes.

S. Maria della Pace. This little church with its beautiful facade is situated in a corner of Rome that many tourists tend to miss. P. da Cortona designed this corner in the Baroque style, using the convex facade of the church as a sort of theatrical backdrop so that the church blends with the nearby houses. At the same time, an indissoluble link is established between the actual square, into which the semi-circular pronaos of the church protrudes, and the interior of the church. The interior has retained its late 15th-century appearance: a short nave with two bays with cross-vaults, and a tribune with a dome. The nave is decorated with *works* by Raphael, B. Peruzzi, A. and G. da Sangallo the Younger, S. Mosca, P. da Cortona, C. Maratta and C. Maderno. The **cloister***, D. Bramante's first project in Rome (1500-1504), is surrounded by a portico with arches resting on pillars with pilaster strips in the Ionic style, supporting an entablature with a long, heavily indented frieze.

Piazza Navona, which occupies the site of Domitian's ancient stadium.

Lazio/Rome

HERITAGE

Via dei Coronari. The name of the street derives from the merchants who sold sacred images and crowns (in Italian *corone*) to pilgrims here. Antique shops have taken their place. This fact, and the small squares added in 1939, are the only changes in this street, which has otherwise retained its Renaissance and Baroque appearance.

S. Agostino. The facade of this church, founded in 1420 and enlarged in 1479-83, is typical of the early Renaissance. It has two orders of pilaster strips joined by volutes, dividing it into three parts, with three doorways. The interior was renovated by Luigi Vanvitelli (1756-61), who replaced the semi-spherical dome with a bowl-shaped vault. P. Gagliardi (1856) painted the frescoes of the *Prophets* on the pillars, except the one on the 3rd pillar on the left (**Isaiah**), which is by Raphael (1512). Below, the **Madonna and Child with St Anne** is by A. Sansovino (1512). On the high altar (1627), designed by G. L. Bernini, is a Byzantine *Madonna*. In the first chapel on the left, the altar-piece of the **Madonna di Loreto** was painted by Caravaggio in 1603-1604. The much revered statue of the **Madonna del Parto** (1521), to the left of the central doorway, is by J. Sansovino.

Palazzo Altemps. It is hard to say whether the success of the annex of the Museo Nazionale Romano is due more to the building or its contents (Renaissance sculptures, including the famous Ludovisi collection). The residence of the Altemps family was built in 1471 over the foundations of medieval houses and other buildings, around a **courtyard** with two loggias, in the typical Renaissance style. Inside the palazzo, the **Sala della Piattaia** was painted in about 1477. The **painted Loggia** or **gallery** reflects the vogue for magnificence and the exotic sparked off by the discovery of the New World. Some **examples of ancient sculpture** are exhibited here, including the famous **Ludovisi throne*** (5C BC) and the **Galatian's suicide***.

Mausoleo di Augusto. The tomb of Octavian, begun in 27 BC, was originally built as a tomb for the emperor and members of his family. It fell into ruin in Late Antiquity but was restored when Piazza Augusto Imperatore was laid out in 1936-38. Little remains of it today. Outside, the massive tumulus was once planted with cypresses. It had obelisks on either side of the entrance, now in Piazza dell'Esquilino and Piazza del Quirinale respectively, and a bronze statue on the top. Inside, the cella once contained the tomb of Au-

gustus, while the most important members of the Julia-Claudia family and the Emperor Nerva were buried around the central pillar.

Ara Pacis Augustae. Today, this monument, the name of which means Altar of Peace, dedicated by the Emperor Augustus in 13 BC, is one of the most significant to survive from that period. He had it built in the heart of Campus Martius, where Palazzo Fiano stands today. Parts of it were rediscovered in the 16th century, but, in the 1930s, they were transferred to the present site on the river, where the altar was reconstructed. Now it is enclosed within a glass pavilion resting on a plinth. The side facing Via di Ripetta bears the inscription *Res Gestae Divi Augusti* (a gesture of the Emperor). The actual altar is inside the rectangular enclosure, the right side of which is decorated on the outside with marvelous reliefs depicting Augustus, Agrippa, Julia and Tiberius. The carving throughout is of an exceptionally high standard.

Via dei Condotti. This street, which is named after the conduits of Acqua Vergine and was laid out in the 16th century, contains many of Rome's most fashionable shops. Tucked among its noble residences, dating mainly from the 16th and 17th centuries, is the church of the Santissima Trinità degli Spagnoli, built in 1741-46. Further along, Caffè Greco is a historic venue and was once the haunt of famous artists, writers and composers (including Goethe and Stendhal).

Piazza di Spagna. Many movies of the 1950s included at least one scene shot in this extraordinary, typically Roman setting. The famous **Boat Fountain**** was designed by P. Bernini, assisted by his son, Gian Lorenzo, in the form of a leaking boat, set slightly below ground level. It stands at the foot of the "Spanish Steps" which lead up to the church of Trinità dei Monti. The cunning design overcame the problem of low water pressure in the piazza. Urban VIII commissioned the fountain in 1629 to commemorate the flood of 1598. The spectacular **Scalinata della Trinità dei Monti**** (known in English as the Spanish Steps was commissioned by Innocent XIII from F. De Sanctis, 1723-26). De Sanctis succeeded in solving the problem of the difference in height between Piazza di Spagna and the church of Trinità dei Monti by building a monumental staircase with a succession of gently curving and converging flights of steps. To make the staircase look more theatrical, he also designed the buildings at each side. The English poet, John Keats, lived and died in the *red house* on the

269

right which, since the early 20th century, has been a museum, the *Keats-Shelley Memorial House*. The building on the opposite side of the steps houses the famous *Babington's* tea-rooms, the first to be opened in Rome and very popular with artists. The square is named after Palazzo di Spagna, residence of the Spanish ambassador to the Vatican since 1622. For once, **Trinità dei Monti*** is a church that was not founded by a pope. In fact it was a French king, Louis XII, who began work on the church in 1502. Pope Sixtus V consecrated it in 1585 and another French king, Louis XVIII, restored it in 1816. As if to highlight the exception to the rule, the pope who commissioned the church asked Domenico Fontana (1587) to design a double staircase in front of it, and a facade with a single order of pilaster strips and a large central semicircular window at the top. Inside, the single nave is divided by a grille in line with the third chapel. It has late Gothic features in the triumphal arch, presbytery and transept and some good *paintings*. Behind the church, **Villa Medici** has spectacular views over the Pincian Hill. On the facade **overlooking** the garden, the two wings protrude slightly from the main building, which has a central portico with a serliana motif. The whole facade is decorated with stuccoes, festoons, bas-reliefs and statues, reflecting the Roman vogue for Antiquity in the late 16th century. The **garden*** has its original layout of straight avenues and beautifully kept hedges.

Via Veneto has retained its distinctive charm. A place where Romans like to stroll, this is where the most elegant shops are located, together with venues like the famous Caffè Doney and exclusive hotels built by the town-planners of the late 19th century for a well-heeled clientele. On the corner with Piazza Barberini is Bernini's *Fontana delle Api*, dedicated to the Barberini family (1644), bees being one of the family symbols.

Palazzo di Propaganda Fide. This building, built in 1586, bears the signature of the two greatest architects working in Rome in the 17th century (Bernini and Borromini). In 1626, it became a college for training missionaries, founded by Gregory XV. In 1644, Bernini worked on the formal brick facade, spanned by pilaster strips, with travertine stringcourses and rustication at the sides. Borromini built the wings overlooking Via di Capo le Case and Via di Propaganda (the latter is a very bold **facade**). The *Column of the Immaculate Conception*, found in 1777 in the ruins of the convent of S. Maria della Con-

cezione in Campo Marzio, was put up in Piazza di Spagna to commemorate the proclamation of the dogma of the Immaculate Conception of the Virgin Mary by Pius IX.

Galleria Nazionale d'Arte Moderna. This gallery (1883) is a must for lovers of 19th- and 20th-century Italian art. It has about 200 *works* by artists such as G. Palizzi, D. Morelli, G. Fattori, C. Monet, G. Balla, G. Klimt, A. Modigliani, P. Mondrian, A. Burri, G. Capogrossi, L. Fontana, J. Lipchitz, G. Paolini, E. Cucchi, M. Paladino.

VIA DEL CORSO

Palazzo Doria Pamphilj, the descendants of this Roman noble family still live in the palazzo, which was built in various phases between the mid-15th and early 18th centuries. The **facade** overlooking Via del Corso dates from the 18th century. The ground and mezzanine floors have unusual cornices above the windows. On either side of the main entrance, the capitals of the columns are decorated with lilies (the heraldic emblem of the family) rather than the usual acanthus leaves. Inside, a monumental staircase (1748-49) leads up to the private apartments, which can also be reached from the doors at either end of the facade.

As you approach the heart of the **Galleria Doria Pamphilj****, the richness of the decor of the reception rooms seems to announce the splendor of the more than 400 paintings in the collection. The paintings are arranged according to criteria established by a document published in the 18th century, mainly according to symmetry, and occasionally according to type and style. The four wings which house the paintings contain *works* by Guercino, P. Bordon, Correggio, L. Lotto, G. Reni, G. Bellini and his workshop, J. Brueghel the Elder, and there is a *bust of Innocent X* by A. Algardi. A room is reserved for the famous **portrait of Innocent X***, by D. Velázquez (1650), and another bust of Innocent X by G. L. Bernini. Four small rooms house groups of paintings arranged according to the century in which they were painted. Here you will find masterpieces such as Caravaggio's **Flight into Egypt***. The Salone Aldobrandini contains a collection of archeological finds from Villa Doria Pamphilj on the Janiculum and some paintings.

S. Ignazio. When Ignatius Loyola, founder of the Jesuits, was canonized in 1622, Gregory XV decided to dedicate this church to him. Work on the church began in 1626. The church of the Gesù was used both as a model for the facade and for the interior. In fact, it has a single nave with three chapels on either side, linked by a passageway. In addition to interesting *works* by A. Algardi, P. Legros the Younger and C. Rusconi, in the center of the nave is a yellow marble disk. From here you can see the amazing perspective of the vaulting and the *trompe l'oeil* "dome" depicted in the **Triumph of the Saint**. A. Pozzo used this technique instead of the planned dome, which was never built. The simulation of depth and light on canvas is quite extraordinary. The three small palazzi with theatrical Rococo facades opposite the facade of the church are called **Burrò**.

Piazza Colonna. In the 19th century, this square was one of the hubs of Roman life. Many cafés were opened and often hosted concerts. The 1873 plan to widen Via del Corso led to the demolition of Palazzo Boncompagni Piombino. Galleria Colonna was built in its place in 1915-22, drawing on similar galleries built in Milan and Naples in the 19th century. In the middle of the square stands the **column of Marcus Aurelius****. Incursions by various Germanic tribes revealed the considerable strategic ability of Marcus Aurelius who, after three years of fighting (172-175), succeeded in driving them back beyond the Danube. To commemorate this victorious campaign, his son Commodus (180-193) erected this column in Luni marble. The spiral frieze depicts the various stages of the conflict. There used to be a statue of Marcus Aurelius on the top, but it was lost in the Middle Ages and replaced by a bronze *statue of St Paul* in 1588-1589, under Sixtus V. The restoration of some of the figures in the central and upper parts of the frieze dates from the same period.

Palazzo di Montecitorio. Most Italians are familiar with this building. Since 1871, it has housed the Italian Chamber of Deputies (parliament). G. L. Bernini was commissioned to build it in 1653 by Innocent X and he designed the convex facade with its Baroque ornamental decoration. In the late 17th century, it was converted into courtrooms by C. Fontana. The brick and travertine facade overlooking Piazza del Parlamento, on the other side of the palazzo, and the *parliamentary chamber* (paneled in oak carved with floral motifs) is by E. Basile (1903-1927). Here you can see works by O. Rosai, C. Carrà, G. De Chirico, L. Viani, G. Boldini and M. Campigli. In front of the palazzo stands the *obelisk of Psammetichus II* (early 6C BC), brought home from Egypt by Augustus, and erected here in 1792.

Via del Corso. The name of the long, straight Via del Corso comes from the races that used to be organized here during Carnival and were moved here from the Testaccio area in the late 15th century. It has been a main thoroughfare since Roman times and follows the line of the old Via Flaminia within the Aurelian walls. It used to cross **Campus Martius**, a vast public area which once comprised the mausoleum of Augustus, the Ara Pacis, the Pantheon and the column of Marcus Aurelius. Some of the oldest early-Christian churches were built on this road, which maintained its role of providing access to the city from the north even after the fall of the Roman Empire. In the 16th century, the popes of the time transformed the houses into palaces and built churches. In the 18th century, Via del Corso became the hub of the intellectual, political and artistic sphere, members of which haunted the numerous cafés (especially Caffè Aragno). In the mid-19th century, the street began to attract commercial buildings. In the early 20th century, it was renamed after King Umberto I, and only regained its original name in 1947.

S. Maria di Montesanto and S. Maria dei Miracoli. They may look like identical twins, but they're not. For a start, there are 13 years between them. The first church was built in 1662 and completed in 1679. Bernini oversaw the work, indeed he designed it, and executed the *statues of saints* which grace its balustrade. The *bell tower* was finished in 1761. Work on the second church began in 1675 and it was completed in 1681. Its balustrade is also decorated with statues in a style similar to that of Bernini, while the elegant 18th-century *bell tower* is by Theodoli.

Piazza del Popolo. Dino Risi's famous movie "Il Sorpasso", made in 1963, a masterpiece

The Spanish Steps below Trinità dei Monti.

of Italian comedy, is just one of many movies incorporating scenes filmed in this theatrical square, formerly the setting for fairs, games and other popular events.

To the north of the square stands Porta del Popolo, and, dominated from the east by the Pincian Hill, in the center of the square, is the **Flaminian obelisk**, the oldest and the second-tallest (25 m) in Rome, after the one erected near the Lateran Palace. This granite monolith was erected in Heliopolis in Egypt in about 1200 BC. It was brought to Rome by Augustus, who placed it in the Circus Maximus. It was moved here in 1589 under the orders of Sixtus V. The semi-circles on each side of the square contain two *fountains* in travertine by Valadier (1818-21), with basins in the shape of huge shells, crowned with statues. Valadier also designed the buildings (1818-24) on the side of the Tridente (the name given to the point where three long, straight roads penetrate the city, forming a trident), which house the famous Caffè Rosati and Caffè Canova. A footpath, also designed by Valadier (1834) and decorated with Neo-classic niches and statues, winds up the Pincian Hill from Piazza del Popolo, ending below the *Casina Valadier*. The large terrace nearby, which overlooks Piazza del Popolo, has incredible **views**** of the city, dominated by the dome of St Peter's.

S. Maria del Popolo. The splendid artworks inside this church add to its appeal. It was built in 1475-77 in the Lombard religious architectural style, on the site of a small chapel erected during the pontificate of Paschal II, with funds raised by the local people (hence its name). In the 16th century, it was altered (Bramante rebuilt the choir and the apse and the Chigi chapel was rebuilt according to a design by Raphael). In the following century, the facade and the interior were decorated in the Baroque style, under the supervision of G. L. Bernini, and the Cybo chapel by C. Fontana was added. The Della Rovere chapel (first chapel, right-hand aisle) contains the *tombs of Cardinals Cristoforo and Domenico Della Rovere* by Bregno and a *Nativity* by Pinturicchio. Bregno was also responsible for the **marble altar** (1473) in the sacristy. Behind the *high altar* (1627) are **monuments to Cardinal Ascanio Sforza*** (1505, on the left) and **Cardinal Girolamo Basso Della Rovere*** (1507, on the right) by A. Sansovino. The **stained glass windows*** in the choir were made by G. de Marcillat in 1509, whereas the beautiful **frescoes** on the ceiling are by Pinturicchio (1508-1510).

In the first chapel of the left transept, on either side of the *Assumption* by A. Carracci (1601), there are two masterpieces by Caravaggio (1600-1601): the **Conversion of St Paul*** (right) and the **Crucifixion of St Peter*** (left). The banker A. Chigi built the **Chigi chapel** (second chapel, left-hand aisle) as a family mausoleum. There is a marked contrast between the chapel's plain outside and the richly decorated interior. Begun in 1513-14 by Lorenzetto, it was completed by Bernini in 1652-56. Raphael prepared the cartoons for the *mosaics* in the dome, executed in 1516.

Porta del Popolo. This gate began as Porta Flaminia, one of the gates in the Aurelian walls. The external facade was renovated in 1561-62 by N. di Baccio Bigio, who based his design on the Arch of Titus. Alexander VII decided to rebuild the internal facade and entrusted the work to G. L. Bernini. The facade is decorated with festoons, oak leaves and ears of wheat, and bears the inscription *Felici faustoque ingressui* (Fortune and happiness to all who enter here). The gate was altered again in 1877-79, when the towers added by Sixtus IV (15C) were demolished in order to make the side-entrances.

FROM TORRE DELLE MILIZIE TO THE TREVI FOUNTAIN

Torre delle Milizie. A leaning tower in Rome! The tower acquired an obvious lean in 1348, when a violent earthquake (which caused the third floor to collapse) caused subsidence. Its history dates back to the lengthy conflicts between the great noble families of the papacy. Built by the Conti in the early 13th century, the tower was acquired by Boniface VIII, who fortified it against the Colonna. Having been restored and consolidated by A. Muñoz in 1914, it was joined to Trajan's markets in 1927. Above the base, built of tufa blocks, there are two floors with brick outer walls and merlons on the top.

Palazzo Colonna. The lines of the present facade date back to 1730, when the building was renovated. There are pavilions with a loggia and large windows at each side (the one accessed from Piazza Ss. Apostoli houses the *Museo delle Cere* (Wax Museum). The same style prevails in the courtyard where the palace proper begins. It was built in 1484 at the wishes of Cardinal G. Della Rovere and now houses the famous **Galleria Colonna***. Together with that of Palazzo Doria Pamphilj, it can be regarded as the most important private collection in Rome. The red marble *column being* watched from the wall by the *Venus*, *Cupid and Satyr* by Bronzino and the *Narcissus* by Tintoretto is the symbol of the Colonna family. The spectacular decoration of the **Great Hall** justifies a visit: stuccoes, frescoes and large Venetian mirrors provide the setting for pictures by Guercino, N. di Liberatore, G. Lanfranco and F. Albani. The *Room of the Apotheosis of Martin V* is named after the subject of the fresco in the center of the ceiling by B. Luti. Also look out for the famous *Peasant Eating Beans* by A. Carracci. Close by, the basilica of **Ss. Apostoli** contains some 15th-century **frescoes**.

Museo Nazionale Romano. This museum will take you on a fascinating journey through the most important aspects of the artistic culture of Imperial Rome. Not surprisingly, this is regarded as one of the world's most important archeological collections. The museum is housed in *Palazzo Massimo alle Terme*, built in the late 19th century in the style of Roman early Baroque residences.

The journey begins with the iconography representing the difficult phase of transition between the late Republican period and the period of Augustus: portraits, inscriptions, and coins from the Republican period gradually give way to works which represent the ideological and political plans of the founder of the Empire. The **statue** found in Via Labicana of **Augustus as Pontefex Maximus*** is one of the finest depictions of the emperor. There are *original Greek* statues in the *Gardens of Sallust*. The exhibits reflect the development of Roman taste from the 1st to 4th centuries with some of the sculptural decoration from the Imperial villas, aristocratic residences and gardens. Masterpieces of the collection include the **Discus-thrower from the Lancellotti** collection (from the An-

tonine period but restored in the 18th century) and another from **Castel Porziano** (1C BC), both copies of the famous sculpture by Myron, the **Apollo found in the Tiber** (copy of a prototype attributed to Pheidias) and the **Chigi Apollo**. A large section of the museum is devoted to official portraits. One room contains the bronzes from the **ships** once moored in Lake Nemi in front of the Caligula's villa (1C BC) which overlooked the lake. Other important finds include the *Portonaccio sarcophagus*, where the battle scenes of Romans fighting Barbarians resemble the reliefs of the Antonine Column, the **sarcophagus of Acilia** with a relief depicting the procession to name the new consul (second half of the 3C), the *sarcophagus of Claudianus* depicting scenes from the Old and New Testaments (ca. 330 AD) and a huge **crater** decorated with one of the earliest images of the Virgin and Child.

The next part of the museum contains wall-paintings and mosaic decoration dating from the 1st century to the late Imperial period. There are splendid **frescoes** (late 1C BC) **from the villa at Gallinas Albas**** at Prima Porta depicting an orchard and flower garden, there are **stuccoes** and **frescoes from Villa della Farnesina****, depicting charming architectural landscapes framed by elegant candelabra, festoons and plants, and the **frescoes** from the villa at Castel di Guido. The basement contains a coin collection and jewelry.

Mura Serviane. When King Servius Tullius decided to build the first set of defensive walls around the town, the future capital of the world was little more than a village. Reinforced by an earth embankment (*agger*), they were about 11 km long, almost 10 m high and an average of 4 m wide. A section of the

HIGHLIGHTS

THE SPECIALTIES OF THE ROMAN CUISINE

Gnocchi alla romana – Smallslices of semolina sprinkled with butter and grated cheese, baked in a hot oven and served piping hot. *Rigatoni co' la Pajata* – The gut of a young calf is chopped up fine and cooked with oil, garlic, parsley, white wine, tomatoes and chili pepper, then served with *rigatoni* (a type of pasta). *Bucatini all'amatriciana* – Bucatini or spaghetti served with a sauce made with lard, pork cheek, white wine, tomatoes, pecorino and chili pepper. *Pasta a cacio e pepe* – once the pasta is cooked, exactly the right amount of the hot pasta water is conserved to make a creamy sauce with pecorino cheese and freshly-ground black pepper. *Fagioli con le cotiche* – Boiled beans are added to boiled pork skin. They are mixed in a pot and cooked gently with lard, ham fat, garlic, parsley and tomato sauce. *Saltimbocca alla romana* – thin slices of veal are fixed to a slice of cooked ham and a sage leaf with a toothpick. They are then cooked with butter and a little white wine.

walls was discovered at Piazza dei Cinquecento when the foundations for the first Termini station were being dug (1869-70). It comprised 17 rows of tufa blocks about 94 m long and 10 m high.

Porta Pia. To begin with, this breach in the **Aurelian Walls** had no external facade. The main facade, commissioned by Pius IV as a background for Strada Pia, faced inwards towards the city. It was designed by Michelangelo (1561-64). The decoration was possibly inspired by the pope's family (the five de' Medici balls, the pateras with hanging ribbons and the square block of marble in the center are associated with the barber's trade because the first de' Medici were barbers). The rooms inside the gate house the *Museo Storico dei Bersaglieri* (Museum of the Bersaglieri, a light-infantry regiment). Not far away is a *commemorative column* crowned with a statue of *Victory*.

Terme di Diocleziano. The Emperor Diocletian was from Dalmatia and he made no secret of the fact that he was not keen on the luxury and intrigues of Rome. In fact, he only visited the city sporadically. However, since he wanted to be remembered in a good light, he gave the Romans this bath complex. It was begun in 298 and finished in 305-306, and was eventually the grandest in Rome (it covered an area of 136,000 m²). It could accommodate about 3,000 people, and the main part of the complex, surrounded by gardens with nymphaeums, exedras and blocks of rooms, was based on the Trajan's Baths. In an extraordinary example of the re-use of building material, part of the complex was converted into the Basilica of S. Maria degli Angeli and another was converted into the building which now houses the Museo Nazionale Romano. What's more, two of the rotundas of the outside walls and the main exedra were incorporated into the buildings erected by G. Koch in Piazza della Repubblica. Long the seat of the Museo Nazionale Romano, a section of the Baths of Diocletian is reserved for the **Inscriptions Department** and the museum's collection of inscriptions.

S. Maria degli Angeli. Shortly after he acceded to the Imperial throne (284) Diocletian began a period of severe repression of the already sizeable Christian community. According to tradition, hundreds of people died building his baths on account of the a palling working conditions. The idea of building a church within part of the bath complex to commemorate those who died emerged in the early 16th century, but not until 1561 did the plan receive the papal seal of approval from Pius IV. The design for it was assigned to Michelangelo, who incorporated the *tepidarium*, the four rooms next to it and those running across it in a complex with a shape similar to a Greek cross with three doors. At the same time, the Carthusian monks, to whom the pope had entrusted the building work, built the adjoining monastery. The complex changed again in the 18th century, when a chapel was built dedicated to St Bruno, founder of the Carthusian order. However, its present appearance dates from the Holy Year of 1750, when L. Vanvitelli renovated the exterior. Those interested in funerary monuments will find plenty to look at in the *shrines* of the internal vestibule and the *sculptures* in the passageway. Note the **Sala della Minerva** or **Aula Ottagona**, which contains some fine statuary, including two bronzes of a **Hellenistic Prince** (2C BC) and a **Boxer Resting** (1C BC), where the wounds have been created with inlay work. Not far from the church are two interesting 19th-century palaces.

Palazzo delle Esposizioni, preceded by a formal flight of steps, is one of the city's most important cultural centers, and is used for exhibitions and other events. The building, designed by P. Piacentini, is unusual because of the complete lack of windows on the walls and the 12 *statues of famous artists* on the top. The **Palazzo della Banca d'Italia** is one of the most successful expressions of the Neo-Classic style of G. Koch. Opposite it is the fine Art-Nouveau exterior of *Teatro Eliseo*.

Palazzo Barberini, Overlooking **Piazza Barberini** and G. L. Bernini's **Triton Fountain** (1642-43), richly decorated with allegorical figures, Palazzo Barberini is an ingenius combination of a patrician city palazzo and a villa with a garden. The most prestigious names of the period worked on this building. It was designed by C. Maderno, while G. L. Bernini designed the loggia-window and the famous *staircase with a square well* which starts at the left-hand side of the portico. On the opposite side of the portico, Borromini designed a *spiral staircase* with pairs of columns. The *mithraeum* in the back garden has an ancient Roman fresco depicting *Mithras in the act of killing the bull* (in the center) and *scenes of myths associated with the god*. The palazzo houses the **Galleria Nazionale d'Arte Antica****, the exhibits of which, dating from the 14th and 18th centuries, trace the development of all the artistic trends: the Giottoesque artists of Rimini, the Mannerists of Rome, painters (some foreign) who imitated the style of Caravaggio and 18th-century painters from the Veneto and Naples. The ground floor of the north wing is devoted to paintings up to the 16th-century, the first floor to the 17th century, the second floor to the 18th century, the library of Cardinal F. Barberini to the cartoons on which the tapestries of the Barberini family are based, the nearby store-rooms to the **decorative** arts, and the ground floor of the south wing to temporary exhibitions. The rooms where the paintings are displayed are beautifully decorated. Highlights include works from the north of Italy and Tuscany of the 16th century, works by Raphael and his workshop (including Raphael's famous portrait, **Fornarina***), the *sketches* by El Greco, two important works by Caravaggio (**Judith and Holofernes** and **Narcissus**), and other works by G. Reni, Guercino, H. Holbein the Younger and Bernini.

S. Carlo alle Quattro Fontane. The creative skills of F. Borromini, who spent 29 years working on this church, are easily recognizable in the facade, the characteristic bell tower and the interior. Four elegant fountains *with statues of the Tiber, the Arno, Diana and Juno* (1588-93) have given the name to the **crossroads of the Quattro Fontane**, laid out under Sixtus V, where Strada Pia intersects with Strada Felice. Further along *Via XX Settembre* are the churches of **S. Susanna**, *S. Bernardo alle Terme* and **S. Maria della Vittoria**. The last church is famous for the **statue of Ecstasy of St Theresa***, a masterpiece by G. L. Bernini (1644-52). Opposite the church is the **Fountain of Moses***, an imposing work by D. Fontana (1587), made in the form of a nymphaeum to celebrate the building of the Acqua Felice aqueduct.

Quirinale. This theatrical setting of papal Rome, **Piazza del Quirinale*** includes the **Fountain of Monte Cavallo**, whose name comes from the Dioscuri (Castor and Pollux). The statues of the gods, depicted standing by their horses, are Imperial Roman copies of 5th-century BC Greek originals found at the Baths of Constantine. Another ancient relic is the obelisk towering above the granite basin (1818), which previously stood by the Mausoleum of Augustus.

Palazzo del Quirinale* was conceived as a summer residence for the pope but, between 1870 and 1945, was occupied by the Royal House of Savoy. An impressive list of artists contributed to the building of this beautiful palazzo, now the official residence of the Italian President. It was begun by M. Longhi the Elder in 1573. He was succeeded by O. Mascherino (who designed the *smaller building* at the far end of the courtyard), D. Fontana, F. Ponzio (who designed the *Grand Staircase* and the *chapel of the Annunciata*), C. Maderno (who designed the doorway and the *chapel of Paolina*) and, finally, G. L. Bernini, who designed the *tower* on the left-hand side of the facade (1626) and the *Loggia delle Benedizioni* (1638). Restoration work has given the palazzo its original 18th-century colors. The right-hand side of the palace (known as the *Manica Lunga*, referring to a long corridor inside) has an unusual facade overlooking Via del Quirinale. The palazzo contains many fine *artworks*: the paintings by G. Reni in the chapel of the Annunciata and by G. Lanfranco and A. Tassi (fresco frieze, 1616) in the Sala Regia. The *gardens*, the Festa della Repubblica, in memory of the referendum of 1946 when Italians voted in favor of the Republic), are laid out in the style of the 16th century and contain a *Coffee House*, created by F. Fuga for Benedict XIV. Near the Quirinal Hill is the **church of S. Andrea al Quirinale***, commissioned by Cardinal C. Pamphilj (1658) from G. L. Bernini, then at the height of his artistic career. The great architect designed an unusual elliptical plan for the church, with the main axis on the shorter side, and a dome with an innovative lantern that would enhance the position of the *altar* of his own design. The church is a masterpiece of religious Baroque architecture. *Paintings* by Baciccia and C. Maratta add to the interest of the interior.

Fontana di Trevi. A. Ekberg's bath in the Trevi Fountain in the movie "La Dolce Vita" made the whole world familiar with this wonderfully theatrical Baroque composition. The fountain, based on the theme of the sea, took 30 years (1732-62) to complete. The style of decoration imitates that of Bernini. At the top of it is a balustrade with allegorical figures, and the crest of Clement XII who commissioned the work. The great *statue of the Ocean* (1759-62) stands in the central niche (on a chariot in the shape of a shell pulled by sea-horses led by tritons), with the personification of *Health* on one side (and a other statue above of the *Virgin Mary*, pointing to the spring) and *Abundance* on the other, both works by F. Della Valle. As they admire this splendid Baroque blend of sculpture and architecture, visitors to Rome should not forget that, according to tradition, if they want to return to Rome, they should throw a coin into the water. Beyond the fountain, **Piazza di Trevi***, named after the meeting of three roads (*tre vie*) in Piazza dei Crociferi, is also enhanced by the colonnade of the 17th-century *church of Ss. Vincenzo e Anastasio*.

THE HISTORIC HEART OF ROME

Palazzo di Venezia. This massive building with its merloned facade was built in 1455-64 by Cardinal P. Barbo as his residence. It was extended by adding the "viridarium" (later Palazzetto Venezia) after he was elected pope (Paul II). This palazzo established the Renaissance model of L. B. Alberti in Rome, with a rectangular plan and porticoes and loggias overlooking the central courtyard (only part of this remains).

Legacies, donations and groups of exhibits from the former Museo Kircheriano and Museo Artistico-industriale now form the collection of the **Museo di Arti Applicate del Palazzo di Venezia****. The extreme diversity of its exhibits is one of the museum's main attractions. An impressive group of paintings from the 13th to 16th centuries from the Veneto, Emilia-Romagna, Lazio, Umbria, the Marches and Tuscany is displayed, region by region. Sala Altoviti contains *ivories* and *jewelry*. Pastels illustrate the popularity of this particular art form in France in the late 18th and mid-19th centuries. The porcelain collection provides an overview of the production of the main European manufacturers from the early 18th to early 20th centuries and there is also a remarkable ceramics collection dating from the 15th to 18th centuries. There are about 800 pieces of silver (17C-19C), 150 items of glassware, and more than 400 pieces of Chinese and Japanese porcelain dating from the 17th to 19th centuries. There are also some interesting bronzes and *terracotta models*.

Basilica di S. Marco. Much of the building material used to construct the facade of the church came from the Colosseum and the Theater of Marcello. Again, the three-arched doorway is influenced by L. B. Alberti. In the second half of the 15th century, this church, founded in 336 and rebuilt for the first time in 792 (but the Romanesque *bell tower* is 12C), became the palatine chapel of Palazzo di Venezia. Despite alterations during the Baroque period, the coffered ceiling has been preserved. This, along with that of S. Maria Maggiore, is the only 15th-century **ceiling** in Rome to have sur-

vived. The **mosaics** of Gregory IV in the apse dated 827-844 belong to the first reconstruction phase, while the *tomb of Leonardo Pesaro* in the right-hand aisle is by A. Canova (1796). Note the interesting reliefs on the altar in the sacristy (1474). The "viridarium" (1464), designed by Alberti as a garden surrounded by a portico, was enlarged in 1466-68 by adding an upper loggia. By blocking up some of the arches, it was converted into **Palazzetto Venezia**, and then, in 1911-13, it was moved to the left of Palazzo di Venezia, following the construction of the Monument to Victor Emmanuel II. In the center of the beautiful **courtyard** is a *well-head* by A. da Brescia.

The Vittoriano. Building the *monument to Victor Emmanuel II*, first king of Italy, took 50 years. However, it was completed in time for the centenary celebrations for the Unification of Italy. The **Altare della Patria** was opened in 1925 to mark the Grave of the Unknown Soldier (1921). The *quadriga* was placed on the top in 1927. Inside the monument is the *Sacrario delle Bandiere delle Forze Armate*, a collection of standards of the branches of the Italian Armed Forces.

S. Maria in Aracoeli. The church acquired its present name after the reconstruction of 1285-87. In 1348 Cola di Rienzo inaugurated the staircase built to honor the image of the *Madonna and Child* (10-11C) which adorns the altar. Behind the simple, 13th-century brick facade, the church is a treasure-trove. Below the *coffered ceiling* (1572-75), the interior was decorated by many artists, including A. Bregno (*funerary monument to Cardinal Ludovico d'Albrecht*, back of the facade), Donatello (*tombstone of Giovanni Crivelli*, back of the facade), Pinturicchio (**Stories from the Life of St Bernardino**, first chapel on the right), Michelangelo (design for the *tomb of Cecchino Bracci*) and A. di Cambio (*tomb of Luca Savelli*, right transept).

The archeological site of the Roman Forum and the Palatine Hill: a stroll through history. Rome, *caput mundi* (head of all the world), the city that became the largest metropolis in the Mediterranean and then dominated much of the ancient world for centuries. It was here that the principles of civilized living, on which modern constitutions are still based, were conceived. Rome was, firstly, the capital of the Roman Empire. In the West, it was the first great unifying power that succeeded in creating a proper state. The Romans advanced thousands of kilometers, colonizing foreign lands and leaving behind them a rich legacy, not only of knowledge but of laws, infrastructures and rules for social organization. Europe today is based on Rome's legacy, despite the fact that its history has a darker side to it, involving the persecution of Christians and slavery. However, throughout its history, many great men have been fascinated by the "dream of Rome": Charlemagne, D. Alighieri, Machiavelli, to name but a few. For the first time, a Western people had organized themselves into a complex social system that was a moral and political entity above particular interests. They left much. All over Europe, we drive along roads that were originally laid by the Romans. The saying that all roads lead to Rome is no coincidence.

This, one of the world's most important archeological sites, has a powerful, fascinating charm which stems from the fact that it was the cradle of our civilization.

Our tour begins with **Trajan's Column****, which is almost 40 m high. After the conquest of the Dacians (from modern Romania) Trajan's empire was at its height. To celebrate, the events of the wars of 101-103 and 107-108 were depicted on the bas-relief frieze which now surrounds the column.

The white Vittoriano.

The base is decorated with trophies of war taken from the enemy. A spiral staircase inside climbs to the top, where, in 1587, the statue of the emperor was replaced by one of *St Peter*.

The majestic complex of the **Forum** and **Trajan's Markets****, designed by Apollodorus of Damascus, was begun in 107 and completed under Hadrian. The tour begins at the **markets**, where business was conducted in the great *hall* overlooking Via IV Novembre. Architectural fragments and statues are displayed in the six *tabernae* (shops) off the hall. From here, a staircase descends to *Via Biberatica*, the *semi-circular* area where the markets were held, which has spectacular views over the whole area. A passageway leads under Via Alessandrina to the **forum**, site of the Greek and Roman libraries, the huge Trajan's temple (the surviving column drums and capitals give you an idea of its size) and the *Basilica Ulpia*, the largest and most sumptuous in Rome. You can still see the columns in the center of the area that has been excavated.

The **Forum of Augustus**** (part of the Imperial Fora), next to Trajan's Markets, was laid out at the wishes of Rome's first emperor, and part of it was excavated in 1924-32. The rest of the site is still under excavation. In the center of the forum, opened in the year 2 BC, stood the *Temple of Mars Ultor*, surrounded by eight columns on each side (three of the ones on the right side survive).

The **Casa dei Cavalieri di Rodi*** built in the 15th century above the left-hand exedra of the forum, was constructed at the wish of Cardinal P. Barbo, and subsequently became the seat of the Order of the Knights of St John of Jerusalem (later of Rhodes and then of Malta, changes reflecting Turkish expansion). In the atrium with its portico you can still see the travertine pillars of the Augustan structure, whereas the *chapel of S. Giovanni Battista* is a 20th-century adaptation of part of the covered structures. On the upper floor is a great *hall* dominated by a tribune (possibly the hall where the knights convened) and an elegant arched loggia (**view**).

The **Forum of Nerva**** was laid out in the narrow space between the Subura and the Roman Forum and contained the Temple of Minerva (hence its other name, "Forum Minervae" or "Palladium"). You can still see part of the base of the temple and the so-called *Colonnacce* (enormous Corinthian columns) which formed the portico and supported the frieze with bas-reliefs. Recent excavations have revealed fragments of another frieze depicting a female figure.

The **Colosseum****, or Flavian Amphitheater (its proper name), is universally regarded as the symbol of Rome, one of the world's most famous monuments. Built at the wish of Vespasian (dedicated in 79 AD) in the area occupied by the artificial lake near the Domus Aurea, it was inaugurated in 80 AD by Titus with games lasting 100 days. Completed by Domitian and restored by A. Severus, in the late empire it was used as a hunting ground. Today, visitors are still amazed by the Colosseum's size and the functional way it was built. It is one of the Roman Empire's great feats of engineering, along with countless bridges and kilometers of aqueducts. The Colosseum is a worthy symbol of the huge size of Imperial Rome and the incredible ability of its architects and engineers.

The arena was the scene of bloody spectsacles which, at the time, were regarded as entertainment. Even today, as you enter the Colosseum, you can almost hear the crowd cheering the gladiators, the cries of the men and the roaring of the animals. In the Middle Ages, the period to which it owes its current name, it was converted into a fortress. In 1312 it passed into the hands of the Roman Senate, and was then consecrated to the Passion of Jesus by Benedict XIV, who put a stop to the devastation and pilfering of the monuments, which had by then become a source of building material. The facade has three orders of arches and is about 50 m high. The elliptical arena, which measures 86x54 m, was separated from the *cavea* (rows of seating) by a podium decorated with niches containing statues, reserved for members of the imperial family and other dignitaries. It had a seating capacity of 50,000. The spectators entered the arena through vaulted corridors which led up to the various floors to the seats (the highest seats were reserved for women). A velarium, or sail, provided shade from the sun. Below the arena, as well as lifts, there were tunnels where the wild animals used in the performances and the "stage scenery" were kept.

The decoration of the **Arch of Constantine**** is a fine example of material recycled from other buildings. This was possibly due to the state of the public finances which, after the emperor's victory over Maxentius in 312, could not afford entirely new decor for the triumphal arch built to mark the occasion. Some of the reliefs date from the Trajan period (the captured Barbarians, the lateral frieze above the cornice and those under the central arch), others from the reign of Hadrian (the medallions above the smaller arches) and others again from the reign of Aurelian (the reliefs above the cornice at either side of the inscription). Other reliefs, made specially for the arch, depict allegorical and historical motifs. It is the largest and best-preserved triumphal arch in Rome, despite having been incorporated into the fortifications of the Colosseum at one time. The arch was restored in 1804.

Retracing our steps, near the *Forum of Peace*, almost at the end of the slope which runs down from Largo Romolo e Remo to the Roman Forum (the buildings on the left belong to the Temple of Antoninus and Faustina), stands the **Basilica Aemilia**, which dates from 179 BC. Its name comes from the Gens Aemilia who, in the 1st century BC, restored the decoration of the basilica. What you see today, partly destroyed by fire, dates from the restoration carried out by Augustus. At that time, the Senators of Rome met in the **Curia** (senate). You can see its plain brick facade and, nearby, the remains of the base of the round *shrine of Venus Cloacina*. This dates from the reconstruction phase under Diocletian after 283 AD, although its foundation is usually attributed to Tullus Hostilius. Inside the Curia, on either side, you can still see the three broad, marble-clad steps on which the 300 members sat. The president's tribune is marked by the figure of a Roman in a toga, which has replaced a statue of Victory. The **Plutei of Trajan** are exhibited here: two finely carved balustrades with reliefs depicting the animals used at *public sacrifices* (a pig,

The unmistakable Colosseum.

a sheep and a bull), food being distributed by the emperor and the burning of registers of outstanding taxes.

The **church of Ss. Luca e Martina*** is an architectural masterpiece by P. da Cortona. It has a striking facade with vertical features and is built on a Greek-cross plan with a dome and a lantern. Although there is no historical evidence that the Apostle Peter was imprisoned in the ancient "Tullianum", in 1726 the **Mamertine Prison*** was consecrated to S. Pietro in Carcere. The travertine facade, dating from 40 BC and preceded by a portico, conceals an earlier facade made of tufa, the same material used inside, dating from the 2nd century BC. Prisoners condemned to death were thrown through a trap-door into a round chamber where they were strangled.

The **Arch of Septimius Severus**** was built to celebrate the tenth anniversary of the emperor's accession to the imperial throne. The inscriptions on the faces of the upper part of the arch refer to the victories over the Parthians, Arabs and Adiabenians. The reliefs above the two smaller arches also refer to the *wars fought by Septimius Severus against the Parthians*, while the frieze below depicts a *triumphal procession*. The iron beaks (*rostra*) of the ships captured at the battle of Antium in 338 BC were placed on the orator's tribune, which has been called the *Rostra* ever since. Caesar moved it from the center of the Comitium to the left-hand side of the Arch of Septimius Severus. The eight granite columns which stand behind the Rostra and the arch belong to the **Temple of Saturn** (497 BC), one of the most revered monuments in Republican Rome. Nearby is a round platform which once supported the Umbilicus Urbis (the symbolic center of Rome) and site of the Miliarum Aureum, a column from which all the distances in the Roman Empire were measured.

The forum stretches out before the Rostra, but, of the many monuments which once stood here, only the *Column of Phocas*, dedicated to the Emperor of the Eastern Empire in 608, has survived. You can still walk along the original polygonal stone paving of the *Via Sacra*, so-called because of the many sanctuaries on either side of it. The street separates the forum from the *Basilica Julia*. This basilica, erected by Caesar and completed by Augustus, comprises a central hall surrounded by a gallery supported by pillars. The street nearby was named *Vicus Tuscus* because an Etruscan community lived be-

tween the forum and the Tiber River. The **Temple of Caesar** was built by Augustus in 29 BC, where the body of the first Julius was cremated. The terrace in front of the pronaos used to be decorated by the *rostra* of the Egyptian ships captured by Octavian during the battle of Antium (31 BC). The nearby **Temple of Castor*** or Temple of the Dioscuri was built in 484 BC. The three surviving grooved columns date from the temple built by Tiberius. The oldest Christian building in the forum, **S. Maria Antiqua**, was once part of the Imperial Palace. The church, dedicated to the Virgin Mary in the 6th century, was embellished by various popes and abandoned after a series of earthquakes. It has an extraordinary collection of murals: a fresco in the right aisle depicts the *Virgin Enthroned with Angels and Saints*. Hadrian I, who commissioned the work, is depicted with a square halo. The left aisle also has interesting frescoes. Those in the chapel left of the apse date from the period of Pope Zachary (8C). There is a **Crucifixion** in the rectangular niche. On one side of the church stands the so-called *Temple of Augustus* where excavations have unearthed commercial buildings dating from the 1st century BC. On the other, the *Oratory of the 40 Martyrs* was founded over a building from the Trajan period, to which an apse was added (the frescoes date from the 8C and 9C). Only the round base and a few architectural fragments are left of the **Temple of Vesta*** where the symbols of the perpetuity of Rome were kept. According to tradition, King Numa Pompilius built the *House of the Vestal Virgins* for the priestesses who kept the sacred fire alight. After a fire in 64 AD, it was rebuilt by Nero and restored and extended several times. The cells of the priestesses were arranged around a large rectangular courtyard with a double portico, and other rooms were possibly used as store-rooms and for sacred furnishings.

The **Temple of Antoninus and Faustina*** is another ancient ruin that adds to the Roman Forum's theatrical splendor. To begin with, the temple was dedicated to the emperor's wife, and, after his death, when he became a god, to Antoninus Pius himself. You can still see the *cipollina* marble columns of the pronaos and the base. The steps were rebuilt during restoration work, while the internal chamber was converted into the *church of S. Lorenzo in Miranda* in the 7th-8th centuries. The grassy areas right of the church mark the edge of the *necropolis* discovered in 1902, attributed to the first inhabitants of the Palatine Hill, who settled there in the late 10th to 8th centuries BC. The lock on the door of the facade of the **Temple of Romulus** is one of the oldest in the world. The temple was begun by Maxentius in honor of his son and completed by Constantine. The huge **Basilica of Maxentius** (also known as the Basilica of Constantine) had a similar fate. You can see the interior with three aisles, and the apse added by Constantine by the new entrance off the Via Sacra (the original one faced the Colosseum).

Titus's seizure of Jerusalem, culminating in the sack of the city (70 AD) marked the beginning of the Jewish diaspora. To commemorate his achievements, Domitian built the **Arch of Titus****, a marble-faced archway with grooved columns. During the Middle Ages, it was incorporated into the fortifications built by Frangipane and was only restored in 1821. Note the reliefs under the arch of the *triumphal procession preceded by the emperor* (right) and *the imperial quadriga carrying Titus* (left). In the middle of the coffered ceiling is the *Apotheosis of Titus*.

The **Farnese gardens** were created in the mid-16th century by Vignola, J. Del Duca and G. Rainaldi. In 1625, they became host to one of the world's first botanical gardens. Today, not much is left of the gardens on the Palatine, except the *birdcages* on the upper terrace, but there are splendid views over the archeological site.

The **"House of Romulus"** lies in a part of the site that is thick with ancient remains. Nearby are the remains of the *Temple of Victory* (294 BC, restored in 1C BC), and the three **Iron-Age** huts which form the first nucleus of the future city of Rome.

The **House of Livia*** is famous for its elegant wall paintings. The *triclinium* has *trompe l'oeil windows* and views, another room has *mythological scenes* in the Pompeian style and, on the right, *Mercury rescuing Io from the clutches of Argos*. The decoration is so luxurious that, for a long time, it was thought to be the **House of Augustus***. However, the latter has been identified as a residence on two levels, part of a complex built in 36 BC. Here the Room of the Masks (theatrical motifs), the Room of Perspectives and the Study are decorated with splendid paintings in the Pompeian style.

The **Domus Flavia** is only the first part of the many *imperial palaces* which occupy the top of the Palatine Hill. But it was effectively the Imperial Palace, since it was here that most of the state functions were held. In the three-aisled *basilica*, the emperor listened to legal cases being discussed. Below it, Caligula consecrated the *Aula of Isis* to the god and decorated it with magnificent wall paintings. The *Aula Regia* was reserved for imperial audiences. The *Lararium* was the emperor's private chapel (the *Casa dei Grifi* below it dates from the 2C BC). A large peristyle separates the three large halls from the imperial banqueting hall where dignitaries were entertained. Note the splendid marble floor. Below this level is the *Domus Transitoria*, where Nero lived.

With regard to the **Palatine Antiquarium**, the Villa Stati Mattei (built above the ruins of the Flavian palace in the 16th century and enlarged by V. Vespignani in 1855) was demolished, except for the so-called *Loggetta Mattei*, which has frescoes attributed to Baldassarre Peruzzi or his workshop, and the 19th-century building which now houses the museum. It contains finds relating to the first settlement on the Palatine, sculptures found between 1870 and the present day and a series of stuccoes and frescoes. The finest examples of statuary are the *head of Meleager* (4C BC), and the **Palladium Palatinum*** (an original of the late 6C BC). The **Campana slabs** (36-28 BC) come from the Temple of Apollo on the hill. The **paintings** in the second Pompeian style (second half of the 1C BC) come from the House of Augustus. The **marble-inlay** wall decoration comes from the Domus Tiberiana and the Domus Transitoria. The **Domus Augustana**, next to the Domus Flavia, was part of the imperial residence. From here, if you look down at the slope of the hill facing Circus Maximus, you can see the *Paedagogium*, built under Domitian to house the school of imperial pages, and the remains of the *Domus Praeconum*, an annex of the imperial palace. The **Palatine Stadium** was built by Domitian, the last of the Flavian emperors, although much restoration was carried out under Septimius Severus. Inside, it had a double portico with the imperial box in the middle of the east side. The oval exterior was possibly built in the early Middle Ages by Theodoric, king of the Ostrogoths, who reigned over Italy between 493 and 526.

S. Clemente. The Basilica of S. Clemente is a real treasure-trove of surprises, an extraordinary conglomeration of superimposed structures which began as a private house in the 2nd century. In the courtyard of the house was a mithraeum which, shortly afterwards, was converted into a place for Christian worship. Having been damaged by the fire started by the Normans in 1084, it was rebuilt on the same lines by Paschal II, and acquired its present appearance in 1713-1719. The interior of the **upper basilica** has preserved its early 12th-century structure, with a nave and two side-aisles with apses separated by columns, and a Cosmatesque **floor**. The **choirstalls** in the center of the nave date from the same period, as do the fine Cosmatesque *ciborium* in the presbytery and the *bishop's throne* in the apse. The mosaic in the bowl of the apse, a **Triumph of the Cross** of the Roman school, dates from the first half of the 12th century. In the right aisle there are two 15th-century *funerary monuments* worthy of note, beside the presbytery. In the left aisle, the chapel of St Catherine contains **frescoes*** painted by M. da Panicale (1428-31), possibly with the assistance of Masaccio. A staircase decorated with architectural fragments from the 4th-century church and the mithraeum leads down to the **lower basilica**. A fresco in the nave depicts the **Legend of Sisinius**: the orders and the names included in the scene are vitally important for scholars of the earliest "vulgar" form of Italian. More frescoes (9C-12C) adorn the walls of the nave and the narthex. A staircase at the end of the left aisle leads down to buildings of Roman date and the 3rd-century *mithraeum*. On the way out, try to spot the *face of the Madonna* dating from the 9th-11th centuries and the early-Christian *baptistery*.

S. Stefano Rotondo, You have to really look for this church, hidden away behind the arches of **Nero's aqueduct**. Rome's oldest church (5C), built on a circular plan, is still quite visible, despite the addition of the 12th-century portico and the elimination of the colonnade and three arms of the Greek cross in the mid-15th century. Note the lovely *frescoes* on the perimeter wall.

S. Maria in Domnica. Paschal I built a church on the site of an earlier place of worship (called a *dominicum*). When the church was rebuilt in the 16th century, the 9th-century basilica form of the interior, with a nave and two side-aisles separated by granite columns, was preserved. The coffered ceiling is 16th century. Below it is a frieze by P. del Vaga based on a design by G. Romano. The **mosaics** in the apse and the triumphal arch both date from the original building.

Parco del Celio. Given its proximity to the Palatine, this precious public garden opened in the early 19th century was certain to contain vestiges from the Neo-Classic period. One of them is the Temple of Claudius, built by Agrippina in 54 AD but converted by her son Nero into a nymphaeum for the nearby Domus Aurea. Inside the park is **Villa Celimontana**, formerly a *casino*, built in the first half of the 19th century by G. Salvi. It contains a selection of material from the former City Antiquarium, including the famous sarcophagus of Crepereia Tryphaena, containing a splendid ivory doll with hinged joints and wearing bracelets.

S. Saba. The church dedicated to founder of an eastern order of monks stands on the top of the "little Aventine" hill. Historical sources confirm there was an early-Christian church here as early as 768. The relief of the *knight with the falcon* (8C) is the most significant of the archeological remains displayed on the portico and in the gallery (both date from 1463) on the facade of the church. A marble *doorway* with mosaic decoration (1205) leads into the bare interior: a nave with two side-aisles separated by 14 Neo-Classic columns. The Cosmatesque *floor* dates from the 13th century, while the frescoes in the apse were executed for the Jubilee of 1575. The *Crucifixion* above the bishop's throne is 14th century, although it has obviously been repainted several times.

S. Sabina. There was already a *titulus* here when Peter of Illyria built his basilica on this site (5C). In 824, Eugenius II added an iconostasis, the ambones and the ciborium. The bell tower and the cloister date from the 13th century. The **wooden doors*** of the main doorway leading into the atrium are from the first basilica. The 18 panels, framed by tendrils, depict *scenes from the Old and New Testaments*. The interior of the church, divided into a nave and two side-aisles, clearly echoes the style of the basilicas in Ravenna. Above the door, a fragment of mosaic bears an *inscription* in gold lettering on a blue background with the names of the founder, Pope Celestine I and depicting the Ecumenical Council held at Ephesus in 431. The *frieze* of red and green mirrors in the spandrels of the arches of the nave date from the 5th-6th centuries. The *choirstalls* have been reconstructed with fragments dating from the 5th-9th centuries, like the bishop's throne in the apse. Finally, the Elci chapel has a *Madonna of the Rosary* by Sassoferrato.

Portico di Ottavia. In BC 23, Augustus dedicated the renovation of the portico, built in 146 BC by Quintus Cecilius Metellus, to his sister, Octavia. Originally it enclosed two temples but it was rebuilt in 203 by Septimius Severus and Caracalla and later became a fish market, a role which lasted from the Middle Ages until the wall of the Jewish ghetto was demolished. An inscription refers to a curious privilege granted to the Conservatori (city magistrates), who had rights over the heads of the largest fish. Not surprisingly, the *church* built behind the portico in the mid-8th century was given the name of *S. Angelo in Pescheria*. The medieval facade of the nearby House of Vallati is mainly the result of restoration carried out since 1927.

S. Maria in Campitelli. This church was built as a votive offering to give thanks for deliverance from the plague of 1656. It was begun in 1662 to house the miraculous image of *S. Maria in Portico Campitelli* (11C) above the *high altar*. This and, indeed, the rest of the church, decorated in the late-Baroque style, is the work of C. Rainaldi. The facade in travertine is decorated with columns and cornices. Inside, the architect has reached a cunning compromise between a central and a longitudinal plan. The chapel of the Reliquaries contains a delightful *portable altar* dating from the 12th century, said to have belonged to St Gregory Nazianzenus.

Piazza del Campidoglio. The square at the top of the Capitoline Hill is pervaded by the genius of Michelangelo. From the outset, he had the idea of turning attention (and, consequently, the symbolic point of reference for town-planning) away from the Roman Forum, the ancient center of the city, and directing it towards the Vatican, the "new" heart of Rome. From this ensued the idea of enclosing the square with three buildings, leaving the side facing St Peter's open, apart from the balustrade bedecked with statues. And finally he imagined the plinth supporting the equestrian statue of Marcus Aurelius as the fulcrum of a pavement with a centrifugal design. The design of the stepped ramp (known as the "Cordonata") leading up to the square is also Michelangelo's. Paul III, the pope who decided to reorganize the area, approved the whole plan, but Michelangelo was only ever able to see it on paper in his preparatory designs. Indeed, other architects built Palazzo Senatorio, Palazzo dei Conservatori and Palazzo Nuovo, paved the square and arranged the *statues* on the balustrade. There is nothing left now to suggest that **Palazzo Senatorio** was once a medieval fortress. After the rebuilding of 1582-1605, the only part of the building conforming to Michelangelo's original plan was the external staircase. The rear facade of the palazzo incorporates 11 arches of the Roman **Tabularium** (included in the tour of the Musei Capitolini), the depository of the state archives of Ancient Rome, built in about 78 BC and used in the Middle Ages as a prison and warehouse. Behind the great portico were various vaulted rooms organized in several layers to overcome the difference in height between the Capitoline Hill and the Roman Forum. There is an unparalleled view over the fora from the terrace behind the right-hand side of Palazzo Senatorio.

Musei Capitolini. In 1563, it was Michelangelo himself who laid the first stone of **Palazzo dei Conservatori**. But he was able to do little else, except leave his designs so that his successors could complete the facade, the portico overlooking the courtyard and the staircase. Roman remains decorate the internal courtyard including the famous gigantic *head of Constantine*, part of a monument to which the fragments of an arm, a leg, a hand and the feet also belong. In 1655, on the opposite side of the square, G. and C. Rainaldi built *Palazzo Nuovo*, again following Michelangelo's design. The Sistine Chapel in the Vatican Museums is proof that Sixtus IV was a patron of the arts. But Rome can also thank this pope, with a passion for painting, for one of the world's most important institutions, the collections known as the **Musei Capitolini**** (Capitoline Museums). Sixtus IV donated the bronzes from the Lateran Palace, the symbols of the power of Ancient Rome. Leo X (1515), Pius V (1566) and, in 1733, Cardinal Albani imitated his example. After that, works discovered during excavations prior to the construction of new buildings after the Unification of Italy increased the collection so that it became one of the most extensive and complete collections of classical sculptures in Europe. This "museum city" comprises the Apartment of the Conservatori, the Museum of Palazzo dei Conservatori, the Pinacoteca Capitolina (art gallery) and the Museo Capitolino. The first three are housed in Palazzo dei Conservatori, while the last occupies the whole of Palazzo Nuovo (since 1997, some of the sculptures from these museums are on display at the converted Montemartini Power Plant). Part of the **Apartment of the Conservatori*** belongs to the Comune di Roma (Rome City Council), which uses it for public ceremonies. In addition to the numerous, splendid **artworks** displayed in its beautiful **rooms**, the museum houses the symbol of the Eternal City: the bronze stat-

Piazza of the Campidoglio.

ue of the **Lupa Capitolina**, or she-wolf of Rome, cast in the early 5th century BC (the twins Romulus and Remus were added in the 15th century); the fragments of the Fasti *Consulares et Trionfales* (records of Roman magistrates and of the great captains of Rome in 13 BC-12 AD) on the walls opposite the windows are all that remain of the Arch of Augustus, which once stood in the Roman Forum. In the center of the adjacent Sala delle Oche is the famous *Head of Medusa* by Bernini (1630) and the magnificent *mastiff* in green spotted serpentina marble (from a Greek 4C BC original). The **Sala delle Guerre Puniche** is the best-preserved, in terms of the original 16th-century decoration of the palace. The **Museo del Palazzo dei Conservatori** contains many fine exhibits, including a **bust of Commodus**, depicting the emperor with the attributes of Hercules (2C), the **Esquiline Venus** (1C BC) and the **crater of Aristonothos** (late 7C BC).

The **Pinacoteca Capitolina*** is a result of Benedetto XIV's passion for Italian and European art from the Middle Ages to the 18th century. A passion which embraced all the schools of painting: from the school of Ferrara to the Venetian school, which, throughout the 15th and 16th centuries produced great *masterpieces*, but also works by foreign painters, such as Rubens and Van Dyck. A valuable porcelain collection shares a room with Caravaggio's *St John the Baptist*, while the huge gilded bronze statue of *Hercules* is a Roman copy of a 2nd-century BC original. Italian 17th-century painting is represented by works by P. da Cortona, G. Lanfranco, Domenichino, G. Reni and L. Carracci, as well as the **Burial and Glory of St Petronilla**, one of Guercino's most famous works (1623). The two exhibits in the courtyard denote the importance of the collections of the **Museo Capitolino***. In the exedra at the

far end of the courtyard is a 1st-century fountain with the colossal figure of a river-god called *Marforio*, one of Rome's "talking statues". The second is the **equestrian statue of Marcus Aurelius*** which graces the right-hand side of the courtyard. This splendid bronze statue depicts the emperor in the act of talking to the people. The raised foreleg of the horse originally rested on the head of a prisoner. According to tradition, when the gilding that originally covered the emperor and his steed returns (only a few traces are left), the tuft of hair between the horse's ears will move, announcing the Last Judgement. During the Imperial period, the eastern cults of Mithras, Isis and Serapis were very popular and widespread. Finds associated with these **cults** (statues, reliefs and inscriptions) are displayed in the rooms on the ground floor. *Hellenistic sculptures* alternate with *Roman copies* of Greek originals in the gallery on the first floor. The Sala delle Colombe has a fine *mosaic* and a child's *sarcophagus* depicting the *myth of Prometheus* (3C) and the *Tavola Iliaca*, or Trojan Tablet, with reliefs representing the Trojan cycle (1C). The nearby Gabinetto della Venere is named after the **Capitoline Venus**, a Roman replica of the Greek original from Cnidos. The 65 *busts of Roman emperors* form a fairly complete "family album" of the emperors, while 79 other *busts depict Greek and Roman philosophers, poets, doctors and writers*, some of whom have yet to be identified. However, some of the most interesting works are exhibited in the great hall on the first floor. They include the famous **Wounded Amazon**, an excellent copy of the 5th-century BC Greek original, and the **Dying Gaul***, regarded as two of the most eloquent expressions of ancient sculpture.

TOWARDS THE LATERAN PALACE...

S. Pietro in Vincoli. The name of the church commemorates the miracle of the chains which bound the Apostle Peter when he was a prisoner in Jerusalem. When they were laid next to those used during Peter's imprisonment in Rome, they were miraculously joined. They are now kept in the reliquary below the altar. The church was begun in 439, on the site of a church that was dedicated to the Apostles in the 4th century but which dated from at least a century earlier. The church was restored in the 15th century, when the beautiful colonnaded portico with arches supported by octagonal stone pillars was added. The marble doorway dates from the same period. Inside, the bases of the 20 Neo-Classic marble columns are an 18th-century addition. When Leo X released him from his commitment, Michelangelo had already worked for three years (1513-16) on the **mausoleum of Julius II**, which stands unfinished in the right transept. He executed the statue of **Moses**, seated, and some of the *figures* in the niches, which were later completed by R. da Montelupo (1542-45). Note the bas-reliefs of the gilded bronze doors in the altar of the Confessio; also the gilded bronze *tabernacle* (1856) containing the presumed chain associated with the saint. A Byzantine mosaic (ca. 680) adorns the second altar of the left aisle.

S. Prassede. Paschal I (817-824) gave orders that the church must be rebuilt. It dates from at least 489 (the remains of the colonnade in the courtyard in front of the facade belong to the early-Christian church). The pope also commissioned the **chapel of St Zeno***, the most important Byzantine monument in Rome. The polychrome marble *floor* is a splendid example of *opus sectile*, a mosaic made with pieces of marble of various shapes and color. Although they have been restored, the **mosaics** in the vault, the right-hand lunette, the lunette below it and the niche of the altar are all very interesting. Paschal I also commissioned the **mosaics** on the triumphal arch and possibly also those in the apse.

S. Maria Maggiore. The patriarchal basilica of the Esquiline has three names: S. Maria Maggiore, S. Maria ad Nives or S. Maria Liberiana. According to the legend, it was built by Pope Liberius on the site of a miraculous snowstorm which occurred on August 3, 356, but, in actual fact, not before the papacy of Sixtus III, who dedicated it to the Motherhood of Mary, defined in 431 by the Ecumenical Council of Ephesus. At that time, the church had a nave, two side-aisles and a central apse. The apse was moved further back during the papacy of Nicholas IV to permit the addition of a transept. The chapels date from the 16th century. Paul V built the palazzo to the right of the facade (1605). Clement XI began the one to the left of it, which was completed by F. Fuga. It was this architect who, in 1741-43, added a new facade. You can see the Romanesque bell tower behind it. Above the portico, Fuga added a loggia with three arches. Behind the arches you can still see two series of the 13th-century mosaics which adorned the original facade. Fuga also contributed to the interior

(1746-50), limiting himself to discreetly rearranging various features and making the church more symmetrical. This is the only one of Rome's patriarchal church interiors that has retained its original appearance. 36 stone columns support the entablature decorated with a 5th-century mosaic frieze. The beautiful coffered ceiling is supposed to have been gilded with the first gold brought from America. Along the side-walls of the nave, above the entablature, the 36 mosaic panels dating from the time of Sixtus III, but restored in 1593, are a rare example of art of the late Roman Empire. The mosaic of the triumphal arch dates from the same period. The splendid mosaic in the apse is the work of Jacopo Torriti (1295). In 1931, the transept from the time of Nicholas IV was partially restored, unveiling frescoes of the prophets attributed to P. Cavallini, Cimabue or the young Giotto. The paintings in the vault of the chapel of Sts Michael and Peter in Chains, accessed through the baptistery from the right aisle, are thought to be by P. della Francesca. But, in this part of the basilica, the eye is drawn to the Sistine Chapel or chapel of the Blessed Sacrement (1584-87). It was D. Fontana, commissioned by Sixtus V, who designed the chapel on a Greek-cross plan, with a dome decorated with ancient marbles. A staircase leads down from the ciborium to the oratory of the Presepio, an old chapel renovated by A. di Cambio (ca. 1290). The Paolina or Borghese chapel (1605-1611), situated at the beginning of the left aisle, is very fine. Michelangelo designed the Sforza chapel just beyond it, between 1564 and 1573.

The **Auditorium of Mecenate**, was probably a summer nymphaeum, in one of the *horti* (gardens) owned by one of Octavia's councilors. Discovered in 1874, the vast rectangular hall has fragments of wall paintings from the 1st century.

The Temple of Minerva Medica, which served as a model for both Renaissance and Baroque architecture, is a large ten-sided hall with niches set below arched windows. It is named after the statue of Minerva with a serpent found nearby (now at the Vatican Museums).

Porta Maggiore, The gate, formed by re-using two arches of the aqueducts carrying the *Acqua Claudia* and the *Anio Novus*, was begun by Caligula in 38 AD and completed by Claudius in 52. The gate in the Aurelian walls marked the beginning of *Via Prenestina* and *Via Casilina*. It has two arches, three niches and a large attic with inscriptions on the side facing Piazzale Labicano commemorating the achievements of Claudius and the restoration of the aqueduct carried out by Vespasian (71) and Titus (81). In 1838, a late-Republican funerary monument in travertine was discovered behind the central niche of Porta Maggiore. The frieze on it depicts scenes in a bakery, leaving no doubt as to the trade of its owner, **Eurisace**.

S. Croce in Gerusalemme. The legalization of the Christian religion did not come about until the reign of Helena's son, Constantine, but it is possible that Helena had already built a small church in her villa. It was rebuilt by Lucius II (1144-45) in the form of a basilica and, having been altered again in the 15th and 16th centuries, was renovated in 1743 by D. Gregorini and P. Passalacqua. The facade, which owes much to Borromini's influence, is one of the finest expressions of Roman Baroque and its curve almost seems to announce the elliptical form of the atrium behind it. The interior is divided into a nave and two side-aisles by huge granite columns (partly incorporated into the pillars added in the 18C) and has a fine Cosmatesque *floor*. Note the *tomb* in the apse and the *fresco* in the bowl of the apse. Stairs lead down from the right of the apse to the chapel of St Helena, which has a fine **mosaic** ceiling. Under the floor of the chapel, according to tradition, is the earth from Calvary and the relics of Christ's Passion, brought to Rome from the Holy Land by St Helena. This legend is the reason for the name of the church.

The Laterano, Piazza di S. Giovanni in Laterano** was another project entrusted by Sixtus V to his favorite architect, D. Fontana. Memories of the beginnings of the Church here were still very vivid. The Emperor Constantine's second wife (of the Gens Laterani) gave the Villa dei Laterani to Pope Melchiades (or Miltiades). This led to the building of a basilica (313-318) and, subsequently, the Palace of the Popes. In 1585-89, Fontana, who was aware of the early history of the site, opened up straight roads leading towards the Basilica of S. Maria Maggiore, the Colosseum and the Appian Way. He raised an obelisk at the confluence of the three roads and added the Palazzo Lateranense, the Loggia delle Benedizioni and the building which houses the Scala Santa. In the 18th century, the facade of the basilica was renovated along with the Triclinium of Leo III, which was the state banqueting hall. In the middle of the square, which is often used for concerts, not to mention the very popular

festival of the patron saints of Rome, stands the **Lateran obelisk** (47 m high including the plinth). It was first erected in Thebes in the 15th century BC and brought to Rome in 357 AD by Constantinus II. Initially, it was placed in the Circus Maximus but it toppled over during an earthquake and was only rediscovered in 1587. The Lateran Treaties signed in **Palazzo Lateranense**** (Lateran Palace) on February 11, 1929 put end to more than 50 years of squabbling between the Italian Government and the Holy See. It resulted in the creation of the State of the Vatican City and, at the time, the Lateran Palace was included in the papal property, with the privileges of an exclave. In his plan for Sixtus V, in 1586-89, D. Fontana imagined the palace as having a representative role. The palace re-acquired this role to some extent in 1967 (having been used as a hospital, an archive and a museum in the interim), when it became the offices of the Cardinal Vicar of Rome. In 1987, the **Museo Storico Vaticano** opened its doors. In the *Papal Apartments*, the late-Mannerist frescoes in the chapel glorify Sixtus V, while those in the other rooms provide a summary of Imperial Roman and Christian history. The actual *Museo Storico* has a section devoted to iconography of the popes and another to papal ceremonial. A balustrade with *twin bell towers* (13C) decorates the top of the *Loggia delle Benedizioni*. To the right of it, S. Giovanni in Fonte, better known as the **Lateran Baptistery**, dates from the same period as the basilica and was altered by Sixtus III, who added an atrium. The baptistery is built on an octagonal plan, with eight columns supporting an architrave and the drum encircling the basalt font. The **church of S. Giovanni in Laterano**** is dedicated to St John the Baptist, St John the Evangelist and the Redeemer, and is the cathedral of Rome. It is the descendant of the basilica founded in 313-318 by Constantine, and has been rebuilt and restored many times. The facade dates from the restoration of 1732-1735, conducted by Alessandro Galilei. It has a single order of pilaster strips and semi-columns supporting an entablature with a tympanum. Above the balustrade are 15 *statues of Christ*, *St John the Baptist*, *St John the Evangelist* and the *Fathers of the Church*. Almost a century before, in 1660, the bronze **doors** of the Curia in the Roman Forum were placed in the central doorway of the church. To the right of it is the *Porta Santa*, which is only ever opened in Jubilee or Holy Years. F. Borromini altered the nave and four aisles twice (1646-50 and 1656-57) but preserved the 16th-century wooden ceiling and the Cosmatesque floor. Before 1718, he made 12 niches in the piers of the **nave** to house huge *statues of the Apostles*. G. di Stefano was responsible for the Gothic *papal altar* (1367) at the end of the nave; the *frescoes* on the outer panels were later altered by A. Romano and F. di Lorenzo. Until 1963, only the pope could officiate at the *high altar*. It incorporates the original wooden altar before which the first popes celebrated mass. The confessio below the high altar contains the *tomb of Martin V* (S. Ghini, 1443). In the **far right-hand aisle**, between the 2nd and 3rd statue, is a *small statue of St James* by A. Bregno (1492); beyond it is the *tomb of Cardinal Antonio Martino De Chaves* (1447). The **inner right-hand aisle** contains the *tomb of Cardinal Ranuccio Farnese*, designed by Vignola; note the **fragment of a fresco** by Giotto on the first pillar. In the **far left-hand aisle**, the Corsini chapel by A. Galilei contains the tomb and the columns of the *monument Clement XII* from the atrium of the Pantheon. The last pillar of the **inner left-hand aisle** contains the *tomb of Elena Savelli* by J. Del Duca (1570). The right arm of the **transept**, which was renovated architecturally and repainted in 1597-1601, leads into the *museum* of the church, which contains some 15th-century jewelry and the *Cross of Constantine* (12C-13C). When F. Vespignani altered the **apse** in the 19th century, the **mosaic** of the previous late 13th-century structure was preserved. The **cloister***, built in 1215-32, is a masterpiece of Cosmatesque art. The arches are supported by small smooth or spiral columns, some of which are decorated with mosaic. The *well-head* in the courtyard is 9th century. Sculptures, architectural fragments and tombstones line the walls of the cloister (note the remains of the **tomb of Riccardo degli Annibaldi** by A. di Cambio) together with Roman and early-Christian artifacts.

Close by is the **Scala Santa*** (Holy Staircase), believed to be the actual steps that Jesus climbed the day he was sentenced to death. Formerly the Monumental Staircase of the Patriarch, it was re-used in the building erected by Sixtus V (1589) for the private chapel of the popes (the *Sancta Sanctorum*), situated on the first floor of Constantine's palace. Since then, the Scala Santa, which may only be ascended by worshippers on their knees, has lead to the chapel of St Lawrence, where the entrance to the "Sanc-

ta Sanctorum" is located. The current appearance of the interior (only visible through a grille) dates from the rebuilding of 1278.

FROM ISOLA TIBERINA TO THE JANICULUM

S. Carlo ai Catinari, the domed church, dedicated to San Carlo Borromeo, is named after the many shops in the vicinity which once sold basins (*catini*). It was built in 1612-20 by R. Rosati. The travertine facade was completed by G.B. Soria (1638). The inside of the church is richly decorated with *works* by 17th-century painters.

Isola Tiberina, If it were really a ship, which is what it seems at first glance, it would be a hospital ship. In fact, according to tradition, during the plague of 293 BC, the serpent consecrated to Aesculapius jumped onto the island from the boat which had brought it here from Epidaurus in Greece, indicating the site where a temple should be dedicated to the god. To commemorate this legend, there is still a *carving of Aesculapius* on the eastern bank, *with the serpent entwined around a stick and a bull's head*. The first nucleus of the *Fatebenefratelli hospital* dates from the 16th century and the healing vocation of the island was confirmed during the plague of 1656, when it was used as a lazzaretto or hospice. It is linked to Lungotevere degli Anguillara by *Ponte Cestio*, a late 19th-century reconstruction of the bridge built in 46 BC by Lucius Cestius, of which only the central arch survives. The **church of S. Bartolomeo all'Isola*** was built above the ruins of the Temple of Aesculapius. It was rebuilt in 1583-85 after the flood of 1557 and altered again in 1623-24. The top of the facade incorporates a *mosaic* fragment from the time of Alexander III (1180) and the *bell tower* dates from the first restoration of the church (1113). The interior is divided into a nave and two side-aisles by columns which probably belonged to the Temple of Aesculapius. The marble *well-head* in the courtyard may belong to a well which was reputed to contain water with miracle-working powers.

The *Torre Caetani*, which controls access to the **Ponte Fabricio***, was part of a medieval fortress. The bridge has two other names: Ponte dei Quattro Capi and Pons Judaeorum because it was used by Jews crossing the Tiber to the ghetto from Trastevere. The bridge, built in 62 BC, seems to have survived the passage of time remarkably well. It was restored once, in the 2nd century, when the original travertine facing was replaced with bricks. The **bridges** of Rome deserve a special mention. They are all wide and monumental and it's hard to decide which is the most beautiful. **S. Cecilia in Trastevere,** A vast garden courtyard lies before the church which, having begun as the *titulus Caeciliae* before the 5th century, was rebuilt as a basilica in the early 9th century under Paschal I. The bell tower and the cloister were added between the 10th and 13th centuries, but, in the 18th century, the church underwent a radical transformation which especially affected the *interior*: the *Apotheosis of St Cecilia* by S. Conca (ca. 1727) which adorns the vault above the nave gives an idea of the lively nature of the decoration applied to the church in the 18th century. A frescoed corridor leads from the right aisle to a room identified as the *calidarium* where St Cecilia was left for three days and was supposed to be scalded to death but miraculously survived. The *Beheading of the Saint* above the altar is by G. Reni. A. di Cambio (1293) made the famous **ciborium** in the center of the presbytery; below the altar, the statue of **St Cecilia** by S. Maderno (1600) depicts the body of the saint as it appeared when her tomb was opened in 1599. Some of the decoration of the original church survives, such as the **mosaic** (ca. 820) in the bowl of the apse. But the masterpiece of the basilica is in the Nuns' Choir: the remains of the fresco of the *Last Judgement* painted by P. Cavallini in 1289-93. This is an exceptional example of Roman painting before Giotto arrived in Rome. The *frescoes* beside the entrance and on the opposite wall are part of the same cycle. **S. Crisogono,** The fairly simple facade of this church does not do justice to its more than 1,000 years of history. The first record of a basilica here dates from the 5th century, but it was not until 1123 that the first church dedicated to St Chrysogonus was built, restored by G.B. Soria in 1620-26. At that time, inside the church, the stucco decoration, the coffered ceiling above the nave and the transept were added, along with the barrel vaults above the side-aisles and the canopy in the presbytery, a re-use of the four alabaster columns of the old ciborium. The 11th-century Cosmatesque *pavement* dates from the 13th-century church. The *chapel of the Blessed Sacrament* at the end of the right aisle is attributed to G. L. Bernini. Below the present church lie the remains of the early-Christian and early medieval basilica, where, between the fragments of *mosaics* are earlier mosaics dating from the 8th and 9th cen-

turies. **S. Pietro in Montorio,** The old name of the Janiculum (*Mons Aureus*, Hill of Gold) is preserved in the name of this church, which was possibly founded in the 9th century but rebuilt in the late 15th century. Its chapels contain many interesting *artworks*. According to tradition (although there is no historical evidence), the cross on which St Peter was martyred once stood on the present site of **Bramante's Tempietto**** (1502-1507), the most eloquent expression of a Renais-

Isola Tiberina.

sance building with a central plan. This monument, placed in the middle of the cloister to the right of the church, consists of a round chamber surrounded by an ambulatory with 16 Tuscan granite columns. It has an elegant, segmented dome supported by a drum with shell-shaped niches. As well as providing a benchmark for early 16th-century Roman architecture, the Tempietto is also remarkable for the use of classical features (for the first time in this building Doric and Tuscan styles are correctly employed together) and the skilful harmony of sculptural decoration and space. **S. Maria in Trastevere.** The material used to construct the basilica (1138-48) was plundered from the Baths of Caracalla. It was built on the site of an early-Christian building (ca. mid-4C). Although, in 1702, the facade of the church was altered and the portico rebuilt, the main structure of the church has not changed significantly. The 13th-century *mosaic* depicting two processions of *female figures* still adorns the facade. In the 18th century, marbles, reliefs and inscriptions previously kept in the basilica or the catacombs were used to decorate the portico. The frames of the three doorways date from the Roman Imperial period. The 22 columns which separate the interior into a nave and

A view of the Trastevere district.

two side-aisles also date from the Neo-Classic period. This is one of the finest buildings to survive from the 12th century. The *ceiling* was designed by Domenichino, while the marble *tabernacle* at the beginning of the nave is by M. da Fiesole. However, all of this is of minor importance compared to what we find in the presbytery and the apse. The presbytery contains the *fons olei*, which marks the spot where, in 38 AD, a miraculous fountain of oil is supposed to have flowed, forcing Callistus I (217-222) to found what was the first official church in Rome. The apse has splendid **mosaics** in the bowl, on the arch, and by the windows. The marble *throne* with a rounded back dates from the 12th century. Notice the *Altemps chapel*, to the left of the apse, where the altar is decorated by a **Madonna della Clemenza**, an encaustic painting of the 6th-7th century. Sculptural decoration adorns the *Avila chapel* (1680), in the left aisle, with a lovely dome.

Palazzo Corsini. It was in this remarkable setting that the Arcadia literary movement, supported by Queen Christina of Sweden, came into being. The movement, whose aim was to eliminate bad literary taste and purify Italian poetry, was very influential in the first half of the 18th century. The memory of the academic life is still kept alive today by the many institutions which have offices there. The palazzo was built in 1510-1512 but rebuilt by F. Fuga (the architectural features on the facade verge towards the Neo-Classic style). The palazzo houses the **Galleria Corsini***, the only 18th-century art collection in Rome which is still intact. It was begun in the 18th century by Cardinal N. M. Corsini, nephew of Clement XII. The paintings, especially those of the Italian schools of the 16th and 17th century, but also a considerable number of paintings by foreign artists, illustrate the first classical trends, steering away from the

Baroque style. The Italian part of the collection begins with works by early painters and continues with *portraits*, especially the one of **Bernardo Clesio** by Joos van Cleve, and *bronze figurines*. Caravaggio's **St John the Baptist** introduces works in the style of Caravaggio while, among the landscapes, note the **Tancred and Erminia** by G. Dughet. The room dedicated to Queen Christina of Sweden contains still life paintings by Christian Berentz. Other works in the gallery include those by C. Maratta, N. Poussin, G.B. Piazzetta and R. Carriera. Note the *Judas and Tamar* by G. Lanfranco, **Salomè with the Head of John the Baptist** by G. Reni and *Ecce Homo* by Guercino, which precede works by Neapolitan painters (M. De Caro, Spagnoletto, D. Gargiulo and L.Giordano). Since 1883, the gardens have been host to a **Botanical Garden**, which has partially retained the layout of the original palace garden. A small artificial lake contains aquatic plants, and the 19th-century glasshouses contain orchids and succulents.

Villa Farnesina. The architectural design of the villa incorporates the principles of balance, harmony and proportion typical of the vogue of Roman Classicism of the early 16th century and contains one of Raphael's most important frescoes. The building is one of the first examples of a villa comprising a central block and a loggia with five arches. They depict the *story of Psyche* and were painted in 1517, over Raphael's cartoons, by his pupils G. Romano, G. da Udine, G. F. Penni and R. del Colle. The mythological scenes in the Sala del Fregio are by B. Peruzzi, as is the ceiling of the **Sala di Galatea****, where Raphael had painted the fresco depicting the sea-nymph on the main wall (1513-14). The *Polyphemus* by S. del Piombo (1512-13) is a typical expression of the Venetian school of painting. Peruzzi painted the frescoes in the Salone delle Prospettive.

Via della Lungara, On this street designed by Bramante is the *Porta Settimiana*, commissioned by Alexander VI, the Borgia pope, to replace a postern gate in the Aurelian walls. According to tradition, the *house* to the right of the gate once belonged to "La Fornarina", the beautiful Roman woman whose portrait Raphael painted.

Passeggiata del Gianicolo. Laid out in 1880-84 on the Janiculum Hill, along with the Pincian Hill, this footpath above the battlements of the walls built by Urban VIII has some of the most beautiful views of Rome. The path meanders up and down through the

Parco Gianicolense (Janiculum Park), dotted with busts of followers of Garibaldi. A *lighthouse* marks one of the highest points. The *equestrian monument to Anita Garibaldi* stands in front of both the splendid **Villa Lante**, built by G. Romano (1518-27) and the *equestrian monument to Giuseppe Garibaldi* (1895). The square in front of the villa has some of the best views over Rome. Not far away, **Villa Doria Pamphilj** is Rome's largest park. It is decorated with the beautiful *Fountains of the Snail* and *the Lily*, and the **Casino di Allegrezze** (an elegant building used by the Italian Government for formal occasions), also known as the Villa del Bel Respiro. Its facade is decorated with ancient marbles and there is a secret garden dotted with statues and bas-reliefs. Part of the *aqueduct* built by Paul V in 1609-1612 runs through the park.

ROME'S, GREEN DIMENSION

Villa Borghese. Rome's most famous public park was created in the 17th century by Cardinal S. Borghese as a park for the Casino Borghese, but, in the following century, was transformed into a picturesque Neo-Classic garden. In 1827, L. Canina extended it and created the Roman Arch, the Greek and Egyptian monumental gateways, and the Fountain of Esculapius. Card*inal* Scipione planned the **Casino Borghese*** as the center of his suburban residence, a setting in which to display his art collections. This is what he had in mind when he entrusted Flaminio Ponzio with the project. In his design (1608-1613), the architect imagined a facade decorated with statues, a fitting introduction to the Neo-Classic works inside, preceded by a double staircase. The portico connects the two symmetrical apartments to the central hall, built to reflect the new NeoClassic lines of the late 18th century. The **Museo and Galleria Borghese**** certainly deserves the definition of "queen of the world's private collections" accorded to the Borghese family's passion for collecting fine things. They loved ancient statuary and the masterpieces of Renaissance and Baroque art, but also the sculptures and paintings of the 16th to 19th centuries. Cardinal Scipione began the collection in 1608. Much of his collection of marbles and sculptures, along with those given to him by Paul V, originating from the old church of St Peter's, was sold to Napoleon Bonaparte by Prince Camillo Borghese in the early 19th century. The collection was reformed with the contents of the Casino, Palazzo Borghese and the Borghese villas

outside Rome. The collection of paintings was more fortunate: the Cardinal brought together works of the great masters, including works from other collections, in particular, that of Olimpia Aldobrandini. In the **Museo Borghese***, the ancient statues, busts and sculptures are still arranged in the early 18th-century manner, which attempted to place them in a suitable background. They are displayed with a "modern" sculpture, often placed in the center of the room, by the Borghese's favorite sculptor, G. L. Bernini. The same combination is found in the portico and in the **great hall**, where the niches contain the busts of 12 Roman Emperors (the huge bust of *Hadrian* is one of the best depictions of the emperor). The floor incorporates fragments of a 4th-century mosaic. The display of masterpieces begins in the former Sala del Vaso: they include the famous **Venus Victrix**** by A. Canova, the dramatic sculpture of **Apollo and Daphne*** by Gian L. Bernini (1624), the **Boy with Basket of Fruit*** (ca. 1593-95) and the **Madonna dei Palafrenieri*** (1605), two masterpieces by Caravaggio. The **Galleria Borghese*** provides an overview of Italian painting from the 15th to 17th centuries. To call the collection exhaustive is almost an understatement. The rooms where the collection is displayed, many of which are frescoed, contain an uninterrupted sequence of paintings by Italy's greatest masters and foreign painters. Raphael's undisputed talent can be seen in his **Deposition***, but all the paintings in this collection are wonderful. To mention just a few examples, Correggio's **Danaë***, **Portrait of a Man*** by Antonello da Messina and Titian's **Sacred and Prophane Love***, a triumphal celebration of Venetian Renaissance painting.

Galleria Nazionale d'Arte Moderna. The style of the building that houses this gallery, Palazzo delle Belle Arti, designed for the International Exhibition of 1911, introduces its visitors to the main subject of the collection. In fact, behind that solemn, Neo-Classic-style facade, decorated with Art-Nouveau motifs and friezes, is Italy's finest collection of 19th- and 20th-century art. The gallery was supposed to house artworks representative of Italian culture and art, but, as a result of additions to the collection, and Italy's increasing ties with other countries, the collection also includes works by foreign artists. The gallery, which now owns an enormous number of works, is currently in the process of reorganizing its collection, part of which has been moved to the new premises in Via Guido Reni. (When the work begun there in 2003 is finished, it will open its doors as the new Museum of 21C Art.) The collection includes works from the Neo-Classic and Romantic periods, by the Tuscan artists known as the *Macchiaioli*, and exponents of the Neapolitan school, Social Realism and Divisionism. 19th-century works by Rodin, Courbet, Degas, Monet and Van Gogh precede masterpieces by foreign artists of the 20th century, such as Klimt and Cézanne. Further on, there are works by Futurist and Cubist artists, works of Metaphysical Painting by Carrà and Morandi, the "*non oggettivo*" movement of Mondrian and the Dadaism of Duchamp. There is quite an extensive collection of works executed between the two World Wars, while the Novecento movement is represented by Casorati and Campigli and works of the Second Futurist movement by Balla, Fillia and Dottori. Works by A. Raphael, M. Mafai and Scipione were painted in reaction to the principles of the Novecento movement. Leoncillo, Basaldella and Sciltian represent the Roman school. The Six from Turin and the Milanese Corrente group, including Guttuso, were opposed to the Novecento movement. After WWII, surrealism was accompanied by more informal artistic trends associated with the expressiveness of materials, color and signs. Foreign trends represented include J. Pollock's American action painting and others by the Cobra group, while movements on a global scale include the kinetic art of Munari and Albers, the pop art of Kounellis and Schifano, arte povera and the Conceptual Art of P. Manzoni.

Villa Giulia. What a contrast there is between the formal facade of the villa, decorated only by the rusticated doorway with Doric columns, and the splendid loggia on three sides of the internal courtyard! The **loggia** was designed by B. Ammannati, who was commissioned to design the building (1551-55) by Julius III, together with G. Vasari (who designed the elegant **nymphaeum**) and Vignola. P. Fontana and T. Zuccari were responsible for inside decoration of the villa. The **Museo Nazionale Etrusco di Villa Giulia*** was created about a century ago to house the finds from the archeological site of *Falerii Veteres*. Today, that small nucleus of archeological material has grown into the largest museum of Etruscan antiquities in the world, with finds from excavations conducted in southern Etruria, including some important Greek finds. The reconstruction of Etruscan history begins with

finds from the necropolis and settlement at Vulci with grave-goods from the Villanovan period (9-8C BC). The site has produced the earliest pottery imported from Greece, a chariot burial marking the transition from the late Villanovan period to the Oriental period (ca. 680 BC) and the bronze weapons from the **Tomb of the Warrior** (6C BC). The polychrome terracotta **statues** of **Hercules fighting Apollo for the Sacred Hind** and the goddess Latoma holding Apollo as a child, decorations from the acroterion of the sanctuary of Portonaccio at Veii (late 6C BC), show Greek and Oriental influences. A large number of Greek vases dating from the 7th-6th centuries BC were found at Cerveteri, as well as the splendid polychrome terracotta sarcophagus of a husband and wife reclining on a couch, known as the **Sarcofago degli Sposi*** (ca. 530 BC). The **Chigi Vase** (640-625 BC) is one of the most important late proto-Corinthian artifacts from Veio. The **shafts** (530-520 BC) of a chariot from a tomb at Castro reflect Ionic influences on Etruscan craftsmanship. The excavations at Pyrgi, the Etruscan port of Cerveteri, have produced some of the most prolific finds, including the **gold tablets*** with an inscription in two languages (Etruscan and Phoenician) referring to the dedication of the sanctuary to the Phoenician divinity Astarte and the Etruscan Uni. A large amount of space is devoted to the towns in the territory around the *Ager Faliscus*, the area between Lake Bracciano and the Tiber, and the area around Capena, culminating in the reconstruction of the terracotta decoration from the **sanctuaries of Falerii Veteres****, built between 480 BC and the late 4th-early 3rd century BC. The architectural terracotta decoration, acroterial friezes and other decorative features are evidence of the extraordinary level of communication between this area of central Italy, Greece and Magno Graecia. The fabulous grave-goods from **tombs** of the Oriental period from the **Barberini** and **Bernardini** collections come from another corner of central Italy. They were discovered at ancient Praeneste (Palestrina), and comprise objects made of precious metals, ivory and bronze (mid-7C BC). The **Cista Ficoroni**, a beautiful toilet box, made in Rome in the late 4th century BC, comes from the same site. An inscription on the handle in Archaic Latin reads *Novios Plautios med Romai fecid, Dindia Malconia fileai dedid*: Novio Plauzio made me in Rome, Dindia Malconia gave me to her daughter.

CASTELLI ROMANI

"I n the morning and evening," wrote Goethe, "a little fog descends upon Rome. On the hills outside of town, however, at Albano, Castel Gandolfo, and Frascati, where I spent three days last week, the air is always clear and pure." He visited the hills more than once. Of one stay, with a marvelous December sunshine, he wrote: "Aside from the evergreens, a number of oak trees are still dense with leaves; likewise the young chestnut trees, though their leaves have yellowed. The landscape has hues of remarkable beauty..." The geography of the Albani Hills can best be glimpsed from an airplane, or else from a topographical map, perhaps an old-fashioned, patiently sketched one. In origin, they are a large volcanic system, with a clearly defined crater area, some 30 km across, broken only to the SW, ripped apart by the eruptions that tore open the lesser craters that are now the lakes of Albano, Nemi, and Ariccia – though the latter is now a dry bed. In the center are Monte Cavo (949 m) and Monte Faete (956 m). The chestnuts and oaks mentioned by Goethe are largely found in the central region, while on the gentle outer slopes are olive groves and vineyards, famed for the "vini dei castelli," or "castle wines." About these wines, Leo XIII (pope from 1878 to 1903) wrote: "exilarant animos, curasque resolvunt," i.e., "they cheer the soul and wipe away cares." The villages and small towns on the slopes are the Castelli Romani, or Roman Castles, properly speaking, 13 in number (Frascati, Grottaferrata, Marino, Castel Gandolfo, Albano, Ariccia, Genzano, Nemi, Rocca di Papa, Rocca Priora, Monte Compatri, Monte Porzio Catone, and Colonna), and called "castles" because noble Roman families and popes owned fortified country houses there. As times became easier, the fortified manors made way for open villas; popes and nobles spent their holidays here, just as the ancient Romans had done (Cicero had a villa at Tusculum, Domitian built one at Castel Gandolfo, the site of ancient Alba Longa). "In the evening" – wrote Goethe, from Frascati, in late September – "by moonlight, we walk around admiring the villas, sketching the most interesting features, even in the dark..."

A panoramic view of Castel Gandolfo.

NOT TO BE MISSED

Frascati (➟ see below): this is the most popular of the Castelli Romani; sumptuous villas have been built here since ancient Roman times. **Monte Porzio Catone** is a 16th-century village built on a hill blanketed with olive groves. **Tusculum***: the ruins of this Latin city can be reached by making a 2 km detour from the route to Grottaferrata; there are the remains of the ampitheater, the theater, the forum and the so called Villa di Tiberio. **Grottaferrata**: the venerable abbey, fortified with walls and moats, is a monastery founded in 1004 by S. Nilo, or St Niles. **Rocca di Papa** has a medieval uphill quarter and a modern, prosperous quarter with gardens; continue along your route, through the woods, and above Lake Albano you will find the Sanctuary of the Madonna del Tufo, built around a boulder frescoed by A. Romano. **Monte Cavo***: with good weather, you can see forever across the Albani Hills, glimpsing Rome, the Tyrrhenian Sea, the Circeo, Monte Terminillo, and the Gran Sasso d'Italia. **Nemi**: the town overlooks the lake, deep blue at the bottom of the crater. **Velletri** lies perched on a spur of the southern slopes of the

Albani Hills, amidst expanses of grapevines. **Genzano di Roma** fans out across the outer slope of the crater of Lake Nemi; a road along the north bank of the lake takes you to the Museo Nemorense, or Museum of Nemi. All that survives of the famous late-imperial Roman ships of Nemi are models and fragments. **Ariccia**: the central square, with fountain and the round church of S. Maria dell'Assunzione, was designed by G. L. Bernini. **Albano Laziale**: it is said that the tombs of the Horatii, early Roman heroes, and their Curiatii opponents, are here; in reality it is an anonymous late-Republic Roman tomb. **Castel Gandolfo** looks out from the rim of the crater of the Lake Albano; the 17th-century summer residence of the pope is in Piazza Plebiscito. **Marino**: "Mole stat sua" is the motto inscribed on the heraldic column of Palazzo Colonna, in the center of this village high above the lake, on a peperino spur.

FRASCATI

This town stands in an area famous for its high-quality wine-production. Its reputation as a holiday destination because of its healthy air dates from the Renaissance, when some of the most important villas outside Rome were built here. The tradition continued until the 19th century, when Frascati was the first town of the Holy See to have a railway connection to the capital (the line was opened in 1857). Villa Aldobrandini* is the most famous noble residence of the area known as the Castelli Romani, a wonderful example of the various types of Mannerist architecture used for building stately homes. The park is scattered with statues and fountains with water features, and the land slopes gracefully down from the villa to the town by means of elegant terraces. The villa was begun in 1598 for Cardinal P. Aldobrandini and finished in 1604, although the monumental entrance and some of the stuccoes were added more than a century later. It contains splendid early 16th-century frescoes which are a remarkable example of the transition from late Mannerism to the Baroque, and a bronze bust of Clement VIII. In the park, note particularly the Teatro delle Acque (Fontana designed the hydraulic system), a large, semi-circular nymphaeum decorated with niches containing water features and statues. The Scuderie Aldobrandini has been created in the former stables of the villa, including the Museo Tuscolano on the ground floor, which has an archeological section with finds dating from proto-history to the medieval period. The Auditorium on the first floor and two other large rooms are used for exhibitions. The tall, richly decorated facade (1698-1700) of the Cathedral has two orders of half-columns, niches containing statues and a relief above the main doorway. The interior, built on a Greek-cross plan, dates from the 16th century. There is a 12th-century wooden Crucifix in the second chapel on the right, a Madonna by Domenichino (third chapel on the right)

The vineyards around Frascati.

and a Madonna del Gonfalone by the 14th-century Roman school (2C chapel on the left). The elegant travertine facade of the 17th-century church of Gesù overlooks the square of the same name. Inside, a white marble line leads to the black circle on the floor at the point where the fake dome can best be admired. Another fake dome is painted above the presbytery, while the walls behind the side-altars and the high altar are frescoed by ingeniously-painted architectural features. The Rocca, now the bishop's palace, was the turreted fort of the town in the Middle Ages and has a 15th-century porticoed courtyard. Many of the rooms are frescoed, those on the ground floor in the Pompeian style. Next to the Rocca is the little church of S. Maria in Vivario. Its bell tower, with three orders of three-light windows (1305), used to belong to the earlier church on this site, dedicated to St Roch. From Frascati, a panoramic road leads to Tuscolo, 5 km away. The ancient Latin town of Tusculum was a popular holiday resort, as you can see from the ruins of villas in the surrounding hills. Remains of the Roman town include Via dei Sepolcri, a shady road with pine-trees and cypresses, a Roman amphitheater and, on a piece of flat ground, the forum and the Roman theater, still well preserved. The remains of the town of the Counts of Tuscolo, razed to the ground by papal troops in 1119, are still visible at the top of the hill. There are marvelous views

over all the Castelli as far as Rome from the Croce di Tuscolo. Near the cross are the ruins of the wall of the ancient acropolis and, close by, a cistern (6-5C BC).

ALBANO LAZIALE

The original settlement, built above the ruins of Domitian's villa and the military camp (the *Castra Albana*) established here by Septimius Severus, was half destroyed during the Barbarian invasions. It came under the Holy See in the late 17th century. Today this residential town is also well-known for its wine-production and is much visited by people from Rome on account of its rich cultural heritage. The main street is *Corso Matteotti* which, together with its extension (*Borgo Garibaldi*), corresponds to the route of the Appian Way through the town. The **Duomo**, the basilica of S. Pancrazio, was founded under Constantine, and you can still see some of the ancient columns. Rebuilt several times over the centuries, its current Baroque style blends well with the buildings surrounding it. From nearby Piazza Mazzini there are

lovely views of the Roman Campagna. Not far away is the **church of S. Maria della Rotonda***. The name of the church refers to its shape, and it is round because it was built above the nymphaeum of Domitian's villa. It has a portico at the front, a dome, and the bell tower dates from the 13th century. The icon of the Madonna inside dates from 475 and, according to tradition, was brought to Albano by nuns from Greece. The **Cisternone***, an enormous underground cistern with a capacity of approximately 10,000 m^3, dates from the 2nd century. It was dug out of the rock for military purposes and is still in use today. It has five aisles supported by pillars and a barrel-vaulted ceiling. Nearby stands the *church of S. Paolo*, situated at the apex of the triangle formed by Via Saffi and Via Murialdo. Behind it you can see the remains of the outer wall of the Roman *amphitheater* (mid-3C), built to entertain the Roman legionaries, with a seating capacity of 15,000. **Porta Pretoria*** was the main entrance to the "Castra Albana". This gate with three arches and a tower on either side re-appeared along with the other Roman ruins you can see on Via Saffi following the air raids of 1944. The Roman ruins also incorporate the **church of S. Pietro***, erected in the 6th century. You can still discern parts of the baths, despite the fact that the church has been altered many times, and there are fragments of Roman marble in the side door, and in the bell tower with its two-light windows. Inside, there are Roman *marble friezes* along the edge of the presbytery, and a 3rd-century *sarcophagus* has been re-used as an altar in the left wall. There are 13th-century frescoes on the right-hand wall and a *painting* by Gherardo delle Notti.

Villa Ferrajoli, built in the 19th century and surrounded by a lovely garden, now houses the *Museo Civico*. Its exhibits range in date from prehistory to the late-Roman period, and it has an Archeological Park attached. Nearby is another Roman monument: the *tomb of the Horatii and the Curatii*. It consists of a rectangular base of stone with a cornice and a frieze, surmounted by two truncated cones, also in stone.

Hidden below the late 16th-century *church of S. Maria della Stella*, the cemetery complex known as the **Catacombe di S. Senatore** probably dates from the 3rd century. The central chamber is decorated with frescoes from the 5th-9th centuries.

FOOD IN LAZIO

Typical Roman specialities, such as spaghetti with cheese and pepper sauce, roast lamb and Jewish-style artichokes, reflect local farming traditions in which stock-breeding provides cheeses and meat products and market gardening provides vegetables. Olives are another important element in local agriculture where they are grown to eat whole or to use for the production of olive oil. Chestnuts and hazelnuts also play an important role in certain areas of the region and the local woods yield delicious truffles. Finally, Pane Casareccio di Genzano, a type of household bread, was the first Italian product to receive IGP status.

LOCAL SPECIALITIES

Gnocchi alla Romana. In international cuisine this dish usually means little semolina dumplings cooked in milk with a cheese and egg yolk sauce. The dumplings are then popped in the oven in a dish with extra butter and cheese to brown. In reality the gnocchi, or dumplings, "alla Romana" are potato dumplings.

Bucatini all'Amatriciana. This sauce originally came from the village of Amatrice, near Rieti. Bucatini or spaghetti are served with a sauce made from lard, cured bacon, white wine, tomatoes and hot chili pepper topped with a generous sprinkling of grated Pecorino cheese. Another spaghetti dish which deserves a mention is the well-known "Spaghetti alla Carbonara"; this may be an evolution of a traditional Roman dish "alla Sangiovannara" which also involved a butter, cheese and egg yolk sauce.

Pajata. Stable companion to "Coda alla Vaccinara", this is one of Rome's true culinary glories. The "pajata" is literally the intestine of an unweaned calf cut into manageable lengths and tied to retain the milk. It is either tossed in an olive oil, garlic, parsley, white wine, chili pepper and tomato sauce and eaten with "rigatoni" pasta, or baked in the oven as a main course with potatoes, lashings of olive oil, fennel seed, rosemary and garlic.

Abbacchio alla Cacciatore. The iconic Roman speciality. Abbacchio is very young, unweaned lamb which is often simply roasted in the oven. When served "alla Cacciatore" (Hunter's Style) the lamb is stewed in white wine with garlic, rosemary, anchovies and chili pepper. Traditionally the meat is taken from the leg and the shoulder.

Carciofi alla Giudia. Artichokes cooked in a traditional recipe from Rome's Jewish community. The tough outer leaves are removed and the artichokes are then gently stewed in oil before being plunged into a sizzling pan of oil that fries them into an open flower-like shape. Artichokes are also served "alla Romana", where the tender parts of the stalk are finely chopped

with mint, garlic, pepper and salt and used to stuff the artichokes which are then gently stewed in water and olive oil.

Coda alla Vaccinara. Oxtail stew, a dish that originated in the trattorias that clustered around Rome's meat market. The local workers were given the unmarketable parts of the meat, jokingly referred to as "the fifth quarter". Once the fat has been trimmed from the tail it is stewed in a tomato sauce flavoured with garlic, onions and herbs, with the addition of sultanas, pine kernels and dark chocolate. Roughly chopped celery is added to complete the stew when it is almost cooked. In the past parts of the cheek and tongue were often thrown into the pot too.

Fagioli con le Cotiche. Boiled beans with thick slices of bacon rind cooked in lard, the fat from a ham, garlic, parsley and tomato sauce.

Porchetta di Arriccia. Roast suckling pork speciality from a village in the hills near Rome. The whole animal is boned and flavoured with herbs and spices before being roast on a spit until its crackling is brown and crispy.

Saltimbocca alla Romana. A Roman speciality that has become internationally famous.

Slices of cured ham are laid over thin slices of veal with a fresh sage leaf and pinned into place with a couple of toothpicks. These are quickly pan fried in butter with a dash of white wine.

Maritozzi. Neo-Classic Roman sweet buns with sultanas, pine kernels and orange peel.

Crostata di Ricotta. A pastry crust pie with a

soft, sheep's cheese ricotta, egg and sugar filling flavoured with spices (usually cinnamon). There are several variations on the basic theme with the addition of candied fruits, cherries, currants, figs or chestnuts.

PRODUCTS

Pecorino Romano DOP. Made from whole sheep's milk from Lazio itself, Sardinia and the neighbouring province of Grosseto. A hard, cooked cheese produced in large wheel-like shapes covered in a thinnish rind with a compact consistency and occasional tiny air bubbles. A very highly-flavoured mature cheese that is also used finely-grated on many local dishes.

Ricotta Romana DOP. One of Lazio's most historical cheeses. The difference from its fellow ricotta cheeses lies in its rather grainy consistency and stronger flavour. It is made from cow's milk.

Coppiette di Cavallo. Top quality, lean horsemeat cut into strips and flavoured with salt and chili pepper. The strips are then tied into pairs (hence its name "coppiette", or couples) and hung to be smoked near the fireplace.

Corallina Romana. Salami made from lean pork traditionally cut from the shoulder. The meat is boned and after the fat has been trimmed off it is roughly minced. Diced lard is added to the mixture which is seasoned with pepper, salt and garlic marinated in wine. This is then stuffed into natural gutskin and cured for 2 to 3 months.

Monte San Biagio Sausages. Sausages produced in the towns and villages of Fondi, Lenola, Itri and Monte San Biagio in the province of Latina. Lean pork is hand-chopped and seasoned with red pepper and coriander.

Romanesque Lazio Artichokes IGP. One of the Roman countryside's prize products. Romanesque artichokes are greeny-purple with large, tender, rounded leaves and no prickles. They are believed to have been cultivated in Lazio since Etruscan times.

Extra Virgin Canino Olive Oil DOP. An emerald green oil shot through with gold produced from Caninese, Leccino, Pendolino, Maurino and Frantoio olives. It combines a fresh, fruity bouquet with a decided flavour and a slightly bitter, tangy after taste. Canino olive oil is produced in northern Lazio in the countryside around Viterbo.

Extra Virgin Sabina Olive Oil DOP. Produced with Carboncella, Leccino, Raja, Pendolino, Olivastrone, Salviana, Olivago and Rosciola olives. Sabina olive oil is golden yellow with occasional green dapples, it has a fruity bouquet and is sweet tasting, although the freshly-pressed oil has a bitter tang. It is produced in the countryside of many towns and villages around Rome and Rieti.

Extra Virgin Tuscia Olive Oil DOP. Pressed from Frantoio, Caninese and Leccino olives, Tuscia oil is emerald green shot through with gold. Its bouquet is reminiscent of healthy, fresh, sun-ripened olives with a fruity flavour and a slightly bitter, tangy after taste.

Genzano Bread IGP. Soft wheat flour milled from top quality cereals and acid yeast to make the dough rise are just two of the secrets that make Genzano bread so special. It is baked in large, cartwheel-shaped loaves or long loaves and has been Rome's favourite bread since the 19th century, thanks to its delicious flavour and week-long freshness.

Latina Kiwis IGP. Cisterna di Latina was one of the first areas in Italy to experiment with growing kiwis back in the 1970s. This was a success story thanks to the soil and climate that are similar to that of the fruit's native land.

WINES

Statistics show clearly that Lazio is white wine country. Three varieties of Malvasia alone account for over half of the regional vineyards, and when a further two strains of Trebbiano are added in, the total nudges two thirds. The region also produces good native-strain reds, red Cori wine and two Cesanese reds, without forgetting newly-introduced grapes such as Sangiovese, Montepulciano, Merlot and Cabernet. Vineyards tend to be concentrated around the area of the Castelli Romani, the Alban Hills area, and the countryside around Viterbo, historically known as the Tuscia. The two best-known wines from the area are Frascati white, an Italian icon, and Est! Est!! Est!!! from Montefiascone, another iconic wine. Colli della Sabina on the cusp of the hills between Rieti and Rome is another well-known wine producing area, as is Frosinone with its Cesanese reds; Latina is the new frontier when it comes to wine producing in Lazio and there are already important producers in Aprilia and Circeo.

FOOD

At the Passo delle Capannelle (1,299 m) you are on the watershed between Aterno and Vomano, two rivers that "envelop" the massif of the Gran Sasso d'Italia. You make your way up here, on the way from L'Aquila to the Adriatic Sea, winding amidst white badlands, along jagged, forest-covered slopes. You also pass by the ruins of "Amiternum," city of the Sabines. The line of descent is along the Vomano Valley, but it makes detours and circles so that you have spectacular views of the Gran Sasso d'Italia: at Campotosto, alongside the great manmade lake with jagged shores, you see the Gran Sasso to the NW, at an angle; at Prati di Tivo, the two peaks of the Corno Grande and the Corno Piccolo stand out clear, harsh, and naked, above rolling meadows and steep pastures gouged with gulleys; at Isola del Gran Sasso d'Italia, in the Mavone Valley, near the Vomano, you can see the peaks glow again just after sunset when the weather is good. As you get closer to the Adriatic, amid the gently rolling hills, you head up to Atri, a two-fold balcony: on the one side you bid farewell to the distant mountain, high over the rows of hills; on the other you greet the approaching sea, vast and fresh, with a long coastline. In the city of Atri, you can see the work of the leading Abruzzese painter, Andrea De Litio. Almost nothing is known of his life, and his work is found almost exclusively here; he is believed to have been active around 1450, and is thought to have been influenced by P. della Francesca. His painting can be seen in the choir of the cathedral.

NOT TO BE MISSED

San Vittorino: beneath the Romanesque church of S. Michele, at the center of town, is a catacomb with the supposed remains of a Christian martyr, Vittorino; at the foot of the hill are the ruins of ancient Sabine and Roman Amiternum, birthplace of Sallust. **Campotosto** is a summer resort near a manmade lake formed by damming the Rio Fucino; the lake reflects the peaks of the Gran Sasso d'Italia. **Pietracamela**, another resort town on the slopes of the Gran Sasso d'Italia, is downhill from Prati di Tivo. From there, you can take a chairlift up to the Madonnina del Gran Sasso (remarkable view of the peaks of the Gran Sasso d'Italia and of the Laga). **Montorio al Vomano**: the modern district lies on the main road, while the medieval one is high on a hill; note the large wooden altars in the parish church. **Tossicia**: venerable houses and a portal by A. Lombardo (1471) at the church of S. Antonio Abate. Sanctuary of S. Gabriele dell'Addolorata: the remains of a 19th-century saint – the patron saint of Abruzzo – are buried here. **Isola del Gran Sasso d'Italia** stands on a ridge of the north slope of the great massif; the windows of the old houses bear sententious Latin mottos. **Castelli**: the production of fine ceramics here dates from the 13th century; the local museum has a ceramics collection and a reproduction of a 16th-century artisan's workshop. S. Giovanni al Mavone is a Romanesque church frescoed in the apse and crypt. S. Maria di Ronzano is a 12th-century church with original frescoes. **S. Clemente al Vomano*** is partly Romanesque, with a noteworthy ciborium by a certain Maestro Ruggero and his son Roberto. S. Maria di Propezzano* is another Romanesque church, built between the 12th-14th century, which commemorates an ancient apparition of the Virgin Mary; note the 15th-century frescoes inside the church. **Atri** looks out from atop a lush spur, to the blue of the Adriatic in the distance; in the celebrated 13th-century. Cathedral are the frescoes by A. De Litio (15C); situated in the piazza is the Teatro Comunale, a reduced version of the Scala opera house in Milan; the Museo Diocesano lies past the adjacent cloister. **Pineto**: a pine grove adorns this beach resort near the mouth of the Vomano River.

L'AQUILA

This ancient city abounds in lovely images: the corners of the castle (16C) built by the Spanish Viceroy, Don Pedro de Toledo; the white-and-red blocks that checker the Romanesque facade of the church of S. Maria di Collemaggio; lastly, the Fountain of 99 Spouts. Rich in monuments, survivor of many earthquakes, L'Aquila is the greatest – if not the largest – city in the region of Abruzzo.

Piazza del Duomo. This is the heart of the city, adorned by two fountains and the site of a daily market. Overlooking it is the Duomo, rebuilt after 1703, with a Neo-Classic facade. Inside, note the Agnifili Tomb, by S. dell'Aquila, an early Christian sarcophagus, bas-reliefs by G. de' Rettori, a painting by F. da Montereale and a handsome painting by V. Mascitelli.

Church of the Suffragio. On the south side of the square, the church's proudest treasure is in the apse: a polyptych by F. and G. C. Bedeschini. To the right, alongside the church, runs Via dei Ramieri, ending at a row of 15th-century warehouses, called the Cancelle.

The little roads in the heart of L'Aquila.

Corso Vittorio Emanuele, the city's main street is a partly porticoed pedestrian mall. Midway along it is the intersection of the Quattro Cantoni; of interest are the 15th-century Palazzo Fibbioni and a 14th-century tower, whose bells chime 99 times, two hours after sunset, to honor the 99 castles that helped build L'Aquila.

S. Bernardino**, towering high above the city, this church was built in 1454-72, and largely rebuilt following the earthquake of 1703. The majestic facade, built by C. dell'Amatrice in 1540, is still intact. Inside, note the handsome gilt carved Baroque ceiling*; the spectacular Baroque organ, by B. Mosca; the terracotta altar-piece* by A. della Robbia; and the tombs of St Bernardino* and Maria Pereira*, both by S. dell'Aquila.

Castle*, surrounded by a large park, this powerful square fort, with stout bastions, was built by the Spanish from 1530 until 1635, and constituted cutting-edge technology in the use of, and defense against, firearms. A monumental portal on the SE side leads into the Museo Nazionale d'Abruzzo, which includes archeological, paleontological, and artistic collections. The archeological collection features Italic and Roman artifacts; noteworthy calendar, from the site of "Amiternum" (after AD 25). The collections of art include works mostly by local artists, ranging from the 12th-18th century. Note the processional cross* by N. da Guardiagrele (1434). Modern artists include R. Guttuso, G. Capogrossi, and D. Cantatore. There is a striking reconstruction of an ancestor of modern elephants, the Archidiskodon meridionalis vestinus (1.5 million years old), unearthed near the city in 1954. **S. Maria di Paganica**, completed in 1308 and repeatedly ravaged by earthquakes, this church boasts a handsome carved Gothic portal (18C interior). A stroll around the church includes three palazzi (Ardinghelli, Camponeschi, and Carli) and two medieval houses (Casa di Buccio and Casa di J. di Notar Nanni).

S. Silvestro, this 14th-century church has a simple facade with a handsome portal and rose window. Inside, the central apse boasts remarkable 15th-century frescoes, as well as paintings by F. da Montereale and G. C. Bedeschini (copy; original now in the Prado, Madrid).

S. Pietro di Coppito. This medieval church was built around 1300-1350 and often restored, consequently the carved architrave over the portal is one of the few original features. Inside, note the 14th-century frescoes and the badly damaged frescoes of St George (right and left apses).

S. Domenico, situated in a steep, largely intact part of the medieval city, this church was rebuilt after the terrible earthquake of 1703; all that survived were the base of the facade, the right wall, and part of the apse. Follow Via Sassa, now Via Buccio di Ranallo, to see a cluster of medieval and Baroque buildings.

S. Maria di Roio, first built in the 15th century, and rebuilt after 1703, this church is surrounded by notable palazzi (Antonelli-Dragonetti, Persichetti, and Rivera).

Fontana delle 99 Cannelle*. A symbol of the city, this fountain has a spout and mascaron for each of the castles that reputedly helped found the city seven centuries ago. Dating from 1272, the fountain has been extensively rebuilt over the years.

S. Giusta, begun in 1257, its solemn facade dates from 1349, with a handsome portal and Gothic rose window. Inside, interesting works are the gilt-wood main altar, inlaid Gothic choir and 15th-century fresco of the Virgin and Child. Around it are Palazzo Centi and Palazzo Dragonetti. Follow Via Fortebraccio, which goes through a charming district, once inhabited by the city Jews.

S. Maria di Collemaggio**, this outstanding monument of Abruzzo architecture stands just outside the Porta Bazzano, in a lovely setting. The church was begun in 1287, on the site of a miraculous vision of the Virgin Mary, at the behest of Pietro da Morrone, the hermit who became Pope Celestine V. The magnificent, early 14th-century facade is adorned with white and pink blocks of stone, arranged in geometric patterns; of the three rose windows and portals, note the central one and the Porta Santa*, on the left side. The huge interior was restored in 1972-74. On the walls, votive frescoes, a polychrome terracotta Virgin and Child, and paintings by C. Ruther; note the tomb of S. Pietro Celestino* (1517).

"**B**ehind the Gran Sasso the setting sun filled the whole springtime sky with a brilliant pinkish light: and, since the moist fields and the river waters and the waters of the sea and the ponds during the day had emitted much vapor, houses and sails and poles and trees and every single thing appeared tinged with pink". This is a glimpse of the Abruzzo coast from "Le Novelle della Pescara" by G. D'Annunzio. The Gran Sasso invariably dominates the horizon throughout this route: through valleys and over hills, along winding secluded roads, down the rolling ridges that drop away to the sea from the high mountains of the Laga and the Gran Sasso d'Italia: this is seaside Abruzzo, east of the Apennine ridges. The rows of hills are divided by rivers that run, more-or-less parallel, down to the Adriatic, like tines raking the length of the beach. The north-south stretch that you will cover is crossed by the rivers Tronto (bordering the Marche), Vibrata, Salinello, Tordino (the valley of Teramo), Vomano (pouring into the sea between Roseto degli Abruzzi and Pineto), Piomba (this river, with the Fino and the Tavo, empties 8 km from the sea into an exceedingly short river, the Saline), and – last stop on this route – Pescara. You head inland just south of the first river, and you will cross the valleys of all the others. Crests, isolated hills, clayey badlands, gravel washes, rows of tremulous poplars, olive groves, the evergreen holm-oaks high on the crags: this road goes through ever-new landscapes, surprising at every turn; the clouds are swept inland by the offshore breeze and even the sky and the light are different. Skirting Pescara, you return to the sea coast, described by the native Pescarese D'Annunzio as extending "in an almost virginal serenity, along the shore that arcs slightly toward the south, in its splendor displaying the bright color of a Persian turquoise"

NOT TO BE MISSED

Giulianova sits atop a low hill to the north of the Tordino River: there is a 15th-century octagonal Duomo and a gallery, chiefly devoted to 19th-century Neapolitan painting; downhill, on the Adriatic coast, extends Giulianova Lido, a fishing town and resort. **Tortoreto Lido**: you can swim among abundant verdant nature, at the foot of gently rolling hills. Tortoreto is a secluded hilltop village; note the 16th-century frescoes in the church of S. Maria della Misericordia. **Civitella del Tronto** is a small town straddling a slope, with a slight late-Renaissance flavor; from the high Fortezza, or fortress, which endured four sieges, you have a vista ranging from the mountains to the sea. **S. Pietro**: take a short detour immediately after Campovalano, and visit the 13th-century church next to the ruins of a 12th-century Benedictine convent. **Campli**: extending across a natural terrace, this little city has medieval and Renaissance architecture and an archeological museum located on the site of a former convent, with artifacts from the necropolis of Campovalano. **Teramo**: most of the city is modern, except for some Roman and medieval parts; in the Cathedral note the frontal by Nicola da Guardiagrele and a polyptych by Jacobello del Fiore, both dating from the 15th century. **Penne** stands on two hills with medieval views and ancient churches; outside of town, on a wooded hill, S. Maria in Colleromano still harbors relics of its 14th-century foundation. **Loreto Aprutino**: the ceramics of Castelli and other towns of the territory are found in the Galleria Acerbo; south of town is the church of S. Maria in Piano, with remarkable 14th-century frescoes. **Pianella**: on a hill outside of town is the Romanesque church of S. Maria Maggiore, with 12th-century pulpit and 12th-15th-century frescoes. **Pescara** (➡ see below): the canal-port, crowded with fishing boats – actually the mouth of the Pescara River – divides the thriving Adriatic town in two, with the pine forest made famous by D'Annunzio to the south, and the long seafront promenade to the north. A renowned international jazz festival takes place in town during the month of July.

PESCARA

At the mouth of the river of the same name, Pescara is a predominantly modern city with two hearts – that of the ancient Pescara (now Portanuova) south of the Porto Canale (port-canal), and that of Castellammare Adriatico to the north. The two municipalities (the first is more business-oriented and less chic, the second more gentlemanly) fused in 1926 to create the capital of a small province. Heavily bombed in WWII, Pescara urbanised and developed from the 1950s on. Tourist areas such as Montesilvano and Città Sant'Angelo, and industrial areas grew up around the fringes towards Chieti, and green spaces were developed around the city, including the Dannunziana pine grove to the south and the Santa Filomena pine grove to the north.

Piazza I Maggio. The piazza houses what the Pescara people consider their most attractive monument, Pietro Cascella's ship (1987), which, with its prow facing the city, symbolises the city's vocation for work, travel and the return home.

Viale Regina Margherita and Viale Bovio. Once Castellammare Adriatico's main thoroughfares lined with residential villas, these two boulevards are now important arteries for the center's residential areas.

Sanctuary of the Madonna dei Sette Dolori*. This was once the central hub of Castellammare Adriatico, as can be seen from the rather rural piazza. The only original element is the church tower (18C), built up around a chapel with a miraculous picture of the Virgin Mary that is now in the right aisle and flanked by an imitation Nostra Signora dei Sette Dolori.

Corso Umberto. Starting in Piazza Rinascita, better known as Piazza Salotto, it is a pivotal point in the urban landscape. It is home to Palazzo della Cassa di Risparmio di Pescara e Loreto Aprutino with mosaics by P. Dorazio. It ends in Piazza Sacro Cuore, with the church of the same name.

Central station. Opened in 1988, the station is on two levels and is one of the most attractive and efficient train stations in Europe.

Corso Vittorio Emanuele. Beautiful boutiques line this wide street, making it extremely dynamic and lively.

Piazza Italia, the square is a product of the desire to inject a monumental appearance into the heart of the new city, born out of the fusion of Castellammare Adriatico and Pescara. The square is somewhat different to the original plan by V. Pilotti (1928). However, the buildings, built before 1936, are a perfect example of fascist architecture. Note the Michetti park and gardens (1997), a fountain with a bronze group representing Pescara (1950s) and the herm of G. D'Annunzio.

Palazzo di Città and Palazzo del Governo. These represent the solemn power of the local government. The four statues representing the River, Sea, Mining and Agriculture on the facade of Palazzo del Governo are by G. Costanzo. In Palazzo di Città, the *Sala Consiliare* is decorated by L. Baldacci. Palazzo del Governo houses numerous artworks, including the famous Il Canto d'Amore*, a sculpture group by C. Barbella, and The daughter of Iorio**, a tempera by F. P. Michetti, bought by the provincial council in 1932 as a representation of the city's soul. In 1943, the tempera was hidden in the Penne cathedral to protect it from bombing.

S. Andrea. A modern church (1964) with three mosaics by A. Sassu (*St Andrew the fisherman*, the Madonna with St Eugene of Mazenod and St Joseph the artisan), who also painted the frescoes of the fathers of the Vatican Council II around St Peter, Pope John XXIII and Pope Paul VI (1964).

Museo delle Meraviglie Marine, features fishing and sailing equipment, an ichthyology section and paleontological finds. The Sala della Marineria Pescarese is important as it houses over 100 period photos.

Museo delle Genti d'Abruzzo*. Housed in the old Bourbonic penitentiary, the museum is one of Italy's key anthropological museums. It features archeological finds, for the most part prehistoric, and documents on the agro-pastoral culture. It has 15 halls with informative, entertaining installations, and a gallery about the Abruzzo territory in Italian and English that provides an insight into understanding the history and traditions of this region.

Museo Casa natale di Gabriele D'Annunzio** was purchased by the parents of the poet, who was born here on 12 March 1863. Only the interior rooms are decorated in the style of the original bourgeois residence. The stables and storerooms have been converted into an exhibition area. Additional areas for the library and museum-house have been added on the balcony. The courtyard features a ceramic portrait of the poet by B.Cascella (1920).

Tempio della Conciliazione. This cathedral was started in 1933 on the site of the old church of S. Cetteo, which was demolished to make way for the Michetti theatre and Palazzo Michetti-Barattucci. It is flanked by the baptistery and bell tower and houses the funerary chapel of L. D'Annunzio*. In 1949, the mortal remains of the poet's mother were laid there, in a sarcophagus decorated with a young sleeping bride by A. Minerbi. Before the chapel is a St Francis bequeathed by D'Annunzio and attributed to Guercino.

Museo Civico Basilio Cascella*. It is located in the chromolithographic works built in the late-19th century by Basilio, the founder of the art and literature magazine Illustrazione Abruzzese. The museum houses over 500 works by Basilio and six other artists from his family. It also features the famous Black Knight by his grandson Andrea, which won praise at the Venezia Biennale in 1964.

Pineta Dannunziana. The tour ends in the city's 350,000 m² green lung, which features the stele of the D'Annunzio theatre, and the former Aurum distillery, designed in the 1930s by Michelucci.

THE MAIELLA MASSIF

When the town of L'Aquila dared to raise its head in rebellion, in 1528, P. de Châlons, Prince of Orange and Viceroy of Naples (French-born but, to repay a slight offered him by Francis I, a turncoat and renegade, in the service of the Holy Roman Emperor, Charles V), sallied furiously forth with his Lansquenet troops. He sacked the town, fined it 100,000 ducats, and set an additional annual tribute toward the construction of a grim castle. He then turned his troops back to Naples; on the way back he lost 500 of his precious German mercenaries in a sudden March blizzard in the Piano delle Cinquemiglia, which stretches south from Sulmona to Isernia. Given the circumstances, the loss of seasoned troops meant more than the usual chance passerby swept away by a flurry of snow. The emperor ordered five strong towers to be built as shelter for lost wayfarers; they are long gone. Stark, deserted, and with only the 19th-century road as a mark of man, this mountainous highland is now highly valued for its vast ski slopes and lush lonely meadows in summer. You will pass through it as you begin to return northward on the circuit of the Maiella. The slopes of this mountain bristle with beech trees and holm-oaks and, higher up, with pine trees; the meadows blossom with flowers in spring and the mountainside yawns with deep, wild gulleys, eroding away into the limestone. Second only to the Gran Sasso d'Italia, this is the most notable mountain group in the central Apennines, running roughly north-south, from Chieti to Sulmona. The valleys of the Pescara River and its tributary, the Orta, bound it to the north and west; then come a series of karstic plains. To the south and SE is the valley of the Aventino, which flows into the Sangro; to the east it is lined by low foothills that level away down to the

Roccaraso is in the Maiella area.

Adriatic Sea. The highest peak, Monte Amaro, stands 2,793 m tall. After the thrills and views of the mountain, you will pass by the two cities of Chieti and Sulmona, the Cistercian church of S. Maria Arabona (incomplete) and the lovely town of Guardiagrele, home of the most celebrated goldsmith of Abruzzo, Ghiberti's student Nicola di Andrea Gallucci, known as Nicola da Guardiagrele.

NOT TO BE MISSED

Chieti (➡ see below) closely follows the contours of the hillside, high over the Pescara River Valley. **Bucchianico**: spread out on an upland, with fine churches, this town has a notable piece of folk tradition, the "Sagra dei Banderesi" honoring St Urban (22-25 May). Blockhaus has a spectacular view from the ridge between the Maielletta and Monte Acquaviva (2,737 m). **Guardiagrele** has a venerable crafts tradition of goldwork and wrought iron; adjacent to the 11th-century Romanesque church of S. Maria Maggiore, the Museo d'Arte Sacra has a processional cross by Nicola da Guardiagrele. **Pennapiedimonte** is a little town with steep stairways and an 18th-century white parish church. **Fara San Martino**, on a terrace on the east slope of the Maiella, was founded in Lombard times; interesting painting in the parish church by T. da Varallo. **Lama dei Peligni**: take a cableway up to the Grotta del Cavallone. **Palena** is an old village with lovely bits of architecture, rebuilt after being devastated by heavy fighting in 1943; go see the 16th-century wooden statue of the Madonna in the churcho of the Rosario. **Pescocostanzo***: this ancient village, with a notable 11th-century basilica, rebuilt in the 15th century and enlarged in 1558, overlooks the highland of Quarto Grande; for centuries, it has produced fine lace and is also a renowned winter skiing resort. **Rivisondoli** is a resort on a spur overlooking the highland. **Roccaraso**: people come here to summer and to ski (highland of Aremogna). **Pettorano sul Gizio**: fine old rustic architecture. **Sulmona**: set against the mountains girding the Valle Peligna, this town with its ancient atmosphere demands a leisurely tour to admire individual monuments (especially the Cathedral and Annunziata) and the elegance of the town itself. **Pacentro** is a village on the slopes of the mountains of Morrone; note the 14th-century towers of the Cantelmo castle. **Caramanico Terme** is a spa; the old town has medieval walls and gates, a castle, and notable churches. **San Valentino in Abruzzo Citeriore** has a parish church by L. Vanvitelli. S. Maria Arabona is a Cistercian Gothic abbey church (13C) with frescoes by Antonio da Atri.

300

CHIETI

In the 1st century AD, Chieti was made a Roman municipality and its orthogonal structure dates from this period. One of the most interesting festivals is a procession held on Good Friday, in which highly artistic statues are paraded.

Cathedral. Extensively reconstructed in the 14th century and remodelled in the 16th century, the cathedral was upgraded in the 18th century. The existing facade and right side date from the 20th century. The bell tower* is lightened by ogival two-mullioned windows and small twin columns. Started by Bartolomeo di Giacomo in 1335, it was completed by Antonio da Lodi in 1498. The portal features a lunette with a mosaic by B. Biagetti. The interior is built to a Latin-cross layout with a nave and two aisles, and a raised presbytery.

S. Francesco della Scarpa. Built in 1239 on the site of a pre-existing church, S. Francesco della Scarpa features a 13th-century rose window with small trefoil arches. The lower part in stone is in the Baroque style. The first chapel on the left houses a wooden bust of St Anthony of Padua by G. Colombo (1706) and the fifth chapel on the left features a painting of the Virgin Mary with Mark the Evangelist, attributed to Padovanino. In the nave there is a lovely wooden pulpit by T. Salvini da Orsogna (18C).

Museo d'Arte Costantino Barbella. The museum houses some very valuable artworks including the Madonna and Child and Crucifixion with Saints, frescoes from the late-14th century; St Jerome and St John the Baptist, paintings on wood by the masters of the Crivelli Polyptychs (15C). 19th-century art is represented by the works of F. Palizzi, B. Cascella (drawings), a collection of sketches by Chieti sculptor C. Barbella and paintings by F. P. Michetti.

S. Domenico. Erected on the site of a medieval church, S. Domenico has a two-storey Baroque (1642) stone facade. The first chapel on the right is St Pompeius Maria Pirotti Teaching the Children by Tommaso Cascella (1949). On the high altar is an altar-piece with the Madonna and Child, St Anne and St Anthony of Padua and St Francis of Paola (17C).

Roman temple. The temple complex north of the ancient forum extended from this area to Corso Marrucino. It comprises three buildings from the 1st century. The religious activities are probably linked to a well that still exists in the space below the pronaos in the middle cell.

Roman theatre. Leave Piazza Trento e Trieste, and follow Via Zecca and Via di Porta Napoli to the remains of the Roman theatre (2C), which is partially built into the hillside. Built in opus reticolatum, the cavea is 84 m in diameter. Part of the left side is visible.

Civitella. The area was the acropolis of Teate Marrucinorum: excavations from 1982 to 1994 uncovered the structure of the sanctuary comprising grandiose Italic temples and an amphitheatre. The 2nd-century BC religious buildings occupied the hillside towards the old center and were decorated with friezes and frontal statues in terracotta.

Museo La Civitella. The museum in Via G. Pianell features Italic and Roman finds from the Chieti area and the Pescara valley. It is divided into three sections. Early urban history, with finds from the Republican era (3C BC). Finds include coins, bronze objects, friezes*, fragments of polychrome terracotta (2C BC). Another section focuses on the Imperial era and large public buildings (portraits of Augustus, Titian, marble statues and fragments of inscriptions). The third section is dedicated to the Land of the Marrucini with bronze and iron weapons, and clay vases from the Palaeolithic to Italic periods.

Museo Archeologico Nazionale d'Abruzzo*. The museum houses interesting finds from the Italic and Roman periods. The upper floor features funerary objects from Abruzzo's most important pre-Roman necropolises (10-4C BC). The funerary bed of Amplero* in wood with ivory inlay is worthy of note. The Sala X houses the imposing funerary statue of the *Warrior of Capestrano***, from the 6th century BC, a vestige of the so-called Picene culture. The warrior was 209 cm high and wore a headdress with a broad brim. His face was masked and two disks on his chest served to protect his heart. In his arms he is clasping an axe and a spade decorated with human and animal figures. On the same floor, the bronze statue of Ercole Curino* (3C BC). The numismatic collection* features about 1000 coins from the 4th century BC to the 19th century AD.

Baths. The baths represent one of the most important complexes remaining from the 1st-century BC Roman city. The baths are divided into nine rooms covered with barrel vaulting that were connected with arches. An ambulatory leads to a room with a mosaic floor, which in turn leads to three ambulatories that were heated with hot air injected below the pavement and along the walls. The last room is a calidarium. The far wall of the mosaic room leads into another room that is now also completely destroyed, with apses on the corners, in one of which there is a basin. To the right of the mosaic room are several service areas.

The ridges of the Sannio mountains are both rugged and rolling, often allowing vast, open views of the distant horizon. The majestic Matese massif rises just beyond the Tammaro River, above Sepino, and runs for 50 km along the Apennine ridge, separating Molise from Campania. The highest point, Mt Miletto (2,050 m), is the birthplace of the only river that runs solely through Molise, the Biferno, which crosses the region before washing into the Adriatic between Termoli and Campomarino. It is to these magic Apennine lands that the predecessors of the Samnites, the Sabines, came in search of new land. Remnants of Samnite worship sites and fortifications are still visible, indicating just how majestic their temples and nearly impenetrable forts were. The Romans also left evidence of their time ruling these lands, a period that culminated in the city of Saepinum. The turbulent times of the Lombards, Normans, Swabians, Angevins and Aragonese can also be discerned in the castles, towers and rings of walls that have become a continuum of buildings. There are the traces of Romanesque, Renaissance and Baroque art in the buildings and churches. Finally, there is the magnificent landscape, which is best explored along the winding, quiet roads.

NOT TO BE MISSED

Campobasso*: the geographical and political center of Molise, this city lies at the foot of the so-called "Monti", a rocky outcrop where the Monforte castle and the church of S. Maria del Monte were built. The heart of this town is the section built in the early 19th century on the orders of Gioacchino Murat, with wide avenues, piazzas and botanic gardens. This section is also home to the key public buildings, businesses and shops. The medieval hamlet** is enclosed by Via Marconi, Via Orefici and Via del Castello, which follow the line of the old town walls (remnants remains of some towers and the S. Paolo, Mancina and the tower-flanked S. Antonio* gates). The towns principal monuments are the church of S. Leonardo*, the church of S. Giorgio* (with a 14C chapel and frescoes) and the Nuovo Museo Provinciale Sannitico* (prehistoric and Roman displays as well as grave goods from Lombard necropolises at Campochiaro, including a reconstruction of a tomb of a horseman and his harnessed horse). The steep steps along Via Chiarizia lead to the castle* built in 1130 over a Samnite fortification. The cast-

le's current appearance is the result of work done after the 1456 earthquake. The square, crenellated keep is imposing, especially with its sloping wall and two towers guarding the entrance. **Sepino**: the countryside around this village is home to some of the most eloquent remnants left by the Samnites and the Romans in the Molise area. The Altilia district lies on the ruins of the Roman city of Saepinum**, surrounded by a nearly complete ring of walls. Note the theater**, the Bojano gate** (in excellent condition) and the paved forum**, which is overlooked by various structures, including the ruins of a triumphal arch, remnants of monuments and the 'griffin' fountain. **S. Maria della Strada****: this church in the Matrice municipality, in the Biferno Valley, was opened way back in 1148. It probably has the best-kept original structure in Molise, especially in the nave and two aisles, the rose window over the main entrance and the tympanum. A monumental, superbly crafted sarcophagus* (14C) has

Campobasso, a panoramic view (above) and the medieval Monforte castle.

wonderful sculpted scenes of epic stories, fantastic animals and symbols.

ISERNIA AND NORTHERN MOLISE

The itinerary through this part of Molise often takes one up into the mountains. Much of this landscape is decidedly mountainous, especially from the section of the Matese massif in Isernia to the "mountain of Frosolone", which is clearly separate from the neighboring hills in Campobasso. Indeed, the only flat section of land in this zone is a thin stretch around Venafro that follows the Volturno River. For the rest, there is the Matese massif to one side and the Mainarde mountain range to the other. This small gap not only leads easily down to the Tyrrhenian coast, but it was also the setting for the first moments in Italian history and it has long been central to the history of Molise. In the Samnite area, major fortifications were built in the surrounding areas to control this gap. Over time, these defensive elements came to be accompanied by temples, with Pietrabbondante being the best example. The fall of the Roman empire was followed by the anarchy of the Barbarian invasions. Eventually, the Lombards conquered much of the Volturno gap, building numerous castles. These castles were later occupied – and altered – by the Normans and the Angevins. Today, many of them still remain, marking the landscape from their perches high on rocky outcrops. Three monks from the Abbey of Farfa also crossed the Volturno gap, building the superb Abbey of S. Vincenzo near the source of the river on a flat section of land at the foot of the Mainarde range. The abbey is a must see for any traveler in this zone.

The Volturno plateau, in the background.

For more than 2,000 years, transhumance was the essence of local economies, ensuring that the coming and goings of men and their herds marked not only the economy but also the culture of Molise. Today, the zone is dotted with traces of the Samnites and the Romans, castles, towers and medieval churches, Renaissance palazzi and ancient hamlets made with local stone. Meanwhile, wide valleys and thick woods filled with Turkey oaks and beech trees are the silent backdrop to any journey in these parts.

NOT TO BE MISSED

Isernia: Corso Marcelli is the axis of the old town. Despite the devastation caused by an earthquake in 1805 and WWII (especially in 1943), the center remains remarkably intact, with narrow, winding alleys running off the main axis. Piazza Celestino V is home to the Fraterna Fountain**, created by an unknown sculptor in the 14th century using, among other elements, Roman tombstones and slabs. The cathedral*, dedicated to St Peter the Apostle, has numerous interesting artworks: paintings by R. Gioia and A. Trivisonno; a silver cross donated by Pope Celestine V; the reliquary of the head of St Nicander (14C); a wooden statue, perhaps 14th century, of the Madonna of the Feet. It is a short walk to Palazzo Pecori-Veneziale*, which has 3 lovely stone portals and is the best conserved example of local noble architecture, and the former convent of S. Maria delle Monache* (the earliest mention of this convent is in 783 AD). The Museo Nazionale del Paleolitico* has finds from excavations in the Isernia-La Pineta area. Numerous finds dating from 736,000 years ago have been made in the Isernia area, making it the oldest Paleolithic site in Europe; the quality and quantity of finds also ensure it is the most important such site on the old continent. **Agnone**: known as the "Samnite Athens", this is an unusual mountain town that has, among its alleys and squares, a notable architectural heritage ranging from the Gothic to the Baroque. **Pietrabbondante***: slightly out of town lies an Italic Sanctuary** built by the Samnites between the 3rd and 1st centuries BC. The site includes two temples and a theater, making it the most important remnant of the Pentri tribe of the Samnites. **Abbey of S. Vincenzo al Volturno****: this abbey lies on a flat area halfway between Rocchetta and Castel San Vincenzo. Excavation work has uncovered various buildings that, in the 8th-9th centuries, were part of not only one of the most important Apennine abbeys but an abbey known across much of Europe. The oldest part of the church of S. Vincenzo Minore, built in the 8th century, perhaps on the ruins of a late Roman church, is home to the chapel of S. Maria in Insula, which has a crypt known as "of the Epiphany". The crypt has an amazing cycle of 9th-century frescoes that explores, with clear Byzantine influences, the Apocalypse.

ABRUZZO NATIONAL PARK

The Parco Nazionale d'Abruzzo (renamed 'd'Abruzzo, Lazio e Molise' in 2002) was created in 1922 to protect the Apennines, and in particular the bears and chamois. Its attraction lies first and foremost with the fauna, which includes bears, chamois, wolves, lynx, golden eagles, and griffon vultures in a wild setting characterised by mountains covered in beech forests. Above 1,700 m the forests give way to pastures, shingle and rocks. The charming medieval villages of Pescasseroli, Civitella Alfedena, Opi, and Barrea watch over the valleys and roads. In and around these villages is an array of animal reserves, nature trails and museums. Those wanting to adventure into the heart of the park can choose from over a hundred marked trails that are transformed into stunning snow-shoeing, skiing and ice-climbing circuits.

Pescasseroli, nestles in a basin surrounded by magnificent beech forests, under the watchful eye of Mt Marsicano, which is the highest peak in the park with an elevation of 2,242 m. This village of Italic origin is a renowned holiday destination and is famous as the birthplace of Benedetto Croce (1866-1952). The interior of the parish church of Ss. Pietro e Paolo, built in Romanesque style in the 12th century and modified after various earthquakes, features a wooden statue of the Black Madonna otherwise known as the Incoronata, and a silver cross from the 15th-century Sulmona school. Also worth seeing is the church of the Carmine dated 1729 and Palazzo Sipari, where Benedetto Croce was born.

Opi. Located on a rocky spur between the Sangro, Fondillo and Fredda valleys, this medieval village is named after a Marsic sanctuary dedicated to Saturn's wife, Ope (the goddess of abundance) that once stood here. Palazzo Baronale (17C) now houses the municipality and Pro Loco. Further up, is the church of S. Maria Assunta, which was founded in the 12th century and was completely remodelled in the 1600s. Behind the church is the Visitors' Center of the Parco Nazionale d'Abruzzo, with the Museo del Camoscio and adjoining chamois reserve.

Fondillo Valley*. The greenest valley in the park features pleasant walking tracks, mountain-bike trails, and cross-country skiing through dense beech forests at the foot of Mt Marsicano and Mt Amaro di Opi.

Camosciara mountain*. The wild amphitheatre In the Camosclara mountain group, dominated by Mt Sterpidalto and Balzo della Chiesa, is one of the most important spots in the park. The cliffs, which were unsuitable for mining and inaccessible to humans, ensured the survival of the Abruzzo chamois.

Villetta Barrea is an important crossroads, built next to the monastery of S. Angelo in Barreggio, of which only a few ruins remain. Villetta Barrea features a number of houses dating from the 16th and 17th centuries. The parish church of S. Maria Assunta, completed in 1720, features a 17th-century portal. The church was damaged during the 1915 earthquake and has been rebuilt. Worth seeing in Via Roma is the Museo della Transumanza and an otter reserve. Between Villetta Barrea and Barrea, the Sangro River pours into Lake Barrea*, a huge artificial lake that blends perfectly into the park's natural environment.

Civitella Alfedena and Rose Valley. Perched on a spur above Lake Barrea, Civitella Alfedena is the flagship of the park. The old center* has remained intact and features several small mansions from the 17th and 18th centuries, a 14th-century tower and 17th-century church of S. Nicola. The lynx reserve is located next to the upper part of the village and the Visitors' Center of the National park can be seen on the facing hillside, along with the museum, Area Faunistica del Lupo, and the sanctuary of S. Lucia. From Civitella, the steep and popular trail 1 leads up through the Rose Valley beech forests*, offering an opportunity to see and photograph the chamois. The Forca Resuni refuge (1,931 m) is a 4h walk out and back. In July and August the trail is only open to groups with an official park guide.

Barrea sits on a rocky outcrop, offering a stunning view over Lake Barrea and the deep Foce limestone gorge. The village was founded in the Samnite period and for many, many years had ties with the abbey of S. Angelo in Barreggio. The old center was restored after the 1983 earthquake and is home to the church of S. Rocco (1527), the church of S. Antonio Abate (founded in the 14C) and the Franciscan monastery of S. Maria delle Grazie. The church of S. Tommaso (16C) is furnished with Baroque altars, crucifixes and wooden statues. A nature trail follows the rim of the gorge and is ideal for observing a variety of birds of prey. On the edge of the lake are the few remains of a Samnite necropolis pillaged by grave robbers.

THE CATTLE-TRACKS OF MOLISE

The *tratturi* – or cattle-tracks – are like ancient highways covered in grass rather than asphalt and bordered by hedges. These are the remnants of the transhumance paths used to move herds between the mountain pastures and those on the plain – pastures that were by no means close together. It is said that, in pre-Roman times, these tracks were part of the Sabine colonization of the Apennines: as part of the "Ver Sacrum" (sacred spring) rite, an entire generation of youths would be consecrated to Mars and then sent out to settle new colonies.

ALONG THE CATTLE-TRACKS

The truth of this rite is uncertain, but it is clear that transhumance was fundamental to the economic and political life of the Pentri tribe of Samnites, who built their major towns and temples (Sepino, Bojano, Pietrabbondante etc.) along these tracks. In the centuries following the Pentri, these tracks remained central to the movement of goods, languages, traditions and cultures. Today, if one superimposes a map of the tracks over a map of Molise, one finds that over half of the 136 towns in the region lie on these ancient routes. This has left these areas with a notable archeological and architectural finds. In the modern world, these tracks have lost their original purpose, practically being transformed into giant "open-air museums" immersed in a splendid landscape of green hills. They are ideal for hiking, horse-riding, mountain biking or off-road biking, especially if one also wants to discover an ancient past. Many of these tracks along the southern Adriatic have given ground to farming, vegetation and even asphalt; however, Molise has the clearest examples, with 6 tracks (and remnants of smaller and side tracks) crossing the region. All of these tracks are protected by the Parco dei Tratturi del Molise, which lies between the Parco Nazionale d'Abruzzo and the Parco Nazionale del Gargano in Puglia.

Tratturo Pescasseroli-Candela: much of this track is on relatively flat land and is one of the best preserved and most easily accessible tracks. It runs along the slopes of the Matese massif, from Bojano to Sepino, covering about 15 km. The route also crosses areas that witnessed some of the most important events in the history of Molise. Beside the Roman settlement of Saepinum, the Sepino area is home to the Samnite temple of St Peter at Cantoni and, in the Terravecchia district, the ruins of Saepins, a fortified town destroyed by the Romans in 293 BC following stiff resistance. It is also worth visiting the WWF protected area in the Guardiaregia and Campochiaro area. It lies quite close to the track and is home to the Quirino gorges, which form one of the most beautiful canyons in the Apennines, Mt Mutria, with steep, beech covered slopes, and various examples of a Karst landscape, including the Cul di Bove and Pozzo della Neve caves.

Tratturo Castel di Sangro-Lucera: This track can be followed for about 15 km between Castel di Sangro and Pescolanciano. There are some wonderful landscapes along the way: in the Molise area, between Civitanova del Sannio and Torella del Sannio; in the central Molise area, around Castropignano and between the Ripalimosani station and Campodipietra.

Tratturo Celano-Foggia: this track is located in northern Molise, a few kilometers northeast of Castel di Sangro-Lucera. It is possible to go along the stretch from Mt Miglio to Castel di Sangro-Lucera. Note the Montedimezzo wood, which the track runs by to the east. If one is in this area it is worth seeing the lovely old center and the Museo storico della campana (history of the bell museum), annexed to the Agnone foundry (one of the oldest in Italy) and the theater and Italic temples at Pietrabbondante, some of the most important monuments in Molise.

A cattle-track that is still used.

FOOD IN ABRUZZO AND MOLISE

There are many products and dishes that are typical of Abruzzo and Molise, including cheeses, cured meats, spiced vegetables, oil and wines. In Abruzzo, praise must be given especially to saffron, which has been grown for centuries in the mountains around Aquila. Even though it is not that widespread in the cuisine, it has risen to became the symbol of the uniqueness of Abruzzo. Molise, a region of hills and mountains, can not only count cured meats and dairy products among its leading foods, but also durum wheat pasta and the truffle. Indeed, in the province of Isernia there are nearly a dozen truffle collection centers.

THE DISHES FROM ABRUZZO

Scapece di Vasto. It is made with fish, perhaps skate or smooth hound, that is fried and kept in a vinegar and saffron marinade.

Scrippelle 'mbusse. Called "wet pancakes", this dish from the Teramo area is made with pancakes that are filled with grated cheese and then plunged into boiling broth before being served with cheese.

Coda di rospo al rosmarino. This dish (angler fish with rosemary), is made by slicing the fish and then frying the pieces in oil, garlic, rosemary and chili. There are regional versions, including one with salt cod in bread crumbs.

Confetti di Sulmona. This is a typical almond praline covered with a layer of sugar. It is normally associated with weddings and the like.

THE DISHES FROM MOLISE

Brodetto di Termoli. This is a classic soup made with various – but fresh – types of fish.

Fusilli alla molisana. Traditionally, the fusilli pasta would have been handmade and served in a tomato sauce flavored with chili pepper. Another famous local pasta dish is maccheroni alla chitarra with a cuttlefish sauce.

Cacio e uovo. Lamb is cooked in an earthenware saucepan with oil, herbs and spices. When cooked, it is covered in a mixture of beaten egg and grated Pecorino cheese.

Picellati. Type of panzerotti cooked in the oven and stuffed with a mixture of bread crumbs, honey, walnuts, and almonds.

THE PRODUCTS OF ABRUZZO

Pecorino di Farindola. The most famous Pecorino cheese is from Farindola. It is made with rennet from a pig's stomach. The cheese is cut into strips, matured for 3 months and soaked in wine, salt and pepper.

Ventricina di Crognaleto. Although a type of sausage, it is ideal for spreading. It is made with chopped cheek, shoulder and pork fat, along with some herbs, rosemary and peppers. Ventricina Vastese is famous variant.

Zafferano dell'Aquila DOP. It is grown on the Navelli plateau. It is hand picked to ensure the fragile stigma is not broken. The stigma is then dried and crushed to make a powder.

Aglio rosso di Sulmona. This sought-after form of garlic is famed for its essential oils. The outside sections are white, but the inner ones are a purple red.

THE PRODUCTS FROM MOLISE

Caciocavallo di Agnone. This cheese is pear shaped with a hard, thin crust. It has a hazelnut color and the matured version is covered in mold. The actual cheese is compact, the smell strong and the taste is sweet, sometimes becoming spicy.

Pecorino di Capracotta. This mountain cheese is made on the slopes of Maiella and in the Matese valleys. It is made with sheep's milk. It is yellow with a hard crust, although the exact appearance depends on how mature it is. The cheese is compact and it has a strong, but aromatic flavor that has hints of spiciness.

Soppressata. This sausage is made with pork and fat that has been cut by hand or roughly minced. It is seasoned with salt, black pepper and saltpeter.

Olio extravergine di oliva Molise DOP. Extra-virgin olive oil made from the following cultivars: Frantoio, Leccino, Moraiolo, Pendolino, Coratina and Gentile di Larino. The oil is yellow with green hints. The smell is fruity and the taste tends to be sweetish.

THE WINES

The Montepulciano grape dominates in Abruzzo and is used for Montepulciano d'Abruzzo, a dry and full-bodied red. Cerasuolo is a rosé wine made from red grapes. Trebbiano d'Abruzzo is a white wine. In Molise, the Montepulciano and Trebbiano grapes are the most common. The main wine is Biferno DOC (white, rosé and red). Other wines are made from the red Aglianico grape and the white Falanghina, Fiano and Greco grapes.

THE CAMPI FLEGREI AND ISLAND OF ISCHIA

"The purity and clarity of that water," wrote the 16th-century Neapolitan historian, Camillo Por-zio, about the Gulf of Naples, "seems to those who see it to be like quicksilver." The wes-tern shores of the gulf in question are the subject of this route, along with the incredible "side-show" of the Phlegraean Fields, in which the phenomena of volcanic activity do some of their less spectacular "numbers." There is the enchanting landscape and there are geological oddities; along-side them, the third attraction for curious sightseers is the aura of classical antiquity, which is so much more intense and evident to the senses here than anywhere else in southern Italy. Here is a brief and far from exhaustive listing of classical sites along this route: at Nisida, Marcus Brutus, assassin of Julius Caesar, before venturing off to the fatal battle of Philippi, where he was defea-ted by Augustus and Mark Antony, bade a last farewell to his wife Portia, daughter of Cato; St Paul debarked in the harbor of Pozzuoli; Virgil set the entrance to the Underworld at Lake Averno; Li-ternum was the site of the country estate to which Publius Cornelius Scipio, Africanus Major, the greatest Roman general before Caesar, retired, disgusted with politics; in Cumae the Sibyl made her prophecies; Lake Miseno was said to be the Stygian swamp across which Charon ferried lost souls; Capo Miseno, according to the ancient historian Strabo, was the land of the Lestrigons, gi-ants who hurled great boulders at the ships of Ulysses; the Gulf of Baiae was without equal on earth in the opinion of the poet Horace (an opinion shared by those who had villas here, among them Marius, Crassus, Caesar, Nero, Pompey, and Varro); in the Lake Lucrino a certain Sergius Ora-ta harvested oysters, while on the banks the architect Cyrus built the Cumanum for Cicero, with a portico extending out into the lake waters; the island of Ischia was also known as Ænaria, and was renowned for its climate and salubrious, curative waters, as much in Roman times as it is today: in Forio, back then, it was customary to try to see the "green ray" created by the steam at sunset.

NOT TO BE MISSED

Naples (⇒ see below): the capital of the south welcomes the tourist with open arms in Piazza del Plebiscito. **Marechiaro**: a village of fishermen and famous trattorias, with the "fenesta" from a clas-sic song by S. Di Giacomo; it lies at the end of a detour from the crossroads of the Capo. **Nisida**: you reach the little island, originally an ancient volcanic crater of almost circular shape, by driving along the embankment, turning off from the coast road just past the promontory of Posillipo. **Poz-zuoli** (⇒ see below): set adjacent to the luminous waters of the gulf are the Roman monuments of the Serapaeum and the amphitheater, while the Rione Terra is perched high on a promontory; nearby, note the surprising volcanic phenomena of the Solfatara** (you pass by here if you take the Via Domiziana) and the dark waters of the **Lake d'Averno***, a great crater with woods on its steep slopes (fine view). **Liternum**: the ruins of the little Roman town lie at the edge of the Lake di Patria. **Cuma***: Neo-Classic ruins and memories are to be found in this great archeological field, where a Greek colony was founded, conveying the alphabet in due time to the rest of the Italian peninsula; go visit the cave of the Sibylla Cumana, or Sybil of Cumae, a sanctuary venerated in an-cient times. **Bacoli**: fishing village, with the Roman ruins of the Cento Camerelle and the Piscina Mirabile. **Miseno**: this small village is located on the cape of the same name; a short detour from Bacoli passes over the dam between the coastal lagoon and the ancient port of Miseno; these two features together made this a major Roman naval base. **Baia***: in the archeological park there are the spectacular Roman ruins, probably part of the palace of the emperors. **Procida** presents a bright-ly colored composition of Mediterranean architecture. **Ischia*** (⇒ see below): you will land at Is-chia Porto (the fishing village of Ischia Ponte, with a bridge linking it to the islet of the Castello, is a couple of km east); the tour of the island, involving steep climbs, seascapes with craggy co-astlines, green vineyards, citrus groves, and pine woods, takes you, among other places, to: **Ca-samicciola Terme**, destroyed by an earthquake at the end of the 19th century; **Lacco Ameno**, a hot springs, with the reef of the Fungo just off the little beach; **Forio**, a dazzling white town on a pro-montory, and renowned for its wines; **Sant'Angelo***, a fishing village, at the base of a small pen-insula; **Barano d'Ischia**, located in a pleasant site, from which you may venture down to the long beach of Lido dei Maronti.

ISCHIA

"The history of Italy comes from the sea," wrote Sabatino Moscati. Ischia (Pithekoussai, as the Greeks called it) was a key site in this history. Archeologists confirm the traditional date of Greek colonization (775 BC), the earliest in Italy; also present were the Phoenicians.

Ischia, the main town on the island, lies at the NE extremity, and has two sections: Ischia Porto and Ischia Ponte. In the former, the inner harbor – where most of the ferries dock – is formed by an ancient volcanic crater, linked to the sea by a channel dug in 1854.
Follow **Via Roma** – with several cafés, restaurants, and shops – and the successive Corso V. Colonna to reach the fishing village of Ischia Ponte. Here is the cathedral of the Assunta, and, beyond the Aragonese bridge, the castle.
In the small village of **Lacco Ameno**, the sanctuary of S. Restituta comprises two churches: the smaller one dates from the 11th century and stands on the site of an Early Christian basilica whose remains lie under the church; under the sacristy there is the **Museo e Scavi archeologici Santa Restituta**, a museum containing finds from the Bronze Age to Byzantine times, Greek kilns and ceramics laboratories (7-2C BC).
In the town of **Forio**, the church of S. Maria di Loreto, built in the 14th century but converted to the Baroque style, has marble decoration; the cylindrical tower (15C) formed of a system of defense against pirates. There are numerous springs yielding mineral water, and beaches, such as Spiaggia di Chiaia and Spiaggia di Citara.
Sant'Angelo is an enchanting little fishing village, with many-colored houses arranged along stepped walkways (cars not allowed). Taxi boats will take you to the Spiaggia dei Maronti, a pleasant beach, or to the Fumarole (hot springs).

POZZUOLI

The phenomenon of bradyseism here can be detected through the holes dug by rock-boring sea mollusks in the columns of the Macellum, indicating that as the land rises and falls, the complex is alternately submerged and lifted out of the water.

The Macellum* – once known as Serapaeum – was the public market of the Roman town of Puteoli under the empire; the sixteen Corinthian columns, with the mollusk-burrowed holes mentioned above, supported a dome.
In the **Anfiteatro****, or amphitheater, built in the 1st century AD, naumachiae (staged sea battles) were held, along with fights and hunts of wild beasts; a tour of the intriguing cellars* includes the shafts up which the cages of the wild beasts were hoisted into the arena.
The Terme di Nettuno, or Neptune's Baths, comprise the impressive remains of a bath structure; the nearby Ninfeo di Diana is actually the ruins of a nymphaeum.
The **Mausolei** di Via Celle are the best preserved funerary complex on the Via Campana. They include 14 buildings with a central hall and elevated funerary chambers, in some of which there are remains of painted or stucco decoration.

The beach at the Sant'Angelo resort on the island of Ischia.

POMPEI, ERCOLANO AND CAPRI

It all began with "a cloud, remarkable in size and appearance," as Pliny the Younger was to write to Tacitus, describing the eruption of 24 August of AD 79, and the death of his uncle, Pliny the Elder, who sailed from Capo Miseno to assist the fleeing population. Its shape "most closely resembled that of a pine tree. It rose straight up as if borne upon a high trunk, and then opened out into numerous branches... here it was bright white, there it was mottled and dirty, where earth and ashes had been carried aloft." For many of the residents of Herculaneum, Stabia, and Pompeii, that was the last thing they ever saw. At the end of this route through another half of the coastline of the Gulf of Naples, a traveller may be tempted to try to rank the remarkable impressions and sights. What ranks first? The dead cities, slain by a volcano, the inimitable island of Capri, the relaxed beauty of Sorrento amid its citrus groves, or the lunar landscape of the crater of Vesuvius? Certainly, there are plenty of powerful impressions here.

NOT TO BE MISSED

Ercolano (➡ see below), or **Herculaneum**: all that you see of this small ancient town, with its charming location, once the exclusive holiday resort of the wealthy and powerful of Imperial Rome, was excavated from a dense, compact slab of lava and mud, from 12 to 25 m high. **Vesuvio***, or Vesuvius, seen from the west: if you turn off from the main route, following the slopes of Mt Vesuvius, you will climb up to the lower station of the chair lift, passing by the observatory on your way (the upper station lies at an elevation of 1,158 m; from there you can walk up to the great tear in the earth, the now deceptively tranquil crater), or else to the 1017 m of the northern slope of the terminal cone. **Torre del Greco**: here, craftsmen fashion exquisite work from coral and mother-of-pearl; you can see their creations in the Museo del Corallo. **Torre Annunziata**: one of the Neapolitan pasta capitals. **Pompei** (➡ see below), or **Pompeii**: the excavations** have unearthed at least three-fifths of the city that was buried by the eruption of Vesuvius in AD 79 (the town probably had a population of about 30,000); nowhere is the voyage backwards in time so entrancing. **Castellammare di Stabia**: note the excavations of the Roman villas of long-vanished Stabiae and the antiquarium. Mt Faito (1,131 m): beech trees, conifers, chestnuts, and cedars crowd its slopes; the view of the Sorrento peninsula and of the gulf is particularly fine from the "belvedere*," or viewpoint; you drive up from Castellammare di Stabia and then down to Vico Equense with its 14th-century Cathedral, the total detour is 30 km. **Sorrento*** lies on a tufa terrace high over the sea, amid gardens and the dark, shiny green leaves of the citrus groves; the exuberant style of the applied arts of the 17th and 18th century can be enjoyed in the Museo Correale di Terranova. **Isola di Capri** (➡ see below): the colors of the sea, sky, rocks and vegetation, the craggy Faraglioni, vineyards, gardens, and breezes: you could easily stay here a lifetime or thereabouts. The Emperor Tiberius was neither the first nor the last to be captivated by the place. You land at Marina Grande; to reach the celestially blue transparency of the Grotta Azzurra**, or Blue Grotto, a marine cave half-filled with sea water, you take a boat. You can take a cableway up to the main town, also called Capri, with its little Mediterranean piazzetta, at once simple and sophisticated: from here, you can walk to see a number of fine sites: the Certosa di S. Giacomo; the Belvedere Cannone, with its view; the ruins of Tiberius's Villa Iovis; a natural arch, the Belvedere di Tragara; and Marina Piccola. The town of **Anacapri*** is white, suspended in the lush greenery; it is located on the western side of the island: you should tour the Villa S. Michele, once owned by a Swedish author, Axel Munthe. The best view is to be had by taking a chairlift to the peak of Mt Solaro (589 m).

POMPEI

Situated on the last low buttress to the SW of Mt Vesuvius not far from the Gulf of Naples, Pompeii is known throughout the world for its tragic destruction and for its miraculous discovery. This is a unique memento of the topography of a city of the ancient world, where life came to a sudden halt on 24 August 79. **The excavations**** have uncovered roughly 60 percent of the city's area, a combination of

Oscan, Etruscan, and Greek cultures, later occupied by the Samnites (late 5C BC) and by the Romans only after 80 BC Pompeii was damaged by an earthquake in 62 AD, before it was buried by the ash and lava of the eruption (79 AD). The entire city seems to leap alive from the shattered ruins.

Of particular note: the rectangular square of the **Forum**** with the podium of the temple of Jupiter, the Building of Eumachia, headquarters of the guild of the "fullones" (cleaners, dyers, and manufacturers of cloth) and the Basilica*, the site of the administration of justice and business; the Hellenistic large theater** (200-150 BC), which was later enlarged, on the hillside slope; the elegant small theater**; the Anfiteatro* dating from 80 BC, the earliest surviving amphitheater known; and the Terme Stabiane** (Baths of Stabia). Among the best-known residential houses are the Casa del Menandro* (House of Menander), richly decorated with frescoes; the Casa di Loreius Tiburtinus* with a triclinium decorated with scenes from the Iliad and the Labors of Hercules; the Praedia di Giulia Felice*, in which, alongside the house of the proprietress (Julia Felix), are a public bath and a rental block with shops; the exemplary Casa dei Vettii**, in which the great triclinium* is decorated with lovely ancient paintings; the Casa degli Amorini Dorati* (House of the Gilded Cupids); the Casa del Fauno* (House of the Faun); the Casa del Poeta Tragico (House of the Tragic Poet) offers a fine example of a middle-class dwelling. Outside the enclosure around the excavations is the Villa dei Misteri**: the huge painting dating from the 1st century BC on the walls of one hall, depicting the Initiation of the Brides to the Dionysian Mysteries**, is a remarkable and exquisite piece of ancient art.

Not far from here, at Boscoreale/Villa Regina, the **Antiquarium** is a museum which features material from the archeological sites of Pompeii and Ercolano.

ERCOLANO

Also located on the Bay of Naples, though less famous than Pompeii, Herculaneum was overwhelmed by the same great eruption of Mt Vesuvius in AD 79. Unlike Pompeii, however, it was buried not by a shower of ashes and lapilli, but by a flowing wall of mud and lava which submerged the town and then solidified, binding it in a dense blanket as hard as tufa-stone and from 12 to 25 meters in depth. Herculaneum is only a third the size of Pompeii; it is now an archeological site of equal importance, but it has somewhat different characteristics. Herculaneum was more of a residential town; Pompeii more of a market town. The modern town has preserved, in its 18th-century villas, the heritage of the town's first rebirth as a holiday spot.

The excavations**. The excavations cover only a minor section of the ancient city, because most of it is under modern houses. If the large public works that have been uncovered tend to follow a traditional layout, the types of residential structures vary widely. Like at Pompeii, in this archeological area as well the ongoing efforts to restore the surviving houses and the work of consolidating the trenches surrounding the ancient city in some cases prevent the public from being able to view all of the houses and complexes. The key monuments are: on the Cardine III, Casa d'Argo, Casa dell'Albergo; on the Cardine IV, Casa dell'Atrio a Mosaico*, Casa a Graticcio*, Casa Sannitica* from pre-Roman times, Terme** (Baths), Casa di Nettuno e Anfitrite*; alongside it stands a well preserved shop, the Casa del Bicentenario**. On the Cardine V: Palestra** (Gymnasium), with a remarkable bronze fountain*; Casa dei Cervi**, one of the richest and most sumptuous houses; Casa del Rilievo di Telefo*; Casa della Gemma*; Terme Suburbane** (Suburban Baths).

CAPRI

The astonishing prodigies of nature, the enchantment of the landscapes, the ineffably lovely light of the sky over this massive block of limestone will always be a siren's lure to travelers. You land at Marina Grande; at the far end of the beach are the ruins of the Palazzo a Mare, possibly inhabited by Augustus; beyond are the enormous ruins of the so-called Bagni di Tiberio, or Baths of Tiberius.

The world-renowned Grotta Azzurra**, or Blue Cave, takes its name from the delightful color the sunlight acquires as it filters through the water. Capri, the main town on the island, is of course quite a haven for jet-setters. The piazzetta, a central square that lends itself admirably to effortless, enjoyable lounging, is enclosed like a courtyard, and is surrounded by an enchanting medieval district. Alongside the square are the Eastern-style domes of the church of S. Stefano.

In the **Certosa di S. Giacomo***, a 14th-century charterhouse, the little cloister dates from the 15th century while the larger one dates from the 16th century. In the halls of the complex there is the Museo Diefenbach.

It takes just 45 min. to reach the archeological excavations of the Villa Iovis*, also known as the Villa of Tiberius. In 30 min., you can reach the Natural Arch*, an arch in a landscape of savage beauty, and the Grotta di Matromania. In 20 min. you can reach the Belvedere di Tragara*, and from there you can descend to the beach of the port of Tragara, to the right of which are the immense shoals and cliffs of the Faraglioni*; note the rare blue lizard that lives on the isolated cliff (the third one) of Scopolo.

THE AMALFI COASTLINE

The coastline faces south here, overlooking sea and bright sunshine. The Mts Lattari plunge sharply down, a rocky bastion broken only by harsh deep valleys, with citrus and olive groves and vegetable gardens on rocky terraces, held up by small, rocky walls created by the back-breaking labor of generations; elsewhere, all you can see is Mediterranean underbrush and stones. The houses all cluster around the mouths of the deep valleys: the steep slopes determine the architectural style, which stacks volume, stairways, and roofs, crisscrossed by intricate lanes, refreshingly shady after the inexorable sunlight that is reflected by the sea and the whitewashed walls. For the entire 10th century and much of the 11th century, Amalfi grew quickly and extensively, taking Pisa's place in Mediterranean trade – later ceding its primacy to Genoa. Amalfi had trading colonies in Naples, Messina, Palermo, in the ports of Puglia, and, outside of Italy, in Durazzo, Tunis, Tripoli, Alexandria, Acre, Antioch, and of course, in the great metropolis of this time, Constantinople. Along with wealth, Amalfi took from the Byzantines and the Muslims a cultural influence that can be seen in the art. The little state of Amalfi, the first of Italy's "maritime republics," included the stretch of coastline from Positano to Cetara, with the islands of Li Galli and Capri; inland, it stretched to Tramonti and, over the crest of the Mts Lattari, it included Gragnano and Lettere. The end came late in the 11th century, as the Normans pushed north, allying themselves with the Pisan fleet in order to rid themselves of the pushy maritime merchants of Amalfi. The sun still shines down on the coastline, the sea breezes still brush the aromatic maquis, and in the little cloister bedecked with intertwined arches the palm trees still cast their shade over the "Paradiso."

NOT TO BE MISSED

Sorrento (➟ see below): the sea of the Sirens, the tufa crags and cliffs, the orange orchards and olive groves that so enchanted the 16th-century poet Torquato Tasso; collections of objects and the applied arts in the aristocratic palazzo of the collectors at the Museo Correale di Terranova; an initial variant on the route offers spectacular views from 18 km of secondary roads; you will pass through Massa Lubrense, a lovely vacation spot on a rolling verdant plateau (you can make your way down to the village, the marina, and the beach of Marina della Lobra) and Termini, a secluded village (by mule-track, 45 minutes to the Punta della Campanella, facing Capri). **Sant'Agata sui Due Golfi**: the name of this little holiday town refers to the two gulfs of Naples and Salerno. **Positano** (➟ see below): the mountain spurs, covered by terraced white houses, run down to the harbor of the old fishing village, long since become an elegant resort. **Grotta di Smeraldo***: the Emerald Grotto, with its surreal green light, is located between Praiano and Conca dei Marini. **Agerola**, this highland of the Lattari Mountains, features resort spots amidst meadows and chestnut groves; fine views of the Amalfi coast, Capri, and the Gulf of Salerno can be enjoyed from the vantage point of San Lazzaro; 18 km detour from Vettica Minore. **Amalfi** (➟ see below): white, stacked in terraces on the steep slopes over the sea; touches of exotic architecture in the Duomo, with its bronze doors from Constantinople (1066), the intertwined arches in the cloister of the Paradiso – all these things are relics of ancient maritime trade with the east, the commerce and glory of the Republic of Amalfi of the 10th and 11th centuries. **Atrani** is magnificently situated in an inlet, between high rock walls; the church of S. Salvatore di Bireto, where the doges of Amalfi were elected, has bronze doors from Constantinople (1087). **Ravello** (➟ see below): the site is perched on cliffs and crags, the roads are rustic at best, the landscape is colorful, and there are simple treasures to be found here; to mention the finest aspects, note the Arab-style architecture and the exotic plants of the garden of Villa Rufolo, the bronze doors by Barisano da Trani in the Duomo, the vista of sea, mountains, and coastline from the high terraced land be-

A panoramic view of Sorrento and the beach.

tween the valleys of the Dragone and the Reginna in the Cimbrone overlook. **Minori**, a beachfront town, formerly an arsenal of the Republic of Amalfi, with the ruins of a Roman villa. **Maiori:** spreading out like an amphitheater in its inlet, at the foot of the majolica dome of the church of S. Maria a Mare; museum. **Cava de' Tirreni**, with a beautiful ancient village. Abbey of the Trinità di Cava: a 7 km detour from Vietri sul Mare, famed for its majolica, will take you to this abbey, founded in the year 1101 and almost completely rebuilt in the 18th century; the Benedictine monastery includes a little 13th-century cloister and a museum. **Salerno***: two rare and exquisite artworks are in the Museo del Duomo: a 12th-century ivory frontal and a 13th-century illuminated "Exultet". The Salerno Duomo itself is one of the most notable monuments in southern Italy, in terms of architecture, history, and artwork; the seafront is lined with palm trees, and is bathed in the light of the gulf.

SORRENTO

The center of the little town is Piazza Tasso (named after the poet T. Tasso, who was born here in 1544); a terrace overlooks the gorge that runs down to the Marina Piccola. The Basilica di S. Antonino has an 11th-century portal on the side. A bell tower, set on an arch atop four columns, stands before the Duomo, rebuilt in the 15th century. Inside, note the choir, a fine piece of intarsia of the Sorrento school. There are ruins of a Roman arch in the 16th-century walls on the side uphill of the town. Near the entrance to the Villa Comunale, note the handsome public park, dotted with palm trees overlooking the sea, and the church of S. Francesco, with a little cloister of Arab-style intertwined arches (14C).

AMALFI

As a Maritime Republic the city wrote a major chapter in the history of Europe, together with Pisa, Genoa, and Venice. Today it stretches along the splendid coastline with its blindingly white houses and intricate narrow lanes, some of them roofed over.

By the seaside is the Piazza Flavio Gioia (named after the man said to have invented the compass). Nearby, with two aisles crowned with Gothic arches, are the remains of the Arsenale della Repubblica.

The **Duomo***, high atop a stairway, dates from the 9th century and was rebuilt in Sicilian Arab-Norman style in 1203, and again in the 18th century. The polychrome facade was redone in the 19th century; the handsome bell tower*, with little towers and interwoven Arab-style arches high atop it, dates from 1180-1276; beneath the Gothic atrium, the central portal features an exquisite bronze door*, cast in Constantinople (1065). In the presbytery are two candelabra and two mosaic ambos (12-13C); in the crypt, with the supposed relics of the apostle Andrew, are statues by M. Naccherino and P. Bernini; alongside the left aisle is the Chapel of the Crucifix, with fragments of the 13th-century church. You can enter the renowned Chiostro del Paradiso* from the far left end of the atrium of the Duomo: it served as the burial place of the noble and illustrious citizens of Amalfi.

RAVELLO

The center of town is the Piazza Vescovado. High atop a stairway is the Duomo*, founded in 1086, built in the 12th century, and drastically renovated in the 18th century; note the bronze door* (1179) and the 13th-century bell tower. Inside: pulpit* decorated with mosaics and reliefs by N. di Bartolomeo da Foggia (1272), and ambo* dating from about 1130. Partly surrounding the Piazza Vescovado is the park of the Villa Rufolo*: in the complex of Moorish-Sicilian style buildings (13C), note in particular the courtyard*, not unlike a small cloister; in a building adjacent to the villa is the Antiquarium; also visit the garden* with exotic plants. After you pass the church of S. Francesco, with its romantic Gothic cloister, you continue on to the Villa Cimbrone*: the courtyard features superb ancient fragments; at the end of the garden, note the famous Belvedere Cimbrone**, a breathtaking view on the gulf and Costiera Amalfitana.

POSITANO

This charming hamlet is said to have been founded by the inhabitants of Paestum as they fled from a Saracen raid. The hamlet was built on the site of a Benedictine abbey dedicated to St. Vitus.

The **parish church of S. Maria Assunta**, which overlooks Piazza Flavio Gioia, has an unmistakable majolica dome. It was founded in the 13th century and it now houses Baroque altars, a 13th-century wooden panel (Madonna with Child, high altar) and a Circumcision by Fabrizio Santafede. Nearby, there are the ruins of a Roman villa. The far side of the village has a large beach (Spiaggia Grande) with a small fishing harbor.

CASERTA AND TERRA DI LAVORO

The name in Italian – Terra di Lavoro – and the appearance of the landscape, would seem to suggest, as the origin of the term, "Land of Labor," the great and fruitful work of a people of tireless farmers. Not so: the original Terra Leboriae refers to the Leborini, the original inhabitants of this area. Nowadays, the term Terra di Lavoro describes the territory of the province of Caserta between Mt Massico and the northern rim of the Phlegraean Fields; in bygone times, the name described a larger portion of Campania. What the 16th-century Neapolitan historian Camillo Porzio once wrote is still true: this territory is "superior to all other lands on earth in fertility and quality and any other thing that can delight or help the human race, rich and abundant." The cities that you will see here – Caserta, Santa Maria Capua Vetere, and Capua – cast bright lights on the history of the region from ancient times, as well as on the history of the entire south of Italy, while the artwork in this area (to mention only a few items, the archaic "mothers" of the Museo Campano in Capua; frescoes, with their Byzantine iconography, painted by local artists in the second half of the 11th century, on the walls of the Benedictine basilica of Sant'Angelo in Formis; and the 18th-century palace, or Reggia, of Caserta) stands out in the body of Italian art. As for the mountain of Roccamonfina, it is a volcano, extinct since antiquity; upon its slopes, softened by the passage of thousands of years, olive trees and vineyards yield to thick dark chestnut groves as you climb: amid the branches and shadows, you will find a classic literary idyll, as is so often the case in southern Italy.

NOT TO BE MISSED

Caserta (➡ see below): the Reggia, or palace, and its grounds are the masterpiece of Luigi Vanvitelli, who expressed in stone and brick the ambitions of the first Bourbon king of Naples, probably inspired in turn by his great-grandfather, Louis XIV, the Sun King: the facade of the building extends for nearly 250 m, the grounds cover 120 hectares. The city grew up around the palace . **Casertavecchia***: the crowning jewel of this medieval town, overlooking the plain from high atop a hill, is the 12th-century cathedral, a rich composite of styles ranging from Romanesque to Sicilian-Arabic and Benedictine. **Santa Maria Capua Vetere** is the town known as Capua to classical antiquity, with Roman ruins: the Campanian amphitheater and the Mithraeum. **Sant'Angelo in Formis***: this basilica from the year 1000 is adorned with remarkable frescoes of the same period. **Capua**: in ancient times, this was Casilinum; it stands in a curve of the Volturno River, enclosed in 16th-century bastions; in the Museo Provinciale Campano note the 200 "madri," archaic votive statues; a Roman bridge stretches over the river. **Carinola**: ruined castle, Romanesque cathedral, and 15th-century Catalonian-Gothic houses. **Sessa Aurunca**: before you enter this small town, take the country road to see the Roman bridge of the Aurunci*, rearing high against the surrounding landscape, with 21 arches; the village occupies the site of the ancient town of Suessa, of which ruins can still be seen; go see the pulpit supported by carved lions and the paschal candelabrum* in the Romanesque Duomo. **Roccamonfina**: this resort town lies amidst chestnut groves on the slopes of an extinct volcano; at a distance of 2.5 km is S. Maria dei Lattani, a 15th-century sanctuary. **Teano**: 12th-century Duomo and the ruins of a Roman theater.

CASERTA

The town is famous for the Reggia, or royal palace (1752) that Charles of Bourbon built upon winning the throne. The exterior was completed in 1774, the interior a century later – after the Bourbons had been expelled. The modern city developed around the "Versailles" of the Bourbon dynasty of the Two Sicilies and is almost a by-product of the royal palace.

The Reggia**, built by Luigi Vanvitelli, has a rectangular plan arranged around four inner courtyards. The lower vestibule*, the main stairway* and the upper vestibule* are the most remarkable sections of the palazzo; the charm of the apartments is given by the Neo-Classic decoration and the memories of court life of the Bourbon dynasty and under Joaquim Murat. The tour includes the royal apartments, new apartment, apartment of the king, old apartment, an 18th-century creche with 1200 figurines, an art gallery, and a vast hall with the Museo dell'Opera (exhibits on Vanvitelli) and the little court theater (1769).

The **splendid park**** has an array of fountains and waterfalls that extend all the way up to the hill and to great waterfall*, with the sculptural group of Diana and Actaeon; the English garden is one of the most noteworthy aspects of this complex.

AMONG THE MOUNTAINS OF IRPINIA

This is a land with scars, where the wounds have healed slowly, where the terrible injures in the architectural and artistic heritage are unmistakable, in some cases irreparable. The earthquake that struck here, in the darkness of an early autumn evening – 23 November 1980 at 7:35 pm – lasted for one long, seemingly endless minute. When seen on a map, the area hit by the earthquake stretches parallel with the overall orientation of the Italian peninsula, elongated, including Naples, Benevento, the Vulture, Potenza, and the Vallo di Diano. The epicenter, the area of the most violent lurches and jolts, straddles the high valleys of the rivers Ofanto and Sele, bounded by Sant'Angelo dei Lombardi and Laviano. There were 3,000 dead, 10,000 injured, some 70 towns and villages wholly destroyed or badly damaged. The enormous quantity of energy that was unleashed in the space of a minute was measured as a 6.4 quake on the Richter scale. The route through the Irpino Mountains recommended here runs entirely through the greenery of mighty and solitary forests, gently rolling landscapes, mountains, hills, the high valleys of gathering streams, the Apennine courses of the rivers Sabato, Calore, Ofanto, and Sele. The earthquake has not damaged the patterns of nature, only the rich landscape wrought by man. Among the areas hardest hit is a diffuse "agrarian" architectural heritage, a body of venerable structures and an artistic fabric – not masterpieces perhaps, but eminently worthy – that had long been neglected and ignored, until the earthquake came, swept much of it away, and finally revealed its true worth.

NOT TO BE MISSED

Avellino (➡ see below) is a modern city located in a verdant hollow of the Sabato Valley, in a mountainous setting, with the Museo Diocesano and the Museo Irpino. **Atripalda**: remains of the Sannites and Roman Abellinum. **Monte Terminio** (1,783 m) is a nature reserve amidst spectacular forests; it extends on the left of the route, and is accessible from Serino. **Bagnoli Irpino** is a resort at the head of the Calore Valley. **Caposele**: above the town are the intake and pumping stations for the great Pugliese aqueduct. **Materdomini** is a resort town, set amid oak groves, with the Sanctuary of S. Gerardo at Maiella, a pilgrimage site. S. Guglielmo al Goleto is a ruined abbey containing the remains of the large and small church, founded in the 12th century by St Guglielmo di Vercelli; this requires a short detour from the SS 7 road, after Lioni. **Sant'Angelo dei Lombardi**: take a short detour; at the head of the Ofanto Valley, this town was devastated by the earthquake of 1980; the 16th-century cathedral with its late Renaissance portal was only partly destroyed; the "Lombardi" were, of course, the Longobards, who founded the town. **Aeclanum** was originally a Samnite town, and later a Roman one: the archeological excavations are just a short way west of the Passo di Mirabella. **Mirabella Eclano**: take a 2.5 km detour from the Passo di Mirabella; a carved and painted wooden 12th-century Crucifix can be seen in the Matrix church on a Saturday in September, during the *Festa del Carro*, a 25 m-tall obelisk is transported into town from a hill, with a statue of Our Lady of Sorrows. **Grottaminarda** is a hilltop farming town, with the 18th-century church of S. Maria Maggiore designed by Vanvitelli. **Basilica dell'Annunciata**: founded in early times, the oldest medieval church in Irpinia was partly carved out of the tufa, near a catacomb, and may have been the headquarters of the earliest bishops of Avellino.

AVELLINO

Reconstruction after WWII and the 1980 earthquake radically changed the face of this city in the valley of the Sabato River. It now looks entirely modern. Above the town, the sanctuary of Montevergine dates from the 12th century.
Cathedral, beneath its cold Neo-Classic facade, the 12th-century church was altered several times. The Romanesque bell tower was built re-using material from an earlier period. Late 18th-century frescoes, and some Roman and medieval capitals have been discovered beneath the stuccoes* (depicting cherubs and flowers) decorating the vaults.

Museo Provinciale Irpino*. It has a fine archeological and art collection (17-19C). It also has Risorgimento exhibits, with documents from the late-18th century to WWI, and a modern art collection, an 18th-century Neapolitan crib and a porcelain collection.
Sanctuary of Montevergine* an archway leads into the new church to the left of the old church. Inside, at the high altar, a richly decorated marble throne with bronze and silver bas-reliefs and statues contains the huge panel of the Madonna of Montevergine*, by Montano d'Arezzo, dating from the late 13th century.

CILENTO, SALERNO AND PAESTUM

"The air was delicately scented by the remarkably large and lovely violet. At last, we glimpsed the sublime and powerful rows of columns hemming in the horizon, in the midst of a desolate wasteland." These are the words in a letter to a friend by the English poet Percy Bysshe Shelley, who saw Paestum in February 1819. "Between one column and the next in this temple – it is called the Temple of Ceres – you can see in one direction the sea, toward which the gentle slope of the hill on which it stands runs down, and in the other direction you can see the vast amphitheatre of the Apennines, dark-colored, purplish mountains with diadems of snow, over which sail thick and leaden cloud banks." The Greeks of Sybaris sailed across the Mediterranean to found this city, calling it Poseidonia, after their sea god; the Lucanians who later descended from the Apennines to take the city for themselves gave it its modern name. Here Shelley was unable to enjoy the excitement of the sacred dances performed by girls depicted on the metopes of the Heraion of the Sele River; he did not see the diver portrayed on a tomb slab, for neither of these artworks, now in the museum, had yet been unearthed. Beyond Paestum, along the route, one is astonished by the nature of the coast of the Cilento, the crags, the cliffs, the inlets, and the glittering light that flashes off the sea, losing itself among the fluttering leaves of the olive groves. Watchtowers are relics of the centuries of Saracen pirate raids, little harbors are reminiscent of the trade in grain, wine, and olive oil once carried on by the sailor-monks from the abbey of Cava de' Tirreni. Midway up the Cilento coast is another Greek city, Elea (or Velia as it was written by Pliny), renowned for the school of philosophy that was begun here by the Ionian Xenophanes of Colophon and continued by Parmenides and Zeno (the latter known for his elegant logical paradoxes, such as that of Achilles being unable to outrun the tortoise; less well known for his participation in an unsuccessful conspiracy against the tyrant Nearchus. When Nearchus interrogated the philosopher, Zeno bit his own tongue off, so as not to betray his fellow-conspirators, and spit it in the tyrant's face. As a result, the tyrant had him crushed to death under a mill stone). Velia, like Paestum, was attacked by the Lucanians, but it withstood the siege. After completing this tour, you will return north along the Vallo di Diano, the highland that separates the Apennine ridge of the Maddalena from the mountains of the Cilento, and then you will head east to Potenza, where you can admire the artifacts of the Lucanians, Italic descendants of the ancient Samnites, in the Museo Archeologico.

NOT TO BE MISSED

Salerno (⟶ see below): between the hills and the coastline, this town boasts the medieval Duomo built by Robert Guiscard; there are a few precious artworks in the Museo diocesano San Matteo, and archeological collections in the Museo Archeologico Provinciale. **Sanctuary of Hera Argiva**: take a 2-km detour from Torre Kernoi, after the Sele River; it is said to have been founded by Jason; among the ruins, not particularly impressive to see nowadays, were the archaic Greek sculptures (metopes) now in Paestum. **Paestum** (⟶ see below), with the ancient Doric columns of the three temples of Greek Poseidonia, the pentagonal walls that mark the perimeter of the vanished city, the excavations, the Museo with the metopes from the Sanctuary of Hera Argiva, and painted Greek and Lucanian slabs, is one of Italy's leading archeological sites, justly famous. **Agropoli**: from the ruins of the Byzantine castle in the old town, perched high over the sea, you can enjoy the vista of the Gulf of Salerno, as far as Capri. **Santa Maria di Castellabate**, whose waters are protected by an underwater park. **Scavi di Velia**: this town, founded as a Phocaean Greek colony, was the town of Elea of the subtle philosophers Xenophanes, Parmenides, and Zeno; the ruins are scattered across the plain and the acropolis. **Palinuro**: located in an inlet at the foot of the promontory; by boat, you can go to the Grotta Azzurra, or Blue Grotto, in 10 minutes, to enjoy the amazingly blue light and water. **Marina di Camerota**, at the beginning of the Golfo di Policastro, with the Calabrian coast in the background. **Sapri**, with its annual commemoration of the landing of the 300 soldiers fighting for a united Italy. **Maratea** (Basilicata), medieval "borgo" perched on a rock, and bathing spots lining the coast; among the numerous grottoes, note the one of Marina di Maratea with its stalactites and stalagmites. **Praia a Mare**: uphill from the beach resort is the Sanctuary of Madonna della Grotta; you can take a boat to the island of Dino, about 1.5 km offshore. **Lagonegro**: this village stands on a slope of Mt Sirino, set in a ring of mountains. It is said that the woman who inspired Leonardo da Vinci's Mona Lisa was laid to rest in the ancient parish church. **Padula**: downhill from the town is the immense Baroque charterhouse, or Certosa di S. Lorenzo, site of the Museo Archeologico della Lucania Occidentale. **Teggiano**: the layout of this medieval town stands high on a secluded hilltop; note the Roman and medieval marble carvings in the former church of S. Pietro. **Sala Consilina**, whose historical center overlooks the ramparts of Diano. **Polla**: 16th-17th-century paintings and the carved choir chancel in the convent church of S. Antonio, in the high part of town; from the square in front of the church, fine view of the entire Vallo di Diano. **Grotta di Pertosa***: once the channel of an underground river, this cavern extends its heavily encrusted walls, with galleries, lakelets, and halls, for more than 2 km.

SALERNO

The old town lies on a slope, with all its Norman landmarks and monuments, overlooking the sea. **Piazza Amendola**. The square is the political heart of the city, lined with the Town Hall to the east, and the Prefettura to the west. A green expanse separates it from the late 19th-century Teatro Verdi.

Via dei Mercanti. The street starts from the Arco di Arechi and is the central thoroughfare of the old town. Follow it and you will reach the Baroque church of S. Giorgio, which has frescoes by Solimena (1675). Of interest are two museums: the Collezione di Ceramiche Alfonso Tafuri, with ceramic works; and the Pinacoteca Provinciale, in Palazzo Pinto.

Duomo**. It was built (1076-85) at the behest of Robert Guiscard, when Salerno was the capital of the Norman realm. It stands at the top of a stairway with, alongside, a bell tower* (12C), surmounted by intertwined arches; with ancient columns; raised Islamic arches; the intarsiate mullioned loggia of the great atrium – all indicate the composite culture of the Norman era. The Romanesque portal has celebrated bronze doors* from Constantinople (1099). In the interior note: the two mosaic-encrusted ambos** (13C, on the right; 12C, on the left) adjacent to the iconostasis* (1175); mosaics in the right apse, where Pope Gregory VII is buried, in the vault of the left apse, and on the marble screen of the main altar; the monument to Queen Margherita di Durazzo* (15C).

The Museo Diocesano contains, among other items, an illuminated Exultet* from the 13th century and an ivory altar frontal** from the 12th century.

Castle of Arechi. High overhead stands the castle built by successive waves of Byzantines, Longobards, and Normans. It boasts a fine view and an exquisite collection of ceramics, ranging from the 8th to the 19th century.

Museo Archeologico Provinciale. It is located inside the S. Benedetto complex. On exhibit are prehistoric stone artifacts, found in the nearby area of Palinuro, funerary furnishings dating from the Iron Age, and several finds of Etruscan origin.

PAESTUM

As you pass through the walls of the Porta Aurea, the area of monuments and excavations is on the right. There are three Greek temples: the Basilica*, from the mid-6th century BC, is the oldest of the temples of Paestum; the Tempio di Nettuno**, or Temple of Neptune (450 BC), is considered by some to be the most beautiful Doric temple in the Greek world; set apart from the others is the smaller Tempio di Cerere*, or Temple of Ceres, dating from the end of the 6th century BC and probably dedicated to the goddess Athena.

The Roman Forum occupies the site of the Greek agora; there is still a building that may have been the Curia, ruins of baths, the Tempio Italico (273 BC, modified in 80 BC), perhaps the Comitium, and the amphitheater.

A natural complement to this tour is a visit to the museum**, of particular importance for the archaic metopes** of the "thesauros" and the six metopes** of the main temple (late 6C BC), which all come from the sanctuary of Hera at the mouth of the Sele River; a seated statue of Zeus** (mid-6C BC); the painted slabs from the Tomba del Tuffatore*, or Tomb of the Diver, an exceedingly rare example of Greek painting.

The Temple of Neptune is the best kept of Paestum's 3 temples.

NAPLES/NAPOLI

T his city, the third largest in Italy and the largest in the "Mezzogiorno," or Southern Italy, was for many centuries the capital of the largest Italian state, prior to the 19th-century Risorgimento and unification. It served as a center of attraction in much the same way that Paris did for France or Madrid for Spain, a role that Rome has played – only recently – for the Italian peninsula. (Indeed, modern Naples' urbanistic and demographic problems are deeply routed in those distant times.) In one of the loveliest natural settings in all of Europe, celebrated throughout history for the variety of panoramic views, the mild weather, the luminous sea, and the gentle breezes, Naples is endowed with a superb heritage of monuments and artistic collections, at the center of an archeological zone that extends from Cumae to Pompeii, and is an attraction that draws visitors from all over the world. "Grand, luminous, and noble city," as one of its most illustrious sons, Giambattista Vico, once called it. Vico, the great historical philosopher, was an example of Naples' cultural and philosophical rigor that has always been the other face of unassuming Neapolitan humanism, immortalized by such actors as Salvatore Di Giacomo and Eduardo De Filippo.

Castel Nuovo, sometimes called Maschio Angioino, was a 14th-century residence of the Anjou family.

FROM THE HARBOR
TO THE MAIN MUSEUMS

Besides maintaining their key role as the centers of political and administrative power in the city, the Municipio (town hall), Castel Nuovo e Palazzo Reale bear interesting testimony to the history of Italy's southern capital. Via Toledo takes us back to the beginnings of Spanish rule; proceeding under another name, it then leads on to the Museo Archeologico Nazionale, commissioned by King Ferdinand IV to house the Farnese Collection and the archeological finds of the Herculaneum and Pompeii digs. The great Farnese Collection of art also led to the foundation of the city's second-largest museum, the Capodimonte Gallery.

Porto. Naples' harbor is one of the most important in the Mediterranean; the Stazione Marittima (terminal) is on the Mo-

lo Angioino; to the north is the Rococo Immacolatella building (D.A. Vaccaro, 18C), to the south is the Calata Beverello.

Piazza del Municipio. At the far end of this lush green square is the 19th-century Palazzo del Municipio, which incorporates the 16th-century church of S. Giacomo degli Spagnoli, built at the behest of the viceroy Pedro da Toledo; inside, behind the main altar, is the sepulcher* by G. da Nola (1539).

Castel Nuovo** or Maschio Angioino (because it was built under Angevin rule; 1279-82) was entirely rebuilt at the behest of Alphonse I of Aragon (15C). It now has the massive 15th-century appearance given it by Catalonian and Tuscan architects, with a trapezoidal plan and round towers. The entrance, flanked by two towers, is the lovely triumphal arch*, a celebrated 15th-century creation by a number of sculptors, including F.

Napoli 1:12 000 (1 cm = 120 m)

0   100   200 m

TANGENZIALE

Via Materdei
Via S. Teresa d. Scalzi
Via Stella
Via Stella
Via Vergini
Via Foria
Via D. Cirillo
S. Giovann a Carbonar

METROPOLITANA F.S. CAVOUR
P.ta S. Gennaro
Museo Madre
Settembrini

S. Teresa d. Scalzi
Museo Archeologico Nazionale
Via S. M. Longo
Gesù d. Monache
Ss. Apos

Via Salvator Rosa
Piazza Cavour
Via dei Tribunali
S. Maria Donnaregina (Museo Diocesano)

MUSEO
Ospedale d. Incurabili
L.go Donna-regina

S. Maria di Costantinopoli
S. Maria d. Grazie a Caponapoli
Duomo
Mus Teso S. Ger

Gall. P. di Napoli
Via Broggia
Accademia di Belle Arti
Via Conte di Ruvo
S. Maria Regina Coeli
V. Pisanelli dell'Anticaglia
Girolamini

la Conigliera
Via Francesco Saverio Correra
Via Enrico Pessina
Via S. Maria di Costantinopoli
Via d. Sapienza
Via del Sole
S. Paolo Maggiore
S. Lorenzo Maggiore
Pio Monte Misericor

Salita Pontecorvo
Pal. Tarsia
Port'Alba
Conservatorio di Musica
P.za V. Bellini
S. Maria Maggiore
Purgatorio ad Arco
Tribunal
Pal. di Filippo di Valois
S. Gennaro all'Olmo
S. Biagio Maggiore

Salita Tarsia
Tarsia
Via Bellini
Cappella Pontano
Capp. Sansevero
Pal. Spinelli di Laurino
S. Gregorio Armeno

Piazza Dante
Convitto nazionale Vittorio Emanuele II
S. Pietro a Maiella
S. Domenico Maggiore
P.za S. Domen.
Pal. d. Panormita
Pal. d. Pietà
Monte d. Pietà
Archivio di Stato
Pal Como (Museo Filang

DANTE
Pal. Filomarino d. Rocca
Pal. Venezia
S. Angelo a Nilo
Ss. Severino e Sossio
S. M. di Monte vergine

Via Roma
S. Michele Arcangelo
Gesù Nuovo
Pal. Carafa d. Spina
Pal. Carafa
V. S. Marcellino
Ss. Marcellino e Festo

Pal. Doria d'Angri
P.za d.Gesù
Spirito Santo
Via Capitelli
Calata Trinità Magg.
S. Chiara
Gesù Vecchio

S. Nicola alla Carità
Via Forno Vecchio
Guglia dell'Immacolata
P.za S. Giovanni Maggiore
Università d. Studi

Pal. Carafa di Maddaloni
Pal. Gravina
S. Giovanni Maggiore
S. Pietro Martire

Monteoliveto
P.za Monteoliveto
S. Maria Donnalbina
S. Maria Donnalbina
Pal. Penna
Via Sedile di Porto

P.za Carità
Pal. d. Poste e Telegrafi
Punto Touring TCI
Via Monteoliveto
S. Maria la Nova
Pal. d. Borsa
Piazza G. Bovio

Via C. Battisti
P.za Matteotti
Via G. Sanfelice
UNIVERSITA

Via A. Diaz
Via dell'Intendenza di Finanza
S. Diego all'Ospedaletto
Via Medina
Via A. De Gasperi

TOLEDO
S. Maria Incoronata
Via Agostino Depretis
Immacolatell

Via S. Giacomo
La Pietà d. Turchini
Fontana d. Nettuno
Teatro Mercadante

Pal. d. Banco di Napoli
S. Giacomo d. Spagnoli
Piazza del Municipio
Via C. Colombo

Pal. S. Giacomo (Municipio)
Via E. Imbriani
MUNICIPIO
Scavi Porto Romano
Nuova calata Piliero
Calata Porta

Pal. Zevallos Stigliano
S. Brigida
Traghetto per: Cagliari, Catania, Eolie, Palermo

Staz. Augusteo
Galleria Umberto
Castel Nuovo
Molo angioin

S. Ferdinando
Teatro S. Carlo
Via S. Carlo
Via Parco di Castello
Stazione marittima

Via Chiaia
Pal. Prefettura
Pza Trieste e Trento
Traghetto per: Capri, Casamicciola, Forio, Ischia, Procida, Sorrento
Bacino angioino

Via Carolina
PLEBISCITO
S. Francesco di Paola
Piazza del Plebiscito
Palazzo Reale
Darsena Ferd. Acton

Pal. del Principe di Salerno
Giardini del Molosiglio

POSILLIPO

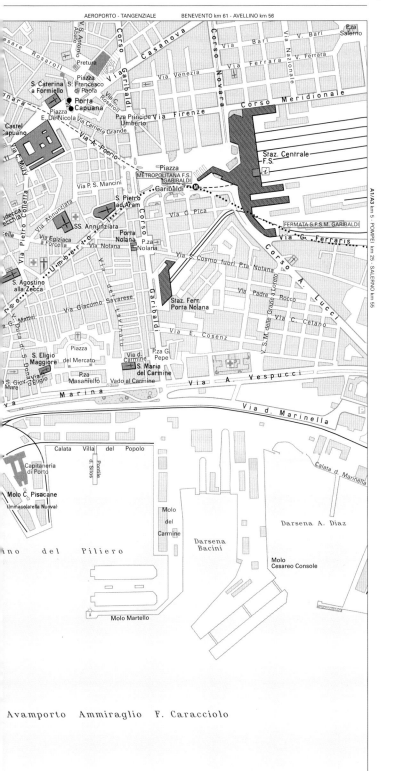

Laurana; note in particular the relief of the triumph of Alphonse. Access to the courtyard, rebuilt in the 18th century, lies beyond the portal; on the far side, opposite the entrance, a 15th-century outside staircase leads to the Sala dei Baroni, where local council sessions are held. Interior. The Museo Civico includes the Palatina chapel (14C), the only surviving feature of the Angevin palace, with a Madonna by F. Laurana (1474). Sculptures from to the 14th-15th centuries and paintings from the 15th-18th centuries are grouped in the two floors of the west wing of the castle; there are many notable works by 19th-century Neapolitan artists.

Palazzo Reale*. It faces the church of S. Francesco di Paola, enclosing the NE side of the Piazza del Plebiscito. It was built by D. Fontana (1600-1602), restored and enlarged in 1743-48, and then subjected to further renovation and restoration. This was the palace of the Bourbons from 1734 to 1860. You can tour the Cortile del Fontana (the Fontana Courtyard, named after the architect) and the Scalone d'Onore (ceremonial stairway) in the atrium (at the base, note the bronze door* by the Parisian Guglielmo Monaco, 1468) with reliefs, originally in the Castel Nuovo.) The Historic Apartment of Palazzo Reale has halls and rooms furnished with genuine 18th- and 19th-centuries furniture and frescoes of the Neapolitan school (17-18C); it houses the Teatro di Corte (Court Theater; F. Fuga, 1768). The Apartment of the Dance is occupied by the Biblioteca Nazionale Vittorio Emanuele III, a library where numerous manuscripts, including those of Tasso and Leopardi, and the burnt papyri* discovered in the Villa dei Papiri at Herculaneum, are preserved.

Piazza Plebiscito. In this harmonious and monumental square, the elliptical curves of the colonnades join the pronaos of the sober Neo-Classic church of S. Francesco di Paola – built at the behest of King Ferdinand I to celebrate the return of the Bourbons (1815) – with its large cupola (P. Bianchi, 1817-46); of the two equestrian statues of Charles III and Ferdinand I, the former is by Canova.

Teatro S. Carlo. This celebrated "temple of the opera" dates from 1737 but was rebuilt in Neo-Classic style during the 19th century. Directly opposite begins the Galleria Umberto I, dating from the end of the 19th century, a chief meeting spot for Neapolitans.

Via Toledo. From Piazza Trieste e Trento, extending up to the Museo Archeologico Nazionale, is the Via Toledo, the lively main thoroughfare of old Naples, the most popular strolling promenade. Note along this route the church of S. Nicola alla Carità (17C), the baroque Palazzo Carafa di Maddaloni, and the church of the Spirito Santo, rebuilt in the 18th century.

Museo Archeologico Nazionale**. Installed in a building that was once a cavalry barracks and later the headquarters of the University, the Museo Archeologico is one of the world's leading archeological museums. Roman replicas of Greek sculpture, unearthed in the cities buried by the eruption of Mt Vesuvius, were one of the great sources of knowledge of Greek art prior to the discovery of the few, rare originals; mosaics and paintings and minor collections complete the wonderful array of objects from Greco-Roman classical antiquity. The number of works is enormous, and they are arranged in over a hundred halls.

Among the marble sculptures**, to mention only the most important: the Tyrannicides*, a funerary stele* from the 5th century BC; an Athena* clearly derived from the work of Phidias; Eurydice and Hermes**, an Augustan-period copy of an original from the school of Phidias; the Aphrodite of the Gardens*; an excellent copy of the renowned Doriforo**, or Offering bearer, by Polyclitus; a Diomedes from Cumae*; the Palestrita*; the Venus Callipige* from a Hellenistic original, a bronze statuette of Herakles; the colossal Farnese Hercules*; torsos of Ares* and Aphrodite*; a Psyche* from Capua; a Venus from Capua*; the renowned Farnese Bull**, the largest surviving group of marble statuary from antiquity; the Diana Ephesina*; a Seated Matron,* believed to depict Agrippina; a bust of Caracalla*; a bronze horse head, possibly dating from the 3rd century BC, once attributed to Donatello; the Augustus of Fondi*; a bust of Homer*; a statuette of a Dancing Faun* from Pompeii; the renowned sculptures of the Sleeping Satyr*, the Drunken Silene*, and Hermes Resting*; a portrait said to be of Seneca*; and, last but not least, the Farnese Atlas*, a Hellenistic sculpture.

Among the paintings and mosaics*, aside from the world-renowned Battle of Alexander versus Darius**, a mosaic based upon an Alexandrian painting, of unique historical and artistic worth, there are also the other major mosaics* from Pompeii, such as the Strolling Musicians*, Plato and His Disciples in the Gardens of Academe*, a bust of a woman* and a Cat Biting a Quail*; a collection of paintings*, including murals from Pompeii, Herculaneum, and Stabia, the most notable items of which are a group of women performing a funerary dance* from Ruvo, women playing astragalomacy* (divination with small bones or dice) in the Neo-Attic style, and Pasquius Proculus with his wife.

A special section contains artworks and other objects unearthed in the 18th century at Herculaneum in the Villa dei Papiri*.

Also note the collection of valuables, among which two gladiatorial helmets*, a vase in dark-blue glass*, a table of 115 pieces from the Casa del Menandro (House of Menander) in Pompeii, and the Tazza Farnese**, a cup in sardonyx from the Alexandrian school.

The exquisite collection of Campanian, Apulian, Lucanian, Etruscan, and Attic vases* can only be seen in part. The Sale del Tempio di Iside (Temple of Isis Halls) are rooms arranged to gather frescoes and archeological finds discovered in Pompeii in 1764-66.

Palazzo Reale di Capodimonte*. On the site of what used to be a small village, King Charles of Bourbon decided to open the famous porcelain factory in 1739. A building to

nificant collections of paintings in Italy, formed mainly by the Farnese collection. Among the masterpieces to be seen here: St Louis of Toulouse Crowns His Brother Robert of Anjou King of Naples** by S. Martini; the Crucifixion** by Masaccio; the Transfiguration** by G. Bellini; the Zingarella**, or Gypsy Girl, by Correggio; Pope Paul III with His Nephews O. and A. Farnese** by Titian; the Parable of the Blind Men* by P. Bruegel; the Flagellation**by Caravaggio. Also worthy of note are the: Galleria dell'Ottocento, or Gallery of the 19th century, with numerous major works by Neapolitan painters; the Historic Apartment and Museum – with a collection of porcelain and majolica, the vast Collezione De Ciccio*, the David* by Pollaiuolo, and the Salottino di Porcellana** (1757-59), a masterpiece of porcelain produced by the factory of Capodimonte, from the palace of Portici. In the handsome park stands the Fabbrica di Porcellane di Capodimonte (porcelain factory; active from 1743 to 1759).

A bird's-eye view of Palazzo Reale di Capodimonte, which houses a national museum.

contain the art collections inherited from his mother, Elisabetta Farnese, was also established there. The manufactory was operative for just 20 years, while the palazzo, commissioned in 1734, has housed the Museo e Gallerie di Capodimonte since 1957. The park is also worth a visit.

Museo e Gallerie Nazionali di Capodimonte*. The Gallerie Nazionali (art galleries) are one of the most versatile and sig-

OLD NAPLES

This caracteristic route covers the heart of the city and the straight district of "Spaccanapoli". Some of the city's most important monuments are located in this area. Apart from renowned churches like S. Chiara and S. Domenico Maggiore, veritable treasure troves of art, the area features some more typical characteristics of the city: jewelry shops, the Christmas creche workshops in

Via San Gregorio Armeno, and the picturesque neighborhood of Forcella.

Incoronata. This church stands along the Via Medina. In its two Gothic aisles, it features frescoes from the 14th-15th century.

S. Maria la Nova. Along Via Monteoliveto, this 15th-century church has two Renaissance cloisters; farther on, the Palazzo Gravina* is built in the Tuscan Renaissance style.

S. Anna dei Lombardi. The nearby church of S. Anna dei Lombardi* can be considered a museum of Renaissance sculpture. Among other things are the marble altarpiece by B. da Maiano (1489); the Pietà in terracotta by G. Mazzoni (1492); a Manger and Saints* by A. Rossellino (1475); the Monument to Maria of Aragon* by A. Rossellino and B. da Maiano; frescoes by G. Vasari and inlaid stalls* in the Old Sacristy.

Spaccanapoli (Via B. Croce and Via S. Biagio dei Librai) runs along an ancient "decumanus." Following this route, you will pass a number of renowned churches and old palazzi, including Palazzo Filomarino, where the philosopher Benedetto Croce lived and died.

Gesù Nuovo. It is a fine example of Neapolitan Baroque, especially in the interior, with its rich colored marble decoration.

S. Chiara*. It was rebuilt in the original style (1310-28), of clear Provençal Gothic inspiration and is one of the foremost monuments of medieval Naples. Inside, note the tomb of Marie de Valois* by Tino di Camaino and assistants (1333-38), and fragments of the funerary monument of Robert I Anjou by G. and P. Bertini from Florence (1343-45); the inscription "Cernite Robertum regem virtute refertum" is said to have been dictated by the poet Petrarch; it comments on the arts of the Trivium and Quadrivium, or pillars of Medieval Scholasticism, who are shown watching over the funerary statue of the dead king. Adjacent are the convent of the Minorites, with a handsome portal* leading into the choir and the Chiostro maiolicato delle Clarisse**, a spacious cloister containing a splendid garden from 1742 at its center; the outside wall of the garden, the seats and the piers are covered with marvelous colored majolica*, hence the name.

S. Domenico Maggiore*. In the convent adjacent to the church, Thomas Aquinas once taught and both Pontano and Giordano Bruno studied. Inside the church are frescoes attributed to Cavallini (ca. 1308) and, in the Cappellone del Crocifisso, a Crucifix* on panel from the 13th century, which

supposedly spoke to St Thomas, and a Deposition attributed to Colantonio.

Sansevero chapel. With 18th-century decoration of colored marble, it is celebrated for the virtuoso statues of Disinganno (Disillusionment, by Queirolo), Pudicizia (Modesty, by A. Corradini) and Christ Veiled* (G. Sammartino, 1735).

S. Angelo a Nilo. Known also as the "Cappella Brancaccio," it is a church in a little square with an ancient statue of the god of the River Nile. It contains the sepulcher of Rinaldo Cardinal Brancaccio*, by Donatello, Michelozzo, and Pagno di Lapo Portigiani (1426-28).

No less interesting is the Via dei Tribunali, another of the ancient "decumani." S. Paolo Maggiore (1583-1603) is a church set high atop a stairway in the Piazzetta S. Gaetano, the site of the ancient Greco-Roman Forum; the interior is richly decorated with marble inlay and frescoes.

S. Lorenzo Maggiore**. One of the most important medieval Neapolitan churches. The first church was built in the 6th century on top of Roman structures which have only recently been brought to light during excavations; this same church was then rebuilt at the express wish of Charles I and Charles II in 1270-75. Of the Baroque renovation, only the facade (1742) remains. The interior of this church is of Provençal Gothic inspiration; note the Gothic sepulcher of Catherine of Austria* by Tino di Camaino and assistants. From the 18th-century cloister you can enter an area of Greek, Roman, and medieval archeological excavations.

Girolamini. The interior of the church of the Girolamini (16-18C) is an interesting composite example of Baroque decoration, though it is badly damaged; adjacent to the main cloister is a small Pinacoteca .

Pio Monte della Misericordia. Such were the confraternity tasks (corporal works of mercy) that, when the building was undergoing construction (1658), the architect was asked to carve out a space for a portico in the lower part of the facade where the needy could be welcomed. In the 17th-century church are sculptures by A. Falcone and paintings by B. Caracciolo, L. Giordano, and the splendid Acts of Mercy** by Caravaggio; the adjacent Pinacoteca, or art gallery, includes paintings from the Neapolitan school of the Pio Monte della Misericordia.

Via del Duomo follows an ancient "cardo" of the Greco-Roman city. The Renaissance Palazzo Como* (1460-90), also called "Cuomo", possibly designed by G. da Maiano, is the site of the Museo Civico Gaetano Filangieri, with an estimable collection of Neapolitan paintings, Italian and Spanish arms and armor (16-18C), European and Oriental ceramics and porcelain, and 16th-century embroideries.

S. Giorgio Maggiore. Rebuilt in the 17th century by C. Fanzago, the church still preserves, at the entrance, the apse of the early Christian building, dating from the 4th-5th centuries.

The Duomo**, still maintains the soaring 13th-century Gothic interior, with pointed arches and piers, against which 110 ancient columns have been placed. The third chapel in the right aisle is the 17th-century chapel of the Tesoro di San Gennaro*, where the Treasury of St Januarius is kept. It features a bronze gate by Fanzago, and frescoes by Domenichino and Lanfranco, a silver altar frontal dating from 1695, silver statues of the Saint and the other patron saints of Naples, little flagons of miracle-working blood, and the saint's cranium, in a 14th-century French reliquary. The Assumption of the Virgin* by Perugino and assistants is in the second chapel in the right transept; frescoes dating from the late 13th-16th centuries, a mosaic floor from the 13th century, a Sienese polyptych from the 14th century and the two tombs of the Minutolo family are in the Minutolo chapel** (to the right of the presbytery); a large 14th-century fresco with a Tree of Jesse is in the second chapel in the left transept. From the left aisle, you can descend to the church of S. Restituta , the first Christian basilica in Naples (4C); in the 5th-century Baptistery, fragments of original mosaics*; in the sixth chapel in the left aisle, Virgin and Saints, in mosaic, by Lello da Orvieto (1322).

S. Maria di Donnaregina. There are two churches named S. Maria di Donnaregina*: the Nuova (or new) is Baroque (1649), and has an interior frescoed and decorated with polychrome marble; the Vecchia (or old) is an important medieval Franciscan Gothic monument, and contains the sepulcher of Mary, Queen of Hungary* by Tino di Camaino and G. Primario (1326) and, in the nuns' choir, frescoes* from the first half of the 14th century, by F. Rusuti and others.

Castel Capuano. At the end of Via dei Tribunali, this castle is also known as the Vicaria; built by the Normans and enlarged by the Swabians, it was the royal palace until the 15th century.

Porta Capuana*, built in 1484 to a plan by G. da Maiano, is one of the great masterpieces of the Renaissance.

S. Giovanni a Carbonara*, which stands high atop an 18th-century staircase, is a church that was founded in 1343, rebuilt at the beginning of the 15th century, and then modified and enlarged. Especially noteworthy are the sculptures, such as the Monumento Miroballo* (16C), the monument to King Ladislaus* (1428) and the sepulcher of Sergianni Caracciolo*. Note also the Caracciolo di Vico chapel, a Renaissance masterpiece.

THE VOMERO

This district may be considered a city within the city; it is hard to believe that the hill slopes were once dotted with farmhouses, patrician residences and villas.

Piazza Vanvitelli. The very center of a district which developed at the end of the 19th century. Once characterized by handsome Art Nouveau architecture, its appearance is that of an anonymous middle-class district, spoilt by real estate speculation.

Villa La Floridiana*. King Ferdinand I gave to his morganatic wife, Lucia Partanna, Duchess of Floridia, the villa (1817-19) now known as La Floridiana. The magnificent park is famous for its abundance of splendid camelias; the Neo-Classic mansion houses the Museo Nazionale della Ceramica Duca di Martina*, an exquisite collection of porcelain and majolica from the main factories of Europe and the East.

Castel S. Elmo. A massive star-shaped fortress, rebuilt in the 16th century. It later became a prison (in 1799 revolutionaries were jailed here, as were many patriots of the Risorgimento). Splendid view** over the city and gulf from the terraces.

Certosa di S. Martino**. It is the genius of C. Fanzago which gave the Certosa di S. Martino, a charterhouse on a ridge of the Vomero hill, its present-day aspect, in the most complete and exquisite 17th-century Neapolitan Baroque. The church*, glittering with marble inlays, is itself a gallery of 17th-century Neapolitan painting. You then pass through the interesting area of the convent; from the square in front of the Certosa, splendid panoramic view*.

Inside the Certosa is the Museo Nazionale di S. Martino**. The museum includes: historical souvenirs and memorabilia of the Kingdom of Naples, the Neapolitan topography section, the section of feasts and costumes, the creche section with the large Cuciniello Creche* and, across the main cloister*, the lavish Pinacoteca, or art gallery, the sculpture section, and the section of applied arts and memorabilia of the Certosa.

A view of Mergellina from Castel dell'Ovo.

THE RIVIERA

The legendary view of Naples was celebrated by painters in the 18th century, only to be followed by photographs and postcards in the 19th century. In touring this part of the Gulf of Naples – perhaps by car along the Posillipo hill – one can understand why people used to say "Once you have seen Naples, you can die in peace."

S. Lucia. Take Via N. Sauro, the first stretch of the magnificent beachfront promenade, or Lungomare, as far as Mergellina, and you will arrive at the Porto di S. Lucia with its quay that leads to the Borgo Marinaro (fishing village); at the end of Via N. Sauro, note the Fontana dell'Immacolatella, a Baroque fountain.

Castel dell'Ovo. It was built in the 12th century (though its current appearance dates from 1691) on the site of a villa that once belonged to Lucullus, a great general of ancient Rome.

Riviera di Chiaia. This elegant road used to be the site of the old Neapolitan promenade, famous for its views and 17th-19th-century houses, important examples of which, especially in the opening stretch, still remain.

Villa Pignatelli. Surrounded by a beautiful garden, it houses the Museo Principe Diego Aragona Pignatelli Cortes, which still preserves the flavor of the original patrician residence; worthy of note are the large araucarias in the garden, as well as the Museo delle Carrozze (Museum of Carriages).

Villa Comunale. The gardens of this municipal villa separate the Riviera di Chiaia from the beachfront promenade, or Lungomare of Via Caracciolo, and enclose the Acquario and Stazione Zoologica*.

Piedigrotta. The Piedigrotta district (so called because it extends from the tunnel – or "grotta" – dug in the 1st century BC underneath the hill of Posillipo) features the church of S. Maria di Piedigrotta, originally built in the 13th century, with a Sienese wooden Madonna from the 14th century.

Parco Virgiliano. Here you can visit the tomb of Giacomo Leopardi and the so-called tomb of Virgil, which was actually a Roman dovecote.

Mergellina. Continuing along Via Caracciolo, you will reach one of the most enchanting sites in Naples: the inlet of Mergellina. In S. Maria del Parto is the tomb of the Neapolitan Humanist poet Jacopo Sannazaro and the famous "Diavolo di Mergellina," a panel from the 16th century showing St Michael besting the Devil.

Posillipo*. A crossroads along the panoramic Via di Posillipo* is the starting point for promenades and walks through the enchanting "region" of Posillipo*, which takes its name from the Greek words for "assuaging pain or grief." The Via di Posillipo will take you to Capo di Posillipo, with a group of houses by the sea, and a little marina; to the little fishing village of Marechiaro, high over the sea, where a plaque on a house on a cliff indicates the "fenesta ca lucive", the window in the famous song by Salvatore Di Giacomo. Lastly, on the Pozzuoli shore, on the island of Nisida, is the ancient volcanic crater, joined to the mainland by a breakwater bridge. The remarkable vistas and views in this area are all of particular note, but perhaps the finest panorama** of Naples is the one from the Belvedere of the Eremo dei Camaldoli (Hermitage of the Camaldolites, elev. 458 m, the highest point in the Campi Flegrei, or Phlegrean Fields, to the NW of the river; exit from A1).

REGGIA DI CASERTA

About 6,000,000 ducats. That is what it cost the Sun King's great-grandson, Charles III of the House of Bourbon and future king of Spain, to build a residence that would rival Versailles. The Reggia di Caserta was declared a UNESCO World Heritage Site in 1997. It took 22 years to build. This huge sum paid for the 1,200 rooms on five floors and the immense garden irrigated by a purpose-built aqueduct. Because of the size of the complex, it proved necessary to bring in extra, forced labor, including galley-slaves and Muslim slaves. Meanwhile, enormous quantities of material were delivered to the site: local tuff, travertine, gray marble, lime, pozzolana and brick, and more expensive marble and iron from the Tuscan quarries of Carrara and Follonica. Charles III wished to emulate the splendor of the French court, raising his court to a European level, but the ruler of Naples also needed a seat that was less exposed to attacks from enemy artillery (in 1742 a British naval squadron had placed the capital under serious threat).

A magical atmosphere pervades the rooms and halls of the palace, which splendidly reflect the transition from the Rococo to the Neo-Classic style. In spring and autumn, the sovereigns would open their doors to illustrious guests, such as Goethe, who were then entertained in the court theater (an exact copy of the San Carlo theater in Naples) by the music of court composers Giovanni Paisiello and Domenico Cimarosa. Once a year, on Easter Monday, the royal subjects were allowed to visit the splendid royal park.

Palazzo Reale*. Luigi Vanvitelli designed the complex and work began in 1752. It was concluded in 1774 under Carlo Vanvitelli, who took over on his father's death (1773). The palace is built on a rectangular plan around four courtyards and covers an area of more than 45,000 m². The rear facade facing the enormous park can be regarded as the main facade. The interior** is a masterpiece of architecture and interior design. The monumental atrium is divided into three aisles and opens onto four courtyards. A statue of Charles Bourbon on a lion looks down from the center of the Grand Staircase*. The elegant vestibule* at the top leads (left) into the Royal Apartments**. One of the finest rooms is the Room of Alexander, with the throne of Joachim Murat. The King's Apartment contains the Council Chamber, Francis II's bedroom and the servants' quarters. The Old Apartment*, designed by Carlo Vanvitelli, decorated with beautiful fabrics and wallpaper, is in the wing of the palace occupied by Ferdinand IV (1780) and Ferdinand II. The ceilings of the first four rooms, named after the four seasons and decorated with luxurious 18th-century and Neo-Classic furnishings, are frescoed with allegorical themes**. The Library houses about 14,000 volumes and is sumptuously furnished and decorated with paintings and frescoes. The Art Gallery contains paintings by 18th- and early 19th-century artists from Italy and abroad.

Park**. At first, apart from its sheer size (120 hectares), what most strikes the visitor is the dramatic visual effect created by Luigi Vanvitelli by placing a succession of pools, fountains and waterfalls all along the

The Grand Staircase in Palazzo Reale.

central axis of the park. The most beautiful features of the park include the Fountain of Eolus* and the Fountain of Ceres*, decorated with statues of dolphins, tritons and two Sicilian rivers, the Simeto and the Oreto, spouting jets of water. From the top of the Great Waterfall**, also called the Fountain of Diana, after the sculpture of Diana and Atheon, there are wonderful views of the park and across the plain to the Phlegrean Fields and Ischia.

Campania is unique in terms of the variety of its food and the fact that some crops, like vines and olive trees, have been cultivated for literally thousands of years. The volcanic soil of the land inland from the coastal strip of this region plays a fundamental role, being very fertile and perfect for growing fruit and vegetables. But farming also takes place on the rocky slopes of the Amalfi Coast, where citrus groves grow on the terraces, and on the slopes of the Apennines, which support a large dairy industry.

TYPICAL LOCAL DISHES

Impepata di cozze. Mussels are cooked in a little boiling water. As soon as they open, they are seasoned with lots of black pepper, lemon juice, parsley and extra virgin olive oil.

Zucchine a scapece. This can be served as a starter or accompany a main dish. Slice the zucchini thinly and fry in oil. Flavor with a little vinegar and fresh mint and serve cold.

Calzone. A circle of pizza dough covered with chopped ham, mozzarella, ricotta and parmesan, folded in half and baked in the oven. The caniscione is similar but has a much richer filling.

Pizza. There are endless varieties of this traditional Campanian fare, but they all involve bread dough. The secret of perfect pizza is a really hot oven.

Sartù. The richest dish in Neapolitan cuisine is served in only a few restaurants in Naples. It is a rice dish with a stuffing of meatballs, sausage, chicken giblets, mozzarella, mushrooms and peas. The number of ingredients make this a very spectacular dish.

Zite ripiene. For this dish use zite (long tubes of dried pasta) or short pasta. When the pasta is half cooked, drain and stuff with a mixture of minced pork fried with suet and onions, salami or sausage meat, caciocavallo cheese, spices and eggs. Scatter grated cheese on top of the dish and bake in the oven.

Coniglio all'ischitana. Many of the inhabitants of Ischia keep rabbits and the meat is widely used in the island's cuisine. The recipe is simple: cut the rabbit into pieces, fry in olive oil to seal and continue cooking with white wine, tomatoes and fresh rosemary.

Gattò di patate. This typical home-made peasant dish is made with mashed potatoes mixed with egg, ham, mozzarella, provolone and other ingredients and cooked in the oven.

Insalata di rinforzo. Traditionally made at Christmas, this is a caponata made with cauliflower, olives, pickles, anchovies and capers, mixed together and flavored with oil and vinegar. The name (it means 'strengthening salad') derives from the fact that the dish was eaten over several days, adding new ingredients each time.

Mozzarella in carrozza. This is a very tasty, simple dish to make. Slices of bread enclosing a slice of mozzarella are dipped in flour and beaten egg and fried.

Babà. This rich, light yeast cake, cooked and drenched with rum syrup, was invented in France.

Pastiera. This cake from Naples was once traditionally made only between Epiphany and Easter. A base of sweet shortcrust pastry is spread with a mixture of fresh ricotta cheese, grains of wheat that have been boiled in milk, chopped candied fruit, eggs, sugar, spices and other ingredients.

Sfogliatelle. There are two types: one with very thick layers of puff pastry, the other with only a covering of sweet shortcrust pastry. In both cases, the filling is made with fresh ricotta, candied fruit, cinnamon and vanilla.

Struffoli. These honey-covered fritters appear on the table at Christmas and are covered with colored sugar.

TYPICAL LOCAL PRODUCTS

Mozzarella di Bufala Campana DOP. Protected by a special consortium, this buffalo milk mozzarella, sold either in plaits or round balls, is most typical of all the region's dairy products. It has been made here since the 12th century. The term mozzarella refers to the technique of cutting the curd with the thumb and index finger.

Pecorino di Laticuda. Made in various areas of the hinterland (in the provinces of Caserta, Avellino and Benevento), this cheese is made with milk from ewes of the Laticuda breed. It is sold fresh after about a month, or mature, when it has a strong taste.

Provolone del Monaco. A semi-hard cow's milk cheese, made entirely by hand, typical of the Sorrento peninsula and the Mts Lattari. The milk comes from top-quality cows of the Agerolese breed, fed exclusively on the aromatic herbs of the Colli Sorrentini.

Salame Napoli. This salami is made all over rural Campania. The ingredients are pork meat and fat, veal, pepper, chili, and garlic cooked in wine.

Pomodoro San Marzano dell'Agro Sarnese-Nocerino DOP. This famous type of tomato, traditionally grown in the countryside between Sarno and Nocera Inferiore, is long and pear-shaped, bright red, has a sweetsour taste, and few seeds or fibrous parts, making it particularly suitable for eating raw. Also excellent for sauces or as preserved skinned tomatoes (pelati).

Carciofo di Paestum IGP. This special breed of artichoke, Tonda di Paestum, is grown in the area around Salerno. The smallest areas of production are Pietrelcina (Benevento) and Schito in the municipality of Castellammare di Stabia (Province of Napoli).

Olio Extravergine d'Oliva. There are various areas of DOP olive-oil production in Campania: olio extravergine Cilento DOP, golden yellow with a fruity taste, slightly bitter and spicy on the tongue; olio extravergine d'oliva Colline Salernitane DOP, with a between green and straw-yellow and its fruity, slightly bitter and spicy taste; olio extravergine d'oliva Penisola Sorrentina DOP, with a color that varies between green and straw-yellow, with a fruity smell and a taste that is slightly spicy and bitter on the tongue.

Castagna di Montella IGP. These chestnuts, the first in Campania to be awarded IGP status, grow in about 3,000 hectares of the Montella area of Irpinia.

Limone Costa di Amalfi IGP and Limone di Sorrento IGP. Lemons are one of the gastronomic delights of Campania. You have to be careful because there are two kinds with IGP status: one is the oval lemon of Sorrento, and the other is the 'pointed' lemon – grown on the peninsula that separates the Bay of Naples from the Bay of Salerno.

Melannurca Campana. A very old species of apple with several distinctive characteristics. It is rather flat with a red striated skin and a rusty color near the stalk; it has white, crunchy pulp with a slightly sour taste.

Nocciola di Giffoni IGP. The Tonda di Giffoni is supposed to be one of Italy's best hazelnuts. It grows in the provinces of Salerno, Avellino, Caserta and Naples.

Noce di Sorrento. Italy's best-quality walnut, also used for making Nocino liqueur. It has a thin shell, white, tender flesh with a pleasant taste, and is not very oily.

WINES

Vine-growing goes back a long way all over Italy, but nowhere has such close links with the origins of wine-production as Campania. Obviously, when the Romans talked about *Campania felix*, they were referring to its fine wines. Then the best wine was reputed to be Falerno, which is still grown in vineyards close to the border with Lazio. In the modern Aglianico we find traces of the ancient vine species Vitis hellenica, and Fiano is reminiscent of the species Vitis apiana.

Today an extraordinary number of wines made here are protected. Taurasi DOCG made from pure Aglianico grapes, is the pride of the region, the first wine in the south of Italy to be awarded this quality label. Recently, the whites Fiano d'Avellino and Greco di Tufo have also been designated DOCG wines. Then there are 17 DOC and 8 IGT wines. There are endless types of wine, including Aglianico del Taburno and Falerno del Massico, sparkling wines like Aversa and Greco di Tufo Spumante, as well as passito and liqueur wines. The most interesting thing about so much variety is that many ancient varieties, based on local grape varietals and traditional farming methods, have been saved from extinction.

Other typical products of the region are Limoncello, a lemon liqueur, and Nocillo, a digestif made with green walnuts.

The Tavoliere is the broadest plain in the entire Italian peninsula, occupying 3000 km², one percent of the nation's surface. In ancient times, this was seabed; in centuries gone by it was winter pasturage, where nomadic sheep herders would lead their flocks. At Foggia there was a "dogana della mena delle pecore," or shepherds' customs station (established in 1447 by Alphonse of Aragon, it provided the royal coffers with an endless stream of cash; it was abolished after Italian unification). Today this is farmland, where grain, forage, vineyards, and fruit orchards grow. It is true that the eye sees only an endless table-

The seaside at Peschici, along the Gargano coast.

land here, but that is not the origin of the name, which refers to the Tabulae Censuariae, the register in which the immense landholdings of the government in this territory were recorded. At a distance, it is surrounded by the outcroppings and spurs of the Samnite Apennines, the rim of the Murgia highlands, and the Gargano. It is from the last elevations of the Apennines as they sink into the plain that Lucera and Troia look out over the Tavoliere from the west: Lucera, where Frederick II gathered the troublesome Saracens of Sicily, a reserve for recruits to his loyal and much feared royal guard; Troia, with its Romanesque cathedral, an outstanding example of the architectural style of the Apulian Middle Ages, veined with Byzantine and Muslim styles. The Gargano, on the other hand, is the other landscape of this route, which virtually follows the entire Gargano coastline before crossing it. This great karstic limestone massif with rounded mountaintops rises from the plain in two successive terraces; extending out into the Adriatic, it plunges into the sea with high, steep coasts, broken here and there by small beaches. At the base of this massif on the southern side are the churches of the Siponto, a region strangled by malarial swamps and earthquakes; on high is the Sanctuary of Arcangelo Michele in Monte Sant'Angelo, dedicated to the Archangel Michael, perched on a high ridge. The coastline has been a relatively recent discovery here. For many years the peninsula was secluded, trapped between the sea and the marshlands of the Tavoliere; today people are drawn here by the shoals and the sands, the olive groves and pine forests, the bright southern light, inland near the scattered remains of the forest that once extended where now only underbrush and pasturage are seen, where white rocks jut out of the arid soil.

NOT TO BE MISSED

Foggia (➡ see below), at the heart of the Tavoliere, is a thoroughly modern town: the Romanesque cathedral was heavily restored in the 18th century; in the Museo Civico there are also exhibits concerning the Foggia-born composer, Umberto Giordano. **S. Leonardo di Siponto***: a 12th-century church, formerly an abbey of the Templar Knights, with a splendid portal decorated with 13th-century reliefs. **S. Maria di Siponto****: a lovely 11th-century Romanesque cathedral, once part of the long-vanished town. **Manfredonia**: the castle (like the city, founded and built by Manfredi, or Manfred, the natural son of the emperor Frederick II), facing the waterfront, is the site of the Museo Archeologico Nazionale. **Monte Sant'Angelo***: in the grotto here, the Archangel Michael was purportedly seen in an apparition in the late 5th century. At that time, the Longobards were particularly devoted to Michael, as a national saint; the sanctuary and town grew together, through the faith of the pilgrims. The so-called tomb of the Longobard king Rotari is actually a later baptistery, in all likelihood; the Museo delle Arti e delle Tradizioni popolari del Gargano "Giovanni Tancredi" features the arts and folkways of the Gargano. **Vieste**: visit the old town, with stepped lanes amid white houses joined by arches; fine view of the coastline and sea from the castle. **Peschici**: high on the coast of the Gargano, perched upon a crag, overlooking the beach below. **Rodi Garganico**: set on a promontory on the north coast of the Gargano; twenty nautical miles away are the Tremiti Islands, with their clear waters, rocky coasts, and aromatic vegetation, the maquis. **Vico del Gargano**: the Trappeto Maratea is an old mill used for producing oil. **Foresta Umbra*** is a vast forest of beech trees, pines, maples, and hornbeams, in the recently established Parco Nazionale del Gargano. **San Giovanni Rotondo**: site of pilgrimages commemorating the Christian virtues of Padre Pio da Pietrelcina. **San Marco in Lamis**, dominated by the like-named convent founded by the Lombards. **San Severo**: site of medieval churches and widely renowned for the production of white wine. **Lucera***: this little town is dense with history, from Roman times, up through the remarkable reigns of Frederick II and of the House of Anjou: the castle that overlooks the plain was enlarged by Charles I d'Anjou with a vast ring of towers and walls; the 14th-century Duomo is also Angevin; the Museo Civico Giuseppe Fiorelli has exhibits chiefly of archeology. **Troia**: the rose window and bronze doors by Oderisio da Benevento embellish the cathedral, a sterling example of Apulian Romanesque; Museo Diocesano and Museo Civico; proto-Romanesque church of S. Basilio.

FOGGIA

The provincial capital lies at the center of the flat land known as the Tavoliere, between the Gargano and the mountains of the Subappennino, at an important junction in the local road and rail system. The name of the modern town probably derives from the Latin foveae, the cisterns used to store grain in Antiquity. Despite considerable rebuilding in the 20th century, the local culture can still be discerned in the urban fabric. Its Baroque and Neo-Classic buildings, and the administrative buildings erected under the Fascism regime stand alongside smaller buildings and churches of ancient foundation.

Cathedral. The cathedral overlooks Piazza De Sanctis. Built in 1172, it was altered in the 17th century and after the 1731 earthquake, and was severely damaged by air raids during WWII. The original Romanesque features of the heavily restored building can only be seen in the bottom of the facade, which is reminiscent of the blind arches decorating the facade of the cathedral of Troia, the diocese to which Foggia once belonged. Above the arches is a finely carved cornice – the work of Bartolomeo da Foggia – which runs along the right side of the church and ends where the bell tower was added in 1740. The interior was decorated in the 18th century. The chapel of the Vetere Icon (right of the presbytery) contains a Byzantine icon of the Virgin. The story goes that some shepherds found the icon illuminated by three flames in the murky waters of a marsh, and that the town was later built here. Below the transept is a large crypt, built on a Greek-cross plan, with a central dome and splendid capitals resting on four columns of red breccia marble, probably carved by Nicola, son of B. da Foggia.

Corso Garibaldi. Both Palazzo della Prefettura and the imposing Town Hall date from the Fascist period. Opposite the Prefecture and overlooking Piazza XX Settembre – Palazzo della Provincia was built by the Bishop of Troia as a seminary. Facing it is Palazzo Perrone, built in the mid-18th century.

Via Arpi. The main street of the old town ends at the Manfredonia gate. Palazzo De Rosa, with its unusual first-floor loggia, stands on one side of Piazza De Sanctis and dates from the Renaissance period.

Palazzo Arpi. The palazzo was rebuilt above the remains of the imperial residence erected by Frederick II in 1223. (All that remains of the original building is the arch of a doorway resting on two eagles which act as brackets – by B. da Foggia – and a plaque). The right part of the building is now the Museo Civico. It has an archeological section (finds from Daunia, red-figure ware and steles, and grave-goods from ancient Arpi), an art gallery with works by local painters, a section on local traditions (with interesting artifacts made by local artisans) and a number of inscriptions and architectural fragments.

Piazza Piano delle Croci. This square stands beyond Porta Arpi, also called Porta Grande, and is better known as 'Piano delle Fosse', because it was here that the ancient grainstores were located. These were replaced by the buildings next to the church of S. Giovanni Battista, erected in 1626.

Church of the Calvario e delle Sette Croci. Situated on a section of the royal path to San Severo, the church was built in the late 17th and early 18th century. It comprises a series of chapels and constitutes a sort of 'Calvary on the plain'. The church complex and the path are now surrounded by a poor area of the town.

TRULLI AND BARI

The Adriatic coast often forms a last little rocky cliffline, in the succession of terraces of "rocky Apulia," as the Murge hills are often called. The "trullo," a remarkable type of dwelling found here, gives its name to another part of the Murge, the SE sector (Murgia dei Trulli). This rolling highland, dark green with crops, drops away toward the Adriatic coastline like a steep rampart, between Mola di Bari and Ostuni, covered with white houses; toward the Gulf of Taranto, on the other hand, it slopes gently in a succession of terraces. The two sections of the Murge differ in terms of agriculture and in terms of population, which is scattered throughout the countryside further south. And there are three notable grottoes or caverns. At Polignano a Mare, the Grotta Palazzese encloses waters of an intense blue-green; it yawns open, with many other marine grottoes, in the steep cliff face, which has been burrowed out by the tireless sea waves. The Grotta di Putignano is a karstic cavity, a treasure chest of alabaster some 20 m tall, covered with pink mineral encrustations. The most notable grottoes however, are the Grotte di Castellana, first explored by a group of local youths in the 18th century. They extend for a good 2 km, some 50 m under the surface of the earth; stalactites and stalagmites dangle and jut, stirring the imagination of cave explorers, and prompting fanciful names such as: Ciclopi (Cyclops), Angelo (Angel), Civetta (Owl), Presepe (Creche), Serpente (Serpent), Altare (Altar), Duomo di Milano (Cathedral of Milan), and Torre di Pisa (Leaning Tower of Pisa). At the end of this succession of caverns you encounter the crystalline whiteness of the Grotta Bianca, which has been described as the world's most beautiful cave. Along the road, there are olive and almond groves, and more than half of the route runs along the seashore. Toward the end of the route, you will be retracing the steps of Horace, in the voyage he describes in his fifth Satire.

NOT TO BE MISSED

Bari (➡ see below): the historical center of this regional capital contains two Romanesque churches, S. Sabino and S. Nicola. **Mola di Bari**: set on a promontory, with a 13th-century cathedral renovated in the Renaissance style by architects from Dalmatia; note the fishing harbor and the Angevin castle, erected in 1278. **Polignano a Mare** overlooks the Adriatic Sea from its jagged cliffs; the light and colors in the Grotta Palazzese are a pale blue: it is the best known grotto in this stretch of coastline, and you can tour it by boat. **Conversano**: on a detour from the main route between Castellana Grotte and Polignano a Mare, with its Duomo, other old churches, and a vista of the coastline from the square in front of the castle. **Grotte di Castellana****: carved by an ancient underground river, this is the largest complex of caves in Italy. **Putignano**, a resort in the Murgia range; in town is the church of Madre di S. Pietro; 1 km away is the grotto, with pink alabastrine encrustations. **Alberobello** (➡ see below): the "trulli," round whitewashed houses with conical grey limestone roofs, line the long steep twisting streets, creating a remarkable townscape. **Martina Franca***: which offers fine views of the valley of Itria, scattered with "trulli"; the city stands on the highest elevation of the southern Murgia range, and has vigorous architecture and a fine Baroque flavor. **Fasano**: resort on a spur of the Murgia range; all around, amidst the Mediterranean vegetation are bright white "trulli" and exotic animals. **Egnazia**: the necropolis, the musem, and the ruins of ancient Gnatia can all be reached via an 11-km detour climbing north along the coast, from Torre Canne. **Ostuni** glitters white among the olive trees on the hills of the Murgia; note the medieval quarters, illuminated at night. **Carovigno**, with a 15th-century castle and the walls of the Messapic town Carbina. **Brindisi**: two Roman columns mark the end of the Via Appia, or Appian Way, on the shore of the peninsula where the modern city stands between two inlets that constitute an excellent natural harbor; the Museo Archeologico Francesco Ribezza and, at a distance of 2 km, the 13th-century church of S. Maria del Casale, the most outstanding monument in the city.

BARI

The old town area of Bari is one of the two parts that make up what is now the second largest city in continental southern Italy. Bari lies on the Adriatic Sea, midway up the coast of Apulia. While the old section lies serried and compact in a labyrinth of twisting lanes, where the entire history of Bari has had its long course, the new section developed during the 19th century on a regular plan made up of broad straight streets. Nowadays, one might mention a third Bari, "Bari Nuovissima", which straddled the railroad line throughout the 20th century, expanding into the industrial section and the Fiera del Levante, the site of a major trade fair.

Basilica di S. Nicola**. This basilica, one of the archetypes of the Romanesque style of Apulia, was built to hold the body of St Nicholas of Lycia, bishop of Myra in Asia Minor, who died in 326 with a reputation for working miracles. In 1087, 62 seafaring men from Bari made off with the saint's 700-year-old relics. A Benedictine abbot named Elia decided to build a new church to contain them, and St Nicholas became the patron saint of the town. Construction lasted from 1087 until 1197. All the features in the Apulian Romanesque style are here: a tripartite facade (here flanked by two truncated towers) with hanging arches under the eaves, two-light windows, three portals, and large blind arches along the sides with little six-light loggias, an immense transept, a single wall enclosing all three apses. Inside, note the nave and aisles lined with columns and pillars.

On the main altar is the 12th-century ciborium*; in the apse is a remarkable marble bishop's throne* and a late-16th-century monument to Bona Sforza; the altar of St Nicholas, in embossed silver foil (1684), can be seen in the right apse; in the left apse, note the panel* by B. Vivarini (1476); beneath the altar of the handsome crypt is the body of St Nicholas. The Treasury is exquisite; note, among other things, the 12th-century candelabra donated by Charles of Anjou. Facing S. Nicola is the Portico dei Pellegrini, rebuilt; to the right, under the 14th-century S. Nicola arch, is the little 11th-century church of S. Gregorio.

Cathedral**. Dedicated to St Sabino, it was built after the Norman king William I, known as "Guglielmo il Malo," practically razed Bari to the ground (1156). It is Romanesque, and was built on the site of the old Byzantine cathedral. This is another notable monument of Apulian Romanesque; note the splendid enormous window* in the apse; the large cylindrical structure along the left side, known as the "trulla," is an old baptistery, made into a sacristy in the 17th century. Of particular interest in the interior: the pulpit, the ciborium, and the bishop's throne, rebuilt from original fragments; also note the crypt, rebuilt in the 18th century. In the Archivi are priceless codices and the renowned scroll of the Exultet I*. Beside the cathedral is the Museo della Cattedrale. The enormous bulk of the castle comprises a keep, or donjon, built on a trapezoidal plan, with two towers left of the original four. Frederick II erected this version, working on the earlier Norman-Byzantine structure. It also comprises the scarps of the ramparts, and the corner towers looming over the moat, added under Spanish rule in the 16th century to the three landward sides; the fourth side, once bathed by sea waves, still has the handsome twin-light mullioned windows of Frederick's project.

The interior is well worth seeing, and features a square Renaissance courtyard, an interesting plaster gallery (Gipsoteca Provinciale), with a collection of casts of the finest and loveliest monuments of the Apulian Romanesque style.

Lungomare Imperatore Augusto. This handsome seafront promenade runs along the old walls on the east side of the Città Vecchia.

The museums. Pinacoteca Provinciale "Corrado Giaquino". Located in the Palazzo della Provincia, on the SE of the Città Vecchia, this art gallery houses a collection touching various aspects of the art of the region, including local medieval statues and paintings. Also noteworthy are the works by the later school of Venetian painters (Bordone, Tintoretto, and Veronese, among others); works by Apulian and Neapolitan painters of the 17th and 18th centuries (C. Giaquinto, O. Tiso); the Neapolitan creches; 18C Apulian ceramics; and a number of 19th-century paintings (Signorini, Induno, and De Nittis).

Acquario Provinciale. This aquarium stands at the foot of the Molo Pizzoli, a large wharf running out into the Gran Porto.

Botanical garden (Via G. Amendola 175). This is particularly interesting for its array of wild plants from Apulia.

S. Felice. In the suburbs of Bari, near Balsignano, this Romanesque church (12C) is made of stone tiles fit one into the other without any linking cement. It testifies to the past richness of this countryside area.

ALBEROBELLO

A forest of grey conical roofs top the massive round buildings of this town, called "trulli." There are about a thousand of these strange round homes in Alberobello; the town's architecture is as unique as it is ancient. The monumental area* comprises the quarters of Monti and Aia Piccola, with the "trulli" aligned along steep and winding lanes. Looking in through the front doors, you can see the interior structure of these remarkable homes (you should have little difficulty in visiting one): a central chamber communicates through archways with the kitchen and the other rooms. The most complete and the tallest "trullo" is the Trullo sovrano, 2 storeys tall. In 1996, Alberobello was inscribed in UNESCO's World Heritage List.

LECCE AND SALENTO

The castle of Otranto is pentagonal, with three round towers. This menacing military construction was erected by Ferdinand of Aragon at the end of the 15th century. This is the extreme tip of
the easternmost cape of the Italian peninsula, surrounded by the waters of the Adriatic, which begins at the channel of Otranto and the waters of the enveloping Ionian sea. The coast is jagged, in
places lined with pine groves; it drops away sheer into the crashing waves, the limestone cliffs studded with marine caves in which humans once lived, in the Paleolithic era. The gently rolling reddish
land supports olive groves and vineyards, amid the jutting white rocks. This route runs from Lecce to Taranto, around the cape of Santa Maria di Leuca – Iapygium promontorium – almost invariably hugging the coast. But we have mentioned Otranto first of all because, in the past, when Apulia was divided into three parts, the Salento peninsula was part of what was then called the Terra
d'Ótranto. This comprised the modern-day provinces of Taranto, Lecce, and Brindisi, but the peninsula nowadays corresponds to the province of Lecce alone. The capital of this province is Lecce,
alluring for its remarkable architecture. Paul Bourget saw it in 1890, and wrote about it in his "Sensations d'Italie," admitting that in Lecce he had discovered new meanings for the terms Baroque
and Rococo: "Lecce showed me that these words could also be synonymous with a light-fingered
fancy, mad elegance, felicitous grace." The city proved to be a "single furor of caprice," even more so in that "its chiseled brightness emanates an almost Eastern light," while "the air is slightly
stirred by the breeze that swells the sails of the ships in the Embarquement pour Cythere, reminiscent of the great and melancholy Watteau."

NOT TO BE MISSED

Lecce (➠ see below): this town, capital of the Salento area, should be toured carefully, unhurried-
ly, and patiently, and not only for the celebrated, flamboyant Baroque architecture of the churches, palazzi, piazzas, and streets. **San Cataldo**: main beach of the province's capital. **Roca Vecchia**:
the ruins of the castle on the cliffs were once a Messapic city. **Otranto** (➠ see below): an enormous
and famous 12th-century mosaic covers the floor of the cathedral*; in the town, mostly enclosed
within walls, also go see the Aragonese castle and the Byzantine-style church of S. Pietro. **Santa Cesarea Terme**; the springs pour forth out of caverns in the cliffs and then drop away into the
sea. **Poggiardo**: a 20 km detour from Santa Cesarea Terme; in a museum you can see the medieval frescoes detached from the crypt of S. Maria; at a distance of 1.5 km is the crypt of S. Stefano, with remains of frescoes dating back to the 12th-15th-centuries. **Grotta Zinzulusa***: this cavern
is outstanding among the caves in the cliffs around Otranto, in terms of encrustations, underground
fauna, and prehistoric finds. **Castro** stands high among the olive groves, with its ancient cathedral, 16th-century walls, and vast view of sea and coast; beneath it is the little port of Castro Marina. **Marina di Leuca**: the lighthouse, the Sanctuary of Finibus Terrae, the caverns in the cliffs,
and the waves of the Ionian sea: this is the far tip of the Salento peninsula. **Patù** (see Marina di
Leuca): the Centopietre is a great Messapic or medieval megalithic construction at the edge of
town, facing the little Romanes-
que church of S. Giovanni. **Usen-
tum**: scanty ruins of the Roman
port can be seen in the inlet of
Marina San Giovanni; a little further along is the islet of Pazzi, inhabited in prehistoric times. **Gallipoli***: the medieval "borgo" with
white terraced houses stands on
an islet, linked by a bridge to the
modern part of town, on a peninsula, jutting into the sea. **Galato-
ne**, interesting examples of Lecce
style Baroque. **Galatina**: Stories
of the Virgin Mary, painted according to an apocryphal Gospel,
and other 15th-century frescoes,
cover the interior of the church of

A section of the facade of the Basilica of S. Croce in Lecce.

S. Caterina. **Nardò** rivaled Lecce as the most important cultural and artistic city in the Salento province during the 17th century. **Porto Cesareo**, situated along the part of the coast which has become a marine protected area. **Manduria**: in this little town in the range of the Murge Tarantine, note the ancient Duomo, the medieval ghetto, the Baroque Palazzo Imperiali, the Messapic walls, and the remarkable Fonte Pliniano. **Taranto** (➠ see below), whose splendid past is hinted at in the golden jewels contained in the Museo Archeologico Nazionale.

LECCE

As Mannerist art and architecture gave way to the Baroque style, Lecce developed its own variant, virtually an original creation due to the city's isolation: the so-called "Barocco Leccese," a welter of spectacular decor, especially on the exterior of buildings: spiral columns, outsized cornices, curving pediments, festoons, swags, vases full of flowers or fruit, ribbons bedecked with putti, mascarons, and caryatids. In any case, a world of spectacular architecture, making the historic center of the city entirely unique. Lecce lies in the Salento plain. It should be visited on foot to appreciate its fame as the "Florence of the Baroque style."

Piazza del Duomo* is a harmonious Baroque setting. The magnificent palazzo of the Seminario* (G. Cino, 1709) encloses an interior courtyard with a lovely Baroque puteal. To the left of the Palazzo Vescovile (1632), with a light loggia along the front, is the Duomo*, rebuilt (1659-70) by G. Zimbalo (known as Zingarello), with a spectacular facade along the side and a slender bell tower* (1682); inside are spiral columns and excellent paintings.

S. Croce**. Further along is the Basilica di S. Croce (1548-1646), considered the most exquisite creation of Lecce Baroque; the facade was the creation of G. Riccardi (lower part), A. Zimbalo (central part) and G. Zimbalo (upper part); the pure and understated interior* is by Riccardi. Here, Baroque decoration triumphs with the wooden ceiling, the rich capitals and the spiraling columns. To the left of the church is the Palazzo del Governo*. It is the former Celestine convent, the facade is by G. Zimbalo and G. Cino, while the enormous courtyard was begun by Riccardi and completed by G. Zimbalo.

To the east of the Duomo, the Baroque church of S. Chiara. The church is attributed to Cino (1694). Not far off is the Roman theater, possibly dating from the reign of Hadrian. Two other typical creations of Lecce Baroque are the church of S. Matteo, by A. Carducci (1667-1700), and the church of the Rosario, the last creation of G. Zimbalo, with odd inventions dotting the elaborate facade and spectacular altars in the interior.

Piazza S. Oronzo*. The center of the Città Vecchia (old town) is in this square, where the Column of S. Oronzo stands. It is considered to be one of the two columns that once marked the terminus of the Appian Way in Brindisi, and was erected here in 1666. The square is partly filled with the excavations of the Roman Anfiteatro*, or amphitheater, dating from the 2nd century AD, one of the best preserved Roman monuments in Lecce. Overlooking the curve of the amphitheater is the Palazzo del Seggio, or Sedile (1592), the ancient seat of communal government.

Castle, with a trapezoid plan and corner lancet bastions, was built at the behest of Emperor Charles V (1539-48). This fortress is the only surviving part of the walls built by Charles V in 1539-49.

Museo Archeologico Provinciale Sigismondo Castromediano*. This provincial museum is divided into three sections: the Antiquarium, with a notable collection of Messapic, Apulian, and Attic vases, terracottas and bronzes; the topographic section, with exhibits concerning towns of ancient Salento (note the sculptures from the local Roman theater); the Pinacoteca, with paintings from the Venetian, Roman, and Neapolitan schools and works by artists and sculptors from the Salento, evangelaries in copper and enamel, 17th-18th century ceramics from manufactories in the Abruzzi and local plants, Murano glass, and ivory.

Arco di Trionfo. The triumphal arch was built in 1548 for Charles V, whose armorial bearings are on the pediment. At the end of the square opening beyond the gate is the Obelisk dedicated to Ferdinand I of Bourbon in 1822.

Ss. Nicolò e Cataldo*. In the enclosure of the cemetery, the church was founded by Tancredi (1180) in a style that shows a clear influence of Burgundian Romanesque architecture. It has a facade rebuilt by G. Cino (1719), with an earlier portal* and strips of floral arabesques, in a clearly Islamic style (12C); in the interior, note the cupola in the middle of the nave, frescoes dating from the 15th century to the 17th century, the cloister (16C) with Baroque aedicula set on spiral columns.

TARANTO

An islet set between two peninsulas almost completely separates the Mar Grande (inlet of the Gulf of Taranto, bounded by the Cheradi islands and by harbor breakwaters) from the inner Mar Piccolo. The city mostly occupies the islet (the Città Vecchia, or old town) and the peninsula to the SE.

Museo Archeologico Nazionale** (reopened in December 2007, after restoration). The museum exhaustively illustrates the history of Magna Graecia from prehistoric times, with finds from most of the territories of southern Italy. The prehistoric section goes from the Paleolithic to the Iron and Bronze Ages, with finds from Torre Castelluccia and Torre Saturo.

The history of Taras and Tarentum is told through many finds discovered in the hundreds of necropolises found in the territory. The statuary comprises pieces dating from the 6th century BC to Roman times, with famous works such as the Ugento Zeus**, a bronze by a local artist. Many local marble statues were inspired by the art of Lysippus, who was active in Taranto. The busts and heads of Roman personages, and the tomb furnishings, are also noteworthy.

Among the other sculptures, the most interesting pieces are the reliefs in local stone which decorated the funerary temples, and the marble sarcophagus of an athlete.

Ceramic production is represented by thousands of vases which testify to the evolution in style and techniques over the centuries. A notable example of this is the Coppa con pesci**, or goblet with fish.

Many works of goldsmithery and jewelry come from the Apulian necropolises, and were probably produced in Taranto, where this craft was active as early as the 4th-3rd century BC. The most outstanding of these are the funerary furnishings** from Canosa, including two caskets in embossed silver, a glass box, a gold-plated tubular sceptre, and many fascinating jewels. Finally, more than 50,000 terracotta figurines complete this extraordinary itinerary inside the second largest archeological museum in southern Italy.

Castel S. Angelo. The castle was built in 1480 by Ferdinand of Aragon on the southwest end of the canal. It features the traditional cylindrical corner towers. From the square behind it starts the Via del Duomo, the main street of the Città Vecchia (old city), which lies almost exactly as it was during the Middle Ages, with, on either side, a labyrinth of alleys and lanes. At the beginning of the road, note three columns, surviving from a Greek temple dating from the 6th century BC. Further along (in Via Paisiello, plaque), note the birthplace of the composer Giovanni Paisiello.

Duomo. The cathedral dates from the 10th-11th centuries, but was modified and renovated on more than an occasion. The facade (1713) is Baroque, while the columns dividing nave and aisles are from pagan temples, with Roman and Byzantine capitals. The coffered ceiling is a 17th-century addition, while on the floor are remains of the ancient mosaics.

S. Domenico Maggiore. In this church, set high atop a long staircase, note the Baroque altars in the Leccese style; facade and presbytery both belong to the original early 14th-century construction.

OTRANTO

Situated on Italy's easternmost promontory, ancient Hydruntum was possibly founded by colonists from Crete and later became a Roman municipium. According to some sources, the town's name comes from The Idro River (ydrous means 'water'), now reduced to a tiny stream which flows into the harbor, while others claim it derives from odronto (meaning 'hill'). The oldest part of Otranto, surrounded by Aragonese walls, with its cobbled streets and white houses, has retained much of its ancient charm.

Cathedral. This silent, somber-looking church was founded in the Romanesque period and dedicated to the Annunciation. It was rebuilt after the Turkish siege of 1480 (the Ottoman hordes used it as a bivouac). The interior has a basilica plan, with a nave and two aisles separated by 14 granite and marble columns. It contains a huge floor mosaic* depicting the Tree of Life, executed in 1163-65 and constitutes an interesting blend of the Western and Eastern cultural traditions.

Aragonese Castle. Rebuilt after 1481 on a pentagonal plan with three round towers around the edge. In the 16th century, a bastion was added stretching almost to the harbor.

Church of S. Pietro. Dating from the 9th and 10th centuries, this was the Otranto's first cathedral. Built on a Greek-cross plan, its has three apses and was once entirely decorated with beautiful frescoes. From the nearby Pelasgi Bastion, there are wonderful views of the harbor and the sea.

TREMITI ISLANDS

This tiny limestone archipelago, situated north of the Gargano peninsula opposite Lake Lesina, consists of a large rock (Il Cretaccio) and the three main islands, described, on account of their extraordinary beauty, as the 'pearls of the Adriatic'. San Domino, with its lush vegetation, is the largest; San Nicola has one town, including an old fortress and an abbey; Capraia is bare and uninhabited. The whole area, and a fourth island, Pianosa, has been designated a Marine Protected Area. As to the origin of the name 'Tremiti', Tacitus refers to 'Trimerum' as the place where Giulia, grand-daughter of Augustus, was banished when she was found guilty of adultery and exiled by Tiberius. Pliny calls them 'Teutria, and it is not until the writings of an anonymous writer from Ravenna that we see the definitive name of 'Tremitis'. This early writer provided a number of names which, with small variations, appear on maps from the Middle Ages onwards. However, the most interesting explanation of the name is the one associated with the myth of the Greek hero Diomedes, who is supposed to be buried on one of these islands, and whose companions were changed into birds by the goddess Venus. In the evening, the haunting calls of these birds (there are large numbers of Cory's shearwaters in the Tremiti islands) are strangely reminiscent of human voices. But, apart from their magical and legendary associations, the unspoiled beauty of these islands, the crystal-clear waters and the ever-changing colors make the Tremiti Islands a must for anyone visiting this part of Apulia.

SAN NICOLA

This is where the islands' history is concentrated, where the main architectural monuments are located and is also the administrative capital. Ferries sail from here to the mainland.

SAN NICOLA DI TREMITI

It is situated on the south-west tip of the smallest island in the archipelago. Visitors disembark at the marina, where fishing-boats are hauled up onto the beach, under the imposing walls of the ancient fortress with its two towers. The town is laid out around Via Diomede. The main street ends at Piazza del Castello, dominated by a round Angevin tower and the castle walls. Beside it, a gate leads into the abbey. First we come to the church of S. Maria a Mare, at the top of a flight of steps (there are splendid views from the top). Inside, there are still several parts of the mosaic executed by the Benedictines. At the high altar is a wooden polyptych of the Venetian School. In the deambulatory on the left is the beautiful Tremiti Cross*, a fine example of Greek Byzantine art. The archeological site is well worth a visit. Set in Mediterranean maquis, it contains the foundations of a votive altar, some rock-cut tombs, a tholos tomb attributed to Diomedes and, on the other side, the grave of Giulia.

SAN DOMINO

The largest island of the group is also the one most visited by tourists. Piazzetta del Belvedere and the main street are full of shops, bars, restaurants hotels and pensions. The best way to admire the lovely coastline is by boat. They leave from Cala delle Arene and sail around the south-east coast of the island, past several beautiful bays and the Grotta delle Viole, so called because of the color of the water in the early hours of the day. Punta di Ponente is the site of a Roman shipwreck and beyond the lighthouse of Punta della Provvidenza is the Grotta del Bue Marino, once famous for its colony of Monk seals.

The solitary landscape of the island of Capraia.

CAPRAIA

Uninhabited and lacking in vegetation apart from a few lentisk and caper bushes, the only sign of life on the island is the lighthouse and a ruined shepherd's hut. Capraia has many pretty bays: Cala del Falconetto (where peregrine and Eleonora's falcons still nest), Cala del Cafone, Cala dei Pesci and Cala dei Vermi.

GARGANO NATIONAL PARK

Whether you are an expert naturalist or merely a nature lover you will be astonished at the variety of the landscape in the Parco Nazionale del Gargano. There are thick forests, marshes, islands off the north coast, deep gorges and valleys, dunes smelling of flowers, arid steppe, pine-forests, rock desert, lagoons with swallow-holes and much more. But it's not only fascinating from a naturalist's point of view. A series of lookout towers was built along the coast to warn local people that the Saracens were coming (some of the towers are perfectly preserved). You may also see the trabucchi, an ancient and complicated system of fishing invented by the Phoenicians, involving sticks stuck into the rock, ropes, pulleys and nets, still used today by local fishermen for fishing from the top of steep cliffs. A colorful land of mountains, sea, forests, Mediterranean maquis and small towns where ancient traditions continue and the tourist facilities are excellent.

FORESTA UMBRA

The forest is situated right in the middle of the park. Covering about 15,000 hectares, this is one of Italy's largest broad-leaved deciduous forests and, since the species that grow here are very like the ones that grew in a primeval forest, going for a walk in it is like taking a step back in time. It is home to numerous animals and birds, including several species of woodpecker, eagle owl, wildcat (now rare) and a herd of roebuck, a species rarely found in the south of Italy.

VIESTE

The tourist symbol of Gargano, with its strange monolith on the beach, is one of the most familiar landmarks on the Apulian coastline. As in other towns on the coast, the white buildings and narrow streets of the old town are reminiscent of the East, with which, for better of for worse, Apulia

has always traded. This is where the coastal landscape varies most. You will be amazed at the succession of creeks, little bays, promontories, high cliffs, stone arches, and beautiful caves.

Monte Sant'Angelo: The spiritual center of Gargano is approached by a steep winding road. Situated 900 m asl, it looks out onto the Bay of Manfredonia on one side and the hinterland of woodland and the flat Tavoliere beyond on the other. Monte Sant'Angelo was the end of the old Lombard Sacred Way, which, for more that 1,500 years, brought pilgrims in search of purification to the shrine of San Michele Arcangelo. It's well worth climbing down to the cave around which this important shrine was built, both for the architectural beauty of the place and the art treasures left here over the centuries by bishops, emperors and other important people who came to worship here.

The island of Faro di S. Eufemia, opposite Vieste.

FOOD IN APULIA

Many of Apulia's typical products are now protected. For example, extra-virgin olive oil, which varies from green to straw-yellow, has a distinctive fruity taste, and is produced mainly around Bari, Brindisi, Foggia and Lecce. The region's salamis and cured meats are just as interesting, especially around Martina Franca, not to mention some of the cheeses made here. Finally, we must not neglect the region's fine pastry-making tradition, with the classic carteddate and other delights.

TYPICAL LOCAL DISHES

Friselle di orzo e di grano. This flat round dried bread made with barley and wheat flour is typical of the area of Lecce. Before eating it is dipped in water and garnished with tomatoes, olive oil and salt.

Taralli. Tiny rings of unleavened bread, scalded in water and baked in the oven. They come in various flavors including wild fennel seeds.

Ciceri e tria. This is a very traditional dish. Boiled chickpeas served with tagliatelle, made with durum wheat, cooked in plenty of water, and tossed in onion fried in oil.

Orecchiette. This is Apulia's most traditional dried pasta dish. Orecchiette, made with durum wheat flour, are still made by hand. They are left to dry for a few hours and served either with a meat sauce or are boiled with turnip heads (cime di rapa), drained and served with chopped anchovies.

Lampascioni. They resemble small onions and have a rather bitter taste. Usually they are boiled and served as a salad with meat dishes, or stewed or baked in the oven.

Rustico leccese. Puff pastry filled with bechamel sauce, mozzarella (made from cow's milk, not buffalo milk) and tomatoes and baked in the oven.

Carteddate. A Christmas sweet: twisted ribbons of puff pastry pinched together, fried, covered with honey or cooked wine, and sprinkled with icing sugar or cinnamon.

Pasticciotto leccese. A sweet from Salento made with sweet shortcrust pastry filled with pastry cream and baked in the oven.

TYPICAL LOCAL PRODUCTS

Canestrato Pugliese DOP. A hard cheese made with raw ewe's milk. It has a distinctive round shape and varies from brown to yellow. The body is compact and crumbly, with very small eyes. It has a spicy, rather strong flavor.

Burrata. This stretched-curd cheese originally came from Andria, but is now made throughout the region. Made with cow's milk, it is unusual because it has an outer part similar to mozzarella and a heart made with the same cheese finely chopped and cream.

Capocollo di Martina Franca. This meat from the nape of the pig is marinated in cooked white wine, then salted and rubbed with local herbs.

Soppressata dell'Appennino Dauno. A mixture of finely chopped best pork and lard, seasoned with salt, whole peppercorns, chili and other spices.

Olio Extravergine di Oliva. Four kinds of olive oils from Apulia have been awarded the DOP label: Collina di Brindisi, Dauno, Terra di Bari and Terra d'Otranto.

Pane d'Altamura DOP. This famous bread made with natural yeast is made with durum wheat, salt and water. Typically it is flat with a nice brown crust and soft white dough full of holes. It keeps for several days.

WINES

In the vineyards of Apulia, red grapes predominate, resulting in wines like Primitivo di Manduria, with a deep color, a distinctive bouquet and a dry or sometimes semi-sweet taste. Another grape, Negroamaro, makes a garnet-red wine, dry on the tongue with a characteristic hint of bitterness, and is also ideal for making the rosé wines which have brought fame to the Salento. More unusual wines include the rare Aleatico, and sweet reddish-purple wines which smell like Moscato.

A specialty of Apulia is vincotto (literally 'cooked wine'), made with must from red grapes that have been left on the vine to wither. The must is cooked over a hot flame for many hours, after which it is put into oak casks and flavored with carob, figs, raspberries or lemons prior to a long period of aging. Delicious with desserts made with almonds or ricotta, creams of various kinds and ice-cream.

FOOD

A s a child, the Latin poet Horace is said to have escaped from his nurse and wandered through the mountain forests until, exhausted, he fell asleep. The tale goes that he was protected by mysterious doves, which covered him with branches of laurel and myrtle, *ut tuto ab atris corpore viperis/dormirem et ursis* (so that he could sleep, his little body safe from black vipers and bears); this remarkable event astounded the woodsmen who later found him. The mountain upon which the infant Horace had his adventure was the Vulture, an ancient volcano with harsh landscapes, covered with forests of beech trees, oaks, chestnuts, lindens, maples, hornbeams, elms, ashes, poplars, and alders – the high point in terms of views of this route over the Ofanto and the Bradano. The birthplace of Horace, of course, is nearby Venosa, or Venusia, once a Roman military colony, and now part of the Basilicata region on the border with Apulia. The poet was born here and completed his early studies under a tutor named Flavius, who taught *magni pueri magnis e centurionibus orti*, or "big boys, the sons of big centurions" (later his father took Horace to study with the best masters in Rome). In the other cities and sites along this route – including Melfi, the castle of Lagopesole, Venosa with the abbey of the Trinità, Acerenza with its large cathedral with a French-style ambulatory around the presbytery – what prevails is the air of medieval history, of the Normans, Swabians, and Angevins, with the great shadow of Frederick II looming over all. Lagopesole, made of reddish limestone, is the largest and the last of this emperor's castles; from another, Norman castle in Melfi – Frederick had restored Melfi's walls – he decreed his "Constitutiones Augustales," which his jurists, including the renowned Pier delle Vigne, had developed to regulate feudal law.

NOT TO BE MISSED

Potenza (➡ see below) occupies the crest of a hill in the high valley of the Basento River; the Museo Archeologico provinciale is devoted to the ancient inhabitants of Lucania, as Basilicata was once called. Castle of **Lagopesole*** is a monumental residence and stronghold, begun by the emperor Frederick II eight years before his death. **Atella**: this village was founded in the 14th century and still has some remains from that period; it is said that Giovanna I, queen of Naples, was held prisoner in the Benedictine monastery. **Monte Vulture** is an extinct volcano: you can drive up to an altitude of 1,245 m with a scenic road, 5.5 km from Rionero

Snow-covered Potenza.

in Vulture, a town alive with history, situated between two hills, or you can take a cableway from the lakes of Monticchio to an altitude of 1,214 m. **Laghi di Monticchio***: the larger of these lakes is on the left of the road, the smaller is to the right; their green waters lie in the crater of a volcano. **Melfi**: this town lies at the foot of the large old castle and is enclosed by ancient walls, relics of the time when this was the residence of Norman kings and, later, of the emperor Frederick Hohenstaufen; go see the renowned sarcophagus of Rapolla in the Museo Nazionale Archeologico. **Rapolla** lies on mountain slopes, with a 13th-century Gothic cathedral whose magnificent portal dates back to 1253 and the Norman church of S. Lucia, with a clear Byzantine influence. At a distance of 6 km is Barile, a village of Albanian traditions (settlers from Scutari and Croya, fleeing the Turks, arrived here around 1460). **Venosa***: in the image of this city, birthplace of Horace (the so-called Casa del Poeta, or House of the Poet, is actually a tepidarium from Roman baths), the monuments of the Middle Ages and the Renaissance, especially the abbey of the Trinità, predominate over the Roman ruins. **Maschito**: beginning in 1467, this town was repopulated by Albanian refugees. Some still speak the dialect. In the Palazzo Comunale is a remarkable collection of paintings by the local artist Mario Cangianelli. **Forenza** is a delightfully situated holiday resort. **Acerenza**, overlooking the high valley of the Bradano River, has a magnificent large Romanesque cathedral with bell tower, whose origins go back to the 11th century; rebuilt in the 16th century, the crypt contains restored frescoes. **Pietragalla**, with old dungeons dug out of the tuff.

POTENZA

Potenza is the capital of the highest Italian region, perhaps explaining why it is so beautiful to arrive there at dusk along the SS 407 Basentana road. You are welcomed by the bridge over the Basento River, a masterpiece of contemporary engineering. Beyond lies the heart of the old city, hidden behind the curtain of high-rise buildings that flank the elegant Via Pretoria and Piazza Pagano. Despite the numerous earthquakes down the years, much interesting evidence of the past remains.

Bridge* over the Basento. This bridge is like a magnificent modern sculpture (1969), having been planned on a commission from Potenza's Consortium of Industrial Areas. It was built to connect the city's industrial area and the road through the valley to the actual city, but visually it looks like an enormous plant where the pillars have been replaced by a gigantic, curled leaf.

Via Pretoria. This street lies in the heart of the old center, with elegant shops, coffee bars and pastry houses. It is very much the place to be seen in Potenza as well as being a favored setting for an evening stroll.

S. Michele Arcangelo*. This church, documented as early as 1178, was enlarged in 1849, but retains its Romanesque appearance. It has a nave and two aisles. In the first bay on the right, note the fresco of the *Madonna with Child and Sts. Ambrose, Nicholas and Archangel Michael*, attributed to the school of Giovanni Luce.

Piazza Mario Pagano. This sizeable, busy piazza was created in the 19th century and is flanked by buildings that house the seats of local power as well as the main theater, Teatro Francesco Stabile, which was opened in 1881 when King Humbert I visited.

S. Francesco d'Assisi. This church with a stone facade was founded in 1274. It has an interesting stone portal in Catalan style as well as intriguing door panels made of walnut that have been carved with plants motifs, musicians and demons. The interior, like most Franciscan buildings, has a single nave. It houses the funerary monument of Donato De Grasis*, which is dated 1534 and is made of limestone.

Duomo*. This old cathedral, built on the ruins of an early-Christian church, was rebuilt in the 12th-13th centuries on the orders of Bishop Andrea Serrao. The current Neo-Classic appearance is the work of A. Magri, one of Vanvitelli's pupils. The tympanum over the main entrance is decorated with the 17th-century coat-of-arms of Bishop B. Claverio. Higher up, note the rose window, which is even older. Work in the late 18th century changed the Latin-cross plan to a single nave. Only a few items give away the cathedral's age: on the right wall of the nave, memorial stones bear Gothic letters and are dated 1200; in the crypt below the apse, there are fragments of a mosaic floor from the 5th-6th century and the ruins of an early-Christian church. The right transept has a chapel dedicated to St Gerardus that bears the remains of the saint in an urn below the altar.

S. Maria del Sepolcro. The church, which is located in the interesting S. Maria district (north of the old center), was founded by the Templar Knights. The facade consists of a portico with three arches: the large wooden door (16C) sits right below a fresco of the *Deposition with the Pious Women* (1658). The interior, originally a single nave, was changed in the 17th century with the addition of the left aisle. The altar of the Holy Sacrament is against the right wall. This stucco work was created by Masillo de Faiella in 1656. It contains a reliquary of the Blood of Christ.

Museo archeologico provinciale*. This museum has finds from the major archeology sites in Basilicata and a good collection of coins ranging from the Classic epoch to the 18th century. The collections explore the history of the ancient inhabitants of the Lucania district and the age of Greek colonization. There are various finds from digs across the region. There is plenty of material related to clay production (6 to 3C BC) in the Greek colonial city of Metapontum (or Metaponto), including architectural, decorative and worship elements. Some of the material is from other towns in the Lucania district.

MATERA

This area is synonymous with long, small stone walls that seem to fade into the undulating horizon, becoming yellow in June from the grain and sometimes being interrupted by the numerous olive trees that cling to the rocks on the Murge plateau. Suddenly, the effect of the landscape is broken by a volcanic rock quarry sparkling under the sun or the famous Sassi. This is how Matera appears, the magic city of the Sassi. It would be worth going there simply to see the caves, rock churches and gorges, but the city offers much more. The old center is filled with Romanesque

The Sassi of Matera is a UNESCO World Heritage Site.

churches from the 13th century and Baroque ones from the late 17th century as well as noble, religious and political buildings.

Piazza Pascoli. This square, created in the 1930s, has one of the postcard views* of the city. It is flanked by Palazzo Lanfranchi*, which is the best example of 17th-century architecture in Matera.

The **Duomo****, surrounded by wonderful 18th-century buildings, was begun in 1230 and completed in 1270 on the orders of Bishop Andrea. The Latin-cross interior is divided into a nave and two aisles by 10 columns with capitals of medieval figures. The church was restored so radically in the 18th century that little of the original sense remains. On the wall to the right of the main entrance is an amazing *Last Judgment**, the last surviving part of a sizeable painting from the Middle Ages attributed to Rinaldo da Taranto. It is worth seeing, in the left aisle, the chapel of the Annunziata, created in the second quarter of the 16th century, perhaps by Altobello Persio. The 1st altar, dedicated to the Virgin Mary, but known locally as the Madonna della Bruna, has a fresco of the Madonna (1270).

The Sassi of Matera**. These have gone from being a source of national shame to a UNESCO World Heritage Site. In little more than 40 years, the perception of these homes along the western wall of a deep gorge has changed completely. In total, they cover 36 hectares, divided between Sasso Caveoso and Sasso Barisano. Although visually they seem rather primordial, they actually contain some quite advanced notions. Winding streets, large staircases, steep steps and narrow alleys lead up to the houses, which sit practically on top of each other around common courtyards where wells are located. Only the facades of these buildings are built, so to speak, with the rest (usually a single, multi-purpose room) being dug into the rock. Finally, there are the churches, where all the key elements – domes, pillars, columns, iconostases, apses – and decorations are actually cut directly into the rock.

Strada dei Sassi*. This road takes in Via Buozzi, Via Madonna delle Virtù and Via D'Addozio. A flight of steps after no. 134 leads onto a rise – the so-called Mt Errone – with one of the most thrilling views* in Matera. This is the setting for the church of Madonna dell'Idris, which is partly cut into the rise and partly built in a more traditional fashion (following the collapse of the barrel vault in the 16C).

S. Lucia alle Malve*. Restoration work in this church, founded around the year 1,000, has brought to light numerous frescoes. The interior is divided into a nave and two aisles, with the entrance in the right aisle. Interestingly, only the right aisle remains a religious building, with the nave and left aisles having been inhabited since 1960.

Church of S. Donato*. This is the most architecturally impressive church in the city. It has pieces of frescoes (St Leonard, St Donatus and two 17C scenes: a bishop on horseback and a miracle). The presbytery has a cross with lilies.

Via Madonna delle Virtù. This is the second part of the Strada dei Sassi, winding its way between the rocky sides of the gorge to the right and the walls of Sasso Caveoso to the left. Along it lies the church of the Madonna delle Virtù, an interesting building that was dug out of the rock in the 11th-12th centuries and then substantially changed in 1674.

Parco archeologico storico e naturale delle Chiese rupestri del Materano**. This park was designed to protect a barren stretch of land that is home to Mediterranean scrubland and the type of oak forests that are common in a limestone landscape. It also protects a superb archeological heritage. There are rock churches (about 160, including genuine churches, places where ascetics lived and various sanctuaries) and medieval frescoes that show just how advanced art and culture was in these parts in the Middle Ages. There are also three Neolithic entrenched villages, an unknown number of prehistoric graves, tanks carved into the rock (and connected to water supply systems) and traditional rural buildings and farmhouses.

MOUNT POLLINO AND SILA

This Calabrian symphony develops in three movements, as it were. The first is the vast Pollino massif, the southern terminus of the Lucanian Apennines, largely stretching east to west, as if it were a barrier warning away would-be visitors to the region. Geographers tell us that this is the southernmost Apennine group to show the marks of glacial activity, and for those who love nature, this is a harsh, powerful, solitary mountain, dotted with secluded and intact settings. The second leg takes us back to classical antiquity. Sybaris was an Achaean colony, wealthy from its silver mines (in what is now San Marco Argentano), a city of refined living, with perhaps the worst reputation in all of Magna Grecia, probably because it was defeated in war. The army of Crotone, in a campaign lasting 70 days, stormed the city, sacked it, and then destroyed it entirely (510 BC). According to tradition, they then shifted the course of the Crati River to submerge the ruins. The search for the actual site of the city impassioned scholars and put archeologists to stern task for many years: now you can see and explore it. It was only discovered several decades ago, in a landscape altered by reclamation: 500 hectares of rolling plains, straddling the modern course of the Crati River about 4 km from its mouth, where it empties into the Gulf of Taranto. The third movement in the symphony involves a drive across the Sila. The first mention we are able to find was in 1812 in the travel journal of the Marquis Adolphe de Custine, who ventured off the beaten track in Italy.

NOT TO BE MISSED

Lagonegro, in a ring of mountains, on a slope of Mt Sirino; at a distance of 2 km in the Noce Valley is a zoological park. **Morano Calabro** is scattered over a morainic hill, with lovely geometric buildings. **Castrovillari**, at the base of Mt Pollino (National park), with a 15th-century castle in the old section, the church of S. Maria di Castello on a hill, and, on the Corso, or main boulevard, the Museo Civico Archeologico. **Cassano all'Ionio** dominates the plain of the Crati River; visit the Museo Diocesano d'Arte Sacra. **Sibari**: the Museo Archeologico Nazionale della Sibaritide is found in the reclaimed village that bears the name of the ancient Greek colony; the archeological digs of Sybaris, Thurii, and Copia are further along, on the right of the road. S. Maria del Patire* is the solitary church of a long-vanished Basilian monastery founded in 1101-05; in the interior is a precious mosaic floor with animal relief carvings of the 12th-century. Take a 7.5-km detour through the woods after **Corigliano Calabro**, with a fine view. **Rossano** overlooks the Ionian Sea from the furthest spur of the Sila Greca: the Byzantine church of S. Marco dates from the 11th century; in the Museo Diocesano d'Arte Sacra is the exquisite and rare Codex Purpureus. **Longobucco** is a village overlooking the wild gorges of the Trionto. **Camigliatello Silano** is a resort area amid the woods of the Sila; you can take a cableway up to Mt Curcio (1,760 m); fine view. **Cosenza** (➡ see below): at the confluence of the Busento and Crati rivers, amid the highlands, with the dense old quarter at the base of the Colle Pancrazio and a Norman castle.

COSENZA

Set in a hilly setting, the town has an ancient quarter, clinging to Colle Pancrazio, and a modern quarter, on the plain below. **Piazza Campanella** lies in the area where the old town meets the modern one. Overlooking the piazza is the church of S. Domenico, a Baroque reconstruction of a 15th-century building. In the interior, note the rich stucco ornamentation, the canvases, and the 17th-century choir. At the center of the old town, with its medieval alleys, the **Duomo*** overlooks the square, with a solemn Gothic facade (3 portals and 3 rose windows). Inside, note the Roman sarcophagus and the funerary monument* to Isabel of Aragon.

The **Museo Interdiocesano** includes paintings dating from the 15th-18th century, gold-smithery, vestments and furnishings, and parchments. One of the most outstanding pieces is the Stauroteca*, an enameled reliquary in the form of a cross, a 13th-century creation of the Sicilian school, donated by Frederick II for the consecration of the cathedral, and ivories by the school of Cellini. Overlooking Piazza XV Marzo, are the Prefettura, or police courts building, the Teatro Comunale and the Palazzo dell'Accademia Cosentina, also the site of the **Museo dei Bretti**, the municipal archeological museum.

S. Francesco d'Assisi. This church was founded in the Gothic period but heavily renovated during the Renaissance and in the Baroque period. High atop the hill stands the mighty square structure of the **castle**, a stronghold built in various phases.

A cluster of gently rounded dome shapes (Montalto, 1,955 m) stands at the center of a starburst-shaped plateau, whose spurs run down to the three coasts along the extremity of the penin-sula. Oaks and holm-oaks blanket the slopes of the mountain; higher up are pine trees and bee-ches. Always, through the straight trunks of the trees, you can glimpse the sparking blue of the sea. The expanse of the Aspromonte area is crossed by this route from south to north in the high secti-ons, and from north to south along the coastline. The non mountainous landscape: vineyard-be-decked hills with chestnut forests, huge hundred-year-old olive trees looking down on little harbors, the arid river beds, flowering with oleanders – all are surprising, "exotic". Here, for instance, are the impressions of the Parisian author Paul-Louis Courier who, as a soldier with a copy of Homer in his rucksack, marched through Calabria with Napoleon Bonaparte's expedition of 1805, which put Jo-seph Bonaparte on the throne of the Two Sicilies. From Reggio di Calabria Courier wrote: "We are triumphant and on the move constantly, and we have stopped only here, where the land came to an end," and: "The cities are in no way notable, at least to my eyes; but the countryside is remar-kable. It resembles nothing I have seen so far. Let us not even consider the orange groves and stands of lemon trees; there are so many other trees and exotic plants, which spring up in great profusi-on under the bright sunlight; you may find the same species found in France, but growing larger and lusher here, giving the landscape an entirely different appearance. And when you see the crags, crowned everywhere with myrtle and aloe and palm trees in great ravines, you might think you we-re on the banks of the Ganges or Nile, except that there are no pyramids, nor elephants; instead there are water buffaloes, looking quite at home amidst the African plants; likewise the color of the inhabitants is not of our world...."

NOT TO BE MISSED
Reggio di Calabria (➡ see below): there is a fine view of both the strait and the Sicilian coast from the seafront promenade; the remarkable bronze statues of Riace are in the Museo Nazionale. **Pentedattilo***: this village is perched atop a sandstone crag with five pinnacles. **Melito di Por-to Salvo**, where Garibaldi twice disembarked, renowned for its production of bergamot and hand-made pipes. **Montalto**: this is the highest peak in the Aspromonte. **Gambarie**: mountain holiday resort in the midst of green forests. Cippo Garibaldi: this stele marks the site on which the ge-neral who united Italy was wounded during a battle between his troops and the royalist soldiers commanded by General Pallavicini, on 29 August 1862. **Delianuova**, a resort amidst the olive gro-ves; note the fine old artwork in the parish church. **Locri**: the museum and the excavations of the Greek colony of Locri Epizefiri can be found at Torre di Gerace, just outside of modern Locri. **Ge-race** is a medieval town high on a crag overlooking the Ionian Sea, with a grand Byzantine-Nor-man-Swabian cathedral, the largest sacred monument in Calabria. **Palmi** overlooks the Marina and the Costa Viola from its high terrace; a remarkable view all the way to Mt Etna and the Aeo-lian Islands from Mt Sant'Elia. **Bagnara Calabra**: a sandy beach and a town set between two rocky spurs. **Scilla**: a crag overlooking the sea, a castle, a lighthouse, and the Homeric reference to Scyl-la, the sea monster foiled by Ulysses.

REGGIO DI CALABRIA
The **Museo Nazionale**** is the first and inter-esting stop in any city tour. The archeological collections, with material from sites in Calabria and Basilicata, are fundamental to under-standing this section of Magna Graecia; a fur-ther attraction is constituted by the world-renowned Bronzes of Riace**, two large stat-ues of warriors, Greek originals (mid 5C BC), attributed to Phidias or his school. Note the ar-tifacts found in ancient Locri with the pinakes* (terracotta tablets) depicting in relief the myth of Persephone, a terracotta group with an Ephebus on Horseback (5C BC) and the mar-

ble group of the Dioscuri (early 5C BC). The section of medieval and modern art boasts two panels by A. da Messina, with *St Jerome* and Abraham and the Angels** (1457), and the *Return of the Prodigal Son** by M. Preti. The **Lungomare*** is a magnificent prome-nade with a view of the Strait of Messina, the Mts Peloritani, and Mt Etna; at its southern ex-tremity, you can see a stretch of Greek walls (4C BC) and ruins of the Roman Baths. The **Duomo** was rebuilt after the 1908 earth-quake. Only two circular towers and a stretch of the curtain walls survive from the Aragonese castle.

THE CALABRIAN COAST

Calabria is nearly entirely made up of mountains and hills, often reaching right to the coast such that the only stretches of flat land are thin seaside patches. This stretch of the Tyrrhenian, between the mouth of the Noce and the Scilla cliffs, is far from homogenous. There are cliffs, underwater ledges, caves with fantastic names, arches eroded into rock, and moon-like stretches of beach, all against a backdrop of olive groves, orange orchards and vineyards. Unfortunately, unregulated building, especially of holiday homes, has ruined parts, blocking access to the sea and hampering any visit. This problem has troubled all of coastal Calabria, but it does not mean there are no unexpectedly beautiful zones. This holds true both along the Strait of Messina, where the land consists of clay and sandstone, and on the Ionian side. On the latter coast, the land is irregular and winding, often marked by the mouths of rivers, expansive beaches, rocky cliffs and charming headlands. In ancient times, this was Magna Graecia. This coast was not only lauded by the poet Pindar, but also the setting for the towns of Sybaris, Crotone and Locri. Over many centuries, this was a center of culture and history. Some wonderful coin collections and archeological finds speak volumes about the Romans and the Bruttii, but there is also much to learn, in these parts, of the Byzantines, the Normans, the time Frederick II passed through, the Angevins and the Aragonese.

PRAIA A MARE

As soon as you cross over the border from the Lucania area, the crystal clear view takes in a magnificent series of sandstone beaches and cliffs that push out along the Scalea headland. As such, it is essential that any visitor makes the trip to Praia a Mare, one of the "historic resorts" in Calabria. The Isola di Dino caves are well worth seeing, especially to enjoy the effect of the sunlight on the sea.

CAPO SCALEA

These beaches can only be reached by boat (which can be hired at Praia a Mare or Scalea). The best spots are the small bays hidden between high cliffs, where the green of the Mediterranean scrubland reaches down to within a few meters of the water.

AMANTEA

The ruins of the castle, in the upper section of the town, are a reminder of the past. The castle was created in Byzantine or Norman times, but then enlarged and strengthened by the Aragonese in the second half of the 15th century. Later, Charles V of Spain also had some work carried out on it. It is also worth seeing the lovely church of S. Bernardino (15C), which has a porticoed facade decorated with ceramic plates in the form of a cross. This echoes a style found in various other southern Italian cities.

TROPEA

The setting is classic Mediterranean: the rugged cliffs tell of the infinite battle between the sea and the land, while the maquis and the palm groves on the plateaus, the strikingly white beaches and the wonderful, playful colors of the sea create a delightful sense of sunny tranquility.

SCILLA

This rocky headland, dominated by the Ruffo castle, separates the charming fishing village from the long, sandy beach. The delightful solidarity between Calabria and the Tyrrhenian is still celebrated here, in an area pervaded by the charm of ancient myths that tell of a terrifying six-headed sea monster that lies waiting to swallow up any boats that venture into this narrow marine passage.

CAPO SPARTIVENTO

Here, at the tip of the boot, there are endless kilometers of white beaches. This is also a special place for dolphin lovers: they can often be seen playing and jumping just a short distance from the shore.

CAPO RIZZUTO

The town, which is home to an important marine reserve, is set on a terraced plateau of the headland that lies between the mouths of the Tacina and Neto rivers, south of Crotona. This land is not only beautiful, but also home to some wonderful archeological treasures. For example, there are the Scifo beaches, overlooked by a column from the temple of Hera Lacinia. In addition, there are Capo Climiti, with the ruins of a villa from the Hellenic-Roman period, and Le Castella, which faces an island bearing that same name that is home to an Aragonese fortress.

MAGNA GRAECIA IN LUCANIA

The Greek colonizers came from the eastern Mediterranean in the early 8th century BC and arrived on the Ionian coast of Basilicata. They had followed a route that had been first outlined centuries before by Mycenaean traders. Perhaps the route had been handed down from father to son, along with tales of fertile land and plentiful, often navigable rivers (Bradano, Basento, Cavone, Agri and Sinni). They bought with them a relatively advanced culture and way of living that merged with local ways to create an autonomous culture. They were far more than just builders of colonial towns, adding temples, agoras and fortified walls. Indeed, the became a political and economic force. This melting pot of ideas and men gave birth to what is known as Western Greece or Magna Graecia, a civilization that has been revealed, through research and excavations, to be filled with relations between different cultures and peoples. Indeed, anyone who truly wants to learn about Magna Graecia must visit the archeological sites of Metaponto and Policoro (the two essential parts of any such visit) as well as spending time looking at the various items on display in the town museums. This is a fragment of bygone times, a journey back in time, filled with culture, history, natural beauty and wonderful landscapes.

The temple of Hera, known as Tavole Palatine, is part of the Metaponto archeological site.

METAPONTO

Once one of the most important cities in Western Greece, it was founded between the mouths of the Bradano and Basento rivers at the end of the 7th century BC. Digs in the "chora", that is the territory tied to the Greek city, have uncovered necropolises, traces of Mycenaean trading centers and, most importantly, the ruins of the temple of Hera, known as Tavole Palatine**. The latter is the most important, non-urban worship site in the colony and the only one that is still "standing". The temple, which is best to visit at sundown, was dedicated to the goddess nearly a century after the site had come to be used for worship. The modern town houses the Museo archeologico nazionale di Metaponto, which gives an archeological overview of the zone from pre-history to late antiquity. Numerous vases, terracotta items and metal objects indicate that the Achaeans came to these parts and that local towns welcomed influences from Greece.

The logical continuation to any visit is the archeology site*. Digs in recent decades have uncovered the ancient layout of Metaponto, allowing reconstructions of ancient buildings using original elements. **Policoro***. The origins of this town lie way back in the mists of time. It sits on the site of "Heraclea", which was, in turn, founded on the site of the older Greek colony of "Siris". The history of this town is told in the Museo nazionale della Siritide*. This museum has a number of interesting finds, including Greek and colonial ceramics from the 7th-6th centuries BC, matrices for terracotta figures from the 4th-3rd centuries BC, items from the tomb of Orafo (2C BC) and, most notably, the grave goods from the tomb of a warrior, with bronze weapons (4C BC), and from the tomb with vases by the Painter of Policoro (5C). The archeology site is near the museum. It includes an area where an archaic temple stood and a sanctuary dedicated to Demeter, from around the 7th century BC.

FOOD IN BASILICATA AND CALABRIA

In Basilicata, many of the typical cheeses, salamis and cured meats have been awarded quality labels, along with local fruits, vegetables and olive oil. In Calabria, the best-known cheeses, salamis and cured meats, sometimes with chili, are made in the wild hills of Aspromonte. But, near the coast, we find the true stars of the region: clementines from Sibari, bergamots and citrons between the Ionian and Tyrrhenian Sea, Zibibbo grapes from Pizzo and liquorice from Rossano and, of course, local olive oil.

BASILICATA: TYPICAL LOCAL DISHES

Pane cotto. Stale bread is added to stock made with leeks and chili, egg and parsley.

Lagane e ceci. Traditional bandit fare. The 'lagane' are a kind of ribbon pasta served with a chickpea, tomato and garlic sauce.

Zuppa di pesce. This rich fish soup from Maratea is unusual since it involves ground dried sweet peppers.

Panzerotti. Tarts filled with a mix of chickpeas, chocolate, sugar and cinnamon, fried or baked in the oven and coated with sugar or honey.

CALABRIA: TYPICAL LOCAL DISHES

Sarde a scapece. Fried sardines are sprinkled with breadcrumbs, oil and vinegar flavored with herbs.

Maccaruni. Rectangles of pasta served with a meat sauce or 'alla pastora', with suet and ricotta, or a sauce made with pork meat and smoked ricotta.

Pesce spada. Swordfish is a classic dish here and cooked in several ways: 'a ghiotta' (fried with bread, olives, pepper and capers, then cooked in the oven with tomatoes) or rolled up (with mozzarella, ham, herbs and cheese inside) and cooked on a hot plate.

Liquirizia. Made from liquorice root to which vegetable carbon and sugar are added.

Pittanchiusa. Also called 'pitta 'mpigliata', a puff pastry cake filled with raisins, walnuts and cooked wine.

BASILICATA: TYPICAL LOCAL PRODUCTS

Pecorino di Filiano DOP. This cheese, made with mixed ewe's and goat's milk, with a strong smell, improves with aging in local caves.

Canestrato di Moliterno. A very strong, hard, straw-yellow cheese made from mixed ewe's and goat's milk.

Soppressata. A salami made with very lean top-quality pork and black pepper.

Fagiolo di Sarconi IGP. Locally grown Borlotto and Cannellino beans.

Peperone di Senise IGP. Three different shapes of bell peppers come under this label: 'appuntito', 'tronco' and 'uncino'.

Olio Extravergine d'Oliva Lucano DOP. The label specifies the area of origin: del Vulture, del Ferrandinese and delle Colline del Materano.

Pane di Matera. This bread made from durum wheat flour is a yellowish color and keeps for a long time.

CALABRIA: TYPICAL LOCAL PRODUCTS

Caciocavallo Silano DOP. This semi-hard cow's milk cheese is made from stretched curd. It is pear-shaped and is tied with string at the top. The flavor varies from mild to strong.

Capocollo di Calabria DOP. Made with the top part of pork loin. The meat is boned and salted, flavored with herbs and sometimes slightly smoked. Other local pork specialties are Pancetta di Calabria DOP (bacon), Salsiccia di Calabria DOP (sausage) and Soppressata di Calabria DOP (salami).

'Nduja. A typical salami made in the towns around Mt Poro, using the fatter parts of the pig, and sweet and chili peppers.

Cipolle rosse di Tropea. Imported by the Phoenicians more than 2,000 years ago, these sweet red onions are grown on the coast between Capo Vaticano and Vibo Valentia.

Olio Extravergine di Oliva. Two types of local olive oil have been awarded the DOP label: Brutium, made near Cosenza, and Lametia, made in the Province of Catanzaro.

WINES

With only a small number of vineyards, Basilicata is mainly known for its red Aglianico del Vulture, which has a dry, fresh, slightly tannic taste which becomes smoother with aging. Champion of the Calabrian wine industry is Cirò (red, white and rosé). Other wines are made with the hardy Gaglioppo grape and a white with Greco.

FOOD

The Tyrrhenian shoreline is the entrance to Sicily. Here the island gives a first taste, a sampling, of many, if not all, its delights, evoking the counterpoint of literary accounts and recollections. Let's consider the plants: the ubiquitous prickly pear, or Indian fig, a harsh and bizarre piece of vegetal architecture, comes from Mexico, and has been here only since the 17th century: in origin, the Mediterranean landscape of this ancient, timeless island is that of grains, olive trees, and vineyards. The orange tree, on the other hand, enclosed with its dark-green foliage in secluded seafront gardens, dates from the Arab occupation: "Rejoice in the oranges that you have plucked," advises a poem of those centuries, "to have them is to have happiness./All hail the pretty cheeks of the branch; all hail the glittering stars of the tree!/You might think that the heavens had rained down pure gold, and that the earth had then moulded that gold into glowing spheres." One of the first places you will encounter is Tindari, profoundly Greek in nature: the features of the island immediately remind the traveller of that other Mediterranean people, who sailed forth from their cramped archipelago in search of boundless horizons. A few lines by the poet Salvatore Quasimodo (Nobel laureate, 1959), were not long ago more famous than the place itself: "Tindari, mite ti so/fra larghi colli pensile sull'acque/dell'isole dolci del dio..." which translates as "Tindari, I know you are mild, among broad hills, above the waters of the gods' soft islands..." Cefalù adds two more pieces to the gameboard: the composite culture – Romanesque-Byzantine-Arab-Norman – of the cathedral, with its hieratic mosaics, and the meticulous 15th-century art of Antonello da Messina, painter of a portrait of a man with a distracting smile ("The interplay of resemblance is a delicate and exceedingly sen-

sitive matter in Sicily, a form of research... Who does the unknown man in the Museo Mandralisca resemble?" – Leonardo Sciascia). Lastly, as you approach Palermo, you can explore the villas of Bagheria, the images of an aristocratic life of the past, "Gattopardi," or Leopards, as in the novel by Tomasi di Lampedusa, and viceroys; the surrealistic sculptures of Villa Palagonia, then as much as today a must for sightseers. Goethe, a traveller who was also a contemporary of the man who ordered the creation of this villa, vents a page of spleen to it: to stroll amongst those "aberrations" gives one the "unpleasant sensation" of receiving "painful blows of madness."

The strait of Messina is key to the Sicilian identity.

NOT TO BE MISSED

Messina (➡ see below): this town overlooking the strait has a modern appearance, the result of bombing and earthquakes; the famed astronomical clock of the Duomo, the Museo Regionale (with among other things the polyptych by Antonello da Messina and canvases by Caravaggio), and the church of the SS. Annunziata dei Catalani are of interest. **Milazzo**: the walls of the old section of this strategically important town enclose the Renaissance style 17th-century Duomo and the castle; at a distance of 6 km from the lighthouse at the tip of the narrow peninsula, there is a fine view from Mt Etna to the Isole Eolie, or Aeolian Islands. **Villa Romana di San Biagio**: the ruins of this Roman villa, with mosaic floors, are uphill from San Biagio, an outlying quarter of Castroreale Terme. **Tindari**: you will turn off the SS road briefly at Locanda; alongside the ruins of Tyndaris, with the 2nd-3rd-centuries BC. Greek theater and a basilica, there is a sanctuary on the site of the acropolis and a fine view of the coast. **Sant'Agata Militello**: beautiful beaches aside, the Museo Etno-Antropologico dedicated to the farming civilization of the Nebrodi is worthy of attention. **Santo Stefano di Camastra**: one of the most famous centers of ceramics production in Sicily. **Mistretta**: you will take a 17-km detour after Santo Stefano di Camastra, on the Mts Nebrodi; a fine altarpiece by Antonello Gagini in the Chiesa Madre; also other important churches, buildings, and artworks. **Cefalù***, at the foot of a massive hill-sized boulder, has a superb Norman cathedral with renowned mosaics, and fine works in the Museo Mandralisca; at a distance of 15 km, note the Sanctuary of Gibilmanna. **Castelbuono** is a small resort town in the Madonie; the Matrice Vecchia is a 14th-century church; in the 14th-century castle, are the Museo Civico and the chapel of S. Anna with stuccoes by Giuseppe and Giacomo Serpotta. **Petralia Sottana** is a little resort town in the Madonie; here and uphill from here, in Petralia Soprana, there are noteworthy artworks and architectural details in the churches; fine view of the Madonie, Mts Nebrodi, and Mt Etna from the Baroque church of S. Maria di Loreto. **Polizzi Generosa** is yet another little resort town in the Madonie: a Flemish triptych in the style of Memling is in the church known as the Chiesa Madre. **Collesano** lies at the base of the Madonie, with the 16th-century. Matrice church and fine artworks. Ruins of Imera, a Greek colony of Zancle (Messina) with an antiquarium; you will take a detour, continuing along the SS 113 road beyond the interchange for the Autostrada at Buonfornello. **Termini Imerese** has Roman ruins in the Villa Palmeri, the public gardens; at a distance of 10 km is Caccamo (a name taken either from the Greek kakkabe, "partridge," or from the Punic caccabe, "horse's head," or from the Latin cacabus, "boiler"), with a large bastioned castle. **Solunto**: the Hellenistic-Roman ruins of this city founded by the Phoenicians stand on a spur of Mt Catalfano, within sight of the sea. **Bagheria**: among the aristocratic villas of this seaside town surrounded by citrus groves and vineyards, of particular architectural note are the Villa Valguarnera and the Villa Palagonia, with its odd statuettes. **Palermo** (➟ see below): the Sicilian capital is an ancient city filled with artistic treasures and natural beauty, but also with unexpected contradictions.

MESSINA

Only the name of Zancle, the 8th-century BC Greek colony, survives; the same is true of Messana, which replaced Zancle in the 5th century BC. The Roman city was described by Cicero as "civitas maxima et locupletissima," high praise indeed for a town. The modern-day city of Messina has a very up-to-date appearance, extending along the shore of the straits; the roads are broad and parallel, and buildings are relatively low, out of fear of earthquakes (though the bell tower of the cathedral stands 60 m tall). In terms of communications, this is the gateway to Sicily, but the narrow strait that separates it from the "continent" may someday soon be spanned by a long-awaited suspension bridge.

Piazza del Duomo. This broad square opens out against a backdrop of hills, and is adorned with the Fontana di Orione*, built by Montorsoli (1547-50).

Duomo*. This cathedral is a painstaking reconstruction of the church that developed over the centuries from its foundation, at the behest of the Norman king, Roger II (it was consecrated in 1197). The lower section of the facade, with bands of mosaics and reliefs, is as old as the three Gothic portals and the two 16th-century portals on the sides. Among the artworks in the interior, note the statue of John the Baptist by Antonello Gagini (1525) and the tomb of the De Tabiatis* by the Sienese Goro di Gregorio (1333).

Santissima Annunziata dei Catalani*. The little square in which this church stands is adorned with a statue by A. Calamecca (1572) of Don John of Austria, the victor of the Battle of Lepanto. The church was built in the second half of the 12th century, and altered in the 13th century; the facade dates from the same period. The transept, dome, and apse with blind arcades and polychrome dressing date from the earlier building.

Via Garibaldi is the main road artery of the city, lined with the Municipio, or Town Hall, and the Teatro Vittorio Emanuele. In Piazza Unità d'Italia is the Fontana del Nettuno, a fountain by Montorsoli (1557) and, just beyond the palace of the Prefettura, the small church of S. Giovanni di Malta, of Renaissance origins.

Museo Regionale*. The most interesting tour in the city, however, is that of the regional museum (along the beach, past the lighthouse. The archeological section is being renovated; the sections on medieval and modern art offer a priceless documentation of the city's art history, with major masterpieces. Note especially: the Madonna degli Storpi*, a sculpture by Goro di Gregorio (1333); the St Gregory polyptych** by Antonello da Messina (1473); Presentation in the Temple, Last Judgement, and Circumcision* by G. Aliprandi, 1519; Scylla*, originally part of the Fountain of Neptune; Adoration of the Shepherds* and Resurrection of Lazarus*, paintings done by Caravaggio while traveling to Messina between 1608 and 1609. One interesting curiosity are the 9 gilt slabs with the Legend of the Sacred Letter (early 19C), which recurs in the clock of the Duomo as well.

Circonvallazione a Monte. Magnificent views can be enjoyed from many different points along these avenues that constitute the "uphill ring road."

PALERMO

On the north coast of Sicily, with the stern Mt Pellegrino as the constant point of reference throughout the landscape, dotted with the citrus groves of the Conca d'Oro, the city of Palermo preserves the memories, monuments, and atmosphere of Arab and Norman times as one of its two urban faces, the more remarkable and original of the two. The other face is that of the Baroque architecture that dates from the 17th-18th century, from the time of the Spanish viceroy and the Bourbon monarchs. The city can be considered as being split in two by the axis of Via Cavour and Via Volturno; to the north, near the port, is the modern section, with rectangular blocks and broad roads; to the south is the intricate and chaotic structure of the old section, once enclosed by medieval and Spanish walls. Two Spanish viceroys, the Duke of Toledo (1565-66) and Maqueda, who governed Sicily from 1598 to 1601, built two straight avenues: the first is Corso Vittorio Emanuele, going from the Marina to the Palazzo dei Normanni; the second avenue runs perpendicular to the first and parallel to the sea: Via Maqueda. These two avenues divide Palermo into four districts, and they meet in the little Piazza Vigliana, or Quattro Canti, once the city center.

THE FIRST FORTIFIED SETTLEMENT

Starting from Quattro Canti, the common name of the little Piazza Vigliena, going along the western stretch of Corso Vittorio Emanuele, the first route takes in the oldest part of the city. This area is called Cassaro (from the Arabic "el Kasr", for castrum or castle) and lay in the heart of the city even in medieval times, when the construction of the Norman palace and the cathedral made it the center of political and religious power.

Corso Vittorio Emanuele, runs from the Marina to the Palazzo dei Normanni. From the Quattro Canti, proceeding eastward, along this street or near it you will find many interesting monuments.

S. Giuseppe dei Teatini, adjacent to the Quattro Canti stands this lavish Baroque church with its remarkable marble-studded interior, bedecked with stuccowork and frescoes.

Via Maqueda, built in 1600 by the viceroy Maqueda, it runs from Porta Vicari, also called Porta S. Antonino, to Piazza Verdi, note the 17th-century church of S. Nicolò da Tolentino and the Palazzo S. Croce (18C).

Gesù*, this was the first church of the Jesuits in Sicily. It was built in 1564 and later enlarged; the dome dates back to the mid-17th century. The interior is covered with wood inlays and marble carvings. It is a sterling example of Sicilian Baroque.

Palazzo Sclafani, a fine example of Gothic civil architecture. Note the facade with its high intertwined archwork, surrounding twin-light mullioned windows.

Cathedral**, this majestic monument of great interest stands at the end of a verdant square. You should pay close attention to the details of its construction, as it is the result of a complex series of rebuildings, ranging from the first structure (by the Normans, in 1185) to renovation and addition of the dome by F. Fuga (1781-1801). It is linked to the bell tower by two pointed arches. On the right side, note the portico, in flamboyant Catalonian Gothic style; the apsidal section* comprises three apses with intertwined arcades and polychrome encrustations.

Palermo's impressive cathedral is one of the city's key architectonic monuments.

Inside. In the Neo-Classic interior, note, in the right aisle the renowned imperial and royal tombs* of Henry VI, Frederick II, Constance, and Roger II; in the chapel to the right of the presbitery, a silver urn (1631) containing the relics of Santa Rosalia, the patron saint of Palermo; in the left aisle, a Madonna* by F. Laurana (1469). Exquisite precious objects are preserved in the treasury, along with the golden tiara of Constance of Aragon, wife of Frederick II. In the sacristy is the Madonna by A. Gagini (1503), the leading member of a family of Palermitan sculptors (originally from Bissone, in the Canton Ticino, birthplace of Antonello's father, Domenico). The crypt dates from the 12th century.

In the Palazzo Arcivescovile, or archbishop's palace, the Museo Diocesano, or diocese museum, has a notable array of sacred art from the 12th-century **Piazza della Vittoria**, immense green space in front of the Norman Palace; its present appearance dates back to the 16th century, when an enormous open area was created for public ceremonies. Its current name commemorates the success of a local revolt against the Bourbon garrison in 1820. It is almost entirely taken up by the palm tree-lined park of Villa Bonanno.

Palazzo dei Normanni*, on the other side of Villa Bonanno stands this vast and majestic building, one of Sicily's most significant monuments. Originally built by the Arabs, later a sumptuous royal palace under Norman rule, hence its name, and then used as the court of Frederick II. During this period, the building lay at the heart of great cultural changes, mingling the ancient classical heritage with Arab and Byzantine traditions (here, the Scuola Siciliana gave birth to Italian poetry).

Palatina chapel**, climbing the majestic staircase in the courtyard of the Norman Palace you reach the Palatine chapel, one of the finest creations of the entire Norman monarchy (Roger II, 1132-40). The structure consists of a nave with two aisles separated by rows of Gothic arches set on ancient columns; note the mosaic floors and exquisite marble lining the lower half of the walls. There is an exceptional wooden ceiling, modeled with stalactite and honeycomb shapes, in distinctly Arab style (ca. 1143), over the nave. Near the sanctuary, the mosaic ambo* on columns, and a 13th-century Paschal candelabrum*; above the marble lower panels, the walls are adorned with splendid 12th-century mosaics** on a gold background, with Bible stories and stories of Saints Peter and Paul; there are Latin writings stretching

the length of the aisles, as well as scenes from the Gospels, with phrases in Greek. Note the Christ Pantocrator, or Almighty Christ, surrounded by Archangels, Prophets, and Evangelists in the dome.

Appartamenti Reali. In the royal apartments (closed to the public) are the Sala di Ercole (or Sala del Parlamento), where the Assembly of Sicily now convenes, and the Sala di Re Ruggero, or King Roger, with mosaics* of hunting scenes (ca. 1170).

S. Giovanni degli Eremiti**. This Norman church stands in a lovely garden and is one of the most enchanting sites in Palermo. In the garden, full of exotic plants, is an exquisite 13th-century cloister*, with lovely little twin columns.

THE SOUTHEASTERN SECTION OF THE OLD TOWN

Starting once again from Quattro Canti, it is possible to explore the sector of the city bounded by the southeastern stretch of Corso Vittorio Emanuele and the southern stretch of Via Maqueda. Following on from Palazzo Abatellis, which houses the important Galleria Regionale (art gallery), the route takes in the ancient Kalsa district, a fortified stronghold built by Muslims in 937.

Piazza Pretoria, adjacent to the Quattro Canti, it is almost entirely occupied by the fanciful Fontana Pretoria*, a great fountain built by the Florentine F. Camilliani (1554-55). S. Cataldo*, this church, with blind arcades on the exterior walls, Arabic crenelation, three little cupolas, and a bare and lovely interior, is a perfect example of pure Norman style (ca. 1160). Martorana**, another gem of the Norman period, this church is also known as S. Maria dell'Ammiraglio (named after an admiral, George of Antioch, who had the church built). It dates from 1143, but it was partly rebuilt in the 16th-17th century; note the addition of a Baroque facade along the side. The bell tower** is original, 4 storeys tall, with mullioned windows, corner columns, and polychrome intarsia. **Inside****, the original Greek cross plan, with the later addition of a series of bays, features two mosaics: Roger II being crowned by Jesus and George of Antioch at the feet of the Virgin Mary, on the pediment of what was a portico. Don't miss the splendid 12th-century. **Byzantine mosaics**** in the sanctuary, with Christ Pantocrator (ruler of the universe), the Archangels, the Prophets, and the Evangelists, in the dome. Note a Birth of Jesus and a Death of the Virgin Mary. Mosaic screens enclose the apses.

S. Lorenzo*. The stucco decoration – with symbolic statues, stories from the lives of Ss. Lorenzo e Francesco (Saints Lawrence and Francis), and rejoicing cherubim – that adorns this oratory is considered to be Serpotta's masterpiece, in terms of expressivity and maturity.

S. Francesco d'Assisi*. This Gothic church, one of the most important in Palermo, was built between 1255 and 1277, altered and enlarged several times; badly damaged during the bombardments of 1943. It features a series of Gothic and Renaissance chapels, flanking the smallest aisle.

Palazzo Chiaramonte*. Set on the vast Piazza Marina, with the palm trees and rare plants of the Giardino Garibaldi at the square's center, is the Palazzo Chiaramonte, also known as the Steri (from the Latin "hosterium," in the sense of fortified palace). This stern and compact structure, with Gothic twin– and triple-light mullioned windows, and tufa-and-pumice intarsias, is a noble example of a medieval Sicilian palazzo. It was the headquarters of the ecclesiastical courts.

Museo Internazionale delle Marionette Antonio Pasqualino. This international museum of marionettes includes in its collections the "pupi siciliani," puppets from the Neapolitan theater, and puppets and marionettes from many nations, as well as Asian shadow-theater puppets. Palazzo Abatellis*, in this palazzo, note the strong architecture, a blend of Catalonian Gothic and Renaissance style (1495). **Galleria Regionale della Sicilia***, housed in Palazzo Abatellis, this gallery has a major art collection. In particular: the marvelous Annunciation** by Antonello da Messina. Other fine masterpieces are three saints*, also by Antonello, the lovely bust of Eleanor of Aragon** by F. Laurana, a famous fresco of the Triumph of Death** from the mid-15th century, originally in Palazzo Sclafani, the Madonna del Latte* by G. di Nicola, the Malvagna Triptych** by the Flemish painter Mabuse, and the exquisite Malaga vase*, a piece of Hispanic-Moorish ceramics.

Foro Italico, opened in the 16th century, this beachfront promenade stretches from Mt Pellegrino to Mt Catafano with a superb view of the Gulf of Palermo. Nearby, the Piazza della Kalsa, whose name comes from the Arabic "el Khalisa," originally given to the surrounding district, a fortified stronghold. At the end of the piazza, the church of S. Teresa is one of the most important examples of Palermo Baroque architecture.

THE NORTHEASTERN SECTION OF THE OLD TOWN

The route leaves again from Quattro Canti, taking in the area to the north of Corso Vittorio Emanuele, running along Via Maqueda towards Piazza Verdi, and the lively Via Roma towards Piazza Olivella. The Museo Archeologico Regionale, one of the most important in Italy, is the highlight of the route. **S. Matteo**, a Baroque church built in 1633-47; the interior boasts marble works and four fine statues by G. Serpotta.

S. Antonio Abate, isolated on an embankment, near the crossroads of Corso Vittorio Emanuele and Via Roma, this church was built in the 12th century and rearranged in the 14th century; the facade dates from the 19th century. Along the left side, you can walk down to Palermo's oldest market, the much loved Bocceria Vecchia, known as the Vucciria. **S. Maria di Porto Salvo**, built in Renaissance style in 1526 and renovated in 1581, when the opening of Corso Vittorio Emanuele resulted in the destruction of the apsidal section, later replaced by a portal.

S. Maria della Catena*, the name comes from the chain, or "catena," used to close off the harbor. In front of the church there is a flight of steps and a portico. The church dates from the late 15th century, stylistically a cross between Catalonian Gothic and the Renaissance. **Oratorio del Rosario di S. Domenico***, Via Bambinai 16). The interior of this oratory is a masterpiece of grace and elegance, especially the stucco decoration** by G. Serpotta; canvases by L. Giordano and the Monreale painter, P. Novelli, considered the greatest Sicilian artist of the 17th century; note also a canvas on the altar by Van Dyck. **S. Cita***, ring for the custodian). The entrance to this oratory is beside the church of S. Cita, known also as S. Zita. Here there is other excellent stuccowork* by Serpotta. **S. Giorgio dei Genovesi**, this fine church dates from the late 16th century and was built for the colony of Genoese people in Palermo. **Museo Archeologico Regionale Antonino Salinas****, this major archeological museum occupies the 17th-century building of a former convent. The entrance is through the lower cloister, with a fountain at its center. Some of the archeological finds discovered beneath the sea are housed here, including a vast and comprehensive collection of stone, lead and iron anchors*. In the hall dedicated to classical sculpture, particularly noteworthy among the enormous collections are the sculptures from Selinunte**, especially the 3 metopes** from

Temple C (mid-6C BC), two half metopes* from Temple F (5C BC), and 4 renowned metopes** from Temple E (460-450 BC). Other sections include prehistoric finds, Greek ceramics, Roman mosaics and frescoes.

THE NEW CITY
AND MOUNT PELLEGRINO

This route takes in the modern areas of the city – whose development began in 1778 and continued into the 19th century with the opening of Viale della Libertà – and areas lying outside the city too; it covers a visit to the Parco della Favorita and a suggested trip up panoramic Mt Pellegrino, where the celebrated sanctuary of S. Rosalia stands.

Piazza Verdi, laid out after the extensive demolition work in the late 19th century, this spacious tree-lined piazza is situated on the border of the new city and the old city. The imposing structure of the Teatro Massimo, built between 1875 and 1897, one of the temples of Italian opera music and one of the largest theaters in Europe (7730 m² surface area), dominates the piazza. **Piazza Castelnuovo,** together with the adjoining Piazza Ruggero Settimo, it forms a vast open space set off with monuments and palm trees. To the right, the vast bulk of the Teatro Politeama stands out. Built between 1867 and 1874 in classical style, the theater houses the Civica Galleria d'Arte Moderna. **Civica Galleria d'Arte Moderna Empedocle Restivo,** this modern art gallery has an interesting collection comprising works by 19th-century and contemporary artists. **Parco della Favorita*,** this magnificent park lies at the base of Mt Pellegrino and was built in 1799 at the behest of the Bourbon king of the Two Sicilies, Ferdinand, when he was forced to take refuge in Sicily after being rudely chased out of Naples by a French army. **Museo Etnografico Siciliano Giuseppe Pitrè,** Alongside the Palazzina Cinese, an early 19th-century. Chinese-style mansion built by a Bourbon king, is the Museo Etnografico Pitrè, one of the leading museums in the field of Sicilian traditions, costumes, and folkways. It comprises 31 halls.

Sanctuary of S. Rosalia*. Set high on the craggy limestone massif of Mt Pellegrino (606 m), this sanctuary of the patron saint of Palermo (13 km north) is made up of a convent and a cave-chapel (with a small natural spring said to flow with holy water that works miracles). In this cavern, the saint lived in penitence until her death (1166); a road leads further on to a broad square, with a colossal statue of S. Rosalia and a splendid view of sea and coastline.

In the outskirts, Villa Giulia*, known also as Villa Flora, this is a lovely 18th-century park with one side overlooking the sea. Adjacent is the Orto Botanico, one of Europe's finest botanical gardens, founded in 1789, with plants from all over the world. **S. Giovanni dei Lebbrosi** in Corso dei Mille, in the southernmost section of Palermo, is this interesting and fine church, which dates from 1070. **S. Spirito*** (in the enclosure of the cemetery of S. Orsola). This squared-off church dates from the 12th century. In the plaza before the church,

The Cuba is part of the Genoardo Norman park.

the anti-Anjou revolt of Palermo against its French garrison, known as the "Vespri Siciliani," was triggered on 31 March 1282. Inside is a 15th-century painted wooden cross. **S. Maria di Gesù*,** this 15th-century church stands on the lower slopes of Mt Grifone in the southernmost section of Palermo.

Zisa**, this building, which stands in the western part of Palermo, was erected in the 12th century by the Norman kings of Sicily, William I and William II, and is a masterpiece of Muslim architecture. Its name derives from the Arabic word for splendid, "aziz," or ceramic tiles; it follows the Muslim architectural tradition of the pleasure house. **Cuba*,** this buildings was one of the pavillions in the park built by William II (1180); its appearance is exquisitely Islamic; there is even an inscription in Arabic in the frieze.

The Arabs first set foot in Sicily in AD 827 at Mazara del Vallo, 205 years after the Hegira, and 116 years after Muslim troops invaded Europe across the Strait of Gibraltar; the conquest of the Byzantine-ruled island took some 75 years (the Norman warrior, Count Roger I of Altavilla, began his attack 234 years after the Saracens first landed, and finally expelled them from Sicily after thirty years of fighting, in 1091). Under Arab rule, the great island was divided into the three "valli" of Mazara, Demone, and Noto. The Val di Mazara comprised the western end of the island; its boundary was a line drawn from a point on the north coast between Termini Imerese and Cefalù and Licata, on the south coast. This route explores the westernmost section of the "vallo." There are three locations in the early part of this route that provide splendid instances of Sicily's originality: Monreale, Segesta, and Erice. In the first of the three, Arab-style stalactites hang down from the cross-vault of the Duomo amidst the glittering gold of the Byzantine style mosaics executed by Sicilian and Venetian master craftsmen. In Segesta the Doric enclosure of the temple of the Elimi features odd, unfluted columns, without any sign of the traditional cella, while in upper Erice you are surrounded by a medieval atmosphere. This route passes through areas that figured in the saga of Garibaldi's unification of Italy: Marsala, where his army of Red Shirts landed; Calatafimi, where they fought their first battle; Alcamo and Partinico, through which the tiny liberation army passed on its way to Palermo to face the 20,000 soldiers under Generale Lanza ("Alcamo: the evocative palm fronds spread over the walls of the gardens here; every house has the appearance of a monastery; a pair of dark eyes flashes down from a high balcony; you stop, you look up, and the lovely apparition has vanished...," writes Giuseppe Cesare Abba, a soldier under Garibaldi). At Mazara, in the narrow lanes of the old town, there is still a flavor of the Arab city; you can hear Arabic spoken by the Algerian and Moroccan sailors who work on the huge fishing fleet.

NOT TO BE MISSED

Monreale*: the Norman Duomo, covered with spectacular mosaics, and with a 12th-century cloister with slender twin columns, is one of the finest medieval monuments in all Italy; at a distance of 10 km is San Martino alle Scale (see Monreale), a resort set amidst pine groves, near a Benedictine abbey. **Alcamo**: this town features classic 14th-century architecture and layout, with remarkable artworks in the old churches (S. Oliva by Antonello Gagini in the 18th-century church of S. Oliva). **Calatafimi**, set on a ridge amongst hills, at the foot of the ruins of a castle; an Ossuary commemorating a battle in Garibaldi's Sicilian campaign (15 May 1860) stands on a rise at a distance of 4.5 km **Segesta** (➡ see below): take a short detour off the road between Calatafimi and the highway entrance; secluded on a high crag is the Doric temple of the ancient city of the Elimi; higher up is a Hellenistic theater overlooking the distant sea; fine view. **Erice** (➡ see below) stands, medieval and silent in the triangle of walls that enclose it, atop a crag: of particular note in the charming setting are the 14th-century church of Matrice and its bell tower; also note the Annunciation by Antonello Gagini in the Museo Civico, views of the sea and of the Isole Egadi from the outer roads; detour of 8 km, on the way to Trapani. **Trapani** (➡ see below), extending over a promontory, boasts the 18th-century. Sanctuary of Annunziata and the impressive Museo Regionale Pepoli (among the items on display are a painting by Titian and a beautiful statue of S. Giacomo by Gagini). **Mozia***: you can take a boat out to the excavations and the museum of the ancient Phoenician city, on the island of San Pantaleo; detour for boat slip after San Leonardo. **Marsala**: the main square has Baroque monuments (the Museo degli Arazzi della Matrice adjacent to the cathedral has Flemish tapestries bestowed by Philip II of Spain); to the west of town, near the sea, are the Roman insula and the Punic liburna (in the Museo di archeologico Biagio Anselmi). **Mazara del Vallo**: this is an exceedingly active fishing port; in the intricate, old Arab town, note the cathedral (with Transfiguration by Antonino Gagini), the little Norman church of S. Nicolò Regale, and the Museo Civico. **Rocche di Cusa**: take a 13 km detour after Mazara del Vallo, passing through Campobello di Mazara; there are tufa quarries, and through the vegetation you can see the cuts where the stones of the temples of Selinunte were extracted. **Castelvetrano**, on a terrace over the coast, with a John the Baptist by Antonello Gagini in the church of S. Giovanni, along with other artworks and examples of sacred architecture; at a distance of 3.5 km to the west, is the 12th-century. Norman church of SS. Trinità di Delia.

ERICE

On the summit of Mt Erice, this lovely, perfectly triangular town has been a favorite stopping place for many centuries, given its perfect climate and astounding views.

Mura. The well preserved walls are made of megalithic blocks (5C BC) in the lower section, and are of Norman material (12C) in the upper section and in the three gates.

Chiesa Matrice/Matrix Church*. This church features an isolated bell tower* with mullioned windows (1312); inside, note the chapels, and a *Virgin*, painted by F. Laurana.

Museo Civico Antonio Cordici, the town museum consists of notable collections of ancient artifacts and art (prehistoric, Punic, Hellenistic, and Roman archeological finds), paintings from the 17th-19th century, local handicrafts and silver, and a marble Annunciation* by A. Gagini (1525).

To the right of the Pepoli castle, at the end of a little road, stands the 12th-13th-centuries Venere castle (12-13C), on the round crag of the acropolis; inside are the ruins of a Temple of Venus, with a sacred well; fine view*.

SEGESTA

Temple**. Standing out in the green landscape, the temple has a peristyle of 36 unfluted Doric columns, supporting a trabeation with flat metopes and two pediments. This construction (5C BC), comprising the single circuit of columns still standing, enclosing the open-air altar of an indigenous cult. Segesta was a rival of Selinunte, and may have had a seaside market town and harbor near what is now Castellammare del Golfo.

Old city. The road that reaches Mt Barbaro (431 m) in less than one kilometer passes thorugh the site where the ancient town lay. The few remains include an imposing square tower, ruins of the old walls, a fortified gate.

Theater*. Datable around the mid-3rd century BC , the theater faces north, perhaps not to distract the spectators with the extraordinary view* which extends all the way to distant Mt Erice. Still visible are the huge hemycicle stalls, while beyond the stage are the remains of pre-existing dwellings.

SELINUNTE

Eastern temples*. This is a group of three temples that are, at this archeological site, each marked with a letter of the alphabet. A single column emerges from the mass of ruins of temple G, probably dedicated to Zeus, one of the largest of Greek antiquity, Doric, with an eight-column peripteros, and a cella; it seems to have been begun in 550 BC and left unfinished, possibly because of the Punic invasion in 409 BC. Temple F is in the middle and is the smallest. It has a six-column peripteros (560-540 BC). Majestically standing out from the landscape, on the other hand, is Temple E**, all of whose columns were raised in the mid-1950s, with part of the trabeation and of the walls of the cella. This magnificent Doric construction dates from the first two decades of the 5th century BC, and has a six-column peripteros; four handsome metopes of its sculptural decoration are now in the Museo Archeologico in Palermo.

Acropolis*, walking for a stretch along the walls made of enormous square blocks of stone, you climb up to the broad, high acropolis*. It was crossed by two intersecting roads, and there are ruins of a number of temples: base of temple O; base and drums of fluted columns of Temple A; fourteen raised columns (1925-27) and part of the trabeation of Temple C, the oldest one in the acropolis (three remarkable metopes from this temple are now in Palermo); pronaos and cella of Temple B; the remains of Temple D; ruins of Punic houses

Temple E at Selinunte was completely rebuilt in the mid-1950s.

(4-3C BC), and the base of a small archaic temple, possibly the source of six other, small metopes, now in Palermo.

At the northern tip of the acropolis is the main gate, or Porta Nord, defended on the outside by magnificent fortifications*.

Old city. On the hill to the north of the acropolis are the ruins of ancient houses and of a site which was probably used as a necropolis after the destruction in 409 BC.

Sanctuary of Malophoros. This sacred precinct, called a sanctuary, lies on the hill beyond the river. Still visible are the ruins of a very ancient small altar, of the altar of sacrifices and of the temple, dedicated to Malophoros, or bearer of pomegranates, probably Demeter.

TRAPANI

Situated on a curved promontory on the west coast of Sicily, Trapani was an important port and a thriving industrial center until quite recently. The fish-processing industry and shipbuilding yards, the salt-pans and business enterprise have thrived here over the centuries, but now it is mainly a services center and the point of departure for tourists heading for the Egadi Islands. However, this part of the island's historical ups and downs over a long period of time have left important testimonials and some real artistic gems. Originally, the Greek colony of Drepanon (meaning "sickle") was founded on a small archipelago

A rose window of the Sanctuary of the Annunziata.

of islands. Over the centuries it has been many things: an Arab town, full of winding narrow streets and courtyards, a craft center during the Norman period, specializing in the working of coral, and a modern fortified peninsula under Spanish rule in the 16th century.

Corso Vittorio Emanuele. The main thoroughfare of the historic center is lined by small, elegant 18th-century palazzi. At its eastern end stands the graceful three-tiered facade of Palazzo Senatorio, built in the Baroque style between 1699 and 1701. Next to it is the

12th-century Torre dell'Orologio (Clock Tower), one of the five depicted in the town's crest. Further along, on the right, is the Chiesa del Collegio (Collegiate Church), begun in 1636, with the Baroque former Collegio dei Gesuiti (Jesuit College) on one side.

Cathedral. Erected in 1635, the cathedral facade (1740) and designed by G. B. Amico, is preceded by a portico. The street opposite the cathedral leads to the 17th-century Chiesa del Purgatorio (Church of Purgatory), where the Misteri (Mysteries), twenty 18th-century wooden statues traditionally paraded round the town on Good Friday, are kept.

S. Agostino. The church dedicated to St Augustine stands in a small square graced by the Fontana di Saturno (Fountain of Saturn), of 1342. Of the original 14th-century building, which was damaged by bombing in 1943, there remains the simple facade with intersecting arches and a sloping roof, a Gothic portal and a rose-window*. Close by, the former church of San Giacomo Maggiore is now the Fardelliana Library, which contains priceless incunabola, manuscripts and illuminated codices from the 14th-15th centuries.

Sanctuary of the Annunziata. This sanctuary dedicated to the Virgin Annunciate is one of Trapani's most interesting monuments, erected between 1315 and 1332 but subsequently altered. The facade dates from the original building, with a huge rose-window and a Gothic portal of Norman influence. Next to it stands the imposing Baroque bell tower. The interior was transformed in 1760 into a single vast nave. On the right of the nave is the Fishermen's Chapel, dating from 1486, with a fine Gothic arch and and an octagonal dome, frescoed in the 16th century. On the left of the presbytery is the entrance to the interesting Sailors' Chapel, which is mainly Renaissance in form but still has Gothic and even Arab-Norman features. Behind the main altar is the 16th-century Chapel of the Madonna, the true sanctuary, decorated with reliefs. Above the altar is the much revered marble statue of the Madonna and Child*, known as the Madonna di Trapani, a work by Nino Pisano or his pupils (14C), at the foot of which is a silver model of the town.

Museo Regionale "Conte Agostino Pepoli". Housed in the premises of a former convent dedicated to the Virgin Annunciate, this museum contains collections of archeological artifacts, sculpture, paintings and sections devoted to the decorative arts, which illustrate the artistic and cultural heritage of Trapani and its surroundings.

COAST OF SICILY – CASTELVETRANO TO GELA

In 1875 Ernest Renan, professor of Hebrew at the College de France, was invited to Palermo to attend a scientific conference; among those present were Prince Umberto di Savoia, or Humbert of Savoy, the heir apparent to the Italian crown, and Ruggero Bonghi, Minister of Public Education. Bonghi asked Renan to join the national commission on antiquities in a tour of "all the major ruins of Sicily," a tour to decide where archeological excavations should be concentrated. Renan accepted, and the scholars and scientists boarded the "Archimede," a steamer that carried them from Trapani to Syracuse. Along the way, Renan and the others landed at Selinunte and travelled inland to Agrigento, the two most important stops on this route along the southern coast of Sicily, from Castelvetrano to Gela. We can only give you an impression of the Sicily that greeted their eyes in that distant year. At Selinunte "a fierce harsh sun (even though it was September), a land dried out by five months of heat, pierced only by a delightful little double white lily." Of the temples and their Doric capitals, he ventured: "In no other place can you so clearly see, step by step, the progress of these divine curves that so nearly reach perfection... Here is the miracle that only the Greeks managed to achieve: to find an ideal and, having found it, stick to it." Concerning a trip inland toward the sulfur-mining area, he wrote: "We saw Africa stretching before us on that day, in a range of hills burnt by sulfureous fumes, without trees, without greenery, without water." At Porto Empedocle Renan landed "under a portico decorated with statues of King Victor Emmanuel and Empedocles"; the name of Empedocles "is scattered through the public places as widely as is that of Garibaldi". The "rude journée" of tours also included a "cordial banquet offered by the people of Agrigento in the very midst of the ruins."

NOT TO BE MISSED

Castelvetrano: amidst olive groves and vineyards, this little town on a natural terrace boasts fine artworks set in its venerable old churches, and a noteworthy Museo Civico; at a distance of 3.5 km, is the Norman church of SS. Trinità di Delia. **Menfi** is a village founded in the 17th century, with an orderly checkerboard layout; its blind alleys and courtyards, however, still breathe the air of the long-ago Arab domination. **Sciacca**: the Steripinto, a remarkable 15th-century construction, was the "testa della corsa," or finish line, for the races run with riderless Berber horses; high atop Mt San Calogero (388 m), at a distance of 7 km, note the pine grove, the sanctuary, and the "stufe vaporose" (caves with steam vapors), and the fine view. **Caltabellotta**, with its intense island atmosphere, extends over three rocky hills: venerable old churches with artworks, excellent view from the ruins of the castle. **Eraclea Minoa**: the ruins of this Greek city founded by the inhabitants of Selinunte and by Spartan settlers stands on the bare upland of Capobianco, overlooking the sea. You will take a 4 km detour just after the bridge over the Platani River. **Agrigento** (➠ see below): the city extends over a spur dominating the Valle dei Templi, or Valley of the Temples, where an archeological walking tour leads you in succession to the Hellenistic-Roman quarter, to the church of S. Nicola, the Museo Archeologico Regionale, and lastly, the renowned Doric temples of Olympian Zeus (Giove Olimpico), Heracles (Ercole), Concord (Concordia), and Hera (Giunone), exquisite relics of the Greek colony, scattered over a beautiful landscape. **Licata**: archeological finds from the entire territory in the Museo archeologico della Badia, fine view from the Castel S. Angelo. **Gela***: the city is modern in appearance although its origins can be traced back to a flourishing Greek colony founded in 689 BC; the relics of classical times are concentrated in the Museo Archeologico Regionale and the fortifications of Capo Soprano.

AGRIGENTO

The main reason for going to Agrigento is to see the amazing array of ancient Greek ruins in the old city; nowhere else on earth, not even in Greece, will you see so many sacred buildings in one place. The Greek colony here was founded around 580 BC by settlers from nearby Gela and by other settlers from Rhodes. In the century that followed, the philosopher Empedocles lived and worked here.

Via Atenea. The crowded and lovely medieval section of Agrigento is crossed by the winding Via Atenea, the main thoroughfare, going from Piazza Aldo Moro, at the boundary of the new addition (near Piazza Marconi), to Piazza Pirandello.

S. Spirito* is a late-13th-century abbey, heavily rebuilt; the stuccoes in the interior are attributed to Serpotta; in the former monastery, note the cloister and various remarkable pieces of medieval architecture.

Cathedral*. It has a complex history, ranging from the 11th to the 17th century, and has interesting architectural details and artworks. Also note the acoustic phenomenon whereby, from the cornice of the apse, it is possible to hear a person whisper at the entrance of the church.

Old city, you can reach the ancient city from Piazza Marconi, following the first stretch of the SS 118 road (Via Crispi) and then driving down into the Valley of the Temples, up to the large square (parking area) facing the enclosure of the Temple of Olympian Zeus. You should then continue east, passing the three main temples and returning to road 118: this route is the archeological tour**.

Ellenistico-Romano quarter*, more than any other, this site offers a sense of just what the ancient city looked like at its Hellenistic foundation (4-2C BC) and on until the fall of the Roman Empire; the area was crossed by 4 parallel roads (cardines) which connected with the *decumanus* (now the SS 118 road at this juncture).

S. Nicola*. The 13th-century Gothic-Romanesque church is of Cistercian construction; the site it occupies has hosted a Greek, a Hellenistic, and a Roman sanctuary, monasteries, and a Norman church. Note the famous sarcophagus* engraved with the myth of Phaedra (2-3C AD). Fine view* of the temples from the square in front of the church.

Oratory of Falaride*, this little temple/oratory represents the Hellenistic phase of the sanctuary, on the site now occupied by the church of S. Nicola.

Museo Archeologico Regionale**. This fine archeological museum is located behind the church. It has collections from the city of Agrigento itself, as well as from the various ancient sites in the provinces of Agrigento and Caltanissetta. Of particular note is the telamon* (male figure used as a column) from the Temple of Olympian Zeus, artifacts* from the excavations of the Roman-Hellenistic quarter, a marble Ephebe* (a beardless youth), dating from about 470 BC , and a red-figured krater* with a scene of Amazon warriors in combat (5C BC).

Temple of Olympian Zeus*. This temple, built after a victory over Carthage (480 BC), was destroyed by earthquakes; you can still see the vast perimeter, heaped with rubble. It did not have the normal circuit of columns; rather, the outer wall was punctuated by half-columns alternating with telamons (male figures used as columns), making it a pseudo-peripteral temple.

The area to the west of the temple is dense with ruins of sacred buildings: the numerous altars, the bases of the temples, sacred enclosures, and "favissae" (dedicatory ditches), all dating from the 6th to the 5th century BC, were part of a sanctuary of the chthonic deities* (or Temple of Demetra and Kore, or Persephone). At the center of this area stand four columns with a fragmentary trabeation from the Temple of Castor and Pollux* (Tempio dei Dioscuri, 5th century BC; the trabeation dates from Hellenistic-Roman times). This notable group of columns is one of the best-known sights in Agrigento; the other temples are arrayed further east along the rocky ridge.

Temple of Heracles*. Eight columns standing in a heap of rubble belong to the Temple of Heracles, a six-column peripteral sanctuary from the late-6th century BC, perhaps the earliest Doric building in Agrigento.

Temple of Concord**, the 6th-century AD transformation of the ancient Temple of Concord into a Christian church probably helped to ensure its survival. It may have been dedicated to Castor and Pollux, sons of Zeus and Leda, and brothers of Helen. The six-column peripteros, built around the middle of the 5th century BC, is intact in its majestic proportions. This is considered to be one of the most perfect works of Greek architecture (the arcades cut into the side walls of the cella date from the adaptation of the temple as church).

Temple of Giunone Lacinia**, now a distinctive feature of this lovely landscape, the Temple of Hera stands alone at the edge of the rocky terrace; it had a six-column peripteros, much like the Temple of Concord, from the same period.

The impressive columns of the Temple of Giunone Lacinia.

FROM SIRACUSA TO CALTANISSETTA

Myths chase each other through the landscape of Trinacria, the ancient name for Sicily. The site where Pluto abducted the young Persephone, daughter of Zeus and Demetra, lies in the heart of the island. Vincent Vivant, the Baron Denon, secretary of the French embassy to Naples, travelling through Sicily in 1788, expected in vain to see, in the area around Castro Giovanni (now Enna), "the plentiful waters form placid lakes, whose cool shores were always enameled with the delicate blooms of the plains," the "delightful" countryside where, for six months of every year, Artemis and Athena were said to have come to live. This route, which begins in Siracusa, leads to Enna, continues on to Caltanissetta, and then goes up over the ridges of the Iblei Mountains, limestone plateaus broken only by the "cave", or gorges, narrow, deep, with sheer rock walls, dug out by rushing streams and mountain rivers. The road then passes over the terraces and rounded peaks of the Erei Mountains, the watershed between the Mar d'Africa, to the south, and the Ionian Sea, to the east. In various spots, you may explore specific sites or themes: at Pantalica, the cliffside necropolis; the ruins of Akrai near Palazzolo Acreide; the 18th-century architectural inventions at Caltagirone. Lastly, at the Casale di Piazza Armerina, you will see other myths depicted in the mosaic floors of the Roman villa: the struggle between Eros and Pan, Hercules, Ulysses and the Cyclops, Daphne, Endymion awaiting Selene, Arion riding a dolphin and playing a lyre.

NOT TO BE MISSED

Siracusa (➟ see below), to defend the town against a besieging force, Archimedes used an array of mirrors to focus the bright sunlight on the Roman ships commanded by Marcellus, setting fire to the fleet. The ancient sites range from the Fonte Aretusa to the Eurialo castle, alongside the well known monuments, the Galleria Regionale of Palazzo Bellomo, the archeological finds in the Museo Archeologico Regionale Paolo Orsi), and the sun-bathed landscape – all offer material for patient, unforgettable explorations. **Necropolis of Pantalica***: there are 5,000 tombs from the long-vanished, indigenous town of Hybla, carved into the rock walls rising sheer over the Anapo and Calcinara rivers. **Palazzolo Acreide***: the archeological area of the Greek town of Akrai, founded by Siracusa in 664 BC. **Grammichele**: the orderly late-17th-century layout of this town extends from the perfect hexagon of the central square. **Caltagirone**: the "queen of the mountains," has an 18th-century appearance and extends over three hilltops; the Palazzetto della Corte Capitaniale was built by A. and G. D. Gagini, while the Gesù and S. Giacomo are Baroque churches. There is a centuries-old local craft tradition of ceramics: the Museo Regionale della Ceramica documents the history of Sicilian ceramics in general, dating back to prehistoric times. **Piazza Armerina** (➟ see below): picturesque town located in the heart of Sicily. **Villa Romana del Casale****: the ruins give some indication of the manifold and vast complexity and luxury of a late-imperial country residence; the mosaic floors are astonishing, both in their expanse and in the variety of depictions. **Lake Pergusa** summons up images of the myth of Persephone – Prosperina abducted by Hades; today a motor racing track encircles the lake. **Enna***: the "belvedere," or vantage point, of Sicily, this town overlooks the Dittaimo Valley from a lofty natural terrace; note the Museo Alessi and the Byzantine-Norman-Swabian Castle of Lombardia. **Caltanissetta**, a modern city set amidst the hills of Sicily's mining region; the Museo Civico, with archeological finds, and the mining museum.

SIRACUSA

Until Roman times, this was the most powerful and magnificent city in all of Sicily. Today, it is an impressive sight, with a mixture of late Baroque architecture – vivid yet damaged by the passage of time, from the reconstruction of the city following the terrible earthquake of 1693 – and ancient classical architecture. It is situated in an exquisite landscape of sea, rocks, Mediterranean vegetation, under a clear blue sky. Recent expansion of the city has largely followed the road leading to Catania.

Parco Archeologico della Neapoli**, the heart of any archeological tour of Syracuse is the archeological park of the Neapolis (Greek for "new city"), which includes most of the classical monuments of Greek and Roman Syracuse. Access is allowed only to the Greek theater and the Latomia del Paradiso (see below). The other ruins are visible from the gates of the park. Nonetheless, the area has retained the fascinating atmosphere of the past.
San Nicolò dei Cordari, the church, near the entrance of the park, dates back to the 11th

century and still has its original apse. Below it is an Imperial Age pool which served as a cistern for the amphitheater.

Ara di Ierone II, the base cut into the rock indicates the altar of Hieron II, which was built for public sacrifices (3C BC); during the Roman Empire, an immense porticoed plaza stood before it, with a large pool in the middle. **Teatro Greco****, this marvelous Greek theater, cut almost entirely out of living rock, appears as it was following the renovation in 230 BC, during the reign of Hieron II. However, the theater existed as early as the 5th century BC, when tragedies by Aeschylus were performed there, and it was further adapted in Roman times. The semicircular cavea is still intact; it was enormous (with a seating capacity of 15,000), and it still has 46 of the original 61 tiers of seats; it encloses the orchestra, behind which was the platform of the skene, little of which remains intact (Charles V used it as a quarry for material with which to fortify Ortigia). Fine view* of the city from the terrace at the top of the tiers of seats.

Latomia del Paradiso**, this the the largest of the many Latomie, or quarries, where the white limestone was extracted to build the town and its walls. The Latomia del Paradiso is interesting for the Orecchio di Dionisio, or Ear of Dionysius, and the Grotta dei Cordari.

Orecchio di Dionisio*, it is an artificial cave, 65 m long, 5 to 11 m wide, and 23 m tall, that tapers almost like a Gothic arch at the top. It was given its name by the painter Caravaggio (1608), who believed the legend that Dionysius, the ruthless "tyrant" of 4th-century BC Syracuse, used this as a prison because of its remarkable acoustic properties of amplification, which allowed the tyrant to hear every word the unwary prisoners uttered.

Grotta dei Cordari*, not open to the public). For centuries, and until just a few decades ago, rope and cable makers (or "cordari") practiced their trade in this long cave supported by narrow pillars, with odd lighting effects and walls decked with moss and maidenhair ferns.

Anfiteatro Romano*, after passing by the small 11th-century church of San Nicolò dei Cordari, an avenue leads to the belvedere from which the amphitheater can be seen. The ellyptical structure was largely carved from the living rock in the 3rd century AD, and was only slightly smaller than the Arena of Verona. In the marble balustrades, the names of the owners of the places of honor are still visible.

S. Giovanni Evangelista*, once you have left the archeological area, the route takes you to the ruins of this little church, razed by the earthquake of 1693. From here you can descend to the Cripta di S. Marciano (the first bishop of Syracuse), a Greek cross plan crypt with fragments of frescoes from various periods on the walls. Also underground is the Catacomba di S. Giovanni*, a 4th-5th-century underground necropolis, with thousands of burial niches, rotundas and crypts in the main gallery.

Museo Archeologico Regionale Paolo Orsi**, housed in the Villa Landolina, this is one of the leading archeological museums in Italy. It is divided into three sections, covering a period of time of more than a millennium.

Section A. It is dedicated to prehistory and also includes a geological section. The evolutionary phases of Sicilian civilizations are explored during the different ages, including the Bronze and Copper Ages.

Section B. This part of the museum documents the centers of Greek colonization, dividing them into Ionic and Doric. Worthy of note are the sculptures found at Megara Hyblaea, and the celebrated Venere Anadiomene**, a statue of Venus found in 1804. Of the same high artistic value is a statue of a Winged Victory**.

Section C. This part features the inland subcolonies of Sicily, among which are Eloro, Akrai, Kasmenai e Kamrina.

Bassa Acradina, this road is flanked by a rocky slope with many caves, some of which were used for the cult of heroes. It leads to the Latomia dei Cappuccini; not open to the public), near the convent of the same name. The huge cave has fascinating areas with vaults and pillars.

S. Lucia, this church, rebuilt in the 17th century with a great tree-lined square before it, was built on the site indicated by tradition as that of the martyrdom of St Lucy, a virgin of 3rd-4th-century Syracuse. Among the remarkable artworks once here, especially the Burial of St Lucy* by Caravaggio, most are now in Palazzo Bellomo.

Ginnasio Romano, (1C AD). Of the quadriporticus that surrounded the ancient Roman gymnasium, only the perimeter is still visible.

Foro Siracusano, a shaft and several bases of columns are all that remain of the ancient agora in this large modern square.

Isola di Ortigia. This is a walking route which explores the little island transformed into a city-fortress over the centuries. Here traces of Greek, Byzantine, Norman, Swabian, Aragonese, Italian Renaissance and Baroque civilization can be seen. **Piazza Archimede**, the square is the heart of the island and is deco-

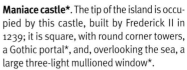
rated with the Fontana di Artemide. Of the many buildings which surround it, to the south is Palazzo Lanza, to the west Palazzo dell'Orologio.

Piazza del Duomo, located in the highest part of the island, this is a handsome Baroque architectural complex.

Duomo**, the cathedral features an 18th-century Baroque facade by A. Palma (1728-54; note the chiaroscuro), but it was built by incorporating the intact outer colonnade of a Doric temple of Athena (5C BC; the capitals and shafts of the columns can be seen protruding from the side wall in Via Minerva). The nave of the church was once the cella of the temple; among the furnishings in the church, note the baptismal font, made of a Hellenistic krater, supported by little bronze 13th-century lions. Also note the painting of St Zosimo*, attributed to Antonello da Messina (removed as a precautionary measure), as well as 16th-century paintings* by A. Gagini.

Fonte Aretusa*. This spring, partly covered by the papyrus plants which grow in abundance, has been bubbling forth into a basin overlooking the sea for millennia. Pindar and Virgil celebrated it in their poems, a fact which lent it a romantic renown linked to the myth of the nymph Arethusa, who threw herself into the sea to elude the pursuit of Alphaeus. According to the myth, she reappeared as a spring, while Alphaeus transformed himself into an underwater river to follow her, till they finally merged their waters; the freshwater spring of the "Occhio della Zillica," feeding into the harbor, is said to be Alphaeus.

Galleria Regionale*, the gallery housed in Palazzo Bellomo boasts fine architecture, a collection of statues, and a good art gallery, with an Annunciation** by A. da Messina (1474) and the Burial of St Lucy* by Caravaggio, plus an enormous 18th-century model of the city.

Maniace castle*. The tip of the island is occupied by this castle, built by Frederick II in 1239; it is square, with round corner towers, a Gothic portal*, and, overlooking the sea, a large three-light mullioned window*.

Via Vittorio Veneto, this is the main street of Spanish Syracuse. Along it are narrow lanes, notable churches, and Baroque palazzi.

PIAZZA ARMERINA

The source of this site's great fame is the extraordinary archeological complex of the Villa Romana del Casale**, a huge Roman country villa (late 3-4C), now inscribed in UNESCO's World Heritage List. It is an intriguing hypothesis, though not at all certain, that this villa belonged to a wealthy importer of wild African animals for the Roman games; the celebrated, brilliant mosaic floors**, some of the largest and most impressive ones surviving from antiquity, are believed to be the work of African master craftsmen, based on certain similarities with mosaic floors found in Roman-occupied North Africa. Numerous elaborate buildings, built in the late Roman architectural style, are arrayed around the large peristyle*, which features a mosaic floor of the imperial family with handmaidens* in a square vestibule, and, on the north side, halls with mosaics of Eroti fishers* and a small game hunt*. The buildings include the baths, with the three classical sections of the frigidarium, the tepidarium, and the calidarium; the Corridoio della Caccia Grossa, or Corridor of the Hunt, with a long mosaic depicting hunting scenes*, the capture of wild beasts* and predatory animals attacking prey in the wild*, a composition that tells a story clearly related to the trade in animals for gladiatorial games in the amphitheaters of ancient Rome; the Sala delle Dieci Ragazze, or Hall of the Ten Girls*, which takes its name from the floor mosaic of ten young girls** intently engaging in athletic pursuits, covered in skimpy two-piece outfits that are surprisingly modern.

On either side of the basilica are numerous rooms many with splendid mosaic floors, including one of Arione on a dolphin with an entourage of naiads and sea monsters*.

An elliptical peristyle lies before the Sala del Triclinium*, with mosaics of the Labors of Hercules*, the Glorification of Hercules*, the Defeated Giants* and Lycurgus and Ambrosia*.

Mosaic in Villa Romana del Casale, Piazza Armerina.

Catania, the second largest city in Sicily is also the birthplace of illustrious men of literature (G. Verga) and music (V. Bellini). It stands on the shores of the Ionian Sea, amid the citrus groves, in the clear Mediterranean light. Mt Etna, with its solemn silhouette, its peak brushed by clouds and snow, forms part of the cityscape and part of Catania's destiny. The volcano made the surrounding land fertile, attracting the original founders; it is also the source of the black lava-stone of which the Roman amphitheater was built, as were the medieval cathedral and the Baroque palazzi.

CATANIA

Piazza del Duomo*. The 18th-century atmosphere of the city strikes the visitor immediately in the central cathedral square, with the remarkable Fontana dell'Elefante (G.B. Vaccarini, 1736), a fountain inspired by Bernini's Fontana della Minerva in Rome. The elephant is called "u liotru".

Duomo*. The facade of the cathedral is also by Vaccarini; of the original 11th-century construction, all that survives are the apses and the transept. In the immense interior, note the Norman structure. In the right apse is the Chapel of S. Agata*, the chapel dedicated to the patron saint of Catania; from here you enter the rich treasury.

Piazza dell'Università the street is interrupted by this university square, a harmonious assembly of buildings by Vaccarini, as well as by Piazza Stesicoro, to the left of which you can see the ruins of the 2nd-century. Anfiteatro Romano, or Roman Amphitheater.

Casa-Museo di Giovanni Verga, to the west of the Duomo runs Via Garibaldi, where, in an 18th-century building, the birthplace of Verga is located, with books, furniture and objects belonging to the great 19th-century writer.

Ursino castle*, the vast solemn square bulk of this castle, built by Frederick II (1239-50) and rebuilt in the 16th century, houses the Museo Civico*. This city museum comprises varied collections of archeology, ancient and modern art, ivory, terracotta, bronze, weapons, and memorabilia of local history.

Museo Civico Belliniano, not far off is the museum dedicated to Bellini and the Teatro Romano, or Roman Theater, with an adjacent, semicircular Odeon.

Via dei Crociferi*, it is one of the monumental arteries of the city, lined with Baroque churches and 18th-century palazzi. Among the former, the sumptuous church of S. Benedetto (1771-77), with a carved wooden portal, and the church of S. Giuliano, a noteworthy example of Catania Baroque attributed to Vaccarini (1739-51).

S. Nicolò. Further west, the church of S. Nicolò, with an unfinished facade, is the lar-

HIGHLIGHTS

THE ITALIAN GENIUS OF "PURE SONG"

Vincenzo Bellini, a unique figure in the history of opera and one of the most original characters in the whole history of music, was born in Catania in 1801 to a family of musicians. He showed a precocious sensitivity to music, completed his studies in Naples and soon established a reputation as a composer. Before long, he had won the approval of Italy's leading opera-houses: San Carlo in Naples, La Scala in Milan, the Fenice in Venice, but also audiences in Vienna, London and Paris. In the French capital, he moved in the main aristocratic, cultural and artistic circles. These were already frequented by composers such as Rossini, Chopin and Liszt, and writers such as Alexandre Dumas and Victor Hugo. Bellini became a great friend of Rossini, and drew attention to himself for his unusual musical style, both because of the content of his music, through which he endeavored to "involve the heart", and for his expressive skills, in particular, the overpowering agility of his melodic expansion. Bellini is recognized as the greatest romantic composer of opera. Some of his most famous works include Il Pirata (The Pirate) (1827), La Sonnambula (The Sleep-walker) (1831), Norma (1831) and I Puritani (The Puritans) (1835). Bellini died a lonely young man at Puteaux, a suburb of Paris, in 1835. In 1876, his remains were finally returned to his native city and have lain in the cathedral of Catania ever since. Many places in Catania are dedicated to his name: the solemn monument in Piazza Stesicoro, the theater and the city's largest public park.

gest one in Sicily. On the pavement of the transept, note the marble sundial with inlaid symbols of the Zodiac. The carved wooden choir in the presbytery, elegant armoirs and rich ecclesiastical garb and ornaments in the Rococo sacristy are noteworthy.

TAORMINA

Palazzo Corvaia*, It stands at the entrance into town, not far from the gate of Porta Messina, and Piazza Vittorio Emanuele, which lies on the former site of the Forum. This 15th-century building features a crenelated facade, mullioned windows with slender columns, and a Catalonian Gothic portal. On the left side of the palace is the little church of S. Caterina d'Alessandria, built in the second half of the 17th century. Behind the church, note the Odeon, a building from Imperial times, with five wedge-shaped arrays of steps; the front of the skene was constituted by the side of a Hellenistic temple; you can still see some of the steps of the temple base.

Teatro Greco**, this theater probably dates from the Hellenistic period (3C BC), and was entirely rebuilt in Roman times (perhaps the 2C AD): the cavea was built in a natural hollow on the side of a hill; of the skene, which had a facade of columns and niches, major ruins survive (something quite rare for an ancient theater), and slender cypresses peek out from among them. The view** from the cavea and the terraces above the skene is as breathtaking as it was described by Goethe. In the house of the custodian a small antiquarium houses architectural marble and stone fragments from the city building, as well as financial documents, and statuary.

Corso Umberto I, pleasant cafés and elegant shops line this main street which runs from one end of the city to the other. Downhill from the first section of this thoroughfare, are the Naumachie* one of the most important Roman monuments in Sicily, an imposing stretch of walls built in imperial times to terrace the hillside where a huge cistern for collecting water lay. Interrupting Corso Umberto is the panoramic terrace of Piazza IX Aprile, with the former Gothic church of S. Agostino (1448). Through Porta di Mezzo and under the Torre dell'Orologio, or clock tower, you enter the medieval district; portals and mullioned windows, in Romanesque and Gothic style, embellish the houses.

Cathedral. Originally built in the 13th century, the cathedral has a long history of construction. The two side portals date from the 15th

century and the 16th century; in the interior are 15th-16th-century polyptychs of the school of Messina (Visitation by A. Giuffrè and Virgin and Saints, by A. De Saliba).

Corso Umberto I ends at Porta Catania. On the left note the vast mullioned windows of the Palazzo dei Duchi di Santo Stefano* (14-15C).

ACIREALE

This is the largest of the seven towns deriving from the ancient city of Akis, a Phoenician colony destroyed during the earthquake of 1169. Known for its mild climate and hot springs, life here moves at a relaxed pace, focusing on pauses at the tables outside the many ice-cream shops. The town owes its Baroque appearance to the fact that it was rebuilt after the earthquake of 1693. The nearby coast, with its citrus groves and the view of the snowy summit of Mount Etna in the distance, is called the "riviera dei Ciclopi" (Riviera of the Cyclops) in memory of the Homeric myth. According to the legend, it was here that a Cyclops (one-eyed giant) named Polyphemus, out of jealousy for his beloved Galatea, killed a young man called Acis, who was then transformed by the compassionate gods into the river that still bears his name. The center of the town is Piazza del Duomo, an elegant "drawing room" surrounded by fine buildings in the flamboyant Baroque style typical of the Catania area. This square is the final destination of the procession of allegorical floats held every year during the carnival.

The Duomo, built in the early 17th century, has a facade reminiscent of the Gothic style dating from the early 20th century. Inside, there are frescoes and paintings by Pietro Paolo Vasta, an 18th-century painter from Acireale, whose works adorn many churches in the town.

Not far away is the Pinacoteca Zelantea, with a collection of artworks and archeological material. Adjoining the art gallery is the very interesting Biblioteca (Library), founded in 1671, one of the finest in the region.

The seaside resort of **Aci Castello** has a small Norman fortress, erected in 1076 and built entirely of black lava. Today it houses the Museo civico, with sections devoted to Sicilian archeology and mineralogy and a botanical garden. A fish market is still held in the little traditional fishing town of **Aci Trezza**. In the sea stand the Faraglioni dei Ciclopi*, which are said to have been thrown by the blinded Poliphemos to destroy Ulysses' fleeing ships.

The distance between the seven islands of the archipelago and the mainland is negligible, yet, here, it is as if time moves at a different pace. Declared a UNESCO World Heritage Site, the islands are named after Eolus, the ancient god of the winds, who made them his home. They are all of volcanic origin, but differ from one another in the colors which make up the landscape. Vulcano (named after the ancient Roman god of fire) is yellowish-green, because of the sulfurous incrustations on the summit and black because of its beaches of black volcanic sand. Lipari is a dazzling contrast of shining black obsidian and white pumice. Strómboli is black during the day and glows an incandescent red at night, on account of its continuous eruptions. Salina is bright green, its now extinct craters being covered with dense woodland. Filicudi, like Alicudi, is dark green, because of the beautiful caper plants which burst out of the basalt rock all over the island. Panarea is a golden color, dotted with the bright green of the vines and the white of the whitewash of the "dammusi", the name given to the houses flat, terrace-roofs large typical of these islands. The water around the islands is crystal-clear and cobalt blue, revealing a rocky sea-bed. The islands have not been inhabited continuously, and their soil, much of which is still virgin, has thrown up a few fragments from early settlements dating from the 5th millenium BC without yielding any further finds from the historic period.

EOLIE

LIPARI

It is the largest and mostly highly populated of the seven islands. A tarred road runs around the coast, while a network of cart-tracks explores the center. It is possible to drive right round the island, passing through tiny villages, making detours to the tops of the hills to enjoy the marvelous views across the archipelago (don't miss the view from Quattrocchi), and dropping down to the shore to admire the pumice caves, little creeks, beaches and the characteristic rocks offshore known as the faraglioni scattered along the coast. The most important town is Lipari, the millenary history of which focuses on its castle.

Having become prosperous in the Middle Ages, thanks to sulfur, alum and pumice mines, in 1544, Lipari was destroyed in a raid led by the Turkish corsair Khair ad-Din, better known as Barbarossa. Within a few years, the Spanish had reconstructed an effective defensive system around the castle, which now houses a small archeological park. The cathedral of San Bartolomeo, built on the site of the ancient acropolis, is of Norman origin.

VULCANO

Vulcano has never been permanently inhabited, but has always attracted people for various reasons. They came for the therapeutic properties of its mud and hot water springs, to exploit its alum and sulfur deposits and to graze their sheep, and, according to some, to bury the dead. Today, the interesting volcanic activity (fumaroles, jets of steam rising out of

The island of Panarea, part of the Eolie islands

the ground) make it possible to enjoy hot-water and mud baths all the year round.

STROMBOLI

Strómboli is the only permanently active volcano in the archipelago. Many people come to the island to watch its spectacular eruptions (there is also an interesting Volcano Center to visit). From the sea, at night, visitors can enjoy the unforgettable spectacle provided by the "sciara del fuoco" (or red-hot lava flow), on the north-west side of the island, where a stream of incandescent lava flows down to meet the sea.

PANAREA

Panarea is the smallest island in the Eolian archipelago. For the last few decades, it has been bombarded by merciless development to build tourist facilities. The best way to enjoy the magical charm of the island is to approach it by sea. Above the delightful bay known as Cala Junco, you can visit the remains of a prehistoric village dating from the Middle Bronze Age.

FILICUDI AND ALICUDI

They are the two islands least visited by mass tourism. Filicudi is a group of craters covered by typical Mediterranean maquis vegetation. Do not miss the chance of going on a nature walk accompanied by a guide who is an expert on the island's plant and animal species. Half of the island of Alicudi is completely uninhabited. Here, the only means of transport available – apart from your feet – is a donkey.

EGADI

The coastlines of these calcareous rock and sandstone islands has many caves and a few enchanting beaches. The inland plateaus are dominated by wheat fields, vineyards and meadows. Its popularity as a tourist destination is on the increase. The designation of the archipelago as a marine and nature reserve is an attempt to slow down development and safeguard the environment.

FAVIGNANA

It is the largest island, nearest to the mainland, less wild and more highly populated than the others of the archipelago. There are numerous interesting buildings, including Villino Florio, the villa belonging to the Florio family of Marsala fame, built in 1876 in the Art Deco Style. There is also a tuna fishery, one of the largest industrial complexes in Europe at the end of the 19th century and, today, a marvelous example of industrial archeology. Favignana also has interesting archeological sites and many tufa quarries, tufa being an ideal building material. But the island's main resource has always been the sea. Tourists come here to enjoy Favignana's splendid beaches, bays and rocks. Tuna fish use the island as a huge buoy, since it lies on the route they use when returning to the coast to reproduce. As a result, many of them are caught in the nets laid by the tuna fisheries.

LEVANZO

Levanzo has an enchanting coastline and clear blue water. Many archeological remains have been discovered in the sea around the island (Punic and Roman ships and Spanish galleons). But Levanzo is worth visiting just for the Grotta del Genovese, a cave famous for its prehistoric wall paintings and incised drawings, dated to between 9,000 and 10,000 BC. They depict human figures in the act of performing a ritual dance and a series of animals, including a deer and are of particular artistic value because of the successful way that movement has been expressed.

MARETTIMO

The island situated furthest from Sicily is a natural paradise. From the wild, steep sides of Mt Falcone, there is a drop down to the sea. There are no hotels, but the islanders who live in the little town between the two small harbors are happy to put tourists up. Every day fishermen set out in little boats to perform the ancient rite of fishing, pitting their strength and skill against the might of the sea.

PELAGIE

Scattered around Italy's southernmost territorial waters (closer to Africa than Sicily), Lampedusa, Linosa and Lampione form the little Pelagian archipelago (from the Greek "pelagos", meaning "high-sea"). The islands differ in geological make-up: Lampedusa and Lampione are calcareous, while Linosa is volcanic. Although they are too small and exposed to have been military bases, their isolation has preserved them from negative environmental transformations. As a result, the diversity of the marine and land species which live there constitute a major attraction for naturalists. The sea around the island of Linosa, which is of volcanic origin, is a paradise for scuba divers. Accommodation can be found in the village of the same name with its picturesque, brightly-colored houses.

LAMPEDUSA

Lampedusa, once famous for its sponges, resembles a rocky platform tipped at an angle. Its steep cliffs overlook water that is crystal-clear and teeming with fish, while its coastline is full of caves and rocks interspersed with little sandy bays.

It has only been permanently inhabited since 1843, when the Bourbon King Ferdinand II established a penal colony here. Until 1940, it was used as a detention center. The population of the island is concentrated in the small town of *Lampedusa*, in the south of the island. In 1995 the **Riserva Naturale Isola di Lampedusa** was created to preserve the Mediterranean maquis and the habitats of certain species of plants and animals on the verge of extinction. The charming **Spiaggia dei Conigli** (Rabbit Beach) is one of the few remaining places where the loggerhead turtle (Caretta caretta) lays its eggs.

Linosa is really the cone of a volcano which has been inactive for almost 2000 years. The sea around the island is deep and full of fish, a true paradise for scuba divers. Accommodation can be found in the village of Linosa, in one of its colorful houses.

RAGUSA AND NOTO

Two important factors have influenced Ragusa: the earthquake in 1693 and the town's relations with the surrounding countryside. After the earthquake the town was rebuilt in two parts: Ragusa "supra", the new Baroque town built on the plateau by the landowning nobility; and Ragusa "iusu", or Ibla, the lower part of the town, also rebuilt in Baroque style after the terrible earthquake, but on the medieval town layout, with stairs and winding alleys. The town's relations with the local peasant farmers of the surrounding countryside were based from the 15th century onwards on "emphyteusis", or perpetual lease: this revolutionary economic arrangement meant that peasants were only required to pay their landlords rent, not a portion of the produce of the land as well. The fields of the small farms were enclosed by the dry-stone walls typical of the area. Over the centuries a strong local culture and sense of identity developed in the people of Ragusa; today it is seen as 'an island within the island'.

From ancient times to Arab and Norman medieval times, the city has always acted as a fortress. The ancient town of Hibla Heraia, at the time of the Greek colonies, had been fortified by the Siculi; the remains of the medieval fortifications may still be seen today.

RAGUSA

San Giorgio, the Duomo, designed in 1739 by Rosario Gagliardi, looks grandly down over a beautiful flight of steps, which lie at an angle to the square. It has an impressive Baroque facade, with a bell tower which is convex in the center, and a Neo-Classic cupola built in 1820; the interior, with nave and two side aisles, is illuminated by stained-glass windows (1926).

Museo Archeologico Ibleo, the Ibleo Archeological Museum has material from excavations carried out in the area of Ragusa, and is divided into six sections: prehistoric sites, Camarina, Archaic Siculian towns, Hellenistic towns, late-Roman settlements, collections and purchases. The prehistoric section includes finds from Bronze Age villages and necropolises; there is interesting ceramic material from Archaic and Classical Siculian towns; particular emphasis is given to pottery production in the Hellenistic towns (a kiln has been reconstructed); and there are numerous objects from Roman and late Roman towns (mosaic floors, epigraphs, glass and bronze objects).

Cathedral, it was built between 1706 and 1760; it stands on a wide terrace on a loggia, overlooking the central Piazza San Giovanni. A cuspidate bell tower makes the monumental facade asymmetrical. The interior is decorated with stuccoes. Below is *Palazzo Zacco*, a Baroque building with grotesque masks.

Le Scale, these picturesque steps (over 300) lead down to the lower part of the town, from the church of Santa Maria delle Scale (St Mary of the Steps). Along the way, among stairs and buttresses, there are interesting examples of Baroque architecture, notably *Palazzo Nicas-*

tro or *Palazzo della Cancelleria* (1760). The Church of Purgatory, with an ornate Baroque doorway, overlooks from the top of a flight of steps *Piazza della Repubblica*.

Santa Maria delle Scale, the church was built in the 14th century and rebuilt in 1693. Parts of the earlier building may still be seen: outside, at the foot of the bell tower, the remains of a doorway and a pulpit; inside, Gothic-Renaissance arches in the chapels on the right aisle.

NOTO

Set in a landscape of quarries and marshes, but also surrounded by citrus groves, almond orchards, and vineyards, Noto is a remarkable town, rebuilt in a lavish Baroque style following the ravages of the earthquake of 1693.

Corso Vittorio Emanuele*. The main street of Noto, which widens into three squares, from which monumental staircases ascend.

Piazza Immacolata. If you enter town from the Porta Nazionale, the first square is the Piazza Immacolata, with a stairway up to the church of S. Francesco all'Immacolata and the convent of the Santissimo Salvatore.

Museo Civico Archeologico. In the above-mentioned convent is the town museum, which comprises an archeological section as well as a modern section.

Piazza del Municipio. In this square stands the elegant Palazzo Ducezio* (V. Sinatra, 18C) and the staircase that climbs up to the cathedral, with a spectacular 18th-century facade.

Piazza XVI Maggio. Continuing along the Corso, you will see this square; note the church of S. Domenico.

ETNA REGIONAL NATURAL PARK

T he park incorporates one of Europe's few active volcanoes, in a spectacular setting in terms of colors, landscapes and human activity. It also protects everything that lives or exists on the volcano, including its volcanic activity: the low walls built of lava, the old farm-houses, the woods of birch and Austrian pine, beech and flowering ash, the striking Etna broom, the plants and animals living in extreme conditions. Just observing the lava shapes, veritable sculptures of Nature, provides scholars with an endless task. One of the wonders of the volcano is Bove Valley, an enormous basin situated on the eastern slope of the volcano with walls as high as 1,000 m, which, according to some theories, is the result of the collapse of the original crater complex.

Although the diversity of wildlife species has diminished in recent times, the fact that humans find much of the environment inhospitable allows many species of birds to survive. Diurnal raptors such as the sparrowhawk, the peregrine falcon and the golden eagle; nocturnal raptors such as the barn owl and the long-eared owl; grey herons, duck and other water birds inhabit Lake Gurrida, the only stretch of water in the mountainous area around Etna. Areas of dense woodland are home to many

Above and below, two views of a volcano.

species of woodland species, such as various species of tit and the common cuckoo. Finally, mushrooms, rare flowers, reptiles, little-known insects and small mammals all add their charm to this strange environment, admired for more than two centuries by travelers on the Grand Tour, possibly the best-known being Goethe and the Englishman, Patrick Brydone.

ASCENDING THE VOLCANO

The **Strada dell'Etna** is the simplest way to ascend the volcano. Leaving Catania by the Via Etnea, follow directions for **Gravina di Catania** and **Nicolosi**, seat of the *Etna Vulcanological Museum*, the base of the Parco dell'Etna. Nearby is the **Astrophysical Observatory of the Università of Catania** and the *Nuova Gussonea Botanical Garden*, then continue on foot or with an off-road vehicle to the *Torre del Filosofo*.

GURRIDA PATH

Of all the walks in the park, the Sentiero Gurrida deserves a special mention. The fact that there are no architectural barriers means that everyone can enjoy the experience.
Suitable for visitors in wheelchairs or on foot, the path winds along for 1.5 km beside Lake Gurrida. A wooden walk-way follows the edge of the lake (dry in summer) and

then continues to the bank of the artificial pool where, two specially-built observation huts (with wheelchair access) enable visitors to birdwatch or enjoy photography. The path starts and finishes at the wine-cellar of an old farm, where visitors can taste and purchase local products.

AMONG THE VESTIGES OF THE PAST

Perhaps the most interesting and pleasurable way to discover the development of Sicily's artistic heritage is to follow an itinerary based on visits to the island's archeological sites. This, after all, was why Sicily was one of the main stops on the Grand Tour during the 18th-19th centuries, of which Goethe's "Italian Journey" is the most famous and most romantic celebration. But, although what most fascinated the German poet about Sicily were the traces of its Greek past (so much so that he wrote that, rather than describing Sicily as Magna Grecia (Greater Greece), that is, a mere colony of Greece, it should be described as one of the most authentic parts of the Greek motherland), we should not forget the important testimonials left here by other cultures and civilizations.

Sites dating from the **Paleolithic** include the rock engravings at Addaura near Palermo and at the Grotta del Genovese on the island of Levanzo. The **Neolithic** is represented by the remains of the villages at Stentinello and Megara Hyblaea. Another aspect of the Neolithic period is the evolution of pottery on the Eolian Islands, providing evidence of the first contact with the Aegean area and Mycenae, and the dissemination of obsidian. Finds from the period are exhibited at that little jewel which is the Lipari Archeological Museum. During the Bronze Age (1800-900 BC), there was an intensification of economic trade and cultural links between Sicily and the Greek and Mycenaean world. Sites associated with this period include the villages on Panarea, Salina, and Lipari, and at Thapsos, whereas later colonization by the Sicani and other Italic peoples finds testimonials in the rock-cut necropolis at Pantalica, and in the excavations conducted at Sabucina and Morgantina.

But the true turning-point in the island's history is the mid-7th century BC, when the **Greek colonization** of the island began. The first Greek "poleis" (cities) were founded at Zancle, Naxos, Catania, Leontinoi, Megara Hyblaea, Siracusa and Gela, which, in turn, led to expansion along the coast or inland, resulting in the foundation of new towns or fortified cities (Himera, Selinunte, Camarina, Agrigento, Akrai and Casmene). During the 7th century BC, the **Punic presence** was also consolidated in Western Sicily, with the founding of settlements at Motya, Palermo and Solunto. In the century that followed, the Greek cities of Sicily reached a level of opulence and power that can be seen in the development of the architecture of the time.

The Selinunte acropolis, with Temple C in the background.

This is documented particularly by the building of sanctuaries and **temples**, for example the first large stone temples at Siracusa and Selinunte. For Sicily, the 5th century BC was a Golden Age which saw the culmination of its political and cultural splendor, leading to urban expansion and architectural development in the cities. Everywhere, new temples were built (Himera, Siracusa, Selinunte, Agrigento). Increasingly, they reflected the architectural canons of classical Greece, which were also adopted – albeit with occasional variations – in the non-Greek settlements on the island (Segesta). Thus Sicily became one of the great centers of the Mediterranean, following the historical and artistic transformations of this cultural area. After the Carthaginian offensive and the destruction which resulted therefrom, in the 4th century BC, we see the resurrection of the most important cities and the foundation of new ones: Gela (whose splendid stone and brick walls on Capo Soprano are still intact), Camarina, Agrigento, Halaesa and Solunto. The 3rd century BC marks the transition, in terms of town-planning and art, to Hellenistic forms: cities such as Tyndaris, Tauromenion (Taormina), Solunto, Akrai (Palazzolo Acreide), Morgantina and Iaitas reflect the new canons of urban planning in the imaginative and scenic layout of their monuments and squares, as shown in the agora at Morgantina. **Stone theaters** suddenly underwent an important phase of development (Siracusa, Segesta, Palazzolo Acreide, Solunto, Morgantina, Tyndaris, Catania, Iaitas, Eraclea Minoa and Taormina).

In 212 BC, Sicily became a **Roman province**. Some of the cities in western Sicily seem to have undergone a certain amount of development, particularly Solunto, Lilybaeum (Marsala) and probably Palermo. In the 1st century AD, the construction of sumptuous residential villas testifies to the development of the latifundium (large estate) system (the most notable example being the Roman villa of at San Biagio). Finally, in the Imperial period, in addition to the restoration of Greek monuments (the theater of Taormina being the prime example), we see the development of important architectural projects

at Tyndaris, Agrigento, the mouth of the Tellaro and at Patti. The economy based on the latifundium system, which also characterized the late Imperial period, gave rise, in terms of architecture and art, to splendid Imperial or senatorial villas, like the one justly celebrated on account of its magnificent mosaics, at Piazza Armerina.

It is therefore clear that an archeological itinerary in Sicily offers great variety and

The archeological zone of Tindari.

potential to visitors. And although we certainly cannot ignore the great monumental complexes such as Siracusa, the Valley of the Temples at Agrigento, Selinunte, Solunto and Piazza Armerina, nor the fabulous collections of the archeological museums of Agrigento, Palermo (with the extraordinary metopes from Selinunte), Siracusa and Catania (to mention only the most important), it is right that we should also consider the marvelous surprises concealed in less well-known sites, often located in superb natural settings. This is certainly the case of the Phoenician settlement on Motya, a tiny island in the Lo Stagnone lagoon off Marsala; Eraclea Minoa, with the remains of its tufa theater built next to a glorious beach; Morgantina, set in the green heart of Sicily, which, despite the fact that it has no great monuments, enables us to understand what a Greek city was really like; and Segesta, where a gravel track leads up from a perfectly preserved Doric temple, to an equally well-preserved theater where, for some years now, performances have been staged at dawn, as the sun rises above the Golfo di Castellammare.

BEACHES

Sicily is the largest island in the Mediterranean and has almost 1,500 kilometers of coastline. The territory of Sicily includes the Island of Ustica, the archipelagoes of the Eolian Islands, the Egadi Islands and the Pelagian Islands (with the islands of Lampedusa and Linosa) and the Island of Pantelleria. In the north and east, the Sicilian coast is high and indented, where the rocks run down to the sea, resulting in a series of promontories interlaced with bays and small flood-plains which make the coast flatter and more sandy. In the west of the island, this uniformity can also be seen in some of the less indented bays. The following is a list of the best beaches for tourists to visit.

Capo Calavà Beach, (Province of Messina). Coming from Messina on the SS 113, you come first to Capo Schino and then to Capo Calavà, the bay of which is entirely occupied by a magnificent beach stretching from one headland to the next. Capo Calavà is 137 m high. On the seaward side, the cliff walls are almost vertical, dropping down to the level of the sea, where there are many caves with gravel or sandy floors. The beach is well preserved because, until now, it has benefited from the supply of sand coming from the erosion of Gioiosa Marea beach just west of it.

San Gregorio Beach, (Province of Messina). Today, the beach of San Gregorio is the most varied section of all the coast around Capo d'Orlando, full of small ravines and inlets. Before you get to Capo d'Orlando, on the eastern slopes of the headland, you will see a tiny salt-water lake formed by the accumulation of sand. The beach was formed in the 1960s behind a jetty built for a harbor project that was never completed. To reach the beach from Messina, follow the A 20, leave the highway at Brolo and continue west along the coast, or take the SS 113. The beach is well sign-posted. Some other notable beaches in the province of Messina include the Santuario and Marinello beaches.

Pollina Beach, (Province of Palermo). The whole coast from Patti Marina to Cefalù is spectacular. State highway 113, which follows the coastline slightly higher up, runs along

very close to this beach, where long sandy stretches alternate with pebbles. Various lanes and good paths lead down onto the beach. At Pollina, park in the large car park on the right before the town of Finale di Pollina. A path leads down to the beach from the left-hand side of the car park, past some imaginative graffiti.

Cala Gallo, (Province of Palermo). The bay lies north-west of Palermo, on a rocky, north-facing part of the coast. Behind it is the splendid reserve of Mt Gallo, its lush Mediterranean vegetation and garrigue dotted with giant fennel, euphorbia, almond and carob trees providing a green lung for the area. This is one of the few sections of coast near Palermo which still has clean water. Although the coast is owned by the State, the area behind it is all privately owned. Access to the sea is therefore forbidden (although a sentence issued by the Supreme Court of Appeal in March 2001 forbids this practice) unless you are prepared to pay a fee to go through a gate. Once you reach the rocks, the greenish-blue water is crystal-clear. The landscape, which was recently designated as a Marine Nature Reserve, consists of at least 3 km of wild coastline.

Beaches of San Vito lo Capo, (Province of Trapani). It is not easy to access these beaches, but they are worth visiting. The long beach, situated in the town, has beautifully clean water. Instead of sand, there is a carpet of tiny shells. Don't be put off by the areas of beach taken over by the hotels, which are some of the finest in the area. In fact, there are still long stretches of open beach which can also be reached from the beach of Lo Zingaro by a path through the Nature Reserve.

River Belice Special Nature Reserve, (province of Trapani). This reserve lies 12 km from Castelvetrano. The final section of the Belice River is an important stopover for birds on migration and the many species which come here to breed, thanks to the wetland and its lush vegetation. Along the coast, the sand dunes provide the ideal

The Zingaro reserve near San Vito Lo Capo.

habitat for a few typical species of flowers and wild animals. The reserve, which is approximately 4 km long, is situated between Marina di Selinunte and the headland of Porto Palo. The western end of the beach has splendid dunes which gradually give way to a limestone ridge with Mediterranean maquis to the east.

The sea is almost always calm, the water is shallow and has a sandy bottom, making it ideal for children. In the Trapani area, it is worth heading to Capo Feto and Cala dei Turchi.

Eraclea Minoa (Capo Bianco) (Province of Agrigento). A wonderful sandy beach more than 5 km long, with several lines of dunes, overhung by cliffs, set on "trubi" (a typical local white sedimentary rock) and on shelves of chalk containing large crystals. The combination of the broad expanse of golden beach, with a thick wood behind the dunes, protected by the splendid white cliffs of "trubi" and gray chalk, makes the beach quite unique.

Scala dei Turchi (Province of Agrigento). This is a real gem of the coast around Agrigento. It is easy to recognize, since it consist of a white promontory which has been carved by the sea and the wind into a stair-like shape, hence its name (the "Turks' Stair"). The beaches lying to the east and west of the promontory are delightful, with their golden sand and white cliffs behind. The province of Agrigento has numerous other beaches, such as Borgo Bonsignore – Mouth of the Platani River, Beaches of Torre Salsa, Gelonardo and Peregole – Torre di Monterosso.

Santa Maria di Focallo Beach (Province of Ragusa). The beaches in the Province of Ragusa are longer than those in the Province of Siracusa. However, the sea is rougher (we are now in the channel called the Stretto di Sicilia) and the sand is much rougher, so much so that the fisherman can drive across it with their vehicles. Some stretches of the long beach at Santa Maria di Focallo (7 km) are quite interesting, with their dunes and rich Mediterranean maquis vegetation. To get there, stop at one of the access-points on the coast road between km 6 and km 8, right opposite Isola dei Porri ("Leek Island").

Vendicari Beach (Province of Siracusa). Perhaps one of Sicily's most beautiful beaches, on a nature reserve dominated by a Swabian tower and the ruins of a tuna fishery. It lies on the road between Pachino and Noto, in a section of the coast which has been successfully preserved, thanks to moves to protect a wetland which hosts large populations of flamingoes. This spotless beach is on a par with those in the Caribbean. The thick Mediterranean maquis vegetation also provides shelter from the heat.

Maddalena Peninsula (Province of Siracusa). To reach the Maddalena Peninsula, drive south from Siracusa for a short distance on la SS 115 and turn off at the junction towards Faro Carrozzieri (lighthouse). When you reach the office of the Guardia di Finanza (Financial Police), turn towards Punta Mole. Here, you must leave the car and proceed on foot for about 3 km along the only footpath, along the top of a cliff. Finally you reach the inlet, with steep cliffs dropping down to the sea and dominated by a cave (Grotta del Pellegrino) which is about 300 m deep. There are plans to make the area of sea off the peninsula into a marine nature reserve.

San Marco Beach at Calatabiano, and the beaches at Fiumefreddo and Mascali (Province of Catania). The area of the coast south of the mouth of the Alcantara River has a broad beach several kilometers long with sand and pebbles. The land behind it has been replanted with eucalyptus and acacias. Development along the coast is still fairly limited (there is a small holiday camp at San Marco, and a paper factory at Fiumefreddo) and citrus groves and fields of crops run down to the edge of the beach. This part of the coast is important from an environmental point of view because it has many springs and water courses with extremely cold water, providing the ideal habitat for acquatic plants of particular importance.

Isolabella Beach (Province of Messina). Sicilians are proud of this beach, with some calling it the most beautiful in Taormina. It is located right in front of Isola Bella: white sand, sparse vegetation. A sizeable section is quite developed, but for about 2 km the sand is free and clean. Once you are at the beach, you can try to head to Isola Bella: many boats, for a fee, make the crossing. The island is covered in vegetation and dominated by an old castle that might be turned into a marine museum.

The same boats will also take you to Giardini Naxos, via the Grotta Azzurra, where the water is stunning and the seabed is lit up to allow you a better view of the underwater creatures.

FOOD IN SICILY

This region dominated by farmland produces a huge number of typical foods and wines, including some that are virtually unique in the Italian scenario. Cheeses, olive oil, fruit and vegetables are the basis of the foods produced on the island, plus Mediterranean specialties like pistachios and prickly pears. For sheer variety, quality and tradition, this region has no equal. Then there are specialties from the sea, like swordfish and tuna from Favignana.

TYPICAL LOCAL DISHES

Arancini di riso. These riceballs, filled with meat sauce and mixed with peas, cubes of soft cheese and other ingredients are served as starters in restaurants, but are also sold in delicatessens and pizzerias.

Caponata di verdure. Caponata is one of Sicily's great vegetable starters. First various vegetables are cooked separately, then fried in oil and sprinkled with vinegar. Olives, anchovies and capers are then added.

Cuscus. This dish is no other than a typical Tunisian couscous that has become a traditional dish around Marsala and Trapani. Cuscus is made with durum wheat grains, left to dry in the sun and preserved. Sicilian cuscus is steamed and served with various types of fish, shellfish and seafood.

Pasta con le sarde. This is Sicily's most exotic pasta dish. When cooked, the pasta is garnished with sardines (boned and chopped into pieces), which are fried in oil, capers, wild fennel seeds, anchovies, pepper, pine nuts, raisins and onions.

Pasta alla Norma. The typical dish of Catania is named after the opera by Vincenzo Bellini, who was born there. Generally the pasta used is spaghetti, which is covered by slices of eggplant fried in oil, topped with a tomato sauce and grated salty ricotta.

The typical Sicilian red orange.

Insalata d'arancia. A delicious orange salad made with thinly sliced oranges tossed in oil, salt and pepper.

Pesce spada a ghiotta. This way of cooking swordfish, typical of the Messina area, involves cooking slices of swordfish with tomatoes, potatoes, olives, capers and celery. Swordfish is also cooked on the grill, or 'alla stimpirata', a sweet-sour recipe from Syracuse.

Sarde a beccafico. These sardines are common all over Sicily. The heads are removed and the fish is slit open, cleaned and flattened. They are placed in a pan with olive oil and sprinkled with a mixture of toasted breadcrumbs, anchovies dissolved in hot oil, pine nuts, cinnamon and lemon or orange juice. They are then baked in the oven and sprinkled with lemon or orange juice.

Cherries decorate the summer *cannolo*, known locally as *ova murin*.

Cannoli siciliani. These sinful Sicilian cakes are famous. First the dough is cooked in the oven, forming short crunchy tubes which are then filled with a mixture of sweet ricotta, pistachios or chopped candied fruit.

Cassata. This famous and very sweet dessert is of Arabic origin. Sponge cake is covered with a ricotta cream with icing sugar, decorated with candied fruit and surrounded with green almond paste.

Frutti di Martorana. Named after a convent in Palermo, these tiny cakes made of ground almonds look like real fruit.

Granita. This Sicilian water-ice comes in many flavors, the most common being coffee and lemon.

TYPICAL LOCAL PRODUCTS

Pecorino siciliano DOP. A hard ewe's milk cheese with a strong flavor made all over Sicily but especially in the hills and mountains between October and June. Sometimes whole black peppercorns are added.

It is also used fresh: before the salting process it is called 'tuma' and, after 2 weeks, becomes 'primusali'.

Ragusano DOP. Made with whole raw milk from cows of the native Sicilian Modicana breed, this rectangular cheese has rounded edges. When young it has a delicate, mild taste and becomes tangy when aged (up to 6 months). Older cheese is used for grating.

Salame Sant'Angelo. This salami from Messina made using only natural ingredients, including finely chopped lean meat, is probably one of Italy's oldest sausages.

Pesce spada. Swordfish are fished in the Straights of Messina using boats with a very tall mast with a lookout post and a long structure protruding beyond the prow. Smoked swordfish is a local delicacy.

Tonno. Tuna fish can be up to 3m long and weigh up to 100kg. The meat is very nutritious and can be preserved in various ways. Tuna roe is used to make bottarga and lattume (fish testicles) is another delicacy. The Alalonga species of tuna has long fins and is particular prized. Shoals of tuna are driven into long nets and channeled into the 'death chamber' where they are killed.

Cappero di Pantelleria IGP. Capers grow on low shrubs in the sun-baked fields of Pantelleria and are one of the island's distinctive features. High-quality capers are also grown on the island of Salina.

Pomodorini di Pachino IGP. These small, round, juicy tomatoes grow on 'vines' trained on the walls of the houses and are preserved in jars for the winter.

Nocellara del Belice DOP. This distinctive eating olive with a firm green pulp is produced in the Belice Valley and especially around Castelvetrano.

Olio Extravergine di Oliva. Extra-virgin olive oil is made all over the island but the characteristics vary depending on the kind of olive. Some oils have been awarded the DOP label, with the following sub-denominations: Mt Etna, Mts Iblei, Valdemone, Mazara Valley, Belice Valley and Trapani valleys.

Arance rosse di Sicilia IGP. Blood oranges, introduced to Sicily by the Arabs in the Middle Ages, grow all over the island and have a particularly red, juicy pulp.

Uva (grapes). This island with a long tradition of wine-making also produces excellent table grapes. For example, uva da tavola di Canicattì IGP, grown in the hinterland of Agrigento; uva da tavola di Mazzarone IGP, used as fruit or for making puddings, jams,

jellies and sorbets; zibibbo from Pantelleria, with large, oval, firm, sweet, white grapes is used to make Passito di Pantelleria, but is also excellent for eating.

Fico d'India dell'Etna DOP. Prickly pears can be yellow or pinky-red, are juicy and full of tiny seeds. Often cultivated using natural methods and used to make an excellent mostarda (type of chutney).

Pistacchio di Bronte. Pistachios, introduced by the Arabs, are only grown at Bronte and a few other towns near Mount Etna and the Province of Enna. The plant thrives on arid ground and grows to a height of 5-6 m.

Tuna fish of Favignana.

WINES

The vineyards of Sicily can be divided into three main areas: the area around Trapani and the famous wines of Marsala in the west, the wines of Etna in the north-east, and the wines from the area of Ragusa in the south-east. This is an ideal habitat for growing vines. The variety of the soil combined with a warm, ventilated climate produces excellent results and guarantees quality. In fact, Sicily has the highest production in Italy and, with its 20 DOC wines, also has the highest development potential.

Many wines are made with traditional grape varietals: for white wine, Catarratto, Ansonica (or Inzolia), Grillo and the renowned Marsala; for red wine, Nero d'Avola, with its intense bouquet and warm, rounded flavor. There are many red and white wines made with grape varietals grown worldwide: white Chardonnay and Sauvignon, and red Syrah, Merlot, and Cabernet Sauvignon. Special wines from this area include Moscato di Noto and Moscato di Siracusa, Malvasia di Lipari and Zibibbo di Pantelleria, perfect companions for puddings.

FOOD

In 1832, at the beginning of a tour of the East, Lamartine landed in the Gulf of Palmas (between the island of S. Antioco and the coast of the Sulcis) and described a beach "at the far end of the gulf," in all likelihood, the littoral strip of the Stagno di S. Caterina: white sand, large thistles, little clumps of aloe vera, and, in his words, "little herds of wild horses roaming free through the heath, galloping up to investigate us, sniffing the air and then, with a wild neighing, tearing off again like flocks of crows; a mile away are grey, bare mountains, with patches of dried-out plants on their slopes; a sky you might expect to see in Africa arches over the limestone peaks; an immense silence hangs over the countryside...." This handsome description may serve as an introduction to this first Sardinian route, more than half of it is coastline, and all of it encompasses vast landscapes, sweeping horizons, with the colors of the sea, cliffs, shoals, and rocks of every mineral family. Let the sea not distract the traveller from the history that came from that sea: Cagliari, originally Karalis, which is now a large town, like Nora and Bithia, along the coast of the great southern gulf of Sardinia, were all cities founded by Phoenicians. Nora, on a spit of land jutting out into the sea, was the first city on Sardinia, according to classical lore, and was founded by Phoenicians from the Iberian Peninsula; like the other Phoenician colonies, it was absorbed by Carthage, itself a Phoenician colony. Bithia was first discovered in 1835 by A. La Marmora, and as late as the reign of Marcus Aurelius was administered by "sufeti," or Punic magistrates. On the western coast of the Iglesiente, Sant'Antioco stands on the island of the same name; it occupies the site of one of the earliest Phoenician cities on Sardinia, Sulcis. During Carthaginian times, it was a major mining center in the Sulcis-Igliesiente area.

NOT TO BE MISSED

Cagliari (➡ see below), clustered around the Pisan-Spanish castle, Su Casteddu, is the chief town in Sardinia. **Nora*** was a Phoenician city that later became Roman; it is still being excavated, and certain parts are now under the waves. Bithia is another city of Phoenician origin, extending out along a small promontory. **Tratalias**: this village on the edge of the reclaimed marshes of Sulcis. Romanesque church, S. Maria di Monserrato. **Sant'Antioco** is the chief town of the island of the same name, which was known as "Sulcis" in Phoenician times; note the Museo Archeologico Ferruccio Barreca and relics of sacrifices. **Carloforte** is the chief town of the nearby island of S. Pietro; settled by exiled Ligurians, from Tunisia, in the 18th century. **Carbonia** was a mining town built in the 1930s; most mining has stopped among the bare mountains. **Masua**, with a handsome and dramatic port, lies between crags and grottoes. Iglesias, in the heart of the mining region, still has medieval details; note the Museo Mineralogico, which boasts a vast collection of minerals. **Siliqua** has traditional houses in the old center; to the south are the ruins of the Castle of Acquafredda. **Villa Speciosa** has a Romanesque church, S. Platano (12C). **Uta** also has a Romanesque church (12C). **Assemini** is known for the cross-shaped Oratory of S. Giovanni, in Byzantine style.

CAGLIARI

Bastione di Saint Remy. The Bastion was built between 1899 and 1902, altering the old Spanish bastions (Sperone and Zecca) at the southern edge of the Castle. It has two terraces: one named after Umberto I, and the other, smaller and higher, dedicated to St Catherine. The Bastion links the Castle to the Villanova quarter; originally it was a promenade and belvedere, enhanced by the impressive Neo-Classic facade in granite and limestone, with triumphal arch and long flight of steps leading towards Piazza Costituzione. It was seriously damaged by bombing in the second world war, and has been faithfully reconstructed. Today, it is the location for the Sunday second-hand market.

Le torri di S. Pancrazio e dell'Elefante. The two twin towers of St Pancras and the Elephant, in limestone ashlar, were built respectively in 1305 and 1307, and are landmarks that really stand out on Cagliari's landscape. The tower of St Pancras on the northern side of the Castle, at its highest point, gave control of all the territory around the city; it was used as a prison from the 17th to the end of the 19th century. The Elephant tower marked entry to the lower part of the quarter; an elephant sculpted on the tower has become a symbol of the city.

Cathedral of S. Maria, was built in Pisan style (along the Romanesque lines which developed in Pisa between the 11th-12th centuries); it was extended at the end of the 13th

A delightful view of Cagliari at night.

century, and then modified to Baroque style in the 17th to 18th centuries. In 1933 a new facade was built, where sculptural work from the original church was recycled. The beautiful transept portals (there is a Roman sarcophagus front above the right portal) and the bell tower also survive from the original building. Inside, on the counter-facade, there are two **pulpits***, originally part of a single ambo (raised platform in the presbytery, for giving readings from the Bible); they were created by Gugliemo da Pisa in 1159-62, for Pisa cathedral, and donated to Cagliari in 1312. The second chapel on the right has a statue of the Black Madonna, in gilded wood (14C). In the right transept, there is a Gothic chapel built under the Aragonese. In the left transept, a chapel from the original Pisan cathedral, and at the back, the magnificent mausoleum of Martin II of Aragon (1676).

Cittadella dei Musei. This modern complex of museums has a great view and occupies a vast area which was used as a military arsenal until 1825; what remains of Pisan, Aragonese, Spanish and Savoy fortifications can be seen here. The museums are: the Museo Archeologico Nazionale (National Archeological Museum), the Pinacoteca Nazionale (National Art Gallery), the Museo d'Arte Siamese (Museum of Siamese Art) and the Raccolta delle Cere Anatomiche (Collection of Anatomic Waxes).

Museo Archeologico Nazionale. In 1993 the National Archeological Museum was moved from its historic site in Piazza Indipendenza, where it had been since 1905. The museum clearly shows the history of Sardinia, from before the development of the Nuraghic Civilisation, with finds from the Su Carroppu cave (5th millennium BC), ranging up to early Christian times, with finds from Corpus and S. Lussorio di Fordongianus. Objects are exhibited which date from pre-historic times, from the Copper and Iron Ages, from Phoenician-Carthaginian and Carthaginian-Roman times, and from Greco-Roman and Roman-Christian times. There is a very important collection of small Nuraghic **bronzes*** (9-8C BC), in the form of votive incense-boats, warriors, workers and priests, which provide valuable information about the social and religious life of the proto-Sardinians. There is also Phoenician material, such as a sacrificial altar and steles, from the Tharros Tophet (Phoenician-Carthaginian sanctuary).

Pinacoteca Nazionale. The National Art Gallery, on three floors, follows the history of Sardinian painting and the spread of the Catalan-Valencian school in the 15th and 16th centuries. The top floor contains retablos from Sardinian churches. Retablos (from the Latin retro tabula, meaning "behind the altar"). They are large wooden structures, placed behind the altar, which were made by assembling various component parts in wood (panels, frames). The oldest were made by Catalan artists who came to Sardinia during the Aragonese occupation; 16th-century retablos are by Sardinian artists, such as Michele Cavaro, with the Triptych of the Consolation and Pietro Cavaro, with his St Augustine in Meditation. The middle floor has 17th-18th-century paintings. On the lower floor, a varied collection ranges from Flemish paintings to works by contemporary Sardinian artists.

Museo d'Arte Siamese Stefano Cardu. This museum has around 1300 pieces, including porcelain, arms, coins, and gold, silver and ivory objects, from Asia.

Raccolta delle Cere Anatomiche di Clemente Susini. This Collection of Anatomic Waxes has 80 models reproducing parts of the human body. The models were made in Florence, between 1803 and 1805, by Clemente Susini (1754-1814), based on dissections by the Sardinian anatomist Francesco Antonio Boi (1767-1855). In recent years, because of their exceptional quality, some waxes have been exhibited in museums in London, Milan, Paris and Tokyo.

Museo di Mineralogia L. De Prunner – Museo Sardo di Geologia e Paleontologia D. Lovisato. The Mineralogy Museum and the Sardinian Geology and Paleontology Museum are located in the Department of Soil Sciences; they were founded in 1802, when Carlo Felice, the Savoy king, exhibited his collections, which he gave to the university in 1806. The mineralogy museum has mineral and rock samples, such as silver from Sarrabus and Carlo Alberto Lamarmora's Sardinian rock collection. The geology and paleontology museum was improved and re-organised at the end of the 19th century, by Domenico Lovisato, who it is named after; it has a rich fossil collection.

S. Michele. This is one of Sardinia's finest examples of Spanish Baroque architecture; it was built by the Jesuits in the 17th century. A portico with three arches leads into the vestibule where the pulpit of Charles V, carved in bas-relief, is located. It is believed that it was here that the Emperor took part in religious ceremonies in 1535 before the expedition against Tunisia, which left from the port of Cagliari. The interior, with beautiful marble and wood ornamentation, has an octagonal ground-plan with radial chapels.

Anfiteatro romano e Villa di Tigellio. The 2nd-century amphitheater is one of the most remarkable Roman buildings in Sardinia. It is almost entirely dug out of the rock; a considerable amount survives of the elliptical rows of seats, the cavea, the barriers and the podium where the town worthies sat. It is believed, although there is no concrete evidence, that Villa di Tigellio is named after Caesar's and Cleopatra's Sardinian musician friend who lived in the 1st century BC. It has three urban Roman houses (1C AD).

Necropoli di Tuvixeddu. The Tuvixeddu necropolis is Phoenician-Carthaginian, and later was used by the Romans. It has over a hundred hypogeum-type tombs, where entry is gained through vertical shafts; burial goods have been found here dating from the 6th century BC to the 1st century AD. One of the best examples of Carthaginian tomb painting can be seen in the tomba dell'Ureo (Tomb of the Uraeus).

Galleria Comunale d'Arte Moderna. The Municipal Modern Art Gallery occupies a late 18th-century building, originally the royal powder magazine. It was converted to become the art gallery in the late 1920s, by a designer from Cagliari, Uboldo Badas. The elegant Neo-Classic facade was built in 1828. The gallery houses the Ingrao Collection and the Sardinian Artists Municipal Collection. The former has of around 500 works including paintings, sculptures and drawings by early 20th-century Italian artists (U. Boccioni, G. Morandi, F. Depero). The latter has paintings and sculptures from 1900 to 1970 by Sardinia's best-known artists. There is also the Biblioteca Ingrao, a library with around 4000 history of art books.

S. Agostino. The church was designed by the Swiss architect, Giorgio Palearo, in 1577, and is one of Sardinia's few Renaissance buildings. Excavation work has revealed Roman and late-Roman remains which suggest that the whole area may have contained an elaborate thermal baths complex.

S. Domenico. The first church of St Dominic, according to tradition, was built in 1254; today almost nothing remains of the late-Gothic church, started in the early 15th century. The damage inflicted during WW II meant that the church had to be rebuilt, in 1954. The crypt contains parts of the late-Gothic building; next to the church, the beautiful cloister is partly late-Gothic (15C) and partly Renaissance (16C).

S. Saturno. The church of St Saturn is also known as the church of Ss Cosmas and Damian; it is one of the oldest and most important of early Christian buildings in Sardinia. It was built in the 5th-6th century, on the site where Saturn of Cagliari was martyred. In 1089 it was converted into a basilica: it consists of an eastern part, with nave and two side aisles, built in Romanesque style in the 11th-12th century by workers from Provence, and of a front section dating from the same time, which was converted into an atrium after the ceiling collapsed. Excavation has revealed a 2nd-5th-century pre-Christian and Christian necropolis.

Sanctuary and basilica of Bonaria. This large 18th-century basilica is dedicated to the Madonna, Protectress of Sailors, and is a place of pilgrimage. It has a modern facade, and stands beside the old 14th-century sanctuary (subsequently altered), the only building that survives to testify the presence of the Aragonese, during the siege of the Pisan Castle. The venerated wood statue of the Madonna dates from the 15th century, but according to legend the statue was washed up on shore in 1370. Next to the sanctuary is the Museo di Nostra Signora di Bonaria; it contains the Treasury, archeological remains and a collection of historical model boats and of ex-votos offered over the centuries by sailors who came to pray here.

FROM ORISTANO TO ALGHERO

Sparse trees, prickly-pear bushes, vast horizons: the hill of Monastir, some twenty km north of Cagliari, offers a vantage point from which to appreciate the size of the Campidani, a broad plain in southern Sardinia. One historian wrote that the view helped him understand the seeds of war between Rome and Carthage, when the fault lines of history and geography became evident before his eyes: it was over the harvests of this vast fertile plain that two great ancient powers of the hungry Mediterranean fought to the death. The Campidani was a historic breadbasket of the region. It was created by the ancient Carthaginians, who chopped down dense forests; as late as the 18th century, by the records of the port of Marseilles, this made Sardinia the fifth-largest producer and exporter of wheat and other crops. After crossing the Campidani – note the reclaimed land around Arborea – you reach the sea, replete with history and bordered by fragmentary relics of ancient peoples from distant lands. In the Gulf of Oristano, set on the slender peninsula of Capo S. Marco, is Tharros, founded by the Phoenicians around 800 BC and later used by the Carthaginians as a stopover base on the route to Massalia (Marseilles). The sea becomes a succession of little "calette," or coves, and rocks at Santa Caterina di Pittinuri; nearby are the insubstantial ruins of Cornus, probably a Carthaginian settlement. From Bosa, a town on an estuary, you can sail down to the sea along the Temo River: coral-diving and fine goldwork are pursued here. Then you drive along a seashore with vivid pink sunsets, a jagged coastline, attractive little beaches, and, at last, Alghero, standing out sharply against the bright waters of the roadstead behind, perched on its small promontory: a fortress with the population and facilities of a town – "Bonita, por mi fé y bien assentada" (Lovely, in faith, and well built) was the imperial opinion of Charles V, according to local lore – and the Catalonian architecture and language left by mid-13th-century Iberian colonists.

NOT TO BE MISSED

Dolianova has a Romanesque church, S. Pantaleo, with remains of 12th-13th-century frescoes in the apse. **Samassi** has another Romanesque church, S. Gemiliano. **Sanluri**: in the middle of this farming village is a 13th-century castle which also houses the Museo "Duca d'Aosta" with relics dating back to the Risorgimento and the two World Wars. Sardara boasts the 14th-century church of S. Gregorio and, to the north, the "nuraghic" well-temple of S. Anastasia. S. Giusta* is a large Romanesque church near the vast pond of the same name. **Oristano** (➡ see below) is a thriving modern town, with few traces of its medieval past. **Tharros*** was a Phoenician city, later Carthaginian and then Roman, now partly underwater and partly on a peninsula near Capo S. Marco. **Santa Caterina di Pittinuri** is a beach resort with

Bosa is a lovely little medieval hamlet.

limestone rocks and, nearby, the archeological sites of Columbaris and Cornus. **Cuglieri**, at the base of the Montiferru, is where you turn off for the detour to San Leonardo de Siete Fuentes, a rustic village with 7 therapeutic springs, amidst holm-oaks, oaks, and elms. **Bosa** is a little town on the north bank of the estuary of the Temo River, beneath the walls of the Serravalle castle; on the other bank is the church of S. Pietro Extra Muros (11C). To the west, the port and beach of Bosa Marina. **Alghero** (➡ see below): 16th-century bastions gird the old town, Catalonian in style, set on a promontory overlooking the brilliant roadstead; across the gulf is Capo Caccia*.

ORISTANO

Oristano is situated just inland from the gulf of Oristano, halfway along the west coast of Sardinia; it lies at the western end of a large, flat flood plain, bounded to the north by the Tirso River, to the west by coastal dunes, and to the south by a lagoon or lake (lo stagno di Santa Giusta). As early as the 7th century, the Byzantine writer George of Cyprus referred to Oristano's lake *(Aristianes limine)*. In the 12th century, the city's name was wrongly assumed to derive from the words "Aureum Stagnum" (meaning "golden pond" in Latin); the city's coat-of-arms shows a piece of land emerging from a golden lagoon. In fact, the names derives from *Aristianum*: in Roman times, large tracts of land here were owned by a man named Aristius. There were three towns in the area inland from the gulf, in ancient times: Tharros on Capo San Marco to the north, Neapolis south-east of Capo Frasca, and Òthoca near today's town of Santa Giusta. The first traces of the new town date from around the 6th century, and the beginning of the Byzantine age: a necropolis developed around the church of S. Maria Assunta (St Mary Assumption), which became the town's cathedral in the 11th century. A number of reasons (ports silting up, piracy, decreasing population) led to the abandonment of Tharros and Neapolis. Othoca, renamed Sancta Justa, became less important than Aristiane which was protected from the sea and lagoons. From the end of the 13th century, the center of the medieval city was surrounded by a turreted city wall. There were two points of entry: Porta Manna (Great Gate) to the north, and Porta Mari (Sea or Lagoon Gate) to the south-west, which was destroyed in 1907, and was near the torre di S. Filippo (tower of St Philip) which once stood in Piazza Manno. In the 12th century Oristano sided with the Aragonese, thus avoiding alliance with the city of Pisa; in 1323 it supported the establishment of the *Regnum Sardiniae et Corsicae (Kingdom of Sardinia and Corsica)*. In the mid 14th century, the great ruler Marianus IV and, subsequently, his children Ugone III and Eleonora d'Arborea were forced to fight against the Catalan-Aragonese armies. The war ended with the defeat of the d'Arborea dynasty at Sanluri (1409). The three centuries of Aragonese and Spanish rule brought about a steep decline in the city's fortunes. In the 18th century (and even more in the 19th) the city underwent a remarkable transformation in terms of building and urban layout. Oristano's new areas (Città Giardino, San Nicola, Torangius) changed the town's appearance, with their enormous buildings in ladiris, surrounded by high walls.

Duomo. The Duomo is dedicated to St Mary Assumption. Although it has an 18th-century appearance, it was built in the 13th century; the bell tower dates from the 15th century. The first chapel on the right has a polychrome wood Annunciation by Nino Pisano (14C) and parts of two 12th-century Romanesque ambos (an ambo is a raised platform in the presbytery, for reading holy texts), which were recycled and used again by a 14th-century Catalan artist. The presbytery has 19th-century paintings by Giovanni Marghinotti, and an 18th-century oval (Assumption) by Vittorio Amodeo Rapous. The 14th-century chapel of Remedy is on the right. The large chapels at the end of the two arms of the transept date from 1830; four standards captured from the French during the 1637 siege hang from the walls.

S. Francesco. The church of St Francis was originally built in the 13th century, and later rebuilt in Neo-Classic style. The left altar has a 15th-century wood Crucifix* of the Catalan school. The central painting in the sacristy altarpiece is by Pietro Cavaro (1533); the others are in the Antiquarium Arborense. There's a superb mid-13th-century Gothic cloister*, modified according to Catalan style in the 16th century. The nearby Piazza Eleonora is named after Eleonora d'Arborea, mistress of the city from 1383 to 1404 and famous for the Logu charter, an important medieval legislative codex.

Antiquarium Arborense. The Antiquarium was founded in 1938, when the State acquired the collection belonging to Efisio Pischedda, an archeologist and lawyer. The collection has been housed since 1992 in the historic Palazzo Parpaglia, which was specially renovated for the purpose. There are three main sections. The first contains prehistoric finds from the Sinis area: Nuraghic bronzes; Etruscan, Greek and Roman pottery; and Phoenician-Carthaginian finds exhibited in a reconstructed Phoenician tomb from Tharros. A large model at the center of the room recreates the ancient town of Tharros. The second section has three retablos from churches in Oristano: one by a 15th-century Catalan painter (St Martin), one by Pietro Cavaro in 1533 (Stigmata of St Francis), and one by Antioco Mainas in 1565 (Madonna of the Councillors). The third section has two late 13th-century inscriptions by Marianus II d'Arborea which refer to the construction of the city tower and walls.

Porta Manna. Porta Manna was the town's main gate. It's also known as the torre di Mariano II (tower of Marianus II), after Marianus II d'Arborea who had it built in 1291, although the upper part dates from later. The gate is also known as the torre di S. Cristoforo (St Christopher's tower), since inside there is a retablo of St Christopher, the patron saint of travellers, which was placed inside possibly in the 15th century.

ALGHERO

Although Alghero is situated in an area which has been inhabited for thousands of years, the town itself only really came into existence after the Catalan-Aragonese conquest of Sardinia in 1323. Once Cagliari and Sassari had been occupied, a firm foothold was required in the north-west of the island. So, in 1354 the king, Peter the Ceremonious, sent a large Catalan-Aragonese force. A few months later, Alghero was entirely populated by peoples from the Iberian peninsula. Over the years, according to military requirements, the many little Genoese towers were demolished, the walls were strengthened and extended, and higher larger towers were built. Alghero was raised to the status of city in 1501 and always enjoyed the privileges the Catalans guaranteed to their overseas colonies. Its worst sufferings were caused by the discovery of America and the plague. In the 16th century the gates were opened to outsiders again; palazzi and churches were crowded on top of each other, in order not to keep within the city walls. In 1720, Sardinia came under the Savoys, but Alghero did not lose its taste for Catalan culture. So much so, that in 1850 a catechism was printed in Catalan for the use of the people of Alghero. In the 19th century the city mushroomed: so in the late 1800s, the walls were demolished on the landward side. It is paradoxical, but it was only when Alghero began to change that the in-

habitants began to take an interest in the old town. It was damaged by allied bombing on 17th May 1943, and by the ravages of uncontrolled building and development. The most important signs of the past are found in the old Mediterranean and Catalan city. By following the walls that once enclosed the town, you can really gain an idea of its history. Many of the towers now are used for exhibitions, and you can still see the remains of the walls in between. They were demolished or swallowed up by buildings on the landward side, but still survive on the seaward side.

Cathedral of S. Maria. It was built in the second half of the 16th century. The late-Gothic Catalan apse and bell tower remain of the original building, as well as, inside, the nave and side aisles, the cupola and the chapels off the presbytery. The cathedral's tetrastyle pronaos dates from 1862. The Museo Diocesano d'Arte Sacra (Diocesan Museum of Sacred Art) is next door. It contains the cathedral's treasury and artworks from the churches of the diocese.

The **chiesa di S. Francesc** or **S. Francesco,** (church of St Francis) is a must to visit. It was built at the end of the 15th century in Catalan Gothic style, as evident in the presbytery, some chapels and the polygonal bell tower with spire, that was saved from collapse in 1593. The single original nave was modified to form a central nave and two side aisles. It has been recently restored, and has a fine 15th-century cloister. The late Baroque main altar (1773) in polychrome marble is noteworthy, as well as the 18th-century wood sculpture of Christ at the Column, originally in the chiesa di S. Croce (church of the Holy Cross), which now no longer exists.

The **Mura catalane,** (Catalan Walls) still surround the old town center, on the seaward side. The walls have towers at regular intervals and are pleasant to walk along. The forte della Maddalena (Magdalen Fort) overlooks the port; it was modified in the 18th century. Behind is the porta a mare (sea gate), one of the points of entry to the old quarter. The towers are: torre della Polvorera is on the north-west corner of the bastions, and the octagonal torre di S. Giacomo in Gothic style, on the south-west corner; to the south-east, the torre di Sulis, or de l'Esperò reial, mentioned as early as 1364, but modified to its current appearance under the Spanish; the 16th century torre de Sant Joan and the 14th-century torre de Portal look towards the new part of Alghero.

HIGHLIGHTS

EVENTS IN ALGHERO: ESTATE MUSICALE INTERNAZIONALE

From July to September, classical music concerts conducted and performed by musicians of international fame are held in the cloister of San Francesco and offer evenings with both classical and folk repertoires. For further information: Tel. 07043621

The area overlooking the northern section of the Gulf of Orosei, around Dorgali, and all the way north along the coast to Siniscola and Posada, constitutes the Baronia, a name that dates from the 14th century. The author S. Satta describes spring there: "What sweet aromas amid the reed beds, in the scrub alive with wild hares and partridges, when the bright sunlight revived the dead and abandoned wood of the low-lying vineyards." As you think back on this route, you will certainly remember the coastline, the blue sea, the rosemary growing against the blinding white limestone of Cala Gonone, the Grotta del Bue Marino. Perhaps you will also think of the low circular stone walls of the prehistoric huts, or "nuraghi" (large, tower-shaped prehistoric stone structures peculiar to Sardinia), of the village of Serra Òrrios, with the sound of wind tossing the olive branches; or the Grotta di Ispinigoli, a great cavern with a deep shaft called the Abisso delle Vergini. Carthaginian jewelry found at the bottom of the shaft, now in the Museo Archeologico di Dorgali, lends some credibility to the legend of bloodcurdling virgin sacrifices. The Ogliastra is another broad plain of eastern Sardinia. A landscape of rocks, harsh but varied, and dotted with pasturage, vineyards, ancient olive groves; you cross the Ogliastra between Tortolì and Lanusei, after fine panoramic views from the high ridge road over the hills. The region may take its name from the little island off S. Maria Navarrese: Isola dell'Ogliastra, or Agugliastra, with reddish boulders of porphyry in the turquoise sea. A timeless scene, with a sense of how it must have looked to the ancient inhabitants. The last leg of this route, on the way back to Nuoro, runs through mountains: you climb to the slopes of the Gennargentu "where amidst white granite the oaks and the dark ilex toss their leaves" (Cardarelli); then you run through the Barbagla dl Ollolai, a stern archaic landscape peopled by shepherds.

NOT TO BE MISSED

Macomer: This town is home to an amazing number of nuraghic constructions. **Nuoro** (➠ see below): a typical inland Sardinian town, birthplace of 1926 Nobel laureate Grazia Deledda. **Oliena** is an old town with traditional houses lining long, narrow, twisting lanes, at the base of the limestone mountain, the Sopramonte; costumes are worn for the feast of S. Lussorio, on 21 August. **Su Gologone** is a karstic stream, the most important in Sardinia, in an idyllic patch of landscape. **Serra Orrios*** is a village of "nuraghe," amidst olive and mastic trees. **Grotta di Ispinigoli**: this cave runs for 10 km, one of Italy's largest; one of the stalagmites is 38 meters high. **Dorgali** is a village sheltered by Mt Bardia; from the nearby fishing village of Cala Gonone, on the Gulf of Orosei, you can take a boat to the Grotta del Bue Marino (or Grotto of the Monk Seal, an animal which perhaps was once found here). **Santa Maria Navarrese**: sand, shoals, islets, and a venerable old wild olive tree by the church, which may have been built in the 11th century, supposedly in thanks for the survival of a shipwrecked princess; note the 17th-century. Spanish tower situated on the coast. **Arbatax** has red porphyry cliffs. **Lanusei** is the capital of Ogliastra. **Fonni** is the highest village in Sardinia (1,000 m), with skiing in winter. **Mamoiada** lies secluded in an oak and chestnut forest. **Orgosolo** is a harsh town of shepherds by the Sopramonte, with fine views. To celebrate Assumption Day on 15 August, a procession is held with knights in costume.

NUORO

Nuoro straddles a rugged granitic ridge which extends out from Mt Ortobene. As the crow flies, the sea is about thirty kms away; the closest port, Olbia, over a hundred kms away. The city is the heart of inland Sardinia's special culture and traditions.

In 1975, a tomb dated some time between the 7th and 8th centuries BC was found during renovation work on an old building in Via Ballero: this is the oldest evidence of human occupation of the site where Nuoro stands today.

The first written documents date from the 14th century: in the *Rationes Decimarum* imposed by Pope John XXII, Nuoro figures as one of the most highly-taxed towns in the diocese of Ottana, and hence one of the most important. The place name Nugor had already been recorded in various 11th-13th-century records. In the 16th century, the town grew considerably; in the 17th century, it had 1600 inhabitants and many churches had been built in addition to those already in existence, church of S. Croce and the late 16th-century church of the Salvatore.

The Tamuli archeological site near Macomer.

es at least 4 anthological contemporary art exhibitions every year.

Museo Deleddiano – Casa Natale di Grazia Deledda, The **Deleddiano Museum*** is in Grazia Deledda's childhood home, a typical 19th-century Nuorese house belonging to a comfortably-off family. Papers and documents relating to the writer and her work are on display in her bedroom: letters, information on films and plays based on her works, Italian and foreign first editions, personal objects, and a copy of her Nobel Prize for literature (1926). The kitchen and portico have been used to recreate environments typical of the agricultural society of her time, furnished with household and work implements and equipment.

Museo della Vita e delle Tradizioni Popolari Sarde**. The Museum of Sardinian Life and Folk Traditions was founded in 1963 but has only been open permanently since 1976. It occupies a building that was specially constructed for the purpose, in Sardinian rural style. The museum shows aspects of domestic and social life. Exhibits include: objects, implements and furniture used in daily life; textile handcrafts (blankets, mats, a funerary rug); and gold and silver jewelry. There is an important collection of traditional costumes, some of which are extremely rare. The museum also has sections on carnival, with displays of costumes and masks, on traditional bread- and cake-making, and on musical instruments.

Museo Archeologico Nazionale. The National Archeological Museum, which opened in July 2002, has a paleontological section with Plio-Pleistocene mammal fossils from the Mt Tattavista vertebrate deposit. There is an interesting hyena skull, and the skull of a type of monkey (Macaca majori) that was widespread in Sardinia at the time. Other rooms show archeological material from the early Neolithic Age up until historical times (stone implements, pottery, bone jewelry, shells, amber), found in areas further inland. The Nuraghic section is the most important; it has reconstructions of various funerary and ceremonial monuments, with mainly bronze materials that were found inside the monuments.

In 1777, with 2782 inhabitants, it was one of the area's largest towns; most inhabitants were shepherds and peasants. Its layout was simple, and it counted 15 churches. The early 19th century was a peaceful time. This came to an end with the royal directives forbidding common use of land (*enclosures decree*, 1820). In the late-19th and early-20th centuries, the town was a center for much original cultural and socio-political activity, which drew inspiration largely from the conflict between traditional Sardinian society and the new society of the nation state. Examples of some of those who were active: the poet S. Satta (1867-1914), the writer G. Deledda (1871-1936, Nobel Prize winner for literature in 1926), and the essayist and politician A. Deffenu (1890-1918). When Nuoro was made a provincial capital in 1927, it grew enormously: the population increased from 8,534 in 1921 to 16,949 in 1951. In the period after the second world war, Nuoro continued to expand, at the same time as it was gradually changing from an agricultural town into a more administrative and service-oriented center.

Duomo, built between 1836 and 1854, has paintings by local 19th-century painters, and a Jesus among the Doctors, perhaps painted by L. Giordano. An attractive nearby square, Piazza Sebastiano Satta, was renovated by C. Nivola in 1967, and named after the poet who was born in a house which still stands there.

Museo dell'Arte della Provincia di Nuoro – MAN. The permanent collection in the gives a good idea of 20th-century Sardinian art, with works by Sardinian artists such as B. Biasi, C. Romagna, Delitala, Floris, Nivola, Pintori and Fancello. The museum organis-

I sola di S. Stefano is one of the seven main islands – the other six being La Maddalena, Caprera, Spargi, Budelli, Razzoli, and S. Maria – in the archipelago that lies just off the NE coast of the Gallura region. It is wedged between Palau on the coast and the island of La Maddalena; the channels that separate it from the two shores are only a few hundred meters across. On February 1793, the 500 soldiers of the Kingdom of Sardinia who were garrisoning the island of La Maddalena saw 23 vessels emerge from the sound of Bonifacio, beyond the Strait of Bonifacio, landing cannon and soldiers on S. Stefano. The purpose and consequences of this expedition are still matters for historical study; it was commanded by a Corsican, C. Cesari, while the artillery – two cannons and a mortar – was commanded by a 23-year-old Corsican captain, Napoleon Bonaparte. Bonaparte began to bombard La Maddalena (a shell is still on display in the mayor's office), but his Provençal marines mutinied when ordered to land. A disgusted Bonaparte hastily departed for Toulon. The remarkable archipelago where this minor chapter of history unfolded, overlooking steep jagged rocks, tufts of maquis, inlets, narrow beaches, and sheer rock walls and shoals churning white amidst the cobalt water and the strong winds of the Strait of Bonifacio, lies halfway along this route on the northern coast of Sardinia. Before you get here, you will have seen the broad gulf of the Asinara, the fortifications of Castelsardo, the red cliffs of the Costa Paradiso, the cluster pines and granite of Capo Testa. It ends with exclusive resort areas among the promontories and inlets of the Costa Smeralda, with their "Neo-Mediterranean" architecture, wild nature, and rich guests.

NOT TO BE MISSED

Porto Torres is a port and Industrial town on the Golfo dell'Asinara, with the 11th-century. Basilica di S. Gavino and Roman ruins. Nostra Signora de Tergu is a 13th-century. Romanesque church which originally belonged to a Benedictine monastery. **Castelsardo**: set on a promontory, surrounded by old walls, this village is crisscrossed with narrow lanes and steep stairs; the castle houses a museum which displays examples of local crafts. **Santa Teresa Gallura** is a fishing village and

Costa Smeralda has crystal-clear water and pristine nature.

a resort town on a deep inlet facing the windy Strait of Bonifacio; to the west is the granite promontory of Capo Testa. **Palau** is a beach town and landing point for ships heading for **La Maddalena** (➡ see below): the handsome town is the only one on the island. You can set out for boat trips through the sunny archipelago; **Caprera** island is where Garibaldi died. **Baia Sardinia** is a fine beach area. **Porto Cervo**: the luxurious village and marina are the best-known resort on the Costa Smeralda. **Cala di Volpe** is an inlet in a glorious setting. **Porto Rotondo** has a famed beach in a cozy little bay. **Olbia** (➡ see below) is a port at the end of the Gulf of Olbia, with a Romanesque church, S. Simplicio.

OLBIA

Olbia is situated on a stretch of coastal plain which slopes towards the inner part of the bay of Olbia; the imposing mass of **isola di Tavolara*** (Tavolara Island) towers over the town. It was an important port in antiquity; with the growth of the tourist industry over the last thirty years, it has recovered its function as the port linking Sardinia with the Italian mainland. Olbia's important sea-

port and airport make it the busiest Italian city in terms of passengers passing through. Its new transport role has produced rapid growth, compromising the town's appearance and layout.

The bay of Olbia was densely populated in pre-Nuraghic and Nuraghic times, as revealed by dozens of nuraghes, giants' tombs, megalithic fortifications and sacred wells found here. The city originated on a square-shaped terrace slightly higher than the sea: it was almost certainly founded by the Carthaginians (5-4C BC). From Roman times, Olbia's growth went hand in hand with the growth of the port. For centuries, it was an important and prosperous town; the area inland from Olbia was farmed intensely and dotted with numerous farming towns. Acte, the emperor Nero's powerful concubine, owned land, villas and a brick factory here.

After the fall of the Roman Empire, Olbia suffered the same destruction and ruin as all coastal Sardinian towns suffered with the barbarian invasions. In the few surviving early-medieval documents, it is referred to as Fausiana. New information about Olbia's history is emerging as a result of an exceptional archeological find made when a tunnel was built in the port area: the remains of around ten Roman boats.

In the 11th century, under Pisan rule, the town was rebuilt on the ancient Carthaginian site. It prospered as Terranova (its name until 1939): sea trade and traffic increased again, and farming flourished on the plain. Terranova was a bishop's see; a number of churches were built here, including the fine Romanesque church of S. Simplicio, built between the 11th-12th centuries, in an unusual position in relation to the town center. There then followed a long period of stagnation compounded by famine, disease and malaria. This continued until the 19th century, when the road linking Olbia to the SS 131 (Carlo Felice) road was built; the railway was opened and streams flowing to the sea were channelled. Again, the city grew as its port gained importance. A number of dairy factories were established, and the mussel-farming industry developed in the 1920s. As the city's economy improved, immigrants arrived from central and southern Italy. In the last thirty years of the 20th century, strong demographic growth has lifted Olbia to its position as Sardinia's fourth largest city, and lent it a distinctive ethnic and cultural mix.

Our itinerary provides a clear picture of Olbia's origins and its development. The town also has a marina, a yacht club (near the old port), and many beautiful beaches both to the south and the north; hence it is a good starting point for trips to tourist resorts on the north-east coast (Golfo Aranci) and south-east to Caletta in the Siniscola area.

S. Paolo, the church is just past the art nouveau town hall. It was built after WWII, in granite ashlar with a majolica-tiled cupola. The urban fabric around Corso Umberto is al-

so noteworthy; many buildings have their original granite architraves. The "Simpliciana" Biblioteca comunale (municipal library) has a collection of Nuraghic finds; it's in an Umbertine-style palazzo at the intersection between Corso Umberto and Via della Terme. In Piazza Regina Margherita, a Carthaginian cistern has been discovered and excavated.

S. Simplicio, the church is one of Sardinia's most interesting examples of Romanesque architecture. It was built in stages between the 11th and 12th centuries on a Christian burial area, entirely in granite ashlar; it's simpler than other large Romanesque churches in Sardinia. The interior has pillars and columns supporting the trussed roof and the side aisle vaults. There is a collection of funerary inscriptions, from necropolises in the area, and of Roman milestones.

Sacred well of Sa Testa. This sacred well is situated a few meters from the scenic road to Golfo Aranci. It is considered to be one of the most interesting monuments of the type in Sardinia, and is dated to the middle Nuraghic period (7-6C BC). The vestibule on the lower floor is reached from the large circular enclosure. A 17-step stairway leads from the vestibule to the tholos chamber, where water gushes from the ground.

LA MADDALENA ARCHIPELAGO

The La Maddalena Archipelago is situated at the far north-eastern tip of Sardinia, and is named after the main island in the group. The islands are granite, covering 49.3 km². They were inhabited in pre-historic time and acquired importance under the Romans as bases for ships sailing the Tyrrhenian Sea. After centuries of abandonment, they were once again used in the 12th century by the Pisans and Genoese; then the first inhabited town was established on La Maddalena in the 16th century, when shepherds migrated from Corsica. When Sardinia came under the Piedmontese, the resistance of the rebellious Corsican community was overcome by a military detachment sent to occupy the archipelago in 1767. La Maddalena became more important, with the presence of the Sardinian navy. The town's main structures were built at this time, starting from the original settlement at Cala Gavetta. In 1887, the Italian government chose the island as a strategic naval base, and as such it was important until the end of WWII. The naval base and dock had a great influence on the town, and the population increased. Since the 1970s, there's been a US base for atomic submarines in the strait between the islands of La Maddalena and Santo Stefano.

The breathtakingly beautiful islands and sea, as well as the various bird species found here, make this stretch of the coast one of the Mediterranean's most outstanding in terms of landscape and nature. The need to protect the area's natural, environmental and historic resources led to the establishment in 1996 of the **Parco nazionale Arcipelago La Maddalena*** (national park). It covers an area of over 20,000 hectares – both land and sea – and 180 km of coastline, and includes all the islands which are part of the La Maddalena administrative area. One especially interesting island is Caprera, which was registered by the European Union as one of Europe's most important nature conservation sites, and has been a nature reserve since 1980. In the last thirty years, tourism in the area has received a boost from facilities on some islands; these include the Caprera Sailing Center and TCI tourist resort.

Four of the seven largest islands (Santo Stefano, Spargi, Maddalena, Caprera) are near the Gallura coast; the other three (Budelli, Razzoli, Santa Maria) are nearer the Bocche di Bonifacio, the strait between Sardinia and Corsica.

La Maddalena. Covering an area of 19.61 kmq, and with a 45 km coastline, this is the largest island. It's triangular in shape, rising to a rugged plateau in the center; its highest point (Guardia Vecchia) reaches 156 m.

Lively Piazza Garibaldi, close to the seafront, is full of crowded bars and cafés, and the island's main official buildings, such as the Municipality. The charming old town is nearby, with the parish church of S. Maria Maddalena: it has two silver candleholders and a silver Crucifix donated by Horatio Nelson who anchored off La Maddalena with the British fleet before the Battle of Trafalgar.

Via V. Emanuele leads to the Cala Gavetta port and marina. Piazza Umberto I, where the Navy buildings are, is past the port.

The Museo Archeologico Navale "Nino Lamboglia" is a naval archeology museum with finds from a Roman boat shipwrecked in 120 BC near Spargi. A reconstruction of the hull contains a remarkable number of amphorae arranged according to the method of loading used by the Romans. Objects displayed include nails, tiles, pieces of hull, and equipment used by the crew, illustrating how sailors lived and methods of navigation. Today the town is the base for the Sardinian Autonomous Navy Command and the Navy Non-commissioned Officers School.

Caprera. The island is believed by geographers to be Ptolemy's ancient Phintonis, and is situated east of La Maddalena. It is the second largest island, with a surface area of 15.75 kmq and a coastline of 34 km. The east coast, where Mt Teialone rises to 212 m, is very rugged; the west coast is flatter, with pastures and pine forests. The island was partially acquired in 1855 by Giuseppe Garibaldi who built a house and some rural buildings here. In 1978 a museum was established here, the Museo Nazionale del Compendio garibaldino. It occupies the west side of a courtyard, over which the pine tree towers that Garibaldi planted on the occasion of his daughter Clelia's birth. The museum consists of a number of intercommunicating rooms, relating to the domestic life and interests of Garibaldi, with doors giving direct access outside. The rooms have been preserved with the functions they originally had, and contain objects, furnishings, paintings and mementos. The bed in the room where Garibaldi died is surrounded by a balustrade donated by the Livorno Veterans Association. The oven and windmill built by Garibaldi can be seen behind the house.

Santo Stefano. Santo Stefano is situated between the town of La Maddalena, and Palau on mainland Sardinia. The fort of St George, also known as Napoleon's fort, can be seen from the ferry. It was part of the fortifications built at the end of the 18th century. Napoleon Bonaparte, who at the time was a young lieutenant-colonel in the Corsican National Guard, directed the bombardment of La Maddalena from here during the 1793 French attack. There are two large cannon balls in the La Maddalena municipality.

Spargi. The island is round, with rugged terrain. Its highest point is Mt Guardia Preposti (155 m). There's a small settlement of shepherds and a lovely, much-visited beach, Cala Corsara.

Budelli. This island lies north of Spargi and is uninhabited. It's known for its pink beach; the color comes from minute coral particles. It's also famous because the Italian director Michelangelo Antonioni shot some scenes for "Red Desert" here. In 1992, there were controversial plans to build a tourist resort. Its uniqueness is now protected as part of the Geo-marine Park of La Maddalena. The islands of **Razzoli** and **Santa Maria** lie to the north-west and north-east, facing the Bocche di Bonifacio, and separated by a passage (Passo degli Asinelli). The former is completely uninhabited; its coastline is steep, and is only accessible on the western side. The latter is almost all flat; it's inhabited and partly cultivated.

Santa Teresa Gallura. The town was once a fishing village but today it is a seaside resort. It lies on a rocky terrace, on the west side of a deep bay called Porto Longonsardo, on the northern tip of Sardinia. The bay lies opposite the windy Bocche di Bonifacio separating Sardinia from Corsica. The town was founded in 1808 under the Savoys (Vittorio Emanuele I's wife was called Teresa), to control smuggling and as a strategic defence against Napoleon.

SASSARI

Sassari lies on a gently sloping calcareous plateau, at the edge of the plain running down to the sea. It is Sardinia's second largest city. In the middle ages, in the place where today's city stands, there was a small village called *Tathari*; it grew as people fled here from the Saracens, the Pisans and the Genoese. In 1378 Sassari was occupied and remained under the control of the d'Arborea family until 1420. In the 15th century it became part of the new institutional and administrative system of Sardinia which, as an independent kingdom, was part of the Catalan-Aragonese federation. The flourishing of the Catalan Gothic style in civil and church architecture dates from this time, and today is still a distinctive feature of the old town. Under Spanish rule, the city suffered hard times, largely due to the Mediterranean wars and stagnating trade and commerce. Sassari, of all the towns and cities in Sardinia, was the closest to humanism and the cultural models of the Italian Renaissance. Echoes of 16th-century classicism can be identified in some buildings in the old town, such as Palazzo d'Usini in the old city square known as the *carra manna* (today Piazza Tola), or in the facade of the Jesuit church of Gesù e Maria (Jesus and Mary), today known as S. Caterina (St Catherine).

In 1652, in the midst of a fierce dispute with Cagliari, Sassari was struck by a terrible plague epidemic which decimated the city's population. The second half of the century, however, was not a period of decline: the population increased and the introduction of new types of agriculture laid the foundations for 18th-century prosperity. Signs of growth in the agricultural economy and in cultural life were evident, especially during

the reign of Carlo Emanuele III (1730-73): new crops were promoted (mulberries, potatoes), the port of Torres was rehabilitated, commerce was encouraged and the University was reopened (1765).

In the first half of the 19th century, the city grew considerably, as a result of the 1836 plan for expansion to the south-west, towards the "royal road" from Sassari to Cagliari, completed in 1829. In the second half of the century, almost all the city walls were demolished and the Aragonese castle (built around 1330) was demolished. The end of the century was a time of much cultural activity, in literature, music, art and politics. The population continued to increase in the twenty years of the Fascist regime and much public and private building was carried out. Three new town development plans, drawn up between 1929 and 1942, provided for suburban expansion and the creation of the new working-class quarter of Monte Rosello, and the residential area of Viale Italia-Porcellana. After the second world war, Sassari was fairly lively culturally and politically, despite the limits and contradictions of its economic growth. Three men from Sassari, A. Segni, E. Berlinguer and F. Cossiga, were key players in Italy's post-war political life.

Piazza Castello, The piazza is named after the old Aragonese castle built around 1330, and once the seat of the Court of the Inquisition. It was demolished in 1877, and the La Marmora barracks (1878-1881) was built in its place. Coats-of-arms from the castle facade can be seen in the courtyard. Inside the barracks, the Museo storico della Brigata Sassari (Sassari Brigade Historical Museum) tells the story of the heroism of the Sardinian infantry in the first world war. The Politeama G. Verdi (theater), built in 1884, is in

The cathedral in Sassari.

nearby Via Politeama. On the left side of the square, the church of Madonna del Rosario has an early 18th-century facade, and inside a superb Baroque main **altar*** in gilded wood, made by local artisans (1686).

Corso Vittorio Emanuele II. The Corso was the main street running through the medieval city from north to south. It was called Platha de Codinas (carved in tufa); Piazza del Comune and Palazzo di Città were halfway along, where the Civic Theater stands today. The Gothic church of S. Caterina and the Palazzo del Podestà were located in the upper part of the Corso. Some 15th-century Gothic houses have survived: one, at 20 Via Canopolo, and especially another, Casa Farris (Farris House), at 23 Via Canopolo. They have lovely Catalan Gothic double windows, and their old porticos can be seen embedded in the walls now. The 15th-century casa di Re Enzo (house of King Enzo) is in similar Catalan style, and has a splendid portico with sculptured capitals. The old municipality was replaced in 1826 by an elegant Neo-Classic building which now houses the Civic Theater. Opposite the theater is the Neo-Classic Palazzo di S. Sebastiano built in the 1820s. To the right, the Baroque facade of the church of S. Andrea was built in 1648 and inspired by Ligurian models. The street then ends as it widens into Piazza S. Antonio; on the left there are some remains of the medieval city walls with a crenelated tower. The church of S. Antonio Abate is in front of the piazza. It was completed in 1709, and has a well-proportioned Baroque facade. The church's furnishings feature the main altar **retablo***, in inlaid gilded wood, by the Genovese artist Bartolomeo Augusto. The Holy Deacon, a painting attributed to Giovanni Muru (early 16C) and Our Lady of Sorrows by Giovanni Marghinotti are in the sacristy.

Medieval walls. The remains of the medieval walls can be seen in Corso Trinità. The walls were started in the 13th century, and completed in the first decades of the 14th century. The walls' interior walkways and an unusual series of small houses built against the walls are visible from Vicolo Godimondo (Godimondo Lane). A tower, only slightly higher than the wall, appears to be a kind of outwork or advance structure. Just beyond, three 14th-century coats-of-arms can be seen embedded into the walls. In front, the chiesa della Trinità (church of the Trinity) has an interesting early 18th-century Baroque facade.

Fonte Rosello. The Rosello Fountain already existed in 1295; it was modified to its current monumental form in 1605-1606. Built in Renaissance style, it consists of two parallelepipeds, one above the other, in white and green marble, crowned by two crossed arches, on top of which was placed an equestrian statue of S. Gavino (St Gavin). The original statue has been lost; the copy there now was made in 1975. At the corners of the base, the statues of the seasons are 1828 copies of the originals which were destroyed.

Palazzo Ducale (or del Comune). The Ducal (or Municipal) Palazzo has been the Municipality since 1900; it's the city's most important example of 18th century civil architecture. It was probably Carlo Valino who oversaw its construction from 1775 to 1805, and who introduced some Piedmont-style features in the process. The austere facade has three levels, horizontally divided by bands and vertically by pilasters; the windows on the first floor are surmounted by rounded gables with cusp, and on the second floor by a rococo motif. The hallway has a double curved staircase, and leads to a well-proportioned courtyard. **Duomo di S. Nicola.** The cathedral of St Nicholas is located in the heart of the medieval town, and was rebuilt over a 12th-century Romanesque church between 1480 and 1505. The facade was built between 1681 and 1715 by skilled workers from Milan. The interior, with its single central nave and cupola on drum, has kept its Gothic appearance. There is a Sienese-school, 14th-century tempera painting at the main altar. A 17th-century silver statue of St Gavin is on the left, in a showcase. The choir was built by Sardinian cabinet-makers in the early 1700s. The adjacent Cathedral Treasury Museum has a standard that was used during processions at the end of the 15th century.

S. Maria di Betlem. The lower part of the facade of St Mary's of Bethlehem is all that remains of the original church, which was built in 1106. The upper part of the facade, with its rose-windows, dates from 1465. The interior was modernised in the 18th-19th-century. However, the Stonemasons' Chapel, left of the entrance, has retained its Aragonese form. The chapel on the left of the high altar has an early 15th-century wood sculpture group (Madonna and Child). The cloister, now almost entirely walled up, has the 16th-century Spurting Fountain: "brillador" in Catalan means "spurt".

Piazza d'Italia. Sassari's growth in the 19th century centered around Piazza d'Italia, which was created in the 1870s. The buildings around the symbolic area of a hectare together create an attractive harmonious environment; in the middle stands the monument to Vittorio Emanuele II by Giuseppe Sartorio (1899). The most impressive building is the majestic and elegant Palazzo della Provincia, designed by Eugenio Sironi and Giovanni Borgnini, and built between 1873 and 1880 in late Neo-Classic style. The facade is massive but well-proportioned, and consists of three orders of windows, and a frieze above. It's possible to visit the aula consiliare (council hall) on the first floor. It was decorated in 1881 with salient episodes from Sassari's past. The royal apartment is next door. Opposite Palazzo della Provincia, at number 19, is the neo-Gothic Palazzo Giordano. It was built in 1878 and has two rooms frescoed by Guglielmo Bilancini.

Museo Archeologico-Etnografico Giovanni Antonio Sanna. Sassari's Museo Archeologico-Etnografico (Archeological and Ethnographic Museum) is the result of a considerable series of acquisitions and donations, such as the collection of paintings left by Senator Giovanni Antonio Sanna, who the museum is named after. It was taken over by the State in 1931. Two artworks worthy of note are a Madonna and Child by Bartolomeo Vivarini, and a St Sebastian by the artist known as Mastro di Ozieri. The archeological section has numerous pre-historic finds from northern and central Sardinia, the altar from Mt d'Accoddi (2450-1850 BC), hypogeian tombs or domus de janas (4-2C millennium BC), and megalithic tombs (1000-900 BC).

In addition there is a Nuraghic hall, with scale models illustrating the two types of nuragh: tholos and corridor nuraghs. There are many displays of pottery and bronze objects for votive use.

The ground floor contains materials from historic times. For the Carthaginian period, there are funerary steles from Sulci, clay objects and numerous amulets. For the Roman period, a considerable collection of oil lamps, pottery, blown glass and gold objects. There are some important pieces of writing, including a bronze tablet from Esterzili (near Seulo). A few steps lead down to the large lower hall, where late-Roman material is exhibited: marble sarcophaguses decorated with figures, and sculptures and mosaics from Turris Libisonis (the Roman colony situated where Porto Torres is now). In Rooms XI and XIII, there is a collection of coins, ranging from rare and precious Carthaginian examples, to coins minted under Vittorio Emanuele I of Savoy (1814-1821).

S. Pietro in Silki. The St Peter's in Silki condaghe, Sassari's oldest manuscript, dates the church of the same name from the 12th century, although the oldest part surviving today is the lower part of the bell tower (13C). The nave masonry dates from around 1477, and the facade from 1675. The interior has a barrel-vaulted roof. The chapel of the Madonna of Graces, the first on the left, is a well-proportioned example of Sardinian Catalan Gothic style (around 1470). The fourth chapel contains the venerated 14th-century simulacrum of the Virgin of Graces.

Piazza d'Italia and the majestic Palazzo della Provincia in Sassari.

In the middle of the Mediterranean sea Sardinia is still wild and mostly rocky with plains, coasts, mountains and hills. Along its 1731 kilometers of shoreline there are some of the most beautiful marine habitats. Its coasts are generally high and rocky, stretching for miles with headlands and deep inlets fringed by islands and islets, extremely long beaches with powdery sand, from dazzling white to pink to granite red. The crystal-clear sea has many different hues: turquoise, cobalt blue, azure, emerald green. Sardinia also has numerous islands: Asinara, La Maddalena and Caprera; Tavolara and Molara in the north east: San Pietro and Sant'Antioco in the south west (actually the latter is joined to the island by an isthmus). There are so many beaches on the island that it is impossible to describe them all in this guidebook, so only the main ones are included below.

CAGLIARI

Poetto Beach. Cagliari's beach, which stretches to the beach of Quartu, is the most famous beach in Sardinia, in the middle of the vast Golfo degli Angeli. Locals and holidaymakers both use this long, spacious and dazzling white beach between the pool of Molentargius, famous for its flamingos, and the sea. Having been exploited for a long time it is now being cleaned up.

Feraxi. Located near Castiadas, this delightful little beach is off the beaten track and therefore quite enchanting.

Costa Rei. The beach is extremely long, about 8 km of limy shore. Beyond the beach there is the pool of Piscina Rei and the fascinating archaeological landscape of the megalithic complex with its string of menhirs (totems dating from the Neolithic age). There has been some unsubtle tourist development in the area but, towards the south, the beach is still intact and secluded.

Chia – Su Giudeu and Cala Cipolla. From Teulada the Costa Sud scenic route leads to the sea where you can see Torre di Chia, built in the 16th century as a defense against Saracen incursions, of which the whole area bears traces. Beneath the tower are the ruins of the Phoenician city of Bithia. West of the tower stretch the splendid beaches of Chia.

Teulada and Capo Malfitano Beaches. The heart of the Costa Sud, Capo Teulada is one of the most beautiful spots in Sardinia, inaccessible and only visible from the sea. Taking a short detour from the Costa Sud scenic route you can instead easily get to the beautiful beach of Teulada, known as Porto Tramatzu. If you continue along the scenic route eastwards towards Domus de Maria you will reach the headland of Capo Malfitano. The headland runs into the sea, creating a sort of marine basin which is extremely picturesque. Below it there are delightful little coves with

pebble beaches, the typical amber color of the "Sulcitano" coast.

Porto Sa Ruxi Beach. The beach of Porto Sa Ruxi, like the other beaches of Giunco and Punta Molentis, is part of the Protected Area of Capo Carbonara which will also include the Islands of Cavoli and Serpentara, in the environs of Villasimius. Actually this stretch of coast has three different little beaches, towered over by soft sand dunes and sheltered from behind by the maquis and juniper shrubs. Some other key beaches in the province of Cagliari are: near Castiadas Costa Rei; near Teulada Nora and Santa Margherita di Pula Beach; near Villasimius Giunco Beach

CARBONIA-IGLESIAS

Porto Pino Beach. Easily reached from Porto Pino in the Sant'Anna Arresi municipality, the beach is unique for its white sand and emerald waters. The beach has numerous facilities, including for fishing, diving and sailing. Some other important beaches in the province of Carbonia-Iglesias are: near Carloforte, Spalmatore Beach and Guidi Beach (both on Isola di San Pietro); near S. Antioco Cala Lunga Beach.

MEDIO-CAMPIDANO

Piscinas Beach. Famous thanks to its wonderful setting but not too crowded. Reaching the shore is not so simple if you are coming from the east, from inland that is. The journey to this stretch of dunes which can reach heights of 20 m is something of an adventure. It is easier to get there if you take the road from Costa Verde. After about 3 km you will reach Piscinas.

Torre dei Corsari and Costa Verde Beaches. A large stretch of sand dotted here and there with the green of juniper shrubs. The sea is emerald green. Other notable beaches in the province of Medio-Campidano area Scivu Dunes and Cala Domestica.

NUORO

Berchidda. Towards Capo Comino, on the coast road which takes you to Posada, you can admire the amazing beach of Berchidda, near a pool. It stretches north to Capo Comino (which you can get to by walking for some distance along the shore) and south almost as far as Orosei. The whiteness of the sand and the light reflected by the crystal-clear sea are dazzling. There are pools along the shoreline, and rolling meadows and hills behind.

Osalla Beach. From the village of Orosei a dirt road heading south leads to the large beach of Osalla, the northern part of the gulf of Orosei. The alluvial beach formed from the mouth of the Cedrino River is made up of fragments of various origin. The 5 km long beach, which is usually deserted even in the summer, is hauntingly empty. Some of the best known beaches in the area are Cala Cartoe, near Dorgali and Capo Comino near Orosei.

OGLIASTRA

Cala Goloritzè. Not far from Baunei which is only 15 km from Tortolì, you can easily get to the coast, where you will find a delightful little cove named Cala Goloritzè, with calm, crystal-clear waters which you can enjoy in the solitude of caves and crags where birds of prey come to nest.

Cala Luna. This is the most famous beach in Sardinia and should preferably be reached by boat from Cala Gonone, skirting 5 km of towering cliffs which have deep caves at their base, a karst system which is one of the most important in the Mediterranean. Cala Luna has a poignant beauty with its dazzling light and its treasured sandy shore between the rocks and cliffs. Behind it a natural freshwater pool provides an alternative to the sea for bathing. Still further back on the edge of the pool there is an exotic copse of oleanders with Polynesian colors.

Torre di Bari. Barisardo is a village in Ogliastra a few miles from the coast which it retreated from in ancient times fearing Saracen incursions. The beach is extremely long, towered over by the Torre di Bari. Built to repel Barbary pirates at the end of the 16th century, it was armed with a garrison to defend the population from Moorish attacks and could send signals to other coastal towers on the eastern shores. The beach is pleasant and easily accessible. The red rocks which surround it make it unique.

OLBIA-TEMPIO

Costa Smeralda. Sand, rock, green maquis and crystal-clear seabeds, so transparent it is often difficult to judge their depth. We are in Costa Smeralda, where reckless development, resorts and "Made in Sardinia" sea are the order of the day. There are a great deal of beaches along the coast, some of which aren't yet overrun with tourists. The most know are Cala Petra Ruja, Razza di Iuncu, and Ulticeddu Beac.

Cala Sabina. Here is a beach you can get to by train. Take one of the trains which leave from Olbia or from Golfo Aranci and alight at Cala Sabina, a few meters from the beach. The view is very easy on the eye: a white beach, blue water and a crown of juniper shrubs close to which you may put up a tent.

Punta Capo Ceraso Beaches. At Punta Capo Ceraso you will find a series of pretty little beaches: Cala sa Figu, Sos, Passizzedos, Por to Lucas and Porto Vitello. These are short stretches of shoreline surrounded by maquis and rocks, as well as pink granite.

Maddalena Archipelago. To visit the beaches of Maddalena you can go by boat from Cannigione, from Palau or from Maddalena, with one of the tours which offer you a whole day at sea, lunch included. The whole archipelago is protected by the Parco Nazionale Geo-

The beach at Cala Luna.

marino and bathing and pleasure boating are regulated by the Park Authority.

Caprera Island. From Palau there are ferries to Maddalena every ten minutes. From there you can drive to Caprera, over a long bridge straddling Passo della Moneta. Cala Brigantino and Cala Coticcio are two small beaches you simply must see.

Cala Li Cossi. Also known as Costa Paradiso Beach. To get there from Santa Teresa Gallura continue along the road to Castelsardo until you reach the fork for Costa Paradiso. This is a piece of authentic Sardinia which stretches from punta Cruzitta to Mt Tinnari, famous for its barren terrain made up of rocks eroded by the wind and the thick vegetation of junipers and tamarisks. You will find a white beach in the shape of an amphitheater on a still rugged stretch of coast, softened by golden sand.

Rena Bianca. This is Santa Teresa's principal beach, located near the outskirts of the town, used by local people and holidaymakers. It is a sandy cove in the shape of a crescent, with granite colored sand, set between cliffs on both sides and dark thickets of maquis behind.

Valle della Luna. The valley is actually a geological fracture, the result of earthquakes some millions of years ago. It meets the sea with Cala Francese. On both sides the eroded rocks create an enchanting environment, unique on the island. The granite appears to be very pale, almost white, as though it were permanently bathed in moonlight. The impression is of an exotic and tough environment, not a pleasant, gentle landscape at all. This uniqueness has given the Valley the reputation of an "alternative" beach, visited by travelers in search of something different.

Impostu Beach. About 8 km north of San Teodoro this is a large beach with white sand, surrounded by oleanders and mimosas. It is quiet except for in the middle of the summer season.

Capo Coda Cavallo Beach. Another white beach with a crystal-clear sea and no facilities, about 20 km from Olbia.

ORISTANO

Compoltitu. Sandy white beach in a partly enclosed roadstead where the water is crystal-clear, framed by a setting of rocks. The surprise is the stretch of lily-white limey rocks worn and smoothed by the sea, which you can sit on to paddle your feet, or which you can use as a diving board to dive into the sea to swim to the isolated white reef which emerges from the roadstead.

S. Caterina di Pittinuri and S'Archittu. The coast is the dark and basaltic coast of Montiferru and the curving beach ends in a headland with the Pittinuri tower, evidence of ancient Barbary raids. The real attraction is the nearby beach of S'Archittu, rather famous due to its splendid monumental arch, hollowed by the sea from limy rock. The rock is smooth and pleasant to the touch, the azure waters contained in circles of rock like natural harbors.

Is Arenas Beach. After the beach of Is Arenas, with its red sand, begins the Sinis peninsula which stretches as far as Marina di Torregrande, in the gulf of Oristano. With pools Is Benas, Sale Porcus and Cabras, the peninsula is ideal for boat-lovers. At sea you can appreciate the thousands of small coves with their high white limestone walls.

SASSARI

Argentiera Beach. You can get there from Alghero on the road of the "Due Mari" heading towards Porto Torres. The sand is limey and quartzose and you will find yourself caught between the magic of the sea and the disquieting thought of the miners' centuries of toil.

Cala Dragunara. This is a delightful rocky inlet where there is a bar and small jetty where you can catch a boat which will take you to the caves of Neptune in just a few, short minutes.

X Beaches. Let's call these gorgeous stretches of sand which lie between Bombarde and Lazzaretto "X Beaches". Indeed, they do not have a name but it would be a pity to miss them. Sunken as though in the middle of a canyon which ends in the sea, they were practically deserted until a few years ago. This is no longer the case in the hottest months of the year but June and September are quiet.

Porticciolo Beach. Equipped with a good pair of walking shoes a day spent in the inlet of Porticciolo will be an unforgettable adventure. Lovely but a little awkward to walk on, the beach and foreshore are scattered with many rocks and detritus. On the right there is small hill with a Saracen tower, built by the Spanish.

Saline Beach. You can get to this rather busy beach from Sassari heading towards Porto Torres. At the entrance to the town leave the main road and continue towards Stintino, following the various signs which follow one another in both the industrial zone and along the B-road. Just before Stintino, near a villa and a little before a Spanish tower, you must turn right onto a recently surfaced road which leads straight to the beach. You will find yourself facing a long stretch of powdery white sand which is well worth the trip.

THE GREAT ROMANESQUE PERIOD

There are two main periods in Sardinian history which set the local architecture: the long "Nuraghic" age, which saw the spread of seven thousand towers throughout the island, and the 'giudicale' period, during which the large Romanesque churches were built. The term 'giudicale' comes from the period between 1000 and the beginning of 1300 when Sardinia, by then already independent from Byzantine rule, was divided into four fairly autonomous regions governed by lords called "iudikes".

One of the most beautiful examples of Romanesque architecture on the island is a group of churches located throughout the island and built high up dominating the surrounding countryside where monks, particularly Benedictine monks from Montecassino and Camaldoli, would pray and where they drained the land, administered farms and taught. Though the areas are now unpopulated the immense Romanesque constructions tend to strike tourists deep down.

Five of these masterpieces are to be found not far from each other in the north-west of the island and can be visited in a few hours. Though no one is really sure, it seems the basilica of SS. Trinità di Saccargia near Sassari was built in two periods by master builders from Pisa, initially between the end of the 11th century and 1116, then a few decades later. This basilica lies beside a former Camaldolesi monastery and is striking for the harmonious way the layers of white limestone and dark basaltic stone alternate around the main building, the bell tower and the front portal. Experts remind us that the basilica as it stands today underwent great renovations between the 19th and 20th centuries. In any case visitors will be awed by the harmony of the entire building. There is a set of frescoes inside, the only entire set remaining from the Sardinian medieval Romanesque period.

Going on towards Olbia (and S. Simplicio), we go by the church of S. Michele di Salvenero, which the Vallombrosani built at the beginning of the 12th century. Turning right we go towards Ardara. The church of S. Maria del Regno, on the edge of the town, was the seat of the "giudici" of Torres; indeed, the church was the lords' palatine chapel. Built by Georgia, the sister of Gonnario-Comita 'giudice' of Torres and Arborea, it was consecrated in 1107; is made entirely of dark Trachyte. One of the most beautiful retables on the island can be seen inside: an enormous altar table dating back to the early 16th century.

Further ahead, on the left of the main road SS 597 there is another masterpiece of Romanesque architecture, S. Antioco di Bisarcio. This was the diocese's cathedral for many years before being transferred to Ozieri and rebuilt before 1000 AD having been damaged by a fire. It is believed the church was built according to the structural and decorative norms of Pisa architecture and the skilful hands of Lombard and Sardinian builders.

The fifth building of this group of Romanesque monuments is not too far from Ardara, in the area of Borutta. Built between the 11th and 12th centuries the basilica of S. Pietro di Sorres was also the seat of the local diocese. The base of the basilica is made of layers of white limestone blocks, whereas the upper part repeats the two-colour bands used in the Trinità di Saccargia. A monastery was added to the basil-

The central vault of the Iglesias cathedral.

Malaspina castle at Bosa.

Tirso Valley and rebuilt in its current position, higher up. There is a very interesting cathedral near Oristano called S. Giusta, a magnificent church of "Pisa-Lombard-Sardinian" architecture built at the beginning of 1100.

The south of the island also boasts magnificent monuments, though the churches are somewhat smaller. There are, though, a few exceptions, like the cathedral in Iglesias, built by count Ugolino, and S. Pantaleo in Dolianova, mostly located inside the towns. However, it is this very difference that makes the area so fascinating and explains why visitors are so surprised to find authentic jewellery with refined architecture being sold on the edges of these farm towns. It is worth mentioning: S. Maria di Monserrato in Tratalias, 1213; S. Platano in Villa Speciosa, built by the Vittorini di Marsiglia around 1144; S. Mariain Uta, also built by the Vittorini, a little earlier; S. Maria di Sibiola in Serdiana, also beginning 12th century.

The book by Coroneo mentions 169 Romanesque churches on the island, plus 9 castles, including the S. Michele castle which was built by Pisa architects in the 13th century, under the domination of Cagliari.

ica, where the Benedictine monks have now started to renovate books. High up on a projection of rock is S. Pietro di Sorres, the last Romanesque building in the north of the island. However, we have to mention two pieces of civil architecture: the Burgos castle, in Goceano, built in the middle of the 12th century, and the Serravalle castle in Bosa, which was started in the same period as the Malaspina family. Even the centre-east of the island, the ancient lordship of Arborea, has some very beautiful Romanesque churches, including the little church of S. Pietro di Zuri, near Ghilarza. Made of pink trachyte rock, it is lit up at dusk.

We know the name of the person who had it built, the "giudice" of Arborea Mariano II. We even know who the architect was, a certain Anselmo from Como, who was by then already "projected towards gothic architecture" – wrote R.Coroneo, author of the book "Architettura romanica dalla metà del Mille al primo '300" (Romanesque architecture from the middle of 1000 to the beginning of 1300) – though he was still sensitive towards the ideas of Romanesque architecture. Initially built between 1923 and 1925, it was dismantled stone by stone when the Omodeo dam was built in the

Olbia, the facade of the church of S. Simplicio.

THE MYSTERY OF THE NURAGHS

The nuraghs have long been an unfathomable mystery. These monumental structures, built in stone in the form of towers, are now a universally-known symbol of Sardinian history and culture; they have for centuries been a real mystery to archeologists and scholars of ancient history. They were widely used as places of worship in Carthaginian and Roman times, and thus it was believed in the past that they may have been large tomb complexes. In the 20th century, a clearer and more complete understanding of the Nuraghic civilisation emerged, especially with knowledge gained from archeological research and excavation campaigns carried out in the fifties. Research by Antonio Taramelli and later by Giovanni Lilliu revealed what the nuraghs really were: dwellings which also had a defensive function, and were the greatest expression of a culture which originated and developed thousands of years ago, in the wake of the great Megalithic civilisations of the Mediterranean.

ROUND FORTRESSES

The first nuraghs were very probably built in pre-historic times, from the second millennium BC. Today, there are over seven thousand nuraghs all over Sardinia, and a large number of them have survived to our times in excellent condition.

If we think of all the activities and works which have been undertaken on the island over the centuries, such as the construction of roads and aqueducts, and the development of towns, it is clear that much evidence of the Nuraghic civilisation must have been destroyed, and thus much precious knowledge lost forever. Most Nuraghic structures are situated in hill areas, but some are found in flat areas, along the coast, on plateaux and in rough, inhospitable terrain, such as for example high in the Gennargentu area, at over 1000 m.

A nuragh consists of a tower which is shaped like a truncated cone; the ground-plan is thus circular. They were built with sedimentary or volcanic rocks and stones, sometimes of considerable size; these are placed in concentric rows that progressively get smaller and smaller as they get higher. Gravity keeps them in place, without any cement or mortar. The entrance is surmounted by an architrave: from here a corridor leads to a room in the shape of a cupola. Sometimes these rooms are on two or more levels, connected by spiral staircases constructed inside the walls. Other structures such as chambers or galleries are sometimes connected to the main tower. In most cases, simple forms prevail. In others, structures were architecturally very complex, such as those with a number of towers. Individual nuraghs were often part of a defence system which was highly structured and organised, within fortified town walls.

Multiple tower nuraghs within fortified walls predominate at "Is Paras", north of the town of Isili, at "Arrubiu", at Orroli, and at "Su Nuraxi" at Barumini, where the Marmilla and Sarcidano regions meet: rich, fertile areas. And this may explain why the nuraghs here are so impressive, and among the largest found on the island. It has also been noted that sometimes villages of round huts with stone foundations developed around the nuraghs.

THE SETTLEMENT OF BARUMINI

Many aspects of the history, life and society of the peoples who inhabited the nuraghs have become clearer since the Nuraghic complex "Su Nuraxi" on the western edge of Barumini was excavated in the early 1950s.

The heart of the settlement is a stronghold formed by a central keep which probably dates from the end of the second millennium BC, and was originally 18 m high. This is surrounded by four towers situated at the points of the compass and built between the 13th-10th centuries BC. The towers in turn are surrounded by a defensive wall with seven towers which appears to date from between the 10th and 8th centuries BC. An Iron Age village (9-6C BC) was found around these structures, with circular stone buildings, probably roofed with branches and leaves, which almost certainly served as dwellings for the soldiers' families. Extremely interesting objects, tools and ornaments have been found here. As Su Nuraxi gradually developed and grew, probably for military reasons, the oldest structures were incorporated and fortified. The Carthaginians made frequent raids into the interior, which meant that there was a strong need for defence.

THE LOSA DI ABBASANTA NURAGH

The word "losa" means "tomb" in the local language of Sardinia. The Losa Nuragh is one of Sardinia's most important nuraghs. It is an example of a complex form of these monuments that were built by the Nuraghic civilization, which lasted almost a thousand years from around 1500 BC to 500 BC. In a sense, these constructions are the most obvious expression of that Sardinian diversity which has always made the culture and history of the island distinctive from the rest of Italy - and the world.

A nuragh is a conical-shaped tower, built of rows of large stones placed one above the other in a drywall contruction, that is, without using any cement or something similar. The towers were normally four to five meters high, although sometimes they reached over ten. Single tower structures normally measured a few meters across at the base. Generally the structures were more complex, and also included bastions, courtyards, ramparts, and smaller towers.

The term nuragh may derive from "nur", a term used in Proto-Sardinian (the language spoken before the Roman conquest); it probably meant "hollow mound of stones, cavity", describing the structure of the monuments.

They may have been castles for tribal leaders, buildings symbolising the aristocratic power of the clan, safe strongholds for the elderly and people of the village, or the temple-tombs of tribal heroes. But whatever they were, the nuraghs survive as evidence of a unique and original culture. The Losa Nuragh consists of a central tower on two levels, and a three-lobed bastion with a concave-convex outline. A wall with two towers surrounds both the small fort and the village of circular or oval huts, which dates from the Nuraghic age. There is a small antiquarium in the area, with exhibits that bear witness to life on the site, from the Nuraghic age up until the time when it was last inhabited, in Roman and early medieval times.

Barumini is home to a famous nuraghic complex.

IN THE CENTER OF THE MEDITERRANEAN

Although there is evidence clearly indicating that the village of Barumini was still inhabited in the early centuries of the Christian era (at least until the 3C AD), the nuraghs appear to have gradually diminished in importance, particularly after the Roman conquest of the island in the 2nd century BC.

The difficulty encountered in attempting to gain an in-depth understanding of the nuraghs is partly due to the fact that the Nuraghic civilisation was totally different from the "classical" Greek civilisation which flourished on the coast of southern Italy and Sicily. However, recent studies have revealed that, although the Nuraghic civilisation was, curiously, extremely self-contained, it did have some important links with the Mycenean culture. And when this culture came to the end of its period of expansion, Nuraghic Sardinia, in the heart of the western Mediterranean, became an important point of reference for both the Etruscan and Phoenician civilisations.

FOOD IN SARDINIA

Sardinia's wild, rugged, mountainous landscape is dominated by sheep and goat farming. As a result, it produces a considerable range of cheeses, meat, salamis and cured meats, although these are not the island's only food resources by any means. It also has many vineyards, olive groves and citrus groves. It produces cereals and vegetables, particularly artichokes and tomatoes. Fish is also in good supply, especially tuna and specialties like bottarga.

TYPICAL LOCAL DISHES

Impanadas. Common all over Sardinia, a sort of pizza or calzone filled with various vegetables and chopped meat.

Maccarrones. Home-made pasta made with durum wheat and water, served with ricotta, fresh cheese and tomato or meat sauce.

Malloreddus. These are typical Sardinian gnocchi made from durum wheat flour and served with a sauce made with meat, tomato and sausage meat.

Agnello. Lamb is cooked on the spit or, around Nuoro, stewed gently with tomatoes and wild fennel.

Burrida. Boiled dogfish is marinated for a day in olive oil, chopped walnuts, vinegar and herbs before eating. It can be served as a starter or a main course.

Porceddu. Suckling pig cooked on the spit over an aromatic wood fire. While cooking it is basted with dripping. It can also be wrapped in myrtle leaves and eaten cold a few days later.

Sebadas. These large, sweet, round, one-portion ravioli are filled with cheese, fried in oil and served with honey.

TYPICAL LOCAL PRODUCTS

Fiore Sardo DOP. Made from raw ewe's milk from Sardinian sheep. When young this cheese has a firm body and is used as a table cheese, eaten fresh or grilled. When mature it has a granular texture and is eaten in wedges.

Pecorino Sardo DOP. This cheese is produced only in Sardinia with whole, raw ewe's milk. The cheese has a compact body and is white or straw-yellow in color. It can be used as a table cheese or the mature version can be used for grating.

Agnello di Sardegna IGP. Prime-quality lamb is the second important contribution of sheep farming to the island's range of food.

Pane Carasau. Typical of the north of Sardinia. Paper-thin leaves of round, crunchy unleavened bread. It keeps for a long time and was once used by shepherds during transhumance. It is also eaten soaked in water and cooked quickly with tomatoes, oil, salt and pepper ('pane guttiau').

Zafferano di Sardegna. Saffron is grown mainly in the Province of Cagliari around San Gavino Monreale. In traditional cuisine, saffron is used to flavor dishes like ravioli di ricotta, desserts and liqueurs.

Bottarga di Muggine. Salted grey mullet roe, pressed and seasoned. It is eaten raw, either in slices as a starter, or grated over pasta. Bottarga is also made from tuna roe.

Miele di Sardegna. Honey is made all over the island, especially in the mountains. There are many different kinds: the usual flavors but also delicate, aromatic honey flavored with asphodel or French honeysuckle; and honey from cardoons and strawberry trees, with an unmistakably bitter taste.

WINES

Like many Italian regions, Sardinia's wine-making tradition goes back thousands of years. Now the local wine industry produces dry white wines with great character, a range of unique dessert wines, and reds which are rapidly gaining recognition. The island's most famous white wine is Vermentino di Gallura DOCG, which has acquired great status over the last ten years. The best red, with plenty of body, is Cannonau. Vernaccia di Oristano, a sweet white liqueur wine, is quite unique. Behind these three giants, there are many wines made with single grape varietals: Nuragus al Torbato and Monica al Cagnulari, the result of local producers' efforts to promote indigenous grapes. Excellent wines inevitably lead to good grappa, sold here under the popular name of 'Filu e ferru'. The island's liqueur made from the berries and leaves of the myrtle plant, Mirto, has recently become very popular on the mainland.

THE A-Z OF WHAT YOU NEED TO KNOW

GETTING TO AND TRANSPORTS

By plane

Below is a list of some of the main international airports in Italy.

ROMA AND LAZIO
Aeroporto Leonardo da Vinci via dell'Aeroporto di Fiumicino tel. 0665951 – www.adr.it

LOMBARDY
Milan Linate and Malpensa airports
www.sea-aeroportimilano.it

VENETO
Aeroporto Valerio Catullo Caselle di Sommacampagna tel. 0458095666
www.aeroportoverona.it

EMILIA-ROMAGNA
Aeroporto G. Marconi
www.bologna-airport.it
tel. 0516479615

TUSCANY
Aeroporto di Firenze
www.aeroporto.firenze.it
tel. 0553061300

CAMPANIA
Aeroporto di Napoli
www.portal.gesac.it

SICILY
Aeroporto Falcone
e Borsellino
Palermo, Punta Raisi –
www.gesap.it

SARDINIA
Aeroporto Costa Smeralda Olbia – tel. 0789563444
www.olbiairport.it

By train

All the main towns in Italy can be reached by train.
For timetables and fares:
TRENITALIA, Tel. 892021, www.trenitalia.com

By boat

Numerous companies serve the various islands. In summer, there tend to be more regular boats, but it is often necessary to book, especially for the more famous destinations. (www.traghettitalia.it):

ALILAURO – Isole Eolie – www.alilauro.it

MOBY LINES – Sardinia, Isola d'Elba – www.mobylines.it

TIRRENIA – Sardinia, Sicily, Isole Tremiti – www.tirrenia.it

GRANDI NAVI VELOCI – Sardinia, Sicily – www2.gnv.it

GRIMALDI LINES – Sicily – www.grimaldi-ferries.com

TOREMAR – Isola d'Elba, Giglio and Capraia – www.toremar.it

CAREMAR – Isole di Ischia,

Capri, Procida and Pontine – www.caremar.it

SNAV – Isole Eolie – www.snav.it

By car

The network of motorways is comprehensive in the north and center of the country, but less so in the south. Note that most motorways (called autostrade) are toll roads.
Motorway information center: freephone 800269269;
www.autostrade.it

Car rental

Most major car hire companies have extensive networks in Italy. Many agencies are located at major airports and train stations.

AVIS
www.avisautonoleggio.it

HERTZ
www.hertz.it

EUROPCAR
www.europcar.it

The most widely used breakdown and roadside assistance service is called **ACI**, Automobile Club d'Italia – via Marsala 8, 00185 Roma – tel. 0649981 – fax 0649982234, www.aci.it

PRACTICAL INFO: MUSEUMS, HOTELS AND RESTAURANTS

Museums and monuments

There is a list – divided region by region and in alphabetical order according to the place – of the museums and monuments indicated in the guidebook, giving the address, telephone number and, potentially, the website. Museums are normally open during the week – and on Sundays and holidays – during office hours (9am-12.30pm and 3-5.30pm). Many museums are closed on Mondays. Note that many museums also operate extended opening hours, often staying open later in the evening. Since exact opening hours often change from zone to zone and from season to season, it is always best to get further information before any visit. For the most famous museums, it is best to book in advance to avoid the queues! Note: it is only possible to visit Leonardo da Vinci's Last Supper in Milan, if you have a booking.

Tourist offices, hotels and restaurants

This section contains a selection – once again divided by region and in alphabetical order according to place – of hotels, restaurants, tourist information centers and so on.

INFO OFFICES

For places where tourist offices exist, the details of the office (address, telephone number and, if it exists, the website) are provided immediately below the name of the place. In some cases, the tourist offices are seasonal, meaning they are only open in high season and not throughout the year. Furthermore, there are various types of tourist offices, which are indicated as follows: for the entire region, **APT** (Azienda Promozione Turistica), **AA(C)ST** (Azienda Autonoma di (Cura) Soggiorno e Turismo), **IAT** (Ufficio di Informazione e di Accoglienza Turistica); on a municipal level, **PRO LOCO**.

HOTELS

There is an official classification system based on stars:

*****L	super-luxury hotel
*****	luxury hotel
****	first level hotel
***	second level hotel
**	third level hotel
*	fourth level hotel

Prices can vary substantially depending on the season and the area. The guidebook contains 4, 3 and 2 star hotels, with prices ranging from € 500 per night (for luxury, well-equipped hotels) to € 50 per night (simple hotel room). However, all the hotels have been selected by Touring Club's experts using strict quality standards (tied to the hotel classification). The entry for each hotel contains the classification, address, website and number of rooms. The term "Meublé" refers to a hotel that does not have a restaurant. The facilities and structures are indicated using symbols (see key).

Practical info

CLIMATE

The climate in Italy is generally temperate, tending to be milder in the coastal zones and harsher as you go inland and into the mountains.

In the north (from the Alps to Emilia), winters tend to be colder, with snow not uncommon in December and January. The summers tend to be hot and the humidity levels high (especially in the cities).

In the center (Liguria to Lazio), the climate is very temperate, with less of a difference between summer and winter. Summers are hot, but not as stuffy as in the north. Likewise, the winters are not as cold. The Apennine areas do, though, tend to be colder than the coast.

The south (including Sicily and Sardinia) enjoys a hot and dry climate, with limited rainfall. In winter, the mercury rarely drops below zero, in autumn things tend to be nice and mild, while in summer the temperatures can soar, almost becoming scorching in July and August. Once again, the mountainous zones tend to be cooler.

INFORMATION

The official Italian state tourist body is Enit:
ENIT
National Tourism Office
via Marghera 2-6
00185 Roma
tel. 0649711 – fax 064463379
www.enit.it

KEY TO SYMBOLS

- ♿ Disabled access
- ♨ Park/garden (hotel)
- ⊕ Outdoor area (restaurant)
- ≋ Private section of beach
- ⊠ Indoor pool
- ⊠ Outdoor pool
- ♨ Own spa center
- ⚕ Wellness center
- ♨ Disco

- ✦ Pets welcome
- Ⓟ Private parking
- ★ TCI member discount

Credit cards accepted:
- AE American Express
- DC Diners Club
- VISA Visa
- MC Mastercard
- JCB JCB
- B Bancomat

Inside

- **Museums and Monuments**
- **Useful addresses: Tourist information Hotels and restaurants**

RESTAURANTS

The TCI classification system uses from 4 to 1 fork, depending on the type and price:

- 🍴🍴🍴🍴 refined atmosphere, elegant, expensive
- 🍴🍴🍴 quite refined and elegant moderate to expensive
- 🍴🍴 good quality with average prices
- 🍴 simple restaurant good prices

Each restaurant entry contains the classification, address, website, and capacity (inside/outside).

The facilities and structures are indicated using symbols (see key). Finally, the type of cuisine is indicated:
- **R** regional/local, typical traditional cuisine
- **C** classical Italian and international cuisine
- **I** innovative, creative

EMERGENCY NUMBERS

112	Military Police (Carabinieri)
113	State Police (Polizia)
115	Fire Department
117	Financial Police
118	Medical Emergencies
1515	Fire-watch
1518	Road Information
803116	Road Assistance

MUSEUMS

This section contains all the museums mentioned in the guidebook. They are listed in "regional" order, starting with Valle d'Aosta and ending with Sardinia. For each region, the list is further divided according to places, which are ordered alphabetically. Each museum listing contains the address, telephone number and, if there is, the website. As indicated on p. 394, it is best to check the opening times and days prior to any visit. To make it easier to find the exact locations, each entry also contains the two-letter code for the province (in brackets). For more information on the province (provinces are administrative sub-areas of a region) and to learn which provinces the codes stand for please look at p. 445.

VALLE D'AOSTA

AOSTA

Complesso monumentale della Collegiata di Sant'Orso
Via Sant'Orso,
Tel. 0165275965-0165275987
www.regione.vda.it

Museo archeologico regionale
Piazza Roncas 12,
Tel. 0165275902-
0165230545 www.regione.vda.it

Museo del Tesoro della Cattedrale
Tel. 016540251-0165340413
www.regione.vda.it

COGNE (AO)

Museo Minerario Alpino
Villaggio dei Minatori 85,
Tel. 0165749264
Temporarily closed

COURMAYEUR (AO)

Museo alpino Duca degli Abruzzi
Strada Villair 2,
Tel. 0165842064
www.guidecourmayeur.com

PIEDMONT

ASTI

Complesso di San Pietro Consavia e Musei paleontologico e archeologico
Corso Alfieri 2,
Tel. 0141353072
www.comune.asti.it/cultura/index.shtml

Cripta e Museo di Sant'Anastasio
Corso Alfieri 365/A,
Tel. 0141437454
www.comune.asti.it/cultura/index.s
html

BAROLO (CN)

Museo della Civiltà Contadina
Castello Falletti, piazza Falletti,
Tel. 017356277

CUNEO

Museo civico
Via S. Maria 10, Tel. 0171634175
www.comune.cuneo.it

GIGNESE (NO)

Museo dell'Obrello e del Parasole
Via Golf Panorama 2,
Tel. 032389622
www.gignese.it/museo/ombrello/info.htm

GRINZANE CAVOUR (CN)

Museo del Castello di Grinzane Cavour
Via Castello 5,
Tel. 0173262159
www.castellogrinzane.com

TURIN/TORINO

Armeria reale
Piazza Castello 191,
Tel. 011543889-0115184358
www.artito.arti.beniculturali.it

Galleria civica d'Arte moderna e contemporanea-GAM
Via Magenta 31, Tel. 0114429518
www.gamtorino.it

Galleria sabauda
Via Accademia delle Scienze 6,
Tel. 0115641755-0115641748
www.artito.arti.beniculturali.it

Museo Civico di Numismatica, Etnografia e Arti Orientali
Via Bricherasio 8,
Tel. 011541557-011541608
www.musei.it/piemonte/torino

Museo di Antichità archeologica
Via XX Settembre 88/C,
Tel. 0114396140
www.museoantichita.it

Museo egizio
Via Accademia delle Scienze 6,
Tel. 0115617776
www.museoegizio.it

Museo nazionale del Cinema
Mole Antonelliana,
via Montebello 20,
Tel. 0118138511-0118138560
www.museocinema.it

Museo nazionale dell'Automobile «Carlo Biscaretti di Ruffia»
Corso Unità d'Italia 40,
Tel. 011677666
www.museoauto.it
Temporarily closed

Museo Pietro Micca e dell'Assedio di Torino del 1706
Via F. Guicciardini 7/A,
Tel. 011546317
www.museopietromicca.it

Museo storico nazionale d'Artiglieria
Corso Galileo Ferraris,
Tel. 0115629223
www.artiglieria.org
Temporarily closed

Palazzo Madama, Museo civico di Arte antica
Piazza Castello, Tel. 0114433501
www.palazzomadamatorino.it

Palazzo Reale Appartamenti reali
Piazzetta Reale, piazza Castello,
Tel. 0114361455
www.ambienteto.arti.beniculturali.it

Pinacoteca della Accademia albertina di Belle Arti
Via Accademia Albertina 8,
Tel. 011889020-0118177862
www.accademialbertina.torino.it

LOMBARDY

BERGAMO

Accademia Carrara-Museo
Piazza G. Carrara 82/A,
Tel. 035399640
www.accademiacarrara.bergamo.it

Civico Orto Botanico "L. ROTA"
P.ggio Torre di Adalberto 2/I,
Tel. 035286060

Galleria d'Arte Moderna e Contemporanea di Bergamo-GAMeC
Via San Tomaso 52,
Tel. 035270272
www.gamec.it

Museo civico archeologico
Piazza Cittadella 9,
Tel. 035242839
www.museoarcheologicobergamo.it

Museo civico di Scienze naturali «Enrico Caffi»
Piazza Cittadella 10,
Tel. 035286011-035286012
www.museoscienzebergamo.it

Museo donizettiano
Via Arena 9,
Tel. 035247116
www.bergamoestoria.it

Museo storico di Bergamo
Rocca di Bergamo,
piazzale Brigata Legnano
Tel. 035226332-035247116
www.bergamoestoria.it

BRESCIA

Museo civico del Risorgimento
Via del Castello 9,
Tel. 03044176
www.bresciamusei.com

Pinacoteca civica Tosio-Martinengo
Piazza Moretto 4,
Tel. 0302977833-0302977834
www.bresciamusei.com

Santa Giulia Museo della Città
Via Musei 81/B,
Tel. 0302977834
www.bresciamusei.com

COMO

Musei civici-Museo archeologico «Paolo Giovio» and Museo storico «Giuseppe Garibaldi»
Piazza Medaglie d'Oro 1,
Tel. 031252550
www.comune.como.it

Pinacoteca di Palazzo Volpi
Via A. Diaz 84,
Tel. 031269869-031252550
www.comune.como.it

CREMONA

Collezione dei Violini di Palazzo comunale
Piazza del Comune 8,
Tel. 037222138
www.aptcremona.it

Museo civico di Storia naturale
Viale Trento e Trieste 35/B,
Tel. 037223766
www.comune.cremona.it

Museo civico «Ala Ponzone» and Museo stradivariano
Via Ugolani Dati 4,
Tel. 0372407269
www.musei.comune.cremona.it

MANTUA/MANTOVA

Casa del Mantegna
Via G. Acerbi 47,
Tel. 0376360506
www.provincia.mantova.it

Museo civico di Palazzo Te
Viale Te,
Tel. 0376323266
www.comune.mantova.it

Museo del Risorgimento
Piazza Sordello 42,
Tel. 0376338645

Museo diocesano «Francesco Gonzaga»
Piazza Virgiliana 55,
Tel. 0376320602
www.museodiocesanomantova.it

Museo di Palazzo d'Arco
Piazza C. d'Arco 4,
Tel. 0376322242
www.museodarco.it

Museo di Palazzo Ducale
Piazza Sordello 40,
Tel. 0376224832-0376352100
www.mantovaducale.it

Museo Tazio Nuvolari e Learco Guerra
Piazza Broletto 9,
Tel. 0376327929
www.tazionuvolari.it

Teatro scientifico o Accademia Nazionale Virgiliana
Via dell'Accademia 47,
Tel. 0376320314
www.accademiavirgiliana.it

MILAN/MILANO

Cappella Portinari
Piazza S. Eustorgio 1,
Tel. 0289402671

Castello Sforzesco-Museo d'Arte antica e Pinacoteca
Piazza Castello,
Tel. 0288463731
www.milanocastello.it

Castello Sforzesco-Museo della Preistoria e Protostoria-Museo Egizio
Piazza Castello,
Tel. 0280539/2
www.milanocastello.it

Castello Sforzesco-Museo delle Arti decorative e Museo degli Strumenti musicali
Piazza Castello,
Tel. 0288463730
www.milanocastello.it

Cenacolo vinciano
Piazza S. Maria delle Grazie 2,
Tel. 0289421146
www.cenacolovinciano.it

Civiche Raccolte archeologiche e numismatiche
Corso Magenta 15,
Tel. 0286450011-028053972
www.milanocastello.it

Civico Museo d'Arte Contemporanea
Palazzo Reale, piazza Duomo 12,
Tel. 0262083219

Civico Planetario (Giardini Pubblici "Indro Montanelli")
Corso Venezia 57,
Tel. 0288463340
www.comune.milano.it

Collezione Studio Treccani
Via Carlo Porta 5,
Tel. 026572627
www.fondazionecorrente.org

Museo Bagatti Valsecchi
Via del Gesù 5,
Tel. 0276006132
www.museobagattivalsecchi.org

Museo civico di Storia naturale
Corso Venezia 55,
Tel. 0288463280
www.comune.milano.it

Musei del Castello
Piazza Castello,
Tel. 0288463837-0288463660
www.milanocastello.it

Museo del Cinema «Gianni Comencini»
Palazzo Dugnani, via Manin 2/B,
Tel. 026554977
www.cinetecamilano.it

Museo del Duomo
Piazza Duomo 14,
Tel. 02860358
www.duomomilano.com

Museo del Giocattolo e del Bambino
Via Pitteri 56,
Tel. 0226411585
www.museodelgiocattolo.it

Museo della Basilica di Sant'Ambrogio
Piazza S. Ambrogio 15,
Tel. 0286450895
www.santambrogio-basilica.it

Museo della Permanente
Via Turati 34,
Tel. 026599803

Museo del Risorgimento
Via Borgonuovo 23,
Tel. 0288464184-0288464177
www.museidelcentro.mi.it

Museo di Milano and di Storia contemporanea
Via S. Andrea 6,
Tel. 0276006245-0288465933
www.museidelcentro.mi.it

Museo manzoniano/ Casa del Manzoni
Via G. Morone 1,
Tel. 0286460403
www.museidelcentro.mi.it

Museo nazionale della Scienza e della Tecnologia «Leonardo da Vinci»
Via S. Vittore 21,
Tel. 02485551
www.museoscienza.org

Museo Poldi Pezzoli
Via Manzoni 12,
Tel. 02794889-02796334
www.museopoldipezzoli.it

Museo Studio «Francesco Messina»
Via S. Sisto 4/A,
Tel. 0286453005-0288463731

Museo teatrale alla Scala
Largo Antonio Ghiringhelli 1,
Tel. 0288797473
www.teatroallascala.org

Pinacoteca ambrosiana
Piazza Pio XI 2,
Tel. 02806921
www.ambrosiana.it

Pinacoteca di Brera
Via Brera 28,
Tel. 02722631
www.brera.beniculturali.it

Tesoro del Duomo
Cattedrale del Duomo di Milano,
via Arcivescovado 1,
Tel. 0272022656
www.duomomilano.com

**Villa Reale Belgiojoso
Bonaparte e Museo
dell'Ottocento**
Via Palestro 16,
Tel. 0276002819-0276340809
www.comune.milano.it/villabelgiojo
sobonaparte

SONDRIO

**Museo valtellinese
di Storia e Arte**
Via Quadrio 27,
Tel. 0342526269
www.comune.sondrio.it

TRENTINO-
ALTO ADIGE

BOLZANO/BOZEN

Museo civico
Via Cassa di Risparmio 14,
Tel. 0471974625
www.comune.bolzano.it/museo_civico
Temporarily closed

**Museo di Scienze naturali
dell'Alto Adige**
Via Bottai 1,
Tel. 0471412964
www.museonatura.it

MERANO/MERAN (BZ)

Castello principesco di Merano
Via Galilei,
Tel. 0473250329
www.comune.merano.bz.it/tuttocitta
/cultura.asp

Museo civico di Merano
Via delle Corse 42/A,
Tel. 0473236015
www.comune.merano.bz.it/tuttocitta
/cultura.asp

Museo della Donna
Via Portici 68,
Tel. 0473231216
www.museia.org

TRENT/TRENTO

**Castello del Buonconsiglio,
Monumenti e Collezioni
provinciali**
Via Bernardo Clesio 5,
Tel. 0461233770
www.buonconsiglio.it

**Mart Trento-Museo di Arte
moderna e contemporanea di
Trento e Rovereto**
Palazzo delle Albere,
via R. da Sanseverino 45,
Tel. 0461234860
www.mart.trento.it

Museo diocesano tridentino
Piazza Duomo 18,
Tel. 0461234419
www.museodiocesanotridentino.it

**Museo tridentino
di Scienze naturali**
Via Calepina 14,
Tel. 0461270311
www.mtsn.tn.it

VENETO

BELLUNO

Museo civico
Piazza del Duomo 16,
Tel. 0437944836
www.comune.belluno.it

PADUA/PADOVA

**Galleria Guglielmo
Tabacchi-Safilo**
Via Settima Strada 15,
Tel. 0496985679
www.safilo.com

Musei civici agli Eremitani
Piazza Eremitani 8,
Tel. 0498204551
padovacultura.padovanel.il

**Museo antoniano e Mostra
antoniana della Devozione
popolare**
Piazza del Santo 11,
Tel. 0498225656
www.basilicadelsanto.org

**Museo del Precinema -
Collezione Minici Zotti**
Prato della Valle 1/A,
Tel. 0498763838
www.minicizotti.it

Museo di Mineralogia
Corso Garibaldi 37,
Tel. 0498272033-0498272000
www.musei.unipd.it

Museo diocesano
Piazza Duomo 12,
Tel. 0498761924-049652855
www.museodiocesanopadova.it

**Museo di Scienze Archeologiche
e d'Arte**
Piazza Capitaniato 7,
Tel. 0498274611-0498274576
www.musei.unipd.it/archeologia

Museo di Storia della Fisica
Via Loredan 10,
Tel. 0498277153
www.musei.unipd.it/fisica

**Museo La Specola INAF Orto
botanico**
Via Orto botanico 15,
Tel. 0498272119
www.ortobotanico.unipd.it

**Osservatorio astronomico di
Padova**
Vicolo dell'Osservatorio 5,
Tel. 0498293469
www.oapd.inaf.it

Palazzo Zuckermann
Corso Garibaldi 33,
Tel. 049665567
padovacultura.padovanet.it

ROCCA PIETORE (BL)

**Museo della Grande Guerra in
Marmolada**
Loc. Malga Ciapela,
forcella Serauta,
Tel. 0437522984
www.museo.marmolada.com

ROVIGO

**Accademia dei Concordi-
Pinacoteca**
Palazzo Roverella, via Laurenti,
Tel. 042527991-042521654
www.concordi.it

TREVISO

Museo civico «Luigi Bailo»
Borgo Cavour 24,
Tel. 0422658442-0422591337
www.comune.treviso.it

Museo diocesano di Arte sacra
Via Canoniche 9,
Tel. 0422416700
www.diocesitv.it

VENICE/VENEZIA

**Arsenale and Museo Storico
Navale**
Riva S. Biasio Castello 2148,
Tel. 0412441399
www.marina.difesa.it/venezia/info.asp

**Ca' Pesaro-Galleria
internazionale d'Arte moderna**
S. Croce 2076,
Tel. 041721127
www.museiciviciveneziani.it

**Ca' Rezzonico-Museo del
Settecento veneziano**
Dorsoduro 3136,
Tel. 0412410100
www.museiciviciveneziani.it

Collezione Peggy Guggenheim
Dorsoduro 701,
Tel. 0412405440-0412405411
www.guggenheim-venice.it

Gallerie dell'Accademia
Dorsoduro 1050,
campo della Carità,
Tel. 0415222247
www.artive.arti.beniculturali.it

**Galleria Giorgio Franchetti
alla Ca' d'Oro**
Cannaregio 3932,
Tel. 0415238790-0415222349
www.artive.arti.beniculturali.it

Museo archeologico nazionale
Piazza S. Marco 17 (entrance from
Museo Correr),
Tel. 0415225978
www.artive.arti.beniculturali.it

Museo civico di Storia naturale
S. Croce 1730,
Fondaco dei Turchi,
Tel. 0412750206
www.museiciviciveneziani.it

Museo Correr
Ala napoleonica, piazza S. Marco,
Tel. 0415209070
www.museiciviciveneziani.it

**Museo d'Arte orientale
a Ca' Pesaro**
S. Croce 2076, S. Stae,
Tel. 0415241173
www.arteorientale.org

**Museo delle Icone bizantine
e postbizantine**
Castello 3412, ponte dei Greci,
Tel. 0415226581
www.istitutoellenico.org

**Museo diocesano d'Arte sacra
di Santa Apollonia**
Castello,
fondamenta della Canonica 4312,
Tel. 0415229166-0412413817
www.museodiocesanovenezia.it

**Museo di Storia del Tessuto e
del Costume- Palazzo Mocenigo**
S. Croce 1992,
Tel. 041721798
www.museicivicivenezia ni.it

Museo ebraico di Venezia
Cannaregio 2902/G,
campo del Ghetto Nuovo,
Tel. 041715359
www.museoebraico.it

Museo Fortuny
S. Marco 3780, campo S. Beneto,
Tel. 0415200995
www.museicivicivenezia ni.it

Palazzo Ducale
S. Marco 1 (entrance from porta del
Frumento),
Tel. 0412715911
www.museicivicivenezia ni.it

Pinacoteca Manfrediniana
Dorsoduro 1, campo della Salute,
Tel. 0412411018
www.seminariovenezia.it

Scuola Grande dei Carmini
Dorsoduro 2617,
Campo dei Carmini,
Tel. 0415289420
www.provincia.venezia.it

VERONA

**Fondazione Museo
Miniscalchi-Erizzo**
Via S. Mammaso 2/A,
tel 0458032484

**Galleria d'Arte moderna
Palazzo Forti**
Vicolo Due Mori 4,
Tel. 0458001903
www.palazzoforti.it

**Museo archeologico
al Teatro romano**
Regaste Redentore 2,
Tel. 0458000360
www.comune.verona.it/Castelvecchi
o/cvsito/mcivici2.htm

**Museo canonicale e
Biblioteca Capitolare**
Piazza Duomo 29,
Tel. 045592813-
0458012890
www.chieseverona.it

**Museo Civico d'arte di
Castelvecchio**
Corso Castelvecchio 2
Tel. 045594734

Museo civico di Storia naturale
Lungadige Porta Vittoria 9,
Tel. 0458079400
www.museostorianaturaleverona.it

**Museo degli Affreschi
«Giovan Battista Cavalcaselle»
alla Tomba di Giulietta**
Via del Pontiere 35,
Tel. 0458000361
www.comune.verona.it/castelvecchi
o/cvsito/mcivici3.htm

Museo Lapidario Maffeiano
Piazza Bra' 28,
Tel. 045590087
www.comune.verona.it/castelvecchi
o/cvsito/mcivici1.htm

VICENZA

**Pinacoteca civica di Palazzo
Chiericati**
Piazza Matteotti 37/39,
Tel. 0444321348-
0444325071
www.comune.vicenza.it/musei/
vicenza.htm

FRIULI
VENEZIA GIULIA

AQUILEIA (UD)

Museo archeologico nazionale
Via Roma 1,
Tel. 043191016-043191035
www.museoarcheo-aquileia.it

Museo civico del Patriarcato
Via Patriarca Popone,
Tel. 0431919451-0431916905
www.comune.aquileia.ud.it

**Museo paleocristiano
nazionale**
Loc. Monastero, piazza Pirano,
Tel. 043191131
www.museoarcheo-aquileia.it

GORIZIA

**Musei provinciali di Gorizia
Sedi di Borgo Castello**
Borgo Castello 13,
Tel. 0481533926
www.provincia.gorizia.it

GRADO (GO)

**Museo Lapidario del Duomo
di Sant'Eufemia**
Campo Patriarchi,
Tel. 043180146

TRIESTE

**Civico Museo del Castello
di San Giusto-Armeria-Lapidario
tergestino al Bastione Lalio**
Piazza della Cattedrale 3,
Tel. 040309362-040310500
www.triestecultura.it

Civico Museo del Mare
Via Campo Marzio 5,
Tel. 040304885
www.triestecultura.it

**Civico Museo del Risorgimento
and Sacrario Oberdan**
Via XXIV Maggio 4,
Tel. 040361675-040310500
www.triestecultura.it

**Civico Museo di Guerra per la
Pace «Diego de Henriquez»**
Via P. Revoltella 29,
Tel. 040948430
www.triestecultura.it

**Civico Museo di Storia e Arte
and Orto Lapidario**
Piazza della Cattedrale 1,
Tel. 040310500-040308686
www.triestecultura.it

Civico Museo di Storia naturale
Piazza Hortis 4,
Tel. 0406758659-
0406758661
www.triestecultura.it

**Civico Museo
«Mario Morpurgo de Nilma»**
Via M.R. Imbriani 5,
Tel. 040636969-040310500
www.triestecultura.it

**Civico Museo «Pasquale
Revoltella» - Galleria di Arte
moderna**
Via Diaz 27,
Tel. 0406754350-0406754158
www.museorevoltella.it

Civico Museo Sartorio
Largo Papa Giovanni XXIII 1,
Tel. 040301479-040310500
www.triestecultura.it

**Civico Museo teatrale
Fondazione «Carlo Schmidl»**
Via G. Rossini 4,
Tel. 0406754072-
040310500
www.triestecultura.it

**Museo della Comunità ebraica
«Carlo e Vera Wagner»**
Via del Monte 5/7,
Tel. 040633819-040371466
www.triestebraica.it

Museo della Farmacia Picciola
Via Caccia 3,
Tel. 040632558
www.retecivica.trieste.it

**Museo Petrarchesco
Piccolomineo**
Piazza Hortis 4,
Tel. 0406758184
www.museopetrarchesco.it

Museo sveviano
Piazza Hortis 4,
Tel. 0406758182-0406758200
www.museosveviano.it

UDINE

**Civici Musei e Gallerie
di Storia e Arte**
Piazzale del Castello 1,
Tel. 0432271591
www.comune.udine.it

**Civica Galleria d'Arte moderna
GAMUD**
Via Ampezzo 2,
Tel. 0432295891
www.comune.udine.it

LIGURIA

BORDIGHERA (IM)

**Museo Biblioteca
«Clarence Bicknell»**
Via Romana 39/bis,
Tel. 0184263694
www.iisl.it

GENOA/GENOVA

Castello D'Albertis
Corso Dogali 18,
Tel. 0102723820-0102723464
www.castellodalbertisgenova.it

**Museo civico di Storia naturale
«Giacomo Doria»**
Via Brigata Liguria 9,
Tel. 010564567
www.museodoria.it

**Museo del Tesoro della
Cattedrale di San Lorenzo**
Cattedrale, piazza S. Lorenzo,
Tel. 0102471831
www.museosanlorenzo.it

Museo di Palazzo Reale
Via Balbi 10,
Tel. 0102710236
www.palazzorealegenova.it

Museo di Sant'Agostino
Piazza Sarzano 35/r,
Tel. 0102511263
www.museosantagostino.it

**Palazzo Doria Pamphilj
o del Principe**
Piazza del Principe 4,
Tel. 010255509
www.palazzodelprincipe.it

IMPERIA

Museo dell'Olivo
Loc. Oneglia,
via Garessio 13,
Tel. 0183295762
www.museodellolivo.com

**Museo navale internazionale del
Ponente ligure**
Loc. Porto Maurizio,
piazza Duomo 11,
Tel. 0183651541-3356399861
www.sullacrestadellonda.it/
museoimperia

Pinacoteca civica
Piazza Duomo 11/A,
Tel. 0183701551-0183701556
www.comune.imperia.it

LA SPEZIA

**Museo civico d'Arte antica,
medievale e moderna
«Amedeo Lia»**
Via Prione 234,
Tel. 0187731100
www.castagna.it/musei/mal

**Museo del Castello di San
Giorgio**
Castello di S. Giorgio,
via XXVII Marzo,
Tel. 0187751142
www.laspeziacultura.it

**Museo civico di Etnografia e
Antropologia «Giovanni
Podenzana» and Museo
diocesano**
Via Prione 156,
Tel. 0187258570
www.laspeziacultura.it

SAVONA

**Civico Museo storico-
archeologico del Priamar**
Corso Mazzini 1,
Tel. 019822708
www.museoarcheosavona.it

Pinacoteca civica
Piazza Chabrol 1/2,
Tel. 019811520-0198387391
www.comune.savona.it

EMILIA-ROMAGNA

BOBBIO (PC)

**Museo dell'Abbazia and Museo
della Città**
Piazza S. Fara 5,
Tel. 0523936219
www.cooltour.it

BOLOGNA

Collezioni comunali d'Arte
Piazza Maggiore 6,
Tel. 0512193526-0512193629
www.comune.bologna.it/iperbole/M
useiCivici

Museo civico archeologico
Via dell'Archiginnasio 2,
Tel. 0512757211
www.comune.bologna.it/museoarch
eologico

Museo civico medievale
Via Manzoni 4,
Tel. 0512193930
www.comune.bologna.it/iperbole/M
useiCivici

Museo di San Domenico
Piazza S. Domenico 13,
Tel. 0516400411

Museo di San Petronio
Piazza Maggiore,
Tel. 051225442

**Museo geologico
«Giovanni Capellini»**
Via Zamboni 63,
Tel. 0512094555-0512094593
www.museocapellini.org

Museo Morandi
Piazza Maggiore 6,
Tel. 0512193332-0512193629
www.museomorandi.it

Pinacoteca nazionale
Via delle Belle Arti 56,
Tel. 0514209411
www.pinacotecabologna.it

BUSSETO (PR)

Casa Barezzi-Museo verdiano
Via Roma 119,
Tel. 0524931117
www.amicidiverdi.it

Villa Pallavicino
Via Provesi 35,
Tel. 052492239
Temporarily closed

CATTOLICA (RN)

Museo della Regina
Via Pascoli 23,
Tel. 0541831464
www.cattolica.net

FERRARA

Casa dell'Ariosto
Via Ariosto 67,
Tel. 0532209988-
0532208564
www.artecultura.fe.it

Casa Romei
Via Savonarola,
Tel. 0532240341
www.beniculturali.it

Civico Museo di Schifanoia
Via Scandiana 23,
Tel. 053264178-053262281
www.artecultura.fe.it

Museo archeologico nazionale
Via XX Settembre 122,
Tel. 053266299
www.archeobo.arti.beniculturali.it/
Ferrara/index.htm

Museo della Cattedrale
Via S. Romano 1/9,
Tel. 0532761299-0532244949
www.comune.fe.it/at

Museo Lapidario civico
Via Camposabbionario 1,
Tel. 053264178-0532209988
www.artecultura.fe.it

Palazzina di Marfisa d'Este
Corso Giovecca 170,
Tel. 0532207450-0532209988
www.artecultura.fe.it

Pinacoteca nazionale
Palazzo dei Diamanti,
corso Ercole I d'Este 21,
Tel. 0532205844
www.pinacotecaferrara.it

MODENA

Galleria estense
Piazza S. Agostino 337,
Tel. 0594395711
www.galleriaestense.it

Musei Civici
Viale Vittorio Veneto 5,
tel 0592033100
www.comune.modena.it

**Museo Lapidario-Musei del
Duomo**
Via Lanfranco 6,
Tel. 0594396969
www.duomodimodena.it

PARMA

**Galleria nazionale di Parma
and Teatro Farnese**
Piazza della Pilotta 5,
Tel. 0521233309
www.artipr.arti.beniculturali.it/htm/
Musei.htm

Museo archeologico nazionale
Piazza della Pilotta 5,
Tel. 0521233718
www.archeobo.arti.beniculturali.it/
Parma/index.htm

PIACENZA

**Musei civici
di Palazzo Farnese**
Piazza Cittadella 29,
Tel. 0523492658
www.musei.piacenza.it

RAVENNA

Museo arcivescovile
Piazza Arcivescovado 1,
Tel. 0544541688
www.ravennamosaici.it

**Museo d'Arte della Città di
Ravenna-MAR**
Via Roma 13,
Tel. 0544482356
www.museocitta.ra.it

Museo nazionale
Complesso di S. Vitale,
via Fiandrini,
Tel. 054434424
www.comune.ra.it/citta/
cultura_biblioteche/
museonazionale.htm

REGGIO NELL'EMILIA

Civici Musei
Via Palazzolo 2,
Tel. 0522456477
musei.comune.re.it

**Galleria civica «Anna e Luigi
Parmeggiani»**
Corso Cairoli 2,
Tel. 0522456477
musei.comune.re.it

RICCIONE (RN)

Museo del Territorio
Via Lazio 10,
Tel. 0541600113
www.comune.riccione.rn.it

RIMINI

Museo della Città
Via L. Tonini 1,
Tel. 05412148 2-0541704421
www.comune.rimini.it

TUSCANY

AREZZO

Museo and Casa Vasari
Via XX Settembre 55,
Tel. 0575409040

**Museo archeologico nazionale
«Gaio Cilnio Mecenate»**
Via Margaritone 10,
Tel. 057520882

Museo diocesano di Arte sacra
Piazzetta dietro il Duomo 12,
Tel. 057523991
Temporarily closed

**Museo statale d'Arte medievale
e moderna**
Via S. Lorentino 8,
Tel. 0575409050-05753776780
www.comunediarezzo.it

CORTONA (AR)

**Museo dell'Accademia etrusca e
della Città di Cortona-MAEC**
Piazza Signorelli 9,
Tel. 0575637235
www.cortonamaec.org

**Museo diocesano
del Capitolo**
Piazza Duomo 1,
Tel. 057562830
www.provincia.arezzo.it/museidentr
olemura/diocesano/home.html

FLORENCE/FIRENZE

**Galleria degli Uffizi and
Corridoio vasariano**
Piazzale degli Uffizi,
Tel. 0552388651-0552388652
www.polomusale.firenze.it/musei/
uffizi

**Museo dell'Opera di Santa
Maria del Fiore**
Piazza Duomo 9,
Tel. 0552302885
www.operaduomo.firenze.it

Museo di San Marco
Piazza S. Marco 3,
Tel. 0552388608
www.polomusale.firenze.it/muse/sa
nmarco/

Museo nazionale del Bargello
Via del Proconsolo 4,
Tel. 0552388606
www.polomusale.firenze.it/bargello

Palazzo Pitti
Piazza Pitti 1,
Tel. 0552388763-
0552388713
www.polomusale.firenze.it/musei

**Palazzo Vecchio Quartieri
monumentali**
Piazza della Signoria,
Tel. 0552768465-0552768325
www.comune.firenze.it/
servizi_pubblici/arte/musei/a.htm

GROSSETO

**Museo archeologico e d'Arte
della Maremma-Museo d'Arte
sacra della Diocesi di Grosseto**
Piazza Baccarini 3,
Tel. 0564488752

**Museo di Storia Naturale
della Maremma**
Strada Corsini 5,
Tel. 0564414701
Temporarily closed

LUCCA

**Complesso museale
e archeologico della Cattedrale**
Piazza Antelminelli,
Tel. 0583490530
www.museocattedralelucca.it

Museo nazionale di Villa Guinigi
Via della Quarquonia,
Tel. 0583496033
www.comune.lucca.it

**Pinacoteca nazionale
di Palazzo Mansi**
Via Galli Tassi 43,
Tel. 058355570
www.comune.lucca.it

PISA

Museo delle Sinopie
Piazza Duomo,
Tel. 0503872210-0503872211
www.opapisa.it

Museo dell'Opera del Duomo
Piazza Duomo,
Tel. 0503872210
www.opapisa.it

**Museo nazionale
di Palazzo Reale**
Lungarno Pacinotti 46,
Tel. 050926540
www.ambientepi.arti.beniculturali.it

Museo nazionale di San Matteo
Lungarno mediceo,
piazza S. Matteo in Soarta,
Tel. 050541865
www.ambientepi.arti.beniculturali.it

PISTOIA

**Musei Rospigliosi-Museo
diocesano Museo del Ricamo**
Via Ripa del Sale 3,
Tel. 057328740
www.sistemamusealipistoiese

Museo civico
Piazza del Duomo 1,
Tel. 05733711

SAN GIMIGNANO (SI)

**Museo civico-Palazzo comunale,
Pinacoteca, Torre Grossa**
Piazza del Duomo,
Tel. 0577990312

Museo d'Arte sacra
Piazza L. Pecori 8,
Tel. 0577940316
www.sangimignano.com/
sgimas.htm

SIENA

Libreria Piccolomini
Piazza del Duomo 8,
Tel. 0577283048
www.operaduomo.siena.it

Museo Archeologico Nazionale
Spedale di Santa Maria della Scala,
piazza Duomo,
Tel. 057749153

Museo civico
Piazza del Campo 1,
Tel. 0577292226
www.comune.siena.it/museocivico/

**Museo dell'Opera
della Metropolitana**
Piazza Duomo 8,
Tel. 0577283048
www.operaduomo.siena.it

Pinacoteca nazionale
Via S. Pietro 29,
Tel. 057746052

VOLTERRA (PI)

Museo diocesano di Arte sacra
Via Roma 13,
Tel. 058886290
www.comune.volterra.pi.it/museiit/
musart.html

Museo etrusco «Guarnacci»
Via Don Minzoni 15,
Tel. 058886347
www.comune.volterra.pi.it/museiit/
metru.html

Pinacoteca e Museo civico
Via dei Sarti 1,
Tel. 058887580
www.comune.volterra.pi.it

MARCHE

ANCONA

**Museo archeologico
nazionale delle Marche**
Via Ferretti 6,
Tel. 071202602
www.archeomarche.it/musarch.htm

Museo diocesano
Piazza Duomo 9,
Tel. 071200391
www.diocesi.ancona.it

**Pinacoteca comunale
«Francesco Podesti» and
Galleria d'Arte moderna**
Via Pizzecolli 17,
Tel. 0712225041
www.comune.ancona.it

ASCOLI PICENO

Galleria d'Arte contemporanea
Corso Mazzini 90,
Tel. 0736248662
www.comune.ap.it/citta/musei.htm

Pinacoteca civica
Piazza Arringo 7,
Tel. 0736298213
www.comune.ap.it

PESARO

Casa Rossini
Via Rossini 34,
Tel. 0721387357-
0721387393
www.comune.pesaro.pu.it

**Musei civici (Pinacoteca e
Museo delle Ceramiche)**
Piazza Toschi Mosca 29,
Tel. 0721387541-0721387474
www.museicivicipesaro.it

Museo archeologico oliveriano
Via Mazza 97, Tel. 072133344
www.archeoprovincia.it

URBINO (PU)

Galleria nazionale delle Marche
Piazza Duca Federico 107,
Tel. 0722322625

Museo archeologico statale
Palazzo Ducale,
piazza Duca Federico,
Tel. 07222760
www.comune.urbino.ps.it

Museo diocesano Albani
Piazza G. Pascoli 1,
Tel. 07222850

Palazzo Ducale
Piazza Duca Federico,
Tel. 0722322625
www.comune.urbino.ps.it

UMBRIA

ASSISI (PG)

**Museo del Foro romano e
Collezione archeologica**
Via Portica,
Tel. 075813053
www.sistemamuseo.it

**Museo della Basilica di San
Francesco, Tesoro e Collezione
Perkins**
Piazza S. Francesco 2,
Tel. 075819001
www.sanfrancescoassisi.org

**Museo diocesano e Cripta
di San Rufino**
Piazza S. Rufino 3,
Tel. 075812712
www.assisimuseocattedrale.com

ORVIETO (TR)

**Museo archeologico
«Claudio Faina»**
Palazzo Faina,
piazza del Duomo 29,
Tel. 0763341216-0763341511
www.museofaina.it

Museo dell'Opera del Duomo
Piazza del Duomo 23,
Tel. 0763343592
www.opsm.it

PERUGIA

Galleria nazionale dell'Umbria
Corso Vannucci 19,
Tel. 0755741400
www.gallerianazionaleumbria.it

**Museo archeologico
nazionale dell'Umbria**
Piazza G. Bruno 10,
Tel. 0755727141
www.archeopg.arti.beniculturali.it

Museo capitolare di San Lorenzo
Piazza IV Novembre,
Tel. 0755724853

SPOLETO (PG)

Galleria Civica d'Arte Moderna
Via Loreto Vittori 11,
Tel. 074346434
www.spoletopermusei.it

**Museo archeologico
nazionale di Spoleto**
Via S. Agata 18/A,
Tel. 0743223277-0743225531
www.archeopg.arti.beniculturali.it

**Museo diocesano di Spoleto,
Norcia e Basilica di Santa
Eufemia**
Palazzo arcivescovile,
via A. Saffi 13,
Tel. 0743231022
www.museiecclesiastici.it

**Museo Nazionale del Ducato
di Spoleto**
Piazza Campello 1,
Tel. 0743223055

Pinacoteca comunale
Palazzo Spada, piazza Sordini,
Tel. 074345940
www.spoletopermusei.it

LAZIO

FRASCATI (RM)

**Scuderie Aldobrandini - Museo
tuscolano**
Piazza Marconi 6,
Tel. 069417195
www.scuderiealdobrandini.it

ROME/ROMA

Galleria Colonna
Via della Pilotta 17,
Tel. 066784350
www.galleriacolonna.it

Galleria Corsini
Via della Lungara 10,
Tel. 0668802323
www.galleriaborghese.it

Galleria Doria Pamphilj
Piazza del Collegio romano 2,
Tel. 066797323
www.doriapamphilj.it

Galleria nazionale d'Arte antica
Via Quattro Fontane 13,
Tel. 064824184
www.galleriaborghese.it/barberini/it/

**Galleria nazionale d'Arte
moderna**
Viale delle Belle Arti 131,
Tel. 0632298328-
0632298221
www.gnam.arti.beniculturali.it

Galleria Spada
Piazza Capo di Ferro 13,
Tel. 066874896-066874893
www.galleriaborghese.it

Musei Vaticani
Viale Vaticano,
Tel. 0669883333
www.vatican.va

Museo and Galleria Borghese
Parco di Villa Borghese,
piazzale Museo Borghese 5,
Tel. 068413979-068417645
www.galleriaborghese.it

Museo Barracco
Corso Vittorio Emanuele II 166,
Tel. 066875657
www2.comune.roma.it/
museobarracco

Musei Capitolini
Piazza del Campidoglio 1,
Tel. 0667102475
www.museicapitolini.org

Museo di Arti Applicate del Palazzo di Venezia
Via del Plebiscito 118,
Tel. 0632810

Museo di Roma in Trastevere
Piazza S. Egidio 1/B,
Tel. 065816563
www.comune.roma.it/museodiroma.trastevere

Museo nazionale di Castel Sant'Angelo
Lungotevere Castello 50,
Tel. 066819111-0639967600

Museo nazionale etrusco di Villa Giulia
Piazzale di Villa Giulia 9,
Tel. 063201951-063226571
www.beniculturali.it

Museo nazionale romano, Crypta Balbi
Via delle Botteghe Oscure 31,
Tel. 0639967700-066977671
www.archeorm.arti.beniculturali.it

Museo Storico Vaticano
Piazza S. Giovanni in Laterano,
Tel. 0669886376-0669886386
www.vatican.va

TARQUINIA (VT)

Museo archeologico nazionale
Palazzo Vitelleschi, piazza Cavour 1,
Tel. 0766856036
www.tarquinia.net

VITERBO

Museo civico
Piazza F. Crispi 2,
Tel. 0761348275
www.comune.viterbo.it

Museo nazionale etrusco
Piazza della Rocca 21/B,
Tel. 0761325929

ABRUZZO

CHIETI

Museo archeologico nazionale d'Abruzzo
Villa Comunale 1,
Tel. 0871331668
www.muvi.org/musarc

Museo d'Arte «Costantino Barbella»
Via De Lollis 10,
Tel. 0871330873-08714083352
www.provincia.chieti.it

Museo La Civitella
Via Pianell, Tel. 087163137
www.lacivitella.it

L'AQUILA

Museo nazionale d'Abruzzo
Via O. Colecchi 1,
Tel. 0862633439
www.muvi.org/museonazionaledabruzzo

PESCARA

Museo Casa natale di Gabriele D'Annunzio
Corso Manthoné 116, Tel. 08560391
www.casadannunzio.beniculturali.it

Museo civico «Basilio Cascella»
Via Marconi 45,
Tel. 0854283515-08542831
www.muvi.org/museocascella

Museo delle Genti d'Abruzzo
Via delle Caserme 22,
Tel. 0854510026-0854511562
www.gentidabruzzo.it

Museo delle Meraviglie marine
Via Paolucci 113, Tel. 0854283516
www.comune.pescara.it/internet/html/citta_info_musei.html

MOLISE

CAMPOBASSO

Nuovo Museo provinciale sannitico
Via Chiarizia 14, Tel. 0874412265

ISERNIA

Museo Nazionale del Paleolitico and Museo archeologico Santa Maria delle Monache
Corso Marcelli 48,
Tel. 0865410500

SEPINO (CB)

Museo archeologico di Saepinum
Loc. Altilia, Tel. 0874790207

CAMPANIA

AVELLINO

Museo provinciale irpino
Palazzo della Cultura,
corso Europa, Tel. 0825790501

BOSCOREALE (NA)

Antiquarium nazionale Uomo e Ambiente nel Territorio vesuviano
Via Sette Termini 15,
Tel. 0815368796
www.pompeiisites.org

CAPUA (CE)

Museo provinciale campano
Via Roma 68,
Tel. 0823620076-0823961402
www.museocampano.it

CASERTA

Appartamenti storici del Palazzo Reale and Museo dell'Opera e del Territorio
Via Douhet 22,
Tel. 0823448084-0823277111
www.reggiadicaserta.org

LACCO AMENO (NA)

Museo Diefenbach
Certosa di S. Giacomo,
Tel. 0818376218-0815781769

Museo e Scavi archeologici Santa Restituta
Piazza S. Restituta,
Tel. 081992442-081991706

MAIORI (SA)

Museo d'Arte sacra «Don Clemente Confalone»
Largo Campo, Tel. 089877090

NAPLES/NAPOLI

Acquario e Stazione zoologica «Anton Dohrn»
Villa Comunale 1,
Tel. 0815833263-0815833111
www.szn.it

Appartamento storico di Palazzo Reale
Piazza Plebiscito 1,
Tel. 0815808111-081400547

Museo archeologico nazionale
Piazza Museo 19,
Tel. 0814422111
www.archeona.arti.beniculturali.it

Museo civico di Castel Nuovo
Maschio angioino, piazza Municipio,
Tel. 081420241-0814201342
www.comune.napoli.it

Museo civico Gaetano Filangieri
Via Duomo 288,
Tel. 081203175

Museo di Capodimonte
Via Miano 2,
Tel. 0817499111
www.capodimonte.spmn.remuna.org

Museo nazionale della Ceramica Duca di Martina nella Villa Floridiana
Via Cimarosa 77, Tel. 0815788418
www.cib.na.cnr.it/remuna/florid/indice.html

Museo Nazionale di San Martino
Largo San Martino 5,
Tel. 0815586408-0812294502
www.beniculturali.it

Museo Principe Diego Aragona Pignatelli Cortes
Via della Riviera di Chiaia 200,
Tel. 0817612356-081669675
www.beniculturali.it

PADULA (SA)

Museo archeologico della Lucania occidentale
Certosa di S. Lorenzo, viale Certosa,
Tel. 097577117

PAESTUM (SA)

Museo narrante del Santuario di Hera Argiva
Via Barizzo Foce Sele 29,
Tel. 0828861440
www.archeosa.beniculturali.it

SALERNO

Museo archeologico provinciale
Via S. Benedetto 38,
Tel. 089231135-089225578

Museo della Ceramica «Alfonso Tafuri»
Largo Cassavecchia 11,
Tel. 089227782

Museo diocesano San Matteo
Largo Plebiscito 12,
Tel. 089239126
www.diocesisalerno.it

Pinacoteca provinciale di Salerno
Palazzo Pinto,
Via Mercanti 62,
Tel. 0892583073
www.pinacoteca.provinciasalerno.org

SORRENTO (NA)

Museo Correale di Terranova
Via Correale 50,
Tel. 0818781846

APULIA

BARI

Museo diocesano della Cattedrale
Palazzo arcivescovile,
via Bianchi Dottula,
Tel. 0805210064

Pinacoteca provinciale «Corrado Giaquinto»
Via Spalato 19,
Tel. 0805412422-0805412423
www.provincia.bari.it

FOGGIA

Museo civico
Piazza V. Nigri 1,
Tel. 0881726245
www.urban.foggia.it

LECCE

Museo archeologico provinciale «Sigismondo Castromediano»
Viale Gallipoli 28,
Tel. 0832683503
www.provincia.le.it

MANFREDONIA (FG)

Museo archeologico nazionale
Castello, corso Manfredi,
Tel. 0884587838

MONTE SANT'ANTANGELO (FG)

Museo delle Arti e Tradizioni popolari del Gargano «Giovanni Tancredi»
Piazza S. Francesco 15,
Tel. 0884562098
www.ecogargano.it

TARANTO

Museo archeologico nazionale
Palazzo Pantaleo,
corso Vittorio Emanuele,
Tel. 0994532112
www.museotaranto.it

BASILICATA

METAPONTO (MT)

Museo archeologico nazionale di Metaponto
Viale Aristea 21, Tel. 0835745327
www.archeobasi.it

POLICORO (MT)

Museo nazionale della Siritide
Via Colombo 8, Tel. 0835972154
www.archeobasi.it/musei

POTENZA

Museo archeologico provinciale
Via Ciccotti, Tel. 0971444820
www.provincia.potenza.it/museo

CALABRIA

CASSANO ALL'IONIO (CS)

Museo diocesano d'Arte sacra
Piazza S. Eusebio da Cassano,
Tel. 098171048

CASTROVILLARI (CS)

Museo civico archeologico
Protoconvento,
via S. Francesco d'Assisi,
Tel. 0981252266
www.comune.castrovillari.cs.it

COSENZA

Museo dei Brettii
Salita S. Agostino,
Tel. 0984813404

REGGIO DI CALABRIA

Museo Nazionale
Piazza De Nava 26,
Tel. 0965812255
www.calabriaweb.it/magnagrecia/ht
ml/presentazionemusei.htm

ROSSANO (CS)

Museo diocesano d'Arte sacra
Piazza Duomo 25,
Tel. 0983525263
www.oldcalabria.org/musei/welcom
e.php

SIBARI (CS)

Museo archeologico nazionale della Sibaritide
Loc. Casabianca,
Tel. 098179391
www.museidellacalabria.com

SICILY

ACI CASTELLO (CT)

Museo civico
Piazza Castello,
Tel. 095271026
www.comune.acicastello.ct.it

ACIREALE (CT)

Pinacoteca Zelantea
Via Marchese di S. Giuliano 17,
Tel. 0957634516
www.zelantea.it

AGRIGENTO

Museo archeologico regionale
Contrada S. Nicola,
Tel. 0922401565
www.regione.sicilia.it

CALTAGIRONE (CT)

Museo regionale della Ceramica
Via Giardino Pubblico,
Tel. 093358418
www.regione.sicilia.it

CASTELVETRANO (TP)

Museo civico
Via Garibaldi 50,
Tel. 0924904932
www.castelvetrano.it

CATANIA

Casa Museo Giovanni Verga
Via S. Anna 8,
Tel. 0957150598
www.regione.sicilia.it

Museo Civico Belliniano
Piazza S. Francesco d'Assisi 3,
Tel. 0957150535
www.comune.catania.it

ERICE (TP)

Museo civico «Antonio Cordici»
Piazza Umberto I,
Tel. 0923860048
www.comune.erice.tp.it

GELA (CL)

Museo archeologico regionale
Corso Vittorio Emanuele 1,
Tel. 0933912626

LICATA (AG)

Museo archeologico della Badia
Via Dante 12,
Tel. 0922772602
www.regione.sicilia.it

MARSALA (TP)

Museo archeologico Baglio Anselmi
Lungomare Boeo 30,
Tel. 0923952535
www.regione.sicilia.it

Museo Degli Arazzi Della Matrice
Via Garraffa 57,
Tel. 0923711327

MAZARA DEL VALLO (TP)

Museo civico
Piazza Plebiscito 2,
Tel. 0923949593
www.comune.mazara-del-vallo.tp.it

MESSINA

Museo Regionale
Viale della Libertà 465,
Tel. 090361292
www.regione.sicilia.it

NOTO (SR)

Museo civico archeologico
Corso Vittorio Emanuele,
Tel. 0931836462

PALERMO

Civica Galleria d'Arte moderna «Empedocle Restivo»
Via Sant'Anna 21,
Tel. 0918431605
www.galleriadartemodernapalermo.it

Galleria regionale della Sicilia Palazzo Abatellis
Via Alloro 4, Tel. 0916230011
www.regione.sicilia.it/beniculturali

Museo archeologico regionale «Antonino Salinas»
Piazza Olivella,
Tel. 0916116805
www.regione.sicilia.it/beniculturali/d
irbenicult/salinas/index.htm

Museo Diocesano
Via M. Bonello 2,
Tel. 0916077215
www.diocesipa.it

Museo etnografico siciliano «Giuseppe Pitrè»
Viale Duca degli Abruzzi 1,
Tel. 0917404879
museopitre.interfree.it

Museo internazionale delle Marionette «Antonio Pasqualino»
Piazzetta Niscemi 5,
Tel. 091328060
www.museomarionettapalermo.it

RAGUSA

Museo archeologico Ibleo
Via Natalelli 107,
Tel. 0932622963
www.regione.sicilia.it

SIRACUSA

Galleria regionale di Palazzo Bellomo
Via Capodieci 14/16,
Tel. 093169511
www.regione.sicilia.it/beniculturali/di
rbenicult/musei/musei2/bellomo.htm

Museo archeologico regionale «Paolo Orsi»
Viale Teocrito 66,
Tel. 0931464022
www.ibmsnet.it/siracusa/
paoloors.html

TRAPANI

Museo regionale «Conte Agostino Pepoli»
Via Conte Agostino Pepoli 180,
Tel. 0923553269
www.regione.sicilia.it

SARDINIA

ALGHERO (SS)

Museo diocesano d'Arte sacra
Piazza Duomo 1,
Tel. 0799733041
www.algheromuseo.it

CAGLIARI

Galleria comunale d'Arte
Giardini Pubblici, l
argo G. Dessì,
Tel. 070490727
www.galleriacomunaledartecagliari.it

Museo archeologico nazionale
Cittadella dei Musei,
piazza Arsenale,
Tel. 070655911-070684000

Museo d'Arte siamese «Stefano Cardu»
Cittadella dei Musei,
piazza Arsenale,
Tel. 070651888

Museo del Santuario di Nostra Signora di Bonaria
Piazza Bonaria,
Tel. 070301747
www.bonaria.eu

Museo di Mineralogia «L. De Prunner» Museo sardo di Geologia e Paleontologia «D. Lovisato»
Via Trentino 51,
Tel. 070757712
www.unica.it/dister

Pinacoteca nazionale
Cittadella dei Musei,
piazza Arsenale,
Tel. 070674054-
070662496
www.pinacoteca.cagliari.benicultur
ali.it

Raccolta delle Cere anatomiche di Clemente Susini
Cittadella dei Musei,
piazza Arsenale 1,
Tel. 0706757627-0706754001
medicina.unica.it/cere

DORGALI (NU)

Museo Archeologico
Via La Marmora,
Tel. 078496243
www.ghivine.com

LA MADDALENA ARCHIPELAGO (OT)

Museo Archeologico Navale "Nino Lamboglia"
La Maddalena Island, loc.
Mongiardino, strada panoramica,
Tel. 0789790660
Temporarily closed

Museo garibaldino nazionale di Caprera
Caprera Island,
Tel. 0789727162
www.compendiogaribaldino.it

NUORO

Museo archeologico nazionale
Via Mannu 3,
Tel. 078431688

Museo Deleddiano Casa Natale di Grazia Deledda
Via Deledda 42,
Tel. 0784258088-0784242900
www.isresardegna.org

Museo dell'Arte della Provincia di Nùoro – M.A.N.
Via Sebastiano Satta 15,
Tel. 0784252110
www.museoman.it

Museo della Vita e delle Tradizioni Popolari Sarde
Via Mereu 56, Tel. 0784257035
www.isresardegna.org

ORISTANO

Antiquarium arborense - Museo archeologico «G. Pau»
Piazzetta Corrias,
Tel. 0783791262

SANLURI

Museo Duca d'Aosta - Castello di Sanluri
Via Generale Nino Villa Santa 1,
Tel. 0709307105
www.sabattalla.it

SANT'ANTIOCO (CI)

Museo archeologico «Ferruccio Barreca»
Piazza Cartagine,
Tel. 078182105
www.archeotur.it

SASSARI

Museo archeologico-etnografico «Giovanni Antonio Sanna»
Via Roma 64,
Tel. 079272203
www.archeossnu.it

Museo diocesano del Tesoro del Duomo
Piazza Duomo, Tel. 079232067
www.diocesi.sassari.it

Museo storico della Brigata Sassari
Piazza Castello 9, Tel. 0792085111
www.assonazbrigatasassari.it/
museo.htm

PRACTICAL INFO

405

This section contains a list in "regional" order of the hotels and restaurants selected by Touring Club Italiano. Like the rest of the guidebook, the section starts with Valle d'Aosta and closes with Sardinia. For each region, the list is in alphabetical order according to place, including practically all the places – providing they have one hotel or restaurant – mentioned in the guidebook. To make it easier to find the general location, each entry also includes, in brackets, the letter code for the relevant province. For more information about the provinces (administrative areas within regions) and a list of which provinces the letter codes stand for, go to p. 445. The key facilities of the hotels and restaurants are indicated using symbols, which are explained on p. 395.

✯✯✯ ✯✯✯ ✯✯✯ ✯✯ ✯ Hotels	⌘ Outdoor pool	▦ American Express
▥▥▥ ▥▥▥ ▥▥ ▥ Restaurants	✿ Own spa center	▦ Diners Club
♿ Disabled access	✿ Wellness center	▦ Visa
♤ Park/garden (hotel)	▥ Disco	▦ Mastercard
❀ Outdoor area (restaurant)	➤ Pets welcome	▦ JCB
♨ Private section of beach	ⓟ Private parking	B Bancomat
♨ Indoor pool	★ TCI member discount	

VALLE D'AOSTA

AOSTA

ℹ AIAT Aosta
Piazza Chanoux 45
Tel. 016533352
www.aiataosta.com

Hotels

ClassHotel Aosta ✯✯✯✯ ♿ ★
Corso Ivrea 146,
Tel. 016541845
www.classhotel.com
Rooms: 105 - ⓟ ✿ - ▦ ▦ ▦ ▦ B

Milleluci ✯✯✯✯ ♿ ★
Meublé,
Loc. Porossan Roppoz 15,
Tel. 0165235278
www.hotelmilleluci.com
Rooms: 31 - ♤ ⌘ ♨ - ▦ ▦ ▦ ▦ ▦

Rayon de Soleil ✯✯✯
Viale Gran San Bernardo al Km 2,
Tel. 0165262247
www.rayondesoleil.it
Rooms: 45 - ♤ ⓟ ♨ - ▦ ▦ ▦ ▦
▦ B

Restaurants

Trattoria degli Artisti ▥▥
Via Maillet 5/7,
Tel. 016540960
Places: 60/24 - R - ▦ ▦ ▦ B

Vecchia Aosta ▥▥
Piazza Porte Pretoriane 4
Tel. 0165361186
www.vecchiaaosta.it
Places: 120/30 - ❀ - R, C - ▦ ▦ ▦
▦ B

Xavier 12 ▥▥
Via Xavier de Maistre 12
Tel. 0165261771
www.ristorantexavier.it
Places: 60- ⓟ - R, C - ▦ ▦ ▦ ▦ B

BREUIL-CERVINIA (AO)

ℹ AIAT Monte Cervino
Via Guido Rey 17
Tel. 0166949136

Hotels

Excelsior-Planet ✯✯✯✯ ♿
Piazzale Planet 1,
Tel. 0166949426
www.excelsiorplanet.com
Rooms: 46 - ⓟ ♨ - ▦ ▦ B

Hermitage ✯✯✯✯
Via Piolet, Tel. 0166948998
www.hotelhermitage.com
Rooms: 36 - ♤ ⓟ ♨ - ▦ ▦ ▦ ▦

Les Neiges d'Antan ✯✯✯
Loc. Perreres 10, Tel. 0166948775
www.lesneigesdantan.it
Rooms: 24 - ♤ ⓟ ✿ ➤ - ▦ ▦ B

Breithorn ✯✯
Piazza G. Rey 10, Tel. 0166949042
www.cervinia.it
Rooms: 24 - ♤ ⓟ ➤ - ▦ ▦ ▦ ▦ B

Restaurants

Hermitage ▥▥▥
Via Piolet , Tel. 0166948998
www.hotelhermitage.com
Places: 80/20 - ❀ ⓟ - R - ▦ ▦
▦ B

Les Neiges d'Antan ▥▥
Loc. Perreres 10,
Tel. 016694877
www.lesneigesdantan.it
Places: 100/10 - ⓟ - R - ▦ ▦ B

COURMAYEUR (AO)

ℹ AIAT
Monte Bianco 13
Tel. 0165842060

Hotels

Romantik Hotel
Villa Novecento ✯✯✯✯ ♿
Viale Monte Bianco 64 ,
Tel. 0165843000
www.villanovecento.it
Rooms: 26 - ♤ ⓟ ✿ - ▦ ▦ ▦ ▦ B

Soglia Hotel Gran Baita ✯✯✯✯ ♿ ★
Strada Larzey 2, Tel. 0165844040
www.sogliahotels.com
Rooms: 53 - ♤ ⓟ ♨ ♨ - ▦ ▦ ▦ ▦

La Grange ✯✯✯ ★
Meublé. Loc. Entrèves, strada La
Brenva 1, Tel. 0165869733
www.lagrange-it.com
Rooms: 21 - ♤ ⓟ - ▦ ▦ ▦

Pilier d'Angle ✯✯✯ ★
Loc. Entrèves,
Via Grandes Jorasses 18,
Tel. 0165869760,
www.pilierdangle.it
Rooms: 23 - ♤ ⓟ ✿ - ▦ ▦ ▦ ▦
▦ B

Miravalle ✯✯
Loc. Planpicieux 20,
Tel. 0165869777
www.courmayeur-hotelmiravalle.it
Rooms: 11 - ♤ ⓟ - ▦ ▦ B

Restaurants

La Clotze ▥▥
Loc. Planpincieux 21,
Tel. 0165869720
www.laclotze.com
Places: 50 - ❀ ⓟ - R - ▦ ▦ ▦ ▦ B

La Grolla ▥▥
Loc. Peindein Val Veny 104,
Tel. 0165869095
www.lagrolla.it
Places: 120/80 - ❀ ⓟ - R - ▦ ▦ B

Pierre Alexis 1877 ▥▥
Via Marconi 50/A,
Tel. 0165843517
pieralexis@hotmail.it
Places: 85/10 - ⓟ - R, C - ▦ ▦ ▦
▦ B

GRESSONEY-LA-TRINITÉ (AO)

£ *AIAT Gressoney-la Trinité* Edelboden Inferiore
Tel. 0125366143
www.aiatmonterosawalser.it

Hotels

Jolanda Sport ★★★★
Loc. Edelboden,
Tel. 0125366140
www.hoteljolandasport.com
Rooms: 33 - ⚙ 🅿 ⛷ 🏊 ♨ - ⒶⒺ ⓪ 🎫 ᴍᴄ

Lo Scoiattolo ★★★
Loc. Tache 6,
Tel. 0125366313
www.htlscoiattolo.com
Rooms: 14 - ⚙ 🅿 - ⒶⒺ ⓪ 🎫 ᴊᴏ8

Restaurants

Castore Lounge b
Loc. Tache,
Tel. 0125366809
www.castorelounge.com
Places: 20/24 - C - 🎫 ᴍᴄ B

GRESSONEY-SAINT-JEAN (AO)

£ *AIAT Monte Rosa Walser*
Villa Deslex
Tel. 0125355185
www.aiatmonterosawalser.it

Hotels

Gressoney ★★★★
Via Lys 3,
Tel. 0125355986
www.hotelsgressoney.eu
Rooms: 25 - ⚙ 🅿 - ⒶⒺ ⓪ 🎫 ᴍᴄ B

La Gran Baita ★★★ A
Strada Castello Savoia 26,
Tel. 0125356441
www.hotelgranbaita.it
Rooms: 12 - 🅿 - 🎫 ᴍᴄ B

Restaurants

Il Braciere b
Loc. Ondrò Verdebio 2,
Tel. 0125355526
ilbaciere@libero.it
Places: 60 - 🅿 - R - ⒶⒺ 🎫 ᴍᴄ

SAINT-VINCENT (AO)

£ *AIAT Saint-Vincent*
Via Roma 62
Tel. 0166512239
www.saintvincentvda.it

Hotels

G. H. Bollia ★★★★
Viale Piemonte 72,
Tel. 01665231
www.grandhotelbillia.com
Rooms: 246 - ⚙ 🅿 ⛷ ♨ - ⒶⒺ ⓪ 🎫 ᴍᴄ

Alla Posta ★★★ A
Piazza 28 Aprile 1,
Tel. 0166512250
www.hotelpostavda.it
Rooms: 36 - ⚙ - ⒶⒺ ⓪ 🎫 ᴍᴄ B

Leon d'Oro ★★★
Via E. Chanoux 26,
Tel. 0166512202
www.leondoro.info
Rooms: 50 - ⚙ 🅿 - ⒶⒺ ⓪ 🎫 ᴍᴄ B

Restaurants

Batezar c ★
Via G. Marconi 1, Tel. 0166513164
Places: 30 - R - ⓪ 🎫 ᴍᴄ B

Del Viale c A
Viale Piemonte 7,
Tel. 0166512569
www.ristorantedelviale.com
Places: 24/46 - ⚙- C - 🎫 ᴍᴄ B

PIEDMONT

ALBA (CN)

£ *Ufficio Turistico*
Piazza Risorgimento 2
Tel. 017335833
www.langheroero.it

Hotels

Locanda del Ponte
Historic House
Loc. Madonna di Como,
Tel. 0173366616
www.locandadelpilone.com
Rooms: 6 - ⚙ 🅿 - ⒶⒺ ⓪ 🎫 ᴍᴄ B

I Castelli ★★★★
Corso Torino 14/1,
Tel. 0173361978
www.hotel-icastelli.com
Rooms: 87 - 🅿 - ⒶⒺ ⓪ 🎫 B

Restaurants

Del Pilone c
Loc. Madonna di Como 34,
Tel. 0173366616
www.locandadelpilone.com
Places: 25/15 - ⚙ 🅿 - R - ⒶⒺ ⓪ 🎫 ᴍᴄ B

Dulcis Vitis b A
Via Rattazzi 7, Tel. 0173364633
www.dulcisvitis.it
Places: 40/20 - 🅿 - R - ⒶⒺ ⓪ 🎫 ᴍᴄ B

Osteria dell'Arco a A
Piazza Savona 5,
Tel. 0173363974
www.osteriadellarco.it
Places: 50 - R - ⒶⒺ 🎫 ᴍᴄ B

ALESSANDRIA

£ *IAT Alessandria*
Via Gagliaudo 2
Tel. 0131234794

Hotels

Mercure Alessandria-Alli Due Buoi Rossi ★★★★ A ★
Via Cavour 32,
Tel. 0131517171
www.mercure.com
Rooms: 47 - ⒶⒺ ⓪ 🎫 ᴍᴄ B

Londra ★★★ A
Meublé. Corso Cavallotti 51,
Tel. 0131251721
www.londrahotel.info
Rooms: 39 - 🅿 ♣ - ⒶⒺ ⓪ 🎫 ᴍᴄ B

Restaurants

La Fermata c A
Loc. Spinetta Marengo,
Via Bolla 2, Tel. 0131251350
www.lafermata-al.it
Places: 35 - ⚙ 🅿 - I - ⓪ 🎫 ᴍᴄ

Grappolo b ★
Via Casale 28,
Tel. 0131253217
www.ristoranteilgrappolo.it
Places: 60/10 - ⚙ -R - ⒶⒺ ⓪ 🎫 ᴍᴄ B

ARONA (NO)

£ *Ufficio Turismo*
Via San Carlo 2
Tel. 0322243601
www.comune.arona.no.it

Hotels

Concorde ★★★★ A
Via Verbano 1, Tel. 0322249321
www.concordearona.com
Rooms: 82 - 🅿 ♣ - ⒶⒺ ⓪ 🎫 ᴍᴄ B

Giardino ★★★
Meublé. Corso della Repubblica 1,
Tel. 032245994
www.giardinoarona.com
Rooms: 56 - ⒶⒺ ⓪ 🎫 ᴍᴄ

Restaurants

La Fermata c A
Piazza del Popolo 39,
Tel. 0322243366
www.ristorantetavernadelpittore.it
Places: 22/28 - ⚙ 🅿 - I -
ⒶⒺ ⓪ 🎫 ᴍᴄ B

Il Grappolo b
Via Pertossi 7, Tel. 032247735
www.ilgrappoloarona.it
Places: 42 - ⚙ 🅿 - R, C - 🎫 ᴍᴄ ᴊᴏ8 B

ASTI

£ *IAT Asti*
Piazza Alfieri 29
Tel. 014153035
www.comune.asti.it

Hotels

Aleramo ★★★ ★
Meublé. Via Emanuele Filiberto 13,
Tel. 0141595661
www.hotel.aleramo.it
Rooms: 42 - 🅿 ♣ - ⒶⒺ ⓪
🎫 ᴍᴄ ᴊᴏ8 B

Antica Dogana ★★★ A ★
Meublé.
Loc. Quarto Inferiore,
Via Dogana 5, Tel. 0141293755
www.albergoanticadogana.it
Rooms: 25 - ⚙ 🅿 - ⒶⒺ ⓪ 🎫 ᴍᴄ

Reale ★★★ A
Piazza Alfieri 6,
Tel. 0141530240
www.hotelristorantereale.it
Rooms: 27 - ⒶⒺ ⓪ 🎫 ᴍᴄ B

Restaurants

Gener New c
Lungotanaro Pescatori 4,
Tel. 0141557270
www.generneuv.it
Places: 63/40 - ⚙ 🅿 - R - ⒶⒺ ⓪ 🎫

Angolo del Beato ⑪ ♿
Via Guttuari 12,
Tel. 0141531668
www.angolodelbeato.it
Places: 35 - R - 🅰🅴 ⑩ 🆅🆉 🅼🅲

CLAVIERE (TO)

> ℹ️ **Proloco Claviere**
> Via Nazionale 30
> Tel. 0122878856

Restaurants

'L Gran Bouc ⑪ ★
Via Nazionale 24/A,
Tel. 0122878830
www.granbouc.com
Places: 95/60 - 🅿 - R - 🅰🅴 ⑩ 🆅🆉 🅼🅲 B

CUNEO

> ℹ️ **IAT Cuneo**
> Piazza Risorgimento 2
> Tel. 0171693258
> www.comune.cuneo.it

Hotels

**Best Western
Hotel Principe** ★★★★
Meublé. Piazza Galimberti 5,
Tel. 0171693355
www.hotel-principe.it
Rooms: 50 - 🅿 ✆ - 🅰🅴 ⑩ 🆅🆉 🅼🅲 🅹🅲🅱 B

Palazzo Lovera ★★★★ ♿ ★
Via Roma 37,
Tel. 0171690420
www.palazzolovera.com
Rooms: 47 - 🅿 ✆ - 🅰🅴 ⑩ 🆅🆉 🅼🅲 B

ClassHotel Cuneo ★★★ ♿ ★
Loc. Madonna dell'Olmo,
Via Cascina Magnina 3/A,
Tel. 0171413188
www.classhotel.com
Rooms: 82 - 🅿 ✆ - 🅰🅴 ⑩ 🆅🆉 🅼🅲 B

Restaurants

Delle Antiche Contrade ⑪ ♿
Via Savigliano 11,
Tel. 0171480488
www.antichecontrade.it
Places: 30/30 - ✿ 🅿 - R, C -
🅰🅴 ⑩ 🆅🆉 🅼🅲 B

San Michele ⑪
Loc. Mondovì 2,
Tel. 0171681962
Places: 30 - R, I - 🅰🅴 ⑩ 🆅🆉 🅼🅲

LIMONE PIEMONTE (CN)

Hotels

G.H. Principe ★★★★ ★
Via Genova 45,
Tel. 017192389
www.alpiemareholidays.com
Rooms: 41 - 🅰 🅿 ⛷ 🛁 -
🅰🅴 ⑩ 🆅🆉 🅼🅲

Le Ginestre ★★★ ★
Via Nizza 68,
Tel. 0171927596,
www.hotelginestre.com
Rooms: 20 - 🅿 - 🆅🆉 B

Restaurants

Lu Taz ⑪ ★
Loc. San Maurizio 5
Tel. 3484446062
www.lutaz.it
Places: 70/10 - ✿ 🅿 - R, C - 🆅🆉 B

SAUZE D'OULX (TO)

> ℹ️ **Pro Loco Sauze d'Oux**
> Piazza Assietta 18

Hotels

G.H. Besson ★★★★
Via del Rio 15,
Tel. 0122859785
www.grandhotelbesson.it
Rooms: 44 - 🅿 ⛷ 🛁

Assietta ★★
Meublé. Piazza Assietta 4,
Tel. 0122850180
www.albergoassietta.it
Rooms: 19 - 🅿 ✆ - 🆅🆉 🅼🅲 B

Restaurants

Capricorno ⑪⑪
Loc. Le Clotes,
Via Case Sparse 21,
Tel. 0122850273
www.chaletilcapricorno.it
Places: 32/30 - ✿ - C - ⑩ 🆅🆉 🅼🅲 B

SESTRIERE (TO)

> ℹ️ **Ass. Turistica Pro-loco Insieme Per Sestriere**
> Piazza Fraiteve 1
> Tel. 012276350

Hotels

Belvedere ★★★★
Via Cesana 18,
Tel. 0122750698
www.newlinehotels.com
Rooms: 36 - 🅿 ⛷ -
🅰🅴 ⑩ 🆅🆉 🅼🅲 B

Sud-Ovest ★★★ ♿
Via Monterotta 17
Tel. 0122755222
www.hotelsud-ovest.it
Rooms: 25 - 🅿 ✆ -
🅰🅴 ⑩ 🆅🆉 🅼🅲 B

Restaurants

Du Grand Père ⑪
Via Forte Seguin 14,
Tel. 0122755970
Places: 60 - 🅿 - R - 🅰🅴 ⑩ 🆅🆉 🅼🅲 B

STRESA (VB)

> ℹ️ **Pro Loco Stresa**
> Piazza Marconi 16
> Tel. 032330150

Hotels

La Palma ★★★★ ♿ ★
Corso Umberto I 33,
Tel. 032332401
www.hlapalma.it
Rooms: 120 - 🅰 🅿 🛁 🛁 ✆ -
🅰🅴 ⑩ 🆅🆉 🅼🅲

Della Torre ★★★
Via Sempione 47,
Tel. 032332555
www.stresa.net/hotel/dellatorre
Rooms: 64 - 🅰 🅿 🛁 - 🅰🅴 ⑩ 🆅🆉 🅼🅲 B

Royal ★★★
Viale Lido 1, Tel. 032332777
www.hotelroyalstresa.com
Rooms: 70 - 🅰 🅿 🛁 - 🆅🆉 🅼🅲 B

Restaurants

Vecchio Tram ⑪ ♿
Via per Vedasco,
Tel. 032331757
www.vecchiotram.net
Places: 35/40 - ✿ 🅿 - I - 🅰🅴 ⑩ 🆅🆉
🅼🅲 B

Casa Bella ⑫
All'Isola dei Pescatori,
Via del Marinaio,
Tel. 032333471
www.isola-pescatori.it
Places: 40/25 - R, C- 🅰🅴 ⑩ 🆅🆉

TURIN/TORINO

> ℹ️ **URP Torino**
> Piazza Palazzo di Città 9/A
> Tel. 011442310-0114423014
> www.comune.torino.org

Hotels

Art Hotel Boston ★★★★ ♿
Via Massena 70, Tel. 011500359
www.hotelbostontorino.it
Rooms: 87 - 🅰 - 🅰🅴 ⑩ 🆅🆉 🅼🅲

Santo Stefano ★★★★ ♿
Via Porta Paltina 19,
Tel. 0115223311
www.nh-hotels.com
Rooms: 125 - 🅰 🅿 ⛷ - 🅰🅴 ⑩ 🆅🆉 🅼🅲

Victoria ★★★★ ♿
Meublé. Via N. Costa 4,
Tel. 0115611909
www.hotelvictoria-torino.com
Rooms: 106 - 🅰 🛁 ✆ -
🅰🅴 ⑩ 🆅🆉 🅼🅲

Villa Sassi ★★★★
Strada Traforo del Pino 47,
Tel. 0118980556
www.villasassi.com
Rooms: 15 - 🅰 🅿 - 🅰🅴 ⑩ 🆅🆉 🅼🅲 B

Amadeus e Teatro ★★★ ★
Meublé.
Via Principe Amedeo 41 bis,
Tel. 0118174951
www.turinhotelcompany.com
Rooms: 28 - ✆ - 🅰🅴 ⑩ 🆅🆉 🅼🅲

Chelsea ★★★ ★
Via Cappel Verde 1/D ang.
Via XX Settembre 79/E,
Tel. 0114360100
www.hotelchelsea.it
Rooms: 15 - 🅿 - 🅰🅴 ⑩ 🆅🆉 🅼🅲 B

Conte Biancamano ★★★ ★
Meublé. Corso Vittorio Emanuele II
73, Tel. 0115623281
www.hotelcontebiancamano.it
Rooms: 24 - 🅰🅴 ⑩ 🆅🆉 🅼🅲 🅹🅲🅱 B

Valentino du Parc ★★★
Meublé. Via Giotto 16,
Tel. 011673932
www.hotelvalentino.it
Rooms: 18 - 🅰 🅿 ✆ - 🅰🅴 ⑩ 🆅🆉 🅼🅲 B

Restaurants

Carignano ¶¶¶ ★
Via Carlo Alberto 35,
Tel. 0115170171
www.sitea.thi.it
Places: 110 - ❀ - R - Ⓐⓔ 🎟 Ⓜⓒ B

Antica Trattoria "Con Calma" ¶¶
Strada comunale del Cartman 59,
Tel. 0118980229
www.concalma.it
Places: 80/70 - ❀ Ⓟ - R - Ⓐⓔ Ⓓ 🎟
Ⓜⓒ B

L'Agrifoglio ¶¶ ♿
Via A. Provana 7/E,
Tel. 0118136837
lagrifoglio@alice.it
Places: 40 - ❀ Ⓟ - R - 🎟 Ⓜⓒ B

Osteria Antiche Sere ¶¶
Via Cenischia 9/A,
Tel. 0113854347
Places: 50/50 - ❀ Ⓟ - R, C - B

Trattoria L'Osto del Borgh Vej ¶¶
Via Torquato Tasso 7,
Tel. 0114364843
www.losto.it
Places: 35/20 - ❀ - R, C - 🎟 Ⓜⓒ B

Tre Galline ¶¶
Via Bellezia 37, Tel. 0114366553
www.3galline.it
Places: 60 - Ⓟ - R - Ⓐⓔ Ⓓ 🎟 Ⓜⓒ B

LOMBARDY

BELLAGIO (CO)

ℹ️ *IAT*
Piazza della Chiesa 14
Tel. 031950204

Hotels

Belvedere ★★★ ♿ ★
Via Valassina 31, 031950410
www.belvederebellagio.com
Rooms: 62 - ♨ Ⓟ ⛷ - Ⓐⓔ 🎟 Ⓜⓒ

Du Lac ★★★
Piazza Mazzini 32,
Tel. 031950320
www.bellagio.info
Rooms: 42 - ⛷ - 🎟 Ⓜⓒ B

Florence ★★★
Piazza Mazzini 46, Tel. 031950342
www.hotelflorencebellagio.com
Rooms: 30 - ⚲ - Ⓐⓔ 🎟 Ⓜⓒ B

Restaurants

Far Out ¶¶ ★
Salita Mella 4,
Tel. 031951743
www.farout.it
Places: 55 - R, C - Ⓐⓔ Ⓓ 🎟 Ⓜⓒ B

Salice Blu ¶¶
Via per Lecco 33,
Tel. 031950535
www.ristorante-saliceblu-bellagio.it
Places: 70/70 - R - ❀ Ⓟ 🎟 Ⓜⓒ B

BERGAMO

ℹ️ *IAT*
Via Gombito, 13
Tel. 035242226
www.apt.bergamo.it

Hotels

Best Western Premier Hotel
Cappello d'Oro ★★★★ ♿ ★
Viale Papa Giovanni XXIII 12,
Tel. 0352289011
www.bestwestern.it/cappellodoro_bg
Rooms: 89 - ♨ Ⓟ 🍴 - Ⓐⓔ Ⓓ 🎟 Ⓜⓒ B

Excelsior San Marco ★★★★ ♿
Piazza della Repubblica 6 ,
Tel. 035366111
www.hotelsanmarco.com
Rooms: 155 - Ⓟ ⚲ ♨ ⛷ 🍴 -
Ⓐⓔ Ⓓ 🎟 Ⓜⓒ B

San Lorenzo ★★★★ ♿
Meublé. Città alta,
piazza Mascheroni 9/A,
Tel. 035237383
www.hotelsanlorenzobg.it
Rooms: 25 - Ⓟ 🍴 - Ⓐⓔ Ⓓ 🎟 Ⓜⓒ ⒿⒸⒷ B

Piazza Vecchia ★★★ ♿
Meublé. Via Colleoni 3,
Tel. 035253179
www.hotelpiazzavecchia.it
Rooms: 13 - Ⓐⓔ Ⓓ 🎟 Ⓜⓒ B

Piemontese ★★★ ★
Meublé. Piazza G. Marconi 11,
Tel. 035242629
www.hotelpiemontese.com
Rooms: 54 - 🍴 - Ⓐⓔ Ⓓ 🎟 Ⓜⓒ B

Restaurants

L'Osteria di Via Solata ¶¶¶¶
Città alta,
Via Solata 8,
Tel. 035271993
www.osteriaviasolata.it
Places: 40 - I - Ⓐⓔ Ⓓ 🎟 Ⓜⓒ ⒿⒸⒷ B

Colleoni & Dell'Angelo ¶¶¶
Città alta,
Piazza Vecchia 7,
Tel. 035232596
www.colleonidellangelo.com
Places: 120/50 - R, I - ❀ -
Ⓐⓔ Ⓓ 🎟 Ⓜⓒ B

Giopì e Margì ¶¶
Via Borgo Palazzo 2,
Tel. 035242366
www.giopimargi.com
Places: 80 - R - ❀ - Ⓐⓔ Ⓓ 🎟 Ⓜⓒ

Gourmet ¶¶
In città alta,
Via S. Vigilio 1,
Tel. 0354373004
www.gourmet-bg.it
Places: 140/130 - R, C - ❀ Ⓟ - Ⓐⓔ Ⓓ
🎟 Ⓜⓒ B

Ol Tiner ¶¶
Loc. San Vigilio,
Via Monte Bastia, Tel. 035258190
Places: 80/30 - R - ❀ Ⓟ

BOARIO TERME (BS)

ℹ️ *Pro Loco Darfo Boario*
Terme
Piazza Lorenzini Colonnello
Tel. 0364536174

Hotels

Rizzi Spa Line ★★★★ ♿
Via Carducci 5/11, Tel. 0364531617
www.rizziaquacharme.it
Rooms: 87 - ♨ ♨ ⚲ ♨ 🍴 - Ⓐⓔ Ⓓ
🎟 Ⓜⓒ B

Diana ★★★
Via Manifattura 12, Tel. 0364531403
www.albergodiana.it
Rooms: 43 - ♨ Ⓟ - 🎟 Ⓜⓒ B

Restaurants

La Storia ¶
Loc. Montecchio, Via Fontanelli 1,
Tel. 0364538787
www.ristorantelastoria.it
Places: 90/90 - R - ❀ Ⓟ - 🎟 Ⓜⓒ B

BORMIO (SO)

ℹ️ *Ufficio Turistico*
Via Roma, 131/B
Tel. 0342903300
www.bormio.to

Hotels

G.H. Bagni Nuovi ★★★★★ ♿ ★
Loc. Bagni Nuovi, S.S. 301,
Tel. 0342910131
www.bagnidibormio.it
Rooms: 74 - ♨ Ⓟ ♨ ♨ - Ⓐⓔ Ⓓ 🎟
Ⓜⓒ B

Palace Hotel ★★★★
Via Milano 54, Tel. 0342903131
www.palacebormio.it
Rooms: 80 - ♨ Ⓟ ⚲ ♨ 🍴 - Ⓐⓔ Ⓓ
🎟 Ⓜⓒ B

Bagni Vecchi ★★★ ★
Loc. Bagni Vecchi, S.S. 301,
Tel. 0342910131
www.bagnidibormio.it
Rooms: 12 - ♨ Ⓟ ♨ ♨ ♨ - Ⓐⓔ 🎟
Ⓜⓒ B

Baita Clementi ★★★
Via Milano 46, Tel. 0342904473
www.baitaclementi.it
Rooms: 42 - ♨ Ⓟ ⚲ - Ⓐⓔ 🎟 Ⓜⓒ B

Miramonti Park ★★★ ♿
Via Milano 5, Tel. 0342903312
www.miramontibormio.it
Rooms: 50 - ♨ Ⓟ ♨ - Ⓐⓔ Ⓓ 🎟 Ⓜⓒ B

Restaurants

Adalgisa ¶¶
Via Milano 90, Tel. 0342904497
Places: 55 - R - Ⓟ - Ⓐⓔ Ⓓ 🎟 Ⓜⓒ B

Al Filò ¶¶
Via Dante 6, Tel. 0342901732
www.bormio.it/viadante/6
Places: 90 - R, I - Ⓟ - 🎟 Ⓜⓒ B

BRESCIA

ℹ️ *APT*
Corso Zanardelli 38
Tel. 03045052/3
www.bresciaholiday.com

Hotels

Best Western Hotel Master
★★★★ ♿ ★
Via L. Apollonio 72,
Tel. 030399037
www.bestwestern.it/master_bs
Rooms: 74 - ♨ Ⓟ - Ⓐⓔ Ⓓ 🎟 Ⓜⓒ B

Park Hotel Ca' Nöa ★★★★
Via Triumplina 66, Tel. 030398762
www.hotelcanoa.it
Rooms: 79 - ♨ Ⓟ ⚲ ♨ -
Ⓐⓔ Ⓓ 🎟 Ⓜⓒ B

Noce *** ★
Via dei Gelsi 5, Tel. 0303542008
www.ristorantehotelnoce.com
Rooms: 13 - P - AE DC VISA MC B

Restaurants

Castello Malvezzi 🍴🍴🍴
Loc. Mompiano,
Via Colle S. Giuseppe 1,
Tel. 0302004224
www.castellomalvezzi.it
Places: 50/40 - ❄ P - I - AE DC VISA MC B

Eden 🍴🍴
Via Zadei 2, Tel. 030303397
www.ristoranteillabirinto.it
Places: 50/25 - ❄ - C - AE DC VISA MC B

La Sosta 🍴🍴
Via S. Martino della Battaglia 20,
Tel. 030295603
www.lasosta.it
Places: 120/80 - ❄ P - R, C - AE DC VISA MC B

Raffa 🍴
Corso Magenta 15, Tel. 03049037
Places: 75 - ❄ P - R, C - AE DC VISA MC

CLUSONE (BG)

i Pro Loco
Piazza Orologio 21
Tel. 034621113

Hotels

Europa *** ★
Viale Gusmini 3, Tel. 034621576
www.htl.europa.it
Rooms: 81 - 🌲 P 🐕 - AE DC VISA MC B

COMO

i APT
Piazza Cavour 17
Tel. 031269712

Hotels

Le Due Corti **** ♿ ★
Piazza Vittoria 12/13, Tel. 031328111
hotelduecorti@virgilio.it
Rooms: 60 - 🌲 P 🏋 🏊 - AE DC VISA MC B

Terminus **** ♿ ★
Lungolario Trieste 14, Tel. 031329111
www.albergoterminus.com
Rooms: 49 - 🌲 P 🐕 - AE DC VISA MC JCB

Villa Flori **** ★
Via per Cernobbio 12, Tel. 03133820
www.hotelvillaflori.it
Rooms: 45 - 🌲 P 🐕 - AE DC VISA MC B

Larius *** ♿ ★
Via F. Anzani 12/C, Tel. 0314038102
www.hlarius.it
Rooms: 21 - 🌲 P 🐕 - AE DC VISA MC B

Restaurants

Ao Storico 🍴🍴🍴 ♿ ★
Via F. Juvara 14,
Tel. 031260193
lostorico@tiscali.it
Places: 30 - ❄ P - C (fish) - AE DC VISA MC B

Oca Bianca 🍴🍴 ♿ ★
Loc. Trecallo, Via Canturina 251,
Tel. 031525605
www.hotelocabianca.it
Places: 50/120 - ❄ P - R, C - AE DC VISA MC B

Osteria Rusticana 🍴
Via Carso 69, Tel. 031306590
www.momsrl.it
Places: 60/54 - ❄ - R - AE DC VISA MC B

CREMONA

i APT
Piazza del Comune 5
Tel. 037223233
www.aptcremona.it

Hotels

Continental **** ★
Piazza della Libertà 26,
Tel. 0372434141
www.hotelcontinentalcremona.it
Rooms: 62 - 🐕 - AE DC VISA MC B

Delle Arti Design Hotel **** ♿ ★
Via Bonomelli 8,
Tel. 037223131
www.dellearti.com
Rooms: 33 - 🌲 - AE DC VISA MC B

Locanda al Carrobbio * ♿
Via Castelverde 54,
Tel. 0372560963
www.casalecarrobbio.it
Rooms: 7 - 🌲 P - AE DC VISA MC B

Restaurants

La Sosta 🍴🍴
Via Sicardo 9,
Tel. 0372456656
claudionevi@libero.it
Places: 60 - R - AE DC VISA MC B

Porta Mosa 🍴🍴
Via S. Maria in Betlem 11,
Tel. 0372411803
www.enotecacatullo.it
Places: 36 - P - R - VISA MC JCB B

Antica Trattoria Bissone 🍴 ★
Via Pecorari 3,
Tel. 037223953
www.bissone.it
Places: 70 - R - AE VISA MC B

LODI

i APT
Piazza Broletto 4
Tel. 0371421391
www.apt.lodi.it

Hotels

UNA Hotel Lodi **** ★
Loc. San Grato,
Via Emilia,
Tel. 0371410461
www.unahotels.it
Rooms: 58 - 🌲 P - AE DC VISA MC JCB B

Concorde Lodi Centro ***
Meublé.
Piazzale della Stazione 2,
Tel. 0371421322
www.hotel-concorde.it
Rooms: 30 - P - AE DC VISA MC B

Restaurants

Isola di Caprera 🍴🍴
Via Isola di Caprera 14,
Tel. 0371421316
www.isolacaprera.com
Places: 200 - ❄ P - R - AE DC VISA MC B

La Quinta 🍴🍴 ♿
Viale Pavia 76,
Tel. 037135041
laquintasnc@tiscali.it
Places: 70 - R - AE DC VISA MC B

MANTUA/MANTOVA

i Uff. Inf. Turistiche
Piazza A. Mantegna 6
Tel. 0376328253
www.provincia.mantova.it

Hotels

Rechigi **** ♿
Meublé. Via Calvi 30,
Tel. 0376320781
www.rechigi.com
Rooms: 55 - 🌲 - AE DC VISA MC

Bianchi Stazione *** ♿ ★
Meublé. Piazza Don Leoni 24,
Tel. 0376326465
www.albergobianchi.com
Rooms: 55 - 🌲 P - AE DC VISA

Mantegna ***
Meublé. Via Filzi 10,
Tel. 0376328019
www.hotelmantegna.it
Rooms: 42 - P - AE DC VISA MC

Restaurants

Aquila Nigra 🍴🍴🍴🍴 ♿
Vicolo Bonacolsi 4,
Tel. 0376327180
www.aquilanigra.it
Places: 45 - ❄ P - R, I - DC VISA MC JCB B

Cento Rampini 🍴🍴
Piazza delle Erbe 11,
Tel. 0376366349
100.rampini@libero.it
Places: 50/50 - R - AE DC VISA MC JCB B

Cigno-Trattoria dei Martini 🍴🍴
Piazza d'Arco 1, Tel. 0376327101
Places: 50 - ❄ - R - AE DC VISA MC JCB B

Grifone Bianco 🍴🍴
Piazza delle Erbe 6,
Tel. 0376365423
www.grifonebianco.it
Places: 60/100 - ❄ - R - AE DC VISA MC

Osteria della Fragoletta 🍴
Piazza Arche 5/A, Tel. 0376323300
lafragoletta@libero.it
Places: 40 - R, I - AE DC VISA MC B

MILAN/MILANO

i APT
Via Marconi 1
Tel. 0272524301
www.milanoinfo.eu

Hotels

Cavour ****
Via Fatebenefratelli 21,
Tel. 02620001
www.hotelcavour.it
Rooms: 113 - P - AE DC VISA MC

Dei Cavalieri ★★★★
Piazza Missori 1,
Tel. 0288571
www.hoteldeicavalieri.com
Rooms: 177 - ᴀᴇ ⱺ 🆅🆉 ᴍᴄ

De la Ville ★★★★ ♿ ★
Via Hoepli 6,
Tel. 028791311
www.delavillemilano.com
Rooms: 109 - 🛏 🛏 -
ᴀᴇ ⱺ 🆅🆉 ᴍᴄ ᴊᴄʙ B

Jolly Hotel President ★★★★ ♿ ★
Largo Augusto 10, Tel. 0277461
www.jollyhotels.com
Rooms: 256 - ᴀᴇ ⱺ 🆅🆉 ᴍᴄ B

Lloyd ★★★★
Meublé.
Corso di Porta Romana 48, Tel.
0258303332
www.lloydhotelmilano.it
Rooms: 57 - ᴘ - ᴀᴇ ⱺ 🆅🆉 ᴍᴄ

Petit Palais
Meublé. Via Molino delle Armi 1,
Tel. 02584891
www.petitpalais.it
Rooms: 18 - 🛏 -
ᴀᴇ ⱺ 🆅🆉 ᴍᴄ ᴊᴄʙ B

Regina ★★★★
Meublé. Via C. Correnti 13,
Tel. 0258106913
www.hotelregina.it
Rooms: 43 - 🛏 ᴘ - ᴀᴇ ⱺ 🆅🆉 ᴍᴄ ᴊᴄʙ B

Sir Edward ★★★★ ♿
Meublé. Via Mazzini 4,
Tel. 02877877
www.hotelsiredward.it
Rooms: 38 - ᴀᴇ ⱺ 🆅🆉 ᴍᴄ ᴊᴄʙ B

Spadari al Duomo ★★★★ ♿
Meublé. Via Spadari 11,
Tel. 0272002371
www.spadarihotel.com
Rooms: 40 - ᴀᴇ ⱺ 🆅🆉 ᴍᴄ B

Starhotels Rosa ★★★★ ♿ ★
Via Pattari 5,
Tel. 028831
www.starhotels.com
Rooms: 243 - ᴀᴇ ⱺ 🆅🆉 ᴍᴄ ᴊᴄʙ

Straf ★★★★ ♿
Via S. Raffaele 3,
Tel. 02805081
www.straf.it
Rooms: 66 - ᴀᴇ 🆅🆉 ᴍᴄ ᴊᴄʙ

UNA Hotel Cusani ★★★★ ♿ ★
Via Cusani 13,
Tel. 0285601
www.unahotels.it
Rooms: 92 - ᴀᴇ ⱺ 🆅🆉 ᴍᴄ ᴊᴄʙ

Ariston ★★★
Meublé. Largo Carrobbio 2,
Tel. 0272000556
www.aristonhotel.com
Rooms: 52 - ᴘ - ᴀᴇ ⱺ 🆅🆉 ᴍᴄ B

Grand Duca di York ★★★ ♿
Meublé. Via Moneta 1/A,
Tel. 02874863
www.ducadiyork.com
Rooms: 33 - ᴀᴇ 🆅🆉 ᴍᴄ

Mercure Milano
Corso Genova ★★★ ★
Meublé.
Via Conca del Naviglio 20,
Tel. 0258104141
www.mercure.com
Rooms: 105 - ᴘ - ᴀᴇ ⱺ 🆅🆉 ᴍᴄ B

Star ★★★
Meublé. Via dei Bossi 5,
Tel. 02801501
www.hotelstar.it
Rooms: 30 - ᴘ - ᴀᴇ ⱺ 🆅🆉 ᴍᴄ ᴊᴄʙ B

Zurigo ★★★ ♿
Meublé. Corso Italia,
Tel. 0272022260
www.brerahotels.it
Rooms: 39 - ᴘ - ᴀᴇ ⱺ 🆅🆉 ᴍᴄ ᴊᴄʙ B

Restaurants

Armani Caffè ❙❙❙ ♿
Via Croce Rossa 2,
Tel. 027231868o
sede@fashion-food.it
Places: 85/70 - I (fusion) - ᴀᴇ ⱺ 🆅🆉
ᴍᴄ B

Boeucc ❙❙❙ ♿
Piazza Belgioioso 2,
Tel. 0276020224
www.boeucc.it
Places: 140 - ᴘ - R, C - ᴀᴇ

Don Lisander ❙❙❙
Via Manzoni 12/A,
Tel. 0276020130
www.ristorantedonlisander.it
Places: 40/150 - ❀ - C -
ᴀᴇ ⱺ 🆅🆉 ᴍᴄ ᴊᴄʙ B

Le Noir ❙❙❙ ♿
Via S. Raffaele 6, Tel. 027208951
www.hotelthegray.com
Places: 28 - I - ᴀᴇ ⱺ 🆅🆉 ᴍᴄ B

L'Opera ❙❙❙ ★
Via Hoepli 6, Tel. 028791311
www.delavillemilano.com
Places: 150 - R - ᴀᴇ ⱺ 🆅🆉 ᴍᴄ ᴊᴄʙ B

L'Ulmet ❙❙❙
Via Disciplini ang. Via Olmetto 21,
Tel. 0286452718
www.lulmet.it
Places: 60 - I - ᴀᴇ 🆅🆉 ᴍᴄ B

Alla Collina Pistoiese ❙❙
Via Amedei 1,
Tel. 0286451085
Places: 100 - ❀ - R (Toscana) - ᴀᴇ ⱺ
🆅🆉 ᴍᴄ B

Artidoro ❙❙ ♿
Via Camperio 15,
Tel. 028057386
www.artidoro.it
Places: 60 - ❀ - R (Emilia) -
ᴀᴇ ⱺ 🆅🆉 ᴍᴄ B

Bagutta
Via Bagutta 14,
Tel. 0276002767
www.bagutta.it
Places: 200/130 - ❀ - R (Toscana) -
ᴀᴇ ⱺ 🆅🆉 B

Emilia e Carlo ❙❙ ♿
Via G. Sacchi 8,
Tel. 02862100
www.emiliaecarlo.it
Places: 60 - ❀ - I - ᴀᴇ ⱺ 🆅🆉 ᴍᴄ B

Gref Food & Charme ❙❙
Via Marco d'Oggiono 6,
Tel. 0258104107
www.gref.it
Places: 40 - C - ᴀᴇ ⱺ 🆅🆉 ᴍᴄ

La Brisa ❙❙ ♿
Via Brisa 15,
Tel. 0286450521
pedrochiara@infinito.it
Places: 55/50 - ❀ - I -
ᴀᴇ ⱺ 🆅🆉 ᴍᴄ B

La Terrazza di Via Palestro ❙❙ ♿
Via Palestro 2,
Tel. 0276002277
www.esperiaristorazione.it
Places: 130/250 - ❀ - I -
ᴀᴇ ⱺ 🆅🆉 ᴍᴄ B

Trattoria Colonna ❙❙
Via S. Maria alla Porta 10,
Tel. 02861812
www.trattorialacolonna.it
Places: 60 - ❀ - C - ᴀᴇ ⱺ 🆅🆉 ᴍᴄ

Setteorti ❙
Via Orti 7,
Tel. 025510852
laurabrett@fastwebnet.it
Places: 26 - ❀ - I - 🆅🆉 ᴍᴄ

Taverna Moriggi ❙
Via Morigi 8,
Tel. 0280582007
www.tavernamoriggi.it - I

MONZA

🛈 **Associazione Turistica**
Piazza Carducci 2
Tel. 039323222

Hotels

De la Ville ★★★★ ♿
Viale Regina Margherita 15,
Tel. 039382581
www.hoteldelaville.com
Rooms: 78 - 🛏 ᴘ - ᴀᴇ ⱺ 🆅🆉 ᴍᴄ

Monza ★★★★
Viale Lombardia 76/78,
Tel. 039272831
www.hotelmonza.com
Rooms: 66 - ᴘ - ᴀᴇ ⱺ 🆅🆉 ᴍᴄ B

Della Regione ★★★ ♿
Via Elvezia 4,
Tel. 039387205
www.hoteldellaregione.it
Rooms: 90 - ᴘ ❧ - ᴀᴇ ⱺ 🆅🆉 B

Restaurants

Alle Grazie ❙❙ ♿
Via Lecco 84,
Tel. 039387903
Places: 32/20 - ❀ ᴘ - C - ᴘ - ᴀᴇ

Lo Chef Giovanni ❙❙ ♿ ★
Via Manara 12,
Tel. 039386462
Places: 50 - ❀ - R, C -
ᴀᴇ ⱺ 🆅🆉 ᴍᴄ B

La Viestana ❙ ♿
Via Mentana 22,
Tel. 039835270
www.colizzi.it/include/viestana.asp
Places: 80 - ❀ - R - 🆅🆉 ᴍᴄ B

SABBIONETA (MN)

🛈 **Pro Loco**
Via Vespasiano Gonzaga 27
Tel. 037552039

Restaurants

Parco Cappuccini ❙ ♿ ★
Via Santuario 30,
Tel. 037552005
www.ristorantecappuccini.com
Places: 250 - ❀ ᴘ - R -
ᴀᴇ 🆅🆉

SALÒ (BS)

i IAT
Piazza S. Antonio
Tel. 036521423
www.provincia.brescia.it

Hotels

Laurin ★★★★
Viale Landi 9,
Tel. 036522022
www.laurinsalo.com
Rooms: 33 - 🅰 🅿 ⚒ - 🔲 💲 🔲 MC B

Salò du Parc ★★★★ ★
Via Cure del Lino 9,
Tel. 0365290043
www.saloduparc.it
Rooms: 43 - 🅰 🅿 ⚒ - 🔲 💲 🔲
MC B

Spiaggia d'Oro ★★★★ ★
Loc. Barbarano,
Via Spiaggia d'Oro 15,
Tel. 0365290034
www.hotelspiaggiadoro.com
Rooms: 36 - 🅰 🅿 ⚒ - 🔲 💲 🔲
MC JCB B

Restaurants

La Veranda ¶¶ ♿
Loc. Barbarano,
Via Spiaggia d'Oro 15,
Tel. 0365290034
www.hotelspiaggiadoro.com
Places: 80/70 - ✦ 🅿 - R - 🔲 💲 🔲
MC JCB B

Osteria di Mezzo ¶¶
Via di Mezzo 10,
Tel. 0365290966
www.osteriadimezzo.it
Places: 35/6 - ✦ - R - 🔲 🔲 MC JCB B

SARNICO (BG)

i Pro Loco Sarnico
Via Lantieri 6
Tel. 035910900

Hotels

Sebino ★★★★ ♿ ★
Piazza Besenzoni 1,
Tel. 035910412
www.hotelsebino.it
Rooms: 24 - 🅿 - 🔲 💲 🔲 MC B

Restaurants

Al Tram ¶¶
Via Roma 1, Tel. 035910117
info@ilcalepino.it
Places: 120/70 - ✦ 🅿 - R - 🔲 MC B

SIRMIONE (BS)

i IAT
Viale Marconi 2
Tel. 030916114-030916245
www.provincia.brescia.it

Hotels

Flaminia ★★★★ ♿
Piazza Flaminia 8,
Tel. 030916078
www.hotelflaminia.it
Rooms: 41 - 🅿 🔲 ✦ -
🔲 💲 🔲 MC B

Sirmione ★★★★ ♿
Piazza Castello 19,
Tel. 030916331
www.termedisirmione.com
Rooms: 101 - 🅰 🅿 ⚒ ✦ 🔲 - 🔲 💲
🔲 MC JCB B

Fonte Boiola ★★★
Viale Marconi 11, Tel. 030916431
www.termedisirmione.com
Rooms: 60 - 🅰 🅿 ⚒ ✦ 🔲 🔲 - 🔲
💲 🔲 MC JCB B

Lugana Parco al Lago ★★★
Loc. Lugana,
Via Verona 69/71,
Tel. 030919003
www.luganaparcoallago.com
Rooms: 17 - 🅰 🅿 🔲 -
🔲 💲 🔲 MC JCB B

Restaurants

La Rucola ¶¶¶
Via Strentelle 3,
Tel. 030916326
www.ristorantelarucola.it
Places: 25 - I - 🔲 💲 🔲 MC B

Signori ¶¶¶
Via Romagnoli 17,
Tel. 030916017
www.ristorantesignori.it
Places: 60/80 - ✦ - R, I - 🔲 💲 🔲
MC B

SONDRIO

i IAT
Via Trieste 12
Tel. 0342512500
www.valtellina.it

Hotels

Vittoria ★★★★ ♿
Meublé. Via Bernina 1,
Tel. 0342533888
www.vittoriahotel.com
Rooms: 39 - 🅿 ✦ - 🔲 💲 🔲 MC B

Europa ★★★ ★
Lungo Mallero Cadorna 27,
Tel. 0342515010
www.albergoeuropa.com
Rooms: 42 - 🅿 ✦ - 🔲 💲 🔲 MC B

Restaurants

Masegra ¶¶
Via de' Capitani Masegra 7/B,
Tel. 0342215970
Places: 130 - 🅿 - R, C -
🔲 💲 🔲 MC B

Sale & Pepe ¶¶
Piazza Cavour 13,
Tel. 0342212210
www.ristorantesalepepe.it
Places: 50/30 - 🅿 - R, I - 💲 🔲 MC B

TRENTINO-ALTO ADIGE

ANDALO (TN)

i APT Dolomiti di Brenta
Piazza Dolomiti 1
Tel. 0461585836
www.aptdolomitipaganella.com

Hotels

Dolomiti Hotel Olimpia ★★★ ♿
Via Paganella 17,
Tel. 0461585715
www.infotrentino.net/hotelolimpia
Rooms: 40 - 🅰 🅿 ⚒ ⚓ - 🔲 MC B

BOLZANO/BOZEN

i Azienda di Soggiorno e Turismo
Piazza Walther 8,
Tel. 0471307000
www.bolzano-bozen.it

Hotels

Four Points Sheraton ★★★★ ♿
Via Buozzi 35,
Tel. 04711950012
www.4p-sheraton-bolzano.it
Rooms: 189 - ⚒ 🔲 -
🔲 💲 🔲 MC B

Parkhotel Laurin ★★★★
Via Buozzi 35,
Tel. 04711950012
www.4p-sheraton-bolzano.it
Rooms: 189 - ⚒ 🔲 -
🔲 💲 🔲 MC B

Parkhotel Werth ★★★★ ♿
Via Maso della Pieve 19,
Tel. 0471250103
www.hotelwerth.com
Rooms: 65 - 🅰 🅿 🔲 - 🔲 💲 🔲 MC

Magdalenerhof ★★★ ♿
Via Rencio 48/A,
Tel. 0471978267
www.magdalenerhof.it
Rooms: 39 - 🅰 🅿 🔲 - 🔲 💲 🔲 MC B

Restaurants

Rastbichler ¶¶
Via Cadorna 1,
Tel. 0471261131
Places: 60/50 - ✦ 🅿 - R, C -
🔲 💲 🔲 MC B

Vögele ¶¶
Via Goethe 3,
Tel. 0471973938
www.voegele.it
Places: 100/20 - R, C - 💲 MC B

BRUNICO/BRUNECK (BZ)

i Associazione Turistica
Piazza Municipio 7,
Tel. 0474555722
www.bruneck.com

Hotels

Royal Hotel Hinterhuber ★★★★
Loc. Riscone/Reischach,
Via Ried 1/A,
Tel. 0474541000
www.royal-hinterhuber.com
Rooms: 49 - 🅰 🅿 ⚒ 🔲 🔲 - 🔲
💲 🔲 MC B

Andreas Hofer ★★★
Via Campo Tures 1,
Tel. 0474551469
www.andreashofer.it
Rooms: 48 - 🅰 🅿 ⚒ ⚓ -
🔲 MC B

412

Restaurants

Langgenhof ⛏ ♿
Loc. Stegona/Stegen,
Via S. Nicolò 11,
Tel. 0474553154
Places: 140/60 - ✿ ℗ - R, C -
▨ ᴍᴄ B

CANAZEI (TN)

> *ℹ APT Val di Fassa*
> *Strèda Roma 36,*
> *Tel. 0462609500*
> *www.fassa.com*

Hotels

Astoria ★★★★ ♿
Via Roma 88,
Tel. 0462601302
www.hotel-astoria.net
Rooms: 39 - ♨ ℗ ⛷ -
ᴀᴇ ▨ ᴍᴄ B

Bellavista ★★★
Loc. Pecol, strada Pordoi 12,
Tel. 0462601165
www.bellavistahotel.it
Rooms: 43 - ♨ ℗ ⛷ - ▨ ᴍᴄ B

Dolomites Inn ★★★
Loc. Penia, Via Antersies 3,
Tel. 0462602212
www.dolomitesinn.com
Rooms: 27 - ♨ ℗ ⛷ - B

Restaurants

La Montanara ⛏
Via Dolomiti 183,
Tel. 0462601352
Places: 60 - R - ▨ ᴍᴄ B

CORVARA IN BADIA CORVARA (BZ)

> *ℹ Consorzio Tur. Alta Badia*
> *Via Col Alt 36,*
> *Tel. 0471836176*
> *www.altabadia.org*

Hotels

Sassongher ★★★★ ♿
Via Sassongher 45,
Tel. 0471836085
www.sassongher.it
Rooms: 53 - ℗ ⛷ ≋ ♥ -
▨ ᴍᴄ B

La Perla ★★★★ ♿
Strada Col Alt 105,
Tel. 0471831000
www.hotel-laperla.it
Rooms: 52 - ♨ ℗ ≋ ⛲ ♥ -
▨ ᴍᴄ B

Sport Hotel Panorama ★★★★
Via Sciuz 1,
Tel. 0471836083
www.sporthotel-panorama.com
Rooms: 35 - ℗ ⛷ ♨ ≋ -
ᴀᴇ ▨ ᴍᴄ B

Restaurants

Stria ⛏ ♿
Loc. Colfosco/Kollfuschg,
Via Val 18, |
Tel. 0471836620
Places: 46 - ℗ - I - ▨ ᴍᴄ B

DOBBIACO/TOBLACH (BZ)

> *ℹ Associazione Turistica*
> *Via Dolomiti 3*
> *Tel. 0474972132*
> *www.dobbiaco.info*

Hotels

Santer ★★★★
Via Alemagna 4,
Tel. 0474972142
www.hotel-santer.com
Rooms: 50 - ♨ ℗ ⛷ ≋ - ▨ B

Sole-Sonne ★★★
Via Dolomiti 1,
Tel. 0474972225
www.dobbiaco.org
Rooms: 40 - ♨ ℗ ≋ - ▨ ᴍᴄ B

Restaurants

Winkelkeller ⛏
Via Conti Künigl 8,
Tel. 0474972022
www.app-pichler.com
Places: 80/14 - ℗ - R

FAI DELLA PAGANELLA (TN)

> *ℹ Ufficio Informazioni*
> *Via Villa, Tel. 0461583130*
> *www.aptdolomitipaganella.*
> *com*

Hotels

Belvedere ★★★
Viale Risorgimento 2,
Tel. 0461583185
www.hotelbelvedere.it
Rooms: 32 - ♨ ℗ ⛷ ♨ ≋ -
⊛ ▨ ᴍᴄ B

LA VILLA/STERN (BZ)

Hotels

Ciasa Antines ★★★★
Via Picenin 18,
Tel. 0471844234
www.hotelantines.it
Rooms: 32 - ♨ ℗ ≋ -
▨ ᴍᴄ B

Dolomiti ★★★
Via Funtanacia 55,
Tel. 0471847143,
www.hotel-dolomiti.com
Rooms: 45 - ♨ ℗ ⛷ ♥ - ▨ ᴍᴄ B

MADONNA DI CAMPIGLIO (TN)

> *ℹ APT*
> *Via Pradalago 4*
> *Tel. 0465447501*
> *www.campiglio.to*

Hotels

Bertelli ★★★★ ♿
Via Cima Tosa 80,
Tel. 0465441013
www.hotelbertelli.it
Rooms: 49 - ♨ ℗ ⛷ ≋ -
ᴀᴇ ⊛ ▨ ᴍᴄ B

Lorenzetti ★★★★ ♿
Viale Dolomiti di Brenta 119,
Tel. 0465441404
www.hotellorenzetti.com
Rooms: 54 - ♨ ℗ ⛷ ≋ -
ᴀᴇ ⊛ ▨ ᴍᴄ B

Touring ★★★ ♿
Via Belvedere 14,
Tel. 0465441051
www.htouring.it
Rooms: 28 - ♨ ℗ ⛷ ≋ ♥ - ᴀᴇ ⊛
▨ ᴍᴄ B

Restaurants

Alfiero ⛏
Via Vallesinella 5,
Tel. 0465440117
www.hotellorenzetti.com
Places: 85 - ℗ - R, C -
ᴀᴇ ⊛ ▨ ᴍᴄ B

MALLES VENOSTA MALS IM VINSCHGAU (BZ)

> *ℹ Ass. Tur. Alta Venosta*
> *Via S. Benedetto 1*
> *Tel. 0473737070*
> *www.altavenostavacanze.it*

Hotels

Garberhof ★★★★
Via Nazionale 25, Tel. 0473831399,
www.garberhof.com
Rooms: 49 - ♨ ℗ ♥ - ▨ ᴍᴄ B

MERANO/MERAN (BZ)

> *ℹ Ass. Tur. Merano*
> *Corso Libertà 45*
> *Tel. 0473272000*
> *www.meraninfo.it*

Hotels

Adria ★★★★
Via H. Gilm 2,
Tel. 0473236610
www.hotel-adria.com
Rooms: 45 - ♨ ℗ ♨ ⛷ ≋ - ▨ ᴍᴄ B

Meranerhof ★★★★ ♿
Via Manzoni 1,
Tel. 0473230230
www.meranerhof.com
Rooms: 70 - ♨ ℗ ⛷ ≋ - ᴀᴇ ⊛ ▨
ᴍᴄ B

Zima ★★★
Meublé. Via Winkel 83,
Tel. 0473230408
www.hotelzima.com
Rooms: 23 - ♨ ℗ ⛷ ≋ ⛲ - ▨ B

Restaurants

Artemis ⛏
Via Verdi 72,
Tel. 0473446282
www.villativoli.it
Places: 40/40 - ✿ ℗ - R - ᴀᴇ ▨ ᴍᴄ

Kallmünz ⛏ ♿
Piazza Rena 12,
Tel. 0473212917
www.kallmuenz.it
Places: 40/20 - ✿ ℗ - I -
ᴀᴇ ⊛ ▨ ᴍᴄ B

MOENA (TN)

i APT
Piazza De Sotegrava 19
Tel. 0462609770
www.fassa.com

Hotels

Alle Alpi ★★★★
Via Moene 47,
Tel. 0462573194
www.hotelallealpi.it
Rooms: 33 - ⚙ 🅿 🔆 ⛄ - 🔲 ⏻ 🎬
🎬 B

Belvedere ★★★
Via Dolomiti 14,
Tel. 0462573233
www.hotelbelvedere.biz
Rooms: 30 - ⚙ 🅿 🔆

Restaurants

Malga Panna ⍩ ♿
Via Strada de Sort 64,
Tel. 0462573489
www.malgapanna.it
Places: 50/20 - ❀ - R, I -
🔲 ⏻ 🎬 🎬 B

ORTISEI/SANKT ULRICH IN GRÖDEN (BZ)

i Ass. Tur. Ortisei
Via Rezia 1
Tel. 0471777600
www.valgardena.il

Hotels

Alpenhotel Rainell ★★★★ ♿
Via Vidalong 19,
Tel. 0471796145, www.rainell.com
Rooms: 27 - ⚙ 🅿 - 🎬 🎬 B

Villa Luise ★★★
Via Grohmann 43,
Tel. 0471796498,
www.villaluise.com
Rooms: 13 - ⚙ 🅿 - 🔲 ⏻ 🎬 🎬

Restaurants

Anna Stuben ⍩⍩⍩
Via Vidalong 3,
Tel. 0471796315
www.annastuben.it
Places: 30 - 🅿 - R, C - 🔲 🎬 🎬 B

Stua Catores ⍩⍩
Via Sacun 49,
Tel. 0471796682
Places: 20/12 - ❀ - 🅿 - R - B

RIVA DEL GARDA (TN)

i Ingarda Trentino
Via Giar. Porta Orientale 8
Tel. 0464554444
www.gardatrentino.it

Hotels

Feeling Hotel Luise ★★★★ ♿ ★
Viale Rovereto 9,
Tel. 0464550858,
www.feelinghotelluise.com
Rooms: 67 - ⚙ 🅿 ⛄ ♦ -
🔲 ⏻ 🎬 🎬 B

Best Western
Hotel Europa ★★★ ★
Piazza Catena 9,
Tel. 0464555433,
www.hoteleuropariva.it
Rooms: 63 - ⚙ ⛄ -
🔲 ⏻ 🎬 🎬 B

Gabri ★★★ ♿
Meublé. Via Longa 6,
Tel. 0464553600
www.hotelgabry.com
Rooms: 39 - ⚙ 🅿 🔆 ⛄ -
🎬 🎬 B

Restaurants

Al Volt ⍩⍩ ♿
Via Fiume 73,
Tel. 0464552570
www.ristorantealvolt.com
Places: 50/8 - 🅿 - R - 🔲 ⏻ 🎬 🎬

SAN CASSIANO SANKT KASSIAN (BZ)

Hotels

Ciasa Salares ★★★★ ♿
Loc. Armentarola,
Via Pre de Vì 31,
Tel. 0471849445
www.siriolagroup.it
Rooms: 42 - ⚙ 🅿 🔆 ⛄ -
🔲 ⏻ 🎬 🎬 B

Gran Ancëi ★★★ ♿
Strada Pre de Costa 10,
Tel. 0471849540
www.granancei.com
Rooms: 35 - ⚙ 🅿 🔆 ⛄ -
⏻ 🎬 🎬 B

Restaurants

St. Hubertus
Via Micurà de Rü 20,
Tel. 0471849500
www.rosalpina.it
Places: 35 - 🅿 - I - 🔲 ⏻ 🎬

SAN MARTINO DI CASTROZZA (TN)

i APT
Via Passo Rolle 165
Tel. 0439768867
www.trentino.to

Hotels

Letizia ★★★ ♿
Via Colbricon 6,
Tel. 0439768615,
www.hletizia.it
Rooms: 38 - ⚙ 🅿 🔆 ♦

TRENT/TRENTO

i APT
Via Manci 2
Tel. 0461216000
www.apt.trento.it

Hotels

Adige ★★★★
Loc. Mattarello, Via Pomeranos 2,
Tel. 0461944545
www.adigehotel.it
Rooms: 80 - 🅿 🔆 ⛄ -
🔲 ⏻ 🎬 🎬 B

America ★★★ ♿
Via Torre Verde 50,
Tel. 0461983010,
www.hotelamerica.it
Rooms: 67 - 🅿 ♦ - 🔲 ⏻ 🎬 🎬

Sporting Trento ★★★ ★
Via R. da Sanseverino 125,
Tel. 0461391215
www.hotelsportingtrento.com
Rooms: 41 - 🅿 - 🔲 ⏻ 🎬 🎬 B

Restaurants

Osteria a le Due Spade ⍩⍩⍩
Via Don Rizzi, Tel. 0461234343
www.leduespade.com
Places: 30/30 - ❀ - R, I -
🔲 ⏻ 🎬 🎬 B

Lo Scrigno del Duomo ⍩⍩
Piazza del Duomo 29,
Tel. 0461220030
www.scrignodelduomo.com
Places: 80/44 - ❀ - ❀ - R -
🔲 ⏻ 🎬 🎬 B

Villa Madruzzo ⍩⍩
Loc. Cognola, Via Ponte Alto 26,
Tel. 0461986220
www.villamadruzzo.it
Places: 100 - ❀ 🅿 - R - 🔲 ⏻ 🎬 🎬 B

VENETO

ABANO TERME (PD)

i IAT
Via Pietro d'Àbano 18
Tel. 0498669055
www.termeeuganeeapt.net

Hotels

Terme Europa ★★★★ ♿ ★
Via V. Flacco 13, Tel. 0498669544,
www.europaterme.it
Rooms: 100 - ⚙ 🅿 ⚇ 🔆 ⛄ ⛄ -
🔲 ⏻

Principe ★★★ ★
Viale delle Terme 87, Tel. 98600844
www.principeterme.com
Rooms: 70 - ⚙ 🅿 ⚇ 🔆 ⛄ ⛄ - ⏻ 🎬

Terme Belvedere ★★★ ♿ ★
Viale delle Terme 21,
Tel. 0498602409
www.termebelvedere.it
Rooms: 100 - ⚙ 🅿 ⚇ 🔆 ⛄ ♦ -
⏻ 🎬

Restaurants

Aubergine ⍩⍩
Via Ghislandi 5, Tel. 0498669910
www.aubergine.it
Places: 80/70 - ❀ 🅿 - C - 🔲 ⏻ 🎬 🎬

BELLUNO

i APT
Piazza Vittorio Emanuele II 2
Tel. 0437940300

Hotels

Europa Executive ★★★★ ♿ ★
Meublé. Via Vittorio Veneto 158/0,
Tel. 0437930196
www.europaexecutive.it
Rooms: 40 - 🅿 - 🔲 ⏻ 🎬 🎬 🎬

Oliver ★★★★
Loc. Nevegal,
Via Col de Gou 341,
Tel. 0437908165
www.dolomiti.it/olivier
Rooms: 54 - ⚐ 🄿 - 🎞 🄼🄲 B

Delle Alpi ★★★
Via Jacopo Tasso 15,
Tel. 0437940545
www.dellealpi.it
Rooms: 40 - 🄿 - 🄰🄴 🄾 🎞 🄼🄲 B

Restaurants

Al Borgo ¶¶ ᕤ ★
Via Anconetta 8,
Tel. 0437926755
www.alborgo.to
Places: 90/90 - ♛ 🄿 - R - 🄰🄴 🎞 🄼🄲

CHIOGGIA (VE)

[𝑖] APT
Piazzetta S. Francesco 8
Tel. 04363231
www.apt-dolomiti-cortina.it

Hotels

Grande Italia ★★★★ ★
Rione S. Andrea 597,
Tel. 041400515
www.hotelgrandeitalia.com
Rooms: 56 - 🄿 - 🄰🄴 🄾 🎞 🄼🄲 B

Ambasciatori ★★★
Loc. Sottomarina, lungomare
Adriatico 30, Tel. 0415540660
www.ambasciatorivenezia.com
Rooms: 63 - 🄿 ᕷ 🎰 - 🄰🄴 🄾 🎞 🄼🄲 B

Restaurants

Garibaldi ¶¶¶
Loc. Sottomarina, Via S. Marco 1924,
Tel. 0415540042
www.ristorantegaribaldi.com
Places: 35 - ♛ 🄿 - R - 🄰🄴 🄾 🎞 🄼🄲 B

CORTINA D'AMPEZZO (BL)

[𝑖] APT
Piazzetta S. Francesco 8
Tel. 04363231
www.apt-dolomiti-cortina.it

Hotels

Park Hotel Faloria ★★★★ ᕤ
Loc. Zuel 46, Tel. 04362959
www.hotel-faloria.it
Rooms: 31 - ⚐ 🄿 🎰 - 🄰🄴 🎞 🄼🄲 B

Franceschi Park Hotel ★★★
Via C. Battisti 86, Tel. 0436867041,
www.franceschiparkhotel.eu
Rooms: 46 - ⚐ 🄿 ᕷ - 🄾 🎞 🄼🄲 B

Menardi ★★★
Via Majon 110, Tel. 04362400,
www.hotelmenardi.it
Rooms: 49 - ⚐ 🄿 - 🄰🄴 🄾 🎞 🄼🄲 B

Restaurants

Tivoli ¶¶¶
Via Lacedel 34,
Tel. 0436866400
www.ristorantetivoli.it
Places: 45/35 - 🄿 - I - 🄰🄴 🄾 🎞 🄼🄲 B

MONTEGROTTO TERME (PD)

[𝑖] APT
Viale Stazione 60
Tel. 049793384

Hotels

Terme Preistoriche ★★★★ ★
Via Castello 5,
Tel. 049793477,
www.termepreistoriche.it
Rooms: 47 - ⚐ 🄿 ♒ ᕷ 🎰 🎰 - 🎞 🄼🄲 B

Continental Terme Hotel ★★★ ᕤ ★
Via Neroniana 8,
Tel. 049793522,
www.continentaltermehotel.it
Rooms: 175 - ⚐ 🄿 ♒ ᕷ 🎰 🎰 - 🄰🄴 🄾 🎞 🄼🄲 B

Restaurants

Da Mario ¶¶
Corso Terme 4,
marco@damarioristorante.191.it
Tel. 049794090
Places: 80/40 - ♛ 🄿 - R, C - 🄰🄴 🄾 🎞 🄼🄲 B

PADUA/PADOVA

[𝑖] APT
Riviera Mugnai 8
Tel. 0498767911
www.apt.padova.it

Hotels

Methis ★★★★ ᕤ ★
Meublé. Riviera Paleocapa 70,
Tel. 0498725555
www.methishotel.com
Rooms: 59 - 🄿 - 🄰🄴 🄾 🎞 🄼🄲 🄹🄾🄱 B

Milano ★★★★ ᕤ
Via P. Bronzetti 62/D,
Tel. 0498712555
www.hotelmilano-padova.it
Rooms: 80 - 🄿 - 🄰🄴 🄾 🎞 🄼🄲 B

Sagittario ★★★ ᕤ ★
Meublé. Loc. Torre,
Via Randaccio 6, T
el. 049725877,
www.hotelsagittario.com
Rooms: 41 - ⚐ 🄿 - 🄰🄴 🄾 🎞 🄼🄲 B

Restaurants

Bastioni del Moro ¶¶ ᕤ ★
Via P. Bronzetti 18,
Tel. 0498710006
www.bastionidelmoro.it
Places: 60/40 - ♛ 🄿 - R, C - 🄰🄴 🄾 🎞 🄼🄲 B

Enoteca Angelo Rasi ¶¶
Riviera Paleocapa 7,
Tel. 0498719797
Places: 25/25 - ♛ - R, I - 🎞 🄼🄲 B

ROVIGO

[𝑖] APT
Via J.H. Dunant 10
Tel. 0425361481
www.apt.rovigo.it

Hotels

Villa Regina Margherita ★★★★ ᕤ
Viale Regina Margherita 6,
Tel. 0425361540
www.hotelvillareginamargherita.it
Rooms: 22 - ⚐ 🄿 - 🄰🄴 🎞 🄼🄲 🄹🄾🄱 B

Best Western Hotel Cristallo★★★
Viale Porta Adige 1,
Tel. 042530701,
www.bestwestern.it/cristallo_ro
Rooms: 48 - 🄿 ♥ - 🄰🄴 🄾 🎞 🄼🄲

TREVISO

[𝑖] Ufficio Informazioni
Piazza Monte di Pietà 8
Tel. 0422547632

Hotels

Maggior Consiglio ★★★★ ᕤ
Via Terraglio 140,
Tel. 04224093,
www.boscolohotels.com
Rooms: 121 - 🄿 🎰 - 🄰🄴 🄾 🎞 🄼🄲 🄹🄾🄱 B

Best Western Al Fogher ★★★ ᕤ
Viale della Repubblica 10,
Tel. 0422432950
www.hotelalfogher.it
Rooms: 55 - 🄿 - 🄰🄴 🄾 🎞 🄼🄲 🄹🄾🄱 B

Restaurants

Alfredo ¶¶¶
Via Collalto 26,
Tel. 0422540275,
www.toula.it
Places: 90 - 🄿 - R - 🄰🄴 🄾 🎞 🄼🄲 B

Basilico ¶¶
Via Bison 34,
Tel. 0422541822
www.ristorantebasilisco.com
Places: 40 - 🄿 - R - 🄰🄴 🄾 🎞 🄼🄲 B

VENICE/VENEZIA

[𝑖] APT
Castello, Fond. S. Lorenzo
Tel. 0415298711
www.turismovenezia.it

Hotels

Al Codega ★★★★ ᕤ ★
Meublé. Piazza San Marco 4435,
Tel. 0412413288
www.nih.it/hotelalcodega
Rooms: 28 - ♥ - 🄰🄴 🎞 🄼🄲 B

Concordia ★★★★ ᕤ
Calle larga S. Marco 367,
Tel. 0415206866
www.hotelconcordia.it
Rooms: 53 - 🄿 - 🄰🄴 🄾 🎞 🄼🄲 🄹🄾🄱

Giorgione★★★★ ᕤ ★
Cannaregio 4587,
campo SS. Apostoli,
Tel. 0415225810
www.hotelgiorgione.com
Rooms: 76 - ⚐ - 🄰🄴 🄾 🎞

La Fenice et Des Artistes★★★★ ★
Meublé. S. Marco 1936,
campiello della Fenice,
Tel. 0415232333
www.fenicehotels.it
Rooms: 69 - ⚐ - 🄰🄴 🄾 🎞 🄼🄲 🄹🄾🄱 B

Londra Palace** ♿**
Castello 4171, riva degli Schiavoni,
Tel. 0415200533
www.hotelondra.it
Rooms: 53 - AE ⊕ VISA MC JCB

Palazzo Sant'Angelo sul Canal Grande** ♿ ★**
Meublé. S. Marco 3488-3478/B,
Tel. 0412411452
www.palazzosantangelo.com
Rooms: 14 - AE ⊕ VISA MC JCB B

Savoia & Jolanda** ♿**
Castello 4187, riva degli Schiavoni,
Tel. 0415206644
www.hotelsavoiajolanda.com
Rooms: 51 - AE ⊕ VISA MC B

Accademia Villa Maravege *
Meublé. Dorsoduro 1058-1060,
fondamenta Bollani,
Tel. 0415210188
www.pensioneaccademia.it
Rooms: 27 - ♣ - AE VISA MC JCB B

Agli Alboretti *
Accademia 884,
rio terrà A. Foscarini,
Tel. 0415230058
www.aglialboretti.com
Rooms: 23 - ♣ - AE VISA MC B

Ca' d'Oro * ♿**
Meublé. Cannaregio 4604,
corte Barbaro, Tel. 0412411212
www.venicehotelcadoro.com
Rooms: 27 - AE ⊕ VISA MC B

Casanova* ♿**
Meublé. S. Marco 1284,
Tel. 0415206855
www.hotelcasanova.it
Rooms: 47 - ✈ - AE ⊕ VISA MC JCB

Do Pozzi *
S. Marco 2373,
calle larga XXII Marzo,
Tel. 0415207855
www.hoteldopozzi.it
Rooms: 29 - ♣ -
AE ⊕ VISA MC JCB

Locanda ai Santi Apostoli*
Meublé. Cannaregio 4391/A,
strada Nuova,
Tel. 0415212612
www.locandasantiapostoli.com
Rooms: 11 - ♣ - AE ⊕ VISA MC JCB B

San Cassiano-Ca' Favretto * ♿**
Meublé. S. Croce 2232,
Tel. 0415241768
www.sancassiano.it
Rooms: 36 - AE ⊕ VISA MC JCB B

Santo Stefano *
Meublé. S. Marco 2957,
campo S. Stefano,
Tel. 0415200166
www.hotelsantostefanovenezia.com
Rooms. 11 - ♣ ✈ - AE VISA MC B

Torino *
Meublé. S. Marco 2356,
calle delle Ostreghe,
Tel. 0415205222
www.hoteltorino.com
Rooms: 37 - AE ⊕ VISA MC JCB B

San Fantin*
Meublé. S. Marco 1930/A,
campiello de la Fenice,
Tel. 0415231401
www.hotelsanfantin.com
Rooms: 14 - VISA MC

Serenissima ★**
Meublé. S. Marco 4486,
calle Goldoni,
Tel. 0415200011
www.nih.i/hotelserenissima
Rooms: 37 - AE VISA MC B

Wildner ** ★
Riva degli Schiavoni 4161,
Tel. 0415227463
www.veneziahotels.com
Rooms: 16 - ✈ - AE ⊕ VISA MC JCB B

Restaurants

Harry's Bar ▯▯▯▯
S. Marco 1323,
calle Vallaresso,
Tel. 0415285777
www.cipriani.com
Places: 80 - R, C - AE ⊕ VISA MC B

Ai Mercanti ▯▯▯
S. Marco 4346/A,
calle dei Fuseri, corte Copo,
Tel. 0415238269
www.aimercanti.com
Places: 50/30 - R, I - VISA MC B

A La Vecia Cavana ▯▯▯
Cannaregio 4624,
rio Terà Ss. Apostoli,
Tel. 0415287106
www.veciacavana.it
Places: 100 - R, I -
AE ⊕ VISA MC B

Al Graspo de Ua ▯▯▯
S. Marco 5094,
calle dei Bombaseri,
Tel. 0415200150
www.algraspodeua.com
Places: 80 - R, C - AE ⊕ VISA MC

Bistrot de Venise ▯▯
S. Marco 4685, calle dei Fabbri,
Tel 0415236651
www.bistrotdevenise.com
Places: 50 - R (historical) - AE VISA MC B

Boccadoro ▯▯▯
Cannaregio 5405/A,
campiello Widmann,
Tel. 0415211021
Places: 45/20 - R - VISA MC

Poste Vecie ▯▯▯ ♿
S. Polo 1608, rialto Pescheria,
Tel. 0411721822
www.postevecie.com
Places: 64/56 - R - AE ⊕ VISA MC

Aciugheta ▯▯
Castello 4357,
campo SS. Filippo e Giacomo,
Tel. 0415224292
www.aciugheta-hotelrio.it
Places: 80/80 - C - AE ⊕ VISA MC

Ai Gondolieri ▯▯ ★
Dorsoduro, San Vio 366,
Tel. 0415286396
www.algondolerl.com
Places: 50 - R - AE ⊕ VISA MC B

Al Conte Pescaor ▯▯ ♿ ★
S. Marco 544,
piscina S. Zulian,
Tel. 0415221483
muosasas@alcontepescaor.199.it
Places: 100/20 - R

Antica Besseta ▯▯
Santa Croce 1395,
salizada de Cà Zusto,
Tel. 0411721687
Places: 46/30 - R - AE ⊕ VISA MC B

Do Forni ▯▯ ★
S. Marco 457, calle dei Specchieri,
Tel. 0415230663
www.doforni.it
Places: 160 - ☉ - R, C -
AE ⊕ VISA MC

Donna Onesta ▯▯ ★
Dorsoduro 3922,
ponte de la Dona Onesta,
Tel. 041710586
www.donaonesta.com
Places: 45 - R - AE VISA MC B

Giardinetto-da Severino ▯▯ ★
Castello 4928, ruga Giuffa,
Tel. 0415285332
www.algiardinetto.it
Places: 100/200 - ☉ - R -
⊕ VISA MC B

Naranzaria ▯▯
S. Polo 130,
Tel. 0417241035
www.naranzaria.it
Places: 30/50 - ☉ - R (and fusion) -
⊕ VISA MC B

Osteria alle Testiere ▯▯
Castello 5801, calle del Mondo Novo, Tel. 0415227220
www.osterialletestiere.it
Places: 25 - R, I - VISA MC

Tre Spiedi ▯▯ ♿ ★
Cannaregio 5906, salizzada
S. Canciano, Tel. 0415208035
www.italiadiscovery.it
Places: 48 - R - AE ⊕ VISA MC JCB B

Vecio Fritolin ▯▯ ★
S. Croce 2262, calle della Regina,
Tel. 0415222881
www.veciofritolin.it
Places: 45 - R, I - AE ⊕ VISA MC

VERONA

> *ⓘ IAT*
> *Piazza Brà, Via degli Alpini 9*
> *Tel. 0458068680*
> *www.tourismverona.it*

Hotels

Victoria ** ♿ ★**
Meublé. Via Adua 8,
Tel. 045590566
www.hotelvictoria.it
Rooms: 71 - P ✈ - AE ⊕ VISA MC JCB B

Bologna * ★**
Piazzetta Scalette Rubiani 3,
Tel. 0458006830
www.hotelbologna.vr.it
Rooms: 32 - AE ⊕ VISA MC B

Giulietta e Romeo *
Meublé. Via Tre Marchetti 3,
Tel. 0458003554
www.giuliettaeromeo.com
Rooms: 34 - AE ⊕ VISA MC B

Restaurants

Arche ▯▯▯ ★
Via Arche Scaligere 6,
Tel. 0458007415
www.ristorantearche.com
Places: 60 - R - AE ⊕ VISA MC

Al Pompiere ▯▯
Vicolo Regina d'Ungheria 5,
Tel. 0458030537
Places: 50 - R - AE VISA MC B

Torcolo ¶¶
Via C. Cattaneo 11,
Tel. 0458033730
www.ristorantetorcolo.com
Places: 120/40 - R - ⑥ 🎫 MC B

VICENZA

> 📋 *APT*
> *Piazza Duomo 5*
> *Tel. 0444544122*
> *www.ascom.vi.it/aptvicenza*

Hotels

Jolly Hotel Tiepolo **** ⅋ ★
Viale S. Lazzaro 110,
Tel. 0444954011
www.jollyhotels.it
Rooms: 115 - 🅿 -
🗚 ⑥ 🎫 MC J⊂B B

Aries *** ⅋ ★
Via L. da Vinci 28,
Tel. 0444239239,
www.arieshotel.it
Rooms: 73 - 🅿 -
🗚 ⑥ 🎫 MC B

Restaurants

Antica Trattoria Tre Visi ¶¶
Corso Palladio 25,
Tel. 0444324868
www.ristorantetrevisi.com
Places: 100/50 - R - **2**
🗚 ⑥ 🎫 MC B

Da Biasio ¶¶
Viale X Giugno 172,
Tel. 0444323363
www.ristorantedabiasio.it
Places: 50 - ❀ 🅿 - I -
🗚 ⑥ 🎫 MC J⊂B B

FRIULI VENEZIA GIULIA

AQUILEIA (UD)

> 📋 *IAT*
> *Piazza del Capitolo 4*
> *Tel. 0431919491*
> *www.aquileiaturismo.info*

Hotels

Patriarchi ***
Via Giulia Augusta 12,
Tel. 0431919595
www.hotelpatriarchi.it
Rooms: 23 - ♨ 🅿 -
🗚 ⑥ 🎫 MC B

Restaurants

Colombara ¶¶ ⅋ ★
Loc. La Colombara,
Via S. Zilli 42,
Tel. 043191513
www.lacolombara.it
Places: 100/40 - R, C -
🗚 ⑥ 🎫 MC B

GORIZIA

> 📋 *AIAT*
> *Via Roma 5*
> *Tel. 0481386222*

Hotels

Best Western
Gorizia Palace ****
Corso Italia 63,
Tel. 048182166
www.goriziapalace.com
Rooms: 70 - 🅿 - 🗚 ⑥ 🎫 MC B

Internazionale *** ⅋ ★
Viale Trieste 173,
Tel. 0481524180
www.hotelinternazionalegorizia.it
Rooms: 49 - 🅿 🚭

Restaurants

Majda ¶¶
Via Duca d'Aosta 71,
Tel. 048130871
Places: 60/40 - ❀ 🅿 - R -
🗚 ⑥ 🎫 MC B

GRADO (GO)

> 📋 *APT*
> *Via Dante Alighieri 72*
> *Tel. 04318991*
> *www.gradoturismo.info*

Hotels

Abbazia **** ⅋ ★
Via Colombo 12, Tel. 043181721,
www.hotel-abbazia.com
Rooms: 51 - 🅿 🚭 🚭 ❦ -
🗚 ⑥ 🎫 MC B

G.H. Astoria **** ⅋ ★
Largo S. Grisogono 3,
Tel. 043183550
www.hotelastoria.it
Rooms: 124 - ☕ ❦ 🚭 🚭 ❦ -
🗚 ⑥ 🎫 MC B

Restaurants

Ai Ciodi ¶¶
Loc. Isola di Anfora,
Tel. 3357522209
Places: 30/140 - ❀ - R

TRIESTE

> 📋 *APT*
> *Via San Nicolò 20*
> *Tel. 04067961*
> *www.triestetourism.it*

Hotels

G.H. Duchi d'Aosta **** ⅋
Piazza Unità d'Italia 2,
Tel. 0407600011
www.magesta.com
Rooms: 55 - ❦ 🚭 🚭 🚭 -
🗚 ⑥ 🎫 MC B

Riviera & Maximilian's **** ⅋
Loc. Grignano,
strada Costiera 22 ,
Tel. 040224551
www.magesta.com
Rooms: 68 - ♨ 🅿 🚭 🚭 -
🗚 ⑥ 🎫 MC B

Restaurants

Antica Trattoria Suban ¶¶ ⅋
Via Comici 2,
Tel. 04054368
www.suban.it
Places: 30/50 - ❀ 🅿 - R -
🗚 ⑥ 🎫 MC J⊂B B

Scabar ¶¶
Erta S. Anna 63,
Tel. 040810368
www.scabar.it
Places: 50/70 - ❀ 🅿 - R, I -
🗚 ⑥ 🎫 MC B

UDINE

> 📋 *APT*
> *Piazza I Maggio 7*
> *Tel. 0342295972*
> *www.regione.fvg.it*

Hotels

Astoria Hotel Italia **** ⅋ ★
Piazza XX Settembre 24,
Tel. 0432505091
www.hotelastoria.udine.it
Rooms: 75 - ❦ - 🗚 ⑥ 🎫 MC B

President *** ⅋ ★
Via Duino 8,
Tel. 0432509905
www.hotelpresident.tv
Rooms: 80 - 🅿 ❦ -
🗚 ⑥ 🎫 MC J⊂B B

Restaurants

Agli Amici ¶¶¶ ⅋
Loc. Gòdia, Via Liguria 250,
Tel. 0432565411
www.agliamici.it
Places: 35/18 - 🅿 - R, I -
🗚 ⑥ 🎫 MC J⊂B B

La' di Moret ¶¶¶ ⅋ ★
Viale Tricesimo 276,
Tel. 0432545096
www.ladimoret.it
Places: 100 - ❀ 🅿 - R, C -
🗚 ⑥ 🎫 MC B

LIGURIA

ALASSIO (SV)

> 📋 *IAT*
> *Via Mazzini 68*
> *Tel. 0182647027*

Hotels

Diana Grand Hotel **** ⅋
Via Garibaldi 110,
Tel. 0182642701
www.hoteldianaalassio.it
Rooms: 57 - ♨ 🅿 ❦ 🚭 🚭 🚭 -
🗚 🎫 MC B

Beau Séjour ***
Via Garibaldi 102,
Tel. 0182646391
www.beausejourhotel.it
Rooms: 45 - ♨ 🅿 🚭 - 🗚 🎫 MC B

Toscana *** ⅋ ★
Via F. Gioia 4, Tel. 0182640657
www.hoteltoscanaalassio.it
Rooms: 55 - 🅿 🚭 - 🗚 ⑥ 🎫 MC B

Restaurants

Baiadelsole ¶¶¶
Corso Marconi 32,
Tel. 0182641814
mirella.porro@tin.it
Places: 35/25 - R, C - 🎫 MC B

GENOA/GENOVA

ℹ️ Genova Turismo
Staz. Ferroviaria Principe
Tel. 0102462633
www.apt.genova.it

Hotels

Jolly Hotel Marina ★★★★ & ★
Molo ponte Calvi 5,
Tel. 01025391
www.jollyhotels.com
Rooms: 143 - ⌷ ⌷ ⌷ B

Novotel Genova Ovest ★★★★ & ★
Via Cantore 8/C,
Tel. 01064841
www.accorhotels.com/italia
Rooms: 223 - ⌷ ⌷ -
⌷ ⌷ ⌷ B

Iris ★★★
Meublé. Via Rossetti Gabriele 4,
Tel. 0103760703
www.hoteliris.it
Rooms: 25 - ⌷ ⌷ - ⌷ ⌷ ⌷ B

Mediterranèe ★★★
A Pegli, Via Lungomare 69,
Tel. 0106973850
www.hotel-mediterranee.it
Rooms: 88 - ⌷ ⌷ ⌷ -
⌷ ⌷ ⌷ ⌷ B

Restaurants

Da Giacomo ❚❚❚ &
Corso Italia 1/r,
Tel. 010311041,
www.ristorantedagiacomo.it
Places: 60/20 - ⌷ ⌷ - R -
⌷ ⌷ ⌷ B

La Bitta nella Pergola ❚❚❚
Via Casaregis 52/r,
Tel. 010588543,
labittanellapergola@libero.it
Places: 30 - ⌷ - I - ⌷ ⌷ ⌷ B

Antica Osteria di Vico Palla ❚❚
Vico Palla 15,
Tel. 0102466575
acap29@libero.it
Places: 95 - R - ⌷ ⌷ ⌷ ⌷

Barisone ❚❚
Loc. Sestri Ponente,
Via Siracusa 2/r,
Tel. 0106049863
Places: 60/50 - ⌷ - R

IMPERIA

ℹ️ Informazioni Turistiche
Via Matteotti 37
Tel. 0183660140

Hotels

Miramare ★★★★ & ★
A Porto Maurizio,
Viale Matteotti 24,
Tel. 0182667120
www.rhotels.it
Rooms: 22 - ⌷ ⌷ ⌷ ⌷ -
⌷ ⌷ ⌷ B

Rossini al Teatro ★★★★ & ★
Meublé.
A Oneglia, Piazza Rossini 14,
Tel. 018374000
www.hotel-rossini.it
Rooms: 49 - ⌷ - ⌷ ⌷ ⌷ ⌷ B

Restaurants

Agrodolce ❚❚❚ &
A Oneglia, Via Des Geneys 34,
Tel. 0183293702
www.ristoranteagrodolce.it
Places: 35/35 - ⌷ - R - ⌷ ⌷ ⌷

Hostaria ❚❚
A Porto Maurizio,
Piazza S. Antonio 9,
Tel. 0183667028
Places: 38/40 - R - ⌷ ⌷ ⌷ ⌷ B

LA SPEZIA

ℹ️ Informazioni Turistiche
Viale Mazzini 45
Tel. 0187770900

Hotels

My Hotels La Spezia ★★★★ &
Meublé. Via XX Settembre 81,
Tel. 0187738848
www.myhotels.it
Rooms: 68 - ⌷ ⌷ - ⌷ ⌷ ⌷ ⌷ B

Genova ★★★
Meublé. Via F.lli Rosselli 84/86,
Tel. 0187732972
www.hotelgenova.it
Rooms: 37 - ⌷ - ⌷ ⌷ ⌷ ⌷ ⌷ B

Restaurants

Antica Trattoria Dino ❚❚
Via Cadorna 18,
Tel. 0187736157
trattoriadino@yahoo.it
Places: 60/60 - ⌷ - C -
⌷ ⌷ ⌷ ⌷ B

Il Centro ❚❚
Loc. Cadimare, Via della Marina 54,
Tel. 0187738832
www.trattoriailcentro.it
Places: 60/80 - ⌷ - R, I - ⌷ ⌷ ⌷ B

PORTOFINO (GE)

ℹ️ APT del Tigullio
Via Roma 35
Tel. 0185269024

Hotels

Piccolo Hotel ★★★★
Via Duca degli Abruzzi 31,
Tel. 0185269015
www.domina.it
Rooms: 22 - ⌷ ⌷ ⌷ ⌷ - ⌷ ⌷

**San Giorgio-Portofino
House** ★★★★ &
Meublé. Via del Fondaco 11,
Tel. 018526991
www.portofinohsg.it
Rooms: 18 - ⌷ ⌷ - ⌷ ⌷ ⌷ B

Restaurants

Da ü Batti ❚❚❚
Vico Nuovo 17,
Tel. 0185269379
vanfop@alice.it
Places: 70 - ⌷ - R - ⌷ ⌷ ⌷ ⌷ ⌷ B

Puny ❚❚❚
Piazza Martiri dell'Olivetta 5,
Tel. 0185269037
Places: 30/60 - R

SANREMO (IM)

ℹ️ Informazioni Turistiche
Largo Nuvoloni 5
Tel. 018450059

Hotels

Eveline Portosole ★★★★ &
Meublé. Corso Cavallotti 111,
Tel. 0184503430
www.evelineportosole.com
Rooms: 22 - ⌷ ⌷ ⌷ - ⌷ ⌷ ⌷ ⌷
⌷ B

Paradiso ★★★
Via Roccasterone 12,
Tel. 0184571211
www.paradisohotel.it
Rooms: 41 - ⌷ ⌷ ⌷ ⌷ -
⌷ ⌷ ⌷ ⌷ B

Restaurants

Da Nicò ❚❚❚❚ &
Piazza Bresca 9,
Tel. 0184501988
Places: 50/50 - R - ⌷ ⌷ ⌷ ⌷ B

SAVONA

ℹ️ Informazioni Turistiche
Corso Italia 157r
Tel. 0198402321

Hotels

Mare Hotel ★★★★
Via Nizza 89/r,
Tel. 019264065,
www.marehotel.it
Rooms: 66 - ⌷ ⌷ ⌷ - ⌷ ⌷ ⌷ ⌷ B

Riviera Suisse ★★★ ★
Via Paleocapa 24,
Tel. 019850853,
www.rivierasuissehotel.it
Rooms: 80 - ⌷ ⌷ ⌷ - ⌷ ⌷ ⌷ ⌷ B

Restaurants

L'Arco Antico ❚❚❚ &
Piazza Lavagnola 26/r,
Tel. 019820938
www.ristorantearcoantico.it
Places: 30 - R, I - ⌷ ⌷ ⌷ ⌷

EMILIA-ROMAGNA

BOLOGNA

ℹ️ IAT
Piazza Maggiore 6
Tel. 051246541
www.comune.bologna.it

Hotels

Al Cappello Rosso ★★★★ & ★
Meublé. Via de' Fusari 9,
Tel. 051261891
www.alcappellorosso.it
Rooms: 33 - ⌷ ⌷ ⌷ ⌷ ⌷ B

Art Hotel Commercianti ★★★★ ★
Meublé. Via de' Pignattari 11,
Tel. 0517457511
www.bolognarthotels.it
Rooms: 34 - ⌷ - ⌷ ⌷ ⌷ ⌷ ⌷ B

Albergo delle Drapperie ***
Meublé. Via Drapperie 5,
Tel. 051223955
www.albergodrapperie.com
Rooms: 21 - 🎫 MC B

Paradise *** ★
Meublé. Vicolo Cattani 7,
Tel. 051231792
www.hotelparadisebologna.it
Rooms: 18 - AE 🎫 MC B

Re Enzo ***
Via Santa Croce 26,
Tel. 051523322
www.hotelreenzo.it
Rooms: 54 - AE 🎫 MC B

Roma ***
Via D'Azeglio 9, Tel. 051231330
www.hotelroma.biz
Rooms: 86 - P - AE 🎫 MC JCB B

Restaurants

Pappagallo ¶¶¶
Piazza Mercanzia 3,
Tel. 051231200,
www.alpappagallo.it
Places: 80 - R - AE 🎫 MC B

Bottega del Vino Olindo Faccioli ¶¶
Via Altabella 15/B,
Tel. 051223171
Places: 20 - R - 🎫 MC JCB B

Franco Rossi ¶¶
Via Goito 3,
Tel. 051238818
www.italiadiscoveri.it/francorossi
Places: 60 - R - AE 🎫 MC B

Grassilli ¶¶
Via dal Luzzo 3,
Tel. 051222961
Places: 25/20 - R -
AE 🎫 JCB B

Trattoria Leonida ¶¶
Vicolo Alemagna 2,
Tel. 051239/42
Places: 60/15 - ✿ - R - AE 🎫 MC B

CESENATICO (FC)

🛈 **IAT**
Viale Roma 112
Tel. 0547673287
www.cesenaticoturismo.com

Hotels

Executive Meeting Place Hotel **** ★
Viale Cesare Abba 90,
Tel. 0547673605
www.michaelhotels.com
Rooms: 140 - P 🎫 MC B

Tridentum ****
Loc. Valverde,
viale Michelangelo 25,
Tel. 054786287,
www.michaelhotels.com
Rooms: 60 - P - 🎫 MC B

Restaurants

Lido Lido ¶¶¶
Via Ferrara 14,
ang. viale Carducci, Tel.
0547673311
www.lidolido.com
Places: 70/30 - ✿ P - I - AE 🎫

FERRARA

🛈 **IAT**
Castello Estense
Tel. 0532209370
www.comune.fe.it

Hotels

Ferrara **** ★
Largo Castello 36,
Tel. 0532205048
www.hotelferrara.com
Rooms: 42 - P - AE 🎫 MC B

Principessa Leonora ****
Meublé. Via Mascheraio 39,
Tel. 0532206020
www.principessaleonora.it
Rooms: 22 - P ✆ - AE 🎫 MC

De Prati ***
Meublé. Via Padiglioni 5,
Tel. 0532241905
www.hoteldeprati.com
Rooms: 16 - AE 🎫 MC B

Restaurants

Al Brindisi ¶¶
Via Adelardi 11, Tel. 0532209142
www.albrindisi.com
Places: 50/30 - R -
AE 🎫 MC B

Osteria della Campana ¶¶
Via Borgo dei Leoni 26,
Tel. 0532241256
www.osteriadellacampana.com
Places: 46/26 - ✿ - R - AE 🎫 MC JCB B

MODENA

🛈 **IAT**
Piazza Grande 14
Tel. 0592032660
www.comune.modena.it

Hotels

Canalgrande ****
Corso Canalgrande 6,
Tel. 059217160
www.canalgrandehotel.it
Rooms: 68 - ✆ -
AE 🎫 MC JCB B

Best Western Hotel Libertà *** ★
Meublé. Via Blasia 10,
Tel. 059222365
www.hotelliberta.it
Rooms: 51 - P - AE 🎫 MC B

Estense ***
Via Berengario 11,
Tel. 059219057,
www.hotelestense.com
Rooms: 60 - P ✆ -
AE 🎫 MC B

Restaurants

Fini ¶¶¶¶
Piazzetta S. Francesco,
Tel. 059223314
www.hotelrealfini.it
Places: 70 - P - R - AE 🎫 MC B

Hosteria Giusti ¶¶¶
Vicolo Squallore 46,
Tel. 059222533
www.osteriadellacampana.com
Places: 24/15 - ✿ - R -
AE 🎫 MC B

Cucina del Museo ¶¶
Via S. Agostino 7,
Tel. 059217429
Places: 24 - P - R, I - AE 🎫 MC B

PARMA

🛈 **IAT**
Via Melloni 1/b
Tel. 0521218889
www.turismo.comune.parma.it

Hotels

Jolly Hotel Stendhal **** ★
Via Bodoni 3,
Tel. 0521208057,
www.hotelstendhal.it
Rooms: 67 - ✆ - AE 🎫 MC B

My Hotels Arte Hotel ***
Meublé. Viale Mansfield 3,
Tel. 0521776926
www.myhotels.it
Rooms: 44 - P ✆ -
AE 🎫 MC JCB B

Tre Ville ***
Strada Benedetta 97/A,
Tel. 0521775309
www.letreville.it
Rooms: 34 - P - AE 🎫 MC B

Restaurants

Parizzi ¶¶¶
Via Repubblica 71,
Tel. 0521285952
www.ristoranteparizzi.it
Places: 45/10 - P - R, I - AE 🎫 MC B

La Filoma ¶¶
Borgo XX Marzo 15,
Tel. 0521206181
www.lafiloma.it
Places: 40 - R - AE 🎫 MC

Parma Rotta ¶¶
Via Langhirano 158,
Tel. 0521966738
www.parmarotta.com
Places: 100/100 - R - AE 🎫 MC B

PIACENZA

🛈 **IAT**
Piazzetta Mercanti 7
Tel. 0523329324

Hotels

ClassHotel Piacenza Fiera **** ★
Loc. Le Mose, Via Caorsana 127/D,
Tel. 0523606091
www.classhotel.com
Rooms: 80 - P - AE 🎫 MC JCB B

City ***
Meublé. Via Emilia Parmense 54,
Tel. 0523579752
www.hotelcitypc.it
Rooms: 60 - P ✆

Restaurants

Antica Osteria del Teatro ¶¶¶¶
Via Verdi 16,
Tel. 0523323777,
www.anticaosteriadelteatro.it
Places: 45 - I - 🎫 MC B

Vecchia Piacenza ¶¶
Via S. Bernardo 1, Tel. 0523305462
www.ristorantevecchiapiacenza.it
Places: 25 - R - 🎫 MC B

RAVENNA

ℹ️ **IAT**
Via Salara 8/12
Tel. 054435404
www.racine.ra.it

Hotels

Mosaico Hotel ★★★★ ♿ ★
Meublé. Via Darsena 9,
Tel. 0544456665
www.mosaicohotels.it
Rooms: 29 - 🅿️ - 🆎 💿 🎫 📵 B

Diana ★★★ ♿ ★
Meublé. Via Rossi 47,
Tel. 054439164
www.hoteldiana.ra.it
Rooms: 33 - ✆ - 🆎 💿 🎫 📵 B

La Reunion ★★★ ♿
Via C. Ricci 29, Tel. 0544212949,
www.lareunion.it
Rooms: 34 - 🅿️ - 🆎 💿 🎫 📵 B

Restaurants

Antica Trattoria al Gallo 1909 🍴🍴
Via Maggiore 87,
Tel. 0544213775
www.anticatrattoriadelgallo.191.It
Places: 25/25 - 🕐 - R - 🆎 💿 🎫 📵

Bella Venezia 🍴🍴
Via IV Novembre 16,
Tel. 0544212746
www.bellavenezia.it
Places: 60/21 - R - 🆎 💿 🎫 📵

REGGIO NELL'EMILIA

ℹ️ **IAT**
Piazza Prampolini 5/c
Tel. 0522451152
www.municipio.re.it/turismo

Hotels

Posta ★★★★ ★
Meublé. Piazza Del Monte 2,
Tel. 0522432944
www.hotelposta.re.it
Rooms: 39

Park Hotel ★★★★ ♿ ★
Via De Ruggero 1,
Tel. 0522292141,
www.parkhotel.re.it
Rooms: 63 - 🔥 🅿️ 🏊 ✆ - 🆎 💿 🎫 📵

Restaurants

Enoteca Morini 🍴🍴🍴
Via Passo Buole 82,
Tel. 0522323986
www.ristoranteenotecamorini.it
Places: 35 - 🅿️ - cucina: R - 🆎 💿

Delle Notarie 🍴🍴 ♿ ★
Via Aschieri 4, Tel. 0522453700
www.albergonotarie.it
Places: 42 - 🅿️- R - 🆎 💿 🎫 📵 B

RICCIONE (RN)

ℹ️ **IAT**
Piazzale Ceccarini 10
Tel. 0541693302
www.comune.riccione.rn.it

Hotels

Luna ★★★★
Viale Ariosto 5,
Tel. 0541692150,
www.lunariccione.it
Rooms: 45 - 🔥 🏊 🎾 🏊 🏊 🏊
🆎 💿 🎫 📵 B

Lungomare ★★★★
Lungomare della Libertà 7,
Tel. 0541692880
www.lungomare.com
Rooms: 56 - 🅿️ 🎾 🏊 🏊 -
🆎 💿 🎫 📵 B

Promenade ★★★★
Via Milano 67,
Tel. 0541600852,
www.hotelpromenade.it
Rooms: 43 - 🔥 🅿️ 🎾 🏊 🏊 🏊 ✆ -
🆎 💿 🎫 📵 B

Atilius ★★★ ♿ ★
Via A. Boito 3,
Tel. 0541647624,
www.atilius.com
Rooms: 51 - 🔥 🅿️ ✆ -
🆎 💿 🎫 📵 B

Novecento ★★★ ♿
Viale D'Annunzio 30,
Tel. 0541644990
www.hotelnovecento.it
Rooms: 35 - 🅿️ 🎾 🏊 - 🆎 💿 🎫 📵 B

Restaurants

Azzurra 🍴🍴
Piazzale Azzarita 2,
Tel. 0541648604
www.ristoranteazzurra.com
Places: 120/40 - 🕐 🅿️ - C - 🆎 💿 🎫
📵 B

Casale 🍴🍴
Viale Abruzzi, Tel. 0541604620
www.ilcasale.net
Places: 120/60 - 🕐 🅿️ - R -
🆎 💿 🎫 📵 B

RIMINI

ℹ️ **IAT**
Piazzale Federico Fellini 3
Tel. 054156902
www.riminiturismo.it

Hotels

Ambasciatori ★★★★ ★
Viale Vespucci 22, Tel. 054155561,
www.hotelambasciatori.it
Rooms: 62 - 🔥 🅿️ 🏊 🏊 -
🆎 💿 🎫 📵 B

Holiday Inn Rimini ★★★★ ★
Viale Vespucci 16, Tel. 054152255,
www.hirimini.com
Rooms: 64 - 🔥 🅿️ 🏊 🏊 🏊 - 🆎 💿
🎫 📵 📵 B

Le Méridien Rimini ★★★★ ♿
Lungomare Murri 13,
Tel. 0541396600
rimini.lemeridien.com
Rooms: 109 - 🅿️ 🎾 🏊 🏊 - 🆎 💿
🎫 📵 📵 B

National ★★★★ ★
Viale Vespucci 42,
Tel. 0541390944,
www.nationalhotel.it
Rooms: 98 - 🅿️ 🎾 🏊 🏊 -
🆎 💿 🎫 📵 📵 B

Villa Lalla ★★★
Viale Vittorio Veneto 22,
Tel. 054155155
www.villalalla.com
Rooms: 33 - 🔥 🅿️ 🏊 -
🆎 💿 🎫 📵 B

Restaurants

Squero 🍴🍴🍴 ♿
Lungomare Tintori 7,
Tel. 054127676
Places: 100/100 - 🕐 🅿️ - fish -
🆎 💿 🎫 📵 B

Taverna degli Artisti 🍴🍴🍴
Viale Amerigo Vespucci 1,
Tel. 054128519
www.tavernadegliartisti.com
Places: 110/150 - 🕐 - R, I - 🆎 💿 🎫
📵 📵 B

TUSCANY

AREZZO

ℹ️ **APT**
Piazza Risorgimento 116
Tel. 057523952
www.apt.arezzo.it

Hotels

AC Arezzo ★★★★ ♿ ★
Via Einstein 4,
Tel. 0575382287
www.ac-hotels.com
Rooms: 79 - 🅿️ - 🆎 💿 🎫 📵 B

Casa Volpi ★★★ ♿
Via S. Martini 29, Tel. 0575354364,
www.casavolpi.it
Rooms: 15 - 🔥 🅿️ - 🆎 💿 🎫 📵 B

Restaurants

Buca di San Francesco 🍴🍴
Via S. Francesco 1,
Tel. 057523271
www.bucadisanfrancesco.it
Places: 40 - R - 🆎 🎫 📵 B

Antica Osteria l'Agania 🍴
Via Mazzini 10,
Tel. 0575295381
www.agania.com
Places: 90 - 🅿️ - R - 🆎 💿 🎫 📵 B

BAGNI DI LUCCA (LU)

ℹ️ **APT**
Piazza Guidiccioni 2
Tel. 058391991

Hotels

Antico Albergo Terme ★★★ ♿ ★
Via del Paretaio 1,
Tel. 058386034,
www.termebagnidilucca.it
Rooms: 27 - 🕐 🎾 🏊

CAPOLIVERI (LI)

ℹ️ **APT Arcipelago Toscano**
Portoferraio - Calata Italia 43
Tel. 0565914671
www.aptelba.it

Hotels

Best Western G.H. Elba International ★★★★
Loc. Naregno,
Via Baia della Fontanella 1,
Tel. 0565946111,
www.elbainternational.it
Rooms: 130 - ♨ 🅿 🏊 🍸 -
AE ⑩ 💯 MC B

Antares ★★★
Loc. Lido di Capoliveri,
Tel. 0565940131
www.elbahotelantares.it
Rooms: 49 - ♨ 🅿 🏊 -
💯 MC B

Restaurants

Il Chiasso ️️️ ★
Vicolo N. Sauro 9,
Tel. 0565968709
ristoranteilchiasso@supereva.it
Places: 35/40 - ❀ - R, C -
AE ⑩ 💯 MC B

CHIANCIANO TERME (SI)

⚹ **APT**
Piazza Italia 67
Tel. 0578671122

Hotels

G.H. Terme ★★★★ ★
Piazza Italia 8,
Tel. 057863254
www.medeahotels.com
Rooms: 72 -♨ 🅿 🏊 -
AE ⑩ 💯 MC B

Moderno ★★★★
Viale Baccelli 10,
Tel. 057863754
www.hotelmodernochianciano.com
Rooms: 70 - ♨ 🅿 🏊 -
AE ⑩ 💯 MC

CORTONA (AR)

⚹ **APT**
Via Nazionale 42
Tel. 0575630352

Hotels

Borgo di Vagli ★★★★
Loc. Borgo di Vagli,
Tel. 057561961
www.borgodivagli.com
Rooms: 21 - 🅿 🏊 -
AE ⑩ 💯 MC B

Relais Villa Petrischio ★★★★ ★
Loc. Farneta,
Via del Petrischio 25,
Tel. 0575610316
www.villapetrischio.it
Rooms: 18 - ♨ 🅿 🏊 -
AE ⑩ 💯 MC B

Restaurants

Osteria del Teatro ️️️ ★
Via Maffei 2,
Tel. 0575630556
www.osteria-del-teatro.it
Places: 80/16 - R -
AE 💯 MC B

FLORENCE/FIRENZE

⚹ **APT**
Via Manzoni 16
Tel. 05523320
www.firenze.turismo.
toscana.it

Hotels

Antica Torre di Via Tornabuoni n. 1 ★ ★
Historic House
Meublé. Via Tornabuoni,
Tel. 0552658161
www.tornabuoni1.com
Rooms: 12 - AE ⑩ 💯 MC B

Residenza Johlea e Antica Dimora Johlea
Historic House
Meublé. Via S. Gallo 76/80,
Tel. 0554633292
www.johanna.it
Rooms: 12 - 🅿

Best Western Hotel Rivoli ★★★★ ★
Meublé. Via della Scala 33,
Tel. 05527861
www.hotelrivoli.it
Rooms: 80 - ♨ 🏊 - AE ⑩ 💯 MC

Lorenzo il Magnifico ★★★★ ★
Meublé.
Via Lorenzo il Magnifico 25,
Tel. 0554630878
www.lorenzoilmagnifico.net
Rooms: 39 - ♨ 🅿 🍸 -
AE ⑩ 💯 MC

Lungarno ★★★★
Borgo S. Jacopo 14,
Tel. 05527261
www.lungarnohotels.com
Rooms: 73 - AE ⑩ 💯 MC JCB B

Plaza Hotel Lucchesi ★★★★ ★
Lungarno della Zecca Vecchia,
Tel. 05526236
www.plazalucchesi.it
Rooms: 97 - AE ⑩ 💯 MC JCB B

Ville sull'Arno ★★★★ ★
Lungarno C. Colombo 3/5,
Tel. 055670971
www.hotelvillesullarno.com
Rooms: 47 - ♨ 🅿 🏊 🍸 -
AE ⑩ 💯 MC

Il Guelfo Bianco ★★★ ★ ★
Meublé. Via Cavour,
Tel. 055288330
www.ilguelfobianco.it
Rooms: 40 - ♨ AE ⑩ 💯 MC B

Loggiato dei Serviti ★★★ ★
Piazza della SS. Annunziata 3,
Tel. 055289592
www.loggiatodeiservitihotel.it
Rooms: 38 - 🍸 - AE ⑩ 💯 MC JCB B

Relais Uffizi ★★★ ★
Meublé. Via Chiasso del Buco 16,
Tel. 0552676239
www.relaisuffizi.it
Rooms: 10 - AE 💯 MC B

Villa Azalee ★★★ ★ ★
Meublé. Viale F.lli Rosselli 44,
Tel. 055214242
www.villa-azalee.it
Rooms: 25 - ♨ 🍸 -
AE ⑩ 💯 MC B

Restaurants

Camillo ️️️
Borgo S. Jacopo 57/r,
Tel. 055212427
cammillo@momax.it
Places: 110 - R -
AE 💯 MC

Cibreo ️️️ ★
Via del Verrocchio 8/r,
Tel. 0552341100
cibreo.fi@tin.it
Places: 70 - 🅿 - R, C - AE ⑩ 💯

Antica Mescita ️️
Via S. Niccolò 60/r,
Tel. 0552342836
Places: 80/20 - R - ⑩ 💯 MC

Boccanegra ️️ ★
Via Ghibellina 124/r,
Tel. 0552001098
www.boccanegra.com
Places: 60/20 - ❀ - R, C-
AE ⑩ 💯 MC B

Frescobaldi & Wine Bar ️️ ★
Via de' Magazzini 2-4/r,
Tel. 055284724
www.frescobaldiwinebar.it
Places: 85/10 - ❀ - R, C-
💯 MC JCB B

Sergio Gozzi ️️ ★
Piazza S. Lorenzo 8/r,
Tel. 055281941
Places: 65 - R - ⑩ 💯 MC

Vinolio ️️
Via S. Zanobi 126/r,
Tel. 055489957
www.vinolio.com
Places: 50 - R - AE 💯 B

FORTE DEI MARMI (LU)

⚹ **Informazioni Turistiche**
Via A. Franceschi 8D
Tel. 058480091

Hotels

Il Negresco ★★★★ ★
Lungomare Italico 82,
Tel 058478820
www.hotelilnegresco.com
Rooms: 39 - ♨ 🅿 🏊 🍸 -
AE ⑩ 💯 MC B

Kyrton ★★★ ★
Via Raffaelli 16, Tel. 0584787461
www.hotelkyrton.it
Rooms: 33 - ♨ 🅿 🏊 🍸 -
AE ⑩ 💯 MC B

Restaurants

La Magnolia ️️️
Viale Morin 46, Tel. 0584787052
www.hotelbyron.net
Places: 60/80 - ❀ 🅿 - R, I -
AE 💯 MC B

GROSSETO

⚹ **APT della Maremma**
Viale Monterosa 206
Tel. 0564462611
www.lamaremma.info

Hotels

Fattoria la Principina
Hotel Centro Congressi ★★★★
Loc. Principina Terra,
S.S. delle Collacchie 465,
Tel. 056444141
www.fattorialaprincipina.it
Rooms: 190 - ♨ 🅿 ⚡ 🏊 🎾 ♨ -
🎔 ᴍᴄ B

Restaurants

Canapone ❙❙
Piazza Dante 3,
Tel. 056424546
Places: 40/40 - R - ᴀᴇ 🎔 ᴍᴄ B

LIVORNO

> ℹ️ **APT Costa degli Etruschi**
> Piazza Cavour 6
> Tel. 0586204611
> www.costadeglietruschi.it

Hotels

Gran Duca ★★★★ ♿
Piazza Micheli 16,
Tel. 0586891024,
www.granduca.it
Rooms: 65 - 🎾 ♥ - ᴀᴇ ⑩ 🎔 ᴍᴄ B

Restaurants

Da Galileo ❙❙
Via della Campana 20,
Tel. 0586889009
Places: 48 - R - ᴀᴇ ⑩ 🎔 ᴍᴄ B

LUCCA

> ℹ️ **APT**
> Piazza S. Maria 35
> Tel. 0583919931
> www.luccaturismo.it

Hotels

Alla Corte degli Angeli ★★★★ ♿
Meublé. Via degli Angeli 23,
Tel. 0583469204
www.allacortedegliangeli.com
Rooms: 11 - 🅿 ♥ - ᴀᴇ ⑩ 🎔 ᴍᴄ ᴊᴏʙ B

Ilaria ★★★★ ♿ ★
Via del Fosso 26,
Tel. 058347615
www.hotelilaria.com
Rooms: 41 - 🅿 ♥ -
ᴀᴇ ⑩ 🎔 ᴍᴄ B

La Luna ★★★ ★
Meublé. Via Fillungo ang. Corte
Compagni 12,
Tel. 0583493634,
www.hotellaluna.com
Rooms: 29 - ᴀᴇ ⑩ 🎔 ᴍᴄ B

Restaurants

Antica Locanda dell'Angelo ❙❙
Via Pescheria 21,
Tel. 0583467711
www.locandadellangelo.it
Places: 60/30 - ● - R -
ᴀᴇ ⑩ 🎔 ᴍᴄ B

Osteria Baralla ❙❙
Via dell'Anfiteatro 5/9,
Tel. 0583440240
www.osteriabaralla.it
Places: 70/40 - R - ⑩ 🎔 ᴍᴄ B

MARCIANA MARINA (LI)

> ℹ️ **APT Arcipelago Toscano**
> Portoferraio - Calata Italia 43
> Tel. 0565914671
> www.aptelba.it

Hotels

Marinella ★★★
Viale Margherita 38,
Tel. 056599018
www.elbahotelmarinella.it
Rooms: 57 - ♨ 🅿 ⚡ ♨ - ᴀᴇ 🎔 ᴍᴄ B

Restaurants

Da Teresina ❙❙
Piazza della Vittoria 15,
Tel. 056599049
Places: 40/50 - R -
ᴀᴇ ⑩ 🎔 ᴍᴄ B

MARINA DI CAMPO (LI)

> ℹ️ **APT Arcipelago Toscano**
> Portoferraio - Calata Italia 43
> Tel. 0565914671
> www.aptelba.it

Hotels

Barracuda ★★★
Viale Elba 46,
Tel. 0565976893
www.hotelbarracudaelba.it
Rooms: 51 - ♨ 🅿 🎾 ♨ - 🎔 ᴍᴄ B

Dei Coralli ★★★
Via degli Etruschi 567,
Tel. 0565976336
www.hoteldeicoralli.it
Rooms: 62 - ♨ 🅿 ♨ ♥ - ᴀᴇ 🎔 ᴍᴄ B

Restaurants

La Lucciola ❙❙
Viale degli Eroi 2,
Tel. 0565976395
www.lalucciola.it
Places: 80 - ● - R - ᴀᴇ 🎔 ᴍᴄ B
www.ducadelmare.it
Rooms: 28 - ♨ 🅿 ♨ - ᴀᴇ 🎔 ᴍᴄ B

MONTECATINI TERME (PT)

> ℹ️ **APT**
> Viale Verdi 66/68
> Tel. 0572772244

Hotels

**Adua & Regina di Saba Wellness
and Beauty** ★★★★ ★
Viale Manzoni 46,
Tel. 057278134
www.hoteladua.it
Rooms: 72 - ♨ 🅿 ⚡ 🏊 ♨ -
ᴀᴇ 🎔 ᴍᴄ B

**Best Western Hotel Cappelli-
Croce di Savoia** ★★★ ★
Viale Bicchierai 139,
Tel. 057271151,
www.hotelcappelli.it
Rooms: 70 - ♨ 🅿 ♨ -
ᴀᴇ ⑩ 🎔 ᴍᴄ B

Restaurants

Enoteca Giovanni ❙❙❙
Via Garibaldi 25-27,
Tel. 057271695
www.enotecagiovanni.it
Places: 60/30 - ● - R, I - ⑩ 🎔 ᴍᴄ B

MONTEPULCIANO (SI)

> ℹ️ **Pro Loco**
> Piazza Don Manzoni 1
> Tel. 0578757341
> www.prolocomontepulciano.it

Hotels

Granducato ★★★
Meublé. Via delle Lettere 62,
Tel. 0578758610
www.nih.it/hotelgranducato
Rooms: 51 - 🅿 - ᴀᴇ ⑩ 🎔 ᴍᴄ ᴊᴏʙ B

Il Marzocco ★★★ ★
Piazza Savonarola 18,
Tel. 0578757262
www.cretedisiena.com/albergomar
zocco
Rooms: 16 - ♨ 🅿 ♥ - ᴀᴇ ⑩ 🎔 ᴍᴄ B

Restaurants

Le Logge del Vignola ❙❙ ★
Via delle Erbe 6,
Tel. 0578717290
www.leloggedelvignola.it
Places: 30 - ● - R, I - ᴀᴇ ⑩ 🎔 ᴍᴄ

PIENZA (SI)

> ℹ️ **Ufficio Turistico**
> Corso Rossellino 59
> Tel. 0578749071

Hotels

Piccolo Hotel La Valle ★★★ ♿
Via Circonvallazione 7,
Tel. 0578749402
www.piccolohotellavalle.it
Rooms: 15 - ♨ 🅿 - ᴀᴇ 🎔 ᴍᴄ ᴊᴏʙ B

Relais il Chiostro di Pienza ★★★ ♿
Corso Rossellino 26,
Tel. 0578748400
www.relaisilchiostrodipienza.com
Rooms: 37 - ♨ ♨ - ᴀᴇ ⑩ 🎔 ᴍᴄ B

Restaurants

Latte di Luna ❙❙
Via S. Carlo 2/4,
Tel. 0578748606
Places: 35/30 - ● - I - 🎔 ᴍᴄ

PISA

> ℹ️ **APT**
> Piazza Vitt. Emanuele II 16
> Tel. 05042291
> www.pisa.turismo.toscana.it

Hotels

Repubblica Marinara ★★★★ ♿ ★
Via Matteucci 81,
Tel. 0503870100
www.hotelrepubblicamarinara.it
Rooms: 55 - 🅿 - ᴀᴇ ⑩ 🎔

Novecento ★★★
Via Roma 37,
Tel. 050500323,
www.hotelnovecento.pisa.it
Rooms: 14 - ĀĒ ⑩ ▥ ᴹᶜ ᴶᶜᴮ B

Restaurants
Osterie dei Mille ¶¶ ★
Via dei Mille 30/32,
Tel. 050556263
icicapri@tin.it
Places: 48 - ℗ - C - ĀĒ ⑩ ▥

PISTOIA
ℹ **APT**
Piazza Duomo 4
Tel. 057321622
www.pistoia.turismo.toscana.it

Hotels
Il Convento ★★★ ♿
Loc. Pontenuovo, Via S. Quirico 33,
Tel. 0573452651
www.ilconventohotel.com
Rooms: 32 - ♨ ℗ ☰ - ▥ ᴹᶜ
Leon Bianco ★★★ ★
Meublé. Via Panciatichi 2,
Tel. 057326675
www.hotelleonbianco.it
Rooms: 27 - ✆ - ĀĒ ⑩ ▥ ᴹᶜ ᴶᶜᴮ B

Restaurants
Lo Storno ¶
Via del Lastrone 8, Tel. 057326193
Places: 50/50 - ❀ - R - ▥ ᴹᶜ B

PORTOFERRAIO (LI)
ℹ **APT Arcipelago Toscano**
Calata Italia 43
Tel. 0565914671
www.aptelba.it

Hotels
Acquaviva Park Hotel ★★★ ★
Loc. Acquaviva,
Tel. 0565915392
www.acquavivaparkhotel.com
Rooms: 38 - ♨ ℗ ☰ - ĀĒ ⑩ ▥ ᴹᶜ B
Paradiso ★★★ ★
Loc. Viticcio, Tel. 0565939034
www.elbaturistica.it
Rooms: 46 - ♨ ℗ ☰ - ▥ ᴹᶜ

Restaurants
Stella Marina ¶¶
Via Vittorio Emanuele II,
Tel. 0565915983
www.ristorantestellamarina.com
Places: 70/50 - ℗ - R - ▥ ᴹᶜ B

PRATO
ℹ **Agenzia per il Turismo**
P.za S. Maria delle Carceri 15
Tel. 057424112
www.prato.turismo.toscana.it

Hotels
Art Hotel Milano ★★★★ ♿
Via Tiziano 15, Tel. 057423371
www.arthotel.it
Rooms: 70 - ♨ ✆ - ĀĒ ⑩ ▥ ᴹᶜ B

Restaurants
Baghino ¶¶
Via Accademia 9,
Tel. 057427920
ristorantebaghino@alice.it
Places: 70 - ❀ - R - ĀĒ ⑩ ▥ ᴹᶜ B

RADDA IN CHIANTI (SI)
ℹ **Pro Loco**
Tel. 0577738494
www.chiantinet.it

Hotels
Il Borgo di Vescine ★★★★ ♿
Loc. Vescine,
Tel. 0577741144,
www.vescine.it
Rooms: 23 - ♨ ℗ ☰ - ĀĒ ⑩ ▥ ᴹᶜ B
Relais Fattoria Vignale ★★★★
Via Pianigiani 8,
Tel. 0577738300
www.vignale.it
Rooms: 42 - ℗ ☰ - ĀĒ ⑩ ▥ ᴹᶜ B

Restaurants
Al Chiasso dei Portici ¶¶ ♿
Chiasso dei Portici 10,
Tel. 0577738774
alchiassodeiportici@libero.it
Places: 30/30 - ❀ - R - ▥ ᴹᶜ

SAN GIMIGNANO (SI)
ℹ **Pro Loco**
Piazza Duomo 1
Tel. 057794008
www.sangimignano.com

Hotels
Villa San Paolo Hotel ★★★★ ♿
S.P. per Certaldo al km 4,
Tel. 0577955100
www.villasanpaolo.com
Rooms: 78 - ♨ ℗ ⚲ ☰ ☰ - ĀĒ ▥
Casolare le Terre Rosse ★★★ ♿
Loc. San Donato,
Tel. 05779021,
www.hotelterrerosse.com
Rooms: 42 - ♨ ℗ ☰ - ĀĒ ⑩ ▥ ᴹᶜ B
La Cisterna ★★★ ★
Piazza della Cisterna 24,
Tel. 0577940328
www.hotelcisterna.it
Rooms: 49 - ĀĒ ⑩ ▥ ᴹᶜ ᴶᶜᴮ B

Restaurants
Cum Quibus ¶¶
Via S. Martino 17,
Tel. 0577943199
info@cumquibus.it
Places: 40/40 - ❀ - R - ĀĒ ⑩ ▥ ᴹᶜ
Dorandò ¶¶
Vicolo dell'Oro 2,
Tel. 0577941862
www.ristorantedorando.it
Places: 35 - R - ĀĒ ⑩ ▥ ᴹᶜ ᴶᶜᴮ B

SIENA
ℹ **Agenzia per il Turismo**
Piazza del Campo 56
Tel. 0577280551
www.terresiena.it

Hotels
Villa Scacciapensieri ★★★★ ♿
Via di Scacciapensieri 10,
Tel. 057741441
www.villascacciapensieri.it
Rooms: 31 - ♨ ℗ ☰ ✆ - ĀĒ ⑩ ▥ ᴹᶜ B
Chiusarelli ★★★ ★
Via Curtatone 15,
Tel. 0577280562
www.chiusarelli.com
Rooms: 49 - ♨ ℗ ✆ - ĀĒ ▥ ᴹᶜ B
Santa Caterina ★★★ ♿ ★
Meublé. Via Piccolomini 7,
Tel. 0577221105
www.hscsiena.it
Rooms: 22 - ♨ ℗ ✆ - ĀĒ ⑩ ▥ ᴹᶜ ᴶᶜᴮ B
Palazzo di Valli ★★ ♿
Meublé. Via Piccolomini 135,
Tel. 0577226102
www.anticatorresiena.it
Rooms: 11 - ♨ ℗ - ĀĒ ⑩ ▥ ᴹᶜ B

Restaurants
Al Mangia ¶¶ ♿
Piazza del Campo 42,
Tel. 0577281121
www.almangia.it
Places: 60/90 - R - ĀĒ ⑩ ▥ ᴹᶜ
La Taverna del Capitano ¶¶
Via del Capitano 6/8,
Tel. 0577288094
*Places: 40/20 - R, I - ĀĒ ⑩ ▥ ᴹᶜ B
Osterie le Logge ¶¶
Via del Porrione 33, Tel. 057748013
www.osterialelogge.it
Places: 60/40 - R - ĀĒ ⑩ ▥ ᴹᶜ

VIAREGGIO (LU)
ℹ **APT della Versilia**
Via Carducci 10
Tel. 0584962233
www.versilia.turismo.toscana.it

Hotels
G.H. Principe di Piemonte ★★★★ ♿
Piazza G. Puccini 1,
Tel. 05844011
www.principedipiemonte.com
Rooms: 106 - ℗ ⚲ ☰ ☰ - ĀĒ ⑩ ▥ ᴹᶜ ᴶᶜᴮ
President ★★★★ ♿ ★
Viale Carducci 5, Tel. 0584962712
www.hotelpresident.it
Rooms: 50 - ☰ - ĀĒ ⑩ ▥ ᴹᶜ B

Restaurants
Oca Bianca ¶¶¶
Via Coppino 409,
Tel. 0584388477
www.oca-bianca.com
Places: 60 - ℗ - C - ĀĒ ⑩ ▥ ᴹᶜ ᴶᶜᴮ B

PRACTICAL INFO

423

Cabreo 🍴 ♿
Via Firenze 14,
Tel. 058454643
Places: 65 - 🌐 - fish - 🎫 🎫 ᴹᶜ B

VOLTERRA (PI)

Hotels
San Lino ★★★★ ♿ ★
Via S. Lino 26, Tel. 058885250,
www.hotelsanlino.com
Rooms: 43 - 🔱 - 🎫 ⓪ 🎫 ᴹᶜ ᴶᴼᴮ B

Villa Nencini ★★★ ♿ ★
Borgo S. Stefano 55, Tel.
058886386
www.villanencini.it
Rooms: 36 - 🛗 📶 🔱 ♥ - 🎫 ⓪ 🎫

Restaurants
Del Duca 🍴
Via di Castello 2, Tel. 058881510
www.enoteca-delduca-ristorante.it
Places: 35/35 - 🌐 - R - 🎫 ⓪ 🎫 ᴹᶜ

Trattoria del Sacco Fiorentino 🍴
Piazza XX Settembre 18, Tel.
058888537
paolodondoli@virgilio.it
Places: 50/14 - R - 🎫 ⓪ 🎫 ᴹᶜ B

MARCHE

ANCONA

Hotels
Fortino Napoleonico ★★★★ ♿
Loc. Portonovo, Via Poggio 166,
Tel. 071801450
www.hotelfortino.it
Rooms: 33 - 🛗 📶 🔱 - 🎫 ⓪ 🎫 ᴹᶜ
B

G.H. Passetto ★★★★ ★
Meublé. Via Thaon de Revel 1,
Tel. 07131307
www.hotelpassetto.it
Rooms: 40 - 🛗 📶 🔱 -
🎫 ⓪ 🎫 ᴹᶜ B

Restaurants
Dina 🍴 ♿
Vicolo Papis 5,
Tel. 07152339
Places: 50/20 - R - B

Trattoria Ulderico 🍴 ♿
Via Mamiani 9, Tel. 0712075237
www.trattoriaulderico.it
Places: 50 - 🌐 - R - 🎫 ⓪ 🎫 ᴹᶜ B

ASCOLI PICENO

Hotels
Palazzo Guiderocchi ★★★★ ♿
Via Cesare Battisti 3,
Tel. 0736244011, z0736243441
www.palazzoguiderocchi.com
Rooms: 40 - 📶 ♥ - 🎫 ⓪ 🎫 ᴹᶜ B

Restaurants
Del Corso 🍴
Corso Mazzini 277,
Tel. 0736256760
Places: 35 - R - 🎫 ᴹᶜ B

NUMANA (AN)

Hotels
Eden Gigli ★★★ ♿
Viale Morelli 11, Tel. 0719330652
www.giglihotels.com
Rooms: 41 - 🛗 📶 🔱 🔱 - 🎫 ᴹᶜ B

Restaurants
Casa Bianca 🍴 ♿
Via Litoranea 4, Tel. 0717390365
casabianca2000@hotmail.com
Places: 120/40 - 📶 - R, I - 🎫 ᴹᶜ B

PESARO

Hotels
Vittoria ★★★★ ♿ ★
Piazzale Libertà 2,
Tel. 072134343
www.viphotels.it
Rooms: 27 - 🛗 📶 🔱 🔱 ♥ - 🎫 ⓪
🎫 ᴶᴼᴮ B

Oasi San Nicola ★★★ ♿
Via S. Nicola 8, Tel. 072150849
www.oasisannicola.it
Rooms: 30 - 🛗 📶 🔱 - 🎫 ⓪ 🎫
ᴶᴼᴮ B

Restaurants
Lo Scudiero 🍴🍴
Via Baldassini 2, Tel. 072164107
www.ristoranteloscudiero.it
Places: 35 - I - 🎫 ⓪ 🎫 ᴹᶜ B

Bristolino 🍴 ♿
Piazza della Libertà 7,
Tel. 072131609
bristolinopesaro@libero.it
Places: 85/25 - I - 🎫 ⓪ 🎫 ᴹᶜ B

SIROLO (AN)

Hotels
Monteconero ★★★
Al monte Conero,
Via Monteconero 26,
Tel. 0719330592
www.hotelmonteconero.it
Rooms: 60 - 🛗 📶 🔱 - 🎫 ⓪ 🎫 ᴹᶜ B

Relais Valcastagno ★★★ ♿
Meublé. Via Valcastagno 10,
Tel. 0717391580
www.valcastagno.it
Rooms: 8 - 🛗 📶 🔱 - 🎫 ⓪ 🎫 ᴹᶜ B

Restaurants
Locanda Rocco 🍴 ♿
Via Torrione 1, Tel. 0719330558
www.locandarocco.it
Places: 20/40 - 📶 - I - 🎫 ᴹᶜ B

URBINO (PU)

Hotels
San Domenico ★★★★ ♿
Piazza Rinascimento 3,
Tel. 07222626
www.viphotels.it
Rooms: 31 - 🛗 📶 ♥ - 🎫 ⓪ 🎫 ᴹᶜ

Fontespino ★★★ ♿
Via Fontespino 10,
Tel. 072257331
www.fontespinohotel.it
Rooms: 15 - 🛗 📶 - 🎫 ᴹᶜ B

Restaurants
Angolo Divino 🍴
Via S. Andrea 12,
Tel. 0722327559
www.angolodivino.com
Places: 40 - 📶 - R - 🎫 🎫 ᴹᶜ B

UMBRIA

ASSISI

Hotels
G.H. Assisi ★★★★ ♿ ★
Via F.lli Canonichetti, Tel. 07581501,
www.grandhotelassisi.com
Rooms: 155 - 🛗 📶 🔱 🔱 - 🎫 ⓪ 🎫
ᴹᶜ ᴶᴼᴮ B

La Terrazza ★★★
Via F.lli Canonichetti,
Tel. 075812368
www.laterrazzahotel.it
Rooms: 26 - 🛗 📶 🔱 - 🎫 ⓪ 🎫 ᴹᶜ

Country House 3 Esse ★★
Meublé. Via di Valecchie 41,
Tel. 075816363
www.countryhousetreesse.com
Rooms: 15 - 🛗 📶 🔱 ♥ - 🎫 ⓪ 🎫

Restaurants
Buca di San Francesco 🍴 ♿
Via E. Brizi 1, Tel. 075812204
bucasanfrancesco@libero.it
Places: 150/60 - 🌐 - R - 🎫 ⓪ 🎫 ᴹᶜ B

Enteca San Pietro 🍴
Via Borgo San Pietro 18/B,
Tel. 075813303
www.enotecasanpietro.com
Places: 45 - R - 🌐 🎫 ᴹᶜ B

GUBBIO (PG)

📋 *IAT*
Viale Repubblica
Tel. 0759220790

Hotels

Bosone Palace **** &
Meublé. Via XX Settembre 22,
Tel. 0759220688
www.mencarelligroup.com
Rooms: 30 - ⒜ ⓪ Ⓜ Ⓜ B

Gattapone *** &
Meublé. Via Ansidei 6,
Tel. 0759272489
www.mencarelligroup.com
Rooms: 18 - ⒜ Ⓟ - ⒜ ⓪ Ⓜ Ⓜ B

Villa Montegranelli ***
Loc. Monteluiano, Tel. 0759220185
www.hotelvillamontegranelli.it
Rooms: 21 - ⒜ Ⓟ ▾ - ⒜ ⓪ Ⓜ Ⓜ B

Restaurants

Federico da Montefeltro 🍴
Via della Repubblica 35,
Tel. 0759273949
www.federicodamontefeltro.it
Places: 160/80 - ⊛ - R, C - ⒜ ⓪ Ⓜ Ⓜ B

La Fornace di Mastro Giorgio 🍴🍴 ★
Via Mastro Giorgio 2,
Tel. 0759221836
www.rosatihotels.com
Places: 120/20 - R - ⒜ ⓪ Ⓜ Ⓜ B

ORVIETO (TR)

📋 *IAT*
Piazza Duomo 24
Tel. 0763341772

Hotels

Fattoria di Titignano &
Historic House - Loc. Titignano 7,
Tel. 0763308000
www.titignano.com
Rooms: 30 - ⒜ Ⓟ ▵ ▾ - Ⓜ Ⓜ Ⓙ B

Palazzo Piccolomini **** & ★
Meublé. Piazza Ranieri 36,
Tel. 0763341743
www.hotelpiccolomini.it
Rooms: 32 - Ⓟ - ⒜ ⓪ Ⓜ Ⓜ B

Picchio *** & ★
Meublé. Via G. Salvatori 17,
Tel. 0763301144
hotelpicchio@tin.it
Rooms: 27 - Ⓟ ▾ - ⒜ ⓪ Ⓜ Ⓜ Ⓙ B

Restaurants

I Sette Consoli 🍴🍴 &
Piazza S. Angelo 1/A,
Tel. 0763343911
www.isetteconsoli.it
Places: 25/25 - ⊛ - R, I - ⒜ ⓪ Ⓜ Ⓜ B

L'Asino d'Oro 🍴🍴 &
Vicolo del Popolo 9,
Tel. 0763344406
luciosforza@hotmail.com
Places: 35/40 - ⊛ - R - ⓪ Ⓜ Ⓜ B

PERUGIA

📋 *IAT*
Piazza Novembre 3
Tel. 0755736458
www.iat.perugia.it

Hotels

Giò Arte e Vini **** &
Via R. D'Andreotto 19,
Tel. 0755731100
www.hotelgio.it
Rooms: 206 - Ⓟ ▵ - ⒜ ⓪ Ⓜ Ⓜ B

Relais dell'Olmo **** & ★
Meublé. Loc. L'Olmo,
strada Olmo-Ellera 4,
Tel. 0755173054
www.relaisolmo.com
Rooms: 32 - ⒜ Ⓟ ⚘ ▵ - ⒜ ⓪ Ⓜ Ⓜ B

Etruscan Chocohotel *** &
Via Campo di Marte 134,
Tel. 0755837314
www.chocohotel.it
Rooms: 94 - ⒜ Ⓟ ▵ - ⒜ ⓪ Ⓜ Ⓜ Ⓙ B

Fortuna *** & ★
Meublé. Via Bonazzi 19,
Tel. 0755722845
www.umbriahotels.com
Rooms: 52 - ⒜ ⓪ Ⓜ Ⓜ B

Rosalba **
Meublé. Piazza del Circo 7,
Tel. 0755728285
www.hotelrosalba.com
Rooms: 11

Restaurants

Cesarino 🍴🍴 &
Piazza IV Novembre 4/5,
Tel. 0755728974
www.isetteconsoli.it
Places: 80/50 - ⊛ - R - ⒜ ⓪ Ⓜ Ⓜ B

Locanda degli Artisti 🍴🍴 ★
Via Campo Battaglia 10,
Tel. 0755735851
www.perugiaonline.com/
locandadegliartisti
Places: 75/100 - R - ⒜ ⓪ Ⓜ Ⓜ B

Osteria del Gambero 🍴🍴
Via Baldeschi 8/A,
Tel. 0755735461
www.osteriadelgambero.it
Places: 55/8 - R - ⒜ ⓪ Ⓜ Ⓜ B

SPOLETO (PG)

📋 *IAT*
Piazza della Libertà 7
Tel. 074349890

Hotels

Convento di Agghielli &
Historic House
Loc. Pompagnano,
Tel. 074325010
www.agghielli.it
Rooms: 16 - ▵ ▵ - ⓪ Ⓜ Ⓜ B

Cavaliere Palace **** &
Corso Garibaldi 49,
Tel. 0743220350
www.cavalierehotels.com
Rooms: 31 - ▵ Ⓟ - ⒜ ⓪ Ⓜ Ⓜ

San Luca **** & ★
Meublé. Via interna delle Mura 21,
Tel. 0743223399
www.hotelsanluca.com
Rooms: 35 - ▵ - ⒜ ⓪ Ⓜ Ⓜ Ⓙ B

Charleston ***
Meublé. Piazza Collicola 10,
Tel. 0743220052
www.hotelcharleston.it
Rooms: 18 - Ⓟ ▾ - ⒜ ⓪ Ⓜ Ⓜ B

Restaurants

Ferretti 🍴🍴
Loc. Monteluco 20,
Tel. 074349849
www.albergoferretti.com
Places: 60/80 - Ⓟ - R - ⒜ Ⓜ Ⓜ B

Pentagramma 🍴🍴
Via T. Martani 2
(piazza della Libertà),
Tel. 0743223141
www.ristorantepentagramma.com
Places: 80/12 - ⊛ - R - ⓪ Ⓜ Ⓜ B

LAZIO

BRACCIANO (RM)

📋 *IAT*
Via Claudia 58
Tel. 0699840062

Hotels

Villa Clementina **** &
Via Traversa Quarto del Lago 12,
Tel. 069986268
www.hotelvillaclementina.it
Rooms: 7 - ▵ Ⓟ ▵ - ⒜ ⓪ Ⓜ Ⓜ Ⓙ B

Restaurants

Vino e Camino 🍴🍴
Piazza Mazzini 11,
Tel. 0699803433
web.tiscalinet.it/vino-e-camino
Places: 55/30 - R - ⒜ ⓪ Ⓜ Ⓜ B

FIUGGI (FR)

📋 *IAT*
Piazza Frascara 4
Tel. 0775515019

Hotels

Ambasciatori **** ★
Via dei Villini 8,
Tel. 0775514351,
www.albergoambasciatori.it
Rooms: 86 - Ⓟ ⚘ - ⒜ ⓪ Ⓜ Ⓜ B

King *** ★
Via Colle della Volpe 6,
Tel. 0775514305
www.kinghotelfiuggi.it
Rooms: 36 - ▵ Ⓟ ▵ ▵ - Ⓜ Ⓜ

Restaurants

La Torre al Centro Storico ¶¶
Piazza Trento e Trieste 29,
Tel. 0775515382
www.ristorantelatorre.biz
Places: 38/20 - R - 🝙 ⓪ 🝙 🝙 B

FRASCATI (RM)

> 🎫 **IAT**
> Piazza Marconi 1
> Tel. 069420331

Hotels

Flora ★★★★ ★
Meublé. Viale Vittorio Veneto 8,
Tel. 069416110
www.hotel-flora.it
Rooms: 37 - 🝙 🝙 - 🝙 ⓪ 🝙 🝙 🝙 B

Colonna ★★★ 👍
Meublé. Piazza del Gesù 12,
Tel. 0694018088
www.hotelcolonna.it
Rooms: 20 - 🝙 - 🝙 ⓪ 🝙 🝙 🝙 B

Restaurants

Cacciani ¶¶
Via A. Diaz 13/15, Tel. 069420378,
www.cacciani.it
Places: 120/80 - R, C- 🝙 ⓪ 🝙

GENZANO DI ROMA (RM)

Hotels

G.H. Primus ★★★★
Via G. Pellegrino 12,
Tel. 069364932
www.grandhotelprimus.it
Rooms: 92 - 🝙 🝙 🝙 - 🝙 ⓪ 🝙 🝙
🝙 B

Restaurants

La Scuderia ¶¶ ★
Piazza Sforza Cesarini 1,
Tel. 069390521
ristorantelascuderia@yahoo.it
Places: 80/70 - ● 🝙 - R - 🝙 ⓪ 🝙
🝙 🝙 B

GROTTAFERRATA (RM)

Hotels

Park Hotel Villa Grazioli ★★★★ 👍
Via U. Pavoni 19,
Tel. 069454001,
www.villagrazioli.com
Rooms: 62 - 🝙 🝙 🝙 - 🝙 ⓪ 🝙 🝙
🝙 B

Restaurants

Taverna dello Spuntino ¶¶ 👍
Via Cicerone 22,
Tel. 069459366
www.tavernadellospuntino.com
Places: 100 - 🝙 - R, C - 🝙 🝙 B

PALESTRINA (RM)

> 🎫 **Pro Loco**
> Piazza S. Maria degli Angeli
> Tel. 069573176

Hotels

La Meridienne ★★★★ 👍
Colle S. Agapito,
Tel. 069534399,
www.hotellameridienne.it
Rooms: 73 - 🝙 🝙 🝙 🝙 🝙 - 🝙 - 🝙 ⓪ 🝙
🝙 B

ROME/ROMA

> 🎫 **APT**
> Via Parigi 11
> Tel. 0636004399
> www.aptroma.com

Hotels

Artemide ★★★★ 👍
Via Nazionale 22, Tel. 06489911
www.hotelartemide.it
Rooms: 85 - 🝙 - 🝙 ⓪ 🝙 🝙 🝙 B

Atlante Garden ★★★★ ★
Meublé. Via Crescenzio 78/A,
Tel. 066872361
www.atlantehotels.com
Rooms: 60 - 🝙 ● -
🝙 ⓪ 🝙 🝙 🝙 B

Barberini ★★★★ 👍 ★
Meublé. Via Rasella 3,
Tel. 064814993
www.hotelbarberini.com
Rooms: 35 🝙 ⓪ 🝙 🝙 🝙 B

Beverly Hills ★★★★ 👍 ★
Largo B. Marcello 220,
Tel. 068542141
www.hotelbeverly.com
Rooms: 183 - 🝙 - 🝙 ⓪ 🝙 🝙 🝙 B

Dei Borgognoni ★★★★
Via del Bufalo 126,
Tel. 0669941505
www.hotelborgognoni.it
Rooms: 51 - 🝙 - 🝙 ⓪ 🝙 🝙 🝙

Delle Nazioni ★★★★ 👍 ★
Via Poli 7,
Tel. 066792441
www.remarhotels.com/nazioni
Rooms: 83 - 🝙 ⓪ 🝙 🝙 🝙 B

Empire Palace Hotel ★★★★
Via Aureliana 39, Tel. 06421281
www.empirepalacehotel.com
Rooms: 110 - 🝙 ⓪ 🝙 🝙 B

Farnese ★★★★ ★
Meublé. Via A. Farnese 30,
Tel. 063212553
www.hotelfarnese.it
Rooms: 23 - 🝙 - 🝙 ⓪ 🝙 🝙 B

Jolly Hotel Leonardo da Vinci ★★★★ 👍 ★
Via dei Gracchi 324,
Tel. 06328481
www.jollyhotels.it
Rooms: 260 - 🝙 🝙 -
🝙 ⓪ 🝙 🝙 🝙 B

Jolly Hotel Vittorio Veneto ★★★★ 👍 ★
Corso d'Italia 1,
Tel. 0684951
www.jollyhotels.com
Rooms: 201 - ● - 🝙 ⓪ 🝙 🝙 B

Locanda Cairoli ★★★★ ★
Meublé. Piazza B. Cairoli 2,
Tel. 0668809278
www.locandacairoli.it
Rooms: 13 - 🝙 - 🝙 ⓪ 🝙 🝙 B

Mascagni ★★★★ ★
Via V. E. Orlando 90,
Tel. 0648904040
www.hotelmascagni.com
Rooms: 40 - 🝙 ⓪ 🝙 🝙 B

Memphis ★★★★ ★
Meublé. Via degli Avignonesi 36,
Tel. 06485849
www.remarhotels.com/memphis
Rooms: 17 - 🝙 ⓪ 🝙 🝙

Mercure Roma Delta Colosseo ★★★★ 👍 ★
Meublé. Via Labicana 144,
Tel. 06770021
www.mercure.com
Rooms: 160 - 🝙 -
🝙 ⓪ 🝙 🝙 B

Mozart ★★★★ 👍 ★
Meublé. Via dei Greci 23/B,
Tel. 0636001915
www.hotelmozart.com
Rooms: 56 - 🝙 ⓪ 🝙

Napoleon ★★★★ ★
Piazza Vittorio Emanuele 105,
Tel. 064467264
www.napoleon.it
Rooms: 75 - 🝙 ⓪ 🝙 🝙 B

Nazionale ★★★★ 👍
Piazza Montecitorio 131,
Tel. 06695001
www.nazionaleroma.it
Rooms: 95 - 🝙 ⓪ 🝙 🝙 B

Oxford ★★★★ ★
Via Boncompagni 89,
Tel. 064203601
www.hoteloxford.com
Rooms: 56 - 🝙 ⓪ 🝙 🝙 B

Piranesi ★★★★ ★
Meublé. Via del Babuino 196,
Tel. 06328041
www.hotelpiranesi.com
Rooms: 32 - 🝙 ⓪ 🝙 🝙 B

Quality Hotel Nova Domus ★★★★ 👍 ★
Via G. Savonarola 38,
Tel. 06399511
www.novadomushotel.it
Rooms: 122 - 🝙 - 🝙 ⓪ 🝙 🝙 B

Raphael ★★★★ 👍 ★
Largo Febo 2,
Tel. 06682831
www.raphaelhotel.com
Rooms: 55 - 🝙 ⓪ 🝙 🝙 B

Sole al Pantheon ★★★★
Meublé. Piazza della Rotonda 63,
Tel. 066780441
www.hotelsolealpantheon.com
Rooms: 25 - 🝙 ⓪ 🝙 🝙 B

Starhotels Michelangelo ★★★★ 👍 ★
Via della Stazione S. Pietro 14,
Tel. 06398739
www.starhotels.com
Rooms: 179 - 🝙 - 🝙 ⓪ 🝙 🝙 🝙

Valadier ★★★★
Via della Fontanella 15,
Tel. 063611998
www.hotelvaladier.com
Rooms: 68 - ● - 🝙 ⓪ 🝙 🝙 B

White ★★★★ 👍 ★
Meublé. Via in Arcione 77,
Tel. 066991242
www.travelroma.com
Rooms: 44 - 🝙 - 🝙 ⓪ 🝙 B

Accademia ✦✦✦ ★
Meublé. Piazza Accademia
di S. Luca 74,
Tel. 0669922607
www.travelroma.com
Rooms: 82 - ⟦AE⟧ ⟦⟧ ⟦VISA⟧ ⟦MC⟧ B

Arcangelo ✦✦✦ ★
Meublé. Via Boezio 15,
Tel. 066874143
www.hotelarcangeloroma.com
Rooms: 33 - ⟦P⟧ -
⟦AE⟧ ⟦⟧ ⟦VISA⟧ ⟦MC⟧ B

Aventino ✦✦✦ &
Via S. Domenico 10,
Tel. 06570057
www.aventinohotels.com
Rooms: 21 - ⟦⟧ ⟦P⟧ - ⟦AE⟧ ⟦⟧
⟦VISA⟧ ⟦MC⟧ ⟦JCB⟧ B

Cesàri ✦✦✦ & ★
Meublé. Via di Pietra 89/A,
Tel. 066749701
www.albergocesari.it
Rooms: 47 - ⟦P⟧ -
⟦AE⟧ ⟦⟧ ⟦VISA⟧ ⟦MC⟧ ⟦JCB⟧ B

Montreal ✦✦✦
Meublé. Via Carlo Alberto 4,
Tel. 064457797
www.hotelmontrealroma.it
Rooms: 27 - ⟦⟧ - ⟦AE⟧ ⟦⟧ ⟦VISA⟧ ⟦MC⟧ B

San Francesco ✦✦✦
Meublé. Via Iacopa dei Settesoli 7,
Tel. 0658300051
www.hotelsanfrancesco.net
Rooms: 24 - ⟦AE⟧ ⟦⟧ ⟦VISA⟧ ⟦MC⟧ B

Teatropace33 ✦✦✦ ★
Meublé. Via del Teatro Pace,
Tel. 066879075
www.hotelteatropace.com
Rooms: 23 - ⟦AE⟧ ⟦⟧ ⟦VISA⟧ ⟦MC⟧ B

Villa del Parco ✦✦✦ & ★
Meublé. Via Nomentana 110,
Tel. 0644237773
www.hotelvilladelparco.it
Rooms: 29 - ⟦⟧ -
⟦AE⟧ ⟦⟧ ⟦VISA⟧ ⟦MC⟧ B

Villa San Pio ✦✦✦ &
Via Santa Melania 19,
Tel. 06570057
www.aventinohotels.com
Rooms: 78 - ⟦⟧ - ⟦AE⟧ ⟦⟧ ⟦VISA⟧ ⟦MC⟧

Restaurants

Il Convivio Troiani ❧❧❧❧ &
Vicolo dei Soldati 31,
Tel. 066869432
www.ilconviviotroiani.com
Places: 50 - R, I - ⟦AE⟧ ⟦⟧ ⟦VISA⟧ ⟦MC⟧ B

L'Altro Mastai ❧❧❧❧ & ★
Via G. Giraud 53,
Tel. 066830129
www.laltromastai.it
Places: 50 - C, I -
⟦AE⟧ ⟦⟧ ⟦VISA⟧ ⟦MC⟧ B

Pagliaccio ❧❧❧❧ &
Via dei Banchi Vecchi 129/A,
Tel. 0668809595
www.ristoranteilpagliaccio.it
Places: 45 - cucina: C, I - ⟦AE⟧ ⟦⟧ ⟦VISA⟧
⟦MC⟧ B

Alberto Ciarla ❧❧❧
Piazza S. Cosimato 40,
Tel. 065818668
www.albertociarla.com
Places: 50/30 - R, fish -
⟦AE⟧ ⟦VISA⟧ ⟦MC⟧ ⟦JCB⟧ B

Al Moro ❧❧❧
Vicolo delle Bollette 13,
Tel. 066783495
Places: 90/20 - R - ⟦AE⟧ ⟦VISA⟧

Al Presidente ❧❧❧
Via in Arcione 95,
Tel. 066797342
www.alpresidente.it
Places: 50/50 - R - ⟦AE⟧ ⟦⟧ ⟦VISA⟧ ⟦MC⟧ B

Checchino dal 1887 ❧❧❧
Via Monte Testaccio 30,
Tel. 065746318
www.checchino-dal-1887.com
Places: 60/30 - R - ⟦AE⟧ ⟦⟧ ⟦VISA⟧ ⟦MC⟧ ⟦JCB⟧ B

Checco er Carettiere ❧❧❧ &
Via Benedetta 10,
Tel. 065800985
www.checcoercarettiere.it
Places: 180/70 - ✿ - R, fish - ⟦AE⟧ ⟦⟧
⟦VISA⟧ ⟦MC⟧ B

Enoteca Capranica ❧❧❧
Piazza Capranica 99/100,
Tel. 0669940992
www.enotecacapranica.it
Places: 70 - C - ⟦AE⟧ ⟦⟧ ⟦VISA⟧ ⟦MC⟧ B

Evangelista ❧❧❧
Via Zoccolette 11/A, Tel. 066875810
ristorantevangelista@infinito.it
Places: 40/20 - ✿ - R, C - ⟦VISA⟧ ⟦MC⟧ B

Il Sanlorenzo ❧❧❧
Via dei Chiavari 4/5, Tel. 066865097
www.ilsanlorenzo.it
Places: 50/16 - ✿ - C - ⟦AE⟧ ⟦⟧ ⟦VISA⟧ ⟦MC⟧
⟦JCB⟧ B

L'Arcangelo ❧❧❧
Via G.G. Belli 59-61,
Tel. 063210992
ristorantelarcangelo@virgilio.it
Places: 35 - R - ⟦AE⟧ ⟦⟧ ⟦VISA⟧ ⟦MC⟧ B

Papà Giovanni ❧❧❧
Via dei Sediari,
Tel. 0668804807
www.ristorantepapagiovanni.it
Places: 40 - ⟦P⟧ - R - ⟦VISA⟧ ⟦MC⟧ B

Sora Lella ❧❧❧
Via di Ponte Quattro Capi 16,
Tel. 066861601
www.soralella.com
Places: 60 - R - ⟦AE⟧ ⟦⟧ ⟦VISA⟧ ⟦MC⟧ B

**Aurora 10 da Pino
il Sommelier** ❧❧❧ ★
Via Aurora 10, Tel. 064742779
www.aurora10.it
Places: 50/30 - R, I - ⟦AE⟧ ⟦⟧ ⟦VISA⟧ B

Caffè Bernini ❧❧
Piazza Navona 44,
Tel. 0668192998
www.caffebernini.com
Places: 40/130 - R, I - ⟦AE⟧ ⟦⟧ ⟦MC⟧ B

Campana ❧❧
Vicolo della Campana 18,
Tel. 066867820
ristlacampana@genie.it
Places: 130 - R - ⟦AE⟧ ⟦⟧ ⟦VISA⟧ ⟦MC⟧ ⟦JCB⟧ B

Dal Cavalier Gino ❧❧
Vicolo Rosini 4,
Tel. 066873434
Places: 50 - R

Da Pancrazio ❧❧
Piazza del Biscione 92,
Tel. 066861246
www.dapancrazio.it
Places: 110/40 - R, C - ⟦AE⟧ ⟦⟧ ⟦VISA⟧ ⟦MC⟧
⟦JCB⟧ B

Gatta Mangiona ❧❧ &
Via Federico Ozanam 30/32,
Tel. 065346702
www.dapancrazio.it
Places: 110/35 - R, C -
⟦VISA⟧ ⟦MC⟧ B

Le Rose ❧❧
Via Sacrofanese 25,
Tel. 0633613050
www.ristorantidiroma.it
Places: 80/100 - ✿ - R

Mamma Angelina &
Viale A. Boito 65,
Tel. 068608928
mammangelina@libero.it
Places: 65/30 - ✿ - ⟦P⟧ - R, C - ⟦AE⟧ ⟦⟧
⟦VISA⟧ ⟦MC⟧

Matricella ❧❧
Via del Leone 3,
Tel. 066832100
www.matricianella.it
Places: 60/28 - ✿ - R -
⟦AE⟧ ⟦⟧ ⟦VISA⟧ ⟦MC⟧ B

**Museo Atelier
Canova Tadolini** ❧❧
Via del Babuino 150/A,
Tel. 0632110702
canova.tadolini@virgilio.it
Places: 80 - R, C -
⟦AE⟧ ⟦⟧ ⟦VISA⟧ ⟦MC⟧ B

Osteria della Frezza ❧❧
Via della Frezza 16,
Tel. 0632111482
www.gusto.it
Places: 200/150 - ✿ - R -
⟦AE⟧ ⟦⟧ ⟦VISA⟧ ⟦MC⟧ B

Osteria del Velodromo Vecchio ❧❧
Via Genzano 139,
Tel. 067886793
velodromo@alice.it
Places: 30/15 - R - ⟦AE⟧ ⟦VISA⟧ ⟦MC⟧ B

Spirito Divino ❧❧
Via dei Genovesi 31/B,
Tel. 065896689
www.spiritodivino.com
Places: 50 - C - ⟦AE⟧ ⟦⟧ ⟦VISA⟧ ⟦MC⟧ B

TARQUINIA (VT)

> ⟦i⟧ **IAT**
> Piazza Cavour 1
> Tel. 0766856384

Hotels

Pegaso Palace Hotel ✦✦✦✦ &
Loc. Marina Velca,
Via Martano,
Tel. 0766810027
www.hpegaso.it
Rooms: 48 - ⟦⟧ ⟦P⟧ ⟦⟧ ⟦⟧ - ⟦AE⟧ ⟦⟧ ⟦VISA⟧

Restaurants

Gradinoro ❧❧❧
Loc. Tarquinia,
lungomare dei Tirreni 17,
Tel. 0766864045
Places: 80/40 - ✿ - ⟦P⟧ - R - ⟦AE⟧ ⟦⟧ ⟦VISA⟧
⟦MC⟧ ⟦JCB⟧

TIVOLI (RM)

> ⟦i⟧ **APT**
> Vicolo Barchetto
> Tel. 0774334522

Hotels

G.H. Duca d'Este ★★★★ &
Loc. Tivoli, Via Tiburtina Valeria
330, Tel. 07743883
www.siriohotel.com
Rooms: 184 - ♨ P ⚒ ⛱ ⚡ - AE ⚫
VISA MC B

Restaurants

Adriano ⛶ ★
Loc. Villa Adriana,
largo Marguerite Yourcenar 2,
Tel. 0774382235
www.hoteladriano.it
Places: 180/150 - ❀ P - C - AE ⚫ VISA
MC JCB B

VITERBO

i **APT**
Piazza S. Carluccio
Tel. 0761304795
www.apt.viterbo.it

Hotels

Balletti Park Hotel ★★★★ ★
Loc. San Martino al Cimino,
Via Umbria 2/A,
Tel. 07613771, www.balletti.com
Rooms: 134 - ♨ P ⛱ -
AE ⚫ VISA MC B

Restaurants

Il Grottino ⛶
Via della Cava 7,
Tel. 0761290088
Places: 40 - cucina: R - VISA MC B

ABRUZZO

CARAMANICO
TERME (PE)

i **APT**
Via Fontegrande 2
Tel. 085922202

Hotels

Maiella e delle Terme ★★★ & ★
Via Roma 29, Tel. 085922301,
www.albergomaiella.it
Rooms: 107 - ♨ P ❀ ⚒ - AE ⚫ VISA
MC B

CHIETI

i **IAT**
Via B. Spaventa
Tel. 087163640
www.regione.abruzzo.it

Hotels

G.A. Abruzzo ★★★
Via Asinio Herio 20,
Tel. 087141940,
www.albergoabruzzo.it
Rooms: 65 - P ❀ - AE ⚫ VISA MC B

Restaurants

Nonna Elisa ⛶
Via per Popoli 265,
Tel. 0871684152
Places: 95 - R - AE ⚫ VISA MC B

CIVITELLA
DEL TRONTO (TE)

Hotels

Zunica ★★★★
Piazza F. Pepe 14,
Tel. 086191319www.hotelzunica.itit
Rooms: 21 - ♥ - AE ⚫ VISA MC

GIULIANOVA (TE)

i **IAT**
Via Mamiani 16
Tel. 0858003013

Hotels

Baltic ★★★ &
Loc. Giulianova Lido,
lungomare Zara,
Tel. 0858008242
www.hotelbaltic.com
Rooms: 75 - ♨ P ⚒ ⛱ ♨ - AE ⚫
VISA MC B

Restaurants

Cesarino ⛶ &
Via Marsala 20,
Tel. 0858004930
Places: 50/40 - R - AE ⚫ VISA MC

L'AQUILA

i **IAT**
Via XX Settembre 8
Tel. 086223306

Hotels

G.H. e del Parco ★★★★
Corso Federico II 74,
Tel. 0862413248
www.grandhotel.it
Rooms: 32 - P ♥ - ⚫ VISA MC B

Castello ★★★ ★
Meublé. Piazza Btg. Alpini,
Tel. 0862419147
www.hotelcastelloaq.com
Rooms: 50 - P - AE ⚫ VISA MC B

Restaurants

Osteria Antiche Mura ⛶
Via XXV Aprile 2,
Tel. 08626242
Places: 45/20 - ❀ P - R - VISA MC B

Osteria la Panarda ⛶
Via G. Valle 18,
Tel. 0862406035
Places: 40 - R - VISA MC B

PESCARA

i **IAT**
Corso Vitt. Emanuele II 301
Tel. 085429001
www.abruzzoturismo.it

Hotels

Esplanade ★★★★ &
Piazza I Maggio 46,
Tel. 085292141
www.esplanade.net
Rooms: 150 - ♨ - AE ⚫ VISA MC B

Ambra Palace ★★★ ★
Via Quarto dei Mille 28,
Tel. 085378247
www.hotelambrapalace.it
Rooms: 61 - ♨ -
AE ⚫ VISA MC JCB B

Restaurants

Grotta del Piccione ⛶
Viale Vittoria Colonna 112,
Tel. 085690731
Places: 110 - ❀ P - fish - AE ⚫ VISA

Taverna 58 ⛶ &
Corso Manthonè 46,
Tel. 085690724
Places: 50/10 - ❀ P - R

PESCASSEROLI (AQ)

i **IAT**
Via Piave
Tel. 0863910461

Hotels

Paradiso ★★★ & ★
Via Fonte Fracassi 4,
Tel. 0863910422
www.albergo-paradiso.it
Rooms: 20 - ♨ P

PESCOCOSTANZO (AQ)

i **IAT**
Vico delle Carceri 4
Tel. 0864641440

Hotels

Archi del Sole ★★★ &
Meublé.
Largo Porta Berardo 9,
Tel. 0864640007
www.archidelsole.it
Rooms: 10 - ♨ -
VISA MC JCB B

RIVISONDOLI (AQ)

i **IAT**
Via Marconi 21
Tel. 086469351

Hotels

Cinque Miglia ★★★ &
Loc. Piano delle Cinquemiglia,
S.S. 17 al km 134,
Tel. 086469627
www.5miglia.it
Rooms: 64 - ♨ P ❀ ⛱

Restaurants

Du Giocondo ⛶
Via Suffragio 2,
Tel. 086469123
www.abruzzoenogastronomico.com
Places: 40 - ❀ P - R -
AE ⚫ VISA MC B

ROCCARASO (AQ)

i **IAT**
Via C. Mori 1
Tel. 086462210

428

Hotels

Pizzalto **** &
Loc. Aremogna,
Via Aremogna 12,
Tel. 0864602383
www.pizzalto.com
Rooms: 53 - ⓟ ☇ - AE ⓪ VISA MC

Restaurants

La Preta ⎮
Loc. Pietransieri, Via Adua 7,
Tel. 08462716
lapreta@interfree.it
Places: 50/20 - R - AE ⓪ VISA MC

SULMONA (AQ)

ⓘ **IAT**
Corso Ovidio 208
Tel. 086453276

Hotels

Santacroce Meeting *** & ★
S.S. 17 al km 95,5,
Tel. 0864251696
www.hotelsantacroce.com
Rooms: 78 - ⚐ ⓟ ⚲ - AE ⓪ VISA MC
B

Restaurants

**Clemente-Osteria della
Quercia** ⎮⎮
Via Quercia 5, Tel. 086452284
Places: 60 - ❀ ⓟ - R - AE ⓪ VISA MC

TERAMO

ⓘ **APT**
Via Oberdan 16
Tel. 0861244222

Hotels

Relais della Corte *** &
Loc. Villa Vomano, S.S. 81,
Tel. 0861319510
www.cortedeitini.com
Rooms: 16 - ⓟ - AE VISA MC B

Restaurants

Antico Cantinone ⎮
Via Ciotti 5, Tel. 0861248863
p.pompa@tiscali.it
Places: 100 - ❀ ⓟ - R - AE ⓪ VISA MC
B

MOLISE

AGNONE (IS)

ⓘ **Pro Loco**
Corso Vittorio Emanuele 78
Tel. 086577246
www.prolocoagnone.com

Hotels

Santo Stefano dei Cavalli &
Historic House
Contrada Castelnuovo 158,
Tel. 330738199
www.santostefanodeicavalli.it
Rooms: 4 - ⚐ ⓟ ⚲ ❧

Restaurants

Selvaggi ⎮
Loc. Staffoli,
S.P. Montesangrina al km 1,
Tel. 086577177
www.staffoli.it
Places: 100 - ❀ ⓟ - R - VISA MC B

CAMPOBASSO

ⓘ **EPT**
Piazza della Vittoria
Tel. 0874415663

Hotels

Eden *** ★
Via Colle delle Api 91,
Tel. 0874698441
www.molisehotels.com
Rooms: 58 - ⚐ ⓟ ⚲ ❧ - AE ⓪ VISA
MC B

Restaurants

**Vecchia Trattoria
da Tonino** ⎮⎮⎮
Corso Vittorio Emanuele II 8,
Tel. 0874415200
vecchiatrattoriadatonino@
hotmail.com
Places: 30/20 - ❀ - R -
AE ⓪ VISA MC B

ISERNIA

ⓘ **EPT**
Via Farinacci 9
Tel. 0865414590

Hotels

G.H. Europa ****
S.S. 17, uscita Isernia Nord,
Tel. 0865212126
www.grandhotel-europa.it
Rooms: 67 - ⓟ ⚲ -
AE ⓪ VISA MC B

Restaurants

Osteria del Paradiso ⎮⎮
Via Occidentale 2,
Tel. 0865414847
Places: 50/20 - R

SEPINO (CB)

Hotels

Dimora al Castello
Historic House
Via Supportici 42,
Tel. 0874790419,
mancinelliangela@virgilio.it
Rooms: 5 - ⚐ ⓟ

CAMPANIA

AMALFI (SA)

ⓘ **AAST**
Corso Rep. Marinare 27
Tel. 089871107
www.amalfitouristoffice.it

Hotels

Luna Convento ****
Via P. Comite 33,
Tel. 089871002
www.lunahotel.it
Rooms: 43 - ⚐ ⓟ ⚲ ⚴ - AE ⓪ VISA
MC JCB B

Miramalfi ****
Via Quasimodo 3,
Tel. 089871588
www.miramalfil.it
Rooms: 49 - ⓟ ⚴ ⚲ - AE ⓪ VISA MC
JCB B

La Bussola *** ★
Lungomare dei Cavalieri 16,
Tel. 089871533
www.labussolahotel.it
Rooms: 58 - ⓟ ⚴ ❧ -
AE ⓪ VISA MC B

Restaurants

La Caravella ⎮⎮⎮⎮
Via M. Camera 12,
Tel. 089871029,
www.ristorantelacaravella.it
Places: 30 - R, I - AE VISA MC B

Marina Grande ⎮⎮⎮
Viale delle Regioni 4,
Tel. 089871129
www.ristorantemarinagrande.com
Places: 40/40 - R, I -
AE ⓪ VISA MC JCB B

ANACAPRI (NA)

ⓘ **AACST**
Via G. Orlandi 59
Tel. 0818371524
www.capritourism.com

Hotels

Al Mulino *** ★
Meublé.
Loc. Grotta Azzurra,
Via La Fabbrica 9,
Tel. 0818382084
www.mulino-capri.it
Rooms: 7 - ⚐ ⓟ - AE ⓪ VISA MC JCB B

San Michele ***
Via G. Orlandi 1/3/5,
Tel. 0818371427
www.sanmichele-capri.com
Rooms: 64 - ⚐ ⓟ ⚲ - AE ⓪ VISA MC B

Senaria ***
Meublé.
Via Follicara 10,
Tel. 0818373222
www.senaria.it
Rooms: 12 - ⓟ ⚲ - AE VISA MC B

Restaurants

Il Cucciolo ⎮⎮⎮
Loc. Damecuta,
Via La Fabbrica 52,
Tel. 0818371917
cucciolosnc@libero.it
Places: 70/60 - ❀ ⓟ - R -
AE ⓪ VISA MC B

AVELLINO

ⓘ **EPT**
Via Due Principati 32/A
Tel. 0825747321
www.eptavellino.it

Hotels

De la Ville ★★★★ ♿
Via Palatucci 20, Tel. 0825780911,
www.hdv.av.it
Rooms: 63 - ♨ 🅿 ⛵ 🐾 🍸 🍴 - 🆎
💿 💳 MC JCB B

Restaurants

La Maschera 🍴
Rampa S. Modestino 1,
Tel. 082537603
www.ristorantelamaschera.com
Places: 40/30 - ⚘ - R -
🆎 💿 💳 MC B

CAPRI (NA)

ℹ️ **AACST**
Piazza Umberto I
Tel. 0818370686
www.capritourism.com

Hotels

Relais Maresca ★★★★
Loc. Marina Grande,
provinciale Marina Grande 284,
Tel. 0818379619
www.relaismaresca.it
Rooms: 27 - ♨ - 🆎 💿 💳 MC B

Weber Ambassador ★★★★
Via Marina Piccola,
Tel. 0818370141,
www.hotelweber.com
Rooms: 81 - 🅿 🐾 - 🆎 💿 💳 MC B

Restaurants

Da Tonino 🍴
Via Dentecala 12,
Tel. 0818376718
Places: 45/45 - ⚘ - C - 🆎 💿 💳 MC
B

CASERTA

ℹ️ **EPT**
Piazza Dante 25
Tel. 0823321137
www.eptcaserta.it

Hotels

Crowne Plaza Hotel ★★★★
Viale delle Industrie,
Tel. 0823523001
www.crowneplaza-caserta.com
Rooms: 320 - 🅿 🍸 - 🆎 💿 💳 MC B
Caserta Antica
Loc. Casertavecchia, Via Tiglio 41,
Tel. 0823371158,
www.hotelcaserta-antica.it
Rooms: 25 - 🅿 🍸

Restaurants

Le Colonne 🍴
Viale Giulio Douhet 7/9,
Tel. 0823467494
www.lecolonnemarziale.it
Places: 75 - 🅿 R - 🆎 💿 💳 MC B

CASTELLAMMARE DI STABIA (NA)

ℹ️ **AACST**
Piazza Matteotti 34/35
Tel. 0818711334
www.stabiatourism.it

Hotels

Crowne Plaza Stabiae Sorrento Coast ★★★★ ♿ ★
S.S. 145 Sorrentina al km 11,
Tel. 0813946700
www.crowneplaza.com
Rooms: 153 - ♨ ⛵ 🍸 🍴 - 🆎 💿 💳
MC JCB B

ERCOLANO (NA)

ℹ️ **Informazioni Turistiche**
Corso Resina 39
Tel. 0817881243

Hotels

Miglio d'Oro Park Hotel ★★★★
Corso Resina 296,
Tel. 0817774097,
www.migliodoroparkhotel.it
Rooms: 52 - ♨ 🅿 ⛵ 🐾 🍸 - 🆎 💿
💳 MC B

Restaurants

Viva lo Re 🍴
Corso Resina 261,
Tel. 0817390207
www.vivalore.it
Places: 55 - R - 🆎 💿 💳 MO B

FORIO (NA)

Hotels

Parco dei Principi ★★★★ ♿ ★
Via Francesco Calise 6,
Tel. 0815071467
www.htlparcodeiprincipi.it
Rooms: 50 - ♨ 🅿 🍸 ⛵ 🍴 🍸 -
🆎 💿 💳 MC JCB

Punta Chiarito ★★★ ★
Loc. Panza,
Via Sorgeto 51,
Tel. 081908102
www.puntachiarito.it
Rooms: 24 - ♨ 🅿 🍸 ⛵ 🍴 🍸 -
🆎 💿 💳 MC

Semiramis ★★
Meublé.
Spiaggia di Citara 236,
Tel. 081907511
www.hotelsemiramisischia.it
Rooms: 41 - ♨ 🅿 🍸 🐾 - 🆎 💿 💳
MC JCB B

Restaurants

Il Melograno 🍴
Via G. Mazzella 110,
Tel. 081998450
www.ilmelogranoischia.it
Places: 36/45 - ⚘ 🅿 - R -
🆎 💿 💳 MC JCB B

Epomeo 🍴
Piazza Pontone 7,
Tel. 081997207
Places: 60/50 - ⚘ - R -
🆎 💿 💳 MC B

ISCHIA (NA)

ℹ️ **AACST**
Via Porto, riva destra
Tel. 0815074231
www.infoischiaprocida.it

Hotels

Jolly Hotel delle Terme ★★★★ ♿ ★
Via De Luca 42,
Tel. 0815070111,
www.jollyhotels.it
Rooms: 194 - ♨ 🅿 🍸 ⛵ 🍴 🍸 -
🆎 💿 💳 MC B

Presidente Terme ★★★★ ★
Via Osservatorio,
Tel. 081993890,
www.president.it
Rooms: 110 - ♨ 🅿 🍸 ⛵ 🍴 🍸 -
🆎 💿 💳 MC B

Il Monastero ★★★
Castello Aragonese,
Tel. 081992435
www.albergoilmonastero.it
Rooms: 22 - 🆎 💿 💳 MC B

Restaurants

Alberto 🍴
Via Cristoforo Colombo 8,
Tel. 081981259
www.albertoischia.it
Places: 54 - 🅿 - R, I - 🆎 💿 💳 MC B

Da Gaetano 🍴
Via M. Mazzella 58,
Tel. 081991807
www.pizzadagaetano.it
Places: 75 - R, C - 🆎 💿 💳 MC B

MARINA DI CAMEROTA (SA)

ℹ️ **Pro Loco**
Via Porto
Tel. 0974932900

Hotels

Pian delle Starze ♿
Historic House
Loc. Starza, Tel. 0974932350
www.hotelrelaispiandellestarze.it
Rooms: 20 - ♨ 🅿 🍸 -
🆎 💿 💳 MC B

Calanca ★★★ ★
Via L. Mazzeo 18,
Tel. 0974932128
www.hotelcalanca-aviresidence.com
Rooms: 20 - ♨ 🅿 🍸 🍸 - 🆎 💿 💳
B

Restaurants

La Maison di Dante 🍴
Via Duca d'Aosta 29,
Tel. 0974932302
www.lamaisondidante.it
Places: 45 - R - 🆎 💿 💳 MC B

NAPLES/NAPOLI

ℹ️ **EPT**
Piazza dei Martiri 58
Tel. 0814107211
www.eptnapoli.info

Hotels

Caravaggio ★★★★ ♿ ★
Piazza Cardinal Sisto
Riario Sforza 157,
Tel. 0812110066
www.caravaggiohotel.it
Rooms: 18 - 🆎 💿 💳 MC B

Mercure Angioino
Napoli Centro **** ★
Meublé.
Via A. Depretis 123,
Tel. 0814910111
www.mercure.com
Rooms: 85 - 🄰🄴 ⓓ 🆅🅸🆂🅰 🅼🄲 🅹🄲🄱 B

Ramada Naples **** ♿
Via G. Ferraris 40,
Tel. 081360211,
www.ramadanaples.com
Rooms: 152 - 🄰🄴 ⓓ 🆅🅸🆂🅰 🅼🄲 B

Renaissance Naples
Hotel Mediterraneo **** ♿
Via Nuova Ponte di Tappia 25,
Tel. 0817970111
www.mediterraneonapoli.com
Rooms: 228 - 🄰🄴 ⓓ 🆅🅸🆂🅰 🅼🄲 🅹🄲🄱

Starhotels Terminus **** ♿ ★
Piazza Garibaldi 91,
Tel. 0817793111
www.starhotels.it
Rooms: 171 - 🄰🄴 ⓓ 🆅🅸🆂🅰 🅼🄲 🅹🄲🄱

Una Hotel Napoli **** ♿ ★
Piazza Garibaldi 9/10,
Tel. 0815636901
www.unahotels.it
Rooms: 89 - 🄰🄴 ⓓ 🆅🅸🆂🅰 🅼🄲 B

Chiaja *** ♿
Meublé. Via Chiaia 216,
Tel. 081415555
www.hotelchiaia.it
Rooms: 27 - 🄰🄴 ⓓ 🆅🅸🆂🅰 🅼🄲 B

Costantinopoli 104 *** ★
Meublé. Via S. Maria di
Costantinopoli 104,
Tel. 0815571035
www.costantinopoli104.it
Rooms: 19 - ♨ ⚘ ♻ -
🄰🄴 ⓓ 🆅🅸🆂🅰 🅼🄲 B

Des Artistes *** ♿ ★
Meublé. Via Duomo 61,
Tel. 081446155
www.hoteldesartistesnaples.it
Rooms: 11 - ♻ - 🄰🄴 ⓓ 🆅🅸🆂🅰 🅼🄲 B

Il Convento *** ♿ ★
Meublé. Via Speranzella 137/A,
Tel. 081403977
www.hotelilconvento.com
Rooms: 14 - ♻ - 🄰🄴 ⓓ 🆅🅸🆂🅰 🅼🄲 B

Marcure Napoli
Garibaldi *** ♿ ★
Meublé. Via G. Ricciardi 33,
Tel. 0816908111
www.accorhotels.com/Italia
Rooms: 88 - ♻ -
🄰🄴 ⓓ 🆅🅸🆂🅰 🅼🄲 🅹🄲🄱 B

Napolit'Amo *** ♿ ★
Meublé. Via S. Tommaso d'Aquino
15, Tel. 0814977110
www.napolitamo.it
Rooms: 17 - ♻ - 🆅🅸🆂🅰 🅼🄲

Nuovo Rebecchino *** ♿ ★
Meublé. Corso Garibaldi 356,
Tel. 0815535327
www.nuovorebecchino.it
Rooms: 58 - ♻ -
🄰🄴 ⓓ 🆅🅸🆂🅰 🅹🄲🄱 B

Prati *** ★
Via Cesare Rosaroll 4,
Tel. 081268898
www.hotelprati.it
Rooms: 43 - ♻ -
🄰🄴 ⓓ 🆅🅸🆂🅰 🅼🄲 🅹🄲🄱 B

Restaurants

Cantinella 🍴🍴🍴
Via Cuma 42 b80132,
Tel. 0817648684
www.lacantinella.it
Places: 90 - 🄿 - R, I - 🄰🄴 ⓓ 🆅🅸🆂🅰 🅼🄲 B

Antica Cantina del Gallo 🍴🍴
Via A. Telesino 21 ,
Tel. 0815441521
Places: 62 - 🄿 - R

Bellini dal 1946 🍴🍴
Via Costantinopoli 79/80,
Tel. 081459774
Places: 90/40 - R, C -
ⓓ 🆅🅸🆂🅰 🅼🄲 B

Ciro a Santa Brigida 🍴🍴 ♿
Via S. Brigida 71/73, Tel.
0815524072
www.ciroasantabrigida.it
Places: 130/20 - 🄿 - R, C - 🄰🄴 ⓓ 🆅🅸🆂🅰
🅼🄲 B

Mimì alla Ferrovia 🍴🍴
Via Alfonso d'Aragona 21,
Tel. 0815538525
www.mimiallaferrovia.it
Places: 180 - 🄿 - R -
🄰🄴 ⓓ 🆅🅸🆂🅰 🅼🄲 B

Pulcinella a Santa Brigida 🍴🍴 ★
Via S. Brigida 49,
Tel. 0815517117
www.pulcinellasantabrigida.it
Places: 40 - ⚘ - R, I -
🄰🄴 🆅🅸🆂🅰 🅼🄲 🅹🄲🄱 B

Tripperia Fiorenzano 🍴🍴
Via Pignasecca 48,
Tel. 0815523663
Places: 60 - R

Osteria la Chitarra 🍴 ★
Rampe S. Giovanni Maggiore 1/B,
Tel. 0815529103
www.osterialachitarra.it
Places: 32/6 - ⚘ - R -
🄰🄴 ⓓ 🆅🅸🆂🅰 🅼🄲 B

PAESTUM (SA)

> ℹ️ **AACST**
> *Via Magna Grecia 887*
> *Tel. 0828811016*
> *www.infopaestum.it*

Hotels

Seliano
Historic House
Via Seliano,
Tel. 0828723634,
www.agriturismoseliano.it
Rooms: 14 - ♨ 🄿 ♻ ♻ - 🄰🄴 ⓓ 🆅🅸🆂🅰
🅼🄲 🅹🄲🄱 B

Calypso *** ★
Loc. Licinella,
Via Mantegna 63,
Tel. 0828811031
www.calypsohotel.com
Rooms: 30 - ♨ 🄿 ⚡ ♻ -
🄰🄴 ⓓ 🆅🅸🆂🅰 B

Paistos *** ★
Loc. Laura,
Via Laura Mare 39,
Tel. 0828851683
www.hotelpaistos.com
Rooms: 10 - ♨ 🄿 -
🄰🄴 🆅🅸🆂🅰 🅼🄲 B

Restaurants

Da Nonna Sceppa 🍴🍴 ♿
Via Laura 45, Tel. 0828851064
www.nonnasceppa.com
Places: 150/150 - ⚘ 🄿 - R - 🄰🄴 ⓓ
🆅🅸🆂🅰 🅼🄲 B

PALINURO (SA)

> ℹ️ **Pro Loco**
> *Piazza Virgilio 1*
> *Tel. 0974938144*
> *www.capopalinuro.it*

Hotels

King's Residence Hotel ****
Baia del Buondormire,
Tel. 0974931324
www.hotelkings.it
Rooms: 66 - ♨ 🄿 🎾 🦌 ♨ ♻ - 🄰🄴
ⓓ 🆅🅸🆂🅰 🅼🄲 B

Best Western Hotel La
Conchiglia ***
Via Indipendenza 52,
Tel. 0974931018
www.hotellaconchiglia.it
Rooms: 30 - 🄿 ♻ - 🄰🄴 ⓓ 🆅🅸🆂🅰 🅼🄲 B

POMPEI (NA)

> ℹ️ **AACST**
> *Via Sacra 1*
> *Tel. 0818507255*
> *www.pompeiturismo.it*

Hotels

Amleto **** ♿ ★
Meublé. Via Bartolo Longo 10,
Tel. 0818631004
www.hotelamleto.it
Rooms: 26 - ♨ 🄿 - 🄰🄴 ⓓ 🆅🅸🆂🅰 🅼🄲 🅹🄲🄱 B

Restaurants

Il Principe 🍴🍴
Piazza B. Longo 8,
Tel. 0818505566
www.ilprincipe.com
Places: 145/45 - cucina: R - 🄰🄴 ⓓ 🆅🅸🆂🅰
🅼🄲 B

POSITANO (SA)

> ℹ️ **AACST**
> *Via Saraceno 6*
> *Tel. 089875067*

Hotels

Buca di Bacco **** ★
Via Rampa Teglia 4,
Tel. 089875699
www.bucadibacco.it
Rooms: 47 - ♨ - 🄰🄴 ⓓ 🆅🅸🆂🅰 🅼🄲 B

Marincanto ****
Via C. Colombo 36, Tel. 089875130,
www.marincanto.it
Rooms: 25 - ♨ 🄿 ♨ ♻ - 🄰🄴 ⓓ 🆅🅸🆂🅰
🅼🄲 B

Casa Albertina *** ★
Via della Tavolozza 3,
Tel. 089875143
www.casalbertina.it
Rooms: 21 - 🄰🄴 🆅🅸🆂🅰 🅼🄲 🅹🄲🄱 B

Restaurants

Santa Croce ¶¶
Loc. Nocelle, Via Nocelle 19,
Tel. 089811260
Places: 90 - ✿ P - R - AE VISA MC B

POZZUOLI (NA)

> ℹ️ **AACST**
> Largo Matteotti 1/A
> Tel. 0815266639
> www.infocampiflegrei.it

Hotels

Villa Luisa ★★★★ ★
Meublé. Via Tripergola 50,
Tel. 0818042870
www.villaluisaresort.it
Rooms: 37 - ♨ P ⚲ ⛷ - AE ⊙ VISA
MC B

Restaurants

La Cucina di Ruggiero ¶¶
Via Intorno al Lago Lucrino 3,
Tel. 0818687473
Places: 50/40 - ✿ - I - VISA MC B

RAVELLO (SA)

> ℹ️ **AACST**
> Via Roma 18/bis
> Tel. 089857096
> www.ravellotime.it

Hotels

Graal ★★★★ ★
Via della Repubblica 8,
Tel. 089857222
www.hotelgraal.it
Rooms: 43 - ♨ ⛷ - AE ⊙ VISA JOB B
Rufolo ★★★★ ★
Via S. Francesco 1, Tel. 089857133,
www.hotelrufolo.it
Rooms: 34 - ♨ P ⛷ -
AE ⊙ VISA MC B
Villa San Michele ★★★ ★
Loc. Castiglione, Via Carusiello 2,
Tel. 089872237
www.amalfi.it/smichele
Rooms: 12 - ♨ P ⛷ - AE ⊙ VISA MC
JOB B

Restaurants

Da Salvatore ¶¶
Via Boccaccio 2,
Tel. 089857227
www.salvatoreravello.com
Places: 90/50 - R - AE VISA MC B

SALERNO

> ℹ️ **EPT**
> Piazza Vittorio Veneto 1
> Tel. 089231432
> www.turismoinsalerno.it

Hotels

G.H. Salerno ★★★★ ♿
Lungomare C. Tafuri 1,
Tel. 0897041111
www.grandhotelsalerno.it
Rooms: 286 - P ⚲ ⛷ ⛷ - AE
⊙ VISA MC B

Jolly Hotel ★★★★ ♿
Meublé. Lungomare Trieste 1,
Tel. 089225222
www.jollyhotels.it
Rooms: 104 - P - AE VISA B

Restaurants

Timone ¶¶
Via Generale Clark2//35,
Tel. 089335111
ristoranteiltimone@hotmail.it
Places: 120 - P - R, C - AE VISA B

SORRENTO (NA)

> ℹ️ **AAS**
> Via De Maio 35
> Tel. 0818074033
> www.sorrentotourism.com

Hotels

Antiche Mura ★★★★
Meublé. Via Fuorimura 7,
Tel. 0818073523
www.hotelantichemura.com
Rooms: 46 - ♨ ⛷ - AE ⊙ VISA MC B
G.H. President ★★★★
Via Colle Parisi 4,
Tel. 0818782262
www.acampora.it
Rooms: 108 - ♨ P ⚲ ⛷ - AE ⊙ VISA
MC B
Gardenia ★★★ ♿
Meublé. Corso Italia 258,
Tel. 0818772365
www.hotelgardenia.com
Rooms: 27 - ♨ P ⛷ - AE ⊙ VISA MC
JOB B

Restaurants

L'Antica Trattoria ¶¶
Via Padre R. Giuliani 33,
Tel. 0818071082
www.lanticatrattoria.com
Places: 50/40 - ✿ - R, I - VISA ⊙ VISA
MC B

APULIA

ALBEROBELLO (BA)

> ℹ️ **Pro Loco**
> Via Montenero 1
> Tel. 0804322822

Hotels

Colle del Sole ★★★
Via Indipendenza 61,
Tel. 0804321814
www.hotelcolledelsole.it
Rooms: 37 - ♨ P - AE ⊙ VISA B
Lanzillotta ★★★
Piazza Ferdinando IV 31,
Tel. 0804321511
www.hotellanzillotta.it
Rooms: 30 - AE VISA MC B

Restaurants

Il Poeta Contadino ¶¶¶
Via Indipendenza 21,
Tel. 0804321917
www.ilpoetacontadino.it
Places: 50 - P - R, I - ⊙ VISA MC B

BARI

> ℹ️ **APT**
> Piazza Moro Aldo 33/A
> Tel. 0805242361
> www.pugliaturismo.com

Hotels

**Mercure Villa Romanazzi
Carducci Bari** ★★★★ ♿ ★
Via G. Capruzzi 326,
Tel. 0805427400
www.villaromanazzi.com
Rooms: 123 - ♨ P ⚲ ⛷ - AE VISA
MC B
Sheraton Nicolaus ★★★★
Via Cardinale A. Ciasca 27,
Tel. 0805682111
www.sheraton.com
Rooms: 175 - ♨ ⛷ - AE ⊙ VISA MC B
Palace Hotel ★★★★ ♿ ★
Via Lombardi 13,
Tel. 0805216551
www.palacehotelbari.it
Rooms: 196 - AE ⊙ VISA MC

Restaurants

Ai 2 Ghiottoni ¶¶¶
Via Putignani 11,
Tel. 0805232240,
ai2ghiottoni@libero.it
Places: 180 - P - R, C -
AE VISA B
Piccinni ¶¶
Via Piccinni 28,
Tel. 0805211227
www.piccinniristorante.it
Places: 70/70 - ✿ P - R, C - AE ⊙
VISA B
Terranima ¶¶
Via Putignani 213/215,
Zo805219725
www.terranima.com
Places: 60/20 - R - AE ⊙ VISA MC B

BRINDISI

> ℹ️ **APT**
> Viale Regina Margherita 43
> Tel. 0831523072
> www.pugliaturismo.com

Hotels

Barsotti ★★★
Meublé. Via Cavour 1,
Tel. 0831560877
www.hotelbarsotti.it
Rooms: 60 - P - AE ⊙ VISA MC JOB B
Minerva ★★★
Via Cardinale A. Ciasca 27,
Tel. 0805682111
www.sheraton.com
Rooms: 175 - ♨ ⛷ - AE ⊙ VISA MC B

Restaurants

Il Giardino ¶¶
Via Tarantini 18,
Tel. 0831564026
Places: 100/100 - ✿ - R - AE ⊙ VISA
MC B
Trattoria Pantagruele ¶¶
Salita di Ripalta 1/3,
Tel. 0831560605
Places: 60/30 - ✿ - R -
AE VISA MC JOB B

FOGGIA

> *📋 APT*
> *Via Perrone 17*
> *Tel. 0881723141*
> *www.pugliaturismo.com*

Hotels

Mercure Cicolella
Foggia ★★★★♿ ★
Viale 24 Maggio 60,
Tel. 0881566111
www.hotelcicolella.it
Rooms: 102 - AE ⑩ ⅦⅡ MC B

White House ★★★★
Meublé.
Via Monte Sabotino 24,
Tel. 0881721644
www.paginegialle.it/whitehouse
Rooms: 40 - P - AE ⑩ ⅦⅡ MC B

Restaurants

Osteria dello Zio Aldo 🍴
Via Arpi 62, Tel. 0881708104
letiziamassimo@tiscali.it
Places: 40 - R, I - AE ⑩ ⅦⅡ MC

Rotarott' 🍴
Loc. La Torretta, centro Incoronata,
Tel. 0881810009
www.rotarott.it
Places: 180/200 - R, I -
AE ⑩ ⅦⅡ MC B

GALLIPOLI (LE)

> *📋 Pro Loco*
> *Via Kennedy*
> *Tel. 0833263007*

Hotels

Bianco ★★★★
Meublé. Via Ravenna 43,
Tel. 0833262685
www.hotelbianco.it
Rooms: 9 - ♿ P - AE ⑩ ⅦⅡ MC B

Ecoresort Le Sirené ★★★♿ ★
Litoranea Gallipoli-S. Maria di
Leuca, Tel. 0833202536
www.attiliocaroli.it
Rooms: 120 - ♿ P ⛱ ⛲ -
AE ⑩ ⅦⅡ MC

Restaurants

La Puritate 🍴
Via S. Elia 18, Tel. 0833264205
Places: 40/40 - R - AE ⑩ ⅦⅡ MC

ISOLE TREMITI (FG)

Hotels

Gabbiano ★★★♿
All'isola San Dòmino,
piazza Belvedere,
Tel. 0882463410
www.hotel-gabbiano.com
Rooms: 40 - ♿ AE ⑩ ⅦⅡ MC JOB B

Restaurants

Il Torrione-da Nonna Sisina †
All'isola San Nicola,
piazza del Castello 73,
Tel. 3475501433
Places: 50 - ❀ - R, C

LECCE

> *📋 APT*
> *Via Monte S. Michele 20*
> *Tel. 0832314117*
> *www.pugliaturismo.com*

Hotels

Casa Elisabetta
Historic House -
Via A. Vignes 15,
Tel. 0832307052
www.beb-lecce.com
Rooms: 12 - AE ⑩ ⅦⅡ MC B

Delle Palme ★★★★
Via Leuca 90, Tel. 0832347171,
www.hoteldellepalmelecce.it
Rooms: 96 - P - AE ⑩ ⅦⅡ MC JOB B

Restaurants

Picton 🍴
Via Idomeneo 14,
Tel. 0832332383
www.acena.it/picton
Places: 70 - R - AE ⑩ ⅦⅡ MC

Trattoria Cucina Casareccia
le Zie 🍴
Via Colonnello Costadura 19,
Tel. 0832245178
Places: 50 - R - ⑩ ⅦⅡ MC B

OSTUNI (BR)

> *📋 APT*
> *Corso Mazzini Giuseppe 8*
> *Tel. 0831301268*

Hotels

Città Bianca ★★★♿
Loc. Vallegna,
S.P. Ostuni-Cisternino al km 4,
Tel. 0831301123
www.cittabiancahotel.com
Rooms: 28 - P ⛱ - ⑩ ⅦⅡ MC B

Restaurants

Osteria del Tempo Perso 🍴
Via Tanzarella Vitale 47,
Tel. 0831304819
www.osteriadeltempoperso.com
Places: 70 - R - AE ⑩ ⅦⅡ MC B

OTRANTO (LE)

> *📋 APT*
> *Piazza Castello 5*
> *Tel. 0836801436*

Hotels

Masseria Panareo ★★★♿ ★
Loc. Parco di Porto Badisco,
litoranea Otranto-S. Cesarea Terme,
Tel. 0836812999
www.masseriapanareo.com
Rooms: 17 - ♿ P ⛱ ⛲ - AE ⑩ ⅦⅡ
MC B

Rosa Antico ★★★♿
Meublé. S.S. 16,
Tel. 0836801563,
www.hotelrosaantico.it
Rooms: 28 - ♿ P - AE ⑩ ⅦⅡ MC B

Restaurants

Acmet Pascià 🍴
Lungomare degli Eroi,
Tel. 0836801282
Places: 40/40 - R - AE ⑩ ⅦⅡ MC B

PESCHICI (FG)

> *📋 APT*
> *Via E. Perrone 17*
> *Tel. 0881723141*
> *www.pugliaturismo.com*

Hotels

D'Amato ★★★★♿
Loc. Spiaggia, Tel. 0884963415
www.hoteldamato.it
Rooms: 90 - ♿ P ⛱ ⛲ - AE ⑩ ⅦⅡ
MC B

Elisa ★★★♿
Via Marina 20, Tel. 0884964012
www.hotelelisa.it
Rooms: 44 - ♿ P ⛱ ⛲ - AE ⑩ ⅦⅡ
MC B

Restaurants

Grotta delle Rondini 🍴
Borgo Marina 30,
Tel. 0884964007
Places: 150/120 - P - R - AE ⑩ ⅦⅡ
MC B

TARANTO

> *📋 APT*
> *Corso Umberto I 121*
> *Tel. 0994532397*
> *www.pugliaturismo.com*

Hotels

Best Western
Hotel Ara Solis ★★★★♿
Loc. Lido Azzurro,
Via Calata penna Dritta 2,
Tel. 0994710809
www.bestwestern.it/arasolis_ta
Rooms: 63 - ♿ P ⛱ -
AE ⑩ ⅦⅡ MC B

Restaurants

Al Gatto Rosso 🍴
Via Cavour 2,
Tel. 3405337800
Places: 48/55 - R - AE ⑩ ⅦⅡ MC JOB B

VIESTE (FG)

> *📋 APT*
> *Piazza Kennedy*
> *Tel. 0884708806*
> *www.pugliaturismo.com*

Hotels

Degli Aranci ★★★★
Piazza S. Maria delle Grazie 10
Tel. 0884708557
www.hotelaranci.com
Rooms: 121 - ♿ P ✕ ⛱ ⛲ - AE ⑩
ⅦⅡ MC B

Gattarella ★★★★
Loc. Lama le Canne,
Tel. 0884703111
www.gattarella.it
Rooms: 117 - ♿ P ✕ ⛱ ⛲

PRACTICAL INFO

433

I Melograni ★★★★ ♿
Lungomare Europa 48,
Tel. 0884701088
www.imelograni.it
Rooms: 110 - ♿ 🅿 💳 🛵 - 🚇 ᴍᴄ B

Vela Velo ★★ ♿
Meublé. Lungomare Europa 55,
Tel. 0884706303
www.velavelo.it
Rooms: 17 - ♿ 🅿 🛵 -
💳 ⬛ 🚇 ᴍᴄ B

Restaurants

Locanda Dragone 🍴🍴
Via Duomo 8, Tel. 0884701212
www.aldragone.it
Places: 85 - R - 💳 ⬛ 🚇

BASILICATA

LIDO DI METAPONTO (MT)

Hotels

Masseria Macchia
& Relais San Pio
Historic House -
Contrada Macchia,
Tel. 0835582193
www.naturgest.it
Rooms: 24 - ♿ 🅿 🏊 🛵 🌊 🛶 -
💳 ⬛ 🚇 ᴍᴄ B

MARATEA (PZ)

ℹ️ **APT**
Piazza del Gesù 32
Tel. 0973876908

Hotels

La Dimora del Cardinale ♿
Historic House -
Via Cardinale Ginnari 1,
Tel. 0973877712
www.ladimoradelcardinale.com
Rooms: 16 - 🅿 🛵 🔌 -
💳 ⬛ 🚇 ᴍᴄ B

Villa del Mare ★★★★
Loc. Acquafredda, S.S. 18,
Tel. 0973878007
www.hotelvilladelmare.com
Rooms: 75 - ♿ 🅿 🏊 🏓 🌊 🛵 -
💳 ⬛ 🚇 ᴍᴄ B

Restaurants

Taverna Rovita 🍴🍴
Via Rovita 13, Tel. 0973876588
Places: 50 - 🅿 - R - 💳 ⬛ 🚇 ᴍᴄ ᴊᴄʙ B

MATERA

ℹ️ **APT**
Via De Viti De Marco 9
Tel. 0835333541

Hotels

Locanda di San Martino ♿
Historic House - Meublé.
Loc. Rioni Sassi, Via Fiorentini 71,
Tel. 0835256600
www.locandadisanmartino.it
Rooms: 28 - 💳 ⬛ 🚇 ᴍᴄ ᴊᴄʙ B

Sant'Angelo ★★★★ ★
Piazza S. Pietro Caveoso,
Tel. 0835314010
www.hotelsantangelosassi.it
Rooms: 16 - 🅿 - 💳 ⬛ 🚇 ᴍᴄ ᴊᴄʙ B

La Casa di Lucio ★★★
Via S. Pietro Caveoso 66,
Tel. 0835312798
www.lacasadilucio.com
Rooms: 10 - 💳 ⬛ 🚇 ᴍᴄ B

Restaurants

Casino del Diavolo 🍴🍴
Via La Martella,
Tel. 0835261986
www.casinodeldiavolo.it
Places: 180/120 - ⬛ 🅿 - R

La Stalla 🍴🍴 ♿
Via Rosario 73, Tel. 0835240455
Places: 52/20 - R - 💳 ⬛ 🚇 ᴍᴄ B

La Villa ⬆️ ♿
loc. Cavallerizza, Tel. 0972236008
Places: 50 - ⬛ 🅿 - R - 🚇 ᴍᴄ

MELFI (PZ)

Hotels

Relais la Fattoria ★★★★ ♿
Loc. Cavallerizza, S.S. 303,
Tel. 097224776
www.relaislafattoria.it
Rooms: 112 - 🅿 🛵 - 💳 ⬛ 🚇

Restaurants

La Villa ⬆️ ♿
Loc. Cavallerizza,
Tel. 0972236008
Places: 50 - ⬛ 🅿 - R - 🚇 ᴍᴄ B

POTENZA

ℹ️ **APT**
Via del Gallitello 89
Tel. 0971507622

Hotels

Park Hotel
Centro Congressi ★★★★ ♿
Raccordo Autostradale
S.S. Basentana,
Tel. 0917472204
www.parkhotelpotenza.com
Rooms: 144 - 🅿 - 💳 ⬛ 🚇 ᴍᴄ B

Vittoria ★★★ ♿
Via Pertini 19, Tel. 097156632
www.hotelvittoriapz.it
Rooms: 46 - 🅿 - 💳 ⬛ 🚇 ᴍᴄ B

Restaurants

Antica Osteria Marconi 🍴🍴
Viale Marconi 233/235,
lel. 097156900
info@vineriaonline.com
Places: 30/30 - ⬛ 🅿 - R - 💳 ⬛ 🚇
ᴍᴄ B

VENOSA (PZ)

Hotels

Il Guiscardo ★★★
Via Accademia dei Rinascenti 106,
Tel. 097232362
www.hotelilguiscardo.it
Rooms: 36 - ♿ 🅿 - 💳 ⬛ 🚇 ᴍᴄ

Restaurants

Al Frantoio 🍴🍴
Via Roma 211,
Tel. 097236925
www.ristorantealfrantoio.it
Places: 70 - 🅿 - R - 💳 ⬛ 🚇 ᴍᴄ B

CALABRIA

BAGNARA CALABRA

ℹ️ **Pro Loco**
Piazza Matteotti 3
Tel. 0966371319

Hotels

Grand Hotel Victoria ★★★★
Piazza Marconi 4,
Tel. 0966376126
www.victoriagrandhotel.it
Rooms: 41 - 🛵 - 🚇 ᴍᴄ B

Restaurants

Kerkyra 🍴🍴🍴 ★
Corso Vittorio Emanuele 217,
Tel. 0966372260
Places: 35 - 🅿 - cucina: R, greca -
💳 ⬛ 🚇 ᴍᴄ B

CAMIGLIATELLO SILANO (CS)

ℹ️ **Pro Loco**
Via Roma
Tel. 0984578159

Hotels

Camigliatello ★★★★
Via Federici,
Tel. 0984578496
www.esperia.it/camigliatello.htm
Rooms: 40 - 🅿 🔌 - 💳 ⬛ 🚇 ᴍᴄ B

Restaurants

Edelweiss 🍴🍴 ★
Viale Stazione 15,
Tel. 0984578044
www.hotelaquilaedelweiss.com
Places: 100 - ⬛ - R, C - 🚇 ᴍᴄ B

COSENZA

ℹ️ **APT**
Corso Mazzini 92
Tel. 098427485

Hotels

Executive ★★★★ ♿
A Rende, Via Marconi 59,
Tel. 800620992
www.hotelexecutivecs.it
Rooms: 98 - ♿ 🅿 🐾 🛵 - 💳 ⬛
🚇 ᴍᴄ B

Best Western
Hotel Centrale ★★★ ♿
Meublé. Via del Tigrai 3,
Tel. 098475750
www.hotelcentralecosenza.it
Rooms: 44 - 🅿 -
💳 ⬛ 🚇 ᴍᴄ B

Restaurants

Osteria dell'Arenella 🍴🍴
Via Arenella 12,
Tel. 098476573
osteria.arenella@virgilio.it
Places: 150/60 - ❀ 🅿 - C - ⒶⒷ �𝐌𝐂 B

Pantagruel
nella Vecchia Rende 🍴🍴
A Rende,
Via Pittore Sant'Anna 2,
Tel. 0984443847
www.pantagruelilristorante.it
Places: 150 - fish - ⒶⒷ 𝐌𝐂 B

GAMBARIE (RC)

ℹ️ **IAT**
Piazzale Mangeruca
S. Stefano in Aspromonte
Tel. 096573295

Hotels

Miramonti ★★★
Via degli Sci 10,
Tel. 0965743048,
www.hotelmiramontigambarie.it
Rooms: 58 - ♨ 🅿 ⛷ 🎿 - ⒶⒷ ⑩ 𝐌𝐂 B

ISOLA DI CAPO RIZZUTO (KR)

Hotels

Fattoria Il Borghetto ★★★★ ♿
Loc. Capo Bianco,
Tel. 0962796223
www.fattoriailborghetto.it
Rooms: 47 - ♨ 🅿 - ⒶⒷ ⑩ 𝐌𝐂 B

MELITO DI PORTO SALVO (RC)

Restaurants

Casina dei Mille 🍴
Loc. Annà, S.S. 106 al km 28,
Tel. 0965787434
Places: 100 - ❀ 🅿 - cucina: R, C - ⒶⒷ ⑩ 𝐌𝐂 B

PALMI (RC)

Hotels

Arcobaleno ★★★★
Loc. Taureana,
Via Provinciale,
Tel. 0966479380
www.hotelresidencearcobaleno.com
Rooms: 55 - ♨ 🅿

Restaurants

Da Gustibus 🍴🍴
Viale delle Rimenbranze 58/60,
Tel. 096625069
Places: 35 - cucina: R -
ⒶⒷ ⑩ 𝐌𝐂 B

PIZZO (VB)

ℹ️ **Pro Loco**
Via S. Francesco 77/79
Tel. 0963531310

Hotels

Marinella ★★★
Riviera Prangi,
Tel. 0963534864
www.hotelmarinella.info
Rooms: 45 - ♨ 🅿 - ⒶⒷ ⑩ 𝐌𝐂 B

Restaurants

Isolabella 🍴🍴
Loc. Marinella,
riviera Prangi,
Tel. 0963264128
Places: 250/100 - ❀ 🅿 - C - ⒶⒷ ⑩ 𝐌𝐂 B

REGGIO DI CALABRIA

ℹ️ **APT**
Via Roma 3
Tel. 096521171

Hotels

G.H. Excelsior ★★★★ ★
Via Vittorio Veneto 66,
Tel. 0965812211
www.montesanohotels.it
Rooms: 84 - 🅿 - ⒶⒷ ⑩ 𝐌𝐂 ᴊᴄʙ B

Palace Masoanri's ★★★
Via Vittorio Veneto 95,
Tel. 096526433
www.montesanohotels.it
Rooms: 65 - ⒶⒷ 𝐌𝐂 B

Restaurants

Baylik 🍴🍴
Vico Leone 3,
Tel. 096548624
www.baylik.it
Places: 80 - I - ⒶⒷ ⑩ 𝐌𝐂 ᴊᴄʙ B

Kalura 🍴🍴 ♿
Loc. Catona, Via Bolano,
Tel. 0965301453
www.ristorante-kalura.it
Places: 300/200 - ❀ 🅿 - R, C - ⒶⒷ ⑩ 𝐌𝐂 B

La Baita 🍴🍴 ♿
Loc. Bocale Secondo,
Via P. renosto 4,
Tel. 0965676017
www.ristorante-kalura.it
Places: 65/50 - ❀ 🅿 - R - ⒶⒷ ⑩ 𝐌𝐂 B

SCILLA (RC)

ℹ️ **Pro Loco**
Piazza S. Rocco
Tel. 0965754266

Hotels

U Bais ★★★★ ♿
Via Nazionale 65,
Tel. 0965704300,
www.hotelubais.it
Rooms: 21 - 🅿 - ⒶⒷ ⑩ 𝐌𝐂 B

Restaurants

Alla Pescatora 🍴🍴
Via Cristoforo Colombo 32,
Tel. 0965754147
Places: 70/30 - R, C - ⒶⒷ ⑩ 𝐌𝐂 B

SIBARI (CS)

Hotels

Oleandro ★★★
Loc. Laghi di Sibari,
Tel. Z0981794928
www.hoteloleandro.it
Rooms: 23 - 🅿 - ⒶⒷ ⑩ 𝐌𝐂 B

TROPEA (VB)

ℹ️ **Pro Loco**
Piazza Ercole
Tel. 096361475

Hotels

Villa Antica ★★★★ ♿
Via Pietro Ruffo di Calabria 37,
Tel. 0963607176
www.villanticatropea.it
Rooms: 20 - ⒶⒷ ⑩ 𝐌𝐂 B

La Pineta ★★★ ★
Via Marina Vescovado 150,
Tel. 096361700
www.albergolapineta.net
Rooms: 60 - 🅿 - ⒶⒷ ⑩ 𝐌𝐂 B

SICILY

ACI CASTELLO (CT)

Hotels

President Park Hotel ★★★★
Via Vampolieri 49,
Tel. 0957116111
www.presidentparkhotel.com
Rooms: 96 - ♨ 🅿 - ⒶⒷ ⑩ 𝐌𝐂 B

Restaurants

Da Federico 🍴🍴
Loc. Aci Trezza, piazza G. Verga 115,
Tel. 095276364 - C

ACIREALE (CT)

ℹ️ **Pro Loco**
Via Oreste Scionti 15
Tel. 095893134
www.acirealeturismo.it

Hotels

Santa Caterina ★★★★ ♿
Via S. Caterina 42/B,
Tel. 0957633735
www.santacaterinahotel.com
Rooms: 20 - 🅿 - ⒶⒷ ⑩ 𝐌𝐂

AGRIGENTO

ℹ️ **AACST**
Via Empedocle 73
Tel. 092220391

Hotels

G.H. dei Templi ★★★★
Loc. Villaggio Mosè,
viale Leonardo Sciascia,
Tel. 0922610175
www.grandhoteldeitempli.com
Rooms: 146 - ♨ 🅿 - ⒶⒷ ⑩ 𝐌𝐂 B

Kore ★★★★ &
Loc. Villaggio Mosè,
viale Leonardo Sciascia,
Tel. 0922653111
www.hotelkore.com
Rooms: 74 - P -
AE ⊚ VISA MC B

Villa Athena ★★★★ ★
Via Passeggiata Archeologica 33,
Tel. 0922596288
www.athenahotels.com
Rooms: 40 - ♨ P ♕ ⸙ ♒ -
AE VISA MC

Restaurants

Kalo's ¶¶
Piazzetta S. Calogero,
Tel. 092226389
ristorantekalos@libero.it
Places: 60/14 - R, C

Leon d'Oro ¶¶ &
Loc. San Leone,
viale Emporium 102,
Tel. 0922414400
vittorio.collura@tin.it
Places: 140/100 - ❀ P - R - AE ⊚
VISA MC

CATANIA

ℹ **APT**
Via Cimarosa 12
Tel. 0957306222
www.apt.catania.it

Hotels

Il Principe ★★★★ & ★
Meublé. Via Alessi 24,
Tel. 0952500345
www.ilprincipehotel.com
Rooms: 19 - P ♒ -
AE ⊚ VISA MC JCB B

Jolly Hotel Bellini ★★★★ & ★
Piazza Trento 13,
Tel. 095316933
www.jollyhotels.it
Rooms: 130 - P -
AE ⊚ VISA MC JCB B

Liberty ★★★★ ★
Meublé. Via S. Vito 40,
Tel. 095311651
www.libertyhotel.it
Rooms: 18 - ♨ -
AE ⊚ VISA MC JCB B

Gresy Hotel ★★
Meublé. Via Pacini 28,
Tel. 095322709
www.gresihotel.com
Rooms: 30 - AE ⊚ VISA MC

Restaurants

I Tre Bicchieri ¶¶ &
Via S. Giuseppe al Duomo 31,
Tel. 0957153540
www.osteriaitrebicchieri.it
Places: 98/16 - C, I -
AE ⊚ VISA MC B

Nievski ¶¶
Via Alessi 13,
Tel. 095313792
Places: 40 - R - AE ⊚ VISA MC B

Trattoria Casalinga ¶¶
Via Biondi 19,
Tel. 095311319
Places: 80/40 - - R, C -
VISA MC B

CEFALÙ (PA)

ℹ **Pro Loco**
Corso Ruggero 77
Tel. 0921421050

Hotels

Alberi del Paradiso ★★★★
Via dei Mulini 18/20,
Tel. 0921423900
www.alberidelparadiso.it
Rooms: 55 - ♒ ♒ -
AE ⊚ VISA MC B

Le Calette ★★★ &
Loc. Caldura,
Via V. Cavallaro 12,
Tel. 0921424144
www.lecalette.it
Rooms: 50 - ♨ P ♕ ♒ ♒ - AE ⊚
VISA MC B

Restaurants

Ostaria del Duomo ¶¶
Via Seminario 5,
Tel. 0921421838
www.osteriadelduomo.it
Places: 40/70 - ❀ - R -
AE ⊚ VISA MC B

ENNA

ℹ **APT**
Via Roma 411
Tel. 0935528288
www.apt-enna.com

Hotels

G.A. Sicilia ★★★
Meublé. Piazza Colaianni 7,
Tel. 0935500850
www.hotelsiciliaenna.it
Rooms: 76 - ♨ -
AE ⊚ VISA MC B

Restaurants

Centrale ¶¶ &
Piazza VI Dicembre 9,
Tel. 0935500963
www.ristorantecentrale.net
Places: 80/50 - R -
AE ⊚ VISA MC B

ERICE (TP)

ℹ **Ufficio Informazioni**
Via C.A. Pepoli 56
Tel. 0923869388

Hotels

I Mulini Resort ★★★★ &
Meublé.
Loc. San Cusumano,
lungomare Dante Alighieri,
Tel. 0923584111
www.imuliniresort.it
Rooms: 19 - ♨ ♒ ♒ -
AE ⊚ VISA MC ♒

Elimo ★★★
Via Vittorio Emanuele 73,
Tel. 0923869377
www.hotelelimo.it
Rooms: 21 - ♨ P -
AE ⊚ VISA MC B

Restaurants

Moderno ¶¶
Via Vittorio Emanuele 63,
Tel. 0923869300
www.hotelmodernoerice.it
Places: 100 - ❀ - R -
AE ⊚ VISA MC B

FAVIGNANA (TP)

ℹ **Pro Loco**
Piazza Matrice 68
Tel. 0923921647

Hotels

Aegusa ★★★ &
Via Garibaldi 11,
Tel. 0923922430,
www.aegusahotel.it
Rooms: 28 - ♨ - AE VISA MC B

Restaurants

La Lampara ¶¶
Via Vittorio Emanuele 2/4,
Tel. 0923921220
Places: 50/100 - ❀ - R -
AE ⊚ VISA MC B

LAMPEDUSA (AG)

ℹ **Ente Turismo Lampedusa**
Via Vittorio Emanuele 87
Tel. 0922971171
www.enteturismolampedus
a.it

Hotels

Il Faro della Guitgia
Tommasino ★★★
Via Lido Azzurro 13,
Tel. 0922970962
www.ilfarodellaguitgia.it
Rooms: 44 - ♒ -
AE VISA MC B

I Dammusi
di Borgo Cala Creta ★★
località Cala Creta,
Tel. 0922970883
www.calacreata.com
Rooms: 25 - ♨ - AE ⊚ VISA MC B

Restaurants

Gemelli ¶¶ &
Via Cala Pisana 2,
Tel. 0922970699
www.ristorantegemelli.it
Places: 50/40 - ❀ P - R, I -
AE ⊚ B

LIPARI (PA)

ℹ **AAST**
Corso Vittorio Emanuele 202
Tel. 0909880095
www.aasteolie.191.it

Hotels

Gattopardo Park Hotel ★★★ ★
Via Diana,
Tel. 0909811035
www.gattopardoparkhotel.it
Rooms: 53 - ♨ ♒ -
AE VISA MC B

Restaurants

Filippino ⚑ ♿ ★
Piazza Municipio,
Tel. 0909811002
www.bernardigroup.it
Places: 100/100 - ⚑ 🅿 - R - ⚏ 🎫
🆔 J0B B

MESSINA

> 🛈 **AAPIT**
> *Via Calabria - isolato 301/bis*
> *Tel. 090674236*
> *www.aptmessina.it*

Hotels

NH Liberty ★★★★♿ ★
Via I Settembre 15,
Tel. 0906409436
www.nh-hotels.com
Rooms: 51 - ⚏ ⚏ 🎫 🆔 B

Villa Morgana ★★★
Loc. Ganzirri,
Via Consolare Pompea 1965,
Tel. 090325575
www.villamorgana.it
Rooms: 15 - ⚑ 🅿 - ⚏ 🎫 🆔 B

Restaurants

Al Padrino ⚑
Via S. Cecilia 54/56,
Tel. 0902921000
Places: 35 - R - 🎫 B

Le Due Sorelle ⚑
Piazza Municipio 4,
Tel. 09044720
Places: 28/16 - ⚑ - C, I - 🎫 B

MONREALE (PA)

> 🛈 **Ufficio Informazioni**
> *Piazza XVI Maggio 12*
> *Tel. 0931836744*

Restaurants

La Botte 1962 ⚑
Contrada Lenzitti 20,
S.S. 186 al km 10,
Tel. 091414051
www.mauriziocascino.it
Places: 75/50 - ⚑ 🅿 - R - ⚏ 🎫
🆔 J0B B

NOTO (SR)

> 🛈 **APT**
> *Piazza Vittorio Emanuele*
> *Tel. 0916564501*

Hotels

Terre di Vendicari
Historic House - Loc. Vaddeddi,
Tel. 3463393845
www.terredivendicari.it
Rooms: 5 - ⚑ 🅿 🏊 ♥ - ⚏ 🎫
🆔 B

La Corte del Sole ★★★♿ ★
Loc. Eloro, contrada Bucachemi,
Tel. 0931820210
www.lacortedelsole.it
Rooms: 24 - ⚑ 🅿 🏊 - ⚏ 🆔 B

Restaurants

Masseria degli Ulivi ⚑ ♿
Loc. Porcari, Tel. 0931813019
www.masseriadegliulivi.com
Places: 80/60 - ⚑ 🅿 - cucina: R -
⚏ 🎫 🆔 B

PALERMO

> 🛈 **AAPIT**
> *Piazza Castelnuovo 35*
> *Tel. 091583847*
> *www.palermotourism.it*

Hotels

Massimo Plaza ★★★★ ★
Meublé. Via Maqueda 437,
Tel. 091325657
www.massimoplazahotel.com
Rooms: 15 - 🔍 - ⚏ ⚏ 🎫 🆔 B

Principe di Villafranca ★★★★
Via G. Turrisi Colonna 4,
Tel. 0916118523
www.principedivillafranca.it
Rooms: 34 - 🅿 - ⚏ ⚏ 🎫 🆔 B

Ucciardhome ★★★★
Via E. Albanese 34/36,
Tel. 091348426
www.hotelucciardhome.com
Rooms: 11 - ⚑ 🅿

Vecchio Borgo ★★★★♿
Meublé. Via Quintino Sella 1/7,
Tel. 0916111446
www.classicahotels.com
Rooms: 38 - ♥ - ⚏ ⚏ 🎫 🆔

Letizia ★★★
Via dei Bottai 30, Tel. 091589110
www.hotelletizia.com
Rooms: 13 - ⚏ ⚏ 🎫 🆔 J0B B

Villa Archirafi ★★ ★
Meublé. Via Lincoln 30,
Tel. 0916168827
www.villaarchirafi.it
Rooms: 40 - ⚑ 🅿 ♥ - ⚏ 🎫 🆔 B

Restaurants

Bye Bye Blues ⚑
Loc. Mondello, Via del Garofalo 23,
Tel. 0916841415
www.byebyeblues.it
Places: 40/40 - ⚑ 🅿 - R, I - ⚏ ⚏
🆔 B

Cucina Papoff ⚑
Via Isidoro la Lumia 32,
Tel. 091586460
www.cucinapapoff.com
Places: 68 - R - ⚏ ⚏ 🎫 🆔 B

Mi Manda Picone ⚑ ♿
Via A. Paternostro 59,
Tel. 0916160660
www.mimandapicone.it
Places: 40/60 - ⚑ R - ⚏ 🎫 🆔

Osteria dei Vespri ⚑
Piazza Croce dei Vespri,
Tel. 0916171631
www.osteriadeivespri.it
Places: 35/40 - ⚑ - R, I - ⚏ ⚏
🆔 B

Il Mirto e la Rosa ⚑
Via Principe Granatelli 30,
Tel. 091324353
www.ilmirtoelarosa.com
Places: 90/45 - ⚑ - R, I - ⚏ ⚏
🆔 B

PANAREA (ME)

Hotels

La Piazza ★★★
Via S. Pietro, Tel. 090983154
www.hotelpiazza.it
Rooms: 31 - ⚑ 🏊 🔍 🏊 - ⚏ ⚏ 🎫
🆔 B

PIAZZA ARMERINA (EN)

> 🛈 **AAST**
> *Via Gen. Muscarà*
> *Tel. 0935680201*

Hotels

Park Hotel Paradiso ★★★♿
Contrada Ramaldo,
Tel. 0935680841
www.parkhotelparadiso.it
Rooms: 95 - ⚑ 🅿 🏊 -
⚏ ⚏ 🎫 🆔 B

Restaurants

Al Fogher ⚑ ♿
Contrada Bellia 1, S.S. 117/bis,
Tel. 0935684123
www.alfogher.net
Places: 40/30 - ⚑ 🅿 - R, I -
⚏ ⚏ 🎫 🆔 B

RAGUSA

> 🛈 **AAPIT**
> *Via Cap. Bocchieri 33*
> *Tel. 0932221511*
> *www.ragusaturismo.it*

Hotels

Poggio del Sole ★★★★♿
S.P. Ragusa, Tel. 0932666452
www.poggiodelsoleresort.it
Rooms: 9 - 🅿

Villa Carlotta ★★★★♿
Via Gandhi 3,
Tel. 0932604140
www.villacarlottahotel.com
Rooms: 26 - ⚑ 🅿 🏊 -
⚏ ⚏ 🎫 🆔 B

Restaurants

Locanda Don Serafino ⚑ ♿
Loc. Ragusa Ibla,
Via Orfanotrofio 39,
Tel. 0932248778
www.locandadonserafino.it
Places: 60/30 - R - ⚏ 🎫 🆔 B

SCIACCA (AG)

> 🛈 **Ufficio Informazioni**
> *Via Vitt. Emanuele 84*
> *Tel. 092522744*

Hotels

G.H. delle Terme ★★★★♿
Viale Nuove Terme 1,
Tel. 092523133
www.grandhoteldelleterme.com
Rooms: 77 - ⚑ 🅿 🏊 🔍 🏊 🏊 - ⚏
⚏ 🎫 🆔 B

Restaurants

Hostaria del Vicolo ⊞ &
Vicolo Sammaritano 10,
Tel. 092523071
www.hostariadelvicolo.com
Places: 38 - R - ⟨AE⟩ ⟨◎⟩ ⟨▦⟩ ⟨MC⟩ B

SELINUNTE (TP)

Hotels

Alceste ★★★ ★
Loc. Marinella, Via Alceste 21,
Tel. 092446184
www.hotelalceste.it
Rooms: 26 - ⟨P⟩ ⟨⟩ - ⟨AE⟩ ⟨◎⟩ ⟨▦⟩ ⟨MC⟩ B

Restaurants

Pierrot ⊞ ★
Loc. Marinella, Via Marco Polo 108,
Tel. 092446205
www.ristorantepierrotselinunte.it
Places: 135/65 - ⟨P⟩ - C

SIRACUSA

Hotels

Caol Ishka ★★★★ &
Loc. Pantanelli, Via Elorina 154,
Tel. 093169057
www.caolishka.com
Rooms: 10 - ⟨⟩ ⟨P⟩ ⟨⟩ -
⟨AE⟩ ⟨◎⟩ ⟨▦⟩ ⟨MC⟩ B

Il Podere ★★★★ &
Traversa Torre Landolina,
Tel. 0931449390
www.ilpodere.it
Rooms: 24 - ⟨⟩ ⟨P⟩ ⟨⟩ ⟨⟩ -
⟨AE⟩ ⟨◎⟩ ⟨▦⟩ ⟨MC⟩ B

Gutkowski ★★ & ★
Traversa Torre Landolina,
Tel. 0931449390
www.ilpodere.it
Rooms: 24 - ⟨⟩ ⟨P⟩ ⟨⟩ ⟨⟩ -
⟨AE⟩ ⟨▦⟩ ⟨MC⟩ B

Restaurants

Archimede ⊞
Via Gemmellaro 8, Tel. 093169701
www.trattoriaarchimede.it
Places: 150/120 - ⊛ - R -
⟨AE⟩ ⟨◎⟩ ⟨▦⟩ ⟨MC⟩ B

Don Camillo ⊞
Via Maestranza 96/100,
Tel. 093167133
www.ristorantedoncamillosiracusa.it
Places: 60 - R - ⟨AE⟩ ⟨◎⟩ ⟨▦⟩ ⟨MC⟩ B

STROMBOLI (ME)

Hotels

La Sciara Residence ★★★ ★
Loc. Piscità, Via Barnao 5,
Tel. 090986004
www.lasciara.it
Rooms: 63 - ⟨⟩ ⟨⟩ ⟨⟩ ⟨⟩ - ⟨AE⟩ ⟨▦⟩ ⟨MC⟩ B

Restaurants

La Locanda del Barbablù ⊞
Loc. San Vincenzo,
Via Vittorio Emanuele 17/19,
Tel. 090986118
www.barbablu.it
Places: 18/35 - R - ⟨AE⟩ ⟨◎⟩ ⟨▦⟩ ⟨MC⟩ B

TAORMINA (ME)

Hotels

Villa Paradiso ★★★★
Via Roma 2, Tel. 094223922
www.hotelvillaparadisotaormina.
com
Rooms: 37 - ⟨⟩ ⟨⟩ ⟨⟩ -
⟨AE⟩ ⟨◎⟩ ⟨▦⟩ ⟨MC⟩ B

Isabella ★★★
Meublé. Corso Umberto 58,
Tel. 094223153
www.gaishotels.com
Rooms: 32 - ⟨⟩ - ⟨AE⟩ ⟨◎⟩ ⟨▦⟩ ⟨MC⟩ B

Villa Belvedere ★★★
Via Bagnoli Croce 79,
Tel. 094223791
www.villabelvedere.it
Rooms: 49 - ⟨⟩ ⟨P⟩ ⟨⟩ - ⟨AE⟩ ⟨▦⟩ ⟨MC⟩ B

Villa Ducale ★★ & ★
Meublé.
Via Leonardo da Vinci 60,
Tel. 094228153
www.villaducale.com
Rooms: 17 - ⟨⟩ ⟨P⟩ -
⟨AE⟩ ⟨▦⟩ ⟨MC⟩ ⟨JCB⟩ B

Villa Schuler ★★
Meublé.
Piazzetta Bastione ang. Via Roma,
Tel. 094223481
www.hotelvillaschuler.com
Rooms: 27 - ⟨⟩ ⟨P⟩ ⟨⟩ - ⟨AE⟩ ⟨▦⟩ ⟨MC⟩ ⟨JCB⟩
B

Restaurants

La Capinera ⊞
Loc. Spisone,
Via Nazionale 177,
Tel. 0942626247
Places: 35/35 - ⊛ ⟨P⟩ - R, I -
⟨AE⟩ ⟨◎⟩ ⟨▦⟩ ⟨MC⟩ ⟨JCB⟩ B

Da Lorenzo ⊞
Via Roma 12,
Tel. 094223480
www.paginegialle.it/
ristorantedalorenzo
Places: 45/60 - R - ⟨AE⟩ ⟨◎⟩ ⟨▦⟩ ⟨MC⟩ B

Il Barcaiolo ⊞
Via Castelluccio 45
(S.S. per Mazzaròl),
Tel. 0942625633
www.barcaiolo.altervista.org
Places: 20/50 - R - ⟨▦⟩ ⟨MC⟩ B

TRAPANI

Hotels

Vittoria ★★★
Meublé. Via Crispi 4,
Tel. 0923873044
www.hotelvittoriatrapani.it
Rooms: 65 - ⟨⟩ - ⟨AE⟩ ⟨◎⟩ ⟨▦⟩ ⟨MC⟩ B

Restaurants

Ai Lumi ⊞ &
Corso Vittorio Emanuele 75,
Tel. 0923872418
www.ailumi.it
Places: 72 - R - ⟨AE⟩ ⟨◎⟩ ⟨▦⟩ ⟨MC⟩ B

SARDINIA

ALGHERO (SS)

Hotels

Calabona ★★★★ &
Loc. Calabona, Tel. 079975728
www.hotelcalabona.it
Rooms: 110 - ⟨⟩ ⟨P⟩ ⟨⟩ ⟨⟩ ⟨⟩ - ⟨AE⟩ ⟨▦⟩
⟨MC⟩ ⟨JCB⟩ B

Florida ★★★
Via Lido 15, Tel. 079950500
www.hotelfloridaalghero.it
Rooms: 76 - ⟨⟩ ⟨P⟩ ⟨⟩ ⟨⟩ - ⟨AE⟩ ⟨◎⟩ ⟨▦⟩
⟨MC⟩ B

Restaurants

La Lepanto ⊞ ★
Via Carlo Alberto 135,
Tel. 079979116
www.lalepanto-ristorante.it
Places: 160 - fish - ⟨AE⟩ ⟨◎⟩ ⟨▦⟩ ⟨MC⟩ B

ARBATAX (OG)

Hotels

Arbatasar Hotel ★★★★ &
Via Porto Frailis 11, Tel. 0782651800
www.arbatasar.it
Rooms: 45 - ⟨⟩ ⟨P⟩ ⟨⟩ ⟨⟩ - ⟨AE⟩ ⟨◎⟩ ⟨▦⟩
⟨MC⟩ B

La Bitta ★★★★ & ★
Località Porto Frailis,
Tel. 0782667080
www.arbataxhotels.com
Rooms: 10 - ⟨⟩ ⟨P⟩ ⟨⟩ ⟨⟩ - ⟨AE⟩ ⟨▦⟩ ⟨MC⟩
B

La Perla ★★★ &
Meublé. Viale Europa 15,
Tel. 0782667800
www.hotel-laperla.it
Rooms: 10 - ⟨⟩ ⟨P⟩ - ⟨AE⟩ ⟨◎⟩ ⟨▦⟩ ⟨MC⟩ B

BAIA SARDINIA (OT)

Hotels

Gran Relais dei Nuraghi ★★★★
Via Tre Monti, Tel. 078999501
www.hotelinuraghi.it
Rooms: 31 - ♨ 🄿 🏊 ♨ - 🄰🄴 ⓪ 🎫
🄼🄲 B

Grazia Deledda ★★★★
Loc. Tilzitta, strada per Baia
Sardinia,
Tel. 078998990
www.hotelristorantegraziadeledda.it
Rooms: 10 - 🄿

BOSA (OR)

> 📖 **Pro Loco**
> Corso Vittorio Emanuele
> Tel. 0785376107

Hotels

Al Gabbiano ★★★
Loc. Bosa Marina,
viale Mediterraneo,
Tel. 0785374123
www.bosa.it/gabbianohotel
Rooms: 30 - ♨ 🄿 🏊 - 🄰🄴 ⓪ 🎫 🄼🄲
B

Corte Fiorita ★★★
Via Lungotemo De Gasperi 45,
Tel. 0785377058
www.albergo-diffuso.it
Rooms: 25 - ♥ - 🎫 🄼🄲 B

CAGLIARI

> 📖 **APT**
> Piazza Giacomo Matteotti
> Tel. 070669255

Hotels

Panorama ★★★★ ♿
Viale Diaz 23, Tel. 070307691
www.hotelpanorama.it
Rooms: 100 - ♨ ♨ - 🄰🄴 ⓪ 🎫 🄼🄲 B

Regina Margherita ★★★★
Meublé. Viale Regina Margherita
44, Tel. 070670342
www.hotelreginamargherita.com
Rooms: 99 - ♨ - 🄰🄴 ⓪ 🎫 🄼🄲 B

Ulivi e Palme ★★★ ★
Via P. Bembo 25,
Tel. 070485861
www.uliviepalme.it
Rooms: 23 - ♨ 🄿 🏊 ♥ - 🄰🄴 ⓪ 🎫
🄼🄲 🄹🄾🄱 B

Restaurants

S'Apposentu ♟♟♟ ♿
Via S. Alenixedda,
Tel. 0704082315
www.sapposentu.it
Places: 40 - 🄿 - R, I - 🄰🄴 ⓪ 🎫 🄼🄲 B

Flora ♟♟ ♿
Via Cavour 60, Tel. 070665870
granchef@tiscali.it
Places: 80 - C - 🄰🄴 ⓪ 🎫 🄼🄲 B

Zenit
Viale Pula 2,
Tel. 070250009
Places: 50/20 - R - 🄰🄴 ⓪ 🎫 🄼🄲

CARLOFORTE (CI)

> 📖 **Pro Loco**
> Corso Tagliafico 2
> Tel. 0781854009
> www.prolococarloforte.it

Hotels

La Valle ★★★ ♿
Loc. Commende,
Tel. 0781857001
www.hotellavalle.com
Rooms: 12 - ♨ 🄿 🏊 -
🄰🄴 ⓪ 🎫 🄼🄲 B

Restaurants

Al Tonno di Corsa ♟♟
Via Marconi 47,
Tel. 0781855106
www.tonnodicorsa.it
Places: 40/60 - R - 🄰🄴 ⓪ 🎫 🄼🄲 B

Dau Bobba ♟♟ ♿
Loc. Segni,
strada delle Saline,
Tel. 0781854037
www.carloforte.net/daubobba
Places: 40/40 - ♠ 🄿 - fish -
⓪ 🎫 🄼🄲 B

CASTELSARDO (SS)

> 📖 **Pro Loco**
> Piazza del Popolo 1
> Tel. 079471506

Hotels

Riviera ★★★★
Lungomare Anglona 1,
Tel. 079470143
www.hotelriviera.net
Rooms: 34 - 🄿 ♥ -
🄰🄴 ⓪ 🎫 🄼🄲 B

Costa Doria ★★★
Loc. Lu Bagnu,
corso Italia 73
Tel. 079474043
www.hotelriviera.net
Rooms: 68 - 🄰🄴 ⓪ 🎫 🄼🄲 B

CASTIADAS (CA)

> 📖 **Pro Loco**
> Località Olia Speciosa
> Tel. 0709949138

Hotels

**Sant'Elmo Beach
Hotel ★★★★** ♿
Loc. Sant'Elmo,
Tel. 070995161
www.hotelphilosophy.net
Rooms: 175 - ♨ 🏊 ♨ -
🄰🄴 ⓪ 🎫 🄼🄲 B

DORGALI (NU)

> 📖 **Pro Loco**
> Via Lamarmora 108
> Tel. 078496243

Hotels

Ispinigoli ★★★ ♿ ★
Loc. Ispinigoli,
Tel. 078495268
www.hotelispinigoli.com
Rooms: 24 - ♨ 🄿 🏊 ♠ -
🄰🄴 🎫 🄼🄲 B

Restaurants

Colibrì ♟
Via Gramsci ang.
Via Floris,
Tel. 078496054
colibri.mereu@tiscali.it
Places: 54 - 🄿 - R - 🎫 🄼🄲 B

LA MADDALENA (OT)

> 📖 **Pro Loco**
> Via Leopardi 11
> www.prolocolamaddalena.it

Hotels

Garibaldi ★★★
Meublé.
Via La Marmora,
Tel. 0789737314
www.hotelgaribaldi.info
Rooms: 44 - ♨ 🄿 - 🄰🄴 ⓪ 🎫 🄼🄲 B

Nido d'Aquila ★★★ ★
Loc. Nido d'Aquila,
Tel. 0789722130
www.hotelnidodaquila.it
Rooms: 19 - ♨ - 🄰🄴 ⓪ 🎫 🄼🄲 B

NUORO

> 📖 **EPT**
> Piazza Italia 19
> Tel. 078430083

Hotels

Grillo ★★★ ♿
Via Mons. Melas 14,
Tel. 078438678
www.grillohotel.it
Rooms: 46 - ♠ - 🄰🄴 ⓪ 🎫 🄼🄲 🄹🄾🄱 B

Paradiso ★★★
Via Aosta 44,
Tel. 078435585
hotelparadisonuoro@tiscali.it
Rooms: 42 - 🄿 - 🄰🄴 ⓪ 🎫 🄼🄲 B

Restaurants

Canne al Vento ♟♟
Via Biasi 123,
Tel. 0784201762
Places: 130/30 - R - 🄰🄴 ⓪ 🎫 🄼🄲 B

Roccas ♟♟
Loc. Monte Ortobene,
contrada Sedda Ortai,
Tel. 3495781623
www.roccas.eu
Places: 70 - ♠ 🄿 - R

OLBIA

> 📖 **AAST**
> Via Catello Piro
> Tel. 078921453

Hotels

Colonna Palace
Hotel Mediterraneo ★★★★
Via Montello 3,
Tel. 078924173
www.itihotels.it
Rooms: 70 - P - AE ① ⅦⅡ MC B

Li Cuncheddi ★★★★
Loc. Capo Ceraso,
Tel. 078936126
www.hotellicuncheddi.com
Rooms: 80 - ♨ P ⚁ ⛱ ♨ - AE ①

Restaurants

Gallura ⅦⅠ
All'Isola Tavolara, Tel. 078958570
Places: 15/200 - R - ⅦⅡ MC B

Da Tonino ⅦⅠ
Corso Umberto 145,
Tel. 078924648
Places: 70 - ● P - R - AE ⅦⅡ MC B

ORISTANO

Pro Loco
Via Vittorio Emanuele II 8
Tel. 078370621

Hotels

Mistral 2 ★★★★
Via XX Settembre 34,
Tel. 0783210389
www.shg.it/mistral2/
Rooms: 132 - ♨ P ♨ -
AE ① ⅦⅡ MC B

I.S.A. ★★★
Piazza Marino 50,
Tel. 0783360101
www.isarose.net
Rooms: 80 - ✆ - AE ① ⅦⅡ MC B

Restaurants

Antica Trattoria del Teatro ⅦⅠ
Via Parpaglia 11,
Tel. 078371672
Places: 30 - R - AE ① ⅦⅡ MC B

Il Giglio ⅦⅠ
Loc. Massama,
S.P. Massama-Siamaggiore,
Tel. 3491447955
www.agriturismoilgiglio.com
Places: 90/20 - ● P - R

PALAU (OT)

Ufficio Turistico
Palazzo Fresi
Tel. 0789707025

Hotels

Palau Hotel ★★★★
Via Baragge, Tel. 0789708468,
www.palauhotel.it
Rooms: 95 - ♨ P ♨ ♨ -
AE ⅦⅡ MC B

La Roccia ★★★
Meublé.
Via dei Mille 15,
Tel. 0789709528,
www.hotellaroccia.com
Rooms: 22 - ♨ P ♨ - AE ⅦⅡ MC B

Restaurants

Da Franco ⅦⅠ
Via Capo d'Orso 1,
Tel. 0789709558
www.ristorantedafranco.it
Places: 105 - R - AE ① ⅦⅡ MC B

PORTO CERVO (OT)

Ufficio Turismo
Arzachena
Palazzo Municipale
Tel. 0789849388

Hotels

Le Ginestre ★★★★
Tel. 078992030
www.leginestrehotel.com
Rooms: 80 - ♨ P ♨ ♨ -
AE ① ⅦⅡ MC

Luci di la Montagna★★★★ ★
Via Sa Conca,
Tcl. 078992051
www.alpitourworld,it
Rooms: 65 - ♨ P ♨ -
AE ① ⅦⅡ MC

Nibaru ★★★★
Meublé. Loc. Cala di Volpe,
Tel. 078996038
www.hotelnibaru.it
Rooms: 60 - ♨ P ⛱ ♨ -
AE ⅦⅡ MC B

Valdiola ★★★ ♿
Loc. Cala di Volpe,
Tel. 078996215
www.hotelvaldiola.com
Rooms: 33 - ♨ P ♨ - AE ⅦⅡ JCB B
B

Restaurants

Gianni Pedrinelli ⅦⅠ ♿
Loc. Piccolo Pevero,
Tel. 078992436
www.giannipedrinelli.it
Places: 130/150 - ● P - R, I -
AE ① ⅦⅡ

SANT'ANTIOCO (CI)

Pro Loco
Piazza Repubblica 31/A
Tel. 0781840592

Hotels

La Rosa dei Venti Resort
Via Goceano 30,
Tel. 0781828010
www.rosaventi.it
Rooms: 3 - ♨

Restaurants

Il Cantuccio ⅦⅠ ♿
Viale Trento 16,
Tel. 078182166
salv.cuccu@tiscali.it
Places: 100 - R,- AE ① ⅦⅡ

SANTA TERESA GALLURA (OT)

AA
Piazza Vittorio Emanuele 24
Tel. 0789754127

Hotels

G.H. Corallaro ★★★★ ♿
Loc. Rena Bianca, 0789755475
www.hotelcorallaro.it
Rooms: 81 - ♨ P ♨ ♨ - AE ⅦⅡ MC B

La Coluccia ★★★★ ♿
Loc. Conca Verde,
Tel. 0789758004
www.hotelphilosophy.net
Rooms: 45 - ♨ ♨ ♨ - AE ① ⅦⅡ MC B

Marinaro ★★★
Via Angioy 48,
Tel. 0789754112
www.hotelmarinaro.it
Rooms: 27 - - AE ⅦⅡ MC

Restaurants

S'Andira ⅦⅠ
Loc. Santa Reparata,
Via Orsa Minore 1,
Tel. 0789754273
www.sandira.it
Places: 60/20 - ● P - C, I - AE ① ⅦⅡ
MC JCB B

SASSARI

AAST
Via Roma 62
Tel. 079231777
www.regione.sardegna.it

Hotels

Grazia Deledda ★★★★
Viale Dante 47,
Tel. 079271235
www.hotelgraziadeledda.it
Rooms: 127 - P - AE ① ⅦⅡ MC B

Leonardo da Vinci ★★★ ★
Via Roma 79,
Tel. 079280744
www.leonardodavincihotel.it
Rooms: 118 - AE ① ⅦⅡ MC B

Restaurants

Liberty ⅦⅠ
Piazza N. Sauro 3,
Tel. 079236361
rliberty@tiscali.it
Places: 80/80 - R, C - AE ① ⅦⅡ MC

GLOSSARY

Acropolis
Fortified high city area or citadel of an ancient city

Acroterion
A sculptural figure or ornament mounted on the apex or corners of a pediment

Aedicule
Small, classical structure, containing a sacred image, either inside a church or building or standing on its own

Altar-frontal
Decorative panel covering the front, lower part of an altar

Altar-piece
Painting or sculpture, placed behind or above an altar

Ambulatory
Open-air walkway flanked by columns or trees; also corridor or passageway in theater, amphitheatre, or catacombs

Ambo, pl. ambones
A raised platform in an early Christian church from which parts of the service were conducted

Amphitheater
An oval or round building with tiers or seats around a central arena, used in Ancient Roman times for gladiatorial contests and spectacles

Anta (pl. Antae)
Pilaster forming the ends of the lateral walls of a temple cella; the facade consists of columns set between two antae, the columns are said to be in antis

Apse
Part of a church at the end of the nave; generally semi-cylindrical in shape; with a semi-spherical roof

Architrave
The lowermost division of a classical entablature, resting directly on the column capitals and supporting the frieze

Archivolt
Molded architrave carried round an arch

Ashlar
Type of external wall covering, made of protruding, roughly-hewn stones

Atrium
The forecourt of an early Christian church, flanked or surrounded by porticoes. Also an open-air central court around which a house is built

Attic
Topmost storey of a classical building (esp. triumphal arches)

Baita
A typical wooden house in the western Alps

Barrel vault
Vault which has a rectangular ground-plan and semicircular cross-section

Basilica
Rectangular-shaped building: in Roman times, used for the administration of justice; in early Christian times, used for worship, and generally with a central nave and side aisles, possibly with apse/s

Bas relief
Type of sculpture (in marble, ivory, bronze or other material) where the carved figures stand out on a flat background to a lesser extent than in a high-relief

Bastion
Projecting part of a fortification, in the form of an irregular pentagon.

Candelabra
Bas relief or painting consisting of fruit, flowers, leaves, or other decorative motifs, used to ornament columns, vaults, walls, etc.

Capital
Part which links a column to the structure above. In classical architecture, capitals were Doric, Ionian, or Corinthian

Cartoon
Full-size, preparatory drawing for a painting, fresco or tapestry

Caryatid
A sculptured female figure used as a column

Cavea
Spectator seating of a theater or amphitheater, usually divided into sections which were assigned to different social classes

Cella
The principal chamber or enclosed part of a classical temple where the cult image was kept

Cenotaph
A monument erected in memory of a deceased person, whose remains are buried elsewhere

Chemin-de-ronde
A continuous gangway providing a means of communication behind the rampart of a fortified wall

Chiaroscuro
Term used to describe paintings which rely on gradations between brightness and darkness

Choir
Area for choir members, either in front of or behind the high altar in a church presbytery

Ciborium
Square structure with four columns supporting an overhead cover; usually containing an altar or tomb; or casket or tabernacle containing the host

Cippus (pl. cippi)
Stone with inscription; sepulchral monument, some-times in the form of an altar

Clipeus
Shield-like frame containing a relief or image

Codex (pl. Codices)
A manuscript book, esp. of Scriptural or Classical texts, usually on vellum

Colonnade
A series of regularly spaced columns supporting an entablature and usually one side of a roof structure

Comacine masters
Skilled Lombard stone-masons

Counter-facade
Internal wall of the facade of a building

Cross vault
Vault consisting of two intersecting barrel vaults, with a square ground-plan

Curtain (wall)
Masonry fortifications, walls and towers, built around castle Depressed Arch
Arch where the curved part consists of a short segment of a circumference

Cusp
Cone- or pyramid-shaped ornamental decoration, and relief work; typical of Gothic period

Deambulatory
An aisle encircling the choir or chancel of a church

Domus de janas
Neolithic Sardinian tombs cut

441

out of the rock; the words mean "houses of the fairies"

Dosseret
Supplementary capital set above a column capital to receive the thrust of the arch

Drum
Part of a cupola, with vertical walls, which the dome extends from

Edicola
Shrine, niche

Embrasure
With a splayed (angled) opening

Encaustic painting
Type of painting in which pigment is mixed with melted beeswax and resin, and the color is fixed by heat after application

Exedra
A large apsidal extension of the interior volume of a church; usually a semi-circular area

Ex-voto
Object given in thanks for grace received from a saint or the Virgin; generally a painting, or wood or silver object, related in some way to the grace received

Forum (pl. fora)
A large flat area in an Ancient Roman town, the center of political life

Greek cross
Cross with arms of equal length

High relief
Type of sculpture where the carved figures protrude substantially from the flat background

Hypogeum
Subterranean excavation for burial of the dead (usually Etruscan)

Incunabulum (pl. incunabula)
Book printed before 1501

Keep
The innermost and strongest structure or tower of a medieval castle

Krater
Ancient Greek and Roman mixing bowl, conical in shape with rounded base

Lacunar ceiling
Ceiling decorated with symmetrically-arranged, embedded panels, usually made of richly-ornamented stucco or wood

Lantern
Topmost part of a cupola, either open or with windows, to allow light inside. It generally resembles a circular temple

Latin cross
Cross with a long vertical arm

Lavabo
Hand-basin usually outside a refectory or sacristy

Loculus (pl. loculi)
Place of burial, rectangular in shape and built into a wall, or found in walls of catacombs

Loggia
A colonnaded or arcaded space within the body of a building but open to the air on one side, often at an upper storey overlooking an open court; also used as a decorative motif

Loop-holes
slits for firing arrows in a medieval castle

Lunette
Semi-circular space on a wall, vault or ceiling, often decorated with a painting or relief

Majolica
A type of early Italian earthenware covered with an opaque tin glaze
Oeil-de-boeuf
Small, round or oval window

Metope
Decorative stone slabs with low reliefs

Narthex
The portico before the nave of an early Christian or Byzantine church

Necropolis
Pre-Christian tombs grouped in or over a particular area, or the area itself

Nymphaeum
Originally a temple of the Nymphs, decorated with the statues of goddesses

Oculus
Circular opening, especially at the top of a dome

Ogival arch
Arch which is pointed at the top, typical of Gothic architecture

Opus sectile
A mosaic or pavement made of thin slabs of colored marble cut in geometrical shapes

Oratory
Place of worship, reserved for certain people or communities

Parvis
The flat ground in front of a church

Pediment
Structure crowning the facade of a building, usually triangular in shape

Pendentive
Concave surface between arches beneath a dome

Pentahedral
Five-sided

Peristyle
A colonnade surrounding a building or courtyard

Piano nobile
Upper floor occupied by the nobility

Pilaster
A shallow, rectangular feature projecting from a wall, having a capital and a base and architecturally treated as a column

Pluteus (pl. plutei)
Reading desk in an early library; decorated square stone slabs in Romanesque churches e.g. used vertically as base for rood screen

Podium
The raised platform encircling the arena of a Roman amphitheater

Polyptych
Altar-piece consisting of a number of panels. A diptych has two panels; a triptych has three

Portal
A doorway, gate or entrance, especially an imposing one emphasized by size and stately architectural treatment

Predella
Small painting or panel, usually in sections, attached below a large altar-piece Presbytery
Part of a church where the main altar is situated; generally raised or separated from the rest of the nave by a balustrade or such like

Presbytery
The part of a church reserved for the officiating clergy

Pronaos
An open vestibule before the cella of a classical temple or porch in front of a church

Putto
Figure of a child sculpted or painted; usually nude

Quadriporticus
A portico running around four sides of a courtyard, especially in front of early Christian or Romanesque churches

Sacellum
In ancient times, a small roofless temple consecrated to a deity; later, a chapel in a church

Sacristy
Part of church where furnishings and vestments are kept, and

where clergy prepare for
services

Sarcophagus
(pl. sarcophagi)
Stone coffin, often with relief
decoration or inscription

Simulacrum
Sacred image or statue,
sometimes central to a
procession

Splayed portal
Portal set into diagonally-sloped
wall facings

Stall
Wide, wooden seat with arm-
rests and back, placed in a row
with others

Stele
Upright stone slab or pillar
bearing a monumental
inscription

Stoup
Vessel for holy water, generally
placed near church entrance

Tambour
The vertical part of a cupola

Tabernacle
Aedicule or niche containing
sacred image, inside or outside
a church, or standing on its

own; also a small, enclosed
aedicule placed on the altar,
containing the host

Terme
Public building complexes for
hot and cold baths. Already
common by the 2nd century BC,
the popularity of bath
complexes reached its height in
the Imperial period, when
swimming-pools, massage
rooms, gymnasiums (palestrae),
gardens and libraries were
added. The actual bath complex
(Terme) consisted of a changing
room, a warm room with a warm
pool (tepidarium), a hot room
with a hot pool (calidarium), a
sauna and a room with pools of
cold water for cold baths
(frigidarium)

Tiburium
Architectural structure enclosing
and supporting a dome, used in
early and Romanesque Lombard
churches

Tondo
Round painting or bas relief

Transenna
Stone slab, sometimes pierced
or sculpted, placed vertically to
close off reserved areas, for
example the presbytery of a
church

Transept
Area perpendicular to the nave,
often extending out at the sides
and giving the building a cross-
shaped ground-plan

Tribune
Area including the presbytery,
choir and apse, in early-
Christian basilicas; in churches
generally, any loggia set into
or protruding from the walls

Tympanum
The triangular space at the top
of the facade of a temple, often
recessed and decorated with
sculpture

Vestibule
Ante-chamber, entrance hall or
lobby

Volute
A spiral, scroll-like ornament

Westwork
The monumental western front
of a Romanesque church

METRIC CONVERSIONS

DISTANCE

Kilometres/Miles

km to mi	mi to km
1 = 0.62	1 = 1.6
2 = 1.2	2 = 3.2
3 = 1.9	3 = 4.8
4 = 2.5	4 = 6.4
5 = 3.1	5 = 8.1
6 = 3.7	6 = 9.7
7 = 4.3	7 = 11.3
8 = 5.0	8 = 12.9

Meters/Feet

m to ft	ft to m
1 = 3.3	1 = 0.30
2 = 6.6	2 = 0.61
3 = 9.8	3 = 0.91
4 = 13.1	4 = 1.2
5 = 16.4	5 = 1.5
6 = 19.7	6 = 1.8
7 = 23.0	7 = 2.1
8 = 26.2	8 = 2.4

WEIGHT

Kilograms/Pounds

kg to lb	lb to kg
1 = 2.2	1 = 0.45
2 = 4.4	2 = 0.91
3 = 6.6	3 = 1.4
4 = 8.8	4 = 1.8
5 = 11.0	5 = 2.3
6 = 13.2	6 = 2.7
7 = 15.4	7 = 3.2
8 = 17.6	8 = 3.6

Grams/Ounces

g to oz	oz to g
1 = 0.04	1 = 28
2 = 0.07	2 = 57
3 = 0.11	3 = 85
4 = 0.14	4 = 114
5 = 0.18	5 = 142
6 = 0.21	6 = 170
7 = 0.25	7 = 199
8 = 0.28	8 = 227

TEMPERATURE

Fahrenheit/Celsius

F	C
0	-17.8
5	-15.0
10	-12.2
15	-9.4
20	-6.7
25	-3.9
30	-1.1
32	0
35	1.7
40	4.4
45	7.2
50	10.0
55	12.8
60	15.5
65	18.3
70	21.1
75	23.9
80	26.7
85	29.4
90	32.2
95	35.0
100	37.8

LIQUID VOLUME

Liters/U.S. Gallons

L to gal	gal to L
1 = 0.26	1 = 3.8
2 = 0.53	2 = 7.6
3 = 0.79	3 = 11.4
4 = 1.1	4 = 15.1

Liters/U.S. Gallons

L to gal	gal to L
5 = 1.3	5 = 18.9
6 = 1.6	6 = 22.7
7 = 1.8	7 = 26.5
8 = 2.1	8 = 30.3

ITALIAN PROVINCES

Italy is divided into 20 regions, which are in turn divided into 110 provinces. In this context, the term province refers to local territorial entities that have their own administrative structure and elected representatives. They are, of course, smaller in size than the regions. Each province is made up of a number of "comuni" or municipalities, with the main municipality also being the local capital. The provinces are identified by two-letter combinations (normally linked to the local capital), as per the list below.

VALLE D'AOSTA
Aosta (AO)

PIEDMONT
Alessandria (AL)
Asti (AT)
Biella (BI)
Cuneo (CN)
Novara (NO)
Turin/Torino (TO)
Verbano-Cusio-Ossola (VB)
Vercelli (VC)

LOMBARDY
Bergamo (BG)
Brescia (BS)
Como (CO)
Cremona (CR)
Lecco (LC)
Lodi (LO)
Mantua/Mantova (MN)
Milan/Milano (MI)
Monza e Brianza (MB)
Pavia (PV)
Sondrio (SO)
Varese (VA)

TRENTINO-ALTO ADIGE
Bolzano/Bozen (BZ)
Trent/Trento (TN)

VENETO
Belluno (BL)
Padua/Padova (PD)
Rovigo (RO)
Treviso (TV)
Venice/Venezia (VE)
Verona (VR)
Vicenza (VI)

FRIULI VENEZIA GIULIA
Gorizia (GO)
Pordenone (PN)
Trieste (TS)
Udine (UD)

LIGURIA
Genoa/Genova (GE)
Imperia (IM)
La Spezia (SP)
Savona (SV)

EMILIA-ROMAGNA
Bologna (BO)
Ferrara (FE)
Forlì-Cesena (FC)
Modena (MO)
Parma (PR)
Piacenza (PC)
Ravenna (RA)
Reggio nell'Emilia (RE)
Rimini (RN)

TUSCANY
Arezzo (AR)
Florence/Firenze (FI)
Grosseto (GR)
Livorno (LI)
Lucca (LU)
Massa-Carrara (MS)
Pisa (PI)
Pistoia (PT)
Prato (PO)
Siena (SI)

MARCHE
Ancona (AN)
Ascoli Piceno (AP)
Fermo*
Macerata (MC)
Pesaro e Urbino (PU)

UMBRIA
Perugia (PG)
Terni (TR)

LAZIO
Frosinone (FR)
Latina (LT)
Rieti (RI)
Rome/Roma (RM)
Viterbo (VT)

ABRUZZO
Chieti (CH)
L'Aquila (AQ)
Pescara (PE)
Teramo (TE)

MOLISE
Campobasso (CB)
Isernia (IS)

CAMPANIA
Avellino (AV)
Benevento (BN)
Caserta (CE)
Naples/Napoli (NA)
Salerno (SA)

APULIA
Bari (BA)
Brindisi (BR)
Barletta-Andria-Trani*
Foggia (FG)
Lecce (LE)
Taranto (TA)

BASILICATA
Matera (MT)
Potenza (PZ)

CALABRIA
Catanzaro (CZ)
Cosenza (CS)
Crotone (KR)
Reggio di Calabria (RC)
Vibo Valentia (VV)

SICILY
Agrigento (AG)
Caltanissetta (CL)
Catania (CT)
Enna (EN)
Messina (ME)
Palermo (PA)
Ragusa (RG)
Siracusa (SR)
Trapani (TP)

SARDINIA
Cagliari (CA)
Carbonia-Iglesias (CI)
Medio Campidano (VS)
Nuoro (NU)
Ogliastra (OG)
Olbia-Tempio (OT)
Oristano (OR)
Sassari (SS)

* New province with letter code still to be determined

GENERAL INDEX

PICTURE CREDITS

Notes

Notes